CASES AND MATERIALS ON
FEDERAL INDIAN LAW
Seventh Edition

■   ■   ■

David H. Getches
Late Dean and Raphael J. Moses Professor of Natural Resources Law
University of Colorado

Charles F. Wilkinson
Distinguished University Professor and
Moses Lasky Professor of Law
University of Colorado

Robert A. Williams, Jr.
E. Thomas Sullivan Professor of Law
University of Arizona

Matthew L.M. Fletcher
Professor of Law
Michigan State University College of Law

Kristen A. Carpenter
Council Tree Professor of Law
University of Colorado Law School

AMERICAN CASEBOOK SERIES®

WEST
ACADEMIC
PUBLISHING

American Casebook Series is a trademark registered in the U.S. Patent and Trademark Office.

Printed in the United States of America

ISBN: 978-1-63459-906-1

Dedicated to

Vine Deloria, Jr. (1933–2005)
Legal scholar, author, mentor, friend

Wilma Mankiller (1945–2010)
Courageous and visionary tribal leader

and

Billy Frank, Jr. (1931–2014)
Treaty rights activist, brilliant orator, and statesman

Whose legacies are celebrated
by this book on Federal Indian Law.

PREFACE

It is difficult to imagine another field of law so dynamic as Indian law. In the thirty-seven years since our first edition was published, Indian law has expanded at warp speed (at least relative to the typical pace for change in the law). Thus, updating a casebook is a more challenging and thorough going task than it is in most other fields. More than eighty percent of the cases in this volume did not exist when the first edition came out in 1978. Moreover, the apparent directions of the law have shifted along with theoretical perspectives offered by the growing number of scholars who contribute to Indian law. A brief history of the evolution of this work is illustrative.

During the mid-1970s, David Getches, Charles Wilkinson, and Daniel Rosenfelt prepared the first edition after several years of representing Indian tribes and groups through legal services programs, particularly the Native American Rights Fund (NARF). The content and organization was based on materials prepared at NARF to train Indian legal services attorneys. At that point the field seemed arcane, but the authors believed it had promise as an intellectually exciting subject, charged with potent implications for a largely forgotten minority group and great symbolic force for our system of law. Teachers in a few law schools, including Professors Wilkinson and Rosenfelt who had become full-time law teachers, were offering Indian law courses. Fortunately, Professor Monroe Price had developed his pioneering casebook which appeared in 1973.

West Publishing Company took a considerable risk in accepting the first edition of this book for publication, doubting that there would be a sufficient market. Everyone's expectations were exceeded as courses proliferated in the nation's law schools and in undergraduate programs, and as enrollments in them increased. The organizing themes of the first edition are preserved here. The book proceeds from the foundational cases in Indian law, standing as landmarks in a rich historical landscape. The periods of history are classified in ways that are now standard and the organization was adopted in other works such as the 1982 edition of Felix S. Cohen's *Handbook of Federal Indian Law*, recently updated in 2012. The analysis of certain issues (e.g., preemption in Indian law) has been accepted by scholars and courts and the analytical approach to criminal jurisdiction has been used widely in classes and teaching materials.

By the time of the second edition in 1986, Professors Getches and Wilkinson found it necessary to integrate a remarkable spate of Supreme Court decisions that had applied the foundational cases in modern contexts—taxation, regulation, water rights, and fishing rights conflicts.

With considerable fealty, the Court carried forward the fundamental principles of federal preemptive powers, tribal sovereignty, and limited state authority in Indian country. A few decisions suggested curious aberrations. Since the second edition, the case law represented in the book has focused almost entirely on United States Supreme Court decisions, with some tribal court cases added to convey an understanding of how the increasingly sophisticated tribal judicial systems function. Provocative, new Indian law scholarship was added, along with materials on applications of Indian law principles to Alaska Natives, Native Hawaiians, and indigenous peoples in other countries.

The third edition saw several major changes. The addition of Professor Williams as an author gave the book greater historical depth and sharpened the moral questions raised in studying the subject, with the inclusion of his original research revealing precedents for the foundations of Indian law tracing to medieval times. Similarly, the growing body of materials in critical race studies could be well-represented because of Professor Williams' leadership in that field. And he also enriched the book's coverage of international and comparative materials.

Most striking in the third edition was the inclusion of new cases that were apparently out of step with the most venerable and reliable principles in the field and seemed to be built on the "aberrations" included in the second edition. This phenomenon, as the first pages in many Indian law articles of this period illustrate, led newcomers to the field to describe it in terms of its complexity and confusion. Indeed, the Supreme Court had become especially active in protecting non-Indian rights and property and began to write opinions that created exceptions to established, two hundred year-old principles; they could be read as carving out new principles.

The fourth edition confirmed a continuing trend of Supreme Court decisions that departed from the foundational cases that constituted most of the first edition and which still dominate the first part of the book. The effect of these decisions was to erode and fragment the territory where tribal law prevails, and suggested a serious undermining of tribal sovereignty, even as tribes were becoming more competent and determined to govern. The fourth edition also added new material on reservation economic development, examining the role and importance of tribal sovereignty in this area where tribes continue to gain ground economically. Legalized gambling, which has proven to be lucrative for many tribes, was also covered in more detail than in earlier editions.

The fifth edition demonstrated that in many ways, Indian law has reached a crossroads. New Supreme Court decisions suggested that the Justices are deeply divided over fundamental questions in the field. One of the Justices has gone so far as to say that Indian law is "schizophrenic," and the decisions added to the fifth edition on important issues such as the scope of the federal trust responsibility to tribes, the extent of congressional plenary power over Indian affairs, and limits on tribal sovereignty over non-members revealed that the Rehnquist Court fomented instability and unpredictability in the field. The fifth edition also added new materials on tribal courts and tribal customary law, protection of Indian sacred sites on public lands, and comparative and international human rights developments.

The sixth edition, with the inclusion of author Matthew L.M. Fletcher, argued for the first time that Native nations have moved into a new era of law and policy—nation-building. Self-determination has helped to propel Native nations into an era of building modern and successful nations, and this edition incorporated materials on the reality of ground-level tribal governance that draw on Professor Fletcher's expertise and experience concerning tribal law and tribal courts. The Supreme Court's dissonance on the foundational principles of federal Indian law—this edition was be the first edition of the casebook unable to report on a significant advance or defense of tribal interests in the federal courts—motivated Native nations to advance the field in legislative and regulatory arenas. Further, given the declaration of support by the Obama Administration of the United Nations Declaration on the Rights of Indigenous Peoples, Native nations may be looking farther outward to assert their basic human rights as indigenous peoples.

In the seventh edition, Kristen A. Carpenter joins the casebook. In conversation with the other co-authors, Professor Carpenter brings insights into the interrelationship of tribal law and international law in advancing federal Indian law's capacity to address human rights. Professor Carpenter also shares particular expertise in American Indian lands, cultural resources, and religious freedoms. Like her co-authors, Professor Carpenter is deeply involved in work with Indian tribes and people throughout the U.S. She has drawn on this experience in her work about the ethical and professional issues facing lawyers for Indian tribes.

In this edition, the authors offer several innovations reflecting developments in Indian Country and in legal education more broadly. First, we expressly acknowledge that the job of Indian lawyers neither begins nor ends with Supreme Court litigation. It has always been the case that lawyers represent tribes in myriad issues, only some of which end up in litigation. Beyond courtroom strategy, lawyers deal with evolving legal rules through negotiation, regulation, and reform, in tribal, state, federal, and international forums alike. Indeed, the project of lawyering for tribes is broad and engaging, filled with promise, as well as special ethical challenges. Today, lawyering for tribes may occur as much in corporate broad rooms and online forums, as in the courts of law or halls of Congress. To the extent that we teach students who may enter the field of Indian law, or other fields that require nimble responses to changing circumstances, along with cross-cultural competencies (that is, all students), we believe that it is worth surfacing certain themes and examples of what we call "Indian Lawyering." To this end, we offer a series of Indian Lawyering Notes, as well as thematic content on lawyering challenges interspersed throughout the text. This material is meant to share contextual information around the cases, as well as to inspire constructive thinking about the lawyer's role in Indian law. In many respects, the job of Indian Lawyering is one of legal reform, a project that respects foundational principles, and improves upon them with critical and innovating thinking. There is ample room for our students to engage in conversations around Indian Lawyering for the future.

Second, in this edition, we build on the book's previous attention to the phenomenon of nation building. Our friends and colleagues Stephen Cornell and Joseph P. Kalt, together with the Harvard Project on American Indian Economic Development, have compellingly identified the current period in Indian affairs as one of "Native American Nation Building." Through their research, it has become apparent that the success of Indian tribes, especially in economic development, may have less to do with federal activity than with tribal norms, values, and institutions. Even more specifically, Cornell and Kalt, along with their colleagues, have shown that sustainable economic development in Indian County correlates heavily with robust assertions of tribal sovereignty (acts of "de facto" tribal sovereignty even where "de jure" tribal sovereignty may be lacking), the creation of capable, accountable governing institutions, and "cultural match" between the tribe's underlying cultural norms and its contemporary governing institutions. While we have long acknowledged the significance of this work in our casebook, we now add a series of "Nation Building Notes" to this edition. These notes reveal the ways in which Indian law and policy are related to governance, economics, and culture in this promising era of tribal development. Indeed, one of the functions of these Nation Building Notes is to emphasize that lawyers cannot go it alone in Indian Country and that they must work with tribal citizens, elected leaders, business people, social workers, religious leaders, and others to accomplish the work of Nation Building in the 21st Century. These are the dynamic, complicated realities facing Indian lawyers, realities that merit serious attention from students and scholars, alike.

As with prior editions, we are deeply indebted to many colleagues who contributed to the content and direction of the book. Among those whose comments, suggestions, and ideas were influential are: Professor Barbara Cosens of the University of Idaho furnished valuable information on tribal water rights settlements. Professor Kate Fort assisted with the Indian Child Welfare Act materials. Gloria Valencia-Weber provided materials on Santa Clara Pueblo tribal citizenship law. Wenona Singel, John Petoskey, and Zeke Fletcher commented on and supplied materials for subjects throughout the book. Thank you to Angela Riley and Eli Wald for allowing Professor Carpenter to share excerpts of articles co-authored with them in this edition. A special thanks goes out to Richard Guest, Lead Attorney for the Native American Rights Fund's Tribal Supreme Court Project, for providing helpful data and assistance on the Court's Indian law decisions.

We also want to acknowledge the fine research and editorial assistance of University of Colorado Law School student Allison Hester, Class of 2017, and colleague Heather Martin,, and University of Arizona Rogers College of Law students Mohammad Moin Uddin, S.J.D., and Michelle Cox, Class of 2017, and Michigan State University Indigenous Law and Policy Center 2015–16 Fellow Leah Jurss.

We give special thanks to The University of Arizona Rogers College of Law, the University of Colorado Law School, and the Michigan State University College of Law for providing funding for research assistants, summer research, and for the substantial overhead necessary to prepare this edition.

A word on our use of excerpted material is in order. In addition to our edited versions of judicial decisions we include abridgements of the copyrighted articles and other material with permission. Our acknowledgments to the authors and other copyright holders begin on the next page. In reprinting excerpts of cases and other materials we have indicated our omissions of text with " * * * " while preserving the author's indication of omissions from quoted material by use of " . . . ". We have, however, omitted citations to cases and other authority without notation. Footnotes in the original work also have been eliminated without notation, although where they are included in the excerpt, we have used the original numbering. Footnotes signaled with an asterisk and the notation "Ed." were added by us.

Finally, we want to express our enduring gratitude and devotion to Dean and Professor David H. Getches, who passed away in 2011. He was a co-author on the first edition of this casebook and a driving force in its evolution through the sixth edition. Founder of the Native American Rights fund, chief counsel in the historic "Boldt decision," and leading Indian law and water law scholar, David was a giant in this field and we, along with Indian people across the country, will always remember and honor his many contributions.

D.H.G.
C.F.W.
R.A.W.
M.L.M.F.
K.A.C.

October 2016

ACKNOWLEDGMENTS

We gratefully acknowledge the following authors and publishers for granting permission to reprint excerpts from copyrighted material:

American Law Institute, Restatement of the Law of American Indians, Addendum to Preliminary Draft No. 4 (Feb. 4, 2016). Copyright © American Law Institute. Reprinted with permission of the American Law Institute.

S. James Anaya and Robert A. Williams, Jr., The Protection of Indigenous Peoples' Rights Over Land and Natural Resources Under the Inter-American Human Rights System, 14 Harvard Human Rights Journal 33 (2001). Reprinted with permission of the authors.

Robert Anderson, Water Rights, Water Quality, and Regulatory Jurisdiction in Indian Country, 34 Stanford Environmental Law Journal 95 (2015). Reprinted with permission of the author.

Raymond D. Austin, ADR and the Navajo Peacemaker Court, 32 Judges Journal 8 (1993). Reprinted with permission.

Raymond D. Austin, Navajo Courts and Navajo Common Law: A Tradition of Tribal Self-Governance (2009). Copyright © 2009 by the University of Minnesota Press. Reprinted with permission.

Kristen A. Carpenter and Angela R. Riley, Indigenous Peoples and The Jurisgenerative Moment in Human Rights Law, 102 California Law Review 163 (2014). Reprinted with permission of the authors.

Kristen A. Carpenter and Eli Wald, Lawyering for Groups: The Case of American Indian Tribal Attorneys 81 Fordham Law Review 3085, (2013). Reprinted with permission of the authors.

Felix S. Cohen, Handbook of Federal Indian Law (1941 ed.) United States Government Publishing Office.

Comment, Tribal Self-Government and The Indian Reorganization Act of 1934, 70 Michigan Law Review 955 (1972). Reprinted with permission of the Michigan Law Review.

Stephen Cornell, The Return of the Native: American Indian Political Resurgence. Copyright © 1988 by Oxford University Press, Inc. Used by permission of Oxford University Press, Inc.

Stephen Cornell and Joseph P. Kalt, American Indian Self-Determination: The Political Economy of a Successful Policy Joint Occasional Papers on Native Affairs Working Paper No. 1. Native Nations Institute for Leadership, Management, and Policy & The Harvard Project on American Indian Economic Development 2010. Reprinted with permission of the authors.

Nancy Costello, Walking Together in a Good Way: Indian Peacemaker Courts in Michigan, 76 University of Detroit Mercy Law Review 875 (1999). Reprinted with permission.

Sandra C. Danforth, Repaying Historical Debts: The Indian Claims Commission, 49 North Dakota Law Review 359 (1973). Reprinted with permission of the North Dakota Law Review.

S. Ehler & J. Morrall (eds. and trans.) Church and State Through the Centuries (1967). Reprinted with permission of Biblo and Tannen Booksellers & Publishers.

Chester E. Eisinger, The Puritan's Justification for Taking the Land, 84 Essex Institute Historical Collections 131 (1948). Reprinted by permission of the Peabody & Essex Museum, Salem Massachusetts.

Ann Laquer Estin, Lone Wolf v. Hitchcock: The Long Shadow, in The Aggressions of Civilization: Federal Indian Policy Since the 1880s (Sandra L. Cadwalader and Vine Deloria, Jr., eds. 1984). Copyright © 1984 by Temple University. Reprinted by permission of Temple University Press.

Matthew L.M. Fletcher, The Eagle Returns: The Legal History of the Grand Traverse Band of Ottawa and Chippewa Indians (2011). Copyright © Michigan State University Press. Reprinted by permission.

Matthew L.M. Fletcher, Indian Courts and Fundamental Fairness: Indian Courts and the Future Revisited, 84 University of Colorado Law Review 59 (2013). Reprinted with permission of the author.

Matthew L.M. Fletcher, Race and American Indian Tribal Nationhood, 11 Wyoming Law Review 295 (2011). Reprinted with permission of the author.

Matthew L.M. Fletcher, Factbound and Splitless: The Certiorari Process as Barrier to Justice for Indian Tribes, 51 Arizona Law Review 933 (2009). Reprinted with permission.

Matthew L.M. Fletcher, Looking to the East: The Stories of Modern Indian People and the Development of Tribal Law, 5 Seattle Journal of Social Justice 1 (2006). Reprinted with permission of the author.

Beth Ganz, Indigenous Peoples and Land Tenure: An Issue of Human Rights and Environmental Protection, 9 Georgetown International Environmental Law Review 173 (1997). Reprinted with permission of the publisher, Georgetown University and Georgetown International Environmental Law Review.

David H. Getches, A Philosophy of Permanence: The Indians' Legacy for the West, Journal of the West 54 (July 1990). Reprinted with permission of the Journal of the West.

Carole E. Goldberg, Public Law 280: The Limits of State Jurisdiction Over Reservation Indians. Originally published in 22 UCLA Law Review 535 (1975). Reprinted with permission of the author.

Carole E. Goldberg-Ambrose, Public Law 280 and The Problem of Lawlessness in California Indian Country. Originally published in 44 UCLA Law Review 1405. Copyright Reprinted with permission of the author.

Sidney L. Harring, Crow Dog's Case: A Chapter in the Legal History of Tribal Sovereignty, 14 American Indian Law Review 191 (1989). Reprinted with permission of the American Indian Law Review.

Dorothy V. Jones, British Colonial Indian Treaties, Handbook of North American Indians, Vol. IV (1988). Copyright © Smithsonian Institution Press. Reprinted with permission.

Francis Jennings, William N. Fenton, Mary A. Druke, David R. Miller (eds.), The History and Culture of Iroquois Diplomacy: An Interdisciplinary Guide to the Treaties of the Six Nations and Their League (1985). Reprinted with permission of Syracuse University Press.

Catharine MacKinnon, Feminism Unmodified (1983). Reprinted with permission of the Harvard University Press.

D'Arcy McNickle, They Came Here First: The Epic of the American Indian (Harper & Row Publishers, Perennial Library edition). Copyright © 1975 by d'Arcy McNickle. Used by permission of Harper Collins, Publishers.

J.G.A. Pocock, Law, Sovereignty and History in a Divided Culture: The Case of New Zealand and the Treaty of Waitangi, The 1992 Iredell Lecture, University of Lancaster. Reprinted with permission of the author.

Francis Paul Prucha, American Indian Policy In The Formative Years: Indian Trade and Intercourse Acts, 1790–1834 (1962). Excerpted by permission of the author.

Francis Paul Prucha (ed.), Documents of United States Indian Policy, Second Edition, Expanded (1990). Copyright © 1995, 1990, 2000 by the University of Nebraska Press. Reprinted with permission of the University of Nebraska Press.

Harold A. Ranquist, The Winters Doctrine and How It Grew: Federal Reservation Of Rights To The Use Of Water, 1975 B.Y.U. Law Review 639. Reprinted with permission.

Douglas Sanders, Aboriginal Rights in Canada: An Overview, 2 Law & Anthropology (1987). Reprinted with permission of the author and Law & Anthropology, Verband der Wissenschaftlichen Gesellschaften Osterreichs.

Wenona R. Singel, Cultural Sovereignty and Transplanted Law: Tensions in Indigenous Self-Rule, 15 Kansas Journal of Law & Public Policy 357 (2006). Reprinted with permission of author.

Edward H. Spicer, Cycles of Conquest: The Impact of Spain, Mexico, and the United States on Indians of the Southwest, 1533–1960 (1962). University of Arizona Press, 1962.

Rina Swentzell, Testimony of a Santa Clara Woman, 14 Kansas Journal of Law and Public Policy 97 (Fall 2004). Reprinted with permission of the Kansas Journal of Law and Public Policy.

Gerald Torres and Kathryn Milun, Translating Yonnondio by Precedent and Evidence: The Mashpee Indian Case, 1990 Duke Law Journal 625. Reprinted with permission of the Duke Law Journal.

S. Lyman Tyler, A History of Indian Policy (1973). Copyright © 1973 by the Bureau of Indian Affairs, Department of the Interior. Reprinted with permission.

Charles F. Wilkinson, American Indians, Time and the Law (1987). Copyright © 1987 by Yale University Press. Reprinted with permission.

Charles F. Wilkinson & Eric R. Biggs, The Evolution Of The Termination Policy, 5 American Indian Law Review 139 (1977). Reprinted with permission of the American Indian Law Review.

Charles F. Wilkinson & John M. Volkman, Judicial Review Of Indian Treaty Abrogation: "As Long As Water Flows Or Grass Grows Upon The Earth"—How Long A Time Is That?, 63 California Law Review 601 (1975). Reprinted with permission.

Robert A. Williams, Jr., The American Indian in Western Legal Thought: The Discourses of Conquest. Copyright © 1990 by Oxford University Press, Inc. Used by permission of Oxford University Press, Inc.

Robert A. Williams, Jr., The Algebra of Federal Indian Law: The Hard Trail of Decolonizing and Americanizing the White Man's Indian Jurisprudence, 1986 Wisconsin Law Review 219. Reprinted with permission of the Wisconsin Law Review.

Robert A. Williams, Jr., Columbus's Legacy: The Rehnquist Court's Perpetuation of European Cultural Racism Against American Indian Tribes, 39 Federal Bar News & Journal 6 (1992). Reprinted with permission of the Federal Bar Association.

Robert A. Williams, Jr., Linking Arms Together: American Indian Treaty Visions of Law and Peace, 1600-1800. Copyright © 1997 by Oxford University Press. Reprinted by permission of Oxford University Press.

SUMMARY OF CONTENTS

PART THREE. THE FRONTIERS OF INDIGENOUS PEOPLES' RIGHTS

TABLE OF CONTENTS

PART TWO. FEDERAL INDIAN LAW AND POLICY
IN CONTEMPORARY PERSPECTIVE

PART THREE. THE FRONTIERS OF
INDIGENOUS PEOPLES' RIGHTS

TABLE OF CASES

The principal cases are in bold type.

CASES AND MATERIALS ON
FEDERAL INDIAN LAW
Seventh Edition

CHAPTER ONE

INTRODUCTION: INDIANS AND INDIAN LAW

■ ■ ■

SECTION A. THE FIELD OF INDIAN LAW

1. WHAT IS FEDERAL INDIAN LAW?

Federal Indian law regulates the legal relationships between Indian tribes and the United States. Comprised of treaties, statutes, regulations, judicial decisions, and other sources, federal Indian law acknowledges tribes as political entities with inherent rights to property and sovereignty, and sets forth a structure in which the federal and tribal governments share in the administration of those rights.

In the history of the United States, the law has been used as both a sword and shield in the quest of tribes to survive the onslaught of conquest and colonization. In its earliest cases, the Supreme Court recognized the ongoing existence of tribes as entities with inherent rights and also "legitimated" a legacy in which European nations claimed Indian lands pursuant to the the "Doctrine of Discovery." See Robert A. Williams, Jr., The American Indian in Western Legal Thought: The Discourses of Conquest (1990).

During the 19th and 20th centuries, federal initiatives removed tribes from their homelands, punished Indians for practicing their religions, and took tribal property, and the courts determined these programs to be either legal or unreviewable. And yet judicial decisions of the 1800's and 1900's also recognized tribal reserved rights to land, water, and self-government, the supremacy of federal treaty rights over state laws, and the duty of the federal government to protect tribal resoources. Throughout U.S. history, federal policy has swung back and forth among programs designed to relocate, assimilate, and reorganize Indian tribes, and even to terminate them altogether.

Today, and for the past sixty years or so, federal lawmakers have generally coalesced around a policy tribal "self-determination" promoting the roles of Indian people and tribes as active participants in the legal processes affecting them. Self-determination appears to have endured in part because it reflects Indian social and cultural perspectives about the vitality of tribal lifeways. While the wellbeing of tribal people is largely attributable to the resilience of Indian people themselves, legal programs allowing tribes to reclaim responsibility from the federal government for Indian education, health care, economic development, and law enforcement have also been successful. See Charles Wilkinson, Blood Struggle: The Rise of Modern Indian Nations (2005).

And yet, many challenges remain, from improving child welfare and community health to alleviating poverty and violence in Indian country. Around the country, many tribes are engaged in a process of "nation building" a term that refers generally to the revitalization of tribal institutions such that they are both grounded in the traditional norms and values of the community and capable of meeting contemporary political, econonomic, and social challenges. See Stephen Cornell and Joseph P. Kalt, *Two Approaches to the Development of Native Nations: One Works, the Other Doesn't*, in Miriam Jorgensen, Rebuilding Native Nations Strategies for Governance and Development (2007).

While these activities are fundamentally about the resilence and determination of Indian people themselves, it is also true that federal Indian law shapes daily life in Indian country. Indeed, the Supreme Court often decides more Indian cases than the numbers of Indians relative to the population as a whole would seem to justify. The proliferation of Indian law suggests three significant points: first, Indians are subject to extensive legal regulation of their rights, second, non-Indian people, lands, governments, and corporations are involved in Indian law cases, and third, Indian law raises difficult questions that go to the very heart of what the rule of law means in the United States.

There are three kinds of sovereigns within the United States—federal, state, and tribal. See Sandra Day O'Connor, *Lessons from the Third Sovereign: Indian Tribal Courts*, 33 Tulsa L. J. 1 (1997). The Constitution delineates the authorities, duties, and limitations of the United States in relation to the state governments, but the structure and text of the Constitution recognizes two other kinds of sovereign entity—foreign nations and Indian tribes.

The Constitutional text, as consistent with the practice of Congress before the ratification of the Constitution, provides for two means by which Indian tribes and the United States will interact. First, the so-called Indian Commerce Clause provides that Congress has authority to regulate commerce with the Indian tribes. One of the first acts of the First Congress was to implement the Indian Commerce Clause in the Trade and Intercourse Act of 1790. Second, the federal government's treaty power provides an additional form by which the United States deals with Indian tribes. There are hundreds of valid and extant treaties between the United States and various Indian tribes. The structure of the Constitution and the treaties established a relationship between sovereigns akin to a trust relationship, with the federal government in the position of trustee and

Indian nations and Indian people in the position of trust beneficiary. The trust relationship is not merely metaphorical, as the federal government holds and administers billions of dollars of Indian and tribal assets in the form of land, natural resources, and cash.

Early jurisprudence of the United States Supreme Court addressed significant aspects of the Indian Commerce Clause and treaty rights in three cases authored by Chief Justice John Marshall—the so-called "Marshall Trilogy" of federal Indian law. In *Johnson v. McIntosh*, 21 U.S. 543 (1823), an early Indian lands case, Chief Justice Marshall held that the federal government had exclusive dominion over affairs with Indian tribes—exclusive as to individual American citizens and, implicitly, as to state government. In *Cherokee Nation v. Georgia*, 30 U.S. 1 (1831), Chief Justice Marshall's lead opinion asserted that while Indian tribes were not state governments as defined in the Constitution, nor were they foreign nations—they were something akin to "domestic dependent nations." And, finally, in *Worcester v. Georgia*, 31 U.S. 515 (1832), Chief Justice Marshall confirmed that the laws of states have "no force" in Indian country, and that the Constitution's Supremacy Clause gave powerful effect to Indian treaties as "the supreme law of the land."

The body of federal Indian law—comprised of the Constitutional text, Indian treaties, Acts of Congress, the Supreme Court's jurisprudence, and other important sources—can be expressed in a few general, fundamental principles. See David H. Getches, *Conquering the Cultural Frontier: The New Subjectivism of the Supreme Court in Indian Law*, 84 Calif. L. Rev. 1573 (1996) (discussing foundational principles of federal Indian law). *First*, Congress's authority over Indian affairs is plenary and exclusive. As a concomitant principle, the federal government holds obligations to Indian tribes and individual Indians known as the trust responsibility. *Second*, state governments have no authority to regulate Indian affairs absent express Congressional delegation or granted in accordance with the federal government's trust obligations. *Third*, the sovereign authority of Indian tribes is inherent, and not delegated or granted by the United States, but can be limited or restricted by Congress in accordance with its trust responsibilities. Congress must clearly express its intent to abrogate any aspect of tribal sovereignty.

A key element in these three principles is the legal term of art, "Indian country," which is defined by Congress to include all reservation lands and certain other kinds of Indian lands. These foundational principles are in strongest force within the boundaries of Indian country.

While this book focuses largely on federal Indian law, it also addresses tribal and international law. By tribal law, we mean the specific law of each tribal nation, such as the law of the Navajo Nation or Cherokee Nation. See Matthew L.M. Fletcher, American Indian Tribal Law (2011). Tribal law, as found in modern-day tribal constitutions and codes, and in tradition and custom as interpreted by tribal courts, affects and in turn is affected by federal Indian law. Historically, of course, tribes broadly regulated the people and lands within their territories, but much of this practice was dismantled by the federal government. Under the current federal policy of tribal self-determination, Congress respects tribal jurisdiction and tribes are, in turn, rebuilding their institutions of government, consistent with both tribal traditions and contemporary expectations of legitimacy and fairness. The legislative codes and judicial decisions, for example, of the Navajo Nation, Cherokee Nation, and others may easily be found online, and there are scholarly works dedicated to the customary and common law traditions of various tribes. Increasingly, federal and state courts enforce tribal law according to general legal principles such as full faith and credit and comity. Congress in recent years has passed specific legislation, including the Tribal Law and Order Act of 2010 and Violence Against Women Reauthorization Act of 2013, restoring certain aspects of tribal law and jurisdictional authority within the United States legal system.

International law is also deeply influential in federal Indian law. As Chief Justice Marshall recognized in the 1800's, the international "law of nations" and "doctrine of discovery" were used historically to justify the colonization and subjugation of indigenous peoples, as well as to recognize tribes as sovereigns with the power to enter into treaties with Europeans. In the post-World War II era, international human rights law has increasingly recognized the rights of racial, ethnic, racial, and political minorities, with ramifications for indigenous peoples. See S. James Anaya, Indigenous Peoples in International Law (2d. ed. 2004).

In 2007, the United Nations General Assembly adopted the Declaration on the Rights of Indigenous Peoples by a vote of 144 to 4. The Declaration recognizes that indigenous peoples have rights, on an individual and collective basis, to self-determination, non-discrimination, property, and equality, among other things. President Obama expressed the United States' support for the Declaration in 2010, and many advocates have turned to the challenge of bringing federal law and policy into compliance with it. See Walter Echo-Hawk, In the Light of Justice: The Rise of Human Rights in Native America and the UN Declaration on the Rights of Indigenous Peoples (2013).

2. WHY STUDY INDIAN LAW?

For the law student, the field of Indian law presents an opportunity to learn about American Indians, their cultures and aspirations, through the realm of law. More broadly, this field of study allows students to deepen their understanding of the U.S. legal system. The foundational cases of Indian law, dealing with the nation's early acquisition of lands and allocation of governance rights, are among the foundational cases of American law.

Indian law integrates legal history and contemporary doctrine across fields of law and other branches of academic inquiry. Treaties and cases hundreds of years old continue to allocate rights and responsibilities among the United States and tribes. Students must understand both the historical context for the treaties and legislative enactments undertaken in certain periods of Congressional policy toward Indians, as well as their broader context in U.S. and global history. How, for example, did the Supreme Court's struggle to gain institutional legitimacy in the 1800's affect the Indian cases that ultimately led to the removal of tribes from their homelands? How should we understand the impact of worldwide concerns about communism and fascism on Congress' policy of tribal "Termination" in the 1940's and 1950's? In what ways did the civil rights movement of the 1960's impact American Indian rights, and how is Indian activism and advocacy changing in today's era of the internet and social media?

Given that treaties and other instruments retain their legal force today, students must also be able to consider and analyze how these historical instruments should apply in contemporary circumstances, a challenge not unlike constitutional law and interpretation, but specific to Indian contexts. The so-called "Boldt decision" of the 1970's had to do exactly that, interpreting language from 1850's treaties reserving to tribes the rights to take fish "at all usual and accustomed grounds and stations * * * in common with all citizens of the Territory." United States v. Washington, 384 F.Supp. 312 (W.D. Wash. 1974). What did that language mean in 1850 and 1970? What does it mean today?

In Indian law, history often meets modernity, and the law often engages with society. Today's tribes and tribal members are engaged in hunting and fishing and the development of technology infrastructure on reservations. They are working to address challenges including domestic violence and the revitalization of tribal languages. As a result, Indian law raises cutting edge questions in criminal law, property and intellectual property, contracts and commercial law, taxation, environmental law, and international human rights. Indian law also demands that the student or lawyer be able to integrate interdisciplinary materials from anthropology (as in religious freedoms cases), sociology (child welfare, juvenile justice, and domestic violence cases), and the sciences (cases about environmental regulation in Indian country), as various cases in this book will reveal.

From a theoretical perspective, Indian law raises some of the most fundamental questions about the American democratic experiment. The Supreme Court's earliest cases had to address the question of whether the Rule of Law would triumph over political expediency, or more explicitly whether treaties and constitutional provisions establishing federal supremacy in Indian affairs, would be able to protect tribal rights against the power and desires of land-hungry states and individuals. Throughout the centuries, Indian law has continued to pose questions of institutionalism, including whether the Court, as the politically insulated branch, or Congress, with its democratic accountability, is better situated to address the vulnerable status of Indian tribes.

Today's tribal advocates are further struggling with seeming tension between the status of tribes as political entities, expressly regulated by the Constitution's Commerce and Treaty Clauses, and notions of equal protection and due process that would seem to require formal equality across races and other protected classes. Does our legal system have room for a pluralistic approach to Indian affairs that recognizes tribes as collective polities while also addressing discrimination against Indians, other groups, and individuals based on race? When it comes to sovereignty, moreover, what does it mean for tribal sovereignty to be both inherent in tribal existence and peoplehood and subject to Congressional adjustment?

From a critical lawyering perspective, how should contemporary lawyers address the fraught history of Indian law, including a set of foundational principles whose articulation by the Supreme Court invoked the Court's perception of Indian "savagery" as a basis for their special "dependent" status and the federal government's attendant obligations to protect them? Can we reconcile, or reform, this colonizing legal history with contemporary norms of non-discrimination and self-determination? See Robert A. Williams, Jr., Like a Loaded Weapon: The Rehnquist Court, Indian Rights, and the Legal History of Racism in America (2005); Savage Anxieties: The Invention of Western Civilization (2012).

And finally, as indigenous peoples increasingly assert themselves in the international legal order, federal Indian law raises major questions of human rights. In realms ranging from land reform to family welfare, indigenous peoples across the world are insisting on rights to equality, property, and self-determination, as well as to be free from violence and oppression. Are these rights best articulated in terms of global struggles for minority rights, defined along lines of race, religion, or class, or as the political claims of "peoples"? How should the United States, with its longstanding commitment to national sovereignty, begin to understand and comply with international norms on the rights of the indigenous peoples within its borders? As in many areas, these pressing questions of Indian law resonate with broader issues facing lawyers and legal institutions. See Stephen Breyer, The World and the Court: American Law and the New Global Realities (2015).

The response of the legal system to Indian issues tells a great deal about that system and about the tenor and contemporary morality of society. Indian legal rights are among the oldest in our society. Before the arrival of explorers and settlers, tribes had their own pre-existing practices of property and self-government. The United States confirmed certain tribal rights, as well as the power of the tribes to bargain away others, as a matter of federal law. This process provided a means for the occupation and sovereignty of the United States to be extended across the continent. Our legal system reveres ancient rights so that challenges to venerable principles tend to be unusual. Nevertheless, politicians and even judges may urge abrogation of Indian rights on the basis that they are "old" or "inequitable." Is it a ground for ignoring or doing away with a family's century old, munificent trust that it is too old or that it unfairly benefits only a few persons? Would Congress take back the huge grants of land given to railroads because the quid pro quo—assistance in opening up transportation to the West—has long since been given?

Ultimately, one should ask whether Felix Cohen, perhaps the greatest of all Indian lawyers, was making an overdrawn point about the old promises when he discussed the role of Indian law in our public law system:

> [T]he Indian plays much the same role in our American society that the Jews played in Germany. Like the miner's canary, the Indian marks the shift from fresh air to poison gas in our political atmosphere; and our treatment of Indians, even more than our treatment of other minorities, reflects the rise and fall in our democratic faith.

Felix S. Cohen, *The Erosion of Indian Rights, 1950–53*, 62 Yale L.J. 348, 390 (1953). We might also ask from whose perspective the Indian appears to be a miner's canary and how Indian people themselves envision their role in the U.S. legal system. See Rennard Strickland, *Yellow Bird's Song: The Message of America's First Native American Attorney*, 29 Tulsa L.J. 247, 247 (1994) (recounting the story of Cherokee attorney John Rollin Ridge (1827–1867)).

3.   INDIAN LAWYERING IN THE ERA OF SELF-DETERMINATION AND NATION BUILDING

Consistent with the intellectual challenges it poses as a course of academic study, Indian law also offers a very rich field in which to consider the practice of law. Lawyers work on Indian law issues in myriad settings, including tribal, state, and federal governments, private law firms of all sizes, small business and multinational corporations. Indian lawyers may be public defenders, prosecutors, deal-makers, or First Amendment lawyers. Indians are hiring attorneys to advance social justice and negotiate complex financial arrangements. As Mohawk tribal member and attorney Dale White recently observed, "Indian law is definitely a 'growth industry.'" See Dale T. White, *Tribal Law Practice: From the Outside to the Inside*, 10 Kan.J.L.&Pub.Pol'y 505, 509 (2000). The growth of Indian lawyering has led scholars to consider professional and ethical aspects of Indian law practice, a major theme of this casebook.

KRISTEN A. CARPENTER AND ELI WALD, LAWYERING FOR GROUPS: THE CASE OF AMERICAN INDIAN TRIBAL ATTORNEYS

81 Fordham L.Rev. 3085, 3091–93, 3108–09, 3126–30, 3162 (2013).

American Indian tribes had, by the time Europeans arrived in the "new world," already been living according to their own traditional laws and cultural norms for thousands of years. Tribal leaders, who traditionally performed internal dispute resolution and external diplomacy functions, found themselves on the front lines in treaty negotiations with European nations in the seventeenth century.

Some of tribes' first experiences with Anglo-American lawyers came in mid-nineteenth century litigation over treaty rights, with mixed results. * * * Today, tribal governments, particularly through their executive and legislative branches, engage lawyers to represent the tribe on a variety of matters, from litigation and business dealings with third parties, to internal legal reform and institution building. Tribes have formed offices of in-house counsel and attorneys general, whose responsibilities may be enumerated in the tribal constitution or legislative code.

* * *

As Judge William Canby has succinctly explained, today's tribal attorney is "often a major influence on tribal affairs." It is against this backdrop that we [consider the professional and ethical challenges facing tribal attorneys]. Many tribal rules of professional responsibility borrow from the ABA's Model Rules, and for the most part they initially seem to work relatively well in guiding lawyers who represent tribes. And yet complex challenges of culture, history, constituency, agency, representation, and identity arise. First, the very understanding of the role of the lawyer as zealous advocate in an adversarial system may be culturally and politically antithetical to tribal societies in which the operative norms favor the collective well-being of the group and values such as harmony and balance. Furthermore, the assumption that the client seeks to pursue its autonomy and advance its goals in an adversarial fashion to the exclusion of others does not always reflect tribal objectives.

Second, any legal representation of American Indian tribes confronts the weight of history in which law has often been used to legitimize egregious moments of European conquest and American colonization— such as the dispossession of Indian lands, relocation of Indian people, and destruction of Indian religions and culture. During various periods of federal Indian policy, the injection of Anglo-American law into tribal communities has been an explicit tool of government "assimilation" programs designed to eradicate tribal cultures and governing structures. [The authors describe a complicated picture of the relationship among tribes and their lawyers during periods of federal Indian policy from the 1800's through the 1970's].

* * *

Yet, in today's period of tribal "self-determination," in which tribal people are revitalizing and decolonizing all aspects of their governments and institutions, the position and responsibilities of the tribal lawyer have also begun to change. Tribal lawyers are now called on to assist with not only treaty rights litigation but also negotiating the contours of government-to-government relationships with states and the federal government; economic development and financial matters; the process of internal legal reform, including the revision of tribal codes and constitutions, and the rebuilding of tribal dispute resolution institutions; and even human rights advocacy in international forums. Through these activities, which constitute the "decolonization" of federal Indian law and the "revitalization" of Indian communities, tribes are identifying the core competencies and values they seek in legal representation and taking the initiative to license and hire attorneys who meet those standards.

* * *

The practice of Indian law is still growing and changing. [The Native American Rights Fund], along with the [Indian Law Resource Center], legal services organizations, and dozens of law firms, both large and small, are providing legal counsel directly to tribes—in tribal, state, federal, and international matters. Many federally recognized tribes have in-house legal counsel, and many have entire legal departments and offices, both on reservations and in Washington, D.C. The number of American Indian lawyers has grown from estimates of twenty-five total in the 1960s to over 3,000 in 2006. The Federal Bar Association and ABA both have sections devoted to American Indian Law, and there is a very active network of professionals in the field, including national, state, and tribal bar associations devoted to Indian law practice.

The self-determination movement continues to thrive in Indian country, shaping both external relations with federal and state governments and the internal revitalization of tribal law, institutions, and societies. There have been major setbacks, such as the Supreme Court's backlash against American Indian rights from 1988 to the present, but overall this is a time of unprecedented growth and opportunity in American Indian law. It is this legal landscape, with all of its professional opportunities and challenges that the contemporary tribal lawyer inhabits.

* * *

Tribal leaders and scholars alike agree that some of the most important work in tribal lawyering is in the project of legal reform and institution building. As Matthew Fletcher has argued, "[T]he days of making pie-in-the-sky arguments in federal court—and winning—are behind us. There has to be another method of preserving and enhancing Indian and Indian tribal rights than pounding down the courthouse door. It is these strategies that Indian lawyers can assist more than any others." In addition to their work "on the front lines" of major litigation, Fletcher argues, tribal lawyers are critically involved in "the development of tribal law and political structures."

During the era of self-determination, tribes are reclaiming historic governing functions and updating them consistent with contemporary circumstances Tribal lawyers may be deeply involved in constitutional reform, setting up court systems and drafting or revising tribal codes. Many current needs directly reflect changes occurring in the self-determination era. Since 1988, tribes have been able to contract with the federal government to administer their own federally funded hospitals, schools, and other programs. They also may be eligible to assume increased regulatory powers over natural resources and environmental regulation within their reservations. As a result of the 2010 passage of the Tribal Law and Order Act, tribes are revising their criminal codes to provide for increased sentences and procedural safeguards for defendants. To these institution-building tasks, tribal lawyers bring important skills of policy analysis, legislative drafting, constitutional and statutory interpretation, contract preparation, and so on.

* * *

To be effective in tribal legal reform in an era of self-determination, tribal lawyers must be mindful of the relationship between tribal culture and government, and the ascendant norm of revitalizing tribal customary law for contemporary contexts. And it is here again that the lawyer's competence, as defined by [the ABA Rules], must include—but regrettably does not incorporate—not only facility with legal institution building but also knowledge about, and respect for, the particular tribal culture. As the Pueblo lawyer and law professor Christine Zuni Cruz has put it, those who seek to work with tribal people must seek "cultural literacy," including the ability to "critically analyze the social and political structures that inform * * * realities."

* * *

[Similarly, in their work on Native American Nation Building] Political economists Joe Kalt and Stephen Cornell coined the term "cultural match" to describe a contemporary tribal government whose structure and values sufficiently correspond with traditional norms to make it functional. As a diagnostic tool, the concept of cultural match is very helpful in explaining why certain forms of government do not work for certain tribes—for example, a model of centralized government with a singular powerful head of state will often present problems for a tribe maintaining a tradition of decentralized, local leadership held by multiple family groups. Even with this insight, however, it is difficult to turn to the challenge of what Kalt and Cornell call "nation building" or the actual work of building institutions that will simultaneously reflect the traditional values of tribes and function in a changing and modern society.

* * *

It is precisely in this most sensitive of functions—the decolonization of tribal law and the reassertion of tribal culture—that tribal lawyers may bring the most to the table. But how can they do it? * * * Robert Porter, a Seneca lawyer and law professor who recently served as President of the Seneca Nation, and then joined an international law firm in New York, * * * explains, "While the tribal client must initiate efforts to revise and reform tribal societies, it is the tribal lawyer who usually does the heavy lifting in terms of effectuating the details of these initiatives." This heavy lifting requires the tribal lawyer to be particularly attentive to certain risks and in some ways to depart from conventional legal training. As Porter articulates:

> If the tribal lawyer does nothing other than, for example, borrow the state domestic relations law when drafting the tribal domestic relations law, the lawyer is doing nothing other than advising the tribe to replicate itself in the image of the dominant society. * * * Because of the way lawyers are trained, this mistake can be easily made. Going to a book answer—a book of state laws—is what the Anglo-American-trained lawyers are taught. Mindlessly borrowing state laws, especially laws governing social behavior, can, in my view, be the equivalent of the forced assimilation efforts to destroy tribal societies seen in the nineteenth century. The difference here is that it is self-induced and perpetually reinforcing, rather than externally imposed.

To realize the potential of decolonization in the law reform process, Porter urges that:

> [T]ribal lawyers should have an added professional obligation to their clients, in addition to their advocating, counseling, and negotiation functions. This obligation is the obligation to help heal the injustice and wrong-doing, the broken social, legal, political, and economic systems within our communities, and the injuries inflicted by colonization.

* * * Professor Duane Champagne notes that for many tribes, there will be resistance to any reform and changes may be modest. Traditional tribal governance may have severely eroded over the generations, such that it is not possible to recover it. Moreover, traditional institutions may not have the capacity or orientation to deal with the market economy or national polity. * * * As Keith Richotte points out, tribal advocates may not be serving their clients well if they project an irreconcilable conflict between "traditional" and "colonial" government. The modern reality of most tribes requires advocates to embrace legal pluralism and the possibility of multiple, contested meanings.

Some tribes will retain their existing constitutions or codes as a base and the lawyer may be constrained to suggesting the places where the tribe is able to make certain provisions more reflective of tribal culture, remove federal influence, or simply to improve administration. Other tribes may attempt more comprehensive reform, for example through a constitutional convention, or the creation of new institutions such as Peacemaker Courts or Elders Council for dispute resolution and juvenile matters.

* * *

As lawyers and clients evaluate how best to use the power of the law and legal profession, there is perhaps something to be learned from the experience of tribal lawyers. In this vein, Rennard Strickland once retold the following story:

> There was an Osage legend or prophecy which said that the white man would bring something with him that was of great value but that he would not know how to use it and that the Indian would take it and add to it and change it and that it would then be good and true and pure. Some say that this was Christianity and that when the Indian joined peyote with this new Christian religion that the prophecy was fulfilled. I think the same may be true of the statute and case law which the white man brought. Our challenge is to take that law and add to it and change it so that law can be good and true and pure not only for Indian people but for all people.

SECTION B. AMERICAN INDIANS TODAY—AN OVERVIEW

An important step in the study of Indian law is to gain some understanding of the state of Indian tribes, Indian individuals, and Indian lands, cultures, resources. American Indians are a heterogeneous group of peoples with many differences of culture, language, land-base, economic development, and other facts. In all of these respects, for example, the Mashpee Wampanoag tribe in Massachusetts, is quite different from, for example, the San Carlos Apache in Arizona. While observing some commonalities among tribes, it is critically important to give attention to the particular circumstances of each and avoid overgeneralizing.

This section and the sources cited in it provide only a starting point for understanding the situation of Indians and Indian tribes. Plainly there is no substitute for spending a great amount of time with Indian people and on the reservations. Students can supplement their studies with internet resources giving them a window into the daily affairs of tribes, from legal developments to cultural events. Daily coverage of legal and news events is available on the websites of TurtleTalk, Indianz.com, and Indian Country Today.

1. *Indian Tribes.* Tribalism remains a driving force in both Indian culture and law. American Indians typically think of themselves as members of a particular tribe first and as Indians second. Treaties were negotiated with tribes, and most Indian land is tribally-owned. The courts have justified special laws for Indians on the ground that Congress is dealing not with a racial minority but rather with political entities—tribes.

There are 567 federally recognized tribes; 229 of them are village groups in Alaska. Altogether, there are 322 federally recognized Indian reservations. The land holdings of the tribes vary widely. Not all Indian tribes in the United States are federally recognized. Congress terminated the federal relationship with more than 100 tribes during the 1950s. In most cases, their land was sold and they were made ineligible for special programs directed toward Indians. Congress has since restored several terminated tribes to federal status but termination remains in force for others. There is another category of tribes without formal ties to the federal government: the tribes and groups referred to as "non-federally recognized," which means either that federal administrators have concluded that they are not entitled to participate in BIA-operated programs or that the tribe is still awaiting a determination of that status through the federal acknowledgement process.

2. *Indian Reservations.* Reservations vary greatly in size and geography. The Navajo reservation consists of more than 17 million acres of high elevation, grazing and red rock land in Arizona, New Mexico, and Utah—an area larger than West Virginia. In North and South Dakota, the four big Sioux reservations amount to about 5 million acres of mostly prairie. In contrast, the smallest reservation is less than 100 acres, and a few small reservations have no residents at all.

The map on these pages shows the location of Indian reservations. Most reservations are west of the one-hundredth meridian, a north-south line running through the center of Nebraska. Consequently, high numbers of Indian law cases are heard by the Eighth, Ninth, and Tenth Circuit Courts of Appeal.

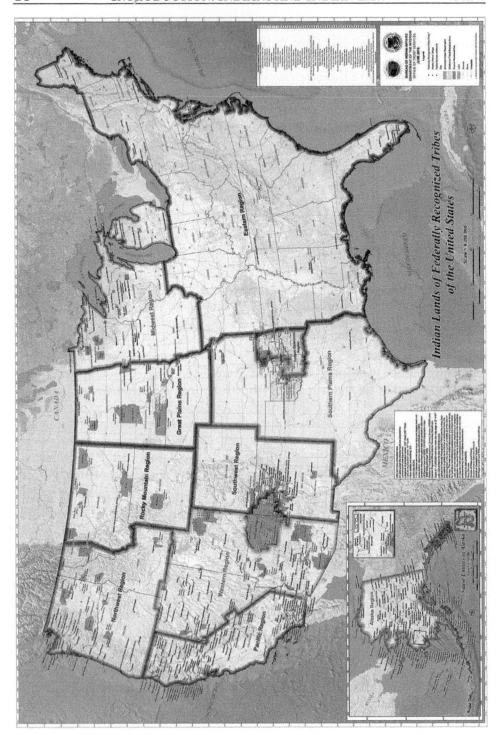

3. *Indian Population.* The 2000 and 2010 censuses collected more data on American Indians than previous censuses, allowing them, for

example, to identify with one or more racial group, and with one or more tribes. Tribes vary widely in population, as the table above reveals. Census data may differ from data from tribal governments and the Bureau of Indian Affairs, however, because the census is based on self-reporting.

The American Indian population has increased dramatically from 357,499 in 1950 to 1.96 million in 1990. In the 2000 census, 2.5 million people, reported as American Indian and an additional 1.6 million people reported as American Indian and at least one other race. To be sure, these enormous increases are based in part on changing census categories and norms of self-identification. But the birth rate among Indians has been very high in recent years as well. For 2000, for example, the birthrate for American Indians was 16.8 per 1000, somewhat higher than the 14.7 for the U.S. population as a whole.

In 2010, the annual population estimate for the American Indian population alone was 2.9 million and in combination with another race the total was 5.2 million. Here are the ways in which individuals identified on the 2010 census.

Table 7.
American Indian and Alaska Native Population by Selected Tribal Groupings: 2010
(For information on confidentiality protection, nonsampling error, and definitions, see www.census.gov/prod/cen2010/doc/sf1.pdf)

Tribal grouping	American Indian and Alaska Native alone		American Indian and Alaska Native in combination with one or more other races		American Indian and Alaska Native tribal grouping alone or in any combination[1]
	One tribal grouping reported	Two or more tribal groupings reported[1]	One tribal grouping reported	Two or more tribal groupings reported[1]	
Total	2,879,638	52,610	2,209,267	79,064	5,220,579
American Indian tribes, specified	1,935,363	96,770	1,211,938	153,180	3,397,251
Apache	63,193	6,501	33,303	8,813	111,810
Arapaho	8,014	388	2,084	375	10,861
Blackfeet	27,279	4,519	54,109	19,397	105,304
Canadian and French American Indian	6,433	618	6,981	790	14,822
Central American Indian	15,882	572	10,865	525	27,844
Cherokee	284,247	16,216	468,082	50,560	819,105
Cheyenne	11,375	1,118	5,311	1,247	19,051
Chickasaw	27,973	2,233	19,220	2,852	52,278
Chippewa	112,757	2,645	52,091	3,249	170,742
Choctaw	103,910	6,398	72,101	13,355	195,764
Colville	8,114	200	2,148	87	10,549
Comanche	12,284	1,187	8,131	1,728	23,330
Cree	2,211	739	4,023	1,010	7,983
Creek	48,352	4,596	30,618	4,766	88,332
Crow	10,332	528	3,309	1,034	15,203
Delaware	7,843	372	9,439	610	18,264
Hopi	12,580	2,064	3,013	680	18,327
Houma	8,169	71	2,438	90	10,768
Iroquois	40,570	1,891	34,490	4,051	81,002
Kiowa	9,437	918	2,947	485	13,787
Lumbee	62,306	651	10,039	695	73,691
Menominee	8,374	253	2,330	176	11,133
Mexican American Indian	121,221	2,329	49,670	2,274	175,494
Navajo	286,731	8,285	32,918	4,195	332,129
Osage	8,938	1,125	7,090	1,423	18,576
Ottawa	7,272	776	4,274	711	13,033
Paiute	9,340	865	3,135	427	13,767
Pima	22,040	1,165	3,116	334	26,655
Potawatomi	20,412	462	12,249	648	33,771
Pueblo	49,695	2,331	9,568	946	62,540
Puget Sound Salish	14,320	215	5,540	185	20,260
Seminole	14,080	2,368	12,447	3,076	31,971
Shoshone	7,852	610	3,969	571	13,002
Sioux	112,176	4,301	46,964	6,669	170,110
South American Indian	20,901	479	25,015	838	47,233
Spanish American Indian	13,460	298	6,012	181	19,951
Tohono O'Odham	19,522	725	3,033	198	23,478
Ute	7,435	785	2,802	469	11,491
Yakama	8,786	310	2,207	224	11,527
Yaqui	21,679	1,516	8,183	1,217	32,595
Yuman	7,727	551	1,642	169	10,089
All other American Indian tribes	270,141	12,606	135,032	11,850	429,629
American Indian tribes, not specified[2]	131,943	117	102,188	72	234,320
Alaska Native tribes, specified	98,892	4,194	32,992	2,772	138,850
Alaskan Athabascan	15,623	804	5,531	526	22,484
Aleut	11,920	723	6,108	531	19,282
Inupiat	24,859	877	7,051	573	33,360
Tlingit-Haida	15,256	859	9,331	634	26,080
Tsimshian	2,307	240	1,010	198	3,755
Yup'ik	28,927	691	3,961	310	33,889
Alaska Native tribes, not specified[3]	19,731	173	9,896	133	29,933
American Indian or Alaska Native tribes, not specified[4]	693,709	—	852,253	1	1,545,963

— Represents zero.

[1] The numbers by American Indian and Alaska Native tribal grouping do not add to the total American Indian and Alaska Native population. This is because the American Indian and Alaska Native tribal groupings are tallies of the number of American Indian and Alaska Native responses rather than the number of American Indian or Alaska Native respondents. Respondents reporting several American Indian or Alaska Native groups are counted several times. For example, a respondent reporting "Cherokee and Navajo" would be included in the Cherokee as well as the Navajo numbers.

[2] Includes respondents who wrote in an American Indian tribe not specified in the American Indian and Alaska Native Tribal Detailed Classification List for the 2010 Census or wrote in the generic term "American Indian."

[3] Includes respondents who wrote in an Alaska Native tribe not specified in the American Indian and Alaska Native Tribal Detailed Classification List for the 2010 Census or wrote in the generic term "Alaska Native."

[4] Includes respondents who checked the "American Indian or Alaska Native" response category on the census questionnaire.

Source: U.S. Census Bureau, 2010 Census special tabulation.

U.S. Census Bureau

In terms of population distribution, significant numbers are found in both urban and reservation communities.

Table 3.

Ten Places With the Largest Number of American Indians and Alaska Natives: 2010
(For information on confidentiality protection, nonsampling error, and definitions, see www.census.gov/prod/cen2010/doc/pl94-171.pdf)

Place	Total population	American Indian and Alaska Native					
		Alone or in combination		Alone		In combination	
		Rank	Number	Rank	Number	Rank	Number
New York, NY	8,175,133	1	111,749	1	57,512	1	54,237
Los Angeles, CA	3,792,621	2	54,236	3	28,215	2	26,021
Phoenix, AZ	1,445,632	3	43,724	2	32,366	7	11,358
Oklahoma City, OK	579,999	4	36,572	7	20,533	3	16,039
Anchorage, AK	291,826	5	36,062	5	23,130	6	12,932
Tulsa, OK	391,906	6	35,990	6	20,617	4	15,173
Albuquerque, NM	545,852	7	32,571	4	25,087	16	7,484
Chicago, IL	2,695,598	8	26,933	10	13,337	5	13,596
Houston, TX	2,099,451	9	25,521	8	14,997	8	10,524
San Antonio, TX	1,327,407	10	20,137	11	11,800	11	8,337
Tucson, AZ	520,116	11	19,903	9	14,154	24	5,749
Philadelphia, PA	1,526,006	13	17,495	25	6,996	9	10,499
San Diego, CA	1,307,402	12	17,865	23	7,696	10	10,169

Source: U.S. Census Bureau, *2010 Census Redistricting Data (Public Law 94-171) Summary File*, Table P1.

Table 4.

Ten Places With the Highest Percentage of American Indians and Alaska Natives: 2010
(For information on confidentiality protection, nonsampling error, and definitions, see www.census.gov/prod/cen2010/doc/pl94-171.pdf)

Place[1]	Total population	American Indian and Alaska Native					
		Alone or in combination		Alone		In combination	
		Rank	Percentage of total population	Rank	Percentage of total population	Rank	Percentage of total population
Anchorage, AK	291,826	1	12.4	1	7.9	1	4.4
Tulsa, OK	391,906	2	9.2	2	5.3	2	3.9
Norman, OK	110,925	3	8.1	3	4.7	3	3.3
Oklahoma City, OK	579,999	4	6.3	7	3.5	4	2.8
Billings, MT	104,170	5	6.0	5	4.4	14	1.5
Albuquerque, NM	545,852	6	6.0	4	4.6	28	1.4
Green Bay, WI	104,057	7	5.4	6	4.1	36	1.3
Tacoma, WA	198,397	8	4.0	16	1.8	5	2.1
Tempe, AZ	161,719	9	3.9	8	2.9	73	1.0
Tucson, AZ	520,116	10	3.8	9	2.7	52	1.1
Sioux Falls, SD	153,888	13	3.6	10	2.7	79	0.9
Spokane, WA	208,916	11	3.8	15	2.0	6	1.8
Eugene, OR	156,185	24	2.8	55	1.0	7	1.8
Topeka, KS	127,473	17	3.1	27	1.4	8	1.7
Sacramento, CA	466,488	23	2.8	46	1.1	9	1.7
Santa Rosa, CA	167,815	15	3.3	18	1.7	10	1.6

[1] Places of 100,000 or more total population. The 2010 Census showed 282 places in the United States with 100,000 or more population. They included 273 incorporated places (including 5 city-county consolidations) and 9 census designated places that were not legally incorporated.

Source: U.S. Census Bureau, *2010 Census Redistricting Data (Public Law 94-171) Summary File*, Table P1.

Table 6.
American Indian Reservations and Alaska Native Village Statistical Areas With Largest American Indian and Alaska Native Populations: 2010
(For information on confidentiality protection, nonsampling error, and definitions, see www.census.gov/prod/cen2010/doc/pl94-171.pdf)

Area		American Indian and Alaska Native				Not American Indian and Alaska Native alone or in combination
	Total population	Alone or in combination	Alone	In combination	
American Indian Reservation					
Navajo Nation Reservation and Off-Reservation Trust Land, AZ–NM–UT . . .	173,667	169,321	166,824	2,497	4,346
Pine Ridge Reservation, SD–NE.	18,834	16,906	16,580	326	1,928
Fort Apache Reservation, AZ	13,409	13,014	12,870	144	395
Gila River Indian Reservation, AZ.	11,712	11,251	10,845	406	461
Osage Reservation, OK.	47,472	9,920	6,858	3,062	37,552
San Carlos Reservation, AZ	10,068	9,901	9,835	66	167
Rosebud Indian Reservation and Off-Reservation Trust Land, SD	10,869	9,809	9,617	192	1,060
Tohono O'odham Nation Reservation and Off-Reservation Trust Land, AZ . . .	10,201	9,278	9,139	139	923
Blackfeet Indian Reservation and Off-Reservation Trust Land, MT	10,405	9,149	8,944	205	1,256
Flathead Reservation, MT.	28,359	9,138	7,042	2,096	19,221
Alaska Native Village Statistical Area					
Knik Alaska Native village statistical area	65,768	6,582	3,529	3,053	59,186
Bethel Alaska Native village statistical area	6,080	4,334	3,953	381	1,746
Kenaitze Alaska Native village statistical area.	32,902	3,417	2,001	1,416	29,485
Barrow Alaska Native village statistical area.	4,212	2,889	2,577	312	1,323
Ketchikan Alaska Native village statistical area.	12,742	2,605	1,692	913	10,137
Kotzebue Alaska Native village statistical area	3,201	2,585	2,355	230	616
Nome Alaska Native village statistical area.	3,681	2,396	1,994	402	1,285
Chickaloon Alaska Native village statistical area.	23,087	2,373	1,369	1,004	20,714
Dillingham Alaska Native village statistical area	2,378	1,583	1,333	250	795
Sitka Alaska Native village statistical area	4,480	1,240	855	385	3,240

Note: In this table, the American Indian and Alaska Native alone-or-in-combination population and the not American Indian and Alaska Native alone-or-in-combination population add to the total population of the reservation or village statistical area. The rankings of the American Indian reservations and Alaska Native village statistical areas are based on the American Indian and Alaska Native alone-or-in-combination population.

Source: U.S. Census Bureau, *2010 Census Redistricting Data (Public Law 94-171) Summary File*, Table P1.

Geographically, many Indian populations remain in the West, though not exclusively so.

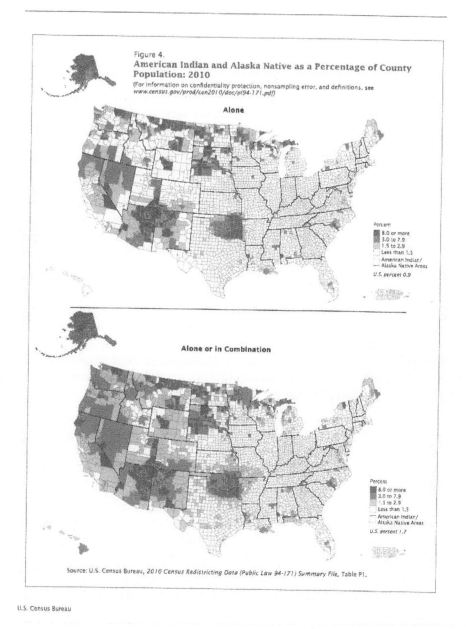

Figure 4.
American Indian and Alaska Native as a Percentage of County Population: 2010
(For information on confidentiality protection, nonsampling error, and definitions, see www.census.gov/prod/cen2010/doc/pl94-171.pdf)

Alone

Alone or in Combination

Source: U.S. Census Bureau, 2010 Census Redistricting Data (Public Law 94-171) Summary File, Table P1.

U.S. Census Bureau

4.   *Economic Conditions*. In 2008, the Census Bureau reported that 24 percent of all Indians (approximately 800,000) were living below the poverty level (based on a 1998–2000 average). However, that figure is down from 1990, when 31 percent of all Indians were below the poverty level. As of 2000, the unemployment rate on reservations was thirteen percent compared to 6.3 percent for the overall US average. However, unemployment rates vary dramatically between reservations. The

Kickapoo reservation in Texas reported a 70 percent unemployment rate, the Navajo Nation's unemployment rate was 25 percent, and the Cherokee Nation's unemployment rate was below the national average at 5.8 percent.

Poverty is evident in the living conditions on most reservations. In 2003, a U.S. Commission on Civil Rights' report revealed that 40 percent of on-reservation housing units were in substandard condition and 50 percent of houses lacked complete plumbing facilities. The report estimated an immediate need for more than 200,000 new housing units for families currently on reservations.

Although the statistics document continued poverty, they also show that economic conditions among Indians are improving. The numbers of Indian businesspeople, doctors, and lawyers, although still relatively small, have surged. The U.S. Department of Commerce reported that, based on 2002 data, there were 201,000 firms owned by American Indians and Alaska Natives. These entities generated 26.9 billion in gross receipts and had 191,000 paid employees.

An analysis by the Harvard Project on American Indian Economic Development identifies some of the economic improvement in Indian country during a period of increasing tribal self-determination and the expansion of gaming activities. Jonathan B. Taylor and Joseph P. Kalt, *American Indians on Reservations: A Databook of Socioeconomic Change between the 1990 and 2000 Censuses* (2005), www.ksg.harvard.edu/hpaied/ key.htm. For the decade ending in 2000 they report:

- Real (inflation-adjusted) per capita income of reservation Indians rose by about one-third. For both gaming and non-gaming tribes, the overall rate of income growth was significantly higher than the 11 percent increase in real per capita income for the U.S. as a whole.

- Family poverty dropped eight-tenths of a percentage point for the U.S. as a whole. But in Indian country, Indian family poverty rates dropped by seven percent or more in non-gaming areas, and by about ten per cent in gaming areas.

- U.S. unemployment dropped by half a percentage point during the period. Indian unemployment rates dropped by about two-and-a-half percent in non-gaming areas and by more than five per cent in gaming areas.

- Housing overcrowding on the reservation decreased and the percentage of American Indians living in homes with plumbing increased significantly in both gaming and non-gaming areas.

- The proportion of adult Indians on reservations with less than a ninth grade education declined substantially and the proportion of Indian adults with college degrees rose substantially.

5. *Health Conditions.* The formal health care system for American Indians, the Indian Health Service (IHS), was established in 1955 as part of the Public Health Service in the Department of Health and Human Services. In 2010, it served approximately 60 percent of the total American Indian population. The federal IHS system consists of 29 hospitals, 59 health centers, 28 health stations, and 4 school health centers. There are also 34 urban Indian health projects, which provide various types of health and referral services. IHS appropriations have not kept pace with health care costs, population growth, and inflation and IHS hospitals are chronically understaffed. Urban Indians are eligible for only limited health services and members of terminated and non-recognized tribes are not eligible for any.

Since the enactment of the 1975 Indian Self-Determination and Education Assistance Act (P.L. 93–638), tribes have had the option of managing IHS programs in their communities with federal funding. The 1976 Indian Health Care Improvement Act (IHCIA) (P.L. 94–437) allowed Medicaid and Medicare reimbursement for services in IHS facilities and authorized IHS to contract with urban Indian health services.

Over the past half century, the general health of American Indians improved. Life expectancy has increased steadily over the past two decades and is now 73.5 years: 69.4 years for men and 77.6 years for women. These statistics are still significantly lower than the life expectancy for Americans of all races. Perhaps the single most hopeful sign in the status of American Indian health is the infant mortality rate, which in 1955 was 62.7 (per 1000 live births) as opposed to 26.4 for the U.S. population as a whole. As of 2010, the infant mortality rate for American Indians was 8.3, contrasted with 6.7 for the entire population.

The number of HIV deaths for American Indians and Alaska Natives in 2005 was 10.6 per 100,000 persons—more than triple the 1999 rate. American Indians have a 40 percent higher rate of AIDS as compared to the white population. IHS has aggressively focused on preventing the spread of HIV/AIDS through policy projects, clinical testing, and education.

The IHCIA, the cornerstone legal authority for the provision of health care to American Indians and Alaska Natives, was made permanent when President Obama signed the the Patient Protection and Affordable Care Act of 2010. The authorization of appropriations for the IHCIA had expired in 2000, and while various versions of the bill were considered by Congress since then, the act now has no expiration date.

6.   *Education.*

With only minor exceptions the history of Indian education has been primarily the transmission of white American education, little altered, to the Indian child as a one-way process. The institution of the school is one that was imposed and controlled by non-Indian society * * * its goals primarily aimed at removing the child from his aboriginal culture and assimilating him into the dominant white culture.

Estelle Fuchs and Robert J. Havighurst, To Live on This Earth: American Indian Education 19 (1973).

Beginning with major legislation passed in the mid-1970s, the situation for Indian education has improved. The 1975 Indian Self-Determination and Education Assistance Act (P.L. 93–638), the 1978 Educational Amendments Act (P.L. 95–561), and the Tribally Controlled Schools Act of 1988 (P.L. 100–297) substantially restructured BIA- and tribally-operated schools, providing for more direct funding and local control. President Clinton's Executive Order 13096 (1998) and President Bush's Executive Order 13336 (2004) both declared support for tribal traditions, languages, and cultures as components of Indian education. Support for Indian education has increased, and the 2008 budget for Indian education was $1 billion, the highest appropriation ever.

At the 2000 census, there were 674,585 Indian children in preschool, kindergarten, elementary or high school. Under the Johnson-O'Malley Act of 1934, the BIA provides funding to public school districts across the nation to meet special needs of more than 271,000 Indian children in their schools.

In 2010, less than 7 percent (48,000) of American Indian students nationwide attended federally operated schools, in contrast to the days when the controversial BIA boarding schools were the only educational institutions available for a large majority of Indian children. As of 2016, the Bureau of Indian Education (BIE) reported that it oversees a total of 183 elementary, secondary, and residential schools, as well as peripheral dormitories, across 23 states. Of these, 130 schools are tribally controlled under P.L. 93–638 Indian Self Determination Contracts or P.L. 100–297 Tribally Controlled Grant Schools Act, and 53 schools are operated by the Bureau of Indian Education. The BIE also oversees two post-secondary schools: Haskell Indian Nations University and Southwestern Indian Polytechnic Institute.

New trends in Indian education policy have paid dividends. Bilingual programs have been instituted. Curricula have been changed—by Indians—to include Indian history and culture. Increased numbers of Indian teachers and teachers' aides have been hired. Tribal elders have been brought into the classrooms as outside experts. These progressive developments, aimed at reversing the negative self-image of Indian children, have been most apparent in the tribal schools and in other "Indian-controlled" schools, but they have also made their mark in most other schools attended by Indians. A long road remains to be traveled before it can be said that Indian children in elementary and secondary schools are receiving quality educations. But a consensus seems to have developed as to the proper approach. In recent years, fully one-third of the BIA's budget has been dedicated to education.

As of 2006, there were 181,100 American Indians enrolled in colleges and universities throughout the country, more than twice the enrollment in 1976. In 2008, according to the U.S. Department of Education, 14 percent of all American Indians over age 25 had completed undergraduate or professional degrees, compared with 24.4 percent for the U.S. population as a whole. Approximately 57,000 Indians have a graduate or professional degree including degrees in medicine and law. For 2010, $34.5 million was appropriated to the BIA for scholarships. In addition, nongovernmental funding for American Indians students has increased substantially over the past ten years.

College enrollment for Indians has been enhanced by the growth of Indian-controlled junior colleges, a movement that began in 1969 when the Navajo Nation opened the Navajo Community College. In 1978, Congress passed the Tribally Controlled Community Colleges Assistance Act (P.L. 95–471) and the BIA now provides grants to tribes for 26 such institutions totaling $64 million in 2010.

One of the longest-running retention programs for minority students in the country is the Pre-Law Summer Institute, administered by the American Indian Law Center at the University of New Mexico School of Law. When the program began in the mid-1960s, an informal survey identified only twenty-five American Indian attorneys nationwide and fifteen law students. Today there are over 3,000 Indian attorneys of whom 1,200 have been assisted by the program. Among the program's alumni and scholarship recipients have been numerous tribal court justices, law professors, tribal attorneys general, a state attorney general, a U.S. Attorney, four Deputy Assistant Secretaries in the Department of the Interior, and three Assistant Secretaries for Indian Affairs. See Mark Fogarty, *AILC Program Jumpstarted Indian Lawyer Boom,* Indian Country Today, June 16, 2003.

Historically, failures in Indian education have been aggravated by the placement of Indian children in non-Indian foster or adoptive homes by private non-Indian organizations and by state agencies. The premise, backed by state courts, which sometimes had jurisdiction over such cases, was that Indian children would benefit by growing up in non-Indian homes leading to a pattern of extensive removal of Indian children from their homes. Major legislation to counteract this pattern and sometimes tragic results was enacted in the form of the far-reaching Indian Child Welfare Act of 1978, recognizing primary jurisdiction over such cases as belonging to tribal courts.

7.   *Indian Land Ownership.* Much of Indian law deals with lands and resources, and jurisdiction over them. Today, tribal land holdings have increased to 67.2 million acres in the lower 48 states, a 34 percent increase in net Indian lands. Approximately 56.2 million acres are held in trust by the United States for various Indian tribes and individuals. There are approximately 326 Indian land areas in the U.S. administered as federal Indian reservations (i.e., reservations, pueblos, rancherias, missions, villages, communities, etc.). The largest is the 16 million-acre Navajo Nation Reservation located in Arizona, New Mexico, and Utah. The smallest is a 1.32-acre parcel in California where the Pit River Tribe's cemetery is located. Many of the smaller reservations are less than 1,000 acres. Alaska Natives hold another 44 million acres as a result of the Alaska Native Claims Settlement Act of 1971. The land is held by twelve Native-run regional corporations and more than 200 Native village corporations. In all, American Indians groups hold about 4.2 percent of the land in the United States.

Land ownership patterns within the exterior boundaries of Indian reservations vary. In some cases, such as the North Carolina Cherokee and the White Mountain Apache in Arizona, all land within the reservation boundaries is owned by the tribe and held in trust by the United States. On other reservations most land within the boundaries is Indian-owned, but some is tribal land while other land has been allotted, i.e., transferred from tribal ownership to individuals, with the United States holding title for the tribe or the individual allottee (or heirs).

The majority of reservations include within their boundaries not only tribal trust land and trust allotments but a third category—land owned in fee title, usually by non-Indians. There are yet other categories on some reservations. The United States owns land and operates some government projects within reservation boundaries. States may sometimes possess inholdings. Non-Indians typically first acquired land within reservations during the 19th and 20th century allotment period when the government acquired and then opened tribal land for homesteading by non-Indians. In a few cases, the non-Indian land predominates. For example, thirty-six percent of the land within the boundaries of the Swinomish Reservation in Skagit County, Washington is owned by non-Indians in fee, and twenty percent of the Indian trust land is leased to non-Indians.

Tribes usually have jurisdiction over "Indian country," which includes all land within the exterior boundaries of the reservation. Thus, tribal regulatory jurisdiction may extend to an area significantly larger than the lands actually in Indian ownership—a significant responsibility for regulation, planning, and law enforcement.

Indian landholdings are growing partly as a result of tribal efforts to reacquire territory lost years ago. Some tribes use economic development revenues to buy back ancestral lands held in fee by non-Indians or allotments held in fractionated ownership by heirs of allottees. In addition, several land claim settlements, such as in the eastern states, have resulted in land transfers and purchases. The Native American Land Conservancy is a non-profit organization that assists in acquiring and protecting sacred lands and the Indian Country Conservancy is dedicated to buying conservation lands important to tribes.

Acquired land is often non-Indian fee land within or adjacent to the reservation borders. The tribes typically seek to place the purchased land in trust with the federal government to ensure that it is not taxed and is removed from the market. Integrating this land eliminates some of the jurisdictional problems caused by checkerboard land patterns. For instance, the Navajo Reservation grew from 15,432,170 acres in 1985 to 17,028,026 acres in 2005. Through efforts of the leadership of the Confederated Salish and Kootenai tribes, the Flathead Reservation in Montana grew from 564,452 acres to 806,699 acres. The Red Lake Band of Chippewa Indians in Minnesota added over 200,000 acres to their reservation resulting in a total landholding of 817,632 acres.

Tribes are also using revenue from natural resource development and gaming to protect cultural resources and restore ancestral lands to their reservations. In 2010, the Swinomish and the Washington State Parks and Recreation Commission worked together to purchase Kiket Island, a formerly privately-owned island within the boundaries of the Swinomish Reservation. The tribe and parks service have agreed to co-manage the area with the goal of protecting the valuable cultural and environmental resources of the island. In 2009, the Zuni Tribe used gaming revenues to reacquire 15,000 acres of land in northeastern Arizona as well as acquiring the rights to the use of an additional 8,500 acres. The land includes part of an ancient pilgrimage trail leading the sacred site, Zuni Heaven. Through the purchase, the Zuni are able to protect the pilgrimage trail from residential development encroaching upon the area.

8. *Tribal Natural Resources.* Indian land is typically thought of as left-over, arid waste land. That stereotype is not wholly accurate. When Congress passed the Wild and Scenic Rivers Act of 1968, the Wolf River on the Menominee Reservation was one of eight rivers designated for immediate inclusion in the National Wild and Scenic Rivers System. Justice Rehnquist has observed that the Wind River Reservation in Wyoming "straddles the Wind River, with its remarkable canyon, and lies in a mile-high basin at the foot of the Wind River Mountains, whose rugged,

glaciated peaks and ridges form a portion of the Continental Divide." The Makah Reservation on the Olympic Peninsula in Washington is located at the awesome entrance to the Strait of Juan de Fuca at the westernmost point of the lower 48 states. Many other such examples can be given.

Tribes own 5.3 million acres of commercial timber land, about one percent of the nation's total. Several tribes, including the Colville in Washington, the Red Lake Chippewa in Minnesota, and the Menominee in Wisconsin, hold valuable timber reserves. Indian timber land has been less intensively managed than Forest Service and Bureau of Land Management holdings. Complaints about poor BIA resource management have been manifested in several successful suits against the agency for mismanagement of tribal timber resources. Today, tribes increasingly are taking over management of their timber.

More than 43 million acres, or 77 percent of all Indian land outside Alaska, is classified as range land. Much of that land has been seriously overgrazed. In addition, most grazing land is leased to non-Indians, often at less than market value. The pattern is similar for the three million acres of agricultural land. However, the most productive crop land is leased to non-Indians, oftentimes at below-market rates.

Tribes have extensive water rights under a doctrine of "reserved rights." These water rights, usually superior to those of other users, have provoked intense conflicts involving the future of water-dependent communities and economic interests. Water rights issues are treated in Chapter 11.

Some tribes (a minority) hold land that is resource rich, and the tremendous potential for development of subsurface mineral rights has only begun to be realized. The Department of the Interior administers over 100,000 mineral leases on Indian lands. In 2010, there were 2,316 oil and gas leases managed by the Bureau of Land Management on tribal lands. The oil and gas leases on 2.3 million acres of land generated over $250 million in revenue to Indian land owners in 2009. With the exception of the Osage Nation, which manages its own leases and collects its own revenues, royalties are collected by the Minerals Revenue Management Service (MRMS) of the Department of the Interior and then distributed to tribes and individuals by the BIA. Indian mineral holders earned more than $350 million in royalties from mineral revenues in 2009.

Fish and wildlife resources are vital to the economy, food supply, and lifestyle on many reservations. In 1905, the United States Supreme Court noted that to Yakima tribal members the right to take fish was "not much less necessary to the existence of the Indians than the atmosphere they breathed," a statement that remains true for many tribes in the Pacific Northwest and the Great Lakes area. Fish propagation facilities have been developed on several reservations in Washington and Oregon. The

Quinault, Lummi, Swinomish, and several other tribes in the Pacific Northwest and Alaska own and operate fish canneries. Big game—primarily deer, elk, bear and antelope—continues to be a staple on dinner tables on the great majority of reservations.

Despite a lack of capital and many disappointments, a growing number of tribes are developing their recreation resources. See generally Stephen Cornell, Tourism and Economic Development: Considerations for Tribal Policy and Planning (Project Rep., The Harv. Project on Amer. Indian Econ. Dev., Energy and Envt'l Pol'y Center, John F. Kennedy Sch. of Gov't, Harv. U., Oct. 1989). The Navajo Nation operates a tribal park, similar to a national park, at the wondrous display of natural statues that is Monument Valley. Skiing facilities are run by the Mescalero Apache Tribe in New Mexico. Kah-Nee-Ta is a luxury resort owned and operated by the Warm Springs Tribe of Oregon. A great many tribes now issue tribal fishing and hunting licenses. The Uintah and Ouray Tribe of Utah offers blue ribbon Rocky Mountain trout streams, and elk from the White Mountain Apache Reservation in Eastern Arizona are prized big game trophies. Indian fishing and hunting rights are discussed in Chapter 12.

9. *Economic Development.* A movement of potentially transcendent force in an era of Native nation building is the growth of tribal economies. Notably, the most robust financial activities today are not directly tied to federal support. As Indians have prevailed in litigation establishing tribal governmental powers and limiting the reach of state tax and regulatory laws in Indian country, tribes have expanded both their sovereign and entrepreneurial functions.

Rapidly increasing numbers of tribes are engaging in major business ventures. As owner of a cement plant, the Passamaquoddy Tribe of Maine developed and patented several new processes; the tribe then sold the plant for a significant profit and kept the patents. The Cherokee of Oklahoma own and operate an electronics manufacturing plant. The Choctaw of Mississippi own and operate a greeting card company and a factory that produces wire harnesses for the auto industry. The Blackfeet Tribe of Montana has operated a nursing home, a bingo hall, and a steel housing frame manufacturing company. Several tribes, including the Gila River Tribe of Arizona, have operated their own office and industrial parks in major metropolitan areas.

For some tribes, though certainly not a majority, gambling has proven to be a lucrative source of revenue to combat sagging reservation economies. Many of the games attract literally thousands of non-Indian customers per evening, and some jackpots approach the millions. Tribes have negotiated over 249 gaming compacts with 28 states to allow gambling on lands held in trust by the federal government.

In 2009, gambling revenues from tribal gaming facilities generated approximately $26.5 billion, an 85 percent increase from 2002. During the late 1980s, after launching a number of tribal ventures including a gravel quarry and a pizza restaurant, the Mashantucket Pequots raised private funding to build Foxwoods, the largest resort casino in the Western Hemisphere. Building on the success of the casino, the Mashantucket Pequots have since invested in the social infrastructure of their reservation, as well as a $15 million waterfront development plan, an industrial park, a shipworks, a pharmaceutical network, and an academy for management and business training. Employment in tribal enterprises increased dramatically, such that at one point, approximately 75 percent of the Mashantucket Pequots' employees were non-Indian. In 1994, the tribe made a $10 million gift to help establish a National Museum of the American Indian. Each year, under an agreement with Connecticut, the tribe contributes 25 percent of its revenues from slot machine operations to the state; in fiscal year 2009, this contribution amounted to over $300 million. During the nation's financial crisis beginning in 2008–2009, however, the Mashantucket Pequots' gaming enterprises experienced a decline in revenues and operational challenges, followed by staff layoffs, debt reorganization, and a credit rating downgrade. The tribe and its enterprises are working to address these challenges now.

Tribes, although not insulated from market trends and other challenges, are beginning to reverse the central pattern of reservation development. Historically, reservation economic activity—when it existed—was typified by non-Indian natural resource development, companies extracting tribal resources with the tribes receiving only royalties, more often than not at below-market rates. That has changed in several respects. First, tribes are now better-equipped to negotiate favorable contractual arrangements. Second, tribes are able to offer inducements for businesses to locate in Indian country because state taxes are often inapplicable. Third, tribes themselves have begun to exercise the judicially validated right to tax reservation businesses as a source of revenue. Tribal economic development is explored in Chapter 9.

10. *Assimilation of Indians.* Federal Indian policy has always dealt, at its nub, with the question of whether and to what extent the United States should permit, encourage, or force the assimilation of American Indians into the majority society. See generally John W. Ragsdale, Jr., *The Movement to Assimilate the American Indians: A Jurisprudential Study,* 57 UMKC L.Rev. 399 (1989).

A prominent force behind assimilationist policy has been the desire for Indian land and resources. But it is not that simple. Many non-Indians unfamiliar with Indian people and Indian reservations presume that Indians would benefit by leaving tribal life behind and sharing in the benefits offered by the majority society. Conflicting perceptions of separatism and assimilation are a constant undercurrent in the study of Indian law.

The quality of life in Indian country depends quite plainly on the eye of the beholder. When Senator Arthur V. Watkins went to the Menominee Reservation during the termination era of the 1950s he likened the experience to visiting "the refugee camps of the Near East." Vine Deloria, Custer Died for Your Sins 73 (1969). Contemporary accounts of Indian country note the persistence of difficult social conditions:

> Contemporary American Indian reservations are notable for, among other things, extreme poverty, a host of related social problems, and economies founded largely on transfer payments and governmental services * * * Most Indians apparently desire to maintain and build upon distinctive tribal identities and communities, yet social pathologies undermine many Indian societies with disheartening results.

Stephen Cornell and Joseph P. Kalt, Pathways from Poverty: Economic Development and Institution-building on American Indian Reservations (Project Rep., The Harv. Project on Amer. Indian Econ. Dev., Energy and Envt'l Pol'y Center, John F. Kennedy Sch. of Gov't, Harv. U., Dec. 1989).

Yet Indians hold fast to their reservations. As Justice Black explained,

> It may be hard for us to understand why these Indians cling so tenaciously to their lands and traditional tribal way of life. The record does not leave the impression that the lands of their reservation are the most fertile, the landscape the most beautiful or their homes the most splendid specimens of architecture. But this is their home—their ancestral home. There, they, their children, and their forebears were born. They, too, have their memories and their loves. Some things are worth more than money and the costs of a new enterprise.

Federal Power Comm'n v. Tuscarora Indian Nation, 362 U.S. 99, 142 (1960).

Tribal leaders and Indian writers are persistent in their efforts to explain to an often ethnocentric majority society the essential goal of preserving tribal cultures and lands. Dr. d'Arcy McNickle, an anthropologist and member of the Flathead Tribe of Montana, explained how tribal knowledge, traditions, and customs survived the pressures of the dominant society:

> What was not anticipated, even by early social scientists, was the tendency of human societies to regenerate themselves, keeping what is useful from the past, and fitting the new into old patterns, sometimes incongruously, to make a working system. Indian societies did not disappear by assimilating to the dominant

white culture, as predicted, but assimilated to themselves bits and pieces of the surrounding cultural environment. And they remained indubitably Indian, whether their constituents lived in a tight Indian community or commuted between the community and an urban job market.

D'Arcy McNickle, They Came Here First 283 (rev. ed. 1975).

Ultimately, externally forced assimilation has faltered in favor of internal cultural evolution, even as tribal people adapt and change to contemporary circumstances in various ways. From traditional Yurok medicine women to young Hopi skate boarders, Alaska Native corporate executives to urban Mohawks in New York City, these are all Indian people today. It is this set of experiences, grounded in tribal life but thoroughly contemporary, from which Indian law emerges.

11. *Political Influence.* Sen. Matthew Stanley Quay, once grand chief of the Delaware tribe, was the first Native American elected to the U.S. Congress, in 1887. Approximately twelve other Native Americans have served in either the Senate or the House since then. Two Native Americans have served in both the U.S. House of Representatives and the U.S. Senate: Charles Curtis, a Kaw-Osage from Kansas, also subsequently served as Vice President under Herbert Hoover; Ben Nighthorse Campbell, a member of the Northern Cheyenne Tribe. U.S. Senator Daniel Kahikina Akaka of Hawaii was the first U.S. Senator of Native Hawaiian ancestry and served in the United States Senate from 1990–2013. In 2016, Congressman Tom Cole is an enrolled citizen of the Chickasaw Nation and Congressman Markwayne Mullin is an enrolled citizen of the Cherokee Nation. Many Native Americans are serving in state legislatures and they hold numerous school board seats and in some cases control local school boards.

Indians, who have been considered United States citizens since 1924, are having greater political influence, impacting state and federal elections. The influence of tribes in national politics is attributable, at least in part, to the economic gains enabling some tribes to make substantial campaign contributions. For instance, in 2002, tribes mounted a successful campaign to oust U.S. Senator Slade Gorton of Washington who had consistently pressed for legislation to diminish Indian sovereignty and rights, and in 2008, 2012, and 2016, Indian tribes were important in presidential campaigns. The National Congress of American Indians (NCAI), based in Washington D.C., serves as the major national tribal lobbying group and advocates on behalf of tribal interests.

———————

The future response of the American legal system to Indian rights will be an important index of the dominant, non-Indian society's ability to tolerate difference and diversity. The separation that is inherent in the

Indians' desire to remain as distinct self-governing and self-determining peoples is not well understood in the dominant society. The inconsistency of having islands of racial groups in a country that fought a civil war and has spent the last one hundred and forty-five years struggling to accept the goal of racial integration is a rallying point for some who would extinguish or revise Indian rights. Is there a basic value in preserving an indigenous culture, even at some cost to the dominant culture? Should the role of the law be to homogenize society? Or should it be flexible enough to preserve difference and diversity?

A student of federal Indian law should look persistently and critically at the theoretical basis for the continuation of the old promises. Is it enough to say that "Indians were here first"? Was Justice Black guilty of oversimplification when he said "Great nations, like great men, should keep their word?" Have the times and the society changed so much that we have sufficiently kept faith with the Indians by having honored the old promises as long as we have? Should we resolve to keep the promises just so long as Indians remain a seriously disadvantaged group or a traditional cultural unit? Is it a realistic, forward-looking justification to say that the promises should be kept because the larger society derives its own benefits from Indians—to say, as one judge has in upholding some of the old rights?

> In a mass society, which presses in at every point toward conformity, the protection of a self-expression, however unique, of the individual and the group becomes ever more important. The varying currents of the subcultures that flow into the main stream of our national life give it depth and beauty.

People v. Woody, 394 P.2d 813, 821–22 (Cal. 1964).

SECTION C. PERSPECTIVES ON INDIAN LAW

ROBERT A. WILLIAMS, JR., COLUMBUS'S LEGACY: THE REHNQUIST COURT'S PERPETUATION OF EUROPEAN CULTURAL RACISM AGAINST AMERICAN INDIAN TRIBES
39 Fed.B. News & J. 358, 358, 358–69 (1992).

Colonization of one race of peoples by another race then, indelibly inscribes a legal system of racial discrimination based on cultural differences, denying rights of self-determination to the colonized race which has been displaced from the territory desired by the colonizer race. This is as true in North America as in all the other colonial encounters between Europeans and indigenous tribal peoples throughout the world.

* * *

Whether it be the denial of rights to self-determination necessitated by colonization of indigenously occupied territory, or the denial of rights to personhood through slavery or Jim Crow segregation laws, the racist focuses on a perceived difference between himself or herself and the intended victim of racial discrimination. The racist perceives this difference as a deficiency: "they" do not use the land as we do and are therefore less "efficient"; or "they" have different skin pigmentation and are therefore genetically inferior. On the basis of this negatively valued and perceived difference, the racist then legislates and enforces a regime of privileges and power discriminating against his or her victim. And so, through the thin veneer of law and the assumed rights of sovereignty and jurisdiction, the racist holding power justifies what otherwise might be regarded as inhumane and irrational treatment of another human being.

* * *

Practitioners and students of United States federal Indian law are all intimately familiar with the three core, fundamental principles in the field from which all Supreme Court Indian law jurisprudence extends: the Congressional Plenary Power doctrine, which holds that Congress exercises a plenary authority in Indian affairs; the Diminished Tribal Sovereignty doctrine, which holds that Indian tribes still retain those aspects of their inherent sovereignty not expressly divested by treaty or statute, or implicitly divested by virtue of their dependent status; and the Trust doctrine, which holds that in exercising its broad discretionary authority in Indian affairs, Congress and the Executive are charged with the responsibilities of a guardian acting on behalf of its dependent Indian wards.

These doctrines all originate in the medieval crusading era legal tradition of Christian European cultural racism and discrimination against non-Christian, normatively divergent peoples, carried to the New World by Columbus and those Europeans who followed him. Because of their lack of familiarity with the racist origins of the core doctrines of modern federal Indian law, most practitioners and students do not realize that every time the current Supreme Court cites to any of the core principles to uphold one of its Indian law decisions, it perpetuates and extends the racist legacy brought by Columbus to the New World of the use of law as an instrument of racial domination and discrimination against indigenous tribal peoples' rights of self-determination.

* * *

The Christian European legal tradition of cultural racism and discrimination against non-Christian peoples, first brought to the New World by Columbus, and translated and adapted by English Protestant monarchs in North America, was formally incorporated into United States federal Indian law by Chief Justice John Marshall in 1823, in the Supreme Court's first major decision on American Indian tribes' self-determining rights and status, *Johnson v. McIntosh*.

* * *

In holding that American Indian tribes had no power to give title to lands to private individuals recognizable in a United States court, Marshall's opinion in *Johnson* relied exclusively and directly upon the medievally-derived legal tradition of Christian European crusading conquest and denial of non-Christian infidel peoples' rights brought to the New World by Columbus. This legal tradition of European cultural racism and discrimination against normatively divergent non-Christian peoples, was, according to Chief Justice Marshall, accepted in the New World by all of the civilized nations of Christian Europe as the "doctrine of discovery." Under this doctrine, recognized and enforced as part of the Law of Nations by the European colonizing nations, discovery of territory in the New World gave the discovering European nation, in Marshall's words, "an exclusive right to extinguish the Indian title of occupancy, either by purchase or by conquest."

* * *

Johnson's candid acknowledgment of the racist assumptions supporting the doctrine of discovery illuminates how deeply embedded European cultural racism is in the foundations of United States Federal Indian law. * * * The doctrine's institutionalization of Christian European cultural racism against normatively divergent and deficient non-Christian peoples was subsequently fashioned into the Trust doctrine's concept of a guardian-ward relationship between the United States and American Indian tribes by the Supreme Court.

CHARLES F. WILKINSON, AMERICAN INDIANS, TIME AND THE LAW
ix–x, 3–4, 13–14, 32, 53–54, 121–22 (1987).

* * *

Four great occurrences dominate Indian law, history, and policy, and they are better understood in terms of time periods than doctrines. They are the existence of aboriginal culture and sovereignty during pre-Columbian times; the location of separate Indian societies on reservations; the imposition of assimilationist policies, including the opening of most reservations to settlement by non-Indians; and the efforts of Indians during the last quarter century to reverse the press of assimilation by reestablishing viable, separate sovereignties in Indian country. In turn, each of these periods needs to be reconciled with the egalitarian and libertarian laws and traditions of the majority society. * * * Indian law encompasses not only Indians and law but also time.

* * *

Federal Indian law presents uniquely formidable obstacles to the development of consistent and unitary legal doctrine. There are a number of scattering forces that push Indian law away from any center. Taken together, these splintering influences have the potential of creating a body of law almost without precedent, of reducing each dispute to the particular complex of circumstances at issue—the tribe, its treaty or enabling statute, the races of the parties, the tract-book location of the land where the case arose, the narrow tribal or state power involved, and other factors. Further, the task of rendering coherent judicial decisions in Indian law is profoundly complicated by the passage of time. In most cases a crucial issue—seldom mentioned in the opinions but implicitly a weighty presence to the parties and judges—is how an old treaty, statute, or court decision should be applied in times bearing little resemblance to the era in which the words of law were originally written.

* * *

Inevitably, Indian policy has been cyclic. This is due in part to the sheer length of time during which it has been made. Even more fundamentally, federal Indian policy has always been the product of the tension between two conflicting forces—separatism and assimilation—and Congress has never made a final choice as to which of the two it will pursue. Thus the laws are not only numerous; they are also conflicting, born of the explicit regimen and implicit tone of the eras in which they were enacted.

As a consequence, Indian law, more than any body of law that regularly comes before the Supreme Court, is a time-warped field. Although there has been ample legislative activity in Indian affairs during the twentieth century, many of the basic rights of Indian tribes depend upon constructions of treaties, statutes, and executive orders promulgated during the nineteenth century or even the eighteenth century. Leaving aside interpretations of the Constitution itself, a large segment of the Court's recent rulings on laws enacted early in the Republic has occurred in the field of Indian law. From 1970 through 1981, for example, the Court directly construed 22 laws enacted before 1800, and 8 of those constructions involved Indian law. Of the 29 recent interpretations of statutes and treaties enacted between 1800 and 1850, 14 were of Indian laws. During the same period (1970 through 1981), the Court ruled on 182 laws passed between 1850 and 1875, 32 of which involved Indian law. In other words, from 1970 to 1981 Indian laws constituted close to one-fourth of the Court's interpretations of laws enacted during the nation's first century. Further, except for the Reconstruction era civil rights statutes, Indian law has been the vehicle for the modern analysis of laws enacted during the nation's first century of existence more frequently than any other body of law. This continual process of drawing meaning from statutes of another age creates much of the distinctiveness of the field.

* * *

A central thrust of the old laws, shared both by the tribes and by the United States, was to create a measured separatism. That is, the reservation system was intended to establish homelands for the tribes, islands of tribalism largely free from interference by non-Indians or future state governments. This separatism is measured, rather than absolute, because it contemplates supervision and support by the United States.

* * *

The modern cases reflect the premise that tribes should be insulated against the passage of time. Inevitably, there are some exceptions, but the mainstream of opinions has built a number of rules that prevent state powers and private rights from expanding to encroach upon tribal prerogatives except by express congressional permission.

* * *

The tribes, then, have sought and obtained a substantial measure of insulation from many of the negative effects of the passage of time. Concurrently, however, they have attempted to make time work in their favor by seeking to establish a vigorous, modern tribal sovereignty with actual powers far beyond those exercised at the time of the treaties and treaty substitutes.

* * *

* * * Ultimately, during the modern era the tribes have used their sovereign status in numerous pragmatic ways to rise from the termination era and gain a place, new though it may now be, in the community of governments in the United States.

* * *

There are no exact answers as to why the law has responded as it has. Surely nothing was inevitable about it. Indian law in, say, 1959, plainly could have moved toward a judicial termination of Indian tribes or toward a legal context in which Indian tribes would be not much more than toy governments.

After my long journey through this body of law, I have reached my own conclusion as to why the field has developed as it has, as to the deepest reasons why the Court has refused to allow American Indian tribes to be engulfed by the passage of time.

These old laws emanate a kind of morality profoundly rare in our jurisprudence. It is far more complicated than a sense of guilt or obligation, emotions frequently associated with Indian policy. Somehow, those old negotiations—typically conducted in but a few days on hot, dry plains between midlevel federal bureaucrats and seemingly ragtag Indian leaders—are tremendously evocative. Real promises were made on those plains, and the Senate of the United States approved them, making them real laws. My sense is that most judges cannot shake that. Their training, experience, and, finally, their humanity—all of the things that blend into the rule of law—brought them up short when it came to signing opinions that would have obliterated those promises.

No, this is no perfect body of law. But the thrust of it has hewed to principle in the face of agonizingly powerful forces to abandon principle in the name of societal change. * * *

This relative stability should now itself be honored. To the tribes, their chief task always has been not just to survive but to build traditional and viable homelands for their people. The original promise of a measured separatism might have allowed that goal to be reached, but the work was interrupted by a century of assimilationist policies and their effects. Perhaps, at last, the tribes can begin to withdraw from the judicial system and train their energies on fulfilling their historic task of creating workable islands of Indianness within the larger society.

DAVID H. GETCHES, A PHILOSOPHY OF PERMANENCE: THE INDIANS' LEGACY FOR THE WEST

J. of the West 54–68 (July 1990).

* * *

Indians survived on the American continents for thousands of years based on a pervasive set of cultural values integrating human life with other forms of life. Today these same values guide tribes in the United States as they move into an era of unprecedented sophistication in managing reservation environments. Most important for the non-Indian West, Indian values are crucial for the future of a region where resource issues are intertwined with economic and social survival.

Tribal peoples have made a wealth of cultural contributions, many of which have gone unnoticed. The Indian legacy most valuable for the future of the American West is a philosophy of permanence. Just as tribes have maintained cohesive societies against incredible odds by living their philosophy, so can the West. Author Vine Deloria argues dramatically that "American society could save itself by listening to tribal people" who have a unique "understanding of the world."

Acceptance of the Indian philosophy means understanding how all human activity relates to the natural world. It requires us to recognize that survival, cultural and physical, demands that we modify and limit human activity when it is not in harmony with the natural world. * * *

A Philosophy of Permanence

The values that enabled American tribes to survive and which have kept them intact reflect a philosophy deeply embedded in aboriginal societies of the Americas. It is a philosophy that commits the people to a permanent existence in harmony with everything around them that explains the success of these people in surviving in America for thousands of years.

* * *

The strength of the Indian philosophy is dramatically shown by the survival of tribal societies in the prehistoric period. But the Indians' record of tenacity since the arrival of Europeans is especially impressive. * * * Typically, tribes were forced to give up their historical homelands and to change their traditional ways.

* * *

In the nineteenth century successive treaties whittled away at Indian reservations to make way for white settlement and to confine tribes to areas where conflict with the settlers could be minimized. Almost systematically the Indians lost their most fertile lands and lands with precious metals.

* * *

A succession of government policies, many ostensibly for the benefit of Indians, has aimed to put an end to tribalism. * * *

* * *

Tribes have struggled to satisfy their basic needs while remaining true to their resource preservation values. Left with vestiges of their ancient homelands, many tribes have had to choose between sacrificing their limited resources for short-term exploitation or conceding some of their economic well-being. They have almost invariably chosen to hold fast to their land base. Expanses of undeveloped land, sometimes rugged stuff out of old cowboy movies, might have been mined, logged, test-bombed, or subdivided if an Indian tribe had not found such ideas repugnant.

Of course many reservations have had their share of resource development and despoliation, often authorized by the Bureau of Indian Affairs with little or no tribal consultation or consent.

* * *

* * * [T]here is no necessary contradiction in Indians' developing coal, cutting timber, fishing with gill nets, and tilling fields and still being touted as stewards of the earth. Indian tribal cultures have survived because they *do* use the earth's resources, but with a sensitive touch. Reservation resources have not always been dealt with sensitively but almost without exception misuse of Indian resources has been counseled by the federal government and undertaken by others.

A NEW ERA IN TRIBAL RESOURCE MANAGEMENT

A long line of Supreme Court cases upholds the legal authority of Indian tribes to govern their members and their territory and to call on the federal government to protect their resources. * * * Indian tribes are now building on legal advances that enable them to guide development and protect their land, water, minerals, and timber. They are engaged in planning resource use, negotiating contracts, passing environmental and land-use laws, and regulating use of reservation resources by both tribal members and non-Indians. They bring to the effort the best of the dominant society's technology and a unique sense of responsibility for those resources.

* * *

Tribes are accelerating their resource management activities also because of recent federal legislation letting them take over administration and enforcement of federal pollution laws on their reservations. They can now set their own standards for how clean water is to be, for waste disposal, and for the use of pesticides.

* * *

The remarkable part of the history of American tribes is not that they were victims of unrelenting attempts to change them. But it is truly astounding that they did manage to hold onto some land and that the core of their culture remains intact. This qualifies them to serve as mentors in resource management and in how to maintain viable communities. Their success is due to the philosophical base of their culture.

* * *

Indian survival for millennia before Europeans arrived and for the few hundred especially difficult years since then can only be explained by a philosophy of life that pervades the otherwise diverse cultures of aboriginal America. The Indians' philosophy of permanence based on an ethical relationship with land was fully developed at the time of white contact. They survived to that point compatibly with the resources around them by living as if they were there to stay. They have since resisted attempts to change them and to part them from their land and culture against apparently insuperable odds by holding fast to the same philosophical anchor. And they are now sophisticated managers in their own right serving as models for their governments. Non-Indian society has not done quite as well.

* * *

MATTHEW L.M FLETCHER, LOOKING TO THE EAST: THE STORIES OF MODERN INDIAN PEOPLE AND THE DEVELOPMENT OF TRIBAL LAW

5 Seattle J. Soc. Just. 1, 1–3, 19 (2006).

For many Indian people the east represents a new beginning. Each day the sun rises and Indian people begin new lives, with new stories and new experiences. East is the direction of young people, of newborns, and creativity. East is the direction of starting over with new and powerful energy. East is the direction of change.

Indian people—scratching and clawing, fighting and dying, sometimes silent, sometimes loud—have survived meticulous and incredible ruin at the hands of outsiders. The stories about these people are the foundation of American Indian law and policy. They are told by tribal attorneys and leaders, academics and judges, and form a great portion of the underlying basis for the rise of tribal self-determination and tribal sovereignty.

The larger story is ongoing, with many tribes running huge money-generating casinos, sophisticated and accountable environmental protection programs, and comprehensive social safety nets, while other tribes struggle to meet basic daily needs. The smaller stories, the stories of individual Indians living on or off the reservation, working or unemployed, educated or illiterate, make up the infrastructure of the remains of tribal cultures. These stories, factual or fictitious, have a great deal to add to the ongoing conversation about where Indian people will go with their newfound self-determination and tribal sovereignty. These new stories are a necessary and integral part of the future of tribal law and governance.

For Indian people to preserve their right of self-determination, their cultures, and their ways of living, they must rely upon their own customs and traditions, whether old or new. They must restore the stories of historic sovereignty and integrate these with contemporary stories of individual Indians, and then incorporate these elements into a modern tribal law.

* * *

Tribal sovereignty is the calling card of tribal leaders—it has been for decades—and the invocation of tribal sovereignty has led to many successes in the courts and before the politicians. It used to be that a tribal attorney could stand before a federal judge with a copy of a treaty . . . page 122 of Felix Cohen's Handbook of Federal Indian Law, and win; but any observer of modern federal Indian law can see that mere invocation of tribal sovereignty is no longer sufficient to persuade. That is not to say that tribal sovereignty is dead. Far from it. * * *

Sovereignty is an Anglo-American legal construct, and as such, that construct is limited. Audre Lorde's warning that the master's house will not be torn down with the master's tools has special relevance to American

Indian law. . . . Accordingly, tribal sovereignty as a tool of Indian advocacy and leadership must be reexamined. If tribes are to recapture the true authority to self-govern, they must move beyond sovereignty.

Although Indian tribes are generally in a better position now than they have been in hundreds of years, they have not taken sufficient advantage of the space [that federal Indian law] recognizes as theirs. Indians and Indian tribes must recognize that the space to make their own laws is equivalent to the right of preserving and making their own culture. Indian leaders fill some of that space from the top down with Anglo-American legal constructs that are necessary for existing in the modern era; but the law of Indian tribes, tribal law, cannot sustain itself without becoming part of the local culture. Or stated another way, tribal culture must permeate tribal law over time in order for that law to survive. Tribal law and culture are inextricably intertwined.

* * *

Tribal governments must seek to govern in a manner that preserves tribal cultures to the maximum extent possible. Modern federal Indian law keeps open a small window for Indian tribes to make their own laws and be governed by them. But the focus of federal Indian policy throughout American history has been one of quashing tribal law and culture. For example, in *United States v. Clapox*, the federal district court described the purpose of Indian reservations as being "in the nature of a school, and the Indians are gathered there, under the charge of an agent, for the purpose of acquiring the habits, ideas, and aspirations which distinguish the civilized from the uncivilized man." The small window of opportunity to declare one's own laws, to determine one's own future and governance, is the question of the next century for tribal advocates.

The notion of an Indian tribe assumes a governmental structure, however limited or simplistic, that does not often exist in reality. Before contact with European conquerors, many, if not most, Indian communities governed themselves through complex kinship relationships. Indian government structures resembling modern governments today, such as hunting or war parties, formed only as necessary. However, due to centuries of treaty-making, federal Indian legislation, and policy culminating in the Indian New Deal (1934's Indian Reorganization Act), the dominant and exclusive Indian governance structure has become the Indian tribe.

Advocacy in favor of a tribal law that is sensitive to tribal cultures and traditions does not mean a return to pre-contact Indian community governance structures. Too much time has passed since Indian people have adopted and adapted to their tribal government structures. Nevertheless, unique tribal custom and tradition must play a part in the continued advancement of tribal governments. Indian tribes are at a critical juncture—the opening for Indian people to make their own laws and be governed by them is here.

Pre-contact, Indian community governance provided social control through a complex arrangement of interconnected relationships dependent on storytelling and mythmaking. Elders passed down mores and other community behavioral norms to younger community members through the telling of stories. Often these stories were tied to the community's traditional territory, such as certain landmarks. The reservation system, the boarding schools and missionaries, and the dispossession of Indian lands guaranteed the loss of most of these stories.

Indian communities today are seeking to restore as many of the old stories as possible, but there is a need to think about new stories. The new stories depict Indian people doing good and evil in recent times, with a realistic bent concerning how Indian communities are now surrounded by a series of often hostile, alien, and dominant cultures. The old stories have translated into a form of Indian community law—the new stories should, in turn, be examined for their relevance to modern tribal law.

* * *

From the east, Indian people look to the south next. The south represents a time of growth, passion, and maturity. The creative labors of earlier times begin to bear fruit. Many Indian people believe that the south represents fire, with both destroying and cleansing properties. South is the direction of fuller understanding.

Tribal governments—and the Indian people that operate them and hold them accountable—must develop a law and tradition of governance that learns from the experiences of individual Indian people and communities, making the new tribal law harmonize with the new (and old) stories of Indian people. Fundamental questions, such as who Indian people are in a legal sense under tribal law, must be answered in light of the modern experiences of Indian people, not the laws and traditions imposed by outsiders.

* * *

Kristen A. Carpenter and Angela R. Riley, Indigenous Peoples and The Jurisgenerative Moment in Human Rights Law
102 Calif.L.Rev. 163, 175–77 (2014)

As indigenous peoples have become actively engaged in the human rights movement around the world, the sphere of international law, once deployed as a tool of imperial power and conquest, has begun to change shape. International human rights law now serves as a basis for indigenous peoples' claims against states and even influences indigenous groups' internal processes of revitalization. Empowered by a growing body of human rights instruments, some as embryonic as the 2007 United Nations Declaration on the Rights of Indigenous Peoples (UNDRIP), indigenous peoples are increasingly recognized in international human rights law as possessing the "right to have rights". From a historic rights vacuum, indigenous peoples have emerged to embrace the evolution of a global "human rights culture" and to articulate rights ranging from individual freedom and equality to collective self-determination, property, and culture.

An examination of these global, if nascent, shifts in indigenous rights reveals a dynamic and complex system that stretches well beyond international legal regimes and into state and indigenous forums alike. This "multiple site" engagement has produced a profound human rights moment, one manifested in the development of interrelated and inter-reliant legal norms and structures.

Events comprising the indigenous rights movement reveal not only "law's migration," but also its generative force and potential to loosen colonization's bind. In 2001, for example, the Inter-American Court on Human Rights held that Nicaragua's obligation to protect property rights under Article 21 of the American Convention on Human Rights encompassed interests defined by the Awas Tingni peoples' own customary law of land tenure. In 2006, Navajo Indians created a tribal human rights commission and later successfully lobbied for the recognition of water and subsistence rights against powerfully aligned federal, tribal, and corporate interests. In 2007, the highest court of Belize ruled in favor of indigenous property rights, based on customary land tenure, citing heavily to the then-draft of the Declaration on the Rights of Indigenous Peoples. Later that year, indigenous groups—having gathered for twenty years at the United Nations in Geneva to press for international studies, hearings, and lawmaking on indigenous rights—witnessed the General Assembly adopt the Declaration on the Rights of Indigenous Peoples by a vote of 144 to 4. Within three years, the most ardent dissenters, Canada, New Zealand, Australia, and the United States, all reversed their opposition and adopted the Declaration.

These examples reflect only a few of the seismic shifts occurring in indigenous rights. For decades, indigenous peoples from across the globe have relied on human rights regimes to challenge the laws of the nation-states in which they reside. They have articulated their claims, pursuant to treaties and other instruments, before the Inter-American Commission and Court on Human Rights as well as before the U.N. Human Rights Council. Their claims often invoke indigenous legal norms that have increasingly received recognition in individual cases and have begun to influence the development of international human rights law itself. Concurrently, nation-states are beginning to accept human rights norms derived from international and indigenous sources in their own judicial decisions, constitutions, and other activities. And indigenous peoples themselves are employing human rights discourse as a tool for internal reflection and reform. These phenomena are inextricably intertwined in substance and form, ultimately reinforcing and reifying a truly indigenous body of human rights law.

* * *

PART ONE

THE HISTORY OF FEDERAL INDIAN LAW AND POLICY

■ ■ ■

If, as Oliver Wendell Holmes said, the life of the common law is experience, then the life of Indian law is history. Authorities have emphasized the crucial role which history has played in Supreme Court opinions in the field. See, e.g., Charles A. Miller, The Supreme Court and the Uses of History 24 (1969). Rather than being just a "backdrop" or "providing perspective," history has been integrated into the case law. This, in turn, reflects Congress' preeminent role in the development of Indian law. Congress is a "trustee" for American Indian tribes and has nearly unfettered power over Indian affairs. Thus, the study of Indian law is essentially a study of what Congress did or did not do.

But in setting Indian policy Congress has almost always acted in response to specific events and conditions in Indian country. Treaties and agreements, for example, were often negotiated in the field and then brought back to Washington, D.C., for ratification. Tribal consent or consultation has sometimes (though not always) been required by Congress before the passage of legislation. In enacting social programs for Indians, Congress has usually based its judgments on trends and conditions on the reservations.

The courts, in assessing past legislative and executive action, have recognized these dynamics. Canons of construction have been developed that look to surrounding circumstances and to the Indians' intent when the treaty or statute is ambiguous—as so often proves the case. The resulting mix necessarily contains a generous dose of history.

Analysis will show that Indian legal history, as made by non-Indians and Indians, cannot properly be viewed in a vacuum. Have the successive Indian policies of the United States reflected policies and events in the dominant society or the concerns and responses of the tribes? Compare the prevailing trends in national policy with prevailing assumptions about the "Indian problem" at the time of the Removal Act, the allotment policy, the Indian Reorganization Act, termination, and during the modern, "self-determination" era. How was an apparent concern for Indians manifested differently in each successive governmental policy? What non-Indian objectives were to be accomplished by each policy? How did Indian people themselves perceive the policy?

There is a comprehensive history of federal Indian policy. See Francis Paul Prucha, The Great Father: The United States Government and the American Indians (1984) (2 volumes). Shorter works include Felix S. Cohen, Handbook of Federal Indian Law, ch. 1 (2012 ed.); N. Bruce Duthu, American Indians and the Law (2008); Walter E. Echo-Hawk: In the Courts of the Conqueror: The 10 Worst Indian Law Cases Ever Decided (2010); David E. Wilkins, Hollow Justice: A History of Indigenous Claims in the United States (2013). The historical origins of the legal intellectual sources shaping modern federal Indian law doctrine are analyzed in Robert A. Williams, Jr., The American Indian in Western Legal Thought: The Discourses of Conquest (1990). Charles F. Wilkinson, American Indians, Time, and the Law (1987) and Frank Pommersheim, Broken Landscape: Indians, Indian Tribes, and the Constitution (2009) assess the history of federal Indian law and policy as shaped by the United States Supreme Court.

CHAPTER TWO

THE EUROPEAN DOCTRINE OF DISCOVERY AND AMERICAN INDIAN RIGHTS

■ ■ ■

The rules and principles of "federal Indian law" have origins that predate even the United States Declaration of Independence. They trace their descent to the centuries-old European legal heritage that also informed the Founders' unprecedented act of separation from Great Britain's colonial empire in 1776. Though radically transformed once transplanted in the New World, that European heritage was unmistakably reflected in the legal system established by the Founders, including the legal system governing the United States' relations with Indian tribes.

The United States itself was an unintended by-product of the colonial designs of European monarchs intent on extending their sovereignty and empire over the vast, unchartered territories of the New World. From the earliest days of colonial encounter with the New World's indigenous peoples, the legal questions that were of principal concern to Europeans focused on the scope and nature of the territorial rights of the Indian tribes that actually occupied the lands so intensely desired by the colonizers from the Old World.

Did the tribes "own" the land? If so, what kinds of title did they hold? If the tribes did hold some kind of title, by what means could they be legally divested of it by "discovering" Europeans? Were tribes "sovereigns" or "nations" capable of transferring dominion of the lands? Did they retain the right to govern themselves once Europeans settled among them? Was their sovereignty, at least as Europeans defined, understood and applied that term, altered?

Even after the colonial era, questions relating to the legal rights of Indian tribes in their lands continued to be of principal concern to the Founders of the United States. Though the Supreme Court provided some early answers in Johnson v. McIntosh, 21 U.S. (8 Wheat.) 543 (1823), page 72, infra, and Worcester v. Georgia, 31 U.S. (6 Pet.) 515 (1832), page 137, infra, unsettled issues and attempts to enforce, revive, or dismiss early precedents persist today.

The Founders liberated themselves from what they regarded as the tyranny of European monarchy, but nonetheless adopted the Old World potentates' rationales for extending their claims of sovereignty and superior rights over the Indian-occupied continent of North America. The answers to the vexing legal questions of the rights of the Indian tribes to the territory of North America accordingly were confronted soon after 1776.

Great Britain based its territorial rights on the fact that it was the first European "discoverer" of the lands occupied by the colonies. The United States, in turn found it convenient to step into Britain's shoes upon its Declaration of Independence. The result that follows from the "doctrine of discovery" under the European Law of Nations sharply diminished the rights of sovereignty and ownership that tribes could assert over their territories under notions of European international law.

The doctrine of discovery was affirmed by the Supreme Court as United States law in *Johnson v. McIntosh*. The following materials show the centuries-old origins of the legal rules and principles perpetuated by the doctrine and its underlying normative assumption that as "infidels, heathens and savages," indigenous tribal peoples like the Indian tribes of North America were racially and culturally inferior to Europeans, and therefore possessed of lesser rights to the lands they occupied. By the time the Supreme Court grappled with the complex set of moral, legal and practical policy issues connected to the doctrine, the old rationalizations sounded harsh and morally questionable. Yet, in the Court's view, the limitations on American Indian rights and property established by the doctrine were too well-entrenched in positive law to allow a departure.

SECTION A. MEDIEVAL AND RENAISSANCE ORIGINS

Legal ideas applied by Europeans to questions of the rights of American Indians in the lands they occupied and possessed in the New World trace to the medieval era. In fact, a legal tradition which justified denying complete rights of self-rule and property to non-Christian peoples was already nearly four centuries old by the time of Christopher Columbus's "discovery" of the New World in 1492. See Robert A. Williams, Jr., The American Indian in Western Legal Thought: The Discourses of Conquest (1990).

1. THE CRUSADING LEGAL TRADITION

Europeans first confronted the question of the rights and status of peoples whose norms, values, and religious traditions differed radically from their own centuries before coming to the New World. The medieval Roman Catholic Church, as the dominant political and legal institution of Western Europe throughout the Middle Ages and early Renaissance, created the legal framework. The Pope in Rome, as divinely designated shepherd of Christ's Universal Flock, was vested with a supreme spiritual jurisdiction over the souls of all humankind. See Williams, *Discourses of Conquest*, supra, at 15–21.

The Crusades to the Holy Lands of the eleventh through thirteenth centuries represented the first large scale effort by the Catholic Church and Christian European military leaders to implement the papacy's theoretical universal authority over non-Christian peoples outside Europe. These papally-proclaimed and directed holy wars were fought under the legal justification that as usurpatious "heathens and infidels," the non-Christian peoples who occupied and possessed Jerusalem and the Levant could be conquered and displaced by Christian European princes and their armies, acting on orders from the Pope in Rome. See James Muldoon, Popes, Lawyers, and Infidels (1979).

The Crusades generated a large corpus of legal opinions and theories on the rights and status of infidel peoples. Extreme defenders of absolute and universal papal sovereignty argued that infidel rulers could not govern lawfully because only a ruler who believed in the true Christian God and received his power directly from the Pope in Rome had legitimate power.

Moderate canon law authorities, such as the great thirteenth century lawyer-Pope Innocent IV, justified the extension of papal sovereignty over infidels on the basis of their divergence from Christian European norms of "natural law:"

> [I]s it licit to invade a land that infidels possess or which belongs to them? * * * [T]he pope has jurisdiction over all men and power over them in law but not in fact, so that through this power which the pope possesses I believe that if a gentile, who has no law except the law of nature [to guide him], does something contrary to the law of nature, the pope can lawfully punish him, as for example in Genesis 19 where we see that the inhabitants of Sodom who sinned against the law of nature were punished by God. Since, however, the judgments of God are examples for us, I do not see why the pope, who is the vicar of Christ, cannot do the same and he ought to do it as long as he has the means to do so. And so some say that if they worship idols [the pope can judge and punish them] for it is natural for man to worship the one and only God, not creatures. Also, the pope can judge the Jews if they violate the law of the Gospel in moral matters if their leaders do not punish them. * * * The pope can order infidels to admit preachers of the Gospel in the lands that they administer, for every rational creature is made for the worship of God * * * . If infidels prohibit preachers from preaching, they sin and so they ought to be punished. In all the aforementioned cases and in all others where it is licit for the pope to command those things, if the infidels do

not obey, they ought to be compelled by the secular arm and war may be declared against them by the pope and not by anyone else.

Innocent IV, *Commentaria Doctissima in Quinque Libros Decretalium,* in The Expansion of Europe: The First Phase 191–192 (James Muldoon ed. 1977). According to Professor James Muldoon, Innocent's discussion of the natural law rights and obligations of infidels represented an important step in the development of international law, and was often quoted in the sixteenth-century debate over the rights of the American Indians in the face of the Spanish conquest of the New World. See James Muldoon, Popes, Lawyers, and Infidels 348 (1979).

Our nation's history of slavery and subsequent *de jure* and *de facto* forms of racial discrimination against African-Americans has tended to define our contemporary notions of what racism is. What about the pope's use of *cultural* differences, as opposed to biological or genetic differences, to justify discrimination against distinct groups of people. Is labelling a group of individuals "infidels" or "heathens" to justify religious wars waged against them in foreign lands also a form of racism? See, e.g., Michael Omi and Howard Winant, Racial Formation in the United States (3rd ed. 2015).

> How should we understand racism today? We have argued that race has no fixed meaning, that it is constructed and transformed sociohistorically through the cumulative convergence and conflict of racial projects that reciprocally structure and signify race. Our emphasis on racial projects allows us to advance a definition of racism as well. A racial project can be defined as racist if it *creates or reproduces structures of domination based on racial significations and identities.*

Id. at 128.

Albert Memmi, a Tunisian Jewish author, wrote one of the most influential works to emerge out of the post-World War II African decolonization movement, The Colonizer and the Colonized (1965). Memmi posits that the "racist attitude" has the following "essential" elements:

> 1)   Stressing *the real or imaginary differences* between the racist and his victim.
>
> 2)   *Assigning values* to these differences, to the advantage of the racist and the detriment of his victim.
>
> 3)   Trying to make them *absolutes* by *generalizing* from them and claiming that they are final.
>
> 4)   *Justifying* any present or possible *aggression* or *privilege.*

See Albert Memmi, *Attempt at a Definition,* in Dominated Man: Notes Toward a Portrait 185–95 (1968).

Consider these attempts at a definition of racism in light of the medieval papal origins of European international law doctrines that justified the denial of equal rights of self-rule and property to non-Christian peoples. These doctrines formed the basis of the doctrine of discovery under the European Law of Nations, and were eventually incorporated into United States law (and the law of every European-derived colonial settler-state). If federal Indian law is "racist" in its origins, how can it escape those origins in its present-day applications by judges, lawyers and policymakers?

2. THE CRUSADING LEGAL TRADITION AND EUROPE'S "AGE OF DISCOVERY"

Although the Crusades to the Holy Lands and territories of the Middle East ended in the thirteenth century, the legal justifications for holy wars against "heathen and infidel" peoples continued to be developed and refined by Church lawyers and theologians. These same ideas were later applied to the "discovery" of new territories by Christian Europeans, first in Africa and then in the New World.

In 1436, King Duarte of Portugal (r. 1433–1438) sought papal permission to conquer the strategically located Canary Islands off the African gold coast, explaining that the inhabitants:

> * * * are not unified by a common religion, nor are they bound by the chains of law, they are lacking normal social intercourse, living in the country like animals. They have no contact with each other by sea, no writing, no kind of metal or money. They have no houses and no clothing except coverlets of palm leaves or goat skins which are worn as an outer garment by the most honored men. They run barefoot quickly through the rough, rocky and steep mountainous regions, hiding * * * in caves hidden in the ground.

Quoted in The Expansion of Europe: The First Phase 54 (James Muldoon ed. 1977).

In response, the Pope issued the bull *Romanus Pontifex,* a legal edict binding on all Christian monarchs, confirming Portugal's exclusive rights to colonize not only the Canaries, but all other parts of Africa as well:

> The Roman Pontiff, successor to the bearer of the keys of the heavenly kingdom and Vicar of Jesus Christ, looking with paternal interest upon all the regions of the world and the specific natures of all the peoples who dwell in them, seeking and desiring the salvation of every one, wholesomely orders and arranges with careful consideration those things which he perceives will be pleasing to the Divine Majesty and by which he may bring the sheep divinely committed to him into the one fold of the Lord, and

> may acquire for them the reward of eternal happiness, and may obtain salvation for their souls.

Quoted in Church and State Through the Centuries 142 (Sidney Ehler & John Morrall trans. and eds. 1967).

Portugal's resulting monopoly over Africa required Europe's other Catholic sovereigns to look elsewhere in pursuing their colonizing ambitions. In 1492, the Spanish Crown accepted the proposal of an itinerant Genoese sailor named Christopher Columbus to sail westward on behalf of Spain in search of a shorter route to the riches of the "Indies." One advantage of Columbus's proposal was that any discoveries of "infidel" held territories he might make on Spain's behalf during his voyage appeared to avoid direct interference with Portugal's papally granted African colonizing monopoly to the south. The Spanish Crown accepted the proposal, and entered into a contract with Columbus. The royal agreement with the Italian sailor was based largely on legal principles developed during the Crusades, providing Columbus with royal authority to discover and make conquests of lands beyond the then-known borders of western Christendom.

Columbus apparently presumed that he could lawfully claim "discoveries" of already inhabited territories for the Spanish Crown wherever he encountered indigenous peoples who diverged from Christian-European cultural norms of religious belief and civilization. He described the Arawaks whom he encountered on a Caribbean island during his first voyage in the New World as follows:

> The people of this island and of all the other islands which I have found and of which I have information, all go naked, men and women * * * They have no iron or steel or weapons * * * They do not hold any creed nor are they idolaters; but they all believe that power and good are in the heavens and were very firmly convinced that I, with these ships and men, came from the heavens, and in this belief they, everywhere, received me after they had mastered their fear.

Quoted in Robert F. Berkhofer, Jr., The White Man's Indian: Images of the American Indian from Columbus to the Present 6 (1978).

Immediately upon learning of Columbus's "discoveries," the Spanish Crown dispatched diplomatic envoys to the incumbent Pope, Alexander VI. Pope Alexander was a Spaniard by birth, a corrupt ecclesiastical politician of the infamous Borgia family who owed not only the papal office but also much of his family's great wealth to the favors of the Castilian Crown. The Pope obligingly issued a series of bulls confirming Columbus's discoveries in the "Indies" on behalf of Spain. Alexander's bulls recited that Columbus and his men

* * * discovered some very remote islands and also mainlands which have not been found by anyone else before and in which several peoples live peacefully, going unclothed—reportedly—and not eating flesh. As far as your above-said envoys could judge, these peoples inhabiting the said islands and lands believe that one God-Creator is in Heaven; they seem to be well fitted to embrace the Catholic faith and to be imbued with good morals; and there is hope that, were they instructed, the name of the Saviour, our Lord Jesus Christ could be easily introduced into these lands and islands.

* * *

And in some islands and lands which have already been discovered gold, spices and very many precious things of various categories and qualities have been found.

* * *

Wherefore, all things considered maturely and, as it becomes Catholic kings and princes, considered with special regard for the exaltation and spread of the Catholic faith—as your forefathers, kings of illustrious memory, used to do—you have decided to subdue the said mainlands and islands, and their natives and inhabitants, with God's grace, and to bring them to the Catholic faith * * * [w]ith the proviso, however, that these mainlands and islands found or to be found, discovered or to be discovered * * * be not actually possessed by some other Christian king or prince.

Bull "Inter caetera Divinae" of Pope Alexander VI dividing the New Continents and granting America to Spain, May 4, 1493. In: Church and State Through the Centuries 153–57 (Sidney Z. Ehler & John B. Morrall trans. & eds. 1967).

Indigenous human rights activists from throughout the Americas have called on the present-day pope in Rome, Pope Francis, to repudiate the doctrine of discovery. See Julian Brave NoiseCat, *Indigenous Leaders Want Pope Francis to Rescind Bull Justifying Imperialism,* The Huffington Post (Sept. 25, 2015), http://www.huffingtonpost.com/entry/pope-francis-doc trine-of-discovery_us_56058eb9e4b0dd8503076c17. As well, the United Nations (UN) Permanent Forum on Indigenous Issues (the UN's central coordinating body for matters relating to the concerns and rights of the world's indigenous peoples), issued a comprehensive study of the contemporary impacts of the doctrine of discovery on indigenous peoples that called on the Holy See, referring to the sovereign entity representing the pope's ecclesiastical jurisdiction of the Catholic Church in Rome, to repudiate the doctrine:

With regard to land dispossessions, forced conversions of non-Christians, the deprivation of liberty and the enslavement of indigenous peoples, the Holy See reported that an "abrogation process took place over the centuries" to invalidate such nefarious actions. Such papal renunciations do not go far enough. There is a pressing need to decolonize from the debilitating impacts and the ongoing legacy of denial by States of indigenous peoples' inherent sovereignty, laws, and title to their lands, territories and resources. At the same time, there is a growing movement among faith-based bodies to repudiate the doctrine of discovery."

Permanent Forum on Indigenous Issues, Study on the impacts of the Doctrine of Discovery on indigenous peoples, including mechanisms, processes and instruments of redress, at ¶ 9, U.N. Doc. E/C. 19/2014/3 (Feb. 20, 2014).

As the UN study noted, a number of religious organizations have formally moved to repudiate the doctrine, including the Episcopal Church, The Unitarian Universalist Association, the World Council of Churches, the United Methodist Church, and the Catholic Sisters of the Loretto Community. In 2016, the Canadian Conference of Catholic Bishops joined the growing movement with this formal statement:

"We acknowledge that many among the Catholic faithful ignored or did not speak out against the injustice, thereby enabling the violation of Indigenous dignity and rights. It is our hope and prayer that by naming and rejecting those erroneous ideas that lie behind what is commonly called the 'Doctrine of Discovery' and *terra nullius*, we may better recognize the challenges we face today so that we may overcome them together."

The "Doctrine of Discovery" and Terra Nullius: A Catholic Response, Canadian Conference of Catholic Bishops 2 (Mar. 29, 2016), http://www. cccb.ca/site/images/stories/pdf/catholic%20response%20to%20doctrine%20 of%20discovery%20and%20tn.pdf.

What if you were Attorney General for a tribe, and the Chairperson and Tribal Council asked for your opinion on passing a resolution calling on the pope to rescind the doctrine of discovery? Would it make a difference in your opinion? In domestic United States law? In global politics? In moral and ethical discussions on the continuing use by domestic courts and legislatures of the doctrine of discovery to justify the superior sovereignty and rights of European-derived nation-states over indigenous peoples? Do you think such "symbolic" gestures are a waste of time and effort for indigenous peoples? If you were asked to draft such a resolution at the request of the tribe for consideration and approval, what major themes and arguments for the papal rescission would you include?

3. SPANISH COLONIAL LAW AND THE RIGHTS OF AMERICAN INDIANS

Pope Alexander's papal donation provided Spain with a relatively secure title to Columbus's discoveries. Few Christian European monarchs of the pre-Reformation era, given the risk of excommunication, would choose to interfere openly with Spain's papally conferred rights to colonize, civilize, and Christianize the indigenous tribal peoples of the New World.

The term "Black Legend" has been used to describe Spain's rapid colonization and resulting destruction of the indigenous cultures and peoples encountered by the Spanish conquistadors in the New World. The noted American historian, Angie Debo, has estimated that the indigenous population of Hispaniola, the first major colony established by Spain in the Americas, was reduced from 250,000 to less than 15,000 in the first two decades of Spanish colonial administration. Similar declines in Indian population are reported in other regions of Spanish America during the early colonial era. Enslavement, European diseases, and superior European military technology resulted in thousands of Indian deaths and the diaspora of hundreds of tribal groups. In many instances, entire Indian populations disappeared. See Angie Debo, A History of the Indians of the United States 20 (1970); Williams, *Discourses of Conquest,*, supra, at 84–85.

Whatever the precise figures and contributing causes of Indian decline that comprise the Spanish "Black Legend" of Indian oppression, Spanish colonial law played an important role in legitimating and energizing the Spanish conquest in the New World. The *Requerimiento* (Requirement) is perhaps the most famous example of the role of law and lawyers in Spain's administration of its New World empire. Promulgated by the Crown's lawyers in 1513, the *Requerimiento* was intended as a charter of conquest, and had to be read aloud to any group of Indians newly discovered by Spanish conquistadors before any hostilities could legally be commenced against them in the New World.

It informed the Indians that God had given charge of "the whole human race" to the Pope in Rome, who had donated their lands to the King and Queen of Spain. All of this was contained in the papal bulls, which the Indians were told they could see if they wished. The *Requerimiento* then explained what was required of the Indians as follows:

> Wherefore, as best we can, we ask and require that you consider what we have said to you, and that you take the time that shall be necessary to understand and deliberate upon it, and that you acknowledge the Church as the ruler and superior of the whole world, and the high priest called Pope, and in his name the king and queen Doña Juana our lords, in his place, as superiors and lords and kings of these islands and this mainland by virtue

of the said donation, and that you consent and permit that these religious fathers declare and preach to you the aforesaid.

* * *

But if you do not do this or if you maliciously delay in doing it, I certify to you that with the help of God we shall forcefully enter into your country and shall make war against you in all ways and manners that we can, and shall subject you to the yoke and obedience of the Church and of their highnesses; we shall take you and your wives and your children and shall make slaves of them, and as such shall sell and dispose of them as their highnesses may command; and we shall take away your goods and shall do to you all the harm and damage that we can, as to vassals who do not obey and refuse to receive their lord and resist and contradict him; and we protest that the deaths and losses which shall accrue from this are your fault, and not that of their highnesses, of ours, or of these soldiers who come with us. And that we have said this to you and made this Requerimiento we request the notary here present to give us his testimony in writing, and we ask the rest who are present that they should be witnesses of this Requerimiento.

Reprinted in The Spanish Tradition in America 58–60 (Charles Gibson ed. 1968).

The Spanish conquistadors' use of the *Requerimiento* was summarized by the leading English-language authority, Lewis Hanke:

A complete list of the events that occurred when the Requirement's formalities ordered by King Ferdinand were carried out in America, more or less according to the law, might tax the reader's patience and credulity, for the Requirement was read to trees and empty huts when no Indians were to be found. Captains muttered its theological phrases into their beard on the edge of sleeping Indian settlements, or even a league away before starting the formal attack, and at times some leather-lunged Spanish notary hurled its sonorous phrases after the Indians as they fled into the mountains.

Lewis Hanke, The Spanish Struggle for Justice in America 34 (1949).

4. SPANISH LEGAL THEORY AND INDIAN RIGHTS

While the theologians and canon law scholars were busy drawing up rules and regulations for the Spanish conquest of the New World, other, more humanistically-inclined legal theorists inside Spain's Catholic universities produced a voluminous literature on questions of the fundamental justice of Spanish rule in the Americas. The most important of the Spanish legal theorists on the rights of the American Indians was Franciscus de Victoria (1480–1546), a Dominican priest and scholar who taught at the University of Salamanca. Victoria's lectures on Indian rights are widely recognized as a primary source of the basic principles of post-sixteenth century Spanish colonial legal theory as well as of the treatment of indigenous colonized peoples under modern international and United States law. See Felix S. Cohen, *The Spanish Origin of Indian Rights in the Law of the United States*, 31 Geo.L.J. 1 (1942). According to international law scholar Anthony Anghie, Victoria's lectures on Indian rights created "a new system of international law which essentially displaces divine law and its administrator, the Pope, and replaces it with natural law administered by a secular sovereign," Imperialism, Sovereignty and the Making of International Law 17–18 (2005).

Victoria's lecture delivered in 1532 entitled "On the Indians Lately Discovered" was the first work by a major Spanish Renaissance writer to explore the Humanist idea of a natural law connection among all nations. His theories contributed to later-developed Enlightenment era ideas on the Law of Nations as a system of international law mutually binding on all nations that remain essentially in a state of nature by virtue of their sovereignty. He developed three arguments that were later reflected in the European Law of Nations.

1)   The inhabitants of the Americas possessed natural legal rights as free and rational people.

2)   Any Spanish claims to title to the Americas on the basis of "discovery" or papal grant were illegitimate and could not affect the inherent rights of the Indian inhabitants.

3)   Transgressions of the universally binding norms of the Law of Nations by the Indians might serve to justify a Christian nation's conquest and colonial empire in the Americas.

See generally Williams, *Discourses of Conquest*, supra, at 96–108.

Victoria's argument that the Indians of the Americas possessed rights under natural law was based on the assertion that Indians were rational beings, and therefore possessed the same natural rights as Christians. With respect to their territories and property they possessed in the New World, the Indians were "true owners alike in public and in private law before the advent of the Spaniards among them." According to Victoria, "just like Christians, * * * neither their princes nor private persons could be despoiled of their property" without just cause. Franciscus de Victoria, De Indis et de Iure Belli Relectiones 128 (Ernest Nys ed., John Pawley Bate trans. 1917).

The only just cause that could be asserted for dispossessing the Indians of their lordship or property according to Victoria was an evident lack of reason on their part. As to those who asserted that the Indians' "barbarous" tribal cultures did not meet European standards of reason, Victoria responded in pointed fashion: "I for the most part attribute their seeming so unintelligent and stupid to a bad and barbarous upbringing, for even among ourselves we find many peasants who differ little from brutes." Id. at 127–28.

Arguing that according to natural law, the Indians whose lands were "discovered" by Spain were free and were therefore "true owners" of the territory they possessed, Victoria dismissed the popular theory of "title by first discovery" as follows:

> Accordingly there is another title which can be set up, namely, by right of discovery: and no other title was originally set up, and it was in virtue of this title alone that Columbus the Genoan first set sail.
>
> Not much, however, need be said about this * * * title of ours, because, as proved above, the barbarians were true owners, both from the public and from the private standpoint. Now the rule of the law of nations is that what belongs to nobody is granted to the first occupant, as is expressly laid down in the [Roman] Institutes. And so, as the object in question was not without an owner, it does not fall under the title which we are discussing * * * [B]y itself it gives no support to a seizure of the aborigines any more than if it had been they who had discovered us.

Id. at 135.

As for the Pope's bulls of donation affirming Columbus's "discoveries" on behalf of Spain, Victoria declared that according to natural law, the Pope "has no temporal power over the Indian aborigines or over other unbelievers," id. at 137, and his asserted superior rights of dominion, therefore, were wholly "baseless." Id. at 132. Attacking the *Requerimiento,* Victoria argued that "even if the barbarians refuse to recognize any lordship of the Pope, that furnished no ground for making war on them and seizing their property." The Indians were free according to natural and divine law, and no human law, whether issued by priest or by king, could bind them without their consent. Such a law "would be void of effect, in as much as law presupposes jurisdiction * * * [T]he law could not bind one who was not previously subject to it." Id. at 135.

Victoria's final argument on Indian rights was that the Indians of the Americas, although free according to natural law, were nonetheless subject to the binding norms of the Law of Nations that was itself derived from natural law. His lectures included citations to Roman law, Holy Scripture, St. Augustine, classical writers, and St. Thomas, all supporting his central thesis that all "civilized" societies recognized an established body of natural law rules binding their conduct as nations. These rules, if breached, could be punished by other states under the Law of Nations.

Although the Law of Nations was completely unknown to the Indians, they supposedly were bound by certain "duties" including that of "natural society and fellowship:"

> [T]he Spaniards have a right to travel in the lands in question and sojourn there, provided they do no harm to the natives, and the natives may not prevent them. Proof of this may in the first place be derived from the Law of Nations (*ius gentium*). For * * * it is reckoned among all nations inhumane to treat visitors and foreigners badly without some special cause, while, on the other hand, it is humane and correct to treat visitors well.

Id. at 151. Victoria cited specifically to the Old and New Testaments to lend support to the universal nature of this natural-law obligation on the part of the Indians to accept the Spaniards into their lands:

> "Every animal loveth its kind" (Ecclesiasticus, ch. 15). Therefore, it appears that friendship among men exists by natural law and it is against nature to shun society of harmless folk. Also * * * there is the passage (St. Matthew, ch. 25): "I was a stranger and ye took me in." Hence, as the reception of strangers seems to be by natural law, that judgment of Christ will be pronounced with universal application.

Id. at 152.

Any laws of the natives denying other nations the right to travel and sojourn in America would be of no effect for "if there were any human law which without any cause took away rights conferred by natural and divine law, it would be inhumane and unreasonable and consequently would not have the force of law." Furthermore, natural law opened the Indian lands to Spanish economic exploits: "[T]he sovereign of the Indians is bound by the law of nature to love the Spaniards. Therefore the Indians may not causelessly prevent the Spaniards from making their profit where this can be done without any injury to themselves." These duties, based on cultural values and norms that were wholly Eurocentric in their origins and application, were to be observed by the Indians under penalty of armed reprisals, such as those authorized by the *Requerimiento*:

> If the Indian natives wish to prevent the Spaniards from enjoying any of their * * * rights under the Law of Nations, * * * the Spaniards can defend themselves and do all that consists with their own safety, it being lawful to repel force by force. And not only so, but, if safety can not otherwise be had, they may build fortresses and defensive works, and if they have sustained a wrong, they may follow it up with war * * * and may avail

themselves of the other rights of war * * * When the Indians deny the Spaniards their rights under the law of nations they do them a wrong. Therefore, if it be necessary, in order to preserve their right, that they should go to war, they may lawfully do so.

Id. at 154.

Victoria was not oblivious to the possibility that the Indians might not be able to understand fully all of the rules of the European Law of Nations. To compensate for their lack of capacity Victoria tentatively suggested that the Indians should be placed under a civilized nation's guardianship. The civilized nation would then hold just title over the property of the Indians and undertake the responsibility for administering their affairs.

The Crown's mandated guardianship responsibilities under the Law of Nations would include the duty of bringing the message of the civilized Christian faith to the natives: "[B]rotherly correction is required by the law of nature, just as brotherly love is. Since then, the Indians are all not only in sin, but outside the pale of salvation, therefore, it concerns Christians to correct and direct them; nay, it seems they are bound to do so * * * ." Id. at 160–61.

If the Indian princes prevented the Spaniards from preaching the gospel, "an obstacle would thereby be put in the way of the welfare of the Indians themselves such as their princes have no right to put there." Thus, "if there is no other way to carry on the work of religion, this furnishes the Spaniards with another justification for seizing the lands and territory of the natives and for setting up new lords * * * with an intent directed more to the welfare of the aborigines than to their own gain." Id. at 157–58.

NOTES

1.   The late Felix Cohen, author of the *Handbook of Federal Indian Law*, who also coined the enduring legal metaphor of the Indian and the miner's canary, page 7, supra, is widely regarded as federal Indian law's most influential scholar. Cohen has written in one of his most frequently cited articles that Victoria was principally responsible for providing "a humane and rational basis for an American law of Indian affairs." Felix S. Cohen, *The Spanish Origin of Indian Rights in the Law of the United States,* 31 Geo.L.J. 1, 11 (1942). To be sure, Victoria professed to be at odds with the harshly stated "discovery" rationales put forward by the likes of Pope Alexander. How was his analysis of Indian rights different in its consequences for the Indians? Do you agree with Cohen or with Professor Anghie, who writes that Victoria "is an extremely complex figure. A brave champion of the rights of the Indians in his time, his work could also be read as a particularly insidious justification of their conquest precisely because it is presented in the language of liberality and even equality"? Anghie, supra at 28.

2.   Philosopher Michel Foucault writes that:

[P]ower is war, a war continued by other means. This reversal of Clausewitz's assertion that war is politics continued by other means * * * implies that the relations of power that function in a society such as ours essentially rest upon a definite relation of forces that is established at a determinate, historically specifiable moment, in war and by war. Furthermore, if it is true that political power puts an end to war, that it installs, or tries to install, the reign of peace in civil society, this by no means implies that it suspends the effects of war or neutralizes the disequilibrium revealed in the final battle. The role of political power, on this hypothesis, is perpetually to reinscribe this relation through a form of unspoken warfare; to reinscribe it in social institutions, in economic inequalities, in language, in the bodies themselves of each and everyone of us.

Michel Foucault, *Two Lectures,* in Power/Knowledge 90 (1980). If political power is simply the continuation of a war by other means, was the use of law in the form of the doctrine of discovery by Pope Alexander and by the Spanish Crown in exercising a brutal form of colonial power over the Indians of the New World one of those means?

SECTION B. THE ENGLISH NORTH AMERICAN COLONIAL ERA INFLUENCE ON UNITED STATES FEDERAL INDIAN LAW AND POLICY

Many of the theoretical influences on federal Indian law and policy may be traced to Spanish colonial era legal sources, but the general framework defining the legal and political relationship between American Indian tribes and the United States emerged out of the English North American colonizing experience. English colonial law struggled with questions of American Indian rights and status for some two centuries prior to the War for Independence.

Most, though by no means, all, of the major English colonizing ventures in the New World focused primarily on acquiring land for agrarian settlement by immigrants from the Old World. In the thirteen original English colonies, this meant that the legal and political relationship between the tribes and the colonies focused almost exclusively on acquiring lands desired by English colonizers. For this, they required a workable, if not completely systematized, legal framework for acquiring Indian land rights.

1. EARLY PRECEDENTS

Like Spain, England was a Catholic country when Europeans commenced their explorations of the New World in the late fifteenth century. King Henry VII of England (r. 1485–1509) issued a charter of discovery to the Italian captain John Cabot in 1497 similar in form and purpose to that issued to Columbus by the Spanish Crown. He was authorized "to seek out, discover, and find whatsoever isles, countries, regions or provinces of the heathen and infidels whatsoever they be, and in what part of the world soever they be, which before this time have been unknown to all Christians * * * ." Reprinted in Documents of American History 5–6 (Henry S. Commager ed. 8th ed. 1968).

With the Reformation and the fall of British Catholicism came major religious and social changes. The Protestant Crown, desperate to catch up with Spain, which had reaped great wealth from its gold-rich colonies, perpetuated the tradition of sanctioning expeditions and conquest of non-Christian lands, and even granted monopolistic privileges to trading companies. Sir Humphrey Gilbert, and after his death at sea, Gilbert's half-brother, Sir Walter Raleigh, were commissioned by Queen Elizabeth I to establish colonies in North America in order to counter Spanish influence in these "heathen and barbarious lands." The Queen's charters to Gilbert and Raleigh were modeled closely after the Royal Charter given by her grandfather, Henry VII, to John Cabot.

Elizabeth's English conquistadors were unable to establish a permanent colony in North America during her reign. The invasion of the Armada in 1588 and war with Spain deflected English interest in overseas colonies. But following Elizabeth's death, a group of English merchants and investors organized the Virginia Company as a joint stock company to establish colonies in North America, and received a patent from King James in 1606.

The justification for the rights of Englishmen to establish what would become the first permanent English colony in North America, Jamestown, was stated in the Crown charter as follows:

> We, greatly commending, and graciously accepting of, their Desire [the Company's] for the furtherance of so noble a Work, which may, by the Providence of Almighty God, hereafter lend to the glory of his divine Majesty, in propagating of Christian Religion to such People, as yet live in Darkness and miserable Ignorance of the true knowledge and worship of God, and may in time bring the Infidels and Savages, living in those Parts, to human Civility, and to a settled and quiet Government, Do, by these our Letters Patent, graciously accept of, and agree to, their humble and well-intended Desires.

Reprinted in Documents of American History, supra, at 8.

Prominent English jurists of England's early discovery era perpetuated and refined the medieval thesis on infidel rights to suit the particular needs of England's own colonizing aspirations in the New World. Alberico Gentili, an Italian Protestant exile who served as Regius Professor of Civil Law at Oxford, published his major treatise on the Law of Nations in 1598 under the title *De iure belli* ("On the Law of War"). Gentili expressed accord with the more temperate views of the Spanish jurist Victoria which required him to search for "honorable reasons for waging war" against peoples who violate natural law and the law of nations:

> Therefore, I approve the more decidedly of the opinion of those who say that the cause of the Spaniards is just when they make war upon the Indians, who practiced abominable lewdness even with beasts, and who ate human flesh, slaying men for that purpose. For such sins are contrary to human nature, and the same is true of other sins recognized as such by all except haply by brutes and brutish men. And against such men, as Isocrates says, war is made as against brutes.

Alberico Gentili, De Iure Belli Libri Tres, 121–22 (J. Rolfe trans. 1964).

Without doubt the greatest common law jurist of the English Renaissance and Enlightenment, Lord Chief Justice Edward Coke, set out the English common law's distinctions regarding an English King's rights of conquest in a Christian versus a non-Christian territory in *Calvin's Case*:

> * * * All infidels are in law *perpetui inimici,* perpetual enemies (for the law presumes not that they will be converted, that being *remota potentia,* a remote possibility) for between them, as with the devils, whose subjects they be, and the Christian, there is perpetual hostility, and can be no peace * * * a Pagan cannot have or maintain any action at all [in the King's courts].

> And upon this ground there is a diversity between a conquest of a kingdom of a Christian King, and the conquest of a kingdom of an infidel; for if a King come to a Christian kingdom by conquest, * * * he may at his pleasure alter and change the laws of that kingdom; but until he doth make an alteration of those laws the ancient laws of that kingdom remain. But if a Christian King should conquer a kingdom of an infidel, and bring them under his subjection, there *ipso facto* the laws of the infidel are abrogated, for that they be not only against Christianity, but against the law of God and of nature, contained in the decalogue; and in that case, until certain laws be established amongst them, the King by himself, and such Judges as he shall appoint, shall judge them and their causes according to natural equity * * * .

77 Eng.Rep. 377, 397–98 (K.B.1608).

Coke's assertions in *Calvin's Case* about infidel kingdoms are *dicta,* since the case had nothing to do with the conquest of an infidel kingdom. Calvin was a "Scotsman born," seeking to assert rights as an alien in English courts. The issue may have been on Coke's mind because he was legal advisor to the Virginia Company that was chartered in 1606 to establish a colony in North America.

Under Coke's formulation, what was the status of an infidel nation's laws relating to territory prior to conquest by a Christian King? Does *Calvin's Case* support the rights granted under the royal charters issued by England's monarchs, authorizing English discoverers of lands not inhabited by Christians to "hold, occupy and enjoy" such lands in seeming disregard of whatever rights the non-Christian peoples occupying those lands might assert?

2.   EARLY ENGLISH COLONIAL PRACTICE RESPECTING INDIAN RIGHTS

The colonies had been left largely free to develop their own systems for regulating the acquisition of territory occupied by the Indian tribes encountered within their chartered limits. Despite the assertions of their charters and the writings of jurists such as Gentili and Coke denying in theory the rights of "savage" Indian tribes to the territories they occupied, in practice the colonies frequently obtained the consent of the tribes through treaties and purchases in order to settle Indian-claimed lands. There are, of course, instances where consent to voluntary purchases could not be freely obtained from the Indians and colonial officials reverted to fraud, duress or outright confiscation in acquiring the lands they desired.

The practice of seeking Indian consent to land cessions instead of using harsher methods ostensibly available to "discoverers" in the name of crusading piety has been explained in various ways. One view is that the values of the Puritans who colonized New England had a tempering influence on their Indian policy. The following excerpt discusses Puritan attitudes and shows considerable agonizing over the moral basis for dispossessing tribes.

CHESTER E. EISINGER, THE PURITAN'S JUSTIFICATION FOR TAKING THE LAND
84 Essex Institute Historical Collections 131, 135–43 (1948).

The question that confronted the Puritans in New England, if not their Anglican contemporaries in the South, was: Can it be morally right for the white man to occupy land that was already occupied by the Indians? The Puritans had to answer this question in the affirmative. And they did, resting their argument on two not unrelated principles. The first was the idea that the American land was *vacuum domicilium*, and the Indians possessed it only by a natural right which was not valid. The second rested on the revealed word of God, in the Bible, ordaining that man occupy the earth, increase, and multiply. These are the ideological bases for the

Puritans' occupation of the land that I wish to examine here. They are, characteristically, theological in nature.

* * *

Among the orthodox New Englanders, John Winthrop, the politically minded leader of Massachusetts Bay, made the most serious effort to think through, in terms of natural rights, the problems of Indian dispossession. In his *Conclusions,* Winthrop lists as one of the objections made against undertaking the plantation in New England: "We have noe warrant to enter upon that land wch hath beene soe long possessed by others." Answering this charge Winthrop distinguished two rights to the earth, a natural and a civil, both God-given.

> [T]he first right was naturall when men held the earth in common every man soweing, and feeding where he pleased; and then as men and the cattle increased they appropriated certaine * * * cells of ground by enclosing, and peculier manurance, and this in tyme gave them a Civil right. . . . And for the Natives in New England they inclose noe land neither have any setled habitation nor any tame cattle to improve the land by, & soe have noe other but a naturall right to those countries.

* * *

One Puritan, who thought uniformity was a stifling form of regimentation and was not long to remain within the fold, Roger Williams, asserted that the Indians were being cheated of their lands. Rebelling against orthodoxy, he also rebelled against the assumption that the white man had any kind of right to territory in America. In December, 1632, Williams wrote a pamphlet attacking the rights of the Plymouth colony to the Indian lands. Neither the King, by whose patent the Pilgrims held the land, nor the Pilgrims themselves had paid for the land. Williams denied the King's power to issue a patent. In *A Key into the Language of America* Williams attempted to discountenance the idea that the Indians do not honor boundaries among themselves or definitely claim possession of any given tracts of land. " . . . I have knowne them make bargaine and sale amongst themselves for a small piece, or quantity of Ground . . . " And this they do, " . . . notwithstanding a sinfull opinion amongst many that Christians have right to *Heathens* Lands." Williams made two points clear. The Indians thought that they owned the land and that it was not *vacuum domicilium.* And the white man, as Williams viewed it, thought that being white and Christian were enough to authorize occupation.

* * *

Winthrop entered the controversy when Williams sent him the 1632 pamphlet discussed above. The governor considered the matter of some moment, and on January 3, 1633, he wrote a letter to Endicott in which he refuted, one by one, the points Williams had made against the English title to the land. The fourth point, according to Winthrop, was that the colonists "lye under a sinne of unjust usurpation upon others possessions." In answer to this charge Winthrop wrote in part:

> But if our title be not good, neither by Patent, nor possession of these parts as *vacuum domicilium,* nor by good liking of the natives, I mervayle by what title Mr. Williams himselfe holdes. & if God were not pleased with our inheritinge these partes, why did he drive out the natives before us? . . . why dothe he still make roome for us, by diminishinge them as we increase? . . . If we had no right to this lande, yet our God hathe right to it, & if he be pleased to give it us . . . who shall controll him or his terms?

NOTE

Regardless of conflicting religious interpretations of Indian rights, when tribes were numerous and relatively powerful, European colonies and colonizing nations found it to their advantage and safety to seek Indian consent to settlement. This meant that Europeans during the North American Encounter era dealt with Indian tribes in practice and in theory, as possessing the degree of sovereignty needed to transfer title to their claimed lands and manage their own affairs. In most cases, acquisition of Indian land was regarded as a matter of exclusive governmental authority. Individual colonists did not have the ability to purchase lands directly from the Indians. These basic principles are reflected throughout the earliest diplomatic relations between Europeans and Indians in colonial North America. In the early seventeenth century, the States General of the United Netherlands instructed the Dutch West India Company to acquire land for settlement only with the consent of the Indians. As enacted into law for the colony of New Netherland: "The Patroons of New Netherland, shall be bound to purchase from the Lords Sachems in New Netherland, the soil where they propose to plant their Colonies, and shall acquire such right thereunto as they will agree for with the said Sachems." The English colonies adopted similar laws requiring the purchase of Indian land for settlement. Thus, both the English and Dutch colonial governments obtained most of their lands from Indians they regarded as being willing to sell, so that for all practical purposes, the tribes were treated as possessing rights of ownership and occupancy over their claimed lands. See Cohen's Handbook of Federal Indian Law § 1.02, at 13–15 (2012 ed.). See *also* Felix S. Cohen, *The Spanish Origin of Indian Rights in the Law of the United States,* 31 Geo.L.J. 1 (1942).

---

3. BRITISH IMPERIAL POLICY AND INDIAN LANDS

The legacy of colonial control of Indian land acquisition came to be regarded as one of the more important components of the English colonies' governmental prerogatives. Indian land sales provided each colonial government with a means of raising capital.

By the mid-eighteenth century, waves of European immigrants had pushed the borders of colonial settlement up to the natural boundaries provided by the eastern mountain ranges. Colonial officials and land speculators began actively exploring opportunities in the "western" territories beyond the Appalachian Mountains in the fertile Ohio and Mississippi River basins. Interest was particularly high in colonies like Virginia, whose charter seemed to give it rights of purchase in Indian-occupied lands stretching across the continent to the Pacific Ocean.

France, England's chief competitor for colonial empire in North America, had designs on the western territories. In 1754, war broke out on the frontier as a result of the conflicting European claims to the territories that were actually in the possession of the numerous Indian tribes of the region. Because of widespread discontent and anger among the tribes over their treatment by the British colonies, most of the Indians on the western frontier were poised to side with France in what became known as the French and Indian War. Most particularly, the tribes were resentful about the continual encroachments onto their lands by English settlers, and fraudulent practices used to cheat them out of their territories.

Recognizing that the colonies' inability or unwillingness to prevent encroachments on Indian lands gravely threatened the Crown's imperial interests in North America, and in order to gain the Indians' alliance in the war against France, the government in England decided to prohibit settlement by English subjects on the lands and hunting grounds belonging to the Indians beyond the eastern mountain ranges. The policy proved successful in securing the strategically valuable alliance of the Iroquois and their tributary tribes to the British cause, and in assuring the Crown's victory over France. By the Treaty of Paris concluding the war in 1763, France ceded its colonial claims in Canada and the western territories between the Mississippi River and the eastern mountain ranges to Great Britain.

Concluding that the colonists could not be trusted to prevent encroachments on this Indian-occupied territory, and that any Indian wars in North America would have to be fought at great expense by the Imperial Crown armies, the government in London formalized the war-time policy of protecting Indian land. King George III's Royal Proclamation of 1763 declared the territory beyond the eastern mountain ranges off limits to settlement and reserved to the tribes of the region.

Widespread colonial resistance greeted the Proclamation of 1763 and its implied assertion that control of Indian lands rested in the King's sovereign prerogatives, and not with the colonial governments' acquisition rights to those lands granted under provisions of their royal charters.

Representative of colonial attitudes was the position expressed by George Washington. As president of the United States many years after the Proclamation, Washington would strongly denounce illegal intrusions and speculation in Indian lands on the western frontier. See pages 99–100, infra. But in 1763, Washington, like many of Virginia's most influential citizens among its ruling elite, was heavily involved in land speculating activities on the frontier. He simply chose to disregard the prohibitions of the King's Proclamation and its unlawfully-regarded interference with colonial aspirations for western settlement. In a 1767 letter, Washington instructed William Crawford, a friend and business associate, to survey two thousand acres of "good rich land" in western Pennsylvania, and other tracts along the Ohio, on the forbidden side of the Proclamation's boundary line:

> * * * I proposed * * * to secure some of the most valuable lands in the King's part, which I think may be accomplished after a while, notwithstanding the proclamation that restrains it at present, and prohibits the settling of them at all; for I can never look upon that proclamation in any other light (but this I say between ourselves), than as a temporary expedient to quiet the minds of the Indians, and must fall, of course, in a few years, especially when those Indians are consenting to our occupying the lands. Any person, therefore, who neglects the present opportunity of hunting out good lands, and in some measure marking and distinguishing them for his own (in order to keep others from settling them), will never regain it.

II The Writings of George Washington 218–24 (Worthington C. Ford ed. 1889), quoted in This Country Was Ours: A Documentary History of the American Indian 57 (Virgil J. Vogel ed. 1972).

Other colonists who were heavily involved in Indian land speculation on the western frontier drew on a variety of arguments to justify their defiance of the King's Proclamation. Some directly challenged the Crown's legal authority to issue a Proclamation which interfered with the colonies' rights to purchase Indian lands within their chartered limits. Others, with perhaps less sincere conviction, asserted the natural law rights of the Indians to sell lands they occupied to whomsoever they pleased. See Williams, *Discourses of Conquest*, supra, at 241–280.

Believing that the British government had no rights to restrict purchases of lands by American colonists directly from the tribes in the western territory, a large number of colonists accordingly continued to speculate heavily in Indian lands after the Proclamation's issuance. In one infamous example, William Murray purchased from the Illinois Indians for $24,000, two prime tracts of land on the frontier for a large colonial land speculation syndicate. These purchases were among the Indian grants involved in the 1823 Supreme Court decision of *Johnson v. McIntosh*, page 72, infra.

4.   THE FOUNDERS' DEBATES ON INDIAN LANDS

Resistance to exercises of Crown power such as the Royal Proclamation of 1763 as unlawful or overbearing was consistent with the spirit of the colonists' famous Declaration of Independence on July 4, 1776, and the Revolutionary War. One of the stated grounds for armed revolt contained in the Declaration of Independence was that Great Britain's King George III "has excited domestic insurrections amongst us, and has endeavoured to bring on the inhabitants of our frontiers, the merciless Indian Savages, whose known rule of warfare, is an undistinguished destruction of all ages, sexes and conditions." See The Declaration of Independence (1776). But the struggle for independence from Great Britain did not diminish the importance of the question of who controlled the right to purchase Indian lands on the frontier. If anything, the prospect of the independent states taking over control of the rich and fertile territories beyond the eastern mountain ranges was, in the minds of many colonists, one of the major reasons for fighting the Revolution. Thus, debates over who would control the sale of Indian lands on the frontier—states that succeeded to the rights of the colonies or a newly formed central sovereign government—intensified during the Revolution.

On June 27, 1776, the eve of the Declaration of Independence, the Virginia constitutional convention resolved that no purchases of Indian lands could be made within Virginia's chartered limits without legislative approval. The state's constitution contained an amendment, which had been drafted by Thomas Jefferson, stipulating that Virginia's western boundary was to remain as it had been defined by the Crown charter of 1609, meaning, to the Virginians at least, that Virginia's borders stretched to the Pacific Ocean.

Such actions by Virginia threatened directly the interests of the land speculating syndicates that had purchased lands from the western tribes prior to the Revolution. The syndicate represented by William Murray, who had purchased lands directly from the Illinois Indians in 1773, was a particular target of Virginia's declaration of jurisdictional control over its western lands.

The issue of control over the western lands became a subject of intense debate within the Continental Congress, the body responsible for drawing up the Articles of Confederation, the first constitution for the thirteen former colonies that had decided to confederate themselves in alliance against Great Britain. That the very fate of the Articles' ratification hinged on the western lands issue is illustrated by the instructions of Maryland's delegates not to agree to the Articles until matters concerning the western lands had been settled. See Oneida Indian Nation v. New York, 860 F.2d 1145 (2d Cir.1988).

The final compromise on Indian lands agreed to by the Continental Congress and eventually ratified by the individual states is contained in Article IX (4), which provides:

> The United States in Congress assembled shall also have the sole and exclusive right and power of * * * regulating the trade and managing all affairs with the Indians, not members of any of the States provided that the legislative right of any State within its own limits be not infringed or violated. * * *

The so-called "legislative right" proviso contained in Article IX (4) was generally understood to guarantee the landed states the right to purchase Indian lands contained within the limits of their boundaries as defined by their original charter-defined boundaries. See *Oneida Indian Nation v. New York*, supra.

The absence of national power to disapprove state Indian land purchases under the Confederation gave the landed states considerable leverage in negotiations with the national government for cession of their western land claims. Virginia, for example, refused to cede its western lands and establish its western boundary, unless the Continental Congress agreed at the same time to declare null and void all pre-Revolutionary purchases of Indian lands by the frontier land speculating companies. The Congress's agreement to such a condition would have, of course, spelled disaster for these companies. William Murray's syndicate, which held valuable land interests purchased by virtue of Indian deeds in the Illinois country, and other speculators who purchased Indian titles in territories bounded by Virginia's vast colonial charter, launched a massive publicity campaign to persuade the Congress to resist Virginia's demands.

Even Thomas Paine, the influential author of the Revolutionary War era pamphlet *Common Sense,* weighed in with a pamphlet invoking the spirit of his earlier work, titled *The Public Good.* The fact that Paine had been given shares in one of the land speculating companies was not mentioned in his spirited defense of the interests of the nation in defeating Virginia's unreasonable claims to control the entire western frontier.

Other influential political figures of the period were invested in land speculating companies. The syndicate holding interests in William Murray's Illinois country purchases, the Illinois-Wabash Company, included a number of prominent shareholders including some members of the Continental Congress. This was typical of other companies such as the Indiana Company that counted Benjamin Franklin as a shareholder.

Congress finally accepted Virginia's terms for ceding its territorial claims north of the Ohio, by agreeing not to investigate the question of conflicting claims in the region. The additional promise by Congress that the ceded lands should be used for the common benefit of the states satisfied the Virginians that their cession did not require a provision which specifically invalidated all private purchases from Indians. The territory ceded by Virginia in 1784 became known as the Old Northwest, and included the lands that had been purchased from the Indians prior to the Revolution by the land speculating companies. Three years later, Congress enacted the Northwest Ordinance of 1787, which promised "the utmost good faith * * * towards the Indians, their lands and property," by the United States to forestall growing fears of wars with the Indians that could inhibit white settlement in the region.

After considerable tension, the Constitutional Convention of 1787 then shifted control of Indian affairs away from the states, facilitated by the bargain struck with Virginia. See Jonathan Elliot, Debates on the Adoption of the Federal Constitution 207 (1845). The commerce clause of the constitution for the new nation vested exclusive authority in Congress to regulate trade and commerce and to make treaties with Indian tribes. This declaration of legislative authority over Indian tribes superseded the vague language of the Articles of Confederation with a broad statement of power that vested Congress with unquestioned authority over the acquisition of lands on the frontier beyond the borders of the states: "The Congress shall have power * * * [t]o regulate Commerce with foreign Nations, and among the several States, and with the Indian Tribes." U.S. Const. art. I, § 8, cl.3.

The new situation with respect to Indian land sales under the Constitution was explained by President Washington to Corn Planter, Chief of the Senecas in 1790. The Iroquois chief had complained to the President of the United States about state purchases of Indian lands, but Washington pointed out that these purchases had occurred before the adoption of the Constitution and added, "But the Case is now entirely altered. The General Government only has the Power to treat with the Indian Nations, * * * No State, nor Person, can purchase your Lands, unless at a general Treaty, held under the Authority of the United States." See Oneida Indian Nation v. New York, 860 F.2d 1145 (2d Cir.1988) (holding that Article IX (4) of the Articles of Confederation did not preclude New York from making purchases of Indian land prior to ratification of the Constitution). The history and evolution of the Indian Commerce Clause is discussed in Robert N. Clinton, *The Dormant Indian Commerce Clause*, 27 Conn.L.Rev. 1055, 1059–1064 (1995).

SECTION C. UNITED STATES COLONIZING LEGAL THEORY

In 1823, the Supreme Court considered the validity of Indian land transfers made before the Revolution. By the time the case arose, many of the same lands purchased from the Indians by speculators were included within lands acquired by the United States itself by the Treaty of Greenville after defeating the tribes in the Battle of Fallen Timbers in 1794. The government then sold the lands to private parties, including an 1818 sale to William McIntosh. The validity of that sale was challenged in the following case by a successor to one of William Murray's pre-Revolutionary land purchases. Daniel Webster argued for the validity of the earlier transfers from the tribes, pointing out that both the English and the French had treated the tribes as sovereigns and as such they should have the power to sell.

JOHNSON V. MCINTOSH

Supreme Court of the United States, 1823.
21 U.S. (8 Wheat.) 543, 5 L.Ed. 681.

MR. CHIEF JUSTICE MARSHALL delivered the opinion of the Court.

The plaintiffs in this cause claim the land, in their declaration mentioned, under two grants, purporting to be made, the first in 1773, and the last in 1775, by the chiefs of certain Indian tribes, constituting the Illinois and the Piankeshaw nations; and the question is, whether this title can be recognized in the Courts of the United States?

The facts, as stated in the case agreed, show the authority of the chiefs who executed this conveyance, so far as it could be given by their own people; and likewise show, that the particular tribes for whom these chiefs acted were in rightful possession of the land they sold. The inquiry, therefore, is, in a great measure, confined to the power of Indians to give, and of private individuals to receive, a title which can be sustained in the Courts of this country.

* * *

On the discovery of this immense continent, the great nations of Europe were eager to appropriate to themselves so much of it as they could respectively acquire. Its vast extent offered an ample field to the ambition and enterprise of all; and the character and religion of its inhabitants afforded an apology for considering them as a people over whom the superior genius of Europe might claim an ascendancy. The potentates of the old world found no difficulty in convincing themselves that they made ample compensation to the inhabitants of the new, by bestowing on them civilization and Christianity, in exchange for unlimited independence. But, as they were all in pursuit of nearly the same object, it was necessary, in order to avoid conflicting settlements, and consequent war with each other, to establish a principle, which all should acknowledge as the law by which the right of acquisition, which they all asserted, should be regulated as between themselves. This principle was, that discovery gave title to the government by whose subjects, or by whose authority, it was made, against all other European governments, which title might be consummated by possession.

The exclusion of all other Europeans, necessarily gave to the nation making the discovery the sole right of acquiring the soil from the natives, and establishing settlements upon it. It was a right with which no Europeans could interfere. It was a right which all asserted for themselves, and to the assertion of which, by others, all assented.

Those relations which were to exist between the discoverer and the natives, were to be regulated by themselves. The rights thus acquired being exclusive, no other power could interpose between them.

In the establishment of these relations, the rights of the original inhabitants were, in no instance, entirely disregarded; but were necessarily, to a considerable extent, impaired. They were admitted to be the rightful occupants of the soil, with a legal as well as just claim to retain possession of it, and to use it according to their own discretion; but their rights to complete sovereignty, as independent nations, were necessarily diminished, and their power to dispose of the soil at their own will, to whomsoever they pleased, was denied by the original fundamental principle, that discovery gave exclusive title to those who made it.

While the different nations of Europe respected the right of the natives, as occupants, they asserted the ultimate dominion to be in themselves; and claimed and exercised, as a consequence of this ultimate dominion, a power to grant the soil, while yet in possession of the natives. These grants have been understood by all, to convey a title to the grantees, subject only to the Indian right of occupancy. * * *

* * *

No one of the powers of Europe gave its full assent to this principle, more unequivocally than England. The documents upon this subject are ample and complete. So early as the year 1496, her monarch granted a commission to the Cabots, to discover countries then unknown to *Christian people,* and to take possession of them in the name of the king of England. Two years afterwards, Cabot proceeded on this voyage, and discovered the continent of North America, along which he sailed as far south as Virginia. To this discovery the English trace their title.

In this first effort made by the English government to acquire territory on this continent, we perceive a complete recognition of the principle which has been mentioned. The right of discovery given by this commission, is confined to countries "then unknown to all Christian people;" and of these countries Cabot was empowered to take possession in the name of the king of England. Thus asserting a right to take possession, notwithstanding the occupancy of the natives, who were heathens, and, at the same time, admitting the prior title of any Christian people who may have made a previous discovery. * * *

* * *

Thus has our whole country been granted by the crown while in the occupation of the Indians. These grants purport to convey the soil as well as the right of dominion to the grantees. * * *

* * *

Further proofs of the extent to which this principle has been recognised, will be found in the history of the wars, negotiations, and treaties, which the different nations, claiming territory in America, have carried on, and held with each other.

* * *

Between France and Great Britain, whose discoveries as well as settlements were nearly contemporaneous, contests for the country, actually covered by the Indians, began as soon as their settlements approached each other, and were continued until finally settled in the year 1763, by the treaty of Paris. * * *

* * *

This treaty expressly cedes, and has always been understood to cede, the whole country, on the English side of the dividing line, between the two nations, although a great and valuable part of it was occupied by the Indians. Great Britain, on her part, surrendered to France all her pretensions to the country west of the Mississippi. It has never been supposed that she surrendered nothing, although she was not in actual possession of a foot of land. She surrendered all right to acquire the country; and any after attempt to purchase it from the Indians, would have been considered and treated as an invasion of the territories of France.

* * *

Thus, all the nations of Europe, who have acquired territory on this continent, have asserted in themselves, and have recognized in others, the exclusive right of the discoverer to appropriate the lands occupied by the Indians. Have the American States rejected or adopted this principle?

By the treaty which concluded the war of our revolution, Great Britain relinquished all claim, not only to the government, but to the "propriety and territorial rights of the United States," whose boundaries were fixed in the second article. By this treaty, the powers of government, and the right to soil, which had previously been in Great Britain, passed definitively to these States. We had before taken possession of them, by declaring independence; but neither the declaration of independence, nor the treaty confirming it, could give us more than that which we before possessed, or to which Great Britain was before entitled. It has never been doubted, that either the United States, or the several States, had a clear title to all the lands within the boundary lines described in the treaty, subject only to the Indian right of occupancy, and that the exclusive power to extinguish that right, was vested in that government which might constitutionally exercise it. * * *

* * *

The United States, then, have unequivocally acceded to that great and broad rule by which its civilized inhabitants now hold this country. They hold, and assert in themselves, the title by which it was acquired. They maintain, as all others have maintained, that discovery gave an exclusive right to extinguish the Indian title of occupancy, either by purchase or by conquest; and gave also a right to such a degree of sovereignty, as the circumstances of the people would allow them to exercise.

* * *

We will not enter into the controversy, whether agriculturists, merchants, and manufacturers, have a right, on abstract principles, to expel hunters from the territory they possess, or to contract their limits. Conquest gives a title which the Courts of the conqueror cannot deny, whatever the private and speculative opinions of individuals may be, respecting the original justice of the claim which has been successfully asserted. The British government, which was then our government, and whose rights have passed to the United States, asserted a title to all the lands occupied by Indians, within the chartered limits of the British colonies. It asserted also a limited sovereignty over them, and the exclusive right of extinguishing the title which occupancy gave to them. These claims have been maintained and established as far west as the river Mississippi, by the sword. The title to a vast portion of the lands we now hold, originates in them. It is not for the Courts of this country to question the validity of this title, or to sustain one which is incompatible with it.

Although we do not mean to engage in the defence of those principles which Europeans have applied to Indian title, they may, we think, find some excuse, if not justification, in the character and habits of the people whose rights have been wrested from them.

The title by conquest is acquired and maintained by force. The conqueror prescribes its limits. Humanity, however, acting on public opinion, has established, as a general rule, that the conquered shall not be wantonly oppressed, and that their condition shall remain as eligible as is compatible with the objects of the conquest. Most usually, they are incorporated with the victorious nation, and become subjects or citizens of the government with which they are connected. The new and old members of the society mingle with each other; the distinction between them is gradually lost, and they make one people. Where this incorporation is practicable, humanity demands, and a wise policy requires, that the rights of the conquered to property should remain unimpaired; that the new subjects should be governed as equitably as the old, and that confidence in their security should gradually banish the painful sense of being separated from their ancient connexions, and united by force to strangers.

When the conquest is complete, and the conquered inhabitants can be blended with the conquerors, or safely governed as a distinct people, public opinion, which not even the conqueror can disregard, imposes these restraints upon him; and he cannot neglect them without injury to his fame, and hazard to his power.

But the tribes of Indians inhabiting this country were fierce savages, whose occupation was war, and whose subsistence was drawn chiefly from the forest. To leave them in possession of their country, was to leave the country a wilderness; to govern them as a distinct people, was impossible, because they were as brave and as high spirited as they were fierce, and were ready to repel by arms every attempt on their independence.

* * *

Frequent and bloody wars, in which the whites were not always the aggressors, unavoidably ensued. European policy, numbers, and skill, prevailed. As the white population advanced, that of the Indians necessarily receded. The country in the immediate neighbourhood of agriculturists became unfit for them. The game fled into thicker and more unbroken forests, and the Indians followed. The soil, to which the crown originally claimed title, being no longer occupied by its ancient inhabitants, was parcelled out according to the will of the sovereign power, and taken possession of by persons who claimed immediately from the crown, or mediately, through its grantees or deputies.

That law which regulates, and ought to regulate in general, the relations between the conqueror and conquered, was incapable of application to a people under such circumstances. The resort to some new and different rule, better adapted to the actual state of things, was unavoidable. Every rule which can be suggested will be found to be attended with great difficulty.

However extravagant the pretension of converting the discovery of an inhabited country into conquest may appear; if the principle has been asserted in the first instance, and afterwards sustained; if a country has been acquired and held under it; if the property of the great mass of the community originates in it, it becomes the law of the land, and cannot be questioned. So, too, with respect to the concomitant principle, that the Indian inhabitants are to be considered merely as occupants, to be protected, indeed, while in peace, in the possession of their lands, but to be deemed incapable of transferring the absolute title to others. However this restriction may be opposed to natural right, and to the usages of civilized nations, yet, if it be indispensable to that system under which the country has been settled, and be adapted to the actual condition of the two people, it may, perhaps, be supported by reason, and certainly cannot be rejected by Courts of justice.

* * *

After bestowing on this subject a degree of attention which was more required by the magnitude of the interest in litigation, and the able and elaborate arguments of the bar, than by its intrinsic difficulty, the Court is decidedly of opinion, that the plaintiffs do not exhibit a title which can be sustained in the Courts of the United States * * * .

NOTES

1. The decision is remarkable from divergent perspectives: 1) it embraced the medievally-originated doctrine of discovery as a root of all land titles under U.S. law, eschewing the need or propriety of questioning its contemporary moral legitimacy; and 2) it applied the doctrine so as to invalidate titles and debase investments like the ones held by politically influential land speculators throughout the country such as George Washington, Ben Franklin, and Thomas Paine. In concluding that discovery gave the United States the exclusive right to extinguish the original tribal right of possession "by purchase or conquest," Marshall avoided the two logical extremes: that discovery erased all Indian title and that Indians held fee title unaffected by discovery. Those positions "produced a cruel dilemma: either Indians had no title and no rights or the Federal land grants on which much of our economy rested were void." Felix S. Cohen, *Original Indian Land Title*, 32 Minn.L.Rev. 28, 48 (1947). *Johnson v. McIntosh* can be read as a blend of Marshall's federalist convictions, an indignant sense of remorse over the way that Indian rights had been treated under the European Law of Nations, and a pragmatic need to fit Indian title into our system of land tenure with a minimum amount of disruption to well-established procedures by which title to millions of acres of Indian lands had already been obtained.

2. Note how Marshall acknowledges the doctrine's premise of the Indians' inferiorly-regarded "character and religion" as the basis for the superior sovereignty of European governments over Indian land as an accepted part of United States law:

> * * * [T]he tribes of Indians inhabiting this country were fierce savages, whose occupation was war, and whose subsistence was drawn chiefly from the forest. To leave them in possession of their country, was to leave the country a wilderness; to govern them as a distinct people, was impossible, because they were as brave and as high spirited as they were fierce, and were ready to repel by arms every attempt on their independence.

Id. at 581. Do you consider Marshall's language in *Johnson* as "racist" toward Indians? How does the pervasiveness of such language in *Johnson* affect the way you believe judges and lawyers should use *Johnson* as a precedent in federal Indian law today?

3.   At different points Marshall uses the terms "sovereignty," "dominion," "the soil," and "title." In the 1803 Louisiana Purchase encompassing the mid-section of what is now the United States, for example, exactly what did the United States obtain, in regard to land title and governmental authority, *vis-á-vis* the European nations and the Indian tribes?

4.   What are the attributes of the real property interest variously called the "Indian right of occupancy," "Indian title," "original Indian title," and "aboriginal Indian title?" In addition to the elements discussed in *Johnson v. McIntosh*, the Court later announced that Indian title is not subject to compensation under the Fifth Amendment if the United States takes the land; compensation is constitutionally required only if a tribal property interest is "recognized" by treaty or other congressional action. See pages 296–303, infra. For other early discussions of the nature of Indian title, see Fletcher v. Peck, 10 U.S. (6 Cranch) 87 (1810); Mitchel v. United States, 34 U.S. (9 Pet.) 711 (1835). Indian property interests are given further treatment in Chapter 5A, infra. Aboriginal title in other countries, and the influence of *Johnson*, is treated in Chapter 14, infra.

5.   How comfortable does Marshall seem with applying the European colonial era doctrine of discovery to the type of Indian rights involved in *Johnson v. McIntosh*? Notice the tension evident between "natural law" and positive law in the opinion, finally resolved in the case by Marshall's resort to the latter. Could Marshall have found a natural law justification for his version of the doctrine of discovery in the case by reference to the writings of Victoria, pages 56–156, supra? To the version of natural law employed by Pope Innocent IV, pages 49–50, supra? The natural law-positive law tension, and Marshall's apparent discomfort with the discovery doctrine were further revealed in a landmark Indian law decision nine years later, *Worcester v. Georgia*, page 137, infra.

5.   Marshall's decision in *Johnson* has spawned a cottage industry among legal scholars on the "meanings" of the decision. Excerpts from two studies by well-respected commentators follow:

> The message of *Johnson v. McIntosh*, then was that the natural rights of human beings to dispose of property that they held by virtue of possession did not apply to Indians in America. While Marshall had intimated that the circumscription of the rights of conquered peoples was a prerogative of conquest he had not suggested that such a circumscription would have occurred if the conquered persons had been other than "fierce savages," incapable of being "incorporated with the victorious nation" and thereby retaining "unimpaired" their rights to property. The special principles of Indian-white property rights were a function of the "character and habit" of the Indians.

* * *

* * * The positive enactments of American states and the federal government, as distinguished from the unwritten principles of natural law, determined the treatment of Indian titles to land. Natural law, Marshall intimated in *Johnson v. McIntosh,* was not designed to apply to cases involving persons whose "character and habits" were so markedly different from "civilized" whites.

G. Edward White, The Marshall Court and Cultural Change: 1815–35, (The Oliver Wendell Holmes Devise History of the Supreme Court, Vols. III–IV) 710–11 (1988).

The acceptance of the Doctrine of Discovery into United States law held profound implications for future relations between the federal government and the Indians. The Doctrine of Discovery's discourse of conquest was now available to legitimate, energize, and constrain as needed white society's will to empire over the North American continent. The doctrine confirmed the superior rights of a European-derived nation to the lands occupied by "infidels, heathens, and savages," encouraged further efforts by white society to acquire the Indians' "waste" lands, and vested authority in a centralized sovereign to regulate the Indians' dispossession according to national interest, security, and sometimes even honor.

Perhaps most important, *Johnson's* acceptance of the Doctrine of Discovery into United States law represented the legacy of 1,000 years of European racism and colonialism directed against non-Western peoples. White society's exercise of power over Indian tribes received the sanction of the Rule of Law in *Johnson v. McIntosh.* The Doctrine of Discovery's underlying medievally derived ideology—that normatively divergent "savage" peoples could be denied rights and status equal to those accorded to the civilized nations of Europe—had become an integral part of the fabric of United States federal Indian law. The architects of an idealized European vision of life in the Indians' New World had successfully transplanted an Old World form of legal discourse denying all respect to the Indians' fundamental human rights. While the tasks of conquest and colonization had not yet been fully actualized on the entire American continent, the original legal rules and principles of federal Indian law set down by Marshall in *Johnson v. McIntosh* and its discourse of conquest ensured that future acts of genocide would proceed on a rationalized, legal basis.

Robert A. Williams, Jr., The American Indian in Western Legal Thought: The Discourses of Conquest 316–17, 325–26 (1990).

6. Whatever subtler meanings and motives underlay Marshall's decision in *Johnson v. McIntosh,* one practical result is clear: it rationalized and girded a legal framework for extinguishing Indian title under the principles of the European colonial era doctrine of discovery. The process was already embodied in U.S. statutes. This gave security to those whose titles

traced to the process and impetus to the method that was used to acquire virtually all the continent from the Indians and to extend the sovereign power of the United States over it. As soon as treaties and other purchases were negotiated with foreign powers claiming lands to the West, the U.S. would begin extinguishing Indian titles using its exclusive prerogatives validated in *Johnson*; only the vestiges—Indian reservations—then would remain in Indian possession and title. Another practical result of Marshall's incorporation of the discovery doctrine into United States law was to constrain the sometimes overbearing and unfair pressures on the Indians from competing purchasers, be they individuals or other governments, not possessed of the rights vested in the superior sovereignty of the United States under the doctrine of discovery. In this sense, can the doctrine of discovery be viewed as "efficient," in terms "of minimizing costs, broadly defined (for example, value of lives, risks borne, and time spent on unproductive warfare) to the European colonizers?" Professor Eric Kades makes this intriguing argument in *The Dark Side of Efficiency: Johnson v. McIntosh and the Expropriation of American Indian Lands*, 148 U.Pa.L.Rev. 1065 (2000). According to Professor Kades, "Johnson v. McIntosh was an essential part of a regime of efficient expropriation because it ensured that Europeans did not bid against each other to acquire Indian lands, thus keeping prices low. * * * " *Id.* at 1071–72.

Professor Matthew L.M. Fletcher offers a rebuttal of Professor Kades' theory, arguing that the transaction costs in the "efficient" world Kades describes are higher under the rule in *Johnson v. McIntosh*:

> * * * In the Kades world, the United States negotiators do not believe that their negotiating partners, the Indians, retain title to their lands. At worst, they treat the negotiations as a joke or a salve to placate the Indians; at best, they drive a hard bargain on price, safe in the knowledge that the Indians don't have a leg to stand on in terms of title or that the Indians would soon die off from disease or starvation. After the sale, the United States and the American citizens still don't think the Indians own title to the land they retain, so they tend to disrespect the borders of retained Indian lands. Moreover, because they sold the land for such a low price and under other harsh terms, the Indians' welfare declines. Conflict ensues, with the Americans feeling righteously indignant because they know that the Indians don't own the land they're claiming. The Indians, having nothing to lose, fight to extermination. Kades, somehow, argues that this is the more efficient outcome.

> In the alternate world, where the *Johnson* rule is reversed, * * * the United States negotiators treat the negotiations as real, as a legitimate attempt to reach a meeting of the minds. The land purchase agreements are more evenly weighted, with higher prices for the land and better terms, allowing the Indians to better fend for themselves on their retained lands. Federal officials, one would hope, respect the land interests of the Indians more because they own their land.

Matthew L.M. Fletcher, *The Iron Cold of the Marshall Trilogy*, 82 N.D.L. Rev. 627, 686–693 (2006).

NATION BUILDING NOTE: DECOLONIZING INDIGENOUS PEOPLES RIGHTS UNDER THE DOCTRINE OF DISCOVERY

Besides the United States, the other major English common law settler-states with large indigenous tribal populations, Australia, Canada and New Zealand, followed Chief Justice Marshall's lead in incorporating the doctrine of discovery into their domestic laws. Their courts have cited and relied upon *Johnson v. McIntosh* to decide major issues of indigenous peoples' rights in their legal systems, even into the present century. Thus, like Indian tribes in the United States, the foremost challenge to the Nation building efforts of indigenous peoples in these countries is decolonizing the limitations on their rights imposed by the doctrine of discovery under domestic law.

Roughly half a century after Chief Justice Marshall incorporated the doctrine of discovery into U.S. law, Chief Justice James Prendergast of New Zealand's Supreme Court relied on the "well known case of *Johnson v. McIntosh*" and its familiar catalog of racist stereotypes of indigenous peoples as lawless, war-like and in a lower state of social organization, to hold that the Maori tribes were incapable of entering into treaties because of their legal incapacity to perform the duties and assume the rights of "a civilized community." Wi Parata v The Bishop of Wellington, 3 JUR. (N.S.) 72 (1877) at 77, 78. The effect of this incapacity, according to *Wi Parata*, was to render the Treaty of Waitangi signed between the English Crown and 512 Maori chiefs in 1840 "a simple nullity." The title of the Crown to New Zealand was not acquired by the treaty, Prendergast explained, but under the European Law of Nations, "by discovery and priority of occupation, as a territory inhabited only by savages." Id. at 78.

It took the Maori nearly a century of sometimes violent, but always persistent struggle, to gain at least formal legal recognition of what they call "te Tiriti o Waitangi," with New Zealand's passage of the Treaty of Waitangi Act of 1975. The Act authorized the creation of the Waitangi Tribunal, charged with investigating legislative or executive actions that violate the principles of the treaty, to report its findings, and make recommendations. Its investigative powers have been extended to include historic claims. See generally P.G. McHugh, *The Constitutional Role of the Waitangi Tribunal*, 1985 N.Z.L.J. 224. The tribunal is not a court, however, and has no sanctioning or enforcement powers, but its recommendations have influenced executive and legislative actions and judicial decisions which recognize the Maori interpretation of the Treaty of Waitangi as protecting their customary and traditional rights. The Tribunal has therefore played an important role in the Maoris' efforts at Nation building, as its recommendations have provided the springboard for multi-million dollar land settlement claims that that have been tranferred to Maori corporate owned and controlled entities. See Robert J. Miller & Jacinta

Ruru, *An Indigenous Lens Into Comparative Law: The Doctrine of Discovery in the United States and New Zealand*, 111 W. Va.L.Rev. 849 (2009).

In Australia, the legal legacy of the doctrine of discovery has been a particularly onerous burden for that country's aboriginal peoples to overcome in their still nascent Nation building efforts. Australian and British colonial authorities early on adopted the theory that Australia was *terra nullius* at the time of Captain James Cook's 1776 "discovery" of the continent, due to the supposed backwards, uncivilized state of its aboriginal inhabitants. It would take Australia's aboriginal peoples nearly two centuries before they were finally able to assert their aboriginal title in an Australian domestic court in Milirrpum v Nabalco Pty Ltd [1971], 17 FLR 141 (Austl.). Justice Blackburn's opinion for the Northern Territory Supreme Court in the infamous "Gove Land Case" unequivocally affirmed Australia's continued adherence to the most extreme application of the doctrine among the English common law settler-states:

> * * * There is a distinction between settled colonies, where the land, being desert and uncultivated, is claimed by right of occupancy, and conquered or ceded colonies. The words "desert and uncultivated" are Blackstone's own; they have always been taken to include territory in which live uncivilized inhabitants in a primitive state of society. The difference between the laws of the two kinds of colony is that in those of the former kind all the English laws which are applicable to the colony are immediately in force there upon its foundation. In those of the latter kind, the colony already having law of its own, that law remains in force until altered."

Id. at 201.

Related to this was the doctrine that discovery was a root of title in international law: that the sovereign whose subjects discovered new territory acquired title to such territory by the fact of such discovery. This principle was repeatedly said to have been the basis of the claims by European sovereigns, including of course the British Crown, to land on the American continent: see, for example, *Johnson and Graham's Lessee v. M'Intosh*, per Marshall C.J.

Id. at 200.

It wasn't until Mabo v. Queensland, 107 A.L.R. 1 (1992), that Australia's High Court finally rejected the doctrine of terra nullius as applied to Australia's aboriginal peoples, and confirmed the possibility that aboriginal title might still exist in some parts of Australia. The High Court's decision in *Mabo* prompted new land rights legislation for Australia's indigenous peoples. Following a lengthy and acrimonious political debate, the federal government passed the Native Title Act, 1993 (Austl.), which established Australia's National Native Title Tribunal ('the Tribunal'), an independent agency empowered to make decisions, conduct inquiries, reviews and mediations, and assist various parties with native title applications, and indigenous land use agreements ('ILUAs'). However, major amendments to the Act were passed in 1997 over fierce opposition of Australia's indigenous communities. See Chapter 14, infra. Critics of the Act in its present form argue that Australia still has a long road to travel in achieving justice for its indigenous peoples with respect to aboriginal land rights and title recognition. See Larissa Behrendt, Achieving Social Justice: Indigenous Rights and Australia's Future 4 (2003).

In Canada, the struggle to decolonize indigenous peoples rights in a legal regime that continues to adhere to the doctrine of discovery has been no less tortuous, or definitively settled at this point in time. The Supreme Court of Canada relied on *Johnson v. McIntosh* as authority for its acceptance of the doctrine of discovery in Canadian law in *St. Catharines Milling and Lumber Co. v. R.* (1887), 13 S.C.R. 577 (Can.):

> At the time of the discovery of America, and long after, it was an accepted rule that heathen and infidel nations were perpetual enemies, and that the Christian prince or people first discovering and taking possession of the country became its absolute proprietor, and could deal with the lands as such. It is a rule of the common law that property is the creature of the law and only continues to exist while the law that creates and regulates it subsists. The Indians had no rules or regulations which could be considered laws."

Id. at 596–97.

Canada, like the United States, originally pursued a policy of extinguishing aboriginal title by treaty for most of the country. But by the time British Columbia's First Nations were being significantly affected by colonization and increases in white settlement and land pressures in the late 19th century, treaties with indigenous peoples, as in the United States, had gone out of fashion. Very few treaties were negotiated by the government with the more than 200 First Nations communities that had been confined to tiny reserves throughout the province, without any recognition of their aboriginal title to their traditional lands.

It wasn't until 1973 that an aboriginal land claim from British Columbia finally made its way to the Supreme Court of Canada in Calder v. Attorney General for British Columbia, [1973] S.C.R. 313, The decision by the Court, though technically a defeat for the Nisga'a Indians, the First Nation involved, played a crucial role in raising the issue of the continuing existence and recognition of unextinguished aboriginal title in Canada in the early 1970s. Three of the seven members of the Supreme Court essentially had supported the Indians' position on the aboriginal title issue. Many Canadian officials, including the Minister of Indian Affairs, recognized that the Supreme Court might not be willing to uphold the status quo on future Indian aboriginal claims cases in British Columbia.

In the wake of *Calder* and other court decisions giving broader recognition to native land rights, government officials began to negotiate aboriginal claims.

The Nisga'a Indians, who had brought the original *Calder* case in the 1970s, finally signed a treaty with Canada in 1998, thereby settling their aboriginal land claims against the government. The treaty provided for a $190 million cash settlement (the Canadian dollar exchanged at a rate of approximately .70 to the U.S. dollar at the time of the settlement) and established a Nisga'a Central Government, with ownership and self-government powers over 1,900 square kilometers of land in the Nass River Valley area of British Columbia. The agreement also contained provisions on Nisga'a entitlements to Nass River salmon stocks and wildlife harvests. See Douglas Sanders, *"We Intend to Live Here Forever": A Primer on the Nisga'a Treaty*, 33 U.Brit.Colum.L.Rev. 103 (1999).

For First Nations in British Columbia, resolving their complex land claims in Canada's courts can be expensive and time-consuming, and there is always the risk of losing, as the Nisga'a experience shows. By some estimates, more than 90 percent of the province is still covered by First Nations' aboriginal title and rights claims, while litigation in the courts grinds on. The experience of the Tsilhqot'in First Nation is illustrative of the struggles indigenous peoples face when the courts of their conqueror continue to rely on the doctrine of discovery in denying them rights in their aboriginal title lands.

Tsilhqot'in Nation v British Columbia, [2014] SCR 256, page 1068, infra, represents the latest chapter in the struggle of British Columbia First Nations for recognition of their aboriginal title and rights in their traditional lands. Overturning a British Columbia Court of Appeals rejection of their claim that had held that a semi-nomadic group like the Tsilhqot'in could not establish title to their territory because they were "too low on the scale of social organization" to establish title to lands on a territorial basis, id. at 715, Canada's Supreme Court recognized the retained rights and title of the Tsilhqot'in to 1900 square kilometers of their traditional territory. But the Court also asserted the Crown's underlying, superior title and rights to the land as well as its unilateral power of extinguishment so long as sufficient "justification" can be provided. See Chaprter 14, supra. Thus, just as in the United States, New Zealand and Australia, as Canadian First Nations legal scholar John Borrows notes; "The doctrine of discovery is alive and well in Canada," John Borrows, *The Durability of Terra Nullius: Tsilhqot'in Nation v British Columbia*, 48 U.B.C.L.Rev. 701 (2015).

CHAPTER THREE

THE FEDERAL-TRIBAL TREATY RELATIONSHIP: THE FORMATIVE YEARS (1789–1871)

■ ■ ■

SECTION A. COLONIAL ERA ORIGINS

Since the earliest colonial encounters, formal dealings with Indian tribes over issues of trade, alliance, and land were conducted almost exclusively by treaty-making. The colonists required the creation of legal and political relationships with the tribes in order to legitimate land transactions, trade, and military partnerships with them, exclusive of other European powers. Choosing this method of dealing itself implied recognition of tribes as self-governing peoples.

The colonial era legacy of treaty-making with the tribes exercised a profound influence on the development of federal Indian law and policy in the post-Revolutionary era. The treaties concluded in the decades immediately following the Revolution negotiated cessions of territory, created reservations, and recognized the internal self-governing powers of tribes. Recognized by the Supreme Court as carrying the force of law under the United States Constitution, these early treaties established the initial framework of United States Indian policy. They also represented the exercise of federal political power over Indians to the exclusion of the states.

Although not every tribe signed a treaty with the United States, the principles drawn from cases analyzing treaties and other aspects of the nation's historic relations with tribes define the nature of tribal legal status. While treaties dealt with acquisition of Indian lands, they also defined the nature of Indian tribes as governments relative to the other sovereigns in the United States—the federal government and the states. The legal and political relationship between tribes and the federal government has been augmented by Congress, the executive branch, the courts, and the tribes themselves largely within this framework. See Matthew L.M. Fletcher, *The Original Understanding of the Political Status of Indian Tribes*, 82 St. John's L.Rev. 153 (2008); Richard B. Collins, *Indian Consent to American Government*, 31 Ariz.L.Rev. 365 (1989). The broad principles derived from the "Marshall Trilogy," *Johnson v. McIntosh*, page 72, supra, and *Cherokee Nation v. Georgia* and *Worcester v. Georgia* (which are in this chapter), are: that Congress exercises plenary power over Indian affairs; that Indian tribes retain sovereign, though diminished inherent powers over their internal affairs and reservation territory; that the United States possesses a trust responsibility toward Indian tribes; and that treaties should be interpreted liberally in favor of the tribes by courts. These principles, which form the jurisprudential foundations of what Professor Robert A. Williams, Jr. has called the "Marshall Model of Indian Rights," Like a Loaded Weapon: The Rehnquist Court, Indian Rights and the Legal History of Racism in America, 49–51 (2005), have structured and informed debate and discussion on federal Indian law and policy in the United States for nearly 200 years. It is doubtful, however, that the tribes and the colonists understood one another's motives or even perceived the treaties as having the same effects. See Colin G. Calloway, Pen and Ink Witchcraft: Treaties and Treaty Making in American Indian History (2013).

DOROTHY V. JONES, BRITISH COLONIAL INDIAN TREATIES
4 Handbook of North American Indians 185–87
(Wilcomb E. Washburn, ed., 1988).

When the British and the Indians met in treaty negotiations during the colonial period, they brought different diplomatic traditions and expectations to the encounter. Out of the interaction between the two groups, over many years and in many different locations, a new kind of diplomacy took shape. The new diplomacy was neither Indian nor European. It was, rather, a complex mix that changed over time according to changing power relationships. No one planned it that way. It was simply the outcome of prolonged and numerous diplomatic encounters between groups who, for the most part, regarded each other with suspicion and hostility but who found it expedient to enter into negotiations in pursuit of their separate goals.

Compounding the conflicts of interests between them was the fact that the Indians and Europeans were strange to each other. This made relations more difficult because they were relations with strangers whose ways were odd and whose words were suspect. It was here that diplomacy played its key role. Diplomacy is the art of dealing with the stranger and, especially, the stranger group. From that fact comes diplomacy's style and mode of operation. In colonial North America the style was intense because of the proximity of the participating groups and their exclusive unbending pride. Out of the almost-daily interaction among Indians and Europeans came a system of treaties that was complex, flexible, completely satisfactory to none, and yet—on the whole—a remarkable achievement for people whose principles and interests were frequently in opposition.

* * *

North American diplomacy was not centralized; it was diffuse. It was not conducted by trained diplomats but by anybody and everybody: by orators, civil leaders, village and provincial councils, missionaries, speculators, traditionalists, dissidents, those with authority and those without. It was a diplomacy that developed its own protocols and ceremonies, and these were rarely European. It was better understood in the centuries when the Indians still had power and the freedom of maneuver than in the centuries when they did not. What happened in the hinterland called colonial North America was the development of a multilateral, multicultural diplomacy unlike the diplomatic tradition of any single participant but partaking of them all. Europeans did not begin with hegemony in the New World. They gained it only gradually, and while they were working toward it, they and their Indian opposites created something new.

American Traditions

In Eastern North America there were at least two different traditions of diplomacy, that of the Mississippi Basin, which centered on the calumet or peace pipe, and that of the Northeast, which centered on the wampum belt or covenant belt. These two traditions can be glimpsed in the work of a remarkable religious figure, Father Joseph Francois Lafitau, who from 1712 to 1717 was stationed at Sault Saint Louis, a Jesuit mission on the south bank of the Saint Lawrence River opposite Montreal.

* * * After comparing the Indians' calumet to the caduceus, Mercury's winged, serpent-entwined staff, Lafitau pointed out that the peace pipe and the caduceus performed similar functions in signaling a diplomatic mission and providing safe conduct, but that the Indians went the ancients one better because they had preserved "the most essential thing in the calumet of peace; it is this pipe, which is I think a veritable altar for the Indians where they offer with all due forms a sacrifice to the sun, a sacrifice which gains for the calumet that respect to which, through a spirit of ancient religion, the sacredness of oaths and the inviolable law of nations are attached, in the same way as these things were formerly attached to Mercury's staff."

By this roundabout route through European antiquity, Lafitau had come to an understanding of one of the essential characteristics of Indian diplomacy. In Indian diplomatic traditions, treaties were not merely temporal agreements. They were sacred collective obligations, to be broken only under peril of divine displeasure. It was a view that had been part of the medieval heritage of European diplomacy. The heritage survived in isolated pockets of the church of which Lafitau was a part, but, in general, European humanists had long since brushed such a view aside.

It was in the New World among the Indians that the sense of sacredness remained strong, informing diplomacy, vivifying it, furnishing the standards of right and wrong, endowing activities with cosmic significance. It is as easy to sentimentalize as to trivialize or ignore this sense of sacredness. * * *

TREATY OF PEACE BETWEEN THE FRENCH, THE IROQUOIS, AND OTHER NATIONS

Reprinted in The History and Culture of Iroquois Diplomacy 137–144
(Francis Jennings ed. 1985).

[The Iroquois tribes, most especially the Mohawks, had been engaged in a decade-long trade war with the French and their major allied tribes, the Hurons and Algonquins, when the French decided to make overtures toward peace with the confederacy in 1645. The 1645 treaty conference at Three Rivers between the Iroquois and the French and their allied tribes of Canada was recorded by a Jesuit priest, Father Barthelemy Vimont. According to Vimont's relation of the events leading up to the treaty, Tokhrahenehiaron, a Mohawk prisoner who had been captured by the Algonquins, had been released by the French with an invitation to the Iroquois to make peace. In July of 1645, he returned to the French fort at Three Rivers accompanied by two principal men from his tribe. Upon the arrival of the Iroquois boat at the bank of the river, Kiotseaeton, the chief diplomat of the Iroquois embassy, declared that he had come on behalf of all the Iroquois to determine if the French, Hurons, and Algonquins were clearly disposed toward peace with his people.]

On the fifth day of July, the Iroquois prisoner who had been set at liberty and sent back to his own country, as I have said in the foregoing Chapter, made his appearance at Three Rivers accompanied by two men of note among those people, who had been delegated to negotiate peace with Onontio (thus they name Monsieur the Governor), and all the French, and all the Savages who are our allies.

A young man name Guillaume Cousture who had been taken prisoner with Father Isaac Jogues, and who had since then remained in the Iroquois country, accompanied them. As soon as he was recognized all threw their arms around his neck; he was looked upon as a man risen from the dead, who brought joy to all who thought him dead,—or, at least, that he was in danger of passing the remainder of his days in most bitter and cruel captivity. As soon as he landed, he informed us of the design of the three Savages with whom he had been sent back. When the most important of the three, named Kiotseaeton, saw the French and the Savages hastening to the bank of the river, he stood up in the bow of the Shallop that had brought him from Richelieu to Three Rivers. He was almost completely covered with Porcelain beads. Motioning with his hand for silence, he called out: "My Brothers, I have left my country to come and see you. At last I have reached your land. I was told, on my departure, that I was going to seek death, and that I would never again see my country. But I have willingly exposed myself for the good of peace. I come therefore to enter into the designs of the French, of the Hurons, and of the Algonquins. I come to make known to you the thoughts of all my country."

* * *

Finally, Monsieur the Governor came from Quebec to Three Rivers; and, after having seen the Ambassadors, he gave audience to them on the twelfth of July. This took place in the courtyard of the Fort, over which large sails had been spread to keep off the heat of the Sun. Their places were thus arranged; on one side was Monsieur the Governor, accompanied by his people and by Reverend Father Vimont, Superior of the Mission. The Iroquois sat at his feet, on a great piece of hemlock bark. They had stated before the assembly that they wished to be on his side, as a mark of the affection that they bore to the French.

* * *

[T]he presents they wished to make us, * * * consisted of seventeen collars of porcelain beads, a portion of which were on their bodies. The remainder were enclosed in a small pouch placed quite near them. When all had assembled and had taken their places, Kiotseaeton who was high in stature, rose and looked at the Sun, then cast his eyes over the whole Company; he took a collar of porcelain beads in his hand and commenced to harangue in a loud voice. "Onontio, lend me ear. I am the mouth for the whole of my country; thou listenest to all the Iroquois, in hearing my words. There is no evil in my heart; I have only good songs in my mouth. We have a multitude of war songs in our country; we have cast them all on the ground; we have no longer anything but songs of rejoicing." Thereupon he began to sing; his countrymen responded; he walked about that great space as if on the stage of a theater; he made a thousand gestures; he looked up to Heaven; he gazed at the Sun; he rubbed his arms as if he wished to draw from them the strength that moved them in war. After he had sung awhile, he said that the present that he held in his hand thanked Monsieur the Governor for having saved the life of Tokhrahenehiaron, when he drew him last Autumn out of the fire and away from the teeth of the Algonquins; but he complained gracefully that he had been sent back all alone to his own country. "If his canoe had been upset; if the winds had caused it to be submerged; if he had been drowned, you would have waited long for the return of the poor lost man, and you would have accused us of a fault which you yourselves would have committed." When he had said this, he fastened his collar in the appointed spot.

Drawing out another, he tied it on the arm of Guillaume Cousture, saying aloud: "It is this Collar that brings you back this prisoner. I would not have said to him, while he was still in our country: 'Go, my Nephew; take a Canoe and return to Quebec.' My mind would not have been at rest; I would always have thought over and over again to myself, 'Is he not lost?'

In truth, I would have had no sense, had I acted in that way. He whom you have sent back had all the difficulties in the world, on his journey."

* * *

The third showed that they had added something of their own to the presents that Monsieur the Governor had given to the captive whom he had sent back to their country; and that those presents had been distributed to the Tribes who are their allies to arrest their hatchets, and to cause the weapons and paddles to fall from the hands of those who were embarking to go to war. He named all those Tribes.

The 4th present was to assure us that the thought of their people killed in war no longer affected them; that they cast their weapons under their feet. "I passed," he said, "near the place where the Algonquins massacred us last Spring. I saw the spot where the fight took place in which they captured the two prisoners who are here. I passed by quickly; I did not wish to see my people's blood that had been shed. Their bodies still lie in that place. I turned away my eyes for fear of exciting my anger; then striking, the earth and listening, I heard the voice of my Forefathers massacred by the Algonquins. When they saw that my heart was capable of seeking revenge they called out to me in a loving voice: 'My grandson, my grandson, be good; do not get angry. Think no longer of us for there is no means of withdrawing us from death. Think of the living,—that is of importance; save those who still live from the sword and fire that pursue them; one living man is better than many dead ones.' After having heard those voices I passed on, and I came to you, to deliver those whom you still hold."

The fifth was given to clear the river and to drive away the enemy's canoes, which might impede navigation. He made use of a thousand gestures, as if he had collected the waves and had caused a calm, from Quebec to the Iroquois country.

The sixth was to smooth the rapids and waterfalls, or the strong currents, that occur in the rivers on which one must sail to reach their country. "I thought that I would perish," he said, "in those boiling waters. This is to appease them;" and with hands and arms he smoothed and arrested the torrents.

The seventh was to produce a profound calm on the great Lake Saint Louys that has to be crossed. "Here," he said, "is something to make it smooth as ice, to appease the winds, and to allay the anger of the waves." Then, after having by his gestures rendered the route easy, he tied a collar of porcelain beads on the arm of a French man, and pulled him straight across the square, to show that our canoes could go to their country without any difficulty.

The eighth performed the whole journey that had to be made on land. You would have said that he felled trees; that he lopped off branches; that he pushed back the bushes; that he put earth in the deepest holes. "There," said he, "is the road, quite smooth and quite straight." He bent toward the ground, looking to see whether there were any more thorns or bushes, and whether there were any mounds over which one might stumble in walking. "It is all finished. We can see the smoke of our villages, from Quebec to the extremity of our country. All obstacles are removed."

The ninth was to tell us that we would find fires all lighted in their houses; that we would not have the trouble of seeking for wood,—that we would find some already cut; and that the fire would never go out, day or night,—that we would see its light, even in our own homes.

The tenth was given to bind us all very closely together. He took hold of a Frenchman, placed his arm within his, and with his other arm he clasped that of an Algonquin. Having thus joined himself to them, "Here," he said, "is the knot that binds us inseparably; nothing can part us." This collar was extraordinarily beautiful. "Even if the lightening were to fall upon us, it could not separate us; for, if it cuts off the arm that holds you to us, we will at once seize each other by the other arm." And thereupon he turned around, and caught the French-man and the Algonquin by their two other arms,—holding them so closely that he seemed unwilling ever to leave them.

The eleventh invited us to eat with them. "Our country is well stocked with fish, with venison, and with game; it is everywhere full of deer, of Elk, of beaver. Give up," said he, "those stinking hogs that run about among your houses, that eat nothing but filth; and come and eat good meat with us. The road is cleared; there is no longer any danger." He accompanied his discourse with appropriate gestures.

He lifted the twelfth collar, to dispel the clouds in the air, so that all might see quite plainly that our hearts and theirs were not hidden; that the Sun and the truth might light up everything.

[Kiotseaeton presented several more belts of a minor nature, before concluding his presentation of treaty terms].

* * *

When this great Iroquois had said all that is mentioned above, he added: "I am going to spend the remainder of the summer in my country in games, in dances, in rejoicing for the good of peace. * * * " That is what occurred at that assembly. Everyone admitted that this man was impassioned and eloquent. I gathered only some disconnected fragments, taken from the mouth of the interpreter who spoke only in a desultory manner and did not follow the order observed by the Barbarian.

He sang some songs between his gifts; he danced for joy; in a word, he showed himself to be a very good Actor, for a man who has learned but what nature has taught him, without rule and without precept.

* * *

On the fourteenth of the same month, Monsieur the Governor replied to the presents of the Iroquois by fourteen gifts, all of which had their meanings and which carried their own messages. The Iroquois accepted them all with great marks of satisfaction, which they manifested by three loud cries, uttered at the same time from the depths of their chests, at each word or at each present that was given them. Thus was peace concluded with them, on condition that they should commit no act of hostility against the Hurons, or against the other Nations who are our allies, until the chiefs of those Nations who were not present had treated with them.

* * *

On Saturday, the fifteenth, they started from Three Rivers. Monsieur the Governor gave them two young French lads, both to help them to take back their canoes and their presents, and to manifest the confidence that he had in those people.

When the Captain Kiotseaeton saw that his people had embarked, he raised his voice, and said to the French and to the Savages who were on the banks of the great river: "Adieu my brothers; I am one of your relatives. I am going to carry back good news to our country." Then, turning to Monsieur the Governor, "Onontio, thy name shall be great throughout the earth; I did not think that I would take back my head that I had risked,— I did not think that it would go forth from your doors; and I am going back loaded with honor, with gifts, and with kindness. * * * " The Savages replied by a fine salvo of musketry, and the Fort fired a canon shot. Thus ended their Embassy. May God cause all this to succeed for his greater glory.

* * *

ROBERT A. WILLIAMS, JR., LINKING ARMS TOGETHER: AMERICAN INDIAN TREATY VISIONS OF LAW AND PEACE, 1600–1800
103–05, 110–13 (1997).

THE PRACTICE OF CONNECTION

In North American indigenous diplomacy, treaties were sacred texts that enabled treaty partners to fulfill a divinely mandated plan of multicultural unity. Indians of the Encounter era also had very practical reasons for making treaties with communities at a distance. Treaties established connections that helped assure survival on a multicultural frontier. The customary bonds of unity created by a treaty could be relied on, at least as far as Indians were concerned, in times of need or crisis. Treaty partners, therefore, as a matter of constitutional principle, were bound to protect each other's interests.

* * *

Those who failed to uphold the customary bonds of unity created by a treaty risked breaching the sacred covenant of peace created by their alliance. In 1756, as the French and Indian War raged on the frontier, the Cherokee chief Culloughculla spoke bluntly to the Virginia commissioners about the failure of the English to live up to their treaty obligations with the tribe. * * * French-allied Indians were committing "horrid murders" on the frontier inhabitants of Virginia. The Cherokees, operating under the obligations of blood feud imposed by their symbolic kinship with the English, were more than willing to help "prevent such massacres" by attacking the French. But, Culloughculla explained, the English had to live up to their reciprocating treaty commitments before the Cherokees could go on the warpath against their common enemy.

> We have had frequent promises from the Governor of South Carolina, to build us a fort; and it was stipulated at a Treaty held at Saludy last summer, when we signed a release for our lands to the Great King George. But we do not find, that Governor has yet made the least Preparations towards performing his engagement. The king, our Father, told me, that we should mutually assist each other, and therefore, as we are not acquainted with the manner of building forts, and had not the necessary materials, we thought ourselves justifiable in making our application to Governor Glen, who, I must again repeat it has forfeited his word. I have a Hatchet ready, but we hope our Friends will not expect us to take it up, till we have a place of safety for our wives and children. When they are secured, we will immediately send a great number of warriors to be employed by your Governor, where he shall think proper.

The Cherokee chief then dutifully explained the consequences of the failure of the English to live up to their treaty responsibilities: "[I]f no steps are taken for our security, the French will extinguish the Friendly Fire between us."

Indians regarded the duty to provide aid and assistance to a treaty partner, like all of the customary bonds of a treaty relationship, as a constitutional obligation. Changes in circumstance or the original bargaining positions of the parties were therefore irrelevant as far as Indians were concerned. Throughout the treaty literature, Indians can be found trying to educate their European-American treaty partners that the duty to provide aid and assistance under a treaty did not change simply because one party became weaker over time in the relationship. If anything, because a treaty connected the two sides together as relatives, the treaty partner who grew stronger over time was under an increased obligation to protect its weaker partner.

The Nanticoke Indians carefully explained in a 1759 council the nature of the continuing obligations of "brotherly" assistance owed them by Governor Horatio Sharpe under their long-standing treaty with the Maryland colony:

> [A]s we love to travel the roads and other places to seek the support of life and as you are our Brother therefore [we] beg and hope you will not suffer us to be trodden down quite for we are as a child just beginning to walk[;] we are so reduced and diminished and are as nothing. . . . When there were great numbers of us Indians and but few white people in this nation we enjoyed our privileges, profits, and customs in quiet but it is quite the contrary now[;] then [we] were not deprived of our freedom and customs for we had the whole nation once under our jurisdiction but now there is but a spot laid out for us not enough for bread for us Indians. . . . [I]f you our trusty Brother suffers us thus to be evilly treated we shall soon be quite destroyed and totally pushed out of this nation, but hope you our Brother will never suffer us thus to be treated.

As the Nanticokes' remonstrance to Maryland's governor illustrates, the different peoples connected by a treaty were expected to abide steadfastly by the sacred principles of multicultural unity sustaining their original agreement. A treaty, as far as Indians were concerned, was entered into precisely to enhance the chance of survival should some calamity or disaster befall the tribe. The constitutionalized connections created by a treaty were a form of assurance and security that could be steadfastly relied on in times of crisis or need as a matter of customary practice.

* * *

"THAT JUSTICE SHOULD BE DONE TO EVERY PERSON"

Throughout the treaty literature, Indian diplomats reiterated a variety of related metaphors and gestures to elaborate their vision of the constitutional principles governing their treaty relationships with Europeans. This customary practice of using the same set of terms to describe the bonds of connection created by a treaty relationship reflected a more general principle of American Indian multicultural constitutionalism. In American Indian visions of law and peace, treaty partners were under a constitutional obligation to continually renew the bonds that made their mutual survival more assured on the North American Encounter era frontier.

Two meetings held in Philadelphia more than twenty years apart between the Conestoga Indians and Pennsylvania colonial officials provide one of the most compelling illustrations in the treaty literature of how the language of Indian diplomacy could draw on a set of customary terms to renew the constitutionalized connections created by a treaty relationship. The first of these meetings occurred in 1712, more than a decade after the departure of William Penn, who had negotiated the initial treaty relationship between the Conestoga tribe and the Pennsylvania colony. At this 1712 meeting, a group of Conestoga chiefs explained to those now in charge of the colony their understanding of the constitutional principles that had been incorporated into their original treaty agreement with Governor Penn:

> [T]he Proprietor, Govr. Penn had at his first Coming amongst them made an agreement with them that they should always Live as friends and Brothers, and be as one Body, one heart, one mind, and as one Eye and Ear; that what the one saw the other should see, and what the one heard the other should hear, and that there should be nothing but Love and friendship between them and us forever.

After this speech the Indians presented a small bundle of furs, stating that they had always abided by this agreement "[a]nd should constantly observe it in all respects."

In the second meeting, some two decades later in 1735, the Conestoga chiefs once again appeared before the Pennsylvania council, now headed by William Penn's son, Thomas, to renew their ancient treaty with the colony. Civility, a Conestoga speaker, made a speech that once again outlined his people's original understanding of their treaty with the senior Penn. In that first treaty, Civility explained, Governor Penn had agreed to purchase the Indians' lands before allowing any "white people" to possess them. But the sale of these lands, according to the legal meanings the Indians attached to their treaty relationship with Pennsylvania, was not intended to separate the two peoples. For the Indians, allowing the white people to possess their lands formed the basis of a continuing constitutional relationship of multicultural unity. As Civility explained to Pennsylvania's colonial officials, when the Indians gave their lands to Penn, they told him that "he and they should live on those Lands like Brethren, in Love and Friendship together, whereby they became all as one People and one Nation, joined together so strongly that nothing should ever disunite them, but that they should continue one People for ever." Civility then restated the customary terms that had been used in the Conestogas' original treaty with the colony:

> [O]ne chief Article then agreed on between William Penn and the Indians was, that if any Mischief or Hurt should befall either, they should assist one another, and constantly have their Eyes open to watch for each other's Safety, and their Ears open that if any News were brought from any Country that might give uneasiness to either, they should carefully inform each other of what they heard.

> That it was further agreed between William Penn and the Indians, that each should bear a share in the other's Misfortunes. That this Country, though it Might be filled with People of different Nations, yet Care should be taken that Justice should be done to every Person, and no Mischief happen without Satisfaction being given when it was necessary.

Civility finished his speech by laying down three bundles of skins "to bind their Words." He declared that "they were now come hither to see William Penn's Sons, to take them by the hand and renew with them the League of Friendship made with their Father."

* * *

Indians, as well, customarily bound their future generations to a treaty relationship. As the Creek speaker Stumpee stated to Georgia's colonial officials at the 1757 Savannah conference:

> You have declared to us that it is your earnest desire to live in the strictest union with us, we cannot but approve these good dispositions. We know that treaties have been made for this purpose by our Fathers and agreed to by many of our Old Men yet living. We are sensible that these treaties are binding not only upon those who signed them but upon our whole people and their posterity. Yet it would be well that they are renewed and confirmed in our days, that the young men may be witnesses to them and transmit a knowledge of them to their children.

* * *

NOTE: THE VIRGINIA COLONY'S TREATY RELATIONS WITH POWHATAN'S CONFEDERACY

The Virginia Company's royal charter from King James I expressed the hope that the establishment of a colony in Virginia would "in time bring the infidels and savages, living in those parts, to human civility, and to a settled and quiet Government." See p. 62, supra. The 145 colonists sent to the New World in 1607 under the Virginia Company's sponsorship were surprised to find that the Indians of Virginia, as related by Captain John Smith, possessed "such government as that their magistrates for good commanding, and their people for due obedience and obeying, excel many places that would be accounted very civil." Quoted in The Jamestown Voyages Under the First Charter 1606–1609, at 369 (Philip L. Barbour ed. 1969).

The site selected for the colony of Virginia was located on lands claimed by the confederacy of Tidewater tribes organized by the Indian emperor Powhatan. Powhatan's early-seventeenth century confederacy included perhaps as many as 9,000 individuals. Shortly after arriving, the vastly outnumbered English colonists purchased rights to settle their colony peacefully from one of Powhatan's tributary tribes, the Paspahegh. They made a payment in copper to the Indians, thus establishing the precedent of dealing with the tribes through formal negotiations and purchasing rights of settlement early on in English-Indian North American colonial relations.

The first-ever formal treaty ceremony recorded between English colonists and an Indian confederacy in North America occurred in 1608 at Powhatan's seat of government in a village on the Chickahominy River, one hundred miles from the Jamestown settlement. Officers of the Virginia Company had originally desired for Powhatan to travel to Jamestown, where he would meet Christopher Newport, the Company's agent. Newport then intended to perform a "coronation" of the Indian emperor. Powhatan insisted on the English coming to his seat of government, and so Newport was required to travel the one hundred miles to the emperor's village. John Smith described the "coronation" ceremony in his "Map of Virginia" as follows:

> All things being fit for the day of his [Powhatan's] coronation, the presents were brought * * * his scarlet cloak and apparel (with much ado) put on him * * * . But a foul trouble there was to make him kneel to receive his crown, he neither knowing the majesty, nor meaning of a Crown, nor bending of the knee, endured so many persuasions, examples, and instructions, as tired them all. At last by leaning hard on his shoulders, he a little stooped, and Newport put the Crown on his head.

Id. at 414.

By accepting the "Crown," Powhatan, at least from the English view, "bent his knee" to the English king and placed himself under his authority. Powhatan presented a cloak and some foot coverings to the English in return for the presents he had received, reflecting his own interpretation of the relation as a reciprocal agreement among, at most, equals. Whatever the misunderstandings between the parties, the Virginia Company nonetheless advertised the treaty in England as proof that the Indian emperor "hath licensed us to negotiate among them, and to possess their country with them." Hundreds of new colonists were recruited to settle in Jamestown amongst the peaceful "savages." See Harry C. Porter, The Inconstant Savage 296 (1979); Robert A. Williams, Jr., The American Indian in Western Legal Thought: The Discourses of Conquest 208–09 (1990).

The death of Powhatan in 1618 resulted in the eventual succession to the head of the confederacy of his more militant brother, Opechancanough, who distrusted the English colonists. Their numbers and encroachments on Indian territory were expanding at a rate never imagined by the Indians during the first decade of English settlement. Opechancanough demanded of the colony's Governor, George Yeardley, the right to approve personally any future grants to colonists of Indian lands, but the Virginia Company directors in England refused to recognize "a sovereignty in that heathen infidel." *Denial by the Virginia Company in London of the Sovereign Rights of the Indians in the Land,* 4 Early American Indian Documents 28 (William S. Robinson ed. 1983). In 1622, Opechancanough, totally frustrated in his dealings with the invading

English, led the confederated Tidewater tribes in a violent assault. Nearly 350 of the 1,240 colonists died in the coordinated surprise attacks on the scattered English settlements outside the immediate region of Jamestown.

The English retaliated with an effective counterattack on Opechancanough's forces, considerably weakening the confederated tribes. Opechancanough managed to organize one final revolt in 1644, but again he was soundly defeated, and this time captured. He was brought to Jamestown and fatally shot in the back by an unnamed soldier before he could be deported to England for trial.

Immediately after Opechancanough's death, a new treaty was negotiated with the confederacy of Tidewater tribes. This was a treaty of surrender and submission to the English Crown forced upon Opechancanough's successor, Necotowance. This 1646 treaty ceded all of the confederacy's lands south of the York River to the English, reserving to the Indians the right to inhabit and hunt on the lands north of the river. The treaty's drawing of a boundary line between the two races, thereby creating a reserved territory to the Indians; its declaration of a duty of protection assumed by a European sovereign over the Indians, and its affirmation of the Indians' diminished legal status and territorial rights, and of the superior rights of a European sovereign to Indian lands all became central features of Indian treaties and policy. See R. Williams, supra, at 214–22. See also Stuart Banner, How the Indians Lost their Land: Law and Power on the Frontier (2005); Nation to Nation: Treaties Between the United States and American Indian Nations (Suzan Shown Harjo ed. 2014).

SECTION B. "THE SAVAGE AS THE WOLF": THE FOUNDERS' FIRST INDIAN POLICY

The Proclamation of 1763, discussed at page 69, supra, asserted the Crown's central authority over Indian land negotiations and a determination to respect existing Indian rights to territory. The Proclamation ceased to have formal legal force once the thirteen original colonies declared their independence from Great Britain in 1776. But the Founders digested and sifted through the legacy represented by the Proclamation in developing their own Indian policy.

A powerful group of tribes who had sided with Great Britain during the Revolution held large claims on the territories between the Appalachians and the Mississippi River ceded to the United States by Great Britain in the Treaty of Paris of 1783. They remained openly hostile to the new nation, and deeply suspicious of its intentions toward their lands. The principles adopted by the Founders to guide the United States' first Indian policy, therefore, responded to the immediate demands of seeking peace and avoiding a costly Indian war with the frontier tribes. But these same principles would come to assume enduring importance for future United States Indian policy, and especially for federal Indian law.

Commander-in-Chief George Washington set out his recommendations in dealing with the frontier Indians in response to a set of reports submitted to him by James Duane, head of the Committee of Indian Affairs of the Continental Congress.

GEORGE WASHINGTON TO JAMES DUANE
(September 7, 1783).
Reprinted from Documents of United States Indian Policy 1–2
(Francis Prucha ed. Second Edition, Expanded, 1990).

* * *

My ideas * * * of the line of Conduct proper to be observed not only towards the Indians, but for the government of the Citizens of America, in their Settlement of the Western Country (which is intimately connected therewith) are simply these.

That the Indians should be informed, that after a Contest of eight years for the Sovereignty of this Country G[reat] Britain has ceded all the Lands of the United States within the limits described by the art[icl]e of the Provisional Treaty [of Paris concluding the Revolutionary War].

That as they (the Indians) maugre all the advice and admonition which could be given them at the commencement; and during the prosecution of the War could not be restrained from acts of Hostility, but were determined to join their Arms to those of G[reat] Britain and to share their fortune; so, consequently, with a less generous People than Americans they would be made to share the same fate; and be compelled to retire along with them beyond the [Great] Lakes. But as we prefer Peace to a state of Warfare, as we consider them as a deluded People; as we persuade ourselves that they are convinced, from experience, of their error in taking up the Hatchet against us, and that their true Interest and safety must now depend upon our friendship. As the Country is large enough to contain us all; and as we are disposed to be kind to them and to partake of their Trade, we will from these considerations and from motives of Comp[assio]n., draw a veil over what is past and establish a boundary line between them and us beyond which we will *endeavor* to restrain our People from Hunting or Settling, and within which they shall not come, but for the purposes of Trading, Treating, or other business unexceptionable in its nature.

In establishing this line, in the first instance, care should be taken neither to yield nor to grasp at too much. But to endeavor to impress the Indians with an idea of the generosity of our disposition to accommodate them, and with the necessity we are under, of providing for our Warriors, our Young People who are growing up, and strangers who are coming from other Countries to live among us, and if they should make a point of it, or appear dissatisfied at the line we may find it necessary to establish, compensation should be made them for their claims within it.

* * * [A] Proclamation in my opinion, should issue, making it Felony (if there is power for the purpose and if not imposing some very heavy restraint) for any person to Survey or Settle beyond the Line * * * [Washington next recommended vesting centralized control of land purchases and the Indian trade in the federal government and discussed the creation of new states out of the western territories ceded by the Indians.]

* * *

[P]olicy and [economy] point very strongly to the expediency of being upon good terms with the Indians, and the propriety of purchasing their Lands in preference to attempting to drive them by force of arms out of their Country; which as we have already experienced is like driving the Wild Beasts of the Forest which will return as soon as the pursuit is at an end and fall perhaps on those that are left there; when the gradual extension of our Settlements will as certainly cause the Savage as the Wolf to retire; both being beasts of prey tho' they differ in shape. In a word there is nothing to be obtained by an Indian War but the Soil they live on and this can be had by purchase at less expense, and without that bloodshed, and those distresses which helpless Women and Children are made partakers of in all kinds of disputes with them * * * .

NOTE

An underlying premise implicit in the boundary-line treaty policy recommended by Washington was that the Indian reservations that would be created on the western side of the boundary line would be temporary in nature. Washington's argument to Congress in support of his policy recommendations that the pressures of advancing white settlement on the frontier would drive the "Savage as the Wolf" westward reflected a highly negative stereotyped view of American Indian tribalism's way of life and use of the land. It was a view widely shared among the Founders and exercised a profound impact on the development of United States Indian policy and, as shall be seen in the *Cherokee* cases, on the development of federal Indian law. See Robert A. Williams, Jr., Savage Anxieties: The Invention of Western Civilization 197–217 (2012).

Homi K. Bhabha has identified the use of racial stereotypes as an important feature of the language used by colonizers to represent the colonized "as a population of degenerate types on the basis of racial origin, in order to justify conquest and to establish systems of administration and instruction." Homi K. Bhabha, *The Other Question: Stereotype, Discrimination and the Discourse of Colonialism,* in The Location of Culture 70 (1994). What do you think Washington had in mind in using the racial stereotype of "the Savage as the Wolf" in his letter to Congress outlining his views as Commander-in-Chief on "the line of Conduct proper to be observed not only towards the Indians, but for the government of the Citizens of America, in their Settlement of the

Western Country (which is intimately connected therewith) * * * "? Given what you have read about Indian treaty and diplomatic traditions in the pre-Revolutionary era, supra, at 85–98, how would Indians view the purpose of the treaties to be negotiated with the United States under Washington's recommended policy proposals?

Washington's recommendations on the United States' first Indian policy, influenced by the British Proclamation of 1763, were adopted almost immediately and virtually unaltered in a set of reports prepared by the Congress's Select Committee on Indian Affairs. A formal Proclamation was issued by the Congress prohibiting unauthorized settlement or purchase of Indian lands. These policies and recommendations established the framework for U.S. Indian treaties and the Trade and Intercourse Acts, pages 103–115, infra, and the underlying principles were embedded in the federal-tribal relationship.

The Treaty of Hopewell with the Cherokees, 1785, is similar to those negotiated throughout the late 1780s with the major tribes and tribal confederacies on the frontiers of the new nation under the boundary line policy outlined by the first President of the United States.

TREATY OF HOPEWELL WITH THE CHEROKEES
(November 28, 1785).
Reprinted from Documents of United States Indian Policy 6–8
(Francis Prucha ed. Second Edition, Expanded, 1990).

The Commissioners Plenipotentiary of the United States, in Congress assembled, give peace to all the Cherokees, and receive them into the favor and protection of the United States of America, on the following conditions:

* * *

* * * ARTICLE III. The said Indians for themselves and their respective tribes and towns do acknowledge all the Cherokees to be under the protection of the United States of America, and of no other sovereign whosoever.

ARTICLE IV. [Describes the frontier boundary line drawn between the Indians and the citizens of the United States.]

ARTICLE V. If any citizen of the United States, or other person not being an Indian, shall attempt to settle on any of the lands westward or southward of the said boundary which are hereby allotted to the Indians for their hunting grounds, or having already settled and will not remove from the same within six months after the ratification of this treaty, such person shall forfeit the protection of the United States, and the Indians may punish him or not as they please: Provided nevertheless, That this article shall not extend to the people settled between the fork of French Broad and Holstein rivers, whose particular situation shall be transmitted to the United States in Congress assembled for their decision thereon, which the Indians agree to abide by.

ARTICLE VI. If any Indian or Indians, or person residing among them, or who shall take refuge in their nation, shall commit a robbery, or murder, or other capital crime, on any citizen of the United States, or person under their protection, the nation, or the tribe to which such offender or offenders may belong, shall be bound to deliver him or them up to be punished according to the ordinances of the United States; Provided, that the punishment shall not be greater than if the robbery or murder, or other capital crime had been committed by a citizen on a citizen.

ARTICLE VII. If any citizen of the United States, or person under their protection, shall commit a robbery or murder, or other capital crime, on any Indian, such offender or offenders shall be punished in the same manner as if the murder or robbery, or other capital crime had been committed on a citizen of the United States; and the punishment shall be in presence of some of the Cherokees, if any shall attend at the time and place, and that they may have an opportunity so to do, due notice of the time of such intended punishment shall be sent to some one of the tribes.

* * *

ARTICLE IX. For the benefit and comfort of the Indians, and for the prevention of injuries or oppression on the part of the citizens or Indians, the United States in Congress assembled shall have the sole and exclusive right of regulating the trade with the Indians, and managing all their affairs in such manner as they think proper.

ARTICLE X. Until the pleasure of Congress be known, respecting the ninth article, all traders, citizens of the United State's shall have liberty to go to any of the tribes or towns of the Cherokees to trade with them, and they shall be protected in their persons and property, and kindly treated.

ARTICLE XI. The said Indians shall give notice to the citizens of the United States, of any designs which they may know or suspect to be formed in any neighboring tribe, or by any person whosoever, against the peace, trade or interest of the United States.

* * *

ARTICLE XIII. The hatchet shall be forever buried and the peace given by the United States, and friendship re-established between the said states on the one part, and all the Cherokees on the other, shall be universal and the contracting parties shall use their utmost endeavors to maintain the peace given as aforesaid, and friendship re-established. * * *

SECTION C.   LEGISLATIVE ENFORCEMENT OF THE TREATY POLICY: TRADE AND INTERCOURSE ACTS

The fateful combination of non-Indians' insatiable desires for the fertile lands reserved to the Indians by the post-Revolutionary series of treaties, and the attitudes of cultural superiority held by a large segment of the population, particularly those along the frontier, rendered enforcement of the boundary lines negotiated in the treaties virtually impossible. Congress sought to back up the policy behind treaties with a series of laws seeking to regulate all aspects of trade and intercourse with the Indians.

FRANCIS PAUL PRUCHA, AMERICAN INDIAN POLICY IN THE FORMATIVE YEARS: INDIAN TRADE AND INTERCOURSE ACTS, 1790–1834

1–3, 43–50 (1962).

The basic Indian policy of the United States was formulated during the first decades of our national existence, as the federal government sought solutions to the problems caused by the presence of the Indians. These problems the new nation inherited from Great Britain when it acquired its independence; they grew out of the given fact that the Indians were here when the white man arrived and that their presence on the land formed an obstacle to the westward advance of the white settlers.

The immediate difficulty facing the United States after the Revolution was the establishment of peace with the tribes, who had been allies of the British, but there were also other basic problems: determining the precise authority of the states and of the national government in managing Indian affairs, extinguishing in an orderly way the Indian title to the land so that the expanding settlements might find unencumbered room, restraining aggressive frontiersmen from encroaching upon country still claimed by the Indians, regulating the contacts between the two races that grew out of trade, providing adequate means to protect the rights of the red man, and fulfilling the responsibility that the Christian whites had to aid the savage pagans along the path toward civilization.

For the management of these Indian affairs the United States by the 1830's had determined a set of principles which became the standard base lines of American Indian policy. The fundamental elements of the federal program were the following:

(1) Protection of Indian rights to their land by setting definite boundaries for the Indian Country, restricting the whites from entering the area except under certain controls, and removing illegal intruders.

(2)   Control of the disposition of Indian lands by denying the right of private individuals or local governments to acquire land from the Indians by purchase or by any other means.

(3)   Regulation of the Indian trade by determining the conditions under which individuals might engage in the trade, prohibiting certain classes of traders, and actually entering into the trade itself.

(4)   Control of the liquor traffic by regulating the flow of intoxicating liquor into the Indian Country and then prohibiting it altogether.

(5)   Provision for the punishment of crimes committed by members of one race against the other and compensation for damages suffered by one group at the hands of the other, in order to remove the occasions for private retaliation which led to frontier hostilities.

(6)   Promotion of civilization and education among the Indians, in the hope that they might be absorbed into the general stream of American society.

This Indian policy of the government was expressed in the formal treaties made with the Indian tribes, but it took shape primarily in a series of federal laws "to regulate trade and intercourse with the Indian tribes, and to preserve peace on the frontier." * * *

* * *

* * * The first of these measures became law on July 22, 1790.* Continuing the pattern set in the Ordinance of 1786 and earlier colonial legislation, the law first of all provided for the licensing of traders and established penalties for trading without a license. Then it struck directly at the current frontier difficulties. To prevent the steady eating away at the Indian Country by individuals who privately acquired lands from the Indians, it declared the purchase of lands from the Indians invalid unless made by a public treaty with the United States. To put a stop to the outrages committed on the Indians by whites who aggressively invaded the Indian Country, the act made provision for the punishment of murder and other crimes committed by whites against the Indians in the Indian Country.

* * *

The genesis of the first trade and intercourse acts is clear. The laws were necessary to provide a framework for the trade—to establish a licensing system which would permit some control and regulation—but this was merely a restatement of old procedures. The vital sections of the laws

---

* [Ed.] 1 Stat. 137.

dealt with the crisis of the day on the frontier. They sought to provide an answer to the charge that treaties with the Indians, which guaranteed their rights to the territory behind the boundary lines, were not respected by the United States. The laws were not "Indian" laws; they touched the Indian only indirectly, as they limited him in his trade and his sale of land. The legislation was, rather, directed against the lawless whites on the frontier and sought to restrain them from violating the sacred treaties made with the Indians. Even when severe crises were resolved by force— by the crushing of the hostile tribes at Fallen Timbers and Horseshoe Bend, for example—the restrictive elements of the intercourse acts were kept, augmented, refined, and applied to later frontiers. [The 1790 Act was a temporary act, and it was re-enacted in somewhat expanded form in 1793, 1 Stat. 329, and 1796, 1 Stat. 469. In 1799, a temporary act substantially followed the 1796 Act. See, 1 Stat. 743.]

* * *

* * * [O]n March 30, 1802, a new trade and intercourse act became law.[17] It was for the most part merely a restatement of the laws of 1796 and 1799, but by now the period of trial was over. The act of 1802 was no longer a temporary measure; it was to remain in force, with occasional additions, as the basic law governing Indian relations until it was replaced by a new codification of Indian policy in 1834.[*]

NOTE

The Trade and Intercourse Acts had some success in controlling private parties' land transactions with Indians like those involved in *Johnson v. McIntosh*. Nevertheless, several states continued to deal directly with tribes, just as they had prior to the Constitution, signing "treaties" and other agreements that purported to extinguish Indian titles and taking possession of tribal lands. Indeed, huge tracts of land in Maine, New York, Connecticut, and other eastern states were acquired by states in transactions with tribes that never were approved by the federal government as required by the Trade and Intercourse Act. Some of those lands were used by the states for roads and parks and others were conveyed to private individuals to become homes, stores, factories, and commercial forests. Tribal leaders often believed these early state transactions were unfair and the bitterness festered over the generations.

Beginning in the late 1960s, tribes, represented in most instances by attorneys in the then-new legal services programs, filed suit. They alleged that the old transactions were not consistent with the principles of *Johnson v. McIntosh* and were void because federal approval had not been obtained as required by the Nonintercourse Acts, so that the tribes still possessed an

---

[17] 2 Stat. 139–146.

[*] [Ed.] 4 Stat. 729. In 1817, provisions on criminal jurisdiction were revised and expanded. See, 3 Stat. 383 and Robert Clinton, *Development of Criminal Jurisdiction over Indian Lands,* 17 Ariz.L.Rev. 951, 959–60 (1975).

ownership interest in their aboriginal lands. They sought to quiet title, usually requesting decrees confirming Indian title. Tribes also usually sought trespass damages for the allegedly unlawful possession. The only federal statute of limitations relating to the subject (28 U.S.C.A. § 2415) did not bar the claims. Citing the doctrine of discovery and *Johnson v. McIntosh* for the proposition that Indians have a federal common-law right to sue to enforce their aboriginal land rights protected by the United States under the Nonintercourse Act, the Supreme Court issued the following landmark decision that continues to generate litigation and controversy, all centered on Indian legislation passed by the first Congress of the United States, more than 225 years ago. See Chapter 5A, infra, where tribal property interests are treated in more detail.

COUNTY OF ONEIDA V. ONEIDA INDIAN NATION

Supreme Court of the United States, 1985.
470 U.S. 226, 105 S.Ct. 1245, 84 L.Ed.2d 169.

JUSTICE POWELL delivered the opinion of the Court.

The Oneida Indian Nation of * * * New York, the Oneida Indian Nation of Wisconsin, and the Oneida of the Thames Band Council (the Oneidas) instituted this suit in 1970 against the Counties of Oneida and Madison, New York. The Oneidas alleged that their ancestors conveyed 100,000 acres to the State of New York under a 1795 agreement that violated the Trade and Intercourse Act of 1793, 1 Stat. 329, and thus that the transaction was void. The Oneidas' complaint sought damages representing the fair rental value of that part of the land presently owned and occupied by the Counties of Oneida and Madison, for the period January 1, 1968, through December 31, 1969.

* * *

II

The respondents in these cases are the direct descendants of members of the Oneida Indian Nation, one of the six nations of the Iroquois, the most powerful Indian Tribe in the Northeast at the time of the American Revolution. * * *

Although most of the Iroquois sided with the British, the Oneidas actively supported the colonists in the Revolution. This assistance prevented the Iroquois from asserting a united effort against the colonists, and thus the Oneidas' support was of considerable aid. After the War, the United States recognized the importance of the Oneidas' role, and in the Treaty of Fort Stanwix, 7 Stat. 15 (Oct. 22, 1784), the National Government promised that the Oneidas would be secure "in the possession of the lands on which they are settled." Within a short period of time, the United States twice reaffirmed this promise, in the Treaties at Fort Harmar, 7 Stat. 33 (Jan. 9, 1789), and of Canandaigua, 7 Stat. 44 (Nov. 11, 1794).

During this period, the State of New York came under increasingly heavy pressure to open the Oneidas' land for settlement. Consequently, in 1788, the State entered into a "treaty" with the Indians, in which it purchased the vast majority of the Oneidas' land. The Oneidas retained a reservation of about 300,000 acres, an area that, the parties stipulated below, included the land involved in this suit.

In 1790, at the urging of President Washington and Secretary of War Knox, Congress passed the first Indian Trade and Nonintercourse Act, ch. 33, 1 Stat. 137. See American State Papers, 1 Indian Affairs 53 (1832); F. Prucha, American Indian Policy in the Formative Years 43–44 (1962). The Act prohibited the conveyance of Indian land except where such conveyances were entered pursuant to the treaty power of the United States.[2] In 1793, Congress passed a stronger, more detailed version of the Act, providing that "no purchase or grant of lands, or of any title or claim thereto, from any Indians or nation or tribe of Indians, within the bounds of the United States, shall be of any validity in law or equity, unless the same be made by a treaty or convention entered into pursuant to the constitution . . . [and] in the presence, and with the approbation of the commissioner or commissioners of the United States" appointed to supervise such transactions. 1 Stat. 330, § 8. Unlike the 1790 version, the new statute included criminal penalties for violation of its terms.[*]

Despite Congress' clear policy that no person or entity should purchase Indian land without the acquiescence of the Federal Government, in 1795 the State of New York began negotiations to buy the remainder of the Oneidas' land. When this fact came to the attention of Secretary of War Pickering, he warned Governor Clinton and later Governor Jay, that New York was required by the Nonintercourse Act to request the appointment of federal commissioners to supervise any land transaction with the Oneidas. The State ignored these warnings, and in the summer of 1795 entered into an agreement with the Oneidas whereby they conveyed virtually all of their remaining land to the State for annual cash payments. It is this transaction that is the basis of the Oneidas' complaint in this case.

The District Court found that the 1795 conveyance did not comply with the requirements of the Nonintercourse Act. In particular, the court stated that "[t]he only finding permitted by the record * * * is that no United States Commissioner or other official of the federal government was present at the * * * transaction." The petitioners did not dispute this finding on appeal. Rather, they argued that the Oneidas did not have a

---

[2] Section four of the 1790 Act declared that "no sale of lands made by any Indians, or any nation or tribe of Indians within the United States, shall be valid to any person or persons, or to any state, whether having the right of pre-emption to such lands or not, unless the same shall be made and duly executed at some public treaty, held under the authority of the United States." 1 Stat. 138.

[*] [Ed.] The current codification, with no material changes, is found at 25 U.S.C.A. § 177.

federal common-law cause of action for this violation. Even if such an action once existed, they contended that the Nonintercourse Act pre-empted it, and that the Oneidas could not maintain a private cause of action for violations of the Act. Additionally, they maintained that any such cause of action was time-barred or nonjusticiable, that any cause of action under the 1793 Act had abated, and that the United States had ratified the conveyance. The Court of Appeals, with one judge dissenting, rejected these arguments. Petitioners renew these claims here; we also reject them and affirm the court's finding of liability.

III

At the outset, we are faced with petitioners' contention that the Oneidas have no right of action for the violation of the 1793 Act. Both the District Court and the Court of Appeals rejected this claim, finding that the Oneidas had the right to sue on two theories: first, a common-law right of action for unlawful possession; and second, an implied statutory cause of action under the Nonintercourse Act of 1793. We need not reach the latter question as we think the Indians' common-law right to sue is firmly established.

A

FEDERAL COMMON LAW

By the time of the Revolutionary War, several well-defined principles had been established governing the nature of a tribe's interest in its property and how those interests could be conveyed. It was accepted that Indian nations held "aboriginal title" to lands they had inhabited from time immemorial. See Cohen, Original Indian Title, 32 Minn.L.Rev. 28 (1947). The "doctrine of discovery" provided, however, that discovering nations held fee title to these lands, subject to the Indians' right of occupancy and use. As a consequence, no one could purchase Indian land or otherwise terminate aboriginal title without the consent of the sovereign. *Oneida Indian Nation v. County of Oneida*, 414 U.S. 661, 667 (1974) (*Oneida I*).

With the adoption of the Constitution, Indian relations became the exclusive province of federal law. *Oneida I, supra,* 414 U.S., at 670 (citing *Worcester v. Georgia*, 6 Pet. 515, 561 (1832)). From the first Indian claims presented, this Court recognized the aboriginal rights of the Indians to their lands. The Court spoke of the "unquestioned right" of the Indians to the exclusive possession of their lands, *Cherokee Nation v. Georgia*, 5 Pet. 1, 17 (1831), and stated that the Indians' right of occupancy is "as sacred as the fee simple of the whites." *Mitchel v. United States*, 9 Pet. 711, 746 (1835). This principle has been reaffirmed consistently. Thus, as we concluded in *Oneida I*, "the possessory right claimed [by the Oneidas] is a *federal* right to the lands at issue in this case." 414 U.S., at 671 (emphasis in original).

Numerous decisions of this Court prior to *Oneida I* recognized at least implicitly that Indians have a federal common-law right to sue to enforce their aboriginal land rights. In *Johnson v. M'Intosh, supra,* the Court declared invalid two private purchases of Indian land that occurred in 1773 and 1775 without the Crown's consent. Subsequently in *Marsh v. Brooks,* 8 How. 223, 232 (1850), it was held: "That an action of ejectment could be maintained on an Indian right to occupancy and use, is not open to question. This is the result of the decision in *Johnson v. McIntosh.*" More recently, the Court held that Indians have a common-law right of action for an accounting of "all rents, issues and profits" against trespassers on their land. *United States v. Santa Fe Pacific R. Co.,* 314 U.S. 339 (1941). Finally, the Court's opinion in *Oneida I* implicitly assumed that the Oneidas could bring a common-law action to vindicate their aboriginal rights. Citing *United States v. Santa Fe Pacific R. Co.,* supra, we noted that the Indians' right of occupancy need not be based on treaty, statute, or other formal Government action. We stated that "absent federal statutory guidance, the governing rule of decision would be fashioned by the federal court in the mode of the common law."

In keeping with these well-established principles, we hold that the Oneidas can maintain this action for violation of their possessory rights based on federal common law.

B

PRE-EMPTION

Petitioners argue that the Nonintercourse Acts pre-empted whatever right of action the Oneidas may have had at common law, relying on our decisions in *Milwaukee v. Illinois,* 451 U.S. 304 (1981) (*Milwaukee II*), and *Middlesex County Sewerage Authority v. National Sea Clammers Assn.,* 453 U.S. 1 (1981). We find this view to be unpersuasive. In determining whether a federal statute pre-empts common-law causes of action, the relevant inquiry is whether the statute "[speaks] *directly* to [the] question" otherwise answered by federal common law. *Milwaukee II, supra,* 451 U.S., at 315 (emphasis added). As we stated in *Milwaukee II,* federal common law is used as a "necessary expedient" when Congress has not "spoken to a *particular* issue." The Nonintercourse Act of 1793 does not speak directly to the question of remedies for unlawful conveyances of Indian land. * * *

Significantly, Congress' action subsequent to the enactment of the 1793 statute and later versions of the Nonintercourse Act demonstrate that the Acts did not pre-empt common-law remedies. In 1822 Congress amended the 1802 version of the Act to provide that "in all trials about the right of property, in which Indians shall be party on one side and white persons on the other, the burden of proof shall rest upon the white person, in every case in which the Indian shall make out a presumption of title in himself from the fact of previous possession and ownership." § 4, 3 Stat.

683; see 25 U.S.C. § 194. Thus, Congress apparently contemplated suits by Indians asserting their property rights.

Decisions of this Court also contradict petitioners' argument for pre-emption. Most recently, in *Wilson v. Omaha Indian Tribe*, 442 U.S. 653 (1979), the Omaha Indian Tribe sued to quiet title on land that had surfaced over the years as the Missouri River changed its course. The Omahas based their claim for possession on aboriginal title. The Court construed the 1822 amendment to apply to suits brought by Indian tribes as well as individual Indians. Citing the very sections of the Act that petitioners contend pre-empt a common-law action by the Indians, the Court interpreted the amendment to be part of the overall "design" of the Nonintercourse Acts "to protect the rights of Indians to their properties." Id., at 664. See also *Fellows v. Blacksmith*, 19 How. 366 (1856).

We recognized in *Oneida I* that the Nonintercourse Acts simply "put in statutory form what was or came to be the accepted rule—that the extinguishment of Indian title required the consent of the United States." Nothing in the statutory formulation of this rule suggests that the Indians' right to pursue common law remedies was thereby pre-empted. Accordingly, we hold that the Oneidas' right of action under federal common law was not pre-empted by the passage of the Nonintercourse Acts.

IV

Having determined that the Oneidas have a cause of action under federal common law, we address the question whether there are defenses available to the counties. We conclude that none has merit.

A

STATUTE OF LIMITATIONS

There is no federal statute of limitations governing federal common-law actions by Indians to enforce property rights. In the absence of a controlling federal limitations period, the general rule is that a state limitations period for an analogous cause of action is borrowed and applied to the federal claim, provided that the application of the state statute would not be inconsistent with underlying federal policies. See *Johnson v. Railway Express Agency, Inc.*, 421 U.S. 454, 465 (1975). We think the borrowing of a state limitations period in these cases would be inconsistent with federal policy. Indeed, on a number of occasions Congress has made this clear with respect to Indian land claims.

* * *

Congress recently reaffirmed this policy in addressing the question of the appropriate statute of limitations for certain claims brought by the United States on behalf of Indians. Originally enacted in 1966, this statute provided a special limitations period of 6 years and 90 days for contract and tort suits for damages brought by the United States on behalf of Indians. 28 U.S.C. §§ 2415(a), (b). The statute stipulated that claims that accrued prior to its date of enactment, July 18, 1966, were deemed to have accrued on that date. § 2415(g). Section 2415(c) excluded from the limitations period all actions "to establish the title to, or right of possession of, real or personal property."

In 1972 and again in 1977, 1980, and 1982, as the statute of limitations was about to expire for pre-1966 claims, Congress extended the time within which the United States could bring suits on behalf of the Indians. The legislative history of the 1972, 1977, and 1980 amendments demonstrates that Congress did not intend § 2415 to apply to suits brought by the Indians themselves, and that it assumed that the Indians' right to sue was not otherwise subject to any statute of limitations. Both proponents and opponents of the amendments shared these views. * * *

With the enactment of the 1982 amendments, Congress for the first time imposed a statute of limitations on certain tort and contract claims for damages brought by individual Indians and Indian tribes. These amendments, enacted as the Indian Claims Limitation Act of 1982, Pub.L. 97–394, 96 Stat. 1976, note following 28 U.S.C. § 2415, established a system for the final resolution of pre-1966 claims cognizable under §§ 2415(a) and (b). The Act directed the Secretary of the Interior to compile and publish in the Federal Register a list of all Indian claims to which the statute of limitations provided in 28 U.S.C. § 2415 applied. The Act also directed that the Secretary notify those Indians who may have an interest in any such claims. The Indians were then given an opportunity to submit additional claims; these were to be compiled and published on a second list. Actions for claims subject to the limitations periods of § 2415 that appeared on neither list were barred unless commenced within 60 days of the publication of the second list. * * *

The legislative history of the successive amendments to § 2415 is replete with evidence of Congress' concern that the United States had failed to live up to its responsibilities as trustee for the Indians, and that the Department of the Interior had not acted with appropriate dispatch in meeting the deadlines provided by § 2415. By providing a 1-year limitations period for claims that the Secretary decides not to pursue, Congress intended to give the Indians one last opportunity to file suits covered by § 2415(a) and (b) on their own behalf. Thus, we think the statutory framework adopted in 1982 presumes the existence of an Indian right of action not otherwise subject to any statute of limitations. It would be a violation of Congress' will were we to hold that a state statute of limitations period should be borrowed in these circumstances.

B

LACHES

The dissent argues that we should apply the equitable doctrine of laches to hold that the Oneidas' claim is barred. Although it is far from clear that this defense is available in suits such as this one,[16] we do not reach this issue today. While petitioners argued at trial that the Oneidas were guilty of laches, the District Court ruled against them and they did not reassert this defense on appeal. As a result, the Court of Appeals did not rule on this claim and we likewise decline to do so.

* * *

D

RATIFICATION

We are similarly unpersuaded by petitioners' contention that the United States has ratified the unlawful 1795 conveyances. Petitioners base this argument on federally approved treaties in 1798 and 1802 in which the Oneidas ceded additional land to the State of New York. There is a question whether the 1802 treaty ever became effective. Assuming it did, neither the 1798 nor the 1802 treaty qualifies as federal ratification of the 1795 conveyance.

The canons of construction applicable in Indian law are rooted in the unique trust relationship between the United States and the Indians. Thus, it is well established that treaties should be construed liberally in favor of the Indians, [citing authority]. "Absent explicit statutory language," *Washington v. Commercial Passenger Fishing Vessel Assn.*, 443 U.S. 658, 690 (1979), this Court accordingly has refused to find that Congress has abrogated Indian treaty rights. *Menominee Tribe v. United States*, 391 U.S. 404 (1968). See generally F. Cohen, Handbook of Federal Indian Law 221–225 (1982 ed.) (hereinafter F. Cohen).

* * *

---

[16] We note * * * that application of the equitable defense of laches in an action at law would be novel indeed. Moreover, the logic of the Court's holding in *Ewert v. Bluejacket*, 259 U.S. 129 (1922), seems applicable here: "the equitable doctrine of laches, developed and designed to protect good faith transactions against those who have slept on their rights, with knowledge and ample opportunity to assert them, cannot properly have application to give vitality to a void deed and to bar the rights of Indian wards in lands subject to statutory restrictions." *Id.*, at 138. Additionally, this Court has indicated that extinguishment of Indian title requires a sovereign act. See, *e.g.*, *Oneida I*, 414 U.S. 661, 670 (1974); *United States v. Candelaria*, 271 U.S. 432, 439 (1926), quoting *United States v. Sandoval*, 231 U.S. 28, 45–47 (1913). In these circumstances, it is questionable whether laches properly could be applied. Furthermore, the statutory restraint on alienation of Indian tribal land adopted by the Nonintercourse Act of 1793 is still the law. See 25 U.S.C. § 177. This fact not only distinguishes the cases relied upon by the dissent, but suggests that, as with the borrowing of state statutes of limitations, the application of laches would appear to be inconsistent with established federal policy. Although the issue of laches is not before us, we add these observations in response to the dissent.

E

NONJUSTICIABILITY

The claim also is made that the issue presented by the Oneidas' action is a nonjusticiable political question. The counties contend first that Art. 1, § 8, cl. 3 of the Constitution explicitly commits responsibility for Indian affairs to Congress. Moreover, they argue that Congress has given exclusive civil remedial authority to the Executive for cases such as this one, citing the Nonintercourse Acts and the 1794 Treaty of Canandaigua. Thus, they say this case falls within the political question doctrine because of "a textually demonstrable constitutional commitment of the issue to a coordinate political department." *Baker v. Carr*, 369 U.S. 186, 217 (1962). * * *

This Court has held specifically that Congress' plenary power in Indian affairs under Art. 1, § 8, cl. 3, does not mean that litigation involving such matters necessarily entails nonjusticiable political questions. *Delaware Tribal Business Committee v. Weeks*, 430 U.S. 73, 83–84 (1977). Accord, *United States v. Sioux Nation*, 448 U.S. 371 (1980). See also *Baker v. Carr, supra*, 369 U.S., at 215–217. If Congress' constitutional authority over Indian affairs does not render the Oneidas' claim nonjusticiable, *a fortiori*, Congress' delegation of authority to the President does not do so either.

We are also unpersuaded that petitioners have shown "an unusual need for unquestioning adherence to a political decision already made." *Baker v. Carr, supra*, at 217. The basis for their argument is the fact that in 1968, the Commissioner of Indian Affairs declined to bring an action on behalf of the Oneidas with respect to the claims asserted in these cases. The counties cite no cases in which analogous decisions provided the basis for nonjusticiability. * * *

* * *

VI

The decisions of this Court emphasize "Congress' unique obligation toward the Indians." *Morton v. Mancari*, 417 U.S. 535, 555 (1974). The Solicitor General, in an *amicus curiae* brief for the United States, urged the Court to affirm the Court of Appeals. The Solicitor General recognized, as we do, the potential consequences of affirmance. He observed, however, that "Congress has enacted legislation to extinguish Indian title and claims related thereto in other eastern States, . . . and it could be expected to do the same in New York should the occasion arise." See Rhode Island Indian Claims Settlement Act, 25 U.S.C. § 1701 et seq.; Maine Indian Claims Settlement Act, 25 U.S.C. § 1721 *et seq.* We agree that this litigation makes abundantly clear the necessity for congressional action.

One would have thought that claims dating back for more than a century and a half would have been barred long ago. As our opinion indicates, however, neither petitioners nor we have found any applicable statute of limitations or other relevant legal basis for holding that the Oneidas' claims are barred or otherwise have been satisfied. The judgment of the Court of Appeals is affirmed with respect to the finding of liability under federal common law,[27] and reversed with respect to the exercise of ancillary jurisdiction over the counties' cross-claim for indemnification. The case is remanded to the Court of Appeals for further proceedings consistent with our decision.

It is so ordered.

JUSTICE STEVENS concurs in the judgment with respect to No. 83–1240.

* * *

JUSTICE STEVENS, with whom THE CHIEF JUSTICE, JUSTICE WHITE and JUSTICE REHNQUIST join, dissenting in No. 83–1065.

In 1790, the President of the United States notified Cornplanter, the Chief of the Senecas, that federal law would securely protect Seneca lands from acquisition by any State or person:

> "If . . . you have any just cause of complaint against [a purchaser] and can make satisfactory proof thereof, the federal courts will be open to you for redress, as to all other persons." 4 American State Papers, Indian Affairs, Vol. 1, p. 142 (1832).

The elders of the Oneida Indian Nation received comparable notice of their capacity to maintain the federal claim that is at issue in this litigation. They made no attempt to assert the claim, and their successors in interest waited 175 years before bringing suit to avoid a 1795 conveyance that the tribe freely made, for a valuable consideration. The absence of any evidence of deception, concealment or interference with the tribe's right to assert a claim, together with the societal interests that always underlie statutes of repose—particularly when title to real property is at stake—convince me that this claim is barred by the extraordinary passage of time. It is worthy of emphasis that this claim arose when George Washington was the President of the United States.

* * *

Today's decision is an unprecedented departure from the wisdom of the common law * * * .

---

[27] The question whether equitable considerations should limit the relief available to the present day Oneida Indians was not addressed by the Court of Appeals or presented to this Court by petitioners. Accordingly, we express no opinion as to whether other considerations may be relevant to the final disposition of this case should Congress not exercise its authority to resolve these far reaching Indian claims.

* * *

* * * The 872 acres of land involved in the instant action includes the principal transportation arteries in the region, and other vital public facilities owned by the Counties of Oneida and Madison. The counties and the private property owners affected by the litigation, without proven notice of the defect in title caused by the State of New York's failure to comply with the federal statute, have erected costly improvements on the property in reliance on the validity of their title. Even if the counties are considered for some purposes to be the alter ego of the State, it is surely a fiction to argue that they are in any way responsible for their predicament, or that their taxpayers, who will ultimately bear the burden of the judgment in this case, are in any way culpable for New York's violation of federal law in 1795.

* * *

The Framers recognized that no one ought be condemned for his forefathers' misdeeds—even when the crime is a most grave offense against the Republic. The Court today ignores that principle in fashioning a common law remedy for the Oneida Nation that allows the tribe to avoid its 1795 conveyance 175 years after it was made. This decision upsets long-settled expectations in the ownership of real property in the Counties of Oneida and Madison, New York, and the disruption it is sure to cause will confirm the common law wisdom that ancient claims are best left in repose. The Court, no doubt, believes that it is undoing a grave historical injustice, but in doing so it has caused another, which only Congress may now rectify.

I respectfully dissent.

NOTES

1.   In Oneida Indian Nation v. County of Oneida, 414 U.S. 661 (1974) (*Oneida I*), the district court had dismissed the Oneidas' case under the well-pleaded complaint rule, which prevents a plaintiff from creating federal question jurisdiction by pleading in the complaint a federal issue that anticipates a defense and is otherwise unnecessary for a well-pleaded complaint. Thus, the lower court reasoned, the Oneidas simply could have alleged continuing possession of the land and did not need to plead the Nonintercourse Act in the complaint; the Nonintercourse Act would properly be raised only in response to the defendant's affirmative defense that the Oneidas did not have legal title due to the 1795 transfer. In a lengthy discussion of federal Indian policy, the Supreme Court emphasized the pervasive ties between the United States and Indian tribes, especially in regard to real property, and concluded that termination of Indian occupancy is "exclusively the province of federal law." Id. at 670. Thus it was appropriate to plead the federal issue in the complaint and the well-pleaded complaint rule did not bar the action.

2.   The eastern Indian land claims cases raised widespread opposition and received considerable media coverage. Many of the defendants were good-faith individual homeowners whose predecessors in interest had long ago received from the states title that they believed to be clear. The most visible case during the 1970s involved the Passamaquoddy and Penobscot Tribes of Maine. Those claims were resolved by a 1980 congressional settlement negotiated among the tribes, the State of Maine, and the affected private landowners. See pages 330–332, infra. Several other disputes were settled in similar fashion. The Oneida Indian Nation and the State of New York, however, were unable to reach a negotiated solution concerning the Oneidas' several claims. The litigation which has ensued has continued to produce important decisions by courts on the eastern Indian land claims, including the Supreme Court's most recent precedent on the Oneidas' claims, City of Sherrill, New York v. Oneida Indian Nation of New York, 544 U.S. 197, 125 S.Ct. 1478, 161 L.Ed.2d 386 (2005). See pages 322–327, infra. See also Charles F. Wilkinson, American Indians Time and the Law 39–41 (1987).

SECTION D. REMOVAL

1.   THE JUSTIFICATIONS FOR INDIAN REMOVAL

Despite the treaties and federal trade and intercourse laws, non-Indians continually encroached on the lands reserved to tribes on the Indian side of the frontier boundary line. Large segments of the white population, particularly in the southern states, desired to control the large treaty-reserved areas of unceded Indian lands within and on their borders. The southern states came to view the treaties themselves as the primary impediments to Euro-American civilization's destined control of all the lands east of the Mississippi River.

Removal of the eastern tribes beyond the Mississippi River was already being proposed as the final solution to the United States "Indian problem" by the close of the eighteenth century. A 1789 report to Congress by Henry Knox, President Washington's Secretary of War, suggested the inevitability of removal as the only honorable policy for the new nation to follow in its relations with the frontier tribes.

> Although the disposition of the people of the states to emigrate into the Indian country cannot be effectually prevented, it may be restrained by postponing new purchases of Indian territory, and by prohibiting the citizens from intruding on the Indian lands * * * . As population shall increase and approach the Indian boundaries, game will be diminished and new purchases may be made for small considerations. This has been and probably will be the inevitable consequence of cultivation. It is, however, painful to consider that all the Indian tribes, once existing in those states now the best cultivated and most populous, have become

extinct. If the same causes continue, the effects will happen and, in a short period the idea of an Indian this side of the Mississippi will be found only in the pages of the historian.

Quoted in Walter Mohr, Federal Indian Relations: 1774–88, at 171 (1933).

The assumed inferiority and inability of American Indians to assimilate with white civilization was also a premise of post-Revolutionary Indian policy. It was not until the Louisiana Purchase in 1803, however, that United States policymakers actually began to debate the tactics of inducing the Indians east of the Mississippi to exchange their remaining ancestral lands for a permanent territory in the West. Professor Prucha credits President Thomas Jefferson with originating the idea of a trans-Mississippi exchange of lands with the eastern tribes. In an "unofficial and private" letter written the year of the Louisiana Purchase to Indiana's territorial governor and famous Indian fighter, William Henry Harrison, Jefferson wrote:

> * * * from the Secretary of War you receive from time to time information and instructions as to our Indian affairs. These communications being for the public records, are restrained always to particular objects and occasions; but this letter being unofficial and private, I may with safety give you a more extensive view of our policy respecting the Indians, that you may the better comprehend the parts dealt out to you in detail through the official channel, and observing the system of which they make a part, conduct yourself in unison with it in cases where you are obliged to act without instruction * * * . [O]ur settlements will gradually circumscribe and approach the Indians, and they will in time either incorporate with us as citizens of the United States, or remove beyond the Mississippi * * * . As to their fear, we presume that our strength and their weakness is now so visible that they must see we have only to shut our hand to crush them, and that all our liberalities to them proceed from motives of pure humanity only. Should any tribe be foolhardy enough to take up the hatchet at any time, the seizing of the whole country of that tribe, and driving them across the Mississippi, as the only condition of peace, would be an example to others, and a furtherance of our consolidation * * * .

President Jefferson to William Henry Harrison (Feb. 27, 1803), in Documents of United States Indian Policy 22 (Francis Prucha ed. 1975). See generally Robert J. Miller, Native America, Discovered and Conquered: Thomas Jefferson, Lewis and Clark, and Manifest Destiny 59–97 (2006).

At about the same time John Quincy Adams gave a speech before the Sons of the Pilgrims. Appealing to the widely-shared belief among Americans of the Post-Revolutionary era that tribalism was incompatible with the spread of a superior Euro-American society, Adams asked his audience rhetorically:

> What is the right of a huntsman to the forest of a thousand miles which he has accidentally ranged in quest of prey? Shall the liberal bounties of Providence to the race of man be monopolized by one of ten thousand for whom they were created. * * * Shall the lordly savage not only disdain the virtues and enjoyments of civilization himself, but shall he control the civilization of a world?

Adams answered his own questions:

> "No, generous philanthropists! Heaven has not been this inconsistent in the works of its hands. Heaven has not thus placed at irreconcilable strife its moral laws with its physical creation."

Quoted in C. Royce, Indian Land Cessions in the United States, 18th Annual Report of the Bureau of American Ethnology: 1896–1897, pt. 2 at 536–37 (1899).

The removal policy eventually gained political support from both the coveters of tribal lands and from non-Indians who were concerned for the Indians' well-being.

2. THE CHEROKEE CASES

During the period when the United States was under the Articles of Confederation, a committee of the Continental Congress condemned the "avaricious" attempts of people in the southern states to get Indian lands "by unfair means," citing it as "the principal source of difficulties with the Indians." Shortly afterwards, in 1788, Henry Knox reported that the intrusions of whites on Cherokee lands were tantamount to war. The Continental Congress responded with a resolution citing the Hopewell Treaty provisions, pages 101–102, supra, and directed Knox to prepare to expel the intruders by force. The states did not respond and the troops were not mobilized, but the dispute delayed North Carolina's ratification of the Constitution.

In 1789, President George Washington personally appeared before the Senate to complain that "the treaty with the Cherokees has been entirely violated by the disorderly white people on the frontiers." Armed invasions of Indian country in the western lands of Georgia and North Carolina took the lives of hundreds of Indians and dispossessed the tribes of their treaty-guaranteed lands.

Finally, North Carolina ratified the Constitution and ceded its western lands to the United States. By then many whites had infiltrated the Indians' lands, and instead of enforcing the Treaty of Hopewell, the United States negotiated the Treaty of Holston with the Cherokees in 1791, which changed the boundary line of the Cherokee territory, ceding more land to the United States. Nor did the government hold this new line against settlement, even with the advantage of federal control over the ceded territory. Deep concern in the Capitol over dishonoring the treaties was insufficient to provoke action over the resistance of the territorial government.

When it turned out that the Holston line did not preserve the settlements of many whites, yet another treaty of land cession was sought by the United States. President Adams was driven by angry settlers and state officials to obtain the additional lands and the objecting Cherokees were overwhelmed by pressure from the federal government. Any hope that the Cherokees' latest acquiescence would finally satisfy the whites' land lust was soon dashed.

By the 1820s, most remaining Cherokee land, once spread over five states, was located in Georgia. Georgia did not cede its western land claims to the United States until 1802 in a compact that required the United States to extinguish Indian title to lands within the state. This was impossible, of course, under the federally negotiated treaties, and the United States government did little to implement the compact for many years. The removal policy was, however, well-formulated by this time as the ultimate solution to this delicate problem of federal-state relations. Then, in 1827 gold was discovered on tribal lands and Georgia increased its demands on the United States to remove the Cherokees west to the Indian territory.

The Cherokees held tenaciously to the vestiges of their domain as the basis of a solid, well-established society. The Cherokee constitution declared that the Cherokee Nation was absolutely sovereign and autonomous on tribal soil. They had a thriving agricultural economy, a written language, and a formal government, including a legislature, and courts. The tribe's 1830 memorial shortly after Congress passed the Removal Act reminded the national government that the Cherokees' sovereignty was secured by treaty and asserted in the Cherokee constitution:

> We wish to remain on the lands of our fathers. We have a perfect and original right to remain without interruption or molestation. The treaties with us and the laws of the United States made in pursuance of treaties, guaranty our residence and privileges, and secures us against intruders. Our only request is, that these treaties may be fulfilled, and these laws executed.

Quoted in Allen Guttman, States' Rights and Indian Removal: *The Cherokee Nation v. Georgia* 58 (1965). See also David W. Miller, The Taking of American Indian Lands in the Southeast: A History of Territorial Cessions and Forced Relocations, 1607–1840, at 172–92 (2011).

Georgia enacted a series of laws beginning in 1827 which, in effect, would have abolished the Cherokee government and distributed Cherokee lands among five Georgia counties. All tribal "laws, usages and customs" were annulled and Georgia law was extended over all Cherokee lands. In addition, the Cherokee legislature and courts were prohibited from meeting.

Advocates of forced Indian removal argued that tribal Indians, stereotyped as primitive hunters, should not retard the advance of civilization. According to some proponents of Indian removal, the territories reserved to the tribes east of the Mississippi were now so surrounded by land hungry whites that destruction of the tribes appeared inevitable and the treaties could therefore no longer be regarded as binding. Conditions had changed so dramatically from the time of the treaties' negotiation that only removal could save the tribes from inevitable destruction.

President John Quincy Adams, in his message to Congress in 1828, described the "Indian problem:"

> [I]n appropriating to ourselves their hunting grounds we have brought upon ourselves the obligation of providing them with subsistence; and when we have had the same good fortune of teaching them the arts of civilization and the doctrines of Christianity we have unexpectedly found them forming in the midst of ourselves communities claiming to be independent of ours and rivals of sovereignty within the territories of the members of our Union. This state of things requires that a remedy should be provided—a remedy which, while it shall do justice to those unfortunate children of nature, may secure to the members of our confederacy their right of sovereignty and soil.

Reprinted in Francis Paul Prucha, The Great Father 190 (1984).

The "remedy" was to breach the Cherokees' treaties and forcibly remove them across the Mississippi River. In 1830, Georgia Governor George Gilmer rationalized the removal policy as follows: "[T]reaties were expedients by which ignorant, intractable, and savage people were induced without bloodshed to yield up what civilized peoples had a right to possess by virtue of that command of the Creator delivered to man upon his formation—be fruitful, multiply, and replenish the earth, and subdue it." Id. at 196. Georgia Congressman, later governor, Wilson Lumpkin put it more gently:

> The practice of buying Indian lands is nothing more than the substitute of humanity and benevolence, and has been resorted to in preference to the sword, as the best means for agricultural and civilized communities entering into the enjoyment of their natural and just right to the benefits of the earth, evidently designed by

Him who formed it for purposes more useful than Indian hunting grounds.

Wilson Lumpkin, The Removal of the Cherokee Indians from Georgia 83 (1969).

The Removal Act was passed by Congress and signed by President Jackson in 1830. It stated:

> That it shall and may be lawful for the President of the United States to cause so much of any territory belonging to the United States, west of the river Mississippi, not included in any state or organized territory, and to which the Indian title has been extinguished, as he may judge necessary, to be divided into a suitable number of districts, for the reception of such tribes or nations of Indians as may choose to exchange the lands where they now reside, and remove there * * * .

> That in the making of any such exchange or exchanges, it shall and may be lawful for the President solemnly to assure the tribe or nation with which the exchange is made, that the United States will forever secure and guaranty to them, and their heirs or successors, the country so exchanged with them; and if they prefer it, that the United States will cause a patent or grant to be made and executed to them for the same: *Provided always,* That such lands shall revert to the United States, if the Indians become extinct, or abandon the same.

* * *

Ch. 148, 4 Stat. 411–12 (1830).

FRANCIS PAUL PRUCHA, AMERICAN INDIAN POLICY IN
THE FORMATIVE YEARS: INDIAN TRADE AND
INTERCOURSE ACTS, 1790–1834
224–48 (1962).

* * *

[A]n uncomfortable fact was becoming increasingly obvious: the contact of the Indians with white civilization had deleterious effects upon the Indians that far outweighed the benefits. The efforts at improvement were vitiated or overbalanced by the steady pressure of white vices, to which the Indians succumbed. Instead of prospering under white tutelage, the Indians were degenerating and disappearing.

It cannot be denied that the land greed of the whites forced the Indians westward and that behind the removal policy was the desire of eastern whites for Indian lands and the wish of eastern states to be disencumbered of the embarrassment of independent groups of aborigines within their boundaries. This selfish drive can explain the radical position and demands of a George M. Troup or a Wilson Lumpkin, and the legislatures of Georgia or Alabama. We know, too, that American frontiersmen developed a peculiar Indian-hating mentality, which, combined with avarice for the Indian lands, made many hope and work for the day when the Indians would disappear. But these selfish economic motives were not the only force behind the removal policy. That men as knowledgeable in Indian ways and as high-minded as Thomas L. McKenney, Lewis Cass, and William Clark were long-time and ardent promoters of Indian removal should give us pause in seeing only Jacksonian villainy behind the policy. The promoters of the program argued with great sincerity that only if the Indians were removed beyond contact with whites could the slow process of education, civilization, and Christianization take place. Insofar as removal was necessary to safeguard the Indian, to that extent the intercourse acts had failed.

* * *

The proposal to move the Indians to a permanent reservation west of the Mississippi * * * was not new and had been gradually gaining momentum in governmental circles. It had originated with Thomas Jefferson in 1803, when the addition of the vast Louisiana Territory created conditions that would make removal feasible. Before the end of Jefferson's administration there was gentle pressure put upon the Cherokees—to introduce to them at least the notion of exchanging their present country for lands west of the Mississippi. The Indian agent was directed by the secretary of war to sound out the chiefs on the idea and to let the subject be talked about the nation, so that the prevailing opinion could be ascertained. Those who chose to live by hunting were to be especially encouraged to emigrate, but care was to be taken that the removal was the result of their own inclinations, and not the result of pressure.

[President James Monroe supported the policy of removal and in 1825, in the face of mounting agitation from Georgia for the removal of the Indians, addressed a special message to Congress on the subject. President John Quincy Adams also approved the policy, but no action was taken during his administration.]

* * *

Then Andrew Jackson became President of the United States. He was a man of forthright views who did not hesitate to speak his mind and a man who had ample Indian experience to give weight to his utterances. He had early decided that it was farcical to treat with the Indian tribes as though they were sovereign and independent nations, and he could point to considerable evidence to show that treaties had never been a success.

* * *

When he entered the White House, Jackson was convinced that the Indians could no longer exist as independent enclaves within the states. Either they must move west or become subject to the laws of the states. Assured of presidential sympathy, Georgia then made a new move against the Cherokees. At the end of 1828 the Georgia legislature passed a law which added Cherokee lands to certain northwestern counties of Georgia. A second law, a year later, extended the laws of the state over these lands, effective June 1, 1830. Thereafter the Cherokee laws and customs were to be null and void.

The Cherokees immediately protested and made representations to the President and to Congress. Jackson, whatever his shortcomings in dealing with the Indians, was not one to hide his realistic intentions behind pleasant phrases, for, as he had written to an Indian commissioner a few years earlier, "with all Indians, the best plan will be to come out with candor." Through the instrumentality of his secretary of war, Jackson answered the Cherokees. Bluntly he told them that they had no hope of succor from the federal government. * * *

* * *

Opposition quickly arose to the treatment of the southern Indians as missionary groups with establishments among the Five Civilized Tribes began to protest the removal of their charges, whom they had been directing along the road toward civilization. Although the secretary of war in 1828 had reprimanded the missionaries for having plans diametrically opposed to those of the government, the opposition did not slacken. Prominent church groups in the North and East began to speak out against the government's policy, working toward that full-throated cry that was to resound in the halls of Congress as the debate on removal got under way in April, 1830. * * *

Jackson moved ahead boldly. In his first message to Congress, on December 8, 1829, he addressed himself to the problem of the "condition and ulterior destiny of the Indian tribes within the limits of some of our States." He called attention to the fact that some of the southern Indians had "lately attempted to erect an independent government within the limits of Georgia and Alabama," that the states had countered this infringement on their sovereignty by extending their laws over the Indians, and that the Indians in turn had appealed to the federal government. Did the federal government have a right to sustain the Indians in their pretensions, he asked. His answer was unequivocal. The Constitution forbade the erection of a new state within the territory of an existing state without the state's permission. Still less, then, could it allow a "foreign and independent government" to establish itself there. On these grounds, he told Congress, he had informed the Indians that their attempt to establish an independent government would not be countenanced by the Executive of the United States, and he advised them either to emigrate beyond the Mississippi or to submit to the laws of the states. He came back to the old argument: if the Indians remained in contact with the whites they would be degraded and destroyed. "Humanity and national honor demand that every effort should be made to avert so great a calamity." The solution was to set apart an ample district west of the Mississippi, to be guaranteed to the Indian tribes as long as they occupied it. There they could be taught the arts of civilization.

Jackson denied any intention to use force. "This emigration should be voluntary, for it would be as cruel as unjust to compel the aborigines to abandon the graves of their fathers and seek a home in a distant land." The protestation had a hollow ring, for the Indians were to be informed that if they remained they would be subject to the state laws and would lose much of their beloved land. With more than a touch of sarcasm, the President pronounced it visionary for the Indians to hope to retain hunting lands on which they had neither dwelt nor made improvements, "merely because they have seen them from the mountain or passed them in the chase."

* * *

When the votes were counted, the removal bill passed by a small majority, but the controversy was not resolved. If anything, the agitation against the administration measure grew stronger as Jackson began to get the movement under way. Memorials continued to pour down upon Congress, and the President was further goaded by the Senate, which demanded an accounting of his enforcement of the intercourse act in Georgia. Jackson replied with a strong vindication of his course of action in withdrawing federal troops from the Cherokee lands as soon as Georgia extended her laws over the area.

* * *

The unwillingness of the Cherokees to emigrate exasperated the secretary of war. "It was hoped that the favorable terms offered by the Government would have been accepted," he wrote to Wilson Lumpkin, who was by then governor of Georgia. "But some strange infatuation seems to prevail among these Indians. That they cannot remain where they are and prosper is attested as well by their actual condition as by the whole history of our aboriginal tribes. Still they refuse to adopt the only course which promises a cure or even an alleviation for the evils of their present condition." * * *

* * *

The Indians could not hold out forever. Those who wished to stay were given small reservations where they were. The rest were moved to the West, amidst inevitable hardships, which have been repeatedly retold.

* * *

NOTES

1.   President Jackson refused the direct request of the Cherokee Nation for federal intervention to uphold tribal treaty rights against Georgia's legislative encroachments on Cherokee territorial sovereignty. Thus, the Cherokees had little choice but to test the Georgia laws in the court.

The Supreme Court had infrequently addressed the issue of Indian rights under United States law. Chief Justice Marshall, in his opinion for the Court in the 1823 case *Johnson v. McIntosh,* page 72, supra, had declared that the legal relationship between the Indians and the discovering nations of Europe was the product of "necessity." Recognition of a right to use and occupy their lands was reserved to the Indians so that this territory later could be purchased or the Indians' rights of occupancy otherwise extinguished exclusively by the sovereign. Indian title was created by the white man's legal institutions to avoid the impracticalities, dangers, and ugliness of forcible expropriation and annihilation. The processes of colonization modified the Indian tribes' relationship to the soil and to the settlers, and European concepts of property were introduced. Land dealings became the sole prerogative of the national government consistent with the new nation's legislation (the Nonintercourse Act), with the British Proclamation of 1763, and with a legal tradition reaching back to the Middle Ages.

Johnson had left many questions unresolved respecting Indian rights. How did the processes of colonization define the federal-tribal relationship beyond the question of land rights? What was the significance of the treaties between tribes and the federal government? What was the relationship between Indians and the states? What was the extent of self-government retained by the Indians? Enduring answers were provided to these questions in the two cases brought about by the Cherokee Nation's challenge to Georgia's exercise of jurisdiction over its reservation.

2.   The *Cherokee* cases, *Cherokee Nation v. Georgia*, and *Worcester v. Georgia*, were the central fury of what was, by all accounts, one of the greatest constitutional crises in the history of the nation. A leading historian of the court, Charles Warren, though he wrote well before Truman's takeover of the steel mills, Watergate, or *Bush v. Gore*, called the Cherokee issue "the most serious crisis in the history of the Court." Charles Warren, 2 The Supreme Court in United States History 189 (1922). Associate Supreme Court Justice Stephen Breyer has devoted an entire chapter to the Cherokee cases in his book, Stephen Breyer, Making Our Democracy Work: A Judge's View 22–31 (2010).

At the height of the Cherokee conflict, former President John Quincy Adams declared that "the Union is in the most imminent danger of dissolution * * * The ship is about to founder." 4 Albert J. Beveridge, The Life of John Marshall 544 (1919). One writer summarized the Cherokee-Georgia conflict this way:

The Governor, legislators, and judges of Georgia had publicly dared the Supreme Court to interfere; and the President of the United States, who had encouraged—or at least winked at—this outrage, now seemed prepared to stand by and watch the State defy the Constitution, laws, and treaties of the United States.

Joseph C. Burke, *The Cherokee Cases: A Study in Law, Politics, and Morality*, 21 Stan.L.Rev. 500 (1969).

By the time the first case reached the court the Justices were apparently aware of the issues:

> The policy of removal * * * and the dire consequences for the Indian population precipitated a growing concern among a segment of educated nineteenth-century Americans for what they termed the "plight" of the Indians * * * caused by their inability to acculturate. Given that fact, most Indians would inevitably be forced to emigrate. Most could not adapt to white customs and institutions: they lacked the inherent qualities of republican yeomen. While civilizing Indians was preferable to dispossessing them, for humanitarian and paternalistic reasons, the civilizing process did not take in most cases. The result was a "plight": dependency and poverty or emigration and dispossession.

> In 1828, in an address commemorating the first settlement of Salem, Massachusetts, [Justice Joseph] Story called attention to the "plight" of the Indians.

* * *

> The westward exodus of the Indians signified for him "the general background of their race." They were "incapable of * * * assimilation" with Western culture: "by their very nature and character, they neither unite themselves with civil institutions, nor can with safety be allowed to remain as distinct communities." Their "ferocious passions, their independent spirit, [and] their wandering life" represented a challenge to white society. By their presence they raised the question "whether the country itself shall be abandoned by civilized man, or maintained by his sword as the right of the strongest." Story knew what the answer to that question would be.

> Story sent a copy of his address to [Chief Justice John] Marshall, who responded with a lengthy discussion of the "Indian question."

> > I have been still more touched with your notice of the red man than of the white. The conduct of our forefathers in expelling the original occupants of the soil grew out of so many mixed motives that any censure which philanthropy may bestow upon it ought to be qualified. The Indians were a fierce and dangerous enemy whose love of war made them sometimes the aggressors, whose numbers and habits made them formidable, and whose cruel system of warfare seemed to justify every

endeavor to remove them to a distance from civilized settlements. It was not until the adoption of our present government that respect for our own safety permitted us to give full indulgence to those principles of humanity and justice which ought always to govern our conduct towards the aborigines when this course can be pursued without exposing ourselves to the most afflicting calamities. That time, however, is unquestionably arrived, and every oppression now exercised on a helpless people depending on our magnanimity and justice for the preservation of character. I often think with indignation on our disreputable conduct (as I think) in the affairs of the Cherokees in Georgia. * * *

G. Edward White, The Marshall Court and Cultural Change: 1815–35 (The Oliver Wendell Holmes Devise History of the Supreme Court, Vols. III–IV) pp. 712–13 (1988).*

3. The Cherokees' lawyer was William Wirt, former United States Attorney General in the administrations of Presidents Monroe and Adams. He was hired by the tribe at the urging of Daniel Webster among others. Wirt decided to represent the Cherokees in the case before the Court. He was worried, however, about the Court's jurisdiction and communicated his concerns through a friend to Chief Justice John Marshall who replied:

I have followed * * * the debate in both houses of Congress, with profound attention and deep interest, and have wished, most sincerely, that both the executive and legislative departments had thought differently on the subject. Humanity must bewail the course which is pursued, whatever may be the decision of policy.

Marshall added, however, that he "thought it his duty to refrain from indicating any opinion" on the jurisdictional issues. Id.

Wirt brought an original action before the Supreme Court arguing that the laws of Georgia could have no force within the Cherokees' treaty-guaranteed reservation. Georgia refused to argue before the Court. While the case was pending, Marshall got a taste of Georgia's attitude. A Cherokee named George Tassel was convicted of murdering another Indian on Cherokee land by a Georgia trial court. Tassel applied to the United States for a writ of habeas corpus on the grounds that under the treaty the Cherokees were entitled to their own courts and that he could not be tried in state court. Marshall issued a writ. The state legislature condemned the Chief Justice's "interference" and Tassel was hanged five days later.

A few months later, *Cherokee Nation v. Georgia* was dismissed because Chief Justice John Marshall ruled, as Wirt had feared, that the Court had no jurisdiction. The Cherokee Nation was not a "foreign nation" within the meaning of Article III, section 2, the constitutional grant of the judicial power.

But in dictum, Marshall laid down principles that, even now, make *Cherokee Nation v. Georgia* an important part of the foundation of the federal-tribal relationship.

CHEROKEE NATION V. GEORGIA
Supreme Court of the United States, 1831.
30 U.S. (5 Pet.) 1, 8 L.Ed. 25.

MR. CHIEF JUSTICE MARSHALL delivered the opinion of the Court.

This bill is brought by the Cherokee nation, praying an injunction to restrain the state of Georgia from the execution of certain laws of that state, which, as is alleged, go directly to annihilate the Cherokees as a political society, and to seize, for the use of Georgia, the lands of the nation which have been assured to them by the United States in solemn treaties repeatedly made and still in force.

If courts were permitted to indulge their sympathies, a case better calculated to excite them can scarcely be imagined. A people once numerous, powerful, and truly independent, found by our ancestors in the quiet and uncontrolled possession of an ample domain, gradually sinking beneath our superior policy, our arts and our arms, have yielded their lands by successive treaties, each of which contains a solemn guarantee of the residue, until they retain no more of their formerly extensive territory than is deemed necessary to their comfortable subsistence. To preserve this remnant, the present application is made.

Before we can look into the merits of the case, a preliminary inquiry presents itself. Has this court jurisdiction of the cause?

The third article of the constitution describes the extent of the judicial power. The second section closes an enumeration of the cases to which it is extended, with "controversies" "between a state or the citizens thereof, and foreign states, citizens, or subjects." A subsequent clause of the same section gives the supreme court original jurisdiction in all cases in which a state shall be a party. The party defendant may then unquestionably be sued in this court. May the plaintiff sue in it? Is the Cherokee nation a foreign state in the sense in which that term is used in the constitution?

The counsel for the plaintiffs have maintained the affirmative of this proposition with great earnestness and ability. So much of the argument as was intended to prove the character of the Cherokees as a state, as a distinct political society, separated from others, capable of managing its own affairs and governing itself, has, in the opinion of a majority of the judges, been completely successful. They have been uniformly treated as a state from the settlement of our country. The numerous treaties made with them by the United States recognize them as a people capable of maintaining the relations of peace and war, of being responsible in their political character for any violation of their engagements, or for any aggression committed on the citizens of the United States by any individual of their community. Laws have been enacted in the spirit of these treaties. The acts of our government plainly recognize the Cherokee nation as a state, and the courts are bound by those acts.

A question of much more difficulty remains. Do the Cherokees constitute a foreign state in the sense of the constitution?

The counsel have shown conclusively that they are not a state of the union, and have insisted that individually they are aliens, not owing allegiance to the United States. An aggregate of aliens composing a state must, they say, be a foreign state. Each individual being foreign, the whole must be foreign.

This argument is imposing, but we must examine it more closely before we yield to it. The condition of the Indians in relation to the United States is perhaps unlike that of any other two people in existence. In the general, nations not owing a common allegiance are foreign to each other. The term *foreign nation* is, with strict propriety, applicable by either to the other. But the relation of the Indians to the United States is marked by peculiar and cardinal distinctions which exist no where else.

* * *

Though the Indians are acknowledged to have an unquestionable, and, heretofore, unquestioned right to the lands they occupy, until that right shall be extinguished by a voluntary cession to our government; yet it may well be doubted whether those tribes which reside within the acknowledged boundaries of the United States can, with strict accuracy, be denominated foreign nations. They may, more correctly, perhaps, be denominated domestic dependent nations. They occupy a territory to which we assert a title independent of their will, which must take effect in point of possession when their right of possession ceases. Meanwhile they are in a state of pupilage. Their relation to the United States resembles that of a ward to his guardian.

They look to our government for protection; rely upon its kindness and its power; appeal to it for relief to their wants; and address the president as their great father. They and their country are considered by foreign nations, as well as by ourselves, as being so completely under the sovereignty and dominion of the United States, that any attempt to acquire their lands, or to form a political connexion with them, would be considered by all as an invasion of our territory, and an act of hostility.

These considerations go far to support the opinion, that the framers of our constitution had not the Indian tribes in view, when they opened the courts of the union to controversies between a state or the citizens thereof, and foreign states.

In considering this subject the habits and usages of the Indians, in their intercourse with their white neighbors, ought not to be entirely disregarded. At the time the Constitution was framed, the idea of appealing to an American court of justice for an assertion of right or a redress of wrong, had, perhaps, never entered the mind of an Indian or of his tribe. Their appeal was to the tomahawk, or to the government. This was well understood by the statesmen who framed the Constitution of the United States, and might furnish some reason for omitting to enumerate them among the parties who might sue in the courts of the Union. Be this as it may, the peculiar relations between the United States and the Indians occupying our territory are such, that we should feel much difficulty in considering them as designated by the term *foreign state,* were there no other part of the constitution which might shed light on the meaning of these words. But we think that in construing them, considerable aid is furnished by that clause in the eighth section of the third article; which empowers congress to "regulate commerce with foreign nations, and among the several states, and with the Indian tribes."

In this clause they are as clearly contradistinguished by a name appropriate to themselves, from foreign nations, as from the several states composing the union. * * *

The counsel for the plaintiffs contend that the words "Indian tribes" were introduced into the article, empowering congress to regulate commerce, for the purpose of removing those doubts in which the management of Indian affairs was involved by the language of the ninth article of the confederation. Intending to give the whole power of managing those affairs to the government about to be instituted, the convention conferred it explicitly; and omitted those qualifications which embarrassed the exercise of it as granted in the confederation. This may be admitted without weakening the construction which has been intimated. Had the Indian tribes been foreign nations, in the view of the convention; this exclusive power of regulating intercourse with them might have been, and most probably would have been, specifically given, in language indicating that idea, not in language contradistinguishing them from foreign nations. Congress might have been empowered "to regulate commerce with foreign nations, including the Indian tribes, and among the several states." This language would have suggested itself to statesmen who considered the Indian tribes as foreign nations, and were yet desirous of mentioning them particularly.

If it be true that the Cherokee nation have rights, this is not the tribunal in which those rights are to be asserted. If it be true that wrongs have been inflicted, and that still greater are to be apprehended, this is not the tribunal which can redress the past or prevent the future.

The motion for an injunction is denied.

* * *

MR. JUSTICE JOHNSON. [concurring]—

* * *

* * * I cannot but think that there are strong reasons for doubting the applicability of the epithet state, to a people so low in the grade of organized society as our Indian tribes most generally are. I would not here be understood as speaking of the Cherokees under their present form of government; which certainly must be classed among the most approved forms of civil government. Whether it can be yet said to have received the consistency which entitles that people to admission into the family of nations is, I conceive, yet to be determined by the executive of these states. Until then I must think that we cannot recognize it as an existing state, under any other character than that which it has maintained hitherto as one of the Indian tribes or nations.

* * *

In the very treaty of Hopewell, the language or evidence of which is appealed to as the leading proof of the existence of this supposed state, we find the commissioners of the United States expressing themselves in these terms. "The commissioners pleni-potentiary of the United States give peace to all the Cherokees, and receive them into the favour and protection of the United States *on the following conditions.*" This is certainly the language of sovereigns and conquerors, and not the address of equals to equals. And again, when designating the country they are to be confined to, comprising *the very territory which is the subject of this bill, they say, "Art. 4. The boundary allotted to the Cherokees for their hunting grounds"* shall be as therein described. Certainly this is the language of concession on our part, not theirs; and when the full bearing and effect of those words "for their hunting grounds," is considered, it is difficult to think that they were then regarded as a state, or even intended to be so regarded. It is clear that it was intended to give them no other rights over the territory than what were needed by a race of hunters; and it is not easy to see how their advancement beyond that state of society could ever have been promoted, or, perhaps, permitted, consistently with the unquestioned rights of the states, or United States, over the territory within their limits. The pre-emptive right, and exclusive right of conquest in case of war, was never questioned to exist in the states, which circumscribed the whole or any part of the Indian grounds or territory. To have taken it from them by direct means would have been a palpable violation of their rights. But every advance, from the hunter state to a more fixed state of society, must have a tendency to impair that pre-emptive right, and ultimately to destroy it altogether, both by increasing the Indian population, and by attaching them firmly to the soil. The hunter state bore within itself the promise of vacating the territory, because when game ceased the hunter would go elsewhere to seek it. But a more fixed state of society would amount to a permanent destruction of the hope, and, of consequence, of the beneficial character of the pre-emptive right.

But it is said, that we have extended to them the means and inducement to become agricultural and civilized. It is true: and the immediate object of that policy was so obvious as probably to have intercepted the view of ulterior consequences. Independently of the general influence of humanity, these people were restless, warlike, and signally cruel in their irruptions during the revolution. The policy, therefore, of enticing them to the arts of peace, and to those improvements which war might lay desolate, was obvious; and it was wise to prepare them for what was probably then contemplated, to wit, to incorporate them in time into our respective governments: a policy which their inveterate habits and deep seated enmity has altogether baffled. But the project of ultimately organizing them into states, within the limits of those states which had not ceded or should not cede to the United States the jurisdiction over the Indian territory within their bounds, could not possibly have entered into the contemplation of our government. Nothing but express authority from the states could have justified such a policy, pursued with such a view.

* * *

Where is the rule to stop? Must every petty kraal of Indians, designating themselves a tribe or nation, and having a few hundred acres of land to hunt on exclusively, be recognized as a state? * * *

* * * [A]t what time did this people acquire the character of a state?

Certainly not by the treaty of Hopewell; for every provision of that treaty operates to strip it of its sovereign attributes; and nothing subsequent adds any thing to that treaty, except using the word *nation* instead of *Indians*. * * *

* * *

They have in Europe sovereign and demi-sovereign states and states of doubtful sovereignty. But this state, if it be a state, is still a grade below them all: for not to be able to alienate without permission of the remainder-man or lord, places them in a state of feudal dependence.

However, I will enlarge no more upon this point; because I believe, in one view and in one only, if at all, they are or may be deemed a state, though not a sovereign state, at least while they occupy a country within our limits. Their condition is something like that of the Israelites, when inhabiting the deserts. Though without land that they can call theirs in the sense of property, their right of personal self government has never been taken from them; and such a form of government may exist though the land occupied be in fact that of another. The right to expel them may exist in that other, but the alternative of departing and retaining the right of self-government may exist in them. And such they certainly do possess; it has never been questioned, nor any attempt made at subjugating them as a people, or restraining their personal liberty except as to their land and trade.

* * *

The argument is that they were states; and if not states of the union, must be foreign states. But I think it very clear that the constitution neither speaks of them as states or foreign states, but as just what they were, Indian tribes; an anomaly unknown to the books that treat of states, and which the law of nations would regard as nothing more than wandering hordes, held together only by ties of blood and habit, and having neither laws or government, beyond what is required in a savage state. The distinction is clearly made in that section which vests in Congress power to regulate commerce between the United States with foreign nations and the Indian tribes.

* * *

MR. JUSTICE BALDWIN [concurring]— * * * I concur in the opinion of the court in dismissing the bill, but not for the reasons assigned.

* * *

* * * [T]he stipulations [of the Treaty of Hopewell] are wholly inconsistent with sovereignty; the Indians acknowledge their dependent character; hold the lands they occupy as an allotment of hunting-grounds; give to congress the exclusive right of regulating their trade and managing all their affairs, as they may think proper. * * *

* * * There can be no dependence so anti-national, or so utterly subversive of national existence as transferring to a foreign government the regulation of its trade, and the management of all their affairs at their pleasure. The nation or state, tribe or village, head men or warriors of the Cherokees, call them by what name we please, call the articles they have signed a definitive treaty or an indenture of servitude; they are not by its force or virtue a foreign state capable of calling into legitimate action the judicial power of this union, by the exercise of the original jurisdiction of this court against a sovereign state, a component part of this nation. Unless the constitution has imparted to the Cherokees a national character never recognized under the confederation; and which if they ever enjoyed was surrendered by the treaty of Hopewell; they cannot be deemed in this court plaintiffs in such a case as this.

* * *

MR. JUSTICE THOMPSON, dissenting.

* * *

That a state of this union may be sued by a foreign state, when a proper case exists and is presented, is too plainly and expressly declared in the constitution to admit of doubt; and the first inquiry is, whether the Cherokee nation is a foreign state within the sense and meaning of the constitution.

The terms *state* and *nation* are used in the law of nations, as well as in common parlance, as importing the same thing; and imply a body of men, united together, to procure their mutual safety and advantage by means of their union. Such a society has its affairs and interests to manage; it deliberates, and takes resolutions in common, and thus becomes a moral person, having an understanding and a will peculiar to itself, and is susceptible of obligations and laws. Vattel, 1. Nations being composed of men naturally free and independent, and who, before the establishment of civil societies, live together in the state of nature, nations or sovereign states; are to be considered as so many free persons, living together in a state of nature. Every nation that governs itself, under what form soever, without any dependence on a foreign power, is a sovereign state. Its rights are naturally the same as those of any other state. Such are moral persons who live together in a natural society, under the law of nations. It is sufficient if it be really sovereign and independent: that is, it must govern itself by its own authority and laws. We ought, therefore, to reckon in the number of sovereigns those states that have bound themselves to another more powerful, although by an unequal alliance. The conditions of these unequal alliances may be infinitely varied; but whatever they are, provided the inferior ally reserves to itself the sovereignty or the right to govern its own body, it ought to be considered an independent state. Consequently, a weak state, that, in order to provide for its safety, places itself under the protection of a more powerful one, without stripping itself of the right of government and sovereignty, does not cease on this account to be placed among the sovereigns who acknowledge no other power. Tributary and feudatory states do not thereby cease to be sovereign and independent states, so long as self-government, and sovereign and independent authority is left in the administration of the state.

Testing the character and condition of the Cherokee Indians by these rules, it is not perceived how it is possible to escape the conclusion, that they form a sovereign state. * * *

NOTES

1. As in *Johnson v. McIntosh,* Marshall took a middle road in structuring the place of American Indians in the federal legal system. His opinion is frequently relied upon today, but it was not even a plurality, much less a majority, opinion. The Court then had seven members, and Justice Duvall was absent, leaving a 2–2–2 split: Marshall and McLean seeing tribes as "domestic dependent nations"; Johnson and Baldwin viewing them as

possessing no sovereignty at all; and Thompson and Story concluding that the Cherokee Nation was a foreign nation possessing sovereignty in the international sense.

While Marshall's opinion is most frequently relied on as the decision of *Cherokee Nation v. Georgia,* the other opinions in the case, because of their substantive views on Indian rights, reveal the deep ideological divisions on the Court (replicating antebellum United States public opinion itself at this time) over the critical issues of tribal sovereignty and self-determination raised by the *Cherokee Cases.* Justice Johnson's concurrence, with its analysis of the Treaty of Hopewell, pages 101–102, supra, recapitulates a variety of arguments for the removal policy. Consider his interpretation of the language relevant to tribal status contained in the Treaty of Hopewell and of the federal government's policy towards Indians at the time the treaty was signed as militating against recognition of the Cherokees as an independent state. Johnson also tackles the toughest philosophical issue for one who seeks to justify denial of the Cherokees' independence. The traditional presumption was that Indians were incapable of assimilation, requiring and legitimating lesser land rights for them than would belong to a conquered "civilized" people. A right of occupancy would suit them until they died out or followed game into the receding wilderness. Johnson grapples with the fact that the Cherokees were disappointing this expectation. Admitting that their government "must be classed among the most approved forms of civil government," he sees their movement from "the hunter state to a more fixed state of society" as an intolerable threat to the sovereignty of the United States and the state. Compare his argument for uprooting the Cherokees from their treaty-secured lands to Adams' justification for removal, page 120 supra.

2.   Significantly, when the original decision of the Court in *Cherokee Nation* was handed down, the concurring opinions of Johnson and Baldwin (who expressed similarly negative racial views of tribes) represented the only substantive discussions by any of the Justices on the issues of tribal status presented by the case. Thus, despite the lack of a clear majority in *Cherokee Nation v. Georgia,* the supporters of President Jackson and the removal policy felt justified in claiming a decisive victory in the case. But Marshall, in his opinion for the Court, had ruled only that the Cherokees were not a "foreign nation" solely for purposes related to the Court's original jurisdictional grant under the Constitution.

Lawyers for the Cherokees faced a conundrum: where to sue? Article III, section 2, clause 1 of the Constitution extended federal judicial *power* over federal questions. However, federal trial court *jurisdiction* was not available until 1875 when Congress passed the general federal question statute. See 28 U.S.C.A. § 1331. Thus, there was no way to initiate the case against Georgia in federal courts unless it fit under another clause 1 category.

An alternative might have been to start the case in state court. Clause 2 of Article III, section 2 says that the Supreme Court has appellate jurisdiction in all other cases (e.g., where there is a federal question). This means that the

Cherokees might have proceeded through the Georgia state courts, arriving at the Supreme Court to raise the federal questions in the case (treaty violations, etc.) on appeal. Besides whatever bias the Cherokees might have encountered in state court, they probably would have confronted the barrier of sovereign immunity under Georgia law.

The Cherokee Nation consequently argued that jurisdiction under clause 1 existed because it was a suit between a state and a foreign state—one of the categories in clause 1. Clause 2 of Article III, section 2 gives the Supreme Court original jurisdiction of cases in which a state is a party, distributing the jurisdiction created under clause 1 between district courts and the Supreme Court. The Supreme Court had already held in Cohens v. Virginia, 19 U.S. (6 Wheat.) 264 (1821) that clause 2 only applies where jurisdiction could be exercised under clause 1.

At the time of *Cherokee,* state sovereign immunity was not thought to be a problem in federal court if the plaintiff were a foreign nation. Though the Eleventh Amendment to the Constitution explicitly bars federal suits against states by citizens of foreign states, dictum in *Cohens* suggested that it does not bar suits by foreign nations themselves. Later the Supreme Court ruled that the Eleventh Amendment also implicitly prevents such suits by foreign nations against states. Monaco v. Mississippi, 292 U.S. 313 (1934). Marshall's decision in *Cherokee Nation* did not have to reach that issue, as the Cherokee Nation, under his analysis, was *not* a foreign nation.

The process of rendering the *Cherokee Nation* opinion was similar to Marbury v. Madison, 5 U.S. (1 Cranch) 137 (1803), where Chief Justice Marshall also held that the Court did not have jurisdiction, but established in dictum the principle of judicial review of congressional acts. Such judicial indirection was necessary at the time of *Marbury* because the authority of the Court was still very much an open question. There was every chance that President Jefferson's administration would refuse to comply with a writ directing Secretary of State Madison to deliver Marbury's commission. The jurisdictional ruling in *Cherokee Nation,* as in *Marbury,* permitted Marshall to set forth important legal principles while, at the same time, rendering no affirmative order; because there was no order to enforce, there was no order to disobey. Such judicial sleight-of-hand would not suffice in the next stage of the Cherokee-Georgia conflict.

Samuel A. Worcester and several other missionaries were arrested for violating a Georgia law which required any non-Indian resident of the Cherokee territory to obtain a license from the governor. The missionaries were convicted and sentenced to four years at hard labor. All were offered pardons, but Worcester and Elizur Butler, anxious to bring a test case, refused. The Supreme Court reviewed the case on a writ of error.

Again, Georgia refused to appear. The proceedings in *Worcester v. Georgia,* and especially the dramatic oral argument, were cloaked with a sense of foreboding due to the very real possibility that Georgia would refuse to obey the Court's order. The case was widely reported and debated in the press. John

Marshall, now seventy-six years old and in poor health, took just two weeks to write the opinion in *Worcester v. Georgia*, which concluded that the Georgia laws were of no effect within the Cherokee territory.

WORCESTER V. GEORGIA

Supreme Court of the United States, 1832.
31 U.S. (6 Pet.) 515, 8 L.Ed. 483.

MR. CHIEF JUSTICE MARSHALL delivered the opinion of the Court.

This cause, in every point of view in which it can be placed, is of the deepest interest.

The defendant is a state, a member of the union, which has exercised the powers of government over a people who deny its jurisdiction, and are under the protection of the United States.

The plaintiff is a citizen of the state of Vermont, condemned to hard labour for four years in the penitentiary of Georgia; under colour of an act which he alleges to be repugnant to the constitution, laws, and treaties of the United States.

The legislative power of a state, the controlling power of the constitution and laws of the United States, the rights, if they have any, the political existence of a once numerous and powerful people, the personal liberty of a citizen, are all involved in the subject now to be considered.

* * *

The indictment charges the plaintiff in error, and others, being white persons, with the offence of "residing within the limits of the Cherokee nation without a license," and "without having taken the oath to support and defend the constitution and laws of the state of Georgia."

* * *

It has been said at the bar, that the acts of the legislature of Georgia seize on the whole Cherokee country, parcel it out among the neighbouring counties of the state, extend her code over the whole country, abolish its institutions and its laws, and annihilate its political existence.

* * *

The extra-territorial power of every legislature being limited in its action, to its own citizens or subjects, the very passage of this act is an assertion of jurisdiction over the Cherokee nation, and of the rights and powers consequent on jurisdiction.

The first step, then, in the inquiry, which the constitution and laws impose on this court, is an examination of the rightfulness of this claim.

America, separated from Europe by a wide ocean, was inhabited by a distinct people, divided into separate nations, independent of each other and of the rest of the world, having institutions of their own, and governing themselves by their own laws. It is difficult to comprehend the proposition, that the inhabitants of either quarter of the globe could have rightful original claims of dominion over the inhabitants of the other, or over the lands they occupied; or that the discovery of either by the other should give the discoverer rights in the country discovered, which annulled the pre-existing rights of its ancient possessors.

After lying concealed for a series of ages, the enterprise of Europe, guided by nautical science, conducted some of her adventurous sons into this western world. They found it in possession of a people who had made small progress in agriculture or manufactures, and whose general employment was war, hunting, and fishing.

Did these adventurers, by sailing along the coast, and occasionally landing on it, acquire for the several governments to whom they belonged, or by whom they were commissioned, a rightful property in the soil, from the Atlantic to the Pacific; or rightful dominion over the numerous people who occupied it? Or has nature, or the great Creator of all things, conferred these rights over hunters and fishermen, on agriculturists and manufacturers?

But power, war, conquest, give rights, which, after possession, are conceded by the world; and which can never be controverted by those on whom they descend. We proceed, then, to the actual state of things, having glanced at their origin; because holding it in our recollection might shed some light on existing pretensions.

* * *

Soon after Great Britain determined on planting colonies in America, the king granted charters to companies of his subjects who associated for the purpose of carrying the views of the crown into effect, and of enriching themselves. The first of these charters was made before possession was taken of any part of the country. They purport, generally, to convey the soil, from the Atlantic to the South Sea. This soil was occupied by numerous and warlike nations, equally willing and able to defend their possessions. The extravagant and absurd idea, that the feeble settlements made on the sea coast, or the companies under whom they were made, acquired legitimate power by them to govern the people, or occupy the lands from sea to sea, did not enter the mind of any man. They were well understood to convey the title which, according to the common law of European sovereigns respecting America, they might rightfully convey, and no more. This was the exclusive right of purchasing such lands as the natives were willing to sell. The crown could not be understood to grant what the crown did not affect to claim; nor was it so understood.

* * *

The charters contain passages showing one of their objects to be the civilization of the Indians, and their conversion to Christianity—objects to be accomplished by conciliatory conduct and good example; not by extermination.

* * *

Certain it is, that our history furnishes no example, from the first settlement of our country, of any attempt on the part of the crown to interfere with the internal affairs of the Indians, farther than to keep out the agents of foreign powers, who, as traders or otherwise, might seduce them into foreign alliances. The king purchased their lands when they were willing to sell, at a price they were willing to take; but never coerced a surrender of them. He also purchased their alliance and dependence by subsidies; but never intruded into the interior of their affairs, or interfered with their self government, so far as respected themselves only.

* * *

Such was the policy of Great Britain towards the Indian nations inhabiting the territory from which she excluded all other Europeans; such her claims, and such her practical exposition of the charters she had granted: she considered them as nations capable of maintaining the relations of peace and war; of governing themselves, under her protection; and she made treaties with them, the obligation of which she acknowledged.

This was the settled state of things when the war of our revolution commenced. The influence of our enemy was established; her resources enabled her to keep up that influence; and the colonists had much cause for the apprehension that the Indian nations would, as the allies of Great Britain, add their arms to hers. This, as was to be expected, became an object of great solicitude to congress. Far from advancing a claim to their lands, or asserting any right of dominion over them, congress resolved "that the securing and preserving the friendship of the Indian nations appears to be a subject of the utmost moment to these colonies."

The early journals of Congress exhibit a most anxious desire to conciliate the Indian nations. * * *

* * *

The first treaty was made with the Delawares, in September 1778.

The language of equality in which it is drawn, evinces the temper with which the negotiation was undertaken, and the opinion which then prevailed in the United States.

* * *

During the war of the revolution, the Cherokees took part with the British. After its termination, the United States, though desirous of peace, did not feel its necessity so strongly as while the war continued. Their political situation being changed, they might very well think it advisable to assume a higher tone, and to impress on the Cherokees the same respect for congress which was before felt for the king of Great Britain. This may account for the language of the treaty of Hopewell. * * *

* * *

When the United States gave peace, did they not also receive it? Were not both parties desirous of it? If we consult the history of the day, does it not inform us that the United States were at least as anxious to obtain it as the Cherokees? We may ask, further: did the Cherokees come to the seat of the American government to solicit peace; or, did the American commissioners go to them to obtain it? The treaty was made at Hopewell, not at New York. The word "give," then, has no real importance attached to it.

* * *

The first and second articles [of the Treaty of Hopewell of 1785] stipulate for the mutual restoration of prisoners, and are of course equal.

The third article acknowledges the Cherokees to be under the protection of the United States of America, and of no other power.

This stipulation is found in Indian treaties, generally. It was introduced into their treaties with Great Britain; and may probably be found in those with other European powers. Its origin may be traced to the nature of their connexion with those powers; and its true meaning is discerned in their relative situation.

The general law of European sovereigns, respecting their claims in America, limited the intercourse of Indians, in a great degree, to the particular potentate whose ultimate right of domain was acknowledged by the others. * * *

* * *

The same stipulation entered into with the United States, is undoubtedly to be construed in the same manner. They receive the Cherokee nation into their favour and protection. The Cherokees acknowledge themselves to be under the protection of the United States, and of no other power. Protection does not imply the destruction of the protected. The manner in which this stipulation was understood by the American government, is explained by the language and acts of our first president.

The fourth article draws the boundary between the Indians and the citizens of the United States. But, in describing this boundary, the term "allotted" and the term "hunting ground" are used.

* * *

To the United States, it could be a matter of no concern, whether their whole territory was devoted to hunting grounds, or whether an occasional village, and an occasional corn field, interrupted, and gave some variety to the scene.

These terms had been used in their treaties with Great Britain, and had never been misunderstood. They had never been supposed to imply a right in the British government to take their lands, or to interfere with their internal government.

The fifth article withdraws the protection of the United States from any citizen who has settled, or shall settle, on the lands allotted to the Indians, for their hunting grounds; and stipulates that, if he shall not remove within six months the Indians may punish him.

The sixth and seventh articles stipulate for the punishment of the citizens of either country, who may commit offences on or against the citizens of the other. The only inference to be drawn from them is, that the United States considered the Cherokees as a nation.

The ninth article is in these words: "for the benefit and comfort of the Indians, and for the prevention of injuries or oppressions on the part of the citizens or Indians, the United States, in congress assembled, shall have the sole and exclusive right of regulating the trade with the Indians, and *managing all their affairs,* as they think proper."

To construe the expression "managing all their affairs," into a surrender of self-government, would be, we think, a perversion of their necessary meaning, and a departure from the construction which has been uniformly put on them. The great subject of the article is the Indian trade. The influence it gave, made it desirable that congress should possess it. The commissioners brought forward the claim, with the profession that their motive was "the benefit and comfort of the Indians, and the prevention of injuries or oppressions." This may be true, as respects the regulation of their trade, and as respects the regulation of all affairs connected with their trade, but cannot be true, as respects the management of all their affairs. The most important of these, are the cession of their lands, and security against intruders on them. Is it credible, that they should have considered themselves as surrendering to the United States the right to dictate their future cessions, and the terms on which they should be made? or to compel their submission to the violence of disorderly and licentious intruders? It is equally inconceivable that they could have supposed themselves, by a phrase thus slipped into an article, on another and most interesting subject, to have divested themselves of the right of self-government on subjects not connected with trade. Such a measure could not be "for their benefit and comfort," or for "the prevention of injuries and oppression." Such a construction would be inconsistent with the spirit of this and of all subsequent treaties; especially of those articles which recognize the right of the Cherokees to declare hostilities, and to make war. It would convert a treaty of peace covertly into an act, annihilating the political existence of one of the parties. Had such a result been intended, it would have been openly avowed.

This treaty contains a few terms capable of being used in a sense which could not have been intended at the time, and which is inconsistent with the practical construction which has always been put on them; but its essential articles treat the Cherokees as a nation capable of maintaining the relations of peace and war; and ascertain the boundaries between them and the United States.

[The opinion similarly reviewed several provisions of the Treaty of Holston of 1791 to show that Cherokee political existence was not extinguished.]

* * *

This relation [under the Treaty of Holston] was that of a nation claiming and receiving the protection of one more powerful: not that of individuals abandoning their national character, and submitting as subjects to the laws of a master.

* * *

This treaty, thus explicitly recognizing the national character of the Cherokees, and their right of self government; thus guarantying their lands; assuming the duty of protection, and of course pledging the faith of the United States for that protection; has been frequently renewed, and is now in full force.

To the general pledge of protection have been added several specific pledges, deemed valuable by the Indians. Some of these restrain the citizens of the United States from encroachments on the Cherokee country, and provide for the punishment of intruders.

From the commencement of our government, congress has passed acts to regulate trade and intercourse with the Indians; which treat them as nations, respect their rights, and manifest a firm purpose to afford that protection which treaties stipulate. All these acts, and especially that of 1802, which is still in force, manifestly consider the several Indian nations as distinct political communities, having territorial boundaries, within which their authority is exclusive, and having a right to all the lands within those boundaries, which is not only acknowledged, but guaranteed by the United States.

* * *

The treaties and laws of the United States contemplate the Indian territory as completely separated from that of the states; and provide that all intercourse with them shall be carried on exclusively by the government of the union.

Is this the rightful exercise of power, or is it usurpation?

While these states were colonies, this power, in its utmost extent, was admitted to reside in the crown. * * * [C]ongress assumed the management of Indian affairs; first in the name of these United Colonies; and, afterwards, in the name of the United States. Early attempts were made at negotiation, and to regulate trade with them. * * *

Such was the state of things when the confederation was adopted. That instrument surrendered the powers of peace and war to congress, and prohibited them to the states, respectively, unless a state be actually invaded, "or shall have received certain advice of a resolution being formed by some nation of Indians to invade such state, and the danger is so imminent as not to admit of delay till the United States in congress assembled can be consulted." This instrument also gave the United States in congress assembled the sole and exclusive right of "regulating the trade and managing all the affairs with the Indians, not members of any of the states: provided, that the legislative power of any state within its own limits be not infringed or violated."

* * * The correct exposition of this article is rendered unnecessary by the adoption of our existing constitution. That instrument confers on congress the powers of war and peace; of making treaties, and of regulating commerce with foreign nations, and among the several states, and *with the Indian tribes*. These powers comprehend all that is required for the regulation of our intercourse with the Indians. They are not limited by any restrictions on their free actions. The shackles imposed on this power, in the confederation, are discarded.

The Indian nations had always been considered as distinct, independent political communities, retaining their original natural rights, as the undisputed possessors of the soil, from time immemorial, with the single exception of that imposed by irresistible power, which excluded them from intercourse with any other European potentate than the first discoverer of the coast of the particular region claimed: and this was a restriction which those European potentates imposed on themselves, as well as on the Indians. The very term "nation," so generally applied to them, means "a people distinct from others." The constitution, by declaring treaties already made, as well as those to be made, to be the supreme law of the land, has adopted and sanctioned the previous treaties with the Indian nations, and consequently admits their rank among those powers who are capable of making treaties. The words "treaty" and "nation" are words of our own language, selected in our diplomatic and legislative proceedings, by ourselves, having each a definite and well understood meaning. We have applied them to Indians, as we have applied them to the other nations of the earth. They are applied to all in the same sense.

* * *

The actual state of things at the time, and all history since, explain these charters; and the King of Great Britain, at the treaty of peace, could cede only what belonged to his crown. These newly asserted titles can derive no aid from the articles so often repeated in Indian treaties; extending to them, first, the protection of Great Britain, and afterwards that of the United States. These articles are associated with others, recognising their title to self-government. The very fact of repeated treaties with them recognises it; and the settled doctrine of the law of nations is, that a weaker power does not surrender its independence—its right to self-government, by associating with a stronger, and taking its protection. A weak state, in order to provide for its safety, may place itself under the protection of one more powerful, without stripping itself of the right of government, and ceasing to be a state. Examples of this kind are not wanting in Europe. "Tributary and feudatory states," says Vattel, "do not thereby cease to be sovereign and independent states, so long as self-government and sovereign and independent authority are left in the administration of the state." At the present day, more than one state may be considered as holding its right of self-government under the guarantee and protection of one or more allies.

The Cherokee nation, then, is a distinct community, occupying its own territory, with boundaries accurately described, in which the laws of Georgia can have no force, and which the citizens of Georgia have no right to enter, but with the assent of the Cherokees themselves, or in conformity with treaties, and with the acts of congress. The whole intercourse between the United States and this nation, is, by our constitution and laws, vested in the government of the United States.

The act of the state of Georgia, under which the plaintiff in error was prosecuted, is consequently void, and the judgment a nullity. Can this court revise, and reverse it?

If the objection to the system of legislation, lately adopted by the legislature of Georgia, in relation to the Cherokee nation, was confined to its extra-territorial operation, the objection, though complete, so far as respected mere right, would give this court no power over the subject. But it goes much further. If the review which has been taken be correct, and we think it is, the acts of Georgia are repugnant to the constitution, laws, and treaties of the United States.

They interfere forcibly with the relations established between the United States and the Cherokee nation, the regulation of which, according to the settled principles of our constitution, are committed exclusively to the government of the union.

They are in direct hostility with treaties, repeated in a succession of years, which mark out the boundary that separates the Cherokee country from Georgia; guaranty to them all the land within their boundary; solemnly pledge the faith of the United States to restrain their citizens from trespassing on it; and recognize the pre-existing power of the nation to govern itself.

They are in equal hostility with the acts of congress for regulating this intercourse, and giving effect to the treaties.

The forcible seizure and abduction of the plaintiff in error, who was residing in the nation with its permission, and by authority of the president of the United States, is also a violation of the acts which authorise the chief magistrate to exercise this authority.

* * *

It is the opinion of this court that the judgment of the superior court for the county of Gwinnett, in the state of Georgia, condemning Samuel A. Worcester to hard labour, in the penitentiary of the state of Georgia, for four years, was pronounced by that court under colour of a law which is void, as being repugnant to the constitution, treaties, and laws of the United States, and ought, therefore, to be reversed and annulled.

MR. JUSTICE MCLEAN.

* * *

With the decision, just given, I concur.

* * *

But the inquiry may be made, is there no end to the exercise of this power over Indians within the limits of a state, by the general government? The answer is, that, in its nature, it must be limited by circumstances.

If a tribe of Indians shall become so degraded or reduced in numbers, as to lose the power of self-government, the protection of the local law, of necessity, must be extended over them. The point at which this exercise of power by a state would be proper, need not now be considered: if indeed it be a judicial question. Such a question does not seem to arise in this case. So long as treaties and laws remain in full force, and apply to Indian nations, exercising the right of self-government, within the limits of a state, the judicial power can exercise no discretion in refusing to give effect to those laws, when questions arise under them, unless they shall be deemed unconstitutional.

The exercise of the power of self-government by the Indians, within a state, is undoubtedly contemplated to be temporary. * * *

At best they can enjoy a very limited independence within the boundaries of a state, and such a residence must always subject them to encroachments from the settlements around them; and their existence within a state, as a separate and independent community, may seriously embarrass or obstruct the operation of the state laws. If, therefore, it would be inconsistent with the political welfare of the states, and the social advance of their citizens, that an independent and permanent power should exist within their limits, this power must give way to the greater power which surrounds it, or seeks its exercise beyond the sphere of state authority.

This state of things can only be produced by a co-operation of the state and federal governments. The latter has the exclusive regulation of intercourse with the Indians; and, so long as this power shall be exercised, it cannot be obstructed by the state. It is a power given by the constitution, and sanctioned by the most solemn acts of both the federal and state governments: consequently, it cannot be abrogated at the will of a state. It is one of the powers parted with by the states, and vested in the federal government. But, if a contingency shall occur, which shall render the Indians who reside in a state, incapable of self-government, either by moral degradation or a reduction of their numbers, it would undoubtedly be in the power of a state government to extend to them the aegis of its laws. Under such circumstances, the agency of the general government, of necessity, must cease.

But, if it shall be the policy of the government to withdraw its protection from the Indians who reside within the limits of the respective states, and who not only claim the right of self government, but have uniformly exercised it; the laws and treaties which impose duties and obligations on the general government should be abrogated by the powers competent to do so. So long as those laws and treaties exist, having been formed within the sphere of the federal powers, they must be respected and enforced by the appropriate organs of the federal government.

* * *

MR. JUSTICE BALDWIN dissented * * * .

NOTES

1.   *Aftermath of Worcester.* The opinion was delivered on March 3, 1832, and a special mandate was issued two days later. Numerous Georgia officials, including the governor, announced that the mandate would not be obeyed. The Court adjourned shortly thereafter.

The opinion and special mandate were not self-executing. Thus, a further order, directing federal marshals to release the two missionaries, was needed when Georgia defied the Court's mandate. But, because of deficiencies in the Judiciary Act of 1789, there was apparently no procedural mechanism to obtain the necessary order to direct the federal marshals. If any way around the procedural road block had existed, it could not have been implemented until the Court reconvened in January, 1833. Thus, arcane procedural rules prevented a direct constitutional clash, at least until early 1833. For a discussion of these procedural technicalities, see Burke, *The Cherokee Cases: A Study in Law, Politics, and Morality,* 21 Stan.L.Rev. 500, 525–26 (1969).

Other events intervened to prevent a head-on conflict among the Court, President Jackson, and the state. During the presidential campaign of 1832, extreme states' rights sentiments had flared up. South Carolina was about to pass its Nullification Ordinance, which contained attacks on the supremacy of the Constitution and on the jurisdiction of the Supreme Court. Jackson came down hard on the side of the Union and the Constitution.

Thus, by early 1833, the *Worcester* case had become a political embarrassment to Jackson. He personally urged the Governor of Georgia to pardon Worcester and Butler, who were now willing to recant from their earlier refusal to accept pardons. Governor Lumpkin's pardon of the missionaries in February 1833 ended the need for a further test of the Court's power.

It is the *Worcester* case of which Jackson purportedly said, "John Marshall has made his decision; now let him enforce it." Though the historians seem to agree that Jackson probably held such thoughts, the statement itself may be apocryphal. The only first-hand report of such a statement is by Horace Greeley. See Horace Greeley, American Conflict 106 (1864). Other authorities doubt that he actually said it. See, e.g., Marquis James, The Life of Andrew Jackson 603–04 (1938); 2 Charles Warren, The Supreme Court in United States History 205–06 (1922).

Jackson plainly helped fuel the Cherokee-Georgia conflict during the late 1820s and early 1830s by supporting Georgia's claimed sovereignty over Cherokee lands. But Jackson may have been unfairly criticized for shirking his constitutional duties to enforce the *Worcester* decision. For examples of such criticisms, see Burke, supra, 21 Stan.L.Rev. at 525 n.143. In fact, as noted above, procedural deficiencies prevented any affirmative order from being directed to the Executive branch, at least until the Court met for its 1833 Term. In addition, reports of Jackson's belief that he could properly refuse to enforce the Court's orders were probably wrong; he apparently believed only that he had the power, as Presidents surely do, to veto proposed legislation on the basis of the President's opinion that the legislation is unconstitutional. See, e.g., 2 C. Warren, supra, at 221–24.

In any event, the nullification furor brought Jackson into the camp of those who wished to avoid a constitutional clash over the *Worcester* decision. As the pardon of Worcester and Butler was imminent, Justice Story was able to report:

> Notwithstanding [that] I am "the most dangerous man in America", the President specially invited me to drink a glass of wine with him. But what is more remarkable, since his last Proclamation and Message, the Chief Justice and myself have become his warmest supporters and shall continue so just as long as he maintains the

principles contained in them. Who would have dreamed of such an occurrence?

See 2 C. Warren, supra, at 237.

2.   *Assimilation and State Power.* McLean's more restrictive view of national power did not exempt him from the ire of President Jackson, who had appointed him three years before. But while McLean concurred in the result, his opinion was read by lower courts as leaving open the possibility of judicial review every so often to determine whether circumstances indicated that a particular tribe had lost the power of self-government so that state law should be extended over them. McLean himself charted the course for state challenges to the exclusivity of federal jurisdiction over Indians. In United States v. Cisna, 25 F. Cas. 422, 424 (C.C.Ohio 1835) (No. 14,795), he ruled, as a circuit judge, that because the small Wyandott reservation in his home state of Ohio was so surrounded by white population and crossed by roads that the federal Nonintercourse acts were "wholly unsuited to the condition of the Wyandott tribe, and it would be impossible to give them a practical operation." Thus, he found that Ohio's newly enacted laws extending state jurisdiction over non-Indians on the reservation, and not federal law, should apply to a non-Indian who stole a horse from an Indian.

The strict limitation placed on the powers of Congress under the Commerce Clause in *Cisna* was consistent with another decision of McLean as a circuit judge: United States v. Bailey, 24 F. Cas. 937 (C.C.Tenn.1834) (No. 14,495). In that case, an 1817 Act extending federal law over crimes in Indian country was held to be unconstitutional because the congressional power, rooted in the Commerce Clause, was limited to the regulation of commercial intercourse. Punishment of one non-Indian for murder of another within Indian country was, therefore, beyond the scope of congressional authority.

Later Supreme Court cases demonstrate that the views of Marshall have prevailed over those of McLean. Congressional power, independent of the apparent commercial limitation seen by McLean, has been consistently upheld by the Court. E.g., United States v. Kagama, 118 U.S. 375 (1886), page 186, infra, United States v. Lara, 541 U.S. 193 (2004) page 589, infra. And McLean's assumption, that the courts should resolve state-federal jurisdictional disputes in the face of congressional inaction by assessing a tribe's progress along the path of "civilization," has never been embraced by the Court. On the contrary, the Court has repeatedly insisted that if federal power and protection over a tribe are terminated, it is for Congress, and not the courts, to say so. E.g., United States v. Holliday, 70 U.S. (3 Wall.) 407 (1865); Moe v. Confederated Salish & Kootenai Tribes of Flathead Reservation, 425 U.S. 463 (1976). Should a court allow the application of state law because a tribe appears to be heavily assimilated?

3.   *Tribal Sovereignty or Federal Power?* Scholars and courts continually debate the true basis of the decision in *Worcester.* Marshall elaborates on the tribe's retained powers of "self-government" (a term used eight times in his opinion), saying that within its territory "the laws of Georgia can have no

force." He uses the opportunity to clarify that the limits on tribal sovereignty discussed in his *Cherokee Nation* opinion relate to land conveyance rights, not to self-government. Notice how he embraces the language of Justice Thompson's dissent in the earlier case to describe the tribe as a sovereign in *Worcester*.

The decision concludes by discussing the extent of federal power in Indian affairs and saying that the exercise of state power would be "repugnant to the constitution, laws, and treaties of the United States." Is federal supremacy, what modern courts have come to call "preemption," the essential basis of the decision? An alternative ground? Or is it raised only because the Court would not have had appellate jurisdiction to review the Georgia state court decision unless a federal question were involved? See William Walters, *Preemption, Tribal Sovereignty, and Worcester v. Georgia,* 62 Or.L.Rev. 127 (1983). Or is Marshall, an adamant Federalist, using the decision as a forum for exerting national control?

Consider how the two rationales relate to one another. Would federal power exist if there was no viable tribal government to exercise sovereignty? That is, would there still be an "Indian tribe" within the meaning of the commerce clause and applicable treaties and statutes? Is this the point that McLean was trying to make?

Modern courts have continued to rely on *Worcester* but, as the Supreme Court explained in a 1973 decision, "the trend has been away from the idea of inherent Indian sovereignty as a bar to state jurisdiction and toward a reliance on federal preemption." McClanahan v. Arizona Tax Commission, 411 U.S. 164, 172 (1973), page 421, infra. Eschewing "platonic notions of Indian sovereignty," the Court sees the sovereignty doctrine today as "a backdrop against which the applicable treaties and federal statutes must be read." Did Marshall use tribal sovereignty as a backdrop to construe the Treaty of Hopewell, or did he use the treaty as confirmation of the tribe's sovereignty?

4.   *Indians as Minorities under United States Law.* Professor White's summary of the decisions in the *Cherokee* cases compares the Marshall Court's treatment of Indians with another racial minority, African Americans:

> * * * The Cherokees, and other Indian tribes, became in effect wards of the federal government. The officials of that government were acknowledged to have the power to do what Georgia had done: place Indians in the position of abandoning their cultural heritage— becoming "civilized"—or being dispossessed of their land and forced to emigrate. Being wards of the government did not mean that Indians in America would have more freedom or more respect. Their "plight," ostensibly solved, remained essentially the same.

* * *

With Jackson's 1830 removal legislation in effect, the federal government began to enter into agreements with southeastern tribes for the cession of their lands. The Creeks, Choctaws, and Cherokees were all forced into signing such treaties, in which the federal government provided them with lands west of the Mississippi * * * .

G. Edward White, supra, at 732, 736.

White concluded: "Racial minorities received a message from the Marshall Court that they were to receive repeatedly in the subsequent course of American history: liberty and equality in America have been regularly contingent on whose freedom and whose equal treatment is at issue." Id. at 740.

3. THE LEGACY OF THE CHEROKEE CASES

The Cherokees, of course, were destined to win their battle but to lose their war. Before the end of his term in office, Jackson was able to succeed in removing the Cherokees to the Indian Territory, an area that later became the state of Oklahoma. As Dean Strickland describes the ultimate outcome of the Cherokee cases for the Cherokees themselves:

> The struggle between the Cherokees and Georgia was climaxed in 1838 by the forcible removal of more than 16,000 Cherokees over a Trail of Tears to what became the state of Oklahoma. The years between 1828 and 1838 were years of chaos in which the Cherokees fought to retain tribal land and law. John Marshall's decisions in *Cherokee Nation v. Georgia* and *Worcester v. Georgia* provided disappointment and then hope, but ultimately it became clear that Marshall might make the law but Jackson enforced the law. So the Cherokees met in council in 1838 and resolved to carry their system of constitutional government with them to the Indian Territory.

Rennard Strickland, Fire and the Spirits—Cherokee Law From Clan to Court 65–67 (1975). See also Theda Perdue & Michael D. Green, The Cherokee Nation and the Trail of Tears (2007).

Jon Meacham, in his Pulitzer Prize winning biography of Andrew Jackson, American Lion: Andrew Jackson in the White House 95–96 (2008), finds a "common theme" in Jackson's thoughts and actions towards Indians:

> As a people Indians were neither autonomous nor independent but were to be manipulated and managed in the context of what most benefited Jackson's America—white America. Missionaries and humanitarian reformers struggled to make the case for the innate rights of the Indians, but the white agenda—more land, fewer Indians, complete control—took precedence in the North and the South (And in the West, too, in the long run).

What are we to make of Jackson on this question, one on which he embodied the attitudes of many of his contemporaries? His was an exaggerated example of the prevailing white view, favoring removal at nearly any cost where his predecessors had spoken in softer terms of "voluntary" emigration. While he took an extreme view of Indian matters, however, he was on the extreme edge of the mainstream, not wholly outside it.

Jackson was neither a humanitarian nor a blind bigot. He thought of himself as practical. And enough Americans believed that Indian removal was necessary in the late 1820s and 1830s that Jackson was able to accomplish it politically.

Id. at 95–96 (2008).

In their book on the processes of racial formation in the United States, see Chapter 2 at p. 50, Professors Michael Omi and Howard Winant make the argument that for "most of its existence, both as a European colony and, as an independent nation, the United States was a *racial despotism.*" Omi and Winant assert that this despotic form of absolute, unchecked rule over select groups of racial minorities over time in the United States had three important and dramatic consequences: American identity has been confirmed as white, "the negation of racialized 'otherness;' " the "color line" created by this form of despotism rendered racial division the fundamental schism in U.S. society, demanding "an ongoing and intensive policing of racial boundaries;" and finally, an oppositional racial consciousness consolidated by this racial despotism "took on permanence and depth as *racial resistance.*" Racial Formation in the United States 130–31 (3rd ed. 2015)

Jackson's words and actions during the Removal crisis do seem to confirm a strongly held cultural belief in American identity as white. The Trail of Tears and other acts of intensive policing of racial boundaries carried out under the Removal policy show the clear contours of the "color line" being enforced by his policy. And the Cherokees steadfast opposition to removal is clearly a form of *racial resistance* to what Jackson sought to accomplish as President during the Removal era. Does the ultimate outcome of the *Cherokee* cases prove the argument made by Omi and Winant, that at least with respect to the treatment of American Indian tribes during the Removal era, the United States was a "racial despotism"?

D'ARCY MCNICKLE, THEY CAME HERE FIRST
199–200 (rev. ed. 1975).

So they all moved, the Cherokees, Choctaws, Chickasaws, Creeks, Seminoles, the Kickapoos, Wyandottes, Ottawas, Pottawatomies Winnebagos, Sac and Fox (after a last-ditch fight led by Black Hawk),

Delawares, Shawnees, Weas, Peorias, Miamis, Kaskaskias, Piankeshaws—all went to the land beyond the Mississippi.

Count de Tocqueville was on hand to witness the beginning of this sorrowful journey, what the Indians afterward would refer to as the Trail of Tears. The Count reported: "At the end of the year 1831, whilst I was on the left bank of the Mississippi, at a place named by Europeans Memphis, there arrived a numerous band of Choctaws. These savages had left their country, and were endeavoring to gain the right bank of the Mississippi, where they hoped to find an asylum which had been promised them by the American government. It was then the middle of the winter, and the cold was unusually severe; the snow had frozen hard upon the ground, and the river was drifting huge masses of ice. The Indians had their families with them; and they brought in their train the wounded and the sick, with children newly born, and old men upon the verge of death. They possessed neither tents nor wagons, but only their arms and some provisions. I saw them embark to pass the mighty river, and never will that solemn spectacle fade from my remembrance. No cry, no sob, was heard amongst the assembled crowd; all were silent. Their calamities were of ancient date, and they knew them to be irremediable. The Indians had all stepped into the bark which was to carry them across, but their dogs remained upon the bank. As soon as these animals perceived that their masters were finally leaving the shore, they set up a dismal howl, and, plunging all together into the icy waters of the Mississippi, swam after the boat."

At a later point in his narrative, de Tocqueville summarized with excellent insight what had taken place on the continent up to that point. "The Indians," he wrote, "in the little which they have done, have unquestionably displayed as much natural genius as the peoples of Europe in their greatest undertakings; but nations as well as men require time to learn, whatever may be their intelligence and their zeal. Whilst the savages were endeavoring to civilize themselves, the Europeans continued to surround them on every side, and to confine them within narrower limits * * * . With their resources and acquired knowledge, the Europeans soon appropriated to themselves most of the advantages which the natives might have derived from the possession of the soil * * * and the Indians have been ruined by a competition which they had not the means of sustaining. They were isolated in their own country, and their race only constituted a little colony of troublesome strangers in the midst of a numerous and dominant people."

NOTES

1.   As the Cherokee Nation moved west, however, it left behind two opinions that would serve as bastions for much of the development of federal Indian law. The second Cherokee case, *Worcester*, would prove to be one of the most enduring opinions in Supreme Court jurisprudence. Of all pre-Civil War

Supreme Court cases, only such venerable decisions as *Marbury v. Madison*, 5 U.S. 137, 2 L. Ed. 60 (1803); *Strawbridge v. Curtiss*, 7 U.S. 267, 2 L. Ed. 435 (1806); *Calder v. Bull*, 3 U.S. 386, 1 L. Ed. 648 (1798); *McCulloch v. Md.*, 17 U.S. 316, 4 L. Ed. 579 (1819); *Gibbons v. Ogden*, 22 U.S. 1, 6 L. Ed. 23 (1824); and *Osborn v. President, Directors & Co. of Bank*, 22 U.S. 738, 6 L. Ed. 204 (1824) have been cited more than *Worcester v. Georgia* from 1970 through 2016. *Cherokee Nation* is ninth on that list.

2.   The term "removal" has come to be associated with the forced migration of the Five Civilized Tribes from the Southeast to the Indian Territory. Actually, the practice of transferring tribes from ancestral lands to reservations in other areas was far more widespread: removals occurred in most parts of the country during the entire nineteenth century. Tribes were transported to the Indian Territory from many Midwestern states and from as far away as the Northern Rockies and the Pacific Northwest. The small coastal tribes in Southwestern Oregon were forcibly marched north along the rugged Oregon coast to the confederated reservations at Siletz and Grand Ronde. See Stephen Dow Beckham, Requiem for a People (1971). The consolidation of separate tribes—usually with diverse cultures and often with backgrounds of outright hostility toward each other—was a method used to establish numerous "confederated" reservations in the Northwest and Great Plains areas. The "Long Walk" of the Navajos is recounted in L.R. Bailey, The Long Walk: A History of The Navajo Wars, 1846–68 (1964). See generally Helen Hunt Jackson's influential exposé, Century of Dishonor (1881).

The leading authority on the removal of the Five Civilized Tribes (the Cherokees, Choctaws, Creeks, Chickasaws, and Seminoles) is the comprehensive work, Grant Foreman, Indian Removal: The Emigration of the Five Civilized Tribes of Indians (1932). See also Angie Debo, And Still the Waters Run (1972) and Angie Debo, The Rise and Fall of the Choctaw Republic (1961).

Counterpoised against the tragedy of those who were removed is the tenacity of those Indians from many tribes who simply refused to budge. Today, for example, the Seminoles hold three federal reservations and one state reservation in southern Florida. The North Carolina Cherokees own approximately 56,000 acres of trust land in the North Carolina hill country. The Choctaws still live on 35,000 acres of their ancestral agricultural land spread out over 10 counties in Mississippi. Deeply traditional, many of the Mississippi Choctaws still speak Choctaw in their homes and learn English as a second language.

SECTION E. THE STATUS OF INDIAN TREATIES IN UNITED STATES LAW

1. CANONS OF CONSTRUCTION

CHARLES F. WILKINSON & JOHN M. VOLKMAN, JUDICIAL
REVIEW OF INDIAN TREATY ABROGATION: "AS LONG AS
WATER FLOWS OR GRASS GROWS UPON THE EARTH"—
HOW LONG A TIME IS THAT?
63 Calif.L.Rev. 601, 608–19 (1975).

When the War of 1812 ended and the British withdrew from the Continent, the tribes lost much of their bargaining leverage. The negotiations became increasingly onesided. After 1815, United States Indian policy became necessarily responsive to the westward expansion, and treaties were used to remove the Indian tribes from the path of the ever-advancing white civilization. From the Indians' point of view, it was a Hobson's choice. Theoretically, they could keep their land and be overrun by white settlers. Or, they could sell their land, their ancestral heritage, and remove to a new site. Certainly no happy solution to such a dilemma could be found under the best of circumstances.

The results of treaty negotiations were almost always unsatisfactory to the Indians. Friendly Indians were commonly selected as chiefs by federal officials and given power and prestige over tribes that had their own methods for selecting leaders. Some treaties purported to bind Indian tribes not present at negotiations by the signatures of unauthorized head men who were unaware that their signatures would bind those tribes. There are numerous accounts of threats, coercion, bribery, and outright fraud by the negotiators for the United States. Given these factors, it is natural that the Indians generally felt ashamed and angry at the close of negotiations.

Indian tribes at treaty negotiations also faced a language barrier. The Indian treaties were written only in English, making it a certainty that semantic and interpretational problems would arise. When several Indian tribes were involved, the government negotiators would sometimes use a language they believed to be common to all tribes but which in fact carried different meanings to each. The very serious language problems have been emphasized by the Supreme Court:

> [T]he negotiations for the treaty are conducted, on the part of the United States, an enlightened and powerful nation, by representatives skilled in diplomacy, masters of a written language, understanding the modes and forms of creating the various technical estates known to their law, and assisted by an interpreter employed by themselves; . . . the treaty is drawn up by

them and in their own language; . . . the Indians, on the other hand, are a weak and dependent people, who have no written language and are wholly unfamiliar with all the forms of legal expression, and whose only knowledge of the terms in which the treaty is framed is that imparted to them by the interpreter employed by the United States. . . .

It is impossible to avoid the conclusion, therefore, that the young nation's ideals were often subservient to its ambitions when it came to honoring the solemn promises contained in the treaties. Breach by the United States was common; in one case a treaty was respected for only 12 days before it was violated by the government negotiator.

In the Indian wars which usually followed, the Indian ranks were punished and debilitated by the United States Army. In turn, new rounds of treaties were negotiated. The Supreme Court has accurately summarized Indian treaty negotiations during this period by concluding that "[t]he Indian Nations did not seek out the United States and agree upon an exchange of lands in an arm's-length transaction. Rather, treaties were imposed upon them and they had no choice but to consent."

To some extent, the practices can be rationalized—at least legally—by the right of conquest or discovery. Nevertheless, Indian treaties were legally binding agreements between real parties. They were agreements that the American Indians rightfully expected to be upheld. Moreover, the rhetorical questions of Chief Justice John Marshall make it clear that the United States received a very real quid pro quo in every Indian treaty:

> When the United States gave peace, did they not also receive it? Were not both parties desirous of it? If we consult the history of the day, does it not inform us that the United States were not at least as anxious to receive it as the [Indians]?

* * *

The unequal bargaining position of the tribes and the recognition of the trust relationship have led to the development of canons of construction designed to rectify the inequality. Although many treaty rights are clearly expressed in Indian treaties, others are not. The courts have been liberal in recognizing the existence of Indian treaty rights in those instances when they are not clearly stated in the treaty. Three primary rules have been developed: ambiguous expressions must be resolved in favor of the Indian parties concerned;[76] Indian treaties must be interpreted as the Indians themselves would have understood them;[77] and Indian treaties must be

---

[76] See, e.g., McClanahan v. State Tax Comm'n, 411 U.S. 164, 174 (1973); Carpenter v. Shaw, 280 U.S. 363, 367 (1930); Winters v. United States, 207 U.S. 564, 576–77 (1908).

[77] See, e.g., Choctaw Nation v. Oklahoma, 397 U.S. 620, 631 (1970); United States v. Shoshone Tribe, 304 U.S. 111, 116 (1938); Starr v. Long Jim, 227 U.S. 613, 622–23 (1913); Worcester v. Georgia, 31 U.S. (6 Pet.) 515, 582 (1832).

liberally construed in favor of the Indians.[78] Thus the construction of Indian treaties is akin to the construction of adhesion contracts, in that Indian treaties, like adhesion contracts, are liberally construed in favor of the weaker party, and their terms are given the meaning attached to them by laymen unversed in the law. The goal is to achieve the reasonable expectations of the weaker party. Many principles of trust law are also applicable.

The courts have put teeth into these rules of construction. For example, the Supreme Court concluded that the treaty phrase "to be held as Indian lands are held" also reserved hunting and fishing rights to the Indians. In construing treaty language reserving to the Indians the right to fish at "usual and accustomed places" on lands relinquished to the United States, it held that the language included an easement to cross over these lands to reach traditional fishing grounds, even after they had become privately settled by whites. Recently, the Court found that general provisions in the Navajo Treaty of 1868, which set aside the reservation "for the use and occupation of the Navajo tribe of Indians" and provided for the exclusion of non-Navajos from the reservation, must be construed as excluding the operation of state laws, including state tax laws, upon Indians living on the reservation.

In the area of water rights, the Court has developed the so-called *Winters* doctrine which provides that implicit in Indian treaties is the reservation of sufficient waters, from streams on and bordering reservations, to fulfill the purposes of establishing the reservation, including irrigation for agriculture. Furthermore, the doctrine provides that Indian water rights date from the establishment of the reservation and are prior and paramount to any other rights subsequently established pursuant to state law. The *Winters* doctrine is essential to the protection of tribal water rights in Western "prior appropriation" states because it establishes an early appropriation date (the date on which the reservation was created) as well as a liberal quantity of reserved water (including the future needs of the reservation). * * *

NOTES

1. In treaty abrogation cases, the Supreme Court has traditionally relied upon the canons of construction if there is "ambiguity" in the legislation that is alleged to have abrogated a treaty right. In South Dakota v. Bourland, 508 U.S. 679 (1993), however, the Court concluded that general provisions in two congressional acts authorizing construction of a dam abrogated the tribe's treaty power to exclude non-Indians from its reservation lands taken by Congress for the dam project and with it the incidental power to regulate non-

---

[78] See, e.g., Choctaw Nation v. United States, 318 U.S. 423, 431–32 (1943); Tulee v. Washington, 315 U.S. 681–684–85 (1942); United States v. Walker River Irrig. Dist., 104 F.2d 334, 337 (9th Cir.1939).

Indian hunting and fishing. The relevant provisions were not explicit as to which treaty right, if any, Congress intended to take, but the Court nonetheless found clear abrogation in the words that took reservation lands for the Oahe Dam and those that broadly opened the lands for public recreational use. Then, in Hagen v. Utah, 510 U.S. 399 (1994), page 521, infra, the Rehnquist Court again failed to invoke the canons in a case involving the effect of congressional legislation on Indian land rights.

> When construing legislation opening Indian country to non-Indian occupancy, the Court has generally resisted diminishing reservation boundaries absent clear evidence that Congress intended to divest the tribe not only of parcels of land but the power to govern the area. * * * The Court now dismisses the canons by declaring that no true ambiguity exists. For instance, *Hagen v. Utah* held that the Ute Indian reservation had been extinguished by statutes that opened some of it up to allotment. *Hagen* involved a 1902 Act that required tribal consent before allotments could be made, with the unallotted land to "be restored to the public domain." When consent was not forthcoming, Congress passed another Act in 1905 allowing allotments to be made without it. This later Act also eliminated the language restoring unallotted lands to the public domain.

> The *Hagen* Court held that the vague phrase in the first Act about restoration to the public domain expressed congressional intent to disestablish the reservation. * * * Next, it found that the 1905 Act not only effectuated allotment without Indian consent, but that it also meant to restore unallotted lands to the public domain, a matter on which it was silent. * * * After drawing these inferences—that restoration was tantamount to disestablishment and that the 1905 Act also removed the requirement of Indian consent to restoration—the Court found there was insufficient ambiguity to warrant applying the canons of construction. * * * Thus, the Utes' reservation was extinguished.

David H. Getches, *Conquering the Cultural Frontier: The New Subjectivism of the Supreme Court in Indian Law*, 84 Calif.L.Rev. 1573, 1620–23 (1996).

2.   One of the canons of treaty construction is that treaty provisions must be read as the Indians themselves would have understood them. The Supreme Court used this canon to interpret an 1837 Treaty and uphold the tribe's rights to hunt, fish and gather on lands ceded to the United States in Minnesota v. Mille Lacs Band of Chippewa Indians, 526 U.S. 172 (1999). The Court said; "In this case, an examination of the historical record provides insight into how the parties to the Treaty understood the terms of the agreement. This insight is especially helpful to the extent it sheds light on how the Chippewa signatories to the Treaty understood the agreement because we interpret Indian treaties to give effect to the terms as the Indians themselves would have understood them." Id. at 196. To determine how the Indians would have understood treaty terms, it is sometimes necessary to recreate the circumstances that existed

when the treaties were negotiated. Testimony is typically taken from tribal members knowledgeable about tribal history and from academicians such as anthropologists and historians. Circumstances among tribes varied widely from region to region, but the following case—the historic "Boldt decision," treated more fully in Chapter 12, pages 911–937—gives the flavor of treaty negotiations and an indication of the way in which courts use history to interpret Indian treaties.

UNITED STATES V. WASHINGTON

United States District Court, Western District of Washington, 1974.
384 F.Supp. 312, affirmed 520 F.2d 676 (9th Cir.1975),
cert. denied 423 U.S. 1086, 96 S.Ct. 877, 47 L.Ed.2d 97 (1976).

BOLDT, SENIOR DISTRICT JUDGE.

* * *

[The litigation involved the extent of off-reservation treaty fishing rights. The Court listed six treaties, between the United States and a total of fourteen tribes in Western Washington, which were entered into between 1854 and 1859.]

* * * Each of said treaties contains a provision securing to the Indians certain off-reservation fishing rights. The following provision from the Treaty of Medicine Creek is typical of these treaty provisions:

"The right of taking fish, at all usual and accustomed grounds and stations, is further secured to said Indians, in common with all citizens of the Territory, and of erecting temporary houses for the purposes of curing * * * ."

* * *

* * * The anthropological reports and testimony of both Dr. Barbara Lane and Dr. Carroll Riley have been thoroughly studied and considered by the court. * * *

* * * In pretreaty times Indian settlements were widely dispersed throughout Western Washington. There was considerable local diversity in the availability and importance of specific animal, plant and mineral resources used for food and artifacts. But one common cultural characteristic among all of these Indians was the almost universal and generally paramount dependence upon the products of an aquatic economy, especially anadromous fish, to sustain the Indian way of life. These fish were vital to the Indian diet, played an important role in their religious life, and constituted a major element of their trade and economy. Throughout most of the area salmon was a staple food and steelhead were also taken, both providing essential proteins, fats, vitamins, and minerals in the native diet. * * *

* * * The major food sources of the Northwest Indians were the wild fish, animal and vegetative resources of the area. It was, therefore, necessary for the people to be on hand when the resources were ready for harvest. These seasonal movements were reflected in native social organization. In the winter, when weather conditions generally made travel and fishing difficult, people remained in their winter villages and lived more or less on stored food. Fresh fish and other foods were harvested during the winter but that season was devoted primarily to ceremonies and manufacturing tasks. During this time people congregated into the largest assemblages and occupied long, multifamily houses. Throughout the rest of the year individual families dispersed in various directions to join families from other winter villages in fishing, clam digging, hunting, gathering roots and berries, and agricultural pursuits. * * *

* * *

* * * The first-salmon ceremony, which with local differences in detail was general through most of the area, was essentially a religious rite to ensure the continued return of salmon. The symbolic acts, attitudes of respect and reverence, and concern for the salmon reflected a ritualistic conception of the interdependence and relatedness of all living things which was a dominant feature of native Indian world view. Religious attitudes and rites insured that salmon were never wantonly wasted and that water pollution was not permitted during the salmon season.

* * * At the time of the treaties, trade was carried on among the Indian groups throughout a wide geographic area. Fish was a basic element of the trade. There is some evidence that the volume of this intra-tribal trade was substantial, but it is not possible to compare it with the volume of present day commercial trading in salmon. Such trading was, however, important to the Indians at the time of the treaties. In addition to potlatching, which is a system of exchange between communities in a social context often typified by competitive gifting, there was a considerable amount of outright sale and trade beyond the local community and sometimes over great distances. * * *

* * *

* * * On December 26, 1853, Isaac Stevens, the first Governor and Superintendent of Indian Affairs of the Washington Territory, wrote to the Commissioner of Indian Affairs suggesting the necessity of making treaties with the Indians west of the Cascade Mountains. * * *

* * * No formal political structure had been created by the Indians living in the Puget Sound area at the time of initial contact with the United States Government. Governor Stevens, acting upon instructions from his superiors and recommendations of his subordinates, deliberately created political entities for purposes of delegating responsibilities and negotiating

treaties. In creating these entities Governor Stevens named many chiefs and sub-chiefs.

* * *

* * * The principal purposes of the treaties were to extinguish Indian claims to the land in Washington Territory and provide for peaceful and compatible coexistence of Indians and non-Indians in the area. The United States was concerned with forestalling friction between Indians and settlers and between settlers and the government. The Indians had received constant assurances from settlers and government representatives that they would be compensated for lands which were being settled by United States' citizens. Settlers had taken up land claims under the Donation Act even though the Indian rights had not yet been extinguished by treaties as required by the act creating the Oregon Territory. Governor Stevens and the treaty commissioners were not authorized to grant to the Indians or treat away on behalf of the United States any governmental authority of the United States.

* * * At the treaty negotiations, a primary concern of the Indians whose way of life was so heavily dependent upon harvesting anadromous fish, was that they have freedom to move about to gather food, particularly salmon, (which both Indians and non-Indians meant to include steelhead), at their usual and accustomed fishing places. The Indians were assured by Governor Stevens and the treaty commissioners that they would be allowed to fish, but that the white man also would be allowed to fish. In 1856, it was felt that the development of the non-Indian fisheries in the case area would not interfere with the subsistence of the Indians.

* * *

* * * There is no record of English having been spoken at the treaty councils, but it is probable that there were Indians at each council who would have spoken or understood some English. One Snohomish Indian who understood English helped translate the Point Elliott treaty. Since, however, the vast majority of Indians at the treaty councils did not speak or understand English, the treaty provisions and the remarks of the treaty commissioners were interpreted by Colonel Shaw to the Indians in the Chinook jargon and then translated into native languages by Indian interpreters. Chinook jargon, a trade medium of limited vocabulary and simple grammar, was inadequate to express precisely the legal effects of the treaties, although the general meaning of treaty language could be explained. Many of those present, however, did not understand Chinook jargon. There is no record of the Chinook jargon phrase that was actually used in the treaty negotiations to interpret the provision "The right of taking fish, at all usual and accustomed grounds and stations, is further secured to said Indians, in common with all citizens of the Territory." A dictionary of the Chinook jargon, prepared by George Gibbs, indicates that

the jargon contains no words or expressions that would describe any limiting interpretation on the right of taking fish.

* * * The treaty language "in common with all citizens of the Territory" was probably introduced by George Gibbs, who was a lawyer and advisor to Governor Stevens. There is no discussion of the phrase in the minutes of the treaty councils, in the instructions to Stevens or to the treaty negotiators, or in Stevens' letters of transmittal of the treaties. There appears to be no phrase in Chinook jargon that would interpret the term in any exact legal sense.

* * * Although there is no evidence of the precise understanding the Indians had of the treaty language, the treaty commissioners probably used the terms "usual and accustomed" and "in common with" in their common parlance, and the meaning of them as found in a contemporaneous dictionary most likely would be what was intended by the government representatives. The 1828 and 1862 editions of Webster's American Dictionary of the English Language define the terms as follows:

> *accustomed:* Being familiar by use; habituated; inured . . . usual; often practiced.

> *common:* Belonging equally to more than one, or to many indefinitely . . . belonging to the public; having no separate owner . . . general; serving for the use of all.

> *usual:* Customary; common; frequent; such as occurs in ordinary practice or in the ordinary course of events.

The Indians who negotiated the treaties probably understood the concept of common ownership interest which could have been conveyed in Chinook jargon. * * *

* * *

* * * There is nothing in the written records of the treaty councils or other accounts of discussions with the Indians to indicate that the Indians were told that their existing fishing activities or tribal control over them would in any way be restricted or impaired by the treaty. The most that could be implied from the treaty context is that the Indians may have been told or understood that non-Indians would be allowed to take fish at the Indian fishing locations along with the Indians.

[In a lengthy opinion, the district judge ruled in favor of the tribes. The state had argued that the treaty right to fish "in common with all citizens of the Territory" meant that the small number of Indian fishers would be subject to all state regulations, including seasons and bag limits. The court rejected that argument, construing the treaty provision liberally and as the Indians themselves would have understood it:]

* * *

* * * By dictionary definition and as intended and used in the Indian treaties and in this decision "in common with" means *sharing equally* the opportunity to take fish at "usual and accustomed grounds and stations"; therefore, nontreaty fishermen shall have the opportunity to take up to 50% of the harvestable number of fish that may be taken by all fishermen at usual and accustomed grounds and stations and treaty right fishermen shall have the opportunity to take up to the same percentage of harvestable fish, as stated above. * * *

* * *

[The opinion was ultimately approved by the Supreme Court in 1979 in a collateral case. See page 911, infra, and the accompanying notes.]

NOTES

1.   The Idaho Supreme Court was called upon to decide whether a treaty with the Shoshone-Bannock Tribe preserved an off-reservation right to fish. The Fort Bridger Treaty recognized the "tribe's right to hunt on the unoccupied lands of the United States so long as game may be found thereon, and so long as peace subsists among the whites and Indians on the borders of the hunting districts." The court held that the right to hunt included the right to fish. It relied on expert testimony of an anthropologist that "hunt" would translate into a word in the Indian language meaning "to obtain wild food" and that salmon fishing was a major part of Indian life at the time of the treaties. Other evidence showed that tribal negotiators expressed concern with hunting and fishing. State v. Tinno, 497 P.2d 1386 (Idaho 1972).

2.   Indian treaties were negotiated in the field by government negotiators and then taken to the Senate for ratification. In many cases, the Senate altered the negotiated terms. In other instances, especially with respect to California and Oregon, the treaties were never ratified at all. In numerous situations, Congress initially ratified a treaty but subsequently modified it or abrogated it totally by subsequent legislation. See pages 350–361, infra.

2.   TREATIES AND RESERVED RIGHTS

The reservations that resulted from Indian treaties (as well as from agreements and other federal actions) were a mixed blessing for Indians. Nearly all tribes vehemently objected to being located on parcels far smaller than their aboriginal domains though they were supposed to be secure enclaves. The diminished territories of reservations established during the expansion era were typically so limited, however, that eking out a livelihood was nearly impossible.

When questions arose over what rights were given up in treaties and what rights were retained, the courts have often taken account of the circumstances and responded favorably to the tribes. "Reservation" has a legal meaning broader than the popular use of the term to describe an area of land set aside for a specific purpose: a reservation is also any property right or power retained by a party to a bilateral agreement. In the following turn-of-the-century opinion written by Justice McKenna, the Court announced substantial tribal reserved rights in an area traditionally claimed to be within state authority, hunting and fishing regulation. The case also has had broad ramifications for non-Indian property rights.

UNITED STATES V. WINANS

Supreme Court of the United States, 1905.
198 U.S. 371, 25 S.Ct. 662, 49 L.Ed. 1089.

MR. JUSTICE McKENNA delivered the opinion of the court.

[A treaty was negotiated in 1859 between the Yakima Nation and the United States. Like many treaties, Article I provided that the tribe would "cede, relinquish, and convey to the United States all their right, title, and interest" in specified land, while Article II "reserved" described land for the "use and occupancy" of the tribe. Article III then provided that the tribe would have the "exclusive right of taking fish" on the reservation. Article III also contained a provision, found in some treaties, that the tribe would have off-reservation fishing rights "at all usual and accustomed places, in common with citizens of the Territory."

The United States brought this action on behalf of the Yakima Nation to enjoin respondents, Winans and other non-Indians, from obstructing off-reservation fishing at usual and accustomed fishing sites. The sites were located on parcels of land along the Columbia River owned in fee by the non-Indian respondents. The respondents operated fish wheels, pursuant to a license from the State of Washington, which were so efficient that they effectively gained "exclusive possession of the fishing places." In addition, the respondents attempted to exclude tribal members from the fishing sites and refused to permit them to cross over other non-Indian fee land to reach the fishing sites. The lower court dismissed the action, finding that the respondents had acquired "perfect absolute title" to the lands in question and therefore had the right to exclude Yakima tribal members from the land.]

* * * The contention of the respondents was sustained. In other words, it was decided that the Indians acquired no rights but what any inhabitant of the Territory or State would have. Indeed, acquired no rights but such as they would have without the treaty. This is certainly an impotent outcome to negotiations and a convention, which seemed to promise more and give the word of the Nation for more. And we have said we will construe a treaty with the Indians as "that unlettered people" understood it, and "as justice and reason demand in all cases where power is exerted by the strong over those to whom they owe care and protection," and counterpoise the inequality "by the superior justice which looks only to the substance of the

right without regard to technical rules." How the treaty in question was understood may be gathered from the circumstances.

The right to resort to the fishing places in controversy was a part of larger rights possessed by the Indians, upon the exercise of which there was not a shadow of impediment, and which were not much less necessary to the existence of the Indians than the atmosphere they breathed. New conditions came into existence, to which those rights had to be accommodated. Only a limitation of them, however, was necessary and intended, not a taking away. In other words, the treaty was not a grant of rights to the Indians, but a grant of rights from them—a reservation of those not granted. And the form of the instrument and its language was adapted to that purpose. Reservations were not of particular parcels of land, and could not be expressed in deeds as dealings between private individuals. The reservations were in large areas of territory and the negotiations were with the tribe. They reserved rights, however, to every individual Indian, as though named therein. They imposed a servitude upon every piece of land as though described therein. There was an exclusive right of fishing reserved within certain boundaries. There was a right outside of those boundaries reserved "in common with citizens of the Territory." As a mere right, it was not exclusive in the Indians. Citizens might share it, but the Indians were secured in its enjoyment by a special provision of means for its exercise. They were given "the right of taking fish at all usual and accustomed places," and the right "of erecting temporary buildings for curing them." The contingency of the future ownership of the lands, therefore, was foreseen and provided for—in other words, the Indians were given a right in the land—the right of crossing it to the river— the right to occupy it to the extent and for the purpose mentioned. No other conclusion would give effect to the treaty. And the right was intended to be continuing against the United States and its grantees as well as against the State and its grantees.

* * *

It is further contended that the rights conferred upon the Indians are subordinate to the powers acquired by the State upon its admission into the Union. In other words, it is contended that the State acquired, by its admission into the Union "upon an equal footing with the original States," the power to grant rights in or to dispose of the shore lands upon navigable streams, and such power is subject only to the paramount authority of Congress with regard to public navigation and commerce. The United States, therefore, it is contended, could neither grant nor retain rights in the shore or to the lands under water.

The elements of this contention and the answer to it are expressed in *Shively v. Bowlby*, 152 U.S. 1. * * * It was said by the court, through Mr. Justice Gray: * * *

"By the Constitution, as is now well settled, the United States, having rightfully acquired the Territories, and being the only Government which can impose laws upon them, have the entire dominion and sovereignty, national and municipal, Federal and State, over all the Territories, so long as they remain in a territorial condition. * * * "

Many cases were cited. And it was further said:

"We cannot doubt, therefore, that Congress has the power to make grants of lands below high water mark of navigable waters in any Territory of the United States, whenever it becomes necessary to do so in order to perform international obligations, or to effect the improvement of such lands for the promotion and convenience of commerce with foreign nations and among the several States, or to carry out other public purposes appropriate to the objects for which the United States hold the Territory."

The extinguishment of the Indian title, opening the land for settlement and preparing the way for future States, were appropriate to the objects for which the United States held the Territory. And surely it was within the competency of the Nation to secure to the Indians such a remnant of the great rights they possessed as "taking fish at all usual and accustomed places." Nor does it restrain the State unreasonably, if at all, in the regulation of the right. It only fixes in the land such easements as enable the right to be exercised.

The license from the State, which respondents plead to maintain a fishing wheel, gives no power to them to exclude the Indians, nor was it intended to give such power. It was the permission of the State to use a particular device. What rights the Indians had were not determined or limited. * * *

Decree reversed and the case remanded for further proceedings in accordance with this opinion.

MR. JUSTICE WHITE dissents.

NOTES

1. What are the elements of the Indian reserved fishing rights recognized in *Winans*? How are the land titles of the non-Indian settlers affected? How is state police power over wildlife limited?

2. Disputes over scarce water supplies have long held a dominant place in natural resource law and policy in the arid western states. Western water law is described more fully at pages 817–819, infra. For our purposes, it is sufficient to state that the prior appropriation doctrine, as applied in western states, grants fixed water rights on a "first in time, first in right" basis: a user can obtain a vested property right, superior to all later users, by (a) diverting water out of a watercourse and (b) putting it to a beneficial use, such as for agricultural, industrial, or domestic purposes. A landowner on a stream

possesses no rights to water based on the location of the property. Such riparian rights have been soundly rejected in favor of the prior appropriation doctrine, which rewards persons who actually put water to use. Traditions of state control over water run deep. In spite of this, three years after *Winans* the Supreme Court handed down the famous *Winters* case. *Winters* upheld a federally-protected reserved tribal right to water independent of state law and touched off a controversy over water that remains at the forefront of resources issues in the American West. See Chapter 12, supra.

The implications of the reserved rights doctrine for state governments and the commensurate limitations imposed on non-Indian property rights have incited adverse reactions, particularly in the area of water rights. Judicial recognition of these rights has led to calls for the elimination of Indian treaties, Indian reservations, and other Indian rights

CHAPTER FOUR

CENTURIES OF SHIFTING
LAW AND POLICY

■ ■ ■

The Indian treaties of the seventeenth-and eighteenth-century colonial era established the idea of "reservations" as a means of confining Indian occupancy and use of land to specific territory. See page 85, supra. The Founders adopted this idea as the centerpiece of the United States' first Indian policy. The reservation concept was perpetuated in a different form and for different motives in the expansion era of the latter half of the nineteenth century.

As the *Cherokee* cases show, it was not enough to keep Indians isolated in the midst of expanding white civilization. The lure of the Indians' land and of gold and other resources within their territory was a temptation too great for the settlers to resist or for the government to pretend to protect. Furthermore, states were jealous of tribal political autonomy within their boundaries.

Thus, the removal policy was designed to sweep tribes westward, farther out of the way of settlement. By the 1850s, the West had large blocks of land reserved for removed tribes, principally located in the Indian Territory (now Oklahoma), which was supposed to become a separate Indian state. In addition, a round of treaties with Indians whose aboriginal territory was in the West had resulted in significant reserves in the Great Plains and elsewhere. In exchange for giving up expansive claims to all their aboriginal lands, tribes accepted these specified tracts with the assurance that they would remain as Indian reservations "forever" or "as long as rivers run" and that the United States would protect the boundaries from incursions by non-Indians.

It was not long before waves of immigrants encountered Indian country in their quest for a new life in the West. They coveted tribal lands and natural resources that were legally off-limits to settlement. So more lands were demanded by homesteaders. The U.S. lacked both the tactical ability and the political will to hold the boundaries of the large western reservations. Instead, federal policy-makers renewed old rationales of civilizing Indians and embodied them in new, ostensibly beneficial programs that required diminishing the reservation land base and exerting greater federal influence within the remainder. Successive treaties resulted in repeated cessions of territory.

Many tribes lost their ability to remain self-sufficient. Deprived of a land base large enough to supply their subsistence, they became dependent on federal rations promised in treaties. With traditional tribal structures undermined by loss of land and growing federal control, self-government was crippled. A syndrome of forced dependence and resulting social and economic decline became the rationale for even greater government domination of Indian life during the late nineteenth and early twentieth centuries.

SECTION A. ALLOTMENTS AND ASSIMILATION (1871–1928)

In the late nineteenth century, Congress expanded its exercise of legislative powers to keep order in Indian country, to protect Indians from hostile non-Indians, and otherwise to legislate for the "national interest." With the enactment of the allotment policy and its accompanying assimilationist efforts came new notions of what was necessary for the "benefit" of tribes.

Shrinking the Indian reservation land base was designed to serve dual goals: to open more land for white settlement and to end Indian tribalism. The allotment policy of the late nineteenth century expansion era was supposed to turn reservations into campuses for training Indians in the "arts of civilization." The Bureau of Indian Affairs took unprecedented control of everyday Indian life, seeking to squeeze out Indian government, religion, and culture. Tribal lands were carved up and parceled out to individual Indians who were to be converted from hunters to farmers. "Surplus" lands were sold for non-Indian settlement; the result was a loss of about two-thirds of all the Indians' lands. The framework created by the early treaty relationship between the tribes and the federal government secured tribal self-government and impeded but ultimately could not prevent an expansive exercise of Congress's power to legislate on behalf of its Indian "wards." The Supreme Court ruled that treaties could be broken if Congress determined that such a breach was in the Indians' best interests. See *Lone Wolf v. Hitchcock*, page 212 infra.

The conflicting legacies of treaty-making and treaty-breaking characterizing the historical relationship between tribes and the federal government are perplexing. Achieving justice between Indians and non-Indians through the reconciliation of the plenary power of Congress in Indian affairs with Congress's duties of trust to the tribes, and at the same time paying due deference to principles of tribal sovereignty, has been a daunting challenge for the United States' legal system over the course of two centuries. The challenge continues today, as tribes carry on their struggle to rebuild their reservations into self-sustaining Native nations within twenty-first century United States society. See generally Rebuilding Native Nations: Strategies for Governance and Development (Miriam Jorgensen ed. 2007).

1. "CIVILIZING" THE INDIAN: THE BIA AND THE RESERVATION SYSTEM

The reservation system was not the result of a conscious decision by a magnanimous or far-sighted federal government to create sanctuaries where Indian people could "perpetuate a radically different heritage from white settlers." G. Edward White: The Marshall Court and Cultural Change: 1815–1835 at 706 (1988). Reservations were created by the federal government as the best means of "civilizing" the Indian. When it became apparent to federal policymakers that the reservations were not fulfilling their intended purposes, an aggressive new approach to the nation's "Indian problem" was implemented. The 1887 Dawes Act provided for "allotment" of the reservations in severalty to individual tribal members as part of an official policy to destroy tribalism through reduction of the treaty-guaranteed tribal land base. Well-intentioned reformers sought to transform Indians and their cultures according to Jeffersonian values of yeoman husbandry. Indian cultural traditions, experiences, and sentiment were often opposed to a sedentary, individualized lifestyle. Yet, small plots in arid lands were inadequate to provide Indians subsistence. These facts did not deter nineteenth century policymakers; the Indian was to be forced to march on "the white man's road."

S. LYMAN TYLER, A HISTORY OF INDIAN POLICY
71–88 (1973).

The new reservation policy after 1850 would again see the Indians placed on isolated lands entirely surrounded by other lands controlled by private landholders, by the States and territories, or by the United States. Within these reservations, legally, the tribes continued to be self-governing bodies. * * * Although we look to California for the beginnings of the experimentation with reservation policy at mid-century, actually it was not at first successful there. Treaties were made in the early 1850's, and some reservations were established, but the Congress refused to ratify the treaties, and thereby nullified the actions of the agents.

In the Mid-1850's, however, reservations were successfully established, and from this early experiment in California the program was extended to other areas west of the Mississippi River. Previously whites had tended to live primarily in the established States and territories in the east, the Indians, predominantly in the unorganized Indian country to the west. In the newly acquired California, New Mexico, and Arizona the

Indians and whites were already intermixed. Thus, Indian reservations entirely surrounded by non-Indians resulted. As the westward movement eventually carried whites into all regions of the United States, whites and Indians also became intermixed in these areas, and the reservation system became the accepted policy to satisfactorily meet the immediate problem. Thus the removal of Indians from inhabited areas and their concentration in an "Indian Country" gradually gave way to their placement on reserved "islands" of land usually within the larger areas they once possessed. * * *

The military were still responsible for maintaining order and for protecting inhabitants and communications lines on the frontier. In practice, a kind of understanding between the military and the civilian agents resulted:

> Indians who did not go willingly to the reservations would be either driven there by force or exterminated in the process. Once on the reservation, the Christian agents and teachers could help them assimilate the white man's culture.

> * * *

> Because Western public opinion was opposed to constructive Indian legislation, to allow the military and the churches to proceed according to their respective ideas, one outside and the other within the reservation, was the best that could be done.

During the period when the Government was attempting to apply this dual policy, settlers and adventurers of various kinds continued their pressure on the areas occupied by the Indians, even entering the established reservations. The Indians protested, but their protests failed to check the flow of non-Indians who seemed intent on "winning the West" from its native occupants. In response to these pressures, dissatisfied Indian leaders attracted bands of followers that left the reservations and tried to solve their problems by the only means that seemed to remain to them, the use of force. The Indians always lost eventually as a result of these encounters, for the numbers arrayed against them proved insurmountable. * * *

When the Nation was welded together by the completion of the transcontinental railroad in 1869, and as spurs were extended from the main line into what had previously been remote areas, the long communication lines that had plagued the Army's attempts to control troublesome Indian bands became less of a problem. The Indians were soon virtually surrounded by their conquerors and newly appointed rulers. The old way under Indian leadership was gradually disappearing. The Indian agent was the new taskmaster bringing a multitude of new programs foreign to Indian ideas of the proper role of man in his society.

Somewhat related to the extension of the railroad was the final disappearance of the buffalo herds that had been the mainstay of the life of the Plains Indian. The buffalo furnished meat for the railroad builders, there was a market for the buffalo hides, eastern hunters and sportsmen from Europe had a drive to kill one of these great animals before they became extinct; all of this resulted in needless slaughter that ended the balance the Indian had maintained with nature by taking only what he needed for food, clothing, and shelter.

* * * The tribe and its leaders had lost their political autonomy. Unable to maintain their own government, they became communities administered from Washington. The administrative structure was the Bureau of Indian Affairs. The local representative was the agent or superintendent given the administrative responsibility to look after the welfare of the Indians in relations with non-Indians, to maintain the resources of the reservation, and to encourage "civilizing" influences. * * *

NOTE

As Tyler explains, the administrative responsibility for the "civilizing" mission of the reservations was placed within the Bureau of Indian Affairs (BIA). Contrary to the promises implicit in the treaties, the BIA never set out to administer the reservations as permanent tribal homelands. Instead, federal Indian policy in essence revived the old assumptions about the Indians' fate that had animated the Founders' original Indian policy: the Indian had to adopt the civilized ways of the white man. United States Indian policy was, therefore, to oversee this civilizing process, as humanely and as cheaply as possible.

As the chief administrative officer of the BIA, the Commissioner of Indian Affairs directed the day-to-day operations of the Bureau, but also framed much of the federal government's Indian policy. The Commissioner's annual reports reveal some of the perceptions and attitudes that sustained and inspired the policy. Those reports put forward a number of consistent themes in advocating for reforms of United States Indian policy. The major reforms associated with the late nineteenth century all acted to some extent upon those themes of white cultural superiority and Indian tribalism's presumed demise.

INDIAN COMMISSIONER MEDILL ON INDIAN COLONIES

From the Annual Report of the Commissioner of Indian Affairs. November 30, 1848.
Reprinted from Documents of United States Indian Policy 77–80
(Francis P. Prucha ed. Second Edition, Expanded, 1990).

* * * Stolid and unyielding in his nature, and inveterately wedded to the savage habits, customs, and prejudices in which he has been reared and trained, it is seldom the case that the full blood Indian of our hemisphere can, in immediate juxtaposition with a white population, be brought farther within the pale of civilization than to adopt its vices; under

the corrupting influences of which, too indolent to labor, and too weak to resist, he soon sinks into misery and despair. The inequality of his position in all that secures dignity and respect is too glaring, and the contest he has to make with the superior race with which he is brought into contact, in all the avenues to success and prosperity in life, is too unequal to hope for a better result. The collision is to him a positive evil. He is unprepared and in all respects unfitted for it; and he necessarily soon sinks under it and perishes. * * * Cannot this sad and depressing tendency of things be checked, and the past be at least measurably repaired by better results in the future? It is believed they can; and, indeed, it has to some extent been done already, by the wise and beneficent system of policy put in operation some years since, and which, if steadily carried out, will soon give to our whole Indian system a very different and much more favorable aspect.

The policy already begun and relied on to accomplish objects so momentous and so desirable to every Christian and philanthropist is, as rapidly as it can safely and judiciously be done, to colonize our Indian tribes beyond the reach, for some years, of our white population; confining each within a small district of country, so that, as the game decreases and becomes scarce, the adults will gradually be compelled to resort to agriculture and other kinds of labor to obtain a subsistence, in which aid may be afforded and facilities furnished them out of the means obtained by the sale of their former possession. To establish, at the same time, a judicious and well devised system of manual labor schools for the education of the youth of both sexes in letters—the males in practical agriculture and the various necessary and useful mechanic arts, and the females in the different branches of housewifery, including spinning and weaving; and these schools, like those already in successful operation, to be in charge of the excellent and active missionary societies of the different Christian denominations of the country, and to be conducted and the children taught by efficient, exemplary, and devoted men and women, selected with the approbation of the Department by those societies; so that a physical, intellectual, moral, and religious education will all be imparted together.

The strongest propensities of an Indian's nature are his desire for war and his love of the chase. * * * His subsistence and dress are obtained principally by means of the chase; and if this resource is insufficient, and it be necessary to cultivate the earth or to manufacture materials for dress, it has to be done by the women, who are their "hewers of wood and drawers of water." Nothing can induce him to resort to labor, unless compelled to do so by a stern necessity; and it is only then that there is any ground to work upon for civilizing and Christianizing him. But little, if any, good impression can be made upon him in these respects, so long as he is able freely to roam at large and gratify his two predominant inclinations. Nor can these be subdued in any other way than by the mode of colonization, to which reference has been made. When compelled to face the stern

necessities of life and to resort to labor for a maintenance, he in a very short time becomes a changed being; and is then willing, and frequently eager, to receive information and instruction in all that may aid him in improving his condition. It is at this stage that he begins to perceive and appreciate the advantages possessed by the white man, and to desire also to enjoy them; and, if too far advanced in life for mental instruction himself, he asks that it may be provided for his children. Such is the experience in the cases of several of the tribes not long since colonized, who a few years ago were mere nomads and hunters; and, when settled in their new countries, were opposed to labor and to anything like schools or missionaries; but who are now desirous of both the latter for the benefit of their children and themselves, and are becoming prosperous and happy from having learned how to provide a certain and comfortable support for themselves and their families by the cultivation of the soil and other modes of labor. The most marked change, however, when this transition takes place, is in the condition of the females. She who had been the drudge and the slave then begins to assume her true position as an equal; and her labor is transferred from the field to her household—to the care of her family and children. This great change in disposition and condition has taken place, to a greater or less extent, in all the tribes that have been removed and permanently settled west of the Mississippi. It is true, that portions of some of them enjoyed a considerable degree of civilization before they were transplanted; but prior to that even they were retrograding in all respects; while now, they and others who have been colonized and confined within reasonable and fixed limits, are rapidly advancing in intelligence and morality, and in all the means and elements of national and individual prosperity; so that before many years, if we sacredly observe all our obligations towards them, they will have reached a point at which they will be able to compete with a white population, and to sustain themselves under any probable circumstances of contact or connexion with it. If this great end is to be accomplished, however, material changes will soon have to be made in the position of some of the smaller tribes on the frontier, so as to leave an ample outlet for our white population to spread and to pass towards and beyond the Rocky mountains; else, not only will they be run over and extinguished, but all may be materially injured. * * *

INDIAN COMMISSIONER MIX ON RESERVATION POLICY

From the Annual Report of the Commissioner of Indian Affairs. November 6, 1858.
Reprinted From Documents of United States Indian Policy 92–94
(Francis P. Prucha ed. Second Edition, Expanded, 1990).

* * * Experience has demonstrated that at least three serious, and, to the Indians, fatal errors have, from the beginning, marked our policy towards them, viz: their removal from place to place as our population advanced; the assignment to them of too great an extent of country, to be held in common; and the allowance of large sums of money, as annuities,

for the lands ceded by them. These errors, far more than the want of capacity on the part of the Indian, have been the cause of the very limited success of our constant efforts to domesticate and civilize him. By their frequent changes of position and the possession of large bodies of land in common, they have been kept in an unsettled condition and prevented from acquiring a knowledge of separate and individual property, while their large annuities, upon which they have relied for a support, have not only tended to foster habits of indolence and profligacy, but constantly made them the victims of the lawless and inhuman sharper and speculator. * * * Our present policy, as you are aware, is * * * to permanently locate the different tribes on reservations embracing only sufficient land for their actual occupancy; to divide this among them in severalty, and require them to live upon and cultivate the tracts assigned to them; and in lieu of money annuities, to furnish them with stock animals, agricultural implements, mechanic-shops, tools and materials, and manual labor schools for the industrial and mental education of their youth. * * *

* * *

The policy of concentrating the Indians on small reservations of land, and of sustaining them there for a limited period, until they can be induced to make the necessary exertions to support themselves, was commenced in 1853, with those in California. It is, in fact, the only course compatible with the obligations of justice and humanity, left to be pursued in regard to all those with which our advancing settlements render new and permanent arrangements necessary. We have no longer distant and extensive sections of country which we can assign them, abounding in game, from which they could derive a ready and comfortable support; a resource which has, in a great measure, failed them where they are, and in consequence of which they must, at times, be subjected to the pangs of hunger if not actual starvation, or obtain a subsistence by depredations upon our frontier settlements. If it were practicable to prevent such depredations, the alternative to providing for the Indians in the manner indicated, would be to leave them to starve; but as it is impossible, in consequence of the very great extent of our frontier, and our limited military force, to adequately guard against such occurrences, the only alternative, in fact, to making such provision for them, is to exterminate them. * * *

INDIAN COMMISSIONER TAYLOR ON INDIAN CIVILIZATION

From the Annual Report of the Commissioner of Indian Affairs. November 23, 1868.
Reprinted from Documents of United States Indian Policy 123–126
(Francis P. Prucha ed. Second Edition, Expanded, 1990).

How can our Indian tribes be civilized? * * *

* * * It so happens that under the silent and seemingly slow operation of efficient causes, certain tribes of our Indians have already emerged from

a state of pagan barbarism, and are to-day clothed in the garments of civilization, and sitting under the vine and fig tree of an intelligent scriptural Christianity.

* * *

The Cherokees, Choctaws, Chickasaws, Creeks, and Seminoles are the tribes to which I refer. They are to-day civilized and Christian peoples. True, there are portions of each tribe still carrying with them the leaven of their ancestral paganism and superstition, but their average intelligence is very nearly up to the standard of like communities of whites.

* * *

What leading or essential causes, then, operated in civilizing the Cherokees and these other tribes?

* * *

* * * [T]he mainsprings of Cherokee civilization were, first, the circumscribing of their territorial domain; this resulted in, second, the localization of the members of the tribe, and consequently in, third, the necessity of agriculture and pastoral pursuits instead of the chase as a means of existence; and as a logical sequence, fourth, the introduction of ideas of property in things, of sale and barter, & c.; and hence, fifth, of course, a corresponding change from the ideas, habits, and customs of savages to those of civilized life; and, sixth, the great coadjutor in the whole work in all its progress, the Christian teacher and missionary, moving *pari passu* with every other cause.

* * *

What, then, is our duty as the guardian of all the Indians under our jurisdiction? To outlaw, to pursue, to hunt down like wolves, and slay? Must we drive and exterminate them as if void of reason, and without souls? Surely, no.

It is beyond question our most solemn duty to protect and care for, to elevate and civilize them. We have taken their heritage, and it is a grand and magnificent heritage. Now is it too much that we carve for them liberal reservations out of their own lands and guarantee them homes forever? Is it too much that we supply them with agricultural implements, mechanical tools, domestic animals, instructors in the useful arts, teachers, physicians, and Christian missionaries? If we find them fierce, hostile and revengeful; if they are cruel, and if they sometimes turn upon us and burn, pillage, and desolate our frontiers, and perpetrate atrocities that sicken the soul and paralyze us with horror, let us remember that two hundred and fifty years of injustice, oppression and wrong, heaped upon them by our race with cold, calculating and relentless perseverance, have filled them with the passion of revenge, and made them desperate.

* * *

2. REFORMS AND THE END OF TREATY-MAKING

By the late 1860s, the idea of large reservations permanently isolated from white settlement where Indians would be relatively autonomous had become unrealistic. Indian lands held under treaties were "needed" to accommodate the rapid expansion of white settlement. It was plain that the Indians could not be civilized sufficiently to merge with the settlers. The reservation system itself was blamed for this failure, along with the treaty system which had created it. A Board of Indian Commissioners, created to aid in reforming the administration of Indian affairs, indicted the government's past dealings with the tribes, and made recommendations that prefigured many of the major changes in Indian policy.

REPORT OF THE BOARD OF INDIAN COMMISSIONERS
November 23, 1869.
Reprinted From Documents of United States Indian Policy 131–34
(Francis P. Prucha ed. Second Edition, Expanded, 1990).

* * *

While it cannot be denied that the government of the United States, in the general terms and temper of its legislation, has evinced a desire to deal generously with the Indians, it must be admitted that the actual treatment they have received has been unjust and iniquitous beyond the power of words to express.

* * *

The history of the government connections with the Indians is a shameful record of broken treaties and unfulfilled promises.

* * *

Paradoxical as it may seem, the white man has been the chief obstacle in the way of Indian civilization. The benevolent measures attempted by the government for their advancement have been almost uniformly thwarted by the agencies employed to carry them out. The soldiers, sent for their protection, too often carried demoralization and disease into their midst. The agent, appointed to be their friend and counsellor, business manager, and the almoner of the government bounties, frequently went among them only to enrich himself in the shortest possible time, at the cost of the Indians, and spend the largest available sum of the government money with the least ostensible beneficial result. The general interest of the trader was opposed to their enlightenment as tending to lessen his profits. * * * The more submissive and patient the tribe, the greater the number of outlaws infesting their vicinity; and all these were the missionaries teaching them the most degrading vices of which humanity is capable. If in spite of these obstacles, a tribe made some progress in agriculture, or their lands became valuable from any cause, the process of civilization was summarily ended by driving them away from their homes with fire and sword, to undergo similar experiences in some new locality.

Whatever may have been the original character of the aborigines, many of them are now precisely what the course of treatment received from the whites must necessarily have made them—suspicious, revengeful, and cruel in their retaliation.

* * *

The policy of collecting the Indian tribes upon small reservations contiguous to each other, and within the limits of a large reservation, eventually to become a State of the Union, and of which the small reservations will probably be the counties, seems to be the best that can be devised. Many tribes may thus be collected in the present Indian territory. The larger the number that can be thus concentrated the better for the success of the plan; care being taken to separate hereditary enemies from each other. When upon the reservation they should be taught as soon as possible the advantage of individual ownership of property; and should be given land in severalty as soon as it is desired by any of them, and the tribal relations should be discouraged. To facilitate the future allotment of the land the agricultural portions of the reservations should be surveyed as soon as it can be done without too much exciting their apprehensions. The titles should be inalienable from the family of the holder for at least two or three generations. The civilized tribes now in the Indian territory should be taxed, and made citizens of the United States as soon as possible.

The treaty system should be abandoned, and as soon as any just method can be devised to accomplish it, existing treaties should be abrogated.

The legal status of the uncivilized Indians should be that of wards of the government; the duty of the latter being to protect them, to educate them in industry, the arts of civilization, and the principles of Christianity; elevate them to the rights of citizenship, and to sustain and clothe them until they can support themselves.

The payment of money annuities to the Indians should be abandoned, for the reason that such payments encourage idleness and vice, to the injury of those whom it is intended to benefit. Schools should be established, and teachers employed by the government to introduce the English language in every tribe. It is believed that many of the difficulties with Indians occur from misunderstanding as to the meaning and intention of either party. The teachers employed should be nominated by some religious body having a mission nearest to the location of the school. The establishment of Christian missions should be encouraged, and their schools fostered. The pupils should at least receive the rations and clothing they would get if remaining with their families. The religion of our blessed Savior is believed to be the most effective agent for the civilization of any people. * * *

INDIAN COMMISSIONER PARKER ON THE TREATY SYSTEM
From the Annual Report of the Commissioner of Indian Affairs. December 23, 1869.
Reprinted from Documents of United States Indian Policy 134–35
(Francis P. Prucha ed. Second Edition, Expanded, 1990).

[Commissioner of Indian Affairs, Ely S. Parker, who was himself a Seneca Indian, opposed negotiating future treaties with the Indians, for the reasons stated in his annual report to Congress of 1869.]

. . . Arrangements now, as heretofore, will doubtless be required with tribes desiring to be settled upon reservations for the relinquishment of their rights to the lands claimed by them and for assistance in sustaining themselves in a new position, but I am of the opinion that *they should not be of a treaty nature.* * * * A treaty involves the idea of a compact between two or more sovereign powers, each possessing sufficient authority and force to compel a compliance with the obligations incurred. The Indian tribes of the United States are not sovereign nations, capable of making treaties, as none of them have an organized government of such inherent strength as would secure a faithful obedience of its people in the observance of compacts of this character. They are held to be the wards of the government, and the only title the law concedes to them to the land they occupy or claim is a mere possessory one. But, because treaties have been made with them, generally for the extinguishment of their supposed absolute title to land inhabited by them, or over which they roam, they have become falsely impressed with the notion of national independence. It is time that this idea should be dispelled, and the government cease the cruel farce of thus dealing with its helpless and ignorant wards. * * *

PRESIDENT GRANT'S PEACE POLICY
From President Grant's Second Annual Message to Congress. December 5, 1870.
Reprinted From Documents of United States Indian Policy 135
(Francis P. Prucha ed. Second Edition, Expanded, 1990).

[President Ulysses Grant sought to respond to the widespread calls for reform by assigning the Indian agencies to religious denominations. Grant's message to Congress in 1870 explained his new "Peace policy" and the reasoning behind this reform.]

* * * I determined to give all the agencies to such religious denominations as had heretofore established missionaries among the Indians, and perhaps to some other denominations who would undertake the work on the same terms—*i.e.,* as a missionary work. The societies

selected are allowed to name their own agents, subject to the approval of the Executive, and are expected to watch over them and aid them as missionaries, to Christianize and civilize the Indian, and to train him in the arts of peace. The Government watches over the official acts of the agents, and requires of them as strict an accountability as if they were appointed in any other manner. I entertain the confident hope that the policy now pursued will in a few years bring all the Indians upon reservations, where they will live in houses, and have school houses and churches, and will be pursuing peaceful and self-sustaining avocations, and where they may be visited by the law-abiding white man with the same impunity that he now visits the civilized white settlements. * * *

NOTES

1.   While the termination of the treaty system had been a major goal of the reformers of Indian policy during this period, the end of treatymaking with the tribes ultimately had more to do with the white man's politics than with the red man's welfare. Treaties had been a defining component of federal-tribal policy during the first ninety-five years of the Republic. The agreements, however, went only to the Senate for ratification. This practice angered many members of the House of Representatives, which appropriated funds to carry out treaty obligations even though it had no say in their negotiation. Finally, in 1871, the House balked altogether: it refused to appropriate funds to meet new treaty obligations until it was given an equal voice in Indian affairs. The Senate capitulated, and a rider was added to the Indian Appropriations Act of 1871 providing as follows:

> * * * hereafter no Indian nation or tribe within the territory of the United States shall be acknowledged or recognized as an independent nation, tribe, or power with whom the United States may contract by treaty: *Provided, further,* That nothing herein contained shall be construed to invalidate or impair the obligation of any treaty heretofore lawfully made and ratified with any such Indian nation or tribe. * * *

16 Stat. 544, 566 (1871).

The 1871 act signaled the beginning of a new period in Indian affairs during which the tribes would experience a long stretch of assimilationist policy and would see the loss of some 90 million acres through the General Allotment Act and other congressional acts. But the end to treaty-making itself has had little direct legal impact. Congress continued to establish reservations and to carry on relationships with the tribes. Agreements were negotiated with the tribes and approved by both houses. Statutes were used for the same purposes. Succeeding presidents also established reservations through executive orders, although the practice was discontinued in 1919. See Indian Appropriations Act of 1919, § 27, 41 Stat. 3, 34. Executive orders are of lesser dignity only in that land set aside by the President can apparently be taken by later federal action without payment of just compensation. See pages 286–290, infra.

In Antoine v. Washington, 420 U.S. 194 (1975), the Supreme Court noted the limited legal effect of the 1871 Act by explaining that agreements and statutes, like treaties, are the "supreme law of the land:"

> [The Act of 1871] meant no more, however, than that after 1871 relations with Indians would be governed by Acts of Congress and not by treaty. The change in no way affected Congress' plenary powers to *legislate* on problems of Indians, including legislating the ratification of contracts of the Executive Branch with Indian tribes to which affected States were not parties. * * * Once ratified by Act of Congress the provisions of the agreements become law, and like treaties, the supreme law of the land.

Id. at 203–04 (emphasis in original).

2.   While the 1871 Act had little direct *legal* impact, what was the *political* effect of Congress' declaration that "hereafter no Indian nation or tribe * * * shall be acknowledged or recognized as an independent nation, tribe, or power * * * "? Did the victory of the reformers amount to a mere symbolic rejection of the prior historical policy of the United States in dealing with tribes in a treaty relationship, or was something more intended by this gesture?

3. EXPANSION OF FEDERAL POWER OVER THE RESERVATION

Consider the role of the late nineteenth century Supreme Court in assessing the lawfulness of Congress' methods in implementing the allotment era "reforms" and in applying the principles derived from the Marshall trilogy. The following landmark case was issued four years prior to the Dawes General Allotment Act of 1887, the culmination of the nineteenth century reformers' efforts to destroy tribalism. *Ex Parte Crow Dog* represents one of the Supreme Court's strongest affirmations of the principle of tribal sovereignty that was announced in the Marshall trilogy.

EX PARTE CROW DOG
Supreme Court of the United States, 1883.
109 U.S. 556, 3 S.Ct. 396, 27 L.Ed. 1030.

MR. JUSTICE MATTHEWS delivered the opinion of the court.

The petitioner is in the custody of the marshal of the United States for the Territory of Dakota, imprisoned in the jail of Lawrence County, in the First Judicial District of that Territory, under sentence of death, adjudged against him by the district court for that district, to be carried into execution January 14th, 1884. That judgment was rendered upon a conviction for the murder of an Indian of the Brule Sioux band of the Sioux nation of Indians, by the name of Sin-ta-ge-le-Scka, or in English, Spotted

Tail, the prisoner also being an Indian, of the same band and nation, and the homicide having occurred as alleged in the indictment, in the Indian country, within a place and district of country under the exclusive jurisdiction of the United States and within the said judicial district. The judgment was affirmed, on a writ of error, by the Supreme Court of the Territory. It is claimed on behalf of the prisoner that the crime charged against him, and of which he stands convicted, is not an offense under the laws of the United States; that the district court had no jurisdiction to try him, and that its judgment and sentence are void. He therefore prays for a writ of habeas corpus, that he may be delivered from an imprisonment which he asserts to be illegal.

The indictment is framed upon section 5339 of the Revised Statutes. That section is found in title LXX., on the subject of crimes against the United States, and in chapter three, which treats of crimes arising within the maritime and territorial jurisdiction of the United States. It provides that "every person who commits murder, . . . within any fort, arsenal, dock-yard, magazine, or in any other place or district of country under the exclusive jurisdiction of the United States, . . . shall suffer death."

Title XXVIII., of the Revised Statutes relates to Indians, and the sub-title of chapter four is, Government of Indian Country. It embraces many provisions regulating the subject of intercourse and trade with the Indians in the Indian country, and imposes penalties and punishments for various violations of them.

* * *

SEC. 2145. Except as to crimes, the punishment of which is expressly provided for in this title, the general laws of the United States as to the punishment of crimes committed in any place within the sole and exclusive jurisdiction of the United States, except the District of Columbia, shall extend to the Indian country.

"SEC. 2146. The preceding section shall not be construed to extend to [crimes committed by one Indian against the person or property of another Indian, nor to] any Indian committing any offence in the Indian country who has been punished by the local law of the tribe, or to any case where by treaty stipulations the exclusive jurisdiction over such offences is or may be secured to the Indian tribes respectively."*

* * *

The argument in support of the jurisdiction and conviction is, that the exception contained in § 2146 Rev. Stat. is repealed by the operation and legal effect of the treaty with the different tribes of the Sioux Indians of

---

*   [Ed.] Currently codified at 18 U.S.C.A. § 1152, page 540, infra.

April 29th, 1868, 15 Stat. 635; and an act of Congress, approved February 28th, 1877, to ratify an agreement with certain bands of the Sioux Indians, & c., 19 Stat. 254.

The following provisions of the treaty of 1868 are relied on:

"ARTICLE I. From this day forward all war between the parties to this agreement shall forever cease. The government of the United States desires peace, and its honor is hereby pledged to keep it. The Indians desire peace, and they now pledge their honor to maintain it.

"If bad men among the whites, or among other people subject to the authority of the United States, shall commit any wrong upon the person or property of the Indians, the United States will, upon proof made to the agent and forwarded to the commissioner of Indian affairs at Washington City, proceed at once to cause the offender to be arrested and punished according to the laws of the United States, and also reimburse the injured person for the loss sustained.

"If bad men among the Indians shall commit a wrong or depredation upon the person or property of any one, white, black, or Indian, subject to the authority of the United States and at peace therewith, the Indians herein named solemnly agree that they will, upon proof made to their agent and notice by him, deliver up the wrong-doer to the United States, to be tried and punished according to its laws; and in case they wilfully refuse so to do, the person injured shall be reimbursed for his loss from the annuities or other monies due or to become due to them under this or other treaties made with the United States * * * "

* * * But it is quite clear from the context that this [second provision] does not cover the present case of an alleged wrong committed by one Indian upon the person of another of the same tribe. The provision must be construed with its counterpart, just preceding it, which provides for the punishment by the United States of any bad men among the whites, or among other people subject to their authority, who shall commit any wrong upon the person or property of the Indians. Here are two parties, among whom, respectively, there may be individuals guilty of a wrong against one of the other—one is the party of whites and their allies, the other is the tribe of Indians with whom the treaty is made. In each case the guilty party is to be tried and punished by the United States, and in case the offender is one of the Indians who are parties to the treaty, the agreement is that he shall be delivered up. In case of refusal, deduction is to be made from the annuities payable to the tribe, for compensation to the injured person, a provision which points quite distinctly to the conclusion that the injured person cannot himself be one of the same tribe. * * *

The second of these provisions, that are supposed to justify the jurisdiction asserted in the present case, is the eighth article of the agreement, embodied in the act of 1877, in which it is declared:

"And Congress shall, by appropriate legislation, secure to them an orderly government; they shall be subject to the laws of the United States, and each individual shall be protected in his rights of property, person, and life."

It is equally clear, in our opinion, that the words can have no such effect as that claimed for them. The pledge to secure to these people, with whom the United States was contracting as a distinct political body, an orderly government, by appropriate legislation thereafter to be framed and enacted, necessarily implies, having regard to all the circumstances attending the transaction, that among the arts of civilized life, which it was the very purpose of all these arrangements to introduce and naturalize among them, was the highest and best of all, that of self-government, the regulation by themselves of their own domestic affairs, the maintenance of order and peace among their own members by the administration of their own laws and customs. They were nevertheless to be subject to the laws of the United States, not in the sense of citizens, but, as they had always been, as wards subject to a guardian; not as individuals, constituted members of the political community of the United States, with a voice in the selection of representatives and the framing of the laws, but as a dependent community who were in a state of pupilage, advancing from the condition of a savage tribe to that of a people who, through the discipline of labor and by education, it was hoped might become a self-supporting and self-governed society. * * * The phrase cannot, we think, have any more extensive meaning than an acknowledgment of their allegiance as Indians to the laws of the United States, made or to be made in the exercise of legislative authority over them as such. The corresponding obligation of protection on the part of the government is immediately connected with it, in the declaration that each individual shall be protected in his rights of property, person, and life; and that obligation was to be fulfilled by the enforcement of the laws then existing appropriate to these objects, and by that future appropriate legislation which was promised to secure to them an orderly government. The expressions contained in these clauses must be taken in connection with the entire scheme of the agreement as framed, including those parts not finally adopted, as throwing light on the meaning of the remainder; and looking at the purpose so clearly disclosed in that, of the removal of the whole body of the Sioux nation to the Indian Territory proper, which was not consented to, it is manifest that the provisions had reference to their establishment as a people upon a defined reservation as a permanent home, who were to be urged, as far as it could successfully be done, into the practice of agriculture, and whose children were to be taught the arts and industry of civilized life, and that it was no part of the design to treat the individuals as separately responsible and amenable, in all their personal and domestic relations with each other, to the general laws of the United States, outside of those which were enacted expressly with reference to them as members of an Indian tribe.

* * *

The nature and circumstances of this case strongly reinforce this rule of interpretation in its present application. It is a case involving the judgment of a court of special and limited jurisdiction, not to be assumed without clear warrant of law. It is a case of life and death. It is a case where, against an express exception in the law itself, that law, by argument and inference only, is sought to be extended over aliens and strangers; over the members of a community separated by race, by tradition, by the instincts of a free though savage life, from the authority and power which seeks to impose upon them the restraints of an external and unknown code, and to subject them to the responsibilities of civil conduct, according to rules and penalties of which they could have no previous warning; which judges them by a standard made by others and not for them, which takes no account of the conditions which should except them from its exactions, and makes no allowance for their inability to understand it. It tries them, not by their peers, nor by the customs of their people, nor the law of their land, but by superiors of a different race, according to the law of a social state of which they have an imperfect conception, and which is opposed to the traditions of their history, to the habits of their lives, to the strongest prejudices of their savage nature; one which measures the red man's revenge by the maxims of the white man's morality. * * *

* * *

To give the clauses in the treaty of 1868 and the agreement of 1877 effect, so as to uphold the jurisdiction exercised in this case, would be to reverse in this instance the general policy of the government towards the Indians, as declared in many statutes and treaties, and recognized in many decisions of this court, from the beginning to the present time. To justify such a departure, in such a case, requires a clear expression of the intention of Congress, and that we have not been able to find.

NOTE

Crow Dog narrowly construed the statutory and treaty provisions at issue in the case in order to avoid an abridgement of tribal sovereignty. The BIA and other policymakers felt a different conclusion should have been reached by the Court, one less sensitive to the treaty provisions and the Indians' own values system as reflected in their exercise of self-government. The Secretary of the Interior used the occasion to renew earlier calls for legislation for federal punishment of reservation crimes. He argued that:

[i]f offenses of this character cannot be tried in the courts of the United States, there is no tribunal in which the crime of murder can be punished . . . If the murder is left to be punished according to the old Indian custom, it becomes the duty of the next of kin to avenge the death of his relative by either killing the murderer or some one of his kinsmen.

Secretary of the Interior, Ann. Rep. at 9 (1884).

The government knew that the Sioux had dealt with Spotted Tail's murder in their traditional way, and that it was not revenge, but restitution. The families involved agreed, following a tribal council meeting and mediation by Brule peacemakers, to a payment of $600, eight horses, and one blanket from Crow Dog's people to Spotted Tail's people. But according to Professor Sidney L. Harring, who has scrutinized and analyzed BIA and other primary source documents on Crow Dog's case, the BIA had been engaged in a carefully orchestrated, decade-long campaign to get Congress to extend federal criminal jurisdiction over Indian country. Crow Dog's case allowed the Bureau the opportunity to foment opinion demanding extension of the white man's criminal law over the reservation. The reformers' pleas for federal legislation were ultimately successful. In 1885, Congress enacted the Major Crimes Act, 18 U.S.C.A. § 1153, page 535, infra, giving the United States jurisdiction to try and punish murder and other serious crimes committed by Indians against other Indians on the reservation.

The common understanding of the context of the Major Crimes Act of 1885, which extended the jurisdiction of federal courts to a list of seven serious crimes when committed among Indians in "Indian country," is that it was passed by Congress as a popular reaction against the *Crow Dog* ruling. * * * The simple truth is that the BIA had been attempting to get such a bill through Congress since 1874. After 1880 this attempt had been in earnest, and had been joined by Eastern Indian reformers, especially the Indian Rights Association, which advocated an aggressive "law for the Indians" statute that would extend full state or territorial criminal and civil law to reservation Indians. The Major Crimes Act passed as a minor part of the Indian Appropriations Bill, with no significant debate, and in response to a "popular outcry" chiefly from powerful and vocal Indian reformers.

* * *

In this context, the Major Crimes Act of 1885 is not difficult to understand. While it was a clear departure from existing practice, it was consistent with the whole general trend of Indian policy, the move from a policy based on treaty rights recognizing Indian sovereignty to one of dependency and forced assimilation. * * *

Sidney L. Harring, *Crow Dog's Case: A Chapter in the Legal History of Tribal Sovereignty*, 14 Am. Indian L.Rev. 191, 223, 230 (1989).

UNITED STATES V. KAGAMA

Supreme Court of the United States, 1886.
118 U.S. 375, 6 S.Ct. 1109, 30 L.Ed. 228.

MR. JUSTICE MILLER delivered the Opinion of the Court.

[In 1885 Congress enacted the Major Crimes Act, making it an offense under the jurisdiction of the United States for one Indian to commit certain enumerated crimes against the person or property of another. Until this Act, the tribes themselves had exclusive jurisdiction to regulate and punish any Indian conduct affecting other Indians within Indian country. See *Ex Parte Crow Dog.* Two Indians were indicted under the Act for murdering another on the Hoopa Valley Reservation in California and challenged the statute as outside of Congress' law-making powers.]

The mention of Indians in the Constitution which has received most attention is that found in the clause which gives Congress "power to regulate commerce with foreign nations and among the several States, and with the Indian tribes."

This clause is relied on in the argument in the present case, the proposition being that the statute under consideration is a regulation of commerce with the Indian tribes. But we think it would be a very strained construction of this clause, that a system of criminal laws for Indians living peaceably in their reservations, which left out the entire code of trade and intercourse laws justly enacted under that provision, and established punishments for the common-law crimes of murder, manslaughter, arson, burglary, larceny, and the like, without any reference to their relation to any kind of commerce, was authorized by the grant of power to regulate commerce with the Indian tribes. * * *

But these Indians are within the geographical limits of the United States. The soil and the people within these limits are under the political control of the Government of the United States, or of the States of the Union. There exist within the broad domain of sovereignty but these two. * * *

* * *

The relation of the Indian tribes living within the borders of the United States, both before and since the Revolution, to the people of the United States has always been an anomalous one and of a complex character.

Following the policy of the European governments in the discovery of America towards the Indians who were found here, the colonies before the Revolution and the States and the United States since, have recognized in the Indians a possessory right to the soil over which they roamed and hunted and established occasional villages. But they asserted an ultimate title in the land itself, by which the Indian tribes were forbidden to sell or transfer it to other nations or peoples without the consent of this paramount authority. When a tribe wished to dispose of its land, or any part of it, or the State or the United States wished to purchase it, a treaty with the tribe was the only mode in which this could be done. The United States recognized no right in private persons, or in other nations, to make such a purchase by treaty or otherwise. With the Indians themselves these relations are equally difficult to define. They were, and always have been, regarded as having a semi-independent position when they preserved their tribal relations; not as States, not as nations, not as possessed of the full attributes of sovereignty, but as a separate people with the power of regulating their internal and social relations, and thus far not brought under the laws of the Union or of the State within whose limits they resided.

* * *

It will be seen at once that the nature of the offence (murder) is one which in almost all cases of its commission is punishable by the laws of the States, and within the jurisdiction of their courts. The distinction is claimed to be that the offence under the statute is committed by an Indian, that it is committed on a reservation set apart within the State for residence of the tribe of Indians by the United States, and the fair inference is that the offending Indian shall belong to that or some other tribe. It does not interfere with the process of the State courts within the reservation, nor with the operation of State laws upon white people found there. Its effect is confined to the acts of an Indian of some tribe, of a criminal character, committed within the limits of the reservation.

It seems to us that this is within the competency of Congress. These Indian tribes *are* the wards of the nation. They are communities *dependent* on the United States. Dependent largely for their daily food. Dependent for their political rights. They owe no allegiance to the States, and receive from them no protection. Because of the local ill feeling, the people of the States where they are found are often their deadliest enemies. From their very weakness and helplessness, so largely due to the course of dealing of the Federal Government with them and the treaties in which it has been promised, there arises the duty of protection, and with it the power. This has always been recognized by the Executive and by Congress, and by this court, whenever the question has arisen.

* * *

The power of the General Government over these remnants of a race once powerful, now weak and diminished in numbers, is necessary to their protection, as well as to the safety of those among whom they dwell. It must exist in that government, because it never has existed anywhere else because the theatre of its exercise is within the geographical limits of the United States, because it has never been denied, and because it alone can enforce its laws on all the tribes. * * *

NOTES

1.   Did the Supreme Court's conception of the relationship between congressional and tribal powers in *Kagama* change dramatically after its decision in *Crow Dog,* handed down three years earlier? What legal differences could explain the apparently disparate outcomes?

2.   In United States v. Lopez, 514 U.S. 549 (1995), the Supreme Court struck down the Gun-Free School Zones Act of 1990, 18 U.S.C. §§ 921, 922, 924, in which Congress, acting under its Commerce Clause grant of authority to regulate interstate commerce, made it a federal criminal offense "for any individual knowingly to possess a firearm" within school zones. The power of Congress to regulate under the Commerce Clause, declared the Court, "is subject to outer limits." 514 U.S. at 557. "To uphold the Government's contentions here, we would have to pile inference upon inference in a manner that would bid fair to convert congressional authority under the Commerce Clause to a general police power of the sort retained by the States." Id. at 567. Can the reasoning of *Lopez* be applied to overturn the present-day prosecution of Indian tribal members under the Major Crimes Act, on the ground that it is beyond the "outer limits" of Congress' authority to regulate Indian commerce? In United States v. Lomayaoma, 86 F.3d 142 (9th Cir.1996), cert. denied, 519 U.S. 909 (1996), the Ninth Circuit held that "Congress did not exceed its powers under the Indian Commerce Clause when it enacted the Indian Major Crimes Act in 1885." Id. at 146. The appeals court held first that Congress' power under the Indian Commerce Clause is more extensive than its power under the Interstate Commerce Clause, id. at 145, and second, the Major Crimes Act "governs an area where Congress has traditionally held plenary and exclusive power." Id. Should the reasoning of the Court in *Lopez* be applied to congressional legislation such as the Indian Child Welfare Act of 1978, which regulates jurisdiction over Indian child placements, an area where Congress had traditionally not legislated extensively, at least prior to 1978? See Chapter 8D.

A recurrent question has been what is necessary to bring a group of people under the broad reach of federal power in Indian affairs.

UNITED STATES V. SANDOVAL

Supreme Court of the United States, 1913.
231 U.S. 28, 34 S.Ct. 1, 58 L.Ed. 107.

MR. JUSTICE VANDEVANTER delivered the opinion of the Court.

[The Court overruled a federal district court decision that a law making it a crime to introduce intoxicating liquor into Indian country was inapplicable to New Mexico Pueblos. The question was whether the pueblo lands were "Indian country" over which the legislative authority of Congress extends. The Pueblos' lands, unlike Indian reservations, were owned communally in fee simple by the Pueblos under grants from the Spanish government, later confirmed by Congress.]

The question to be considered, then, is, whether the status of the Pueblo Indians and their lands is such that Congress competently can prohibit the introduction of intoxicating liquor into those lands notwithstanding the admission of New Mexico to statehood. * * *

The people of the pueblos, although sedentary rather than nomadic in their inclinations, and disposed to peace and industry, are nevertheless Indians in race, customs, and domestic government. Always living in separate and isolated communities, adhering to primitive modes of life, largely influenced by superstition and [fetishism], and chiefly governed according to the crude customs inherited from their ancestors, they are essentially a simple, uninformed and inferior people. * * * [T]hey have been regarded and treated by the United States as requiring special consideration and protection, like other Indian communities. Thus, public moneys have been expended in presenting them with farming implements and utensils, and in their civilization and instruction * * * .

With one accord the reports of the superintendents charged with guarding their interests show that they are dependent upon the fostering care and protection of the Government, like reservation Indians in general; that, although industrially superior, they are intellectually and morally inferior to many of them; and that they are easy victims to the evils and debasing influence of intoxicants. We extract the following from published reports of the superintendents:

[The reports from Indian Service officials in the field disclosed, among other things, "debauchery," "intemperance," and "heathen customs" among the Pueblo Indians.]

* * *

[I]t is not necessary to dwell specially upon the legal status of this people under either Spanish or Mexican rule, for whether Indian communities within the limits of the United States may be subjected to its guardianship and protection as dependent wards turns upon other considerations. Not only does the Constitution expressly authorize Congress to regulate commerce with the Indian tribes, but long continued legislative and executive usage and an unbroken current of judicial decisions have attributed to the United States as a superior and civilized nation the power and the duty of exercising a fostering care and protection over all dependent Indian communities within its borders, whether within its original territory or territory subsequently acquired, and whether within or without the limits of a State. * * * In Tiger v. Western Investment Co., 221 U.S. 286, 315, prior decisions were carefully reviewed and it was further said: "Taking these decisions together, it may be taken as the settled doctrine of this court that Congress, in pursuance of the long-established policy of the Government, has a right to determine for itself when the guardianship which has been maintained over the Indian shall cease. It is for that body, and not for the courts, to determine when the true interests of the Indian require his release from such condition of tutelage."

Of course, it is not meant by this that Congress may bring a community or body of people within the range of this power by arbitrarily calling them an Indian tribe, but only that in respect of distinctly Indian communities the questions whether, to what extent, and for what time they shall be recognized and dealt with as dependent tribes requiring the guardianship and protection of the United States are to be determined by Congress, and not by the courts.

As before indicated, by [a] uniform course of action beginning as early as 1854 and continued up to the present time, the legislative and executive branches of the Government have regarded and treated the Pueblos of New Mexico as dependent communities entitled to its aid and protection, like other Indian tribes, and, considering their Indian lineage, isolated and communal life, primitive customs and limited civilization, this assertion of guardianship over them cannot be said to be arbitrary but must be regarded as both authorized and controlling. * * *

It is said that such legislation cannot be made to embrace the Pueblos, because they are citizens. As before stated, whether they are citizens is an open question, and we need not determine it now, because citizenship is not in itself an obstacle to the exercise by Congress of its power to enact laws for the benefit and protection of tribal Indians as a dependent people.

It also is said that such legislation cannot be made to include the lands of the Pueblos, because the Indians have a fee simple title. It is true that the Indians of each pueblo do have such a title to all the lands connected therewith, excepting such as are occupied under executive orders, but it is a communal title, no individual owning any separate tract. * * * Considering the reasons which underlie the authority of Congress to prohibit the introduction of liquor into the Indian country at all, it seems plain that this authority is sufficiently comprehensive to enable Congress to apply the prohibition to the lands of the Pueblos.

* * *

NOTES

1.   How are tribal and federal powers conceptualized in *Kagama* and *Sandoval* as compared with *Cherokee Nation, Worcester,* and *Crow Dog*?

2.   Almost a half century before *Sandoval,* the Territorial Court of New Mexico had concluded that the Pueblos could not possibly be Indians. They were not "savages" but rather were some of the "most law-abiding, sober, and industrious people of New Mexico." United States v. Lucero, 1 N.M. 422, 444–45 (1869). The United States Supreme Court quickly agreed in United States v. Joseph, 94 U.S. (4 Otto) 614, 616 (1876). The "history" and "domestic habits" of other American Indians were "matters of public notoriety." The Pueblos, on

the other hand, were "peaceable, industrious, intelligent, honest, and virtuous people. They are Indians only in feature, complexion, and a few of their habits * * * ." As a result, the *Joseph* Court found that the Nonintercourse Act of 1834 did not apply to the Pueblos and that the United States had no authority to bring an ejectment action on their behalf against alleged trespassers on their lands. By the time *Sandoval* was handed down in 1913, however, the BIA had compiled enough information of intoxication, debauchery, and "moral inferiority" (all described at great length in the full *Sandoval* opinion) to prove that the Pueblos were Indians after all.

The deeply traditional and religious Pueblo Indians were doubtless puzzled by the Court's reasoning in *Sandoval*, but the result effectively overruled *Joseph* and implicitly vindicated the Pueblos' long-standing position that any prior transfers of their lands were invalid as being in violation of the Nonintercourse Act. The Pueblo Lands Act, 43 Stat. 636, was passed in 1924 to provide a vehicle for resolving the thousands of claims by non-Indians to Pueblo lands. A board was established to determine the exterior boundaries of Pueblo lands. The Attorney General was directed to bring actions to quiet title to all such lands, but good faith non-Indian claimants were permitted to establish adverse possession defenses under rules set forth in the Pueblo Lands Act. Supplemental statutes then brought the complex process to a resolution generally acceptable both to the Pueblos and the non-Indian claimants. See generally Charles T. Du Mars, et al., Pueblo Indian Water Rights 55–67 (1984); Mountain States Tel. & Tel. Co. v. Pueblo of Santa Ana, 472 U.S. 237 (1985). Today, nineteen pueblos own approximately two million acres which are held in fee, not in trust, but which are Indian country under 18 U.S.C.A. § 1151(b). See Chapter 7A.

NOTE: INDIAN CITIZENSHIP AND TRIBALISM

One question that was carefully avoided by the Court in *Sandoval* was whether the Pueblos were citizens. The Court said that: "whether they are citizens is an open question, and we need not determine it now, because citizenship is not in itself an obstacle to the exercise by Congress of its power to enact laws for the benefit and protection of tribal Indians as a dependent people."

The issue of Congress's continuing guardianship over Indians who had been made citizens but who had not abandoned their tribal relations and ways of life proved troubling for the Court during the nineteenth century. In the infamous pre-Civil War case of Dred Scott v. Sanford, 60 U.S. 393 (1856), which denied rights of United States citizenship to members of the African race, Chief Justice Roger Taney, writing for the Court, noted that tribal Indians were in a "state of pupilage" in relation to the United States:

> But they may, without doubt, like the subjects of any other foreign Government, be naturalized by the authority of Congress, and become citizens of a State, and of the United States, and if an individual should leave his nation or tribe and take up his abode

among the white population, he would be entitled to all the rights and privileges which would belong to an emigrant from any other foreign people.

Id. at 404.

Decisions following the Civil War interpreted the Fourteenth Amendment's blanket grant of citizenship to "[a]ll persons born or naturalized in the United States, and subject to the jurisdiction thereof" as excluding Indians. In McKay v. Campbell, 16 F. Cas. 161 (D.Or.1871) (No. 8,840), the court held that Indians could not come within the sweep of the Amendment because "the Indian tribes within the limits of the United States have always been held to be distinct and independent political communities, retaining the right of self-government, though subject to the protecting power of the United States." 16 F.Cas. at 166.

The view that Indians were not "subject to the jurisdiction" of the United States was sustained by the Supreme Court in Elk v. Wilkins, 112 U.S. 94 (1884), in which an Indian living in Omaha, Nebraska apart from his tribe was held not to have been made a citizen by the Fourteenth Amendment. Perhaps the restrictive interpretation on citizenship for Indians could be explained because the Court had not yet fully analyzed and announced the now familiar doctrine of far-reaching federal guardianship control and jurisdiction over Indians that was articulated in cases beginning with *United States v. Kagama*, page 186, supra. But denial of citizenship under the Fourteenth Amendment could be sustained upon another ground. In *Elk v. Wilkins,* the Court pointed out that section 2 of the Fourteenth Amendment retained an exclusion of "Indians not taxed" in referring to apportionment of the House of Representatives in Article I, § 2, cl. 3 of the Constitution. The inference was drawn, not unreasonably, that Congress would have removed the exclusion, just as it removed the three-fifths formula for counting slaves when it enacted the Fourteenth Amendment, had it intended that Indians be made citizens.

In fact, until the Citizenship Act of 1924 naturalized all "Indians born within the territorial limits of the United States," 43 Stat. 253, 8 U.S.C. § 1401(a)(2), Congress pursued a policy of extending citizenship to Indians only selectively through treaties and statutes. Some of these laws uniformly conditioned Indian citizenship upon Indians conforming their individual behavior to the dominant society's norms and renouncing tribal culture and traditions. For instance, the 1861 Treaty with the Pottawatomies, 12 Stat. 1191, 1192, allowed male heads of families to become citizens if the President of the United States was satisfied that they were "sufficiently intelligent and prudent to conduct their affairs and interests." Other treaties conditioned citizenship upon acceptance of an allotment or removal to a new reservation. Statutes enabling certain Indians to become citizens also typically required that the eligible Indians abandon their tribal relations, adopt the habits of civilized life, become self-supporting, and learn to read and write the English language. See, e.g., Act of March 3, 1865, 13 Stat. 541, 562, discussed in Oakes v. United States, 172 F. 305 (C.C.A.Minn.1909). A statute allowing naturalization of Winnebago Indians required proof to the satisfaction of the federal district court that Indian applicants were sufficiently intelligent and prudent to control their affairs, had adopted the habits of civilized life, and for the preceding five years had supported themselves and their families. 16 Stat. 335, 361–62. If these requirements were met, the court would grant a certificate enabling the Secretary of the Interior to issue patents in fee to lands held by the Indians and to pay them for their shares of tribal property. The Indians would then cease to be members of their tribe, and their land would be subject to taxation. One statute made Indians who enlisted and fought in World War I citizens. 41 Stat. 350. Another, which is still codified, made citizens of Indian women who married non-Indian men. 25 U.S.C. § 182.

The General Allotment Act of 1887, discussed in the next section, bestowed citizenship upon all Indians who received allotments. In addition, citizenship was conferred upon Indians who had taken up residence apart from any tribe and adopted the habits of civilization. A 1906 amendment to the Allotment Act deferred granting of citizenship to allottees until the expiration of the twenty-five year period of trust rather than simply upon allotment. According to the Supreme Court, "Congress, in granting full rights of citizenship to Indians, believed that it had been hasty." United States v. Celestine, 215 U.S. 278, 291 (1909). Many Indian allottees, despite the bestowal of the benefits of citizenship and the accompanying array of "civilizing" assimilationist programs and pressures, clung tenaciously to their tribal ways and traditions. This was intolerable to policymakers who assumed that Indian tribalism was incompatible with United States citizenship.

It was also conceptually troubling that Indian citizens remained wards of the federal government at least so long as their land was in trust and the allottees had not abandoned their tribal relations. In 1905, the Court had found that citizenship under the Allotment Act made the laws prohibiting liquor traffic inapplicable to sales to allotted Indians because citizen-Indians were beyond the reach of congressional power. Matter of Heff, 197 U.S. 488 (1905). But Congress's retreat from automatic citizenship in the 1906 Act and the federal government's policy of continuing to recognize the tribal relations and wardship of Indians who were granted allotments and trust patents led the Court to reconsider its decision in *Heff.* In United States v. Nice, 241 U.S. 591 (1916), the Court expressly overruled *Heff,* relying on the "familiar rule" that legislation affecting Indians, even naturalized Indians, "is to be construed in their interest and a purpose to make a radical departure is not lightly to be inferred. * * * As, therefore, these allottees remain tribal Indians and under national guardianship, the power of Congress to regulate or prohibit the sale of intoxicating liquor to them, as is done by the act of 1897, is not debatable."

In the early twentieth century the Court decided a number of other cases that in essence, simply ignored many of the earlier perceived problems about the supposed incompatibility of Indian citizenship with continued tribal relations and federal guardianship. See, e.g., Winton v. Amos, 255 U.S. 373 (1921); Tiger v. Western Inv. Co., 221 U.S. 286 (1911); *Celestine,* supra, 215 U.S. at 288–90. While no doubt should have lingered on the question, the 1924

Citizenship Act specified that "citizenship shall not in any manner impair or otherwise affect the right of any Indian to tribal or other property."

4. THE GENERAL ALLOTMENT ACT

Larger national events occurring at mid-century took their inevitable toll in Indian country by the 1880s. The United States acquired the Pacific Northwest through the Treaty with Great Britain of 1846. By the Treaty of Guadalupe Hildalgo with Mexico of 1848, the United States annexed California, Nevada, Utah, most of Arizona, and large areas of New Mexico and Colorado. Gold was discovered at Sutter's Mill in California in 1848, spurring the largest human migration in history. California (1852), Oregon (1859), and Nevada (1864) achieved early statehood. The transcontinental railroad was completed in 1869. The General Homestead Act of 1862, the Desert Land Act of 1877, and other federal land disposition programs lured settlers west.

As the West began to fill up, it was no longer convenient for the federal government to keep Indian reservations separate and apart under tribal ownership. Before the 1850s, almost all Indian land had been held communally by the tribes. A few treaties had provided for the allotment of lands, i.e., the conversion of some tribal land into parcels of land held by individual tribal members. One such provision was in the 1798 Treaty with the Oneida Indian Nation. In 1853, however, Commissioner of Indian Affairs George Manypenny instituted a general policy of attempting to negotiate allotment provisions in treaties. Allotment became a principal device in the program to assimilate Indians at the same time as tribal lands were made available for non-Indian settlement. Indian policy thus became merged with Manifest Destiny.

The purpose of some early allotments was to reserve tracts then occupied by tribal members from the large tribal land cessions. More commonly, however, allotments were used as a means to break up tribal land holdings. Some statutes also authorized the allotment of federal lands to individual Indians. See, e.g., 25 U.S.C.A. § 334 (Indians not residing on reservations); 25 U.S.C.A. § 336 (Indians settling on public domain); 25 U.S.C.A. § 337 (Indians occupying national forests); 43 U.S.C.A. § 189 (repealed 1976) (Indians abandoning tribal relations). In addition, those Indians who were citizens were authorized to homestead unappropriated public lands in the same manner as non-Indians pursuant to 43 U.S.C.A. § 161 (repealed 1976). Finally, there were several allotment acts that applied to a single tribe. But the General Allotment Act of 1887, or Dawes Act, was the vehicle through which Congress systematically allotted lands on most Indian reservations—some 41 million acres of former tribal land were allotted. In addition to diminishing the tribal land estate, the Act opened many reservations to extensive settlement by non-Indians, and marked a major turn in Indian law and policy.

DELOS SACKET OTIS, HISTORY OF THE ALLOTMENT POLICY, HEARINGS ON H.R. 7902 BEFORE THE HOUSE COMM. ON INDIAN AFFAIRS

73d Cong., 2d Sess., pt. 9, at 428–85 (1934).

* * *

President [Cleveland] signed the Dawes Act on February 8, 1887. The chief provisions of the act were: (1) a grant of 160 acres to each family head, of 80 acres to each single person over 18 years of age and to each orphan under 18, and of 40 acres to each other single person under eighteen;* (2) a patent in fee to be issued to every allottee but to be held in trust by the Government for 25 years, during which time the land could not be alienated or encumbered; (3) a period of 4 years to be allowed the Indians in which they should make their selections after allotment should be applied to any tribe—failure of the Indians to do so should result in selection for them at the order of the Secretary of the Interior; (4) citizenship to be conferred upon allottees and upon any other Indians who had abandoned their tribes and adopted "the habits of civilized life." * * *

AIMS AND MOTIVES OF THE ALLOTMENT MOVEMENT

That the leading proponents of allotment were inspired by the highest motives seems conclusively true. A Member of Congress, speaking on the Dawes bill in 1886 said, "It has * * * the endorsement of the Indian rights associations throughout the country, and of the best sentiment of the land." * * *

* * *

The supreme aim of the friends of the Indian was to substitute white civilization for his tribal culture, and they shrewdly sensed that the difference in the concepts of property was fundamental in the contrast between the two ways of life. That the white man's way was good and the Indian's way was bad, all agreed. So, on the one hand, allotment was counted on to break up tribal life. This blessing was dwelt upon at length. The agent for the Yankton Sioux wrote in 1877:

"As long as Indians live in villages they will retain many of their old and injurious habits. Frequent feasts, community in food, heathen ceremonies, and dances, constant visiting—these will continue as long as the people live together in close neighborhoods and villages * * * I trust that before another year is ended they will generally be located upon individual lands [or] farms. From that date will begin their real and permanent progress."

---

* [Ed.] There were demands for equalization and in 1891 the original Act was amended to provide for allotments of 160 acres of grazing land, or 80 acres of farming land, to each Indian. See 25 U.S.C.A. § 331.

On the other hand, the allotment system was to enable the Indian to acquire the benefits of civilization. The Indian agents of the period made no effort to conceal their disgust for tribal economy. * * *

But voices of doubt were here and there raised about allotment as a wholesale civilizing program. "Barbarism" was not without its defenders. Especially were the Five Civilized Tribes held up as an example of felicity under a communal system in contrast to the deplorable condition of certain Indians upon whom allotment had been tried. A minority report of the House Committee on Indian Affairs in 1880 went so far as to state that Indians had made progress only under communism. At this point it is worth remarking that friends and enemies of allotment alike showed no clear understanding of Indian agricultural economy. Both were prone to use the word "communism" in a loose sense, in describing Indian enterprise. It was in the main an inaccurate term. Gen. O.O. Howard told the Lake Mohonk Conference in 1889 about a band of Spokane Indians who worked their lands in common in the latter part of the 1870's, but certainly in the vast majority of cases Indian economic pursuits were carried on directly with individual rewards in view. This was primarily true even of such essentially group activities as the Omahas' annual buffalo hunt. Agriculture was certainly but rarely a communal undertaking. The Pueblos, who had probably the oldest and most established agricultural economy, were individualistic in farming and pooled their efforts only in the care of the irrigation system. What the allotment debaters meant by communism was that the title to land invariably vested in the tribe and the actual holding of the land was dependent on its use and occupancy. They also meant vaguely the cooperativeness and clannishness—the strong communal sense—of barbaric life, which allotment was calculated to disrupt.

* * *

The believers in allotment had another philanthropic aim, which was to protect the Indian in his present land holding. They were confident that if every Indian had his own strip of land, guaranteed by a patent from the Government, he would enjoy a security which no tribal possession could afford him. If the Indian's possession was further safeguarded by a restriction upon his right to sell it they believed that the system would be foolproof. * * *

It must also be noted that while the advocates of allotment were primarily and sincerely concerned with the advancement of the Indian they at the same time regarded the scheme as promoting the best interest of the whites as well. For one thing, it was fondly but erroneously hoped that setting the Indian on his own feet would relieve the Government of a great expense.

* * *

It must be reported that the using of these lands which the Indians did not "need" for the advancement of civilization was a logical part of a whole and sincerely idealistic philosophy. The civilizing policy was in the long run to benefit Indian and white man alike. But doubters of the allotment system could see nothing in the policy but dire consequences for the Indian. Senator Teller in 1881 called the Coke bill "a bill to despoil the Indians of their lands and to make them vagabonds on the face of the earth." At another time he said,

"If I stand alone in the Senate, I want to put upon the record my prophecy in this matter, that when 30 or 40 years shall have passed and these Indians shall have parted with their title, they will curse the hand that was raised professedly in their defense to secure this kind of legislation and if the people who are clamoring for it understood Indian character, and Indian laws, and Indian morals, and Indian religion, they would not be here clamoring for this at all."

* * *

* * * Senator Teller had charged that allotment was in the interests of the land-grabbing speculators, but the minority report of the House Indian Affairs Committee in 1880 had gone even further in its accusations. It said:

"The real aim of this bill is to get at the Indian lands and open them up to settlement. The provisions for the apparent benefit of the Indian are but the pretext to get at his lands and occupy them * * * . If this were done in the name of greed, it would be bad enough; but to do it in the name of humanity, and under the cloak of an ardent desire to promote the Indian's welfare by making him like ourselves whether he will or not, is infinitely worse."

* * *

It is probably true that the most powerful force motivating the allotment policy was the pressure of the land-hungry western settlers. * * *

* * *

There were many expressions of Indian opposition to allotment in the early 1880's. * * * The Senecas and the Creeks made bold to memorialize Congress against disrupting with allotment their systems of common holding. * * *

Certain tribes had specific objections to allotment. A memorial from the Creeks, Choctaws, and Cherokees in 1881 read: "The change to an individual title would throw the whole of our domain in a few years into the hands of a few persons." * * *

What can be said * * * is that there was no apparent widespread demand from the Indians for allotment.

THE APPLICATION OF ALLOTMENT

The application of allotment to the reservations was above all characterized by extreme haste.

* * *

[In addition to the General Allotment Act, Congress also passed special legislation dealing with individual tribes.] In 1888 Congress had ratified five agreements with different Indian tribes providing for allotment and for the sale of surplus lands. The following year Congress passed eight such laws. A member of the Board of Indian Commissioners in 1891 estimated that the 104,314,349 acres of Indian reservations in 1889 had been reduced by 12,000,000 acres in 1890 and by 8,000,000 acres in the first 9 months of 1891. * * *

* * *

In the years prior to 1887 the Government had approved 7,463 allotments with a total acreage of 584,423; from 1887 through 1900 it approved a total of 53,168 [pursuant to the General Allotment Act] with an acreage of nearly 5,000,000. * * *

* * *

ADMINISTRATION AND CHANGES IN POLICY: LEASING

* * *

Those who were dissatisfied with the results achieved by the Dawes Act saw various causes of failure. For one thing, the whole emphasis of the allotment policy was laid upon farming, and critics from time to time pointed out that large sections of the Indians' lands were not suitable for agriculture. * * *

* * *

It was not true that the Government made no efforts whatever to equip the Indians for farming. But it made very slight efforts. The appropriation act passed in 1888 provided for the allocation of $30,000 to the purchase of seed, farming implements, and other things "necessary for the commencement of farming". In 1888 alone 3,568 allotments had been made. The appropriation, therefore, granted less than $10 to every new allottee setting out on his farming career. There is, furthermore, no way of knowing how much of this money was expended for this purpose. * * *

The following year the same amount was provided but in 1890 no such appropriation was made. In 1891 Congress raised $15,000 for the purpose and this sum was continued through the next 2 years. After 1893 the appropriation acts up to 1900 included no such items. * * *

* * *

Defects in the system which * * * occupied the attention of the friends of the Indian were those resulting from the fact that allotted lands must be free from State taxation. The Dawes Act, providing for the 25-year Federal trust period during which time the land might not be encumbered, meant, it was clear, that no State could tax the allottee's holdings. As a result, the friends of the Indian were noting in 1889, States were refusing to assume any responsibilities for Indian communities and were withholding such services as the up-keep of schools and roads. It was also apparent that this situation was a source of great hostility to Indians on the part of white neighbors. * * *

The decision to allow the Indian to lease his land was fraught with grave consequences for the whole allotment system. Probably it was the most important decision as to Indian policy that was made after the passage of the Dawes Act. * * *

* * *

RESULTS OF ALLOTMENT TO 1900

Analysis of the achievements of the allotment system requires first some appraisal of the leasing practice which vitally affected allotment results. There were defenders of the leasing system all through the 1890's. It had certain immediate consequences which recommended it to friends of the Indian who were sincere if lacking in vision. There was the simple fact of allotted lands lying idle which the Indians either could not or would not cultivate. Such waste seemed wicked to a generation that was coming increasingly to set store by efficiency. How much better it was for the lands to be used and the Indians to be deriving an income from them. * * *

* * * [Leasing] took care of minors, women, and the old folks, and it was economically profitable. One agent said the Indians got more out of the leased lands than if they worked them themselves. * * * Leasing was undoubtedly a spur to the taking of allotments. But it seems hardly to have been a spur to the Indian becoming a farmer. * * *

* * * General Whittlesey, of the Board of Indian Commissioners, said to the Mohonk Conference in 1891, "Another hindrance [to the allotting of lands] is the influence brought to bear by surrounding white settlers, who are waiting to get possession of the lands that may be reserved after allotments are completed. If there are valuable tracts of land, they try to prevent those lands from being allotted, and to prevent Indians from selecting them, by bribery and by other means." * * *

JOHN COLLIER, MEMORANDUM, THE PURPOSES AND
OPERATION OF THE WHEELER-HOWARD INDIAN RIGHTS
BILL, HEARINGS ON H.R. 7902 BEFORE THE SENATE
AND HOUSE COMMITTEES ON INDIAN AFFAIRS

73d Cong., 2d Sess., 15, 15–18 (1934).

* * *

The individualized parcels of [allotted] land have been held under Government trust over longer or shorter periods. Sometimes, where the land was agricultural, the Indian family has lived upon and has used one or more of the allotments attached to its several members. Where the land was of grazing character, or was timberland, allotment precluded the integrated use of the land by individuals or families, even at the start.

Upon the allottees' death, it has been necessary to partition the land equally among heirs, or to sell it, and in the interim it has been leased.

Most likewise of the land of living allottees has been leased to whites.

Through sales by the Government of the fictitiously designated "surplus" lands; through sales by allottees after the trust period had ended or had been terminated by administrative act; and through sales by the Government of heirship land, virtually mandatory under the allotment act: Through these three methods, the total of Indian land holdings has been cut from 138,000,000 acres in 1887 to 48,000,000 acres in 1934.

These gross statistics, however, are misleading, for, of the remaining 48,000,000 acres, more than 20,000 acres are contained within areas which for special reasons have been exempted from the allotment law; whereas the land loss is chargeable exclusively against the allotment system.

Furthermore, that part of the allotted lands which has been lost is the most valuable part. Of the residual lands, taking all Indian-owned lands into account, nearly one half, or nearly 20,000,000 acres, are desert or semidesert lands.

* * *

The above statement relates solely to land losses. The facts can be summarized thus:

Through the allotment system, more than 80 percent of the land value belonging to all the Indians in 1887 has been taken away from them; more than 85 percent of the land value of all the allotted Indians has been taken away.

And the allotment system, working down through the partitionment or sale of the land of deceased allottees, mathematically insures and practically requires that the remaining Indian allotted lands shall pass to whites. The allotment act contemplates total landlessness for the Indians of the third generation of each allotted tribe.

* * *

[E]qually important with the outright loss of land is the effect of the allotment system in making such lands as remain in Indian ownership unusable.

There have been presented to the House Indian Committee numerous land maps, showing the condition of Indian-owned lands on allotted reservations. The Indian-owned lands are parcels belonging (a) to allottees and (b) to the heirs of deceased allottees. Both of these classes of Indian-owned land are checkerboarded with white-owned land already lost to the Indians, and on many reservations the Indian-owned parcels are mere islands within a sea of white-owned property.

Farming, at least at the subsistence level, and commercial farming within irrigated areas, is still possible on those parcels belonging to living allottees. But grazing, upon the grazing land of living allottees, and businesslike or conservative forest operation, upon the allotted forest land of living allottees, are largely, often absolutely, impossible.

On the checkerboarded land maps, the heirship lands each year become a greater proportion of the total of the remaining Indian land. These heirship lands belong to numerous heirs, even up to the number of hundreds.

And one heir possessed equities in numerous allotments, up to the number of hundreds.

The above conditions force some of the Indian allotted land out of any profitable use whatsoever, and they force nearly all of it into the condition of land rented to whites, and rented under conditions disadvantageous to the Indians. The denial of financial credit to Indians is of course, an added influence.

The Indians are practically compelled to become absentee landlords with petty and fast-dwindling estates, living upon the always diminishing pittances of lease money.

And here there becomes apparent the administrative impossibility created by the allotment system.

* * *

The Indian Service is compelled to be a real-estate agent in behalf of the living allottees; and in behalf of the more numerous heirs of deceased allottees. As such real-estate agent, selling and renting the hundreds of thousands of parcels of land and fragmented equities of parcels, and disbursing the rentals (sometimes to more than a hundred heirs of one parcel, and again to an individual heir with an equity in a hundred parcels), the Indian Service is forced to expend millions of dollars a year. The expenditure does not and cannot save the land, or conserve the capital accruing from land sales or from rentals.

The operation gets nowhere at all; under the existing system of law it cannot get anywhere; it creates between the Indians and the Government a relationship barren, embittered, full of contempt and despair; it keeps the Indians' own minds focused upon petty and dwindling equities which inexorably vanish to nothing at all.

For the Indians the situation is necessarily one of frustration, of impotent discontent. They are forced into the status of a landlord class, yet it is impossible for them to control their own estates; and the estates are insufficient to yield a decent living, and the yield diminishes year by year and finally stops altogether.

* * *

NOTES

1.   The heart of the Allotment Act was 25 U.S.C.A. § 331:

In all cases where any tribe or band of Indians has been or shall be located upon any reservation created for their use by treaty stipulation, Act of Congress, or Executive order, the President shall be authorized to cause the same or any part thereof to be surveyed or resurveyed whenever in his opinion such reservation or any part may be advantageously utilized for agricultural or grazing purposes by such Indians, and to cause allotment to each Indian located thereon to be made in such areas as in his opinion may be for their best interest not to exceed eighty acres of agricultural or one hundred and sixty acres of grazing land to any one Indian. * * *

There was no provision for tribal consent or consultation on the question of reservation allotment. The acreage requirements in the statute lacked flexibility to distinguish among allottees based on differing quality of lands and climates. There was no provision for making allotments of equal value as opposed to equal acreage, except to make allotments smaller than the maximum acreages in the allottee's "best interest." The allotment program was effectively ended in 1934. However, many allotments are still held in trust because the original 25 year trust periods were extended, first by secretarial order, and then by operation of the Indian Reorganization Act of 1934. See pages 216–235, infra. Some reservations, it should be noted, escaped allotment entirely or had very little land allotted. The allotment policy is explored in Jay P. Kinney, A Continent Lost—A Civilization Won: Indian Land Tenure in America (1937). Dr. Otis's report, supra, has been reprinted by the University of Oklahoma Press in The Dawes Act and the Allotment of Indian Lands (Francis Paul Prucha ed. 1973). See also Frederick E. Hoxie, A Final Promise: The Campaign to Assimilate the Indians, 1880–1920 (1984); Judith V. Royster, The Legacy of Allotment, 27 Ariz.St.L.J. 1 (1995).

2.   During the period of trust, Indian allotments may not be taxed by the state or county, but when fee patents issue they are fully taxable and may be sold for non-payment. States may, however, condemn allotted lands for any public purpose. 25 U.S.C.A. § 357.

3.   Indians have long complained of so-called "forced fee patents," i.e., patents (the terminology for a deed from the federal government) issued to "competent" Indian allottees before the expiration of the 25-year trust period without their application or express consent. See, e.g., 25 U.S.C.A. § 357. Many of these late-nineteenth and early-twentieth century patents, of which there were thousands, resulted from the recommendations of competency commissions that declared certain Indian allottees competent to receive their land in fee; in addition, government policy called for the issuance of fee patents to allottees of one-half or less Indian blood. See, e.g., LeAnn Larson LaFave, *South Dakota's Forced Fee Land Claims: Will Landowners Be Liable for Government's Wrongdoing?*, 30 S.D.L.Rev. 59 (1985). In circumstances of fractionated interests (multiple allottee heirs owning equal, undivided interests in a single parcel), the Secretary engaged in "Secretarial transfers" in accordance with 25 U.S.C. § 372, which authorized the Secretary to sell Indian lands held in trust where the Secretary concludes that one of the heirs is "incompetent." See Wenona T. Singel & Matthew L.M. Fletcher, *Power, Authority, and Tribal Property*, 41 Tulsa L.Rev. 21 (2005).

Several suits have been filed to set aside forced fee patents but have typically been barred by statutes of limitations. E.g., United States v. Mottaz, 476 U.S. 834 (1986).

4.   One pervasive legacy of the allotment policy is the matter of fractionated heirships, where dozens or even hundreds of heirs to the original allottee own partial interests in an allotment, due to an allottee having died intestate. It is not uncommon for inherited fractional interests in allotments to be measured in thousandths. In addition to many other problems, it is difficult for all the heirs to agree on a use for the land. See generally Jessica A. Shoemaker, *Like Snow in the Springtime: Allotment, Fractionation, and the Indian Land Tenure Problem*, 2003 Wis.L.Rev. 729.

Congress responded to the problem in 1982 by enacting the Indian Land Consolidation Act of 1982, 25 U.S.C.A. §§ 2201–2211, allowing tribes to adopt, with the consent of the Secretary, plans providing for the sales and exchanges of tribal lands in order to eliminate fractional interests and consolidate tribal holdings, to purchase allotments with the consent of at least 50 percent of the owners, and to provide for escheat to the tribe of individual interests that represent less than 2 percent of the tract and which failed to earn $100, in the year before death. The escheat provision was held to be an unconstitutional taking in Hodel v. Irving, 481 U.S. 704 (1987). The fractional ownership resulted in less than $.01 per year in rent for some of the heirs, but the Court was persuaded that the value of the property may substantially exceed its income-producing ability. While *Hodel* was pending on appeal, Congress amended the escheat provision of the Act to narrow the class of land subject to escheat. The definition of "fractional interest" was changed to a 2 percent or less interest in a parcel which did not earn $100 in any of the five years (instead of one year) prior to the date of the decedent's death, and allowed the decedent to devise his or her interest to any other owner of an undivided fractional interest. Babbitt v. Youpee, 519 U.S. 234 (1997), held, however, that the amended escheat provision failed to cure the constitutional deficiency identified in the original version of the Act, and, as in *Hodel*, therefore, constituted an unconstitutional taking without just compensation.

The Indian Land Consolidation Act was amended again in 2000 and 2004. See American Indian Probate Reform Act of 2004, P.L. 108–374 (codified at 25 U.S.C.A. § 2201 *et. seq.*). It encourages the development of tribal probate codes approved by the Secretary of the Interior under guidelines set out by Congress in the legislation. In the absence of a will, trust property descends according to an approved tribal code but if there is no tribal probate code, a uniform probate code will be applied to replace the problematic automatic escheat provisions of earlier versions of the legislation. Surviving spouses receive a life estate in the decedent's trust lands. If there is no surviving spouse then only after a list of potential eligible heirs, including lineal descendants down to great grandchildren, parents, and siblings, is exhausted, does the land escheat to the tribe. The 2004 amendments do provide however for a co-owner of the property to acquire the decedent's interest by paying fair market value to the estate. In addition to these consolidating mechanisms, the amendments also authorize funding for Bureau of Indian Affairs Land Consolidation Offices to acquire fractional interests and legal services corporations to write wills for individual Indians. A 2011 report of the Department of the Interior noted that 267,000 owners held approximately 4.1 million interests in over 10 million acres of land. Office of Inspector General, U.S. Department of the Interior, Coordination of Efforts to Address Indian Land Fractionation, Report No.: WR–EV–BIA–0002–2010 at 2 (January 2011). For further discussion of the issues generated by fractionation and the Indian Land Consolidation Act, see Kathleen R. Guzman, *Give or Take an Acre: Property Norms and the Indian Land Consolidation Act*, 85 Iowa L.Rev. 595 (2000).

How should the problem of fractionated ownership of allotted lands be handled? Is this an area that should be left to Indian tribes and their own laws? Prior to European contact, Indian tribes had their own systems of regulating land use, land ownership, and property inheritance. A good deal of this traditional knowledge has survived into modern times and, for a number of tribes, is relied upon to supplement tribal land and probate codes. Can this type of tribal common law be applied to the problem of fractionated interests in allotted lands? For an in-depth discussion of tribal common law property rights systems, see Professor Kenneth Bobroff's article, *Retelling Allotment: Indian Property Rights and the Myth of Common Ownership*, 54 Vand.L.Rev. 1559 (2001).

5.   Did the Allotment Act single out Indian lands for sacrifice to westward expansion? During the same period that the Allotment Act was passed, "our public land policy was basically one of disposal [of lands owned by

the United States but not reserved for any specific purpose] into non-Federal ownership to encourage settlement and develop the country." Public Land Law Review Comm'n, One Third of the Nation's Land, A Report to the President and to the Congress 28 (1970). Homestead acts were passed, beginning in 1862, to open public land for settlement. The railroads received grants of some 91 million acres, of which only a small part was Indian land. Large conveyances were made to new states and mineral, timber, and range resources were opened to settlers' use.

These facts suggest that the opening of Indian lands was one aspect of a broad-based national policy to open the West for settlement—a movement that some historians view as being at the core of our national prosperity and character. Does that justify the allotment policy in whole or in part? Should Congress, rather than treating Indian lands much like the public domain lands, have followed one policy for public domain lands and another for Indian lands? Are there legal differences between public domain lands and Indian lands that would justify such a course?

The term "public lands" excludes Indian lands. See generally Cohen's Handbook of Federal Indian Law § 5.01, at 385 (Nell Jessup Newton ed. 2012). Thus, for example, in 1964 Congress established the Public Land Law Review Commission to recommend policy for the "public lands," which were defined as all lands in federal ownership except Indian lands. See 43 U.S.C.A. § 1400. The American Indian Policy Review Commission was then established in 1975 to review Indian policy, including Indian land policy. See 25 U.S.C.A. § 174.

ANN LAQUER ESTIN, LONE WOLF V. HITCHCOCK: THE LONG SHADOW, IN THE AGGRESSIONS OF CIVILIZATION: FEDERAL INDIAN POLICY SINCE THE 1880'S

(Sandra L. Cadwalader & Vine Deloria, Jr., eds. 1984), at 215, 216–34.

* * * For the Kiowas and Comanches, the 1867 treaty of Medicine Lodge Creek was still in effect, with annuity payments due until 1898. Article XII of the treaty provided that any further cessions of tribal land required the signatures of "at least three-fourths of all the adult male Indians occupying the same." Collecting these signatures on the proposed allotment agreements was the primary task of the [Cherokee] commission [in 1892].

Commissioner David H. Jerome addressed the Kiowa, Comanche, and Apache in council at Fort Sill. He began with a description of the changes in Indian Territory during the twenty-four years since the Medicine Lodge Treaty: the disappearance of the buffalo and other game from the southern plains, growing dependence on government rations, and significantly, a doubling in the region's white population while the three tribes had not increased in number. Jerome then presented allotment as the means of alleviating the hardships of the past decades.

If the Indians will do what the Great Father wants them to do, and do their part well, it will result in your having plenty of food and clothing; and instead of having, as you sometimes do, only one meal a day, you will have three meals a day and have plenty of clothing and things that will make you comfortable through the winter. Instead of having to wait for an issue of beef every two weeks, you can go out and kill a beef of your own and have a feast every day if you please. I told you a little while ago that for twenty-four years the Indians had increased very little if any in numbers. Now, if you follow the plan that we have told you about you will not have your babies die from the cold, but you will have them grow up good, strong, healthy men and women, instead of putting them in the ground.

Jerome's cynical reliance on this sort of appeal reflected the increasingly desperate situation of the Plains tribes. During the early reservation years, the Indians had been able to supplement their treaty annuity income and the unreliable government rations with hunting (and periodic raids on Texas ranches). Within a decade of the Medicine Lodge Treaty, however, their subsistence economy had been destroyed, and the tribes were kept under tight control by the Indian agents and military at Fort Sill. * * *

* * *

* * * With prodding from Quanah Parker, Commissioner Jerome presented a proposal to give every member of the three tribes a 160-acre allotment and to pay $2 million for the [2,150,000 acres of] surplus land remaining after allotment.

* * *

After Jerome presented the offer, Commissioner Warren Sayre made certain that the Indians assembled in council understood the iron fist in the velvet glove: he claimed that under the Dawes Act the President could order tribes to take allotments whether they wanted to or not. Sayre admitted that the President had not made such an order for the Kiowa, Comanche, and Apache reservation, and might never do so, but he cited the examples of other tribes: "The Shawnees, Pottawatomies, Tonkawas, the Pawnees, the Otoes, the Missourias, and Poncas have been required to take allotments of land whether they desired to or not."

Despite their desperate condition and the strong inducements offered by the commissioners, the three tribes decided in a council held before the third day's session to keep their treaty land. Although willing to move in the direction which Jerome was urging, Lone Wolf and the others foresaw that allotment could not be forced on their people without disastrous results. At the start of the third day of meetings, Lone Wolf addressed the three commissioners and made the tribes' position clear.

* * *

> Very few of our young men and women are educated or partially educated. Here is Joshua Givens, myself, Quanna Parker, and a few others, you can talk to them and they will answer you in English. Look at them; the rest are not dressed as well as they are. When the worst comes, they will be the only ones that will be able to cope with the white man when he comes to this country. The rest will not know what to do.

With the other members of the three tribes, Lone Wolf knew that the ultimate danger was the loss of their last remaining tribal lands and their identity as a people.

Lone Wolf's pleadings were not intended to turn back the clock or attempt to avoid change. The Kiowa chief agreed that the road set out by the Medicine Lodge Treaty "is about the best that we can travel." He described the "good advice" he had received in Washington and the progress the tribes were making in building schools and houses, concluding: "For that reason, because we are making such rapid progress, we ask the commission not to push us ahead too fast on the road we are to take."

* * *

Iseeo, a young Kiowa sergeant in the U.S. Calvary, rose to speak to the commissioners at the request of the chiefs * * *

> * * * Mother earth is something that we Indians love. The Great Father in Washington told us that this reservation was ours; that we would not be disturbed; that this place was for our use, and when you told us the purpose of the Government it made us uneasy. We do not know what to do about selling our mother to the Government. That makes us scared.

Quanah Parker, who had grown rich from his own farm and from dealings with Texas cattlemen, asked pointed questions about the business aspects of the deal: "How much will be paid for one acre, what the terms will be, and when it will be paid." * * *

* * *

Given the tribes' overwhelming opposition to the selling of the reservation, it is surprising how quickly the Cherokee Commission completed its task.

* * *

Throughout the proceedings, Quanah was the most frequent speaker and most aggressive negotiator. On the fourth day of the meeting, Quanah broke the impasse with an announcement that he had sent for a lawyer and proposed that a representative of each tribe meet with the lawyer and the commissioners to examine the proposed agreement. Quanah also requested that once the tribes understood the agreement the commissioner adjourn for two months to let the tribes consider.

Without agreeing to Quanah's plan, Jerome set a time the following morning to meet with the representatives and the lawyer. Several days later, the council reconvened; it was announced that the lawyer was unable to help the tribes at this point, and Quanah offered a compromise proposal that the differences between the tribes and the Commission be resolved directly with Congress by a delegation from the tribes. Quanah thought the tribes should be paid a half million dollars more than the commissioners had offered, and asked the Commission to present both figures to Congress.

Quanah got Lone Wolf and White Man to support his proposal, and the three commissioners announced the following day that they would accept Quanah's proposal. Despite this assurance, the document Jerome prepared for signatures was little different than the terms he had originally offered. The agreement as drafted and signed included the original $2 million figure, and gave the tribes only "an opportunity to be heard" in Congress for the balance. * * *

* * *

Before the commissioners left Fort Sill, they were already fighting rumors of foul play. Jerome denied that the commission had tried to coerce and "bull-doze" Indians into signing, or that the interpreters had been promised special favors or benefits and were therefore not translating properly. * * *

* * *

Although Lone Wolf was among the Kiowas who had initially agreed to sign, he reverted to opposition almost immediately. Before the commissioners left the reservation, Lone Wolf paid them a visit with a group of other signers. The Indians suspected that they had been deceived by incorrect translation of the terms of the agreement. Their request to see the document was denied, as was their request to have their names erased.

When they left the reservation, Jerome and his colleagues had collected 456 signatures. This was well over three-fourths of the adult male population as certified by Agent George Day. * * *

* * *

Congress received the Jerome agreement in January 1893, three months after the commissioners had finished collecting signatures. Transmitted by President Benjamin Harrison, the text of the agreement was accompanied by a letter from Commissioner Atkins as well as Agent Day's certification that 456 of 562 eligible Indians had signed the document. The report did acknowledge the tribes' position on the price of the land, but made no effort to urge Congress to consider it.

> * * * [I]n compliance with their request, we report that they desire to be heard through an attorney and a delegation to Washington upon that question, the agreement signed, however, to be effective upon ratification no matter what Congress may do with their appeal for the extra half million dollars.

* * *

* * * In October, anthropologist James Mooney of the Bureau of American Ethnology wrote to the Indian Rights Association to enlist their support in the fight to prevent ratification. Mooney noted that "the need is urgent and immediate, as boomer organizations are already made up in all the important border towns of Texas, Oklahoma, and Kansas, and resolutions calling for immediate ratification are already before Congress."

The three tribes held a general council in the same month and sent another memorial to Congress, this one crafted by a Washington, D.C. attorney, W.C. Shelley. Signed by 323 members of the tribe, the memorial set forth the history of "mendacity, fraud and coercion" in the dealings of the Cherokee Commission, and repudiated the agreement. * * *

* * *

* * * Lone Wolf, Quanah, and a delegation representing the tribes arrived in Washington March 1894 to meet with congressional committees about the bill. Lone Wolf and Quanah testified before a subcommittee of the House Indian Affairs Committee.

* * *

* * * Although the [House committee] reports acknowledged the strong Indian opposition to the bills, the committee's sentiment seemed closer to the views expressed by the governor of the Oklahoma Territory, with which the reports ended: "I cannot refrain from urging . . . that these reservations be at once opened to settlement. They embrace some of the finest land in Oklahoma and would be capable of supporting a large population."

* * *

* * * Two Senate resolutions in January 1899 requested more information about the matter from the Secretary of Interior. * * * In response to the Senate request, Secretary C.M. Bliss and Indian Affairs Commissioner W.A. Jones sent letters expressing their view that the agreement should not be ratified because of the tribes' persistent opposition and because the allotments as proposed were too small to support families by livestock grazing and the land too poor to be suitable for agriculture. Bliss recommended that a new agreement be negotiated

through an Indian inspector, and suggested that in any event the size of the allotments be doubled.

Secretary Bliss also enclosed reports received from the Kiowa and Comanche reservation during the past five years which illustrated the depth of the tribes' opposition. A report dated August 1893 by Captain Hugh G. Brown, who was then acting agent on the reservation, described the aftermath of the Jerome Commission's visit very simply: "The Kiowas, Comanches and Apaches are almost without exception, now that they understand it, uniformly opposed to the agreement."

Two days later Secretary Bliss reported the census figures that indicated that less than three-fourths of the adult Indian men had signed the agreement. A tribal roll, prepared less than three months after Agent Day's count of 562 adult men, listed 725 Indian men over age 18 and 639 men over 21.

* * *

* * * The tribes held another council in October, and drafted another petition to Congress, signed this time by 571 Indian men, 25 percent more than the original number of signatures on the Jerome document.

The tribes' final memorial was transmitted to the House and Senate when the Fifty-Sixth Congress convened in January 1900. Accompanied by letters from Commissioner Jones and Ethan A. Hitchcock, the new Interior Secretary, the petition was a clear and simple statement of the Indians' repudiation.

> [E]ach and every one of us who signed the treaty do solemnly declare that if we had not been deceived we would never have signed it. . . .
>
> We now realize that if this treaty is ratified we are doomed to destruction as a people and brought to the same impoverished condition to which the Cheyenne and Arapaho and other Indian tribes have been brought from the effects of prematurely opening their reservations for the settlement of white men among them.

* * *

In February 1900, the House proponents of ratification tried a new approach, and added their two-year-old bill as a rider to another Senate Indian bill that concerned the Fort Hall Reservation in Idaho. After the amended Fort Hall bill passed the House, it returned to the Senate, where Senator O.H. Platt of Connecticut, a loyal sympathizer of the Indian Rights Association, requested a conference on the amendment. Platt lost his bid to stop the legislation, however, and the bill passed the Senate without debate at the end of the session. No words in the title of the Act of June 6, 1900 indicated that Section VI was a ratification of the long-disputed

Jerome agreement. The ratification legislation amended the original Jerome agreement in several critical ways, but the amendments were never submitted to the three tribes for their approval.

* * *

A month after Congress ratified the revised Jerome agreement, a delegation from the three tribes visited Washington to argue for a better bill. The group met briefly with President McKinley, but were informed that the matter would not be reconsidered * * *

* * *

[Lone Wolf next retained former Congressman and federal Judge William Springer as attorney to challenge the allotment of his tribe's reservation in federal court.]

Springer had filed a complaint for Lone Wolf in the equity division of the Supreme Court of the District of Columbia on June 6, naming Hitchcock a defendant. The suit sought to restrain the Interior Department from carrying out the provisions of the allotment act, arguing that the acts of Congress were "unconstitutional and void" and a violation of "solemn treaty provisions." * * *

* * *

In a ruling handed down on June 20, the court denied a preliminary injunction and rejected Springer's contention that the acts deprived the tribes of their property without due process of law. The opinion by Justice A.C. Bradley in *Lone Wolf v. Hitchcock* described the history of the allotment legislation as "the usual process," and held that misunderstanding, deception, and lack of tribal consent were not relevant to the court's determination, the matter being one for exclusive consideration by Congress. As for the process due the tribes in Congress, "It is to be assumed that they [the tribes' objections] were carefully considered and determined with due regard to the public interests of and the rights of the Indian."

* * *

* * * By proclamation of President McKinley on July 4, 1901, the date of opening was set for August 6, 1901.

The three tribes' reservation was one of the last to be opened in the "twin territories," and generated enormous interest. Registration of land-hungry whites began on July 10, and after two weeks more than 150,000 people had registered for the 13,000 allotments available. Before the date of opening, a lottery was held to select those who would be allowed to claim 160-acre homesteads at a price of $1.75 per acre.

The *fait accompli* of 13,000 non-Indian homesteads cannot have helped Lone Wolf and Springer in their uphill legal battle. On December 4, 1901, the Court of Appeals of the District of Columbia rejected their appeal, with a broad holding about the legal effect of treaties and the status of Indian property rights. [Lone Wolf and the other tribal members then brought their contention that Congress had unlawfully violated the Medicine Lodge Treaty of 1867 to the United States Supreme Court].

* * *

LONE WOLF V. HITCHCOCK
Supreme Court of the United States, 1903.
187 U.S. 553, 23 S.Ct. 216, 47 L.Ed. 299.

MR. JUSTICE WHITE * * * delivered the opinion of the Court:

* * *

The contention [that Congress could not divest the tribes of their lands except according to the terms of the treaty] in effect ignores the status of the contracting Indians and the relation of dependency they bore and continue to bear towards the government of the United States. To uphold the claim would be to adjudge that the indirect operation of the treaty was to materially limit and qualify the controlling authority of Congress in respect to the care and protection of the Indians, and to deprive Congress, in a possible emergency, when the necessity might be urgent for a partition and disposal of the tribal lands, of all power to act, if the assent of the Indians could not be obtained.

Now, it is true that in decisions of this court, the Indian right of occupancy of tribal lands, whether declared in a treaty or otherwise created, has been stated to be sacred, or, as sometimes expressed, as sacred as the fee of the United States in the same lands. But in none of these cases was there involved a controversy between Indians and the government respecting the power of Congress to administer the property of the Indians. * * *

* * *

Plenary authority over the tribal relations of the Indians has been exercised by Congress from the beginning, and the power has always been deemed a political one, not subject to be controlled by the judicial department of the government. Until the year 1871 the policy was pursued of dealing with the Indian tribes by means of treaties, and, of course, a moral obligation rested upon Congress to act in good faith in performing the stipulations entered into on its behalf. But, as with treaties made with foreign nations (Chinese Exclusion Case, 130 U.S. 581, 600), the legislative power might pass laws in conflict with treaties made with the Indians.

The power exists to abrogate the provisions of an Indian treaty, though presumably such power will be exercised only when circumstances arise which will not only justify the government in disregarding the stipulations of the treaty, but may demand, in the interest of the country and the Indians themselves, that it should do so. When, therefore, treaties were entered into between the United States and a tribe of Indians it was never doubted that the *power* to abrogate existed in Congress, and that in a contingency such power might be availed of from considerations of governmental policy, particularly if consistent with perfect good faith towards the Indians. (The opinion then quoted from *United States v. Kagama,* page 186, supra.) * * *

In view of the legislative power possessed by Congress over treaties with the Indians and Indian tribal property, we may not specially consider the contentions pressed upon our notice that the signing by the Indians of the agreement of October 6, 1892, was obtained by fraudulent misrepresentations, and concealment, that the requisite three fourths of adult male Indians had not signed, as required by the twelfth article of the treaty of 1867, and that the treaty as signed had been amended by Congress without submitting such amendments to the action of the Indians since all these matters, in any event, were solely within the domain of the legislative authority, and its action is conclusive upon the courts.

The act of June 6, 1900, which is complained of in the bill, was enacted at a time when the tribal relations between the confederated tribes of Kiowas, Comanches, and Apaches still existed, and that statute and the statutes supplementary thereto dealt with the disposition of tribal property, and purported to give an adequate consideration for the surplus lands not allotted among the Indians or reserved for their benefit. Indeed, the controversy which this case presents is concluded by the decision in Cherokee Nation v. Hitchcock, 187 U.S. 294, decided at this term, where it was held that full administrative power was possessed by Congress over Indian tribal property. In effect, the action of Congress now complained of was but an exercise of such power, a mere change in the form of investment of Indian tribal property, the property of those who, as we have held, were in substantial effect the wards of the government. We must presume that Congress acted in perfect good faith in the dealings with the Indians of which complaint is made, and that the legislative branch of the government exercised its best judgment in the premises. In any event, as Congress possessed full power in the matter, the judiciary cannot question or inquire into the motives which prompted the enactment of this legislation. If injury was occasioned, which we do not wish to be understood as implying, by the use made by Congress of its power, relief must be sought by an appeal to that body for redress, and not to the courts. The legislation in question was constitutional, and the demurrer to the bill was therefore rightly sustained.

* * *

Affirmed.

NOTES

1.   The *Lone Wolf* Court relied in part on the *Chinese Exclusion Case,* upholding the abrogation of a treaty with a foreign nation. Should international treaty law be applied *in toto* in this context, or are there reasons that different rules should apply to the abrogation of Indian treaties? How persuasive are these other justifications of the *Lone Wolf* rule: a) Strict adherence to the terms of treaties would distribute an undue share of the nation's wealth to Indians; b) Treaties are frequently too imprecise to permit rigorous judicial enforcement; c) The *Lone Wolf* rule preserves necessary flexibility in the formulation of public policy? See Reid Peyton Chambers, *Judicial Enforcement of the Federal Trust Responsibility to Indians,* 27 Stan.L.Rev. 1213, 1225–30 (1975). See also Angela R. Riley, *The Apex of Congress' Plenary Power over Indian Affairs: The Story of* Lone Wolf v. Hitchcock, *in* Indian Law Stories 189 (Carole Goldberg, Kevin K. Washburn & Philip P. Frickey, eds. 2011).

2.   The effect of *Lone Wolf* has been somewhat ameliorated by subsequent case law. It is now established that treaty land cannot be taken without just compensation. See page 282, infra. The Court in the 1980 *Sioux Nation* opinion had strong words for *Lone Wolf* and restricted several aspects of the decision, yet the holding remains a valid precedent. See pages 402–410, infra.

5.   ASSIMILATIONIST POLICIES

Gradual assimilation, the theory went, would benefit Indians by eliminating the reservations which, even in the 1880s, were becoming visible pockets of poverty. A consensus developed—among non-Indians, at least—in favor of assimilation as the only politically viable alternative to the strong push for the wholesale destruction of Indian culture and Indian reservations. See generally Angelique Eaglewoman, *Tribal Nations and Tribalist Economics: The Historical and Contemporary Impacts of Intergenerational Poverty and Cultural Wealth Within the United States,* 49 Washburn L.J. 805 (2010); Henry Eugene Fritz, The Movement for Indian Assimilation, 1860–1890 (1963).

Assimilation was furthered during this era by a number of laws and policies related to the broad "civilizing" goals of the General Allotment Act. Education, for example, became central to assimilationist thinking in the late nineteenth century. A military man, Captain R.H. Pratt, was named the first superintendent of the new Carlisle Indian Boarding School in Pennsylvania. He let his views on Indian education be known:

> * * * A great general had said that the only good Indian is a dead one * * * . I agree with the sentiment, but only in this: that all the Indian there is in the race should be dead. Kill the Indian in him and save the man.

Richard H. Pratt, *The Advantages of Mingling Indians with Whites*, in Americanizing the American Indians 260–61 (Francis Paul Prucha ed. 1973).

> The BIA boarding school system was expanded and modeled after the Carlisle example: The children usually were kept at boarding school for eight years, during which time they were not permitted to see their parents, relatives or friends. Anything Indian—dress, language, religious practices, even outlook on life * * * was uncompromisingly prohibited. Ostensibly educated, articulated in the English language, wearing store bought clothes, and with their hair short and their emotionalism toned down, the boarding-school graduates were sent out either to make their way in a White world that did not want them, or to return to reservations to which they were now foreign.

Peter Farb, Man's Rise to Civilization 257–59 (1968).

As Farb indicates, the pressures to do away with Indian culture, including religion, became part of federal assimilationist policy. A notorious example is the Wounded Knee massacre of 1890, where some 146 Sioux Indians were killed by the Seventh Cavalry. Federal troops would never have been in the area in the absence of a preoccupation with stifling the Ghost Dance, a native religious practice. Such overt federal regulation of the free exercise of Indian religion, not unique to Wounded Knee or to the boarding schools, has seldom if ever been duplicated in our nation's history. See generally Angie Debo, A History of the Indians of the United States 290–94 (1970); Jennings C. Wise, The Red Man in the New World Drama 289–91 (Vine Deloria, Jr. ed. 1971).

The so-called "Five Civilized Tribes" that had been removed to Oklahoma Indian Territory in the early nineteenth century, the Cherokees, Choctaws, Creeks, Chickasaws, and Seminoles, originally had been excepted from the General Allotment Act of 1887. Then, Congress passed the Curtis Act in 1898, followed by the Five Tribes Act of 1906, which extended forced allotments and other assimilation programs sponsored by the federal government to these tribes as well. The historical experience of the Creeks under the reform policies and legislation applied generally to all of the tribes removed to the Oklahoma Indian territory is described at length in Harjo v. Kleppe, 420 F.Supp. 1110 (D.D.C.1976).

Crow Dog, Kagama, and Lone Wolf, while members of different tribes from different parts of the country, all seem to have shared at least one common characteristic: resistance. Each of them took a stand and fought against federal policies aimed at assimilating them to "the white man's road." Why did United States courts and policymakers fail to hear their voices?

A notorious federal habeas corpus case, decided in 1879, demonstrates some of the difficulties tribal Indians encountered in the post-Civil War era when attempting to have their rights recognized through the United States legal system. Standing Bear, a Ponca tribal leader, led a small band from the Indian Territory (now Oklahoma) back to the tribe's traditional homeland in northern Nebraska. The United States Army incarcerated the group and prepared to march them back to the Indian Territory. Standing Bear, with the encouragement of an Omaha newspaperman, filed a writ of habeas corpus. The issue of the case revolved around the status of tribal Indians in federal court. The habeas statutes of the time referred to "persons" being held in custody in violation of the constitution, laws, or treaties of the United States. Thus, the judge in the case had to turn to Webster's dictionary to determine whether Indians were "persons" under United States law: "Webster describes a person as 'a living soul; a self-conscious being; a moral agent; especially a living human being; a man, woman, or child; an individual of the human race.' This is comprehensive enough, it would seem, to include even an Indian." United States ex rel. Standing Bear v. Crook, 25 F.Cas. 695, 697 (C.C.D.Neb.1879) (No. 14,891).

SECTION B. THE PERIOD OF INDIAN REORGANIZATION (1928–1945)

President Theodore Roosevelt once aptly described the General Allotment Act as "a mighty pulverizing engine to break up the tribal mass." By the beginnings of the twentieth century, that engine had ground hard on the land base and governments of Indian country. The practical result of allotment era reforms was to undermine the tribal sovereignty principles of the Marshall trilogy. Supreme Court cases such as *United States v. Kagama*, page 186, supra, *Lone Wolf v. Hitchcock*, page 212, supra, and *United States v. Sandoval*, page 188, supra, all stood for the idea that federal power would be exercised to supplant rather than secure the role of tribes as sovereigns. They implied that Indian tribes had withered away under the weight of non-Indian society and thus, tribal governments were anachronisms.

The Great Hunkpapa Sioux medicine man, Sitting Bull, reacting to an 1889 agreement by his people to cede yet another remnant of Sioux ancestral lands to the United States government, understood the pressures of historical forces on Indian tribal identity as well as any of the reform-minded policy-makers in Washington. "Indians?" the Sioux patriot proclaimed despairingly; "There are no Indians left now but me." Quoted in Stephen Cornell, Return of the Native 51 (1988).

Remarkably, despite decades of military assaults, followed by the political and legal efforts to dismantle American Indian tribes during the late nineteenth century, tribal culture and tribal traditions were not completely destroyed by the allotment era reforms and assimilative pressures. Reservations in the early twentieth century were still "Indian country"—places where a "measured separatism" had been maintained between Indians and the dominant society. See Charles F. Wilkinson, American Indians, Time, and the Law 14–19 (1987).

The reasons for American Indian tribalism's perpetuation and persistence are varied and complex. Professor Stephen Cornell notes that the community and political organization of the Pueblos, Navajos, and Tohono O'odham of the Southwest generally were less affected by United States control through most of the allotment era. Their lands were not subject to any extensive allotments and the traditional systems of local autonomy that had been maintained by these relatively more isolated tribal groups therefore managed to survive. In parts of Indian country that had undergone intensive allotment, the traditional structures of tribal religious and political authority survived by going underground, out of sight of the BIA Indian agents and missionaries. And everywhere in Indian country, large numbers of Indians persisted in holding on to their identities as tribal peoples by maintaining their kinship relations, ways of thinking about and acting in the world, systems of meaning, and tribal languages. Finally, though many reservations had undergone extensive allotment, in most cases, the reservations had not been completely disestablished by the allotment era reforms. Survival of the reservations meant survival of the tribal unit. The federal government continued its focus on the reservation as the principal unit of Indian administration. In the process, the geographical consolidation of tribal peoples initiated earlier by Indian-white conflict continued on apace. American Indian tribalism was radically transformed in some ways but remained deeply embedded in Indian culture. See Cornell, *The Return of the Native* 80–82.

Predictably perhaps, the persistence of American Indian tribalism attracted a new generation of non-Indian reformers in the 1920s. These reformers, led by John Collier, commissioner of the BIA during the New Deal administration of President Franklin Roosevelt, envisioned a dramatic departure from the federal government's previous Indian policies. Rather than aiming to destroy tribalism, Collier and the other New Deal era reformers sought to revive tribal governing structures through the Indian Reorganization Act (IRA) of 1934. See generally Lawrence C. Kelly, The Assault on Assimilation: John Collier and the Origins of Indian Policy Reform (1983); Kenneth R. Philp, John Collier's Crusade for Indian Reform, 1920–1954 (1977).

1. THE INDIAN REORGANIZATION ACT: DESIGN FOR MODERN TRIBAL GOVERNMENTS

The underlying premise of the reformers who designed and administered the IRA was that the forced assimilation of Indians through the Allotment Act legislation and related policies worked to destroy Indians as individuals and Indian communities. The reformers believed that the tribe itself, organized as a self-governing community, was better equipped to deal with the outside influences of the dominant society. See Edward H. Spicer, Cycles of Conquest 352 (1962). The reforms of the 1920s and 1930s thus were different from those previously employed by the United States in attempting to implement a final solution to the nation's "Indian problem." Tribal self-government was to be encouraged, rather than discouraged.

The IRA has generated a great deal of debate and discussion among scholars, Indian and non-Indian, and among Indian peoples themselves, as to whether, on balance, the transformations wrought in Indian country by this landmark legislation of twentieth century federal Indian policy were beneficial or detrimental to American Indian tribalism's survival. Modern-day critics of the IRA contend that in many ways, the goals of the IRA era reforms ultimately were not all that different from the goals of previous Indian policies. The IRA was yet another incorporative program, established through policies designed by non-Indians.

COMMENT, TRIBAL SELF-GOVERNMENT AND THE INDIAN REORGANIZATION ACT OF 1934
70 Mich.L.Rev. 955, 955–79 (1972).

The Indian Reorganization (Wheeler-Howard) Act of 1934 (IRA) was, by all accounts, one of the most significant single pieces of legislation directly affecting Indians ever enacted by the Congress of the United States. It has been "equalled in scope and significance only by the legislation of June 30, 1834, and the General Allotment Act of February 8, 1887." A major reversal of governmental policy and approach toward Indian affairs was effectuated by the IRA.

* * *

The allotment era extended from 1887 to 1934, when the IRA ended the practice completely in so far as it applied to tribally owned lands. Publication of the *Meriam Report*[33] in 1928 caused a significant slowdown of allotment parceling, but by then the damage had been done. * * *

During the period preceding the enactment of the IRA there was some recognition that Indians were living in grinding poverty, that Indian health and education were in an abominable state, and that government policies were not working. As early as 1881 books like Helen Hunt Jackson's crusading *A Century of Dishonor* had exposed these conditions to public view and made people aware of broken treaties and other unfulfilled

---

[33] Institute for Govt. Research, Studies in Administration, The Problem of Indian Administration.

promises. But it was not until publication of the *Meriam Report* that a movement toward change began. The *Report* is an extremely detailed document, describing and analyzing the entire spectrum of Indian life and the problems of governmental administration of Indian affairs. It brought these problems into sharp focus, and in so doing presaged more than any other work the enactment of the IRA six years later.

The basic position taken by the Meriam staff was that

> [t]he object of work with or for the Indians is to fit them either to merge into the social and economic life of the prevailing civilization as developed by the whites or to live in the presence of that civilization at least in accordance with a minimum standard of health and decency.

If this goal were accomplished, as the staff saw it, there would be no need for further governmental supervision. This position did not imply automatic cultural assimilation, however. The authors of the *Report* recognized explicitly that many Indians wished to maintain a separate cultural identity, although they also admitted this would be difficult in so far as the economic underpinnings of the old culture had been destroyed.

The process of allotment as historically administered was criticized, as were other approaches to the "Indian problem":

> The work of the government directed toward the education and advancement of the Indian himself . . . is largely ineffective. The chief explanation . . . lies in the fact that the government has not appropriated enough funds to permit the Indian Service to employ an adequate personnel properly qualified for the task before it.

The Meriam staff sought to redirect the approach to Indian affairs by development of the social services necessary to enable Indians to reach a level of self-support.

* * *

The recommendations of the *Meriam Report* fell short of the broad-ranging goals later expressed by the IRA. For example, decentralization of authority was recommended, but to local Indian agents rather than to the tribes themselves. Still, the publication of this work was an event of major importance in the history of Indian affairs and was a significant stimulus in the direction the IRA was later to follow.

* * *

B.   *The Act's Objectives: An Analytical Look Behind the Scenes*

The thrust of the IRA can be gathered from its operative provisions. Every section in some way affects tribal self-government, although obviously not all are equally relevant to this discussion.

Section 1 of the IRA [25 U.S.C.A. § 461] ended the policy of allotment: "No land of any Indian reservation . . . shall be allotted in severalty to any Indian." This provision, while not going directly to self-government, was a key factor in making it possible; it alone assures the Act's historical significance.

Section 4 [25 U.S.C.A. § 464] related to alienation. In general, it prohibited any transfer of Indian land or shares in the assets of tribal corporations otherwise than to the tribe, except that the Secretary could authorize voluntary exchanges of such lands or interests of equal value when it would be "expedient and beneficial for or compatible with the proper consolidation of Indian lands." This provision has had the desirable effect of further strengthening the tribal land base and tribal control over it.

Section 10 [25 U.S.C.A. § 470] set up a revolving fund from which the Secretary of Interior could make loans to chartered corporations for purposes of economic development. This reversed an earlier policy by which loans were made to individual Indians and under which there had been problems in repayment. Under the IRA, loans are made only to the tribes, with individual loans being arranged between the tribe and the individual. Also, section 11 appropriated a small amount of funds to be used for loans to Indians for tuition payment and other expenses in "recognized vocational and trade schools" and in high schools and colleges.

Section 18 [25 U.S.C.A. § 478] provided that the Act would not apply to any reservation wherein a majority of the adult Indians voted against its application at a special election to be held within one year after the Act's approval. This section marked a significant change in approach to Indian legislation. Formerly, legislation had been either special, applying by its terms to only one tribe or group of tribes, or general, applying to all Indians without consideration of tribal differences. Through section 18, the IRA became a type of enabling act, giving each tribe the opportunity to determine for itself whether it wanted to come under the Act. There was, however, a major flaw in the approach: a tribe could hold the election only once. If it voted against application, it did not have the option of later reconsideration.

The essence of the IRA lay in those provisions relating directly to tribal organization, viz., sections 16 [25 U.S.C.A. § 476] and 17. The former provided:

> Any Indian tribe, or tribes, residing on the same reservation, shall have the right to organize for its common welfare, and may adopt an appropriate constitution and bylaws . . . [Procedure is then established for ratification by members and approval by the Secretary of Interior].

> In addition to all powers vested in any tribe or tribal council by existing law, the constitution adopted by said tribe shall also vest in such tribe or its tribal council the following rights and powers: To employ legal counsel, the choice of counsel and fixing of fees to be subject to the approval of the Secretary of the Interior; to prevent the sale, disposition, lease, or encumbrance of tribal lands, interests in lands, or other tribal assets without the consent of the tribe; and to negotiate with the Federal, State, and local governments. . . .

Section 17 [25 U.S.C.A. § 477] first provided for issuance of a charter of incorporation to a tribe and established procedures for petition and ratification. It continued:

> Such charter may convey to the incorporated tribe the power to purchase, take by gift, or bequest, or otherwise, own, hold, manage, operate, and dispose of property of every description, real and personal, including the power to purchase restricted Indian lands and to issue in exchange therefor interests in corporate property, and such further powers as may be incidental to the conduct of corporate business, not inconsistent with law; but no authority shall be granted to sell, mortgage, or lease for a period exceeding ten years any of the land included in the limits of the reservation. Any charter so issued shall not be revoked or surrendered except by Act of Congress.

The purpose of adopting a charter is different than that of adopting a constitution, the charter being oriented more toward business than toward governmental organization.

Perhaps the prime objective of the IRA, which was crucial to any effective establishment of self-government, was elimination of the "absolutist" executive discretion previously exercised by the Interior Department and the Office of Indian Affairs. During the hearings, Commissioner of Indian Affairs John Collier presented to the House Committee examples which revealed the vastness of this discretionary power. Not only had administrative power grown beyond control, but its exercise and the effects of its exercise also changed from year to year, depending on the attitude or whim of a given commissioner. Further, this discretionary power was also exercised by local agency superintendents, a situation that led Senator Wheeler to refer to the local agent as "a czar." So all-encompassing was this power that "the Department [had] absolute discretionary powers over all organized expressions of the Indians. . . . [T]ribal councils exist[ed] by [the Department's] sufferance and [had] no authority except as . . . granted by the Department." Consequently, the IRA sought to eliminate this boundless discretion or at least place a damper on its exercise. "This bill * * * seeks to get away from the bureaucratic control of the Indian Department, and it seeks further to give the Indians the control of their own affairs. . . ."

It was not entirely clear, however, precisely what changes were to be made. Commissioner Collier was the moving force behind the new administrative approach. Of course, as Commissioner, he already possessed broad powers to move the Indian Office in the desired direction. Apparently, however, he was one of that rare breed of administrators who seek actively to undermine their own powers through legislation. To be sure, the Office would not become powerless under the Act. Subsequent developments have shown that it can and will exercise much power, often to the detriment of its constituency. And the Commissioner himself, in a memorandum to the House Committee, said, "The bill does not bring to an end, or imply or contemplate, a cessation of Federal guardianship. . . . On the contrary, it makes permanent the guardianship services, and reasserts them. . . ." He sharply distinguished between these "guardianship services," which he sought to retain, and administrative absolutism. Commissioner Collier's goal was to move toward the elimination of the Office of Indian Affairs in its present capacity and he hoped that it would "ultimately exist as a purely advisory and special service body [as is] the Department of Agriculture [vis-a-vis] American farmers," a goal as yet unrealized.

* * *

The IRA did not, however, accomplish all that was promised toward granting autonomy to the tribes. Even under the final Act, the Secretary was empowered to review many actions of the tribal governments, and still retains close control over tribal government. The rationale for this federal control was that at the time of the adoption of tribal constitutions and charters under the IRA, most Indians had had little experience in managing their own affairs. In large part, of course, this was true of the generation of Indian leaders in the 1930's primarily because of the application of administrative authority in harsh form during the preceding years.

The sponsors and supporters of the IRA saw in it a major change in the pattern of Indian governance. It would be incorrect, however, to assume that constitutional self-government was a new phenomenon in Indian affairs in an historical or legal sense. A survey of the Indian legal experience suggests that the IRA was really resurrecting and revitalizing older forms and concepts. * * *

D.   Experience under the IRA

During the two-year period within which tribes could accept or reject the IRA, 258 elections were held. In these elections, 181 tribes (129,750 Indians) accepted the Act and 77 tribes (86,365 Indians, including 45,000 Navajos) rejected it. The IRA also applies to 14 groups of Indians who did not hold elections to exclude themselves. Within 12 years, 161 constitutions and 131 corporate charters had been adopted pursuant to the IRA. The experience of these tribes has been as varied as the tribes themselves. * * *

The constitutions and charters themselves vary considerably, especially with respect to the forms of government adopted, "ranging from ancient and primitive forms in tribes where such forms have been perpetuated, to models based on progressive white communities." Likewise, the powers vested in the tribes through these documents "vary in accordance with the circumstances, experience, and resources of the tribe." On the other hand, there are provisions which appear in most constitutions in nearly identical terms. Most governments established under the IRA, unlike federal and state governments, have no provision for the separation of powers. The governing body is the tribal council, and in many instances it acts in a legislative as well as executive capacity. The council members, acting either in their capacity as elected political officials or as directors of the tribal corporation, also manage the common resources of the tribe. While it is often assumed that such a unification of powers is undesirable, most tribes have operated well under a unified system.

* * *

A by-product of the IRA has been better control and management of tribal property. Under the earlier allotment policy the tribal land base was consistently diminished through the parceling of land to individual Indians; consequently, management of land use was difficult. Even after the IRA land management remained a problem on some reservations because of the earlier parceling. However, IRA funds have been used to reacquire much of this previously allotted land. Out of the renewed land base such developments as livestock cooperatives and tribal farming enterprises have arisen.

* * *

* * * In the end it must be concluded that the experience of the tribes under the IRA has been positive. The Act provided a powerful stimulus to tribal governmental organization and in many cases so strengthened that organization as to enable continued development despite fluctuations in administrative policy.

* * *

EDWARD H. SPICER, CYCLES OF CONQUEST
351–52 (1962).

* * *

The Indian Reorganization Act of 1934 proposed, for the first time in United States history, to make a beginning at political integration of Indian communities. In substance, what it proposed was a transitional community, something like the Jesuit mission community in which Indians maintained a form of Spanish local government but in which they were exempt for a specific period from paying tribute (taxes) and could continue to hold land as a corporate body. The IRA proposed * * * a plan for tribal representative government on the reservations. The form proposed was constitutional, the constitutions to be written with special reference to each tribe's social structure with the aid of technicians in government from the Indian Bureau. The tribal councils formed on this basis had jurisdiction within their reservations, except with respect to ten major crimes which since 1885 had been handled in federal courts. They had powers of taxation and many other powers over the tribal members, whose qualifications they defined. They had no formal working relations with local and state governments, their only channels of communication being through the Indian Bureau. They were thus a peculiar form of isolated institution, not actually a working part of the political structure of the United States. They nevertheless were considered a means for gaining experience in the type of constitutional, representative government which existed in the United States generally. Together with their powers as a managing body for the tribal resources in land, timber, minerals, etc., they constituted a school for learning to work together politically in the Anglo-American way. It had taken nearly one hundred years for the Indian Bureau to devise this transitional mechanism. It was applied only after Indians had lived for generations under the superintendent system, and moreover the latter was not abolished.

In providing this new form of organization for communities of Indians on the reservations, the IRA brought about a fundamental change in what had become the structure of those communities. As settlers had pressed around the reservations, the Indian Bureau had become aware of the necessity for some sort of political organization for the tribes. The need for agreements by tribes as wholes in regard to use of such reservation resources as oil and minerals by Anglo entrepreneurs had resulted in the Indian Bureau setting up groups of Indians to act as legal spokesman for the tribes. These were Indians, hand-picked by superintendents, who acted as their "advisers" in tribal matters and signed legal papers when necessary as in the case of oil exploration leases on the Navajo Reservation. They were in no sense representative bodies, but, consistent with the paternalistic regime of the superintendents, were groups selected by the latter to function in name as the tribe. They increased the hold of the superintendent over reservation affairs. The IRA plan in principle, and as it turned out to some extent in practice, instituted a more representative system which in some measure modified the control of the superintendents.

In addition, the IRA established new means for breaking down the social isolation of the reservation populations. The most important of such means consisted of the Johnson-O'Malley Act which enabled the Indian Bureau or the tribal councils to make contracts for services with state governments or with private corporations. Under this act it became possible to contract with state governments for the education of Indian children in state and county schools, thus throwing the Indian children in closer contact with non-Indians in their own localities. Similarly, health and other services were contracted for with state governments or private groups. Although still quite separate from the local governments of their areas, Indians on reservations came to participate more in the society surrounding them, and the virtual limitation of contact to federal bureau officials began to change.

NOTES

1. Criticism of the IRA has come from traditional Indians who feel that the IRA has resulted in the substitution of "white man's laws" for the old tribal ways. The point is illustrated by a 1971 suit brought by traditional members of the Hopi Tribe in northeastern Arizona. They sought to set aside the Secretary of the Interior's approval of a major coal lease between the Hopi Tribal Council and Peabody Coal. The lease permitted strip mining on Black Mesa, a sacred area on one of the most traditional of all reservations. According to the plaintiffs' complaint:

> Carving up Black Mesa by the process known as strip mining is a desecration, a sacrilege, contrary to the instruction of the Great Spirit and to the essential relationship to the land that is embodied in Hopi culture, life and religion; contrary, in short, to everything that Hopi culture and religion mean.

The Hopi Tribal Council was established pursuant to an IRA constitution adopted in 1936. As was typically the case, the BIA had made great efforts to "sell" the constitution to the tribe. But a constitution granting broad powers to one central tribal council was, as the BIA acknowledged at the time, contrary to the Hopi way: most Hopi decisions had always been made by the individual villages and their respective Kikmongwi, or traditional religious leaders. The village system and certification of all representatives to the central tribal council by the Kikmongwi were provided for in the 1936 IRA constitution as a special concession designed by Collier and his colleagues to make the IRA form more attractive to skeptical Hopis. Only a few Hopis voted in the required election, however. Traditional Hopis were prevented by their religious beliefs from taking part in political activity. Thus, it was a handful of non-traditionalists whose vote adopted the constitution for all Hopis.

The plaintiffs in the Black Mesa lawsuit alleged that the Hopi Tribe had not delegated to the tribal council, by means of the IRA constitution, the right to enter into the strip mining lease. The constitution does not on its face grant the tribal council the authority to lease tribal resources—only the power to *prevent* their disposition. Other objections were raised, including the fact that the tribal council was improperly constituted because several members had not been certified by Kikmongwi as the constitution required.

The traditionalists were never able to reach the merits in court. The tribe had not been joined as a defendant because of the doctrine of tribal sovereign immunity. The suit was dismissed because of the failure to join an indispensable party, the tribe. Lomayaktewa v. Hathaway, 520 F.2d 1324 (9th Cir.1975), cert. denied 425 U.S. 903 (1976). See also Charles F. Wilkinson, *Home Dance, The Hopi, and Black Mesa Coal: Conquest and Endurance in the American Southwest*, 1996 BYU L.Rev. 449 (1996).

Thus, although the IRA has been accepted more widely by Indians than most earlier policies, complaints that IRA constitutions vested overly broad powers in tribal councils and that Indian traditional governmental forms had been ignored were (and still are) widespread. The point seems to be that notwithstanding the more enlightened perceptions of the "Indian problem" during the New Deal, the solutions were tainted with the non-Indians' cultural bias. How should tribes amend their constitutions or reform their governing laws to utilize effectively their cultural and legal traditions in developing and operating their own forms of self-government? See Eric Lemont, American Indian Constitutional Reform and the Rebuilding of Native Nations (2006).

2.   There has been relatively little litigation concerning the IRA. Tribes have established business corporations under Section 17, 25 U.S.C.A. § 477, and waived sovereign immunity in regard to those corporations. A waiver of sovereign immunity however is not implied because the tribal corporation is chartered under Section 17. Such waivers must be express and comply with the by-laws of the corporation. See Memphis Biofuels, LLC v. Chickasaw Nation Industries, Inc., 585 F.3d 917 (6th Cir.2009). Such express waivers generally have been limited to the operations and assets of the Section 17 business corporation, so that other tribal assets have not been affected by the waivers. See generally pages 135–138, infra. The Act requires secretarial approval of tribal constitutions for those tribes choosing to organize governments under Section 16 of the IRA, 25 U.S.C.A. § 476. Many IRA constitutions include additional provisions that all or certain specified tribal ordinances must also be approved by the Secretary. The Supreme Court has said: "the most that can be said about this period of constitution writing is that the Bureau of Indian Affairs, in assisting the drafting of tribal constitutions, had a policy of including provisions for Secretarial approval; but that policy was not mandated by Congress." Kerr-McGee Corp. v. Navajo Tribe of Indians, 471 U.S. 195, 198 (1985). The Court also found that non-IRA tribes were not subject to secretarial approval of their constitutions or codes, and that IRA tribes "are free, with the backing of the Interior Department, to amend their constitutions to remove the requirement of Secretarial approval" as to ordinances. Id. at 199.

What powers does a tribe acquire under Section 16, 25 U.S.C.A. § 476, that are not already possessed as a result of inherent tribal sovereignty? No case has construed definitely the right of IRA tribes to prevent disposition of their lands.

2. THE CONTRIBUTIONS OF FELIX COHEN

In 1941, seven years after the passage of the IRA, the Department of the Interior published the *Handbook of Federal Indian Law*, authored by Felix Cohen, Associate Solicitor of the Interior Department in the Roosevelt Administration during the IRA era. Cohen, who penned the famous "miner's canary" analogy to underscore the unique role the Indian plays in American society, see page 7, supra, was a highly respected legal scholar and a leader of the legal realism movement, one of the most important reform movements in American law of the twentieth century. See generally Dalia Tsuk, *The New Deal Origins of American Legal Pluralism*, 29 Fla.St.U.L.Rev. 189 (2001).

As a legal realist and innovative thinker, Cohen's far-ranging ideas and intellect are reflected throughout his legal work within the Interior Department and particularly his drafting and administration of the IRA. The Realists focused on the close connection between law and policy, and the *Handbook* is illustrative of realist scholarship and its reliance on legal analysis to advocate progressive social policies. Cohen, as the Interior Department's attorney, was an advocate and architect of the reform policies of John Collier, and in that sense, the *Handbook* represents one of the more voluminous lawyer's briefs ever produced for the revival of tribal sovereignty—the overarching policy goal of the IRA. As the *Handbook* itself declared: "The most basic of all Indian rights, the right of self-government, is the Indian's last defense against administrative oppression * * * ." Id. at 122.

Cohen's prestige as a scholar, the massive research effort that went into compiling the work, and the brilliant synthesis of case law and historical precedents reflected throughout the text enshrined the *Handbook* as the principal scholarly resource for lawyers and judges in the field of Indian law. Felix Frankfurter, a Roosevelt appointee to the Supreme Court, referred to Cohen's work as bringing "meaning and reason out of the vast hodgepodge of treaties, statutes, judicial and administrative rulings, and unrecorded practice in which the intricacies and perplexities, confusion and injustices of the law governing Indians lay concealed." Felix Frankfurter, Of Law and Men 298 (1956).

The *Handbook* represents a rigorous defense of tribal sovereignty and like the IRA itself, promoted the revival of American Indian tribalism within the context of federal power over Indian tribes. As Cohen and the other non-Indian architects of the IRA clearly recognized, the federal-tribal relationship had been recast by a half century's worth of government efforts aimed at destroying tribalism. Whatever the original pristine theoretical nature of the principles of tribal sovereignty that could be derived from the Marshall trilogy, practical realities taught that tribal powers affirmed by treaties and a long line of Supreme Court decisions could be swept away at the whim of Congress without the consent of Indians, as had happened in the allotment era. But the genius of Cohen also realized that to the extent that inherent powers survived the destructive forces of the allotment era reforms in *theory*, they could be revived in *practice*, and encouraged by the Congress' express recognition of those powers in legislation such as the IRA. The following excerpt from the original 1941 edition of the *Handbook* represents, without question, the single most influential passage ever written by an Indian law scholar.

FELIX S. COHEN, HANDBOOK OF FEDERAL INDIAN LAW
122–23 (1941).

* * * Indian self-government, the decided cases hold, includes the power of an Indian tribe to adopt and operate under a form of government of the Indians' choosing, to define conditions of tribal membership, to regulate domestic relations of members, to prescribe rules of inheritance, to levy taxes, to regulate property within the jurisdiction of the tribe, to control the conduct of members by municipal legislation, and to administer justice.

Perhaps the most basic principle of all Indian law, supported by a host of decisions hereinafter analyzed, is the principle that *those powers which are lawfully vested in an Indian tribe are not, in general, delegated powers granted by express acts of Congress, but rather inherent powers of a limited sovereignty which has never been extinguished.* Each Indian tribe begins its relationship with the Federal Government as a sovereign power, recognized as such in treaty and legislation. The powers of sovereignty have been limited from time to time by special treaties and laws designed to take from the Indian tribes control of matters which, in the judgment of Congress, these tribes could no longer be safely permitted to handle. The statutes of Congress, then, must be examined to determine the limitations of tribal sovereignty rather than to determine its sources or its positive content. What is not expressly limited remains within the domain of tribal sovereignty.

The acts of Congress which appear to limit the powers of an Indian tribe are not to be unduly extended by doubtful inference.

* * *

From the earliest years of the Republic the Indian tribes have been recognized as "distinct, independent, political communities," and, as such, qualified to exercise powers of self-government, not by virtue of any delegation of powers from the Federal Government, but rather by reason of their original tribal sovereignty. Thus treaties and statutes of Congress have been looked to by the courts as limitations upon original tribal powers, or, at most, evidences of recognition of such powers, rather than as the direct source of tribal powers. This is but an application of the general principle that "It is only by positive enactments, even in the case of conquered and subdued nations, that their laws are changed by the conqueror."

* * *

The whole course of judicial decision on the nature of Indian tribal powers is marked by adherence to three fundamental principles: (1) An Indian tribe possesses, in the first instance, all the powers of any sovereign state. (2) Conquest renders the tribe subject to the legislative power of the United States and, in substance, terminates the external powers of sovereignty of the tribe, *e.g.*, its power to enter into treaties with foreign nations, but does not by itself affect the internal sovereignty of the tribe, *i.e.*, its powers of local self-government. (3) These powers are subject to qualification by treaties and by express legislation of Congress, but, save as thus expressly qualified, full powers of internal sovereignty are vested in the Indian tribes and in their duly constituted organs of government.

NOTE

Cohen's assessment of the "whole course of judicial decisions on the nature of Indian tribal powers," contained in the 1941 edition of the *Handbook,* was a restatement of an Opinion of the Solicitor of the Interior Department (Cohen was Associate Solicitor) requested by Congress four months after passage of the IRA in 1934. Congress asked whether the phrase it had enacted into law under § 16 of the IRA—"all powers vested in any Indian tribe or tribal council by existing law"—operated as a legislative grant or a recognition of tribal powers. The bold thesis that an Indian tribe possesses "all the powers of any sovereign state" had not been promoted in any of the testimony by Interior Department officials who advocated the bill before Congress earlier in the year.

Some scholars do not view the Interior Department's official interpretation of the IRA as recognizing inherent sovereign powers of the tribe as unalloyed support for autonomous Indian self-government, because it is accompanied by the restraining principle stated in the opinion that "Conquest renders the tribe subject to the legislative power of the United States." Russel Barsh and James Henderson call it a "two-edged sword", and ask what is the meaning of residual sovereignty "if the residuum can be confiscated by Congress at any time without recourse? Congress continued to enjoy as much power over tribes as previously, but had been cautioned to exercise it, if at all, only in express acts." Russell Barsh and James Youngblood Henderson, The Road: Indian Tribes and Political Liberty 112 (1980).

Some members of Congress, within a decade, became anxious once again to make radical reforms to the nation's Indian policy. A 1943 Senate Report called for immediate abolition of the BIA and unrestricted citizenship for all

Indians, in tones reminiscent of an earlier generation's attitudes toward solving the "Indian problem."

> While the original aim [of federal policy] was to make the Indian a citizen, the present aim appears to be to keep the Indian an Indian and to make him satisfied with all the limitations of a primitive life. We are striving mightily to help him recapture his ancient, worn-out cultures which are now a vague memory to him and are absolutely unable to function in his present world.

SECTION C. THE TERMINATION ERA (1945–1961)

A turnaround in congressional Indian policy resulted in the dramatic departure from the reforms spearheaded by John Collier that began in the earlier decades of the twentieth century. There were calls from Capitol Hill to repeal the IRA and to move away from the encouragement of tribal self-government as official federal policy. Collier, Commissioner of the BIA since 1933, resigned in 1945. Felix Cohen resigned from the Interior Department in 1948. In 1949 the Hoover Commission issued its Report on Indian Affairs, recommending an about-face in federal policy: "complete integration" of Indians should be the goal so that Indians would move "into the mass of the population as full, taxpaying citizens." Three dissenters, led by vice-chairman Dean Acheson, objected to the commission's recommendation of rapid assimilation on the basis of existing data. See generally Comm'n on Organization of the Executive Branch of the Government, Indian Affairs: A Report to Congress (1949).

The termination policy adopted by the federal government following these events had a major impact on the attitudes of subsequent generations of Indian leadership. Though now formally repudiated by the federal government, the memory of congressional committees and bureaucrats in Washington "terminating" the existence of hundreds of tribes across Indian country stands as a chilling reminder to Indian peoples that Congress can unilaterally decide to extinguish the special status and rights of tribes without Indian consent.

1. PASSAGE OF THE TERMINATION PROGRAM

Some described the new direction in Indian affairs as "emancipation" because it would "free" Indians from the oppressive, day-to-day control of the BIA over life on the reservations. The termination program was implemented in the 1950s and proved to bring many things other than "freedom" to Indian country.

GARY ORFIELD, A STUDY OF THE TERMINATION POLICY

(1966), Reprinted in Senate Comm. on Labor and Public Welfare, 91st Cong., 1st Sess.,
The Education of American Indians, Vol. 4 at 674–90.
(Comm. Reprint 1970).

"In view of the historic policy of Congress favoring freedom for the Indians, we may well expect future Congresses to continue to endorse the principle that 'as rapidly as possible' we should end the status of Indians as wards of the Government and grant them all the rights and prerogatives pertaining to American citizenship.

"With the aim of 'equality before the law' in mind our course should rightly be no other. Firm and constant consideration for those of Indian ancestry should lead us all to work diligently and carefully for the full realization of their national citizenship with all other Americans. Following in the footsteps of the Emancipation Proclamation of 94 years ago, I see the following words emblazoned in letters of fire above the heads of the Indians—" 'These people shall be free!' "

—SENATOR ARTHUR V. WATKINS

There is something un-American about the idea of reservations. In many parts of the country people feel a vague guilt about the "Indian problem" of their region. It is disturbing that a society which has achieved such a high degree of success in assimilating many minority groups has so often failed with the Indian peoples. Perhaps, some argue, the Government has been too protective, keeping the Indians apart from the rest of the country in reservations. Possibly it would be better if they were to enter the life of the cities, following the path of other ethnic groups. Perhaps Government paternalism should be ended, and the people should be given the same opportunity for successful assimilation which was offered to our ancestors.

The new Republican President took office in 1953 and carried with him majorities in both Houses of Congress. Seriously concerned with the danger of big government, Eisenhower warned, "Those who would stay free must stand eternal watch against excessive concentration of power in government." This sentiment was strongly echoed in Congress. The first year of the new administration saw the beginning of an extensive congressional effort to reduce the involvement of the Federal Government in Indian affairs, and thus to "free" the Indian people.

Congress did not long delay action. On June 9, 1953, Representative Harrison introduced House Concurrent Resolution 108. The resolution was seemingly innocuous, but actually a highly important statement expressing the "sense of Congress" in support of ending Federal supervision of Indian people "as rapidly as possible."

RESOLUTION 108

"Whereas it is the policy of Congress, as rapidly as possible to make the Indians within the territorial limits of the United States subject to the same laws and entitled to the same privileges and responsibilities as are applicable to other citizens of the United States, and to grant them all the rights and prerogatives pertaining to American citizenship; and

"Whereas the Indians within the territorial limits of the United States should assume their full responsibilities as American citizens: Now, therefore be it

"*Resolved by the House of Representatives (the Senate concurring),* That it is declared to be the sense of Congress that, at the earliest possible time, all of the Indian tribes and the individual members thereof located within the States of California, Florida, New York, and Texas, and all of the following named Indian tribes and individual members thereof, should be freed from Federal supervision and control and from all disabilities and limitations specially applicable to Indians. It is further declared to be the sense of Congress that the Secretary of the Interior should examine all existing legislation dealing with such Indians, and treaties between the Government of the United States and each such tribe, and report to Congress at the earliest practicable date, but not later than January 1, 1954, his recommendations for such legislation as, in his judgment, may be necessary to accomplish the purposes of this resolution."

The resolution was not controversial. It was considered by the Indian Affairs Subcommittee and the Interior Committee and favorably reported on July 15. The resolution was placed on the unanimous-consent calendar and reached the House floor on July 27. The measure aroused very little discussion. The committee accepted the one amendment offered, and there was no further debate. No one spoke in opposition to the resolution, and it was passed amid a long series of private bills. The resolution reached the Senate on July 28, and a total of 4 days was required for referral, committee action, and the submission of a committee report. Obviously the ground was well prepared. The Senate endorsed the resolution the day it was submitted, without a word spoken either in support or in opposition.

* * *

The Indian witnesses.—Deeply concerned with the proposed legislation, tribal delegates played an important role in most of the hearings. Members of the tribe under consideration participated in nine of the 13 hearings, some coming as tribal delegates and some on their own initiative. Tribes with large resources were able to pay the way of delegates and to send large groups. Three of the poorest tribes were unable to send a single member. "After an Indian tribe is far enough in poverty," said Senator Young, "you automatically do not hear from them any more, because they cannot come to Washington to testify."

* * *

Although the great majority of Indian spokesmen were opposed to the legislation, five of the hearings saw a division of opinion among the Indian witnesses. None of the tribes took a position clearly supporting the legislation, but there were substantial groups within several of the tribes which favored termination. Indian supporters and opponents of the legislation each developed several lines of argument. Those supporting the policy relied heavily upon the following arguments:

(1) That they desired to liquidate the reservation and to receive their personal share of the tribal property.

(2) That they wished freedom from Government control and regulation.

(3) That they wanted their property removed from trust status to allow them to mortgage or sell.

(4) That tribal or community ownership was socialistic or communistic.

* * *

The bulk of Indian testimony, however, was overwhelmingly in opposition to the legislation. The arguments presented can be classified into the following broad categories: (1) Financial concerns, (2) loss of rights and privileges established by treaties or by Federal law, (3) concern for the state of tribal preparedness, (4) procedural issues, and (5) emotional ties to their lands.

* * *

Academic experts.—The massive record of testimony on the termination bills is perhaps most surprising for what it fails to contain. In more than 1,700 pages of testimony there is no statement by a sociologist, an anthropologist, a social worker, or anyone else trained in the social sciences. Although most reservations have been studied by social scientists concerned with Indian acculturation, the only evidence presented to the committee was a letter from an economics student who had spent a summer on one reservation. Academics failed to either participate in the hearings or to submit written statements for the record.

* * *

NOTE

Termination policy is often equated with House Concurrent Resolution 108 and the acts terminating individual tribes. In fact, there were many other programs, all implementing the push toward rapid assimilation that had dramatic impacts on the tribes that were not singled out for termination. The best example of other assimilationist legislation during the termination era is

"Public Law 280," passed in 1953, in which Congress took the unprecedented step of passing general legislation extending state civil and criminal jurisdiction into Indian country. See Chapter 7C, infra. Other aspects of the comprehensive program enacted during the termination era include: the transfer of many educational responsibilities from the tribes and the federal government to the states; the transfer of Indian health responsibilities from the BIA to the Department of Health, Education and Welfare (now Health and Human Services); the establishment of the Indian Claims Commission in 1946, pages 306–312, infra; legislative and administrative inaction regarding reservation economic development; and continued relocation programs to encourage Indian migration from the reservations to urban areas. See generally II Francis Paul Prucha, The Great Father: The United States Government and the American Indians 1023–24, 1060–84 (1984).

Another episode of the termination era involved the "updating" of Felix Cohen's *Handbook of Federal Indian Law*. The original *Handbook*, described at pages 227–235, supra, proved to be one of the great treatises in all of the law; like Blackstone, Cohen sorted, analyzed, and compiled a mass of diffuse authorities in order to give Indian law a coherency and purpose it had previously lacked. It became, in Justice Frankfurter's words, "an acknowledged guide for the Supreme Court in Indian litigation." Felix Frankfurter, Of Law and Life and Other Things That Matter 143 (Philip B. Kurland, ed. 1965).

In the 1950s, Cohen's work became "embarrassing" because it so clearly recognized many tribal powers, including the power of self-government. In the termination years, the solution to such a problem was to "rewrite Cohen's book and discredit the original under the guise of a revision * * * . From a well-reasoned, balanced discussion of the countless undecided questions (most of which are still unresolved), the book deteriorated into a volume with a new and constant theme: the Federal Government's power over Indian affairs is plenary." *Foreword* to Felix S. Cohen, *Handbook of Federal Indian Law* v–vi (1941) (U.N.M. reprint, 1971).

The 1958 revision soon fell into disuse. A facsimile of the original 1941 work, which had become virtually unobtainable, was reprinted in its entirety by the University of New Mexico in 1971. A full revision of the treatise was completed in 1982. Felix S. Cohen, *Handbook of Federal Indian Law* (1982 ed.) The treatise has been most recently revised in Cohen's Handbook of Federal Indian Law (Nell Jessup Newton ed. 2012).

2. THE EFFECTS OF TERMINATION: SOME RIGHTS LOST; SOME RETAINED

CHARLES F. WILKINSON & ERIC R. BIGGS, THE EVOLUTION OF THE TERMINATION POLICY

5 Am. Indian L.Rev. 139, 151–54 (1977).

* * * Since HCR 108 was a statement of policy only, individual acts were needed to implement the policy in regard to specific tribes. The following table shows the individual acts in chronological order.

Group	Number	Acres	State	Authorizing statute (date)	Effective date
Menominee	3,270	233,881	Wisconsin	68 Stat. 250 (1954)	1961
Klamath	2,133	862,662	Oregon	68 Stat. 718 (1954)	1961
Western Oregon*	2,081	2,158	Oregon	68 Stat. 724 (1954)	1956
Alabama-Coushatta	450	3,200	Texas	68 Stat. 768 (1954)	1955
Mixed-blood Utes	490	211,430	Utah	68 Stat. 868 (1954)	1961
Southern Paiute	232	42,839	Utah	68 Stat. 1099 (1954)	1957
Lower Lake Rancheria	Unk.	Unk.	California	70 Stat. 58 (1956)	1956
Peoria	Unk.	Unk.	Oklahoma	70 Stat. 937 (1956)	1959
Ottawa	630	0	Oklahoma	70 Stat. 963 (1957)	1959
Coyote Valley Rancheria	Unk.	Unk.	California	71 Stat. 283 (1957)	1957
California Rancheria Act**	1,107	4,317	California	72 Stat. 619 (1958)	1961–70
Catawba	631	3,388	South Carolina	73 Stat. 592 (1959)	1962
Ponca	442	834	Nebraska	76 Stat. 429 (1962)	1966

* 61 tribes and bands. Figures listed are aggregates.

** 37 to 38 rancherias. Figures listed are aggregates.

This means that approximately 109 tribes and bands were terminated. A minimum of 1,362,155 acres and 11,466 individuals were affected. Statistics on Indian population are notoriously inaccurate, but no more than 3 per cent of all federally recognized Indians were involved. The total amount of Indian trust land was diminished by about 3.2 per cent.

After an individual termination act was passed, a third step was required before termination finally took effect. Each act directed the Secretary of Interior to develop a detailed termination plan for the tribe. Usually the difficult questions in the plans revolved around the transfer of land from trust status into private ownership. As is seen from the above chart, plans were often completed for the smaller tribes within a year or two after the individual acts were passed. The three tribes with the largest land holdings—the Menominee, the Klamaths, and the mixed-blood Utes— all had plans with lengthy provisions for complicated trusts or private corporations. The Menominee plan, for example, was enormously complex: it was 30 pages long (miniscule type, three columns to a page) in the *Federal Register*. Those three plans were not made final until 1961, seven years after the individual acts were passed.

The effects of the termination program can be best appreciated by analyzing these individual acts and plans. Those documents were very different from the glossy euphemisms used by Congress to describe termination: it was purportedly a program to "free" Indians from federal supervision and to eliminate "restrictions deemed discriminatory" against Indians. In fact, termination did little to promote "freedom" or to root out "discrimination." Termination ended the special federal-tribal relationship almost completely and transferred almost all responsibilities for, and powers over, affected Indians from the federal government to the states. The historic special Indian status came to an abrupt end for terminated individual Indians and tribes.

More specifically, these basic elements were common to all of the individual congressional acts and administrative plans:

1.   *Fundamental changes in land ownership patterns were made.* For most of the smaller tribes, all land was simply appraised and sold to the highest bidder, with the proceeds going to the tribe. For the Klamaths, members were given a choice between immediate payment and participation in a private trust. Most Klamaths chose immediate sale and 600,000 acres were sold in 1961. Most of the remaining private trust land has also now been sold. For the mixed-blood Utes and the Menominee, state corporations were established. The Ute land has now been sold. The Menominee land is now back in trust, as a result of the tribe's restoration in 1973, but 9,500 acres were sold in the 1960's to pay corporate bills.

2.   *The trust relationship was ended.* This means that federal expertise would be unavailable for land and resource management. There would no longer be federal protections against the sale of land.

3.   *State legislative jurisdiction was imposed.* With few exceptions, on federally recognized reservations only tribal

councils and Congress have power to pass laws. After termination, state legislatures and county boards would have broad authority over such basic matters as education, adoptions, alcoholism, land use, and other fundamental areas of social and economic concern.

4. *State judicial authority was imposed.* On federally recognized reservations, except for so-called "Public Law 280" reservations, federal and tribal courts hear almost all cases; state courts have extremely limited jurisdiction. After termination, all criminal and civil cases went to state court. The imposition of state legislative and judicial authority is an especially crucial factor. Indians have always argued for federal and tribal authority over reservation Indians because of long-standing discriminatory practices by local officials. Reliable authorities indicate that those claims of local hostility are warranted. Termination took away the buffer of federal and tribal law.

5. *All exemptions from state taxing authority were ended.* The power to tax is part of the state's legislative jurisdiction, discussed above, but is so important that it deserves to be treated separately. Indian tribes and individual members enjoy almost total immunity from state tax laws when in Indian country, which usually means within the boundaries of a federally recognized reservation. The states do not suffer financially—the federal government provides substantial *in lieu* payments to compensate for the lost tax revenue. That immunity, which often resulted from federal treaties and meant much to Indian tribes and individuals, was abolished by termination.

6. *All special federal programs to tribes were discontinued.* There are an increasing number of federal programs available only to federally recognized tribes. They include training, housing, recreation, and business grants and contracts.

7. *All special federal programs to individuals were discontinued.* These substantial programs provide members of federally recognized tribes much-needed health, education, and welfare assistance. These programs, like the tribal programs, are available only to federally recognized Indians, not to the general non-Indian population. Neither are they available to terminated tribes and individuals.

8. *Tribal sovereignty was effectively ended.* Indian tribes have inherent sovereignty and nothing in the termination acts expressly extinguished that governmental authority. Nevertheless, the loss of the land base meant that in most cases the tribe had no geographic area over which to exert jurisdiction. * * * Thus the terminated tribes were effectively

stripped of their broad powers to act as governments. Tribal sovereignty, more than any single legal doctrine, has contributed to the exciting developments on Indian reservations in the 1970's; one writer has aptly described tribal sovereignty as a "cornucopia"—but not for terminated tribes.

In return, individual tribal members received a check for the value of their land. In most instances, the payments amounted to little, although the withdrawing Klamaths received payments of $43,000 in 1961. The check did not compensate for the loss of federal benefits or the new tax burdens. It could not pay for the loss of tribal governmental authority, or compensate for the discrimination that followed in the state agencies and courts. Perhaps most tragic of all, the check could not possibly pay for the psychological costs of "not being an Indian any more."

* * *

MENOMINEE TRIBE OF INDIANS V. UNITED STATES

Supreme Court of the United States, 1968.
391 U.S. 404, 88 S.Ct. 1705, 20 L.Ed.2d 697.

MR. JUSTICE DOUGLAS delivered the opinion of the Court.

The Menominee Tribe of Indians was granted a reservation in Wisconsin by the Treaty of Wolf River in 1854. By this treaty the Menominees retroceded certain lands they had acquired under an earlier treaty and the United States confirmed to them the Wolf River Reservation "for a home, to be held as Indian lands are held." Nothing was said in the 1854 treaty about hunting and fishing rights. Yet we agree with the Court of Claims[1] that the language "to be held as Indian lands are held" includes the right to fish and to hunt. The record shows that the lands covered by the Wolf River Treaty of 1854 were selected precisely because they had an abundance of game. The essence of the Treaty of Wolf River was that the Indians were authorized to maintain on the new lands ceded to them as a reservation their way of life which included hunting and fishing.

What the precise nature and extent of those hunting and fishing rights were we need not at this time determine. For the issue tendered by the present decision of the Court of Claims is whether those rights, whatever their precise extent, have been extinguished.

That issue arose because, beginning in 1962, Wisconsin took the position that the Menominees were subject to her hunting and fishing regulations. Wisconsin prosecuted three Menominees for violating those regulations and the Wisconsin Supreme Court held that the state regulations were valid, as the hunting and fishing rights of the

---

[1] *Menominee Tribe of Indians v. United States*, 179 Ct.Cl. 496, 503–504, 388 F.2d 998, 1002.

Menominees had been abrogated by Congress in the Menominee Indian Termination Act of 1954. 25 U.S.C. §§ 891–902.

Thereupon the tribe brought suit in the Court of Claims against the United States to recover just compensation for the loss of those hunting and fishing rights. The Court of Claims by a divided vote held that the tribe possessed hunting and fishing rights under the Wolf River Treaty; but it held, contrary to the Wisconsin Supreme Court, that those rights were not abrogated by the Termination Act of 1954. We granted the petition for a writ of certiorari in order to resolve that conflict between the two courts. On oral argument both petitioner and respondent urged that the judgment of the Court of Claims be affirmed. The State of Wisconsin appeared as *amicus curiae* and argued that the judgment be reversed.

In 1953 Congress by concurrent resolution instructed the Secretary of the Interior to recommend legislation for the withdrawal of federal supervision over certain American Indian tribes, including the Menominees. Several bills were offered, one for the Menominee Tribe that expressly preserved hunting and fishing rights. But the one that became the Termination Act of 1954, viz., H.R. 2828, did not mention hunting and fishing rights. Moreover, counsel for the Menominees spoke against the bill, arguing that its silence would by implication abolish those hunting and fishing rights. It is therefore argued that they were abolished by the Termination Act.

The purpose of the 1954 Act was by its terms "to provide for orderly termination of Federal supervision over the property and members" of the tribe. Under its provisions, the tribe was to formulate a plan for future control of tribal property and service functions theretofore conducted by the United States. On or before April 30, 1961, the Secretary was to transfer to a tribal corporation or to a trustee chosen by him all property real and personal held in trust for the tribe by the United States.

The Menominees submitted a plan, looking toward the creation of a county in Wisconsin out of the former reservation and the creation by the Indians of a Wisconsin corporation to hold other property of the tribe and its members. The Secretary of the Interior approved the plan with modifications; the Menominee Enterprises, Inc., was incorporated; and numerous ancillary laws were passed by Wisconsin integrating the former reservation into its county system of government. The Termination Act provided that after the transfer by the Secretary of title to the property of the tribe, all federal supervision was to end and "the laws of the several States shall apply to the tribe and its members in the same manner as they apply to other citizens or persons within their jurisdiction."

It is therefore argued with force that the Termination Act of 1954, which became fully effective in 1961, submitted the hunting and fishing rights of the Indians to state regulation and control. We reach, however, the opposite conclusion. The same Congress that passed the Termination Act also passed Public Law 280, as amended, 18 U.S.C. § 1162. The latter came out of the same committees of the Senate and the House as did the Termination Act; and it was amended in a way that is critical here only two months after the Termination Act became law. As amended, Public Law 280 granted designated States, including Wisconsin, jurisdiction "over offenses committed by or against Indians in the areas of Indian country" named in the Act, which in the case of Wisconsin was described as "All Indian country within the State." But Public Law 280 went on to say that "Nothing in this section . . . shall deprive any Indian or any Indian tribe, band, or community of any right, privilege, or immunity afforded under Federal treaty, agreement, or statute *with respect to hunting, trapping, or fishing* or the control, licensing, or regulation thereof." (Emphasis added.) That provision on its face contains no limitation; it protects any hunting, trapping, or fishing right granted by a federal treaty. Public Law 280, as amended, became the law in 1954, nearly seven years *before* the Termination Act became fully effective in 1961. In 1954, when Public Law 280 became effective, the Menominee Reservation was still "Indian country" within the meaning of Public Law 280.

Public Law 280 must therefore be considered *in pari materia* with the Termination Act. The two Acts read together mean to us that, although federal supervision of the tribe was to cease and all tribal property was to be transferred to new hands, the hunting and fishing rights granted or preserved by the Wolf River Treaty of 1854 survived the Termination Act of 1954.

This construction is in accord with the overall legislative plan. The Termination Act by its terms provided for the "orderly termination of Federal *supervision* over the property and members" of the tribe. 25 U.S.C. § 891. (Emphasis added.) The Federal Government ceded to the State of Wisconsin its power of supervision over the tribe and the reservation lands, as evident from the provision of the Termination Act that the laws of Wisconsin "shall apply to the tribe and its members in the same manner as they apply to other citizens or persons within [its] jurisdiction."

The provision of the Termination Act (25 U.S.C. § 899) that "all statutes of the United States which affect Indians because of their status as Indians shall no longer be applicable to the members of the tribe" plainly refers to the termination of federal supervision. The use of the word "statutes" is potent evidence that no *treaty* was in mind.

We decline to construe the Termination Act as a backhanded way of abrogating the hunting and fishing rights of these Indians. While the power to abrogate those rights exists (see Lone Wolf v. Hitchcock, 187 U.S. 553, 564–567) "the intention to abrogate or modify a treaty is not to be lightly imputed to the Congress." Pigeon River, etc., Co. v. Charles W. Cox, Limited, 291 U.S. 138, 160. See also Squire v. Capoeman, 351 U.S. 1.

Our conclusion is buttressed by the remarks of the legislator chiefly responsible for guiding the Termination Act to enactment, Senator Watkins, who stated upon the occasion of the signing of the bill that it "in no way violates any treaty obligation with this tribe."

We find it difficult to believe that Congress, without explicit statement, would subject the United States to a claim for compensation by destroying property rights conferred by treaty, particularly when Congress was purporting by the Termination Act to settle the Government's financial obligations toward the Indians.[15]

Accordingly the judgment of the Court of Claims is

Affirmed.

MR. JUSTICE MARSHALL took no part in the consideration or decision of this case.

MR. JUSTICE STEWART, with whom MR. JUSTICE BLACK joins, dissenting.

* * *

The statute is plain on its face: after termination the Menominees are fully subject to state laws just as other citizens are, and no exception is made for hunting and fishing laws. Nor does the legislative history contain any indication that Congress intended to say anything other than what the unqualified words of the statute express.[2] In fact two bills which would have explicitly preserved hunting and fishing rights were rejected in favor of the bill ultimately adopted—a bill which was opposed by counsel for the Menominees because it failed to preserve their treaty rights.[5]

---

[15] Compare the hearings on the Klamath Termination bill, which took place shortly before the Menominee bills were reached, in which Senator Watkins expressed the view that perhaps the Government should "buy out" the Indians' hunting and fishing rights rather than preserve them after termination. See Joint Hearings, Subcommittees of the Committees on Interior and Insular Affairs, 83d Cong., 2d Sess., Pt. 4, on S. 2745 and H.R. 7320, pp. 254–255.

[2] I cannot attach any significant weight to an offhand remark in a speech made by one Senator after the enactment of the bill. [Ed. The reference is to Senator Watkins' remark quoted near the end of the majority opinion.]

It is, of course, irrelevant that the legislative history reveals no intention by the Congress to incur a financial obligation to the Menominees. If what the Congress did took away the Menominees' property rights, then regardless of congressional intent they are entitled to compensation from the United States for the taking.

[5] "I think it is clear that [the bill] does affect those treaty rights and that those treaties are abrogated. Certainly it abolishes the tribal right to exclusive hunting and fishing privileges, because automatically upon the final termination date, the Menominee Reservation so far as hunting and fishing is concerned, would become subject to the laws of Wisconsin." Joint Hearings on S. 2813, H.R. 2828, and H.R. 7135, Subcommittees of Committees on Interior and Insular Affairs, 83d Cong., 2d Sess., Pt. 6, pp. 692, 708.

The Court today holds that the Termination Act does not mean what it says. The Court's reason for reaching this remarkable result is that it finds "*in pari materia*" another statute which, I submit, has nothing whatever to do with this case.

That statute, Public Law 280, 18 U.S.C. § 1162 and 28 U.S.C. § 1360, granted to certain States, including Wisconsin, general jurisdiction over "Indian country" within their boundaries. Several exceptions to the general grant were enumerated, including an exception from the grant of criminal jurisdiction for treaty-based hunting and fishing rights. 18 U.S.C. § 1162(b). But this case does not deal with state jurisdiction over Indian country; it deals with state jurisdiction over Indians after Indian country has been terminated. Whereas Public Law 280 provides for the continuation of the special hunting and fishing rights while a reservation exists, the Termination Act provides for the applicability of all state laws without exception after the reservation has disappeared.

The Termination Act by its very terms provides:

> "[A]ll statutes of the United States which affect Indians because of their status as Indians shall no longer be applicable to the members of the tribe . . . " 25 U.S.C. § 899.

Public Law 280 is such a statute. It has no application to the Menominees now that their reservation is gone.

The 1854 Treaty granted the Menominees special hunting and fishing rights. The 1954 Termination Act, by subjecting the Menominees without exception to state law, took away those rights. The Menominees are entitled to compensation.

I would reverse the judgment of the Court of Claims.

NOTES

1.   Was there a case or controversy in light of the fact that both the tribe and the United States agreed that the tribe should receive no compensation? Was it appropriate for an *appellant* (the Menominee Tribe) to request that the decision of the lower court (the Court of Claims) be *affirmed*?

2.   In Kimball v. Callahan, 493 F.2d 564 (9th Cir.1974), cert. denied 419 U.S. 1019 (1974) (*Kimball I*), five members of the Klamath Tribe who had withdrawn under the tribe's termination plan claimed that they retained treaty rights to hunt, trap, and fish free from state regulation on their former reservation lands. The lands had been sold, mostly to the United States for national forest purposes, in order to pay withdrawing members for their share in tribal property. The court held, following the decision in *Menominee Tribe v. United States*, that the claimed rights were created by treaty and "that a Klamath Indian possessing such rights on the former reservation at the time of its enactment retains them even though he relinquishes his tribal

membership or the reservation shrinks pursuant to the Act." 493 F.2d at 569. In so doing the court refused to distinguish *Menominee* on the grounds that, unlike the Menominees, the Klamaths were given a choice whether or not to withdraw and, further, that the Klamaths no longer occupied the former reservation lands. The opinion found that the reasoning of *Menominee* transcended these differences, bolstering its conclusion by adding that Congress had refused to heed Senator Watkins' suggestion that it "buy out" Klamath's hunting and fishing rights after termination rather than preserving them. *Kimball I* expressly overruled Klamath and Modoc Tribes v. Maison, 338 F.2d 620 (9th Cir.1964), a pre-*Menominee* decision rejecting claims of certain remaining (non-withdrawing) Klamaths to a right to hunt and fish on former reservation lands.

In *Kimball II,* the Court of Appeals resolved further questions of tribal authority and membership. The court held that the Klamath Tribe continued to exist in spite of the termination legislation, that termination did not affect the sovereign authority of the tribe to regulate the exercise of tribal treaty rights, and that descendants of persons on the "final" 1957 tribal roll were entitled to exercise treaty rights as tribal members. But the court went on to say that state regulation of hunting and fishing would be permitted if it were required for conservation. Kimball v. Callahan, 590 F.2d 768 (9th Cir.1979), cert. denied 444 U.S. 826 (1979). The tribe reopened its tribal rolls and began to regulate its treaty rights through the Klamath Indian Game Commission. It has not been necessary for the state to regulate Klamath hunting for conservation.

3.   The Ute Termination Act of 1954, 25 U.S.C.A. §§ 677–677aa, divided the tribe into two groups—the mixed bloods, who were terminated, and the full bloods, who were not. The full bloods continue as a federally-recognized tribe and possess the Uintah and Ouray Reservation in Utah. The Tenth Circuit, following *Menominee* and *Kimball I,* upheld the right of mixed blood Utes to hunt and fish on the reservation. Both the United States and the Ute Tribe— the full bloods—had argued that the rights had been abrogated. See United States v. Felter, 752 F.2d 1505 (10th Cir.1985).

4.   Several termination acts authorized the creation of individual trusts, administered by banks, to manage the financial affairs of tribal members who were minors or found to be "incompetent" by the BIA. Members of the Klamath and Menominee Tribes attacked the trusts as being beyond the scope of Congress' power and as constituting racial discrimination. Those arguments were rejected, the courts finding that Congress can determine whether termination shall be "complete or only partial" and that the trusts were aspects of a "continuing partial guardianship" over the affairs of those individuals. The mandatory trusts were not, therefore, discrimination on the basis of race because they were set up under laws enacted by Congress in its capacity as "guardian" for its Indian "wards." See Crain v. First National Bank, 324 F.2d 532 (9th Cir.1963), and Otradovec v. First Wisconsin Trust, 454 F.2d 1258 (7th Cir.1972).

It may be that a "continuing, partial guardianship" exists after termination in areas other than these individual trust arrangements. Since *Menominee* and *Kimball I* held that treaty rights to hunt and fish survived termination, does that mean that the federal government is a trustee and that a terminated tribe, like a federally recognized tribe, is entitled to federal protection of its fish and game resources? Such reasoning was apparently the basis of a contract entered into by the Department of Interior and the Klamath Tribe; the United States provided funds so that the tribe could establish a game code, court system, and a corps of tribal police to implement the tribal hunting and fishing rights recognized in *Kimball I*.

5.   "Termination" of a tribe, if applied literally, may suggest that a terminated tribe no longer exists as a cultural or legal entity. Does this mean that a terminated tribe no longer has standing in court, eligibility for grants, or contractual capacity? One answer is that Congress can terminate only the federal-tribal relationship, not the tribe itself. See Menominee Tribe v. United States, 388 F.2d 998, 1000–01 (Ct.Cl.1967), affirmed 391 U.S. 404 (1968). The fact that tribal existence is independent of current federal administrative recognition is also supported by Joint Tribal Council of the Passamaquoddy Tribe v. Morton, 528 F.2d 370 (1st Cir.1975), pages 330–331, infra, where the court found that the Passamaquoddy Tribe is a "tribe" within the meaning of the Non-Intercourse Act whether or not the tribe had ever been officially recognized by some action of federal officials. Thus the Ninth Circuit said in *Kimball II*:

> Although the [Klamath Termination] Act terminated federal supervision over trust and restricted property of the Klamath Indians, disposed of federally owned property, and terminated federal services to the Indians, it specifically contemplated the continuing existence of the Klamath Tribe. It did not affect the power of the tribe to take any action under its constitution and bylaws consistent with the Act. The Klamaths still maintain a tribal constitution and tribal government, which among other things establishes criteria for membership in the Tribe. The tribal roll created by the Act was for purposes of determining who should share in the resulting distribution of property. [*Kimball I*] held that the Act did not abrogate tribal treaty rights of hunting, fishing, and trapping. Neither did the Act affect the sovereign authority of the Tribe to regulate the exercise of those rights.

6.   In California, several tribes and bands directly attacked the California Rancheria Act of 1958, 72 Stat. 619, which contemplated the termination of 38 rancherias, i.e., reservations. Section 3(c) of the Act provided that the Secretary was required, among other things, to install irrigation and domestic water systems for the rancherias before implementing the Act. Such facilities were not installed at the Robinson Rancheria. A district judge held that the installation of proper facilities was a condition precedent to termination and that the 1964 secretarial plan for terminating the rancheria was void. Duncan v. Andrus, 517 F.Supp. 1 (N.D.Cal.1977). Other California

cases ordering "judicial restoration" include Table Bluff Band of Indians v. Andrus, 532 F.Supp. 255 (N.D.Cal.1981); Smith v. United States, 5 Indian L.Rep. F–73, 5 Indian L.Rep. F–157 (N.D.Cal.1978); and Daniels v. United States, 5 Indian L.Rep. F–73 (N.D.Cal.1978). The latter two cases both involved the Hopland Rancheria. The United States in 1980 acknowledged its formal relationship with the Hopland Band and the next year the band adopted a constitution and created a governing body. It then brought an action in the Court of Claims for money damages against the United States for losses of lands conveyed and of federal benefits. The Court of Appeals held the action should be dismissed because it was not brought within the six-year statute of limitations (before 1980, while the tribe was unrecognized). Hopland Band of Pomo Indians v. United States, 855 F.2d 1573 (Fed.Cir.1988).

7.   The Menominees sued in the Court of Claims for damages caused by termination. The court ruled that relief could be based only on improper administrative action, not on Congress's passage of the act itself because the court did not have jurisdiction over a claim for a congressional breach of trust when the act was valid and constitutional under Congress's broad power over Indian affairs. Menominee Tribe v. United States, 607 F.2d 1335 (Ct.Cl.1979), cert. denied 445 U.S. 950 (1980). The Federal Circuit later held that the Interior Department's restrictions on land use, such as the administrative implementation of the Act's requirement of sustained-yield management of the tribe's timber resource, did not conflict with the Termination Act. Menominee Tribe v. United States, 726 F.2d 712 (Fed.Cir.1983), cert. denied 469 U.S. 826 (1984).

REPEALING THE ACT TERMINATING FEDERAL SUPERVISION OVER THE PROPERTY AND MEMBERS OF THE MENOMINEE INDIAN TRIBE OF WISCONSIN
H.R. Report 93–572, 93d Cong., 1st Sess. (1973).

* * *

By the Act of June 18, 1954, as amended, the Congress provided that the termination of special Federal services and the grant to the Menominee Indians of full control over their affairs would be accomplished no later than April, 1961.

The plan adopted by the tribe provided for the incorporation of a profit corporation under Wisconsin State law, known as Menominee Enterprises, Inc., to take title to the lands and assets of the tribe and to operate the tribal sawmill. One hundred shares of stock in the Corporation and one income bond was issued to each member of the tribe on the final roll. The stock was held and voted by an eleven-member Menominee Common Stock and Voting Trust elected by the membership.

This plan brought the Menominee people to the brink of economic, social and cultural disaster. The sawmill operation, which supported the tribe and most of the Federal services prior to termination, is now only marginally successful. Menominee Enterprises, Inc., saddled with a huge corporate indebtedness, a difficult management scheme, and high county and state taxation, is on the verge of bankruptcy. In order to meet its tax burden, pay interest on the income bonds, and continue to operate the mill on a marginal basis, the Corporation has had to sell portions of its land, which has had a traumatic effect on the tribe.

Only recently have the Menominee people been able to gain some measure of control of their own affairs from a corporate structure that has been dominated and controlled by non-Menominee persons. With a growing awareness of the state to which termination has brought them, the Menominee people have mounted a forceful effort to reimpose a Federal trust on their remaining lands and to restore special Federal services. Among those tribes that were subjected to the termination policy, the Menominee have uniquely retained intact most of their land base and have maintained a cohesive tribal identity and community.

Unless this bill is enacted, the dim future of the tribe is made clear in the concluding paragraph of an extensive report of the Bureau of Indian Affairs to the 93d Congress. The Report states:

> The economic instability of MEI (Menominee Enterprises, Incorporated) combined with the elimination of public funds to the county make the situation perilous. Unless relief is made immediately available in the form of either a massive infusion of public funds or restoration, MEI will no longer be economically viable and Menominee County will go under.

Repeal of the Menominee termination act and restoration of Federal services and the Federal trust will prevent the collapse predicted in the Bureau of Indian Affairs report.

* * *

NOTES

1.   The Menominee Restoration Act was enacted on December 22, 1973. 25 U.S.C.A. §§ 903–903f. The Klamath Tribe of Oregon, which possessed the largest reservation terminated by Congress (68 Stat. 718 (1967)), was restored in 1986. 25 U.S.C.A. §§ 566 et seq. Numerous other tribes have also been restored.

2.   Termination provides an especially good opportunity for analyzing the variations in the relationship between Indian tribes and the federal government depending on current policy. For instance, the Menominee Tribe in 1954 (the year the Termination Act was passed but before it became effective) was effectively run by the BIA. There was a tribal General Council, but it was only advisory to the BIA. An "advisory committee" of tribal members was established to make minor decisions and to provide advice to the BIA when the General Council was not in session. BIA employees administered all federal

programs. Once termination became effective in 1961, there was no tribal council. The tribe's land holdings of some 234,000 acres came under the ownership of Menominee Enterprises, Inc. (MEI), a Wisconsin corporation. MEI was the business arm of the tribe. Because full jurisdiction had been transferred to the State of Wisconsin, there was no role for a tribal political entity during the years of termination. Once the tribe was restored by act of Congress in 1973, the federal-tribal relationship was reinstituted. Tribal and federal jurisdiction was re-established, and the tribe and its members became eligible for federal services. A new constitution was adopted and a tribal legislature and tribal business enterprise began operating. Today, the tribal court handles thousands of cases, including civil actions with non-Indian parties as plaintiffs or defendants. The BIA plays a much more limited role: under a "trust agreement" negotiated by the tribe with the BIA, most decisions are made by the tribe and most BIA services are delivered by the tribe under contract with the BIA.

SECTION D. THE ERA OF SELF-DETERMINATION (1961–PRESENT)

1. A REACTION TO TERMINATION

Ironically, termination, which was originally designed as an effort once and for all to detribalize the American Indian, worked precisely the opposite effect. The policy awakened Indians to the historical realization that more often than not, federal policy had been directed toward the destruction of tribalism, and that only tribal control of Indian policy and lasting guarantees of sovereignty could assure tribal survival in the United States.

The crises in Indian country engendered by the threat of termination thus galvanized Indian leadership nationally, demonstrating the vital necessity of united action and organizational structures. The effect was to create what Professor Stephen Cornell has called, a "supratribal consciousness." The National Congress of American Indians (NCAI) was a "supratribal" entity organized in the Mid-1940s. It convened an emergency conference in Washington in 1954 to protest the congressional move toward termination, seen by many Indians as the greatest threat to tribal existence since the end of military action against them.

* * * Both substance and method were at issue. Not only did many Indians oppose the overtly assimilationist nature of termination, with its attendant losses of land and federal protection, but they were incensed at the lack of Indian input into either policy making or implementation, a mockery of the spirit of the Indian New Deal. The IRA may not have been satisfactory, but termination was no improvement. On the contrary, in its disregard for Indian

viewpoints, treaty rights, and the survival of tribal communities, it seemed a colossal step backward.

The result was a major shot in the supratribal arm. Nancy Lurie has argued that it was not until the 1950s and termination that many Indians became fully aware of "the diametrical opposition between Indian and white objectives," of the essentially ideological confrontation between assimilationism on the one hand and the commitment many Indians still felt to preservation of nation and community on the other. "A common Indian opposition was spontaneously evoked" as the implications of the new policy became clear. Termination had touched a nerve, drawing Indian groups and leadership together in a concerted effort—much of it waged through the NCAI—to defeat or modify the termination program. In the summer of 1961, when nearly five hundred Indians from seventy tribes gathered in Chicago for the American Indian Chicago Conference, they had in common, wrote d'Arcy McNickle, an anthropologist who was one of them, "a sense of being under attack, and it was this shared experience which drew them together." In its concluding statement the conference rejected termination and asserted the right of Indian communities to choose their own ways of life. It was the largest multitribal gathering in decades, the most striking evidence to date of a supratribal consciousness making its way into politics.

And it had an effect. It was a long struggle, but the opposition to termination gradually grew. State governments, at first in favor, had second thoughts once they realized what was involved in assuming responsibilities once borne by the feds, while other critics attacked the lack of Indian input and the haste with which the policy was adopted. In 1958, signaling the beginnings of retreat, the secretary of the interior called termination without tribal consent—once official practice—"unthinkable," although termination remained government policy for another decade. But by the early 1960s Indian and non-Indian protest, coupled with the policy's failure to deal effectively with Indian problems, had killed its momentum.

Stephen Cornell, The Return of the Native 123–24 (1988).

With the abandonment in practice of the termination policy in the early 1960s—the Kennedy Administration took no affirmative action to terminate tribes—federal Indian policy once more entered a period of gradual transformation. The Great Society programs of the Johnson years in the Mid-1960s embraced Indian tribes and invested millions of dollars in reservation social programs and infrastructure. Programs such as the Economic Opportunity Act recognized the permanency of Indian tribes and the importance of social investment in reservation communities. In 1968, President Johnson delivered a special message to Congress entitled "The Forgotten Americans." This was apparently the first special message by any President to Congress solely on Indian affairs. See generally S. Lyman Tyler, A History of Indian Policy 200–14 (1973); Angie Debo, A History of the Indians of the United States 405–13 (1970).

In 1970, Richard M. Nixon issued a landmark statement calling for a new federal policy of "self-determination" for Indian nations.

2.　PRESIDENT NIXON'S MESSAGE TO CONGRESS

MESSAGE FROM THE PRESIDENT OF THE UNITED STATES TRANSMITTING RECOMMENDATIONS FOR INDIAN POLICY

H.R.Doc. No. 91–363, 91st Cong., 2d Sess. (July 8 1970).

To the Congress of the United States:

* * *

It is long past time that the Indian policies of the Federal government began to recognize and build upon the capacities and insights of the Indian people. Both as a matter of justice and as a matter of enlightened social policy, we must begin to act on the basis of what the Indians themselves have long been telling us. The time has come to break decisively with the past and to create the conditions for a new era in which the Indian future is determined by Indian acts and Indian decisions.

SELF-DETERMINATION WITHOUT TERMINATION

The first and most basic question that must be answered with respect to Indian policy concerns the historic and legal relationship between the Federal government and Indian communities. In the past, this relationship has oscillated between two equally harsh and unacceptable extremes.

On the one hand, it has—at various times during previous Administrations—been the stated policy objective of both the Executive and Legislative branches of the Federal government eventually to terminate the trusteeship relationship between the Federal government and the Indian people. As recently as August of 1953, in House Concurrent Resolution 108, the Congress declared that termination was the long-range goal of its Indian policies. This would mean that Indian tribes would eventually lose any special standing they had under Federal law: the tax exempt status of their lands would be discontinued; Federal responsibility for their economic and social well-being would be repudiated; and the tribes themselves would be effectively dismantled. Tribal property would be divided among individual members who would then be assimilated into the society at large.

This policy of forced termination is wrong, in my judgment * * * .

* * *

This * * * must be the goal of any new national policy toward the Indian people: to strengthen the Indian's sense of autonomy without threatening his sense of community. We must assure the Indian that he can assume control of his own life without being separated involuntarily from the tribal group. And we must make it clear that Indians can become independent of Federal control without being cut off from Federal concern and Federal support. My specific recommendations to the Congress are designed to carry out this policy.

1. Rejecting termination.

Because termination is morally and legally unacceptable, because it produces bad practical results, and because the mere threat of termination tends to discourage greater self-sufficiency among Indian groups, I am asking the Congress to pass a new Concurrent Resolution which would expressly renounce, repudiate and repeal the termination policy as expressed in House Concurrent Resolution 108 of the 83rd Congress. * * *

2. The right to control and operate Federal programs * * * .

Federal support programs for non-Indian communities—hospitals and schools are two ready examples—are ordinarily administered by local authorities. There is no reason why Indian communities should be deprived of the privilege of self-determination merely because they receive monetary support from the Federal government. Nor should they lose Federal money because they reject Federal control.

For years we have talked about encouraging Indians to exercise greater self-determination, but our progress has never been commensurate with our promises. Part of the reason for this situation has been the threat of termination. But another reason is the fact that when a decision is made as to whether a Federal program will be turned over to Indian administration, it is the Federal authorities and not the Indian people who finally make that decision.

This situation should be reversed. In my judgment, it should be up to the Indian tribe to determine whether it is willing and able to assume administrative responsibility for a service program which is presently administered by a Federal agency. * * *

* * *

4. Indian Education

* * * Consistent with our policy that the Indian community should have the right to take over the control and operation of federally funded programs, we believe every Indian community wishing to do so should be able to control its own Indian schools. This control would be exercised by

school boards selected by Indians and functioning much like other school boards throughout the nation. * * *

* * *

THE WHITE HOUSE, JULY 8, 1970
RICHARD NIXON

NOTE

The ideas in Nixon's text were not new, but the widely cited message, with its remarkable force and specificity, served as a catalyst. Several of the proposals were adopted by Congress, in a form surprisingly close to Nixon's guidelines. See generally Daniel H. Israel, *The Reemergence of Tribal Nationalism and Its Impact on Reservation Resource Development*, 47 U.Colo.L.Rev. 617, 624–29 (1976). The Indian Education Act of 1972, 20 U.S.C.A. §§ 241aa, 887c, 1211a, and other reforms in the area of Indian education are discussed in Daniel M. Rosenfelt, *Toward a More Coherent Policy for Funding Indian Education*, Law & Contemp.Probs., (Winter 1976) at 190. Several Nixon proposals not included in the above excerpt were also carried out. The Indian Financing Act of 1974, codified at 25 U.S.C.A. § 1451–1453 and other scattered sections of 25 U.S.C.A., sought to enhance tribal economies through tribal economic development. The Taos Pueblo of New Mexico regained its sacred Blue Lake. Act of December 15, 1970, Pub.L. No. 91–550, 84 Stat. 1437.

The principal legislative initiative to emerge from the Nixon proposals, the Indian Self-Determination and Education Assistance Act of 1975, 25 U.S.C.A. §§ 450a–450n, gives express authority to the Secretaries of Interior and Health and Human Services to contract with, and make grants to, Indian tribes and other Indian organizations for the delivery of federal services. The Act reflects a fundamental philosophical change concerning the administration of Indian affairs: tribal programs are funded by the federal government, but the programs should be planned and administered by the tribes themselves; federal "domination" should end. See Declaration of Policy, 25 U.S.C.A. § 450a. The most important features of the Act are found at 25 U.S.C.A. § 450f (as amended):

> (a)(1) The Secretary is directed, upon the request of any Indian tribe by tribal resolution, to enter into a self-determination contract or contracts with a tribal organization to plan, conduct, and administer programs, or portions thereof * * * for the benefit of Indians because of their status as Indians * * * .

> (b) Whenever the Secretary declines to enter into a contract or contracts pursuant to subsection (a) of this section, he shall (1) state any objections in writing to the tribal organization, (2) provide assistance to the tribal organization to overcome the stated objections, and (3) provide the tribal organization with a hearing on

the record and the opportunity for appeal on the objections raised, under such rules and regulations as the Secretary may promulgate.

3. CONGRESSIONAL RESPONSE AND NEW TRIBAL RESPONSIBILITIES

Despite some critics' skeptical views of the new federal policy of Indian self-determination formally inaugurated by President Nixon's 1970 Message to Congress, see, e.g., Jack Forbes, Native Americans and Nixon 120–24 (1981), Indian tribes benefited significantly on many fronts during this era of reform. The social, political, and legal activism of Indian leaders and their advocates in the 1950s, 60s and 70s resulted in an unprecedented volume of Indian legislation, most of it favorable to Indian interests, and all of it enacted at the behest of tribes or at least with their participation.

The Indian Child Welfare Act of 1978, 25 U.S.C.A. §§ 1901–1963 (ICWA), is by any standard, one of the most significant and meaningful pieces of legislation addressing indigenous peoples' human rights concerns. The ICWA provides a comprehensive scheme for the adjudication of child custody cases involving Indian children that defers heavily to tribal governments. See pages 680–718, infra.

The American Indian Religious Freedom Act of 1978, section 2, codified at 42 U.S.C.A. § 1996, as a policy statement on traditional Indian religions has proven much less significant than originally hoped in terms of providing protection to Indian religious practices and beliefs harmed by federal land use decisions. It is a largely unenforceable vehicle for recognition by federal policymakers of the continuing existence and vitality of Indian religions. It constitutes, nevertheless, a symbolically important acknowledgment of Indian religious tenets. See page 769, infra.

Since the 1970s, Indian tribal governments also have been more frequently incorporated within the general legislative and regulatory framework of the federal system. For example, Congress has treated tribes as states for purposes of administering major federal environmental statutes on their reservations. See page 613, infra.

While tribes have not completely escaped the legacy of federal paternalism when it comes to control of their natural resources, they now have more participation and say in how their resources are protected, developed and managed. In 1990, Congress passed the National Indian Forest Resources Management Act, 25 U.S.C.A. §§ 3101–3120, to allow the federal government and an Indian tribe landowner jointly to protect, conserve, utilize, manage, and enhance the tribe's forest lands. The Act also provides for civil actions for trespass on Indian forest lands which can be brought in the tribal court, and federal and state courts are required to extend full faith and credit to the tribal court judgment. 25 U.S.C.A. §§ 3106. In 1993, Congress passed the American Indian Agricultural

Resource Management Act, 25 U.S.C.A. §§ 3701–3713, to carry out the federal government's trust duty to protect, conserve, utilize, and manage Indian agricultural lands and related renewable resources with the active participation of the tribal landowner. This Act also gives tribes concurrent jurisdiction with the federal government to enforce civil trespass actions and the tribal court judgment is entitled to full faith and credit in federal and state courts. 25 U.S.C.A. §§ 3713. The Indian Mineral Development Act, 25 U.S.C.A. §§ 2101–2108, was enacted in 1982 to authorize Indian tribes, with approval of the Interior Secretary, to enter into joint ventures, operating, production sharing, service, managerial, lease or other agreements for the extraction, processing or other development of oil, gas, uranium, coal, geothermal or other energy or non-energy mineral resources. See, e.g., Cohen's Handbook of Federal Indian Law § 17.01, at 1107 (Nell Jessup Newton ed. 2012).

Nearly 400 Indian treaties, and several statutes and court decisions spell out the federal government's obligation for Indian education. Congress initially addressed the dismal state of Indian education by providing for small loans to individual Indian students pursuing vocational and higher education in the 1934 Indian Reorganization Act, 25 U.S.C.A. §§ 470, and funding for Indians attending state public schools in the 1934 Johnson O'Malley Act, 48 Stat. 596. Several major laws that have advanced Indian education followed. These include the Navajo Community College Act, 25 U.S.C.A. §§ 640a–640c–3, the Indian Education Act, 25 U.S.C.A. §§ 2601–2651, the Indian Self-Determination and Educational Assistance Act, 25 U.S.C.A. §§ 450a–450n, the Tribally Controlled College or University Assistance Act, 25 U.S.C.A. §§ 1801–1852, and the Vocational and Technical Education Assistance to the States Act, 20 U.S.C.A. § 2327.

In 1988 the Indian Self-Determination Act (ISDA) was amended to make contracting easier. It also created a self-governance demonstration project to allow up to twenty tribes to enter into self-governance "compacts" with the federal government under which tribes that have successfully managed other ISDA contracts can plan and administer virtually all functions and activities now performed for them by the BIA or Indian Health Service. Unlike the usual ISDA contracts, tribes are free to redesign the programs and reallocate funds among them. This is similar to block grants, allowing tribes to decide what services they need and to carry them out as they wish. In 1991, the ISDA was again amended to extend the demonstration project from five to eight years, expand the number of eligible tribes to thirty, and increase funding. In 1994, Congress passed the Indian Self-Determination Contract Reform Act, 25 U.S.C.A. §§ 450b, 450c, 450e, 450f, 450j, 450j–1, 450k to 450m–1, 450n, to address several problems in implementation which emerged after the 1988 Amendments. Congress also enacted the Tribal Self-Governance Act of 1994, 25 U.S.C.A. §§ 450n, 450aa note, 458aa to 458gg, to make permanent the self-governance demonstration project. The Act authorized the Secretary to select twenty new tribes per year from the applicant pool to participate in self-governance. It was amended in 1996 to increase the number of new tribes to be selected each year to fifty. See 25 U.S.C.A. § 458bb.

With respect to law and order on the reservation and tribal criminal jurisdiction, Congress amended the Indian Civil Rights Act (ICRA) in 1986 to increase the criminal penalties available to Indian tribal courts from $500 to $5000 and from six months to one year in jail. Since then, Congress has struggled with the best approach to improving tribal courts and justice systems. It enacted the Indian Law Enforcement Reform Act of 1990, 25 U.S.C.A. §§ 2801–2809, to sharpen and increase the responsibilities of the BIA and the Department of Justice concerning Indian country crimes. In 1993, Congress passed the Indian Tribal Justice Act, 25 U.S.C.A. §§ 3601–3631, to authorize increased federal funding of Indian tribal courts. The Indian Tribal Justice Technical and Legal Assistance Act of 2000, 25 U.S.C.A. §§ 3651–3681, gives the United States Attorney General the authority to award grants and provide technical assistance to Indian tribal justice systems. See 25 U.S.C.A. § 3681. In 2010, Congress passed the Tribal Law and Order Act, which includes a number of provisions requested by tribes such as increased sentencing authority for tribal courts in criminal prosecutions. See 25 U.S.C.A. § 1302 (3)(a)–(f).

The Violence Against Women Reauthorization Act of 2013 recognizes tribes' inherent power to exercise "special domestic violence criminal jurisdiction" over non-Indian defendants, who commit acts of domestic violence or dating violence against Indian women, or who violate certain protection orders in Indian country. Pub. L. No. 113–4, sec. 904, 25 USCA § 1304. See page 586.

Indian reservations usually have the highest rates of unemployment in the nation. Economic development on Indian reservations is therefore a high priority for Indian tribal governments and the federal government. In 1974, Congress passed the Indian Financing Act, 25 U.S.C.A. § 1451 et seq., "to provide capital on a reimbursable basis to help develop and utilize Indian resources, both physical and human, to a point where the Indians will fully exercise responsibility for the utilization and management of their own resources" and improve their standard of living. Pub. L. No. 93–262, § 2. The 1974 Act has been amended several times, most recently in 2002, see Pub. L. No. 107–331, and now authorizes the Interior Secretary to guarantee and insure commercial loans to individual Indians and Indian organizations to effectuate economic development on Indian reservations. Several other laws were passed to spur economic development on Indian reservations: the Indian Tribal Regulatory Reform and Business Development Act of 1999, Pub. L. No. 106–447 (authorizes creation of an authority to review laws and regulations that affect business and investment on Indian reservations and report findings to congressional committees and Indian tribes); the Indian Tribal Economic Development and Contract Encouragement Act of 2000, Pub. L. No. 106–179, 25 U.S.C.A. § 81 (provides that contracts with Indian tribes that encumber Indian lands for seven or more years are invalid unless approved by the Interior Secretary); the Native American Business Development, Trade Promotion, and Tourism Act of 2000, Pub. L. No. 106–464, 25 U.S.C.A. §§ 4301–4307 (provides for financial and technical assistance and administrative services for business development to enhance economies of Indian tribes and requires Secretary to conduct tourism demonstration projects to promote tourism on Indian lands); and the Indian Arts and Crafts Enforcement Act of 2000, Pub. L. No. 106–497, 25 U.S.C.A. §§ 305–305e (authorizes recovery of damages to include all gross profits accrued by seller of fake Indian arts and crafts). After finding that a significant amount of products and jewelry labeled "Native American" were inauthentic, Congress passed the Indian Arts and Crafts Amendment Act of 2010, Pub. L. No. 111–211, which allows any federal law enforcement officer to investigate violations of the Indian Arts and Crafts Act. The addition of the Indian Gaming Regulatory Act, 25 U.S.C.A. §§ 2701–2721, made clear the conditions under which tribes can establish gambling businesses on their reservations. See pages 741–761, infra.

Congress has taken steps to protect the cultures of Native Americans. The 1990 Native American Graves Protection and Repatriation Act (NAGPRA), 25 U.S.C.A. §§ 3001–3013, pages 801–817, infra, directs federal agencies and museums to return Native American human remains and sacred objects to appropriate native entities if they can be identified. The NAGPRA "safeguards the rights of Native Americans by protecting tribal burial sites and rights to items of cultural significance to Native Americans. * * * Cultural items protected * * * include Native American human remains, sacred objects, and objects of cultural patrimony." Pueblo of San Ildefonso v. Ridlon and Regents of the University of California, 103 F.3d 936, 938 (10th Cir.1996). The Act also has protective provisions for cultural objects that are inadvertently discovered. The National Museum of the American Indian, pages 817–805, infra, is required to inventory and repatriate Native American funerary objects, sacred objects and objects of cultural patrimony to Indian tribes or Native Hawaiians who can show cultural affiliation. See National Museum of the American Indian Act Amendments of 1996, Pub. L. No. 104–278, 20 U.S.C.A. §§ 80q et seq. The Native American Languages Act, 25 U.S.C.A. §§ 2901–2906, encourages the use and teaching of indigenous languages. The Act encourages elementary, secondary and higher education institutions "to include Native American languages in the curriculum in the same manner as foreign languages and grant proficiency in Native American languages the same full academic credit as proficiency in foreign languages." 25 U.S.C.A. § 2903. The term Native American includes "Indian, Native Hawaiian, or Native American Pacific Islander." 25 U.S.C.A. § 2902.

Congress is aware of the magnitude of social problems on Indian reservations and has passed several laws to address them. These laws include the Indian Child Protection and Family Violence Act, 25 U.S.C.A. §§ 3201–3211, the Indian Alcoholism and Substance Abuse Prevention and Treatment Act, 25 U.S.C.A. §§ 2401–2478, and the Indian Health Care Act, 25 U.S.C.A. §§ 1613–1682. Each of these acts has been amended to allow Indian participation and input into plans addressing reservation social problems.

The increased acceptance of Indian initiatives in Congress has been facilitated by the aggressive and active role of tribal leaders in the lobbying process.

> One of the greatest developments in Indian policy since termination has gone relatively unnoticed in many quarters: Indians have learned how to lobby. Highly effective legislative campaigns have been pursued by individual tribes and by national organizations. Indians and their advocates hold a range of well-placed staff positions in Congress. A skilled network exists to identify opposition proposals and to react to them promptly and professionally. Nonetheless tribal rights remain vulnerable to initiatives backed by well-organized interest groups. At the same time, the Indian presence in Washington is incomparably superior to that which existed, for example, just two decades ago. No Indian legislation has been passed over Indian opposition since the Indian Civil Rights Act of 1968.

> * * * The higher sovereign, faced with few practical constraints, holds nearly full sway in its ability to sap or energize Indian sovereignty. The power exists to enact everything from the debilitating allotment and termination programs to the beneficent child welfare and tax status laws that offer so much promise to Indian people. With ultimate primacy in Indian law and policy lodged firmly in Congress, Indian leaders know full well that whether tribal sovereignty will decline or progress will depend in important part on the tribes' skill in presenting their views in the legislative forum.

Charles F. Wilkinson, American Indians, Time and the Law 82–83, 86 (1987).

4. THE SUPREME COURT AND THE MODERN INDIAN RIGHTS MOVEMENT

Our survey of the history of early federal Indian policy to the present reveals that inconsistency characterizes the diverse programs and reforms of the dominant society for resolving its ongoing 200-year-old "Indian problem." Congress and the Executive branch have embraced treaties and reservations as the best way to "civilize" Indians, then rejected those solutions in favor of breaking treaties and establishing allotments. Legislation was crafted to reorganize and revitalize tribal governments, only to be followed by resolutions implementing tribal termination. Later, a President announced a new program of "self-determination" for Indian tribes, and new legislation incorporated tribal governments as permanent players in the federal system.

Such shifts and changes in policy are not wholly unexpected in dealing with the political branches of the federal government. But inconsistency is not something ordinarily expected from the only unelected (presumably "non-political") branch of government, the judiciary. Courts are fundamentally conservative institutions by design, relying on *stare decisis* and evolving precedent to reach decisions consistent with prior decisions.

For many years, the Supreme Court had only rare occasions to decide Indian cases. Then, in 1959, the Court issued its landmark decision in Williams v. Lee, 358 U.S. 217 (1959), pages 418–420, infra, inaugurating the modern era of Indian rights. Professor Charles Wilkinson has called *Williams* "a ringing endorsement of tribal sovereignty" and "the first favorable modern opinion" issued by the Court. Charles F. Wilkinson, Blood Struggle: The Rise of Modern Indian Nations 107 (2005). Following *Williams*, and throughout the turbulent period of the 1960s and 1970s, the Justices accepted an unprecedented number of cases involving Indian rights, and tribes generally won those cases, largely by arguing upon the foundations of the Marshall trilogy, as updated and given jurisprudential rigor by Felix Cohen's *Handbook*. See pages 232–235, supra. As will be seen in the final section of this chapter, the judicial fealty to these principles was broken.

The following landmark case of the modern Indian rights movement, decided, by the Supreme Court in 1974, raises a host of difficult questions on the special continuing relationship between Indian tribes and the United States.

MORTON V. MANCARI

Supreme Court of the United States, 1974.
417 U.S. 535, 94 S.Ct. 2474, 41 L.Ed.2d 290.

MR. JUSTICE BLACKMUN delivered the opinion of the Court.

* * *

I

Section 12 of the Indian Reorganization Act, 25 U.S.C.A. § 472, provides:

"The Secretary of the Interior is directed to establish standards of health, age, character, experience, knowledge, and ability for Indians who may be appointed, without regard to civil-service laws to the various positions maintained, now or hereafter, by the Indian Office, in the administration of functions or services affecting any Indian tribe. Such qualified Indians shall hereafter have the preference to appointment to vacancies in any such positions."

In June 1972, pursuant to this provision, the Commissioner of Indian Affairs, with the approval of the Secretary of the Interior, issued a directive stating that the BIA's policy would be to grant a preference to qualified Indians not only, as before, in the initial hiring stage, but also in the situation where an Indian and a non-Indian, both already employed by the BIA, were competing for a promotion within the Bureau. The record indicates that this policy was implemented immediately.

Shortly thereafter, appellees, who are non-Indian employees of the BIA at Albuquerque, instituted this class action, on behalf of themselves and other non-Indian employees similarly situated, in the United States District Court for the District of New Mexico, claiming that the "so-called 'Indian Preference Statutes,'" were repealed by the 1972 Equal Employment Opportunity Act and deprived them of rights to property without due process of law, in violation of the Fifth Amendment. * * *

II

The federal policy of according some hiring preference to Indians in the Indian service dates at least as far back as 1834.[7] Since that time, Congress repeatedly has enacted various preferences of the general type here at issue. The purpose of these preferences, as variously expressed in the legislative history, has been to give Indians a greater participation in their own self-government,[9] to further the Government's trust obligation toward the Indian tribes; and to reduce the negative effect of having non-Indians administer matters that affect Indian tribal life.

The preference directly at issue here was enacted as an important part of the sweeping Indian Reorganization Act of 1934. The overriding purpose of that particular Act was to establish machinery whereby Indian tribes would be able to assume a greater degree of self-government, both politically and economically. Congress was seeking to modify the then-

---

[7]   Act of June 30, 1834, § 9, 4 Stat. 737, 25 U.S.C. § 45:

"[I]n all cases of the appointments of interpreters or other persons employed for the benefit of the Indians, a preference shall be given to persons of Indian descent, if such can be found, who are properly qualified for the execution of the duties."

[9]   Senator Wheeler, cosponsor of the 1934 Act, explained the need for a preference as follows:

"We are setting up in the United States a civil service rule which prevents Indians from managing their own property. It is an entirely different service from anything else in the United States, because these Indians own this property. It belongs to them. What the policy of this Government is and what it should be is to teach these Indians to manage their own business and control their own funds and to administer their own property, and the civil service has worked very poorly so far as the Indian Service is concerned * * * ."

existing situation whereby the primarily non-Indian-staffed BIA had plenary control, for all practical purposes, over the lives and destinies of the federally recognized Indian tribes. * * *

One of the primary means by which self-government would be fostered and the Bureau made more responsive was to increase the participation of tribal Indians in the BIA operations. In order to achieve this end, it was recognized that some kind of preference and exemption from otherwise prevailing civil service requirements was necessary. * * *

Congress was well aware that the proposed preference would result in employment disadvantages within the BIA for non-Indians. Not only was this displacement unavoidable if room were to be made for Indians, but it was explicitly determined that gradual replacement of non-Indians with Indians within the Bureau was a desirable feature of the entire program for self-government. Since 1934, the BIA has implemented the preference with a fair degree of success. The percentage of Indians employed in the Bureau rose from 34 percent in 1934 to 57 percent in 1972. This reversed the former downward trend, and was due, clearly, to the presence of the 1934 Act. The Commissioner's extension of the preference in 1972 to promotions within the BIA was designed to bring more Indians into positions of responsibility and, in that regard, appears to be a logical extension of the congressional intent.

III

It is against this background that we encounter the first issue in the present case: whether the Indian preference was repealed by the Equal Employment Opportunity Act of 1972. Title VII of the Civil Rights Act of 1964, 78 Stat. 253, was the first major piece of federal legislation prohibiting discrimination in *private* employment on the basis of "race, color, religion, sex, or national origin." 42 U.S.C. § 2000e–2(a). Significantly, §§ 701(b) and 703(i) of that Act explicitly exempted from its coverage the preferential employment of Indians by Indian tribes or by industries located on or near Indian reservations. 42 U.S.C. §§ 2000e(b) and 2000e–2(i). This exemption reveals a clear congressional recognition, within the framework of Title VII, of the unique legal status of tribal and reservation-based activities. The Senate sponsor, Senator Humphrey, stated on the floor by way of explanation:

> "This exemption is consistent with the Federal Government's policy of encouraging Indian employment and with the special legal position of Indians." 110 Cong.Rec. 12723 (1964).

The 1964 Act did not specifically outlaw employment discrimination by the Federal Government. Yet the mechanism for enforcing longstanding Executive Orders forbidding Government discrimination had proved ineffective for the most part. In order to remedy this, Congress, by the 1972

Act, amended the 1964 Act and proscribed discrimination in most areas of federal employment. * * *

* * *

* * * For several reasons we conclude that Congress did not intend to repeal the Indian preference and that the District Court erred in holding that it was repealed.

First: There are the above-mentioned affirmative provisions in the 1964 Act excluding coverage of tribal employment and of preferential treatment by a business or enterprise on or near a reservation. 42 U.S.C. §§ 2000e(b) and 2000e–2(i). These 1964 exemptions as to private employment indicate Congress' recognition of the longstanding federal policy of providing a unique legal status to Indians in matters concerning tribal or "on or near" reservation employment. * * *

Second: Three months after Congress passed the 1972 amendments, it enacted two *new* Indian preference laws. These were part of the Education Amendments of 1972, 86 Stat. 235, 20 U.S.C. §§ 887c(a) and (d), and § 1119a (1970 ed., Supp. II). The new laws explicitly require that Indians be given preference in Government programs for training teachers of Indian children. * * *

Third: Indian preferences, for many years, have been treated as exceptions to Executive Orders forbidding Government employment discrimination. The 1972 extension of the Civil Rights Act to Government employment is in large part merely a codification of prior anti-discrimination Executive Orders that had proved ineffective because of inadequate enforcement machinery. * * *

Fourth: Appellees encounter head-on the "cardinal rule * * * that repeals by implication are not favored." * * *

* * *

IV

We still must decide whether, as the appellees contend, the preference constitutes invidious racial discrimination in violation of the Due Process Clause of the Fifth Amendment. *Bolling v. Sharpe*, 347 U.S. 497 (1954). The District Court, while pretermitting this issue, said, "[W]e could well hold that the statute must fail on constitutional grounds."

Resolution of the instant issue turns on the unique legal status of Indian tribes under federal law and upon the plenary power of Congress, based on a history of treaties and the assumption of a "guardian-ward" status, to legislate on behalf of federally recognized Indian tribes. The plenary power of Congress to deal with the special problems of Indians is drawn both explicitly and implicitly from the Constitution itself. Article I, § 8, cl. 3, provides Congress with the power to "regulate Commerce . . . with the Indian Tribes," and thus, to this extent, singles Indians out as a proper subject for separate legislation. Article II, § 2, cl. 2, gives the President the power, by and with the advice and consent of the Senate, to make treaties. This has often been the source of the Government's power to deal with the Indian tribes. The Court has described the origin and nature of the special relationship:

> In the exercise of the war and treaty powers, the United States overcame the Indians and took possession of their lands, sometimes by force, leaving them an uneducated, helpless and dependent people, needing protection against the selfishness of others and their own improvidence. Of necessity, the United States assumed the duty of furnishing that protection, and with it the authority to do all that was required to perform that obligation and to prepare the Indians to take their place as independent, qualified members of the modern body politic . . . *Board of County Comm'rs v. Seber*, 318 U.S. 705, 715 (1943).

See also *United States v. Kagama*, 118 U.S. 375, 383–384 (1886).

Literally every piece of legislation dealing with Indian tribes and reservations, and certainly all legislation dealing with the BIA, single out for special treatment a constituency of tribal Indians living on or near reservations. If these laws, derived from historical relationships and explicitly designed to help only Indians, were deemed invidious racial discrimination, an entire Title of the United States Code (25 U.S.C.) [25 U.S.C.A.] would be effectively erased and the solemn commitment of the Government toward the Indians would be jeopardized. See *Simmons v. Eagle Seelatsee*, 244 F.Supp. 808, 814, n. 13 (E.D.Wash.1965), affd, 384 U.S. 209 (1966).

It is in this historical and legal context that the constitutional validity of the Indian preference is to be determined. As discussed above, Congress in 1934 determined that proper fulfillment of its trust required turning over to the Indians a greater control of their own destinies. The overly paternalistic approach of prior years had proved both exploitative and destructive of Indian interests. Congress was united in the belief that institutional changes were required. An important part of the Indian Reorganization Act was the preference provision here at issue.

Contrary to the characterization made by appellees, this preference does not constitute "racial discrimination." Indeed, it is not even a "racial" preference.[24] Rather, it is an employment criterion reasonably designed to further the cause of Indian self-government and to make the BIA more

---

[24] The preference is not directed towards a "racial" group consisting of "Indians"; instead, it applies only to members of "federally recognized" tribes. This operates to exclude many individuals who are racially to be classified as "Indians." In this sense, the preference is political rather than racial in nature. * * *

responsive to the needs of its constituent groups. It is directed to participation by the governed in the governing agency. The preference is similar in kind to the constitutional requirement that a United States Senator, when elected, be "an Inhabitant of that State for which he shall be chosen," Art. I, § 3, cl. 3, or that a member of a city council reside within the city governed by the council. Congress has sought only to enable the BIA to draw more heavily from among the constituent group in staffing its projects, all of which, either directly or indirectly, affect the lives of tribal Indians. The preference, as applied, is granted to Indians not as a discrete racial group, but, rather, as members of quasi-sovereign tribal entities whose lives and activities are governed by the BIA in a unique fashion. See n. 24, supra. In the sense that there is no other group of people favored in this manner, the legal status of the BIA is truly *sui generis*. Furthermore, the preference applies only to employment in the Indian service. The preference does not cover any other Government agency or activity, and we need not consider the obviously more difficult question that would be presented by a blanket exemption for Indians from all civil service examinations. Here, the preference is reasonably and directly related to a legitimate, nonracially based goal. This is the principal characteristic that generally is absent from proscribed forms of racial discrimination.

On numerous occasions this Court specifically has upheld legislation that singles out Indians for particular and special treatment. *See, e.g., Board of County Comm'rs v. Seber*, 318 U.S. 705 (1943) (federally granted tax immunity); *McClanahan v. Arizona State Tax Comm'n*, 411 U.S. 164 (1973) (same); *Simmons v. Eagle Seelatsee*, 384 U.S. 209 (1966), aff'g 244 F.Supp. 808 (E.D.Wash.1965) (statutory definition of tribal membership, with resulting interest in trust estate); *Williams v. Lee*, 358 U.S. 217 (1959) (tribal courts and their jurisdiction over reservation affairs). Cf. *Morton v. Ruiz*, 415 U.S. 199 (1974) (federal welfare benefits for Indians "on or near" reservations). This unique legal status is of long standing, see *Cherokee Nation v. Georgia*, 5 Pet. 1 (1831); *Worcester v. Georgia*, 6 Pet. 515 (1832), and its sources are diverse. See generally U.S. Dept. of Interior, Federal Indian Law (1958). As long as the special treatment can be tied rationally to the fulfillment of Congress' unique obligation toward the Indians, such legislative judgments will not be disturbed. Here, where the preference is reasonable and rationally designed to further Indian self-government, we cannot say that Congress' classification violates due process.

* * *

NOTES

1.   The Indian preference statute, 25 U.S.C.A. § 472, has been held to apply to promotions and lateral transfers where a vacancy is being filled within the BIA. Freeman v. Morton, 499 F.2d 494 (D.C.Cir.1974). See Carole Goldberg, *What's Race Got to Do with It?: The Story of* Morton v. Mancari, *in*

Race Law Stories 237 (Rachel F. Moran & Devon W. Carbado eds. 2008). But in Mescalero Apache Tribe v. Hickel, 432 F.2d 956 (10th Cir.1970), cert. denied 401 U.S. 981 (1971), it was held that the preference does not apply to reductions in force because there are no "vacancies" to be filled. The hiring preference also applies to the Indian Health Service, located in the Department of Health and Human Services. See Preston v. Heckler, 734 F.2d 1359 (9th Cir.1984).

2. The Court's several references to the federal-tribal relationship in such terms as "unique" and "special" were doubtless due in part to the preferential college admissions issues that the Court was facing when *Morton v. Mancari* was handed down. See, e.g., DeFunis v. Odegaard, 416 U.S. 312 (1974) (dismissed on the basis of mootness). Later, it distinguished the Indian employment preference from state attempts to use race as a factor in college admissions. Regents of the University of California v. Bakke, 438 U.S. 265, 304 n.42 (1978).

The Court continued to stress the special status of Indians in cases decided after *Morton v. Mancari* that raised the issue of reverse discrimination in violation of the Constitution's Equal Protection clause. In Fisher v. District Court of Rosebud County, 424 U.S. 382 (1976), the Court held that Montana state courts had no jurisdiction over an adoption proceeding involving persons who were tribal members and reservation residents:

> [W]e reject the argument that denying [respondents] access to the Montana courts constitutes impermissible racial discrimination. The exclusive jurisdiction of the Tribal Court does not derive from the race of the plaintiff but rather from the quasi-sovereign status of the Northern Cheyenne Tribe under federal law.

424 U.S. at 390. See also, e.g., Moe v. Confederated Salish & Kootenai Tribes, 425 U.S. 463 (1976). In United States v. Antelope, 430 U.S. 641 (1977), page 551, infra, the Court said:

> The decisions of this Court leave no doubt that federal legislation with respect to Indian tribes, although extending to Indians as such, is not based upon impermissible racial classifications. Quite the contrary, classification singling out Indian tribes as subjects of legislation are expressly provided for in the Constitution and supported by the ensuing history of the Federal Government's relations with Indians. [Citing authority] * * * Legislation with respect to these "unique aggregations" has repeatedly been sustained by this Court against claims of unlawful racial discrimination.

430 U.S. at 645.

3. *Morton v. Mancari* and its holding that Indians constitute a "political" rather than "racial" category that therefore is not subject to the same type of equal protection analysis used by courts to protect the rights of other minority groups in the United States is one of the most important decisions of the modern Indian rights movement. As Professor Addie C. Rolnick, in *The*

Promise of Mancari: Indian Political Rights as Racial Remedy, 86
N.Y.U.L.Rev. 958 (2011), explains:

> Although the *Mancari* opinion itself leaves room for several different
> interpretations of the relationship between Indian race and Indian
> political status, it has since been invoked to stand for the idea that
> Indian refers solely to a political category. That is, being Indian is a
> matter of membership in a political group, a status that is framed as
> oppositional or unrelated to race. Federal Indian law—the body of
> federal statutes, court decisions, and regulations that recognizes the
> unique legal status of Indian nations and authorizes special rules or
> benefits for Indians because of that unique status—has been upheld
> against constitutional challenges based in part on this idea.

Id. at 964–65.

Not surprisingly, Justice Blackmun's opinion has generated a voluminous
law review literature. For a lively scholarly exchange on *Morton*'s "political"
versus "racial" approach to characterizing Indians for purposes of
constitutional review under the Equal Protection clause of the Fourteenth
Amendment, see David C. Williams, *The Borders of the Equal Protection
Clause: Indians as Peoples*, 38 UCLA L.Rev. 759 (1991) and Professor Carole
Goldberg-Ambrose's pointed response, *Not "Strictly" Racial: A Response to
"Indians as Peoples,"* 39 UCLA L.Rev. 169 (1991).

4.   Do the principles of *Morton v. Mancari* apply only to federal
legislation? *Morton v. Mancari* was given a broad reading by a federal court of
appeals the very next year in Livingston v. Ewing, 601 F.2d 1110 (10th
Cir.1979), cert. denied 444 U.S. 870 (1979). The case involved a challenge to
the Indian preference policies implemented by the State of New Mexico and
the City of Santa Fe that permitted Indians to display and sell handcrafted
jewelry, arts, and crafts on the grounds of the Museum of New Mexico and the
Palace of the Governors in downtown Santa Fe. The policies specifically
prohibited sales by persons other than Indians. After non-Indian jewelers
sought and were denied authorization to sell crafts in the area assigned on an
exclusive basis to the Indians, they challenged the state policy. The Livingston
court first held that the policy was covered by 42 U.S.C.A. § 2000e–2(i) of the
Equal Employment Opportunities Act, which provides:

> Nothing   contained   in   this   subchapter   [prohibiting
> discrimination in employment] shall apply to any business or
> enterprise on or near an Indian reservation with respect to any
> publicly announced employment practice of such business or
> enterprise under which a preferential treatment is given to any
> individual because he is an Indian living on or near a reservation.

The appeals court interpreted the term "employment practice" broadly to
include the exclusive concession through which the Indians render a service to
the state museum by attracting tourists. The court ruled that the square in the
City of Santa Fe is "on or near an Indian reservation" within the meaning of

the statute, since it is only eight miles from the nearest Indian pueblo and within a short distance of others. Relying heavily on the Supreme Court's conclusion in *Morton v. Mancari* that Indians are an allowable class for purposes of protective legislation, the *Livingston* court further held that the Indian preference did not constitute reverse discrimination in violation of the Equal Protection clause. Finding no facial, stigmatized discrimination against non-Indians in the application of the preference, the court held that the educational, cultural, and artistic interests that the state was fostering far outweighed the right claimed by the non-Indian artists. "The exclusive franchise given the Indians," said the court, "is one element of a comprehensive program designed to allow the general public to meet the Indians and to gain information as to the character and quality of the Indians' work." Livingston v. Ewing, 601 F.2d at 1116. See Cohen's Handbook of Federal Indian Law § 14.03, at 948 (Nell Jessup Newton ed. 2012).

5.   During the 1990s, the Rehnquist Court increased its scrutiny of government affirmative action programs and struck down the use of racial preferences on constitutional grounds in several high profile cases that drew intense national attention. In one of those cases, Adarand Constructors v. Pena, 515 U.S. 200 (1995), Justice Stevens, in dissent, opined that the majority's position that strict scrutiny must be applied with "consistency" to all racial preference legislation would equate "the special preferences that the national government has provided to Native Americans since 1834 as comparable to the official discrimination against African Americans that was prevalent for much of our history." 515 U.S. at 244.

Although the Supreme Court has never directly questioned the continuing validity of *Morton v. Mancari* since its decision in *Adarand*, the Ninth Circuit has suggested a narrower view of Congress's power to legislate for the benefit of Indians. In Williams v. Babbitt, 115 F.3d 657 (9th Cir.1997), cert. denied 523 U.S. 1 117 (1998), the court upheld a constitutional challenge to the Reindeer Industry Act, which was passed by Congress in 1937 to benefit Alaska Natives. The influx of white settlers to Alaska early in the century increased competition for fish and game, making it difficult for Alaska Natives to subsist. In order to provide a more stable food supply the government imported reindeer from Russia for the Natives to raise. Non-Indians then began to raise and trade in reindeer themselves. The Reindeer Industry Act provided funds to buy out the non-Natives, restricted trade in reindeer owned by the United States or the Natives to Native purchasers, and denied non-Natives the privilege of grazing reindeer on federal lands.

In 1986, the BIA advised a non-Native that he could import and raise reindeer. Native reindeer herders appealed the matter to the Interior Board of Indian Appeals (IBIA), which held the agency's interpretation was incorrect. It said that the purpose of the act was to preserve the Native character of the reindeer industry in Alaska, and therefore "the act must be construed to prohibit non-Native entry into the reindeer industry * * * ." The federal district court upheld this interpretation.

On appeal, the Ninth Circuit found nothing in the act to support the IBIA interpretation, but said that it was constrained by administrative law principles to defer to the agency's interpretation of the statute unless the interpretation was unreasonable. Given the canons of construction applicable to ambiguous statutes in Indian affairs, it said that an interpretation favoring natives was not unreasonable. The court said deference to the agency could only be limited if it raised grave constitutional problems.

Judge Kozinski, writing for the majority, said: "Under strict scrutiny, the IBIA's interpretation would almost certainly render the Reindeer Act unconstitutional." The court therefore interpreted the Act "as not precluding non-natives in Alaska from owning and importing reindeer." Id. at 666. Judge Kozinski, quoting Justice Stevens' dissent in *Adarand* in which Stevens had raised doubts about the viability of *Mancari*, supra, said; "If Justice Stevens is right about the logical implications of *Adarand*, *Mancari*'s days are numbered." 115 F.3d at 665. See also Dawavendewa v. Salt River Project Agricultural Improvement & Power District, 154 F.3d 1 117, 1120 (9th Cir.1998), cert. denied 528 U.S. 1098 (2000) (refusing to apply *Morton v. Mancari* to a contract between the Navajo Nation and a non-Indian employer requiring a preference for hiring Navajos).

6.   In 2000, the Supreme Court, in another case originating from the Ninth Circuit, was asked to apply *Morton* to the unique situation of Native Hawaiians and their congressionally-delegated trust relationship with the state of Hawaii. Rice v. Cayetano, 528 U.S. 495 (2000), page 1045, infra, involved a challenge to Hawaii's voting scheme for election to the board of trustees for the Office of Hawaiian Affairs (OHA), a state agency which administers programs designed for the benefit of "Hawaiians" and "native Hawaiians." The terms are defined by state statute as follows:

> "Hawaiian" means any descendant of the aboriginal peoples inhabiting the Hawaiian Islands which exercised sovereignty and subsisted in the Hawaiian Islands in 1778, and which peoples thereafter have continued to reside in Hawaii.

> * * *

> "Native Hawaiian" means any descendant of not less than one-half part of the races inhabiting the Hawaiian Islands previous to 1778, as defined by the Hawaiian Homes Commission Act, 1920, as amended; provided that the term identically refers to the descendants of such blood quantum of such aboriginal peoples which exercised sovereignty and subsisted in the Hawaiian Islands in 1778 and which people thereafter continued to reside in Hawaii.

The state law allowing only these two classes of person in elections for OHA trustees was challenged by a non-Hawaiian as violating the Fifteenth Amendment to the U.S. Constitution which states in part: "The right of citizens of the United States to vote shall not be denied or abridged by the United

States or by any State on account of race, color, or previous condition of servitude."

Hawaii defended its exclusion of non-Hawaiians from voting by invoking *Morton v. Mancari*, arguing that like the BIA, OHA trustees are charged directly with protecting the interests of native Hawaiians. In a 7–2 decision, the Court declared that it was unnecessary for it to "take the substantial step of finding authority in Congress, delegated to the State, to treat Hawaiians or native Hawaiians as tribes." 528 U.S. at 520, citing *Morton v. Mancari*, 417 U.S. at 554. In any event, Congress had not taken such action and the Court held that Hawaii's law was barred by the direct language of the Fifteenth Amendment.

Concluding his opinion for the Court, Justice Kennedy offered the following advice to "all the citizens of Hawaii:"

> When the culture and way of life of a people are all but engulfed by a history beyond their control, their sense of loss may extend down through generations; and their dismay may be shared by many members of the larger community. As the State of Hawaii attempted to address these realities, it must, as always, seek the political consensus that begins with a sense of shared purpose. One of the necessary beginning points is this principle: The Constitution of the United States, too, has become the heritage of all the citizens of Hawaii.

Id. at 524.

7. *Rice v. Cayetano* and its implications for the rights of Native Hawaiians are discussed more fully in Chapter 13B. Aside from its impact on Native Hawaiian claims to special rights and status under *Morton v. Mancari*, does *Rice* limit the reach of that landmark 1974 decision on Indian rights beyond the context of the Fifteenth Amendment's prohibition on state-imposed elector qualifications?

In Malabed v. North Slope Borough, 335 F.3d 864 (9th Cir.2003), the North Slope Borough, a political subdivision of the state of Alaska, enacted an ordinance giving a preference in Borough employment to members of federally recognized Indian tribes. The Court rejected the Borough's argument that *Morton v. Mancari* justified the ordinance:

> *Mancari* held only that when Congress acts to fulfill its unique trust responsibilities toward Indian tribes, such legislation is not based on a suspect classification. Indeed, in its more recent case of Rice v. Cayetano, 528 U.S. 495 (2000), the Supreme Court expressly stated that the *Mancari* "opinion was careful to note . . . that the case was confirmed to the authority of the BIA, an agency described as 'sui generis.'"

Id. at 868, n.5.

8.   Gregory Smith and Caroline Mayhew write of a "concerted effort by some interests to limit *Mancari's* application or even have the case overturned in its entirety." Such efforts, if successful they warn, could lead to years of litigation on the question of whether congressional legislation establishing a host of federal Indian programs is constitutional under a strict scrutiny standard of review. *Apocalypse Now: The Unrelenting Assault on Morton v. Mancari*, 60 Fed.Law. 47, 55 (2013). They also note that while a decision of such far-ranging consequences may seem unlikely:

> * * * [A]t least one justice has indicated a willingness to review the fundamentals of federal Indian law. Writing in concurrence in the judgment in *United States v. Lara* [see Chapter 7, infra], Justice Clarence Thomas stated that "federal Indian law is at odds with itself" and called upon the Court to "examine more critically our tribal sovereignty case law." He stated that he does "not necessarily agree that the tribes have any residual inherent sovereignty,"a view which if adopted by the Court could significantly impact the political/racial distinction established in *Mancari*.

Id. If you were a lawyer arguing for tribal interests before the Supreme Court, how would you respond to Justice Thomas's doubts on "residual tribal sovereignty"?

The End of an Era

Rice v. Cayetano was one of a number of Supreme Court cases in recent decades that dealt significant setbacks to the struggles by Native Americans to vindicate their rights. The Court, first under Chief Justice William Rehnquist, and now under Chief Justice John Roberts, has issued a series of decisions that have been viewed as serious curtailments of tribal sovereignty and rights and reversals of long-established precedents protective of important tribal religious and cultural rights. Recall that congressional plenary power, tribal sovereignty, the trust doctrine and the Indian law canons of construction are foundational concepts traceable to the Marshall trilogy. Legal scholars and others have criticized the Court's apparent disregard of long-established precedents based on the trilogy when it comes to deciding cases involving Indian rights.

In Duro v. Reina, 495 U.S. 676 (1990), pages 597–598, infra, the Supreme Court ruled there was no tribal court jurisdiction over the crimes of non-member Indians committed on the reservation. The Court cited no precedent and overcame Congress's own consistent treatment of the dividing line for criminal jurisdiction as pertaining to "Indians," not tribal members. The *Duro* Court's concern with the "special nature of the [Indian] tribunals" was prominent among the motives it cited for curbing tribal power. The decision noted that "while modern tribal courts include many familiar features of the judicial process, they are influenced by the unique customs, languages, and usages of the tribes they serve." 495 U.S. at 693.

Other major decisions adverse to tribal governments include Nevada v. Hicks, 533 U.S. 353 (2001), page 641, infra (holding that tribal courts may not assert jurisdiction over civil claims against state officials who enter tribal land to execute a search warrant on a tribal member suspected of having violated state law outside the reservation), and Atkinson Trading Company v. Shirley, 532 U.S. 645 (2001) (holding that the Navajo Nation could not impose its hotel occupancy tax on a non-Indian business operating on non-Indian owned fee land located within the boundaries of the Navajo Indian Reservation).

In City of Sherrill v. Oneida Indian Nation, 544 U.S. 197 (2005), page 328 infra, the Court ruled that an Indian tribe could not revive its "ancient sovereignty" by purchasing parcels of historic reservation land now located within the borders of a non-Indian local government. In so ruling, the Court rejected the tribe's argument that the parcels it now owns are exempt from local tax rolls. In 2009, the Court handed down Carcieri v. Salazar, 555 U.S. 379 (2009), overturning more than 70 years of DOI practice of taking land into trust for Indian tribes recognized after passage of the IRA in 1934. The decision sent shock waves throughout Indian country, and tribes immediately began to lobby Congress to reverse the decision.

The Court's 2013 decision in Adoptive Couple v. Baby Girl, 133 S.Ct. 2552 (2013), pages 703, infra, generated intense controversy and concern in Indian country and in the national press as well. The Indian Child Welfare Act (ICWA) was found not to apply in a case where the biological father, a Cherokee citizen, had never acquired legal or physical custody of the child as defined by the Court under the Act. Justice Samuel Alito's majority opinion for the Court devoted significant attention to the low percentage of Cherokee "blood" the child was determined to possess, and drew a sharp rebuke in dissent from Justice Sonia Sotomayor.

Examples of the Court's adverse decisions touching on Indian religious freedom and rights include Lyng v. Northwest Indian Cemetery Protective Association, 485 U.S. 439 (1988), page 771, infra, and Employment Division, Department of Human Resources v. Smith, 485 U.S. 660 (1988) (*Smith I*), and Employment Division, Department of Human Resources of Oregon v. Smith, 494 U.S. 872 (1990) (*Smith II*), page 800, infra.

The trend of these cases departing from basic principles of Indian law is striking. From the beginning of the modern era of Indian law in 1959 until what some commentators regard as its demise with the elevation of William Rehnquist to Chief Justice and appointment of Antonin Scalia as Associate Justice in 1986, tribes and tribal interests prevailed before the Court in 47 out of 80 cases, or 59% of the time. Since 1986, tribal interests have prevailed in less than a third of the cases heard by the Court. The Tribal Supreme Court Project for the Native American Rights Fund (NARF) keeps close track of the current Court's Indian law decisions. NARF reports that at the end of the Court's October 2015 term, "the overall win-loss record of Indian country before the Roberts' Court stands at 5-wins and 10-losses." NARF does note that this figure marks a substantial improvement from the 0-wins and 7-losses suffered by tribal interests at the hands of the Roberts' Court during the October 2005 through 2010 terms. See *The Tribal Supreme Court Project Memorandum*, Narf.org, July 14, 2016, http://sct.narf.org/updatememos/2016/07-14-16.pdf

The Court's decisions in recent decades denying tribes important rights while veering away from long-established precedents have led noted scholars in the field of federal Indian law to publish critical assessments of the Justices, some recommending that tribes avoid bringing any cases before the Court if at all possible.

Professor Robert N. Clinton has charged the Court with "neo-colonialism," seeming concerned only with protecting the "right of non-Indian political processes to control the rights, destinies, and interests of Indian minorities, but not the right of Indian governments to affect the rights and interests of non-Indians or non-member Indians who reside within their reservation and affect the lives of tribal members." Clinton, *Peyote and Judicial Political Activism: Neo-Colonialism and the Supreme Court's New Indian Law Agenda*, 38 Fed. B. News & J. 92, 98–100 (1991).

Dean David Getches observes:

> Courts have generally served as the conscience of federal Indian law, protecting tribal powers and rights at least against state action, unless and until Congress clearly states a contrary intention. The Supreme Court has recently begun to depart from this traditional standard, abandoning entrenched principles of Indian law in favor of an approach that bends tribal sovereignty to fit the Court's perceptions of non-Indian interests.

David H. Getches, *Conquering the Cultural Frontier: The New Subjectivism of the Supreme Court in Indian Law*, 84 Calif.L.Rev. 1573, 1574 (1996).

Getches labeled the Rehnquist Supreme Court's approach to Indian rights as "subjectivism," with the Court defining the rights of Indians, including the powers of tribal government, according to the preferences of a majority of the Justices' as to what the result ought to be. Rather than relying on foundational principles that go back to the Marshall trilogy and requiring clear expressions of Congress to set Indian policy, members of the Court have started writing their own policy in some recent cases. In order to resuscitate the foundational principles, Dean Getches believes that some members of the Court or future appointees "must take sufficient interest and at least one of them must assert intellectual leadership in Indian cases." Id. at 1652. In a more recent law review article, he had this to say about the Supreme Court's "ethnocentric" direction in Indian law:

> [I]n Indian law, the Court has been engaged in a search for meaning that involves it in a hands-on project of finding legislative purpose and doing what the Justices believe to be the best under the circumstances. In that context, I find the most troubling aspect of the inquiry to be the importation of current social values, an essentially ethnocentric enterprise that challenges even the wisest judge.

* * *

The Justices must also understand that their recent decisions have begun to dismantle Indian policy, and that this inevitably will cause confusion among state, local, and tribal governments, heighten tensions among Indians and their non-Indian neighbors, undermine reservation economic development efforts, and frustrate lower federal and state courts.

David H. Getches, *Beyond Indian Law: The Rehnquist Court's Pursuit of States' Rights, Color-Blind Justice and Mainstream Values*, 86 Minn.L.Rev. 267, 301, 360 (2001).

Professor Matthew L.M. Fletcher has suggested that the *certiorari* process by which the Supreme Court decides which cases to hear may discriminate against tribal interests.

* * * Something extraordinary has been happening in federal Indian law. From 1959, the generally recognized beginning of the modern era of federal Indian law, to 1987, when the Supreme Court decided the major Indian gaming case California v. Cabazon Band of Mission Indians, Indians and Indian tribes (to whom this Article will often call "tribal interests") won nearly 60% of federal Indian law cases decided by the Supreme Court. But since Cabazon, tribal interests have lost more than 75% of their cases. The sample under study—from 1986 to 1993—covers the first years of this radical turnaround. Consistent with the overall pattern of the period, tribal interests lost about 75% of their cases during the period under study.

The research presented in this Article reveals powerful evidence that the Supreme Court's certiorari process harshly discriminates against the interests of Indian tribes and individual American Indians. During the period analyzed in this study—October Terms (OT) 1986 through 1993—the Supreme Court granted certiorari once out of ninety-two Indian tribe and tribal interest petitions (excluding three unpaid in forma pauperis prisoner petitions involving indigent Indians in which the Court granted certiorari). During the same period of time, the Court granted cert fourteen times out of a mere thirty-seven petitions filed by states and local units of government against tribal interests—more than a third of the petitions. Other petitioners opposing tribal interests did not fare as well as state governments, but the Court still granted their petitions significantly more often than tribal parties (four grants out of twenty-eight petitions). This difference is statistically significant. Because so few tribal petitions are granted, and relatively so many petitions filed by opposing parties are granted, the number of cases where a tribal party is the respondent—and at a clear disadvantage statistically—is overwhelming.

* * *

The import, of course, of a grant of certiorari is that the Court has agreed to review a lower court decision adverse to the petitioner. It is well-established that the Court grants certiorari and reverses the lower court decision far more than it affirms. Of the twenty-two petitions granted, the tribal interest was a respondent in twenty of the cases, was the petitioner once, and was not present once.

The bare statistics are incredible. The question remains—how does the Court's certiorari process discriminate so wildly against tribal interests? The Supreme Court's certiorari process, which includes the clerks that do much of the Court's work, discriminates against Indians and Indian tribes in two ways. First, the Court undervalues the merits and importance of petitions filed by tribal interests. Second, the Court overvalues the merits and importance of petitions filed by the traditional opponents of tribal interests—state governments and, to a lesser extent, the federal government and private entities. In shorthand, if a tribe or an Indian loses in the federal courts of appeal, the Court will almost never review the case, but if a state loses against a tribe or an Indian, the Court often grants certiorari. This imbalance skews the development of federal Indian law doctrine.

Matthew L.M. Fletcher, *Factbound and Splitless: The Certiorari Process as a Barrier to Justice for Indian Tribes*, 51 Ariz.L.Rev. 933, 933–37 (2009).

The disarray imposed on Indian law by many of the Supreme Court's decisions in the last thirty years has surely been unsettling on tribal efforts to protect land, sovereignty and other rights. But those decisions can also be seen partly as a reaction to aggressive use of the tools of sovereignty by tribes growing in their determination to govern all the territory and people who come within their boundaries. The backlash of non-Indians affected by these assertions of sovereignty may explain the challenges to tribal jurisdiction that have found their way to the courts, if not the failure of judicial adherence to precedent. But the resilience of tribes through the assaults of past federal policies suggests that they will not be deterred in their efforts.

If commentators are correct that the Supreme Court should be avoided by Indian tribes seeking to assert their sovereignty and rights, what alternative paths to rebuilding Native nations are available to tribes emboldened by their successes over the last half-century? One answer has been to appeal to Congress to exercise its plenary power to reverse the Court's limitation on tribal rights. In egregious situations, Congress has responded. After *Duro*, supra, Congress passed remedial legislation reaffirming tribal jurisdiction over nonmember Indians on the reservation. United States v. Lara, 541 U.S. 193 (2004), page 589, infra, held that Congress has the constitutional power to remove restrictions imposed on the exercise of a tribe's inherent legal authority. Congress also attempted to provide greater protection to religious freedom after *Smith II*, supra. It passed the Religious Freedom Restoration Act, 42 U.S.C.A. §§ 2000bb to 2000bb–4 restoring a stricter standard of review on all religious freedom cases—not just involving Indian religion—but the Act's application to state laws was found beyond Congress's authority. See City of Boerne v. Flores, 521 U.S. 507 (1997).

NOTE: NATION BUILDING: THE THEME FOR THE CURRENT ERA?

The Self-determination era was launched by the congressional repudiation of the termination policy and the declarations of President Nixon. The self-determination policy was anchored by multiple legislative acts reaffirming a national commitment to preserve and strengthen tribal governments. It was propelled by the Supreme Court's 1959 landmark decision in *Williams v. Lee* and enriched by numerous Supreme Court decisions. That trend continued at least until about thirty years ago.

The self-determination policy is far more deeply entrenched than past federal Indian policies. Indeed, just the fact that a policy has remained constant for half a century provides a degree of stability. Moreover, since the 1960s, Congress's power over Indian affairs has been exercised almost exclusively to further tribal sovereignty and economic self-sufficiency. In some cases, Congress has even reversed or modified the Court's anti-Indian decisions, after listening to the concerns of tribal leaders and their advocates that the Justices' untethered approach to Indian rights threatens the health, safety and welfare of reservation communities.

The combined effects of the modern Indian rights movement's achievements of legislative reforms in Congress, legal victories in the courts, and increased tribal governmental responsibility for day-to-day life on the reservation are evident throughout modern-day Indian country. Native nations themselves have seized these tools and are using them to build and protect their political and economic power. They have turned this into a new, self-created era of nation building.

Tribes today possess greater economic and political power than they have had at any time in our history since before the early treaties were negotiated. The vindication of treaty rights has led to sustainable commercial activities and re-enriched cultural practices and traditions. Tribes in the Northwest and the Great Lakes states, for instance, now have fishing ventures that employ thousands of tribal members in traditional pursuits and that produce revenues that can provide benefits for the tribal communities and the individuals within them. Tribes operate fishing boats, fish packing plants, and tourism and guiding businesses.

The legal victories of the twentieth century that defined the jurisdictional attributes of Indian country and immunities from state laws within reservations have enabled some tribes near population centers or highways to open profitable gambling parlors and casinos. These businesses have produced literally hundreds of millions of dollars in profits and create jobs on the reservation. Economic activity also enables tribes to increase their governing capacity and their influence in the political systems of the dominant society.

Tribal prerogatives to impose taxes on activities occurring on the reservation, including on profitable non-Indian businesses such as those that develop minerals and oil and gas on the reservation, raise significant revenues. The Supreme Court's decisions of the modern era approved these taxes and tribes are now regularly collecting these revenue streams to finance the government of their territory and the provision of services to tribal members.

Twenty-first century tribal governments are increasingly complex entities, with major departments and subdivisions to administer laws for controlling land use, environmental protection, water allocation, fish and wildlife regulation, education, social welfare benefits, and more. Greater responsibility than ever before has been handed over to the tribes to administer programs formerly run by the BIA. Tribes and their subdivisions are often the largest employers on reservations. Tribal governments coupled with the tribal enterprises like farms, fish packing industries, manufacturing, and other businesses employ tens of thousands of people nationally.

State legislatures have also enacted legislation designed to accommodate and facilitate the role of Indian tribes in the federal system. Hundreds of bills involving state relations with Native Americans have been passed, including authorizations for cooperative agreements between state agencies and tribes in a variety of policy areas such as law enforcement, hazardous and solid waste disposal, allocation of tax revenue, economic development, and allocation of water rights.

It can be said with some assurance that Indian tribes of the 21st century have truly and meaningfully achieved the status of "the third sovereign" in our federal system. See Sandra Day O'Connor, *Lessons from the Third Sovereign: Indian Tribal Courts*, in Navajo Nation Peacemaking: Living Traditional Justice (Marianne O Nielsen, ed. 2005). The challenge confronting tribes today is to find ways to continue to build upon the sovereignty and rights secured by the victories won in the courts and in Congress during the modern era to gain even greater economic and political control of the reservation in the 21st century.

Professor Stephen Cornell of the Native Nations Institute at the University of Arizona and Professor Joseph Kalt of the Harvard Project on American Indian Economic Development have described this challenge in their pathbreaking research on the successful strategies used by tribes over the past several decades to achieve greater autonomy and self-sufficiency as the task of "rebuilding Native nations." They describe a "revolution that is underway in Indian country:"

> * * * As much of the world knows, many of the more than five hundred America Indian nations are poor, and those nations' poverty tears at their social fabrics and cultures. What much of the world doesn't know is that in the last quarter century, a growing number of those nations have broken out of the prevailing pattern of poverty. They have moved aggressively to take control of their futures and

rebuild their nations, rewriting constitutions, reshaping economies, and reinvigorating Indigenous communities, cultures and families.

Rebuilding Native Nations 6–7, supra.

As Professors Cornell and Kalt have recognized in their research and work in the field with literally hundreds of tribes over the past several decades, successful reservation economic and community development poses a number of significant challenges for American Indian tribes. Building a sustainable economy, competing with federal and state governments for jurisdiction and control over reservation resources and business activity, training the reservation workforce, respecting tribal beliefs, traditions and values—these are just a few of the major problems that confront tribes as they struggle to achieve economic self-sufficiency in Indian country.

Given the formidable barriers that every tribe confronts in achieving successful reservation development, there are a surprising number of success stories in Indian country of tribes meeting the challenges and implementing strategies aimed at self-sufficiency. Finding the keys to unlock the development potential of their reservation resources in a culturally appropriate manner represents perhaps the greatest challenge confronting American Indian tribes in the 21st century as they enter a new era of Native nation building.

As Professors Cornell and Kalt note, in the past, most efforts at understanding reservation economic and social problems have focused on the role of federal policies and laws in promoting or frustrating Indian country development. But such approaches have not been very helpful in understanding why some tribes have been relatively successful in achieving reservation development, while other tribes, working under the same set of laws and federal policies, and similarly situated in terms of development potential, have achieved a much lower level of economic performance and community cohesion.

Professors Cornell and Kalt have developed an impressive body of research and data on Indian country development, focused on the role of tribal structures and policies in explaining variations in economic performance and community vitality among different tribes. Their work has yielded a number of important insights into how tribes can successfully meet the challenges of achieving self-sufficiency. See Stephen Cornell and Joseph P. Kalt, *Reloading the Dice: Improving the Chances for Economic Development on American Indian Reservations*, in What Can Tribes Do? Strategies and Institutions in American Indian Economic Development (S. Cornell & J. Kalt eds. 1992). Their extensive field work and research has involved literally hundreds of tribes ranging from the small Muckleshoot Tribe in suburban Seattle, to the White Mountain Apache Tribe, located in eastern Arizona on one of the largest and most populated reservations in the nation. They have even extended their study of successful tribal development to Canada, Australia New Zealand and other countries with significant indigenous tribal populations. Their research in this country and around the world has confirmed that sustainable economic and community development for tribal communities in the United States and elsewhere is consistently preceded by assertions of tribal sovereignty, the creation of capable and accountable institutions of self-government, and a "match" between the tribe's underlying cultural norms and the institutions of government by which tribes seek to manage and promote economic and community development. See Chapter 9, supra.

NATION BUILDING NOTE: REBUILDING TRADITIONAL PUEBLO DWELLINGS TO REVITALIZE CULTURE THROUGH HOUSING

The Nation building challenges of the 21st century are multiple and diverse for each Indian reservation community in the United States. Research by Professors Cornell and Kalt shows that careful prioritization and deliberate planning, with an understanding of what tribal initiatives will have the support and commitment of the people and its leadership over time, are essential elements of many of the contemporary tribal success stories at Nation building. See Chapter 9.

One such success story is provided by Ohkay Owingeh, the "Place of the Strong People," one of the 19 federally recognized pueblos in New Mexico that were at the center of the controversy in *United States v. Sandoval*. See page 188. A major nation building challenge taken on by the 3,500 community members of Ohkay Owingeh literally involves physically rebuilding their historic village center known as Owe'neh Bupingeh.

Occupied for over 700 years, Owe'neh Bupingeh serves as the cultural heart of the community with its historic pueblo-style homes surrounding the four village plazas. These plazas are where the pueblo's most important dances and ceremonies take place throughout the year. Over the years, however, many of the homes surrounding the plaza had fallen into disrepair and been abandoned, or used only during the village ceremonies and left vacant the rest of the year. As described by the Harvard Project, for the people of Ohkay Owingeh, the "depopulation of the historic village center wasn't just a pueblo version of urban decay, it was threatening the cultural integrity, language transmission, and life-ways of Ohkay Owingeh." The Harvard Project on American Indian Economic Development, *Honoring Nations 2014: Celebrating Excellence in Tribal Governance* 12 (2014), http://hpaied.org/sites/default/files/HN2014%20Report%202015.pdf.

Through the tribal council and tribal housing authority, the pueblo sought to revitalize the houses in Owe'neh Bupingeh by bringing families back to live around the plazas. Community meetings were held to help to identify the kinds of changes that could make Owe'neh Bupingeh homes more appealing and livable. A consensus soon emerged that the buildings should be repaired, but modern amenities should be added as part of the renovations.

The pueblo worked closely with the United States Office of Housing and Urban Development Office of Native American Programs and other federal and state agencies to raise $9 million for the rehabilitation project from over 20 different sources. As of 2014, 34 of the homes in Owe'neh Bupingeh had been renovated with modern kitchens, bathrooms, and laundry rooms. The traditional layout of the village center with connected homes surrounding the plazas has been maintained. Historic mud-plaster adobe has been used on outer walls and the project has won numerous architectural awards. Demand for village housing is on the rise, and there is increased interest and participation in traditional practices and ceremonies. As one tribal member observes, "The weakness and sadness that once existed is now laughter, voices, and aromas, which makes it a living pueblo. You can feel its strength and power as though you have entered a space that requires its highest form of respect." Id. at 15.

Professor Charles F. Wilkinson, one of the original authors on the first edition of this casebook, published in 1978 at the highpoint of the modern Indian rights movement, has chronicled the remarkable successes and achievements of that movement in his book, Blood Struggle: The Rise of Modern Indian Nations (2005). Professor Wilkinson has fittingly reminded us that the advances made by tribal communities like Ohkay Owingeh, the "Place of the Strong People," over the past half century are the product, not of the courts and legislature of the conqueror, but of "the Indian tribal leaders of the historic post-World War II era, who have made their reservations into homelands." Id. at v. The legacy of the achievements of that generation, one of Indian country's greatest, is reflected in the court decisions and legislation of the modern era. But as Wilkinson explains, the foundation for rebuilding Native nations in the 21st century is to be found, as it has since the beginnings of the earliest colonial encounters, in the desire of Indian peoples "to make their own laws and be ruled by them," *Williams v. Lee*, at page 426, supra.

> The current legal structure, largely the result of tribal initiatives, does not afford Indian people all they would wish, but it sets a generally favorable context for an expansive tribal self-determination. Of course, tribal leaders must always keep a watchful eye on Washington, D.C. Congress has nearly unlimited power to adjust or eliminate Indian rights, and the Supreme Court has encompassing authority to interpret treaties and old and new statutes. That is why, although a major event over the past half century has been the resurrection and creation of laws favorable to American Indians, perhaps an even larger advance has been the underlying reason for the progress: the tribes' surprising ability to influence their own destiny in the courts and Congress—an ability the tribes are determined to preserve and enhance in the future.

Id. at 242.

PART TWO

FEDERAL INDIAN LAW AND POLICY IN CONTEMPORARY PERSPECTIVE

■ ■ ■

The history of federal Indian law and policy has generated a number of still vibrant legacies shaping contemporary policy debates and legal doctrines that define the federal-tribal relationship. The Marshall trilogy of early Indian law decisions, *Johnson v. McIntosh, Cherokee Nation v. Georgia*, and *Worcester v. Georgia*, provide foundational principles for guiding the deliberations of Congress and the decisions of courts on the nature of federal powers over tribes, Indian self-government, issues of jurisdiction in Indian country, and the special rights of tribal Indians as groups. Yet, those principles themselves have not remained static. The effects of the allotment policy on the tribal land base and the introduction of a non-Indian presence in Indian country have continuing significance. Although considerable revitalization of tribal governments was achieved by the Indian Reorganization Act, the termination policy's chilling lessons on the precariousness of tribalism haunt Indians even today. And the self-determination era has incorporated Indian tribes as legitimate and recognized governmental entities in the federal system.

Now, Native nations are entering into the period of nation building, a dynamic era of tribal government revitalization. For the first time since the early decades of American history, Native nations are expected and encouraged to govern themselves, pursue business ventures of their own, and decide how they want to utilize the natural and economic resources of the reservation.

CHAPTER FIVE

THE FEDERAL-TRIBAL RELATIONSHIP

■ ■ ■

SECTION A. TRIBAL PROPERTY INTERESTS

In 1823, the Supreme Court ruled in Johnson v. McIntosh, 21 U.S. (8 Wheat.) 543 (1823), page 137, supra, that tribes did not own fee title to their lands but held a lesser interest that the Court characterized as a right of occupancy under the doctrine of discovery. The United States, under the doctrine, had the exclusive right to purchase or extinguish Indian title. By that time, Congress had enacted the Nonintercourse Act, 25 U.S.C.A. § 177, prohibiting the conveyance of Indian lands except as authorized by Congress. Thus, Congress and the Court attempted to establish a legal foundation for the orderly disposition and recognition of Indian property interests.

For more than two hundred years the government has undertaken to resolve Indian property interests according to the principles of the doctrine of discovery. In most instances, it has extinguished Indian title through purchase. While some land has been retained by the federal government, most has been made available for non-Indian acquisition. The extinguishment of Indian title often occurred through treaties or agreements in which Indians ceded a large tract of land to the United States and retained a smaller parcel that the United States recognized and agreed to protect.

Today, Indians still hold substantial and, in some instances, valuable tracts of land. The source of Indian rights in the property may be traced to aboriginal possession, treaty, agreement, statute, executive action, purchase, or action of a colony, state, or foreign nation. In some cases, the source of title may be important. For example, land holdings that have been "recognized" or "confirmed" by Congress differ from the right of occupancy derived from aboriginal title in that the government must pay compensation under the Fifth Amendment when it takes recognized title while it need not do so in the case of aboriginal title. See Tee-Hit-Ton Indians v. United States, 348 U.S. 272 (1955), page 296, infra. In some cases, one can find within a single Indian reservation considerable variation in the types of land holdings. A portion of the reservation may have been reserved by treaty, another tract added by executive order, and still another parcel acquired by purchase. This section examines the status of Indian land holdings established by treaty, statute, executive order, or other means.

UNITED STATES V. SHOSHONE TRIBE OF INDIANS

Supreme Court of the United States, 1938.
304 U.S. 111, 58 S.Ct. 794, 82 L.Ed. 1213.

MR. JUSTICE BUTLER delivered the opinion of the Court.

The Shoshone Tribe brought this suit to recover the value of part of its reservation taken by the United States by putting upon it, without the tribe's consent, a band of Arapahoe Indians.

* * *

The sole question for decision is whether, as the United States contends, the Court of Claims erred in holding that the right of the tribe included the timber and mineral resources within the reservation.

The findings show: The United States, by the treaty of July 2, 1863, set apart for the Shoshone Tribe a reservation of 44,672,000 acres located in Colorado, Utah, Idaho and Wyoming. By the treaty of July 3, 1868, the tribe ceded that reservation to the United States. And by it the United States agreed that the "district of country" 3,054,182 acres definitely described "shall be and the same is set apart for the absolute and undisturbed use and occupation of the Shoshone Indians * * *, and the United States now solemnly agrees that no persons," with exceptions not important here, "shall ever be permitted to pass over, settle upon, or reside in" that territory. The Indians agreed that they would make the reservation their permanent home.

* * *

When the treaty of 1868 was made, the tribe consisted of full blood blanket Indians, unable to read, write, or speak English. Upon consummation of the treaty, the tribe went, and has since remained, upon the reservation. It was known to contain valuable mineral deposits—gold, oil, coal and gypsum. It included more than 400,000 acres of timber, extensive well-grassed bench lands and fertile river valleys conveniently irrigable. It was well protected by mountain ranges and a divide, and was the choicest and best-watered portion of Wyoming.

In 1904 the Shoshones and Arapahoes ceded to the United States 1,480,000 acres to be held by it in trust for the sale of such timber lands, timber and other products, and for the making of leases for various purposes. The net proceeds were to be credited to the Indians. From 1907 to 1919 there were allotted to members of the tribes 245,058 acres.

The court's finding of the ultimate fact is: "The fair and reasonable value of a one-half undivided interest of the Shoshone or Wind River

Reservation of a total of 2,343,540 acres, which was taken by the United States on March 19, 1878, from the Shoshone Tribe of Indians for the Northern Arapahoe Tribe, was, on March 19, 1878, $1,581,889.50." That is $1.35 per acre for 1,171,770 acres, one-half of the reservation in 1878, at the time of taking. The United States does not challenge the principle or basis upon which the court determined the amount to be added to constitute just compensation.

The substance of the Government's point is that in fixing the value of the tribe's right, the lower court included as belonging to the tribe substantial elements of value, ascribable to mineral and timber resources, which in fact belonged to the United States.

It contends that the Shoshones' right to use and occupy the lands of the reservation did not include the ownership of the timber and minerals and that the *opinion* of the court below departs from the general principles of law regarding Indian land tenure and the uniform policy of the Government in dealing with Indian tribes. It asks for reversal with "directions to determine the value of the Indians' right of use and occupancy but to exclude therefrom 'the net value of the lands' and 'the net value of any timber or minerals.' "

* * *

In this case we have held [in an earlier opinion], 299 U. S. 476, 484, that the tribe had the right of occupancy with all its beneficial incidents; that, the right of occupancy being the primary one and as sacred as the fee, division by the United States of the Shoshones' right with the Arapahoes was an appropriation of the land *pro tanto;* that although the United States always had legal title to the land and power to control and manage the affairs of the Indians, it did not have power to give to others or to appropriate to its own use any part of the land without rendering, or assuming the obligation to pay, just compensation to the tribe, for that would be, not the exercise of guardianship or management, but confiscation.

It was not then necessary to consider, but we are now called upon to decide, whether, by the treaty, the tribe acquired beneficial ownership of the minerals and timber on the reservation. The phrase "absolute and undisturbed use and occupation" is to be read, with other parts of the document, having regard to the purpose of the arrangement made, the relation between the parties, and the settled policy of the United States fairly to deal with Indian tribes. In treaties made with them the United States seeks no advantage for itself; friendly and dependent Indians are likely to accept without discriminating scrutiny the terms proposed. They are not to be interpreted narrowly, as sometimes may be writings expressed in words of art employed by conveyancers, but are to be construed in the sense in which naturally the Indians would understand them.

The principal purpose of the treaty was that the Shoshones should have, and permanently dwell in, the defined district of country. To that end the United States granted and assured to the tribe peaceable and unqualified possession of the land in perpetuity. Minerals and standing timber are constituent elements of the land itself. For all practical purposes, the tribe owned the land. Grants of land subject to the Indian title by the United States, which had only the naked fee, would transfer no beneficial interest. * * *

The treaty, though made with knowledge that there were mineral deposits and standing timber in the reservation, contains nothing to suggest that the United States intended to retain for itself any beneficial interest in them. The words of the grant, coupled with the Government's agreement to exclude strangers, negative the idea that the United States retained beneficial ownership. The grant of right to members of the tribe severally to select and hold tracts on which to establish homes for themselves and families, and the restraint upon cession of land held in common or individually, suggest beneficial ownership in the tribe. As transactions between a guardian and his wards are to be construed favorable to the latter, doubts, if there were any, as to ownership of lands, minerals or timber would be resolved in favor of the tribe. The cession in 1904 by the tribe to the United States in trust reflects a construction by the parties that supports the tribe's claim, for if it did not own, creation of a trust to sell or lease for its benefit would have been unnecessary and inconsistent with the rights of the parties.

Although the United States retained the fee, and the tribe's right of occupancy was incapable of alienation or of being held otherwise than in common, that right is as sacred and as securely safeguarded as is fee simple absolute title. *Cherokee Nation v. Georgia*, 5 Pet. 1, 48. *Worcester v. Georgia*, 6 Pet. 515, 580. Subject to the conditions imposed by the treaty, the Shoshone Tribe had the right that has always been understood to belong to Indians, undisturbed possessors of the soil from time immemorial. Provisions in aid of teaching children and of adult education in farming, and to secure for the tribe medical and mechanical service, to safeguard tribal and individual titles, when taken with other parts of the treaty, plainly evidence purpose on the part of the United States to help to create an independent permanent farming community upon the reservation. Ownership of the land would further that purpose. In the absence of definite expression of intention so to do, the United States will not be held to have kept it from them. The authority of the United States to prescribe title by which individual Indians may hold tracts selected by them within the reservation, to pass laws regulating alienation and descent and for the government of the tribe and its people upon the reservation detracts nothing from the tribe's ownership, but was reserved for the more convenient discharge of the duties of the United States as guardian and sovereign.

United States v. Cook, 19 Wall. 591, gives no support to the contention that in ascertaining just compensation for the Indian right taken, the value of mineral and timber resources in the reservation should be excluded. That case did not involve adjudication of the scope of Indian title to land, minerals or standing timber, but only the right of the United States to replevin logs cut and sold by a few unauthorized members of the tribe. We held that, as against the purchaser from the wrongdoers, the United States was entitled to possession. It was not there decided that the tribe's right of occupancy in perpetuity did not include ownership of the land or mineral deposits or standing timber upon the reservation, or that the tribe's right was the mere equivalent of, or like, the title of a life tenant.

The lower court did not err in holding that the right of the Shoshone Tribe included the timber and minerals within the reservation.

Affirmed.

NOTES

1.   *Shoshone Tribe* removed considerable confusion over the extent of tribal property interests relative to the interests of the United States. *United States v. Cook*, distinguished by the Court in *Shoshone*, dealt specifically with the limitations on rights of Indians as beneficial owners of the reservation land to cut and sell timber and the prerogatives of the United States as superior sovereign under the doctrine of discovery to protect the land, including the timber. *Cook* had held that the United States could bring an action of replevin to recover possession of reservation timber cut and sold by tribal members to a non-Indian. Because of Cook's emphasis on the government's right to pursue legal remedies and the absence of language acknowledging that this action was, after all, for the benefit and protection of the tribe's interests, it was misinterpreted. The decision was read to imply that tribes held no property interest in reservation timber. E.g., 19 Op.Atty.Gen. 194 (1888); 19 Op.Atty.Gen. 710 (1890); Pine River Logging & Improvement Co. v. United States, 186 U.S. 279 (1902). *Shoshone Tribe* remains the law and tribes are presumed to hold full beneficial ownership of the land, minerals, timber, and other associated property interests. See White Mountain Apache Tribe v. Bracker, 448 U.S. 136, 145–46 n. 12 (1980), page 655, infra. There are exceptions. A few treaty and statutory provisions expressly recognize lesser interests in a particular tribe.

2.   While title to most tribal land is held by the United States in trust, tribes such as the Pueblos of New Mexico and the Tuscarora of New York hold fee title to their land. In both instances, however, the tribes may not convey title without the consent of the United States. Mountain States Tel. & Tel. Co. v. Pueblo of Santa Ana, 472 U.S. 237, 252–55 (1985) (Pueblo land transactions

covered by Section 17 of Pueblo Lands Act of 1924, 43 Stat. 641); Oneida Indian Nation v. Oneida County, 414 U.S. 661, 674–75 n. 9 (1974) (Tuscarora Nation land transactions covered by Nonintercourse Act, 25 U.S.C.A. § 177).

SIOUX TRIBE V. UNITED STATES
Supreme Court of the United States, 1942.
316 U.S. 317, 62 S.Ct. 1095, 86 L.Ed. 1501.

MR. JUSTICE BYRNES delivered the opinion of the Court.

[In 1875 and 1876 the President issued executive orders setting aside four tracts of lands for the use of the Sioux Tribe.]

* * *

About two and half years after the last of these four executive orders withdrawing lands from sale and setting them apart for the use of the Sioux, the Commissioner of Indian Affairs submitted to the Secretary of the Interior a report upon a suggestion that the orders be modified so as to permit the return of the lands to the public domain. The report, dated June 6, 1879, reviewed the problems arising from the liquor trade during the years following the Fort Laramie treaty, recalled that the purpose of the four executive orders of 1875 and 1876 had been to eliminate this traffic, observed that they had "to a great extent accomplished the object desired, viz: the prevention of the sale of whiskey to the Indians." * * *

* * *

* * * Accordingly, he recommended that the lands withdrawn from sale by the President in 1875 and 1876 be returned to the public domain, with the exception of three small tracts directly opposite the Cheyenne, Grand River, and Standing Rock agencies. On August 9, 1879, an executive order to this effect was promulgated and the land, with the exceptions indicated, was "restored to the public domain." Five years later, the Commissioner informed the Secretary that the Grand River Agency had ceased to exist and that the agents at Cheyenne and Standing Rock considered it no longer necessary to withhold the tracts opposite their agencies from the public domain "for the purpose for which they have thus far been retained." Consequently, an executive order was prepared and signed by the President on March 20, 1884, restoring these three small pieces of land to the public domain, "the same being no longer needed for the purpose for which they were withdrawn from sale and settlement."

One additional event remains to be noted. In the Indian Appropriation Act for 1877, approved August 15, 1876, Congress provided:

" . . . hereafter there shall be no appropriation made for the subsistence of said Indians [i.e., the Sioux], unless they shall first agree to relinquish all right and claim to any country outside the boundaries of the permanent reservation established by the treaty of eighteen hundred and sixty-eight [the Fort Laramie treaty] for said Indians; and also so much of their said permanent reservation as lies west of the one hundred and third meridian of longitude [the western boundary set by the Fort Laramie treaty had been the 104th meridian], and shall also grant right of way over said reservation to the country thus ceded for wagon or other roads, from convenient and accessible points on the Missouri River . . . [.]"

On September 26, 1876—a date subsequent to the first three of the four executive orders setting apart additional lands for the use of the Sioux, but about two months prior to the last of those orders—the Sioux Tribe signed an agreement conforming to the conditions imposed by Congress in the Indian Appropriation Act and promised to "relinquish and cede to the United States all the territory lying outside the said reservation, as herein modified and described . . . [.]"

* * *

Section 3 of Article IV of the Constitution confers upon Congress exclusively "the power to dispose of and make all needful rules and regulations respecting the territory or other property belonging to the United States." Nevertheless, "from an early period in the history of the government it has been the practice of the President to order, from time to time, as the exigencies of the public service required, parcels of land belonging to the United States to be reserved from sale and set apart for public uses." *Grisar v. McDowell*, 6 Wall. 363, 381. As long ago as 1830, Congress revealed its awareness of this practice and acquiesced in it. By 1855 the President had begun to withdraw public lands from sale by executive order for the specific purpose of establishing Indian reservations. From that date until 1919, hundreds of reservations for Indian occupancy and for other purposes were created by executive order. Although the validity of these orders was occasionally questioned, doubts were quieted in *United States v. Midwest Oil Co.*, 236 U. S. 459. In that case, it was squarely held that, even in the absence of express statutory authorization, it lay within the power of the President to withdraw lands from the public domain.

The Government therefore does not deny that the executive orders of 1875 and 1876 involved here were effective to withdraw the lands in question from the public domain. It contends, however, that this is not the issue presented by this case. It urges that, instead, we are called upon to determine whether the President had the power to bestow upon the Sioux Tribe an interest in these lands of such a character as to require compensation when the interest was extinguished by the executive orders of 1879 and 1884. Concededly, where lands have been reserved for the use and occupation of an Indian Tribe by the terms of a treaty or statute, the tribe must be compensated if the lands are subsequently taken from them.

Shoshone Tribe v. United States, 299 U. S. 476; *United States v. Shoshone Tribe*, 304 U. S. 111; *United States v. Klamath Indians*, 304 U. S. 119. Since the Constitution places the authority to dispose of public lands exclusively in Congress, the executive's power to convey any interest in these lands must be traced to Congressional delegation of its authority. The basis of decision in *United States v. Midwest Oil Co.* was that, so far as the power to withdraw public lands from sale is concerned, such a delegation could be spelled out from long continued Congressional acquiescence in the executive practice. The answer to whether a similar delegation occurred with respect to the power to convey a compensable interest in these lands to the Indians must be found in the available evidence of what consequences were thought by the executive and Congress to flow from the establishment of executive order reservations.

It is significant that the executive department consistently indicated its understanding that the rights and interests which the Indians enjoyed in executive order reservations were different from and less than their rights and interests in treaty or statute reservations. The annual reports of the Commissioner of Indian Affairs during the years when reservations were frequently being established by executive order contain statements that the Indians had "no assurance for their occupation of these lands beyond the pleasure of the Executive," that they "are mere tenants at will, and possess no permanent rights to the lands upon which they are temporarily permitted to remain," and that those occupying land in executive order reservations "do not hold it by the same tenure with which Indians in other parts of the Indian Territory possess their reserves."

Although there are abundant signs that Congress was aware of the practice of establishing Indian reservations by executive order, there is little to indicate what it understood to be the kind of interest that the Indians obtained in these lands. However, in its report in 1892 upon a bill to restore to the public domain a portion of the Colville executive order reservation, the Senate Committee on Indian Affairs expressed the opinion that under the executive order "the Indians were given a license to occupy the lands described in it so long as it was the pleasure of the Government that they should do so, and no right, title, or claim to such lands has vested in the Indians by virtue of this occupancy."

* * * Petitioner urges that, by including executive order reservations within the provisions of [the General Allotment] Act, Congress revealed its belief that the degree of ownership enjoyed by Indian tribes is identical whether the reservation is created by treaty, statute, or executive order. * * *

* * * We think that the inclusion of executive order reservations meant no more than that Congress was willing that the lands within them should be allotted to individual Indians according to the procedure outlined. It did

not amount to a recognition of tribal ownership of the lands prior to allotment. Since the lands involved in the case before us were never allotted—indeed, the executive orders of 1879 and 1884 terminated the reservation even before the Allotment Act was passed[ ]—we think the Act has no bearing upon the issue presented.

Perhaps the most striking proof of the belief shared by Congress and the Executive that the Indians were not entitled to compensation upon the abolition of an executive order reservation is the very absence of compensatory payments in such situations. It was a common practice, during the period in which reservations were created by executive order, for the President simply to terminate the existence of a reservation by canceling or revoking the order establishing it. * * *

We conclude therefore that there was no express constitutional or statutory authorization for the conveyance of a compensable interest to petitioner by the four executive orders of 1875 and 1876, and that no implied Congressional delegation of the power to do so can be spelled out from the evidence of Congressional and executive understanding. The orders were effective to withdraw from sale the lands affected and to grant the use of the lands to the petitioner. But the interest which the Indians received was subject to termination at the will of either the executive or Congress and without obligation to the United States. The executive orders of 1879 and 1884 were simply an exercise of this power of termination, and the payment of compensation was not required.

Affirmed.

NOTES

1. The Court in *Sioux Tribe* distinguished Shoshone Tribe v. United States, 299 U.S. 476 (1937), in which the Court held that tribal title had been confirmed by establishing federal schools on the reservation granting allotments, and paying the tribe for earlier cessions of land. Beyond an explicit act of Congress, what kind of federal actions are sufficient to "ratify" an executive order reservation and make its taking compensable? When is legislation not sufficient confirmation? See Confederated Bands of Ute Indians v. United States, 330 U.S. 169 (1947) (rejecting tribe's attempt to distinguish its case from *Sioux Tribe* arguing on grounds than an 1880 Act confirmed the Indians' understanding that the White River Valley was always part of their reservation and therefore compensable).

2. Under the Property Clause, U.S. Const. art. IV, § 3, cl. 2, Congress possesses authority over the public lands. But in *Midwest Oil*, cited in *Sioux Tribe,* the Court upheld President Taft's extensive withdrawals of oil and gas deposits under public lands on the ground that Congress had "impliedly acquiesced" in unilateral executive withdrawals of public lands, a prominent example being Indian reservations. If Congress "acquiesced" in the creation of

executive order Indian reservations with all of the attributes of treaty reservations, how does that affect compensability for takings?

3. The first executive order Indian reservations were established in 1855 but it was not until 1919 that Congress insisted that only it, and not the Executive acting alone, had authority to create Indian reservations. 43 U.S.C.A. § 150. A similar law affecting only Arizona and New Mexico had been passed in 1918. 25 U.S.C.A. § 211. Subsequent to these statutes, additions to reservations were made by temporary secretarial withdrawals later confirmed by Congress. E.g., Arizona v. California, 373 U.S. 546, 596 n.100 (1963).

4. In 1927, as a part of the oil and gas leasing act, Congress prohibited any changes in the boundaries of reservations created by executive order except by an act of Congress. 25 U.S.C.A. § 398d. See Sekaquaptewa v. MacDonald, 448 F.Supp. 1183, 1192 (D.Ariz.1978), affirmed in part and reversed in part on other grounds 619 F.2d 801 (9th Cir.1980), cert. denied 449 U.S. 1010 (1980) (rejecting claim that Congress intended the oil and gas leasing act of 1927 to constitute recognition of Indian property interests in reservations established by Executive order).

5. In the Indian Claims Commission Act of 1946, Congress provided that takings of executive order lands before the effective date of the Act would be compensable in the Commission, 25 U.S.C.A. § 70a, discussed at pages 306–312, infra. Fort Berthold Reservation v. United States, 390 F.2d 686, 696–97 (Ct.Cl.1968). Takings of executive order lands after 1946 are apparently compensable in the Court of Claims under 28 U.S.C.A. § 1505. Both kinds of claims, however, involve "nonrecognized" title under existing law and are subject to the "no-interest" rule, pages 300–301, infra, so that awards bear interest only from the date of the award rather than from the date of taking. As a policy matter in modern times, Congress has compensated tribes when executive order land has been taken. See, e.g., the Hoopa-Yurok Settlement Act, 25 U.S.C.A. § 1300i.

MONTANA V. UNITED STATES
Supreme Court of the United States, 1981.
450 U.S. 544, 101 S.Ct. 1245, 67 L.Ed.2d 493.

JUSTICE STEWART delivered the opinion of the Court.

This case concerns the sources and scope of the power of an Indian tribe to regulate hunting and fishing by non-Indians on lands within its reservation owned in fee simple by non-Indians. Relying on its purported ownership of the bed of the Big Horn River, on the treaties which created its reservation and on its inherent power as a sovereign, the Crow Tribe of Montana claims the authority to prohibit all hunting and fishing by non-members of the Tribe on non-Indian property within reservation boundaries. We granted certiorari, to review a decision of the United States Court of Appeals for the Ninth Circuit that substantially upheld this claim.

* * *

II

The respondents seek to establish a substantial part of their claim of power to control hunting and fishing on the reservation by asking us to recognize their title to the bed of the Big Horn River. The question is whether the United States conveyed beneficial ownership of the riverbed to the Crow Tribe by the Treaties of 1851 or 1868, and therefore continues to hold the land in trust for the use and benefit of the Tribe, or whether the United States retained ownership of the riverbed as public land which then passed to the State of Montana upon its admission to the Union. *Choctaw Nation v. Oklahoma*, 397 U. S. 620, 627–628.

Though the owners of land riparian to *nonnavigable* streams may own the adjacent riverbed, conveyance by the United States of land riparian to a *navigable* river carries no interest in the riverbed. Rather, the ownership of land under navigable waters is an incident of sovereignty. As a general principle, the Federal Government holds such lands in trust for future States, to be granted to such States when they enter the Union and assume sovereignty on an "equal footing" with the established States. After a State enters the Union, title to the land is governed by state law. The State's power over the beds of navigable waters remains subject to only one limitation: the paramount power of the United States to ensure that such waters remain free to interstate and foreign commerce. It is now established, however, that Congress may sometimes convey lands below the high water mark of a navigable water,

> "[and so defeat the title of a new State,] in order to perform international obligations, or to effect an improvement of such lands for the promotion and convenience of commerce with foreign nations and among the several States, or to carry out other public purposes for which the United States hold the Territory." *Shively v. Bowlby*, 152 U. S. 1, 48.

But because control over the property underlying navigable waters is so strongly identified with the sovereign power of government, it will not be held that the United States has conveyed such land "except because of some special duty or exigency." *United States v. Holt State Bank*, 270 U. S., at 55. See also *Shively v. Bowlby, supra*, at 48. A court deciding a question of title to the bed of a navigable water must, therefore, begin with a strong presumption against conveyance by the United States, and must not infer such a conveyance "unless the intention was definitely declared or otherwise made plain," *United States v. Holt State Bank, supra*, at 55, or was rendered "in clear and *especial* words," *Martin v. Waddell*, 41 U. S., at 411, or "unless the claim confirmed in terms embraces the land under the waters of the stream," *Packer v. Bird*, 137 U. S., at 672.

In *United States v. Holt State Bank, supra,* this Court applied these principles to reject an Indian Tribe's claim of title to the bed of a navigable lake. The lake lay wholly within the boundaries of the Red Lake Indian reservation, which had been created by treaties entered into before Minnesota joined the Union. In these treaties the United States promised to "set apart and withhold from sale, for the use of" the Chippewas, a large tract of land, Treaty of Sept. 30, 1854, 10 Stat. 1109, and to convey "a sufficient quantity of land for the permanent homes" of the Indians, Treaty of Feb. 22, 1855, 10 Stat. 1165. The Court concluded that there was nothing in the treaties "which even approaches a grant of rights in lands underlying navigable waters; nor anything evincing a purpose to depart from the established policy * * * of treating such lands as held for the benefit of the future State." *United States v. Holt State Bank, supra,* at 58–59. Rather, "[t]he effect of what was done was to reserve in a general way for the continued occupation of the Indians what remained of their aboriginal territory."

The Crow treaties in this case, like the Chippewa treaties in *Holt State Bank,* fail to overcome the established presumption that the beds of navigable waters remain in trust for future States and pass to the new States when they assume sovereignty. The 1851 treaty did not by its terms formally convey any land to the Indians at all, but instead chiefly represented a covenant among several tribes which recognized specific boundaries for their respective territories. Treaty of Fort Laramie, 1851, 11 Stat. 749, Art. 5. It referred to hunting and fishing only insofar as it said that the Crow Indians "do not surrender the privilege of hunting, fishing, or passing over any of the tracts of country heretofore described," a statement that had no bearing on ownership of the riverbed. By contrast, the 1868 treaty did expressly convey land to the Crow Tribe. Article 2 of the treaty described the reservation land in detail and stated that such land would be "set apart for the absolute and undisturbed use and occupation of the Indians herein named. . . ." Second Treaty of Fort Laramie, May 7, 1868, 15 Stat. 649, Art. 2. The treaty then stated:

> "[T]he United States now solemnly agrees that no persons, except those herein designated and authorized to do so, and except such officers, agents, and employees of the Government as may be authorized to enter upon Indian reservations in discharge of duties enjoined by law, shall ever be permitted to pass over, settle upon, or reside in the territory described in this article for the use of said Indians. . . ." *Ibid.*

Whatever property rights the language of the 1868 treaty created, however, its language is not strong enough to overcome the presumption against the sovereign's conveyance of the riverbed. The treaty in no way expressly referred to the riverbed, nor was an intention to convey the riverbed expressed in "clear and *especial* words," or "definitely declared or otherwise made plain." Rather, as in *Holt*, "[T]he effect of what was done was to reserve in a general way for the continued occupation of the Indians what remained of their aboriginal territory."

Though Article 2 gave the Crow Indians the sole right to use and occupy the reserved land, and, implicitly, the power to exclude others from it, the respondents' reliance on that provision simply begs the question of the precise extent of the conveyed lands to which this exclusivity attaches. The mere fact that the bed of a navigable water lies within the boundaries described in the treaty does not make the riverbed part of the conveyed land, especially when there is no express reference to the riverbed that might overcome the presumption against its conveyance. In the Court of Appeals' * * * decision, on which recognition of the Crow Tribe's title to the riverbed rested in this case, that court construed the language of exclusivity in the 1868 treaty as granting to the Indians all the lands, including the riverbed, within the described boundaries. *United States v. Finch*, 548 F. 2d, at 829. Such a construction, however, cannot survive examination. As the Court of Appeals recognized, *ibid.*, and as the respondents concede, the United States retains a navigational easement in the navigable waters lying within the described boundaries for the benefit of the public, regardless of who owns the riverbed. Therefore, such phrases in the 1868 treaty as "absolute and undisturbed use and occupation" and "no persons except those herein designated . . . shall ever be permitted," whatever they seem to mean literally, do not give the Indians the exclusive right to occupy all the territory within the described boundaries. Thus, even if exclusivity were the same as ownership, the treaty language establishing this "right of exclusivity" could not have the meaning that the Court of Appeals ascribed to it.[5]

---

[5] In one recent case, *Choctaw Nation v. Oklahoma*, 397 U. S. 620, supra, this Court did construe a reservation grant as including the bed of a navigable water, and the respondents argue that this case resembles *Choctaw Nation* more than it resembles the established line of cases to which *Choctaw Nation* is a singular exception. But the finding of a conveyance of the riverbed in *Choctaw Nation* was based on very peculiar circumstances not present in this case.

Those circumstances arose from the unusual history of the treaties there at issue, a history which formed an important basis of the decision. Choctaw Nation v. Oklahoma, supra, 397 U.S., at 622–628. Immediately after the Revolutionary War, the United States had signed treaties of peace and protection with the Cherokee and Choctaw tribes, reserving them lands in Georgia and Mississippi. In succeeding years the United States bought large areas of land from the Indians to make room for white settlers who were encroaching on tribal lands, but the Government signed new treaties guaranteeing that the Indians could live in peace on those lands not ceded. The United States soon betrayed that promise. It proposed that the tribes be relocated in a newly acquired part of the Arkansas Territory, but the new territory was soon overrun by white settlers, and through a series of new cession agreements the Indians were forced to relocate farther and farther west. Ultimately, most of the tribes' members refused to leave their eastern lands, doubting the reliability of the government's promises of the new western land, but Georgia and Mississippi, anxious for the relocation westward so they could assert jurisdiction over the Indian lands, purported to abolish the tribes and distribute the tribal lands. The Choctaws and Cherokees finally signed new treaties with the United States aimed at rectifying their past suffering at the hands of the Federal Government and the States.

Under the Choctaw treaty, the United States promised to convey new lands west of the Arkansas territory in fee simple, and also pledged that "no Territory or government shall ever

Moreover, even though the establishment of an Indian reservation can be an "appropriate public purpose" within the meaning of *Shively v. Bowlby*, 152 U. S., at 48, justifying a congressional conveyance of a riverbed, see, *e.g., Alaska Pacific Fisheries v. United States*, 248 U. S. 78, the situation of the Crow Indians at the time of the treaties presented no "public exigency" which would have required Congress to depart from its policy of reserving ownership of beds under navigable waters for the future States. See *Shively v. Bowlby, supra*, at 48. As the record in this case shows, at the time of the treaty the Crows were a nomadic tribe dependent chiefly on buffalo, and fishing was not important to their diet or way of life.

For these reasons, we conclude that title to the bed of the Big Horn River passed to the State of Montana upon its admission into the Union, and that the Court of Appeals was in error in holding otherwise.

* * *

[The Court then held that the tribe could not regulate non-Indian fishing and duck hunting on the Big Horn River. That portion of the opinion is reprinted at page 602, infra.]

NOTES

1.   What kind of language in an Indian treaty (or statute or executive order) would be "strong enough to overcome the presumption against" the federal government's pre-statehood conveyance of a riverbed? What should be the role of the canons of construction?

2.   How important are the "circumstances" surrounding the treaty? See footnote 5 discussing the *Choctaw* case. Suppose evidence had been introduced in *Montana* that the Crows depended heavily on the river and its resources for their livelihoods at the time of the treaty?

In Puyallup Tribe of Indians v. Port of Tacoma, 717 F.2d 1251, 1258 (9th Cir.1983), cert. denied 465 U.S. 1049 (1984), the court distinguished *Montana* to uphold tribal ownership of a riverbed:

[W]here a grant of real property to an Indian tribe includes within its boundaries a navigable water and the grant is made to a tribe dependent on the fishery resource in that water for survival, the

---

have a right to pass laws for the government of the Choctaw Nation . . . and that no part of the land granted to them shall ever be embraced in any Territory or State." Treaty of Dancing Rabbit Creek, Sept. 17, 1830, 7 Stat. 333–334, quoted in *Choctaw Nation v. Oklahoma, supra*, 397 U.S., at 625. In 1835, the Cherokees signed a treaty containing similar provisions granting reservation lands in fee simple and promising that the tribal lands would not become part of any State or Territory. Id., at 626. In concluding that the United States had intended to convey the riverbed to the tribes before the admission of Oklahoma to the Union, the *Choctaw* court relied on these circumstances surrounding the treaties and placed special emphasis on the Government's promise that the reserved lands would never become part of any State. Id., at 634–635. Neither the special historical origins of the Choctaw and Cherokee treaties nor the crucial provisions granting Indian lands in fee simple and promising freedom from state jurisdiction in those treaties have any counterparts in the terms and circumstances of the Crow Treaties of 1851 and 1868.

grant must be construed to include the submerged lands if the Government was plainly aware of the vital importance of the submerged lands and the water resource to the tribe at the time of the grant.

Accord Muckleshoot Indian Tribe v. Trans-Canada Enterprises, Ltd., 713 F.2d 455 (9th Cir.1983), cert. denied 465 U.S. 1049 (1984). See also Confederated Salish & Kootenai Tribes v. Namen, 665 F.2d 951 (9th Cir.1982), cert. denied 459 U.S. 977 (1982) (treaty description of reservation included boundary line bisecting Flathead Lake, showing intent to convey the lakebed; also evidence of the Indians' reliance on fishing).

3. The Coeur d'Alene Tribe attempted to sue Idaho state officials to prevent violations of its property rights in Lake Coeur d'Alene, a navigable lake within the reservation. The Court said the suit was barred by the state's sovereign immunity under the Eleventh Amendment to the U.S. Constitution which prohibits suits "against one of the United States by Citizens of another State." Idaho v. Coeur d'Alene Tribe, 521 U.S. 261 (1997). The Court had earlier extended the effect of this provision beyond the limits of its text to prevent suits by tribes against states in Blatchford v. Village of Noatak, 501 U.S. 775 (1991), adding such litigation to a list of Court-made extensions of immunity pursuant to the provision. The Court has historically allowed litigants to circumvent the bar of sovereign immunity, however, by suing state officials in their official capacity instead of naming the state as a defendant. See Ex parte Young, 209 U.S. 123 (1908). Narrowing the *Ex parte Young* exception, the Court found that the injunction sought by the tribe against state officials was "close to the functional equivalent of quiet title" because it would effectively extinguish the state's control over the land. Four Justices dissented, perpetuating the Court's sharp philosophical division over matters involving sovereign immunity.

Of course, the Eleventh Amendment does not apply to the United States and so the federal government still can bring quiet title suits against states on behalf of tribes. The United States, in fact, did bring such a suit in federal district court, acting in its own capacity and as Trustee for the Coeur d'Alene Tribe. In Idaho v. United States, 533 U.S. 262 (2001), the Supreme Court held that the federal government held title in trust for the tribe to lands underlying portions of Lake Couer d'Alene and part of the St. Joe River within the reservation.

Justice Souter's majority opinion held that the negotiating history between the tribe and Congress and subsequent events plainly evidenced that Congress recognized the Executive Order reservation lying within boundaries it ultimately confirmed by legislation, and that it did not intend to pass title to the submerged lands within the reservation boundaries to Idaho absent "negotiated consensual transfer." Chief Justice Rehnquist, writing a dissent joined by Justices Scalia, Kennedy, and Thomas, argued that the evidence of congressional intent was insufficient to defeat the presumption under the equal footing doctrine that Idaho had a right as an incoming state to all submerged lands within its borders.

4.   Tribes whose riverbed interests were damaged by federal navigation improvements on the Arkansas River have been denied compensation because of the United States' navigation servitude. United States v. Cherokee Nation of Oklahoma, 480 U.S. 700 (1987). The servitude is invoked to deny compensation for takings of property within navigable waterways. Justice Rehnquist, writing the majority opinion for the court, stated:

> * * * we cannot conclude that respondent [the tribes]—though granted a degree of sovereignty over tribal lands—gained an exemption from the servitude simply because it received title to the riverbed interests. Such a waiver of sovereign authority will not be implied, but instead must be surrendered in unmistakable terms [citations omitted.] * * * Respondent can point to no such terms. * * *

Id. at 707. Justice Rehnquist also rejected arguments that the federal trust responsibility protected any rights of the Cherokee Nation in the riverbed.

TEE-HIT-TON INDIANS V. UNITED STATES

Supreme Court of the United States, 1955.
348 U.S. 272, 75 S.Ct. 313, 99 L.Ed. 314.

MR. JUSTICE REED delivered the opinion of the Court.

This case rests upon a claim under the Fifth Amendment by petitioner, an identifiable group of American Indians of between 60 and 70 individuals residing in Alaska, for compensation for a taking by the United States of certain timber from Alaskan lands allegedly belonging to the group. The area claimed is said to contain over 350,000 acres of land and 150 square miles of water. The Tee-Hit-Tons, a clan of the Tlingit Tribe, brought this suit in the Court of Claims under 28 U.S.C. § 1505. The compensation claimed does not arise from any statutory direction to pay. Payment, if it can be compelled, must be based upon a constitutional right of the Indians to recover. This is not a case that is connected with any phase of the policy of the Congress, continued throughout our history, to extinguish Indian title through negotiation rather than by force, and to grant payments from the public purse to needy descendants of exploited Indians. The legislation in support of that policy has received consistent interpretation from this Court in sympathy with its compassionate purpose.[2]

* * * [In the proceedings below, the Court of Claims adopted the Commissioner's findings of fact and] held that petitioner was an identifiable group of American Indians residing in Alaska; that its interest in the lands prior to purchase of Alaska by the United States in 1867 was

---

[2]   See Indian Claims Commission Act [analyzed at pages 306–307, infra]; *Worcester v. Georgia*, 6 Pet. 515, 582; *Alaska Pacific Fisheries v. United States*, 248 U. S. 78, 87, 89; *United States v. Santa Fe Pacific R. Co.*, 314 U. S. 339, 354.

"original Indian title" or "Indian right of occupancy." It was further held that if such original Indian title survived the Treaty of 1867, 15 Stat. 539, Arts. III and VI, by which Russia conveyed Alaska to the United States, such title was not sufficient basis to maintain this suit as there had been no recognition by Congress of any legal rights in petitioner to the land in question. The court said that no rights inured to plaintiff by virtue of legislation by Congress. * * * The Tee-Hit-Tons' petition was thereafter dismissed.

* * *

The Alaskan area in which petitioner claims a compensable interest is located near and within the exterior lines of the Tongass National Forest. By Joint Resolution of August 8, 1947, 61 Stat. 920, the Secretary of Agriculture was authorized to contract for the sale of national forest timber located within this National Forest "notwithstanding any claim of possessory rights." The Resolution defines "possessory rights" [to include "aboriginal occupancy or title"] and provides for all receipts from the sale of timber to be maintained in a special account in the Treasury until the timber and land rights are finally determined. Section 3(b) of the Resolution provides:

> "Nothing in this resolution shall be construed as recognizing or denying the validity of any claims of possessory rights to lands or timber within the exterior boundaries of the Tongass National Forest."

The Secretary of Agriculture, on August 20, 1951, pursuant to this authority contracted for sale to a private company of all merchantable timber in the area claimed by petitioner. This is the sale of timber which petitioner alleges constitutes a compensable taking by the United States of a portion of its proprietary interest in the land.

The problem presented is the nature of the petitioner's interest in the land, if any. Petitioner claims a "full proprietary ownership" of the land; or, in the alternative, at least a "recognized" right to unrestricted possession, occupation and use. Either ownership or recognized possession, petitioner asserts, is compensable. If it has a fee simple interest in the entire tract, it has an interest in the timber and its sale is a partial taking of its right to "possess, use and dispose of it." *United States v. General Motors Corp.*, 323 U. S. 373, 378. It is petitioner's contention that its tribal predecessors have continually claimed, occupied and used the land from time immemorial; that when Russia took Alaska, the Tlingits had a well-developed social order which included a concept of property ownership; that Russia while it possessed Alaska in no manner interfered with their claim to the land; that Congress has by subsequent acts confirmed and recognized petitioner's right to occupy the land permanently and therefore the sale of the timber off such lands constitutes a taking *pro tanto* of its asserted rights in the area.

The Government denies that petitioner has any compensable interest. It asserts that the Tee-Hit-Tons' property interest, if any, is merely that of the right to the use of the land at the Government's will; that Congress has never recognized any legal interest of petitioner in the land and therefore without such recognition no compensation is due the petitioner for any taking by the United States.

I.   *Recognition.*—The question of recognition may be disposed of shortly. Where the Congress by treaty or other agreement has declared that thereafter Indians were to hold the lands permanently, compensation must be paid for subsequent taking. The petitioner contends that Congress has sufficiently "recognized" its possessory rights in the land in question so as to make its interest compensable. Petitioner points specifically to two statutes to sustain this contention. The first is § 8 of the Organic Act for Alaska of May 17, 1884, 23 Stat. 24.[10] The second is § 27 of the Act of June 6, 1900, which was to provide for a civil government for Alaska, 31 Stat. 321, 330.[11] * * *

We have carefully examined these statutes and the pertinent legislative history and find nothing to indicate any intention by Congress to grant to the Indians any permanent rights in the lands of Alaska occupied by them by permission of Congress. Rather, it clearly appears that what was intended was merely to retain the *status quo* until further congressional or judicial action was taken. There is no particular form for congressional recognition of Indian rights of permanent occupancy. It may be established in a variety of ways but there must be the definite intention by congressional action or authority to accord legal rights, not merely permissive occupation. *Hynes v. Grimes Packing Co.*, 337 U. S. 86, 101.

This policy of Congress toward the Alaskan Indian lands was maintained and reflected by its expression in the Joint Resolution of 1947 under which the timber contracts were made.

II.   *Indian Title.*—(a) The nature of aboriginal Indian interest in land and the various rights as between the Indians and the United States dependent on such interest are far from novel as concerns our Indian inhabitants. It is well settled that in all the States of the Union the tribes who inhabited the lands of the States held claim to such lands after the coming of the white man, under what is sometimes termed original Indian title or permission from the whites to occupy. That description means mere

---

[10] " . . . That the Indians or other persons in said district shall not be disturbed in the possession of any lands actually in their use or occupation or now claimed by them but the terms under which such persons may acquire title to such lands is reserved for future legislation by Congress. . . ."

[11] "The Indians or persons conducting schools or missions in the district shall not be disturbed in the possession of any lands now actually in their use or occupation, . . ."

possession not specifically recognized as ownership by Congress. After conquest they were permitted to occupy portions of territory over which they had previously exercised "sovereignty," as we use that term. This is not a property right but amounts to a right of occupancy which the sovereign grants and protects against intrusion by third parties but which right of occupancy may be terminated and such lands fully disposed of by the sovereign itself without any legally enforceable obligation to compensate the Indians.

This position of the Indian has long been rationalized by the legal theory that discovery and conquest gave the conquerors sovereignty over and ownership of the lands thus obtained. 1 Wheaton's International Law, c. V. The great case of *Johnson v. McIntosh*, 8 Wheat. 543, denied the power of an Indian tribe to pass their right of occupancy to another. It confirmed the practice of two hundred years of American history "that discovery gave an exclusive right to extinguish the Indian title of occupancy, either by purchase or by conquest."

* * *

In *Beecher v. Wetherby*, 95 U. S. 517, a tract of land which Indians were then expressly permitted by the United States to occupy was granted to Wisconsin. In a controversy over timber, this Court held the Wisconsin title good.

> "The grantee, it is true, would take only the naked fee, and could not disturb the occupancy of the Indians: that occupancy could only be interfered with or determined by the United States. It is to be presumed that in this matter the United States would be governed by such considerations of justice as would control a Christian people in their treatment of an ignorant and dependent race. Be that as it may, the propriety or justice of their action towards the Indians with respect to their lands is a question of governmental policy, and is not a matter open to discussion in a controversy between third parties, neither of whom derives title from the Indians. The right of the United States to dispose of the fee of lands occupied by them has always been recognized by this court from the foundation of the government."

In 1941 a unanimous Court wrote, concerning Indian title, the following:

> Extinguishment of Indian title based on aboriginal possession is of course a different matter. The power of Congress in that regard is supreme. The manner, method and time of such extinguishment raise political, not justiciable, issues. *United States v. Santa Fe Pacific R. Co.*, 314 U. S. 339, 347.

No case in this Court has ever held that taking of Indian title or use by Congress required compensation. The American people have compassion for the descendants of those Indians who were deprived of their homes and hunting grounds by the drive of civilization. They seek to have the Indians share the benefits of our society as citizens of this Nation. Generous provision has been willingly made to allow tribes to recover for wrongs, as a matter of grace, not because of legal liability. 60 Stat. 1050.

(b) There is one opinion in a case decided by this Court that contains language indicating that unrecognized Indian title might be compensable under the Constitution when taken by the United States. *United States v. Alcea Band of Tillamooks*, 329 U. S. 40.

Recovery was allowed under a jurisdictional Act of 1935, 49 Stat. 801, that permitted payments to a few specific Indian tribes for "legal and equitable claims arising under or growing out of the original Indian title" to land, because of some unratified treaties negotiated with them and other tribes. The other tribes had already been compensated. Five years later this Court unanimously held that none of the former opinions in Vol. 329 of the United States Reports expressed the view that recovery was grounded on a taking under the Fifth Amendment. *United States v. Alcea Band of Tillamooks*, 341 U. S. 48. Interest, payable on recovery for a taking under the Fifth Amendment, was denied.[*]

Before the second *Tillamook* case, a decision was made on Alaskan Tlingit lands held by original Indian title. *Miller v. United States*, 159 F. 2d 997. That opinion holds such a title compensable under the Fifth Amendment on reasoning drawn from the language of this Court's first *Tillamook* case. After the *Miller* decision, this Court had occasion to consider the holding of that case on Indian title in *Hynes v. Grimes Packing Co.*, 337 U. S. 86, 106, note 28. We there commented as to the first *Tillamook* case: "That opinion does not hold the Indian right of occupancy compensable without specific legislative direction to make payment." We further declared "we cannot express agreement with that [compensability of Indian title by the *Miller* case] conclusion."

Later the Government used the *Hynes v. Grimes Packing Co.* note in the second *Tillamook* case to support its argument that the first *Tillamook* opinion did not decide that taking of original Indian title was compensable under the Fifth Amendment. Thereupon this Court in the second *Tillamook* case, 341 U. S. 48, held that the first case was not "grounded on a taking under the Fifth Amendment." Therefore no interest was due. This later *Tillamook* decision by a unanimous Court supported the Court of Claims in its view of the law in this present case. See *Tee-Hit-Ton Indians v. United*

---

[*]   [Ed.] Interest, which often far exceeds the value of the land when old takings are involved, can be recognized against the United States only when a property right recognizable under the Fifth Amendment is involved. Otherwise, the United States is protected by the "no-interest" rule. See page 300 infra.

States, 128 Ct. Cl., at 87, 120 F. Supp., at 204–205. We think it must be concluded that the recovery in the *Tillamook* case was based upon statutory direction to pay for the aboriginal title in the special jurisdictional act to equalize the Tillamooks with the neighboring tribes, rather than upon a holding that there had been a compensable taking under the Fifth Amendment. This leaves unimpaired the rule derived from *Johnson v. McIntosh* that the taking by the United States of unrecognized Indian title is not compensable under the Fifth Amendment.

This is true, not because an Indian or an Indian tribe has no standing to sue or because the United States has not consented to be sued for the taking of original Indian title, but because Indian occupation of land without government recognition of ownership creates no rights against taking or extinction by the United States protected by the Fifth Amendment or any other principle of law.

* * *

In considering the character of the Tee-Hit-Tons' use of the land, the Court of Claims had before it the testimony of a single witness who was offered by plaintiff. He stated that he was the chief of the Tee-Hit-Ton tribe. He qualified as an expert on the Tlingits, a group composed of numerous interconnected tribes including the Tee-Hit-Tons. His testimony showed that the Tee-Hit-Tons had become greatly reduced in numbers. Membership descends only through the female line. At the present time there are only a few women of childbearing age and a total membership of some 65.

The witness pointed out that their claim of ownership was based on possession and use. * * * The ownership was not individual but tribal. As the witness stated, "Any member of the tribe may use any portion of the land that he wishes, and as long as he uses it that is his for his own enjoyment, and is not to be trespassed upon by anybody else, but the minute he stops using it then any other member of the tribe can come in and use that area."

When the Russians first came to the Tlingit territory, the most important of the chiefs moved the people to what is now the location of the town of Wrangell. Each tribe took a portion of Wrangell harbor and the chief gave permission to the Russians to build a house on the shore.

The witness learned the alleged boundaries of the Tee-Hit-Ton area from hunting and fishing with his uncle after his return from Carlisle Indian School about 1904. From the knowledge so obtained, he outlined in red on the map, which petitioner filed as an exhibit, the territory claimed by the Tee-Hit-Tons. * * *

* * *

* * * From all that was presented, the Court of Claims concluded, and we agree, that the Tee-Hit-Tons were in a hunting and fishing stage of civilization, with shelters fitted to their environment, and claims to rights to use identified territory for these activities as well as the gathering of wild products of the earth. We think this evidence introduced by both sides confirms the Court of Claims' conclusion that the petitioner's use of its lands was like the use of the nomadic tribes of the States Indians.

The line of cases adjudicating Indian rights on American soil leads to the conclusion that Indian occupancy, not specifically recognized as ownership by action authorized by Congress, may be extinguished by the Government without compensation. Every American schoolboy knows that the savage tribes of this continent were deprived of their ancestral ranges by force and that, even when the Indians ceded millions of acres by treaty in return for blankets, food and trinkets, it was not a sale but the conquerors' will that deprived them of their land. * * *

In the light of the history of Indian relations in this Nation, no other course would meet the problem of the growth of the United States except to make congressional contributions for Indian lands rather than to subject the Government to an obligation to pay the value when taken with interest to the date of payment. Our conclusion does not uphold harshness as against tenderness toward the Indians, but it leaves with Congress, where it belongs, the policy of Indian gratuities for the termination of Indian occupancy of Government-owned land rather than making compensation for its value a rigid constitutional principle.

The judgment of the Court of Claims is

Affirmed.

MR. JUSTICE DOUGLAS, with whom THE CHIEF JUSTICE and MR. JUSTICE FRANKFURTER concur, dissenting.

The first Organic Act for Alaska became a law on May 17, 1884, 23 Stat. 24. It contained a provision in § 8 [quoted in note 10 of the majority opinion, supra] * * *

* * *

It is said that since § 8 contemplates the possible future acquisition of "title," it expressly negates any idea that the Indians have any "title." That is the argument; and that apparently is the conclusion of the Court.

There are, it seems to me, two answers to that proposition.

First. The first turns on the words of the Act. The general land laws of the United States were not made applicable to Alaska. § 8. No provision was made for opening up the lands to settlement, for clearing titles, for issuing patents. * * *

Second. The second proposition turns on the legislative history of § 8. * * * The words "or now claimed by them" were added by an amendment offered during the debates by Senator Plumb of Kansas. 15 Cong. Rec. 627–628. Senator Benjamin Harrison, in accepting the amendment, said, " . . . it was the intention of the committee to protect to the fullest extent all the rights of the Indians in Alaska and of any residents who had settled there, but at the same time to allow the development of the mineral resources . . . "

* * *

The conclusion seems clear that Congress in the 1884 Act recognized the claims of these Indians to their Alaskan lands. What those lands were was not known. Where they were located, what were their metes and bounds, were also unknown. Senator Plumb thought they probably were small and restricted. But all agreed that the Indians were to keep them, wherever they lay. It must be remembered that the Congress was legislating about a Territory concerning which little was known. No report was available showing the nature and extent of any claims to the land. No Indian was present to point out his tribe's domain. Therefore, Congress did the humane thing of saving to the Indians all rights claimed; it let them keep what they had prior to the new Act. The future course of action was made clear—conflicting claims would be reconciled and the Indian lands would be put into reservations.

That purpose is wholly at war with the one now attributed to the Congress of reserving for some future day the question whether the Indians were to have any rights to the land.

* * *

NOTES

1.   Does anything in *Johnson v. McIntosh,* page 72, supra, suggest the result in *Tee-Hit-Ton?* Assuming the validity of the holdings in *Shoshone Tribe* and *Sioux Tribe,* should Indian title be compensable? The issues in *Tee-Hit-Ton* are analyzed comprehensively in Nell Jessup Newton, *At the Whim of the Sovereign: Aboriginal Title Reconsidered,* 31 Hastings L.J. 1215 (1980).

2.   Justice Reed in footnote 17 of the *Tee-Hit-Ton* opinion pointed to the government's assertion in the *Tillamook* case "that if aboriginal Indian title was compensable without specific legislation to that effect, there were claims with estimated interest already pending under the Indian jurisdictional act [establishing the Indian Claims Commission] aggregating $9,000,000,000." Some scholars, including Dean Newton, see 31 Hasting L.J. 1215, 1249, supra, have charged that the Justice Department attorneys "cooked the books" in the *Tillamook* case. See Donald Craig Mitchell, Sold America, The Story of Alaska Natives and Their Land, 1867–1959, 403 (2003).

In an appendix to the brief it filed in *Alcea Band of Tillamooks*, the Department of Justice represented to the U.S. Supreme Court that if the Indian Claims Commission determined that all claims of Indian tribes pending before the Commission were valid, the United States would be obligated to pay $1 billion as compensation for the unlawful abrogation of the tribes' aboriginal titles. But if aboriginal title were Fifth Amendment "private property," the United States would be required to pay the tribes an additional $8 billion in interest. Brief for Petitioner at 55–56, *United States v. Alcea Band of Tillamooks,* 341 U.S. 48 (1951). In fact, the U.S. liability for Indian Claims Commission judgments was slightly less than $150 million. If the United States had been required to pay interest on the judgments, the total interest payment would have been slightly more than $1 billion.

Id.

3.   The Court of Federal Claims has strictly limited findings of takings. In Zuni Tribe of New Mexico v. United States, 16 Cl.Ct. 670 (1989), the court held that the Zuni Tribe had failed to prove that its claim was for "recognized title" which had to be based upon evidence of specific congressional intent. Congress had acted to recognize the Pueblos' land titles by assigning the Surveyor-General the task of surveying them and reporting back about the ownership and possession of the land so that Congress could act further. The Surveyor-General failed to carry out the congressional mandate with regard to the Zuni and therefore the court said the Zuni Tribe had only aboriginal title because there was not formal congressional recognition of its title.

4.   Despite Justice Reed's assertion in *Tee-Hit-Ton* that "[e]very American schoolboy knows that the savage tribes of this continent were deprived of their ancestral ranges by force * * * it was not a sale but the conquerors' will that deprived them of their land," the historical record suggests otherwise. Felix Cohen, writing in 1947, challenged "the common impression" that the United States took the land from "the original Indian owners of the continent * * * by force and proceeded to lock them up in concentration camps called 'reservations.'" Felix S. Cohen, *Original Indian Title,* 32 Minn.L.Rev. 28, 34–35 (1947). As Cohen sought to show in his article, most takings of Indian land were compensated in some fashion by negotiated treaties or agreements, by special legislation permitting individual tribal claims, or by claims brought pursuant to the Indian Claims Commission Act of 1946:

> * * * While nobody has ever calculated the total sum paid by the United States to Indian tribes as consideration for more than two million square miles of land purchased from them, and any such calculation would have to take account of the conjectural value of a myriad of commodities, special services, and tax exemptions, which commonly took the place of cash, a conservative estimate would put

the total price of Indian lands sold to the United States at a figure somewhat in excess of 800 million dollars.

Id. at 36.

While Cohen acknowledged that the United States' record of dealings with the tribes is not "without its dark pages," he also noted that the "purchase of more than two million square miles of land from the Indian tribes represents what is probably the largest real estate transaction in the history of the world. It would be miraculous if, across a period of 150 years, negotiations for the purchase and sale of these lands could be carried on without misunderstandings and inequities. We have been human, not angelic, in our real-estate transactions." Felix S. Cohen, *Original Indian Title*, 32 Minn.L.Rev. 28, 42 (1947).

5.   While *Tee-Hit-Ton* has never been overruled, there have been subsequent developments on Native property and sovereignty in Alaska. As described more fully in Ch. 13, infra, Congress passed the Alaska Native Claims Settlement Act (ANCSA) in 1971. See 43 U.S.C.A. §§ 1601–1628. In return for relinquishing their claims to aboriginal title to most of the state (365 million acres), Alaska Natives agreed to accept land selection rights to 44 million acres along with money payments totaling $962.5 million. ANCSA set up a system of regional and village corporations to hold and manage the assets of Native peoples. In *State of Alaska v. Native Village of Venetie*, the U.S. Supreme Court held that land transferred in fee simple to a village corporation, pursuant to ANCSA, and then back to the native village was not "Indian country" as a matter of federal law, and thus subject to state instead of tribal or federal jurisdiction.

6.   In recent years, Alaska Natives have fought successfully for the right to petition the Secretary of the Interior to take land into trust for them. In Akiachak Native Community v. Salazar, 935 F.Supp.2d 195 (D.D.C.2013), aff'd 827 F.3d 100 (D.C. Cir. 2016), a federal district court held ANCSA did not repeal the Secretary's authority under the IRA, 25 U.S.C, § 465 and 25 U.S.C § 473a, to take land into trust for Alaska Natives. The court also found that the exclusion of Alaska Natives from the fee-into-trust program was void under 25 U.S.C. § 467(g), which nullifies regulations that discriminate among Indian Tribes. In 2014, the Department of Interior published a final rule deleting the "Alaska Exclusion," 25 C.F.R. § 151.1, for taking land into trust. 79 FR 76.888–02.

7.   Scholars have argued that *Tee-Hit-Ton*, decided in the year after Brown v. Board of Education, is a difficult case to square with the concept of racial equality in the U.S. See Stacy L. Leeds, *The More Things Stay the Same: Waiting on Indian Law's* Brown v. Board of Education, 38 Tulsa L.Rev. 73, 73–74 (2002); see also Joseph William Singer, *Well Settled?: The Increasing Weight of History in American Indian Land Claims*, 28 Ga.L.Rev. 481, 483–84 (1994) ("*Tee-Hit-Ton* amounts to a formal declaration that American Indian citizens remain, to a significant extent, outside the normal protection of the Federal Constitution and can therefore be subjected to formally unequal treatment

under the law."). What does it mean for our system of law that *Tee-Hit-Ton* has never been overruled and may be inconsistent with otherwise applicable norms of property and equality in the U.S. and around the world?

NOTE: TRIBAL PROPERTY RIGHTS, THE INDIAN CLAIMS COMMISSION, AND CONTEMPORARY INTERNATIONAL HUMAN RIGHTS LAW

Justice Reed's opinion in *Tee-Hit-Ton* noted specifically that the tribe's claim was not connected with "any phase of the policy of the congress, continued throughout our history, to extinguish Indian title" through various legislative acts. Reed specifically cited to the Indian Claims Commission Act of 1946, 25 U.S.C.A. §§ 70–70v, as an example of Congress' policy "to grant payments from the public purse to needy descendents of exploited Indians." 348 U.S. at 273.

The Indian Claims Commission

Before passage of the Indian Claims Commission Act in 1946, Indian claims against the United States could be litigated only if Congress had passed special legislation authorizing suit to be brought by a particular tribe. The Court of Claims had been established in 1855 to permit many types of claims against the United States, thus affording a partial waiver of sovereign immunity. 10 Stat. 612. In 1863, however, all claims based on treaty violations were excluded from the jurisdiction of the Court of Claims. 12 Stat. 765, 767. Statutes of limitations also were impediments to most non-treaty Indian claims.

By the 1940s, a consensus had been reached that a better mechanism was needed to resolve Indian claims. The process of enacting special legislation for each Indian claim had proved cumbersome—a total of 142 such acts had been passed. There was also widespread sentiment among Indians and in Congress that past moral wrongs should be legally redressed. Further, the idea of a "final settling" of obligations to Indians complemented the mounting pressure for termination.

In 1946, Congress enacted the Indian Claims Commission Act which established a three-member (later five-member) commission to adjudicate Indian claims. Tribes were allowed to prosecute specified claims arising before the passage of the Act. All claims were required to be filed with the Commission by August 13, 1951, but old claims would not be subject to any other statute of limitations or to the defense of laches. Review of Commission decisions was to be by the Court of Claims and then by the Supreme Court. Claims arising after the passage of the Act were to be filed in the Court of Claims. Initially, the Commission was to complete its work within five years. But the complex cases moved slowly and Congress continually extended the life of the Commission. Finally, Congress dissolved the Commission and transferred all pending cases to the Court of Claims as of September, 1978. The former Court of Claims is now the United States Court of Federal Claims. 28 U.S.C.A. § 1505.

Substantive grants for relief, applicable only to groups and not to individual Indians, are set forth in section 2 of the Act, 25 U.S.C.A. § 70a:

> The Commission shall hear and determine * * * (1) claims in law or equity arising under the Constitution, laws, treaties of the United States, and Executive orders of the President; (2) all other claims in law or equity, including those sounding in tort, with respect to which the claimant would have been entitled to sue in a court of the United States if the United States was subject to suit; (3) claims which would result if the treaties, contracts, and agreements between the claimant and the United States were revised on the ground of fraud, duress, unconscionable consideration, mutual or unilateral mistake, whether of law or fact, or any other ground cognizable by a court of equity; (4) claims arising from the taking by the United States, whether as the result of a treaty of cessation or otherwise, of lands owned or occupied by the claimant without the payment for such lands of compensation agreed to by the claimant; and (5) claims based upon fair and honorable dealings that are not recognized by any existing rule of law or equity.

Sandra C. Danforth, *Repaying Historical Debts: The Indian Claims Commission,* 49 N.D.L.Rev. 359 (1973), notes that while clauses 1 and 2 cover typical claims cases in law or equity, based on the Constitution, laws, treaties or executive orders or sounding in tort, clauses 3 to 5 provided the Commission with jurisdiction beyond that allowed in a regular claims court.

> In clause 3, Congress gave the Commission authority to perform the political function of going behind a treaty, necessary in hearing any case where provisions of the treaty itself formed the basis of the claim. Clause 4 acknowledges government liability in transactions involving land held by so-called "Indian title" or "aboriginal title," which had never been specifically recognized by Congress. In writing the fifth clause, Congress created a new cause of action, assessed as the most unique feature of the Act, appearing to be an "unprecedented jurisdiction for any court." This clause confers broad jurisdiction on the Commission to hear cases which arise from moral wrongs. Although some cases dealt with under clauses 3 and 4 could also be argued on the basis of "fair and honorable dealing," the particular purpose of this clause was to give claims with no other basis an opportunity to be heard.

Id. at 388–89.

As Danforth notes, the great majority of claims filed involved disputes about land, and typically focused upon the issue of whether inadequate compensation or no compensation was paid when Indian groups ceded territory to the government or were forcibly removed. A number of claims involved the failure of the government to fulfill specific treaty obligations, such as providing reservation schools, annuity payments, or equipment. Other claims sounded in tort and required the government to account for its mismanagement of tribal funds held under its fiduciary duty to the Indians. Id. at 389. Particularly in regard to clause 5, Danforth makes the point that the provisions of Section 2 were narrowly construed and thus the full potential of the Act was not realized.

The most important reason for the limited variety in the claims filed was related to the nature of compensation to be awarded and to the novel character of parts of Section 2. Although nowhere in the Act is it explicitly stated that recoveries were to be monetary, the wording of the Act indicated that this was the legislative intent.

* * *

* * * Claims typically arose from the taking of Indian land by the government to facilitate the westward movement of the white population across the continent. Given the strong attachment to land which has remained one of the persistent characteristics of Indian societies, just compensation would involve return of at least some of the land which was taken, not a monetary substitute.

Id. at 390, 392.

Indian claimants also had quarrels with the "no-interest" rule that governed the claims process established by the Act. The rule provides that interest is not generally recoverable against the United States. Although exceptions to the rule require interest payments under some circumstances, such as when a Fifth Amendment taking is involved, takings of unrecognized Indian title were found not to give rise to liability for interest in claims cases. United States v. Alcea Band of Tillamooks, 341 U.S. 48 (1951) (Alcea II).[3] Commission awards were valued as of the date of the taking. Some tribes, therefore, were left with judgments—without interest—for one or two dollars per acre for takings of original Indian title for land worth several hundred, or even a thousand, times that much today. Rulings by the courts on these and other issues relating to interest meant that interest was allowed "on only small classes of claims." See Howard M. Friedman, *Interest on Indian Claims: Judicial Protection of the Fisc,* 5 Val.U.L.Rev. 26, 46 (1970). Even for takings of recognized title, only simple, not compound, interest was awarded.

These rules on valuation and on interest apply generally in suits against the government. The issue is whether they are appropriate in the context of the Indian Claims Commission. In any event, the courts seem to have been guided in part by pragmatic concerns; many billions of dollars of federal expenditures were at stake. Cf., note 17 of *Tee-Hit-Ton,* page 296, supra.

Most special acts before 1946 required that judgments be reduced by the value of "gratuities" rendered to the tribes by the United States. Such "gratuitous off-sets" significantly reduced many awards by subtracting the

---

[3] The courts did hold that claims for loss of original Indian title were compensable if brought under the provisions of the Indian Claims Commission Act. Otoe and Missouria Tribe v. United States, 131 F.Supp. 265 (Ct.Cl.1955), cert. denied 350 U.S. 848 (1955). *Tee-Hit-Ton,* page 296, supra, held to the contrary because the claim arose after 1946 and thus was not within the jurisdiction of the Indian Claims Commission.

value of health services, education services, blankets, tools, farm implements, and the like. For the twenty years before the Commission was established, interlocutory awards before off-sets were $49,000,000. Off-sets were $29,000,000, thus diminishing total awards by almost sixty percent.

The 1946 Act was more favorable to the tribes regarding gratuitous off-sets. 25 U.S.C.A. § 70a exempts many "gratuities" (including health and educational expenditures and federal expenses in connection with removal) and provides that off-sets shall be awarded only when the Commission finds that the "entire course of dealings * * * in good conscience warrants such action." See generally Ponca Tribe of Oklahoma v. United States, 183 Ct.Cl. 673 (1968), and United States v. Pueblo De Zia, 474 F.2d 639 (Ct.Cl.1973). But any provision for off-sets raises the greater question of why services provided by a trustee should be considered at all in connection with legislation supposedly designed to right old wrongs against the beneficiaries of the trust.

Another problem with the workings of the Commission was the posture of the Justice Department attorneys in charge of defending the claims. They took a consistently hard stand on settlement and most claims required lengthy trials and appeals. The turtle's pace of the claims process was not due solely to the defense attorneys, but the chronology is staggering, even by the standards of complex modern litigation: the original deadline for filing claims, remember, was 1951 and 227 of the 611 dockets remained unresolved as of 1972. The Commission expedited its work during its last years but 68 dockets were still pending when the Court of Claims took over in 1978. See generally United States Indian Claims Comm'n, Final Report (1978).

Monetary Awards and Extinguishment of Aboriginal Title

Traditionally, Congress provided that claims awards would be distributed by means of per capita payments to individual tribal members. Payments are now governed by the Distribution of Judgment Funds Act of 1973, 25 U.S.C.A. §§ 1401–07, which calls for a distribution plan to be developed by the tribe and approved by the Secretary of the Interior. At least twenty percent of the award must be set aside for tribal needs, unless the circumstances "clearly warrant otherwise." Id. § 1403(b)(5). Ten percent is typically deducted for attorney's fees as are expenses incurred by the BIA in connection with the distribution of the judgment. Was Danforth correct in assuming that legislative intent was to limit claims under the Act to monetary damages? Prospects of big monetary awards may have led some tribes—on advice of claims counsel—to claim damages instead of pressing their claims to continuing land rights. Indian tribal lawyers were not inclined to raise claims to unextinguished occupancy rights because they were out to recover the highest sum of damages possible and this required alleging a taking. (The attorneys are typically paid on a contingent fee.)

Claims based on "live" aboriginal title raise serious potential problems for the federal government. If Indians still occupy aboriginal lands without a treaty, statute, or executive order to define their rights, their occupancy would be in competition with public land uses or private land claims. As a practical matter, was there any realistic prospect of achieving restoration of aboriginal use and occupancy on lands populated by non-Indians? Should tribes have sought only trespass damages based on interference with use and occupancy and claimed unextinguished aboriginal title even if greater damages were available for an extinguishment of title? How would you explain to tribal clients the choice of remedies available to them?

If a tribe did not seek compensation for loss of possession of its land, can it later assert title to those lands? One court has ruled that the *failure* to assert a claim that such lands were still subject to unextinguished tribal title (based on an executive order) in an Indian Claims Commission case precluded any claim from being asserted later. Navajo Tribe of Indians v. New Mexico, 809 F.2d 1455 (10th Cir.1987). The Navajo Tribe claimed that some two million acres of land in northwest New Mexico had been added to its reservation by executive order. Subsequently, hundreds of private parties entered the lands and occupied them with the permission of the government, many receiving patents. The tribe's title to the land had never been formally extinguished. The Tenth Circuit held that the tribe's claim to aboriginal title should have been filed under the Indian Claims Commission Act. The court said that if the Indian Claims Commission had found that the tribe's title was viable, the Commission would have compensated the tribe (effectively extinguishing future rights).

This is a unique twist of judicial interpretation of the Indian Claims Commission Act, seeing it as an engine for extinguishing Indian titles, with compensation if timely claims are brought, without compensation if they are not. *Navajo* has been criticized as "unsupported by anything in the language of the [Indian Claims Commission] Act or the entire mass of litigation under the Act." Richard W. Hughes, *Indian Law,* 18 N.M.L.Rev. 403, 410 (1988). Hughes comprehensively and insightfully reviews the law of Indian land claims to demonstrate that live title disputes were never intended to be confined to adjudication under the Indian Claims Commission Act. He further explains how practice under the Act has been dominated by a pattern of finding, and tribes accepting, extinguishment of title and compensation for it.

A number of tribes have realized belatedly that they were being relegated to awards of money damages by the Indian Claims Commission Act cases rather than being able to seek a later adjudication that they retained rights to tribal lands, either because the United States never extinguished their aboriginal title or because the tribes never lawfully ceded the land. Michelle Smith and Janet C. Neuman, in their article, *Keeping Indian Claims Commission Decisions in Their Place: Assessing the Preclusive Effect of ICC Decisions in Litigation Over Off-Reservation Treaty Fishing Rights,* 31 Haw.L.Rev. 475 (2009), have argued that because usual and accustomed fishing sites were not limited to a tribe's exclusive aboriginal territory, Indian Claims Commission decisions regarding a tribe's "aboriginal territory" should not have a preclusive effect on the locations where a tribe may assert retained rights.

In some cases, tribes trying to preserve their rights have refused to accept payments of judgment funds appropriated by Congress pursuant to awards of the Commission or Claims Court. In others, they have tried to change their lawyers' strategy late in the litigation.

In the 1970s, claims of the eight Sioux tribes were in the final stages of adjudication of rights in the sacred Black Hills of South Dakota. See *United States v. Sioux Nation*, page 402, infra. They realized they stood to lose all their future rights or claims to the lands. The Indian Claims Commission had entered an award subject to certain "off-sets." The amount of the off-sets was subject to settlement negotiations. The largest of the tribes notified its attorney and the court that the attorney's contract had expired and that he was not authorized to act for them. The tribe also sought to be dismissed from the litigation and informed the court that it did not want to seek damages but rather wanted a return of land. By that time, attorney contracts with tribes representing a majority of the Sioux had expired and the attorneys and the court were aware that many Sioux opposed the settlement. Nevertheless, the Indian Claims Commission and Claims Court approved a stipulation signed by the attorneys settling the case on behalf of all the tribes and entered judgment.

Six of the eight tribes appealed the judgments saying that their attorneys acted without authority in obtaining the award and they sought the attorneys' dismissal from the case. The Court of Appeals upheld the Claims Court's denial of the motion based on the argument that the settlement of the off-set amount (without which a determination of final judgment would have been impossible) "was a ministerial act." The court also noted that throughout the lengthy litigation the tribes had not objected to the way their lawyers handled the case:

> The Claims Court was fully justified in refusing to terminate the authority of the attorneys who had been handling this complex litigation for 30 years and were at the point of successfully completing it, unless and until the appellant tribes moved to substitute new counsel who could continue to handle the case without significant delay.

Sioux Tribe of Indians v. United States, 862 F.2d 275, 281 (Fed.Cir.1988).

A dissenting judge disagreed:

> Most of these [attorney] contracts have terminated and are no longer in effect. It is inconceivable to me that, with over half the clientele in loud revolt, nominal counsel has the authority to bind these tribes, against their intentions and instructions. Further, the United States as well as the Claims Court had full knowledge, throughout the past years of these proceedings, that most of the principals objected to the negotiations and to the purported settlement.

862 F.2d at 282.

What alternatives were open to the tribes late in the litigation? Do the Indians now have any hope of arguing that their aboriginal title has not been extinguished?

Every Indian claim involved consideration of the history of an Indian group's dealings with the United States. In order to present claims to the Commission, many tribes hired anthropologists, historians, sociologists and other experts. The decisions of the Commission, which have been published by the Native American Rights Fund, provide a documentation of the histories of some tribes.

The Dann Case

Many Indian tribes and individuals have long asserted that the Indian Claims Commission Act failed as a matter of law and policy in fairly compensating them for their land claims or even recognizing their existing rights in their aboriginal lands. In an unprecedented report issued by the Inter-American Commission on Human Rights of the Organization of American States in 2002, an international human rights body for the first time agreed with those assertions, concluding that the processes of the Indian Claims Commission as applied to the Dann sisters, two Western Shoshone cattle ranchers, "were not sufficient to comply with contemporary international human rights norms, principles and standards that govern the determination of indigenous property interests." Mary and Carrie Dann, United States, Case 11.140, Inter-Am. C.H.R., Report No. 75/02, para. 139 (Dec. 27, 2002).

The *Dann* case was originally litigated in United States courts under familiar and well-established principles of federal Indian law. The Western Shoshone were among a number of tribal groups with claims before the Commission with aboriginal "title" rights that had never been expressly extinguished by treaty or statute. The tribe could have asserted aboriginal rights and sought damages against the government for tortious interference with rights of use and occupancy without conceding loss of title. But the Western Shoshone claims, like all other claims before the Commission, were pursued as if the aboriginal rights of the Indians had been extinguished. The Western Shoshone claim was one of several Indian claims decisions based on little or no evidence in the form of statutes or official government acts extinguishing Indian rights of use and occupancy. The only "evidence" of extinguishment of aboriginal title was the "gradual encroachment" of settlers or simply the historical result that Indian populations have been drastically reduced relative to numbers of non-Indians.

In United States v. Dann, 470 U.S. 39 (1985), Mary and Carrie Dann, members of the Western Shoshone, were cited by the Bureau of Land Management for grazing cattle on the public lands without a federal permit. The Dann sisters claimed that the land had been in possession of their family since time immemorial. The Western Shoshone, however, had obtained a final award from the Indian Claims Commission for the extinguishments of tribal claims to aboriginal title in those same lands. A $26 million award for the taking had been deposited in an interest-bearing trust account in the United States Treasury, but a plan of distribution had not yet been approved. The Court held that the deposit in the trust account, in light of the United States' trust obligation, amounted to "payment" and that any tribal claim to aboriginal title had been extinguished. See also Western Shoshone National Council v. Molini, 951 F.2d 200 (9th Cir.1991), cert. denied 506 U.S. 822 (1992) (holding that an Indian Claims Commission award constituted a general determination of title which bars the Shoshone from asserting title against the state of Nevada, and that hunting and fishing rights are extinguished along with the extinguishment of aboriginal title). The *Dann* case specifically involved a provision of the Indian Claims Commission Act that provided that "payment of any claim * * * shall be a full discharge of the United States * * * ." 25 U.S.C.A. § 70v.

While the *Dann* court held that the claims award precluded the tribe from asserting that no taking had ever occurred, the decision expressed no opinion on whether the Dann sisters' individual aboriginal title rights claims had been also extinguished by the ruling of the Indian Claims Commission.

> The Danns also claim to possess individual as well as tribal aboriginal rights and that because only the latter were before the Indian Claims Commission, the "final discharge" of § 22(a) does not bar the Danns from raising individual aboriginal title as a defense in this action. Though we have recognized that individual aboriginal rights may exist in certain contexts, this contention has not been addressed by the lower courts and, if open, should first be addressed below. We express no opinion as to its merits.

470 U.S. at 50.

On remand, the Ninth Circuit considered whether individual aboriginal title existed. United States v. Dann, 865 F.2d 1528 (9th Cir.1989). The Court cited Cramer v. United States, 261 U.S. 219 (1923), holding the individual Indians' right of occupancy on public land (not "aboriginal title" in the usual sense) superior to the rights of a railroad which was later granted some of the same land. The Court concluded that the Danns had individual aboriginal rights to occupy one section of land and to graze stock on others. The rights were implied from the policy of public land settlement during that era which respected Indian occupancy. Individual Indians' rights were subject to changes in public land policy, however, and since the 1934 Taylor Grazing Act withdrew all unappropriated land from settlement, it ended the possibility of later affirming individual "aboriginal" title through the implied consent of the government.

In 1993, having exhausted their domestic remedies in U.S. courts, the Danns decided to pursue a different strategy in a different type of legal forum. They petitioned the Inter-American Commission on Human Rights (IACHR) of the Organization of American States (OAS) to hear their complaint against the United States, an OAS member, that denial of their aboriginal property rights violated their human rights as indigenous peoples, protected under the American Declaration of the Rights and Duties of Man. In December 2002, the IACHR issued a formal report, concluding that based on facts established by the *Dann* petition and subsequent submissions, including the U.S. State

Department's formal reply to the IACHR, the United States had violated the Dann sisters' human rights under international law.

CASE OF MARY AND CARRIE DANN V. UNITED STATES
Case No. 11.140 (Judgment on the Merits)
Inter-Am. C. H.R. No. 75/02.
December 27, 2002.

I. Summary

* * *

5. In the present report, having examined the evidence and arguments presented on behalf of the parties to the proceedings, the Commission concluded that the State has failed to ensure the Danns' right to property under conditions of equality contrary to Articles II, XVIII and XXIII of the American Declaration in connection with their claims to property rights in the Western Shoshone ancestral lands.*

* * *

B. Pertinent Facts

* * *

2. U.S. Domestic Process for Determining Indigenous Land Claims—the Indian Claims Commission

113. The Commission notes that according to information on the record, publicists have over the years since its establishment and dissolution criticized the ICC on various grounds. Among the subjects of these criticisms have been the fact that the ICC Act permitted an individual or small group of Indians to present a claim on behalf of a whole tribal group without requiring proof of the consent of that tribe, the absence of rules permitting the intervention of interested persons in the proceedings before the ICC, and the narrowing of the ICC jurisdiction to award only monetary compensation and accordingly to preclude claimants from recovering lands.

* * *

---

*   [Ed.] Article II. Right to equality before the law

All persons are equal before the law and have the rights and duties established in this Declaration, without distinction as to race, sex, language, creed or any other factor.

Article XVIII—Right to a fair trial

Every person may resort to the courts to ensure respect for his legal rights. There should likewise be available to him a simple, brief procedure whereby the courts will protect him from acts of authority that, to his prejudice, violate any fundamental constitutional rights.

Article XXIII—Right to property

Every person has a right to own such private property as meets the essential needs of decent living and helps to maintain the dignity of the individual and of the home.

130. Of particular relevance to the present case, the Commission considers that general international legal principles applicable in the context of indigenous human rights to include:

- the right of indigenous peoples to legal recognition of their varied and specific forms and modalities of their control, ownership, use and enjoyment of territories and property;

- the recognition of their property and ownership rights with respect to lands, territories and resources they have historically occupied; and

- where property and user rights of indigenous peoples arise from rights existing prior to the creation of a state, recognition by that state of the permanent and inalienable title of indigenous peoples relative thereto and to have such title changed only by mutual consent between the state and respective indigenous peoples when they have full knowledge and appreciation of the nature or attributes of such property. This also implies the right to fair compensation in the event that such property and user rights are irrevocably lost.

131. Based upon the foregoing analysis, the Commission is of the view that the provisions of the American Declaration should be interpreted and applied in the context of indigenous petitioners with due regard to the particular principles of international human rights law governing the individual and collective interests of indigenous peoples. Particularly pertinent provisions of the Declaration in this respect include Article II (the right to equality under the law), Article XVIII (the right to a fair trial), and Article XXIII (the right to property). As outlined above, this approach includes the taking of special measures to ensure recognition of the particular and collective interest that indigenous people have in the occupation and use of their traditional lands and resources and their right not to be deprived of this interest except with fully informed consent, under conditions of equality, and with fair compensation. The Commission wishes to emphasize that by interpreting the American Declaration so as to safeguard the integrity, livelihood and culture of indigenous peoples through the effective protection of their individual and collective human rights, the Commission is respecting the very purposes underlying the Declaration which, as expressed in its Preamble, include recognition that "[s]ince culture is the highest social and historical expression of that spiritual development, it is the duty of man to preserve, practice and foster culture by every means within his power."

D. Application of International Human Rights Norms and Principles in the Circumstances of Mary and Carrie Dann

* * *

138. * * * [T]he Commission first wishes to expressly recognize and acknowledge that the State, through the development and implementation of the Indian Claims Commission process, has taken significant measures to recognize and account for the historic deprivations suffered by indigenous communities living within the United States and commends the State for this initiative. As both the Petitioners and the State have recognized, this process provided a more efficient solution to the sovereign immunity bar to Indian land claims under U.S. law and extended to indigenous communities' certain benefits relating to claims to their ancestral lands that were not available to other citizens, such as extended limitation periods for claims.

139. Upon evaluating these processes in the facts as disclosed by the record in this case, however, the Commission concludes that these processes were not sufficient to comply with contemporary international human rights norms, principles and standards that govern the determination of indigenous property interests.

140. The Commission first considers that Articles XVIII and XXIII of the American Declaration specially oblige a member state to ensure that any determination of the extent to which indigenous claimants maintain interests in the lands to which they have traditionally held title and have occupied and used is based upon a process of fully informed and mutual consent on the part of the indigenous community as a whole. This requires at a minimum that all of the members of the community are fully and accurately informed of the nature and consequences of the process and provided with an effective opportunity to participate individually or as collectives. In the case of the Danns, however, the record indicates that the land claim issue was pursued by one band of the Western Shoshone people with no apparent mandate from the other Western Shoshone bands or members. There is also no evidence on the record that appropriate consultations were held within the Western Shoshone at the time that certain significant determinations were made. This includes in particular the ICC's finding that the entirety of the Western Shoshone interest in their ancestral lands, which interests affect the Danns, was extinguished at some point in the past.

* * *

142. The insufficiency of this process was augmented by the fact that, on the evidence, the issue of extinguishment was not litigated before or determined by the ICC, in that the ICC did not conduct an independent review of historical and other evidence to determine as a matter of fact whether the Western Shoshone properly claimed title to all or some of their

traditional lands. Rather, the ICC determination was based upon an agreement between the State and the purported Western Shoshone representatives as to the extent and timing of the extinguishment. In light of the contentions by the Danns that they have continued to occupy and use at least portions of the Western Shoshone ancestral lands, and in light of the findings by the Ninth Circuit Court of Appeals as to the merits of the ICC's extinguishment finding, it cannot be said that the Danns' claims to property rights in the Western Shoshone ancestral lands were determined through an effective and fair process in compliance with the norms and principles under Articles XVIII and XXIII of the American Declaration.

143. Further, the Commission concludes that to the extent the State has asserted as against the Danns title in the property in issue based upon the ICC proceedings, the Danns have not been afforded their right to equal protection of the law under Article II of the American Declaration. The notion of equality before the law set forth in the Declaration relates to the application of substantive rights and to the protection to be given to them in the case of acts by the State or others. Further, Article II, while not prohibiting all distinctions in treatment in the enjoyment of protected rights and freedoms, requires at base that any permissible distinctions be based upon objective and reasonable justification, that they further a legitimate objective, regard being had to the principles which normally prevail in democratic societies, and that the means are reasonable and proportionate to the end sought.

144. The record before the Commission indicates that under prevailing common law in the United States, including the Fifth Amendment to the U.S. Constitution, the taking of property by the government ordinarily requires a valid public purpose and the entitlement of owners to notice, just compensation, and judicial review. In the present case, however, the Commission cannot find that the same prerequisites have been extended to the Danns in regard to the determination of their property claims to the Western Shoshone ancestral lands, and no proper justification for the distinction in their treatment has been established by the State. In particular, as concluded above, any property rights that the Danns may have asserted to the Western Shoshone ancestral lands were held by the ICC to have been "extinguished" through proceedings in which the Danns were not effectively represented and where the circumstances of this alleged extinguishment were never actually litigated nor the merits of the finding finally reviewed by the courts. And while compensation for this extinguishment was awarded by the ICC, the value of compensation was calculated based upon an average extinguishment date that does not on the record appear to bear any relevant connection to the issue of whether and to what extent all or part of Western Shoshone title in their traditional lands, including that of the Danns, may no longer subsist. Further, the Commission understands that the amount of compensation awarded for the

alleged encroachment upon Western Shoshone ancestral lands did not include an award of interest from the date of the alleged extinguishment to the date of the ICC decision, thus leaving the Western Shoshone uncompensated for the cost of the alleged taking of their property during this period.

* * *

VI. Conclusions

* * *

172. Based upon the foregoing analysis, the Commission hereby concludes that the State has failed to ensure the Danns' right to property under conditions of equality contrary to Articles II, XVIII and XXIII of the American Declaration in connection with their claims to property rights in the Western Shoshone ancestral lands.

VII. Recommendations

173. In accordance with the analysis and conclusions in the present report,

THE INTER-AMERICAN COMMISSION ON HUMAN RIGHTS REITERATES THE FOLLOWING RECOMMENDATIONS TO THE UNITED STATES:

1. Provide Mary and Carrie Dann with an effective remedy, which includes adopting the legislative or other measures necessary to ensure respect for the Danns' right to property in accordance with Articles II, XVIII and XXIII of the American Declaration in connection with their claims to property rights in the Western Shoshone ancestral lands.

2. Review its laws, procedures and practices to ensure that the property rights of indigenous persons are determined in accordance with the rights established in the American Declaration, including Articles II, XVIII and XXIII of the Declaration. * * *

* * *

NOTES

1. Under the Commission's rules, the United States was requested to provide information "as to measures adopted by the state to implement the Commission's recommendation." In its response the United States reiterated its position that the Danns' claim "is, fundamentally, not a human rights claim, but an attempt by two individual Indians to reopen the question of collective Western Shoshone tribal property rights to land—a question that has been litigated to finality in the U.S. courts." Based upon these submissions, the United States stated that it "respectfully declines to take any further actions to comply with the Commission's recommendations." After having been informed of the Commission's findings on the petition, the United States seized

and confiscated approximately 225 head of cattle from the Danns' ancestral land, which were subsequently auctioned off to the highest bidder several days later. These events took place despite a direct request by the Commission for the United States to return the livestock to the Danns and refrain from impounding any additional livestock belonging to the Danns until the procedure before the Commission was complete, including implementation of any final recommendations that the Commission might adopt in the matter.

In light of this response by the United States government, what advice would you give as an attorney to a tribal client about pursuing an Indian rights claim before the international human rights system? What have the Dann sisters "won" if anything, by virtue of this favorable "judgment on the merits" by the IACHR of their human rights complaint against the government of the United States? The *Dann* case, as well as other indigenous human rights complaints that have been brought before the IACHR, are discussed in S. James Anaya and Robert A. Williams, Jr., *The Protection of Indigenous Peoples' Rights Over Lands and Natural Resources Under the Inter-American Human Rights System*, 14 Harv.Hum.Rts.J. 33 (2001).

2.   The IACHR is not the only international human rights body to take note of the United States' treatment of the Dann sisters. In August 2001, the United Nations Committee on the Elimination of Racial Discrimination (CERD) expressed "concern" over the situation involving the Danns and their Western Shoshone ancestral lands, and recommended that the United States "should ensure effective participation by indigenous communities in decisions affecting them, including those on their land rights," as required by the United Nations International Convention on the Elimination of All Forms of Racial Discrimination, to which the United States is a signatory. See Concluding Observations of the Committee on the Elimination of Racial Discrimination: United States of America. 14/08/2001, at para. 21, U.N. Doc. CERD/C/59/Misc.17/Rev.3. Then, in 2006, CERD issued an Early Warning and Urgent Action Procedure Decision, restating the concerns outlined in the Concluding Observations and expressing concern about legislative efforts to privatize Western Shoshone ancestral land for transfer to multinational extractive industries. It recommended that the United States freeze any plan to privatize these lands and to desist from all activities which were being carried out without consultation of the Western Shoshone peoples. See Early Warning and Urgent Action Procedure Decision 1(68): United States of America. 11/04/2006, U.N. Doc. CERD/C/USA/DEC/1. Despite CERD's 2006 Early Warning Decision, the United States has refused to alter policies on mining on Western Shoshone ancestral lands.

3.   Professors James Anaya and Siegfried Wissner, citing the Inter-American Commission's *Dann* report and other precedents from international human rights bodies and domestic courts around the world, have pointed to an evolving international norm that recognizes indigenous peoples' property and ownership rights with respect to lands, territories and resources they have historically occupied. Therefore, according to Professors Anaya and Wiessner, indigenous peoples have a right to "demarcation, ownership, development,

control and use of the lands they have traditionally owned or otherwise occupied and used." S. James Anaya & Siegfried Wiessner, *The U.N. Declaration on the Rights of Indigenous Peoples: Towards Re-Empowerment*, in International Human Rights and Indigenous Peoples, 99–102 (2009). If the United States Supreme Court were to hear a case with facts similar to *Tee-Hit-Ton* today and sought to apply this international law norm, would the case come out differently?

4. Tribes have lost their lands through various circumstances, including the courts' failure to accord tribal property full protection under the law as in *Tee-Hit-Ton* and *Dann*. Even when tribal rights have been acknowledged, as in the Supreme Court's recognition of tribal rights in *Oneida I* and *II,* see Ch. 3, supra, there has been no remedy of land or money. Therefore, tribes have sometimes worked to recover their lands through other means.

NOTE ON NATION BUILDING: LAND ACQUISITION

One of the hardest blows to Indian tribes after the arrival of Europeans was the loss of land. Through the treaties and then allotment, termination, relocation, and other unsavory means, the government found ways to deprive Indian people of their homelands. The all-time low for tribal land holdings in the lower 48 states was 50.2 million acres, during the early 1960s, after termination laws took effect.

But the ties of Indian people to the land are too strong for them not to rebound from this tragedy. And rebound they have. Today, tribal land holdings have increased to 67.2 million acres in the lower 48 states, a 34% increase in net Indian lands. They have added to their reservations, in other words, an area nearly three times the size of the state of Massachusetts.

The campaign of the Taos Pueblo to reclaim Blue Lake in 1970 was one of the first early victories in tribal land acquisition. Since this historic breakthrough, tribes have brought lawsuits, advocated in Congress and the land agencies, and engaged in old-fashioned bargaining with willing sellers. Some tribes, like the Passamaquoddy in Maine, have been successful in bringing claims under the Nonintercourse Act. Others, like the Warm Springs Tribe in central Oregon, lobbied for legislation correcting survey errors and returning the McQuinn Strip to their reservation. As part of the Cobell Settlement, the Land Buy Back Program provided $1.9 billion for tribes to purchase fractionated interests and consolidate that land back into trust. Almost every tribe has an active land acquisition program. Day by day they are acquiring land and increasing their land bases.

Not all efforts have been successful. Courts have barred the Western Shoshone from land recovery because of monetary Indian Claims Commission (ICC) settlements. The Great Sioux Nation, working for the return of the Black Hills, also was barred by ICC settlements. It has refused to touch the ICC money judgment. The settlement now amounts to more than a billion dollars, sitting in the federal treasury. The Sioux, taking the long view, are unwilling to relent, and are willing to wait.

The Confederated Salish and Kootenai Tribes, located in western Montana on the Flathead Reservation, are a leading example of proactive and determined work to regain land. The 1855 Treaty of Hellgate reserved 1.25 million acres of aboriginal land. The magnificent Flathead Reservation was opened for homesteading in 1910. Allotment led to the loss of 60% of the reservation—over half a million acres. Congressional acts left the tribe with just 245,000 acres.

But then, in 1935 the Confederated Salish and Kootenai Tribes ratified an IRA constitution, and the tribal government voted to stop the removal of reservation land. For the past three generations, the tribes' active Tribal Lands Department has administered an ambitious Land Acquisition Program with the goal of purchasing back 62% of the tribe's original reservation land. Every year, the tribe dedicated as much budget money to land acquisition as possible. The tribes won $4 million in an ICC settlement in 1955 and $7.4 million in the U.S. Court of Claims for a treaty violation. The tribes participated in the Cobell Land Buy Back Program and purchased $5.2 million worth of fractionated interests. In all, tribally owned lands in the reservation have almost tripled to 600,000 acres.

Pat Smith, former in-house attorney for the tribes, recalls with admiration that when he started working in 1984, the tribes owned less than 35% of the reservation in tribal trust land and allotments, and now they own more than 60%. Pat Smith explained that "the tribe took its priorities, and went out and bought the land back acre by acre with cold hard cash." And they are not finished yet.

Land acquisition continues to be a major priority for virtually every tribe. They are working daily to recover lands through all means available. The sense of pride, connection to the land, redemption for the ancestors, and hope for generations is palpable. As tribes expand their land holdings, they are truly nation-building in all senses of the word, for the future of their people.

See generally Charles Wilkinson, *Blood Struggle* 206–40 (2005); *An Introduction to Indian Nations in the United States*, Nat'l Cong. of Am. Indians, 13–15, http://www.ncai.org/about-tribes/indians_101.pdf; *Land Buy-Back Program for Tribal Nations*, U.S. Dept. of Interior, https://www.doi.gov/buybackprogram; Armen H. Merjian, *An Unbroken Chain of Injustice: The Dawes Act, Native American Trusts, and* Cobell v. Salazar, 46 Gonz.L.Rev. 609 (2011); Timothy Williams, *Sioux Racing to Find Millions to Buy Sacred Land in Black Hills*, N.Y. Times, Oct. 3, 2012; *Flathead Reservation Timeline: Confederated Salish and Kootenai Tribes*, Mont. Off. of Pub. Instruction, http://opi.mt.gov/pdf/IndianEd/iefa/FlatheadTimeline.pdf.

Twenty years after *Oneida I* and *II,* the Oneida Nation used proceeds from economic development activities to purchase land within the boundaries of its original treaty reservation. On the theory that these were Indian lands, the Nation claimed certain tax immunities, leading to the following litigation.

CITY OF SHERRILL, NEW YORK V. ONEIDA
INDIAN NATION OF NEW YORK

Supreme Court of the United States, 2005.
544 U.S. 197, 125 S.Ct. 1478, 161 L.Ed.2d 386.

JUSTICE GINSBURG delivered the opinion of the Court.

This case concerns properties in the city of Sherrill, New York, purchased by the Oneida Indian Nation of New York (OIN or Tribe) in 1997 and 1998. The separate parcels of land in question, once contained within the Oneidas' 300,000-acre reservation, were last possessed by the Oneidas as a tribal entity in 1805. For two centuries, governance of the area in which the properties are located has been provided by the State of New York and its county and municipal units. In *County of Oneida v. Oneida Indian Nation of N. Y.*, 470 U. S. 226 (1985) *(Oneida II)*, this Court held that the Oneidas stated a triable claim for damages against the County of Oneida for wrongful possession of lands they conveyed to New York State in 1795 in violation of federal law. In the instant action, OIN resists the payment of property taxes to Sherrill on the ground that OIN's acquisition of fee title to discrete parcels of historic reservation land revived the Oneidas' ancient sovereignty piecemeal over each parcel. Consequently, the Tribe maintains, regulatory authority over OIN's newly purchased properties no longer resides in Sherrill.

Our 1985 decision recognized that the Oneidas could maintain a federal common-law claim for damages for ancient wrongdoing in which both national and state governments were complicit. Today, we decline to project redress for the Tribe into the present and future, thereby disrupting the governance of central New York's counties and towns. Generations have passed during which non-Indians have owned and developed the area that once composed the Tribe's historic reservation. And at least since the middle years of the 19th century, most of the Oneidas have resided elsewhere. Given the longstanding, distinctly non-Indian character of the area and its inhabitants, the regulatory authority constantly exercised by New York State and its counties and towns, and the Oneidas' long delay in seeking judicial relief against parties other than the United States, we hold that the Tribe cannot unilaterally revive its ancient sovereignty, in whole or in part, over the parcels at issue. The Oneidas long ago relinquished the reins of government and cannot regain them through open-market purchases from current titleholders.

I

A

OIN is a federally recognized Indian tribe and a direct descendant of the Oneida Indian Nation (Oneida Nation), "one of the six nations of the Iroquois, the most powerful Indian tribe in the Northeast at the time of the American Revolution." *Id.*, at 230. At the birth of the United States, the

Oneida Nation's aboriginal homeland comprised some six million acres in what is now central New York. *Ibid.; Oneida Indian Nation of N. Y.* v. *County of Oneida,* 414 U. S. 661, 664 (1974) *(Oneida I).*

In the years after the Revolutionary War, "the State of New York came under increasingly heavy pressure to open the Oneidas' land for settlement." *Oneida II,* 470 U. S., at 231. Reflective of that pressure, in 1788, New York State and the Oneida Nation entered into the Treaty of Fort Schuyler. For payments in money and kind, the Oneidas ceded to New York "all their lands." [Pet. for Cert]. Of the vast area conveyed, "[t]he Oneidas retained a reservation of about 300,000 acres," *Oneida II,* 470 U. S., at 231, "for their own use and cultivation." [Pet. for Cert.].[4]

* * *

B

* * *

This * * * present case * * * concerns parcels of land in the city of Sherrill, located in Oneida County, New York. According to the 2000 census, over 99% of the population in the area is non-Indian: American Indians represent less than 1% of the city of Sherrill's population and less than 0.5% of Oneida County's population. OIN owns approximately 17,000 acres of land scattered throughout the Counties of Oneida and Madison, representing less than 1.5% of the counties' total area. OIN's predecessor, the Oneida Nation, had transferred the parcels at issue to one of its members in 1805, who sold the land to a non-Indian in 1807. The properties thereafter remained in non-Indian hands until OIN's acquisitions in 1997 and 1998 in open-market transactions. OIN now operates commercial enterprises on these parcels: a gasoline station, a convenience store, and a textile facility.

Because the parcels lie within the boundaries of the reservation originally occupied by the Oneidas, OIN maintained that the properties are exempt from taxation, and accordingly refused to pay the assessed property taxes. The city of Sherrill initiated eviction proceedings in state court, and OIN sued Sherrill in federal court. * * * OIN sought equitable relief prohibiting, currently and in the future, the imposition of property taxes. * * * [T]he District Court concluded that parcels of land owned by the Tribe in Sherrill and Madison are not taxable.

A divided panel of the Second Circuit affirmed. * * *

---

[4] Under the "doctrine of discovery," *Oneida II,* 470 U. S., at 234, "fee title to the lands occupied by Indians when the colonists arrived became vested in the sovereign—first the discovering European nation and later the original States and the United States," *Oneida I,* 414 U. S., at 667.). In the original 13 States, "fee title to Indian lands," or "the pre-emptive right to purchase from the Indians, was in the State." *Id.,* at 670. Both before and after the adoption of the Constitution, New York State acquired vast tracts of land from Indian tribes through treaties it independently negotiated, without National Government participation.

* * *

We granted the city of Sherrill's petition for a writ of certiorari, and now reverse the judgment of the Court of Appeals.

II

OIN and the United States argue that because the Court in *Oneida II* recognized the Oneidas' aboriginal title to their ancient reservation land and because the Tribe has now acquired the specific parcels involved in this suit in the open market, it has unified fee and aboriginal title and may now assert sovereign dominion over the parcels. When the Oneidas came before this Court 20 years ago in *Oneida II* they sought money damages only. The Court reserved for another day the question whether "equitable considerations" should limit the relief available to the present-day Oneidas. *Id.*, at 253, n. 27.

* * *

* * * In this action, OIN seeks declaratory and injunctive relief recognizing its present and future sovereign immunity from local taxation on parcels of land the Tribe purchased in the open market, properties that had been subject to state and local taxation for generations.[7] We now reject the unification theory of OIN and the United States and hold that "standards of federal Indian law and federal equity practice" preclude the Tribe from rekindling embers of sovereignty that long ago grew cold.[8]

The appropriateness of the relief OIN here seeks must be evaluated in light of the long history of state sovereign control over the territory. From the early 1800's into the 1970's, the United States largely accepted, or was indifferent to, New York's governance of the land in question and the validity vel non of the Oneidas' sales to the State. In fact, the United States' policy and practice through much of the early 19th century was designed to dislodge east coast lands from Indian possession. Moreover, the properties here involved have greatly increased in value since the Oneidas sold them 200 years ago. Notably, it was not until lately that the Oneidas sought to regain ancient sovereignty over land converted from wilderness to become part of cities like Sherrill.

This Court has observed in the different, but related, context of the diminishment of an Indian reservation that "[t]he longstanding assumption of jurisdiction by the State over an area that is over 90% non-

---

[7] The dissent suggests that, compatibly with today's decision, the Tribe may assert tax immunity defensively in the eviction proceeding initiated by Sherrill. We disagree. The equitable cast of the relief sought remains the same whether asserted affirmatively or defensively.

[8] We resolve this case on considerations not discretely identified in the parties' briefs. But the question of equitable considerations limiting the relief available to OIN, which we reserved in *Oneida II*, is inextricably linked to, and is thus "fairly included" within, the questions presented. See this Court's Rule 14.1(a) ("The statement of any question presented is deemed to comprise every subsidiary question fairly included therein.").

Indian, both in population and in land use," may create "justifiable expectations." *Rosebud Sioux Tribe v. Kneip*, 430 U. S. 584, 604–605 (1977). Similar justifiable expectations, grounded in two centuries of New York's exercise of regulatory jurisdiction, until recently uncontested by OIN, merit heavy weight here.

The wrongs of which OIN complains in this action occurred during the early years of the Republic. For the past two centuries, New York and its county and municipal units have continuously governed the territory. The Oneidas did not seek to regain possession of their aboriginal lands by court decree until the 1970's. And not until the 1990's did OIN acquire the properties in question and assert its unification theory to ground its demand for exemption of the parcels from local taxation. This long lapse of time, during which the Oneidas did not seek to revive their sovereign control through equitable relief in court, and the attendant dramatic changes in the character of the properties, preclude OIN from gaining the disruptive remedy it now seeks. The principle that the passage of time can preclude relief has deep roots in our law, and this Court has recognized this prescription in various guises. It is well established that laches, a doctrine focused on one side's inaction and the other's legitimate reliance, may bar long-dormant claims for equitable relief. * * *

* * *

Finally, this Court has recognized the impracticability of returning to Indian control land that generations earlier passed into numerous private hands. See *Yankton Sioux Tribe v. United States*, 272 U. S. 351, 357 (1926) ("It is impossible . . . to rescind the cession and restore the Indians to their former rights because the lands have been opened to settlement and large portions of them are now in the possession of innumerable innocent purchasers. . . "). * * *

In this case, the Court of Appeals concluded that the "impossibility" doctrine had no application because OIN acquired the land in the open market and does not seek to uproot current property owners. But the unilateral reestablishment of present and future Indian sovereign control, even over land purchased at the market price, would have disruptive practical consequences similar to those that led this Court in *Yankton Sioux* to initiate the impossibility doctrine. The city of Sherrill and Oneida County are today overwhelmingly populated by non-Indians. A checkerboard of alternating state and tribal jurisdiction in New York State—created unilaterally at OIN's behest—would "seriously burde[n] the administration of state and local governments" and would adversely affect landowners neighboring the tribal patches. 510 U. S at 42 (quoting *Solem v. Bartlett*, 465 U. S. 463, 471–72, n. 12 (1984)). If OIN may unilaterally reassert sovereign control and remove these parcels from the local tax rolls, little would prevent the Tribe from initiating a new generation of litigation to free the parcels from local zoning or other regulatory controls that protect all landowners in the area.

* * *

In sum, the question of damages for the Tribe's ancient dispossession is not at issue in this case, and we therefore do not disturb our holding in *Oneida II*. However, the distance from 1805 to the present day, the Oneidas' long delay in seeking equitable relief against New York or its local units, and developments in the city of Sherrill spanning several generations, evoke the doctrines of laches, acquiescence, and impossibility, and render inequitable the piecemeal shift in governance this suit seeks unilaterally to initiate.

* * *

For the reasons stated, the judgment of the Court of Appeals for the Second Circuit is reversed, and the case is remanded for further proceedings consistent with this opinion.

* * *

[JUSTICE SOUTER, concurring]

* * *

JUSTICE STEVENS, dissenting.

This case involves an Indian tribe's claim to tax immunity on its own property located within its reservation. It does not implicate the tribe's immunity from other forms of state jurisdiction, nor does it concern the tribe's regulatory authority over property owned by non-Indians within the reservation.

* * *

Without the benefit of relevant briefing from the parties, the Court has ventured into legal territory that belongs to Congress. Its decision today is at war with at least two bedrock principles of Indian law. First, only Congress has the power to diminish or disestablish a tribe's reservation. Second, as a core incident of tribal sovereignty, a tribe enjoys immunity from state and local taxation of its reservation lands, until that immunity is explicitly revoked by Congress. Far from revoking this immunity, Congress has specifically reconfirmed it with respect to the reservation lands of the New York Indians.[4] Ignoring these principles, the Court has done what only Congress may do—it has effectively proclaimed a diminishment of the Tribe's reservation and an abrogation of its elemental right to tax immunity. Under our precedents, whether it is wise policy to

---

[4] In providing New York state courts with jurisdiction over civil actions between Indians, Congress emphasized that the statute was not to be "construed as subjecting the lands within any Indian reservation in the State of New York to taxation for State or local purposes." 25 U.S.C. § 233. See *Oneida Indian Nation of N.Y. v. County of Oneida*, 414 U. S. 661, 680–681, n. 15 (1974).

honor the Tribe's tax immunity is a question for Congress, not this Court, to decide.

* * *

In any event, as a matter of equity I believe that the "principle that the passage of time can preclude relief," should be applied sensibly and with an even hand. It seems perverse to hold that the reliance interests of non-Indian New Yorkers that are predicated on almost two centuries of inaction by the Tribe do not foreclose the Tribe's enforcement of judicially created damages remedies for ancient wrongs, but do somehow mandate a forfeiture of a tribal immunity that has been consistently and uniformly protected throughout our history. In this case, the Tribe reacquired reservation land in a peaceful and lawful manner that fully respected the interests of innocent landowners—it purchased the land on the open market. To now deny the Tribe its right to tax immunity—at once the most fundamental of tribal rights and the least disruptive to other sovereigns— is not only inequitable, but also irreconcilable with the principle that only Congress may abrogate or extinguish tribal sovereignty. I would not decide this case on the basis of speculation about what may happen in future litigation over other regulatory issues. For the answer to the question whether the City may require the Tribe to pay taxes on its own property within its own reservation is pellucidly clear. Under settled law, it may not.

Accordingly, I respectfully dissent.

NOTES

1.   In a post-*Sherrill* decision, Cayuga Indian Nation of N.Y. v. Pataki, 413 F.3d 266 (2d Cir.2005), cert. denied, 547 U.S. 1128 (2006), a divided panel of the Second Circuit interpreted *Sherrill* as precluding the tribe's "disruptive" possessory land claim based on a violation of the Nonintercourse Act, regardless of whether it was equitable or legal in nature with respect to the relief sought, and applied equitable defenses to bar the tribe's ejectment *and* damages claims. The damages claim barred by the appeals court had resulted in a $248 million judgment for the tribe in the federal district court. Stating that the *Sherrill* holding had "dramatically" altered the legal landscape of Indian land claims throughout New York, the court also held that the federal law of laches "can apply against the United States [joined as a plaintiff in the *Cayuga* case] in these particular circumstances." The United States is not normally subject to laches as a defense. *See* Kathryn E. Fort, *The (In)Equities of Federal Indian Law*, The Federal Lawyer, Mar./Apr. 2007, 32, 35. See also Kathryn E. Fort, *The New Laches: Creating Title Where None Existed*, 16 Geo. Mason L.Rev. 357 (2009).

2.   In Oneida Indian Nation of N.Y. v. State of New York, 500 F.Supp.2d 128 (N.D.N.Y.2007), the State argued that *Cayuga* foreclosed land claims brought by the Oneida Indian Nation as well. But the district court rejected that argument, explaining that nonpossessory land claims—unlike the

trespass claim in *Cayuga*—would not be subject to the laches defense. But the Second Circuit reversed, applying *Sherrill*'s equitable defenses. See Oneida Indian Nation of N.Y. v. County of Oneida, 617 F.3d 114 (2d Cir.2010). In a telling portion of the opinion, the majority agreed that the *Sherrill* defenses were not really "laches"-related, but a sui generis defense, uniquely tailored to curtail disruptive Indian claims:

> We have used the term "laches" here, as did the district court and this Court in *Cayuga*, as a convenient shorthand for the equitable principles at stake in this case, but the term is somewhat imprecise for the purpose of describing those principles. The Oneidas assert that the invocation of a purported laches defense is improper here as the defendants have not established the necessary elements of such a defense. It is true that the district court in this case did not make findings that the Oneidas unreasonably delayed the initiation of this action or that the defendants were prejudiced by this delay-both required elements of a traditional laches defense. This omission, however, is not ultimately important, as the equitable defense recognized in *Sherrill* and applied in *Cayuga* does not focus on the elements of traditional laches but rather more generally on the length of time at issue between an historical injustice and the present day, on the disruptive nature of claims long delayed, and on the degree to which these claims upset the justifiable expectations of individuals and entities far removed from the events giving rise to the plaintiffs' injury.

Id., 617 F.3d 114, at 127.

3.   In a related case, the Second Circuit concluded that the Oneida Indian Nation was immune from a foreclosure suit involving fee land located within the Oneida reservation boundaries. Oneida Indian Nation of New York v. County of Madison, N.Y., 605 F.3d 149, 159 (2d Cir.2010). The Supreme Court had granted a petition for certiorari on the questions "whether tribal sovereign immunity from suit, to the extent it should continue to be recognized, bars taxing authorities from foreclosing to collect lawfully imposed property taxes" and "whether the ancient Oneida reservation in New York was disestablished or diminished." However, shortly after the county filed for certiorari, the Oneidas informed the Court that the Nation had passed a tribal ordinance waiving "its sovereign immunity to enforcement of real property taxation through foreclosure by state, county and local governments within and throughout the United States." The Justices then vacated and remanded the case back to the Second Circuit, instructing the court to address, "in the first instance, whether to revisit its ruling on sovereign immunity in light of this new factual development, and—if necessary—proceed to address other questions in the case consistent with its sovereign immunity ruling." 562 U.S. 42, 43 (2011)(per curiam). Why do you think the Oneidas adopted this ordinance? Based on the Court's decision in *Sherrill*, can you predict how the Justices would rule on the questions presented on certiorari in the case?

On May 16, 2013, after many years of litigation, the Oneida Indian Nation, the State of New York and Madison and Oneida counties signed an agreement to resolve land, tax, and gaming disputes among them. The agreement recognized the right of the Oneida Nation to petition the U.S. to take 25,000 acres of land into federal trust status and gave the Oneida Nation exclusive gaming rights in a ten county Central New York region. The agreement also obligated the Nation to invest 25 percent of its net gaming revenue from its slot machines (roughly $50 million a year) in the state and surrounding counties, and to match tribal taxes on cigarettes and gasoline to state rates. The agreement was ratified by the New York legislature in 2013.

4. In Mohegan Tribe v. Connecticut, 638 F.2d 612 (2d Cir.1980), cert. denied 452 U.S. 968 (1981), the court rejected an argument that the provisions of the Nonintercourse Act restricting transfers of land applied only in "Indian Country," an area that was described in versions of the Act passed in 1796, 1799, and 1802. The state's theory would have distinguished the settled areas of original states from the geographic area defined as Indian country. The court found that Congress had been clear in its intention to place geographic limits on the application of various provisions of the Acts that related to trading, liquor, and other matters, but not the nonintercourse (land transaction) restrictions, which used language suggesting general applicability. Thus, it would be improper to infer such a limitation upon the entire statute.

Some eastern claims have been blocked on procedural grounds. The Supreme Court held that the 1959 Act terminating the Catawba Tribe of South Carolina subjected the tribe's land claim to the state statute of limitations. South Carolina v. Catawba Indian Tribe, 476 U.S. 498 (1986). The First Circuit affirmed the dismissal of the complaint of the Mashpee Tribe of Massachusetts on the basis of a jury verdict finding that the Mashpee Tribe did not exist when the suit was filed. Mashpee Tribe v. New Seabury Corp., 592 F.2d 575 (1st Cir.1979), cert. denied 444 U.S. 866 (1979). See also Epps v. Andrus, 611 F.2d 915 (1st Cir.1979) (individual Chappaquiddick Indians lack standing to bring Nonintercourse Act claim).

5. Ultimately, tribal land claims are usually resolved by negotiations among the tribe, the state, private parties, and the federal government, and yet these settlements have also led to further lawsuits. The Narragansett claim was settled in 1978 through an arrangement in which the tribe's claim for 3200 acres in Rhode Island was resolved by a transfer of 1800 acres, 900 from the state and 900 from private owners willing to sell at fair market value. Congress provided a fund of $3.5 million in order to purchase land from the private landowners. See Rhode Island Indian Claims Settlement Act of 1978, 25 U.S.C.A. §§ 1701–1712. In Carcieri v. Salazar, 555 U.S. 379 (2009), however, the Supreme Court rejected the authority of the Bureau of Indian Affairs' to take land into trust for the tribe on grounds that the tribe had not been "under Federal jurisdiction" in 1934, the year that the Indian Reorganization Act's land re-acquisition provisions were passed.

6.   The extensive land claims of the Maine Indians were settled in 1980 with the passage of the Maine Indian Claims Settlement Act, 25 U.S.C.A. §§ 1721–1735. The Act approved an agreement between the state and the three tribal groups with land claims, the Passamaquoddy Tribe, the Penobscot Nation, and the Houlton Band of Maliseet Indians. The negotiations leading to the congressional settlement act were instituted after the First Circuit Court of Appeals issued its decision in Joint Tribal Council of Passamaquoddy Tribe v. Morton, 528 F.2d 370 (1st Cir.1975):

> The central issue in this action is whether the Secretary of the Interior was correct in finding that the United States has no "trust relationship" with the Tribe and, therefore, should play no role in the Tribe's dispute with Maine. Whether, even if there is a trust relationship with the Passamaquoddies, the United States has an affirmative duty to sue Maine on the Tribe's behalf is a separate issue that was not raised or decided below and which consequently we do not address. The district court held only that defendants "erred in denying plaintiffs' request for litigation on the sole ground that no trust relationship exists between the United States and the Passamaquoddy Tribe." It was left to the Secretary to translate the finding of a "trust relationship" into concrete duties.

> Over the years, the federal government has recognized many Indian tribes, specifically naming them in treaties, agreements, or statutes. The general notion of a "trust relationship," often called a guardian-ward relationship, has been used to characterize the resulting relationship between the federal government and those tribes. It is the defendants' and the intervenor's contention here that such a relationship may only be claimed by those specifically recognized tribes.

> The Tribe, however, contends otherwise. It rests its claim of a trust relationship on the Nonintercourse Act, enacted in its original form by the First Congress in 1790 to protect the lands of "any . . . tribe of Indians." Plaintiffs argue, and the district court found, that the unlimited reference to "any . . . tribe" must be read to include the Passamaquoddy Tribe as well as tribes specially recognized under separate federal treaties, agreements or statutes. As the Act applies to them, plaintiffs urge that it is sufficient to evidence congressional acknowledgement of a trust relationship in their case at least as respects the Tribe's land claims.

* * *

> * * * That the Nonintercourse Act imposes upon the federal government a fiduciary's role with respect to protection of the lands of a tribe covered by the Act seems to us beyond question, both from the history, wording and structure of the Act and from the cases cited above and in the district court's opinion. The purpose of the Act has been held to acknowledge and guarantee the Indian tribes' right of

occupancy, and clearly there can be no meaningful guarantee without a corresponding federal duty to investigate and take such action as may be warranted in the circumstances.

We emphasize what is obvious, that the "trust relationship" we affirm has as its source the Nonintercourse Act, meaning that the trust relationship pertains to land transactions which are or may be covered by the Act, and is rooted in rights and duties encompassed or created by the Act. Congress or the executive branch may at a later time recognize the Tribe for other purposes within their powers, creating a broader set of federal responsibilities; and we of course do not rule out the possibility that there are statutes or legal theories not now before us which might create duties and rights of unforeseen, broader dimension.

* * *

Id. at 372–76, 379–80.

The ruling by the unanimous First Circuit Court of Appeals panel stunned the state's government, real estate industry, and its congressional delegation. In passing the Maine Indian Claims Settlement Act, supra, the land conveyances from the three tribes to the state of Maine were deemed by Congress to be in conformity with the Nonintercourse Act. Accordingly, all aboriginal title and Indian claims were retroactively extinguished. The Act's provisions were made effective upon appropriation of $81.5 million by Congress. The funds were to be used partly to purchase 305,000 acres for the tribes. The balance, $27 million, was to be held in trust and invested by the United States, with quarterly payments of income to the Passamaquoddies and Penobscots. The Act also made the tribes eligible for federal services to Indians and included detailed provisions concerning state and tribal jurisdiction on tribal land.

7.   In State of Vermont v. Elliott, 616 A.2d 210 (Vt.1992), cert. denied 507 U.S. 911 (1993), a group claiming to be members of the Western Abenaki Tribe were charged with fishing without a license at a 1987 "fish-in" demonstration in Vermont. Their defense was based on the doctrine of "aboriginal rights." The tribal members claimed that they were members of a currently viable Indian tribe which had from "time immemorial" continuously occupied the land where the offenses occurred and, because they held "aboriginal title" to the land, they were not subject to state regulation for fishing without a license. The Vermont Supreme Court disagreed, holding that the Abenakis' aboriginal rights were extinguished by "a series of historical events." These events included colonial land grants made to white settlers, a rebellion by the grantees between 1770 and 1775 in reaction to New York's attempt to remove the New Hampshire grantees, Vermont's 1777 declaration of independence as a "republic," and Vermont's admission to the Union in 1791 by which the grants were confirmed. The court was further persuaded by what it called "the phenomenon of white settlement * * * and appropriation to the exclusion of other competing claims," although it recognized "that the Abenakis

never voluntarily abandoned the area and that they were never completely removed * * * ."

At what point in time did history act to extinguish Abenaki aboriginal rights? The Vermont Supreme Court's decision in *Elliott* has been the subject of pointed academic criticism. See Joseph William Singer, *Well Settled?: The Increasing Weight of History in American Indian Land Claims,* 28 Ga.L.Rev. 481 (1994); John P. Lowndes, *When History Outweighs Law: Extinguishment of Abenaki Aboriginal Title,* 42 Buff.L.Rev. 77 (1994).

NOTE: TRIBAL RECOGNITION, PROPERTY, AND PEOPLEHOOD

The definition of the term "tribe" is fundamental to Indian law and particularly to Indian tribal property interests. Congress has broad power to recognize tribes, thereby extending its Commerce Clause powers over tribes and their lands. Recognition is easy to establish for those tribes with a federally-created reservation. In addition, under the Federally Recognized Tribe List Act, tribes may be recognized by judicial action as well as by treaty, legislation, or executive branch action. 25 U.S.C. §§ 479, 479a–1.

Some older cases suggest that decisions on recognition of an Indian tribe, like similar decisions in the international sphere, are "political questions" left solely to Congress. See United States v. Holliday, 70 U.S. (3 Wall.) 407 (1865). Are congressional determinations in this area likely to be virtually immune from judicial review? See Judge Posner's opinion in Miami Nation of Indians of Indiana, Inc. v. United States Dept. of Interior, 255 F.3d 342 (7th Cir.2001), suggesting that federal court deference to Interior's federal acknowledgment decisions may be equivalent to a nonjusticiable political question.

During the removal era, Congress often moved different ethnological groups to a single reservation and called the consolidated group a single "tribe." Conversely, Congress has sometimes taken an ethnological tribe and divided it into separate bands, treating each band as a tribe.

In United States v. John, 437 U.S. 634 (1978), the state of Mississippi challenged the exercise of federal jurisdiction over certain crimes committed on lands within the area of the state designated as a reservation for the Choctaw Indians. The reservation was created for the Mississippi Choctaws who had refused to remove to the west of the Mississippi River with the rest of their tribe in the early nineteenth century. In holding that federal law, not state law, applied to the crime of assault with intent to kill when committed by a Choctaw Indian on Choctaw land, the Supreme Court stated:

> The Mississippi lands in question here were declared by Congress to be held in trust by the Federal Government for the benefit of the Mississippi Choctaw Indians who were at that time under federal supervision. There is no apparent reason why these lands, which had been purchased in previous years for the aid of those Indians, did not become a "reservation," at least for the purposes of federal criminal jurisdiction at that particular time. See United

States v. Celestine, 215 U.S. 278, 285 (1909). But if there were any doubt about the matter in 1939 when, as hereinabove described, Congress declared that title to lands previously purchased for the Mississippi Choctaws would be held in trust, the situation was completely clarified by the proclamation in 1944 of a reservation and the subsequent approval of the constitution and bylaws adopted by the Mississippi Band.

* * *

We assume for purposes of argument, as does the United States, that there have been times when Mississippi's jurisdiction over the Choctaws and their lands went unchallenged. But, particularly in view of the elaborate history, recounted above, of relations between the Mississippi Choctaws and the United States, we do not agree that Congress and the Executive Branch have less power to deal with the affairs of the Mississippi Choctaws than with the affairs of other Indian groups. Neither the fact that the Choctaws in Mississippi are merely a remnant of a larger group of Indians, long ago removed from Mississippi, nor the fact that federal supervision over them has not been continuous, destroys the federal power to deal with them.

Id. at 649, 652.

When Congress has not clearly indicated the reach of its legislation the courts have had to address whether a group is properly included as a "tribe." A commonly used definition is found in Montoya v. United States, 180 U.S. 261, 266 (1901): "a body of Indians of the same or a similar race, united in a community under one leadership or government, and inhabiting a particular though sometimes ill-defined territory." This test can be an imposing barrier, as evidenced by Mashpee Tribe v. New Seabury Corp., 592 F.2d 575 (1st Cir.1979), cert. denied 444 U.S. 866 (1979).

The Mashpee Tribe brought suit under the Nonintercourse Act, asserting that its tribal land was taken from it between 1834 and 1870 without the required federal consent. It claimed to be a tribe of Indians that had lived in and around the town of Mashpee, Massachusetts, continuously since time immemorial. The defendant landowners in the town of Mashpee denied that the group claiming to be the Mashpee Tribe "is or was a tribe," and therefore lacked standing to bring a suit under the Act.

A trial on whether the Mashpee was an Indian tribe lasted 40 days and was submitted to the jury on special interrogatories. The jury found that the Mashpee had been a tribe at certain times in its history, but was not an Indian tribe at the date of the enactment of the first Nonintercourse Act, nor on certain other relevant dates when land allegedly passed out of tribal ownership, nor on the date of the commencement of the law suit in 1976. Citing Montoya, the district court dismissed the suit, and the First Circuit affirmed:

Plaintiff must prove that it meets the definition of "tribe of Indians" as that phrase is used in the Nonintercourse Act both in order to establish any right to recovery and to establish standing to bring this suit. This issue is particularly difficult in this case because the Mashpees differ from most other groups who have sought to assert rights as Indian tribes. The federal government has never officially recognized the Mashpees as a tribe or actively supported or watched over them. Moreover, the Mashpees have a long history of intermarriage with non-Indians and acceptance of non-Indian religion and culture. These facts do not necessarily mean that the Mashpees are not a tribe protected by federal law, but they do make the issue of tribal existence a difficult factual question for the jury.

* * *

* * * That the Mashpees have lost this case represents not a failure of the law to protect Indians in changing times, but a failure of the evidence to show that this group was an object of the protective laws. In future cases if the issue of tribal status is raised, the court, with the aid of the parties and expert witnesses, will be able to shape instructions responsive to the special problems presented at that time. * * *

592 F.2d at 581–82, 587–88. Writing about the *Mashpee* case, Professor Martha Minow observed:

> The jury's resistance to the question posed may reflect problems with the notion of "tribe," especially as a concept defined by whites to describe and regulate nonwhites. Or the jury's result may express discomfort with the pretense of a singular history, given the complex and competing narratives offered by the witnesses. An alternative account offered by the anthropologist watching the trial suggests that the idea of any cultural group as distinctive is no longer meaningful—if, indeed, it ever was—given the varieties of contacts and mutual interactions among groups. The American understanding of Indian tribes includes nineteenth-century photographs of individual Native Americans—but * * * the clothing and even the poses in the photographs were contributed by the white photographer. The Mashpee plaintiffs saw themselves as members of a tribe; how should that count in the assessment of difference?

Gerald Torres and Kathryn Milun, in *Translating Yonnondio by Precedent and Evidence: The Mashpee Indian Case,* 1990 Duke L.J. 625, conclude that:

> In response to the Mashpee's claims, attorneys for the Town of Mashpee argued that the Tribe lacked racial purity, that it failed to retain a sufficient degree of self-government. It exercised little if any "sovereignty" over specific territory; it maintained no perceivably coherent sense of "community," and therefore was not a Tribe as defined by the Supreme Court in *Montoya.* * * *

> * * * According to the defendants, the Mashpee could be "self-governed" only if the Tribe adopted political forms susceptible to

documentary proof. * * * [B]ecause the Mashpee Indian culture is rooted in large measure on the passing of an oral record, their history could only signify silence. * * * The stories that members of the Mashpee Tribe told were stories that legal ears could not hear. Thus the legal requirements of relevance rendered the Indian storytellers mute and the culture they were portraying invisible. * * *

Id. at 647–49, 651. *Mashpee* illustrates the complex problem of asserting group identity in the face of overwhelming outside cultural influence. As the Mashpee Tribe discovered, claims of self-identity are not always recognized by outsiders. After nearly three decades of struggle, the Mashpee Wampanoag Indian Tribal Council was acknowledged by the Office of Federal Acknowledgment, 72 Fed.Reg. 80007–1 (Feb. 22, 2007).

During the early 1960s, the BIA began distinguishing between "recognized" and "nonrecognized" tribes. Federal contacts had been broken off or never initiated with many tribes. Decisions had been made over the years to furnish or deny services to various groups in *ad hoc* fashion by administrators. In spite of the arbitrary way in which these decisions were often made, federal officials took the position that tribes not "served" by the BIA were not covered by the federal-tribal relationship.

When the United States brought suit against the State of Washington, asserting the fishing rights of several tribes under a series of 1854 and 1855 treaties, the Stillaguamish Tribe asked for government representation. The tribe was a named party to one of the treaties, but federal officials refused to protect its rights on the ground that it was not a tribe "recognized" by the BIA. The tribe then intervened, represented by its own attorney, and the case proceeded to a successful conclusion. The court held that "[n]onrecognition of the tribe by the federal government * * * may result in the loss of statutory benefits, but can have no impact on vested treaty rights." United States v. Washington, 520 F.2d 676, 693 (9th Cir.1975), cert. denied 423 U.S. 1086 (1976).

The Stillaguamish Tribe then petitioned the Secretary of Interior to establish that it was entitled to federal services. The petition alleged that the Stillaguamish were ethnologically an Indian tribe, that Congress had never terminated the federal-tribal relationship, and that any administrative refusal to "recognize" the tribe was arbitrary. When the Secretary refused to rule on the petition, the tribe obtained an order directing the Secretary to act. Stillaguamish Tribe v. Kleppe, No. 75–1718 (D.D.C. Aug. 24, 1975). The Secretary then concluded that there was ample authority under the broad provisions of the Snyder Act, 25 U.S.C.A. § 13, and the Johnson-O'Malley Act, 25 U.S.C.A. §§ 452–454, to provide federal services to the tribe.

As a result of this litigation, the BIA promulgated its first set of rules in 1978 to determine which groups are entitled to be federally acknowledged as tribes. These rules were substantially modified in 1994 to expedite the review process. 25 C.F.R. Part 83 (1997). The rules allow any "Indian group in the continental United States that believes it should be acknowledged as an Indian tribe" to submit a petition, called a "letter of intent," to the Interior Department's Assistant Secretary for Indian Affairs. 25 CFR 83.4. The criteria for acknowledgment of tribes generally track the evidence that the Stillaguamish submitted when the tribe petitioned the Secretary before any formal procedures had been proscribed.

The mandatory criteria are set forth in section 83.7:

(a)   The petitioner has been identified as an American Indian entity on a substantially continuous basis since 1900. * * * Evidence to be relied upon in determining a group's Indian identity may include one or a combination of the following, as well as other evidence * * *

(1)   Identification as an Indian entity by Federal authorities.

(2)   Relationships with State governments based on identification of the group as Indian.

(3)   Dealings with a county, parish, or other local government in a relationship based on the group's Indian identity.

(4)   Identification as an Indian entity by anthropologists, historians, and/or other scholars.

(5)   Identification as an Indian entity in newspapers and books.

(6)   Identification as an Indian entity in relationships with Indian tribes or with national, regional, or state Indian organizations.

(b)   A predominant portion of the petitioning group comprises a distinct community and has existed as a community from historical times until the present.

* * *

(c)   The petitioner has maintained political influence or authority over its members as an autonomous entity from historical times until the present.

* * *

(d)   A copy of the group's present governing document, including its membership criteria. In the absence of a written document, the petitioner must provide a statement describing in full its membership criteria and current governing procedures.

(e)   The petitioner's membership consists of individuals who descend from a historical Indian tribe or from historical Indian tribes which combined to function as a single political entity.

* * *

(f)   The membership of the petitioning group is composed principally of persons who are not members of any acknowledged North American Indian tribe.

* * *

(g) Neither the petitioner nor its members are the subject of congressional legislation that has expressly terminated or forbidden the Federal relationship.

Under these rules, the Department has acknowledged the existence of 18 tribes. The process has been slow, in part because it requires the evaluation of extensive historical and anthropological evidence, but in recent years the pace of review has increased. Once active review of a petition has commenced, the Assistant Secretary must publish an acknowledgment decision in the Federal Register within one year. If a tribe disagrees with the BIA's finding, it may file an appeal with the Interior Board of Indian Appeals. 25 CFR 83.11.

Nearly 70 of the tribes that are not currently recognized by the federal government had their tribal relationship with the United States terminated in the 1950s. The Lumbee Indian Tribe of North Carolina numbers approximately 62,000 members. In 1988 the BIA rejected the tribe's petition for recognition citing a 1956 Act of Congress which explicitly barred the Lumbees from receiving services as an Indian tribe from the BIA. In response, the tribe lobbied Congress. A recognition bill passed in the House in 1993, but was stalled in the Senate over concerns that the Lumbees had not gone through the federal recognition process. The BIA, which runs the process, says it cannot act until Congress changes the 1956 law. New Lumbee recognition bills have been introduced in Congress in recent years, but none have been enacted.

On June 29, 2015, the Department of the Interior (Department) released its final rule to reform the process for Federal acknowledgment ("Part 83") criticized by many as "broken" and in need of reform. The rule claims to promote efficiency through several procedural reforms. Substantively, it contains two modifications to Part 83. First, the final rule retains the current criterion (a), requiring identification of the petitioner as an Indian entity, but does not limit the evidence in support of this criterion to observations by those external to the petitioner. In other words, the final rule allows the Department to accept any and all evidence, such as the petitioner's own contemporaneous records, as evidence that the petitioner has been an Indian entity since 1900. Second, the rule reviews the number of marriages in support of criterion (b) (community)—past Departmental practice has been to count the number of marriages within a petitioner; this rule instead provides that the Department count the number of petitioner members who are married to others in the petitioning group.

What is the best way to determine who is a "people?" This question has long occupied political philosophers, John Rawls, The Law of Peoples (1999) (describing the role of peoples in democratic societies), and American Indian studies scholars alike. See Tom Holm, The Great Confusion in Indian Affairs: Native Americans and Whites in the Progressive Era xiv, xvii (2005) (postulating aspects of American Indian peoplehood); Kristen A. Carpenter, *Real Property and Peoplehood*, 27 Stan.Env.L.J. 313 (2008) (linking American Indian peoplehood to the relationship with the tribal land base).

Robert A. Williams, Jr., in *Encounters on the Frontiers of International Human Rights Law: Redefining the Terms of Indigenous Peoples' Survival in the World,* 1990 Duke L.J. 660, 663 n. 4, writes that "indigenous peoples have insisted on the right to define themselves." Isaiah Locklear, a Lumbee elder, has said: "The old people, you see, they knew they was Indians. That wasn't a question. But up until the turn of the century, there was no particular name for our Indian people. We were just Indians." Jose Barreiro, *Lumbee Country,* 2 Ne. Indian Q. 13, 33 (1988).

As described above, the UN General Assembly adopted the Declaration on the Rights of Indigenous Peoples, G.A. Res 61/295, in 2007. Article 33 recognizes the right of indigenous peoples to "determine their identity or membership in accordance to their customs and traditions." This approach underlines the importance of "self-identification" among indigenous peoples. See Chapter 14B, infra for a discussion of the U.N. Declaration, and further materials on the protection of indigenous peoples' rights within the international human rights system.

Consider the reforms to the federal acknowledgment process as articulated at http://www.bia.gov/WhoWeAre/AS-IA/ORM/83revise/index.htm. In what ways do these reforms bring federal law into compliance with the Declaration and various conceptions of indigenous peoplehood described above?

SECTION B. THE FEDERAL-TRIBAL RELATIONSHIP AS A SOURCE OF FEDERAL POWER

The cases involving tribal property in the first section of this chapter illustrate the struggle to sort out the trustee obligations of the United States government that demand protection of Indian property from the trustee's discretion to take, use, manage and sell the property. Cases often turned on neat, hypertechnical rules of Indian property and trust law. Claims cases versus the United States yielded both high sounding rationales for doing justice to tribes and crabbed legal theories for limiting Indian recovery. Some decisions did award compensation for rights or property taken from or lost by the Indians, others did not, but no court has ever set aside a congressional action as unwise or unlawful under the "plenary power" doctrine.

As cases like *Kagama,* page 186, supra, and *Lone Wolf,* page 212, supra, illustrate, congressional authority to legislate over Indian affairs was oftentimes vigorously challenged by Indians or tribes. Such legislation was always upheld, even when it unilaterally abrogated an Indian treaty. The Court, in stressing the idea of Congress's plenary power in Indian affairs, declined to invade powers assigned to a coordinate branch of government. These decisions paid only lip service to the trust obligation in which the plenary power theoretically was rooted.

The idea that federal power over Indian affairs stems from protective obligations to the tribes is rooted in the Marshall trilogy. Its application in *Johnson v. McIntosh* invested the United States, as successor to the colonies and their European predecessors who "discovered" the lands, with oversight of all land transactions.

Then in the *Cherokee* cases Marshall connected the prerogatives of the discovery doctrine to duties of the nation to ensure the sovereignty and independence of Indian nations by protecting them from outsiders, even the states. Calling the discovery doctrine an "extravagant and absurd idea," he said that it had nevertheless become institutionalized through international law, treaties, and the U.S. Constitution. The U.S. had inherited powers and duties under the doctrine, and enshrined ultimate authority over Indian affairs in the federal government through the Indian Commerce Clause of the Constitution. Thus, the federal government stood in a protective relationship over tribal governments. And since the doctrine so embodied in the law resulted in preserving a tribe's "right to self-government" as a "distinct community," any state laws contrary to a tribe's sovereignty over territory were unconstitutional.

Later the Supreme Court used the notion of a protective duty to tribal governments to uphold equally broad powers over them. In challenges to state assertions of authority over Indians, however, the existence of congressional plenary power has proved to be a formidable shield guarding the reservations as enclaves for the exercise of tribal governing authority. A tension persists between the federal trusteeship obligation, with its preemptive exclusion of state intrusions that could impede tribal sovereignty, and exercises of congressional powers that often remove or denigrate Indian rights and tribal sovereignty. The Court has alluded variously to several federal constitutional powers, including the Treaty Clause, the War Power, and Property Clause, as supporting legislative and executive authority over Indian affairs. See generally Felix S. Cohen, Handbook of Federal Indian Law §§ 5.01–5.01 (2012 ed.). Today federal power over Indian affairs is accepted as tracing primarily to the Indian Commerce Clause, art. I, Sec. 8, cl. 3, the only express grant of federal power over Indians, where Congress is authorized "to regulate Commerce * * * with the Indian Tribes."

1. THE MARSHALL MODEL OF INDIAN RIGHTS AND CONGRESSIONAL PLENARY POWER IN INDIAN AFFAIRS

As Dean Newton has aptly put it in her study of the subject, "[t]he mystique of plenary power has pervaded federal regulation of Indian affairs from the beginning." Nell Jessup Newton, *Federal Power Over Indians: Its Sources, Scope, and Limitations*, 132 U.Pa.L.Rev. 195, 199 (1984). Since the publication of Dean Newton's article on the plenary power doctrine, a number of Indian law scholars, noted practitioners, and respected scholars from other fields such as constitutional law have continued to carry on a spirited debate over whether federal Indian law, owing to the base motives in its colonialist history, must be rejected and a new order sought. This debate continues to raise a set of vital questions and issues for students, practitioners, and judges about the very nature of the federal-tribal relationship. See generally, Milner S. Ball, *Constitution, Court, Indian Tribes*, 1987 Am.B.Found.Res.J. 1; Robert N. Clinton, *There is No Federal Supremacy Clause for Indian Tribes*, 34 Ariz.St.L.J. 113 (2002); Sarah H. Cleveland, *Powers Inherent in Sovereignty: Indians, Aliens, Territories, and the Nineteenth Century Origins of Plenary Power over Foreign Affairs*, 81 Tex.L.Rev. 1 (2002).

In reading the cases and materials in this section, consider the basis, the wisdom and the consequences of the foundational concepts of Indian law laid out in the Marshall trilogy. Whose interests have been served by invoking the "mystique of plenary power" and the federal trusteeship for Indian tribes? Has what Professor Robert A. Williams, Jr. called "the Marshall Model of Indian Rights," Robert A. Williams, Jr., Like a Loaded Weapon: The Rehnquist Court, Indian Rights, and the Legal History of Racism in America 49 (2005) been faithfully applied by courts in the modern era? Were the models' roots corrupt *ab initio*? What alternative theories were available and how would they have affected the outcome of specific cases? Can a legal doctrine traceable to racial prejudice against Indian people ever serve as a vehicle for achieving racial justice between Indian tribes and the dominant society in the United States?

ROBERT A. WILLIAMS, JR., THE ALGEBRA OF FEDERAL INDIAN LAW: THE HARD TRAIL OF DECOLONIZING AND AMERICANIZING THE WHITE MAN'S INDIAN JURISPRUDENCE

1986 Wis.L.Rev. 219, 260–65.

* * *

A. The Development of Modern United States Colonial Legal Theory: 1900 Through the Present

* * *

This notion of unquestioned plenary power in Congress to deal with Indian Nations rested squarely upon the foundations laid out in Chief Justice Marshall's early articulations of the dependent status and rights of Indians within the domestic law of the United States under the doctrine of discovery. Numerous late nineteenth and early twentieth century Supreme Court opinions freely extended Marshall's original limited recognition of an overriding sovereignty of the federal government in Indian affairs to entail a superior and unquestionable power on the part of Congress unrestrained by normal constitutional limitations. In case after case, the Court simply refused to check Congress' free reign in matters where it was thought that broad discretionary powers were vital to the solution of the immensely difficult "Indian problem." * * *

* * *

Throughout the late nineteenth and early twentieth centuries, Congress unilaterally abrogated numerous Indian treaties under the plenary power doctrine. These congressional actions were unquestioningly presumed by the Court to be "in perfect good faith" under the domestic law of the United States as derived from the doctrine of discovery. * * *

* * *

Besides justifying unquestioned abrogation and unilateral determination of tribal treaty and property rights, the plenary power paradigm has been interpreted to permit the denial of other fundamental human rights of Indian people in the United States. Violent suppression of Indian religious practices and traditional forms of government, separation of Indian children from their homes, wholesale spoliation of treaty-guaranteed resources, forced assimilative programs and involuntary sterilization of Indian women, represent but a few of the practical extensions of a * * * legal consciousness that at its core regards tribal peoples as normatively deficient and culturally, politically and morally inferior to Europeans. For half a millennium, whether articulated in this notion of plenary power possessed by Congress in Indian affairs, or through the Law of Nations * * *, European-derived legal thought has sought to erase the difference presented by the Indian in order to sustain its own discursive context; European norms and value structures. Animated by a central orienting myth of its own universalized, hierarchical position among all other discourses, the white man's archaic, European-derived law respecting the Indian is ultimately genocidal in both its practice and intent. * * *

* * *

NOTE

Williams' article inspired a lively debate with Robert Laurence on the contours and palatability of the plenary power doctrine. *See* Robert Laurence, *Learning to Live With the Plenary Power of Congress Over the Indian Nations: An Essay in Reaction to Professor Williams'* Algebra· 30 Ariz.L.Rev. 413 (1988) (arguing, among other things, that plenary power does not mean absolute but rather without subject matter limitation and that plenary power is critical to the protection of tribal sovereignty).

Professor Williams renewed his racial critique of federal Indian law in *Like a Loaded Weapon*, supra:

We have identified four principal elements of the Marshall Model of Indian Rights as it arises out of *Johnson* and the two *Cherokee* cases. First, the Marshall model is based upon a foundational set of beliefs in white racial superiority and Indian racial inferiority. Second, the model defines the scope and content of the Indian's inferior legal and political rights by reference to the doctrine of discovery and its organizing principle of white racial supremacy over the continent of North America. Third, the model relies on a judicially validated language of Indian savagery to justify the asserted privileges. Finally, the Court's role as a creature and instrument of these originating sources makes it impossible for the justices to do anything meaningful or lasting to protect Indian rights from the continuing rights-denying jurispathic force of the language of racism used to justify the discovery doctrine's racially discriminatory legal principles.

Id. at 70.

In his book, In The Courts of The Conqueror: The 10 Worst Indian Law Cases Ever Decided (2010), Walter R. Echo-Hawk, former staff attorney for the Native American Rights Fund, joined Professor Williams' call to challenge the Supreme Court Justices about their continued adherence to the racist principles of the Marshall Model:

* * * Even though colonialism was rejected as repugnant by the international community shortly after World War II, the legal underpinnings of colonialism remain implanted in the domestic law of the United States. In addition, the Supreme Court continues to rely upon legal doctrines infected with bare race notions as it decides contemporary Indian cases, long after the ideology of race has been discarded by virtually every other governmental institution in the country. Thus, the legal system ironically remains one of the last to perpetuate a form of racism. These fundamental problems in federal Indian law have prompted a call for reform among a growing number of prominent legal scholars who present a powerful case for decolonizing federal Indian law and confronting the Supreme Court about its continued legal precedent tainted with racism. * * * [H]ow can legal advocates expect to win lawsuits by citing cases that call Native Americans "savages" and by relying upon legal principles founded on the racial inferiority of their clients?

* * * [T]he Court needs to find some theory other than conquest, colonization, or racial superiority to justify its decisions. That change would entail a paradigm shift in American legal thinking similar to that which prompted the Court to overturn the legal basis for segregating America. Such a sea change for Indians has not yet emerged. Until change is demanded by society at large, the Court will continue to apply outmoded rules to Indians that "the Courts of the conqueror cannot deny. . . .

Id. at 5.

Other scholars, expressing profound disapproval with the Supreme Court's Indian law decisions of the past thirty years, have focused on the Court's departures from foundational principles of the Marshall Model. See, e.g., Hope M. Babcock, *A Civic-Republican Vision of "Domestic Dependent Nations" in the Twenty-First Century: Tribal Sovereignty Re-envisioned, Reinvigorated, and Re-empowered*, 2005 Utah L.Rev. 443 (2005) (criticizing the Court's invention of what she calls a "prudential plenary power doctrine," that in many ways, is far worse than the congressional version of the doctrine).

Dean Getches has pointed out that during the modern era of Indian law "[t]he foundational cases of the Marshall trilogy, adapted only slightly to reflect evolving national policy, were invoked in virtually every case to support the Court's decisions * * *. Using the Marshall trilogy as its linchpin, the Court honored the tradition of upholding tribal self-governance unless Congress had spoken to the contrary." David H. Getches, *Beyond Indian Law: The Rehnquist Court's Pursuit of States' Rights, Color-Blind Justice and Mainstream Values,* 86 Minn.L.Rev. 267, 272–73 (2001). He is sharply critical of "a spate of cases beginning about the time Rehnquist became Chief Justice in 1986," opining that the problem was that "the Court veered away from the foundations of Indian law." Id. at 273–74. He says of the "Marshall Model":

> As broad as the extension of congressional power over Indian affairs was intended to be, it was not the purpose of the government, in claiming or exercising that power, to destroy tribal sovereignty. * * * Exclusive congressional power, and its preemptive force, was necessary to implement laws and treaties created to protect tribal government within tribal territory.

Id. at 271–72. He goes on to argue that fixing the Supreme Court's departures from foundational principles is better left to Congress—using plenary power— than to the courts:

> To be sure, these Rehnquist-era decisions departing from, but not overruling, venerable principles have created a veneer of confusion over a historically complex but consistent body of law. * * * Moreover, it could be self-fulfilling for scholars and judges to overstate the degree of confusion and hopelessness in Indian law. * * * It may imply that it is up to the Court to wade in and "do justice." Nice though this may sound, licensing courts to reinvent Indian law based on the judges' notions of justice and what is right for society could add legitimacy to an ethnocentric judicial foray into Indian policy. Indian law has always been based on the assumption that separate societies could exist exempt from the American melting pot, preserving customs, values, and governance of the vestiges of traditional tribal territory. Judges who are not steeped in the culture and values of Indian tribalism are ill-equipped to rework these complex and anomalous traditions case by case.

Id. at 275–77.

In reading Indian law cases, consider whether the foundational principles of *Worcester* and its progeny have generally favored or disfavored tribes. Consider what alternatives there are to the plenary power doctrine, whether as applied by Congress or by the Supreme Court. If Congress is displeased with what it regards as judicial tampering with its constitutionally-delegated power over Indian affairs and interference with its policy of Indian self-determination, can the plenary power doctrine ultimately prove to be beneficial to tribes and tribal sovereignty? See United States v. Lara, page 589, infra.

2.   TREATY ABROGATION

UNITED STATES v. DION
Supreme Court of the United States, 1986.
476 U.S. 734, 106 S.Ct. 2216, 90 L.Ed.2d 767.

JUSTICE MARSHALL delivered the opinion of the Court.

Respondent Dwight Dion, Sr., a member of the Yankton Sioux Tribe, was convicted of shooting four bald eagles on the Yankton Sioux reservation in South Dakota in violation of the Endangered Species Act.

* * *

I

The Eagle Protection Act by its terms prohibits the hunting of the bald or golden eagle anywhere within the United States, except pursuant to a permit issued by the Secretary of the Interior. The Endangered Species Act imposes an equally stringent ban on the hunting of the bald eagle. The Court of Appeals for the Eighth Circuit, however, sitting en banc, held that members of the Yankton Sioux Tribe have a treaty right to hunt bald and golden eagles within the Yankton reservation for noncommercial purposes. It further held that the Eagle Protection Act and Endangered Species Act did not abrogate this treaty right. It therefore directed that Dion's convictions for shooting bald eagles be vacated, since neither the District Court nor the jury made any explicit finding whether the killings were for commercial or noncommercial purposes.[3]

The Court of Appeals relied on an 1858 treaty signed by the United States and by representatives of the Yankton Tribe. Treaty with the Yancton [1858 spelling] Sioux, Apr. 19, 1858, 11 Stat. 743. Under that treaty, the Yankton ceded to the United States all but 400,000 acres of the land then held by the Tribe. The treaty bound the Yanktons to remove to,

---

[3]   On remand from the en banc court, an Eighth Circuit panel rejected a religious freedom claim raised by Dion. Dion does not pursue that claim here, and accordingly we do not consider it.

* * *

and settle on, their reserved land within one year. The United States in turn agreed to guarantee the Yanktons quiet and undisturbed possession of their reserved land, and to pay to the Yanktons, or expend for their benefit, various moneys in the years to come. The area thus reserved for the Tribe was a legally constituted Indian reservation. The treaty did not place any restriction on the Yanktons' hunting rights on their reserved land.

All parties to this litigation agree that the treaty rights reserved by the Yankton included the exclusive right to hunt and fish on their land. As a general rule, Indians enjoy exclusive treaty rights to hunt and fish on lands reserved to them, unless such rights were clearly relinquished by treaty or have been modified by Congress. F. Cohen, Handbook of Federal Indian Law 449 (1982 ed.) (hereinafter Cohen). These rights need not be expressly mentioned in the treaty. See *Menominee Tribe v. United States*, 391 U. S. 404 (1968); *Alaska Pacific Fisheries v. United States*, 248 U. S. 78 (1918). Those treaty rights, however, little avail Dion if, as the Solicitor General argues, they were subsequently abrogated by Congress. We find that they were.

II

It is long settled that "the provisions of an act of Congress, passed in the exercise of its constitutional authority, . . . if clear and explicit, must be upheld by the courts, even in contravention of express stipulations in an earlier treaty" with a foreign power. *Fong Yue Ting v. United States*, 149 U. S. 698, 720 (1893); cf. *Goldwater v. Carter*, 444 U. S. 996 (1979). This Court applied that rule to congressional abrogation of Indian treaties in *Lone Wolf v. Hitchcock*, 187 U. S. 553, 566 (1903). Congress, the Court concluded, has the power "to abrogate the provisions of an Indian treaty, though presumably such power will be exercised only when circumstances arise which will not only justify the government in disregarding the stipulations of the treaty, but may demand, in the interest of the country and the Indians themselves, that it should do so." *Ibid.*

We have required that Congress' intention to abrogate Indian treaty rights be clear and plain. Cohen 223; see also *United States v. Santa Fe Pacific R. Co.*, 314 U. S. 339, 353 (1941). "Absent explicit statutory language, we have been extremely reluctant to find congressional abrogation of treaty rights. . . ." *Washington v. Commercial Passenger Fishing Vessel Assn.*, 443 U. S. 658, 690 (1979). We do not construe statutes as abrogating treaty rights in "a backhanded way," *Menominee Tribe v. United States*, 391 U. S. 404, 412 (1968); in the absence of explicit statement, " 'the intention to abrogate or modify a treaty is not to be lightly imputed to the Congress.' " *Id.*, at 413, quoting *Pigeon River Improvement, Slide & Boom Co. v. Cox Ltd.*, 291 U. S. 138, 160 (1934). Indian treaty rights are too fundamental to be easily cast aside.

We have enunciated, however, different standards over the years for determining how such a clear and plain intent must be demonstrated. In some cases, we have required that Congress make "express declaration" of its intent to abrogate treaty rights. See *Leavenworth, Lawrence & Galveston R. Co. v. United States*, 92 U. S. (2 Otto) 733, 741–742 (1875); see also Wilkinson & Volkman 627–630, 645–659. In other cases, we have looked to the statute's "legislative history" and "surrounding circumstances" as well as to "the face of the Act." *Rosebud Sioux Tribe v. Kneip*, 430 U. S. 584, 587 (1977), quoting *Mattz v. Arnett*, 412 U. S. 481, 505 (1973). Explicit statement by Congress is preferable for the purpose of ensuring legislative accountability for the abrogation of treaty rights, cf. *Seminole Nation v. United States*, 316 U. S. 286, 296–297 (1942). We have not rigidly interpreted that preference, however, as a *per se* rule; where the evidence of congressional intent to abrogate is sufficiently compelling, "the weight of authority indicates that such an intent can also be found by a reviewing court from clear and reliable evidence in the legislative history of a statute." Cohen 223. What is essential is clear evidence that Congress actually considered the conflict between its intended action on the one hand and Indian treaty rights on the other, and chose to resolve that conflict by abrogating the treaty.

A

The Eagle Protection Act renders it a federal crime to "take, possess, sell, purchase, barter, offer to sell, purchase or barter, transport, export or import, at any time or in any manner any bald eagle commonly known as the American eagle or any golden eagle, alive or dead, or any part, nest, or egg thereof." 16 U. S. C. § 668(a). The prohibition is "sweepingly framed"; the enumeration of forbidden acts is "exhaustive and careful." *Andrus v. Allard*, 444 U. S. 51, 56 (1979). The Act, however, authorizes the Secretary of the Interior to permit the taking, possession, and transportation of eagles "for the religious purposes of Indian tribes," and for certain other narrow purposes, upon a determination that such taking, possession or transportation is compatible with the preservation of the bald eagle or the golden eagle. 16 U. S. C. § 668a.

Congressional intent to abrogate Indian treaty rights to hunt bald and golden eagles is certainly strongly suggested on the face of the Eagle Protection Act. The provision allowing taking of eagles under permit for the religious purposes of Indian tribes is difficult to explain except as a reflection of an understanding that the statute otherwise bans the taking of eagles by Indians, a recognition that such a prohibition would cause hardship for the Indians, and a decision that that problem should be solved not by exempting Indians from the coverage of the statute, but by authorizing the Secretary to issue permits to Indians where appropriate.

The legislative history of the statute supports that view. The Eagle Protection Act was originally passed in 1940, and did not contain any explicit reference to Indians. Its prohibitions related only to bald eagles; it cast no shadow on hunting of the more plentiful golden eagle. In 1962, however, Congress considered amendments to the Eagle Protection Act extending its ban to the golden eagle as well. As originally drafted by the staff of the Subcommittee on Fisheries and Wildlife Conservation of the House Committee on Merchant Marine and Fisheries, the amendment simply would have added the words "or any golden eagle" at two places in the Act where prohibitions relating to the bald eagle were described.

Before the start of hearings on the bill, however, the Subcommittee received a letter from Assistant Secretary of the Interior Frank Briggs on behalf of the Interior Department. The Interior Department supported the proposed bill. It noted, however, the following concern:

> The golden eagle is important in enabling many Indian tribes, particularly those in the Southwest, to continue ancient customs and ceremonies that are of deep religious or emotional significance to them.

The House Committee reported out the bill. In setting out the need for the legislation, it explained in part:

> Certain feathers of the golden eagle are important in religious ceremonies of some Indian tribes and a large number of the birds are killed to obtain these feathers, as well as to provide souvenirs for tourists in the Indian country. In addition, they are actively hunted by bounty hunters in Texas and some other States. As a result of these activities if steps are not taken as contemplated in this legislation, there is grave danger that the golden eagle will completely disappear." H. R. Rep. No. 1450, 87th Cong., 2d Sess., 2 (1962).

The Committee also reprinted Assistant Secretary Briggs' letter in its Report, and adopted an exception for Indian religious use drafted by the Interior Department. The bill as reported out of the House Committee thus made three major changes in the law, along with other more technical ones. It extended the law's ban to golden eagles. It provided that the Secretary may exempt, by permit, takings of bald or golden eagles "for the religious purposes of Indian tribes." And it added a final proviso: "Provided, That bald eagles may not be taken for any purpose unless, prior to such taking, a permit to do so is procured from the Secretary of the Interior." *Id.*, at 7. The bill, as amended, passed the House and was reported to the Senate Committee on Commerce. At the Senate hearings, representatives of the Interior Department reiterated their position that, because "the golden eagle is an important part of the ceremonies and religion of many Indian tribes," the Secretary should be authorized to allow the use of eagles for religious purposes by Indian tribes. The Senate Committee agreed, and passed the House bill with an additional amendment allowing the Secretary to authorize permits for the taking of golden eagles that were preying on livestock. That Committee again reprinted Assistant Secretary Briggs' letter and summarized the bill as follows: "The resolution as hereby reported would bring the golden eagle under the 1940 act, allow their taking under permit for the religious use of the various Indian tribes (their feathers are an important part of Indian religious rituals) and upon request of a Governor of any State, be taken for the protection of livestock and game." The bill passed the Senate, and was concurred in by the House, with little further discussion.

It seems plain to us, upon reading the legislative history as a whole, that Congress in 1962 believed that it was abrogating the rights of Indians to take eagles. Indeed, the House Report cited the demand for eagle feathers for Indian religious ceremonies as one of the threats to the continued survival of the golden eagle that necessitated passage of the bill. Congress expressly chose to set in place a regime in which the Secretary of the Interior had control over Indian hunting, rather than one in which Indian on-reservation hunting was unrestricted. Congress thus considered the special cultural and religious interests of Indians, balanced those needs against the conservation purposes of the statute, and provided a specific, narrow exception that delineated the extent to which Indians would be permitted to hunt the bald and golden eagle.

Respondent argues that the 1962 Congress did not in fact view the Eagle Protection Act as restricting Indian on-reservation hunting. He points to an internal Interior Department memorandum circulated in 1962 stating, with little analysis, that the Eagle Protection Act did not apply within Indian reservations. Memorandum from Assistant Solicitor Vaughn, Branch of Fish and Wildlife, Office of the Solicitor to the Director, Bureau of Sport Fisheries and Wildlife, April 26, 1962. We have no reason to believe that Congress was aware of the contents of the Vaughn memorandum. More importantly, however, we find respondent's contention that the 1962 Congress did not understand the Act to ban all Indian hunting of eagles simply irreconcilable with the statute on its face.

Respondent argues, and the Eighth Circuit agreed, that the provision of the statute granting permit authority is not necessarily inconsistent with an intention that Indians would have unrestricted ability to hunt eagles while on reservations. Respondent construes that provision to allow the Secretary to issue permits to *non*-Indians to hunt eagles "for Indian religious purposes," and supports this interpretation by pointing out testimony during the hearings to the effect that large-scale eagle bounty hunters sometimes sold eagle feathers to Indian tribes. We do not find respondent's argument credible. Congress could have felt such a provision necessary only if it believed that Indians, if left free to hunt eagles on reservations, would nonetheless be unable to satisfy their own needs and would be forced to call on non-Indians to hunt on their behalf. Yet there is nothing in the legislative history that even remotely supports that patronizing and strained view. Indeed, the Interior Department immediately after the passage of the 1962 amendments adopted regulations authorizing permits *only* to "individual Indians who are authentic, bona fide practitioners of such religion." 28 Fed. Reg. 976 (1963).[8]

Congress' 1962 action, we conclude, reflected an unmistakable and explicit legislative policy choice that Indian hunting of the bald or golden eagle, except pursuant to permit, is inconsistent with the need to preserve those species. We therefore read the statute as having abrogated that treaty right.

B

Dion also asserts a treaty right to take bald eagles as a defense to his Endangered Species Act prosecution. He argues that the evidence that Congress intended to abrogate treaty rights when it passed the Endangered Species Act is considerably more slim than that relating to the Eagle Protection Act. The Endangered Species Act and its legislative history, he points out, are to a great extent silent regarding Indian hunting rights. In this case, however, we need not resolve the question of whether the Congress in the Endangered Species Act abrogated Indian treaty rights. We conclude that Dion's asserted treaty defense is barred in any event.

Dion asserts that he is immune from Endangered Species Act prosecution because he possesses a treaty right to hunt and kill bald eagles. We have held, however, that Congress in passing and amending the Eagle Protection Act divested Dion of his treaty right to hunt bald eagles. He therefore has no treaty right to hunt bald eagles that he can assert as a defense to an Endangered Species Act charge.

We do not hold that when Congress passed and amended the Eagle Protection Act, it stripped away Indian treaty protection for conduct not expressly prohibited by that statute. But the Eagle Protection Act and the Endangered Species Act, in relevant part, prohibit exactly the same conduct, and for the same reasons. Dion here asserts a treaty right to engage in precisely the conduct that Congress, overriding Indian treaty rights, made criminal in the Eagle Protection Act. Dion's treaty shield for that conduct, we hold, was removed by that statute, and Congress' failure to discuss that shield in the context of the Endangered Species Act did not revive that treaty right.

---

[8] Respondent's argument that Congress in amending the Eagle Protection Act meant to benefit nontreaty tribes is also flawed. Indian reservations created by statute, agreement, or executive order normally carry with them the same implicit hunting rights as those created by treaty. See Cohen 224; Antoine v. Washington, 420 U.S. 194 (1975).

It would not promote sensible law to hold that while Dion possesses no rights derived from the 1858 treaty that bar his prosecution under the Eagle Protection Act for killing bald eagles, he nonetheless possesses a right to hunt bald eagles, derived from that same treaty, that bars his Endangered Species Act prosecution for the same conduct. Even if Congress did not address Indian treaty rights in the Endangered Species Act sufficiently expressly to effect a valid abrogation, therefore, respondent can assert no treaty defense to a prosecution under that Act for a taking already explicitly prohibited under the Eagle Protection Act.

III

We hold that the Court of Appeals erred in recognizing Dion's treaty defense to his Eagle Protection Act and Endangered Species Act prosecutions. * * *

NOTE: INDIAN TREATY ABROGATION, CONGRESSIONAL INTENT, AND THE CLEAR STATEMENT RULE

As *Dion* shows, the search for standards to measure "clear and plain" congressional intent to abrogate Indian treaty rights has had a long and uneven history. One of the most famous cases on this issue is FPC v. Tuscarora Indian Nation, 362 U.S. 99 (1960).

Tuscarora: "clear expression to the contrary"

The eminent domain power in the Federal Power Act enables licensees of the Federal Power Commission to condemn lands needed for a project. The Court held the power to apply to Tuscarora lands. Because the Tuscaroras held fee lands, provisions in the Act, preventing condemnation where it would "interfere or be inconsistent with the purpose for which [an Indian] reservation was created or established," did not protect them. The Tuscarora majority found that the tribal fee land could be taken because "general Acts of Congress apply to Indians as well as to all others in the absence of a clear expression to the contrary." 362 U.S. at 120. In one of the most frequently quoted statements in all of Indian law, Justice Black began his dissent: "Great nations, like great men, should keep their word," id. at 142, and went on to launch a stinging critique of the reasoning in the case.

Seneca: "sufficiently clear and specific"

Another strongly worded dissent was provoked by the *Seneca Nation* cases. Here as well, a United States court found congressional intent to abrogate without also finding an explicit statement in the record that Congress knew it was extinguishing an Indian treaty right by its action. The *Seneca Nation* cases involved the oldest active Indian treaty with the United States. See Seneca Nation of Indians v. Brucker, 262 F.2d 27 (D.C.Cir.1958), cert. denied 360 U.S. 909 (1959) (*Seneca I*); Seneca Nation of Indians v. United States, 338 F.2d 55 (2d Cir.1964), cert. denied 380 U.S. 952 (1965) (*Seneca II*). The Treaty of Nov. 11, 1794, 7 Stat. 4, promised that the tribe would hold its land in perpetuity and that the United States would "never claim the same, nor disturb the Seneca Nation." Nonetheless, in *Seneca I*, the court refused to enjoin construction of the Allegheny Reservoir Project, while recognizing that the project would flood more than 10,000 acres of the land reserved by treaty, leaving fewer than 2,300 acres of the reservation habitable. More convenient and inexpensive sites were available, but the Army Corps' "incredible political power" beat back all movements for alternative sites. Arthur Ernest Morgan, Dams and Other Disasters, 310–67 (1971). See also Alvin M. Josephy, Jr., *Cornplanter Can You Swim?*, Am. Heritage, Dec. 1968, at 4, 106.

While there was evidence in the legislative record that Congress was aware that Seneca land would be flooded by the project, no evidence was cited demonstrating that Congress knew that the flooding would violate the treaty. Nonetheless the *Seneca I* court reasoned that Congress had, "in a sufficiently clear and specific way, shown an intention" to authorize the taking of Seneca land. To support its conclusions about what "Congress knew," the court cited a Senate Committee report. The full Committee report, as it dealt with the Senecas, provided this:

> The committee has approved the budget estimate of $1 million to initiate construction of this project. The Corps of Engineers has indicated a willingness to accept flowage easements over land owned by the Seneca Indians, in order that the reservation may be kept intact. The committee desires that the Corps of Engineers cooperate to the maximum extent practicable with the Seneca Indians, in order to minimize the effect of the Allegheny River Reservoir on the Indian lands. It is recognized that if the Seneca Indian Nation elects to grant easements for this purpose, they will control the reservoir area within the boundaries of their reservation, and that recreational benefits will inure to the Seneca Nation as a result of the development of this project. The committee recognizes that this procedure may not be entirely satisfactory to all the Seneca Indians, but also realizes that they have rights in the courts if they insist on determining the issues involved in the courts.

S.Rep. No. 609, 85th Cong., 1st Sess. 26 (1957).

In *Seneca II*, the tribe sought to block condemnation of a strip of its land through the remaining part of its reservation for a four lane highway to service the reservoir project. The *Seneca II* court relied on "delegated administrative discretion" rather than on explicit congressional intent to uphold the action.

> The replacement or relocation of existing highways unquestionably is a part of the reservoir project authorized by Congress. Act of June 28, 1938, 52 Stat. 1215. The land involved in this action is land necessary to extend the rerouted Route 17 from a two-lane to a four-lane limited access highway. The decision to make this extension was made by the Secretary of the Army and Congress delegated this authority to the Secretary. * * * Congress need not itself specifically and expressly authorize by "special enactment" each

particular taking of Indian land, but can choose to delegate some of its authority to administrative offices and agencies. We see no reason to interfere with this reasonable exercise of delegated administrative discretion as to the amount of land required for the relocation of the road.

388 F.2d at 56–57.

Judge Moore wrote a vigorous dissent in *Seneca II*, beginning his assault on the majority opinion with Justice Black's famous quotation that "Great Nations, like great men, should keep their word," and harshly criticizing the majority's lax standard for finding congressional intent to abrogate:

> Would it not be far more consistent with the Indian policy so frequently expressed by Congress and the Supreme Court to let Congress decide whether . . . to condemn land for a superhighway rather than to impute to Congress an intent to vest the Secretary of the Army with such powers?

Id. at 59

Menominee: "explicit statement"

Federal Indian law changed dramatically in tone and result following the *Seneca* cases. The Supreme Court set a high standard with its opinion in Menominee Tribe of Indians v. United States, 391 U.S. 404 (1968), page 238, supra. Justice Douglas, one of the dissenters in *Tuscarora*, now was able to write the majority opinion in this landmark case, posing the important issue of whether the Termination Act of 1954 abrogated the treaty hunting and fishing rights of the Menominee Indians, one of the major tribes terminated by the legislation. *Menominee* held that it did not:

> We decline to construe the Termination Act as a backhanded way of abrogating the hunting and fishing rights of these Indians. While the power to abrogate those rights exists (see *Lone Wolf v. Hitchcock*) "the intent to abrogate or modify a treaty is not to be lightly imputed to the Congress." (citations omitted.)

> * * *

> We find it difficult to believe that Congress, without explicit statement, would subject the United States to a claim for compensation by destroying property rights conferred by treaty, particularly when Congress was purporting by the Termination Act to settle the Government's financial obligations toward the Indians.

Id. at 412–13.

Menominee's explicit statement standard was adopted by a number of lower courts, producing highly favorable results for some tribes. United States v. Winnebago Tribe, 542 F.2d 1002 (8th Cir.1976), for example, applied the standard to stop efforts of the Army Corps of Engineer to acquire treaty lands of the Winnebago Indians by eminent domain for a recreation project. Hearings before Congress and a letter from the Chief of Engineers of the Corps evidenced an "awareness" that the acquisition of Indian lands would be necessary for the project, but the court found no indication of "the clear intent of Congress to abrogate the Treaty." The court, citing *Menominee*, refused to sanction "the taking of treaty lands without express congressional authorization."

This strict judicial approach to requiring express legislative action before finding an Indian treaty abrogation was also supported by Professor Charles Wilkinson and John Volkman in a widely cited law review article published in 1975:

> The relationship of Congress toward the American Indian is characterized by uniquely broad power and a fiduciary's duty. At issue is the level congressional dealings should attain to be consistent with that power and duty. Today, although most courts have come to recognize that many substantive rights cannot be guaranteed unless procedural amenities are provided, some decide questions of Indian treaty abrogation by tests not markedly different from those they use to repeal statutes by implication. Yet surely it is reasonable to treat Indian treaties, which define important substantive rights and are stamped with a trust relationship, by a stricter standard. Under the highly unusual circumstances in which treaty abrogation claims arise, applying the rule of express legislative action would ensure that these decisions are made in a manner consonant with "the most exacting fiduciary standards" to which the federal government must be held in its dealings with Indians. * * *

> * * *

> Importantly, the rule proposed here would not unduly hamper Congress. If the courts found that Congress had not appropriately provided for an abrogation it wished to accomplish, Congress could act quickly to rectify the matter:

>> If, as has been argued here, Congress has already impliedly authorized the taking, there can be no reason why it would not pass a measure at once confirming its authorization. It has been known to pass a Joint Resolution in one day where this Court interpreted an Act in a way it did not like * * *. Such action would simply put this question of authorization back into the hands of the Legislative Department of the Government where the Constitution wisely reposed it.

> Thus the proposed rule does not conflict with the established power of Congress to abrogate Indian treaties. On the contrary, the rule deals only with the procedures that must be followed in the proper exercise of congressional power.

> Moreover, and this point cannot be overemphasized, this test would be fully consistent with the Nation's recognized obligations to Indian tribes. The Court has consistently characterized the

relationship between Congress and the American Indian as "solemn," "unique" or "special," and "moral." The case that established the right of Congress to abrogate treaties, *Lone Wolf v. Hitchcock*, cautioned that abrogations should be made only "if consistent with perfect good faith towards the Indians." Other cases have stated that Indian treaties represent "the word of the Nation" and "should be so construed as to uphold the sanctity of the public faith." Similarly, Presidents from Washington to Nixon have characterized the Nation's commitments to Indians in moral terms.

Morality and good faith are not notions which can be dispensed with lightly, for they have played a major part in the development of our jurisprudence. No judge should be reluctant to consider such factors in analyzing the duty the federal government owes American Indians. Indeed, there is perhaps no area of public law in which such considerations should play a larger part. The rule of express legislative action suggested here is consistent with these principles. Although abrogation would be permitted in furtherance of the national interest, no abrogation would occur without full notice and disclosure to the affected tribes.

Charles F. Wilkinson and John M. Volkman, *Judicial Review of Indian Treaty Abrogation: "As Long as Water Flows or Grass Grows Upon the Earth"—How Long a Time Is That?*, 63 Calif.L.Rev. 601, 655–56, 658–59 (1975).

Until the *Dion* decision in 1986, the Supreme Court itself generally followed a consistent approach in its post-*Menominee* opinions, usually requiring a clear and specific statement by Congress—in a statute or in reliable legislative history—before finding an intention to extinguish treaty rights. This is evidenced, among many other examples, by County of Oneida v. Oneida Indian Nation, 470 U.S. 226, 247–48 (1985) (page 106, supra): "[T]he Court has held that congressional intent to extinguish Indian title must be 'plain and unambiguous * * * Absent explicit statutory language,' this Court accordingly has refused to find that Congress has abrogated Indian rights." See generally Felix S. Cohen, *Handbook of Federal Indian Law* § 2.02 (2012 ed.). Further, while the Court stopped short of announcing a rule of express abrogation, it often commented on the absence of an explicit statement by Congress in the many cases upholding Indian rights against asserted treaty abrogations. See Washington v. Commercial Passenger Fishing Vessel Ass'n, 443 U.S. 658 (1979), page 925, infra. To be sure, opinions sometimes eschewed any such requirement. See, e.g., DeCoteau v. District County Court, 420 U.S. 425, 444 (1975), page 512, infra (intent of Congress to extinguish Indian country may be found "on the face of the act *or be clear from the surrounding circumstances and legislative history*."). In some instances, such as Montana v. United States, 450 U.S. 544 (1981), page 290, supra, the states benefited from opposing principles of construction that, like the Indian rules, are bottomed in a trust duty. Nevertheless, the existence of an express statutory statement, if not a requisite, had been the usual benchmark for analysis, at least until *Dion*, which held that Congress's intent to abrogate a treaty can be demonstrated by "clear evidence" that Congress: (1) considered the impact of its actions on the Indian treaty right; and, (2) consciously chose to resolve any conflicts with the statute by abrogating the treaty.

Post-Dion: "clear evidence"

The Supreme Court's next major opinion after *Dion* on Indian treaty abrogation was South Dakota v. Bourland, 508 U.S. 679 (1993). *Bourland* involved the Cheyenne River Sioux Tribe's attempts to regulate hunting and fishing by non-Indians on lands and overlying waters located within the tribe's reservation in South Dakota but acquired by the United States for the operation of the Oahe Dam and Reservoir. The Fort Laramie Treaty of 1868 promised that the tribe's reservation was to be held by the United States for its "absolute and undisturbed use and occupation," and that no non-Indians (except authorized government agents) would "ever be permitted to pass over, settle upon, or reside in" the Indian lands.

In 1944, Congress passed the Flood Control Act, which authorized the construction of the Oahe Dam and Reservoir Project, and the taking of tribal trust lands belonging to the Cheyenne River Sioux Tribe. Then in 1954, Congress passed the Cheyenne River Act, by which the United States formally acquired 104,420 acres of tribal land, but certain rights were reserved to the tribe, including "without cost, the right of free access to the shoreline of the reservoir including the right to hunt and fish in and on the aforesaid shoreline and reservoir, subject however to regulations governing the corresponding use by other citizens of the United States." The tribe asserted that this language reserved to it the right to regulate hunting and fishing in the taken area, including by non-Indians who came into that part of the reservation.

The Supreme Court, in a majority opinion written by Justice Thomas, invoked its decision in *Dion* to conclude that Congress had abrogated the tribe's original treaty right to regulate non-Indian hunting and fishing on lands taken for the federal water project.

> [T]he clear effect of the Flood Control Act is to open the lands taken for the Oahe Dam and Reservoir project for the general recreational use of the public. Because hunting and fishing are "recreational purposes," the Flood Control Act affirmatively allows non-Indians to hunt and fish on such lands, subject to federal regulation. The Act also clearly prohibits any "use" of the lands "which is inconsistent with the laws for the protection of fish and game of the State in which such area is situated" or which is determined by the Secretary of the Army to be "contrary to the public interest."
>
> If the Flood Control Act leaves any doubt whether the Tribe retains its original treaty right to regulate non-Indian hunting and fishing on lands taken for federal water projects, the Cheyenne River Act extinguishes all such doubt. Section 2 of that Act declares that the sum paid by the Government to the Tribe for former trust lands taken for the Oahe Dam and Reservoir Project, "shall be in final and

complete settlement of all claims, rights, and demands" of the Tribe or its allottees. This provision reliably indicates that the Government and the Tribe understood the Act to embody the full terms of their Agreement, including the various rights that the Tribe and its members would continue to enjoy after conveying the 104,420 acres to the Government. The Tribe's § IX* "right of *free access* to the shoreline of the reservoir includ[es] *the right to hunt and fish*" but is "*subject . . . to regulations governing the corresponding use by other citizens of the United States.*" If Congress had intended by this provision to grant the Tribe the additional right to regulate hunting and fishing, it would have done so by a similarly explicit statutory command. The rights granted the Tribe in § IX stand in contrast to the expansive treaty right originally granted to the Tribe of "absolute and undisturbed use," which *does* encompass the right to exclude and to regulate.

* * *

Our decision in [*Dion*] supports this conclusion. In *Dion*, we considered whether an Indian who takes an eagle on tribal land violates the Bald Eagle Protection Act. We demanded "clear evidence that Congress actually considered the conflict between its intended action on the one hand and Indian treaty rights on the other, and chose to resolve that conflict by abrogating the treaty." The Bald Eagle Protection Act contains an exemption allowing the Secretary of the Interior to permit the taking of an eagle "for the religious purposes of Indian tribes" and for other narrow purposes found to be compatible with the goal of eagle preservation. We found this exemption "difficult to explain except as a reflection of an understanding that the statute otherwise bans the taking of eagles by Indians." Likewise, we cannot explain § X of the Cheyenne River Act and § 4 of the Flood Control Act except as indications that Congress sought to divest the Tribe of its right to "absolute and undisturbed use and occupation" of the taken area. When Congress reserves limited rights to a tribe or its members, the very presence of such a limited reservation of rights suggests that the Indians would otherwise be treated like the public at large.

508 U.S. at 689–90, 693–94.

In the tradition of Justice Black in *Tuscarora*, Justice Blackmun, joined by Justice Souter, vigorously dissented from the majority's application of the *Dion* standard:

The land at issue in this case is part of the Cheyenne River Sioux Reservation. The United States did not take this land with the purpose of destroying tribal government or even with the purpose of limiting tribal authority. It simply wished to build a dam. The Tribe's

---

*   [Ed.] The correct section is X.

authority to regulate hunting and fishing on the taken area is consistent with the uses to which Congress has put the land, and, in my view, that authority must be understood to continue until Congress clearly decides to end it.

* * *

The majority, however, points not even to a scrap of evidence that Congress actually considered the possibility that by taking the land in question it would deprive the Tribe of its authority to regulate non-Indian hunting and fishing on that land. Instead, it finds Congress' intent *implicit* in the fact that Congress deprived the Tribe of its right to exclusive use of the land, that Congress gave the Army Corps of Engineers authority to regulate public access to the land, and that Congress failed explicitly to reserve to the Tribe the right to regulate non-Indian hunting and fishing. Despite its citation of [*Dion* and other authority], the majority adopts precisely the sort of reasoning-by-implication that those cases reject. . . .

* * *

In its search for a statement from Congress abrogating the Tribe's right to regulate non-Indian hunting and fishing in the taken area, the majority turns to a provision in the Cheyenne River Act that the compensation paid for the taken area "shall be in final and complete settlement of all claims, rights, and demands of said tribe." Quoting Pub. L. 776, § II, 68 Stat. 1191. But this provision simply makes clear that Congress intended no further compensation for the rights it took from the Tribe. It does not address the question of *which* rights Congress intended to take or, more specifically, whether Congress intended to take the Tribe's right to regulate hunting and fishing by non-Indians. The majority also relies on the fact that § X of the Act expressly reserved to the Tribe the right to hunt and fish but not the right to regulate hunting and fishing. To imply an intent to abrogate Indian rights from such congressional silence once again ignores the principles that "Congress' intention to abrogate Indian treaty rights be clear and plain." *Dion*, and that "statutes are to be construed liberally in favor of the Indians, with ambiguous provisions interpreted to their benefit." *County of Yakima*, [quoting *Montana*]. Congress' failure to address the subject of the Tribe's regulatory authority over hunting and fishing means that the Tribe's authority survives and not the reverse.

Id. at 698, 700–01, 703. The dueling majority and dissenting opinions in *Bourland* suggest that *Dion*'s "clear evidence" standard failed to maintain the apparent clarity of *Menominee*'s "explicit statement" rule.

In Minnesota v. Mille Lacs Band of Chippewa Indians, 526 U.S. 172 (1999), page 942, infra, the state argued that the tribe had relinquished its

1837 Treaty rights to hunt, fish and gather in its 1855 treaty. But according to the Court:

> [T]he 1855 Treat] is devoid of any language expressly mentioning—much less abrogating—usufructuary rights. Similarly, the [1855] Treaty contains no language providing money for the abrogation of previously held rights. These omissions are telling because the United States treaty drafters had the sophistication and experience to use express language for the abrogation of treaty rights.

Id. at 195. The state also argued that the tribe's 1837 Treaty rights "were extinguished when Minnesota was admitted to the Union in 1858." Id. at 202. Using *Dion*'s "clear evidence" test, the Court wrote:

> There is no such "clear evidence" of congressional intent to abrogate the Chippewa Treaty rights here. The relevant statute [Minnesota Enabling Act] * * * makes no mention of Indian treaty rights; it provides no clue that Congress considered the reserved rights of the Chippewa and decided to abrogate those rights when it passed the Act. The State concedes that the Act is silent in this regard * * * and the State does not point to any legislative history describing the effect of the Act on Indian treaty rights.

Id. at 203.

Non-treaty rights cases; Canons of construction

Consider those cases, unlike *Dion*, where treaty rights are not directly involved. The practice of using treaty construction rules in non-treaty situations has been followed with respect to determining whether other important Indian rights have been extinguished. The courts generally have required express action by Congress, or something close to it. Montana v. Blackfeet Indian Tribe, 471 U.S. 759 (1985), page 678, infra ("[T]he Court consistently has held that it will find the Indians' exemption from state taxes lifted only when Congress has made its intention to do so unmistakably clear."); Bryan v. Itasca County, 426 U.S. 373 (1976), page 565, infra (Public Law 280, applying state "civil law of general application" to Indian country, does not extend state regulatory laws, including tax statutes, because Congress "would have expressly said so" if extension of regulatory laws were contemplated by the statute); and Santa Clara Pueblo v. Martinez, 436 U.S. 49 (1978), page 434, infra (Indian Civil Rights Act of 1968, imposing certain Bill of Rights limitations on tribal governments, construed not to permit judicial review for declaratory and injunctive relief because only habeas corpus is "provided for expressly in [25 U.S.C.A.] § 1303.")

The Indian law rules of construction applicable to such cases are not complex; they vary according to the setting, but all are derivations of (1) very liberal construction to determine whether Indian rights exist, and (2) very strict construction to determine whether Indian rights are to be abridged or abrogated. As with principles of statutory construction generally, no pat formulations will solve the tough cases. The specific statutory language and the factual setting often have heavy bearing, but rules of construction plainly fashion results in Indian litigation to a far greater extent than in most other areas of law.

A primary reason for the toughness of the rules is the development of over 180 years of law, explored in the following section, dealing with the trust relationship. Ultimately, it is that relationship, not the designation of a document as a treaty, that is the policy foundation upon which the rules are premised.

Federal statutes of general applicability

More difficult cases arise when a federal "statute of general applicability" conflicts with Indian rights. One such statute is the Freedom of Information Act (FOIA), which requires broad public disclosure of government documents in the public interest. In Department of the Interior and Bureau of Indian Affairs v. Klamath Water Users Protective Association, 532 U.S. 1 (2001), the United States Supreme Court held that the FOIA applies to communications between a tribal government and federal agencies, even when those documents were submitted by the tribe at the request of the Department of Interior in the course of administrative and adjudicative proceedings in which the tribe had a direct interest.

The Court's unanimous decision, written by Justice Souter, flatly rejected the Government's request to read an "Indian trust" exemption into the statute. "There is simply no support for the exemption in the statutory text, which we have elsewhere insisted be read strictly in order to serve FOIA's mandate of broad disclosure." Id. at 16.

Lower courts have at times had difficulty in determining whether other federal statutes include an implied "Indian exemption." Courts have said that the principle announced in *Tuscarora* that "a general statute in terms applying to all persons includes Indians and their property interests" is subject to certain exceptions:

> A federal statute of general applicability that is silent on the issue of applicability to Indian tribes will not apply to them if: (1) the law touches "exclusive rights of self-governance in purely intramural matters"; (2) the application of the law to the tribe would "abrogate rights guaranteed by Indian treaties"; or (3) there is proof "by legislative history or some other means that Congress intended [the law] not to apply to Indians on their reservations. . . ."

Donovan v. Coeur d'Alene Tribal Farm, 751 F.2d 1113, 1116 (9th Cir.1985). The announced exceptions, have opened the door to case-by-case examinations of the circumstances of particular tribes and tribal businesses in determining whether a federal statute applies.

There is a conflict in the circuits concerning applicability of the Occupational Safety and Health Act (OSHA) to tribal businesses. In Donovan v. Navajo Forest Products Industries, 692 F.2d 709 (10th Cir.1982), the Tenth Circuit found that OSHA could not be applied to the Navajo in derogation of the exclusivity guaranteed in the Navajo Treaty. However, the Ninth Circuit reached an opposite result in the above quoted *Coeur d'Alene* case, distinguishing *Navajo Forest Products Industries* because the Coeur d'Alene Tribe had no treaty and the other exceptions were not applicable. Then in U.S. Department of Labor v. Occupational Safety & Health Review Comm'n, 935 F.2d 182 (9th Cir.1991), the same court held that OSHA also applied to the tribal sawmill on the Warm Springs Reservation in spite of the existence of a treaty with a right of "exclusive use." The court said that such a "generalized right of exclusion" may exist independent of a treaty and is insufficient to bar application of OSHA. In Reich v. Mashantucket Sand & Gravel, 95 F.3d 174 (2nd Cir.1996), the Second Circuit held that OSHA applied to the tribe's construction company because (1) it engaged in activities that were "commercial and service" in nature and not governmental; (2) it employed non-Indians; and (3) its work on expanding the Foxwoods Casino had a direct affect on interstate commerce.

Disagreements among courts are expecially apparent in labor and employment cases. The Seventh Circuit found that wildlife officers employed by a tribe performed "governmental" functions and therefore the Fair Labor Standards Act did not apply to the tribe. Reich v. Great Lakes Indian Fish and Wildlife Comm'n, 4 F.3d 490 (7th Cir.1993). But the Ninth Circuit held that none of the exceptions contained in *Donovan v. Coeur d'Alene Tribal Farm* prevented application of the federal Employment Retirement Income Security Act (ERISA) to the Warm Springs tribal sawmill. The tribe therefore was required to contribute to the Lumber Industry Pension Fund on behalf of employees even though the tribe had its own pension plan. Lumber Industry Pension Fund v. Warm Springs Forest Products Industries, 939 F.2d 683 (9th Cir.1991) Cf. Smart v. State Farm Insurance Co., 868 F.2d 929 (7th Cir.1989) (denial of ERISA benefits to tribal member has no effect on tribal self-governance.)

The Eleventh Circuit found in Florida Paraplegic Association, Inc. v. Miccosukee Tribe, 166 F.3d 1126 (11th Cir.1999), that the Americans with Disabilities Act (ADA) applied to a restaurant and entertainment facility owned and operated by the Miccosukee Tribe. The court went on to hold, however, that Congress did not unequivocally express its intent to abrogate tribal sovereign immunity from private suits under the Act. Thus, the plaintiffs could not pursue their ADA claims against the tribe, absent a waiver of sovereign immunity. The court went out of its way to note that the Act does authorize the Attorney General of the United States to bring actions under the ADA against tribes. In Equal Opp'ty Comm'n v. Fond du Lac Heavy Equipment, 986 F.2d 246 (8th Cir.1993), the court refused to apply the "general applicability" rule to the Age Discrimination in Employment Act (ADEA) because "the tribe's specific right of self-government would be affected." Id. at 249. The tribe was the employer and the complainant was an Indian applicant.

In 2004, the National Labor Relations Board, overruling 30 years of its own precedent, ruled that "Indian owned and operated enterprises" are subject to federal labor law and the board's jurisdiction. For the board, the tipping point was when tribes became significant employers of non-Indians and their businesses compete with non-Indian businesses. Under these circumstances the National Labor Relations Act, which does not mention tribes, becomes applicable to them. On appeal by the tribe the D.C. Circuit affirmed the decision of the National Labor Relations Board. San Manuel Indian Bingo and Casino v. NLRB, 475 F.3d 1306 (D.C.Cir.2007).

> [W]e need not choose between *Tuscarora*'s statement that laws of general applicability apply also to Indian tribes and *Santa Clara Pueblo*'s statement that courts may not construe laws in a way that impinges upon tribal sovereignty absent a clear indication of Congressional intent. Even applying the more restrictive rule of *Santa Clara Pueblo*, the NLRA does not impinge on the Tribe's sovereignty enough to indicate a need to construe the statute narrowly against application to employment at the Casino. First, operation of a casino is not a traditional attribute of self-government. Rather, the casino at issue here is virtually identical to scores of purely commercial casinos across the country. Second, the vast majority of the Casino's employees and customers are not members of the Tribe, and they live off the reservation. For these reasons, the Tribe is not simply engaged in internal governance of its territory and members, and its sovereignty over such matters is not called into question. Because applying the NLRA to San Manuel's Casino would not impair tribal sovereignty, federal Indian law does not prevent the Board from exercising jurisdiction.

475 F.3d at 1315.

SECTION C. THE FEDERAL-TRIBAL RELATIONSHIP AS A SOURCE OF INDIAN RIGHTS

1. EXECUTIVE ACCOUNTABILITY UNDER THE TRUST RELATIONSHIP

SEMINOLE NATION V. UNITED STATES

Supreme Court of the United States, 1942.
316 U.S. 286, 62 S.Ct. 1049, 86 L.Ed. 1480.

MR. JUSTICE MURPHY delivered the opinion of the Court.

[Under an 1856 treaty, the federal government promised to establish a $500,000 trust fund, the annual interest ($25,000) to be paid to the members of the Seminole Nation per capita as an annuity. The tribe sued in the Court of Claims for alleged violations of the treaty, including the manner in which the payments were made. One question before the Supreme Court on certiorari to the Court of Claims was whether amounts paid from 1870 through 1874 directly to the tribal treasurer ($37,500) and to creditors ($28,922.64), at the request of the Seminole General Council (the tribal council), satisfied the treaty requirement that the annuity be disbursed directly to the individual tribal members.]

* * *

The Government contends that, since those payments were made at the request of the tribal council, the governing body of a semi-autonomous political entity, possessing the power to enter into treaties and agreements with the United States, the tribe is not now entitled to receive payment a second time; and that, despite the fact that the Treaty of 1856 provided that the payments were to be made per capita for the benefit of each individual Indian, these payments at the request of the General Council discharged the treaty obligation, because the agreement was one between the United States and the Seminole Nation and not one between the United States and the individual members of the tribe.

The argument for the Government, however sound it might otherwise be, fails to recognize the impact of certain equitable considerations and the effect of the fiduciary duty of the Government to its Indian wards. The jurisdictional act, 43 Stat. 133, expressly confers jurisdiction on the Court of Claims to adjudicate "all legal and equitable claims," arising under treaty or statute, which the Seminole Nation may have against the United States, and the second amended petition avers:

"That since the passage of said Act of April 15, 1874, it was reported by the officers of defendant [the United States] that the Seminole tribal officials were misappropriating the Seminole tribal funds entrusted to them, and robbing the members of the tribe of an equal share of the tribal income. That the reports of the Dawes Commission show conclusively that the governments of the Five Civilized Tribes were notoriously and incurably corrupt, that every branch of the service was infested with favoritism, graft and crookedness, and that by such methods the tribal officers acquired large fortunes, while the other members entitled to share in the tribal income received little benefit therefrom."

It is a well established principle of equity that a third party who pays money to a fiduciary for the benefit of the beneficiary, with knowledge that the fiduciary intends to misappropriate the money or otherwise be false to his trust, is a participant in the breach of trust and liable therefor to the beneficiary. See Bogert, Trusts and Trustees (1935), vol. 4, §§ 901, 955; Scott, Trusts (1939), vol. 3, § 321.1; American Law Institute, Restatement of the Law of Trusts (1935), § 321. The Seminole General Council, requesting the annuities originally intended for the benefit of the individual members of the tribe, stood in a fiduciary capacity to them. Consequently, the payments at the request of the Council did not discharge the treaty obligation if the Government, for this purpose the officials administering Indian affairs and disbursing Indian moneys, actually knew that the Council was defrauding the members of the Seminole Nation.

Furthermore, this Court has recognized the distinctive obligation of trust incumbent upon the Government in its dealings with these dependent and sometimes exploited people. In carrying out its treaty obligations with the Indian tribes, the Government is something more than a mere contracting party. Under a humane and self imposed policy which has found expression in many acts of Congress and numerous decisions of this Court, it has charged itself with moral obligations of the highest responsibility and trust. Its conduct, as disclosed in the acts of those who represent it in dealings with the Indians, should therefore be judged by the most exacting fiduciary standards. Payment of funds at the request of a tribal council which, to the knowledge of the Government officers charged with the administration of Indian affairs and the disbursement of funds to satisfy treaty obligations, was composed of representatives faithless to their own people and without integrity would be a clear breach of the Government's fiduciary obligation.[12] If those were the circumstances, either historically notorious so as to be judicially noticed or otherwise open to proof, when the $66,422.64 was paid over at the request of the Seminole General Council during the period from 1870 to 1874, the Seminole Nation is entitled to recover that sum, minus such amounts as were actually expended for the benefit of the Nation by the Council. * * *

* * *

Accordingly, this phase of the case must be remanded [to] the Court of Claims

* * *

NOTES

1.   The *Seminole Nation* decision has been cited in numerous cases as authority for the application of fiduciary principles to the government in the administration of Indian affairs. Such cases usually concern the manner in which the United States has managed Indian property. Some hold, as does *Seminole Nation*, that the federal trust duty extends to protection of Indians from their own improvidence. Thus, in Menominee Tribe v. United States, 101 Ct.Cl. 22 (1944), a tribe recovered for the negligent management of tribal timber resources, even though part of the management had been delegated to the tribal business committee, and some members of the tribe profited in the process. Allowing some individuals to profit from the tribe's property was itself

---

[12] As was well said by Chief Judge (later Mr. Justice) Cardozo in Meinhard v. Salmon, 249 N.Y. 458, 464, 164 N.E. 545, 546:

"Many forms of conduct permissible in a workaday world for those acting at arm's length, are forbidden to those bound by fiduciary ties. A trustee is held to something stricter than the morals of the market place. Not honesty alone, but the punctilio of an honor the most sensitive, is then the standard of behavior. As to this there has developed a tradition that is unbending and inveterate. Uncompromising rigidity has been the attitude of courts of equity when petitioned to undermine the rule of undivided loyalty by the 'disintegrating erosion' of particular exceptions. * * * Only thus has the level of conduct for fiduciaries been kept at a level higher than that trodden by the crowd."

mismanagement. To what extent can or should federal officials deny or withhold control of tribal assets from tribal members and governments on the ground that they may mismanage, and thereby expose the government to liability?

2.   In Morton v. Ruiz, 415 U.S. 199 (1974), members of the Tohono O'odham Tribe challenged the BIA's decision to limit general assistance benefits under the Snyder Act, 25 U.S.C. § 13, to Indians living on reservations. Mr. Ruiz had moved his family off the reservation in order to live closer to his job at a copper mine. When the mine workers went on strike he applied for welfare. The state denied him benefits under a policy of not paying welfare to strikers. The BIA denied him assistance, too, because of an eligibility requirement in the BIA Manual that limited benefits to Indians living on reservations. In fact, however, benefits regularly had been extended to Indians living "on or near" reservations and during the annual appropriations process the agency had represented to Congress that funds would be expended for the benefit of the wider class of beneficiaries.

The Supreme Court noted that the same BIA Manual stating the limitation of benefits to Indians living on reservations contained a requirement that eligibility requirements be published. However, no formal regulations were ever published under the Administrative Procedure Act (APA) to publicize the limitation and the manual itself was not "published" according to the APA. The Court found this procedural deficiency to be fatal.

The denial of benefits to these respondents under such circumstances is inconsistent with "the distinctive obligation of trust incumbent upon the Government in its dealings with these dependent and sometimes exploited people." Seminole Nation v. United States, 316 U.S., at 296. Before benefits may be denied to these otherwise entitled Indians, the BIA must first promulgate eligibility requirements according to established procedures.

> The same reasoning—that the BIA's internal policy requiring notice to beneficiaries must be followed before the agency denies benefits even if the APA would not require it—was followed in Yankton Sioux Tribe v. Kempthorne, 442 F.Supp.2d 774 (D.S.D.2006) (closure of reservation schools enjoined until BIA could consult with tribe as required by BIA policy). The court invoked the "canons of construction applicable in Indian law [that] are based on the unique trust relationship between the United States and Indian Tribes."

In Lincoln v. Vigil, 508 U.S. 182 (1993), the Court ruled that the Indian Health Service (IHS) need not engage in "notice and comment rulemaking" under § 553 of the APA before discontinuing clinical mental health services to handicapped Indian children because the result in *Ruiz* was driven by an internal BIA procedure in the Indian Affairs Manual subjecting the agency to rulemaking procedures even when the APA did not require it. Since IHS had no such rule, the Court looked to the basic notice and comment rulemaking requirements of the APA which do not apply to "general statements of policy" which it said includes "an announcement like the one before us, that the agency will discontinue a discretionary allocation of unrestricted funds from a lump-sum appropriation." The Court later held that tribes that take over administering health services may enforce a specific contractual provision allowing them "contract support costs" even where the lump-sum appropriations for the program are inadequate. See Cherokee Nation of Oklahoma v. Leavitt, 543 U.S. 631 (2005). The decision represents a major victory for tribes that have taken on provision of government services. The two tribes that brought the case had several million dollars at stake. The Court rejected the government's curious argument that tribes' took their chances that the federal government would not keep its contractual promise because of the "unique government-to-government nature" of the contract.

3.   The trust relationship was given further definition in two cases dealing with the government's liability for its management of Indian natural resources, United States v. Mitchell, 445 U.S. 535 (1980) (*Mitchell I*) and United States v. Mitchell, 463 U.S. 206 (1983) (*Mitchell II*). The two cases involved a claim for money damages by members of the Quinault Tribe for federal mismanagement of the timber on their allotments. In *Mitchell I*, the Court held that the allottees had not established liability under the General Allotment Act, because it contemplated that "the allottee, and not the United States, was to manage the land." The Act "created only a limited trust relationship between the United States and the allottee that does not impose any duty upon the Government to manage timber resources." 445 U.S. at 542–43.

In *Mitchell I*, the Court remanded the case to determine whether liability could be based on statutes other than the General Allotment Act. The Claims Court found an enforceable duty in the Indian timber management statutes, 25 U.S.C.A. § 406–07, 466, and in *Mitchell II* the Supreme Court agreed:

> * * * In contrast to the bare trust created by the General Allotment Act, the statutes and regulations now before us clearly give the Federal Government full responsibility to manage Indian resources and land for the benefit of the Indians. They thereby establish a fiduciary relationship and define the contours of the United States' fiduciary responsibilities.

* * *

> Moreover, a fiduciary relationship necessarily arises when the Government assumes such elaborate control over forests and property belonging to Indians. All of the necessary elements of a common-law trust are present: a trustee (the United States), a beneficiary (the Indian allottees), and a trust corpus (Indian timber, lands, and funds).[30] "[W]here the Federal Government takes on or has control or supervision over tribal monies or properties, the fiduciary relationship normally exists with respect to such monies or properties (unless Congress has provided otherwise) even though

---

[30] See Restatement (Second) of the Law of Trusts § 2, Comment *h*, at 10 (1959).

nothing is said expressly in the authorizing or underlying statute (or other fundamental document) about a trust fund, or a trust or fiduciary connection." Navajo Tribe of Indians v. United States, 224 Ct.Cl. 171, 183, 624 F.2d 981, 987 (1980).

Our construction of these statutes and regulations is reinforced by the undisputed existence of a general trust relationship between the United States and the Indian people. This Court has previously emphasized "the distinctive obligation of trust incumbent upon the Government in its dealings with these dependent and sometimes exploited people." Seminole Nation v. United States, 316 U.S. 286, 296 (1942). This principle has long dominated the Government's dealings with Indians. [citing authority]

Because the statutes and regulations at issue in this case clearly establish fiduciary obligations of the Government in the management and operation of Indian lands and resources, they can fairly be interpreted as mandating compensation by the Federal Government for damages sustained. Given the existence of a trust relationship, it naturally follows that the Government should be liable in damages for the breach of its fiduciary duties. It is well established that a trustee is accountable in damages for breaches of trust. See Restatement (Second) of the Law of Trusts §§ 205–212 (1959); G. Bogert, The Law of Trusts & Trustees § 862 (2d ed. 1965); 3 A. Scott, The Law of Trusts § 205 (3d ed. 1967). This Court and several other federal courts have consistently recognized that the existence of a trust relationship between the United States and an Indian or Indian tribe includes as a fundamental incident the right of an injured beneficiary to sue the trustee for damages resulting from a breach of the trust. * * *

463 U.S. at 224–26.

After a hiatus of nearly two decades, the Court returned to the questions raised by *Mitchell I* and *II* of whether a particular federal statute involving Indian trust property gives rise to a cause of action for an alleged breach of trust by the Secretary of Interior.

UNITED STATES v. NAVAJO NATION

Supreme Court of the United States, 2003.
537 U.S. 488, 123 S.Ct. 1079, 155 L.Ed.2d 60.

JUSTICE GINSBURG delivered the opinion of the Court.

This case concerns the Indian Mineral Leasing Act of 1938 (IMLA), and the role it assigns to the Secretary of the Interior (Secretary) with respect to coal leases executed by an Indian Tribe and a private lessee. The controversy centers on 1987 amendments to a 1964 coal lease entered into by the predecessor of Peabody Coal Company (Peabody) and the Navajo Nation (Tribe), a federally recognized Indian Tribe. The Tribe seeks to recover money damages from the United States for an alleged breach of trust in connection with the Secretary's approval of coal lease amendments negotiated by the Tribe and Peabody. This Court's decisions in United States v. Mitchell, 445 U. S. 535 (1980) *(Mitchell I)*, and *United States v. Mitchell*, 463 U. S. 206 (1983) *(Mitchell II)*, control this case. Concluding that the controversy here falls within *Mitchell I*'s domain, we hold that the Tribe's claim for compensation from the Federal Government fails, for it does not derive from any liability-imposing provision of the IMLA or its implementing regulations.

I

A

The IMLA, which governs aspects of mineral leasing on Indian tribal lands, states that "unallotted lands within any Indian reservation," or otherwise under federal jurisdiction, "may, with the approval of the Secretary . . . , be leased for mining purposes, by authority of the tribal council or other authorized spokesmen for such Indians, for terms not to exceed ten years and as long thereafter as minerals are produced in paying quantities." § 396a.

* * *

Peabody mines coal on the Tribe's lands pursuant to leases covered by the IMLA. This case principally concerns Lease 8580 (Lease or Lease 8580), which took effect upon approval by the Secretary in 1964. The Lease established a maximum royalty rate of 37.5 cents per ton of coal, but made that figure "subject to reasonable adjustment by the Secretary of the Interior or his authorized representative" on the 20-year anniversary of the Lease and every ten years thereafter.

As the 20-year anniversary of Lease 8580 approached, its royalty rate of 37.5 cents per ton yielded for the Tribe only "about 2% of gross proceeds." This return was higher than the ten cents per ton minimum established by the then-applicable IMLA regulations. It was substantially lower, however, than the 12 1/2 percent of gross proceeds rate Congress established in 1977 as the minimum permissible royalty for coal mined on federal lands under the Mineral Leasing Act. For some years starting in the 1970's, to gain a more favorable return, the Tribe endeavored to renegotiate existing mineral leases with private lessees, including Peabody.

In March 1984, the Chairman of the Navajo Tribal Council wrote to the Secretary asking him to exercise his contractually conferred authority to adjust the royalty rate under Lease 8580. On June 18, 1984, the Director of the Bureau of Indian Affairs for the Navajo Area, acting pursuant to authority delegated by the Secretary, sent Peabody an opinion letter raising the rate to 20 percent of gross proceeds.

Contesting the Area Director's rate determination, Peabody filed an administrative appeal in July 1984, pursuant to 25 CFR § 2.3(a) (1985). The appeal was referred to the Deputy Assistant Secretary for Indian Affairs, John Fritz, then acting as both Commissioner of Indian Affairs and Assistant Secretary of Indian Affairs. In March 1985, Fritz permitted Peabody to supplement its brief and requested additional cost, revenue, and investment data. He thereafter appeared ready to reject Peabody's appeal (undated draft letter). By June 1985, both Peabody and the Tribe anticipated that an announcement favorable to the Tribe was imminent.

On July 5, 1985, a Peabody Vice President wrote to Interior Secretary Donald Hodel, asking him either to postpone decision on Peabody's appeal so the parties could seek a negotiated settlement, or to rule in Peabody's favor. A copy of Peabody's letter was sent to the Tribe, which then submitted its own letter urging the Secretary to reject Peabody's request and to secure the Department's prompt release of a decision in the Tribe's favor. Peabody representatives met privately with Secretary Hodel in July 1985, no representative of the Tribe was present at, or received notice of, that meeting.

On July 17, 1985, Secretary Hodel sent a memorandum to Deputy Assistant Secretary Fritz. The memorandum "suggest[ed]" that Fritz "inform the involved parties that a decision on th[e] appeal is not imminent and urge them to continue with efforts to resolve this matter in a mutually agreeable fashion." "Any royalty adjustment which is imposed on those parties without their concurrence," the memorandum stated, "will almost certainly be the subject of protracted and costly appeals," and "could well impair the future of the contractual relationship" between the parties. Secretary Hodel added, however, that the memorandum was "not intended as a determination of the merits of the arguments of the parties with respect to the issues which are subject to the appeal."

The Tribe was not told of the Secretary's memorandum to Fritz, but learned that " 'someone from Washington' had urged a return to the bargaining table." 46 Fed. Cl., at 223. Facing "severe economic pressure," 263 F. 3d, at 1328; the Tribe resumed negotiations with Peabody in August 1985.

On September 23, 1985, the parties reached a tentative agreement on a package of amendments to Lease 8580. They agreed to raise the royalty rate to 12 1/2 percent of monthly gross proceeds, and to make the new rate retroactive to February 1, 1984. The 12 1/2 percent rate was at the time customary for leases to mine coal on federal lands and on Indian lands. The amendments acknowledged the legitimacy of tribal taxation of coal production, but stipulated that the tax rate would be capped at eight percent. In addition, Peabody agreed to pay the Tribe $1.5 million when the amendments became effective, and $7.5 million more when Peabody began mining additional coal, as authorized by the Lease amendments. The agreement "also addressed ancillary matters such as provisions for future royalty adjustments, arbitration procedures, rights of way, the establishment of a tribal scholarship fund, and the payment by Peabody of back royalties, bonuses, and water payments." 46 Fed. Cl., at 224. "In consideration of the benefits associated with these lease amendments," the parties agreed to move jointly to vacate the Area Director's June 1984 decision, which had raised the royalty to 20 percent.

In August 1987, the Navajo Tribal Council approved the amendments. The parties signed a final agreement in November 1987, and Secretary Hodel approved it on December 14, 1987. Shortly thereafter, pursuant to the parties' stipulation, the Area Director's decision was vacated.

In 1993, the Tribe brought suit against the United States in the Court of Federal Claims, alleging, *inter alia,* that the Secretary's approval of the amendments to the Lease constituted a breach of trust. The Tribe sought $600 million in damages.

* * *

The Tribe's principal contention is that the IMLA's statutory and regulatory scheme, viewed in its entirety, attaches fiduciary duties to each Government function under that scheme, and that the Secretary acted in contravention of those duties by approving the 12 1/2 percent royalty contained in the amended Lease. We read the IMLA differently. As we see it, the statute and regulations at issue do not provide the requisite "substantive law" that "mandat[es] compensation by the Federal Government." *Mitchell II,* 463 U. S., at 218.

The IMLA and its implementing regulations impose no obligations resembling the detailed fiduciary responsibilities that *Mitchell II* found adequate to support a claim for money damages. The IMLA simply requires Secretarial approval before coal mining leases negotiated between Tribes and third parties become effective, and authorizes the Secretary generally to promulgate regulations governing mining operations. * * * The endeavor to align this case with *Mitchell II* rather than *Mitchell I,* however valiant, falls short of the mark. Unlike the "elaborate" provisions before the Court in *Mitchell II,* 463 U. S., at 225, the IMLA and its regulations do not "give the Federal Government full responsibility to manage Indian resources . . . for the benefit of the Indians," *id.,* at 224. The Secretary is neither assigned a comprehensive managerial role nor, at the time relevant here, expressly invested with responsibility to secure "the needs and best interests of the Indian owner and his heirs." *Ibid.*

Instead, the Secretary's involvement in coal leasing under the IMLA more closely resembles the role provided for the Government by the GAA [General Allotment Act] regarding allotted forest lands. See *Mitchell I,* 445 U. S., at 540–544. Although the GAA required the Government to hold allotted land "in trust for the sole use and benefit of the Indian to whom such allotment shall have been made," *id.*, at 541, that Act did not "authoriz[e], much less requir[e], the Government to manage timber resources for the benefit of Indian allottees," *Mitchell I*, 445 U. S., at 545. Similarly here, the IMLA and its regulations do not assign to the Secretary managerial control over coal leasing. Nor do they even establish the "limited trust relationship," *id.*, at 542, existing under the GAA; no provision of the IMLA or its regulations contains *any* trust language with respect to coal leasing.

Moreover, as in *Mitchell I*, imposing fiduciary duties on the Government here would be out of line with one of the statute's principal purposes. The GAA was designed so that "the allottee, and not the United States, . . . [would] manage the land." *Id.*, at 543. Imposing upon the Government a fiduciary duty to oversee the management of allotted lands would not have served that purpose. So too here. The IMLA aims to enhance tribal self-determination by giving Tribes, not the Government, the lead role in negotiating mining leases with third parties. As the Court of Federal Claims recognized, "[t]he ideal of Indian self-determination is directly at odds with Secretarial control over leasing." 46 Fed. Cl., at 230.

* * *

Citing 25 U. S. C. § 396a,* the IMLA's general prescription, the Tribe next asserts that the Secretary violated his "duty to review and approve any proposed coal lease with care to promote IMLA's basic purpose and the [Tribe's] best interests." To support that assertion, the Tribe points to various Government reports identifying 20 percent as the appropriate royalty, and to the Secretary's decision, made after receiving *ex parte* communications from Peabody, to withhold departmental action.

In the circumstances presented, the Tribe maintains, the Secretary's eventual approval of the 12 1/2 percent royalty violated his duties under § 396a in two ways. First, the Secretary's approval was "improvident," because it allowed the Tribe's coal "to be conveyed for what [the Secretary] knew to be about half of its value." Second, Secretary Hodel's intervention into the Lease adjustment process "skewed the bargaining" by depriving the Tribe of the 20 percent rate, rendering the Secretary's subsequent approval of the 12 1/2 percent rate "unfair."

The Tribe's vigorously pressed arguments headlining § 396a * * * fail, for they assume substantive prescriptions not found in that provision. As to the "improviden[ce]" of the Secretary's approval, the Tribe can point to no guides or standards circumscribing the Secretary's affirmation of coal

---

*   [Ed.] Section 396a states that "unallotted lands within any Indian reservation," or otherwise under federal jurisdiction, "may, with the approval of the Secretary * * * be leased for mining purposes, by authority of the tribal council or other authorized spokesmen for such Indians, for terms not to exceed ten years and as long thereafter as minerals are produced in paying quantities."

mining leases negotiated between a Tribe and a private lessee. Regulations under the IMLA in effect in 1987 established a minimum royalty of ten cents per ton. See 25 CFR § 211.15(c) (1985). But the royalty contained in Lease 8580 well exceeded that regulatory floor. At the time the Secretary approved the amended Lease, it bears repetition, 12 1/2 percent was the rate the United States itself customarily received from leases to mine coal on federal lands. Similarly, the customary rate for coal leases on Indian lands issued or readjusted after 1976 did not exceed 12 1/2 percent.

In sum, neither the IMLA nor any of its regulations establishes anything more than a bare minimum royalty. Hence, there is no textual basis for concluding that the Secretary's approval function includes a duty, enforceable in an action for money damages, to ensure a higher rate of return for the Tribe concerned. Similarly, no pertinent statutory or regulatory provision requires the Secretary, on pain of damages, to conduct an independent "economic analysis" of the reasonableness of the royalty to which a Tribe and third party have agreed. 263 F. 3d, at 1340 (concurring opinion below, finding such a duty).

The Tribe's second argument under § 396a concentrates on the "skew[ing]" effect of Secretary Hodel's 1985 intervention, *i.e.,* his direction to Deputy Assistant Secretary Fritz to withhold action on Peabody's appeal from the Area Director's decision setting a royalty rate of 20 percent. The Secretary's actions, both in intervening in the administrative appeal process, and in approving the amended Lease, the Tribe urges, were not based upon an assessment of the merits of the royalty issue; instead, the Tribe maintains, they were attributable entirely to the undue influence Peabody exerted through *ex parte* communications with the Secretary. Underscoring that the Tribe had no knowledge of those communications or of Secretary Hodel's direction to Fritz, the Tribe asserts that its bargaining position was seriously compromised when it resumed negotiations with Peabody in 1985. The Secretary's ultimate approval of the 12 1/2 percent royalty, the Tribe concludes, was thus an outcome fundamentally unfair to the Tribe.

Here again, as the Court of Federal Claims ultimately determined, the Tribe's assertions are not grounded in a specific statutory or regulatory provision that can fairly be interpreted as mandating money damages. Nothing in § 396a, the IMLA's basic provision, or in the IMLA's implementing regulations proscribed the *ex parte* communications in this case, which occurred during an administrative appeal process largely unconstrained by formal requirements. * * *

We note, moreover, that even if Deputy Assistant Secretary Fritz had rendered an opinion affirming the 20 percent royalty approved by the Area Director, it would have been open to the Secretary to set aside or modify his subordinate's decision. As head of the Department of the Interior, the

Secretary had "authority to review any decision of any employee or employees of the Department." 43 CFR § 4.5(a)(2) (1985). Accordingly, rejection of Peabody's appeal by the Deputy Assistant Secretary would not necessarily have yielded a higher royalty for the Tribe.

* * *

* * * The judgment of the United States Court of Appeals for the Federal Circuit is accordingly reversed, and the case is remanded for further proceedings consistent with this opinion.

It is so ordered.

[JUSTICE SOUTER, with whom JUSTICE STEVENS and JUSTICE O'CONNOR join, dissenting.]

* * *

NOTES

1. On remand, the Court of Appeals for the Federal Circuit agreed with the Navajo Nation that "the Supreme Court did not address the question of whether, apart from IMLA, 'a network of other statutes and regulations,' [*Navajo Nation*,] 123 S.Ct. at 1090, imposes 'judicially enforceable fiduciary duties upon the United States,' *id.*, in connection with the Peabody lease." Navajo Nation v. United States, 347 F.3d 1327, 1331–32 (C.A.Fed.2003). The case was remanded by the Court of Appeals to the Court of Federal Claims to determine whether the tribe had preserved its argument regarding other federal statutes not rejected or held inapplicable by the Supreme Court's decision in the case and whether such statutes "can fairly be read as money-mandating in light of the Supreme Court's decisions" applying *Mitchell I* and *Mitchell II*.

On remand, the Federal Circuit Court of Appeals, reversing a Federal Court of Claims decision, held that the Navajo Nation had stated a cognizable claim under the Indian Tucker Act and federal common law by invoking a "network" of laws that showed the comprehensive federal control of Navajo coal leasing matters under treaties and several statutes including the Navajo-Hopi Rehabilitation Act of 1950, U.S.C. §§ 635(a) (allowing certain leases) and 638 (providing for surveys and studies of resources including coal). *Navajo Nation v. United States*, 501 F.3d 1327 (Fed.Cir.2007). The Supreme Court unanimously reversed saying that the lease in question was not under the Rehabilitation Act and that to read the requirement of making studies as a money-mandating duty to follow the requests of the tribe "would simply be too far a stretch." United States v. Navajo Nation, 556 U.S. 287 (2009).

More broadly, the Court said:

The Federal Government's liability cannot be premised on control alone. * * * In *Navajo I* we reiterated that the analysis must begin with "specific rights—creating or duty—imposing statutory or regulatory prescriptions." *If* a plaintiff identifies such a prescription, and *if* that prescription bears the hallmarks of a "conventional fiduciary relationship," *White Mountain, then* trust principles (including any such principles premised on "control") could play a role in "inferring that the trust obligation [is] enforceable by damages." But that must be the second step of the analysis, not (as the Federal Circuit made it) the starting point.

* * * Because the Tribe cannot identify a specific, applicable, trust-creating statute or regulation that the Government violated, we do not reach the question whether the trust duty was money mandating. Thus, neither the Government's "control" over coal nor common-law trust principles matter.

556 U.S. at 302.

2. On the same day that it issued its decision in *United States v. Navajo Nation*, the Court decided United States v. White Mountain Apache Tribe, 537 U.S. 465 (2003). The historic former military post of Fort Apache was established in 1870 in territory that eventually became part of the White Mountain Apache Tribe's reservation. In 1922, Congress transferred control of the fort to the Secretary of the Interior and in 1923 set aside about 400 acres for use as an Indian school. Congress enacted a statute declaring that Fort Apache would be "held by the United States in trust for the White Mountain Apache Tribe, subject to the right of the Secretary of the Interior to use any part of the land and improvements for administrative or school purposes for as long as they are needed for the purpose." Pub.L. 86–392, 74 Stat. 8 (1960 Act). The Secretary exercised that right, and as Justice Souter's majority opinion for the Court in *White Mountain* explained, allowed the fort to fall into disrepair; "Although the National Park Service listed the fort as a national historical site in 1976, the recognition was no augury of fortune, for just over 20 years later the World Monuments Watch placed the fort on its 1998 List of 100 Most Endangered Monuments." Id. at 469.

In 1993, the tribe commissioned an engineering assessment of Fort Apache, finding that it would cost about $14 million to rehabilitate the property occupied by the Government in accordance with standards for historic preservation. The tribe sued the United States in the Court of Federal Claims, alleging breach of fiduciary duty to "maintain, protect, repair and preserve" the trust property.

The federal government, citing *Mitchell I*, contended that the 1960 Act had not even created the "bare trust" found to exist under the General Allotment Act. The Supreme Court disagreed:

> The 1960 Act goes beyond a bare trust and permits a fair inference that the Government is subject to duties as a trustee and liable in damages for breach. The statutory language, of course, expressly defines a fiduciary relationship in the provision that Fort Apache be "held by the United States in trust for the White Mountain Apache Tribe." 74 Stat. 8. Unlike the Allotment Act, however, the

statute proceeds to invest the United States with discretionary authority to make direct use of portions of the trust corpus. The trust property is "subject to the right of the Secretary of the Interior to use any part of the land and improvements for administrative or school purposes for as long as they are needed for the purpose," and it is undisputed that the Government has to this day availed itself of its option. As to the property subject to the Government's actual use, then, the United States has not merely exercised daily supervision but has enjoyed daily occupation, and so has obtained control at least as plenary as its authority over the timber in *Mitchell II*. While it is true that the 1960 Act does not, like the statutes cited in that case, expressly subject the Government to duties of management and conservation, the fact that the property occupied by the United States is expressly subject to a trust supports a fair inference that an obligation to preserve the property improvements was incumbent on the United States as trustee. This is so because elementary trust law, after all, confirms the commonsense assumption that a fiduciary actually administering trust property may not allow it to fall into ruin on his watch. "One of the fundamental common-law duties of a trustee is to preserve and maintain trust assets," *Central States, Southeast & Southwest Areas Pension Fund v. Central Transport, Inc.*, 472 U.S. 559, 572 (1985) (citing G. Bogert & G. Bogert, Law of Trusts and Trustees § 582, p. 346 (rev.2d ed.1980)). Given this duty on the part of the trustee to preserve corpus, "it naturally follows that the Government should be liable in damages for the breach of its fiduciary duties." *Mitchell II.*

Id. at 474–75.

Justice Ginsburg, who had authored the Court's 6–3 majority opinion in *United States v. Navajo Nation*, wrote a concurrence in *White Mountain*, joined by Justice Breyer (also in the majority in *Navajo Nation)*, which sought to reconcile the applications of the *Mitchell* cases in the two decisions.

> In this case [*White Mountain*], the threshold set by the *Mitchell* cases is met. The 1960 Act provides that Fort Apache shall be "held by the United States in trust for the White Mountain Apache Tribe" and, at the same time, authorizes the Government to use and occupy the fort. * * *

> *Navajo*, in contrast, turns on the threshold question whether the Indian Mineral Leasing Act (IMLA) and its regulations impose any concrete substantive obligations, fiduciary or otherwise, on the Government. *Navajo* answers that question in the negative. The "controversy . . . falls within *Mitchell I*'s domain," *Navajo* concludes, for "the Tribe's claim for compensation . . . does not derive from any liability-imposing provision of the IMLA or its implementing regulations." 123 S. Ct. at 1084. The coal-leasing provisions of the IMLA and its allied regulations, *Navajo* explains, lacked the

characteristics that typify a genuine trust relationship: Those provisions assigned the Secretary of the Interior no managerial role over coal leasing; they did not even establish the "limited trust relationship" that existed under the law at issue in *Mitchell I.*

Id. at 480–81.

Four Justices who had been in the majority in *Navajo Nation* dissented in *White Mountain.* Justice Thomas wrote the dissent, joined by Chief Justice Rehnquist and Justices Scalia and Kennedy. They insisted that since "there is nothing in the statute that 'clearly establish[es] fiduciary obligations of the Government in the management and operation of Indian lands,' the 1960 Act creates only a 'bare trust.' " Id. at 484.

3.   After these cases, finding a "network" of statutes to base a breach of trust damages claim depends on: 1) express statutory language supporting a fiduciary relationship; and 2) comprehensive control over government property. The rule has been applied in lower courts. Claims have proceeded in some cases (e.g., Osage Tribe of Indians v. United States, 68 Fed.Cl. 322 (2005) (U.S had specific duty to verify royalties are collected and deposit them for tribe); Shoshone Indian Tribe v. United States, 364 F.3d 1339 (Fed.Cir.2004) (Tribe may assert claim for failure to collect lease proceeds under Mineral Leasing Act)). They have been rejected in other cases (e.g., Samish Indian Nation v. United States, 82 Fed.Cl. 54 (2008) (rejecting claim for damages for lost federal benefits during period tribe was wrongfully denied federal recognition for lack of statutory basis); Marceau v. Blackfeet Housing Auth., 540 F.3d 916 (9th Cir.2008) (Claim for shoddy housing built under U.S. Housing Act because statute did not give federal agency a managerial role and property was not held in trust by U.S.); Nulankeyutmonen Nkihtaqmikon v. Impson, 503 F.3d 18 (1st Cir.2007) (Tribal members had no enforceable fiduciary relationship where land was owned by tribe, not individual plaintiffs)).

NOTE: THE COBELL LITIGATION

A highly-publicized class action suit filed in 1996 alleged gross mismanagement by the federal government of at least 300,000 trust accounts of individual Indian beneficiaries. See Cobell v. Norton, 240 F.3d 1081 (D.C.Cir.2001). Recall that government policy in the 1880s was intended to break up the tribally-owned lands and distribute them to heads of families so they would emulate the contemporary Jeffersonian ideal of the yeoman farmer. What was left over after each head of family got an allotment of land was distributed as homesteads to white settlers. The latter goal was achieved. But the Allotment policy led to the loss of 100 million acres of once-tribal land. The lands that remained in individual Indian hands passed from generation to generation, with individual interests in land becoming more fractionated through intestate succession to a multiplicity of heirs. The government was to lease the lands and to hold and distribute the proceeds to the owners. Funds were placed in Individual Indian Money (IIM) accounts. In *Cobell*, plaintiffs contended that the federal government was unable to account for hundreds of millions of dollars owed to individual Indian beneficiaries who did not receive what they were due from IIM accounts.

Judge Royce Lamberth, presiding over the class action suit in the D.C. federal district court, held that the federal government had breached its fiduciary duties and announced that the court would oversee the federal government's efforts to overhaul the antiquated trust account system:

> It would be difficult to find a more historically mismanaged federal program than the Individual Indian Money (IIM) trust. The United States, the trustee of the IIM trust, cannot say how much money is or should be in the trust. As the trustee admitted on the eve of trial, it cannot render an accurate accounting to the beneficiaries, contrary to a specific statutory mandate and the century-old obligation to do so. More specifically, as Secretary Babbitt testified, an accounting cannot be rendered for most of the 300,000-plus beneficiaries, who are now plaintiffs in this lawsuit. Generations of IIM trust beneficiaries have been born and raised with the assurance that their trustee, the United States, was acting properly with their money. Just as many generations have been denied any such proof, however. "If courts were permitted to indulge their sympathies, a case better calculated to excite them could scarcely be imagined." Cherokee Nation v. Georgia, 30 U.S. (5 Pet.) 1 (1831).

> * * *

> The United States' mismanagement of the IIM trust is far more inexcusable than garden-variety trust mismanagement of a typical denotive trust. For the beneficiaries of this trust did not voluntarily choose to have their lands taken from them; they did not willingly relinquish pervasive control of their money to the United States. The United States imposed this trust on the Indian people. As the government concedes, the purpose of the IIM trust was to deprive plaintiffs' ancestors of their native lands and rid the nation of their tribal identity. The United States reaped the "benefit" of this imposed program long ago—sixty-five percent of what were previously tribal land holdings quickly opened up to non-Indian settlement. But the United States has refused to act in accordance with the fiduciary obligations attendant to the imposition of the trust, which are not imposed by statute.

> The defendants cannot provide an accounting of plaintiffs' money, which the United States has forced into the IIM trust. * * *

> Plaintiffs bring this lawsuit to force the government to abide by its duty to render an accurate accounting of the money currently held within the IIM trust. But plaintiffs must remember that this is a lawsuit. They cannot treat the court as a grievance committee for the United States' mishandling of the trust. Whether plaintiffs like it or

not, only Congress can play that type of role. For everyone involved must consider not only plaintiffs' rights, but also the constitutional role of courts in American government. This court can consider only plaintiffs' soundly grounded causes of action, and it cannot provide relief beyond them. The component of the case currently before the court concerns the issue of whether defendants are in breach of any trust duties such that plaintiffs should be afforded some prospective relief to prevent further injury of their legal rights. Plaintiffs have stated and proved certain valid legal claims that entitle them to relief.

* * * [T]he court finds that the United States government, by virtue of the actions of defendants and their predecessors, is currently in breach of certain trust duties owed to plaintiffs. The government recently has taken substantial steps toward bringing itself into compliance in several respects. Nonetheless, given the long and sorry history of the United States' trusteeship of the IIM trust, the defendants' recalcitrance toward remedying their mismanagement despite decades of congressional directives, and the consequences of allowing these enumerated breaches of trust to continue, the court will retain continuing jurisdiction over this matter. It would be an abdication of duty for this court to do anything less.

91 F.Supp.2d 1, 6–7 (D.D.C.1999).

The D.C. Circuit Court of Appeals held that the district court's decision "that government officials breached their obligations to IIM beneficiaries is in accordance with the law and well-supported by the evidentiary record." Cobell v. Norton, 240 F.3d 1081, 1110 (D.C.Cir.2001).

Judge Lamberth then appointed a Court Monitor to review the Interior Department's trust reform activities and file written reports to the Court. The Monitor's reports, "were, to say the least, unflattering to the DOI [Department of Interior]." 334 F.3d at 1136. Discussions with DOI officials could not explain why there had been a one and one-half year hiatus between beginning the process to determine the method of accounting and the first steps to an accounting.

During the litigation Judge Lamberth held various federal officials "in civil contempt of court." The D.C. Circuit Court of Appeals reviewed the contempt citations:

The district court used some harsh words in the *Contempt Opinion*, expressing its dissatisfaction with the defendants' conduct. *See, e.g.*, 226 F.Supp.2d at 125 ("The Department of Interior is truly an embarrassment to the federal government in general and the executive branch in particular. The 300,000 individual Indian beneficiaries deserve a better trustee-delegate than the Secretary of Interior"); *id.* at 113 ("The Court is both saddened and disgusted by the Department's intransigence"). Of particular note are the district court's statement that "Secretary Norton and Assistant Secretary McCaleb can now rightfully take their place alongside former-Secretary Babbitt and former Assistant Secretary Gover in the pantheon of unfit trustee-delegates," *id.* at 161, and the court's invitation to Secretary Norton or any other individual at the Department who "feel[s] that as a result of th[e] Court's ruling they are unable or unwilling to perform their duties to the best of their ability" to "leave the Department forthwith." *Id.* at 133.

334 F.3d. at 1136.

The Court of Appeals set aside some of the contempt findings and twice rejected Judge Lamberth's appointments of a "judicial monitor" in the case to oversee Interior's compliance with his orders. The appeals court held that the appointment exceeded the district court's authority. Cobell v. Norton, 392 F.3d. 461, 477 (D.C.Cir.2004). It also reversed his injunction requiring the Department of Interior to disconnect most of its computer systems from the Internet in light of concerns about the security of individual Indian trust account data "housed on an unknown number of Interior's computer systems." *Cobell v. Norton*, 391 F.3d 251, 253 (D.C.Cir.2004)

Judge Lamberth's orders continued and, after one particularly scathing condemnation of Interior officials, see *Cobell v. Norton*, 229 F.R.D. 5 (D.D.C.2005), the government asked to have him removed from the case alleging bias against the government. In July 2006, the D.C. Circuit Court of Appeals took the extraordinary step of reassigning the case to another judge. Cobell v. Kempthorne, 455 F.3d 317 (D.C.Cir.2006).

The new judge, James Robertson, held a trial and issued an opinion stating that although the lack of available funding means:

> Interior is unable to perform an adequate accounting of the IIM trust does not mean that a just resolution of this dispute is hopeless. It does mean that a remedy must be found for the Department's unrepaired, and irreparable, breach of its fiduciary duty over the last century.

Cobell v. Kempthorne, 532 F.Supp.2d 37, 103 (D.D.C.2008).

Judge Robertson proceeded and, after hearings, ordered the government to pay $455 million. He noted that although exhibits in the case showed a shortfall of $3 billion, the award represented a plausible estimate of the funds due. Cobell v. Kempthorne, 569 F.Supp.2d 223 (D.D.C.2008). On appeal, the D.C. Circuit vacated, differing with Judge Robertson's finding that an accounting was impossible. It remanded with directions "to provide the trust beneficiaries the best accounting possible, in a reasonable time" and said the "district court should exercise its equitable power to ensure that Interior allocates its limited resources in rough proportion to the estimated dollar value of payments due to class members. It should also consider low-cost statistical methods of estimating benefits across class sub-groups." Cobell v. Salazar, 573 F.3d 808, 815 (D.C.Cir.2009).

In December 2009, the *Cobell* plaintiffs and the federal government reached a sweeping settlement that was subject to congressional approval. See Settlement Agreement, Cobell v. Salazar, No. 96–CV01285–JR, U.S. District Court for the District of Columbia. The agreement includes provisions for:

- A $1.4 billion fund to be distributed to holders of Individual Indian Money accounts

- A $2 billion Trust Land Consolidation Fund for purchase of fractional individual interests in allotments and transfer of the titles to tribes

- A scholarship fund of up to $60 million comprised of balances of funds left after these payments and purchases to be used for Indian scholarships

- Establishment of an Indian Trust Responsibility Commission.

The Secretary promptly issued a Secretarial Order creating a "Secretarial Commission on Indian Trust Administration and Reform" upon enactment of legislation approving the settlement. The commission will be charged with "conducting a comprehensive evaluation of the Department's management and administration of the trust administration system." See Secretary of the Interior, Order No. 3292 (Dec. 8, 2009).

A year later, on December 8, 2010, President Obama signed the settlement into law. Its implementation remains subject to the lower court's approval, a process in which individual parties may raise objections.

INDIAN LAWYERING NOTE: SETTLING THE TRIBAL TRUST CLAIMS

Following the settlement of the Individual Indian Monies accounts case, the federal government turned to tribal claims that the Department of the Interior had also mismanaged tribal trust fund accounts going back to the allotment era. This case was resolved by settlement. The United States agreed to pay forty-two tribes over one billion dollars to resolve these claims. Individual tribes, some of which were represented by individual counsel and others by NARF, received major monetary awards. These settlements brought a certain degree of closure to claims that had been a major stain on the federal tribal relationship and vindication for the tribes that had been raising the issue for so long.

Yet when the tribal trust settlements reached the tribal communities, questions arose about how to use the money. Some tribal leaders were pressured to release the funds on a per capita basis to individuals. When, in some instances, tribal leaders chose to spend or invest funds on behalf of the collective, they became unpopular or were voted out of office. Tribal attorneys found themselves caught in the middle. In addition to the upheaval in certain tribes, the trust fund settlement also inspired a dispute over fees among tribal lawyers who represented tribes at various stages in the litigation.

As a lawyer for tribal government, how would you discuss with your clients the pros and cons of settling historic cases and the potentially competing interests of individuals and tribal members?

UNITED STATES V. JICARILLA APACHE NATION

Supreme Court of the United States, 2011
564 U.S. 162, 131 S.Ct. 2313, 180 L.Ed.2d 187

JUSTICE ALITO delivered the opinion of the Court.

The attorney-client privilege ranks among the oldest and most established evidentiary privileges known to our law. The common law, however, has recognized an exception to the privilege when a trustee obtains legal advice related to the exercise of fiduciary duties. In such cases, courts have held, the trustee cannot withhold attorney-client communications from the beneficiary of the trust.

In this case, we consider whether the fiduciary exception applies to the general trust relationship between the United States and the Indian tribes. We hold that it does not. Although the Government's responsibilities with respect to the management of funds belonging to Indian tribes bear some resemblance to those of a private trustee, this analogy cannot be taken too far. The trust obligations of the United States to the Indian tribes are established and governed by statute rather than the common law, and in fulfilling its statutory duties, the Government acts not as a private trustee but pursuant to its sovereign interest in the execution of federal law. The reasons for the fiduciary exception—that the trustee has no independent interest in trust administration, and that the trustee is subject to a general common-law duty of disclosure—do not apply in this context.

I

The Jicarilla Apache Nation (Tribe) [brought claims against the United States, alleging that "the Government failed to maximize returns on its trust funds, invested too heavily in short-term maturities, and failed to pool its trust funds with other tribal trusts." During discovery, the "Government turned over thousands of documents but withheld 226 potentially relevant documents as protected by the attorney-client privilege, the attorney work-product doctrine, or the deliberative-process privilege." Later, the government turned over some of the documents, but still "continued to assert the attorney-client privilege and attorney work-product doctrine with respect to the remaining 155 documents." The lower court held that the documents relating to the management of the trust funds fell within the "fiduciary exception" to the attorney-client privilege doctrine. In common law trust doctrine, the trustee may not assert the privilege against the beneficiary as to trust management. The

Court of Federal Claims held that the Indian trust assets in this case were sufficiently analogous to a common law trust. The United States appealed that decision, arguing that the federal trust responsibility, at least in this context, is not analogous to a common law trust.]

II

The Federal Rules of Evidence provide that evidentiary privileges "shall be governed by the principles of the common law . . . in the light of reason and experience." Fed. Rule Evid. 501.

* * *

The objectives of the attorney-client privilege apply to governmental clients. "The privilege aids government entities and employees in obtaining legal advice founded on a complete and accurate factual picture." 1 Restatement (Third) of the Law Governing Lawyers § 74, Comment *b*, pp. 573–574 (1998). Unless applicable law provides other-wise, the Government may invoke the attorney-client privilege in civil litigation to protect confidential communications between Government officials and Government attorneys. *Id.*, at 574 ("[G]overnmental agencies and employees enjoy the same privilege as nongovernmental counterparts"). The Tribe argues, however, that the common law also recognizes a fiduciary exception to the attorney-client privilege and that, by virtue of the trust relationship between the Government and the Tribe, documents that would otherwise be privileged must be disclosed. As preliminary matters, we consider the bounds of the fiduciary exception and the nature of the trust relationship between the United States and the Indian tribes.

* * *

The leading American case on the fiduciary exception is *Riggs Nat. Bank of Washington, D.C. v. Zimmer*, 355 A. 2d 709 (Del. Ch. 1976). In that case, the beneficiaries of a trust estate sought to compel the trustees to reimburse the estate for alleged breaches of trust. The beneficiaries moved to compel the trustees to produce a legal memorandum related to the administration of the trust that the trustees withheld on the basis of attorney-client privilege. * * * Applying the common-law fiduciary exception, the court held that the memorandum was discoverable.

* * *

The Federal Courts of Appeals apply the fiduciary exception based on the same two criteria. * * * Not until the decision below had a federal appellate court held the exception to apply to the United States as trustee for the Indian tribes.

In order to apply the fiduciary exception in this case, the Court of Appeals analogized the Government to a private trustee. . . . We have applied that analogy in limited contexts, *see, e.g., United States v. Mitchell*,

463 U.S. 206, 226 . . . (1983) (*Mitchell II*), but that does not mean the Government resembles a private trustee in every respect. On the contrary, this Court has previously noted that the relationship between the United States and the Indian tribes is distinctive, "different from that existing between individuals whether dealing at arm's length, *as trustees and beneficiaries,* or otherwise." *Klamath and Moadoc Tribes v. United States,* 296 U. S. 244, 254 . . . (1935) (emphasis added). "The *general* relationship between the United States and the Indian tribes is not comparable to a private trust relationship." *Cherokee Nation of Okla. v. United States,* 21 Cl. Ct. 565, 573 (1990) (emphasis added).

The Government, of course, is not a private trustee. Though the relevant statutes denominate the relationship between the Government and the Indians a "trust," *see, e.g.,* 25 U. S. C. § 162a, that trust is defined and governed by statutes rather than the common law. *See United States v. Navajo Nation,* 537 U. S. 488, 506 (2003) (*Navajo I*) ("[T]he analysis must train on specific rights-creating or duty-imposing statutory or regulatory prescriptions"). As we have recognized in prior cases, Congress may style its relations with the Indians a "trust" without assuming all the fiduciary duties of a private trustee, creating a trust relationship that is "limited" or "bare" compared to a trust relationship between private parties at common law.

The difference between a private common-law trust and the statutory Indian trust follows from the unique position of the Government as sovereign. The distinction between "public rights" against the Government and "private rights" between private parties is well established. The Government consents to be liable to private parties "and may yield this consent upon such terms and under such restrictions as it may think just." *Murray's Lessee v. Hoboken Land & Improvement Co.,* 18 How. 272, 283, 15 L. Ed. 372 (1856). This creates an important distinction "between cases of private right and those which arise between the Government and persons subject to its authority in connection with the performance of the constitutional functions of the executive or legislative departments." *Crowell v. Benson,* 285 U. S. 22, 50 (1932).

Throughout the history of the Indian trust relationship, we have recognized that the organization and management of the trust is a sovereign function subject to the plenary authority of Congress. See *Merrion v. Jicarilla Apache Tribe,* 455 U.S. 130, 169, n. 18 (1982) ("The United States retains plenary authority to divest the tribes of any attributes of sovereignty"); *United States v. Wheeler,* 435 U.S. 313, 319 (1978) ("Congress has plenary authority to legislate for the Indian tribes in all matters, including their form of government"); *Winton v. Amos,* 255 U. S. 373, 391 (1921) ("Congress has plenary authority over the Indians and all their tribal relations, and full power to legislate concerning their tribal property"); *Lone Wolf v. Hitchcock,* 187 U.S. 553, 565 (1903) ("Plenary authority over the tribal relations of the Indians has been exercised by Congress from the beginning, and the power has always been deemed a political one, not subject to be controlled by the judicial department of the government"); *Cherokee Nation v. Hitchcock*, 187 U.S. 294, 308 (1902) ("The power existing in Congress to administer upon and guard the tribal property, and the power being political and administrative in its nature, the manner of its exercise is a question within the province of the legislative branch to determine, and is not one for the courts"). * * *

Because the Indian trust relationship represents an exercise of that authority, we have explained that the Government "has a real and direct interest" in the guardianship it exercises over the Indian tribes; "the interest is one which is vested in it as a sovereign." *United States v. Minnesota*, 270 U.S. 181, 194 (1926). This is especially so because the Government has often structured the trust relationship to pursue its own policy goals. Thus, while trust administration "relat[es] to the welfare of the Indians, the maintenance of the limitations which Congress has prescribed as a part of its plan of distribution is distinctly an interest of the United States." * * *

We do not question "the undisputed existence of a general trust relationship between the United States and the Indian people." *Mitchell II*, 463 U.S., at 225. The Government, following "a humane and self imposed policy * * * has charged itself with moral obligations of the highest responsibility and trust," *Seminole Nation v. United States*, 316 U.S. 286, 296–297 (1942), obligations "to the fulfillment of which the national honor has been committed[.]" Congress has expressed this policy in a series of statutes that have defined and redefined the trust relationship between the United States and the Indian tribes. In some cases, Congress established only a limited trust relationship to serve a narrow purpose [citing *Mitchell I*, 445 U.S., at 544 and *Navajo I*, 537 U.S., at 507–508]. * * *

In other cases, we have found that particular "statutes and regulations . . . clearly establish fiduciary obligations of the Government" in some areas. *Mitchell II, supra*, at 226. * * * Once federal law imposes such duties, the common law "could play a role." *United States v. Navajo Nation*, 129 S. Ct. 1547, 1558 (2009) (*Navajo II*). We have looked to common-law principles to inform our interpretation of statutes and to determine the scope of liability that Congress has imposed. * * * But the applicable statutes and regulations "establish [the] fiduciary relationship and define the contours of the United States' fiduciary responsibilities." * * * When "the Tribe cannot identify a specific, applicable, trust-creating statute or regulation that the Government violated, . . . neither the Government's 'control' over [Indian assets] nor common law trust principles matter." * * * The Government assumes Indian trust responsibilities only to the extent it expressly accepts those responsibilities by statute.

Over the years, we have described the federal relationship with the Indian tribes using various formulations. The Indian tribes have been called "domestic dependent nations," *Cherokee Nation v. Georgia*, 5 Pet. 1, 17 (1831), under the "tutelage" of the United States, * * * and subject to "the exercise of the Government's guardianship over * * * their affairs," *United States v. Sandoval*, 231 U. S. 28, 48 (1913). These concepts do not necessarily correspond to a common-law trust relationship. * * * That is because Congress has chosen to structure the Indian trust relationship in different ways. We will apply common-law trust principles where Congress has indicated it is appropriate to do so. For that reason, the Tribe must point to a right conferred by statute or regulation in order to obtain otherwise privileged information from the Government against its wishes.

III

In this case, the Tribe's claim arises from 25 U. S. C. §§ 161–162a and the American Indian Trust Fund Management Reform Act of 1994, § 4001 *et seq.* These provisions define "the trust responsibilities of the United States" with respect to tribal funds. § 162a(d). * * *

As we have discussed, the Government exercises its carefully delimited trust responsibilities in a sovereign capacity to implement national policy respecting the Indian tribes. The two features justifying the fiduciary exception—the beneficiary's status as the "real client" and the trustee's common-law duty to disclose information about the trust—are notably absent in the trust relationship Congress has established between the United States and the Tribe.

The Court of Appeals applied the fiduciary exception based on its determination that the Tribe rather than the Government was the "real client" with respect to the Government attorneys' advice. . . . In cases applying the fiduciary exception, courts identify the "real client" based on whether the advice was bought by the trust corpus, whether the trustee had reason to seek advice in a personal rather than a fiduciary capacity, and whether the advice could have been intended for any purpose other than to benefit the trust. . . . Applying these factors, we conclude that the United States does not obtain legal advice as a "mere representative" of the Tribe; nor is the Tribe the "real client" for whom that advice is intended. * * *

Here, the Government attorneys are paid out of congressional appropriations at no cost to the Tribe. Courts look to the source of funds as a "strong indicator of precisely who the real clients were" and a "significant factor" in determining who ought to have access to the legal advice. * * * We similarly find it significant that the attorneys were paid by the Government for advice regarding the Government's statutory obligations.

The payment structure confirms our view that the Government seeks legal advice in its sovereign capacity rather than as a conventional fiduciary of the Tribe. Undoubtedly, Congress intends the Indian tribes to benefit from the Government's management of tribal trusts. That intention represents "a humane and self imposed policy" based on felt "moral obligations." * * * This statutory purpose does not imply a full common-law trust, however. Cf. Restatement 2D, § 25, Comment b ("No trust is created if the settlor manifests an intention to impose merely a moral obligation"). Congress makes such policy judgments pursuant to its sovereign governing authority, and the implementation of federal policy remains "distinctly an interest of the United States." [citations][5] We have said that "the United States continue[s][6] as trustee to have an active interest" in the disposition of Indian assets because the terms of the trust relationship embody policy goals of the United States. * * *

We cannot agree with the Tribe and its amici that "[t]he government and its officials who obtained the advice have no stake in [the] substance of the advice, beyond their trustee role," Brief for Respondent 9, or that "the United States' interests in trust administration were identical to the interests of the tribal trust fund beneficiaries," Brief for National Congress of American Indians et al. as Amici Curiae 5. The United States has a sovereign interest in the administration of Indian trusts distinct from the private interests of those who may benefit from its administration. Courts apply the fiduciary exception on the ground that "management does not manage for itself." * * * But the Government is never in that position. While one purpose of the Indian trust relationship is to benefit the tribes, the Government has its own independent interest in the implementation of federal Indian policy. For that reason, when the Government seeks legal advice related to the administration of tribal trusts, it establishes an attorney-client relationship related to its sovereign interest in the execution of federal law. In other words, the Government seeks legal advice in a "personal" rather than a fiduciary capacity * * *

Moreover, the Government has too many competing legal concerns to allow a case-by-case inquiry into the purpose of each communication. When "multiple interests" are involved in a trust relationship, the equivalence between the interests of the beneficiary and the trustee breaks down. * * * That principle applies with particular force to the Government. Because of the multiple interests it must represent, "the Government cannot follow

---

[5]   Chief Justice Hughes, writing for a unanimous Court, insisted that the "national interest" in the management of Indian affairs "is not to be expressed in terms of property, or to be limited to the assertion of rights incident to the ownership of a reversion or to the holding of a technical title in trust." *Heckman*, 224 U. S. [413,] 437.

[6]   Congress has structured the trust relationship to reflect its considered judgment about how the Indians ought to be governed. [The majority goes on to summarize Congressional goals under the policies of allotment, reorganization, and self-determination]. * * * The control over the Indian tribes that has been exercised by the United States pursuant to the trust relationship— forcing the division of tribal lands, restraining alienation—does not correspond to the fiduciary duties of a common-law trustee. Rather, the trust relationship has been altered and administered as an instrument of federal policy.

the fastidious standards of a private fiduciary, who would breach his duties to his single beneficiary solely by representing potentially conflicting interests without the beneficiary's consent." *Nevada v. United States*, 463 U. S. 110, 128 (1983).

As the Court of Appeals acknowledged, the Government may be obliged "to balance competing interests" when it administers a tribal trust.* * * The Government may need to comply with other statutory duties, such as the environmental and conservation obligations that the Court of Appeals discussed, * * * The Government may also face conflicting obligations to different tribes or individual Indians. * * * And sometimes, we have seen, the Government has enforced the trust statutes to dispose of Indian property contrary to the wishes of those for whom it was nominally kept in trust. The Government may seek the advice of counsel for guidance in balancing these competing interests. Indeed, the point of consulting counsel may be to determine whether conflicting interests are at stake.

The Court of Appeals sought to accommodate the Government's multiple obligations by suggesting that the Government may invoke the attorney-client privilege if it identifies "a specific competing interest" that was considered in the particular communications it seeks to withhold. * * * But the conflicting interests the Government must consider are too pervasive for such a case-by-case approach to be workable.

* * *

The Court of Appeals also decided the fiduciary exception properly applied to the Government because "the fiduciary has a duty to disclose all information related to trust management to the beneficiary." * * *

The United States, however, does not have the same common-law disclosure obligations as a private trustee. As we have previously said, common-law principles are relevant only when applied to a "specific, applicable, trust-creating statute or regulation." *Navajo II*, 129 S. Ct., at 1550. The relevant statute in this case is 25 U.S.C. § 162a(d), which delineates "trust responsibilities of the United States" that the Secretary of the Interior must discharge. The enumerated responsibilities include a provision identifying the Secretary's obligation to provide specific information to tribal account holders: The Secretary must "suppl[y] account holders with periodic statements of their account performance" and must make "available on a daily basis" the "balances of their account." § 162a(d)(5). The Secretary has complied with these requirements by adopting regulations that instruct the Office of Trust Fund Management to provide each tribe with a quarterly statement of performance, 25 CFR § 115.801 (2010), that identifies "the source, type, and status of the trust funds deposited and held in a trust account; the beginning balance; the gains and losses; receipts and disbursements; and the ending account balance of the quarterly statement period," § 115.803. Tribes may request more frequent statements or further "information about account transactions and balances." § 115.802.

The common law of trusts does not override the specific trust-creating statute and regulations that apply here. Those provisions define the Government's disclosure obligation to the Tribe. The Tribe emphasizes, Brief for Respondent 34, that the statute identifies the list of trust responsibilities as nonexhaustive. See § 162a(d) (trust responsibilities "are not limited to" those enumerated). The Government replies that this clause "is best read to refer to other statutory and regulatory requirements" rather than to common-law duties. Brief for United States at 8. Whatever Congress intended, we cannot read the clause to include a general common-law duty to disclose all information related to the administration of Indian trusts. When Congress provides specific statutory obligations, we will not read a "catchall" provision to impose general obligations that would include those specifically enumerated. * * * Reading the statute to incorporate the full duties of a private, common-law fiduciary would vitiate Congress' specification of narrowly defined disclosure obligations.

By law and regulation, moreover, the documents at issue in this case are classed "the property of the United States" while other records are "the property of the tribe." 25 CFR § 115.1000 (2010); see also §§ 15.502, 162.111, 166.1000. Just as the source of the funds used to pay for legal advice is highly relevant in identifying the "real client" for purposes of the fiduciary exception, we consider ownership of the resulting records to be a significant factor in deciding who "ought to have access to the document." *See Riggs*, 355 A. 2d, at 712. In this case, that privilege belongs to the United States.[7]

* * *

Courts and commentators have long recognized that "[n]ot every aspect of private trust law can properly govern the unique relationship of tribes and the federal government." Cohen § 5.02[2], at 434–435. The fiduciary exception to the attorney-client privilege ranks among those aspects inapplicable to the Government's administration of Indian trusts. The Court of Appeals denied the Government's petition for a writ of mandamus based on its erroneous view to the contrary. We leave it for that court to determine whether the standards for granting the writ are met in light of our opinion. We therefore reverse the judgment of the Court of

---

[7]   The dissent tells us that applying the fiduciary exception is even more important against the Government than against a private trustee because of a "history of governmental mismanagement." Post, at 2342. While it is not necessary to our decision, we note that the Indian tribes are not required to keep their funds in federal trust. See 25 U. S. C. § 4022 (authorizing tribes to withdraw funds held in trust by the United States); 25 CFR pt. 1200(B). If the Tribe wishes to have its funds managed by a "conventional fiduciary," post, at 2336, it may seek to do so.

Appeals and remand the case for further proceedings consistent with this opinion.

It is so ordered.

JUSTICE KAGAN took no part in the consideration or decision of this case.

JUSTICE GINSBURG, with whom JUSTICE BREYER joins, concurring in the judgment.

* * *

JUSTICE SOTOMAYOR, dissenting.

Federal Indian policy, as established by a network of federal statutes, requires the United States to act strictly in a fiduciary capacity when managing Indian trust fund accounts. The interests of the Federal Government as trustee and the Jicarilla Apache Nation (Nation) as beneficiary are thus entirely aligned in the context of Indian trust fund management. Where, as here, the governing statutory scheme establishes a conventional fiduciary relationship, the Government's duties include fiduciary obligations derived from common-law trust principles. Because the common-law rationales for the fiduciary exception fully support its application in this context, I would hold that the Government may not rely on the attorney-client privilege to withhold from the Nation communications between the Government and its attorneys relating to trust fund management.

The Court's decision to the contrary rests on false factual and legal premises and deprives the Nation and other Indian tribes of highly relevant evidence in scores of pending cases seeking relief for the Government's alleged mismanagement of their trust funds. But perhaps more troubling is the majority's disregard of our settled precedent that looks to common-law trust principles to define the scope of the Government's fiduciary obligations to Indian tribes. Indeed, aspects of the majority's opinion suggest that common-law principles have little or no relevance in the Indian trust context, a position this Court rejected long ago. Although today's holding pertains only to a narrow evidentiary issue, I fear the upshot of the majority's opinion may well be a further dilution of the Government's fiduciary obligations that will have broader negative repercussions for the relationship between the United States and Indian tribes.

* * *

The majority's conclusion employs a fundamentally flawed legal premise. We have never held that all of the Government's trust responsibilities to Indians must be set forth expressly in a specific statute or regulation. To the contrary, where, as here, the statutory framework establishes that the relationship between the Government and an Indian tribe "bears the hallmarks of a conventional fiduciary relationship," *Navajo II*, 556 U.S. at 301 (internal quotation marks omitted), we have consistently looked to general trust principles to flesh out the Government's fiduciary obligations.

For example, in *United States v. White Mountain Apache Tribe*, 537 U.S. 465 (2003), we construed a statute that vested the Government with discretionary authority to "use" trust property for certain purposes as imposing a concomitant duty to preserve improvements that had previously been made to the land. *Id.*, at 475 (quoting 74 Stat. 8). Even though the statute did not "expressly subject the Government to duties of management and conservation," we construed the Government's obligations under the statute by reference to "elementary trust law," which "confirm[ed] the commonsense assumption that a fiduciary actually administering trust property may not allow it to fall into ruin on his watch." 537 U. S., at 475,. Similarly, in *Seminole Nation*, we relied on general trust principles to conclude that the Government had a fiduciary duty to prevent misappropriation of tribal trust funds by corrupt members of a tribe, even though no specific statutory or treaty provision expressly imposed such a duty. *See* 316 U. S., at 296.

Accordingly, although the "general 'contours' of the government's obligations" are defined by statute, the "interstices must be filled in through reference to general trust law." *Cobell*, 240 F. 3d, at 1101 (quoting *Mitchell II*, 463 U. S., at 224). This approach accords with our recognition in other trust contexts that "the primary function of the fiduciary duty is to constrain the exercise of discretionary powers which are controlled by no other specific duty imposed by the trust instrument or the legal regime." * * * Indeed, "[i]f the fiduciary duty applied to nothing more than activities already controlled by other specific legal duties, it would serve no purpose." * * *

* * *

Contrary to the majority's view, the Government's disclosure obligations are not limited solely to the "narrowly defined disclosure obligations" set forth in § 162a(d)(5) and its implementing regulations, ante, at 2329–2330; rather, given that the statutory regime requires the Government to act as a conventional fiduciary in managing Indian trust funds, the Government's disclosure obligations include those of a fiduciary under common-law trust principles. *See supra*, at 2326–2327. Instead of "overrid[ing]" the specific disclosure duty set forth in § 162a(d)(5) and its implementing regulations, general trust principles flesh out the Government's disclosure obligations under the broader statutory regime, consistent with its role as a conventional fiduciary in this context.

This conclusion, moreover, is supported by the plain text of the very statute cited by the majority. Section 162a(d), which was enacted as part of the American Indian Trust Fund Management Reform Act of 1994 (1994 Act), 108 Stat. 4239, sets forth eight "trust responsibilities of the United States." But that provision also specifically states that the Secretary of the Interior's "proper discharge of the trust responsibilities of the United States shall include (but are not limited to) "those specified duties. 25 U. S. C. § 162a(d) (emphasis added). By expressly including the italicized language, Congress recognized that the Government has pre-existing trust responsibilities that arise out of the broader statutory scheme governing the management of Indian trust funds. Indeed, Title I of the 1994 Act is entitled "Recognition of Trust Responsibility," 108 Stat. 4240 (emphasis added), and courts have similarly observed that the Act "recognized and reaffirmed . . . that the government has longstanding and substantial trust obligations to Indians." *Cobell*, 240 F. 3d, at 1098; see also H. R. Rep. No. 103–778, p. 9 (1994) ("The responsibility for management of Indian Trust Funds by the [Government] has been determined through a series of court decisions, treaties, and statutes"). That conclusion accords with common sense as not even the Government argues that it had no disclosure obligations with respect to Indian trust funds prior to the enactment of the 1994 Act.

The majority requires the Nation to "point to a right conferred by statute" to the attorney-client communications at issue, ante, at 2325, and finding none, denies the Nation access to those communications. The upshot of that decision, I fear, may very well be to reinvigorate the position of the dissenting Justices in *White Mountain Apache* and *Mitchell II*, who rejected the use of common-law principles to inform the scope of the Government's fiduciary obligations to Indian tribes. *See White Mountain Apache*, 537 U.S., at 486–487 (THOMAS, J., dissenting); *Mitchell II*, 463 U.S., at 234–235 (Powell, J., dissenting). That approach was wrong when *Mitchell II* was decided nearly 30 years ago, and it is wrong today. Under our governing precedents, common-law trust principles play an important role in defining the Government's fiduciary duties where, as here, the statutory scheme establishes a conventional fiduciary relationship. Applying those principles in this context, I would hold that the fiduciary exception is fully applicable to the communications in this case.

III

We have described the Federal Government's fiduciary duties toward Indian tribes as consisting of "moral obligations of the highest responsibility and trust," to be fulfilled through conduct "judged by the most exacting fiduciary standards." *Seminole Nation*, 316 U. S., at 297; *see also Mitchell II*, 463 U. S., at 225–226 (collecting cases). The sad and well-documented truth, however, is that the Government has failed to live up to its fiduciary obligations in managing Indian trust fund accounts. See, e.g., *Cobell*, 240 F. 3d, at 1089.

* * *

As Congress has recognized, "[t]he Indian trust fund is more than balance sheets and accounting procedures. These moneys are crucial to the daily operations of native American tribes and a source of income to tens of thousands of native Americans." *Id.*, at 5. Given the history of governmental mismanagement of Indian trust funds, application of the fiduciary exception is, if anything, even more important in this context than in the private trustee context. The majority's refusal to apply the fiduciary exception in this case deprives the Nation—as well as the Indian tribes in the more than 90 cases currently pending in the federal courts involving claims of tribal trust mismanagement—of highly relevant information going directly to the merits of whether the Government properly fulfilled its fiduciary duties. Its holding only further exacerbates the concerns expressed by many about the lack of adequate oversight and accountability that has marked the Government's handling of Indian trust fund accounts for decades.

* * * By rejecting the Nation's claim on the ground that it fails to identify a specific statutory right to the communications at issue, the majority effectively embraces an approach espoused by prior dissents that rejects the role of common-law principles altogether in the Indian trust context. Its decision to do so in a case involving only a narrow evidentiary issue is wholly unnecessary and, worse yet, risks further diluting the Government's fiduciary obligations in a manner that Congress clearly did not intend and that would inflict serious harm on the already-frayed relationship between the United States and Indian tribes. Because there is no warrant in precedent or reason for reaching that result, I respectfully dissent.

NOTES

1.   What remains of the United States' "general" trust obligations to Indian tribes and Indian people? Does Justice Sotomayor's dissent, which characterizes the majority's view of the trust relationship as one that "must be set forth expressly in a specific statute or regulation," give notice of the end of the trust relationship as we know it? Recall Justice Thomas' dissent in *White Mountain*, where he asserted that the "general" trust relationship is defined in the earliest Supreme Court cases: "We have recognized a general trust relationship since 1831. *Cherokee Nation v. Georgia*, 5 Pet. 1, 16, 8 L.Ed. 25 (1831) (characterizing the relationship between Indian tribes and the United States as *"a ward to his guardian"*) * * * ." 537 U.S. 465, 474 n.3 (2003) (emphasis added).

2.   The *Jicarilla* decision generated an unusual amount of national press coverage. *E.g.*, Andrew Cohen, *You Can't Verify the Trust, Supreme Court Tells the Apache Nation*, The Atlantic, June 13, 2011 ("[T]he law may call the government a "trustee" over Indian tribes and may require the feds from time to time to undertake certain fiduciary obligations on behalf of the various Nations. But when push comes to shove, the law only rarely is going to force the feds to do something they don't want to do in the first place for reasons of their own. Where, as here, a Tribe comes to court looking for monetary damages, well, you get a 7–1 ruling from the Court that transcends traditional ideological lines.").

3.   In a case decided earlier in the 2010 Term, *United States v. Tohono O'odham Nation*, 131 S.Ct. 1723 (2011), the Supreme Court held that tribal money claims for breach of trust may not be brought in the Court of Federal Claims under 28 U.S.C. § 1500 where the tribe also has sued in federal district court for a trust accounting.

2. EXECUTIVE AGENCY CONFLICTS IN THE ADMINISTRATION OF THE FEDERAL TRUST RESPONSIBILITY TO INDIANS

Indian trust issues have also arisen with respect to federal agencies other than the BIA. The Department of the Interior oversees several agencies charged with administering the federal government's public land and resource management responsibilities. There are numerous examples of conflicts between Indian interests and other Interior agencies. The Bureau of Mines, attempting to develop helium for national military purposes, was found liable for withholding information from the Navajo Tribe concerning one of the tribe's mineral leases. Navajo Tribe of Indians v. United States, 364 F.2d 320 (Ct.Cl.1966). A variety of other conflicts between the national interest and Indian interests have arisen, not always with relief for the Indian parties. The Bureau of Land Management has been a competitor with tribes for title to public domain lands. See, e.g., United States v. Dann, 470 U.S. 39 (1985), page 312, supra. The National Park Service and the Fish and Wildlife Service have often opposed Indian hunting and fishing rights on lands they managed. The Bureau of Reclamation, which has developed large water projects across the West, has effectively represented a non-Indian constituency against the tribes in the competition for western water. See the statement by the National Water Commission, page 877, infra. The Office of the Solicitor, general counsel to the Department, is in the near-impossible position of reconciling the trust duty to Indians with the agency's responsibilities to the other agencies. On occasion, the Solicitor's Office has received heavy criticism. See the leading study, Reid Peyton Chambers, *Discharge of the Federal Trust Responsibility to Enforce Legal Claims of Indian Tribes: Case Studies of Bureaucratic Conflict of Interest,* Subcomm. on Administrative Practice and Procedure of the Senate Comm. on the Judiciary, 91st Cong., 2d Sess. (Comm.Print.1971).

The Forest Service, in the Department of Agriculture, and the Defense Department are other federal agencies with substantial public land management duties. The United States Department of Justice likewise has been criticized for its practice of representing opposing federal and tribal interests simultaneously. See Ann C. Juliano, *Conflicted Justice: The Department of Justice's Conflict of Interest in Representing Native American Tribes*, 37 Ga.L.Rev. 1307 (2003).

PYRAMID LAKE PAIUTE TRIBE OF INDIANS V. MORTON

United States District Court, District of Columbia, 1972.
354 F.Supp. 252.

GESELL, DISTRICT JUDGE.

[Pyramid Lake is located 20 miles northeast of Reno, Nevada, within the reservation boundaries of the Pyramid Lake Tribe of Paiute Indians. Derby Dam was built in 1905 as part of a federal water development project intended to benefit non-Indian irrigators. The dam diverts water from the Truckee River, which feeds Pyramid Lake, to lands irrigated by the Newlands Reclamation Project. With its only source of water diminished, the lake level steadily dropped over the decades, and large expanses of former lake bottom became exposed. The impacts on the lake led to the destruction of Pyramid Lake's once thriving fishery, which had been relied on traditionally by the tribe as a primary food source.]

This is an action by a recognized Indian tribe challenging a regulation issued by the Secretary of the Interior. The matter came before the Court for trial without a jury following an extended period of pretrial activity during which issues were narrowed and efforts to resolve the controversy by negotiation failed. Claiming that the regulation should be set aside as arbitrary, capricious, and an abuse of the Secretary's authority, the Tribe invokes applicable provisions of the Administrative Procedure Act, 5 U.S.C. § 706. A declaration of rights and affirmative injunctive relief is also sought on the ground the Secretary has unlawfully withheld and unreasonably delayed required actions, 5 U.S.C. § 706(1).

* * *

The regulation was signed by the Secretary on September 14, 1972, appears in the Federal Register, 37 Fed.Reg. 19838, and became effective November 1, 1972. It is designed to implement pre-existing general regulations by establishing the basis on which water will be provided during the succeeding twelve months to the Truckee-Carson Irrigation District, which is located in Churchill County, Nevada, some 50 miles east of Reno. The Tribe contends that the regulation delivers more water to the

District than required by applicable court decrees and statutes, and improperly diverts water that otherwise would flow into nearby Pyramid Lake located on the Tribe's reservation.

This Lake has been the Tribe's principal source of livelihood. Members of the Tribe have always lived on its shores and have fished its waters for food. Following directives of the Department of Interior in 1859, which were confirmed by Executive Order signed by President Grant in 1874, the Lake, together with land surrounding the Lake and the immediate valley of the Truckee River which feeds into the Lake, have been reserved for the Tribe and set aside from the public domain. The area has been consistently recognized as the Tribe's aboriginal home.

Recently, the United States, by original petition in the Supreme Court of the United States, filed September, 1972, claims the right to use of sufficient water of the Truckee River for the benefit of the Tribe to fulfill the purposes for which the Indian Reservation was created, "including the maintenance and preservation of Pyramid Lake and the maintenance of the lower reaches of the Truckee as a natural spawning ground for fish and other purposes beneficial to and satisfying the needs" of the Tribe. United States v. States of Nevada and California.

* * * The area involved is a water shortage area characterized by seasonal and yearly variations in available supply. Beneficial irrigation for farming and other uses within the District are accommodated through some 600 miles of main water ditches and drains and the water is ultimately parcelled out through 1,500 delivery points. The water fed into this system comes from the Carson River following storage in Lahontan Reservoir and by diversion of water from the Truckee River at Derby Dam where it passes through the Truckee Canal to be stored in the Lahontan Reservoir for subsequent or simultaneous release. The Secretary entered into a contract with the District in 1926 and this contract is still in effect.

* * * [A]ny water diverted from the Truckee at Derby Dam for the District is thereby prevented in substantial measure from flowing further north into Pyramid Lake. The Lake is a unique natural resource of almost incomparable beauty. It has no outflow, and as a desert lake depends largely on Truckee River inflow to make up for evaporation and other losses. It is approximately five miles wide and twenty-five miles long and now has a maximum depth of 335 feet. Although the Lake has risen a few feet in recent years, it has dropped more than 70 feet since 1906. A flow of 385,000 acre feet of water per year from the Truckee River into the Lake is required merely to maintain its present level. The decreased level and inflow have had the effect of making fish native to the Lake endangered protected species, and have unsettled the erosion and salinity balance of

the Lake to a point where the continued utility of the Lake as a useful body of water is at hazard.[8]

The regulation under attack is the most recent of a series of regulations issued from year to year since 1967 pursuant to general policies established by the Secretary. The Tribe contends that the Secretary's action is an arbitrary abuse of discretion in that the Secretary has ignored his own guidelines and failed to fulfill his trust responsibilities to the Tribe by illegally and unnecessarily diverting water from Pyramid Lake.

The focus of the inquiry has been to determine whether the 378,000 acre feet of water which the regulation contemplates will be diverted from the Truckee River at Derby Dam may be justified on a rational basis. This determination must be made in the light of three major factors which necessarily control the Secretary's action: namely, the Secretary's contract with the District, certain applicable court decrees, and his trust responsibilities to the Tribe. The Secretary and the Tribe are in substantial agreement that these are the factors to be weighed. The issue, therefore, comes down to whether or not the Secretary's resolution of conflicting demands created by these factors was effectuated arbitrarily rather than in the sound exercise of discretion.

The Court has carefully reviewed the processes by which the Secretary arrived at the disputed regulation. The Secretary had before him various written recommendations from interested agencies and experts, including responsible expert studies presented by the Tribe. There was a wide variation in these recommendations suggesting diversion of water in varying amounts ranging from 287,000 acre feet to 396,000 acre feet. All purported to be made on the basis of guidelines and policies previously set by the Secretary. After reviewing these written submissions, the Secretary conferred with the Assistant Secretary for Water and Power Resources (with authority over the Bureau of Reclamation) and the Assistant Secretary for Public Land Management (with authority over Indian Affairs) and made what one of these Assistants characterized as a "judgment call." * * *

Furthermore, while the Secretary's good faith is not in question, his approach to the difficult problem confronting him misconceived the legal requirements that should have governed his action. A "judgment call" was simply not legally permissible. The Secretary's duty was not to determine a basis for allocating water between the District and the Tribe in a manner that hopefully everyone could live with for the year ahead. This suit was pending and the Tribe had asserted well-founded rights. The burden rested

---

[8]   Native fish which naturally spawn in the Truckee can no longer do this and the Lake must be stocked at least until 1974 when construction to permit the fish again to pass into the river for spawning is to be completed.

on the Secretary to justify any diversion of water from the Tribe with precision. It was not his function to attempt an accommodation.

In order to fulfill his fiduciary duty, the Secretary must insure, to the extent of his power, that all water not obligated by court decree or contract with the District goes to Pyramid Lake. The United States, acting through the Secretary of Interior, "has charged itself with moral obligations of the highest responsibility and trust. Its conduct, as disclosed in the acts of those who represent it in dealings with the Indians, should therefore be judged by the most exacting fiduciary standards."

* * *

The Secretary was obliged to formulate a closely developed regulation that would preserve water for the Tribe. He was further obliged to assert his statutory and contractual authority to the fullest extent possible to accomplish this result. Difficult as this process would be, and troublesome as the repercussions of his actions might be, the Secretary was required to resolve the conflicting claims in a precise manner that would indicate the weight given each interest before him. Possible difficulties ahead could not simply be blunted by a "judgment call" calculated to placate temporarily conflicting claims to precious water. The Secretary's action is therefore doubly defective and irrational because it fails to demonstrate an adequate recognition of his fiduciary duty to the Tribe. This also is an abuse of discretion and not in accordance with law.

The record before the Court clearly establishes the underlying defects and arbitrary nature of the challenged regulation. The Secretary erred in two significant respects. First, he disregarded interrelated court decrees, and, second, he failed to exercise his authority to prevent unnecessary waste within the District. The effect of this is to deprive the Tribe of water without legal justification. * * * [Two interrelated Nevada District Court decrees, the *Orr Ditch* and *Alpine* decrees, governed the allocation of water for beneficial uses in the irrigation district. About two-thirds of the district's water was covered by the *Alpine* decree that allowed a maximum of 2.92 acre-feet of water per acre of land, while the *Orr Ditch* decree allowed 4.5 acre-feet per acre.] * * * The evidence demonstrates conclusively that the Secretary formulated the regulation by totally ignoring the Alpine decree and must have reached his calculations by relying solely on larger quantities provided by the Orr Water Ditch decree.

In addition, the evidence conclusively showed that the regulation is wholly inadequate to prevent waste within the District, causing substantial and wholly unnecessary diversion of water from the Truckee River to the obvious detriment of the Tribe. It was amply demonstrated that water could be conserved for Pyramid Lake without offending existing decrees or contractual rights of the District through better management which would prevent unnecessary waste. * * *

Under the contract between the Secretary and the District the Secretary has the right to require the District to conduct its affairs in a non-wasteful manner but no such action was taken or is contemplated in the regulation. * * *

* * *

Accordingly, the Court directs that on or before January 1, 1973, the Secretary shall submit to this Court a proposed amended regulation which is in conformity with the findings of fact and conclusions of law set forth in this Memorandum Opinion. The amendment shall provide, among other things, an effective means to measure water use, to minimize unnecessary waste, to end delivery of water within the District to land not entitled under the decrees, and to assure compliance by the District. Proper weight shall be given to both the Orr Water Ditch and Alpine decrees and the amount of water diverted shall be wholly consistent with the Secretary's fiduciary duty to the Tribe.

* * *

In the event the amended regulation fails to assure at least the delivery of 385,000 acre feet of water to Pyramid Lake, the Secretary shall accompany the regulation with a full, detailed, factual statement of the reasons why this result has not been achieved * * * .

* * *

NOTES

1.   After the decision in *Pyramid Lake* the Secretary of the Interior failed to issue new regulations that would sufficiently limit the amount of Truckee River water that could be diverted to the Newlands Reclamation Project. The judge ultimately adopted regulations proposed by the tribe that would protect the fishery. When the operators of the reclamation project, the Truckee-Carson Irrigation District (TCID), refused to comply with the new regulations, the Secretary terminated the operating contract with TCID. In 1974, the district sued the Secretary to set aside the regulations and to prevent termination of the contract. The tribe intervened in the case. Ten years later, the Ninth Circuit upheld the Secretary's action. Truckee-Carson Irrig. Dist. v. Secretary of Department of Interior, 742 F.2d 527 (9th Cir.1984). The tribe also prevailed in litigation upholding the Secretary's decision to operate Stampede Dam mainly to protect the cui-ui and Lahontan cutthroat trout, now both protected by the Endangered Species Act, rather than to provide water for consumptive use. Carson-Truckee Water Conservancy Dist. v. Clark, 741 F.2d 257 (9th Cir.1984), cert. denied 470 U.S. 1083 (1985).

2.   The tribe lost, however, in perhaps the most significant case in the flurry of litigation that followed *Pyramid Lake,* supra. In his opinion, Judge Gesell ruled that the Secretary should assume that the so-called *Orr Ditch* decree, which purported to adjudicate all water rights to the Truckee River,

was invalid as to the tribe. The *Orr Ditch* litigation, filed in 1913 and made final in 1944, had awarded the tribe no reserved water rights for fisheries purposes. Since there was a substantial question as to the applicability of the *Orr Ditch* decree, Judge Gesell reasoned that the Secretary should give the benefit of the doubt to the tribe.

The tribe and the United States filed suit to set aside the *Orr Ditch* decree. The Supreme Court, reversing the Ninth Circuit, held that the attack was barred by *res judicata.* Nevada v. United States, 463 U.S. 110 (1983), page 864, infra. The opinion emphasized the importance of the policy of finality embedded in the *res judicata* doctrine, saying that "[t]he policies advanced by the doctrine of *res judicata* perhaps are at their zenith in cases concerning real property, land, and water." Id. at 129 n. 10. The lower court opinion had set out in considerable detail the facts concerning the conflict of interest in the *Orr Ditch* litigation; the United States Attorney had represented both the tribe and the planned Newlands Reclamation Project, the tribe's chief competitor for water, which was awarded extensive water rights in the *Orr Ditch* decree. Nevertheless, the Court, in an opinion by Justice Rehnquist, found that both the tribe and the United States, as trustee, were barred by *res judicata* from reopening the litigation:

> Both the briefs of the parties and the opinion of the Court of Appeals focus their analysis of *res judicata* on provisions relating to the relationship between private trustees and fiduciaries, especially those governing a breach of duty by the fiduciary to the beneficiary. While these undoubtedly provide useful analogies in a case such as this, they cannot be regarded as finally dispositive of the issues. This Court has long recognized "the distinctive obligation of trust incumbent by the Government" in its dealings with Indian tribes, see, e.g., Seminole Nation v. United States, 316 U.S. 286, 296 (1942). These concerns have been traditionally focused on the Bureau of Indian Affairs within the Department of the Interior.

> But Congress in its wisdom, when it enacted the Reclamation Act of 1902, required the Secretary of the Interior to assume substantial obligations with respect to the reclamation of arid lands in the western part of the United States. Additionally, in § 26 of the Act of April 21, 1904, ch. 1402, 33 Stat. 225, Congress provided for the inclusion of irrigable lands of the Pyramid Lake Indian Reservation within the Newlands Project, and further authorized the Secretary, after allotting five acres of such land to each Indian belonging to the Reservation, to reclaim and dispose of the remainder of the irrigable Reservation land to settlers under the Reclamation Act.

> Today, particularly from our vantage point nearly half a century after the enactment the Indian Reorganization Act of 1934, it may well appear that Congress was requiring the Secretary of the Interior to carry water on at least two shoulders when it delegated to him both

the responsibility for the supervision of the Indian tribes and the commencement of reclamation projects in areas adjacent to reservation lands. But Congress chose to do this, and it is simply unrealistic to suggest that the Government may not perform its obligation to represent Indian tribes in litigation when Congress has obliged it to represent other interests as well. In this regard, the Government cannot follow the fastidious standards of a private fiduciary, who would breach his duties to his single beneficiary solely by representing potentially conflicting interests without the beneficiary's consent. The Government does not "compromise" its obligation to one interest that Congress obliges it to represent by the mere fact that it simultaneously performs another task for another interest that Congress has obligated it by statute to do.

463 U.S. at 127–28.

After *Nevada*, classic trust principles applicable to a private trustee continue to apply without modification in situations such as *Seminole Nation*, page 361, supra, where the United States is holding funds for a tribe, a lesser standard necessarily applies to the Indian trust duty when the Secretary has to serve competing legitimate public interests. Cf. In re United States, 590 F.3d 1305 (Fed.Cir.2009) (fiduciary exception to attorney client privilege did not apply to tribe's request for discovery of documents from the United States where no competing governmental interest). How specific must Congress's directive to a federal official be for it to excuse the Secretary from fiduciary standards in protection of Indian lands and resources? Could a truly independent federal office be established that would realistically eliminate or ameliorate such conflicts?

3.　　The decision in *Nevada v. United States* undermines Judge Gesell's premise that the tribe could ultimately enforce extensive reserved water rights. Does Judge Gesell's reasoning, that the government is a trustee with special obligations to the tribe and that exacting judicial scrutiny is required concerning the ongoing administration of a multi-purpose federal project, still apply after the above-quoted language from *Nevada v. United States*? Does the Secretary, pursuant to this trust, have authority to take protective measures in favor of the tribe? Note that the tribe argued that the Secretary's regulations allowed more water to be delivered to the district than the earlier decrees actually required. See Truckee-Carson Irrig. Dist. v. Secretary of Department of Interior, supra, the 1984 decision upholding the operating criteria adopted by the Secretary of the Interior in response to Judge Gesell's opinion:

> The Secretary did not exceed his authority when he adopted the operating criteria. In the 1926 contract, the Secretary explicitly reserved the right to issue regulations governing the operation of the Newlands Project. This reservation allowed the Secretary to issue the regulation restricting the amount of water that would be diverted. Similarly, even if the operating criteria were more restrictive than similar conditions under the 1926 contract, this change was within the Secretary's authority.

The Secretary's promulgation of the operating criteria was neither arbitrary nor capricious. See 5 U.S.C. § 706(2)(A). The criteria were adopted under the direction of the *Tribe v. Morton* court after the court and the Secretary considered the Secretary's obligations to TCID, to the water rights' owners, and to the Tribe. See 364 F.Supp. at 255. After "consider[ing] whether the [promulgation of the operating criteria] was based on a consideration of the relevant factors and whether there has been a clear error of judgment," as required by Citizens to Preserve Overton Park, Inc. v. Volpe, 401 U.S. 402, 416 (1971), we cannot say that the promulgation of the operating criteria was arbitrary or capricious.

742 F.2d at 532.

4. The *Pyramid Lake* case marked an important departure in the type of relief available to Indians in lawsuits based on the federal trust obligation. Affirmative enforcement of federal fiduciary duties could be a significant means of protecting Indian rights and resources and is potentially more valuable to Indians than merely being able to sue for money damages long after rights have been lost. In *Judicial Enforcement of the Federal Trust Responsibility to Indians*, 27 Stan.L.Rev. 1213 (1975), Reid Chambers examined the issue of granting of equitable relief against the federal trustee:

If, as the *Cherokee* cases suggest, a chief objective of the trust responsibility is to protect tribal status as self-governing entities, executive extinguishment of the tribal land base diminishes the territory over which tribal authority is exercised and thereby imperils fulfillment of the guarantee of tribal political and cultural autonomy. If this is the correct interpretation of the trust responsibility, equitable relief in appropriate cases seems essential. Such relief is particularly vital to accommodate the conflicts between Indian trustee responsibilities and competing government projects that affect countless federal agencies.

Id. at 1248.

Chambers traces the "enduring teaching of the *Cherokee* cases"—the treaties contain a basic guarantee of the United States to protect the territorial and governmental integrity of the tribes—through two important early-20th century opinions, Lane v. Pueblo of Santa Rosa, 249 U.S. 110 (1919) (enjoining the Secretary of the Interior from disposing of tribal lands under the general public land law), and Cramer v. United States, 261 U.S. 219 (1923) (voiding a federal land patent issued nineteen years earlier, purporting to convey Indian lands to a railroad); and to modern cases such as *Pyramid Lake* and Manchester Band of Pomo Indians v. United States, 363 F.Supp. 1238 (N.D.Cal.1973) (imposing upon the BIA a duty to make trust funds productive of income).

Chambers acknowledges that this approach to the trust relationship has not always been followed by Congress and the courts: "The courts have upheld congressional power to terminate the trust relationship or constrict its purposes, and while the *Lone Wolf* doctrine seems questionable, it is unlikely to be overruled." Yet, according to Chambers, the different approaches to the purposes of the trust responsibility can be reconciled to permit judicial enforcement as long as a distinction is observed between executive and congressional action. "Reading all the cases together, the principle that emerges is that Congress intends specific adherence to the trust responsibility by executive officials unless it has expressly provided otherwise. Such a formulation preserves the role of Congress as the ultimate umpire of the purposes of the trust relationship while requiring strict executive compliance with the terms of the trust." Id. at 1248.

Under Chambers' distinction between congressional and executive accountability under the trust relationship administrative actions are not shielded by plenary power and are subject to judicial review under the provisions of the Administrative Procedure Act, 5 U.S.C.A. §§ 701–706. While criticizing general language in the cases about Congress' plenary power, Chambers concluded that "[t]his power of Congress recognized under the *Lone Wolf* rendition of the trust responsibility is manifestly awesome, perhaps unlimited. * * * For while courts recognize that Congress has a trust responsibility, they uniformly regard it as essentially a moral obligation, without justiciable standards for its enforcement." 27 Stan.L.Rev. at 1226–27. There are important procedural limitations on Congress: compensation must be paid for Fifth Amendment takings and Congress must clearly state any intended abridgements of treaty rights or other rights protected by the trust duty. But no substantive exercises of congressional power in Indian affairs have ever been struck down.

5.   Being able to rely upon a trustee to bring litigation, as the Pyramid Lake tribe was able to do in many of the cases filed after Judge Gesell's opinion, is an important asset in itself. This is especially true when the trustee has the wealth and litigation advantages of the federal government. The United States represents tribes in numerous cases but courts have seldom ordered the government to undertake representation after it has declined to do so. One federal law states: "In all States and territories where there are reservations or allotted Indians, the United States Attorney shall represent them in all suits at law and in equity." 25 U.S.C.A. § 175. In spite of the mandatory tone of the statute, courts have generally ruled that it imposes a discretionary duty in cases where the government has a potential conflict of interest.

Congress has explicitly conferred jurisdiction on the district courts over federal question actions brought by any "Indian tribe or band with a governing body duly recognized by the Secretary of the Interior * * * " 28 U.S.C.A. § 1362. Today, when major cases are brought by the United States as trustee, the affected tribe usually will join as a co-plaintiff or intervenor.

An extensive study of the modern role of the trust doctrine can be found in two companion articles by Mary Christina Wood, *Indian Land and the Promise of Native Sovereignty: The Trust Doctrine Revisited*, 1994 Utah L.Rev. 1471, and *Protecting the Attributes of Native Sovereignty: A New Trust*

Paradigm for Federal Actions Affecting Tribal Lands and Resources, 1995 Utah L.Rev. 109.

3. CONGRESSIONAL ACCOUNTABILITY UNDER THE TRUST RELATIONSHIP

UNITED STATES V. SIOUX NATION OF INDIANS

Supreme Court of the United States, 1980.
448 U.S. 371, 100 S.Ct. 2716, 65 L.Ed.2d 844.

MR. JUSTICE BLACKMUN delivered the opinion of the Court.

This case concerns the Black Hills of South Dakota, the Great Sioux Reservation, and a colorful, and in many respects tragic, chapter in the history of the Nation's West.

* * *

For over a century now the Sioux Nation has claimed that the United States unlawfully abrogated the Fort Laramie Treaty of April 29, 1868, 15 Stat. 635, in Art. II of which the United States pledged that the Great Sioux Reservation, including the Black Hills, would be "set apart for the absolute and undisturbed use and occupation of the Indians herein named." *Id.*, at 636. The Fort Laramie Treaty was concluded at the culmination of the Powder River War of 1866–1867, a series of military engagements in which the Sioux tribes, led by their great chief, Red Cloud, fought to protect the integrity of earlier-recognized treaty lands from the incursion of white settlers.

The Fort Laramie Treaty included several agreements central to the issues presented in this case. First, it established the Great Sioux Reservation, a tract of land [comprising most of South Dakota west of the Missouri River] in addition to certain reservations already existing east of the Missouri. The United States "solemnly agree[d]" that no unauthorized persons "shall ever be permitted to pass over, settle upon, or reside in [this] territory." *Ibid.*

* * *

Fourth, Art. XII of the treaty provided:

No treaty for the cession of any portion or part of the reservation herein described which may be held in common shall be of any validity or force as against the said Indians, unless executed and signed by at least three fourths of all the adult male Indians, occupying or interested in the same. *Ibid.*

The years following the treaty brought relative peace to the Dakotas, an era of tranquility that was disturbed, however, by renewed speculation that the Black Hills, which were included in the Great Sioux Reservation, contained vast quantities of gold and silver. In 1874 the Army planned and undertook an exploratory expedition into the Hills, both for the purpose of establishing a military outpost from which to control those Sioux who had not accepted the terms of the Fort Laramie Treaty, and for the purpose of investigating "the country about which dreamy stories have been told." D. Jackson, Custer's Gold 14 (1966) (quoting the 1874 annual report of Lieutenant General Philip H. Sheridan, as Commander of the Military Division of the Missouri, to the Secretary of War). Lieutenant Colonel George Armstrong Custer led the expedition of close to 1,000 soldiers and teamsters, and a substantial number of military and civilian aides. Custer's journey began at Fort Abraham Lincoln on the Missouri River on July 2, 1874. By the end of that month they had reached the Black Hills, and by mid-August had confirmed the presence of gold fields in that region. The discovery of gold was widely reported in newspapers across the country. Custer's florid descriptions of the mineral and timber resources of the Black Hills, and the land's suitability for grazing and cultivation, also received wide circulation, and had the effect of creating an intense popular demand for the "opening" of the Hills for settlement. The only obstacle to "progress" was the Fort Laramie Treaty that reserved occupancy of the Hills to the Sioux.

* * *

* * * [T]he Secretary of the Interior, in the spring of 1875, appointed a commission to negotiate with the Sioux. The commission was headed by William B. Allison. The tribal leaders of the Sioux were aware of the mineral value of the Black Hills and refused to sell the land for a price less than $70 million. The commission offered the Indians an annual rental of $400,000, or payment of $6 million for absolute relinquishment of the Black Hills. The negotiations broke down.

In the winter of 1875–1876, many of the Sioux were hunting in the unceded territory north of the North Platte River, reserved to them for that purpose in the Fort Laramie Treaty. On December 6, 1875, for reasons that are not entirely clear, the Commissioner of Indian Affairs sent instructions to the Indian agents on the reservation to notify those hunters that if they did not return to the reservation agencies by January 31, 1876, they would be treated as "hostiles." Given the severity of the winter, compliance with these instructions was impossible. On February 1, the Secretary of the Interior nonetheless relinquished jurisdiction over all hostile Sioux, including those Indians exercising their treaty-protected hunting rights, to the War Department. The Army's campaign against the "hostiles" led to Sitting Bull's notable victory over Custer's forces at the battle of the Little Big Horn on June 25. That victory, of course, was short-lived, and those Indians who surrendered to the Army were returned to the reservation, and deprived of their weapons and horses, leaving them completely dependent for survival on rations provided them by the Government.

In the meantime, Congress was becoming increasingly dissatisfied with the failure of the Sioux living on the reservation to become self-sufficient.[11] The Sioux' entitlement to subsistence rations under the terms of the Fort Laramie Treaty had expired in 1872. Nonetheless, in each of the two following years, over $1 million was appropriated for feeding the Sioux. In August 1876, Congress enacted an appropriations bill providing that "hereafter there shall be no appropriation made for the subsistence" of the Sioux, unless they first relinquished their rights to the hunting grounds outside the reservation, ceded the Black Hills to the United States, and reached some accommodation with the Government that would be calculated to enable them to become self-supporting. Act of Aug. 15, 1876, 19 Stat. 176, 192. Toward this end, Congress requested the President to appoint another commission to negotiate with the Sioux for the cession of the Black Hills.

This commission, headed by George Manypenny, arrived in the Sioux country in early September and commenced meetings with the head men of the various tribes. The members of the commission impressed upon the Indians that the United States no longer had any obligation to provide them with subsistence rations. The commissioners brought with them the text of a treaty that had been prepared in advance. The principal provisions of this treaty were that the Sioux would relinquish their rights to the Black Hills and other lands west of the one hundred and third meridian, and their rights to hunt in the unceded territories to the north, in exchange for subsistence rations for as long as they would be needed to ensure the Sioux' survival. In setting out to obtain the tribes' agreement to this treaty, the commission ignored the stipulation of the Fort Laramie Treaty that any cession of the lands contained within the Great Sioux Reservation would have to be joined in by three-fourths of the adult males. Instead, the treaty was presented just to Sioux chiefs and their leading men. It was signed by only 10% of the adult male Sioux population.

Congress resolved the impasse by enacting the 1876 "agreement" into law as the Act of Feb. 28, 1877 (1877 Act). 19 Stat. 254. The Act had the effect of abrogating the earlier Fort Laramie Treaty, and of implementing

---

[11] * * *

One historian has described the ration provisions of the Fort Laramie Treaty as part of a broader reservation system designed by Congress to convert nomadic tribesmen into farmers. Hagan, The Reservation Policy: Too Little and Too Late, in Indian-White Relations: A Persistent Paradox 157–169 (J. Smith & R. Kvasnicka, eds., 1976). In words applicable to conditions on the Sioux Reservation during the years in question, Professor Hagan stated:

* * *

"The quantity of food supplied by the government was never sufficient for a full ration, and the quality was frequently poor. * * *

"That starvation and near-starvation conditions were present on some of the sixty-odd reservations every year for the quarter century after the Civil War is manifest." *Id.*, at 161 (footnotes omitted).

the terms of the Manypenny Commission's "agreement" with the Sioux leaders.

The passage of the 1877 Act legitimized the settlers' invasion of the Black Hills, but throughout the years it has been regarded by the Sioux as a breach of this Nation's solemn obligation to reserve the Hills in perpetuity for occupation by the Indians. One historian of the Sioux Nation commented on Indian reaction to the Act in the following words:

> "The Sioux thus affected have not gotten over talking about that treaty yet, and during the last few years they have maintained an organization called the Black Hills Treaty Association, which holds meetings each year at the various agencies for the purpose of studying the treaty with the intention of presenting a claim against the government for additional reimbursements for the territory ceded under it. Some think that Uncle Sam owes them about $9,000,000 on the deal, but it will probably be a hard matter to prove it." F. Fiske, The Taming of the Sioux 132 (1917).

Fiske's words were to prove prophetic.

* * *

[In 1920 Congress passed a special jurisdictional act under which the Sioux brought suit in the Court of Claims alleging that by the 1877 Act the government had taken the Black Hills without just compensation in violation of the Fifth Amendment. The court dismissed the claim in 1942 saying that it was a moral claim not covered by the just compensation clause and not authorized by the jurisdictional statute.

After Congress established the Indian Claims Commission in 1946, the tribe again raised the Black Hills claim. The Commission allowed them to reopen the case because the dismissal had been caused partly by the failings of their attorney in the earlier case. The Commission found that the 1877 Act constituted a taking under the Fifth Amendment to the Constitution and that the Black Hills had been acquired through unfair and dishonorable dealings. It ruled that the Indians were entitled to $17.55 million for the land and gold taken. On appeal the Court of Claims held that the taking claim was barred by the *res judicata* effect of the 1942 decision. The damage award stood, nevertheless, because only the decision on the taking claim was appealed by the government. Under cases construing the 1946 Act, only a taking (as opposed to relief based on the statutory "fair and honorable dealings" cause of action) would entitle the Sioux to interest on the damages award—another approximately $90 million.

In 1978, while the case was before the Commission on remand, Congress passed a statute allowing the Court of Claims to review the taking claim without regard to the defenses of *res judicata* and collateral estoppel. The Court of Claims found that there had been a taking and that the tribe was entitled to recover the principal sum with annual interest at 5% since 1877. The Supreme Court granted the United States' petition for certiorari.]

* * *

In reaching its conclusion that the 1877 Act effected a taking of the Black Hills for which just compensation was due the Sioux under the Fifth Amendment, the Court of Claims relied upon the "good faith effort" test developed in its earlier decision in *Three Tribes of Fort Berthold Reservation v. United States*, 182 Ct. Cl. 543, 390 F. 2d 686 (1968). The *Fort Berthold* test had been designed to reconcile two lines of cases decided by this Court that seemingly were in conflict. The first line, exemplified by *Lone Wolf v. Hitchcock*, 187 U. S. 553 (1903), recognizes "that Congress possesse[s] a paramount power over the property of the Indians, by reason of its exercise of guardianship over their interests, and that such authority might be implied, even though opposed to the strict letter of a treaty with the Indians." Id., at 565. The second line, exemplified by the more recent decision in *Shoshone Tribe v. United States*, 299 U. S. 476 (1937), concedes Congress' paramount power over Indian property, but holds, nonetheless, that "[t]he power does not extend so far as to enable the Government 'to give the tribal lands to others, or to appropriate them to its own purposes, without rendering, or assuming an obligation to render, just compensation.' " Id., at 497 (quoting *United States v. Creek Nation*, 295 U. S. 103, 110 (1935)). In *Shoshone Tribe*, Mr. Justice Cardozo, in speaking for the Court, expressed the distinction between the conflicting principles in a characteristically pithy phrase: "Spoliation is not management." 299 U. S., at 498.

The *Fort Berthold* test distinguishes between cases in which one or the other principle is applicable:

"It is obvious that Congress cannot simultaneously (1) act as trustee for the benefit of the Indians, exercising its plenary powers over the Indians and their property, as it thinks is in their best interests, and (2) exercise its sovereign power of eminent domain, taking the Indians' property within the meaning of the Fifth Amendment to the Constitution. In any given situation in which Congress has acted with regard to Indian people, it must have acted either in one capacity or the other. Congress can own two hats, but it cannot wear them both at the same time.

"Some guideline must be established so that a court can identify in which capacity Congress is acting. The following guideline would best give recognition to the basic distinction between the two types of congressional action: Where Congress makes a good faith effort to give the Indians the full value of the land and thus merely transmutes the property from land to money, there is no taking. This is a mere substitution of assets or change of form and is a traditional function of a trustee." 182 Ct. Cl., at 553, 390 F. 2d, at 691.

Applying the *Fort Berthold* test to the facts of this case, the Court of Claims concluded that, in passing the 1877 Act, Congress had not made a good-faith effort to give the Sioux the full value of the Black Hills. The principal issue presented by this case is whether the legal standard applied by the Court of Claims was erroneous.

* * *

The Government contends that the Court of Claims erred insofar as its holding that the 1877 Act effected a taking of the Black Hills was based on Congress' failure to indicate affirmatively that the consideration given the Sioux was of equivalent value to the property rights ceded to the Government. It argues that "the true rule is that Congress must be assumed to be acting within its plenary power to manage tribal assets if it reasonably can be concluded that the legislation was intended to promote the welfare of the tribe." Brief for United States 52. The Government derives support for this rule principally from this Court's decision in *Lone Wolf v. Hitchcock.*

* * *

* * * We must presume that Congress acted in perfect good faith in the dealings with the Indians of which complaint is made, and that the legislative branch of the government exercised its best judgment in the premises.* In any event, as Congress possessed full power in the matter, the judiciary cannot question or inquire into the motives which prompted the enactment of this legislation. If injury was occasioned, which we do not wish to be understood as implying, by the use made by Congress of its power, relief must be sought by an appeal to that body for redress and not to the courts. The legislation in question was constitutional.

Ibid. (Emphasis supplied.)

The Government relies on the italicized sentence in the quotation above to support its view "that Congress must be assumed to be acting within its plenary power to manage tribal assets if it reasonably can be concluded that the legislation was intended to promote the welfare of the tribe." Brief for United States 52. Several adjoining passages in the paragraph, however, lead us to doubt whether the *Lone Wolf* Court meant to state a general rule applicable to cases such as the one before us.

* * *

* * * [I]t seems significant that the views of the Court in *Lone Wolf* were based, in part, on a holding that "Congress possessed full power in the matter." Earlier in the opinion the Court stated: "Plenary authority over the tribal relations of the Indians has been exercised by Congress from the beginning, and the power has always been deemed a political one, not

subject to be controlled by the judicial department of the government." 187 U.S., at 565. Thus, it seems that the Court's conclusive presumption of congressional good faith was based in large measure on the idea that relations between this Nation and the Indian tribes are a political matter, not amenable to judicial review. That view, of course, has long since been discredited in takings cases, and was expressly laid to rest in *Delaware Tribal Business Comm. v. Weeks*, 430 U .S. 73, 84 (1977).[28]

* * * [F]ollowing up on the political question holding, the *Lone Wolf* opinion suggests that where the exercise of congressional power results in injury to Indian rights, "relief must be sought by an appeal to that body for redress and not to the courts." Unlike *Lone Wolf*, this case is one in which the Sioux have sought redress from Congress, and the Legislative Branch has responded by referring the matter to the courts for resolution. * * * Where Congress waives the Government's sovereign immunity, and expressly directs the courts to resolve a taking claim on the merits, there would appear to be far less reason to apply *Lone Wolf*'s principles of deference. See *United States v. Alcea Band of Tillamooks*, 329 U. S. 40, 46 (1946) (plurality opinion).

The foregoing considerations support our conclusion that the passage from *Lone Wolf* here relied upon by the Government has limited relevance to this case. More significantly, *Lone Wolf*'s presumption of congressional good faith has little to commend it as an enduring principle for deciding questions of the kind presented here. In every case where a taking of treaty-protected property is alleged, a reviewing court must recognize that tribal lands are subject to Congress' power to control and manage the tribe's affairs. But the court must also be cognizant that "this power to control and manage [is] not absolute. While extending to all appropriate measures for protecting and advancing the tribe, it [is] subject to limitations inhering in . . . a guardianship and to pertinent constitutional restrictions." *United States v. Creek Nation*, 295 U. S. 103, 109–110 (1935).

---

[28] For this reason, the Government does not here press *Lone Wolf* to its logical limits, arguing instead that its "strict rule" that the management and disposal of tribal lands is a political question, "has been relaxed in recent years to allow review under the Fifth Amendment rational-basis test." Brief for United States 55, n. 46. The Government relies on Delaware Tribal Business Comm. v. Weeks, 430 U. S. 73, at 84–85 (1977) and Morton v. Mancari, 417 U. S. 535, 555 (1974), as establishing a rational-basis test for determining whether Congress, in a given instance, confiscated Indian property or engaged merely in its power to manage and dispose of tribal lands in the Indians' best interests. But those cases, which establish a standard of review for judging the constitutionality of Indian legislation under the Due Process Clause of the Fifth Amendment, do not provide an apt analogy for resolution of the issue presented here—whether Congress' disposition of tribal property was an exercise of its power o eminent domain or its power of guardianship. As noted earlier,* the Sioux concede the constitutionality of Congress' unilateral abrogation of the Fort Laramie Treaty. They seek only a holding that the Black Hills "were appropriated by the United States in circumstances which involved an implied undertaking by it to make just compensation to the tribe." United States v. Creek Nation, 295 U. S. 103, 111 (1935). The rational-basis test proffered by the Government would be ill-suited for use in determining whether such circumstances were presented by the events culminating in the passage of the 1877 Act.

Accord: *Menominee Tribe v. United States*, 391 U. S. 404, 413 (1968); [citing additional authority].

As the Court of Claims recognized in its decision below, the question whether a particular measure was appropriate for protecting and advancing the tribe's interests, and therefore not subject to the constitutional command of the Just Compensation Clause, is factual in nature. The answer must be based on a consideration of all the evidence presented. We do not mean to imply that a reviewing court is to second-guess, from the perspective of hindsight, a legislative judgment that a particular measure would serve the best interests of the tribe. We do mean to require courts, in considering whether a particular congressional action was taken in pursuance of Congress' power to manage and control tribal lands for the Indians' welfare, to engage in a thoroughgoing and impartial examination of the historical record. A presumption of congressional good faith cannot serve to advance such an inquiry.

* * *

We turn to the question whether the Court of Claims' inquiry in this case was guided by an appropriate legal standard. We conclude that it was. In fact, we approve that court's formulation of the inquiry as setting a standard that ought to be emulated by courts faced with resolving future cases presenting the question at issue here:

> In determining whether Congress has made a good faith effort to give the Indians the full value of their lands when the government acquired [them], we therefore look to the objective facts as revealed by Acts of Congress, congressional committee reports, statements submitted to Congress by government officials, reports of special commissions appointed by Congress to treat with the Indians, and similar evidence relating to the acquisition. . . .

> The "good faith effort" and "transmutation of property" concepts referred to in *Fort Berthold* are opposite sides of the same coin. They reflect the traditional rule that a trustee may change the form of trust assets as long as he fairly (or in good faith) attempts to provide his ward with property of equivalent value. If he does that, he cannot be faulted if hindsight should demonstrate a lack of precise equivalence. On the other hand, if a trustee (or the government in its dealings with the Indians) does not attempt to give the ward the fair equivalent of what he acquires from him, the trustee to that extent has taken rather than transmuted the property of the ward. In other words, an essential element of the inquiry under the *Fort Berthold* guideline is determining the adequacy of the consideration the government gave for the Indian lands it acquired. That inquiry cannot be avoided by the government's simple assertion that it acted in good faith in its dealings with the Indians.

220 Ct. Cl., at 452, 601 F. 2d, at 1162.

* * *

In sum, we conclude that the legal analysis and factual findings of the Court of Claims fully support its conclusion that the terms of the 1877 Act did not effect "a mere change in the form of investment of Indian tribal property." *Lone Wolf v. Hitchcock*, 187 U. S., at 568. Rather, the 1877 Act effected a taking of tribal property, property which had been set aside for the exclusive occupation of the Sioux by the Fort Laramie Treaty of 1868. That taking implied an obligation on the part of the Government to make just compensation to the Sioux Nation, and that obligation, including an award of interest, must now, at last, be paid.

The judgment of the Court of Claims is affirmed.

It is so ordered.

MR. JUSTICE REHNQUIST, dissenting.

* * *

Although the Court refrains from so boldly characterizing its action, it is obvious from these facts that Congress has reviewed the decisions of the Court of Claims, set aside the judgment that no taking of the Black Hills occurred, set aside the judgment that there is no cognizable reason for relitigating this claim, and ordered a new trial. I am convinced that this is nothing other than an exercise of judicial power reserved to Art. III courts that may not be performed by the Legislative Branch under its Art. I authority.

Article III vests "the judicial Power . . . of the United States" in federal courts. Congress is vested by Art. I with *legislative* powers, and may not itself exercise an appellate-type review of judicial judgments in order to alter their terms, or to order new trials of cases already decided. * * *

* * * Congress has exceeded the legislative boundaries drawn by these cases and the Constitution and exercised judicial power in a case already decided by effectively ordering a new trial.

* * *

It is therefore apparent that Congress has accomplished more than a private litigant's attempted waiver, more than legislative control over the general jurisdiction of the federal courts, and more than the establishment of a new rule of law for a previously decided case. What Congress has done is uniquely judicial. It has reviewed a prior decision of an Art. III Court, eviscerated the finality of that judgment, and ordered a new trial in a pending case.

* * *

* * * There were undoubtedly greed, cupidity, and other less-than-admirable tactics employed by the Government during the Black Hills episode in the settlement of the West, but the Indians did not lack their share of villainy either. It seems to me quite unfair to judge by the light of "revisionist" historians or the mores of another era actions that were taken under pressure of time more than a century ago.

Different historians, not writing for the purpose of having their conclusions or observations inserted in the reports of congressional committees, have taken different positions than those expressed in some of the materials referred to in the Court's opinion. This is not unnatural, since history, no more than law, is not an exact (or for that matter an inexact) science.

* * *

Ray Billington, a senior research associate at the Huntington Library in San Marino, Cal., since 1963, and a respected student of the settlement of the American West, emphasized in his introduction to the book Soldier and Brave (National Park Service, U. S. Dept. of the Interior, 1963) that the confrontations in the West were the product of a long history, not a conniving Presidential administration:

> "Three centuries of bitter Indian warfare reached a tragic climax on the plains and mountains of America's Far West. Since the early seventeenth century, when Chief Opechancanough rallied his Powhatan tribesmen against the Virginia intruders on their lands, each advance of the frontier had been met with stubborn resistance. At times this conflict flamed into open warfare: in King Phillips' rebellion against the Massachusetts Puritans, during the French and Indian Wars of the eighteenth century, in Chief Pontiac's assault on his new British overlords in 1763, in Chief Tecumseh's vain efforts to hold back the advancing pioneers of 1812, and in the Black Hawk War. . . .

* * *

Another history highlights the cultural differences which made conflict and brutal warfare inevitable:

> "The Plains Indians seldom practiced agriculture or other primitive arts, but they were fine physical specimens; and in warfare, once they had learned the use of the rifle, [were] much more formidable than the Eastern tribes who had slowly yielded to the white man. Tribe warred with tribe, and a highly developed sign language was the only means of intertribal communication. The effective unit was the band or village of a few hundred souls, which might be seen in the course of its wanderings encamped by a watercourse with tipis erected; or pouring over the plain, women and children leading dogs and packhorses with their trailing travois, while gaily dressed braves loped ahead on horseback. They lived only for the day, recognized no rights of property,

robbed or killed anyone if they thought they could get away with
it, inflicted cruelty without a qualm, and endured torture without
flinching." S. Morison, The Oxford History of the American People
539–540 (1965).

That there was tragedy, deception, barbarity, and virtually every other
vice known to man in the 300-year history of the expansion of the original
13 Colonies into a Nation which now embraces more than three million
square miles and 50 States cannot be denied. But in a court opinion, as a
historical and not a legal matter, both settler and Indian are entitled to the
benefit of the Biblical adjuration: "Judge not, that ye be not judged."

NOTES

1.   Is history, in the context of modern litigation, subject to substantial
manipulation? To what extent should history be a source of law? A compelling
historical, social, and legal account of the United States' taking of *Paha Sapa*
(the Sioux name for the sacred Black Hills) can be found in John P. LaVelle,
Rescuing Paha Sapa: *Achieving Environmental Justice by Restoring the Great
Grasslands and Returning the Sacred Black Hills to the Great Sioux Nation*, 5
Great Plains Nat. Resources J. 42 (2001).

2.   Shortly after the decision, the Oglala Sioux Tribe, the largest of the
tribes in the Sioux Nation, brought suit challenging the legality of the taking
that was involved in *Sioux Nation.* The litigation sought to reject the damage
award and to restore the tribe's rights in the Black Hills based upon the
allegation that Congress had acted unconstitutionally in taking the Black
Hills. The action was dismissed on the ground that Congress had provided an
exclusive remedy for wrongful taking of Indian lands in passing the Indian
Claims Commission Act. Oglala Sioux Tribe v. United States, 650 F.2d 140 (8th
Cir.1981), cert. denied 455 U.S. 907 (1982).

3.   Congress's action in abrogating the Fort Laramie Treaty was
strikingly similar to its action in approving an agreement ceding Indian lands
without approval of three-fourths of the adult males in *Lone Wolf v. Hitchcock*,
page 212, supra. The Court stated in *Sioux Nation* that a principal holding in
Lone Wolf, that there is congressional power to abrogate Indian treaties, was
"not at issue." 448 U.S. at 411 n. 27. Has the rule of *Lone Wolf* nevertheless
been qualified?

4.   *Sioux Nation* also cited Delaware Tribal Business Committee v.
Weeks, 430 U.S. 73 (1977), as having "laid to rest" *Lone Wolf's* view "that
relations between this Nation and the Indian tribes are a political matter, not
amenable to judicial review." *Delaware Tribal Business Committee* involved a
challenge to congressional legislation excluding a group of non-federally
recognized Kansas Delaware Indians who had agreed to dissolve their
relations with the Delaware Nation under an 1866 treaty from the distribution
of an Indian Claims Commission judgment in favor of the modern day
descendants of members of the historical Delaware Nation. The Kansas
Delawares alleged that Congress' distribution of the award constituted a denial

of the equal protection of the laws guaranteed by the Due Process Clause of the Fifth Amendment. Justice Brennan's opinion for a unanimous Court rejected the argument of the federally recognized tribal groups favored by Congress' distribution plan that *Lone Wolf* precluded the Court from reviewing the legislation.

> The statement in *Lone Wolf* that the power of Congress "has always been deemed a political one, not subject to be controlled by the judicial department of the government," however pertinent to the question then before the Court of congressional power to abrogate treaties, has not deterred this Court, particularly in this day, from scrutinizing Indian legislation to determine whether it violates the equal protection component of the Fifth Amendment. *See, e.g., Morton v. Mancari.* "The power of Congress over Indian affairs may be of a plenary nature; but it is not absolute." *United States v. Alcea Band of Tillamooks,* 329 U.S. 40, 54 (1946) (plurality opinion).

Id. at 84.

CHAPTER SIX

TRIBAL SOVEREIGNTY AND THE
CHALLENGE OF NATION-BUILDING

■ ■ ■

American Indian tribes existed long before the arrival of European nations and the founding of the American Republic. After centuries of upheaval and repression in which most tribal governments often had no way to survive except by going underground, tribal nations are now embracing and asserting their sovereignty. Federal Indian law allows for space, albeit limited, for "reservation Indians to make their own laws and be ruled by them." Williams v. Lee, 358 U.S. 217, 220 (1959). Indian tribes retain inherent sovereignty that has not been extinguished by the United States or negotiated away by tribes in treaties and other agreements. In recent decades, Indian tribes have exercised this sovereignty by engaging in the difficult, arduous, and rewarding process of nation-building.

The United States' legal recognition of tribal sovereignty followed the leads of England, France, Holland, and Spain before it in acknowledging Indian tribes as nations. Whatever misunderstandings the new nation and the prior European colonial powers held about Indians, their treatment of the tribes as political entities capable of entering treaties set a pattern for their continuing recognition as sovereigns over their traditional lands.

Though the federal government often ignored or repressed the tribes, tribal sovereignty has survived in a relatively robust form throughout the history of federal Indian law and policy. The Marshall trilogy established that inherent tribal sovereign authority, coupled with federal authority, trumped state law producing a kind of pragmatic federalism. Further, federal Indian law recognizes and requires a form of dependence by Indian tribes upon the the United States for the protection of Indian lands and rights.

Indian tribal sovereignty remains a doctrine of considerable vitality because of its internal significance for tribal governments and the resulting external consequences for the states and for non-members of the tribe within Indian country. Defined by Chief Justice Marshall as "domestic dependent nations," Cherokee Nation v. Georgia, 30 U.S. 1, 17 (1831), Indian tribes have long been recognized under the principles of federal Indian law as possessing the right to self-government, free of most state law strictures over their own territory and members. Tribal sovereignty thus protects and affirms the right of tribes to exercise criminal and civil jurisdictional authority over their own members. By virtue of their inherent sovereignty, tribes, as recognized and affirmed by Congress, exercise criminal jurisdiction over non-member Indians on the reservation as well. In addition, the tribes have also been recognized as possessing a degree of civil jurisdictional authority over all nonmembers, Indian or non-Indian, who enter the reservation, and engage in certain proscribed forms of conduct.

As Professors Stephen Cornell and Joseph P. Kalt have demonstrated in their research on successful Indian country economic and community development, tribal governments and law-making institutions are flourishing throughout Indian country, mainly because of the commitment of Indians to one of the fundamental principles of federal Indian law, tribal sovereignty. Significantly, the most successful tribal nations are those that exercise what they describe as " 'de facto' sovereignty * * * [or] genuine decision-making control over the running of tribal affairs and the use of tribal resources" through these institutions. Stephen Cornell and Joseph P. Kalt, *Reloading the Dice: Improving the Chances for Economic Development on American Indian Reservations*, in What Can Tribes Do? Strategies and Institutions in American Indian Economic Development 14 (Stephen Cornell and Joseph P. Kalt, eds. 1992). Thus, the academic research of Cornell and Kalt simply confirms what the history of federal Indian law and policy has demonstrated time and time again. Indian tribes fight to protect and assert their inherent sovereignty as among the most important tools that they possess to address the challenges of Native nation building in the United States.

SECTION A. INHERENT TRIBAL SOVEREIGNTY

Federally recognized Indian tribes in the United States retain inherent sovereignty unless divested by consent or by Act of Congress. In general, tribal sovereignty includes the power of Indian tribes to govern Indian reservations and their members. Tribal sovereignty is not granted by the United States, or by treaty or statute, but instead flows from the status of Indian tribes as sovereigns that pre-existed the United States.

The Supreme Court first articulated the doctrine of retained sovereignty (or reserved rights) in the Marshall Trilogy, Johnson v. McIntosh, 21 U.S. 543 (1832); Cherokee Nation v. Georgia, 30 U.S. 1 (1831); and Worcester v. Georgia, 31 U.S. 515 (1832). There, the Supreme Court held that tribal sovereignty flows from the status of Indian tribes under international common law, recognized by the United States through hundreds of Indian treaties and federal statutes. Indian tribes are "domestic" nations, *Cherokee Nation*, 30 U.S. at 17. Domestic nationhood means that Indian tribes agreed to come under the protection of the United States, usually through the treaty process. Justice Thompson's dissent in

Cherokee Nation explicitly referenced international law in describing the status of Indian tribes: "Consequently, a weak state, that, in order to provide for its safety, places itself under the protection of a more powerful one, without stripping itself of the right of government and sovereignty, does not cease on this account to be placed among the sovereigns who acknowledge no other power. Tributary and feudatory states do not thereby cease to be sovereign and independent states, so long as self government, and sovereign and independent authority is left in the administration of the state." Id. at 53 (Thompson, J., dissenting). In *Worcester*, Chief Justice Marshall expressly adopted that framework in the majority opinion: "The [United States] receive the Cherokee nation into their favor and protection. The Cherokees acknowledge themselves to be under the protection of the United States, and of no other power. Protection does not imply the destruction of the protected." *Worcester*, 31 U.S. at 552. Instead, the federal government's duty of protection to Indian tribes expressly allows for the retention of inherent tribal sovereignty. Id. at 581–82 ("By various treaties, the Cherokees have placed themselves under the protection of the United States: they have agreed to trade with no other people, nor to invoke the protection of any other sovereignty. But such engagements do not divest them of the right of self government, nor destroy their capacity to enter into treaties or compacts.").

In numerous instances, the Supreme Court has acknowledged inherent tribal powers to prosecute crimes, e.g., Talton v. Mayes, 163 U.S. 376 (1896); tax, e.g., Merrion v. Jicarilla Apache Tribe, 455 U.S. 130 (1982); and determine tribal membership criteria, Santa Clara Pueblo v. Martinez, 436 U.S. 49 (1978). In the first edition of Cohen's Handbook on Federal Indian Law, Felix S. Cohen expressed comprehensively this theory of inherent sovereignty:

> Perhaps the most basic principle of all Indian law, supported by a host of decisions hereinafter analyzed, is the principle that those *powers which are lawfully vested in an Indian tribe are not, in general, delegated powers granted by express acts of Congress, but rather inherent powers of a limited sovereignty which has never been extinguished.* Each Indian tribe begins its relationship with the Federal Government as a sovereign power, recognized as such in treaty and legislation. The powers of sovereignty have been limited from time to time by special treaties and laws designed to take from the Indian tribes control of matters which in the judgment of Congress, these tribes could no longer be safely permitted to handle. The statutes of Congress, then, must be examined to determine the limitations of tribal sovereignty rather than to determine its sources or its positive content. What is not expressly limited remains within the domain of tribal sovereignty.

Felix S. Cohen, Handbook of Federal Indian Law 122 (1941 ed.).

This section of the book details the theory behind the inherent powers of Indian tribes. The following landmark decision involving the jurisdictional authority of the Navajo Nation's tribal court system helped launch what Professor Charles Wilkinson has called a distinctive "modern era of Indian law." Charles Wilkinson, American Indians, Time and the Law 1 (1987).

WILLIAMS V. LEE

Supreme Court of the United States, 1959.
358 U.S. 217, 79 S.Ct. 269, 3 L.Ed.2d 251.

MR. JUSTICE BLACK delivered the opinion of the Court.

Respondent, who is not an Indian, operates a general store in Arizona on the Navajo Indian Reservation under a license required by federal statute. He brought this action in the Superior Court of Arizona against petitioners, a Navajo Indian and his wife who live on the Reservation, to collect for goods sold them there on credit. Over petitioners' motion to dismiss on the ground that jurisdiction lay in the tribal court rather than in the state court, judgment was entered in favor of respondent. The Supreme Court of Arizona affirmed, holding that since no Act of Congress expressly forbids their doing so Arizona courts are free to exercise jurisdiction over civil suits by non-Indians against Indians though the action arises on an Indian reservation. Because this was a doubtful determination of the important question of state power over Indian affairs, we granted certiorari.

[The opinion describes the background of the decision in Worcester v. Georgia, 31 U.S. 515 (1832).] * * * Rendering one of his most courageous and eloquent opinions, Chief Justice Marshall held that Georgia's assertion of power was invalid. * * *

Despite bitter criticism and the defiance of Georgia which refused to obey this Court's mandate in Worcester the broad principles of that decision came to be accepted as law. Over the years this Court has modified these principles in cases where essential tribal relations were not involved and where the rights of Indians would not be jeopardized, but the basic policy of Worcester has remained. * * * Essentially, absent governing Acts of Congress, the question has always been whether the state action infringed on the right of reservation Indians to make their own laws and be ruled by them. Cf. Utah & Northern Railway v. Fisher, 116 U.S. 28.

Congress has also acted consistently upon the assumption that the States have no power to regulate the affairs of Indians on a reservation. To assure adequate government of the Indian tribes it enacted comprehensive statutes in 1834 regulating trade with Indians and organizing a Department of Indian Affairs. Not satisfied solely with centralized government of Indians, it encouraged tribal governments and courts to become stronger and more highly organized. See, e.g., the Wheeler-Howard Act, 25 U.S.C. §§ 476, 477. Congress has followed a policy calculated eventually to make all Indians full-fledged participants in American society. This policy contemplates criminal and civil jurisdiction over Indians by any State ready to assume the burdens that go with it as soon as the educational and economic status of the Indians permits the change without disadvantage to them. See H.R.Rep. No. 848, 83d Cong., 1st Sess. 3, 6, 7 (1953). Significantly, when Congress has wished the States to exercise this power it has expressly granted them the jurisdiction which *Worcester v. Georgia* had denied.

No departure from the policies which have been applied to other Indians is apparent in the relationship between the United States and the Navajos. On June 1, 1868, a treaty was signed between General William T. Sherman, for the United States, and numerous chiefs and headmen of the "Navajo nation or tribe of Indians." At the time this document was signed the Navajos were an exiled people, forced by the United States to live crowded together on a small piece of land on the Pecos River in eastern New Mexico, some 300 miles east of the area they had occupied before the coming of the white man. In return for their promises to keep peace, this treaty "set apart" for "their permanent home" a portion of what had been their native country, and provided that no one, except United States Government personnel, was to enter the reserved area. Implicit in these treaty terms, as it was in the treaties with the Cherokees involved in *Worcester v. Georgia*, was the understanding that the internal affairs of the Indians remained exclusively within the jurisdiction of whatever tribal government existed. Since then, Congress and the Bureau of Indian Affairs have assisted in strengthening the Navajo tribal government and its courts. The Tribe itself has in recent years greatly improved its legal system through increased expenditures and better-trained personnel. Today the Navajo Courts of Indian Offenses exercise broad criminal and civil jurisdiction which covers suits by outsiders against Indian defendants. No Federal Act has given state courts jurisdiction over such controversies. In a general statute Congress did express its willingness to have any State assume jurisdiction over reservation Indians if the State Legislature or the people vote affirmatively to accept such responsibility. [citing Public Law 280] To date, Arizona has not accepted jurisdiction, possibly because the people of the State anticipate that the burdens accompanying such power might be considerable.

There can be no doubt that to allow the exercise of state jurisdiction here would undermine the authority of the tribal courts over Reservation affairs and hence would infringe on the right of the Indians to govern themselves. It is immaterial that respondent is not an Indian. He was on the Reservation and the transaction with an Indian took place there. The cases in this Court have consistently guarded the authority of Indian governments over their reservations. Congress recognized this authority in the Navajos in the Treaty of 1868, and has done so ever since. If this power is to be taken away from them, it is for Congress to do it. Lone Wolf v. Hitchcock, 187 U.S. 553, 564–566.

Reversed.

NOTES

1. Professor Wilkinson described the historical context of this landmark decision as follows:

> The rendering of the *Williams* decision can fairly be set as a watershed for several reasons. For decades before, Indian law decisions had been rendered fitfully by the Supreme Court. The tribes and the federal government instituted few cases to establish or expand tribal powers. Most of the litigation to reach the Court during the twentieth century before 1959 arose out of disputes involving individual Indians or even non-Indians; as a result the decisions lacked the public law overtones of either the modern era or the nineteenth century. * * * After *Williams,* the pace of decisions began to accelerate, with the result that the Court has become more active in Indian law than in fields such as securities, bankruptcy, pollution control and international law.

Charles F. Wilkinson, American Indians, Time and the Law 1–2 (1987).

2. Justice Black cites the "courageous and eloquent" opinion of Chief Justice Marshall in *Worcester* as the source of the "basic policy" informing the infringement test announced by the Court in *Williams*: "Absent governing acts of Congress, the question has always been whether the state action infringed on the right of reservation Indians to make their own laws and be ruled by them." Did *Williams* depart from the basic *legal* analysis of tribal jurisdiction in *Worcester*? How would you state the *Williams* approach if you were an advocate asserting state jurisdiction over reservation Indians? Or if you were a tribal judge asserting exclusive tribal court civil adjudicatory jurisdiction over a nonmember on the reservation?

3. The *Williams* decision was a test case for the Navajo Nation. In 1957, the Arizona legislature introduced and nearly enacted legislation that would extend state law and state court jurisdiction into Navajo Indian country under Public Law 280, a federal statute enacted in 1953 that authorized state governments to assert criminal and civil jurisdiction over Indian reservations if they chose to do so—and without tribal consent. See Raymond D. Austin, Navajo Courts and Navajo Common Law: A Tradition of Tribal Self-Governance 26–27 (2009). The Navajo Tribal Council quickly formulated a strategy to preempt attempts by Arizona unilaterally to invoke Public Law 280.

> The strategy was pursued along two complimentary paths. First, the Navajo Nation tapped the federal courts to define its sovereign rights,

and second, the Navajo Nation took control of police and court functions—services typically provided by sovereigns—that were then under the administration of the Bureau of Indian Affairs.

Id. After Paul and Lorena Williams won their case before the Supreme Court, the Tenth Circuit granted the Navajo Nation a second critical victory in Native American Church v. Navajo Tribal Council, 272 F.2d 131 (10th Cir.1959) (holding that the First Amendment did not prohibit the Navajo legislature from enacting statutes banning the peyote). These two cases helped to lay the legal foundation for the establishment of the Navajo Nation's modern tribal judiciary, which took over the caseload from the Nation's CFR court on April 1, 1959. Austin, supra, at 27–28.

By the late 1960s and early 1970s, for the first time Indian country had begun to develop a significant capability for comprehensive legal reform. Most of the new attorneys were young lawyers in legal services firms. There was a good deal of interaction among the different offices, and one central priority became clear to both the lawyers and tribal leaders: it was imperative to establish clear legal rulings about the existence and extent of tribal sovereignty. Most basically, the sovereignty announced by Chief Justice Marshall in *Worcester v. Georgia* had to be reaffirmed by modern courts. *Williams v. Lee* definitely helped, but the legal doctrine needed to be expanded and the justification deepened. The idea gradually developed that, as a foundation stone, as something to build upon, a "bright line" rule needed to be established: state regulatory laws do not apply to reservation Indians. Then an opportunity presented itself at the Navajo reservation where the DNA-People's Legal Services firm was willing to press ahead with a test case. The amount in controversy was $16.20.

MCCLANAHAN V. ARIZONA STATE TAX COMMISSION

Supreme Court of the United States, 1973.
411 U.S. 164, 93 S.Ct. 1257, 36 L.Ed.2d 129.

MR. JUSTICE MARSHALL delivered the opinion of the Court.

* * *

I.

Appellant is an enrolled member of the Navajo tribe who lives on that portion of the Navajo Reservation located within the State of Arizona. Her complaint alleges that all her income earned during 1967 was derived from within the Navajo Reservation. [Appellant challenged the withholding of state income tax from her pay check, and the Arizona Court of Appeals rejected her claim.]

* * *

II.

* * *

The principles governing the resolution of this question are not new. On the contrary, "[t]he policy of leaving Indians free from state jurisdiction and control is deeply rooted in the Nation's history." Rice v. Olson, 324 U.S. 786, 789 (1945). This policy was first articulated by this Court 141 years ago [by] Mr. Chief Justice Marshall [in] Worcester v. Georgia, 6 Pet. 515, 557 (1832). * * *

* * *

This is not to say that the Indian sovereignty doctrine, with its concomitant jurisdictional limit on the reach of state law, has remained static during the 141 years since *Worcester* was decided. Not surprisingly, the doctrine has undergone considerable evolution in response to changed circumstances. * * *

Finally, the trend has been away from the idea of inherent Indian sovereignty as a bar to state jurisdiction and toward reliance on federal pre-emption. . . . The modern cases thus tend to avoid reliance on platonic notions of Indian sovereignty and to look instead to the applicable treaties and statutes which define the limits of state power. Compare, e.g., United States v. Kagama, 118 U.S. 375 (1886), with Kennerly v. District Court, 400 U.S. 423 (1971).

The Indian sovereignty doctrine is relevant, then, not because it provides a definitive resolution of the issues in this suit, but because it provides a backdrop against which the applicable treaties and federal statutes must be read. It must always be remembered that the various Indian tribes were once independent and sovereign nations, and that their claim to sovereignty long predates that of our own Government. Indians today are American citizens. They have the right to vote, to use state courts, and they receive some state services. But it is nonetheless still true, as it was in the last century, that "[t]he relation of the Indian tribes living within the borders of the United States * * * [is] an anomalous one and of a complex character * * * . They were, and always have been, regarded as having a semi-independent position when they preserved their tribal relations; not as States, not as nations, not as possessed of the full attributes of sovereignty, but as a separate people, with the power of regulating their internal and social relations, and thus far not brought under the laws of the Union or of the State within whose limits they resided." *United States v. Kagama*, 118 U.S., at 381–382.

III

When the relevant treaty and statutes are read with this tradition of sovereignty in mind, we think it clear that Arizona has exceeded its lawful authority by attempting to tax appellant. The beginning of our analysis must be with the treaty which the United States Government entered with the Navajo Nation in 1868. The agreement provided, in relevant part, that a prescribed reservation would be set aside "for the use and occupation of the Navajo tribe of Indians" and that "no persons except those herein so authorized to do, and except such officers, soldiers, agents, and employés of the government, or of the Indians, as may be authorized to enter upon Indian reservations in discharge of duties imposed by law, or the orders of the President, shall ever be permitted to pass over, settle upon, or reside in, the territory described in this article." 15 Stat. 668.

The treaty nowhere explicitly states that the Navajos were to be free from state law or exempt from state taxes. But the document is not to be read as an ordinary contract agreed upon by parties dealing at arm's length with equal bargaining positions. We have had occasion in the past to describe the circumstances under which the agreement was reached. "At the time this document was signed the Navajos were an exiled people, forced by the United States to live crowded together on a small piece of land on the Pecos River in eastern New Mexico, some 300 miles east of the area they had occupied before the coming of the white man. In return for their promises to keep peace, this treaty 'set apart' for 'their permanent home' a portion of what had been their native country." *Williams v. Lee*, 358 U.S., at 221.

It is circumstances such as these which have led this Court in interpreting Indian treaties, to adopt the general rule that "[d]oubtful expressions are to be resolved in favor of the weak and defenseless people who are the wards of the nation, dependent upon its protection and good faith." Carpenter v. Shaw, 280 U.S. 363, 367 (1930). When this canon of construction is taken together with the tradition of Indian independence described above, it cannot be doubted that the reservation of certain lands for the exclusive use and occupancy of the Navajos and the exclusion of non-Navajos from the prescribed area was meant to establish the lands as within the exclusive sovereignty of the Navajos under general federal supervision. It is thus unsurprising that this Court has interpreted the Navajo treaty to preclude extension of state law—including state tax law— to Indians on the Navajo Reservation. See Warren Trading Post Co. v. Arizona Tax Comm'n, 380 U.S., at 687, 690; *Williams v. Lee*, supra, at 221– 222.

* * *

IV

[The Court then rejected the State's claim that taxing individual Indians does not infringe on tribal sovereignty.]

Reversed.

NOTE

Is a state's taxation of income earned by a tribal member on the reservation always barred? Williams v. Lee, 358 U.S. 217 (1959), is sometimes credited with introducing the "infringement test" to federal Indian law, where state laws or regulations or taxes that "infringe" on tribal sovereignty are categorically barred. That categorical bar extended in *Williams* to stop state courts from asserting jurisdiction over a civil suit brought against tribal members for a case arising on Indian lands. In Oklahoma Tax Comm'n v. Sac and Fox Nation, 508 U.S. 114 (1993), the Supreme Court essentially restated *McClanahan* to stand for the proposition that a state is categorically barred from taxing on-reservation income of tribal members residing on trust land.

SECTION B. INHERENT TRIBAL SOVEREIGNTY AND THE CONSTITUTION

As a baseline, inherent tribal sovereignty flows from Indian tribes themselves. But due to misunderstandings about the federal government's duty of protection over Indian tribes, courts often assumed that tribal sovereignty is a "grant" from the United States to Indian tribes, or that Indian tribes were "arms" of the federal government. These assumptions were rampant during the 19th century and much of the 20th century, a period of federal coercion in Indian affairs, where tribal sovereignty appeared to exist at the sufferance of the United States.

The following leading cases establish that Indian sovereignty is not sourced from the federal government or the United States, but is inherent and independent from the United States Constitution's Bill of Rights.

TALTON V. MAYES

Supreme Court of the United States, 1896.
163 U.S. 376, 16 S.Ct. 986, 41 L.Ed. 196.

MR. JUSTICE WHITE, after stating the case, delivered the opinion of the court.

* * *

Appellant and the person he was charged with having murdered were both Cherokee Indians, and the crime was committed within the Cherokee territory. [The case was prosecuted in Cherokee tribal court.]

To bring himself within the statute, the appellant asserts, 1st, that the grand jury, consisting only of five persons, was not a grand jury within the contemplation of the Fifth Amendment to the Constitution, which it is asserted is operative upon the Cherokee nation in the exercise of its legislative authority as to purely local matters * * * .

By treaties and statutes of the United States the right of the Cherokee nation to exist as an autonomous body, subject always to the paramount authority of the United States, has been recognized. And from this fact there has consequently been conceded to exist in that nation power to make laws defining offences and providing for the trial and punishment of those who violate them when the offences are committed by one member of the tribe against another one of its members within the territory of the nation.

[The treaty of 1835 with the Cherokee Nation provided that tribal lands would never be included within any territory or state of the United States. This guarantee was reaffirmed in the treaty of 1868. The 1890 act establishing the Territory of Oklahoma provided that the Indian nations in the Indian Territory would retain exclusive jurisdiction over crimes committed by tribal members in Indian country. Thus the crime in question was not a federal offense.*]

* * *

The question, therefore, is, does the Fifth Amendment to the Constitution apply to the local legislation of the Cherokee nation so as to require all prosecutions for offences committed against the laws of that nation to be initiated by a grand jury organized in accordance with the provisions of that amendment. * * *

The case in this regard therefore depends upon whether the powers of local government exercised by the Cherokee nation are Federal powers created by and springing from the Constitution of the United States, and hence controlled by the Fifth Amendment to that Constitution, or whether they are local powers not created by the Constitution, although subject to its general provisions and the paramount authority of Congress. The repeated adjudications of this court have long since answered the former question in the negative. * * *

True it is that in many adjudications of this court the fact has been fully recognized, that although possessed of these attributes of local self government, when exercising their tribal functions, all such rights are subject to the supreme legislative authority of the United States. But the existence of the right in Congress to regulate the manner in which the local powers of the Cherokee nation shall be exercised does not render such local powers Federal powers arising from and created by the Constitution of the United States. It follows that as the powers of local self government enjoyed by the Cherokee nation existed prior to the Constitution, they are not operated upon by the Fifth Amendment, which, as we have said, had for its sole object to control the powers conferred by the Constitution on the National Government. * * *

---

* After this decision, the tribal courts of the Cherokee Nation and of the other Five Civilized Tribes were abolished by the Curtis Act of 1898. State law was extended to their lands at the time of Oklahoma statehood in 1906. Eds.

* * *

NOTES

1.   *Talton's* premises that tribal sovereign powers pre-dated and therefore were not limited by the Constitution can be traced to *Worcester* and the Supreme Court's 1883 decision in Ex parte Crow Dog, 109 U.S. 556 (1883), page 180, supra. The reasoning of the *Worcester-Crow Dog-Talton* line of cases survived into the modern era, thanks partly to the contributions of Felix Cohen and his formulation of the tribal sovereignty doctrine in the Handbook of Federal Indian Law. Cohen's highly respected review of a "host" of judicial decisions concluded that tribal sovereign authority was "inherent" and subject to limitation only by Congress or by the agreement of the tribes. Felix S. Cohen, Handbook of Federal Indian Law 122 (1941 ed.).

2.   The 1968 Indian Civil Rights Act mandated extension of many Bill of Rights provisions to tribal governments. See 25 U.S.C. § 1302. The Indian Civil Rights Act is discussed more fully in Section C of this chapter. But the existence of such limitations on tribal governments under federal statute does not lessen the vitality of *Talton v. Mayes* and its progeny. They are not *constitutional* restrictions and often may not be enforced by a private right of action in federal court. Santa Clara Pueblo v. Martinez, 436 U.S. 49 (1978). The only remedies for an aggrieved individual are those available in tribal forums and a federal writ of habeas corpus (25 U.S.C. § 1303). In addition, some key requirements (e.g., no establishment of religion, grand jury indictment) were not included in the Act.

3.   The evolving versions of the Indian Civil Rights Act, enacted in 1968, and significantly amended in 1986 and again in 2010, can be understood as snapshots in time of Congress's views on the Bill of Rights. In 1968, for example, the right to counsel for indigent criminal defendants had only recently been established in Gideon v. Wainwright, 372 U.S. 335 (1963), and so Congress apparently did not see the need to codify it in the Indian Civil Rights Act. The 2010 Tribal Law and Order Act that significantly strengthened criminal procedure rights, especially in the right to counsel context, see 25 U.S.C. § 1302(c)(1), can be seen as a more modern Congressional understanding of due process.

Could the legacy of *Worcester* as expressed in cases like *Talton* survive modern conditions and pressures? The following case, decided at a key moment in the modern era of Indian law, see Ezekiel J.N. Fletcher, *Trapped in the Spring of 1978: The Continuing Impact of the Supreme Court's Decisions in* Oliphant, Wheeler, *and* Martinez, 55 Fed.Law. 34 (March/April, 2008), affirmed the continuing vitality of the tribal sovereignty doctrine as a fundamental principle of the Supreme Court's Indian rights decisions.

UNITED STATES V. WHEELER

Supreme Court of the United States, 1978.
435 U.S. 313, 98 S.Ct. 1079, 55 L.Ed.2d 303.

MR. JUSTICE STEWART delivered the opinion of the Court.

[The Indian defendant here pled guilty in Navajo Tribal Court to disorderly conduct and to contributing to the delinquency of a minor. Under federal statutes discussed more thoroughly in Chapter 7B, infra, federal courts have jurisdiction over certain major crimes committed by Indians in Indian country. Rape is one of those crimes. A year after the tribal prosecution, the defendant was indicted in federal court for rape arising out of the same incident.]

The question presented in this case is whether the Double Jeopardy Clause of the Fifth Amendment bars the prosecution of an Indian in a federal district court under the Major Crimes Act, 18 U.S.C. § 1153, when he has previously been convicted in a tribal court of a lesser included offense arising out of the same incident.

* * *

II

In Bartkus v. Illinois, 359 U.S. 121, and Abbate v. United States, 359 U.S. 187, this Court reaffirmed the well-established principle that a federal prosecution does not bar a subsequent state prosecution of the same person for the same acts, and a state prosecution does not bar a federal one. The basis for this doctrine is that prosecutions under the laws of separate sovereigns do not, in the language of the Fifth Amendment, "subject [the defendant] for the same offence to be twice put in jeopardy." * * *

* * *

Bartkus and *Abbate* rest on the basic structure of our federal system, in which States and the National Government are separate political communities. State and Federal Governments "[derive] power from different sources," each from the organic law that established it. Each has the power, inherent in any sovereign, independently to determine what shall be an offense against its authority and to punish such offenses, and in doing so each "is exercising its own sovereignty, not that of the other." And while the States, as well as the Federal Government, are subject to the overriding requirements of the Federal Constitution, and the Supremacy Clause gives Congress within its sphere the power to enact laws superseding conflicting laws of the States, this degree of federal control over the exercise of state governmental power does not detract from the fact that it is a State's own sovereignty which is the origin of its power.

III

It is undisputed that Indian tribes have power to enforce their criminal laws against tribe members. Although physically within the territory of the United States and subject to ultimate federal control, they nonetheless remain "a separate people, with the power of regulating their internal and social relations." United States v. Kagama, [118 U.S. 375,] 381–382 [1886]; Cherokee Nation v. Georgia, 5 Pet. 1, 16 [1832].[18] Their right of internal self-government includes the right to prescribe laws applicable to tribe members and to enforce those laws by criminal sanctions. * * * [T]he controlling question in this case is the source of this power to punish tribal offenders: Is it a part of inherent tribal sovereignty, or an aspect of the sovereignty of the Federal Government which has been delegated to the tribes by Congress?

* * *

The powers of Indian tribes are, in general, *"inherent powers of a limited sovereignty which has never been extinguished."* F. Cohen, Handbook of Federal Indian Law 122 (1945) (emphasis in original). Before the coming of the Europeans, the tribes were self-governing sovereign political communities. See McClanahan v. Arizona State Tax Comm'n, 411 U.S. 164, 172. Like all sovereign bodies, they then had the inherent power to prescribe laws for their members and to punish infractions of those laws.

Indian tribes are, of course, no longer "possessed of the full attributes of sovereignty." *United States v. Kagama,* supra, at 381. Their incorporation within the territory of the United States, and their acceptance of its protection, necessarily divested them of some aspects of the sovereignty which they had previously exercised. By specific treaty provision they yielded up other sovereign powers; by statute, in the exercise of its plenary control, Congress has removed still others.

But our cases recognize that the Indian tribes have not given up their full sovereignty. We have recently said that "Indian tribes are unique aggregations possessing attributes of sovereignty over both their members and their territory. . . . [They] are a good deal more than 'private, voluntary organizations.'" United States v. Mazurie, 419 U.S. 544, 557. The sovereignty that the Indian tribes retain is of a unique and limited character. It exists only at the sufferance of Congress and is subject to complete defeasance. But until Congress acts, the tribes retain their existing sovereign powers. In sum, Indian tribes still possess those aspects of sovereignty not withdrawn by treaty or statute, or by implication as a

---

[18] Thus, unless limited by treaty or statute, a tribe has the power to determine tribe membership, Cherokee Intermarriage Cases, 203 U.S. 76; Roff v. Burney, 168 U.S. 218, 222–223; to regulate domestic relations among tribe members, Fisher v. District Court, 424 U.S. 382, cf. United States v. Quiver, 241 U.S. 602; and to prescribe rules for the inheritance of property. Jones v. Meehan, 175 U.S. 1, 29; Mackey v. Coxe, 18 How. 100.

necessary result of their dependent status. See Oliphant v. Suquamish Indian Tribe[, 435 U.S. 191 (1978)].

* * *

It is evident that the sovereign power to punish tribal offenders has never been given up by the Navajo Tribe and that tribal exercise of that power today is therefore the continued exercise of retained tribal sovereignty. * * *

* * *

Moreover, the sovereign power of a tribe to prosecute its members for tribal offenses clearly does not fall within that part of sovereignty which the Indians implicitly lost by virtue of their dependent status. The areas in which such implicit divestiture of sovereignty has been held to have occurred are those involving the relations between an Indian tribe and nonmembers of the tribe. Thus, Indian tribes can no longer freely alienate to non-Indians the land they occupy. Oneida Indian Nation v. County of Oneida, 414 U.S. 661, 667–668; Johnson v. McIntosh, 8 Wheat. 543, 574. They cannot enter into direct commercial or governmental relations with foreign nations. Worcester v. Georgia, 6 Pet. 515, 559; Cherokee Nation v. Georgia, 5 Pet., at 17–18; Fletcher v. Peck, 6 Cranch 87, 147 (concurring opinion of Mr. Justice Johnson). And, as we have recently held, they cannot try nonmembers in tribal courts. Oliphant v. Suquamish Indian Tribe.

* * *

In sum, the power to punish offenses against tribal law committed by Tribe members, which was part of the Navajos' primeval sovereignty, has never been taken away from them, either explicitly or implicitly, and is attributable in no way to any delegation to them of federal authority. It follows that when the Navajo Tribe exercises this power, it does so as part of its retained sovereignty and not as an arm of the Federal Government.

* * *

The conclusion that an Indian tribe's power to punish tribal offenders is part of its own retained sovereignty is clearly reflected in a case decided by this Court more than 80 years ago, Talton v. Mayes, 163 U.S. 376. * * *

The relevance of *Talton v. Mayes* to the present case is clear. The Court there held that when an Indian tribe criminally punishes a tribe member for violating tribal law, the tribe acts as an independent sovereign, and not as an arm of the Federal Government. Since tribal and federal prosecutions are brought by separate sovereigns, they are not "for the same offence," and the Double Jeopardy Clause thus does not bar one when the other has occurred.

* * *

Reversed.

NOTES

1.   *Wheeler* references cases in which the Supreme Court has held that Indian tribes have lost sovereign powers "by virtue of their dependent status." Two years later, the Supreme Court clarified its statement by holding in a tax case:

> Tribal powers are not implicitly divested by virtue of the tribes' dependent status. This Court has found such a divestiture in cases where the exercise of tribal sovereignty would be inconsistent with the overriding interests of the National Government, as when the tribes seek to engage in foreign relations, alienate their lands to non-Indians without federal consent, or prosecute non-Indians in tribal courts which do not accord the full protections of the Bill of Rights.

Washington v. Confederated Tribes of Colville Indian Reservation, 447 U.S. 134, 153–54 (1980). The Court in *Colville* suggests that Indian tribes may be divested of powers where those powers conflict with the "overriding interests of the National Government." Which is it? By virtue of dependent status or in the overriding interests of the federal government? What is the usefulness of a test like that? Does the test give the Supreme Court too much authority to do mischief in Indian law? We will return to this question in Chapter 7(D).

2.   The Supreme Court refused to extend the theory of inherent sovereignty to the Commonwealth of Puerto Rico in Commonwealth of Puerto Rico v. Sanchez Valle, 136 S. Ct. 1863 (2016). The Court wrote that Indian tribes as sovereigns are to be contrasted with territories like Puerto Rico, which do not retain inherent sovereignty and cannot exercise criminal jurisdiction without Congressional authorization. Justice Breyer in dissent suggested that Congress, by not acting to limit tribal sovereignty, had therefore effectively authorized tribal prosecutorial authority, a notion the majority quickly rejected:

> [T]he dissent's contrary reasoning is deeply disturbing. According to the dissent, Congress is in fact "the 'source' of the Indian tribes' criminal enforcement power" because it has elected not to disturb the exercise of that authority. Post, at 5. But beginning with Chief Justice Marshall and continuing for nearly two centuries, this Court has held firm and fast to the view that Congress's power over Indian affairs does nothing to gainsay the profound importance of the tribes' pre-existing sovereignty. See Worcester v. Georgia, 6 Pet. 515, 559–561 (1832); Talton v. Mayes, 163 U. S. 376, 384 (1896); Michigan v. Bay Mills Indian Community, 572 U. S. ___, ___–___ (2014) (slip op., at 4–5). And once again, we have stated in no uncertain terms that the tribes are separate sovereigns precisely because of that inherent authority.

Sanchez Valle, 136 S. Ct. at 1873 n.5. Why would Justice Breyer's theory of tribal sovereignty be concerning for tribal interests?

NATION BUILDING NOTE: HEALTH

First contact with colonizers from the West immediately created cataclysmic health consequences for Indian people, with many effects continuing today. Epidemics of infectious diseases such as smallpox and influenza killed more than 90% of all Indian people on the continent by 1900. Although those epidemics eventually relented, the new foods, economics, and stresses of the new arrivals bred a long-term health crisis in Indian country. The leading causes of illness and death for Indian populations include heart disease, diabetes, liver disease, and suicide. Social determinants—poverty and inadequate education, insufficient infrastructure, processed foods, and lack of running water—combined with assimilationist practices and historical trauma, led to poor health conditions and created barriers to improvement.

However, if we have learned anything from the history of Indian people, it is their perseverance. Native Americans have the strength within their communities to protect and heal their people, and that power is increasingly being recognized. Ever since treaty time, the federal government has provided some health benefits to Indian people through the Indian Health Service. For a century and a half, IHS provided all direct services but, since the early 1970s, tribes have steadily become more engaged. Using contracting and self-governance laws, they have taken over management of many IHS programs and facilities as well as responsibility for constructing new health facilities. There now are 17 tribally-run hospitals and 249 tribally-run clinics in Indian Country. This tends to create a more welcoming atmosphere for Native American patients and also facilitates healing through the use of medicine men and women, traditional medicines, and creative cultural programs, trends that have begun to spread to IHS facilities and health providers beyond Indian country.

Tribal assertion of control over their own health care has led to steady and better results than when responsibility rested with outsiders. The incidence of heart disease, diabetes, obesity, alcoholism, cirrhosis, cancer, food scarcity, and mental health issues all remain higher in Indian populations than in the larger population, but all health indicators are on the upswing with the exception of obesity and diabetes. The infant mortality rate has dropped from 25.0 (per 1000 births) in 1973 to 7.6 in 2013, a decrease of 70%. The Indian heart disease death rate has decreased from 318.8 (per 100,000 population) in 1980 to 128 for 2013. Tribes have been meeting the scourge of alcohol head on and have made impressive progress. Most, if not all tribes have alcohol treatment programs, usually with strong cultural components, and some have voted to keep alcohol off reservations entirely. The alcohol-related death rate for Indian populations decreased from 77.5 in 1980 to 49.6 in 2008. The chronic liver disease and cirrhosis death rate decreased from 72.4 to 43.1 over the same period.

The Tohono O'odham Nation in southwestern Arizona and part of northern Mexico provides a vivid example of tribes taking responsibility over critical health matters. Traditionally, the O'odham farmed corn, squash, chilies, and importantly, tepary beans with floodwaters. They were fully acclimated to living off of the sparse but captivating desert landscape. As Tucson grew nearby, water that would normally reach the reservation dried up, traditional farmers were pushed off their land, and BIA officials pressed farmers and other members to join the labor force on industrial cotton fields.

Western dietary and lifestyle influences like fast food restaurants then moved in. As a result, the Tohono O'odham have faced one of the worst adult-onset diabetes crises in the country. This menace has cost the already impoverished community many limbs and lives. Nutritionists have linked this diabetes epidemic to the shift from traditional foods to fatty and sugary western foods. Studies have shown that traditional foods like tepary beans had regulated blood sugar and held diabetes in check. The Tohono O'odham were used to their traditional desert foods, not fundamentally different western foods.

Recognizing the need for a shift back to traditional foods, the Tohono O'odham Nation has engaged in a broad-based effort to change dietary habits and raise tepary beans and other traditional foods. The Tohono O'odham has a Health and Human Services Department, working with farmers, the tribal communities, and non-profits, with many subdivisions running programs on the reservation from woman, infant and children programs to senior health services and meals on wheels. The tribe has secured Central Arizona Project water rights for farming traditional crops. O'odham people also formed an ambitious, multi-faceted nonprofit, Tohono O'odham Community Action that for more than 20 years has developed all manner of programs to bring back traditional foods and educate native people about their value. TOCA's founder, Terrol Dew Johnson, who notes that tepary beans are part of the Tohono O'odham creation story, explains that "many Native communities are reclaiming their food traditions by revitalizing agricultural and cultural practices and advocating for food sovereignty. There cannot be a return to health and strength without this deep understanding of place and cultural roots." He adds "I don't have to die of diabetes."

Other tribes have responded in the same spirit and, across Indian country, there is growing interest in food sovereignty. They look to traditional belief systems including the concepts of harmony and balance in respect to food, and how these values can motivate individuals and communities to increase their use of traditional foods and adopt healthier lifestyles. Examples of such foods include: wild rice (Upper Great Lakes); blue corn, squash, and beans (Southwest); berries, salmon, and whale (Pacific Northwest); and beaver and bison (Plains). Most of these traditional foods are high in protein and low in fat and sugar. Although the relationship between Native people and their traditional foods has been battered, one study reported that the extent and continued use of traditional foods and harvesting practices is often unrecognized or underestimated by non-Native health care providers.

Improving the health of Native people is a daunting task. After generations of federal control, the momentum has finally shifted toward allowing Native communities to heal themselves, using traditional methods when they find it appropriate. Progress has been gradual. Still, virtually all the indicators are improving. Crucially, this progress derives from the tribes themselves, and they continue to keep at it, on their own terms, day by day.

For more detail, see generally *Health of American Indian or Alaska Native Population*, Ctr. for Disease Control & Prevention (Apr. 27, 2016), http://www. cdc.gov/nchs/fastats/american-indian-health.htm; David H. DeJong, *Plagues, Politics, and Policy: A Chronicle of the Indian Health Service 1955–2008* (2011); Joseph E. Trimble and Fred Beauvais, *Prevention of Alcoholism, Drug Abuse, and Health Problems Among American Indians and Alaska Natives: An Introduction and Overview*, in *Health Promotion and Substance Abuse Prevention Among American Indian and Alaska Native Communities: Issues in Cultural Competence* 2–28 (2001); Herb Nabigon, *The Hollow Tree: Fighting Addiction with Traditional Native Healing* (2006); Julia Guarino, *Tribal Food Sovereignty in the American Southwest*, 11 J. Food L. & Pol'y 31 (2015).

SECTION C. THE CONTEMPORARY SCOPE OF TRIBAL SOVEREIGNTY UNDER THE INDIAN CIVIL RIGHTS ACT

Wheeler cites the Court's 1896 decision in *Talton v. Mayes* as still "relevant" to the question of the source of tribal self-governing powers in United States law. As *Talton* holds, those powers originate in the tribes' retained inherent sovereignty and are not considered as delegated to the tribes from the federal government.

In 1968, after seven years of sporadic legislative effort, Congress exercised its plenary power to pass the Indian Civil Rights Act, 25 U.S.C. § 1301 et seq. (ICRA). According to extensive historical research conducted by Professor Angela R. Riley, despite congressional intent to extend civil rights laws to tribal citizens, ICRA's sponsor, Senator Sam Ervin, a Southern segregationist, may have intended the ICRA's limitation of tribal authority to promote the assimilation of Indian people into the larger society. Angela R. Riley, *(Tribal) Sovereignty and Illiberalism*, 95 Calif.L.Rev. 799, 809 (2007). In the years preceding the final enactment of the ICRA, dozens of American Indians testified about civil rights abuses they suffered, mostly at the hands of state and local government officials. While some Indians testified about the lack of religious freedom and tribal government abuses, most witnesses complained that federal and state officials were the primary causes and perpetrators of these abuses. John R. Wunder, "Retained by the People": A History of American Indians and the Bill of Rights 132–36 (1994). Of course the ICRA was directed at tribal governments alone.

Indian response was mixed during the legislative process. Some tribes had no objection in principle but believed that the legislation was unnecessary. Others argued that the legislation would unduly formalize tribal court systems. Still others, including the traditional pueblos of the Southwest, opposed any incursions whatsoever on their tribal sovereignty. In retrospect, it seems certain that the lack of organized tribal opposition to the legislation was a result of the era in which it was passed. Senate hearings were held in the early and mid-1960s, at a time when Indian political power was not at the level it is today. In any event, the House held only one day of hearings on the bill in its final form, providing little time to organize opposition.

The resulting legislation imposed on tribes a set of requirements tracking many of the constitutional restraints on states and the federal government. Notably absent are limitations similar to the establishment of religion clause, the guarantee of a republican form of government, the privileges and immunities clauses, the provisions involving the right to vote, the requirement of free counsel for an indigent accused, and the right to a jury trial in civil cases.

For the first ten years after the enactment of the ICRA, federal courts often took jurisdiction over suits against tribal governments to enforce the Act. E.g., Dodge v. Nakai, 298 F.Supp. 26 (D.Ariz.1969) (striking down a Navajo Nation banishment action as denying due process, abridging freedom of speech, and constituting a bill of attainder). Additionally, the United States Department of Justice sued or threatened to sue numerous Indian tribes for violations of ICRA. These cases reached settlement prior to a court decision. Lawrence R. Baca, *Reflections on the Role of the United States Department of Justice in Enforcing the Indian Civil Rights Act*, in The Indian Civil Rights Act at Forty 1 (Kristen A. Carpenter, Matthew L.M. Fletcher, and Angela R. Riley, eds. 2012). Then, in the following landmark decision issued in 1978 (the same year in which *Wheeler* was decided), the Supreme Court significantly circumscribed federal judicial review of tribal action under the ICRA.

SANTA CLARA PUEBLO V. MARTINEZ

Supreme Court of the United States, 1978.
436 U.S. 49, 98 S.Ct. 1670, 56 L.Ed.2d 106.

MR. JUSTICE MARSHALL delivered the opinion of the Court. * * *

This case requires us to decide whether a federal court may pass on the validity of an Indian tribe's ordinance denying membership to the children of certain female tribal members.

Petitioner Santa Clara Pueblo is an Indian tribe that has been in existence for over 600 years. Respondents, a female member of the tribe and her daughter, brought suit in federal court against the tribe and its Governor, petitioner Lucario Padilla, seeking declaratory and injunctive relief against enforcement of a tribal ordinance denying membership in the tribe to children of female members who marry outside the tribe, while extending membership to children of male members who marry outside the tribe. Respondents claimed that this rule discriminates on the basis of both sex and ancestry in violation of Title I of the Indian Civil Rights Act of 1968 (ICRA), 25 U.S.C. §§ 1301–1303 (1970), which provides in relevant part that "[n]o Indian tribe in exercising powers of self-government shall * * * deny to any person within its jurisdiction the equal protection of its laws." Id., § 1302(8).

Title I of the ICRA does not expressly authorize the bringing of civil actions for declaratory or injunctive relief to enforce its substantive provisions. The threshold issue in this case is thus whether the Act may be interpreted to impliedly authorize such actions, against a tribe or its officers, in the federal courts. For the reasons set forth below, we hold that the Act cannot be so read.

I

Respondent Julia Martinez is a full-blooded member of the Santa Clara Pueblo, and resides on the Santa Clara Reservation in Northern New Mexico. In 1941 she married a Navajo Indian with whom she has since had several children, including respondent Audrey Martinez. Two years before this marriage, the Pueblo passed the membership ordinance here at issue, which bars admission of the Martinez children to the tribe because their father is not a Santa Claran.[2] Although the children were raised on the reservation and continue to reside there now that they are adults, as a result of their exclusion from membership they may not vote in tribal elections or hold secular office in the tribe; moreover, they have no right to remain on the reservation in the event of their mother's death, or to inherit their mother's home or her possessory interests in the communal lands.

[On a motion to dismiss, the District Court held that the ICRA impliedly waived tribal sovereign immunity and conferred jurisdiction under 28 U.S.C. § 1343(4).]

* * *

Following a full trial, the District Court found for petitioners on the merits. While acknowledging the relatively recent origin of the disputed rule, the District Court nevertheless found it to reflect traditional values of patriarchy still significant in tribal life. The court recognized the vital

---

[2] "1. All children born of marriages between members of the Santa Clara Pueblo shall be members of the Santa Clara Pueblo.

"2. . . . [C]hildren born of marriages between male members of the Santa Clara Pueblo and non-members shall be members of the Santa Clara Pueblo.

"3. Children born of marriages between female members of the Santa Clara Pueblo and non-members shall not be members of the Santa Clara Pueblo. * * * "

importance of respondents' interests,[5] but also determined that membership rules were "no more or less than a mechanism of social ... self-definition," and as such were basic to the tribe's survival as a cultural and economic entity. In sustaining the ordinance's validity under the "equal protection clause" of the ICRA, 25 U.S.C § 1302 (8), the District Court concluded that the balance to be struck between these competing interests was better left to the judgment of the Pueblo:

> "[The] equal protection guarantee of the Indian Civil Rights Act should not be construed in a manner which would require or authorize this Court to determine which traditional values will promote cultural survival and should therefore be preserved. . . . Such a determination should be made by the people of Santa Clara; not only because they can best decide what values are important, but also because they must live with the decision every day. . . .

> " . . . To abrogate tribal decisions, particularly in the delicate area of membership, for whatever 'good' reasons, is to destroy cultural identity under the guise of saving it." 402 F.Supp., at 18–19.

[The Tenth Circuit affirmed the jurisdiction of the district court but reversed on the merits.] Because of the ordinance's recent vintage, and because in the [Tenth Circuit panel]'s view the rule did not rationally identify those persons who were emotionally and culturally Santa Clarans, the court held that the tribe's interest in the ordinance was not substantial enough to justify its discriminatory effect.

We granted certiorari and we now reverse.

II

* * *

As separate sovereigns pre-existing the Constitution, tribes have historically been regarded as unconstrained by those constitutional provisions framed specifically as limitations on federal or state authority. Thus, in Talton v. Mayes, 163 U.S. 376 (1896), this Court held that the Fifth Amendment did not "operat[e] upon" "the powers of local self-government enjoyed" by the tribes. Id., at 384. In ensuing years the lower federal courts have extended the holding of *Talton* to other provisions of the Bill of Rights, as well as to the Fourteenth Amendment.

As the Court in *Talton* recognized, however, Congress has plenary authority to limit, modify or eliminate the powers of local self-government which the tribes otherwise possess. * * * Title I of the ICRA, 25 U.S.C. §§ 1301–1303, represents an exercise of that authority. In 25 U.S.C. § 1302,

---

[5] The court found that "Audrey Martinez and many other children similarly situated have been brought up on the Pueblo, speak the Tewa language, participate in its life, and are, culturally, for all practical purposes, Santa Claran Indians."

Congress acted to modify the effect of *Talton* and its progeny by imposing certain restrictions upon tribal governments similar, but not identical, to those contained in the Bill of Rights and the Fourteenth Amendment. In 25 U.S.C. § 1303, the only remedial provision expressly supplied by Congress, the "privilege of the writ of habeas corpus" is made "available to any person, in a court of the United States, to test the legality of his detention by order of an Indian tribe."

* * *

III

Indian tribes have long been recognized as possessing the common-law immunity from suit traditionally enjoyed by sovereign powers. * * *

It is settled that a waiver of sovereign immunity " 'cannot be implied but must be unequivocally expressed.' " United States v. Testan, 424 U.S. 392, 399 (1976), quoting United States v. King, 395 U.S. 1, 4 (1969). Nothing on the face of Title I of the ICRA purports to subject tribes to the jurisdiction of the federal courts in civil actions for injunctive or declaratory relief. Moreover, since the respondent in a habeas corpus action is the individual custodian of the prisoner, see, e.g., 28 U.S.C. § 2243, the provisions of § 1303 can hardly be read as a general waiver of the tribe's sovereign immunity. In the absence here of any unequivocal expression of contrary legislative intent, we conclude that suits against the tribe under the ICRA are barred by its sovereign immunity from suit.

IV

As an officer of the Pueblo, petitioner Lucario Padilla is not protected by the tribe's immunity from suit. See Puyallup Tribe, Inc. v. Washington Dept. of Game, supra, 433 U.S., at 171–172; cf. Ex parte Young, 209 U.S. 123 (1908). We must therefore determine whether the cause of action for declaratory and injunctive relief asserted here by respondents, though not expressly authorized by the statute is nonetheless implicit in its terms.

In addressing this inquiry, we must bear in mind that providing a federal forum for issues arising under § 1302 constitutes an interference with tribal autonomy and self-government beyond that created by the change in substantive law itself. Even in matters involving commercial and domestic relations, we have recognized that "subject[ing] a dispute arising on the reservation among reservation Indians to a forum other than the one they have established for themselves," Fisher v. District Court, 424 U.S. 382, 387–388 (1976), may "undermine the authority of the tribal court . . . and hence . . . infringe on the right of the Indians to govern themselves." *Williams v. Lee*, supra, 358 U.S., at 223. A fortiori, resolution in a foreign forum of intratribal disputes of a more "public" character, such as the one in this case, cannot help but unsettle a tribal government's ability to maintain authority. Although Congress clearly has power to authorize civil actions against tribal officers, and has done so with respect to habeas corpus relief in § 1303, a proper respect both for tribal sovereignty itself and for the plenary authority of Congress in this area cautions that we tread lightly in the absence of clear indications of legislative intent. Cf. Antoine v. Washington, 420 U.S. 194, 199–200 (1975); Choate v. Trapp, 224 U.S. 665, 675 (1912).

[In analyzing congressional intent, the Court referred to the general policy of "self-determination" and to other titles of the ICRA which were designed to strengthen tribal courts and tribal government.]

* * *

* * * This commitment to the goal of tribal self-determination is demonstrated by the provisions of Title I itself. Section 1302, rather than providing in wholesale fashion for the extension of constitutional requirements to tribal governments, as had been initially proposed, selectively incorporated and in some instances modified the safeguards of the Bill of Rights to fit the unique political, cultural, and economic needs of tribal governments. Thus, for example, the statute does not prohibit the establishment of religion, nor does it require jury trials in civil cases, or appointment of counsel for indigents in criminal cases.

* * *

Moreover, * * * implication of a federal remedy in addition to habeas corpus is not plainly required to give effect to Congress' objective of extending constitutional norms to tribal self-government. Tribal forums are available to vindicate rights created by the ICRA, and § 1302 has the substantial and intended effect of changing the law which these forums are obliged to apply. Tribal courts have repeatedly been recognized as appropriate forums for the exclusive adjudication of disputes affecting important personal and property interests of both Indians and non-Indians.[21] See, e.g., Fisher v. District Court, 424 U.S. 382 (1976); Williams v. Lee, 358 U.S. 217 (1959). See also Ex parte Crow Dog, 109 U.S. 556 (1883). Nonjudicial tribal institutions have also been recognized as competent law-applying bodies. See United States v. Mazurie, 419 U.S. 544 (1975).[22] Under these circumstances, we are reluctant to disturb the

---

[21] * * * Judgments of tribal courts, as to matters properly within their jurisdiction, have been regarded in some circumstances as entitled to full faith and credit in other courts. See, e.g., Mackey v. Coxe, 59 U.S. 100 (1855); Standley v. Roberts, 59 F. 836, 845 (C.A.8 1894), appeal dismissed, 17 S.Ct. 999 (1896).

[22] By the terms of its Constitution, adopted in 1935 and approved by the Secretary of the Interior in accordance with the Indian Reorganization Act of 1934, 25 U.S.C. § 476, judicial authority in the Santa Clara Pueblo is vested in its tribal council.

Many tribal constitutions adopted pursuant to 25 U.S.C. § 476, though not that of the Santa Clara Pueblo, include provisions requiring that tribal ordinances not be given effect until the Department of Interior gives its approval. See I American Indian Policy Review Commission, supra, at 187–188; 1961 Hearings (Pt. I), supra, at 95. In these instances, persons aggrieved by

balance between the dual statutory objectives which Congress apparently struck in providing only for habeas corpus relief.

* * *

Our reluctance is strongly reinforced by the specific legislative history underlying 25 U.S.C. § 1303. This history, extending over more than three years, indicates that Congress' provision for habeas corpus relief, and nothing more, reflected a considered accommodation of the competing goals of "preventing injustices perpetrated by tribal governments, on the one hand, and, on the other, avoiding undue or precipitous interference in the affairs of the Indian people."

* * * After considering numerous alternatives for review of tribal convictions, Congress apparently decided that review by way of habeas corpus would adequately protect the individual interests at stake while avoiding unnecessary intrusions on tribal governments.

* * *

* * * [G]iven Congress' desire not to intrude needlessly on tribal self-government, it is not surprising that Congress chose at this stage to provide for federal review only in habeas corpus proceedings.

By not exposing tribal officials to the full array of federal remedies available to redress actions of federal and state officials, Congress may also have considered that resolution of statutory issues under § 1302, and particularly those issues likely to arise in a civil context, will frequently depend on questions of tribal tradition and custom which tribal forums may be in a better position to evaluate than federal courts. * * * [E]fforts by the federal judiciary to apply the statutory prohibitions of § 1302 in a civil context may substantially interfere with a tribe's ability to maintain itself as a culturally and politically distinct entity.[32]

As we have repeatedly emphasized, Congress' authority over Indian matters is extraordinarily broad, and the role of courts in adjusting relations between and among tribes and their members correspondingly restrained. See Lone Wolf v. Hitchcock, 187 U.S. 553, 565 (1903). Congress retains authority expressly to authorize civil actions for injunctive or other relief to redress violations of § 1302, in the event that the tribes themselves prove deficient in applying and enforcing its substantive provisions. But unless and until Congress makes clear its intention to permit the

---

tribal laws may, in addition to pursuing tribal remedies, be able to seek relief from the Department of Interior.

[32] A tribe's right to define its own membership for tribal purposes has long been recognized as central to its existence as an independent political community. See Roff v. Burney, 168 U.S. 218, 18 S.Ct. 60, 42 L.Ed. 442 (1897); Cherokee Intermarriage Cases, 203 U.S. 76, 27 S.Ct. 29, 51 L.Ed. 96 (1906). Given the often vast gulf between tribal traditions and those with which federal courts are more intimately familiar, the judiciary should not rush to create causes of action that would intrude on these delicate matters.

additional intrusion on tribal sovereignty that adjudication of such actions in a federal forum would represent, we are constrained to find that § 1302 does not impliedly authorize actions for declaratory or injunctive relief against either the tribe or its officers.

The judgment of the Court of Appeals is, accordingly,

Reversed.

MR. JUSTICE BLACKMUN took no part in the consideration or decision of this case.

MR. JUSTICE WHITE, dissenting. * * *

NOTES

1.   In 2014, the Santa Clara Pueblo Tribal Council repealed the 1939 membership ordinance, 1944 and 1982 membership resolutions, and "unwritten law" on tribal membership. Tribal Resolution 2014–81. The Council also enacted a resolution establishing interim membership procedures allowing for persons of mixed parentage previously excluded (such as persons similarly situated to Julia Martinez's children) to be admitted. Tribal Resolutions 2014–82 & 2014–83. In 2007, the Council enacted the Non-Member Residence Code. The Code provided that all persons then residing and those who wished to reside on Pueblo lands must apply to be a nonmember resident. The Council began implementation of the Code in 2015.

2.   The cases decided before *Santa Clara* had split on the extent to which principles developed in federal cases arising under the Constitution would apply under similar provisions in the ICRA. See generally National American Indian Court Judges Ass'n, Indian Courts and the Future 17–20 (David Getches ed. 1978). The answer seems to be that in criminal cases, federal courts are more likely to apply federal constitutional principles because the writ of habeas corpus is an Anglo-American legal principle. In Wounded Knee v. Andera, 416 F.Supp. 1236, 1241–42 (D.S.D.1976), the court found that due process under the ICRA required a prosecutor in tribal court and remarked: "The [tribal] judicial system is Anglo-American and assuredly not Indian; adding the safeguards guaranteed in Anglo-American law certainly is no more of an encroachment upon the Indian way of life than the tribal court itself." More recently, the Second Circuit explicitly asserted that Congress must have intended to force federal courts to apply federal criminal procedure principles in habeas review of tribal court convictions. See Poodry v. Tonawanda Band of Seneca Indians, 85 F.3d 874, 900 (1996) ("Congress did not intend with § 1303 to enact a special variety of habeas review. Habeas corpus is, of course, a peculiarly Anglo-American remedy.").

In 2010, Congress enacted the Tribal Law and Order Act, which allows for tribes to sentence offenders for up to three years, so long as the tribal court guarantees and provides a right to counsel for indigent defendants and other criminal procedure rights afforded under United States law. See 25 U.S.C.

§§ 1302(b), (c). It is helpful to look at the "incorporation" cases under the Fourteenth Amendment. In those cases, the Supreme Court was asked to decide which of the basic Bill of Rights protections were within the states' Fourteenth Amendment obligation to provide "due process" to citizens. Although the Court ultimately found that most Bill of Rights limitations should extend to the states through the Fourteenth Amendment due process clause, this result was driven more by the nature of the legal traditions than by basic concepts of justice and equity. In the early cases, the Court said the question was whether the protection is "necessarily fundamental to fairness in every criminal system that might be imagined." In the later cases, the Court asked more specifically whether the protection was "fundamental in the context of the criminal processes maintained by the American States." Duncan v. Louisiana, 391 U.S. 145, 149–50 n.14 (1968). The Court in *Duncan*, at some length, explained that its interpretation of due process was specific to the traditions of the "Anglo-American regime of ordered liberty," and that it was not saying that "a fair and enlightened system of justice would be impossible without them." If tribes create "fair and equitable" justice systems that do not behave exactly as their federal and state counterparts, do they pass muster under the due process standard of the ICRA?

Beyond fundamental definitions of rights, the Bill of Rights has been heavily embellished with prescribed requirements for federal and state justice systems. *Miranda* warnings and the exclusionary rule have become standard. Are those procedures the only way to ensure that such rights are realized? The best ways? Should tribes be able to adopt their own approaches?

3.   Ordinarily federal courts will hold, as a matter of comity, that tribal remedies must be exhausted before a hearing on a habeas writ by a tribal member under the ICRA. See Selam v. Warm Springs Tribal Corr. Facility, 134 F.3d 948, 953 (9th Cir.1998). The 1-year limitation on tribal sentencing authority meant as a practical matter that few tribal court convictions would be reviewed by federal courts because, more likely than not, the prisoner's release would moot the habeas petition before effective review. The enhanced sentencing provisions of the Tribal Law and Order Act will undoubtedly subject tribal court criminal convictions to additional federal court review.

4.   Certain rights guaranteed under the U.S. Constitution may appear to be so fundamental as to override the rule in *Talton v. Mayes* that the Bill of Rights does not apply to tribal governments. Consider the decision in Vann v. Kempthorne, 467 F.Supp.2d 56, 69 (D.D.C.2006), rev'd, 534 F.3d 741 (D.C.Cir.2008), in which the court suggested that the Cherokee Nation's decision to amend its constitution to exclude from tribal citizenship the so-called Cherokee Freedmen may have been a violation of the Thirteenth Amendment's prohibition on slavery.

NATION BUILDING NOTE: FEMINIST LEGAL THEORY AND THE DEFINITION OF "MEMBERSHIP" IN NATIVE NATIONS

Several prominent feminist legal scholars have expressed concern over the Court's decision in *Santa Clara* favoring tribal sovereignty. In the words of Professor Judith Resnik, the principle of sovereignty "trumped inquiry about the legality, under federal law, of rules that (at least from a feminist perspective) subordinate women." *Dependent Sovereigns: Indian Tribes, States, and the Federal Courts*, 56 U.Chi.L.Rev. 671, 702 (1989). Professor Resnik's article conceded that the Supreme Court's protection of the tribe's ability to maintain itself as a culturally and politically distinct entity through its membership rule "has a good deal of appeal." But, she asked, "How comfortable should the federal judges (all men) who decided the case have been as they worked with an implied distinction between the" Santa Claran "membership rule and perhaps—but never reached in *Santa Clara Pueblo*—a federal norm of non-subordination?" Id. at 703.

The Santa Clara membership provisions in the pueblo's 1935 constitution did not expressly draw distinctions on the basis of gender. The pueblo retained discretion under this constitution to admit members. But, in that same year, Professor Resnik notes, the Department of the Interior made a "declaration" of its views on "Membership in Indian Tribes" in a circular addressed to all "engaged in Indian Reorganization Act." That "declaration" stated that "Congress [has] a definite policy to limit the application of Indian benefits." The department therefore planned "to urge and insist that any constitutional provision conferring automatic tribal membership upon children hereafter born, should limit such membership to persons who reasonably can be expected to participate in tribal relations and affairs." The department suggested several tests for membership, such as having both parents be recognized tribal members or be residents of the reservation or that an individual possess a "certain degree of Indian blood." Four years later, in 1939, the pueblo adopted its new ordinance on membership that reflected patrilineal traditions.

Professor Resnik professes sensitivity to the dangers of imposing her own cultural values onto the membership rules chosen by the Pueblo: "But," she adds, "I cannot share the ease with which the Supreme Court in *Santa Clara Pueblo* assumed the 1939 Ordinance to be an artifact of Santa Clara sovereignty. The emergence of a codified, written, non-discretionary, gender-based membership rule is linked to the Pueblo's decision to organize under guidance of the Department of the Interior, is linked to the Pueblo as a recipient of federal funds, and is linked to the Pueblo as situated in a United States culture that has made patrilineal and patriarchal rules so familiar that, to some, they seem uncontroversial." Id.

Another influential legal scholar, Catharine MacKinnon, likewise found *Santa Clara* to be a hard case.

> The Santa Clara rule was passed to prevent women who married out from passing land out, in an attempt to secure the survival of a culture for which land is life. Without knowing this, which I have by

word of mouth, it is hard to understand what the Supreme Court meant when it said that this rule was " 'no more or less than a mechanism of social * * * self-definition,' and as such [was] basic to the tribes' survival as a cultural and economic entity." The rule was seen as basic to survival because it discouraged Native women from marrying white men—or white men from marrying Native women, depending on how you see who does what—because that was taking away Native land. When Native men married white women, the experience apparently had been that white women more often integrated with the tribe.

Catharine A. MacKinnon, Feminism Unmodified 67 (1987).

For Professor MacKinnon, "cultural survival" is as contingent upon equality between women and men as it is upon equality among peoples. Thus, the tribe should not have been willing to sacrifice Julia Martinez's tribal connection and full membership in the tribal community when confronted by what Professor MacKinnon regarded as "a white male supremacist threat." "Why," she asks, "is excluding women always an option for solving problems men create between men? Maybe women's loyalty would be more reliable if their communities were more equitable." Id. at 68. Professor Angela P. Harris responds to Professor MacKinnon's analysis of *Santa Clara* by offering a much different type of feminist perspective on the Court's decision. *Race and Essentialism in Feminist Legal Theory*, 42 Stan.L.Rev. 581 (1990). Professor Harris charges that Professor MacKinnon's discussion of *Santa Clara* is an example of *essentialism;* that is, describing and analyzing the experiences of persons different than ourselves, and assuming that their perspectives on issues of equality and oppression are the same as our own.

In recent years, Indian women have spoken on their own behalf about the importance of the rules adopted in the *Martinez* case. Santa Clara member Rina Swentzell, similarly situated with Julia Martinez, defended the *Martinez* decision:

> I am a woman from Santa Clara Pueblo. I was born there. I lived with my great-grandmother on the main plaza next to the Winter kiva until she died when I was thirteen years old. My formal education began there where I went to the Bureau of Indian Affairs school at the Pueblo through the sixth grade. I was 39 years old when the Supreme Court ruled on the Santa Clara v. Martinez case. Even then, I wanted the courts to rule in favor of the tribe—to rule for tribal sovereignty. My desire was not because I was not concerned about my children who would not be considered members of the Pueblo, because I am a woman married to a non-Santa Clara person. It was not because I did not know that my cousin would have his children considered members because he is a man, though he was not born in the Pueblo, did not grow up there, and was married to a non-Santa Clara person. Of course, I also knew that it did not make sense; that

it was not just or fair. I knew that what was happening in the community was blatant gender discrimination.

* * *

At Santa Clara Pueblo, the social order was not traditionally either/or, not matriarchical or patriarchical. It was both. Even today, every child is born as a Winter person or a Summer person with the option to become the other if the sensibilities are of the other. To know and acknowledge both is encouraged, because ultimately, the goal is to embrace the whole—to be a part of the larger context, to be a part of society. But, more importantly, one should be part of the whole within which society operates—the natural world. That is why we wear cloud and mountain *tablitas* on our heads, skunk skins on our ankles, branches around our necks as we honor the forces of nature of which we are a part. The ultimate effort is to see the interactive quality of the world, of society, of family, of self. It is believed that every person has feminine and masculine, warm and cold, dark and light qualities. And, living is about acknowledging the other, the opposite, and balancing those forces within us and within our human society because that is what the natural world does.

Rina Swentzell, *Testimony of a Santa Clara Woman*, 14 Kan.J.L. & Pub.Pol'y, 97, 97–99 (2004).

At a conference at Michigan State University, several American Indian women joined Rina Swentzell in addressing the question of whether they would choose a federal solution to the problem of sex discrimination in Indian communities. The women unanimously chose to support the *Martinez* decision; they would choose tribal and indigenous solutions, rather than federal solutions.

Rina Swentzell: "[My children, who are not members] live in houses that everybody in the community acknowledges are theirs and we know nobody is going to throw them out. That's just the way it is. How do we work from this? We work through this thing within our own time. And it will happen. It will happen in such a way that we can feel like we have not given ourselves over to being the other."

Francine [Jaramillo], Isleta Pueblo member and tribal judge: "[Tribal court litigants] want to be treated fairly. And do we need ICRA or the federal government to tell us how to do it and this is the way you have to do it? I'd have to say no, we don't."

Eva Petoskey, Grand Traverse Band of Ottawa and Chippewa Indians member and former tribal council vice-chair: "I'm a strong advocate for strengthening our tribal governments. * * * I like the *Martinez* case. I can tell you that right now. I think that * * * even though the comment in [the MacKinnon article] was that the only time the Supreme Court has upheld sovereignty was at the expense of an Indian woman. And I say *I would pay that price. I would pay* *that price.* I would pay that price because I know a slightly different world. * * * I don't really have a life without the tribe's sovereignty. We don't have our land without the tribe's sovereignty. We don't have much hope of preserving our language. We don't have much hope of being able to live at home and raise our children where they can know about who they are."

Rebecca Miles, Nez Perce Tribe member and tribal council member: "[As a tribal leader] I'm protecting what was guaranteed to us. * * * I would always choose the tribe over myself, in any case. And I think that's been the difficulty and the success of tribes since the Indian Civil Rights Act."

Michigan State University College of Law, Indigenous Law and Policy Center 5th Annual Indigenous Law Conference, Forty Years of the Indian Civil Rights Act—History, Tribal Law, and Modern Challenges (Oct. 10–11, 2008). See also Gloria Valencia-Weber, Rina Swentzell, and Eva Petoskey, *40 Years of the Indian Civil Rights Act: Indigenous Women's Reflections*, in The Indian Civil Rights Act at Forty 39 (Kristen A. Carpenter, Matthew L.M. Fletcher, and Angela R. Riley, eds. 2012).

Professor MacKinnon revisited the *Martinez* decision, and tempered her views somewhat and stated that "indigenous tribunals, in an important outpost of sovereignty upon which all Native peoples can build, won power over Native women's equality claims." Catharine A. MacKinnon, *Martinez Revisited*, in The Indian Civil Rights Act at Forty, 27 (Kristen A. Carpenter, Matthew L.M. Fletcher, and Angela R. Riley, eds. 2012). Still, she argued that "having sovereignty achieved at the expense of equality is disheartening." Id. at 35. She recommended international fora to resolve these concerns.

Anthropologists have long described Indian tribes as being either patrilineal or matrilineal (i.e., tracing lineage either through the father's line or the mother's line), though many Indian communities do not view lineage as a matter of gender, but through clan structures or even the seasons. As we have seen, for many tribes distinctions based upon gender do influence membership, inheritance, and other important rules of tribal life. For instance, the Cherokees are categorized as a matrilineal society because they traditionally recognized tribal membership for children of Cherokee women who married white men (but not the children of Cherokee men who married white women). Though the rule was changed in the 1892 Constitution, many of the great Cherokee leaders like John Ross were in fact products of such unions.

In Tewa communities like Santa Clara, the summer and winter moieties (an anthropological term, derived from a French word meaning "halves") form the prime units of social and ceremonial organization within the pueblo and provide the governmental divisions for the management of virtually all practical tasks and religious activities of village communal life. In traditional Santa Clara society, individuals inherit their moiety association almost always from their father. Furthermore, a woman marrying a man of opposite affiliation must join her husband's moiety, "shaking off her blossom petals and replacing them with icicles" if she is a summer moiety member; or shaking off her icicles if she is of the winter moiety. 9 Handbook of North American Indians: Vol. 9, Southwest 296 (Alfonso Ortiz, vol. ed. 1979).

Alfonso Ortiz, the preeminent expert on Tewa anthropology and Tewa himself, has written that the "two most meaningful things one can say about the Tewa life cycle are, first, one is not born a Tewa but rather one is made a Tewa and second, once made, one has to work hard continuously throughout one's life to remain a Tewa." Id. at 277. According to Ortiz, the moieties play a critical role in this process of becoming and remaining a Tewa. All of the major ceremonial rites of passage are, as Ortiz notes, "undergone by all Tewa children through their father's moiety." Id. at 287–88.

Tewa traditions on moiety "membership," in theory at least, would seem to make it impossible for any child born to Martinez and her Navajo husband to become a Tewa, or stay one through participation in the complex series of rituals and ceremonies that comprise social, religious, and even political life in the village. Nevertheless, "there is no clear and unalterable role of recruitment into the moieties, because there is no clear and unambiguous rule of descent." Alfonso Ortiz, Tewa World 58 (1969). Because religious beliefs and ceremonies are more important than kinship and marriage in organizing Pueblo village life, exceptions to formal moiety membership rules can sometimes be made. See 9 Handbook of North American Indians, Southwest, supra, at 281–85.

We are left, of course, with the "hard" question of how to understand the particular situation of Martinez and her daughter Audrey, fathered by a member of the Navajo tribe (a tribe, by the way, which traditionally determines membership matrilineally, at least according to the categories used by anthropologists). The lower court decisions in *Santa Clara* showed how over time, the village had developed flexible methods for dealing with these troubling types of membership issues. The record at trial discloses that Martinez had made her troubling situation known to the Pueblo Council. As the federal district court judge who issued the initial decision in the case wrote:

> Julia Martinez first attempted to have Audrey recognized as a member of the Pueblo in 1946, shortly after Audrey was born. Since 1963 her efforts have been vigorous and constant. Julia Martinez has met with her representative to the Council, to request that he present the request that Audrey be enrolled to the Council. When her representative refused to bring the matter up in Council, she obtained special permission from the Governor to address the Council herself. She and other women in her situation have formed a committee which as a group petitioned representatives and, with special permission, the Council. Julia Martinez, individually and with the committee, succeeded in having a special meeting of the entire Pueblo convened to discuss the situation. Julia Martinez, individually and with the committee of similarly situated women attended meetings with various BIA officials, and with the All-Pueblo

Agency in Albuquerque. She and her husband Myles attempted to have Myles Martinez naturalized as a member of the Pueblo, in which case their children would have automatically been recognized as members. Mrs. Martinez also met with her State Representative concerning the recognition of her children as members of Santa Clara. Finally, Mrs. Martinez attended the hearings held by the Subcommittee on Constitutional Rights of the United States Senate Committee on the Judiciary, where she sought the help of then Senator Sam Ervin, Jr. In most instances there has been more than one attempt to resolve the matter through a particular channel; in particular, meetings with the Council representatives, the Governor and the Council have occurred four or five times over the last ten years. Finally, in 1971, Julia and Audrey Martinez sought legal advice. This suit was filed only after attempts by their lawyer to gain recognition for Audrey had failed. Plaintiffs have exhausted available remedies with the Pueblo.

Martinez v. Santa Clara Pueblo, 402 F.Supp. 5, 10–11 (D.N.M.1975).

Some tribal communities are matriarchal, with the Haudenosaunee perhaps the most famous. Haudenosaunee women had control over the community's economic resources, and therefore had more political power. See Judith K. Brown, *Economic Organization and the Position of Women among the Iroquois*, 17 Ethnohistory 151 (Summer–Autumn 1970); Renée Jacobs, Note, *Iroquois Great Law of Peace and the United States Constitution: How the Founding Fathers Ignored the Clan Mothers*, 16 Am. Indian L.Rev. 497, 498–507 (1991). The power of women in Haudenosaunee communities is also strongly expressed in tribal law. See id. at 507–09. Clause 44 of the Haudenosaunee Great Law provided that: "The lineal descent of the people of the Five Nations shall run in the female line. Women shall be considered the progenitors of the Nation. They shall own the land and the soil. Men and women shall follow the status of the mother." A.C. Parker, The Constitution of the Five Nations or The Iroquois Book of the Great Law 42 (1916). That law has import to this day. The children of Seneca men, for example, are not eligible for citizenship with the Seneca Nation of Indians unless their mothers are Seneca citizens.

SECTION D. TRIBAL SOVEREIGN IMMUNITY

In Part III of the *Santa Clara* majority opinion, the Court held that in the absence of any unequivocal expression of contrary legislative intent, "suits against the tribe under the ICRA are barred by its sovereign immunity." *Santa Clara* thus upholds one of the most important elements of the tribal sovereignty doctrine in the Supreme Court's modern Indian law decisions, the principle of tribal sovereign immunity. Tribal sovereign immunity protects tribes from suits in much the same manner as the United States is shielded from liability in its domestic courts. An Indian tribe is subject to suit only as expressly authorized by Congress or where the tribe itself has effectively waived its immunity.

The Supreme Court's acknowledgement of tribal sovereign immunity dates back at least to 1850 in Parks v. Ross, 52 U.S. 362 (1850), where the Court held that a suit against John Ross, Cherokee Nation tribal leader, could not proceed in federal court due to the status of the Cherokee Nation as a nation. Id. at 374. See generally William Wood, *It Wasn't An Accident: The Tribal Sovereign Immunity Story*, 62 Am.U.L.Rev. 1587, 1640–41 (2013); Catherine Struve, *Tribal Immunity and Tribal Courts*, 36 Ariz.St.L.J. 137, 148–155 (2004); Andrea M. Seielstad, *The Recognition and Evolution of Tribal Sovereign Immunity under Federal Law: Legal, Historical, and Normative Reflections on a Fundamental Aspect of American Indian Sovereignty*, 37 Tulsa L.Rev. 661 (2002). At one time viewed by the Court as a rule intended to protect the federal government from liability as trustee and guardian of the tribes as much as the tribes themselves, sovereign immunity is now regarded by tribal governments as an important adjunct of their sovereignty, required both to sustain tribal self-determination and encourage economic development.

KIOWA TRIBE OF OKLAHOMA V. MANUFACTURING TECHNOLOGIES, INC.

Supreme Court of the United States, 1998.
523 U.S. 751, 118 S.Ct. 1700, 140 L.Ed.2d 981.

JUSTICE KENNEDY delivered the opinion of the Court.

In this commercial suit against an Indian Tribe, the Oklahoma Court of Civil Appeals rejected the Tribe's claim of sovereign immunity. Our case law to date often recites the rule of tribal immunity from suit. While these precedents rest on early cases that assumed immunity without extensive reasoning, we adhere to these decisions and reverse the judgment.

I

Petitioner Kiowa Tribe is an Indian Tribe recognized by the Federal Government. The Tribe owns land in Oklahoma, and, in addition, the United States holds land in that State in trust for the Tribe. Though the record is vague about some key details, the facts appear to be as follows: In 1990, a tribal entity called the Kiowa Industrial Development Commission agreed to buy from respondent Manufacturing Technologies, Inc., certain stock issued by Clinton-Sherman Aviation, Inc. On April 3, 1990, the then-chairman of the Tribe's business committee signed a promissory note in the name of the Tribe. By its note, the Tribe agreed to pay Manufacturing Technologies $285,000 plus interest. The face of the note recites it was signed at Carnegie, Oklahoma, where the Tribe has a complex on land held in trust for the Tribe. According to respondent, however, the Tribe executed and delivered the note to Manufacturing Technologies in Oklahoma City, beyond the Tribe's lands, and the note obligated the Tribe to make its payments in Oklahoma City. The note does not specify a governing law. In a paragraph entitled "Waivers and Governing Law," it does provide: "Nothing in this Note subjects or limits the sovereign rights of the Kiowa Tribe of Oklahoma."

The Tribe defaulted; respondent sued on the note in state court; and the Tribe moved to dismiss for lack of jurisdiction, relying in part on its sovereign immunity from suit. The trial court denied the motion and entered judgment for respondent. The Oklahoma Court of Civil Appeals affirmed, holding Indian tribes are subject to suit in state court for breaches of contract involving off-reservation commercial conduct. The Oklahoma Supreme Court declined to review the judgment, and we granted certiorari.

II

***

Though the doctrine of tribal immunity is settled law and controls this case, we note that it developed almost by accident. The doctrine is said by some of our own opinions to rest on the Court's opinion in Turner v. United States, 248 U.S. 354 (1919). Though *Turner* is indeed cited as authority for the immunity, examination shows it simply does not stand for that proposition. The case arose on lands within the Creek Nation's "public domain" and subject to "the powers of [the] sovereign people." 248 U.S., at 355. The Creek Nation gave each individual Creek grazing rights to a portion of the Creek Nation's public lands, and 100 Creeks in turn leased their grazing rights to Turner, a non-Indian. He built a long fence around the land, but a mob of Creek Indians tore the fence down. Congress then passed a law allowing Turner to sue the Creek Nation in the Court of Claims. The Court of Claims dismissed Turner's suit, and the Court, in an opinion by Justice Brandeis, affirmed. The Court stated: "The fundamental obstacle to recovery is not the immunity of a sovereign to suit, but the lack of a substantive right to recover the damages resulting from failure of a government or its officers to keep the peace." Id., at 358. "No such liability existed by the general law." Id., at 357.

The quoted language is the heart of *Turner*. It is, at best, an assumption of immunity for the sake of argument, not a reasoned statement of doctrine. One cannot even say the Court or Congress assumed the congressional enactment was needed to overcome tribal immunity. There was a very different reason why Congress had to pass the Act: "The tribal government had been dissolved. Without authorization from Congress, the Nation could not then have been sued in any court; at least without its consent." Id., at 358. The fact of tribal dissolution, not its sovereign status, was the predicate for the legislation authorizing suit.

Turner, then, is but a slender reed for supporting the principle of tribal sovereign immunity.

Turner's passing reference to immunity, however, did become an explicit holding that tribes had immunity from suit. We so held in *USF & G,* saying: "These Indian Nations are exempt from suit without Congressional authorization." 309 U.S., at 512 (citing *Turner,* supra at 358). As sovereigns or quasi sovereigns, the Indian Nations enjoyed immunity "from judicial attack" absent consent to be sued. 309 U.S., at 513–514. Later cases, albeit with little analysis, reiterated the doctrine. E.g., *Puyallup,* 433 U.S., at 167, 172–173; *Santa Clara Pueblo,* 436 U.S., at 58; *Blatchford,* supra, at 782.

* * *

There are reasons to doubt the wisdom of perpetuating the doctrine. At one time, the doctrine of tribal immunity from suit might have been thought necessary to protect nascent tribal governments from encroachments by States. In our interdependent and mobile society, however, tribal immunity extends beyond what is needed to safeguard tribal self-governance. This is evident when tribes take part in the Nation's commerce. Tribal enterprises now include ski resorts, gambling, and sales of cigarettes to non-Indians. See Mescalero Apache Tribe v. Jones, 411 U.S. 145 (1973). In this economic context, immunity can harm those who are unaware that they are dealing with a tribe, who do not know of tribal immunity, or who have no choice in the matter, as in the case of tort victims.

These considerations might suggest a need to abrogate tribal immunity, at least as an overarching rule. Respondent does not ask us to repudiate the principle outright, but suggests instead that we confine it to reservations or to noncommercial activities. We decline to draw this distinction in this case, as we defer to the role Congress may wish to exercise in this important judgment.

Congress has acted against the background of our decisions. It has restricted tribal immunity from suit in limited circumstances. See, e.g., 25 U.S.C. § 450f(c)(3) (mandatory liability insurance); § 2710(d)(7)(A)(ii) (gaming activities). And in other statutes it has declared an intention not to alter it. See, e.g., § 450n (nothing in financial-assistance program is to be construed as "affecting, modifying, diminishing, or otherwise impairing the sovereign immunity from suit enjoyed by an Indian tribe"); see also *Potawatomi,* 498 U.S., at 510 (discussing Indian Financing Act of 1974, 88 Stat. 77, 25 U.S.C. § 1451 et seq.).

* * *

Like foreign sovereign immunity, tribal immunity is a matter of federal law. Although the Court has taken the lead in drawing the bounds of tribal immunity, Congress, subject to constitutional limitations, can alter its limits through explicit legislation. See, e.g., *Santa Clara Pueblo,* supra, at 58.

* * *

In light of these concerns, we decline to revisit our case law and choose to defer to Congress. Tribes enjoy immunity from suits on contracts, whether those contracts involve governmental or commercial activities and whether they were made on or off a reservation. Congress has not abrogated this immunity, nor has petitioner waived it, so the immunity governs this case. The contrary decision of the Oklahoma Court of Civil Appeals is Reversed.

JUSTICE STEVENS, WITH WHOM JUSTICE THOMAS and JUSTICE GINSBURG JOIN, DISSENTING. [omitted]

* * *

NOTES

1. The tribe specified in a paragraph entitled "Waivers and Governing Law" that: "Nothing in this Note subjects or limits the sovereign rights of the Kiowa Tribe of Oklahoma." Is such a clause sufficient notice to non-Indian corporations that federal Indian law principles of tribal sovereign immunity will apply to this off-reservation contract? Perhaps the need to know such basic principles of Indian law explains why some states now require the subject to be tested on the state's bar exam, and other states are considering including Indian law on theirs. See Gloria Valencia-Weber & Sherri Nicole Thomas, *When the State Bar Exam Embraces Indian Law: Teaching Experiences and Observations,* 82 N.D.L.Rev. 741 (2006).

The Indian Tribal Economic Development and Contract Encouragement Act of 2000, P.L. 106–179, includes among its provisions a requirement of disclosure of Indian tribal sovereign immunity in contractual situations covered under 25 U.S.C. § 81, the major Indian contracting statute.

2. Indian tribes have begun to waive their sovereign immunity strategically. Some tribes have enacted a tribal tort claims act, in which the tribe adopts a statute similar to the Federal Tort Claims Act, waiving immunity in tribal court for a specific damage amount. See David D. Haddock & Robert J. Miller, *Can a Sovereign Protect Investors from Itself? Tribal Institutions to Spur Reservation Investment,* 8 J. of Small and Emerging Bus.L. 173, 194 (2004) ("[T]he Grand Ronde, Umatilla, Siletz, and Warm Springs Tribes in Oregon, the Grand Traverse Band of Ottawa and Chippewa Indians in Michigan, and the Mashantucket Pequot Tribal Nation in Connecticut have all adopted tort claims ordinances.").

Indian law practitioner and scholar Kaighn Smith theorizes that Indian tribes use sovereignty both "affirmatively" and "defensively":

Affirmative sovereignty is the positive assertion of tribal authority, including the enactment of tribal law, to govern matters within the jurisdiction of a given tribe. Defensive tribal sovereignty involves the use of sovereign immunity "to shield tribes, their reservation affairs, and their reservation enterprises from the imposition of state or federal authority."

Kaighn Smith, Jr., *Ethical "Obligations" and Affirmative Tribal Sovereignty: Some Considerations for Tribal Attorneys*, in 31st Annual Federal Bar Association Indian Law Conference, Active Sovereignty in the 21st Century, Course Materials, 532, 534 (Apr. 6–7, 2006).

3. The doctrine of sovereign immunity incorporates a hierarchy of sovereign powers within the American constitutional system. For example, tribal sovereign immunity defenses are not a shield against suit by the United States against the tribe. United States v. Yakima Tribal Court of the Yakima Indian Nation, 794 F.2d 1402 (9th Cir.1986); United States v. Red Lake Band of Chippewa Indians, 827 F.2d 380, 383 (8th Cir.1987), cert. denied 485 U.S. 935 (1988) ("[J]ust as a state may not assert sovereign immunity as against the federal government, neither may an Indian tribe, as a dependent nation, do so.").

State and tribal governments, however, may assert sovereign immunity from suit by each other. Tribal suits against state governments are barred by the Eleventh Amendment to the Constitution. See Blatchford v. Native Village of Noatak, 501 U.S. 775 (1991). States may sue other states based upon consent, implied by their acceptance of the Constitution, but the *Blatchford* Court saw no such mutuality between tribes and states. Except under the Fourteenth Amendment, even Congress cannot abrogate the states' immunity by legislation, like the Indian Gaming Regulatory Act, to allow suits by tribes and others against states. See Seminole Tribe of Florida v. Florida, 517 U.S. 44 (1996).

Indian tribes are immune from suit from state governments. See Oklahoma Tax Comm'n v. Citizen Band Potawatomi Indian Tribe, 498 U.S. 505, 509 (1991). However, tribal sovereign immunity can be abrogated or waived in limited circumstances by Congress. See Public Service Co. of Colorado v. Shoshone-Bannock Tribes, 30 F.3d 1203 (9th Cir.1994) (holding that Congress abrogated tribal sovereign immunity in the Hazardous Materials Transportation Act, 49 U.S.C. § 1801, § 1811(c)(2)).

4. Tribal sovereign immunity may be waived by an Indian tribe or abrogated by an Act of Congress. Courts disfavor implied waivers of sovereign immunity. Santa Clara Pueblo v. Martinez, 436 U.S. 49, 58 (1978) ("It is settled that a waiver of sovereign immunity " 'cannot be implied but must be unequivocally expressed.' ") (quoting United States v. Testan, 424 U.S. 392, 399 (1976)).

In C & L Enterprises, Inc. v. Citizen Band Potawatomi Indian Tribe of Oklahoma, 532 U.S. 411 (2001), the United States Supreme Court, in a unanimous decision written by Justice Ginsburg, held that an Indian tribe waived its immunity from suit in Oklahoma state court when it expressly agreed to an arbitration clause in a tribal contract with a non-Indian contractor. The contractor was hired to install a roof on a building owned by the tribe off the reservation on non-trust lands. The contract clause was contained in a standard form agreement that was proposed by the tribe and accepted by the contractor. The clause provided that all disputes arising out of the contract "shall be decided by arbitration in accordance with the Construction Industry Arbitration Rules of the American Arbitration Association. . . . The award rendered by the arbitrator . . . shall be final, and judgment may be entered upon in accordance with applicable law in any court having jurisdiction thereof." 532 U.S. 411 at 415. The Court held that under the terms of the contract "the Tribe clearly consented to arbitration and to the enforcement of arbitral awards in Oklahoma state court." Id. at 423.

5.   Does a tribe waive its immunity from suit to the extent that it carries insurance? See Evans v. McKay, 869 F.2d 1341 (9th Cir.1989) (tribal sovereign immunity was not waived by Indian Self-Determination Act provision vesting Secretary with power to require tribes to carry insurance). The Navajo Nation Supreme Court has held that the tribe's waiver of immunity through an insurance exception in the Navajo Sovereign Immunity Act was effective although the insurance company had become insolvent. Johnson v. Navajo Nation, 5 Navajo Rptr. 192, 14 Indian L.Rep. 6037 (Navajo Supreme Court 1987). Other tribal courts have held that a tribe waives its immunity in tribal court to the extent it carries insurance. E.g., Kalantari v. Spirit Mountain Gaming, Inc., 2004 WL 5606419 (Grand Ronde Tribal Court, Mar. 24, 2004), appeal dismissed, 2005 WL 6165553 (Grand Ronde Ct.App., May 16, 2005).

6.   The doctrine of sovereign immunity derives from English common law—loosely, "the King can do no wrong." Many tribal court judges have been reluctant to apply tribal sovereign immunity in some cases on the grounds that the doctrine is not consistent with tribal customs and traditions. The following opinion by Michael Petoskey, chief judge of the Pokagon Band of Potawatomi Indians tribal court, articulates the issues as he applies the doctrine:

> The difficulty of this case, in viewing the pleadings in the light most favorable to Plaintiff, is that Plaintiff **may** not have been treated fairly. There are indications that such was the case. However, they are **only indications** as the facts have not been established. Application of the law of sovereign immunity will deny Plaintiff the opportunity to be heard and to make his arguments against all Defendants.
>
> Although justice may be "in the eye of the beholder", there can be no doubt that justice is and has been a basic human struggle throughout history. It is striking how "law" has been used by those in power to suppress others. The post-contact history of American Indians stands as a strong testament for that proposition.

"Great nations, like great men, should keep their word." See Federal Power Commission v. Tuscarora Indian Nation, 362 U.S. 99 (1960), quoting Justice Black in dissent. American Indians have suffered greatly at the hands of a dominant power that did not keep its treaty-making words to them. Plaintiff says Defendants did not keep their word. . . . Defendants argue that they did keep their word. However, the truth will not be revealed in public because of the protections of sovereign immunity. The Court can't help but wonder how the *Seven Grandfathers* would judge the actions/inactions of the principal actors in this matter. Would they demand as a matter of cultural traditions that one treat others as he or she would have them treat him or her?

* * *

It is unfortunate for Plaintiff that he did not bargain for a waiver of sovereign immunity. Given his position and length of employment with the Band, he had to have known of the protections provided by law, the important public policy considerations implicated and how to protect "the benefits of the bargain".

Soderburg v. Pokagon Band of Potawatomi Indians Tribal Council, No. 07–150, at 5–7 (Pokagon Band of Potawatomi Indians Tribal Court, Sept. 23, 2008) (emphases in original).

7.   One case seemed to sweep aside well-established sovereign immunity principles. Dry Creek Lodge, Inc. v. Arapahoe and Shoshone Tribes, 623 F.2d 682 (10th Cir.1980), cert. denied, 449 U.S. 1118 (1981). The court granted damages and injunctive relief against the tribes and in favor of non-Indian plaintiffs who had built a guest lodge within the reservation with the encouragement of the BIA superintendent and then were denied access to the property on a road that was blocked by the tribe. The tribal court refused to hear the matter without the consent of the tribal council. The court distinguished *Santa Clara,* by finding that "there has to be a forum where the dispute can be settled * * * to hold that they have access to no court is to hold they have constitutional rights which have no remedy."

Dry Creek Lodge is of limited validity. It has been limited and distinguished often by the court that decided it, but has not been either followed or overruled. E.g., Ramey Construction Co. v. Apache Tribe of the Mescalero Reservation, 673 F.2d 315, 319 n. 4 (10th Cir.1982). It has not been adopted by any other jurisdiction. E.g., Demontiney v. United States ex rel. Dept. of Interior, Bureau of Indian Affairs, 255 F.3d 801, 815 n.6 (9th Cir.2001).

8.   Attacks on the facial validity of tribal sovereign immunity have followed repeatedly since *Dry Creek Lodge,* including challenges to tribal immunity in state court dram shop actions, compare. Filer v. Tohono O'Odham Nation Gaming, 129 P.3d 78 (Ariz.App.2006) (upholding tribal sovereign immunity); Holguin v. Ysleta Del Sur Pueblo, 954 S.W.2d 843 (Tex.App.1997)

(same); Foxworthy v. Puyallup Tribe of Indians, 169 P.3d 53 (Wash.App.2007) (same), appeal dismissed 2009; with Bittle v. Bahe, 192 P.3d 810 (Okla.2008) (rejecting the tribal sovereign immunity defense); tribal sovereign lending, e.g., Colorado ex rel. Suthers v. Cash Advance and Preferred Cash Loans, 242 P.3d 1099 (Colo.2010) (affirming immunity); and tribal gaming compact interpretation, compare Cossey v. Cherokee Nation Enters. LLC, 212 P.3d 447 (Okla.2009) (rejecting immunity); Dye v. Choctaw Casino of Pocola, 230 P.3d 507 (Okla.2009) (same); Griffith v. Choctaw Casino of Pocola, 230 P.3d 488 (Okla.2009) (same); with Choctaw Nation of Oklahoma v. State of Oklahoma, 724 F. Supp. 2d 1182 (W.D.Okla.2010) (enjoining the Oklahoma courts from asserting jurisdiction after the tribe and the State of Oklahoma prevailed in arbitration on the immunity question).

The *Kiowa Tribe* majority plaintively requested that Congress reconsider the validity of tribal sovereign immunity, but Congress did not abrogate tribal immunity in the way the Court recommended. However, the State of Michigan asked the Court to reconsider *Kiowa Tribe* in a case where an Indian nation opened a gaming facility on off-reservation lands owned in fee.

MICHIGAN V. BAY MILLS INDIAN COMMUNITY

Supreme Court of the United States, 2014.
___ U.S. ___, 134 S. Ct. 2024, 188 L.Ed.2d 1071.

JUSTICE KAGAN delivered the opinion of the Court.

The question in this case is whether tribal sovereign immunity bars Michigan's suit against the Bay Mills Indian Community for opening a casino outside Indian lands. We hold that immunity protects Bay Mills from this legal action. Congress has not abrogated tribal sovereign immunity from a State's suit to enjoin gaming off a reservation or other Indian lands. And we decline to revisit our prior decisions holding that, absent such an abrogation (or a waiver), Indian tribes have immunity even when a suit arises from off-reservation commercial activity. Michigan must therefore resort to other mechanisms, including legal actions against the responsible individuals, to resolve this dispute.

I

[In 2010, the Bay Mills Indian Community opened a small casino on fee lands owned by the tribe located about 125 miles from the tribe's reservation. The State of Michigan sued the tribe in federal court, alleging violations of the Indian Gaming Regulatory Act and the Class III gaming compact with the tribe. The tribe raised its sovereign immunity. The Sixth Circuit held that neither the gaming compact nor the Indian Gaming Regulatory Act abrogated tribal immunity, and dismissed the State's complaint.]

II

* * *

Among the core aspects of sovereignty that tribes possess—subject, again, to congressional action—is the "common-law immunity from suit traditionally enjoyed by sovereign powers." * * * That immunity, we have explained, is "a necessary corollary to Indian sovereignty and self-governance." * * * And the qualified nature of Indian sovereignty modifies that principle only by placing a tribe's immunity, like its other governmental powers and attributes, in Congress's hands. [United States v. United States Fidelity & Guaranty Co.] ("It is as though the immunity which was theirs as sovereigns passed to the United States for their benefit"). Thus, we have time and again treated the "doctrine of tribal immunity [as] settled law" and dismissed any suit against a tribe absent congressional authorization (or a waiver). * * *

In doing so, we have held that tribal immunity applies no less to suits brought by States (including in their own courts) than to those by individuals. * * * While each State at the Constitutional Convention surrendered its immunity from suit by sister States, "it would be absurd to suggest that the tribes"—at a conference "to which they were not even parties"—similarly ceded their immunity against state-initiated suits. Blatchford v. Native Village of Noatak, 501 U.S. 775, 782 * * * (1991).

Equally important here, we declined in *Kiowa* to make any exception for suits arising from a tribe's commercial activities, even when they take place off Indian lands. [Our precedents] had established a broad principle, from which we thought it improper suddenly to start carving out exceptions. Rather, we opted to "defer" to Congress about whether to abrogate tribal immunity for off-reservation commercial conduct. * * *

Our decisions establish as well that such a congressional decision must be clear. The baseline position, we have often held, is tribal immunity; and "[t]o abrogate [such] immunity, Congress must 'unequivocally' express that purpose." * * * That rule of construction reflects an enduring principle of Indian law: Although Congress has plenary authority over tribes, courts will not lightly assume that Congress in fact intends to undermine Indian self-government. * * *

The upshot is this: Unless Congress has authorized Michigan's suit, our precedents demand that it be dismissed. And so Michigan, naturally enough, [argues] that if it does not, we should revisit—and reverse—our decision in Kiowa, so that tribal immunity no longer applies to claims arising from commercial activity outside Indian lands. * * *

* * *

IV

Michigan argues that tribes increasingly participate in off-reservation gaming and other commercial activity, and operate in that capacity less as governments than as private businesses. * * * Further, Michigan contends, tribes have broader immunity from suits arising from such conduct than other sovereigns—most notably, because Congress enacted legislation limiting foreign nations' immunity for commercial activity in the United States. * * * It is time, Michigan concludes, to "level[ ] the playing field." * * *

But this Court does not overturn its precedents lightly. * * * [T]his Court has always held that "any departure" from the doctrine "demands special justification." * * *

And that is more than usually so in the circumstances here. First, *Kiowa* itself was no one-off: Rather, in rejecting the identical argument Michigan makes, our decision reaffirmed a long line of precedents, concluding that "the doctrine of tribal immunity"—without any exceptions for commercial or off-reservation conduct—"is settled law and controls this case." * * * Second, we have relied on Kiowa subsequently: In another case involving a tribe's off-reservation commercial conduct, we began our analysis with Kiowa's holding that tribal immunity applies to such activity (and then found that the Tribe had waived its protection). * * * Third, tribes across the country, as well as entities and individuals doing business with them, have for many years relied on Kiowa (along with its forebears and progeny), negotiating their contracts and structuring their transactions against a backdrop of tribal immunity. * * * And fourth * * * , Congress exercises primary authority in this area and "remains free to alter what we have done"—another factor that gives "special force" to stare decisis. * * *

* * *

[I]t is fundamentally Congress's job, not ours, to determine whether or how to limit tribal immunity. The special brand of sovereignty the tribes retain—both its nature and its extent—rests in the hands of Congress. * * * Congress, we said—drawing an analogy to its role in shaping foreign sovereign immunity—has the greater capacity "to weigh and accommodate the competing policy concerns and reliance interests" involved in the issue. * * * And Congress repeatedly had done just that: It had restricted tribal immunity "in limited circumstances" (including, we noted, in § 2710(d)(7)(A)(ii)), while "in other statutes" declaring an "intention not to alter" the doctrine. * * * So too, we thought, Congress should make the call whether to curtail a tribe's immunity for off-reservation commercial conduct—and the Court should accept Congress's judgment.

All that we said in *Kiowa* applies today, with yet one more thing: Congress has now reflected on *Kiowa* and made an initial (though of course not irrevocable) decision to retain that form of tribal immunity. Following *Kiowa*, Congress considered several bills to substantially modify tribal immunity in the commercial context. Two in particular—drafted by the chair of the Senate Appropriations Subcommittee on the Interior—expressly referred to Kiowa and broadly abrogated tribal immunity for most torts and breaches of contract. See S. 2299, 105th Cong., 2d Sess. (1998); S. 2302, 105th Cong., 2d Sess. (1998). But instead of adopting those reversals of *Kiowa*, Congress chose to enact a far more modest alternative requiring tribes either to disclose or to waive their immunity in contracts needing the Secretary of the Interior's approval. See Indian Tribal Economic Development and Contract Encouragement Act of 2000, § 2, 114 Stat. 46 (codified at 25 U.S.C. § 81(d)(2)); see also F. Cohen, Handbook of Federal Indian Law § 7.05[1][b], p. 643 (2012). Since then, Congress has continued to exercise its plenary authority over tribal immunity, specifically preserving immunity in some contexts and abrogating it in others, but never adopting the change Michigan wants. So rather than confronting, as we did in Kiowa, a legislative vacuum as to the precise issue presented, we act today against the backdrop of a congressional choice: to retain tribal immunity (at least for now) in a case like this one.

Reversing *Kiowa* in these circumstances would scale the heights of presumption: Beyond upending "long-established principle[s] of tribal sovereign immunity," that action would replace Congress's considered judgment with our contrary opinion. * * * As Kiowa recognized, a fundamental commitment of Indian law is judicial respect for Congress's primary role in defining the contours of tribal sovereignty. See [*Kiowa*]; see also [*Santa Clara Pueblo*] ("[A] proper respect * * * for the plenary authority of Congress in this area cautions that [the courts] tread lightly"); Cohen, supra, § 2.01[1], at 110 ("Judicial deference to the paramount authority of Congress in matters concerning Indian policy remains a central and indispensable principle of the field of Indian law"). That commitment gains only added force when Congress has already reflected on an issue of tribal sovereignty, including immunity from suit, and declined to change settled law. And that force must grow greater still when Congress considered that issue partly at our urging. See [*Kiowa*] (hinting, none too subtly, that "Congress may wish to exercise" its authority over the question presented). Having held in *Kiowa* that this issue is up to Congress, we cannot reverse ourselves because some may think its conclusion wrong. Congress of course may always change its mind—and we would readily defer to that new decision. But it is for Congress, now more than ever, to say whether to create an exception to tribal immunity for off-reservation commercial activity. As in *Kiowa*—except still more so—"we decline to revisit our case law[,] and choose" instead "to defer to Congress." * * *

V

As "domestic dependent nations," Indian tribes exercise sovereignty subject to the will of the Federal Government. *Cherokee Nation*, 5 Pet., at 17. Sovereignty implies immunity from lawsuits. Subjection means (among much else) that Congress can abrogate that immunity as and to the extent it wishes. If Congress had authorized this suit, Bay Mills would have no valid grounds to object. But Congress has not done so: The abrogation of immunity in IGRA applies to gaming on, but not off, Indian lands. We will not rewrite Congress's handiwork. Nor will we create a freestanding exception to tribal immunity for all off-reservation commercial conduct. This Court has declined that course once before. To choose it now would entail both overthrowing our precedent and usurping Congress's current policy judgment. Accordingly, Michigan may not sue Bay Mills to enjoin the Vanderbilt casino, but must instead use available alternative means to accomplish that object.

We affirm the Sixth Circuit's judgment and remand the case for further proceedings consistent with this opinion.

It is so ordered.

JUSTICE SOTOMAYOR, concurring.

The doctrine of tribal immunity has been a part of American jurisprudence for well over a century. See, e.g., Parks v. Ross, 11 How. 362, 13 L.Ed. 730 (1851); Struve, Tribal Immunity and Tribal Courts, 36 Ariz. St. L.J. 137, 148–155 (2004) (tracing the origins of the doctrine to the Mid-19th century); Wood, It Wasn't An Accident: The Tribal Sovereign Immunity Story, 62 Am. U.L.Rev. 1587, 1640–1641 (2013) (same). And in more recent decades, this Court has consistently affirmed the doctrine. * * *

* * *

II

* * *

B

The principal dissent contends that Tribes have emerged as particularly "substantial and successful" commercial actors. * * * The dissent expresses concern that, although tribal leaders can be sued for prospective relief, * * * Tribes' purportedly growing coffers remain unexposed to broad damages liability. * * * These observations suffer from two flaws.

First, not all Tribes are engaged in highly lucrative commercial activity. * * *

Second, even if all Tribes were equally successful in generating commercial revenues, that would not justify the commercial-activity exception urged by the principal dissent. * * * [T]ribal business operations are critical to the goals of tribal self-sufficiency because such enterprises in some cases "may be the only means by which a tribe can raise revenues," Struve, 36 Ariz. St. L.J., at 169. This is due in large part to the insuperable (and often state-imposed) barriers Tribes face in raising revenue through more traditional means.

For example, States have the power to tax certain individuals and companies based on Indian reservations, making it difficult for Tribes to raise revenue from those sources. * * * States may also tax reservation land that Congress has authorized individuals to hold in fee, regardless of whether it is held by Indians or non-Indians. * * *

As commentators have observed, if Tribes were to impose their own taxes on these same sources, the resulting double taxation would discourage economic growth. Fletcher, In Pursuit of Tribal Economic Development as a Substitute for Reservation Tax Revenue, 80 N.D. L.Rev. 759, 771 (2004). * * *

* * *

Moreover, Tribes are largely unable to obtain substantial revenue by taxing tribal members who reside on non-fee land that was not allotted under the Dawes Act. As one scholar recently observed, even if Tribes imposed high taxes on Indian residents, "there is very little income, property, or sales they could tax." Fletcher, supra, at 774. The poverty and unemployment rates on Indian reservations are significantly greater than the national average. * * * As a result, "there is no stable tax base on most reservations." Fletcher, supra, at 774; see Williams, Small Steps on the Long Road to Self-Sufficiency for Indian Nations: The Indian Tribal Governmental Tax Status Act of 1982, 22 Harv. J. Legis. 335, 385 (1985).

* * *

JUSTICE SCALIA, dissenting.

In Kiowa Tribe of Okla. v. Manufacturing Technologies, Inc., 523 U.S. 751, 118 S.Ct. 1700, 140 L.Ed.2d 981 (1998), this Court expanded the judge-invented doctrine of tribal immunity to cover off-reservation commercial activities. Id., at 760, 118 S.Ct. 1700. I concurred in that decision. For the reasons given today in Justice THOMAS's dissenting opinion, which I join, I am now convinced that *Kiowa* was wrongly decided; that, in the intervening 16 years, its error has grown more glaringly obvious; and that stare decisis does not recommend its retention. Rather than insist that Congress clean up a mess that I helped make, I would overrule *Kiowa* and reverse the judgment below.

* * *

JUSTICE THOMAS, with whom JUSTICE SCALIA, JUSTICE GINSBURG, and JUSTICE ALITO join, dissenting.

* * *

In the 16 years since *Kiowa*, the commercial activities of tribes have increased dramatically. This is especially evident within the tribal gambling industry. Combined tribal gaming revenues in 28 States have more than tripled—from $8.5 billion in 1998 to $27.9 billion in 2012. National Indian Gaming Commission, 2012 Indian Gaming Revenues Increase 2.7 Percent (July 23, 2013). * * * But tribal businesses extend well beyond gambling and far past reservation borders. In addition to ventures that take advantage of on-reservation resources (like tourism, recreation, mining, forestry, and agriculture), tribes engage in "domestic and international business ventures" including manufacturing, retail, banking, construction, energy, telecommunications, and more. Graham, An Interdisciplinary Approach to American Indian Economic Development, 80 N.D. L.Rev. 597, 600–604 (2004). Tribal enterprises run the gamut: they sell cigarettes and prescription drugs online; engage in foreign financing; and operate greeting cards companies, national banks, cement plants, ski resorts, and hotels. * * * These manifold commercial enterprises look the same as any other—except immunity renders the tribes largely litigation-proof.

As the commercial activity of tribes has proliferated, the conflict and inequities brought on by blanket tribal immunity have also increased. Tribal immunity significantly limits, and often extinguishes, the States' ability to protect their citizens and enforce the law against tribal businesses. This case is but one example: No one can seriously dispute that Bay Mills' operation of a casino outside its reservation (and thus within Michigan territory) would violate both state law and the Tribe's compact with Michigan. Yet, immunity poses a substantial impediment to Michigan's efforts to halt the casino's operation permanently. The problem repeats itself every time a tribe fails to pay state taxes, harms a tort victim, breaches a contract, or otherwise violates state laws, and tribal immunity bars the only feasible legal remedy. Given the wide reach of tribal immunity, such scenarios are commonplace. * * *

In the wake of *Kiowa*, tribal immunity has also been exploited in new areas that are often heavily regulated by States. For instance, payday lenders (companies that lend consumers short-term advances on paychecks at interest rates that can reach upwards of 1,000 percent per annum) often arrange to share fees or profits with tribes so they can use tribal immunity as a shield for conduct of questionable legality. Martin & Schwartz, The Alliance Between Payday Lenders and Tribes: Are Both Tribal Sovereignty and Consumer Protection at Risk? 69 Wash. & Lee L.Rev. 751, 758–759, 777 (2012). * * *

* * *

JUSTICE GINSBURG, dissenting.

[Omitted]

NOTES

1.   Justice Thomas's dissenting opinion encourages petitioners to bring yet more cases before the Supreme Court when he warns that tribal immunity is a problem "every time a tribe fails to pay state taxes, harms a tort victim, breaches a contract, or otherwise violates state laws, and tribal immunity bars the only feasible legal remedy." 134 S. Ct. at 2051 (Thomas, J., dissenting). Cf. Matthew L.M. Fletcher, *(Re)Solving the Tribal No-Forum Conundrum:* Michigan v. Bay Mills Indian Community, 123 Yale L.J. Online 310 (2013).

2.   Tribal sovereign immunity does not bar suit where the plaintiff requests injunctive or declaratory relief against individual tribal government officials who allegedly violated federal law in federal courts. The *Bay Mills* Court suggests that tribal officials violating state law might also be sued, but the Court has not yet expressly held as such.

The Ninth Circuit held in Maxwell v. County of San Diego, 708 F.3d 1075 (9th Cir. 2013), that tribal public safety officials (police and ambulance workers) are not immune from suit under the tribal official immunity doctrine because any damages arising from the claim would come from the tribal workers' pockets. Id. at 1090. This decision worked an end-around of tribal sovereignty for the benefit of nonmember tort claimants. The tribe argued unsuccessfully that the tribe would indemnify the workers in the event of a damages award, and therefore tribal immunity should have been affirmed. Is the tribe's argument persuasive? What if anything can the tribe to do prevent these types of claims in the future?

3.   Another area where tribal immunity is under attack is in the context of tribal sovereign lending. In 2010, the Colorado Supreme Court decided a major tribal sovereign immunity case involving the efforts of the Colorado Attorney General to investigate payday lender franchises allegedly operated by the Miami Tribe of Oklahoma and the Santee Sioux Tribe of Nebraska, affirming that the tribes (and more specifically, their business arms) are immune from the state's investigative process. See Colorado ex rel. Suthers v. Cash Advance and Preferred Cash Loans, 242 P.3d 1099 (Colo.2010). The court noted:

> The modern realities of tribal sovereignty explain the broad applicability of the doctrine of tribal sovereign immunity. As Indian law scholar Robert A. Williams, Jr. recognized twenty-five years ago, "[t]erritorial remoteness, an inadequate public infrastructure base, capital access barriers, land ownership patterns, and an underskilled labor and managerial sector combine with paternalistic attitudes of federal policymakers to stifle Indian Country development and investment." Robert A. Williams, Jr., Small Steps on the Long Road

> to Self-Sufficiency for Indian Nations: The Indian Tribal Government
> Tax Status Act of 1982, 22 Harv. J. on Legis. 335, 335–36 (1985).
> Because of these barriers and tribes' virtual lack of a tax base, tribal
> economic development-often in the form of tribally owned and
> controlled businesses-is necessary to generate revenue to support
> tribal government and services. See generally Matthew L.M.
> Fletcher, In Pursuit of Tribal Economic Development as a Substitute
> for Reservation Tax Revenue, 80 N.D.L.Rev. 759 (2004).

Id. at 1107. Prominent scholars are beginning to weigh in on this phenomenon, worried about the potential long-term impact to tribal sovereignty. See Nathalie Martin & Joshua Schwartz, *The Alliance Between Payday Lenders and Tribes: Are Both Tribal Sovereignty and Consumer Protection at Risk?*, 69 Wash. & Lee L.Rev. 751 (2012).

NATION BUILDING NOTE:
SELF-DETERMINATION CONTRACTING

Modern tribal governance is built upon the Indian Self-Determination and Education Assistance Act (ISDEAA), enacted in 1975, and its progeny. 25 U.S.C. §§ 450 et seq. As the United States appropriates funds to the Interior Department to administer federal services in Indian country, Indian tribes may compel the federal government to enter into government contracts to administer those programs themselves, replacing the federal agencies. Four decades after the initial statute, more than 50 percent of all federal Indian programs are administered by Indian tribes instead of the federal government. Geoffrey D. Strommer & Stephen D. Osborne, *The History, Status, and Future of Tribal Self-Governance under the Indian Self-Determination and Education Assistance Act*, 39 Am. Indian L.Rev. 1, 1 (2014–2015).

Under ISDEAA, Indian tribes can enter into 638 (or self-determination) or self-governance contracts. The first type of contracts, named after the original Act's Public Law number, 93–638, involves tribes choosing from a menu (of sorts) of federally administered tribal programs, for example, membership, courts, education services, job training, law enforcement and public safety. Housing and health care are covered under separate statutes. The tribes agree to administer those programs through annual funding agreements, and leave the rest to the federal government. The tribe then will receive as a pass-through from the federal government Congressionally-appropriated funds to be spent on those programs. The tribes may supplement the federal money with tribal money, but once a tribe accepts the contract, it steps into the federal government's shoes to administer the service. Many tribes choose to leave law enforcement and public safety duties, for example, with the United States due to the excessive cost of that service. In any event, 638 contracting tribes become federal contractors and must comply with fairly onerous requirements in the administration of federal programs.

The other kind of contracts are self-governance contracts, first introduced in 1988 and more formally codified in 1994, whereby an Indian nation will accept the obligation to perform *all* of the federal Indian programs for the tribe. The tribe must apply for this status by demonstrating a strong track record in its 638 contracting.

The origin of the theory of tribal self-determination and self-governance contracting likely was Felix S. Cohen's original draft of the Indian Reorganization Act. H.R. 7902, 73rd Cong., 2d Sess., § 4, reprinted in The Indian Reorganization Act: Congresses and Bills 9–10 (Vine Deloria, Jr., ed. 2002). That section of the bill did not survive the cut, and it took several more decades before the United States would enact a similar provision in the ISDEAA.

The ISDEAA has not ended all disputes between tribes and the government over federal Indian programs. In Lincoln v. Vigil, 508 U.S. 182 (1993), the Court ruled that the Indian Health Service (IHS) need not engage in "notice and comment rulemaking" under § 553 of the Administrative Procedure Act (APA) before discontinuing clinical mental health services to handicapped Indian children.

Of far more critical importance to the administration of self-determination and self-governance contracts was the issue of contract support costs. Contract support costs, also known as indirect costs, are basically overhead. Whenever a contractor or a grantee receives money from the federal government (or anyone else), the recipient must either establish or have already in place an administrative arm to actually do the work of the contract or the grant. For a 638 or self-governance contractor, that includes money to pay for a building and infrastructure, salaries to pay workers, and whatever else is needed to administer the contract. Normally, the contract award would include funds for indirect costs, and the tribe and the government can negotiate that amount. But for decades, the United States did not appropriate funds for indirect costs, and so tribes were never reimbursed for their start-up and administration costs like other federal contractors.

Eventually, tribes began to bring class action suits against the BIA and the IHS, seeking reimbursement. The dollar figures for large class actions involving several years' worth of unpaid indirect costs was often staggering. The United States fought the tribes all of the way. Eventually, one suit reached the Supreme Court, Cherokee Nation of Oklahoma v. Leavitt, 543 U.S. 631 (2005). There, the Court held that tribes that take over administering health services may enforce a specific contractual provision allowing them "contract support costs" even where the lump-sum appropriations for the program are inadequate. The decision represented a major victory for tribes that have taken on provision of government services. The two petitioning tribes that brought the case had several million dollars at stake. The Court rejected the government's curious argument that tribes' took their chances that the federal government would not keep its contractual promise because of the "unique government-to-government nature" of the contract.

In a sequel to *Leavitt*, the Supreme Court held (5–4) in Salazar v. Ramah Navajo Chapter, 132 S. Ct. 2181 (2012), that federal agencies with self-determination contracts must pay full indirect contract costs even where Congress has not appropriated funds for those costs. Congress may set an annual appropriations limit on contract support costs (as indirect costs are also called) for Indian self-determination contracts (for example, in fiscal year 2000 that amount was more than $120 million), but if a tribal organization successfully proves entitlement to indirect costs, the government must pay those funds even if the agency's appropriations have been exhausted.

Going forward, the federal government now agrees to pay indirect costs in full. But some cases remain pending. In early 2016, the federal government settled Ramah Navajo Chapter v. Jewell, No. 90 CV 957 JAP/KBM (D.N.M., Feb. 23, 2016), for $940 million, with 8.5 percent of that total being paid to counsel for the class. Another case, Menominee Indian Tribe of Wisconsin v. United States, 136 S. Ct. 750 (2016), reached the Supreme Court, which held that the tribe's contract support costs claims had been brought too late, and must be dismissed.

SECTION E. TRIBAL JUSTICE SYSTEMS IN HISTORICAL AND CULTURAL CONTEXT

1. CUSTOMARY AND TRADITIONAL AMERICAN INDIAN LEGAL SYSTEMS

Traditional tribal governments in what is now the territory of the United States differed from the feudalized, hierarchical governmental systems endemic to the Old World. Most were far more decentralized and based on consensus and rule by the people rather than by a monarch who ruled by divine right. Tribal leaders rarely dictated their decisions; their power to lead depended on their ability to persuade and the respect they earned among the people. See Sharon O'Brien, American Indian Tribal Governments 15–16 (1989). Nevertheless, the tribes had established modes of governance that were not, at first, obvious to the Europeans who colonized the continent. "[T]hough it appeared to the casual white observer that anarchy reigned in Indian [reservations], those societies had evolved their own patterns of law and order." William T. Hagan, Indian Police and Judges 11 (1966).

The major tribal groups first encountered by Europeans in Eastern North America, such as the Powhatan Confederacy of Virginia, the Haudenosaunee (Iroquois) Confederacy, and the Cherokees, each possessed a system of fundamental laws and well-understood principles of self-government. The Haudenosaunee Confederacy governed itself in accordance with the Great Law of Peace established in the 18th century. A. C. Parker, The Constitution of the Five Nations or The Iroquois Book of the Great Law (1916). For other Indian tribes, written law "weakened their power by limiting accessibility to a few and losing the value of rhythm and intonation." Sarah Deer, The Beginning and End of Rape: Confronting Sexual Violence in Native America 16 (2015).

Many Indian tribes of North America adapted their traditional forms of government and laws in order to counter more effectively the Europeans who sought their lands. The Cherokee Nation's adoption of a written constitution and a formal, Anglo-style government structure in the early nineteenth century helped hold off the desires of white settlers and the new states for a while.

Clan and Kinship Systems. For most North American Indian tribes, clan and kinship systems are the source of many of the traditions, customs, and practices that define the rules and norms of political, legal, and social life. The Cherokees, for example, relied on their clan system to provide what has been called the "constitutional fabric" for their nation. John Phillip Reid, A Law of Blood: The Primitive Law of the Cherokee Nation 37 (1970). The Cherokees divided themselves into some fifty different towns spread throughout the Southern Appalachian range (in the area today forming the borderlands of North and South Carolina, Georgia, Tennessee, and southwestern Virginia). Because the Cherokees spoke three sectional dialects, intratribal communication and relations across village and regional boundaries could be difficult at times. Yet, "the legal and social structure of clanship, while providing less than perfect governmental unity, conjoined the Cherokees into one nation and one people." Id.

There were seven Cherokee clans organized along "matrilineal" lines, meaning that a Cherokee son, for example, belonged to his mother's clan. Upon divorce, Cherokee children followed the mother, not the father, and if the mother died, her eldest brother claimed her offspring. Even while the mother was alive, her brother, according to tribal custom, rightfully instructed and disciplined her children; not the biological father.

For the Cherokees, clanship provided order and security in tribal life. The pre-eminent Cherokee legal historian, Professor Rennard Strickland, explained that the clan was "the major institution exercising legal powers." Rennard Strickland, Fire and the Spirits: Cherokee Law from Clan to Court 27 (1975). The Cherokee clan system divided Cherokee society into easily identifiable groups of connection. Clanship terms like "brother," "uncle," "younger brother," and so on were vitally important to the Cherokees because they impressed a binding scheme of reciprocal rights and duties, effectively giving them legal force and significance among the Cherokee as a people.

A Cherokee on a hunt away from his town could visit another Cherokee town and know that clan relations would welcome him, defend his rights, and perform other duties owed a member of his clan. This knowledge of clanship rights and duties provided the Cherokees with a sense of "legal cohesiveness" as a people, uniting each individual to the tribal nation as a whole. Robert A. Williams, Jr., Linking Arms Together: American Indian Treaty Visions of Law and Peace, 1600–1800, 66–67 (1997).

An example of this "legal cohesiveness" is found in the Cherokee law of blood feud. The commission as well as punishment of a homicide were clan responsibilities. "The ghost of the murdered clansman could not pass from the earth until the blood had been revenged." Strickland, supra, at 27. Thus, if a member of the Bird clan was killed by a member of the Paint clan, a surviving member of the Bird clan could avenge the murder and release the ghost of his kin by killing any member of the Paint clan, thus satisfying the clan's group responsibility for the crime. Under Cherokee law, members of the Paint clan could protect the innocent in their own clan by themselves killing the guilty clan member. That act, under Cherokee law, ended the potential for any cycle of retaliatory killings. There was one retaliation, and that finished the matter as far as tribal law was concerned. Reid, supra, at 78–79; Strickland, supra, at 27–28.

Other North American Indian tribes each possessed their own distinctive forms of tribal law and complex systems of self-governance, organized in most instances according to well-established relationships of family, clan and kinship. E.g., Bruce G. Miller, The Problem of Justice: Tradition and Law in the Coast Salish World (2001); Michael Witgen, An Infinity of Nations: How the Native New World Shaped Early North America (2012) (describing Upper Great Lakes Anishinaabeg—Odawa, Ojibwe, and Bodewadmi—governance).

Law and Order. The legal systems of most tribes regarded enforcement of tribal law primarily as a family affair, with serious consequences for the peace and harmony of tribal society at large. We have already seen one example of tribal customary law at work in an Indian society in the famous nineteenth century case of Ex parte Crow Dog, 109 U.S. 556 (1883). The Brule Sioux had dealt with Crow Dog's murder of Spotted Tail according to their own legal traditions. As mediated by a tribal council and Brule Sioux peacemakers, the families involved agreed to a settlement of $600, eight horses, and one blanket. The offering of property to one side by the other did not indicate any substantive resolution of the merits of the case, nor was it a "blood money" payment to avoid revenge. "It was more of an offer of reconciliation, a symbolic continuing of tribal social relations." Often, in fact, the recipients would refuse the offered property; "a position that showed the tribe both their pride and their wealth." Sidney L. Harring, *Crow Dog's Case: A Chapter in the Legal History of Tribal Sovereignty*, 14 Am. Indian L.Rev. 191, 236–37 (1989).

Other tribal communities imposed wide varieties of sanctions, with many focused on restitution and material remedies, and others relying more on corporal punishments. For example, the Zuni Pueblo's punishments changed depending on the crimes committed. If the crime was one of simple theft or a physical assault, the Pueblo council would be more likely to assess a monetary or material penalty. See Watson Smith & John M. Roberts, Zuni Law: A Field of Values, Papers of the Peabody Museum of American Archaeology and Ethnology, Harvard University, Vol. 31, no. 1, at 121–22 (1954). However, individuals convicted of witchcraft or revealing secrets of the kachina could be hanged, clubbed, or flogged. See Smith & Roberts at 122. Some tribes dealt with domestic violence and sexual assault harshly, but not necessarily through violence. The Kiowas practiced a form of extreme humiliation for sexual assault, enforced by Kiowa women, that "was perhaps more chastening in its effect than the threat of the electric chair * * * ." Jane Richardson, Law and Status among the Kiowa Indians (1940), quoted in Andrea Smith, Conquest: Sexual Violence and American Indian Genocide 19 (2005).

Property Rights. Indian tribes also possessed sophisticated property rights regimes. The Michigan Anishinaabek (or the Three Fires Confederacy of Ottawa, Chippewa, and Potawatomi tribes) developed a complex system of hunting, fishing, farming, and trading territories. For example, Ottawa trade routes "could be used only by the family who pioneered them and who maintained a gift-exchange and kinship ties which assured safe passage for traders and a supply of goods when they reached their destination." James M. McClurken, The Ottawa, in People of the Three Fires: The Ottawa, Potawatomi, and Ojibway of Michigan 1, 11 (1986). Each family had its own hunting territories. Alexander Henry, a British fur trader who participated in the 1763 battle at Fort Michilimackinac, described Ottawa familial hunting rights as running with the land. Alexander Henry, Travels and Adventures 149 (University of Michigan 1968). Johann Kohl added: "The beaver dams—so persons conversant with the subject assured me—all have owners among the Indians, and are handed down from father to son. The sugar camps . . . have all an owner, and no Indian family would think of making sugar at a place where it had no right. Even the cranberry patches, or places in the swamp and bush where that berry is plucked, are family property; and the same with many other things.' " Johann Kohl, Kitchi Gami: Life Among the Lake Superior Ojibway 421 (1860) (Minnesota Historical Society Press 1985).

Puget Sound and Pacific northern Indian tribes also developed sophisticated property rights structures and legal regimes. See generally Russel Lawrence Barsh, *Coast Salish Property Law: An Alternative Paradigm for Environmental Relationships*, 12 Hastings W.–N.W. J. Envt'l L. & Pol'y 1 (2005). The Makah seafaring fishers, for example, actually divided the ocean into exclusive family territories, territories passed down through the generations. Use rights included those materials that floated up onto the beach. Vine Deloria, Jr., Indians of the Pacific Northwest 26, 62 (1977). Moreover, only a few could be chosen to become the owner of the community's whaling canoes, which reached 50 feet long. Made of cedar trees, the single log vessels were often harvested from high in the mountains. Id. at 32–33. Inland, the river-based tribes like the Skagit Indians "strictly controlled who could fish and at which sites." Fay G. Cohen, Treaties on Trial 22 (1986). Leaders of Pacific Northwest Indian communities "are still known for their potlatches—the social gatherings where special events are commemorated and where a leader can affirm his position by a great sharing of his goods and possessions." Cohen at 19. Cf. Ronald L. Trosper, *Traditional American Indian Economic Policy*, 19:1 Am. Indian Culture & Res. J. 65, 80–81 (1995) (detailing "generosity as fundamental in traditional Indian societies" such as in New England and in the South).

2. TRIBAL COURTS IN THE MODERN ERA: ORIGINS, GROWTH AND DEVELOPMENT

One of the most significant developments to occur during the modern era of federal Indian law has been the growing importance of tribal courts as vital law-making institutions of contemporary Indian self-government. The incipient efforts of tribes to revitalize their sovereign, self-governing powers over their reservations that were nurtured by the Supreme Court's landmark 1959 decision in Williams v. Lee, 358 U.S. 217 (1959), have given birth to the contemporary renaissance of American Indian tribal law within the United States legal system. Tribal law, or tribal customary law as it is sometimes called, is being interpreted and enforced by hundreds of tribal courts across Indian country. And, with increasing frequency, many of those authoritative interpretations of tribal law by tribal courts are being recognized and given legal force by state and federal court judges in cases involving Indian tribes and Indian individuals under principles of full faith and credit and comity.

The development of tribal courts in the modern era has been encouraged by congressional legislation and Executive Branch policies, favorable Supreme Court decisions such as *Williams*, and the commitment of Indian tribes, tribal judges, and tribal court personnel to create more effective institutions governed by an Indian vision of law and justice. The increased level of legislative and judicial activity on the part of tribes has been accompanied by growing pains and concerns about the administration of justice in Indian country by tribal courts. This section takes a closer look at the complex and difficult questions raised by the growth and revitalization of American Indian tribal law making authority during the modern era of Indian law.

MATTHEW L.M. FLETCHER, INDIAN COURTS AND FUNDAMENTAL FAIRNESS: *INDIAN COURTS AND THE FUTURE* REVISITED

84 U.Colo.L.Rev. 59, 63–64, 66–67, 70–73 (2013).

* * *

I.   The Getches Report and the Present

* * *

A.   The Historical Context of the Getches Report

In 1979, the National American Indian Court Judges Association ("NAICJA") published a report entitled Indian Courts and the Future: Report of the NAICJA Long Range Planning Project. The project involved surveys of twenty-three tribal courts from around the country about their structure, jurisdiction, day-to-day operations, procedures, and relations with state and federal courts.

* * *

B.   The State of Indian Courts Circa 1978

At this time, Indian courts suffered from a lack of legal infrastructure—constitutional texts, statutory texts, tribal customary law, and traditional law—upon which to draw and interpret. Tribal judges usually applied state and federal precedents in their 1970s and early 1980s opinions. They did so despite the fact that those opinions were derived from federal and state statutes that did not apply in the tribal context and involved common law from the Anglo-American tradition that also did not apply to tribal communities. Statutorily, with the exception of a few tribal constitutions, courts had little to draw upon except ICRA. Until 1978, when the Supreme Court decided Santa Clara Pueblo v. Martinez, holding that ICRA did not provide a federal cause of action to adjudicate those claims, litigants could access federal courts to litigate ICRA complaints.

* * *

C.   The State of Indian Courts Circa 2012

Each year, tribal justice systems grow in numbers, quality, and sophistication, and they grow in a manner many would never have contemplated or expected in 1978. * * * Despite having their civil and criminal jurisdiction over nonmembers handcuffed by United States Supreme Court decisions before most even began accepting cases, tribal courts have developed in some of the most creative and progressive ways. Examples include developing cooperative arrangements with state courts, civil remedies against non-Indian criminal offenders, peacemakers courts (traditional dispute resolution practices), and drug courts.

But, just as in 1978, many tribal courts remain undeveloped and often inefficient because of a lack of resources and a lack of functional judicial independence. Concerning resources, tribal judges face the reality of limited governmental social services for families and children in need and limited tribal court operations resources. Furthermore, many tribal judges and their staff members have little or no access to electronic legal research and law clerks, although some law schools with Indian law programs are now serving as sources for tribal courts seeking low-cost court clerks. On the structural side, many tribal judges face overt and covert attacks on their independence (although the extent of interference with the judicial function by tribal policymakers is debated). For example, many tribal constitutions provide express or implied tribal council control over appointments and retention of tribal judges. Additionally, some tribal judges face threats from tribal legislatures on budgets. Many tribal courts have virtually no authority to review tribal government actions—even where tribal independence is assured by constitution or statute—because of tribal sovereign immunity.

* * *

II. Fundamental Fairness and Indian Courts

What guarantees fundamental fairness in Indian courts? Is it ICRA? Is it unwritten tribal customary and traditional law? Is it tribal statutory and constitutional protections? For each tribe, the answer may be different. [The Getches Report] focused the discussion about these questions by placing the onus on tribal justice systems and away from how state or federal courts and legislatures could guarantee fairness in Indian country. Rather than recommending another federal solution, Dean Getches, on behalf of the National American Indian Court Judges Association, recommended positive tribal law, a return to tribal traditions, and guarantees of procedural due process. In other words, Dean Getches argued that eventually tribal jurisprudence on due process and equal protection should not be based on American jurisprudence but instead on tribal law.

And yet, tribal judges and litigants rely almost exclusively on American jurisprudence concerning due process and equal protection as introduced into tribal law by ICRA. In our 2008 study of tribal court decisions applying ICRA to civil rights claims, we found that ninety-five percent of tribal courts applied American law.

Of the 120 cases involving an ICRA issue, tribal court judges cited federal and state case law as persuasive (and often controlling law) in 114 cases (95 percent). And, of the six cases in which the tribal court explicitly refused to apply federal or state case law, either the parties included tribal members in a domestic dispute or the tribal court held that its interpretations of the substantive provisions of ICRA were stronger or more protective of individual rights than would otherwise be available in analogous federal or state cases.

Of course, the selection of these cases likely dictated the result in that every case involved an allegation relating to, or reasoning based upon, application of ICRA.

In my view, and this is terribly preliminary, tribal courts will soon rely less on ICRA and the related American jurisprudence on due process and equal protection and more on their own customs and traditions for insight. American law was (and still is) a necessary crutch to establishing a tribal common law that effectively guarantees fundamental fairness to litigants in Indian courts as tribes continue to reestablish and adapt their customs and traditions to meet modern needs. Tribal courts have long recognized a need for a legal foundation that would help them guarantee fundamental fairness for all litigants, and American law, as imposed by Congress in ICRA, provides that foundation. Tribal justice systems can proceed in a manner that builds upon that foundation, as many have. Or tribal courts can dispense with ICRA and federal and state law altogether and choose to rely exclusively on their own common law. As Vine Deloria and Clifford Lytle once wrote, "The greatest challenge faced by the modern tribal court system is in harmonizing of past Indian customs and traditions with the dictates of contemporary jurisprudence."

NOTES

1.   In 1978, the National American Indian Court Judges Association reported that there were 71 tribal courts, and 32 "CFR" courts which trace their descent from the nineteenth century Courts of Indian Offenses. Today, as many as 400 tribal courts exercise some form of jurisdiction. National American Indian Court Judges Assn., National Directory of Tribal Justice Systems (2013). The numbers, however, tell only part of the story of the growth and diversity of these unique and evolving institutions that are in the forefront of modern tribal efforts to define the meanings and scope of tribal sovereignty in United States society. For surveys describing the diversity of tribal law and tribal justices systems, see Matthew L.M. Fletcher, American Indian Tribal Law (2011); Frank Pommersheim, Tribal Justice: Twenty-Five Years as a Tribal Appellate Justice (2015); and Justin B. Richland & Sarah Deer, Introduction to Tribal Legal Studies (3rd ed. 2016).

2.   A key question for modern tribal courts in the United States is the question of legitimacy, within and without the tribal community:

> Much remains to be done in the building of Indian nations' judicial systems. For a number of reasons, many are currently far from establishing complete legitimacy in the eyes of non-Indian governments, individuals, and court systems. First, tribal courts tend to be less specialized that state and federal courts. For example, the court on many reservations does not have a distinct probate division.

Second, the capacity of tribal courts is lacking for certain types of litigation—empaneling a jury that is comprised entirely of tribal members who have no connection to a given proceeding is exceedingly difficult in reservations that are sparsely populated. By the same token, tribal judges often have had little experience in certain areas of the law; topics such as business law are relative newcomers to their venues. Third, some tribal courts continue to lack independence from the political processes of Native nations.

The Harvard Project on American Indian Economic Development, The State of Native Nations: Conditions Under U.S. Policies of Self-Determination 46–47 (2008).

The legitimacy of tribal court judgments and orders in federal and state courts may depend on whether the tribal court takes the Indian Civil Rights Act seriously, and applies it in accordance with federal precedents. Cf. Matthew L.M. Fletcher, *Contract and (Tribal) Jurisdiction*, 126 Yale L.J. Forum 1, 5 (2016) (noting that some members of the Supreme Court worried that tribal courts were not constrained by the Federal Constitution).

3. TRIBAL COURT DECISION MAKING IN MODERN TRIBAL LEGAL SYSTEMS

Because of the diversity among Indian country tribal justice systems, it would be impossible to synthesize the decisions of all of the tribal courts into an "American Indian tribal law" on a particular topic. Each of the tribal courts operating in Indian country represents a unique response to the need felt by a particular tribal community to make its own laws and to be governed by its own customs and traditions. The materials in this section focus attention on the development of tribal law in just a few areas.

a. The Preservation and Restoration of Tribal Customs and Traditions in Tribal Common Law

One of the twentieth century's most influential legal scholars, Robert Cover, coined the term "jurisgenesis" to describe a process whereby a community engages in "the creation of legal meanings." Robert M. Cover, *Nomos and Narrative*, 97 Harv.L.Rev. 4, 11 (1983). Tribal courts throughout Indian country are engaging in the creation of legal meanings by relying on tribal customs and traditions as important sources of tribal law.

Tribal courts often encounter conflicting jurisdictional and conflict of laws situations. When does tribal custom prevail over other forms of conflicts of laws situations? Many tribes have statutes in their tribal codes that determine the order in which laws should be applied by the tribal court. The Code of the Winnebago Tribe of Nebraska is fairly typical in this regard: "[T]he court shall apply the tribal constitution, and the provisions of all statutory law here forth or hereafter adopted by the tribe in matters not covered by tribal statute. The court shall apply traditional tribal customs and usages, which shall be called common law." Code of Winnebago Tribe of Nebraska, Section 1–109.

Where do tribal courts find tribal customary law? Tribal elders may be called upon to testify on customs that can be applied as law. Tribal courts may also turn to academic works on tribal customs and traditions as sources of tribal common law. Many tribal judges take judicial notice of well-known customs and traditions and apply them to issues before the court. For example, the Hopi Tribal Court said it "may dispense with proof of the existence of a Hopi custom, tradition or culture if it finds the custom, tradition or culture to be generally known and accepted within the Hopi Tribe [and] take judicial notice of the custom or tradition." Hopi Indian Credit Ass'n v. Thomas, No. AP–001–84 (Hopi Tribal Court 1996). Some tribal courts, however, are less receptive to taking judicial notice, and require the parties to present affirmative evidence of tribal customs or cultural practices. See, e.g., Healy v. Mashantucket Pequot Gaming Enterprise, 3 Mash. Rptr. 64, 71 (Mash. Pequot Tribal Ct. 1999) ("This court is mindful of its duty to honor the customs, traditions and cultural practices of the Mashantucket Pequot Tribal Nation. The defendant in this case, however, does not offer any Mashantucket Pequot tribal custom, tradition or cultural practice as support for the amendment to the Board of Review policy. Where there is no evidence of a tribal custom, tradition or cultural norm that will be disrupted, the court may apply general federal and state principles of due process.").

Many tribal codes permit the tribal court on its own motion to seek the advice of elders or counselors on the tribe's customary law. The Winnebago Tribe of Nebraska, for example, permits its tribal court to call on tribal members with knowledge of the tribe's customs and traditions for advice: "When in doubt as to the tribal common law, the court may request the advice of counselors and tribal elders familiar with it." Code of the Winnebago Tribe of Nebraska § 1–109.

Special problems of identifying, validating, and applying tribal customary and traditional law are examined in Matthew L.M. Fletcher, *Rethinking Customary Law in Tribal Court Jurisprudence*, 13 Mich.J. Race & L. 57, 88–93 (2007).

Navajo Nation. The courts of the Navajo Nation were at the center of the jurisdictional dispute in the landmark 1959 Supreme Court decision in Williams v. Lee, 358 U.S. 217 (1959). The Navajo Nation operates the largest tribal court system in Indian country, located on the most populous reservation in the United States. The broad range of major issues that tribal courts deal with on a daily basis are all regularly handled by the Navajo Nation courts. Separation of powers and judicial independence, impeachment and removal of elected officials, election controversies, employment relations, family law, probate and inheritance of property, paternity and child support, enrollment, land tenure rights on the reservation, tribal bills of rights and protection of individual rights under the Indian Civil Rights Act, 25 U.S.C. §§ 1301–1304, tribal sovereign immunity, contracts and commercial transactions are all part of the regular business of the Navajo Nation court system. The Navajo Nation docket exceeds 100,000 cases per year, providing a line of precedents large enough to constitute a common law of the tribe.

The Navajo courts have approached the difficult task of "blending the old with the new" by integrating traditional tribal dispute resolution methods with Anglo-American judicial methods. They have exemplified professionalism, independence, and institutional competence, while maintaining an abiding and rigorous respect for the integrity of the Navajo way.

RAYMOND D. AUSTIN,* ADR AND THE NAVAJO PEACEMAKER COURT

32 Judges Journal 8, 8–11, 47–48 (1993).

Long before Europeans set foot on the Americas, the Navajo Nation had its own unique legal structure and dispute settlement traditions. Some of these traditional legal concepts have survived and have now been incorporated into modern Navajo methods of dispute resolution by the Courts of the Navajo Nation.

* * *

FREEDOM WITH RESPONSIBILITY

One fundamental value of Navajo society is complete equality among people. Navajos have what some call "permissive" child-rearing techniques, but Navajo children are treated as equals who have their own identities. This reflects the value that equals are free to do what they please, without others telling them what they can or cannot do. When asked if another Navajo will do something or if that person's property may be used, a tribe member will reply "it's up to him." Navajos do not believe in making decisions for others. Navajo common law rejects coercion. That creates difficulties for any legal system which is built upon coercion, authority, and levels of power, such as the adversary system.

The high respect for individual freedom is balanced by concepts of responsibility and duty. Navajos have an ingrained respect for *ke'e*, or kinship. *Ke'e* encompasses extensive responsibilities to others and respect for them. The others include spouses, children, immediate blood relations,

---

*   [Ed.] Justice Austin served as Associate Justice on the Navajo Supreme Court from 1985–2001.

clan relations, Navajos in general, and people at large. Even Father Heaven, Mother Earth, and the plants and animals are included.

Navajo families live in groups, with each person having a role for family survival. Men have duties to women, women to men, and parents have responsibilities to their children. The family, which includes extended family members, works as an economic unit. The Navajo clan system, where people trace their lineage through their mothers, is a legal system. Navajo relations and responsibilities to clan members are part of a sophisticated system that defines rights, duties, and mutual obligations in relationships. Navajos are taught their responsibilities to clan members, which they carry out, and there is a saying that "One should act towards others as if they were your relatives." Shaming is an important part of discipline, and Navajos say to a wrongdoer, "You act as if you had no relatives." Mutual dependence, cooperation, and the ethic of family and clan are the framework for freedom with responsibility.

The Navajo culture stresses *hozho*, which when generally translated means "harmony." It is, however, broader than that, with a meaning something like "a reality with a place for everything, and everything in its place, functioning well with everything else." In other words, the "Perfect State." Wrongdoing and offenses occur when something or someone is out of harmony. Navajo religious ceremonies are directed to regaining and maintaining harmony.

Another Navajo legal value, which supplements notions of freedom and responsibility, is a great respect for tradition. Navajo traditions reflect freedom, responsibility, and dealing with the things that get in the way of a good and prosperous life. Those things are "monsters" in the Navajo way of thinking. Abstract Navajo values found in religious ceremonies, the creation stories, and past Navajo practices become concrete guides for daily life. They give real meaning to ideas of equality, responsibility, and duty.

These are the primary foundations for the traditional Navajo legal system.

* * *

TRADITIONAL PROCEDURE

A great deal of the Navajo common law is built upon relationships, and Navajo civil procedures utilize them. When someone does wrong, or injures another, there is "talking." The Navajo word for "trial" is *ahwiniti*, which roughly translated means, "Someone (or more than one person) is the focus of discussion." Navajo civil procedure requires talking things out to reach consensus. During the process of talking, it is easy to identify duties, responsibilities, and relationships, as well as examining approaches to resolve disputes. The procedural goals are to reach consensus and harmony, with plans to maintain it. Continuing relationships, a key to modern alternative dispute resolution, are a central part of the process.

* * *

APPLICABILITY TO MODERN SETTINGS

Throughout the history of modern courts of adjudication in the Navajo Nation, Navajo judges have used these principles in cases before them. The Navajo Court of Indian Offenses was created by the United States government in 1892 to destroy Navajo culture, but history shows that the Navajo judges of that court resisted imposed methods and instead used Navajo common law to resolve disputes. Following the creation of the Navajo Tribal Courts in 1958, Navajo judges have strived to reconcile adjudication with Navajo common-law methods. * * *

* * *

In 1981, the chief justice of the Navajo courts started a project to use the Navajo common law in the Navajo courts. That led to several initiatives. Written court opinions use Navajo common law, and it is now the law of preference. * * *

* * *

Navajos see their common law as the base upon which their society functions. Not only does it have relevance for approaches to alternative dispute resolution, but it also has relevance to all aspects of modern Navajo law and legal institutions. Indian courts should be leery about the miracles of modern alternative dispute resolution, because Indians had it long before the United States government imposed the adjudication system on the Indian tribes in 1883. Indian courts do not need more imposed systems, including non-Indian methods, theories, or procedures of alternative dispute resolution. While they may have value to help focus upon elements of traditional systems, the traditional values are the most important for Indians.

* * *

TSOSIE V. DESCHENE

Supreme Court of the Navajo Nation, 2014.
Nos. SC–CV–57–14, SC–CV–58–14, 12 Am. Tribal Law 55.

* * *

The Navajo Nation primary election was held on August 26, 2014 after a number of public debates. Out of a total of 17 candidates for the office of the Navajo Nation President, Joe Shirley, Jr. and Christopher C. Deschene (Deschene) prevailed as the top two candidates to be placed on the ballot for the general election. The Navajo Election Administration (NEA) had certified both candidates as eligible to run for the position prior to the primary election.

[Appellants] filed written complaints * * * asserting that on April 14, 2014 Deschene submitted a candidate application with a false statement that he met all qualifications for the position, including the requirement in 11 N.N.C. § 8(A)(4) that he "must *fluently* speak and understand Navajo."1 (Emphasis added). The requirement for fluency in Navajo is a statutory requirement that was enacted by the Navajo Nation Council in 1990 as part of the 1990 Election Code. Res. CAP–23–90. The Election Code does not define "fluently" and the Navajo Board of Election Supervisors did not adopt rules or regulations to implement and interpret this provision. The Appellants further assert Deschene has been open about his inability to fluently speak and understand Navajo at a number of public forums held in the months leading up to the primary election. Despite Deschene's disclosures, it is undisputed that no challenges to his qualifications were filed by the Appellants prior to the primary election.

V.

We now address the requirement for fluency in the Navajo language. Deschene argues the requirement for fluency in Navajo should be disregarded in favor of the 9,831 voters (19% of all voters of the primary election), who voted for him because the qualification is vague, ambiguous, subjective and discriminating against young and educated Navajos. We strongly disagree.

The law that a candidate for the office of the Navajo Nation President "[m]ust fluently speak and understand Navajo and read and write English," 11 N.N.C. § 8(A)(4), is clear and unambiguous, and a reasonable regulation of a candidate's right to political liberty. Candidates have a "Fundamental Law right to participate in the political system by running for office." In re Grievance of Wagner, 7 Am. Tribal Law 528, 532 (Nav.Sup.Ct.2007) (citing Begay v. NEA, 8 Nav. R. 241, 249, 4 Am. Tribal Law 604 (Nav.Sup.Ct.2002)). "While the right or privilege of placing one's name in nomination for public elective office is a part of political liberty, thus making it a due process right, that liberty may be restricted by statute. Any such restriction must be reasonable and forward some important governmental interest." Bennett v. Navajo Board of Election Supervisors, 6 Nav. R. 319, 325 (Nav. Sup. Ct. 1990).

As Diné, we are the image of our ancestors and we are created in connection with all creation. Upon our creation, we are identified by:

Our Diné name,

Our clan,

Our language,

Our life way,

Our shadow,

Our footprints.

Therefore, we were called the Holy Earth-Surface-People [Diyin Nohookáá Diné],

* * *

Different thinking, planning, life ways, languages, beliefs, and laws appear among us, But the fundamental laws [Diné bi beehaz'áanii bitsé siléí] placed by the Holy People remain unchanged.

1 N.N.C. § 201 (emphasis added).

Diné bi beenahaz'áanii is the foundation of Diné bi nahat'á (providing leadership through developing and administering policies and plans utilizing these laws as guiding principles) and Diné sovereignty. In turn, Diné bi nahat'á is the foundation of the Diné bi naat'á (government). Diné bi beenahaz'áanii recognizes the freedoms of the individual Diné but it also firmly supports "the [collective] right and freedom of the people that the sacred Diné language (nihiinéí') be taught and preserved. * * *" See 1 N.N.C. § 204(C). The individual freedoms of each Diné have long been respected but restricted by the collective rights of the Diyin Nohookáá Diné, the fundamental values and principles of Diné Life Ways, and our inherent right to self-govern.

So long as there is a reasonable basis for the restriction and an important governmental interest is advanced, in this case the collective right that the sacred Diné language (nihiinéí') be preserved by requiring fluency in Navajo as a requirement of the highest elected official, this Court will presume that the Council will not enact legislation which would deny civil rights. *Sandoval* [*v. NEA*], 11 Am. Tribal Law [112,] 119–20 [Navajo Sup. Ct. 2013)]. The legal requirement applies generally to all presidential candidates. There is no evidence to show the law was intended to discriminate against the young person who may not be fluent and who may aspire to be a leader. There is no indication from the legislative history of this provision that would overcome the presumption in Navajo law that duly enacted laws are presumed to be valid. From the policy enunciated in Title 1, the reasonableness of the fluency qualification in Title 11 is beyond question. The law was enacted to preserve, protect, and promote self-determination, for which language is essential. Diné binanita'í jíliigo nábináhaazláago Diné bizaad bee yájíłtti' dóó bik'izhdiitiihdoo háálá Diné bina'nitiní jíli dóó Diné bájizi dóó bich'ááh jizi. Therefore, we find the requirement for fluency in the Navajo language is a reasonable regulation of a candidate's right to participate in the political system. We therefore reject Deschene's arguments to simply disregard the explicit requirement for fluency as specified in 11 N.N.C. § 8(A)(4).

* * *

In accordance with our duty to interpret Navajo statutory law using Diné bi beenahaz'áanii, we therefore interpret the meaning and adopt a standard for "fluently" as offered by the Appellants as follows:

> Da dilkoohgo, t'áá k'idahineezláago, t'áá chánahgo, diits'a'go, háálá Diné Binanit'a'í ídlíigo éí łahdóó baa yájíłti' (talk about), nabík'í yájíłti' (analysis speech), bich'i' yájíłti' (to talk about), hach'i'yáłti' (to be talked to), and Diné k'ehgo bik'izhdii'tiih (comprehending the substance in the iné language).

* * *

NOTES

1.   The Navajo language fluency requirement and the disqualification of Chris Deschene from the 2014 tribal election for president were extremely controversial. E.g., Andrew Curley, *The Dark Side of Navajo Traditionalism*, Al-Jazeera America, Nov. 3, 2014. Deschene, who was a lawyer, had already campaigned during the presidential primary season, finished second in voting, and qualified for the general election. He argued that the voters should decide whether his lack of fluency in the language would disqualify him. Is that persuasive?

The Navajo Supreme Court did not actually disqualify Deschene. The court merely upheld the requirement, allowing Deschene to prove fluency. Deschene declined to do so. Note the procedural posture at the start of the opinion, in which the petitioners claimed Deschene had falsified his application for candidacy. In a subsequent opinion, the Navajo Supreme Court explained that Deschene had not challenged the falsification allegation. Tsosie v. Navajo Board of Election Supervisors, 12 Am. Tribal Law 73 (Navajo Nation Supreme Court 2014). Does the falsification allegation complicate the case?

There was enormous pressure from within and without the tribal community to allow Deschene to run. The Navajo Nation Council amended the code to allow for non-fluent speakers to run for office, but the sitting Navajo President vetoed the bill. The Navajo Supreme Court, split 2–1, later issued a writ of mandamus ordering the Navajo Board of Election Supervisors to immediately print ballots without Deschene's name on them. Tsosie v. Navajo Board of Election Supervisors, 12 Am. Tribal Law 64, 70 (Navajo Nation Supreme Court 2014). Two weeks later, the court held the election board in civil contempt for failing to comply. Tsosie v. Navajo Board of Election Supervisors, 12 Am. Tribal Law 73 (Navajo Nation Supreme Court 2014). In 2015, Deschene was announced as the Department of Energy's Director of the Office of Indian Energy.

2. Former Navajo Nation Supreme Court Justice Raymond Austin explained in greater detail the legal concept of *Diné bibee haz'áanii*:

> Traditional Navajos understand *Diné bibee haz'áanii* as values, norms, customs, and traditions that are transmitted orally across generations and which produce and maintain right relations, right relationships, and desirable outcomes in Navajo society. In the modern Navajo world, the term *Diné bibee haz'áanii* is understood as Navajo statutory law, administrative regulations, court-made law, and Navajo common law (values, norms, customs, and traditions). Thus, the standard translation of *Diné bibee haz'áanii* is law and that is how the Navajo courts have described the term.

> In 1990, the Navajo Nation Supreme Court explained the legal aspects and legal understanding of the word *haz'áanii* in *Bennett v. Navajo Board of Election Supervisors*:

> > The Navajo word for "law" is *haz'áanii*. While we hear that word popularly used in the sense of laws enacted by the Navajo Nation Council . . . it actually refers to higher law. It means something which is "way at the top"; something written in stone so to speak; something which is absolutely there; and, something like the Anglo concept of natural law. In other words, Navajos believe in a higher law, and as it is expressed in Navajo, there is a concept similar to the idea of unwritten constitutional law. [*Bennett*, 6 Nav. R. 319, 324 (1990).]

> The Supreme Court went on to explain that Navajo higher law includes "fundamental customs and traditions, as well as substantive rights found in the Treaty of 1868, the Navajo Nation Bill of Rights, the Judicial Reform Act of 1985, and the Title Two Amendments of 1989." [Id.] Although the Supreme Court did not identify any fundamental customs and traditions that would constitute higher law, Navajo thinking would place the doctrines of *hózhó*, *k'é*, and *k'éí* into that category.

> These three doctrines are not basic legal principles in the sense that they can be applied directly to legal questions in litigation. They essentially describe conditions generated through law when we speak of them in the legal context. They also describe other conditions, such as, for example, when they are spoken of in the spiritual context. The three fundamental Navajo doctrines are like the Anglo concept of natural law. They are also Diné philosophical doctrines. They are integral to the Navajo Creation Scripture and Journey Narratives and undergird, along with other doctrines, Navajo culture (including customs, traditions, and philosophy), language, spirituality, sense of place, and identity.

Raymond D. Austin, Navajo Courts and Navajo Common Law: A Tradition of Tribal Self Governance 40–41 (2009).

3.   Dr. Austin cautions both Navajos and non-Navajos, particularly legal counsel, about the importance of Navajo custom and about the application of Navajo custom in legal cases:

> Although a party may not follow customs or traditions, when any is pleaded in the initial pleadings or anytime thereafter, it becomes relevant and can be considered by the judge and those litigating. Moreover, not all Navajo customs are law, and the individual contributing common-law knowledge may refuse to testify on custom in open court due to its sacred nature or object on other grounds. Participants should understand that the adversarial process is not a traditional Navajo method of dispute resolution. An in camera disclosure of the sacred custom is a possible solution. Problems sometimes arise when litigants attempt to introduce Indian common law into tribal, state, and federal courts, but under most circumstances any problem can be alleviated through respectful discussion and understanding.

> Legal practitioners who are not familiar with Navajo culture, including language, etiquette, and spiritual beliefs and practices, would do well to associate with a court advocate or attorney who is Navajo and a member of the Navajo Nation Bar Association. The Navajo legal practitioner can help locate sources of Navajo common law, including knowledgeable persons, and advise on introducing customs into court proceedings. Although being Navajo does not guarantee a person will know Navajo common law, Navajo legal counselors are usually culturally embedded. They know Navajo spiritual and social practices, can speak the Navajo language, and possess an insider's view of Navajo court practice.

Austin, supra, at 46–47.

Hopi Tribe. Like the Navajo Nation, the tribal courts of the Hopi Tribe are leaders in applying tribal customary and traditional law as embodied in the Hopi language and oral teachings in deciding legal disputes. See generally Justin B. Richland, Arguing with Tradition: The Language of Law in Hopi Tribal Court (2008).

The origins of the Hopi Tribal Court are at least as dramatic as that of the Navajo courts. In 1940, Bureau of Indian Affairs area superintendent Seth Wilson helped to create the Hopi Court of Indian Offenses, "largely an agency-run institution." Id. at 37. The Hopi Tribal Council enacted Hopi Ordinance 21 in 1972, abolishing the court of Indian offenses, and creating the Hopi Tribal Court. Id. at 39–40. A Navajo man had threatened to invoke the Indian Civil Rights Act in federal court against the Hopi Tribe in a dispute over livestock, and the Hopi counsel recommended the creation of a Hopi tribal court to deal with the matter. Id. at 40–41.

The Hopi Tribe is not a uniform group. The federally recognized Indian nation is a grouping together of several disparate and formerly independent tribal groups. The following case addresses the conflict between the federally-guided creation of the tribe and the tribal villages, which retain significant autonomy within the federally recognized tribal structure.

IN THE MATTER OF THE CERTIFIED QUESTION OF LAW RE: VILLAGE AUTHORITY TO REMOVE TRIBAL COUNCIL REPRESENTATIVES

Hopi Appellate Court 2010
No. 2008–AP–0001, 11 Am. Tribal Law 80.

ROBERT N. CLINTON, ASSOCIATE JUSTICE.

* * *

CERTIFIED QUESTION OF LAW

[3] Do Villages, regardless of their form of government, have the authority to remove or decertify their duly-certified Tribal Council Representatives?

ANSWER

* * *

[5] This Court unanimously finds that, under both the Constitution and Hopi custom and tradition, the Hopi and Tewa Villages, regardless of their form of government, have authority to remove, recall or decertify their duly certified Tribal Council Representatives during their term of office by whatever process the Village selects and that Article IV, section 4 of the Constitution governs both selection and removal, recall, or decertification of Tribal Council Representatives.

Village Authority to Remove or Decertify Tribal Council Representatives

A. Constitutional Background

[8] Prior to the initial drafting and adoption of the Hopi Constitution in 1936 there was no central Hopi government. Rather, the people comprising the Hopi Tribe lived in 12 self-governing Villages, each of which retained its own aboriginal sovereignty. Each was an autonomous, sovereign city-state. The historical letters and records filed with this Court as part of the record in this case demonstrate that the creation of a central Hopi government and the drafting of the Constitution, significantly promoted by the federal government through Oliver La Farge, was highly controversial, a fact well understood by Mr. La Farge. Accordingly, unlike many of the tribal constitutions drafted pursuant to section 16 of the Indian Reorganization Act of 1934 (IRA), codified as amended at 25 U.S.C. § 476, the Hopi Constitution avoided boilerplate legal clauses and was carefully drafted to preserve the Hopi way of life. In particular, the Hopi Constitution advances a very different theory of the source of power of the Hopi Tribe than most of the tribal constitutions drafted during this period.

While most of the tribal constitutions drafted at the same time suggest the source of power of the central tribal government rests with delegation from the people of the affected tribe,1 the Hopi Constitution expressly rejects that approach. Instead, the Preamble to the Hopi Constitution states:

> This Constitution, to be known as the Constitution and By-Laws of the Hopi Tribe, *is adopted by the self-governing Hopi and Tewa Villages of Arizona* to provide a way of working together for peace and agreement between the villages, and of preserving the good things of Hopi life, and to provide a way of organizing to deal with modern problems, with the United States Government and with the outside world generally.

(Emphasis supplied).

[9] Furthermore, the entire structure of the Hopi Constitution indicates that the authority of the central government of the Hopi Tribe rests on the bedrock of the aboriginal sovereignty of the Hopi and Tewa Villages. The Villages delegated limited powers to the central Hopi government. Under Article II, section 4 of the Constitution the Villages determine Village membership. As already noted, the Constitution expressly reserves certain powers of dispute resolution to the Villages in Article III, section 2. The only officials in the current government of the Hopi Tribe selected by all members of the Hopi Tribe are the Chairman and Vice Chairman, who, pursuant to Article IV, section 7 of the Constitution are elected in at-large elections. All members of the Tribal Council Representatives, according to the express language of the Constitution, constitute "representatives from the various villages." Const. Art. IV, sec. 1. The Tribal Council Representatives are apportioned among the Villages, not the population generally, under a formula set forth in Article IV, section 1 of the Constitution. Under Article IV, section 3, each Tribal Council representative "must be a member of the Village he represents." And, of course, Article IV, section 4, the most critical provision for purposes of resolving this certified question of law, provides:

> Each village shall decide for itself how it chooses its representatives, subject to the provisions of SECTION 5. Representatives shall be recognized by the Tribal Council only if they are certified by the Kikmongwi of their respective villages, Certifications may be in writing or in person.

[10] * * * The bedrock constitutional authority upon which the tribal sovereignty of the Hopi Tribe therefore rests is the inherent aboriginal sovereignty of the Hopi and Tewa Villages that comprise the Hopi Tribe. As in the Articles of Confederation, the Hopi Villages retain all aspects of their inherent aboriginal sovereignty not exclusively delegated by the Constitution to the central government of the Hopi Tribe.

[11] * * * Thus, the Hopi Constitution, therefore leaves both the selection and the manner of selection of the Tribal Council Representatives entirely to the unfettered discretion of the Hopi and Tewa Villages. * * *

* * *

C. The Problem of Constitutional Interpretation

[13] The certified question of law presented by the Village of Bacavi poses an important constitutional question which seems to implicate a potential conflict between various clauses in the Hopi Constitution. On the one hand, the entire structure of the Constitution indicates that the Tribal Council Representatives are selected by and represent the Villages and Article IV, section 4 expressly provides that "[e]ach village shall decide for itself how it chooses its representatives." On the other hand, Article IV, section 2 provides an express term of office for representatives of two years and the only express provision for discretionary removal before the expiration of that two year term is found in Article V, section 2. * * *

* * *

D. Village Powers to Remove, Recall or Decertify Tribal Council Representatives

[14] Prior to adoption of the Hopi Constitution there was no central Hopi government and therefore each of the Hopi and Tewa Villages unquestionably possessed inherent aboriginal powers of self-government. In re Komaquaptewa, No. 01–AP–00013 (Hopi Ct.App. 8/16/2002). * * * Those inherent aboriginal powers logically must have included the power to select, remove, recall or decertify spokespersons to negotiate or otherwise deal with other Villages and the outside world because without such powers the Villages would have lacked the authority to create the Hopi Constitution and By-Laws. Thus, selection, removal, recall or decertification of political spokespersons constitutes part of the inherent aboriginal sovereignty of each of the Hopi and Tewa Village.

[15] The problem posed by the certified question of law in this matter involves the question of whether the adoption of the Hopi Constitution operated to deprive the Hopi and Tewa Villages of their pre-existing sovereign right to select, remove, recall or decertify political representatives. * * * Clearly, the manner of selection of Tribal Council Representatives set forth in Article IV, section 4 of the Constitution expressly reaffirms the pre-existing sovereign right of the Hopi and Tewa Villages to select their Tribal Council Representatives in whatever manner they choose. It constitutes a reaffirmation of preexisting sovereign power, not a delegation of new authority to the Villages. * * * [The] Villages did have pre-existing inherent aboriginal sovereign rights to select, remove, recall, or decertify their political spokespersons and representatives.

[16] * * * Thus, if any limitation on this pre-existing sovereign power of the Hopi and Tewa Villages is to be found in the Constitution, the argument must derive from implied constitutional limitations on Village authority derived from the structure or clauses in the Constitution. The only obvious source for such an implied limitation on Village authority would be found in the combined effect of the two year term for Tribal Council Representatives set forth in Article IV, section 2 of the Constitution and the grant of a removal for cause authority to the Tribal Council in Article V, section 2. * * * The Constitution established a new central government for the Hopi Tribe and its powers needed to be and were expressly delegated by the Hopi and Tewa Villages in the Constitution. Thus, if the Tribal Council was to exercise any authority to remove officials and Village representatives for cause, such powers needed to be expressly delegated in the Constitution and they were in Article V, section 2. By contrast, the Villages possessed pre-existing aboriginal sovereignty over the selection, removal, recall and decertification of political spokespersons. No express delegation was required to reaffirm that sovereignty since they already possessed it. Article IV, section 2 simply reaffirms that view for purposes of the selection of the Tribal Council Representatives but is otherwise silent on the question of removal, recall, and decertification. * * * Since nothing in the Constitution suggests that the pre-existing sovereign power of the Hopi and Tewa Villages to remove, recall, or decertify their representatives was removed from them or exclusively delegated to the Tribal Council by Article V, section 2 of the Constitution, this Court finds that the Villages continue to retain that authority under the Hopi Constitution.

* * *

[18] * * * [The] right of abstention constitutes an important political part of Hopi customs and traditions. It permits Hopi, whether individual Hopi members or whole Villages, to preserve harmony and consensus by not outright disruptively casting dissenting votes, while still politely manifesting their disagreement by declining to participate. It provides a way of preserving political civility while providing an outlet for political dissent—a tradition and custom from which the United States government could learn much. While this Court need not, and on the record before us cannot, trace the cultural origins of the right of abstention, it is sufficient to say that it clearly constitutes an essential part of the Hopi Way that is far older than the Constitution itself. * * * Some villages have always refused to send representatives to the Tribal Council. This Court is informed that currently Old Oraibi, Lower Meoncopi and Shongopavi continue to exercise their right of abstention by declining to participate in the central Hopi government. Whatever else this history suggests, it plainly demonstrates that the right of political abstention constitutes a pre-existing and enduring part of the Hopi Way. Accepting the view that the

removal for cause power established by Article V, section 2 constitutes the exclusive manner in which Tribal Council representatives can be removed or recalled during their term of office, would deny the Hopi and Tewa Villages and each member of those villages their longstanding right of abstention and force them to participate in the central Hopi government after they had concluded either that their Tribal Council Representatives no longer were serving their interests or positions or that they no longer wished to participate in the central government. * * *

* * *

Unlike the removal for cause provisions of Article V, section 2, removal, recall or decertification by the Villages does not even require any showing of cause, just as recall by the electorate in the tribes which use this device does not require any such showing. This observation answers the due process concerns expressed by some Villages and by the majority in the Interim Answer. If removal, recall or decertification of a Tribal Council Representative constitutes a political act that does not require any showing of cause, no notice, hearing or other due process is required since it is not a fact-finding process or other form of adjudication. Removal, recall, or decertification of a Tribal Council Representative is simply a political act reflecting a lack of continuing political confidence of the Village in the ability of the Tribal Council Representative to fairly and fully represent the interests of the Village.

[22] In some cases, the Villages will be in a superior position to the Tribal Council in knowing whether any particular Tribal Council Representative is fully performing his or her job. As noted above, the role of the Tribal Council Representative involves bilateral communication— representing the Village interests to the Tribal Council and informing and explaining to the Village the issues before and actions of the Tribal Council. Certainly, the Tribal Council will be fully aware of any failure of a Tribal Council Representative to perform the first duty and, as Article V, section 2, recognizes will be authorized to remove any Representative for "serious neglect of duty." By contrast, the Villages, not the Tribal Council, will be aware of failures by any Tribal Council Representative to inform and explain to the Village the issues before and actions taken by the Tribal Council. Failure to do so may never come to the attention of the full Tribal Council. Thus, the Villages need the continuing ability to remove, recall or decertify Tribal Council Representatives who fail to perform this role or who fail in their actions and votes on the Tribal Council to fully and fairly represent the views and interests of their Village.

[23] For all of these reasons, this Court unanimously concludes that the removal power of the Tribal Council contained in Article V, section 2 is not exclusive and that the Hopi and Tewa Villages, regardless of their form of government, have authority to remove, recall, or decertify their duly

certified Tribal Council Representatives during their term of office by whatever process the Village selects.

* * *

NOTES

1.   At Hopi, this decision is known as the "Final Decision." The appellate judges had been specially appointed to handle this case. Previously, a panel of regular appellate judges had issued an "Interim Decision." That panel, split 2–1, reached the opposite conclusion. The Final Decision reaches an outcome that appears to contradict the text of the Hopi Constitution, enacted in 1936. Article V establishes that a Hopi council member may be removed for cause (certain crimes of dishonesty, felonies, and "serious neglect of duty"). There is no provision for removal by a village government, and Article V's structure and text suggest that removal may only be accomplished by the tribal council. In the "Interim Decision," the majority wrote:

> The Constitution sets out the explicit ground rules governing the relationship between tribal and village sovereigns. It would be ill-advised to initiate the practice of reading meaning into the silences of the primary document *mediating* the relationship between the tribal and village sovereigns. It is out of deep respect for both that we decline to effect a Constitutional Amendment by plenary judicial review.

Interim Decision, slip op. at 4 (emphasis in original).

Note that the Hopi appellate court concludes that a village representative could be recalled without due process. Perhaps there are some "Indian political questions" that should not be decided in court?

2.   Courts, even tribal courts, are courts of persuasive—and coercive—power. Robert Cover called this "violence." Robert Cover, *Violence and the Word*, 95 Yale L.J. 1601, 1601 (1986) ("Legal interpretive acts signal and occasion the imposition of violence upon others: A judge articulates her understanding of a text, and as a result, somebody loses his freedom, his property, his children, even his life."). Relatively few pre-contact Indian communities used coercive force in government. Should modern Indian tribes? Pat Sekaquaptewa wrote about the use of "sanction" in Hopi traditional law and in Hopi tribal court:

> At Hopi we have a complex persisting set of traditional sanctions, religious and secular. Maqastutavo ["fear teaching"] persists and influences peoples' actions but equally effective is the making of examples of bad behavior with all the attendant chastisement and public ridicule. Some breaches of norms * * * are sanctioned by both the traditional and tribal systems. * * *
>
> The important considerations for policymaking purposes with respect to sanction include: (1) What were/are the traditional

sanctions and when should they apply; (2) Whether the traditional sanctions are sufficient or whether tribal sanctions "backing them up" are desired; (3) Whether innovative tribal sanctions of a nature similar to traditional sanctions are desired, such as outing bad behavior in the tribal newspaper for example; and (4) When and how tribal courts and police should recognize and enforce the decisions, remedies, and/or sanctions issued by traditional authorities?

Pat Sekaquaptewa, *Key Concepts in the Finding, Definition, and Consideration of Custom Law in Tribal Lawmaking*, 32 Am. Indian L.Rev. 319, 367–69 (2007–2008).

3. In disputes between citizens and residents of an insular Indian community that involve internal subject matters, such as inheritance or use of property, and parties and judges that speak the indigenous language and are conversant, the law applied and the procedures used may be dramatically different from standard Anglo-American legal cases. Justin B. Richland, *"What are You Going to Do With the Village's Knowledge?" Talking Tradition, Talking Law in Hopi Tribal Court*, 39 Law & Soc'y Rev. 235, 252–53 (2005).

b. Alternative Tribal Dispute Resolution Mechanisms: Peacemaker Courts and Sentencing Circles

Since at least 1982, with the establishment of the Navajo Nation's peacemaker courts, many Indian tribes have been attempting to apply traditional and customary law to discrete areas of civil and criminal law parallel to the more Anglo-American style of justice dispensed by tribal courts.

NANCY A. COSTELLO, WALKING TOGETHER IN A GOOD WAY: INDIAN PEACEMAKER COURTS IN MICHIGAN

76 U.Det. Mercy L.Rev. 875, 879–80, 888–89 (1999)

The Peacemaker Court of the Grand Traverse Band essentially recreated traditional Indian justice methods practiced by Indians long before European settlers imposed the Anglo-European justice system on tribes in the late 1800s. * * * Unlike the Anglo-European legal system, traditional Indian peacemaking focuses not on the guilt of the wrongdoer, but on solving the problems the dispute presents. Heavy emphasis is placed on the spirit and the feelings of the perpetrator and victim, and the restoration of relationships in the family and community. Peacemaker Courts recognize that when the feelings of parties are separated from the legal process and a judge's decision does not address those feelings, dissatisfaction follows. Peacemakers recognize that when a legal system ignores the emotions of the parties, tribal relationships cannot be restored. In contrast to the dominant culture's justice system, peacemaking is an educational device that attempts to mend relationships and teach tribe members correct behavior.

"Peacemaking focuses on maintenance of relationships. If people treat each other with respect and people accept their responsibility, things move toward a feeling of harmony, and justice has really been done," said Chief Judge [Michael] Petoskey. "If justice happens in the adversarial legal system it seems to be by accident. The adversarial system relies on who has the best lawyer, who understands the technicalities, and who can beat up on the other more."

The focus on problem solving rather than guilt makes peacemaking an effective method to penetrate the denial of a wrongdoer. The absence of coercion or punishment allows all parties to freely discuss a problem. Wrongdoers, therefore, are more likely to overcome the psychological barrier that holds them back from acknowledging substance abuse and other problems.

The involvement of relatives and friends in the peacemaking process also assures that weak victims or silent, ashamed perpetrators have someone who can speak for them and in support of them. If an abused victim is afraid to speak, relatives can describe the victim's pain and protect that person's interests. Likewise, if a perpetrator feels shame for committing an act and is therefore hesitant to speak, relatives may speak to show mitigation of the harm and offer restitution.

* * *

For the Grand Traverse Band, peacemaking is as much about building community as it is about resolving conflicts. The Peacemaker Court, which emphasizes the involvement of family and friends in dispute resolution, promotes tribal traditions and community harmony for a tribe that is reconstituting after a century of dislocation.

* * *

Following federal recognition, scattered tribe members moved to the Peshawbestown region seeking newly-established health services, low-income housing, jobs, and a long-lost sense of tribal community. Tribal government provided local leadership and has spearheaded successful economic development. In 1974, the only public enterprise the Grand Traverse Band owned was a coin-operated laundry. By 1984, four years after federal recognition, the Grand Traverse Band opened a bingo hall. A casino-motel complex soon followed, as well as an Indian art store and other commercial buildings and businesses. The millions of dollars generated by these enterprises were directed back into housing, human services, and plumbing for the Tribe, and created annual payments for each tribe member. Tribe members returning to the fold sought jobs at the casinos and government agencies, and welcomed an annual dividend check provided by gaming profits.

But those who were moving to Peshawbestown were returning to a socially complex tribe. Some were familiar with Indian culture and traditions. Many were not. Some members returning to tribal territory who sought jobs and homes had brushes with the law. As tribal membership increased, juvenile wrongdoing escalated. Juveniles who got into trouble entered a tribal court system modeled after the impersonal Anglo-European system. In creating its Peacemaker Court, the Grand Traverse Band pulled together as a community to decide what would be the best justice method to govern disputes involving tribal youths.

NOTES

1.   More and more Indian tribes are developing and relying upon peacemaker courts, and other indigenous justice systems such as sentencing circles, to handle many different types of disputes, including juvenile and adult misdemeanors, petty theft, and many kinds of civil cases between individual tribal citizens. However, peacemaker courts and sentencing circles have met with mixed outcomes in dealing with one kind of community problem—violence against women.

> Because an adversarial model and a restorative model seem, at first glance, incompatible, there may be a tendency to reject one approach in favor of the other. * * * Extreme caution is warranted to ensure that a peacemaking or restorative approach does not replicate traditional Anglo-American constructs of victim blaming, shame, and secrecy. * * * One of the potential weaknesses of an approach like restoration/restorative justice is the assumption of some degree of preexisting equality between the parties—and clearly a rape survivor and her perpetrator are at unequal places. Moreover, * * * a victim of sexual assault may feel as though she has failed if she has not "made peace" with her rapist.

Sarah Deer, The Beginning and End of Rape: Confronting Sexual Violence in Native America 124–25 (2015).

2.   At least one commentator has argued that the resort to peacemaker courts or other indigenous justice systems in certain cases does not go far enough, and that any kind of American-style justice system is damaging to tribal societies:

> [I]n every significant aspect, the American legal system is in conflict with the manner in which native people have traditionally resolved disputes. As a result, tribes that have embraced litigation subject their citizens to a dispute resolution process that precipitates and requires a radical change in their behavior in order to obtain justice from the system. While behaving like an American may not seem problematic (especially for Americans), the resulting effect is that native people end up relinquishing traditional cultural values, particularly those relating to community and relationship. As native

people lose their connectedness to one another, the fragmentation of their societies soon follows.

Robert B. Porter, *Strengthening Tribal Sovereignty through Peacemaking: How the Anglo-American Legal Tradition Destroys Indigenous Societies*, 28 Colum.Hum.Rts.L.Rev. 235, 280–81 (1997).

NATION BUILDING NOTE: ON MARRIAGE EQUALITY IN INDIAN COUNTRY

Obergefell v. Hodges, 135 S. Ct. 2071 (2015), may have effectively eliminated legal barriers to same-sex marriage, but Indian tribes retain plenary authority over their internal, domestic relations. In absence of controlling federal law, Indian tribes have authority to make tribal laws relating to marriage without federal or state interference. See, e.g., United States v. Quiver, 241 U.S. 602 (1916); Kobogum v. Jackson Iron Co., 43 N.W. 602 (Mich.1889).

In 2005 and 2006, the Navajo Nation and the Cherokee Nation of Oklahoma enacted laws defining marriage as between a man and a woman in attempts to prohibit same-sex marriage. See Matthew L.M. Fletcher, *Same-Sex Marriage, Indian Tribes, and the Constitution*, 61 U. Miami L.Rev. 53, 70 (2006). However, since then, at least a dozen Indian tribes have enacted laws or take steps to ensure marriage equality within their jurisdictions. Ann E. Tweedy, *Tribes, Same-Sex Marriage, and* Obergefell v. Hodges, 62 Fed.Law. 6 (Oct./Nov.2015) ("Besides three tribes that have tied their marriage laws to state law (and which now allow same sex marriage because states must), at least 13 tribes are known to allow same-sex marriages under tribal law."). See also Ann E. Tweedy, *Tribal Laws & Same-Sex Marriage: Theory, Process, and Content*, 46 Colum.Hum.Rts.L.Rev. 104 (2015) (cataloguing various tribal laws).

The Cherokee ban came in response to the successful attempt by two Cherokee women to apply for a tribal marriage license. See Fletcher, Same-Sex Marriage, supra, at 70. The Cherokee Nation Judicial Appeals Tribunal (now Supreme Court) rejected the petitions of the Nation's general counsel and the Nation's tribal council to challenge the application on grounds that neither party had standing to sue. See In re Adverse Order of Dist. Ct. against Reynolds, 2005 WL 6171271 (Cherokee Nation Supreme Court 2005); Anglen v. McKinley, 2005 WL 6169010 (Cherokee Judicial Appeals Tribunal) 2005). The Nation's application form for a marriage certificate through the Cherokee courts now reads:

> A man and woman wishing to have their marriage certificate filed in the Cherokee Nation District Court must be married within the Cherokee Nation and have their marriage vows solemnized by a Minister, Spiritual leader, or Justice/Judge of the Cherokee Nation who has a license to perform marriage issued by the Cherokee Nation Court Clerk.

The plaintiff coupled declined to pursue an affirmative appeal to enforce their marriage equality rights, disappointed by the Cherokee Nation's intolerance.

In 2012, the Native American Program of Legal Aid Services of Oregon, the Indigenous Ways of Knowing Program at Lewis & Clark Graduate School of Education and Counseling, the Western States Center, the Pride Foundation, and Basic Rights Oregon published the Tribal Equity Toolkit: Tribal Resolutions and Codes to Support Two Spirit & LGBT Justice in Indian Country. The toolkit, available online, suggested statutory language for Indian tribes to consider adopting to guarantee marriage equality:

The Tribe's [domestic relations; family; marriage] [code; ordinance; statute], [cite to specific provision], is amended by adding three new sections, to read as follows:

[§ 1] Parties to a Marriage.

1. Marriage is the legally recognized union of two persons. A marriage that is otherwise valid shall be valid regardless of whether the parties to the marriage are of the same sex or different sexes.

2. No Tribal government treatment or legal status, effect, right, benefit, privilege, protection, or responsibility related to marriage, whether deriving from a statute, resolution, administrative or court rule, regulation, policy, common law, or any other source of law, shall differ based on whether the parties to the marriage are or have been of the same sex or different sexes.

[§ 2] Equal Access to Marriage License. No application for a marriage license shall be denied on the grounds that the parties are of the same sex.

* * *

[§ 3] Recognition of Marriages, Domestic Partnerships, and Civil Unions from Other Jurisdictions. All marriages, domestic partnerships, and civil unions performed under the laws of another jurisdiction, which are valid under the laws of the jurisdiction when and where performed, shall be recognized as valid by the Tribe, provided that such marriage, domestic partnership, or civil union is not otherwise expressly prohibited by Tribal law.

Id. at 18–19.

The toolkit offers additional model codes relating to domestic partnerships and civil unions, adoptions, child welfare and juvenile justice codes for LGBT youth, and numerous other areas. It is now clear that mere marriage equality is only a first step in ridding a tribe's laws of implicit bias against LGBT persons.

4.   TRIBAL CONSTITUTIONS

Tribal constitutions and codes form the foundation of most tribal court litigation, with the exception of tribes like the Navajo Nation that have not adopted a written tribal constitution. Many tribal constitutions originated in the 1934 Indian Reorganization Act that provided the framework for the creation of Indian tribes as constitutional governments. 25 U.S.C. § 476. The drafters of the Act, especially Felix S. Cohen, recognized that the adoption of a constitutional system of government was foreign to tribal governments, and took pains to give tribes great deference to Indian tribes in crafting their own indigenous constitutions. See generally Felix S. Cohen, On the Drafting of Tribal Constitutions (David E. Wilkins, ed. 2006). However, many of these IRA-era tribal constitutions included provisions designed to consolidate tribal governmental power in the hands of federal bureaucrats. Most of these tribal constitutions included provisions requiring that each and every tribal governmental act receive the approval of the Secretary of Interior, or his designee, before they would become effective. E.g., Const. and Bylaws of the Hannahville Indian Community art. V, § 1 cl. 6, 7, and 11 (July 23, 1936); id. art. VI, § 5; Const. and By-laws of the Keweenaw Bay Indian Community art. VI, §§ 1(b), (j), (k), (l), (n), (o), (p), and (r) (Dec. 17, 1936) (requiring Secretarial approval for certain council actions); id. art. VI, § 2 (detailing the process for presenting tribal council actions to the Secretary for approval); Const. and Bylaws of the Bay Mills Indian Community art. VI, §§ 1(b) and (f) (Nov. 4, 1936) (requiring Secretarial approval of tribal attorney hires and ordinances relating to tribal lands); see also id. Amend. II, § 3 (Aug. 7, 1959) (requiring Secretarial approval of certain tribal "adoptions" into membership). See generally Timothy W. Joranko & Mark C. Van Norman, *Indian Self-Determination at Bay: Secretarial Authority to Disapprove Tribal Constitutional Amendments*, 29 Gonz.L.Rev. 81 (1993–1994).

Modern tribal constitutions allow for far less federal control, and many could be said to be much closer to truly indigenous constitutions. Consider the preamble of the Constitution of the Little Traverse Bay Bands of Odawa Indians, ratified in 2007:

IN THE WAYS OF OUR ANCESTORS, to perpetuate our way of life for future generations, we the Little Traverse Bay Bands of Odawa Indians, called in our own language the WAGANAKISING ODAWAK, a sovereign, self-governing people who follow the Anishinaabe Traditions, Heritage, and Cultural Values, set forth within this Constitution the foundation of our governance. This Constitution is solemnly pledged to respect the individuality of all our members and their spiritual beliefs and practices, while recognizing the importance of preserving a strong, unified Tribal identity in accordance with our Anishinaabe Heritage. We will work together in a constructive, cooperative spirit to preserve and protect our lands, resources and Treaty Rights, and the right to an education and a decent standard of living for all our people. In keeping faith with our Ancestors, we shall preserve our Heritage while adapting to the present world around us.

Const. of the Little Traverse Bay Bands of Odawa Indians preamble (Jan. 26, 2007).

Other tribal constitutions suffered from the heavy hand of the federal government. In Snowden v. Saginaw Chippewa Indian Tribe of Michigan, 32 Indian L.Rep. 6047 (Saginaw Chippewa Indian Tribe Appellate Court, Jan. 7, 2005), a case involving the highly controversial efforts of the then-tribal council to disenroll deceased members of the tribe, Justice Frank Pommersheim wrote:

This case is not just about the meaning of the Saginaw Chippewa Tribal Constitution of 1986, but it is also a story about a People and a Tribe enmeshed in the coils of an unknowing and meddlesome Bureau of Indian Affairs and Federal Government. This destabilizing federal force is amply demonstrated in the history leading up to the adoption of the first Saginaw Chippewa Tribal Constitution in 1937. * * *

* * *

* * * The Tribe's desire to include all of its communities— even those communities outside the Isabella Reservation—met strong resistance from Assistant Commissioner of Indian Affairs, William Zimmerman. Commissioner Zimmerman took the position that a tribe could only organize under the IRA if it had a reservation and its only members could be tribal people residing on the reservation.

With this dubious interpretation at the forefront of his review of the proposed Constitution, he changed the preamble to read, "We, the Indians residing on the Isabella Reservation in the State of Michigan. . . ." In addition, he changed the proposed Tribal Council representation to require all council members be elected from within the Reservation, and required that all tribal members *reside* on the Reservation. Commissioner Zimmerman further advised the Tribe that subsequent to the referendum to accept the constitution the Tribe could "adopt" those individuals living off the reservation. In fact, this "adoption" language appears in Sec. 2 of Art. III—Membership of the 1937 Constitution.

All these "recommendations" were accepted by the Business Committee and incorporated into the proposed Tribal Constitution that was voted on and accepted by tribal members on March 27, 1937. Unfortunately, the 1937 Constitution—

whatever its intent—sowed the seeds of membership confusion
and discontent that yielded the bitter harvest at the core of this
most challenging, even heart wrenching, litigation about the
cultural and legal aspects of tribal belonging.

Id. at 6048–49. For Pommersheim's commentary on the case, see Frank
Pommersheim, Tribal Justice: Twenty-Five Years as a Tribal Appellate
Justice 171–75 (2016).

INDIAN LAWYERING NOTE: INTERNAL POLITICAL
DISPUTES & MASS DISENROLLMENT

In recent decades, Indian country has confronted multiple legal issues of
national concern—intractable internal political disputes and mass
disenrollment of tribal members. The legal framework for these disputes is the
lack of federal court jurisdiction to hear internal tribal governance disputes
involving elections and membership.

Intractable Internal Political Disputes

In recent years, dozens of Indian tribes have been embroiled in internal
political disputes with no easy or even viable resolution. Often, these disputes
arise out of regular tribal elections where the sitting elected officials refuse to
leave office, creating a "holdover council." The holdover council might or might
not have legitimate reasons to challenge the validity of the election, and
usually these disputes are resolved through tribal court decisions. E.g.,
Snowden v. Saginaw Chippewa Indian Tribe of Michigan, 32 Indian L.Rep.
6047 (Saginaw Chippewa Indian Tribe Appellate Court, Jan. 7, 2005); Pete v.
Lac Vieux Desert Band of Lake Superior Chippewa Indians Tribal Council, No.
10–AP–02 (Lac Vieux Desert Appellate Court, Dec. 20, 2010). However, in both
of the above instances, enormous controversy and perhaps unlawful actions by
one or both parties preceded the tribal court decisions.

The Lac Vieux Desert Band tribal court initially ruled against the sitting
council in the election dispute, and when the council members refused to vacate
their offices, Judge Bradley Dakota had them jailed for contempt of court.
Ultimately, before the federal court could rule on a petition for a writ of habeas
corpus, the county sheriff holding the council members released them. Lac
Vieux Desert Band of Lake Superior Chippewa Indians Tribal Council v. Lac
Vieux Desert Band of Lake Superior Chippewa Indians Tribal Court, 2010 WL
3909957 (W.D.Mich., Sept. 14, 2010).

Normally, the federal government has no interest in a tribal election, and
federal courts would have no jurisdiction to resolve internal tribal political
disputes. However, in the Saginaw Chippewa dispute, the Assistant Secretary
for Indian Affairs, Kevin Gover, was forced to intervene in order to ascertain
which faction of tribal government was authorized to administer federal self-
determination money. Saginaw Chippewa Indian Tribe of Michigan v. Gover,
1999 WL 33266029 (E.D.Mich., Aug. 19, 1999).

This is the rub in the 21st century. Where there are two or more tribal political factions claiming to be the proper elected tribal government, the federal government is forced quickly to make a determination of which faction the United States will acknowledge as the proper contractor in the federal self-determination contracts. The current federal process is strongly supportive of tribal sovereignty and the lack of federal authority to decide tribal disputes, but it also virtually guarantees that the "holdover" council will be rewarded with federal recognition likely until the next election period. How this works is like this: a tribal faction institutes a process with the regional Bureau of Indian Affairs official to force the office to acknowledge the proper winner of the election; the federal official makes a determination; the losing faction appeals that decision to the Interior Board of Indian Appeals (IBIA). The IBIA has followed the Bureau's policies favoring "non-interference in internal tribal matters and of support of tribal self-governance and self-sufficiency. * * *" Tarbell v. Eastern Regional Director, Bureau of Indian Affairs, 50 IBIA 219 (Sept. 17, 2009). Further, federal regulations require the IBIA to issue a stay of the regional BIA official's decision. 43 CFR 4.314; Wadena v. Acting Minneapolis Area Director, Bureau of Indian Affairs, 30 IBIA 139 (Dec. 11, 1996). Once the decision below is stayed, the "holdover" council remains in office with the power of the purse until the IBIA renders a decision. Typically, the IBIA, again in deference to tribal sovereignty, will hold an appeal until the next election cycle, rendering the case moot. E.g., Smoke v. Eastern Area Director, Bureau of Indian Affairs, 31 IBIA 99 (July 31, 1999). The "holdover" council effectively "wins," based on these procedures and practices.

Imagine you are counsel to a sitting tribal council that becomes a "holdover" council that asks you to pursue a strategy that effectively allows them to take advantage of this legal regime. There are deep ethical concerns to agreeing, are there not?

What solutions are there? Should the federal government alter its policies on internal tribal political disputes? In what way should the United States change its approach? What impacts could that have on tribal sovereignty?

Mass Disenrollments

It is well-settled, blackletter law that Indian tribes retain the power to decide their own membership criteria. E.g., Santa Clara Pueblo v. Martinez, 436 U.S. 49 (1978). See also Restatement of the Law of American Indians § 25 (Preliminary Draft, Jan. 27, 2016). The power to decide membership also includes the power to exclude persons from membership or to disenroll current members. Couple these inherent tribal powers with the requirement that civil rights claims be heard in tribal forums, and with sovereign immunity, and suddenly tribal disenrollment decisions are not reviewable in federal or state courts.

Mass disenrollment is when an Indian tribe terminates the tribal membership of a significant number of enrolled members. Ironically, the Supreme Court's decision in Santa Clara Pueblo v. Martinez, 436 U.S. 49 (1978), affirming that the Indian Civil Rights Act may only be enforced in tribal forums and that tribes retain the inherent right to decide membership criteria, establishes the legal framework for mass disenrollment. In too many cases, it appears that tribal leaders have pushed through disenrollment actions to enhance the tribal gaming per capita revenue sharing for remaining tribal members, or to settle longstanding political scores within the tribe.

Moreover, federal judges in California and the Ninth Circuit Court of Appeals have harshly criticized Indian tribes defending their disenrollment decisions. In one case involving the Table Mountain Rancheria, Judge Karlton wrote that "somebody ought to warn the tribe that this is the kind of facts where some court is going to say 'we're outraged' and put it to them." Wenona T. Singel, *Indian Tribes and Human Rights Accountability*, 49 San Diego L.Rev. 567, 610 (2012). On appeal, the Ninth Circuit panel affirmed the tribe's immunity from suit, but also suggested that the problem was one that Congress or the Supreme Court should consider fixing:

> We agree with the district court's conclusion that this case is deeply troubling on the level of fundamental substantive justice. Nevertheless, we are not in a position to modify well-settled doctrines of tribal sovereign immunity. This is a matter in the hands of a higher authority than our court.

Lewis v. Norton, 424 F.3d 959, 963 (9th Cir.2005).

In general, Indian tribes that engage in mass disenrollments have not created an independent forum to allow the disenrollees to challenge the government's actions. However, some tribes do move forward even where there is a tribal court forum. In a long series of decisions involving multiple tribal court cases, as well as federal court litigation, hundreds of Nooksack tribal members have been fighting their proposed disenrollment by the tribal government. See generally Gabriel S. Galanda & Ryan D. Dreveskracht, *Curing the Tribal Disenrollment Epidemic: In Search of a Remedy*, 57 Ariz.L.Rev. 383, 422–29 (2015).

Fortunately for the Nooksack members facing disenrollment, they are represented by counsel and there is a tribal court where judicial review may be had. Unfortunately for the proposed disenrollees, the tribal government has legislative jurisdiction to restrict the tribal court's authority to review membership matters. However, the Nooksack appellate court did strike down the procedures provided for the disenrollments on the grounds that tribal ordinances are, under the tribe's constitution, "subject to approval of the Secretary of the Interior." Roberts v. Kelly, 12 NICS App. 33, 35 (Nooksack Tribal Court of Appeals, Mar. 18, 2014). Since the tribe had not yet sought and received the federal government's approval, the disenrollment procedures could not be enforced. However, that same court also held that the procedures, once approved, would comply with the tribe's due process obligations. Id. at 39–41. The procedures allowed disenrollees up to 10 pages of written argument and up to 10 minutes of oral argument, by telephone, to contest their disenrollment. Id. at 40. The Nooksack matters are pending.

Some commentators claim that thousands of tribal members have been disenrolled by Indian tribes during this time. Suzanne D. Painter-Thorne, *If You Build It, They Will Come: Preserving Tribal Sovereignty in the Face of Indian Casinos and the New Premium on Tribal Membership*, 14 Lewis & Clark L.Rev. 311, 320 (2010). Commentators charge some of these Indian tribes with greed and political factionalism. E.g., Galanda & Dreveskracht, *supra*.

The remedy for mass disenrollment is unclear. Three federal courts have distinguished *Martinez* by taking jurisdiction under the habeas corpus provision in ICRA in cases where a tribe has banished or expelled persons from the tribe's territory. See Poodry v. Tonawanda Band of Seneca Indians, 85 F.3d 874 (2d Cir.1996) (holding that the Tonawanda Band could not expel members of the tribe for "treason" who were residents of the tribe's reservation without due process of law); Sweet v. Hinzman, 2009 WL 1175647 (W.D.Wash.2009) (holding that the Snoqualmie tribal council violated ICRA by banishing tribal members without due process); Quair v. Sisco, 359 F.Supp.2d 948 (E.D.Cal.2004) (accepting jurisdiction over a dispute involving the banishment of several members of the Santa Rosa Rancheria Tachi Indian Tribe who had been stripped of membership). But these cases are rare, and it is far from clear that these decisions prevented disenrollment.

One activist group drafted legislation titled the "California Indian Legacy Act" that was intended to require California tribes to "accept as members anyone certified by the BIA to be a descendant of the band." Singel, supra, at 610.

Professor Wenona T. Singel suggests that the remedy for mass disenrollment must come from within tribal communities first, and then perhaps through inter-tribal human rights accords. What solution would you suggest? Tribal? Intertribal? Federal? International? What would be the strengths or weaknesses of each? Are any of them practical?

The Cherokee Nation of Oklahoma has repeatedly sought to disenroll the African-American descendants of former slaves—the Freedmen—that had intermarried with and in some cases were owned by American Indians in the southeast, including the Cherokees and the Seminoles, have been a part of those tribal communities since at least the early 19th century. In large part, this relationship has been imposed on the tribal communities by actions taken by the United States.

In 2006, the Cherokee Nation Judicial Appeals Tribunal overruled its own precedent and held that a tribal statute purporting to expel from tribal citizenship many of the descendants of the Cherokee Freedmen, former slaves of the Cherokees, was unconstitutional under tribal law. See Allen v. Cherokee Nation Tribal Council, 6 Am. Tribal Law 18 (Cherokee Nation Judicial Appeals Tribunal 2006), overruling Riggs v. Ummerteskee, 3 Am. Tribal Law 10 (Cherokee Nation Judicial Appeals Tribunal 2001). After that decision, perhaps 45,000 persons once again became eligible for citizenship in the Cherokee Nation. See S. Alan Ray, *A Race or Nation? Cherokee National*

Identity and the Status of Freedmen's Descendants, 12 Mich.J. Race &L. 387, 392–94 (2007). The tribal legislature acted quickly in proposing a tribal constitutional amendment providing that Cherokee citizenship required at least a minimum degree of Cherokee *Indian* blood—individuals tracing their ancestry only to the Cherokee Freedmen would no longer be eligible for tribal membership. In 2007, the Cherokees voted and overwhelmingly adopted this constitutional amendment. See id. The Freedmen brought suit in federal court on a theory that the Thirteenth Amendment abrogates the sovereign immunity of the Cherokee Nation and its officials. They have been partially successful. See Vann v. Kempthorne, 534 F.3d 741 (D.C.Cir.2008). Litigation continues in the D.C. district court, the tribal court, and in an Oklahoma federal court.

Tiya Miles, focusing on one nineteenth century Cherokee Freedmen family started by a Cherokee Indian man named Shoeboots and a free black woman named Doll, highlights the arbitrariness of the legal lines that the Cherokee Nation is trying to draw to this day:

> The Cherokee lawyer's response tolerates little ambiguity. It maps out two straightforward routes to Cherokee citizenship, one for "Cherokees," and one for "Negroes." A Cherokee could trace his or her lineage to a parent or forebear on the "authenticated rolls." A black person formerly owned by Cherokees could appeal to the Treaty of 1866, which granted citizenship to freed slaves who had returned to the Cherokee Nation within six months. The Cherokee lawyers indicated that because the Shoeboots claim to be free-born Cherokees, they could not appeal to the Treaty of 1866, and because they were also descended from a black mother, they were ineligible for Cherokee citizenship though routes external to that treaty. A family like the Shoeboots that was black *and* Cherokee and had been both enslaved *and* free had no place within the streamlined, race-conscious categories designated by the Cherokee and American governments. William Shoeboots' strategy of deemphasizing slavery had failed. The very freedom that he claimed for his Afro-Cherokee family made that family inconceivable in the view of the Cherokee Nation. To be a black citizen of the Cherokee Nation, the attorneys seemed to say, required always having been a slave. For reasons of clarity and expediency, and in keeping with the Cherokee Nation's fixed definitions of racial categorization and tribal belonging, no other possibility would be entertained.

Tiya Miles, Ties That Bind: The Story of an Afro-Cherokee Family in Slavery and Freedom 202 (2005).

The dispute between the Cherokee Nation and the Cherokee Freedmen is played out in tribal governments virtually every day, but usually in a context somewhat different than the stark Black-White-Indian racial dynamics. Almost invariably, tribal citizenship depends on race, typically referred to as "blood quantum" or lineage. It may be time for Indian tribes to define tribal citizenship to include non-Indian tribal community members:

Whatever the circumstances, these American Indian tribal nations have one element in common—nationhood—and they should behave as nations. Most nations around the world adopt membership rules and criteria without regard to race and ancestry, and Indian nations should consider doing the same. Membership is a two-way street: both parties must expressly consent to the relationship (although, ironically, many American Indians who became citizens of the United States through an act of Congress in 1924 did not have that option).

There are two ways for Indian nations to proceed in this vein. The first is to change tribal membership criteria to immediately create an avenue for nonmembers to become members, regardless of race or ancestry. This may not be palatable for a host of reasons. First, the federal government, from Congress to the executive branch to the federal judiciary, might not be ready for such a radical change in how the United States deals with Indian nations. Second, Indian nations might not be ready for this change, either. The Grand Traverse Band, for example, has zealously defended the decisions of its enrollment committee to deny membership to community members who do not meet the current membership criteria. The Band is not alone in this regard, with other Indian nations involved in similar litigation.

There is a second way, one that requires Indian nations to follow the old maxim to plan seven generations into the future. This way could potentially incorporate nonmembers into the tribal membership without destroying the Indian or tribal character of American Indian nations. It can be done, but it will take a great deal of time, perhaps even generations.

Matthew L.M. Fletcher, *Race and American Indian Tribal Nationhood*, 11 Wyo.L.Rev. 295, 324–25 (2011).

5. TRIBAL CODE DEVELOPMENT

In recent years, Indian tribes have also begun the process of modernizing their tribal codes for purposes of transitioning into a modern global economy. In particular, the National Conference of Commissioners on Uniform State Laws, the authors of statutes such as the Uniform Commercial Code, have contributed model codes for tribes to consider adopting. The first code is the Model Tribal Secured Transactions Act. Another model code relating to tribal probate law is under development.

WENONA T. SINGEL, CULTURAL SOVEREIGNTY AND TRANSPLANTED LAW: TENSIONS IN INDIGENOUS SELF-RULE

15 Kan.J.L.&Pub.Pol'y 357, 360–62 (2006)

In the past five years, many tribes have developed a growing interest in enacting a form of secured transactions code as tribal law. This is because tribes have developed a growing recognition of the fact that secured transactions codes are often critical tools for promoting economic growth in Indian country. Without a secured transactions code enacted as tribal law, lenders remain wary of extending credit in Indian country because they cannot predict whether or how any security interest they may take in goods will be recognized or enforced under tribal law. This problem is exacerbated because Article 9 includes a choice of law provision providing that that the secured transactions law that governs the perfection of any security interest is generally the law of the location of the debtor. Under this choice of law rule, if the debtor is an individual or entity or Indian nation located in Indian country, then the law that governs the making and enforcement of security interests is always the tribe with jurisdiction over the Indian country in question. The result is that under the law of nearly every state, whenever a debtor is located in an area of Indian country where the relevant tribe with jurisdiction lacks a secured transactions code on the books, there is no definite set of rules that will govern the making and enforcement of a security interest. The uncertainty that results from this phenomenon creates a disincentive for lender investment in Indian country generally, and the effects of this disincentive are felt by individuals, by small and large businesses, and by tribal governments.

In response to the threat to economic growth that the absence of tribal secured transactions codes presents, many Indian nations have responded by enacting tribal secured transactions codes as tribal law. In addition, a few law schools have devoted resources to helping tribes develop tribal secured transactions codes, and the National Conference of Commissioners on Uniform State Laws (NCCUSL) also became involved in the effort to develop and promote the tribal enactment of this code. NCCUSL is a national organization that develops a wide variety of uniform laws for state enactment. In particular, NCCUSL monitors state law UCC developments and considers whether developments merit revision of the model form of the UCC. When NCCUSL creates or revises a uniform law, it combines the expertise of academics and practitioners from each of the fifty states and ultimately issues an official form of the model law in question which it then endorses for state adoption. The American Law Institute (ALI) also reviews and decides whether to endorse the model laws that NCCUSL develops. Once the model form is endorsed by NCCUSL and ALI, both organizations then encourage each state legislature to adopt the model law with as few changes as possible. A guiding principle that informs the NCCUSL's development of model codes generally is that uniformity of the law from state to state promotes greater certainty, predictability, and efficiency in the law. In the area of commercial law, this uniformity encourages efficient economic transactions because parties are able to contract with each other without a significant investment of time and resources each time a party engages in commerce in a new state law jurisdiction.

* * *

As the interest in enacting secured transactions codes in Indian country grew, so too did the number and variety of problems associated with successful tribal incorporation of the code. The first problem occurred at the outset, with tribes' failure to properly integrate the code into tribal law. In many cases, tribes adopted secured transactions codes by simply cutting and pasting either the model Article 9 of the UCC or an enacted state version of Article 9 and incorporating the cut-and-pasted product as tribal law. This method of tribal incorporation was the least likely to be successful, since it often failed to take into account previously-enacted tribal laws to ensure that the incorporated code did not conflict with existing tribal law. This method also suffered because the model Article 9 of the UCC and the various state-enacted versions of Article 9 are each laden with cross-references to other bodies of law which the drafters of Article 9 presume to be enacted by each respective jurisdiction. For example, Article 9 refers to other portions of the UCC governing sales and leases, debtor-creditor law, and commercial paper. If none of these other portions of the UCC are enacted as tribal law, then a tribe that adopts a model secured transactions code with references to concepts embedded in these other codes will ultimately enact a law that cross-references itself to a series of dead-ends, or non-existent law.

* * * Finally, a fourth problem that the adoption of secured transactions codes may trigger is the introduction of new meanings, norms and values regarding relationships between individuals that may not comport with and may even directly conflict with the meanings, norms and values that are integral to the community's identity and the cohesiveness of its members' relationships.

Among the various difficulties associated with the enactment of secured transactions codes as tribal law, the potential for conflict with cultural sovereignty is especially worthy of attention. As mentioned earlier, the project to promote cultural sovereignty includes efforts to develop tribal legal systems in a way that reflects tribal histories, cultures and community norms. In contrast to the goals of cultural sovereignty, transplanted law represents a further step toward modeling tribal legal systems after Anglo legal systems. Transplanted law also represents a failure to organically develop tribal legal systems to fit the unique cultures, communities, territories, and traditions of indigenous peoples. In the case of a secured transactions code modeled after Article 9 of the UCC, the code challenges the development of cultural sovereignty to the extent that it displaces or modifies tribal norms and values that relate to the ownership of property and the relationship between debtors and creditors.

NOTE

In National Labor Relations Board v. Pueblo of San Juan, 276 F.3d 1186 (10th Cir.2002), the court held that the National Labor Relations Act did not preempt the Pueblo's "right to work" ordinance, which provided:

> No person shall be required, as a condition of employment or continuation of employment on Pueblo lands, to: (i) resign or refrain from voluntary membership in, voluntary affiliation with, or voluntary financial support of a labor organization; (ii) become or remain a member of a labor organization; (iii) pay dues, fees, assessments or other charges of any kind or amount to a labor organization; (iv) pay to any charity or other third party, in lieu of such payments any amount equivalent to or a pro-rata portion of dues, fees, assessments or other charges regularly required of members of a labor organization; or (v) be recommended, approved, referred or cleared through a labor organization.

San Juan Pueblo Tribal Ordinance No. 96–63, quoted in *Pueblo of San Juan*, 276 F.3d at 1189. According to the court:

> A "right-to-work" law, as the term is used here, is a statute which § 14(b) of the NLRA permits states and territories to enact to invalidate agreements establishing "union shops." A closed shop, originally permitted under the NLRA, is created when an employer and a union agree that only people who are already union members may be hired. This was outlawed in 1947 by the Taft Hartley Act's amendment of the NLRA, 29 U.S.C. § 158(a)(3). A union shop is created when an employer and a union agree to require employees, as a condition of their continued employment, to have membership in a labor union "on or after the thirtieth day following the beginning of such employment." 29 U.S.C. § 158(a)(3). Such an agreement between an employer and a union is a union security agreement. Provided they comply with other requirements of 29 U.S.C. § 158, and provided no right-to-work law forbids them, the NLRA permits union shops and union security agreements.

Id. at 1190 n.3. Other Indian tribes have adopted "right-to-work" laws in order to lessen the powers of labor unions in Indian country. E.g., Siletz Tribal Code § 5.200 (2008); 5 Grand Traverse Band Code § 801 (2004). See generally Wenona T. Singel, *Labor Relations and Tribal Self-Governance*, 80 N.D.L.Rev. 691, 727–29 (2004). Still other tribes have reacted to the presence of union activity in their communities by establishing a tribal code paralleling the federal labor laws. E.g., Little River Band of Ottawa Indians, Fair Employment Practices Code, Ordinance No. 05–600–03 (2008).

Are Indian tribes acting in accordance with their customs and traditions by taking action to reduce the political and economic power of workers, at least some of whom are tribal citizens? According to Professor Singel, "[T]his strategy [of enacting right-to-work laws] is at bottom a reactive and insufficient approach that will thwart the ability of tribes to develop more progressive and comprehensive labor policies that satisfy the specific needs of tribal communities." Id. at 728.

NATION BUILDING NOTE: INDIAN LAWYER REGULATION

Indian tribes have been remarkably lax in regulating lawyer conduct in Indian country. Save a few tribal nations, notably the Navajo Nation, the Crow Nation, the Hoopa Valley Tribe, Mashantucket Pequot Tribal Nation, the Tulalip Tribes, and a handful of others, tribal courts rarely require lawyers to take a tribal bar exam. Even fewer tribal nations boast a bar association; perhaps only the Navajo Nation has a large and active bar association.

This is unsettling given the number of attorneys practicing law in Indian country and on behalf of Indian tribes. The National Native American Bar Association has recently engaged more substantively with the practicing bar, issuing a critically important report on a study titled *The Pursuit of Inclusion: An In-Depth Exploration of the Experiences and Perspectives of Native American Attorneys in the Legal Profession* in 2015 and issuing its first formal ethics opinion, *Duties of Tribal Court Advocates to Ensure Due Process Afforded to All Individuals Targeted for Disenrollment* (adopted June 26, 2015). Moreover, in recent years, attorneys Andrew Adams, Venus McGhee-Prince, Doreen McPaul, and several others formed the Tribal In-House Counsel Association.

Largely, Indian country lawyer regulation in specific cases of alleged misconduct is ad hoc, with tribal courts and tribal elected officials both asserting power to discipline or even disbar attorneys. In recent years, several high-profile matters have attracted attention. In 2010, for example, the Navajo Nation Supreme Court disciplined the Navajo Chief Legislative Counsel, Frank Seanez, for recommending actions in defiance of Navajo court decisions:

> In legal opinions and memoranda that he issued as Chief Legislative Counsel to the Council, Mr. Seanez intentionally and knowingly advised the Council to act contrary to what he, a government practitioner of his experience, knows or ought to know to be law. He informed the Council that our holdings should not be followed, and presented his own arguments as the law that the Council must follow. Specifically, he dismissed our unambiguous holding that the People have ultimate authority to determine their governmental structure and amend all provisions that concern doctrines of separation of powers, checks and balances, accountability to the people, and service of the anti-corruption principle. Shirley v.

Morgan, No. SC.CV–02–10, p. 25, 9 Am. Tribal Law 46, 76 (Nav.Sup.Ct. May 28, 2010) clarified in Shirley v. Morgan, supra, 9 Am. Tribal Law 78, 85 (Nav.Sup.Ct. July 16, 2010). In the face of our unambiguous holding, he persisted in advising the Council that they have "unquestioned" authority to amend Titles 2, 7 and 11 without restriction. This legal opinion of Mr. Seanez alone constitutes gross misconduct of a Navajo Nation Bar member.

In re Seanez, 9 Am. Tribal Law 329, 333 (Navajo Nation Supreme Court, Oct. 18, 2010), on reconsideration, Nov. 24, 2010. The Court suspended Mr. Seanez's tribal license to practice for 49 months. After Mr. Seanez continued to advise the Navajo council, the Navajo Supreme Court disbarred him, and ordered him to pay $72,612 in sanctions. In re Seanez, 9 Am. Tribal Law 377, 387 (Navajo Nation Supreme Court, Jan. 25, 2011).

In-house tribal counsel are in a unique position to advise Indian tribes, and in many ways are the most critical and important attorneys in Indian country. But despite their best efforts, in-house counsel's work is all-too-often politicized, and their retention as civil servants is occasionally jeopardized. In Lomayesva v. Talayumptewa, No. 2015–CR–0088 (Hopi Tribal Court, Nov. 6, 2015), the tribal court ordered the reinstatement of the Hopi Tribe's General Counsel after he was terminated in violation of the tribe's employee manual:

> In short, the Tribal Council must follow its own laws, and not conveniently "re-interpret" a Hopi Tribal Council Resolution when the political winds change. Here, not one notion of Hopi fundamental fairness, not one attempt at due process, and not a single attempt to provide notice and an opportunity to be heard can be gleaned from the record and testimony before this Court. If this Court were to endorse and condone this abrogation of Hopi law, then all of the Hopi Tribe, the Hopi people, would suffer a terrible precedent in the Hopi way of life.

> This is not to say that Plaintiff cannot be terminated. He does not have a lifetime expectation of employment under any circumstance that may arise. Rather, the Employee Manual must be followed properly as required by the Resolution. Hopi law must be respected. If Tribal Council wishes to remove and terminate Plaintiff's employment, it must follow the terms of the Resolution that the Hopi Tribal Council, on its own accord, adopted.

Id. at 21–22. An appeal is pending.

Indian tribes are often slow to learn from the Jack Abramoff experience, where several Indian tribes retained Mr. Abramoff's firm, who billed millions of dollars in tribal money fraudulently and unethically. Deborah Solomon, *Lobbying Reservations*, N.Y. Times Mag., Feb. 26, 2006. Professor Wenona Singel recommends that Indian tribes adopt guidelines for the retention of outside counsel similar to the procurement rules that many states apply. Wenona T. Singel, Address, Outside Counsel and Internal Control Systems,

12th Annual Indian Law Conference, Michigan State University College of Law (Nov. 6, 2015).

CHAPTER SEVEN

TRIBAL SOVEREIGNTY AND JURISDICTION: CONGRESSIONAL AND JUDICIAL RECOGNITION AND LIMITATIONS

■ ■ ■

Federal Indian law at its core is about jurisdiction, which derives from the sovereignty of the government asserting it. Subject to federal statutes or treaties divesting power, Indian tribes have inherent power to control their own lands and people residing and doing business on those lands. The United States has responsibility for enforcing and protecting Indian treaty rights and broad power to regulate commerce with the Indian tribes. State governments and their political subdivisions seek to assert jurisdiction throughout their borders although their authority over Indian lands and people is limited by federal law.

These three sovereigns have contended for power and authority in Indian country since the Founding of the American Republic, leading to numerous Supreme Court decisions adjudicating disputes over jurisdiction and sovereignty between the three. Whenever Congress speaks clearly, its assumption of jurisdiction or allocation to the states or tribes of jurisdiction will prevail. Thus, the federal government has taken jurisdiction over major crimes and crimes between Indians and non-Indians in Indian country. And some states have been given jurisdiction over crimes and civil causes of action, but the general rule tracing back to Worcester v. Georgia, 31 U.S. 515 (1832), is that Indian tribes have primary and often exclusive civil and criminal jurisdiction except to the extent it has been assumed by the federal government. The Supreme Court, however, in a number of cases has allowed state governments to assert jurisdiction, and essentially limited tribal jurisdiction, over non-Indians in Indian country.

But for Indian tribes, jurisdiction and sovereignty are about survival. Jurisdiction can give the tribes protection from sometimes hostile state law enforcement. It also gives them the governmental power required to operate cultural and economic programs essential to nation building. Tribes see their ability to make their own laws and be governed by them as a critical force necessary to preserve a geographic and cultural core, and perpetuate their survival as peoples. Thus, jurisdictional disputes may mean more to a tribe than to a competing state government.

This Chapter covers the criminal and civil jurisdiction of the United States, Indian tribes, and state governments in Indian country. To analyze a jurisdictional dispute, one must determine first, whether the area in question is "Indian country." If it is not, the special jurisdictional rules of Indian law do not apply. If it is Indian country, and a tribal member engaged in on-reservation activities is the object of the assertion of jurisdiction by the state, the tribe presumptively has jurisdiction to the exclusion of the state. However, Congress has altered the rules covering many situations, making it necessary to look at federal legislation to be sure. When nonmembers of the tribe are the object of the assertion of jurisdiction, a variety of rules apply as a result either of congressional action or Supreme Court decisions.

This chapter treats, first, perhaps the most important legal term of art in federal Indian law—"Indian country."

SECTION A. THE ARENA OF FEDERAL AND TRIBAL JURISDICTION: "INDIAN COUNTRY"

1. LITIGATING "INDIAN COUNTRY": RESERVATION DIMINISHMENT AND DISESTABLISHMENT

The term "Indian country" is the starting point for analysis of jurisdictional questions in Indian law, because it defines the geographic area in which tribal and federal laws normally apply and state laws normally do not apply. 18 U.S.C. § 1151, adopted in 1948, defines Indian country as follows:

> * * * [T]he term "Indian country," as used in this chapter, means (a) all land within the limits of any Indian reservation under the jurisdiction of the United States government, notwithstanding the issuance of any patent, and, including rights-of-way running through the reservation, (b) all dependent Indian communities within the borders of the United States whether within the original or subsequently acquired territory thereof, and whether within or without the limits of a state, and (c) all Indian allotments, the Indian titles to which have not been extinguished, including rights-of-way running through the same.

Section 1151 is a criminal statute, but the Supreme Court has found that it "generally applies as well to questions of civil jurisdiction." DeCoteau v. District Court, 420 U.S. 425, 427 n.2 (1975).

The phrase "Indian country" was used as early as the eighteenth century as a reflection of the then prevailing concept that a separate territory would be set aside for Indians. The early nonintercourse acts used the term, but there was no statutory definition. As the policy of removing tribes west began to take effect, a statutory definition was provided in the Nonintercourse Act of 1834:

> [A]ll that part of the United States west of the Mississippi, and not within the states of Missouri and Louisiana, or the territory of Arkansas, and, also, that part of the United States east of the Mississippi river, and not within any state to which the Indian title has not been extinguished, for the purposes of this act, [shall be] deemed to be the Indian country.

4 Stat. 729. That definition remained on the books until the general statutory revision of 1874 when it was deleted, reflecting the fact that the westward expansion had made the earlier definition obsolete. In the absence of a statutory definition the courts then proceeded to define Indian country judicially. Those decisions were incorporated into the 1948 statute and are of assistance in understanding the current statutory definition of Indian country. See Marc Slonim, *Indian Country, Indian Reservations, and the Importance of History in Federal Indian Law*, 45 Gonz.L.Rev. 517 (2009/2010).

Jurisdictional disputes between tribes and non-Indian governments, as well as claims by convicted criminals that the locus of their crime was not Indian country, generated numerous cases involving the question of whether a particular reservation either had been "diminished" or even "disestablished" by acts of Congress, treaties or other agreements. The Supreme Court also tackled complex questions concerning the jurisdictional status of reservations where large blocks of land were opened to homesteading during the allotment era. These cases were notable for the Court's scrutiny of ancient statutes and an often sparse and vague legislative history. The Court often decided these cases by trying to avoid "checkerboarding"—where state and tribal jurisdictional lines became dependent on the ownership of individual parcels of land. Later, the Court emphasized the current demographics of a particular reservation.

Seymour v. Superintendent, 368 U.S. 351 (1962), first identified the problem of reservation "checkerboarding," as hampering the enforcement of criminal laws because of jurisdictional confusion. The Supreme Court interpreted a 1906 statute transferring a large part of the southern half of the Colville Reservation from tribal ownership to non-Indian ownership. The Court found that § 1151 intended to avoid "an impractical pattern of checkerboard jurisdiction" that would require "law enforcement officers operating in the area * * * to search tract books in order to determine" jurisdiction. 368 U.S. at 358. The Court held that a crime occurring on land owned in fee simple by a non-Indian in the township of Omak in the "open" area of the Colville Reservation remained Indian country.

Seymour was followed in Mattz v. Arnett, 412 U.S. 481 (1973), which held that the Klamath River Reservation in California was not terminated by an 1892 Act that allotted some reservation land to Indians and opened other reservation land to settlement by non-Indian homesteaders. Two years after *Mattz*, however, the Court held in DeCoteau v. District County Court, 420 U.S. 425 (1975), that the Lake Traverse Reservation of the Sisseton and Wahpeton bands of the Sioux in South Dakota was terminated by Congress by an 1891 Act that ceded and conveyed all of the reservation's 780,000 acres of unallotted lands to the United States, and resulted in the return of those lands to the public domain. Then in Rosebud Sioux Tribe v. Kneip, 430 U.S. 584 (1977), the Court held that Congress intended to disestablish Indian country in most of four counties in South Dakota over which the tribe asserted jurisdiction. In these cases, the Court searched for indicators of congressional intent to terminate the reservation. The *Mattz* court was "not inclined to infer an intent to terminate the reservation" in absence of "clear termination language." But the latter two cases said that the rule in *Mattz* allowed congressional intent to terminate to be found if it was "clear from the surrounding circumstances and legislative history." Thus, in *DeCoteau* where the statute was rather vague the record of negotiations leading up to the tribe's agreement to "cede, sell, relinquish, and convey" all the unallotted lands to the government for a sum certain was enough to find termination of reservation status. Then, in *Rosebud* the same kind of vague statute without evidence of legislative history was still found sufficient to disestablish a reservation.

In *DeCoteau*, Justice Douglas, joined in dissent by Justices Brennan and Marshall, sought to illustrate what he called the "dimensions of the tragedy inflicted" by the majority's decision. First, he explained, the case involved an Indian child's placement in a foster home, "which goes to the heart of tribal self-government. The question of a child's welfare cannot be decided without reference to his family structure. This involves both sympathetic knowledge of the individuals involved, and knowledge of the background culture. The tribe is fearful that if South Dakota has jurisdiction over tribal children it will place them with non-Indian families where they will lose their cultural identity." Next, he pointed to the practical problems of the majority's decision for civil and criminal jurisdiction over Indians:

> * * * Jurisdiction dependent on the "tract book" promises to be uncertain and hectic. Many acts are ambulatory. In a given case, who will move—the State, the tribe, or the Federal Government? The contest promises to be unseemly, the only beneficiaries being those who benefit from confusion and uncertainty. Without state interference, Indians violating the law within the reservation would be subject only to tribal jurisdiction, which puts the responsibility where the Federal Government can supervise it. Checkerboard jurisdiction cripples the United States in fulfilling its fiduciary responsibilities of guardianship and protection of

Indians. It is the end of tribal authority for it introduces such an element of uncertainty as to what agency has jurisdiction as to make modest tribal leaders abdicate and aggressive ones undertake the losing battle against superior state authority. * * *

Id. at 467–68.

The Court's decisions did little to dispel the uncertainty in defining "Indian country" on the ground. In the following case, the Court once again returned to the issue of reservation diminishment and the judicial search for evidence of congressional intent to change reservation boundaries during the nineteenth century allotment era.

SOLEM V. BARTLETT
Supreme Court of the United States, 1984.
465 U.S. 463, 104 S.Ct. 1161, 79 L.Ed.2d 443.

JUSTICE MARSHALL delivered the opinion of the Court.

* * *

I

In 1979, the State of South Dakota charged respondent John Bartlett, an enrolled member of the Cheyenne River Sioux Tribe, with attempted rape. Respondent pleaded guilty [but] contended that the crime for which he had been convicted occurred within the Cheyenne River Sioux Reservation, established by Congress in the Act of March 2, 1889, ch. 405, § 4, 25 Stat. 889; that, although on May 29, 1908, Congress opened for settlement by non-Indians the portion of the Reservation on which respondent committed his crime, the opened portion nonetheless remained Indian country; and that the State therefore lacked criminal jurisdiction over respondent.

* * *

II

In the latter half of the 19th century, large sections of the western States and Territories were set aside for Indian reservations. Towards the end of the century, however, Congress increasingly adhered to the view that the Indian tribes should abandon their nomadic lives on the communal reservations and settle into an agrarian economy on privately owned parcels of land. This shift was fueled in part by the belief that individualized farming would speed the Indians' assimilation into American society and in part by the continuing demand for new lands for the waves of homesteaders moving west. As a result of these combined pressures, Congress passed a series of surplus land Acts at the turn of the century to force Indians onto individual allotments carved out of reservations and to open up unallotted lands for non-Indian settlement. * * *

* * *

Unfortunately, the surplus land Acts themselves seldom detail whether opened lands retained reservation status or were divested of all Indian interests. When the surplus land Acts were passed, the distinction seemed unimportant. The notion that reservation status of Indian lands might not be coextensive with tribal ownership was unfamiliar at the turn of the century. Indian lands were judicially defined to include only those lands in which the Indians held some form of property interest: trust lands, individual allotments, and, to a more limited degree, opened lands that had not yet been claimed by non-Indians. See Bates v. Clark, 95 U.S. 204 (1877); Ash Sheep Co. v. United States, 252 U.S. 159 (1920). Only in 1948 did Congress uncouple reservation status from Indian ownership, and statutorily define Indian country to include lands held in fee by non-Indians within reservation boundaries. 18 U.S.C. § 1151.

Another reason why Congress did not concern itself with the effect of surplus land Acts on reservation boundaries was the turn-of-the-century assumption that Indian reservations were a thing of the past. Consistent with prevailing wisdom, Members of Congress voting on the surplus land Acts believed to a man that within a short time—within a generation at most—the Indian tribes would enter traditional American society and the reservation system would cease to exist. Given this expectation, Congress naturally failed to be meticulous in clarifying whether a particular piece of legislation formally sliced a certain parcel of land off one reservation.

Although the Congresses that passed the surplus land acts anticipated the imminent demise of the reservation and, in fact, passed the acts partially to facilitate the process, we have never been willing to extrapolate from this expectation a specific congressional purpose of diminishing reservations with the passage of every surplus land act. Rather, it is settled law that some surplus land acts diminished reservations, and other surplus land Acts did not. The effect of any given surplus land Act depends on the language of the act and the circumstances underlying its passage.

Our precedents in the area have established a fairly clean analytical structure for distinguishing those surplus land acts that diminished reservations from those acts that simply offered non-Indians the opportunity to purchase land within established reservation boundaries. The first and governing principle is that only Congress can divest a reservation of its land and diminish its boundaries. * * *

Diminishment, moreover, will not be lightly inferred. Our analysis of surplus land acts requires that Congress clearly evince an "intent . . . to change . . . boundaries" before diminishment will be found. *Rosebud Sioux Tribe v. Kneip*. The most probative evidence of congressional intent is the statutory language used to open the Indian lands. Explicit reference to cession or other language evidencing the present and total surrender of all tribal interests strongly suggests that Congress meant to divest from the reservation all unallotted opened lands. *DeCoteau v. District County Court*; *Seymour v. Superintendent*. When such language of cession is buttressed by an unconditional commitment from Congress to compensate the Indian tribe for its opened land, there is an almost insurmountable presumption that Congress meant for the tribe's reservation to be diminished. See *DeCoteau v. District County Court*.

As our opinion in *Rosebud Sioux Tribe* demonstrates, however, explicit language of cession and unconditional compensation are not prerequisites for a finding of diminishment. When events surrounding the passage of a surplus land Act—particularly the manner in which the transaction was negotiated with the tribes involved and the tenor of legislative Reports presented to Congress—unequivocally reveal a widely held, contemporaneous understanding that the affected reservation would shrink as a result of the proposed legislation, we have been willing to infer that Congress shared the understanding that its action would diminish the reservation, notwithstanding the presence of statutory language that would otherwise suggest reservation boundaries remained unchanged. To a lesser extent, we have also looked to events that occurred after the passage of a surplus land Act to decipher Congress' intentions. Congress's own treatment of the affected areas, particularly in the years immediately following the opening, has some evidentiary value, as does the manner in which the Bureau of Indian Affairs and local judicial authorities dealt with unallotted open lands.

On a more pragmatic level, we have recognized that who actually moved onto opened reservation lands is also relevant to deciding whether a surplus land act diminished a reservation. Where non-Indian settlers flooded into the opened portion of a reservation and the area has long since lost its Indian character, we have acknowledged that *de facto*, if not *de jure*, diminishment may have occurred. See *Rosebud Sioux Tribe v. Kneip*, supra; *DeCoteau v. District County Court*. In addition to the obvious practical advantages of acquiescing to *de facto* diminishment,[12] we look to the subsequent demographic history of opened lands as one additional clue as to what Congress expected would happen once land on a particular reservation was opened to non-Indian settlers.[13]

---

[12] When an area is predominately populated by non-Indians with only a few surviving pockets of Indian allotments, finding that the land remains Indian country seriously burdens the administration of state and local governments. Conversely, problems of an imbalanced checkerboard jurisdiction arise if a largely Indian opened area is found to be outside Indian country.

[13] Resort to subsequent demographic history is, of course, an unorthodox and potentially unreliable method of statutory interpretation. However, in the area of surplus land Acts, where

* * *

III

A

We now turn to apply these principles to the Act of May 29, 1908. We begin with the Act's operative language, which reads:

> "[T]he Secretary of the Interior . . . is hereby . . . authorized and directed, as hereinafter provided, to sell and dispose of all that portion of the Cheyenne River and Standing Rock Indian reservations in the States of South Dakota and North Dakota lying and being within the following described boundaries. . . .

> "[F]rom the proceeds arising from the sale and disposition of the lands aforesaid, exclusive of the customary fees and commissions, there shall be deposited in the Treasury of the United States, to the credit of the Indians belonging and having tribal rights on the reservation aforesaid in the States of South Dakota and North Dakota the sums to which the respective tribes may be entitled. . . ." Ch. 218, §§ 1, 6, 35 Stat. 460–61, 463.

These provisions stand in sharp contrast to the explicit language of cession employed in the Lake Traverse and 1904 Rosebud Acts discussed in our opinions in *DeCoteau* and *Rosebud Sioux Tribe*. Rather than reciting an Indian agreement to "cede, sell, relinquish and convey" the opened lands, the Cheyenne River Act simply authorizes the Secretary to "sell and dispose" of certain lands. This reference to the sale of Indian lands, coupled with the creation of Indian accounts for proceeds, suggests that the Secretary of the Interior was simply being authorized to act as the Tribe's sales agent. * * *

* * *

This case is made more difficult, however, by the presence of some language in the Cheyenne River Act that indirectly supports petitioner's view that the reservation was diminished. For instance, in a provision permitting Indians already holding allotment on the opened lands to obtain new allotments in the unopened territories, the Act refers to the unopened territories as "within the respective reservations thus diminished." § 2, 35 Stat. 461. Elsewhere, the Act permits tribal members to harvest timber on certain parts of the opened lands, but conditions the grant for "only as long as the lands remain part of the public domain." § 9, 35 Stat. 464. On the assumption that Congress would refer to opened lands as being part of the public domain only if the lands had lost all vestiges of reservation status, petitioners and several amici point to the term "public domain" as well as the phrase "reservations thus diminished" as evidence that Congress

---

various factors kept Congress from focusing on the diminishment issue, the technique is a necessary expedient.

understood the Cheyenne River Act to divest unallotted open lands of their reservation status.

Undisputedly, the references to the opened areas as being in "the public domain" and the unopened areas as comprising "the reservation thus diminished" support petitioner's view that the Cheyenne River Act diminished the reservation. These isolated phrases, however, are hardly dispositive.[17] And, when balanced against the Cheyenne River Act's stated and limited goal of opening up reservation lands for sale to non-Indian settlers, these two phrases cannot carry the burden of establishing an express congressional purpose to diminish. The Act of May 29, 1908, read as a whole, does not present an explicit expression of congressional intent to diminish the Cheyenne River Sioux Reservation.

B

The circumstances surrounding the passage of the Cheyenne River Act also fail to establish a clear congressional purpose to diminish the reservation. In contrast to the Lake Traverse Act and 1904 Rosebud Act, the Cheyenne River Act did not begin with an agreement between the United States and the Indian Tribes, in which the Indians agreed to cede a portion of their territory to the Federal Government. The Cheyenne River Act had its origins in "[a] bill to authorize the sale and disposition of a portion of the surplus and unallotted lands in the Cheyenne River and Standing Rock reservations," * * * .

* * *

C

The subsequent treatment of the Cheyenne River Sioux Reservation by Congress, courts, and the Executive is so rife with contradictions and inconsistencies as to be of no help to either side. * * * Moreover, both parties have been able to cite instances in which state and federal courts exerted criminal jurisdiction over the disputed area in the years following opening. Neither sovereign dominated the jurisdictional history of the opened lands in the decades immediately following 1908.

What is clear, however, is what happened to the Cheyenne River Sioux Tribe after the Act of May 29, 1908, was passed. Most of the members of the Tribe obtained individual allotments on the lands opened by the Act. Because most of the tribe lived on the opened territories, tribal authorities and Bureau of Indian Affairs personnel took primary responsibility for policing and supplying social services to the opened lands during the years

---

[17] There is also considerable doubt as to what Congress meant in using these phrases. In 1908, "diminished" was not yet a term of art in Indian law. When Congress spoke of the "reservation thus diminished," it may well have been referring to diminishment in common lands and not diminishment of reservation boundaries. Similarly, even with diminishment, unallotted opened lands could be conceived of as being in the "public domain" inasmuch as they were available for settlement.

following 1908. The strong tribal presence in the opened area has continued until the present day. Now roughly two-thirds of the Tribe's enrolled members live in the opened area. The seat of tribal government is now located in a town in the opened area, where most important tribal activities take place.

Also clear is the historical fact that the opening of the Cheyenne River Sioux Reservation was a failure. Few homesteaders perfected claims on the lands, due perhaps in part to the price of the land but probably more importantly to the fact that the opened area was much less fertile than the lands in southern South Dakota opened by other surplus land Acts. As a result of the small number of homesteaders who settled on the opened lands and the high percentage of tribal members who continue to live in the area, the population of the disputed area is now evenly divided between Indian and non-Indian residents. Under these circumstances, it is impossible to say that the opened areas of the Cheyenne River Sioux Reservation have lost their Indian character.

* * *

NOTES

1.   What was "the fairly clean analytical structure" identified by the Court? Is this a structure that tribes, states, and local units of government can effectively use to deal with jurisdictional concerns? If you were an Indian country law enforcement officer or prosecutor, for state, federal, or tribal jurisdictions, does the *Solem* test help you? Following *Solem*, can you determine whether the following types of land are Indian country? Homesteaded land owned in fee by a non-Indian within a reservation? A town, established under state law, within an Indian reservation? A state highway or railroad route through an Indian reservation? A trust allotment beyond the boundaries of a reservation? A former allotment, now owned by an Indian in fee, within a reservation? A former allotment, now owned by an Indian in fee, not within the exterior limits of a reservation?

The lack of precision and predictability in the Court's Indian country disestablishment and diminishment cases has exacerbated law enforcement problems on Indian reservations especially when non-Indian perpetrators of crime are involved. Federal prosecutors who must prove the location of a crime in order to determine whether it occurred in Indian country sometimes simply decline to prosecute rather than enter into the complex jurisdictional maze. See Examining Federal Declinations to Prosecute Crimes in Indian Country, Hearing before the Indian Affairs Committee of the United States Senate, 110th Cong. 37–39 (Sept. 18, 2008) (prepared testimony of Thomas B. Heffelfinger, former United States Attorney for the District of Minnesota).

2.   In addition to reservations and allotments covered by subsections (a) and (c) of 18 U.S.C. § 1151, Indian country also includes "dependent Indian communities." The Supreme Court has said that the term "dependent Indian

community" as used in 18 U.S.C. § 1151(b) covers any "area * * * validly set apart for the use of the Indians as such, under the superintendence of the Government." Oklahoma Tax Comm'n v. Citizen Band Potawatomi Indian Tribe, 498 U.S. 505, 511 (1991). The Court seemed to recognize that Congress intended to eschew technical distinctions in land tenure and "defined Indian country broadly, . . . [intending] to designate as Indian country all lands set aside by whatever means for the residence of tribal Indians under federal protection, together with trust and restricted Indian allotments." Oklahoma Tax Comm'n v. Sac and Fox Nation, 508 U.S. 114, 125 (1993) (citing Felix Cohen, Handbook of Federal Indian Law 34 (1982 ed.)).

The term "dependent Indian community" was taken from the Supreme Court's decision in United States v. Sandoval, 231 U.S. 28 (1913). In that case and others following it, the Court had held that distinctly Indian communities outside established reservations were sufficiently similar to communities on reservations to be included within the meaning of Indian country. E.g., United States v. South Dakota, 665 F.2d 837 (8th Cir.1981) (holding that a tribal housing project on trust land was a "dependent Indian community"), cert. denied 459 U.S. 823 (1982).

Some 229 Alaska Native villages arguably fit the definition of dependent Indian communities. With one exception (Metlakatla), there are no reservations in Alaska but predominantly Native villages have lived for many generations in cohesive communities. These communities have longstanding relationships with the federal government, including the receipt of substantial federal assistance under Indian programs. Many of the villages are federally recognized tribes organized under the Indian Reorganization Act. Most have selected land traditionally used by them in and around their villages to be patented to them under the Alaska Native Claims Settlement Act (ANCSA). See Chapter 13A, infra. The Act recognized the villages' historic ties to land in the vicinity of their settlements and issued title to the selected lands to be held in the name of native-owned corporations. The Supreme Court, however, held that Alaska Native lands conveyed under ANCSA were not "set aside by the Federal Government for the use of the Indians as Indian land," and second, were not "under federal superintendence." Alaska v. Village of Venetie Tribal Government, 522 U.S. 520, 527 (1998).

More recently, a sharply divided Tenth Circuit Court of Appeals, sitting en banc, held that the Indian lands in the Churchrock Chapter of the Navajo Nation in Utah could not be "Indian country." Hydro Resources, Inc. v. United States Environmental Protection Agency, 608 F.3d 1131 (10th Cir.2010) (en banc). The majority rejected the EPA's argument that the relevant Navajo lands were "dependent Indian communities:"

> In our case, it is undisputed that HRI's Section 8 land hasn't been explicitly set aside by Congress (or the Executive) for Indian use since the brief period when it was appended to the Navajo Reservation nearly a century ago. * * * It is likewise undisputed that the land isn't under federal superintendence, and hasn't been since

the government sold it in 1970. * * * McKinley County and the State of New Mexico provide all essential public services to HRI's Section 8 land, including roads, law enforcement, and emergency and school services. The Navajo Church Rock Chapter recognizes that private lands within its boundaries, like HRI's, are subject to state jurisdiction and control. And state authorities have long assessed tax on HRI's property. Under *Venetie*'s interpretation of § 1151(b), it would seem unavoidable that the land in question is not Indian country.

HRI, 608 F.3d at 1137.

The majority also rejected EPA's efforts to inject an "anti-checkerboarding" public policy interest into the Indian country statute:

> EPA attempts to overcome this by arguing that § 1151 as a whole is imbued with an "anti-checkerboard" purpose. * * * But this argument overstates the statutory case against checkerboarding. In *Seymour*, the Court simply observed the obvious: subsection (a), by its express terms, includes within the definition of Indian country *all* lands within the congressionally prescribed boundaries of a reservation, including private fee lands.

Id. at 1157.

The dissent objected that the majority departed from Tenth Circuit precedents that defined a "community of reference" before applying the *Venetie* factors to decide whether a specific parcel was part of a dependent Indian community. Instead, the majority isolated the specific land owned by HRI from the larger community in which it was located:

> The Church Rock Chapter of the Navajo Nation was formally certified as a local governmental unit by the Navajo Nation Council in 1955, although residents built a Chapter House for local governance purposes in 1946. The Chapter, which is located just east of the town of Gallup, New Mexico, consists of over 57,000 acres. The federal government holds approximately 52% of this land in trust for the Navajo nation, and holds an additional 26% in trust in the form of allotments to individual Indians. The Bureau of Land Management ("BLM") owns an additional 10% of the land, which is subject to grazing leases granted to Navajos. In addition, the state of New Mexico owns about 4% the remaining land, and private interests own approximately 6%.

Id. at 1168 (Ebel, C.J., dissenting).

3.   Tribes with checkerboard jurisdiction have joined with state and local law enforcement agencies to find practical solutions. One solution gaining credibility and credence is the development of cross-deputization or mutual help agreements. See generally Hannah Bobee, Allison Boisvenu, Anderson Duff, Kathryn E. Fort & Wenona T. Singel, *Criminal Jurisdiction in Indian Country: The Solution of Cross-Deputization*, Michigan State University

College of Law, Indigenous Law and Policy Center Working Paper 2008–1 (July 2008).

2.　POST-*SOLEM* RESERVATION BOUNDARY CASES

Influential factors in the *Solem* Court's analysis were "events that occurred after the passage of a surplus land Act to decipher Congress' intentions" including "who actually moved onto opened reservation lands." This means of imputing intentions to earlier congressional actions by looking at the subsequent demographics has led to *de facto* diminishment. In two major reservation diminishment cases decided by the Court since *Solem*, the Justices have given weight to such post hoc factors to determine congressional intent to find reservation diminishment. In Hagen v. Utah, 510 U.S. 399 (1994), and South Dakota v. Yankton Sioux Tribe, 522 U.S. 329 (1998), the Court focused on growth of non-Indian population and land ownership following passage of a surplus land act.

In the 1994 *Hagen* decision, the Court found that Congress had intended to diminish the Uintah Reservation in the state of Utah by passage of a 1902 Act which provided that if a majority of the adult male members of the Uintah and White River Indians consented, the Secretary of the Interior should make allotments by October 1, 1903, out of the Uintah Reservation. The Act also provided that when the deadline for allotments passed, "all the unallotted lands within said reservation shall be restored to the public domain" and subject to homesteading at $1.25 per acre. The proceeds from the sale of lands restored to the public domain were to be used for the benefit of the Indians.

Justice O'Connor's majority opinion reviewed the tri-factor test relied upon by the Court in *Solem* to determine congressional intent to diminish a reservation. Particular attention was focused upon the statutory language of the 1902 Act providing that the lands "shall be *restored to the public domain*."

> * * * Statutes of the period indicate that Congress considered Indian reservations as separate from the public domain. Likewise, in *DeCoteau* we emphasized the distinction between reservation and public domain lands: "That the lands ceded in the other agreements were *returned to the public domain, stripped of reservation status*, can hardly be questioned.... The sponsors of the legislation stated repeatedly that the ratified agreements would return the ceded lands to the 'public domain.'" 420 U.S. at 446 (emphasis added).

Id. at 413. The *Hagen* Court held that restoration of unallotted reservation lands to the public domain evidenced "a congressional intent with respect to those lands inconsistent with the continuation of reservation status. Thus, the existence of such language in the operative section of a surplus land Act indicates that the Act diminished the reservation."

Justice O'Connor also relied on *Solem*'s contemporary historical context factor to support the Court's conclusion in *Hagen* that Congress intended to diminish the Uintah Reservation:

> * * * As we have noted, the plain language of the 1902 Act demonstrated the congressional purpose to diminish the Uintah Reservation. Under the 1902 Act, however, the consent of the Indians was required before the Reservation could be diminished; that consent was withheld by the Indians living on the Reservation. After this Court's *Lone Wolf* decision in 1903, Congress authorized the Secretary of the Interior to proceed unilaterally. The Acting Commissioner for Indian Affairs in the Department of the Interior directed Indian Inspector James McLaughlin to travel to the Uintah Reservation to "endeavor to obtain [the Indians'] consent to the allotment of lands as provided in the law, and to the restoration of the surplus lands." Letter from A. C. Tonner to James McLaughlin (April 27, 1903), reprinted in S. Doc. No. 159, 58th Cong., 3d Sess., 9 (1905). The Acting Commissioner noted, however, that the effect of the 1903 Act was "that if the [Indians] do not consent to the allotments by the first of June next the allotments are to be made notwithstanding, and the unallotted lands . . . are to be opened to entry" according to the terms of the 1902 Act.

> Inspector McLaughlin explained the effect of these recent developments to the Indians living on the Reservation:

> > " 'By that decision of the Supreme Court, Congress has the legal right to legislate in regard to Indian lands, and Congress has enacted a law which requires you to take your allotments.

> > . . .

> > " 'You say that [the Reservation boundary] line is very heavy and that the reservation is nailed down upon the border. That is very true as applying to the past many years and up to now, but congress has provided legislation which will pull up the nails which hold down that line and after next year there will be no outside boundary line to this reservation.' " Minutes of Councils Held by James McLaughlin, U.S. Indian Inspector, with the Uintah and White River Ute Indians at Uintah Agency, Utah, From May 18 to May 23, 1903.

> Inspector McLaughlin's picturesque phrase reflects the contemporaneous understanding, by him conveyed to the Indians, that the Reservation would be diminished by operation of the 1902 and 1903 Acts notwithstanding the failure of the Indians to give their consent.

Id. at 416–17.

Completing the three-factor checklist approach derived from *Solem*, the Court noted that the current population of the area is approximately 85 percent non-Indian. The population of the largest city in the area—Roosevelt City, named for the President who opened the Reservation for settlement—is about 93 percent non-Indian, as the Court noted. This demographic factor, combined with the fact that the State of Utah had exercised jurisdiction over the opened lands from the time of the Reservation's opening, convinced the *Hagen* majority that the Uintah Indian Reservation had been diminished by Congress.

Justice Blackmun, joined by Justice Souter, wrote a sharply worded dissent to the majority's holding that Congress had intended to diminish the Uintah reservation, noting particularly that the 1902 Act relied upon by the majority never became effective because the Indians never consented to diminishment as required by the terms of the statute.

> "Great nations, like great men, should keep their word," FPC v. Tuscarora Indian Nation, 362 U.S. 99, 142 (1960) (Black, J., dissenting), and we do not lightly find that Congress has broken its solemn promises to Indian tribes. The Court relies on a single, ambiguous phrase in an Act that never became effective, and which was deleted from the controlling statute, to conclude that Congress must have intended to diminish the Uintah Valley Reservation. I am unable to find a clear expression of such intent in either the operative statute or the surrounding circumstances and am compelled to conclude that the original Uintah Valley Reservation boundaries remain intact.

Id. at 422.

In *Yankton*, decided by the Court in 1998, the tribe had initiated litigation to block state approval of a landfill on non-Indian fee lands within the boundaries of the original Yankton Reservation. The Court interpreted an 1894 surplus lands act as effecting a congressional diminishment of the Yankton Sioux Reservation in South Dakota, and therefore found that the landfill was located on lands no longer within the Reservation boundary. Justice O'Connor, this time writing the opinion for a unanimous Court in *Yankton*, found that the statutory language of the 1894 Act, providing that the tribe will "cede, sell, relinquish, and convey to the United States all their claim, right, title, and interest in and to all the unallotted lands within the limits of the reservation" for a fixed payment of $600,000, evidenced the requisite congressional intent to diminish the Yankton Sioux Reservation.

> This "cession" and "sum certain" language is "precisely suited" to terminating reservation status. See *DeCoteau*, 420 U.S. at 445. Indeed, we have held that when a surplus land Act contains both explicit language of cession, evidencing "the present and total surrender of all tribal interests," and a provision for a fixed-sum payment, representing "an unconditional commitment from Congress to compensate the Indian tribe for its opened land," a "nearly conclusive," or "almost insurmountable," presumption of

diminishment arises. *Solem,* supra, at 470; see also *Hagen,* 510 U.S. at 411.

522 U.S. at 344.

The Court also found that the manner in which the transaction was negotiated with the Yankton Tribe and " 'the tenor of legislative Reports presented to Congress' reveal a contemporaneous understanding that the proposed legislation modified the reservation. * * * In terms that strongly suggest a reconception of the reservation, Commissioner Cole admonished the Tribe."

> "This reservation alone proclaims the old time and the old conditions . . . the tide of civilization is as resistless as the tide of the ocean, and you have no choice but to accept it and live according to its methods or be destroyed by it. To accept it requires the sale of these surplus lands and the opening of this reservation to white settlement.

> "You were a great and powerful people when your abilities and energies were directed in harmony with the conditions which surrounded you, but the wave of civilization which swept over you found you unprepared for the new conditions and you became weak. . . . You must accept the new life wholly. You must break down the barriers and invite the white man with all the elements of civilization, that your young men may have the same opportunities under the new conditions that your fathers had under the old."

Id. at 352–53.

In closing, Justice O'Connor offered the following judicial lament for tribes like the Yankton, whose reservation lands were diminished by Congress during the nineteenth century Allotment era of federal Indian policy.

> The allotment era has long since ended, and its guiding philosophy has been repudiated. Tribal communities struggled but endured, preserved their cultural roots, and remained, for the most part, near their historic lands. But despite the present-day understanding of a "government-to-government relationship between the United States and each Indian tribe," see, e.g., 25 U.S.C. § 3601, we must give effect to Congress' intent in passing the 1894 Act. * * *

Id. at 357. How far should courts go in attempting to resuscitate a failed policy such as the Allotment Act through interpretations of contemporaneous statutes? See Judith V. Royster, *The Legacy of Allotment,* 27 Ariz.St.L.J. 1 (1995). If the intent of the particular statute is not readily apparent should the courts search for the "widely shared assumptions" of the era when the law was passed? If attitudes differed substantially between Indians and non-Indians at the time, whose assumptions should carry the greater weight?

The Court's decisions in *Hagen* and in *Yankton* have changed the negotiating position of many states in regards to their relationships with

Indian tribes. For example, the State of Michigan had entered into negotiations over an omnibus tax agreement with most of the Michigan Indian tribes. Part of the compulsion for these tribes to negotiate on these tax issues was the implied threat that the State would pursue litigation to extend their taxing jurisdiction over Michigan reservations by asking the courts to find that the reservations had been disestablished. See Matthew L.M. Fletcher, *The Power to Tax, the Power to Destroy, and the Michigan Tribal-State Tax Agreements*, 82 U.Det. Mercy L.Rev. 1, 17–18 (2004).

In Smith v. Parker, 774 F.3d 1166 (8th Cir.2014), aff'd sub nom., Nebraska v. Parker, 136 S. Ct. 1072 (2016), the Omaha Tribe of Nebraska attempted to enforce tribal liquor licensing regulations and taxes on nonmember-owned businesses that sold alcohol in the Village of Pender, located within the exterior boundaries of the tribe's reservation. The Secretary of the Interior approved the tribe's liquor laws, an act that effectively delegated federal authority to enforce tribal liquor laws in accordance with United States v. Mazurie, 419 U.S. 544 (1975).

Since tribal authority over nonmembers was confirmed, nonmembers and the village, later joined by the State of Nebraska, challenged the reservation boundaries, arguing that the tribe's reservation had been diminished, and therefore there could be no tribal authority over the portion of the reservation where the village lay.

NEBRASKA V. PARKER
Supreme Court of the United States, 2016.
__ U.S. __, 136 S.Ct. 1072, 194 L.Ed.2d 152.

JUSTICE THOMAS delivered the opinion of the Court.

The village of Pender, Nebraska sits a few miles west of an abandoned right-of-way once used by the Sioux City and Nebraska Railroad Company. We must decide whether Pender and surrounding Thurston County, Nebraska, are within the boundaries of the Omaha Indian Reservation or whether the passage of an 1882 Act empowering the United States Secretary of the Interior to sell the Tribe's land west of the right-of-way "diminished" the reservation's boundaries, thereby "free[ing]" the disputed land of "its reservation status." Solem v. Bartlett, 465 U.S. 463, 467, 104 S.Ct. 1161, 79 L.Ed.2d 443 (1984). We hold that Congress did not diminish the reservation in 1882 and that the disputed land is within the reservation's boundaries.

I

A

Centuries ago, the Omaha Tribe settled in present-day eastern Nebraska. By the mid-19th century, the Tribe was destitute and, in exchange for much-needed revenue, agreed to sell a large swath of its land to the United States. In 1854, the Tribe entered into a treaty with the

United States to create a 300,000-acre reservation. Treaty with the Omahas (1854 Treaty), Mar. 16, 1854, 10 Stat. 1043. * * *

In 1865, after the displaced Wisconsin Winnebago Tribe moved west, the Omaha Tribe agreed to "cede, sell, and convey" an additional 98,000 acres on the north side of the reservation to the United States for the purpose of creating a reservation for the Winnebagoes. Treaty with the Omaha Indians (1865 Treaty), Mar. 6, 1865, 14 Stat. 667–668. The Tribe sold the land for a fixed sum of $50,000. Id., at 667.

* * *

Then came the 1882 Act, central to the dispute between petitioners and respondents. In that Act, Congress again empowered the Secretary of the Interior "to cause to be surveyed, if necessary, and sold" more than 50,000 acres lying west of a right-of-way granted by the Tribe and approved by the Secretary of the Interior in 1880 for use by the Sioux City and Nebraska Railroad Company. Act of Aug. 7, 1882 (1882 Act), 22 Stat. 341. The land for sale under the terms of the 1882 Act overlapped substantially with the land Congress tried, but failed, to sell in 1872. Once the land was appraised "in tracts of forty acres each," the Secretary was "to issue [a] proclamation" that the "lands are open for settlement under such rules and regulations as he may prescribe." §§ 1, 2, id., at 341. Within one year of that proclamation, a nonmember could purchase up to 160 acres of land (for no less than $2.50 per acre) in cash paid to the United States, so long as the settler "occup[ied]" it, made "valuable improvements thereon," and was "a citizen of the United States, or . . . declared his intention to become such." § 2, id., at 341. The proceeds from any land sales, "after paying all expenses incident to and necessary for carrying out the provisions of th[e] act," were to "be placed to the credit of said Indians in the Treasury of the United States." § 3, id., at 341. Interest earned on the proceeds was to be "annually expended for the benefit of said Indians, under the direction of the Secretary of the Interior." Ibid.

The 1882 Act also included a provision, common in the late 19th century, that enabled members of the Tribe to select individual allotments, §§ 5–8, id., at 342–343, as a means of encouraging them to depart from the communal lifestyle of the reservation. * * * The 1882 Act provided that the United States would convey the land to a member or his heirs in fee simple after holding it in trust on behalf of the member and his heirs for 25 years. § 6, 22 Stat. 342. Members could select allotments on any part of the reservation, either east or west of the right-of-way. § 8, id., at 343.

After the members selected their allotments—only 10 to 15 of which were located west of the right-of-way—the Secretary proclaimed that the remaining 50,157 acres west of the right-of-way were open for settlement by nonmembers in April 1884. One of those settlers was W.E. Peebles, who "purchased a tract of 160 acres, on which he platted the townsite for Pender." Smith v. Parker, 996 F.Supp.2d 815, 828 (D.Neb.2014).

B

The village of Pender today numbers 1,300 residents. Most are not associated with the Omaha Tribe. Less than 2% of Omaha tribal members have lived west of the right-of-way since the early 20th century.

Despite its longstanding absence, the Tribe sought to assert jurisdiction over Pender in 2006 by subjecting Pender retailers to its newly amended Beverage Control Ordinance. The ordinance requires those retailers to obtain a liquor license (costing $500, $1,000, or $1,500 depending upon the class of license) and imposes a 10% sales tax on liquor sales. Nonmembers who violate the ordinance are subject to a $10,000 fine.

The village of Pender and Pender retailers, including bars, a bowling alley, and social clubs, brought a federal suit against members of the Omaha Tribal Council in their official capacities to challenge the Tribe's power to impose the requirements of the Beverage Control Ordinance on nonmembers. Federal law permits the Tribe to regulate liquor sales on its reservation and in "Indian country" so long as the Tribe's regulations are (as they were here) "certified by the Secretary of the Interior, and published in the Federal Register." 18 U.S.C. § 1161. The challengers alleged that they were neither within the boundaries of the Omaha Indian Reservation nor in Indian country and, consequently, were not bound by the ordinance.

* * *

II

We must determine whether Congress "diminished" the Omaha Indian Reservation in 1882. If it did so, the State now has jurisdiction over the disputed land. Solem, 465 U.S., at 467, 104 S.Ct. 1161. If Congress, on the other hand, did not diminish the reservation and instead only enabled nonmembers to purchase land within the reservation, then federal, state, and tribal authorities share jurisdiction over these "opened" but undiminished reservation lands. Ibid.

The framework we employ to determine whether an Indian reservation has been diminished is well settled. Id., at 470–472, 104 S.Ct. 1161. "[O]nly Congress can divest a reservation of its land and diminish its boundaries," and its intent to do so must be clear. Id., at 470, 104 S.Ct. 1161. To assess whether an Act of Congress diminished a reservation, we start with the statutory text, for "[t]he most probative evidence of diminishment is, of course, the statutory language used to open the Indian lands." Hagen v. Utah, 510 U.S. 399, 411, 114 S.Ct. 958, 127 L.Ed.2d 252 (1994). Under our precedents, we also "examine all the circumstances surrounding the opening of a reservation." Id., at 412, 114 S.Ct. 958. Because of "the turn-of-the-century assumption that Indian reservations were a thing of the past," many surplus land Acts did not clearly convey "whether opened lands retained reservation status or were divested of all Indian interests." Solem, supra, at 468, 104 S.Ct. 1161. For that reason, our precedents also look to any "unequivocal evidence" of the contemporaneous and subsequent understanding of the status of the reservation by members and nonmembers, as well as the United States and the State of Nebraska. South Dakota v. Yankton Sioux Tribe, 522 U.S. 329, 351, 118 S.Ct. 789, 139 L.Ed.2d 773 (1998).

A

As with any other question of statutory interpretation, we begin with the text of the 1882 Act, the most "probative evidence" of diminishment. [Solem] * * * Common textual indications of Congress' intent to diminish reservation boundaries include "[e]xplicit reference to cession or other language evidencing the present and total surrender of all tribal interests" or "an unconditional commitment from Congress to compensate the Indian tribe for its opened land." * * * Such language "providing for the total surrender of tribal claims in exchange for a fixed payment" evinces Congress' intent to diminish a reservation, * * * and creates "an almost insurmountable presumption that Congress meant for the tribe's reservation to be diminished," * * *. Similarly, a statutory provision restoring portions of a reservation to "the public domain" signifies diminishment. * * * In the 19th century, to restore land to the public domain was to extinguish the land's prior use—its use, for example, as an Indian reservation—and to return it to the United States either to be sold or set aside for other public purposes. * * *

The 1882 Act bore none of these hallmarks of diminishment. The 1882 Act empowered the Secretary to survey and appraise the disputed land, which then could be purchased in 160-acre tracts by nonmembers. 22 Stat. 341. The 1882 Act states that the disputed lands would be "open for settlement under such rules and regulations as [the Secretary of the Interior] may prescribe." Ibid. And the parcels would be sold piecemeal in 160–acre tracts. Ibid. So rather than the Tribe's receiving a fixed sum for all of the disputed lands, the Tribe's profits were entirely dependent upon how many nonmembers purchased the appraised tracts of land.

From this text, it is clear that the 1882 Act falls into another category of surplus land Acts: those that "merely opened reservation land to settlement and provided that the uncertain future proceeds of settler purchases should be applied to the Indians' benefit." * * * Such schemes allow "non-Indian settlers to own land on the reservation." * * * But in doing so, they do not diminish the reservation's boundaries.

* * *

B

We now turn to the history surrounding the passage of the 1882 Act. The mixed historical evidence relied upon by the parties cannot overcome the lack of clear textual signal that Congress intended to diminish the reservation. That historical evidence in no way "unequivocally reveal[s] a widely held, contemporaneous understanding that the affected reservation would shrink as a result of the proposed legislation." * * *

Petitioners rely largely on isolated statements that some legislators made about the 1882 Act. Senator Henry Dawes of Massachusetts, for example, noted that he had been "assured that [the 1882 Act] would leave an ample reservation " for the Tribe. 13 Cong. Rec. 3032 (1882) (emphasis added). And Senator John Ingalls of Kansas observed "that this bill practically breaks up that portion at least of the reservation which is to be sold, and provides that it shall be disposed of to private purchasers." Id., at 3028. Whatever value these contemporaneous floor statements might have, other such statements support the opposite conclusion—that Congress never intended to diminish the reservation. Senator Charles Jones of Florida, for example, spoke of "white men purchas[ing] titles to land within this reservation and settl [ing] down with the Indians on it." Id., at 3078 (emphasis added). Such dueling remarks by individual legislators are far from the "clear and plain" evidence of diminishment required under this Court's precedent. * * *

More illuminating than cherry-picked statements by individual legislators would be historical evidence of "the manner in which the transaction was negotiated" with the Omaha Tribe. * * * In Yankton Sioux, for example, recorded negotiations between the Commissioner of Indian Affairs and leaders of the Yankton Sioux Tribe unambiguously "signaled [the Tribe's] understanding that the cession of the surplus lands dissolved tribal governance of the 1858 reservation." * * * No such unambiguous evidence exists in the record of these negotiations. In particular, petitioners' reliance on the remarks of Representative Edward Valentine of Nebraska, who stated, "You cannot find one of those Indians that does not want the western portion sold," and that the Tribe wished to sell the land to those who would " 'reside upon it and cultivate it' " so that the Tribe members could "benefit of these improvements," 13 Cong. Rec. 6541, falls short. Nothing about this statement or other similar statements unequivocally supports a finding that the existing boundaries of the reservation would be diminished.

C

Finally, we consider both the subsequent demographic history of opened lands, which serves as "one additional clue as to what Congress expected would happen once land on a particular reservation was opened to non-Indian settlers," * * * as well as the United States' "treatment of the affected areas, particularly in the years immediately following the opening," which has "some evidentiary value," * * *. Our cases suggest that such evidence might "reinforc[e]" a finding of diminishment or nondiminishment based on the text. * * * But this Court has never relied solely on this third consideration to find diminishment.

As petitioners have discussed at length, the Tribe was almost entirely absent from the disputed territory for more than 120 years. Brief for Petitioners 24–30. The Omaha Tribe does not enforce any of its regulations—including those governing businesses, fire protection, animal control, fireworks, and wildlife and parks—in Pender or in other locales west of the right-of-way. 996 F.Supp.2d, at 832. Nor does it maintain an office, provide social services, or host tribal celebrations or ceremonies west of the right-of-way. Ibid.

This subsequent demographic history cannot overcome our conclusion that Congress did not intend to diminish the reservation in 1882. And it is not our role to "rewrite" the 1882 Act in light of this subsequent demographic history. * * * After all, evidence of the changing demographics of disputed land is "the least compelling" evidence in our diminishment analysis, for "[e]very surplus land Act necessarily resulted in a surge of non-Indian settlement and degraded the 'Indian character' of the reservation, yet we have repeatedly stated that not every surplus land Act diminished the affected reservation." * * *

Evidence of the subsequent treatment of the disputed land by Government officials likewise has "limited interpretive value." * * * Petitioners highlight that, for more than a century and with few exceptions, reports from the Office of Indian Affairs and in opinion letters from Government officials treated the disputed land as Nebraska's. * * * It was not until this litigation commenced that the Department of the Interior definitively changed its position, concluding that the reservation boundaries were in fact not diminished in 1882. * * * For their part, respondents discuss late-19th-century statutes referring to the disputed land as part of the reservation, as well as inconsistencies in maps and statements by Government officials. * * * This "mixed record" of subsequent treatment of the disputed land cannot overcome the statutory text, which is devoid of any language indicative of Congress' intent to diminish. * * *

Petitioners' concerns about upsetting the "justifiable expectations" of the almost exclusively non-Indian settlers who live on the land are compelling, Rosebud Sioux, supra, at 605, 97 S.Ct. 1361 but these expectations alone, resulting from the Tribe's failure to assert jurisdiction, cannot diminish reservation boundaries. Only Congress has the power to diminish a reservation. DeCoteau, 420 U.S., at 449, 95 S.Ct. 1082. And though petitioners wish that Congress would have "spoken differently" in 1882, "we cannot remake history." Ibid.

* * *

In light of the statutory text, we hold that the 1882 Act did not diminish the Omaha Indian Reservation. Because petitioners have raised only the single question of diminishment, we express no view about whether equitable considerations of laches and acquiescence may curtail the Tribe's power to tax the retailers of Pender in light of the Tribe's century-long absence from the disputed lands. Cf. City of Sherrill v. Oneida Indian Nation of N.Y., 544 U.S. 197, 217–221, 125 S.Ct. 1478, 161 L.Ed.2d 386 (2005).

SECTION B. FEDERAL CRIMINAL JURISDICTION

The United States federalized Indian country criminal jurisdiction in the First Congress with the enactment of the first Trade and Intercourse Act. 1 Stat. 137 (1790). Through this and related trade and intercourse act enacted through 1834, the federal government hoped to prevent hostilities between American citizens and Indian tribes. In general, throughout most of the 19th century, the United States' criminal jurisdiction in Indian country involved policing Indian country borders, and prosecuting non-Indians that committed crimes against Indians and others on Indian lands. Criminal jurisdiction over each reservation was governed by specific treaty terms.

That changed dramatically in the 1880s when Congress affirmatively authorized federal prosecutors to prosecute Indian-on-Indian crimes that occurred on Indian lands through the Major Crimes Act in 1885. Act of Mar. 3, 1885, ch. 341, 23 Stat. 385, codified as amended at 18 U.S.C. § 1153. From that time on, the federal government became been the primary law enforcement organization in Indian country. In the mid-20th century, the United States authorized many states to assume criminal jurisdiction over Indian country, excluding the federal government. See Chapter 7(C).

There are numerous laws vesting the United States with jurisdiction over crimes by and against Indians, in and out of Indian country. Many deal with liquor violations (18 U.S.C. §§ 1154, 1156, 1161, 3055, 3113, 3488, 3618, 3619). Others prohibit such things as non-Indian entry on Indian land to take fish or game without permission (18 U.S.C. § 1165), destruction of boundary or warning signs on a reservation (18 U.S.C. § 1164), land transactions with Indians without federal authority (25 U.S.C. § 177), possession of gambling devices (15 U.S.C. § 1175), theft or embezzlement from a tribe (18 U.S.C. § 1163), and counterfeiting government trademarks for or misrepresenting crafts or goods to be Indian products (18 U.S.C. §§ 1158, 1159).

The most important statutes, however, are the Indian Country Crimes Act (18 U.S.C. § 1152), extending federal enclave law to interracial crimes in Indian country; the Major Crimes Act (18 U.S.C. §§ 1153, 3242), punishing Indian offenders for commission in Indian country of several felonies; and the Assimilative Crimes Act (18 U.S.C. § 13), allowing federal prosecutions for state law violations. A suggested approach for analyzing the complex area of criminal jurisdiction is found at the end of this section. Many of the rules are highly technical but they raise a number of central policy issues as to the proper roles of the three sets of governments in Indian country.

1. THE INDIAN COUNTRY CRIMES ACT,
18 U.S.C. § 1152

The Indian Country Crimes Act, also referred to as the General Crimes Act, the Interracial Crime Provision, and the Federal Enclave Statute, provides for federal jurisdiction over crimes committed by non-Indians in Indian country:

> Except as otherwise expressly provided by law, the general laws of the United States as to the punishment of offenses committed in any place within the sole and exclusive jurisdiction of the United States, except the District of Columbia, shall extend to the Indian country.

> This section shall not extend to offenses committed by one Indian against the person or property of another Indian, nor to any Indian committing any offense in the Indian country who has been punished by the local law of the tribe, or to any case where, by treaty stipulations, the exclusive jurisdiction over such offenses is or may be secured to the Indian tribes respectively.

18 U.S.C. § 1152.

The Act originated in the Trade and Intercourse Act of 1790 and was amended several times during the early nineteenth century, but only minor wording changes have been made since 1854. This statute, which was discussed in Ex parte Crow Dog, 118 U.S. 556 (1883), applies to Indian reservations the federal statutes applicable to federal enclaves such as military installations and national parks. The statute covers crimes committed by non-Indians against Indians and crimes by Indians against non-Indians.

The second paragraph of the Act creates several exceptions to the broad provisions of the first paragraph. Crimes by an Indian against another Indian are exempted, but many such offenses go to federal court under the Major Crimes Act, 18 U.S.C. § 1153. The statute's reference to punishment "by the local law of the tribe" allows for exclusive jurisdiction by tribal courts, so long as the tribe wins a race to prosecution. E.g., United

States v. Smith, 562 F.2d 453 (7th Cir.1977), cert. denied, 434 U.S. 1072 (1978). The last clause is likely operative only if a tribe can point to an extant treaty provision authorizing exclusive tribal criminal jurisdiction. The statute has on its face no exception for crimes by a non-Indian against a non-Indian. And it was applied in such cases in Indian country during the pre-statehood era. As states were admitted to the Union, however, new interests arose and the statute was interpreted differently in United States v. McBratney, 104 U.S. 621 (1881) (holding that Colorado courts, not federal or tribal courts, have jurisdiction over non-Indian on non-Indian crimes committed in Indian country). The case turned on the equal footing doctrine, and apparently upon the lack of a disclaimer clause in Colorado's Constitution. Colorado, unlike some other western states admitted to the Union in the latter half of the nineteenth century, was not required to disclaim jurisdiction over Indian lands within state boundaries as the price of its statehood. Under the equal footing doctrine, Colorado is admitted to the Union with a status equal to the original states. But then the Court held that the murder of a non-Indian by another non-Indian in the Crow Reservation in Montana—a state that had disclaimed jurisdiction as a condition of statehood—was subject to state jurisdiction. Draper v. United States, 164 U.S. 240 (1896). The Court later extended that rule to the original 13 states. New York ex rel. Ray v. Martin, 326 U.S. 496 (1946).

As the *McBratney* decision affirmatively forbids federal prosecution of non-Indian-on-non-Indian crime under the Act, the Act only applies when an Indian perpetrator commits a crime against a non-Indian victim, or when a non-Indian perpetrator commits a crime against an Indian victim. United States v. Reza-Ramos, 816 F.3d 1110, 1190–20 (9th Cir.2016). See also United States v. Bruce, 394 F.3d 1215, 1221 (9th Cir.2005); United States v. Johnson, 637 F.2d 1224, 1231 n.11 (9th Cir.1980).

2. THE ASSIMILATIVE CRIMES ACT, 18 U.S.C. § 13

The Assimilative Crimes Act has been held to be one of the "general laws of the United States" made applicable in Indian country by the Indian Country Crimes Act. The statute permits federal prosecutions by "assimilating" substantive state law. No state judicial jurisdiction is involved. The Assimilative Crimes Act reads:

(a) Whoever within or upon any of the places now existing or hereafter reserved or acquired as provided in section 7 of this title, is guilty of any act or omission which, although not made punishable by any enactment of Congress, would be punishable if committed or omitted within the jurisdiction of the State, Territory, Possession, or District in which such place is situated, by the laws thereof in force at the time of such act or omission, shall be guilty of a like offense and subject to a like punishment.

(b) * * * [F]or purposes of subsection (a) of this section, that which may or shall be imposed through judicial or administrative action under the law of a State, territory, possession, or district, for a conviction for operating a motor vehicle under the influence of a drug or alcohol, shall be considered to be a punishment provided by that law. Any limitation on the right or privilege to operate a motor vehicle imposed under this subsection shall apply only to the special maritime and territorial jurisdiction of the United States.

18 U.S.C. § 13.

The legislative history of the Act, originally passed in 1825, gives no indication that Congress intended it to apply within Indian reservations. Essentially, the statute was designed to supplement the applicable law in federal enclaves (such as military bases and national parks) where there is no "local law." But the Supreme Court in Williams v. United States, 327 U.S. 711 (1946), assumed it applied to Indian lands by virtue of the incorporation of federal enclave law for Indian country through the predecessor to the Assimilative Crimes Act.

Lower federal courts also hold that the Assimilative Crimes Act applies to Indian country. In United States v. Marcyes, 557 F.2d 1361 (9th Cir.1977), the court upheld the federal criminal convictions of Indians under the Assimilative Crimes Act for selling fireworks on the Puyallup Reservation in Washington, in violation of state law. The court, citing Williams, stated that Congress' purpose in enacting the Assimilative Crimes Act was to fill in the gaps in the criminal law applicable to federal enclaves created by the failure of Congress to pass specific criminal statutes. See also United States v. Billadeau, 275 F.3d 692 (8th Cir.2001).

If, as the Marcyes court found, Congress's purpose was gap filling, is it necessary or appropriate where a tribe has laws of its own to punish minor crimes? It is particularly problematic when application of victimless or consensual crimes as defined by the state are at issue, as in United States v. Sosseur, 181 F.2d 873 (7th Cir.1950). There, a federal appeals court allowed a Wisconsin anti-gambling statute to be applied in Indian country to a tribally licensed slot machine operator. Professor Clinton called the implications of Sosseur "troubling":

> Victimless or consensual crime statutes enacted by the states generally involve legislation of morals in one sense or another. To allow the states, through the Act, to make moral judgments for the tribes, undermines the purpose for continuing reservation policy—permitting the Indian tribes to maintain their own separate, evolving, cultural traditions and government. The result in Sosseur, insofar as it applies to victimless or consensual crimes, is an aberration in terms of Indian policy.

Robert N. Clinton, *Criminal Jurisdiction Over Indian Lands: A Journey Through a Jurisdictional Maze*, 18 Ariz.L.Rev. 503, 536 (1976).

3. THE MAJOR CRIMES ACT, 18 U.S.C. § 1153

Within two years after the *Crow Dog* decision, 118 U.S. 556 (1883), Congress passed the original Major Crimes Act (MCA). Act of Mar. 3, 1885, ch. 341, 23 Stat. 385, codified as amended at 18 U.S.C. § 1153. The Act overturned *Crow Dog*'s rule of exclusive tribal jurisdiction over crimes among Indians and mandated federal jurisdiction over seven enumerated crimes; it grants no state jurisdiction. It has been amended numerous times, most recently in 1988, and now covers more than a dozen major crimes. As amended, 18 U.S.C. § 1153 now reads:

(a) Any Indian who commits against the person or property of another Indian or other person any of the following offenses, namely, murder, manslaughter, kidnapping, maiming, a felony under chapter 109A [rape and related offenses], incest, assault with intent to commit murder, assault with a dangerous weapon, assault resulting in serious bodily injury * * * , an assault against an individual who has not attained the age of 16 years, arson, burglary, robbery, and a felony under section 661 of this title within the Indian country, shall be subject to the same law and penalties as all other persons committing any of the above offenses, within the exclusive jurisdiction of the United States.

(b) Any offense referred to in subsection (a) of this section that is not defined and punished by Federal law in force within the exclusive jurisdiction of the United States shall be defined and punished in accordance with the laws of the State in which such offense was committed as are in force at the time of such offense.

In the constitutional challenge to the Major Crimes Act that followed, the Supreme Court sustained the power of Congress to extend federal criminal laws over Indian country as a function of its "guardianship" of Indians. United States v. Kagama, 118 U.S. 375 (1886).

The Major Crimes Act applies only when the perpetrator (the criminal defendant) is an Indian. The victim can be an Indian "or other person."

4. AN ANALYTICAL APPROACH TO FEDERAL CRIMINAL JURISDICTION IN INDIAN COUNTRY

The jurisdictional maze can be walked with some confidence if a step-by-step approach is followed. See generally Robert N. Clinton, *Criminal Jurisdiction Over Indian Lands: A Journey Through a Jurisdictional Maze*, 18 Ariz.L.Rev. 503 (1976). We do not treat here the applicability of general federal statutes within Indian country. Rather, this analysis applies to the federal criminal laws dealing specially with Indians.

The federal government has helpfully published charts online created by Arvo Q. Mikkanen, an Assistant United States Attorney for the Western District of Oklahoma, that details whether federal, state, and tribal governments have criminal jurisdiction over a particular crime in Indian country. We borrow heavily from those charts here, but focus solely on federal criminal jurisdiction. As such, this section does not apply in states where the United States has authorized state criminal jurisdiction over Indian country, as in Public Law 280 states.

We begin with a blank chart to allow students to fill it in as we go:

Indian Perpetrator

Who was the victim?	What was the crime?	Jurisdiction

Non-Indian Perpetrator

Who was the victim?	What was the crime?	Jurisdiction

Was the Locus of the Crime in Indian Country?

The first determination is whether the crime occurred in Indian country. If it did not, the inquiry is over: the state courts have jurisdiction; the federal and tribal courts have none.

If the crime did occur in Indian country, the analysis continues.

Does "Public Law 280" or a Specific Jurisdictional Statute Apply?

The United States has enacted a number of statutes that cede criminal jurisdiction to specific states. The most important of these is Public Law 280, discussed in the next subsection of this chapter. If Public Law 280 or one of the specific statutes applies, state courts have jurisdiction. Federal courts have no jurisdiction if Public Law 280 applies but may continue to have jurisdiction if the particular law being enforced so provides.

If the crime occurred in Indian country and neither Public Law 280 nor a specific statute applies, then the analysis continues.

Was the Crime Committed by an Indian?

The federal statutory scheme is based in large part on racial identity as an Indian or non-Indian. Thus, the next step is to determine the races of the criminal defendant and the victim.

Federal authorities may prosecute any Indian country crime in which the perpetrator (the criminal defendant) is an Indian; the victims can be either Indian or non-Indian. If the victim is an Indian, then only the Major Crimes Act applies. Since the Major Crimes Act enumerates a short list of crimes eligible for prosecution by federal authorities, if the Indian commits a crime not enumerated, the tribal government has exclusive jurisdiction.

If the Indian commits a crime against a non-Indian, then again the Major Crimes Act applies. But if the crime is listed in the federal criminal code that applies to the special maritime and territorial jurisdiction of the United States under the United States Code, then the Indian may be prosecuted under the Indian Country Crimes Act. If the crime is not a Major Crimes Act crime, or is not listed in the Indian Country Crimes Act, then federal prosecutors may "assimilate" (or borrow) state criminal laws and prosecute the Indian under the Assimilative Crimes Act.

Indian Perpetrator

Who was the victim?	What was the crime?	Jurisdiction
Indian	Crimes enumerated in the Major Crimes Act, 18 U.S.C. § 1153	Federal
Non-Indian	Crimes enumerated in the Major Crimes Act, 18 U.S.C. § 1153	Federal
	Other federal crimes punishable in accordance with the Indian Country Crimes Act, 18 U.S.C. § 1152, or state law crimes punishable under the Assimilative Crimes Act, 18 U.S.C. § 13	Federal

Was the Crime Committed by a Non-Indian?

If the criminal perpetrator is a non-Indian, the Major Crimes Act is inapplicable. If the victim is an Indian, then the perpetrator may be punished under either the Indian Country Crimes Act or the Assimilative Crimes Act. If the crime is listed in the federal criminal code that applies to the special maritime and territorial jurisdiction of the United States under the United States Code, then the Indian Country Crimes Act applies. If the crime is not listed in the federal criminal code, then federal prosecutors may "assimilate" (or borrow) state criminal laws and prosecute the perpetrator under the Assimilative Crimes Act.

If the victim is a non-Indian, then there is no federal criminal jurisdiction. The state will retain jurisdiction over these crimes. State criminal jurisdiction is discussed in the next section.

Non-Indian Perpetrator

Who was the victim?	What was the crime?	Jurisdiction
Indian	Crimes punishable in accordance with the Indian Country Crimes Act, 18 U.S.C. § 1152, or state law crimes punishable under the Assimilative Crimes Act, 18 U.S.C. § 13, where there is no applicable federal criminal statute	Federal
Non-Indian	Any crime cognizable under state law	State

NOTES

1. "Indian status" is often an element of the offense, meaning that federal prosecutors must prove beyond a reasonable doubt to a federal jury (which will almost always consist entirely of non-Indians) that the defendant or a victim is an "Indian." The federal criminal statutes do not define "Indian," leaving it to the courts to define the term. Despite the fact that it is usually a simple matter of determining whether the person is a member of a federally recognized Indian tribe, there are both perpetrators and victims that are "Indian" under the statute who are not tribal members. As to be expected, there are ambiguities as to who is an "Indian," leading to controversy as to the meaning of "Indian."

In United States v. Stymiest, 581 F.3d 759 (8th Cir.2009), the Eighth Circuit reaffirmed its test for determining whether a criminal defendant is an "Indian" for purposes of prosecution under the Major Crimes Act. The court's test—"whether the defendant (1) has some Indian blood, and (2) is recognized as an Indian by a tribe or the federal government or both"—derives from United States v. Rogers, 45 U.S. 567, 572–73 (1846). *Stymiest*, 581 F.3d at 762.

The Ninth Circuit recently reexamined its Indian status test in United States v. Zepeda, 792 F.3d 1103 (9th Cir.2015) (en banc), cert. denied, 136 S. Ct. 1712 (2016). The court parsed through several of its cases and articulated a test that more closely conforms to the Eighth Circuit's test: "We hold that proof of Indian status under the [MCA] requires only two things: (1) proof of some quantum of Indian blood, whether or not that blood derives from a member of a federally recognized tribe, and (2) proof of membership in, or affiliation with, a federally recognized tribe." *Zepeda*, 792 F.3d at 1113. Concurring in the judgment alone, Judge Kozinski blasted the test, arguing that the test "transforms the Indian Major Crimes Act into a creature previously unheard of in federal law: a criminal statute whose application turns on whether a defendant is of a particular race." Id. at 1116 (Kozinski, C.J., concurring in the judgment). Judge Ikuta also wrote separately to argue that the first prong of the test was unnecessary: "In holding that a person is not an Indian unless a federal court has determined that the person has an acceptable Indian 'blood quantum,' we disrespect the tribe's sovereignty by refusing to defer to the tribe's own determination of its membership rolls." Id. at 1190 (Ikuta, C.J., concurring in the judgment).

In an earlier case, United States v. Cruz, 554 F.3d 840 (9th Cir.2009), Judge Kozinski also dissented from the majority's conclusion that a defendant who was a non-tribal member but had once received tribal government services was not an Indian for purposes of the Major Crimes Act:

> The record discloses that the Blackfeet tribal authorities have accorded Cruz "descendant" status, which entitles him to many of the benefits of tribal membership, including medical treatment at any Indian Health Service facility in the United States, certain educational grants, housing assistance and hunting and fishing privileges on the reservation.

> That Cruz may not have taken advantage of these benefits doesn't matter because the test is whether the tribal authorities recognize him as an Indian, not whether he considers himself one. That they do is confirmed by the fact that, when he was charged with an earlier crime on the reservation, the tribal police took him before the tribal court rather than turning him over to state or federal authorities. How that case was finally resolved is irrelevant; what matters is that the tribal authorities protected him from a state or federal prosecution by treating him as one of their own. Finally, Cruz was living on the reservation when he was arrested, another piece of evidence supporting the jury's verdict.

Id. at 852 (Kozinksi, C.J., dissenting).

Is the first prong of the *Stymiest* and *Zepeda* test necessary? *Rogers* is a pre-Civil War decision holding that a white man who was enrolled in the Cherokee Nation as a tribal member could not avoid federal prosecution in the pre-Major Crimes Act era. Is this precedent relevant, or even legitimate?

2. For years, federal enforcement of major crimes violations on reservations has been limited by the high rate of declinations to prosecute by U.S. Attorneys and a dearth of law enforcement officers in Indian country. In response to these conditions, Congress enacted the Tribal Law and Order Act (TLOA) of 2010. Pub.L. 111–211, Title II, July 29, 2010, 124 Stat. 2262, a statute intending to improve cooperation between tribal and federal law enforcement departments, provide better training for tribal law enforcement officers, increase the criminal penalties that tribal courts could impose, and force federal prosecutors to explain reasons for declining to prosecute Indian country crimes. Congress made the following findings in enacting this important legislation:

* * *

(3) less than 3,000 tribal and Federal law enforcement officers patrol more than 56,000,000 acres of Indian country, which reflects less than 1/2 of the law enforcement presence in comparable rural communities nationwide;"(4) The complicated jurisdictional scheme that exists in Indian country—

"(A) has a significant negative impact on the ability to provide public safety to Indian communities;

"(B) has been increasingly exploited by criminals; and

"(C) requires a high degree of commitment and cooperation among tribal, Federal, and State law enforcement officials;

"(5)(A) domestic and sexual violence against American Indian and Alaska Native women has reached epidemic proportions;

"(B) 34 percent of American Indian and Alaska Native women will be raped in their lifetimes; and

"(C) 39 percent of American Indian and Alaska Native women will be subject to domestic violence;

"(6) Indian tribes have faced significant increases in instances of domestic violence, burglary, assault, and child abuse as a direct result of increased methamphetamine use on Indian reservations; and

"(7) crime data is a fundamental tool of law enforcement, but for decades the Bureau of Indian Affairs and the Department of Justice have not been able to coordinate or consistently report crime and prosecution rates in tribal communities.

Pub.L. 111–211, § 202.

TLOA also created the Indian Law and Order Commission to study Indian country criminal jurisdiction in detail. In its report, *A Roadmap for Making Native America Safer: Report to the President & Congress of the United States* (Nov. 2013), the Commission recommended radical reform of Indian country criminal justice. The Commission's factual findings mirrored that of Congress in TLOA, but added that conditions in Alaska Native tribal communities are actually much worse. The Commission recommended that the United States allow Indian tribes to opt-out of a criminal justice system that relies on federal or state governments as the primary law enforcers, and take over the policing of their reservations.

3. Under the Major Crimes Act, a defendant may be entitled to a jury instruction on a lesser included offense even though such lesser included offense is not enumerated in the Major Crimes Act. Keeble v. United States, 412 U.S. 205 (1973). In other words, a defendant may be charged and convicted

of an offense not listed in the Major Crimes Act, such as the lesser included offense of child abuse in a murder case. United States v. Ganadonegro, 854 F. Supp.2d 1068 (D.N.M.2012).

4.　Does the Major Crimes Act divest the tribal courts of concurrent jurisdiction? In Wetsit v. Stafne, 44 F.3d 823 (9th Cir.1995), the defendant, a member of the Fort Peck Tribes, stabbed to death her common law husband, also a tribal member, within the boundaries of the reservation. A federal jury acquitted her of the crime of voluntary manslaughter under the Major Crimes Act. She was then charged with manslaughter by the tribe for the killing, and convicted, sentenced, and fined in tribal court in a jury trial. She brought a habeas corpus action in federal district court under the Indian Civil Rights Act, 25 U.S.C. § 1303, alleging that the federal courts have exclusive jurisdiction of manslaughter under the Major Crimes Act. The Ninth Circuit affirmed the district court's dismissal of the petition based on a failure to exhaust her tribal remedies by appealing the conviction in tribal courts, noting that a tribal court is competent to try a tribal member for a crime also prosecutable under the Major Crimes Act, in compliance with the Indian Civil Rights Act.

5.　In United States v. Mitchell, 502 F.3d 931 (9th Cir.2007), the court upheld the death sentence imposed on a Navajo Nation tribal member who was convicted of a carjacking on the reservation resulting in death. At the order of the United States Attorney General, the United States Attorney for the District of Arizona chose to prosecute Mitchell under the Federal Death Penalty Act rather than the Major Crimes Act. A different federal law—the Violent Crime Control and Law Enforcement Act of 1994—allows tribal governments "to elect whether to have to death penalty apply to first degree murders occurring on that tribe's land." Tova Indritz, *Reflections on the State of Criminal Law*, 33rd Annual Federal Bar Association Indian Law Conference Course Materials 549 (2008) (citing 18 U.S.C. § 3598). The Navajo Nation had not chosen to "opt-in" to the death penalty. United States Attorney General Alberto Gonzales ordered the local federal prosecutor to proceed under the Federal Death Penalty Act, making thetribal preference irrelevant.

6.　The Organized Crime Control Act, 18 U.S.C. § 1955, was intended to curtail the organized crime that feeds on unlawful gambling activity. Several Indians and non-Indians were convicted of participating in an "illegal gambling business," which was defined as a business involving five or more persons that "is in violation of the law of a state or political subdivision in which it is conducted." The Indian defendants appealed, claiming that they could not be "in violation" of a *state* law for their on-reservation conduct and thus they were not guilty of violating the Organized Crime Control Act. The court agreed that the state could not have enforced its gambling law against the Indian defendants, but held that because the laws were applicable to non-Indians on the reservation the activity nevertheless was "a violation of the law of a State" and thus was unlawful gambling activity prohibited by the Act. United States v. Farris, 624 F.2d 890, 897 (9th Cir.1980), cert. denied 449 U.S. 1111 (1981).

In California v. Cabazon Band of Mission Indians, 480 U.S. 202 (1987), the Supreme Court declined to decide the coverage of the Organized Crime Control Act (OCCA), 18 U.S.C. § 1955, but rejected a state argument that it made the tribal bingo enterprise unlawful. In dictum that seems to disapprove the Ninth Circuit approach in *Farris,* the Court said:

> There is nothing in OCCA indicating that the States are to have any part in enforcing federal criminal laws or are authorized to make arrests on Indian reservations that in the absence of OCCA they could not effect. We are not informed of any federal efforts to employ OCCA to prosecute the playing of bingo on Indian reservations, although there are more than 100 such enterprises currently in operation, many of which have been in existence for several years, for the most part with the encouragement of the Federal Government.

480 U.S. at 213–14. The federal government has, at times, acted to curb Indian gaming. In one case the U.S. sued to enjoin five tribes from operating casinos, arguing that they would violate OCCA as well as the Assimilative Crimes Act. The court refused relief. Apparently, if crimes are involved, the correct procedure for the government is to prosecute, not to seek an injunction, although the decision left open the difficult question of whether the United States can criminally prosecute an Indian tribe, a sovereign government. United States v. Bay Mills Indian Community, 727 F. Supp. 1110 (W.D.Mich.1989). Did the Indian Gaming Regulatory Act, 25 U.S.C. § 2701 et seq., discussed in Chapter 9, infra, preempt or repeal OCCA? Several Indian defendants who were convicted of possessing gambling devices and conducting illegal gambling in Indian country in violation of 15 U.S.C. § 1175 (possession and use) and 18 U.S.C. § 1955 (OCCA) challenged their convictions claiming that the IGRA, 25 U.S.C. § 2701, and 18 U.S.C. § 1166 "preempted" OCCA. The court held that the IGRA did not "preempt" or implicitly repeal 18 U.S.C. § 1955 (OCCA) and, because the IGRA permits for the continuing application of 15 U.S.C. § 1175, there was no repeal of that section. United States v. Cook, 922 F.2d 1026 (2d Cir.1991), cert. denied 500 U.S. 941 (1991).

7.   United States v. Blue, 722 F.2d 383 (8th Cir.1983), upheld the applicability of another general criminal law, 21 U.S.C. § 841(a)(1), prohibiting sales of certain drugs. The court found that the holding does not represent any further infringement upon tribal sovereignty or self-government and that, in the light of the low penalties permissible in tribal courts under the ICRA, "Congress must have assumed that Indians on reservations would generally be subject, as all other citizens are, to federal criminal sanctions which apply to all persons." Id. at 385–86. Should such general laws be extended over Indians within Indian country by an inference? Would the court find differently after Congress substantially increased allowable penalties in tribal courts in the Tribal Law and Order Act of 2010?

UNITED STATES V. ANTELOPE

Supreme Court of the United States, 1977.
430 U.S. 641, 97 S.Ct. 1395, 51 L.Ed.2d 701.

MR. CHIEF JUSTICE BURGER delivered the opinion of the Court.

The question presented by our grant of certiorari is whether, under the circumstances of this case, federal criminal statutes violate the Due Process Clause of the Fifth Amendment by subjecting individuals to federal prosecution by virtue of their status as Indians.

(1)

On the night of February 18, 1974, respondents, enrolled Coeur d'Alene Indians, broke into the home of Emma Johnson, an 81-year-old non-Indian, in Worley, Idaho; they robbed and killed Mrs. Johnson. Because the crimes were committed by enrolled Indians within the boundaries of the Coeur d'Alene Indian Reservation, respondents were subject to federal jurisdiction under the Major Crimes Act, 18 U.S.C. § 1153. They were, accordingly, indicted by a federal grand jury on charges of burglary, robbery and murder. Respondent William Davison was convicted of second-degree murder only. Respondents Gabriel Francis Antelope and Leonard Davison were found guilty of all three crimes as charged, including first-degree murder under the felony-murder provisions of 18 U.S.C. § 1111, as made applicable to enrolled Indians by 18 U.S.C. § 1153.

(2)

In the United States Court of Appeals for the Ninth Circuit, respondents contended that their felony-murder convictions were unlawful as products of invidious racial discrimination. They argued that a non-Indian charged with precisely the same offense, namely the murder of another non-Indian within Indian country, would have been subject to prosecution only under Idaho law, which in contrast to the federal-murder statute, 18 U.S.C. § 1111, does not contain a felony, murder provision. To establish the crime of first-degree murder in state court, therefore, Idaho would have had to prove premeditation and deliberation. No such elements were required under the felony-murder component of 18 U.S.C. § 1111.

Because of the difference between Idaho and federal law, the Court of Appeals concluded that respondents were "put at a serious racially-based disadvantage," since the Federal Government was not required to establish premeditation and deliberation in respondents' federal prosecution. This disparity, so the Court of Appeals concluded, violated equal protection requirements implicit in the Due Process Clause of the Fifth Amendment. * * * [W]e reverse.

(3)

The decisions of this Court leave no doubt that federal legislation with respect to Indian tribes, although relating to Indians as such, is not based upon impermissible racial classifications. Quite the contrary, classification expressly singling out Indian tribes as subjects of legislation are expressly provided for in the Constitution and supported by the ensuing history of the Federal Government's relations with Indians.

* * *

Both *Mancari* and *Fisher* involved preferences or disabilities directly promoting Indian interests in self-government, whereas in the present case we are dealing not with matters of tribal self-regulation, but with federal regulation of criminal conduct within Indian country implicating Indian interests. But the principles reaffirmed in *Mancari* and *Fisher* point more broadly to the conclusion that federal regulation of Indian affairs is not based upon impermissible classifications. Rather, such regulation is rooted in the unique status of Indians as "a separate people" with their own political institutions. Federal regulation of Indian tribes, therefore, is governance of once-sovereign political communities; it is not to be viewed as legislation of a " 'racial' group consisting of 'Indians'." Morton v. Mancari, 417 U.S., at 553 n. 24. Indeed, respondents were not subjected to federal criminal jurisdiction because they are of the Indian race but because they are enrolled members of the Coeur d'Alene Tribe. We therefore conclude that federal criminal statutes enforced here are based neither in whole nor in part upon impermissible racial classifications.

(4)

The challenged statutes do not otherwise violate equal protection. We have previously observed that Indians indicted under the Major Crimes Act enjoy the same procedural benefits and privileges as all other persons within federal jurisdiction. Keeble v. United States, 412 U.S. 205, 212 (1973). See 18 U.S.C. § 3242. Respondents were, therefore, subjected to the same body of law as any other individual, Indian or non-Indian, charged with first-degree murder committed in a federal enclave. They do not, and could not, contend otherwise.

There remains, then, only the disparity between federal and Idaho law as the basis for respondents' equal protection claim. Since Congress has undoubted constitutional power to prescribe a criminal code applicable in Indian country, United States v. Kagama, 118 U.S. 375 (1886), it is of no consequence that the federal scheme differs from a state criminal code otherwise applicable within the boundaries of the State of Idaho. Under our federal system, the National Government does not violate equal protection when its own body of law is evenhanded,[11] regardless of the laws of States with respect to the same subject matter.

The Federal Government treated respondents in the same manner as all other persons within federal jurisdiction, pursuant to a regulatory scheme that did not erect impermissible racial classifications; hence, no violation of the Due Process Clause infected respondents' convictions.

* * *

NOTE

In footnote 11, the Court "intimated no views" on United States v. Cleveland, 503 F.2d 1067 (9th Cir.1974), and other cases. In *Cleveland,* the Ninth Circuit upheld the dismissal, on equal protection grounds, of an indictment for assault by an Indian against an Indian. The federal punishment was more severe than the Arizona punishment for the same offense. An amendment to § 1153 made Arizona law applicable to prosecutions for assault with a deadly weapon. The Major Crimes Act applies, of course, to crimes against either an Indian or a non-Indian. But § 1152 (the Indian Country Crimes Act) would apply federal law to a non-Indian who committed the same act (assault) against the same person (an Indian) in the same place (the reservation). The prosecutor's burden of proof was also reduced under the Arizona statute. The court found that: "The sole distinction between the defendants who are subjected to state law and those to whom federal law applies is the race of the defendant. No federal or state interest justifying the distinction has been suggested, * * * and we can supply none."

The court also refused to lower the federal punishment in order to bring it into line with the Arizona provision: "We firmly reject the Government's invitation to rewrite the penalty provisions of the applicable statutes to equalize the punishment of Indians and non-Indians charged with assaulting Indians. Fixing the punishment for crimes is a legislative rather than a judicial function." 503 F.2d at 1071.

---

[11] It should be noted, however, that this Court has consistently upheld federal regulations aimed *solely* at tribal Indians, as opposed to all persons subject to federal jurisdiction. See, e.g., United States v. Holliday, 3 Wall. 407, 417–418 (1865); Perrin v. United States, 232 U.S. 478, 482 (1914). See also Rosebud Sioux Tribe v. Kneip, 430 U.S. 584, 613–615, n. 47 (1977). Indeed, the Constitution itself provides support for legislation directed specifically at the Indian Tribes. As the Court noted in Morton v. Mancari, the Constitution therefore "singles Indians out as a proper subject for separate legislation." 417 U.S. at 552.

In this regard, we are not concerned with instances in which Indians tried in federal court are subjected to differing penalties and burdens of proof from those applicable to non-Indians charged with the same offense. Compare United States v. Big Crow, 523 F.2d 955 (C.A.8 1975), cert. denied, 424 U.S. 920, 96 S.Ct. 1126, 47 L.Ed.2d 327 (1976), and United States v. Cleveland, 503 F.2d 1067 (C.A.9 1974), with United States v. Analla, 490 F.2d 1204 (C.A.10), vacated and remanded, 419 U.S. 813, 95 S.Ct. 28, 42 L.Ed.2d 40 (1974). See 18 U.S.C. § 1153 (1976 ed.) (which provides for uniform penalties for both Indians and non-Indians charged with assault resulting in serious bodily injury). That issue is not before us, and we intimate no views on it.

Congress responded in 1976, amending federal law to reduce or eliminate the chance for Indian and non-Indian co-defendants to be punished for the same crimes with widely varying sentences. The Major Crimes Act specifies that crimes not "defined and punished" by federal law "shall be defined and punished in accordance with the law of the State." Burglary is listed in the Act but is not a federal crime. Upon conviction for burglary in Indian country in Minnesota under the Major Crimes Act, should an Indian defendant be sentenced according to the federal sentencing guidelines or the state guidelines? United States v. Norquay, 905 F.2d 1157 (8th Cir.1990), held that the state guidelines should determine the range of the sentence (which was higher than the federal) but the federal guidelines (which were tougher than the state's in this respect) would determine how the sentence would be calculated. The court cited the goal of the federal sentencing act of promoting uniform sentencing with the federal system. Congress responded by amending the federal guidelines, 18 U.S.C. § 3551, to apply to persons convicted under the Major Crimes Act and the Assimilative Crimes Act. Pub.L. No. 101–647 (Nov. 29, 1990). Procedural guidelines for sentencing promulgated by the United States Sentencing Commission now require that the "sentence imposed may not exceed any maximum sentence and may not fall below any mandatory minimum sentence that is required under the law of the state in which the crimes occur." United States v. Garcia, 893 F.2d 250, 252 (10th Cir.1989), cert. denied 494 U.S. 1070 (1990).

UNITED STATES V. BRYANT

Supreme Court of the United States, 2016.
___ U.S. ___, 136 S.Ct. 1954, 195 L.Ed.2d 317.

JUSTICE GINSBURG delivered the opinion of the Court.

[18 U.S.C. § 117(a)] makes it a federal crime for any person to "commi[t] a domestic assault within . . . Indian country" if the person has at least two prior final convictions for domestic violence rendered "in Federal, State, or Indian tribal court proceedings." * * * Respondent Michael Bryant, Jr., has multiple tribal-court convictions for domestic assault. For most of those convictions, he was sentenced to terms of imprisonment, none of them exceeding one year's duration. His tribal-court convictions do not count for § 117(a) purposes, Bryant maintains, because he was uncounseled in those proceedings.

The Sixth Amendment guarantees indigent defendants, in state and federal criminal proceedings, appointed counsel in any case in which a term of imprisonment is imposed. Scott v. Illinois, 440 U. S. 367, 373–374 (1979). But the Sixth Amendment does not apply to tribal-court proceedings. See Plains Commerce Bank v. Long Family Land & Cattle Co., 554 U. S. 316, 337 (2008). The Indian Civil Rights Act of 1968 (ICRA), Pub. L. 90–284, 82 Stat. 77, 25 U.S.C § 1301 et seq., which governs criminal proceedings in tribal courts, requires appointed counsel only when a sentence of more than one year's imprisonment is imposed. § 1302(c)(2). Bryant's tribal-court convictions, it is undisputed, were valid when entered. This case presents the question whether those convictions, though uncounseled, rank as predicate offenses within the compass of § 117(a). Our answer is yes. Bryant's tribal-court convictions did not violate the Sixth Amendment when obtained, and they retain their validity when invoked in a § 117(a) prosecution. That proceeding generates no Sixth Amendment defect where none previously existed.

I

A

"[C]ompared to all other groups in the United States," Native American women "experience the highest rates of domestic violence." 151 Cong. Rec. 9061 (2005) (remarks of Sen. McCain). According to the Centers for Disease Control and Prevention, as many as 46% of American Indian and Alaska Native women have been victims of physical violence by an intimate partner. * * * American Indian and Alaska Native women "are 2.5 times more likely to be raped or sexually assaulted than women in the United States in general." Dept. of Justice, Attorney General's Advisory Committee on American Indian and Alaska Native Children Exposed to Violence, Ending Violence So Children Can Thrive 38 (Nov. 2014) * * * . American Indian women experience battery "at a rate of 23.2 per 1,000, compared with 8 per 1,000 among Caucasian women," and they "experience 7 sexual assaults per 1,000, compared with 4 per 1,000 among Black Americans, 3 per 1,000 among Caucasians, 2 per 1,000 among Hispanic women, and 1 per 1,000 among Asian women." * * *

* * *

The "complex patchwork of federal, state, and tribal law" governing Indian country, Duro v. Reina, 495 U. S. 676, 680, n. 1 (1990), has made it difficult to stem the tide of domestic violence experienced by Native American women. Although tribal courts may enforce the tribe's criminal laws against Indian defendants, Congress has curbed tribal courts' sentencing authority. At the time of § 117(a)'s passage, ICRA limited sentences in tribal court to a maximum of one year's imprisonment. 25 U.S.C § 1302(a)(7) (2006 ed.). Congress has since expanded tribal courts' sentencing authority, allowing them to impose up to three years' imprisonment, contingent on adoption of additional procedural safeguards. 124 Stat. 2279–2280 (codified at 25 U.S.C § 1302(a)(7)(C), (c)). To date, however, few tribes have employed this enhanced sentencing authority. * * *

States are unable or unwilling to fill the enforcement gap. Most States lack jurisdiction over crimes committed in Indian country against Indian victims. See United States v. John, 437 U. S. 634, 651 (1978). In 1953, Congress increased the potential for state action by giving six States "jurisdiction over specified areas of Indian country within the States and provid[ing] for the [voluntary] assumption of jurisdiction by other States." California v. Cabazon Band of Mission Indians, 480 U. S. 202, 207 (1987) (footnote omitted). See Act of Aug. 15, 1953, Pub. L. 280, 67 Stat. 588 (codified, as amended, at 18 U.S.C § 1162 and 25 U.S.C §§ 1321–1328, 1360). States so empowered may apply their own criminal laws to "offenses committed by or against Indians within all Indian country within the State." *Cabazon Band of Mission Indians*, 480 U. S., at 207; see 18 U.S.C § 1162(a). Even when capable of exercising jurisdiction, however, States have not devoted their limited criminal justice resources to crimes committed in Indian country. Jimenez & Song, *Concurrent Tribal and State Jurisdiction Under Public Law 280*, 47 Am. U. L.Rev. 1627, 1636–1637 (1998); Tribal Law and Policy Inst., S. Deer, C. Goldberg, H. Valdez Singleton, & M. White Eagle, Final Report: Focus Group on Public Law 280 and the Sexual Assault of Native Women 7–8 (2007) * * * .

That leaves the Federal Government. * * * [W]hen § 117(a) was before Congress, Indian perpetrators of domestic violence "escape[d] felony charges until they seriously injure[d] or kill[ed] someone." 151 Cong. Rec. 9062 (2005) (remarks of Sen. McCain).

As a result of the limitations on tribal, state, and federal jurisdiction in Indian country, serial domestic violence offenders, prior to the enactment of § 117(a), faced at most a year's imprisonment per offense—a sentence insufficient to deter repeated and escalating abuse. To ratchet up the punishment of serial offenders, Congress created the federal felony offense of domestic assault in Indian country by a habitual offender. * * * The section provides in pertinent part:

> "Any person who commits a domestic assault within . . . Indian country and who has a final conviction on at least 2 separate prior occasions in Federal, State, or Indian tribal court proceedings for offenses that would be, if subject to Federal jurisdiction any assault, sexual abuse, or serious violent felony against a spouse or intimate partner . . . shall be fined . . . , imprisoned for a term of not more than 5 years, or both. . . ." § 117(a)(1).

Having two prior convictions for domestic violence crimes—including tribal-court convictions—is thus a predicate of the new offense.

B

This case requires us to determine whether § 117(a)'s inclusion of tribal-court convictions is compatible with the Sixth Amendment's right to counsel. * * *

"As separate sovereigns pre-existing the Constitution, tribes have historically been regarded as unconstrained by those constitutional provisions framed specifically as limitations on federal or state authority." Santa Clara Pueblo v. Martinez, 436 U. S. 49, 56 (1978). The Bill of Rights, including the Sixth Amendment right to counsel, therefore, does not apply in tribal-court proceedings. * * *

In ICRA, however, Congress accorded a range of procedural safeguards to tribal-court defendants "similar, but not identical, to those contained in the Bill of Rights and the Fourteenth Amendment." * * *

The right to counsel under ICRA is not coextensive with the Sixth Amendment right. If a tribal court imposes a sentence in excess of one year, ICRA requires the court to accord the defendant "the right to effective assistance of counsel at least equal to that guaranteed by the United States Constitution," including appointment of counsel for an indigent defendant at the tribe's expense. § 1302(c)(1), (2). If the sentence imposed is no greater than one year, however, the tribal court must allow a defendant only the opportunity to obtain counsel "at his own expense." § 1302(a)(6). In tribal court, therefore, unlike in federal or state court, a sentence of imprisonment up to one year may be imposed without according indigent defendants the right to appointed counsel.

* * *

In Nichols v. United States, 511 U. S. 738 (1994), * * * Nichols pleaded guilty to a federal felony drug offense. 511 U. S., at 740. Several years earlier, unrepresented by counsel, he had been convicted of driving under the influence (DUI), a state-law misdemeanor, and fined $250 but not imprisoned. Ibid. Nichols' DUI conviction, under the then mandatory Sentencing Guidelines, effectively elevated by about two years the sentencing range for Nichols' federal drug offense. Ibid. We rejected Nichols' contention that, as his later sentence for the federal drug offense involved imprisonment, use of his uncounseled DUI conviction to elevate that sentence violated the Sixth Amendment. Id., at 746–747. "[C]onsistent with the Sixth and Fourteenth Amendments of the Constitution," we held, "an uncounseled misdemeanor conviction, valid under Scott because no prison term was imposed, is also valid when used to enhance punishment at a subsequent conviction." Id., at 748–749.

C

Respondent Bryant's conduct is illustrative of the domestic violence problem existing in Indian country. During the period relevant to this case, Bryant, an enrolled member of the Northern Cheyenne Tribe, lived on that Tribe's reservation in Montana. He has a record of over 100 tribal-court convictions, including several misdemeanor convictions for domestic assault. Specifically, between 1997 and 2007, Bryant pleaded guilty on at least five occasions in Northern Cheyenne Tribal Court to committing domestic abuse in violation of the Northern Cheyenne Tribal Code. On one occasion, Bryant hit his live-in girlfriend on the head with a beer bottle and attempted to strangle her. On another, Bryant beat a different girlfriend, kneeing her in the face, breaking her nose, and leaving her bruised and bloodied.

For most of Bryant's repeated brutal acts of domestic violence, the Tribal Court sentenced him to terms of imprisonment, never exceeding one year. When convicted of these offenses, Bryant was indigent and was not appointed counsel. Because of his short prison terms, Bryant acknowledges, the prior tribal-court proceedings complied with ICRA, and his convictions were therefore valid when entered. Bryant has never challenged his tribal-court convictions in federal court under ICRA's habeas corpus provision.

In 2011, Bryant was arrested yet again for assaulting women. In February of that year, Bryant attacked his then girlfriend, dragging her off the bed, pulling her hair, and repeatedly punching and kicking her. During an interview with law enforcement officers, Bryant admitted that he had physically assaulted this woman five or six times. Three months later, he assaulted another woman with whom he was then living, waking her by yelling that he could not find his truck keys and then choking her until she almost lost consciousness. Bryant later stated that he had assaulted this victim on three separate occasions during the two months they dated.

Based on the 2011 assaults, a federal grand jury in Montana indicted Bryant on two counts of domestic assault by a habitual offender, in violation of § 117(a). * * * Bryant entered a conditional guilty plea, reserving the right to appeal that decision. Bryant was sentenced to concurrent terms of 46 months' imprisonment on each count, to be followed by three years of supervised release.

* * *

II

Bryant's tribal-court convictions, he recognizes, infringed no constitutional right because the Sixth Amendment does not apply to tribal-court proceedings. Brief for Respondent 5. Those prior convictions complied with ICRA, he concedes, and therefore were valid when entered. But, had his convictions occurred in state or federal court, Bryant observes, [the Sixth Amendment's protections] would have rendered them invalid because he was sentenced to incarceration without representation by court-appointed counsel. Essentially, Bryant urges us to treat tribal-court convictions, for § 117(a) purposes, as though they had been entered by a federal or state court. We next explain why we decline to do so.

* * *

Nichols' reasoning steers the result here. Bryant's 46-month sentence for violating § 117(a) punishes his most recent acts of domestic assault, not his prior crimes prosecuted in tribal court. Bryant was denied no right to counsel in tribal court, and his Sixth Amendment right was honored in federal court, when he was "adjudicated guilty of the felony offense for which he was imprisoned." Alabama v. Shelton, 535 U. S. 654, 664 (2002). It would be "odd to say that a conviction untainted by a violation of the Sixth Amendment triggers a violation of that same amendment when it's used in a subsequent case where the defendant's right to appointed counsel is fully respected." 769 F. 3d [671,] 679 [(9th Cir. 2015)] (Watford, J., concurring).

Bryant acknowledges that had he been punished only by fines in his tribal-court proceedings, Nichols would have allowed reliance on his uncounseled convictions to satisfy § 117(a)'s prior-crimes predicate. Brief for Respondent 50. We see no cause to distinguish for § 117(a) purposes between valid but uncounseled convictions resulting in a fine and valid but uncounseled convictions resulting in imprisonment not exceeding one year. "Both Nichols's and Bryant's uncounseled convictions 'comport' with the Sixth Amendment, and for the same reason: the Sixth Amendment right to appointed counsel did not apply to either conviction." * * *

* * *

* * * Because a defendant convicted in tribal court suffers no Sixth Amendment violation in the first instance, "[u]se of tribal convictions in a subsequent prosecution cannot violate [the Sixth Amendment] 'anew.'" [United States v.] Shavanaux, 647 F. 3d, [993,] 998 [8th Cir. 2011)]. Bryant observes that reliability concerns underlie our right-to-counsel decisions and urges that those concerns remain even if the Sixth Amendment itself does not shelter him. * * * Nichols, however, counter[s] the argument that uncounseled misdemeanor convictions are categorically unreliable, either in their own right or for use in a subsequent proceeding. Bryant's recognition that a tribal-court conviction resulting in a fine would qualify as a § 117(a) predicate offense, we further note, diminishes the force of his reliability-based argument. There is no reason to suppose that tribal-court proceedings are less reliable when a sentence of a year's imprisonment is imposed than when the punishment is merely a fine. No evidentiary or procedural variation turns on the sanction—fine only or a year in prison—ultimately imposed.

Bryant also invokes the Due Process Clause of the Fifth Amendment in support of his assertion that tribal-court judgments should not be used as predicate offenses. But, as earlier observed, ICRA itself requires tribes to ensure "due process of law," § 1302(a)(8), and it accords defend ants specific procedural safeguards resembling those contained in the Bill of Rights and the Fourteenth Amendment. * * * Further, ICRA makes habeas review in federal court available to persons incarcerated pursuant to a tribal-court judgment. § 1303. By that means, a prisoner may challenge the fundamental fairness of the proceedings in tribal court. Proceedings in compliance with ICRA, Congress determined, and we agree, sufficiently ensure the reliability of tribal-court convictions. Therefore, the use of those convictions in a federal prosecution does not violate a defendant's right to due process. See *Shavanaux*, 647 F. 3d, at 1000; cf. State v. Spotted Eagle, 316 Mont. 370, 378–379, 71 P. 3d 1239, 1245–1246 (2003) (principles of comity support recognizing uncounseled tribal-court convictions that complied with ICRA).

* * *

JUSTICE THOMAS concurring.

* * *

[T]he only reason why tribal courts had the power to convict Bryant in proceedings where he had no right to counsel is that such prosecutions are a function of a tribe's core sovereignty. See United States v. Lara, 541 U. S. 193, 197 (2004); United States v. Wheeler, 435 U. S. 313, 318, 322–323 (1978). By virtue of tribes' status as " 'separate sovereigns pre-existing the Constitution,' " tribal prosecutions need not, under our precedents, comply with " 'those constitutional provisions framed specifically as limitations on federal or state authority' " (quoting Santa Clara Pueblo v. Martinez, 436 U. S. 49, 56 (1978)).

On the other hand, the validity of Bryant's ensuing federal conviction rests upon a contrary view of tribal sovereignty. Congress ordinarily lacks authority to enact a general federal criminal law proscribing domestic abuse. See United States v. Morrison, 529 U. S. 598, 610–613 (2000). But, the Court suggests, Congress must intervene on reservations to ensure that prolific domestic abusers receive sufficient punishment. The Court does not explain where Congress' power to act comes from, but our precedents leave no doubt on this score. Congress could make Bryant's domestic assaults a federal crime subject to federal prosecution only because our precedents have endowed Congress with an "all-encompassing" power over all aspects of tribal sovereignty. *Wheeler*, supra, at 319. Thus, even though tribal prosecutions of tribal members are purportedly the apex of tribal sovereignty, Congress can second-guess how tribes prosecute domestic abuse perpetrated by Indians against other Indians on Indian land by virtue of its "plenary power" over Indian tribes. See United States v. Kagama, 118 U. S. 375, 382–384 (1886); accord, *Lara*, 541 U. S., at 200.

I continue to doubt whether either view of tribal sovereignty is correct. See id., at 215 (THOMAS, J., concurring in judgment). Indian tribes have varied origins, discrete treaties with the United States, and different patterns of assimilation and conquest. In light of the tribes' distinct histories, it strains credulity to assume that all tribes necessarily retained the sovereign prerogative of prosecuting their own members. And by treating all tribes as possessing an identical quantum of sovereignty, the Court's precedents have made it all but impossible to understand the ultimate source of each tribe's sovereignty and whether it endures. See

Prakash, Against Tribal Fungibility, 89 Cornell L. Rev. 1069, 1070–1074, 1107–1110 (2004).

Congress' purported plenary power over Indian tribes rests on even shakier foundations. No enumerated power—not Congress' power to "regulate Commerce . . . with Indian Tribes," not the Senate's role in approving treaties, nor anything else—gives Congress such sweeping authority. See *Lara*, supra, at 224–225 (THOMAS, J., concurring in judgment); Adoptive Couple v. Baby Girl, 570 U. S. ___, ___–___ (2013) (THOMAS, J., concurring).

Indeed, the Court created this new power because it was unable to find an enumerated power justifying the federal Major Crimes Act, which for the first time punished crimes committed by Indians against Indians on Indian land. See *Kagama*, supra, at 377–380. The Court asserted: "The power of the General Government over these remnants of a race once powerful, now weak and diminished in numbers, is necessary to their protection. . . . It must exist in that government, because it has never existed anywhere else." *Kagama*, supra, at 384. Over a century later, *Kagama* endures as the foundation of this doctrine, and the Court has searched in vain for any valid constitutional justification for this unfettered power. See, e.g., Lone Wolf v. Hitchcock, 187 U. S. 553, 566–567 (1903) (relying on *Kagama*'s race-based plenary power theory); *Wheeler*, supra, at 319; *Lara*, supra, at 224 (THOMAS, J., concurring in judgment) ("The Court utterly fails to find any provision of the Constitution that gives Congress enumerated power to alter tribal sovereignty").

It is time that the Court reconsider these precedents. Until the Court ceases treating all Indian tribes as an undifferentiated mass, our case law will remain bedeviled by amorphous and ahistorical assumptions about the scope of tribal sovereignty. And, until the Court rejects the fiction that Congress possesses plenary power over Indian affairs, our precedents will continue to be based on the paternalistic theory that Congress must assume all-encompassing control over the "remnants of a race" for its own good. *Kagama*, supra, at 384.

NOTES

1.   *Antelope* and *Bryant* involve federal constitutional challenges to convictions of American Indians under federal criminal statutes for crimes committed in Indian country. The Court disposed of the constitutional questions in *Antelope* by relying on the theory developed in Morton v. Mancari, 417 U.S. 535 (1974), that federal statutory classifications based on Indian status are not race or ancestry based, but instead based on the political status of Indian people as members or descendants of members of Indian tribes. The *Bryant* Court relied on the theory advanced in cases such as Talton v. Mayes, 163 U.S. 376 (1896), that the federal constitution is inapplicable to Indian tribes.

It now seems well settled that federal criminal jurisdiction in Indian country, as well as tribal criminal jurisdiction over Indians (at least) pass federal constitutional muster. But commentators have argued that federal prosecutions of Indians for crimes committed in Indian country *do* violate the constitution. E.g., Troy A. Eid & Carrie Covington Doyle, *Separate But Unequal: The Federal Criminal Justice System in Indian Country*, 81 U.Colo.L.Rev. 1067 (2010) (arguing federal prosecutions are unconstitutional). See also Kevin K. Washburn, *American Indians, Crime, and the Law*, 104 Mich.L.Rev. 709 (2006) (arguing federal prosecutions are at least constitutionally suspect).

If you represented an Indian person criminally charged in federal court, your client likely would not enjoy a jury that included even a single Indian person. The prosecution likely would be forced to prove to that same jury beyond a reasonable doubt that your client was an "Indian" under federal law, which is relatively easy when the defendant is a tribal member, but not so much when the defendant is not. The prosecution might also ask for sentence enhancement under the federal sentencing guidelines for your client's prior uncounseled tribal court convictions. In short, there are seemingly some constitutional infirmities. But what are the alternatives to federal criminal jurisdiction?

2.   The *Bryant* decision prompted critical commentary from those knowledgeable about tribal criminal defense. Barbara L. Creel and John P. Lavelle, *High Court Denies Rights of Natives*, Albuquerque J., June 26, 2016. Professors Creel and LaVelle argue that tribal court criminal defendants are "routinely" sentenced to imprisonment without the assistance of legal counsel. The authors also note that non-Indians subject to tribal prosecution are guaranteed the right to counsel, but Indians are not. 25 U.S.C. § 1304 (tribal jurisdiction provisions of the Violence Against Women Act).

SECTION C. STATE CRIMINAL JURISDICTION

In general, states do not possess criminal jurisdiction over Indian country crimes absent a grant of authority to do so by the United States. However, in numerous instances, the United States has authorized states to exercise complete or partial criminal jurisdiction. The federal government has only done so on an ad hoc basis, and often has allowed states to pick and choose their jurisdiction. As a result, state criminal jurisdiction frequently is even more complicated than federal criminal jurisdiction.

1. THE SPECIAL CASE OF NON-INDIAN ON NON-INDIAN CRIME IN INDIAN COUNTRY

It is now well established that state governments have jurisdiction to prosecute crime committed by non-Indians against other non-Indians in Indian country. How states acquired that jurisdiction is perplexing, and an interesting study of the gradual encroachment of state power into Indian country.

In 1881, the Supreme Court decided United States v. McBratney, 104 U.S. 621 (1881), forbidding the federal government from prosecuting a non-Indian for a crime committed against another non-Indian on the Ute Reservation. An 1861 federal statute enacted before Colorado's statehood acknowledged federal criminal jurisdiction over Indian country crimes. 12 Stat. 172, 176 (1861). The 1868 treaty that created the Ute Reservation included a so-called "bad men" clause that required the tribe to turn over non-Indians that committed on-reservation crimes to the federal government for prosecution. 15 Stat. 619, 621 (1868).

In 1875, Colorado achieved statehood. The Act of Congress extending statehood to Colorado included an "equal footing clause," a standard clause placing the new state on the same footing under the Constitution as other states. The Supreme Court read that provision as effectively extending state criminal jurisdiction into Indian country:

> The act of March 3, 1875 [the statehood act], necessarily repeals the provisions of any prior statute, or of any existing treaty, which are clearly inconsistent therewith. The Cherokee Tobacco, 11 Wall. 616. Whenever, upon the admission of a State into the Union, Congress has intended to except out of it an Indian reservation, or the sole and exclusive jurisdiction over that reservation, it has done so by express words. The Kansas Indians, 5 Wall. 737. . . . The State of Colorado, by its admission into the Union by Congress, upon an equal footing with the original States in all respects whatever, without any such exception as had been made in the treaty with the Ute Indians and in the act establishing a territorial government, has acquired criminal jurisdiction over its own citizens and other white persons throughout the whole of the territory within its limits, including the Ute Reservation, and that reservation is no longer within the sole and exclusive jurisdiction of the United States. The courts of the United States have, therefore, no jurisdiction to punish crimes within that reservation, unless so far as may be necessary to carry out such provisions of the treaty with the Ute Indians as remain in force. But that treaty contains no stipulation for the punishment of offences committed by white men against white men. It follows that the Circuit Court of the United States for the District of Colorado has no jurisdiction of this indictment, but, according to the practice heretofore adopted in like cases, should deliver up the prisoner to the authorities of the State of Colorado to be dealt with according to law.

McBratney, 104 U.S. at 623–24.

Note that the Court cited to The Kansas Indians, 72 U.S. 737 (1866), a decision affirming tribal tax immunity from state taxation on reservation lands. There, the State of Kansas' statehood act had included what is known as a disclaimer, a provision in which the new state agrees not to assert its authority in Indian country. 12 Stat. 127 (1861).

The Colorado statehood act did not include a disclaimer. The *McBratney* Court took that omission as an affirmative statement that the new state had instead acquired jurisdiction over Indian country. Normally, there is no state authority in Indian country absent an express federal statement to that effect. Cf. Worcester v. Georgia, 31 U.S. 515, 561 (1832) (holding that state law has "no force" in Indian country). The Court's reasoning ignored that principle, and instead reversed the normal presumption favoring federal and tribal authority in favor of the subjective principles underlying the equal footing doctrine.

In Draper v. United States, 164 U.S. 240 (1896), the Supreme Court extended the *McBratney* holding to Montana, which had disclaimed jurisdiction over Indian country in its enabling act. There, the Court more explicitly referenced the equal footing doctrine as justification to strip federal criminal jurisdiction:

> As equality of statehood is the rule, the words relied on here to create an exception cannot be construed as doing so, if, by any reasonable meaning, they can be otherwise treated. The mere reservation of jurisdiction and control by the United States of 'Indian lands' does not of necessity signify a retention of jurisdiction in the United States to punish all offenses committed on such lands by others than Indians or against Indians.

Id. at 244–45. The Court further buttressed its analysis by reference to the General Allotment Act of 1887, 24 Stat. 33, arguing that since the United States fully expected to transfer Indian country to state jurisdiction through the allotment process, the disclaimer did not preserve federal criminal jurisdiction:

> From these enactments it clearly follows that at the time of the admission of Montana into the Union, and the use in the enabling act of the restrictive words here relied upon, there was a condition of things provided for by the statute law of the United States, and contemplated to arise, where the reservation of jurisdiction and control over the Indian lands would become essential to prevent any implication of the power of the state to frustrate the limitations imposed by the laws of the United States upon the title of lands once in an Indian reservation, but which had become extinct by allotment in severalty, and in which contingency the Indians themselves would have passed under the authority and control of the state.

Id. at 246.

In New York ex rel. Ray v. Martin, 326 U.S. 496 (1946), the Court later extended that rule to the original 13 states, states that never would have enjoyed criminal jurisdiction in Indian country absent federal authorization. Justice Black's majority opinion simply announced that the presumption favoring state jurisdiction: "[I]n the absence of a limiting treaty obligation or Congressional enactment, each state had a right to exercise jurisdiction over Indian reservations within its boundaries." Id. at 499. This conclusion flies in the face of Worcester v. Georgia, 31 U.S. 515, 561 (1832), which held that Georgia, one of the original 13 states, did not have jurisdiction over a state law crime committed by a non-Indian, relying exclusively on inapposite Supreme Court precedents involving the equal footing doctrine. The outcome is circular reasoning writ large.

The modern wrinkle in modern cases applying *McBratney* is that "state courts have jurisdiction with respect to criminal prosecutions in cases involving non-Indian defendants who committed offenses on Indian lands against non-Indians or non-Indian defendants who committed offenses described as 'victimless' on Indian lands." People v. Collins, 826 N.W.2d 175, 175 (Mich.Ct.App.2012). Any first year law student could ask what a "victimless" crime is, since all crimes involve a "victim," the sovereign of the jurisdiction in which the crime is committed. A crime committed on a tribe's reservation is a crime committed against the tribe and the United States, not a state.

We reproduce the chart earlier noting criminal jurisdiction over crimes committed by non-Indians:

Non-Indian Perpetrator

Who was the victim?	What was the crime?	Jurisdiction
Indian	Crimes punishable in accordance with the Indian Country Crimes Act, 18 U.S.C. § 1152, or state law crimes punishable under the Assimilative Crimes Act, 18 U.S.C. § 13, where there is no applicable federal criminal statute	Federal
Non-Indian	Any crime cognizable under state law	State

2. PUBLIC LAW 280 AND OTHER FEDERAL AUTHORIZATIONS OF STATE JURISDICTION IN INDIAN COUNTRY

The termination era produced several assimilationist policies other than the termination acts themselves. The principal example is Public Law 280, which alters the traditional dominance of federal and tribal law as to those reservations affected by the Act. Public Law 280 is thus an exception to the general jurisdictional structure in Indian country.

CAROLE E. GOLDBERG, PUBLIC LAW 280: THE LIMITS OF STATE JURISDICTION OVER RESERVATION INDIANS

22 UCLA L.Rev. 535, 537–59 (1975).

* * *

* * * Passed in 1953, PL–280 was an attempt at compromise between wholly abandoning the Indians to the states and maintaining them as federally protected wards, subject only to federal or tribal jurisdiction. The statute originally transferred to five willing states[11] and offered all others, civil and criminal jurisdiction over reservation Indians regardless of the Indians' preference for continued autonomy. PL–280 did not, however, terminate the trust status of reservation lands.

From the outset, PL–280 left both the Indians and the states dissatisfied, the Indians because they did not want state jurisdiction thrust upon them against their will, the states because they resented the remaining federal protection which seemed to deprive them of the ability

---

[11] * * * In regard to criminal jurisdiction in the mandatory states the Act provides:

Each of the States or Territories [sic] shall have jurisdiction over offenses committed by or against Indians in the areas of Indian country listed opposite the name of the State or Territory to the same extent that such State or Territory has jurisdiction over offenses committed elsewhere within the State or Territory, and the criminal laws of such State or Territory shall have the same force and effect within such Indian country as they have elsewhere within the State or Territory:

State or Territory of	Indian country affected
Alaska	All Indian country within the State, except that on Annette Islands, the Metlakatla Indian community may exercise jurisdiction over offenses committed by Indians in the same manner in which such jurisdiction may be exercised by Indian tribes in Indian country over which State jurisdiction has not been extended.
California	All Indian country within the State.
Minnesota	All Indian country within the State, except the Red Lake Reservation.
Nebraska	All Indian country within the State.
Oregon	All Indian country within the State, except the Warm Springs Reservation.
Wisconsin	All Indian country within the State.

[18 U.S.C. § 1162(a). The parallel provision for civil jurisdiction is 28 U.S.C. § 1360(a). Ed.]

to finance their newly acquired powers. Predictably, disagreement between the Indians and the states erupted over the scope of jurisdiction offered by PL–280 and the means by which transfers of jurisdiction were to be effected. Among the matters in dispute were whether states assuming jurisdiction under PL–280 acquired the power to tax and zone on Indian reservations, and whether states asserting PL–280 jurisdiction had satisfied the procedural prerequisites for doing so.

Recent social, economic, and political developments have made the Indians and states especially anxious that their respective interpretations of PL–280 prevail. The expansion of metropolitan areas near Indian reservations has increased the states' interest in regulating and exploiting residential and recreational development on trust land. States have been notably desirous of acquiring pollution and subdivision control. The discovery of substantial energy resources on reservations, and consequent industrial development, have spurred similar state interest in regulating and taxing those activities. At the same time, tribal governments have been receiving encouragement from the federal government to develop tribal enterprises and strengthen their administrative apparatus, increasing their interest in freedom from state power. Finally, growing demands on the part of Indians that they receive their share of state services and their share of representation in state legislatures have produced concomitant demands on the part of the states that Indians submit to state jurisdiction.

The jurisdictional stakes are considerably higher today than they were when PL–280 was enacted; at the same time federal Indian policy is more devoted to fulfilling federal responsibility for Indians and building effective tribal governments. Broadly speaking, the model for federal Indian policy seems to be changing from one favoring state power with minimum protection for Indian interest to one favoring tribal autonomy with minimum protection for state interests. Nevertheless, since PL–280 is the most direct evidence of congressional intent with respect to state jurisdiction, the debate over the scope of state power on Indian reservations must contend with policy choices Congress made when PL–280 was enacted. Amendments to the Act adopted in 1968 did, however, bring PL–280 more in conformity with current policy by rendering all *future* assertions of state jurisdiction under the Act subject to the affected Indians' consent, and authorizing states to return jurisdiction to the federal government. But controversies persist over jurisdiction claimed by the states prior to these amendments.

* * *

PL–280 differed from earlier relinquishments of federal Indian jurisdiction in that it authorized every state to assume jurisdiction at any time in the future. Previous transfers had been limited to some or all the reservations in a single state, and had followed consultation with the individual state and affected tribes by the Bureau of Indian Affairs (hereinafter referred to as B.I.A.). Although PL–280 itself had begun as an attempt to confer jurisdiction on California only, by the time it was reported out of the Senate, the prevailing view was that "any legislation in [the] area should be on a general basis, making provision for all affected States to come within its terms. . . ." The Senate Report of the bill in committee suggests why Congress was concerned with effectuating a general transfer of jurisdiction after years of an ad hoc policy which had involved careful evaluation in each case from the point of view of both Indians and the states. The Report indicates the foremost concern of Congress at the time of enacting of PL–280 was lawlessness on the reservations and the accompanying threat to Anglos living nearby. * * *

Of course, conferring jurisdiction on the states was not the only available solution to the very real law enforcement problem. * * * State criminal jurisdiction was preferred to other alternatives however, because it was the cheapest solution; Congress was interested in saving money as well as bringing law and order to the reservations.

There is much less evidence of the congressional rationale for conferring civil jurisdiction on the states, and much less factual support for that decision. * * * In this context, the Senate Report on PL–280 declared that the Indians "have reached a stage of acculturation and development that makes desirable extension of State civil jurisdiction. . . ." The implication of this and similar statements was that Indians were just as socially advanced as other state citizens, and should therefore be released from second-class citizenship as well as the paternalistic supervision of the B.I.A.

Considering the absence of any significant investigation of the Indians' stage of social development prior to the broad delegation of jurisdiction to every state by PL–280, it seems unlikely that Congress knew or cared about the Indians' readiness for state jurisdiction. Furthermore, it is difficult to reconcile this theme of advanced acculturation with the prevailing notion that state criminal jurisdiction was necessary because the Indians were disorderly and incapable of self-government. Most likely, civil jurisdiction was an afterthought in a measure aimed primarily at bringing law and order to the reservations, added because it comported with the pro-assimilationist drift of federal policy, and because it was convenient and cheap.

The choice Congress made in PL–280 did not wholly satisfy either the tribes or the states. The source of the Indians' displeasure was the absence of a provision for tribal consent prior to state assumption of jurisdiction. The states, on the other hand, were unhappy about the absence of a provision either granting federal subsidies to states that accepted jurisdiction or removing reservation lands from tax-exempt trust status. * * *

* * *

The five, later six, states that were granted PL–280 jurisdiction immediately and irrevocably (mandatory states) lacked the flexibility to condition their jurisdiction on Indian consent. * * * In contrast, the states merely authorized to assume jurisdiction at their discretion (optional states) could take the Indians' wishes into account before asserting their power, and many did so, either formally or informally. For some states, this recognition of Indian sovereignty was spontaneous; in others, it was formed by the bitter experience of states such as Wyoming, South Dakota, Washington, and New Mexico, in which the Indians had waged vigorous and successful battles against bills and constitutional amendments imposing state jurisdiction unilaterally. Although Arizona and Iowa simply asserted jurisdiction without seeking concurrence of the affected Indians, and Idaho and Washington ignored Indian preferences as to some subject matters, Florida first solicited the consent of the Seminole tribe, Nevada consulted with every tribe in the state prior to assuming jurisdiction, and Idaho, Montana, North Dakota, South Dakota, and Washington established some form of Indian consent procedure despite the absence of a requirement in PL–280.

* * *

In 1968, Congress eliminated the need for self-imposed limits on state jurisdiction in the future by establishing a tribal consent provision in PL–280 itself. Congress provided in the Civil Rights Act of 1968 that henceforth no state could acquire PL–280 jurisdiction over the objections of the affected Indians.[79] Furthermore, in an action which most legislators believed did no more than make explicit existing law, the 1968 Act declared that state jurisdiction could be acquired one tribe at a time, so long as a majority of the adult enrolled members of the tribe expressed their consent in a special election. Finally, in a more controversial action, it allowed acceptance of jurisdiction over some subject matters, but not others.[81]

* * *

---

[79] 25 U.S.C. § 1326 (1970) provides:

State jurisdiction acquired pursuant to this subchapter with respect to criminal offenses or civil causes of action, or with respect to both, shall be applicable in Indian country only where the enrolled Indians within the affected area of such Indian country accept such jurisdiction by a majority vote of the adult Indians voting at a special election held for that purpose. The Secretary of the Interior shall call such special election * * * when requested to do so by the tribal council or other governing body, or by 20 per centum of the such enrolled adults.

[81] 25 U.S.C. § 1321(a) provides that states may assume criminal jurisdiction "over any or all . . . offenses"; 25 U.S.C. § 1322(a) provides that states may assume civil jurisdiction over "any or all . . . civil causes of action arising within . . . Indian country . . . "

[No tribe has consented to state jurisdiction under Public Law 280 under the 1968 provision. Ed.]

The significance of the addition of a tribal consent provision to PL–280 lies not only in its recognition of the principle of Indian self-determination, but also in its new conception of the role of state jurisdiction on reservations. The tribal consent provision transformed PL–280 from a law which justified state jurisdiction on law enforcement, budgetary, and assimilationist grounds to one which justified state jurisdiction as a means of providing services to Indian communities. Among the strongest arguments in favor of the 1968 Act's amendment was that the institution of state jurisdiction under PL–280, far from improving reservation law and order and elevating Indians from second-class citizenship, had subjected them to discriminatory treatment in the courts, as well as discrimination in the provision of state services. * * *

The beneficial impact of the 1968 amendments to PL–280 should not be overemphasized, however. The Indian consent provision was not made retroactive, and thus earlier assumptions of state jurisdiction over Indian objections were not affected. Moreover, it did not enable Indians who had consented to state jurisdiction under a state-initiated consent provision to reconsider their decisions.

* * *

The absence of an Indian consent provision in PL–280 reflected insensitivity to the interests of the Indians; the absence of federal subsidies to PL–280 states demonstrated similar insensitivity to the dilemma of states handed jurisdiction but simultaneously denied the means to finance it. This financial dilemma derives from a basic inconsistency in federal policy. On the one hand, Congress wished to satisfy state demands for improved law and order on the reservation; on the other hand, Congress was itself unwilling to pay for such improvements or to enable the states to do so by lifting the tax-exempt status of Indian trust lands.

The failure to resolve this inconsistency had disastrous consequences for states acquiring PL–280 jurisdiction. Local governments acquiring jurisdiction were required to hire more police, more judges, more prison guards, more probation and parole officers, and more juvenile aid officers, and to build new police stations, courthouses, and jails. It could have been predicted that a state which undertook law enforcement on the reservation as vigorously as elsewhere in the state would incur higher expenses than the federal government, even allowing for the greater expense of operating a federal as opposed to a municipal court. The new resources available to the states under PL–280 such as fines and court costs were clearly inadequate; estimates based on federal experience indicated such funds would cover only about 10 percent of all newly-acquired law enforcement expenses. The mandatory PL–280 states were hardest hit; they could not avoid the economic consequences of federal withdrawal from the reservations by refusing jurisdiction under the Act.

Financial hardship for the states translated into inadequate law enforcement for the reservations. The most notable failure among the mandatory states was Nebraska, where the Omaha and Winnebago reservations were left without any law enforcement at all once federal officers withdrew. This bitter experience made Indians and local governments alike wary of state assumption of jurisdiction under the Act in the optional PL–280 states. * * *

* * *

Had PL–280 originally contained a provision permitting the states and the tribes to demand the return or "retrocession" of state PL–280 jurisdiction to the federal government, much of the dissatisfaction with the Act would have been avoided, though federal dissatisfaction might have been greater. Retrocession would have allowed both states and tribes to experiment with state jurisdiction, the states to determine whether it was too costly, the tribes to determine whether it fairly met their needs. In addition, retrocession would have permitted jurisdictional arrangements to reflect changed circumstances. If a tribe subject to PL–280 jurisdiction developed new economic resources, or a new generation of tribal members wished to establish strong tribal governing institutions, the state could be required to relinquish jurisdiction.

* * *

Eventually, however, Congress extended the advantages of retrocession to the states, although not to the Indians. By 1968, the states' financial difficulties with PL–280 had become so apparent that relief was provided in the form of a section of the 1968 Civil Rights Act [25 U.S.C. § 1323] enabling any state which had previously assumed jurisdiction under PL–280 to offer the return of all or any measure of its jurisdiction to the federal government by sending a resolution to the Secretary of the Interior. The Secretary could accept or reject the retrocession in his discretion. Under this provision, the Indians could not participate in the retrocession decision, although they might attempt to do so informally through appeals directly to the Secretary.

* * *

NOTES

1.　Beyond the six mandatory states, several "optional states" asserted jurisdiction over a variety of subject matter before the Act was amended to require tribal consent: Arizona (air and water pollution); Florida (full P.L. 280 jurisdiction); Idaho (7 subject areas; full, if tribes consent); Iowa (civil jurisdiction over Sac and Fox Reservation); Montana (criminal jurisdiction over Flathead Reservation; full, where tribes request, counties consent, and governor proclaims); Nevada (full, but counties may opt out; later amendment required tribal consent); North Dakota (civil only, subject to tribal consent);

South Dakota (criminal and civil matters arising on highways; full if U.S. reimburses costs of enforcement); Utah (full, if tribes consent); Washington (8 subject areas on Indian trust land; full as to non-Indians and Indians on non-trust land).

2.   In addition to the grant in Public Law 280, Congress has passed individual acts that grant state courts jurisdiction over all Indian country within New York (62 Stat. 1224) and Kansas (54 Stat. 249). See also, e.g., Maine Indian Claims Settlement Act of 1980, 25 U.S.C. § 1725. Other acts have dealt with particular kinds of jurisdiction on specific reservations, such as the Agua Caliente Reservation in California (63 Stat. 705), the Devil's Lake Reservation in North Dakota (60 Stat. 229), and the Sac and Fox Reservation in Iowa (62 Stat. 1161). See Matthew L.M. Fletcher, Federal Indian Law § 7.5, at 329–30 (2016).

3.   Washington v. Confederated Bands and Tribes of the Yakima Indian Nation, 439 U.S. 463 (1979), resolved several basic procedural issues arising under Public Law 280. Washington, an optional state, enacted a law described by the Court as follows:

> The most significant feature of the new statute was its provision for the extension of at least some jurisdiction over all Indian lands within the State, whether or not the affected tribe gave its consent. Full criminal and civil jurisdiction to the extent permitted by Pub.L. 280 was extended to all fee lands in every Indian reservation and to trust and allotted lands therein when non-Indians were involved. Except for eight categories of law, however, state jurisdiction was not extended to Indians on allotted and trust lands unless the affected tribe so requested. The eight jurisdictional categories of state law that were thus extended to all parts of every Indian reservation were in the areas of compulsory school attendance, public assistance, domestic relations, mental illness, juvenile delinquency, adoption proceedings, dependent children, and motor vehicles.

Id. at 475–76.

The Supreme Court found that the terms of Public Law 280 did not require an "all or nothing" assumption of jurisdiction in optional states and thus upheld the constitutionality of the "partial geographic and subject-matter jurisdiction" approach taken by Washington. The Court rejected a lower court ruling that the state law was a denial of equal protection because there was no rational basis for the land ownership and racial distinctions. The state action was entitled to the deference given to congressional action in Indian affairs since "Washington was legislating under explicit authority granted by Congress" and the state statute met the rational basis test. Id. at 501–02. The Court also found that Washington's approach was not barred as a matter of federal law by the clause in the state constitution in which Washington disclaimed all title to Indian lands and recognized that such lands would remain under the "absolute jurisdiction" of Congress. Public Law 280 granted congressional consent to the extension of state jurisdiction and the question of whether the state constitution must be amended was purely a matter of state law. In State v. Pink, 186 P.3d 634 (Wash.Ct.App.2008), the court held that it had no jurisdiction over criminal evidence discovered during a vehicle stop under Washington's limited acceptance of P.L. 280 jurisdiction.

4.   The Menominee Restoration Act did not speak directly to the question of whether Public Law 280 would apply to the restored reservation. Cf. Application of Nacotee, 389 F. Supp. 784 (E.D.Wis.1975). After protracted negotiations among the tribe, the state, and the Department of Interior, Governor Lucey retroceded jurisdiction on February 19, 1976, so as to render the ambiguity moot. Several other tribes have negotiated with the states and have achieved partial or complete retrocession under 25 U.S.C. § 1323.

5.   Because Public Law 280 fundamentally changes the jurisdictional arrangements in Indian country the Supreme Court has insisted on exacting compliance with its procedures. In 1967, the Blackfeet Tribal Council in Montana passed a resolution stating that the "Tribal Court and the State shall have concurrent and not exclusive jurisdiction of all suits wherein the defendant is a member of the tribe." After a state court adjudicated a debt collection matter brought by a reservation grocery store against tribal members, the Montana Supreme Court purported to apply the rule in Williams v. Lee, 358 U.S. 217 (1959), a case involving a nearly identical fact situation, and held that there was no infringement of tribal self-government because of the resolution. The United States Supreme Court reversed, saying that the infringement test announced in *Williams* applied only "absent governing Acts of Congress." Kennerly v. District Court of Montana, 400 U.S. 423 (1971). Here Public Law 280 was a "governing act" and it required that assumption of state jurisdiction be based on affirmative state legislation which was lacking. It also noted that the tribal consent requirements required under the act as amended would not be satisfied if the Montana legislature now passed affirmative legislation because the amendments say that consent must be manifested in a majority vote of tribal members, not simply a resolution of the tribal council.

BRYAN V. ITASCA COUNTY
Supreme Court of the United States, 1976.
426 U.S. 373, 96 S.Ct. 2102, 48 L.Ed.2d 710.

MR. JUSTICE BRENNAN delivered the opinion of the Court.

* * *

Petitioner Russell Bryan, an enrolled member of the Minnesota Chippewa Tribe resides in a mobile home on land held in trust by the United States for the Chippewa Tribe on the Leech Lake Reservation in Minnesota. In June of 1972, petitioner received notices from the auditor of respondent Itasca County, Minn., that he had been assessed personal property tax liability on the mobile home totaling $147.95. Thereafter, in September 1972, petitioner brought this suit in the Minnesota District Court seeking a declaratory judgment that the State and county were without authority to levy such a tax on personal property of a reservation Indian on the reservation and that imposition of such a tax was contrary to federal law. The Minnesota District Court rejected the contention and entered judgment for respondent County. The Minnesota Supreme Court affirmed. We granted certiorari and now reverse.

I

[Our precedents] preclude any authority in respondent County to levy a personal property tax upon petitioner's mobile home in the absence of congressional consent. Our task therefore is to determine whether § 4 of Pub.L. 280, 28 U.S.C. § 1360, constitutes such consent.

Section 4(a), 28 U.S.C. § 1360(a), provides:

"Each of the States . . . listed . . . shall have jurisdiction over civil causes of action between Indians or to which Indians are parties which arise in the areas of Indian country listed . . . to the same extent that such State . . . has jurisdiction over other civil causes of action, and those civil laws of such State . . . that are of general application to private persons or private property shall have the same force and effect within such Indian country as they have elsewhere within the State . . .:

"Minnesota . . . All Indian country within the State, except the Red Lake Reservation."

The statute does not in terms provide that the tax laws of a State are among "civil laws . . . of general application to private persons or private property." The Minnesota Supreme Court concluded, however, that they were, finding in § 4(b) of the statute a negative implication of inclusion in § 4(a) of a general power of tax. Section 4(b), 28 U.S.C. § 1360(b), provides:

"Nothing in this section shall authorize the alienation, encumbrance, or taxation of any real or personal property, including water rights, belonging to any Indian or any Indian tribe, band, or community that is held in trust by the United States or is subject to a restriction against alienation imposed by the United States; or shall authorize regulation of the use of such property in a manner inconsistent with any Federal treaty, agreement, or statute or with any regulation made pursuant thereto; or shall confer jurisdiction upon the State to adjudicate, in probate proceedings or otherwise, the ownership or right to possession of such property or any interest therein."*

The Minnesota Supreme Court reasoned that "unless paragraph (a) is interpreted as a general grant of the power to tax, then the exceptions contained in paragraph (b) are limitations on a non-existent power."

---

    *   [Ed.] The similar, but not identical, criminal provision is found at 18 U.S.C. § 1162(b).

Therefore, the state court held: "Public Law 280 is a clear grant of the power to tax." We disagree. That conclusion is foreclosed by the legislative history of Pub.L. 280 and the application of canons of construction applicable to congressional statutes claimed to terminate Indian immunities.

II

The primary concern of Congress in enacting Pub.L. 280 that emerges from its sparse legislative history was with the problem of lawlessness on certain Indian reservations, and the absence of adequate tribal institutions for law enforcement. See Goldberg, Public Law 280: The Limits of State Jurisdiction over Reservation Indians, 22 U.C.L.A.Rev. 535, 541–542 (1975). * * * Thus, provision for state criminal jurisdiction over offenses committed by or against Indians on the reservations was the central focus of Pub.L. 280 and is embodied in § 2 of the Act, 18 U.S.C. § 1162.

In marked contrast in the legislative history is the virtual absence of expression of congressional policy or intent respecting § 4's grant of civil jurisdiction to the States. * * *

Piecing together as best we can the sparse legislative history of § 4, subsection (a) seems to have been primarily intended to redress the lack of adequate Indian forums for resolving private legal disputes between reservation Indians, and between Indians and other private citizens, by permitting the courts of the States to decide such disputes; this is definitely the import of the statutory wording conferring upon a State "jurisdiction over civil causes of action between Indians or to which Indians are parties which arise in . . . Indian country . . . to the same extent that such State . . . has jurisdiction over other civil causes of action." With this as the primary focus of § 4(a), the wording that follows in § 4(a)—"and those civil laws of such State . . . that are of general application to private persons or private property shall have the same force and effect within Indian country as they have elsewhere within the State"—authorizes application by the state courts of their rules of decision to decide such disputes. Cf. 28 U.S.C. § 1652. This construction finds support in the consistent and uncontradicted references in the legislative history to "permitting" "*State courts to adjudicate* civil controversies" arising on Indian reservations, H.R.Rep. No. 848, pp. 5, 6, (emphasis added), and the absence of anything remotely resembling an intention to confer general state civil regulatory control over Indian reservations. In short, the consistent and exclusive use of the terms "civil causes of action," "aris[ing] in," "civil laws of general application to private persons and private property," and "adjudicat[ion]," in both the Act and its legislative history virtually compels our conclusion that the primary intent of § 4 was to grant jurisdiction over private civil litigation involving reservation Indians in state court.

* * *

Our construction is also more consistent with Title IV of the Civil Rights Act of 1968, 25 U.S.C. §§ 1321–1326. Title IV repeals § 7 of Pub.L. 280 and requires tribal consent as a condition to further state assumptions of the jurisdiction provided in 18 U.S.C. § 1162 and 28 U.S.C. § 1360. Section 402 of Title IV, 25 U.S.C. § 1322, tracks the language of § 4 of Pub.L. 280. Section 406 of Title IV, 25 U.S.C. § 1326, which provides for Indian consent, refers to "State jurisdiction acquired pursuant to this subchapter with respect to criminal offenses or civil causes of action. . . ." It is true, of course, that the primary interpretation of § 4 must have reference to the legislative history of the Congress that enacted it rather than to the history of Acts of a later Congress. Nevertheless, Title IV of the 1968 Act is intimately related to § 4, as it provides the method for further state assumptions of the jurisdiction conferred by § 4. . . . It would be difficult to suppose that Congress in 1968 intended the meaning of § 4 to vary depending upon the time and method by which particular States acquired jurisdiction. And certainly the legislative history of Title IV makes it difficult to construe § 4 jurisdiction acquired pursuant to Title IV as extending general state civil regulatory authority, including taxing power, to govern Indian reservations. Senator Ervin, who offered and principally sponsored Title IV, see *Kennerly v. District Court of Montana*, 400 U.S., at 429 n. 5, referred to § 1360 civil jurisdiction as follows:

> "Certain representatives of municipalities have charged that the repeal of [§ 7 of] Public Law 280 would hamper air and water pollution controls and provide a haven for undesirable, unrestricted business establishments within tribal land borders. Not only does this assertion show the lack of faith that certain cities have in the ability and desire of Indian tribes to better themselves and their environment, but, *most importantly, it is irrelevant, since Public Law 280 relates primarily to the application of state civil and criminal law in court proceedings,* and has no bearing on programs set up by the States to assist economic and environmental development in Indian territory." (Emphasis added.) Hearing before the Subcommittee on Indian Affairs of the House Committee on Interior and Insular Affairs, No. 90–23, 90th Cong., 2d Sess., 136 (1968).

III

Other considerations also support our construction. Today's congressional policy toward reservation Indians may less clearly than in 1953 favor their assimilation, but Pub.L. 280 was plainly not meant to effect total assimilation. . . . [T]here is notably absent any conferral of state jurisdiction over the tribes themselves, and § 4(c), 28 U.S.C. § 1360(c), providing for the "full force and effect" of any tribal ordinances or customs "heretofore or hereafter adopted by an Indian tribe . . . if not inconsistent with any applicable civil law of the State," contemplates the continuing vitality of tribal government.

Moreover, the same Congress that enacted Pub.L. 280 also enacted several termination Acts—legislation which is cogent proof that Congress knew well how to express its intent directly when that intent was to subject reservation Indians to the full sweep of state laws and state taxation. * * * Thus, rather than inferring a negative implication of a grant of general taxing power in § 4(a) from the exclusion of certain taxation in § 4(b), we conclude that construing Pub.L. 280 *in pari materia* with these Acts shows that if Congress in enacting Pub.L. 280 had intended to confer upon the States general civil regulatory powers, including taxation, over reservation Indians, it would have expressly said so.

IV

Additionally, we note that § 4(b), excluding "taxation of any real or personal property . . . belonging to any Indian or any Indian tribe . . . that is held in trust by the United States or is subject to a restriction against alienation imposed by the United States," is not obviously the narrow exclusion of state taxation that the Minnesota Supreme Court read it to be. On its face the statute is not clear whether the exclusion is applicable only to taxes levied directly on the trust property specifically, or whether it also excludes taxation on activities taking place in conjunction with such property and income deriving from its use. And even if read narrowly to apply only to taxation levied against trust property directly, § 4(b) certainly does not expressly authorize all other state taxation of reservation Indians.

Moreover, the express prohibition of any "alienation, encumbrance, or taxation" of any trust property can be read as prohibiting state courts, acquiring jurisdiction over civil controversies involving reservation Indians pursuant to § 4, from applying state laws or enforcing judgments in ways that would effectively result in the "alienation, encumbrance, or taxation" of trust property. Indeed, any other reading of this provision of § 4(b) is difficult to square with the identical prohibition contained in § 2(b) of the Act, which applies the same restrictions upon States exercising criminal jurisdiction over reservation Indians. It would simply make no sense to infer from the identical language of § 2(b) a general power in § 2(a) to tax Indians in all other respects since § 2(a) deals only with criminal jurisdiction.

Indeed, § 4(b) in its entirety may be read as simply a reaffirmation of the existing reservation Indian-Federal Government relationship in all respects save the conferral of state-court jurisdiction to adjudicate private civil causes of action involving Indians. * * *

Finally, in construing this "admittedly ambiguous" statute, *Board of County Comm'rs v. Seber*, 318 U.S., at 713, we must be guided by that "eminently sound and vital canon," Northern Cheyenne Tribe v.

Hollowbreast, 425 U.S. 649 (1976), that "statutes passed for the benefit of dependent Indian tribes ... are to be liberally construed, doubtful expressions being resolved in favor of the Indians." Alaska Pacific Fisheries v. United States, 248 U.S. 78, 89 (1918). * * * What we recently said of a claim that Congress had terminated an Indian reservation by means of an ambiguous statute is equally applicable here to the respondent's claim that § 4(a) of Pub.L. 280 is a clear grant of power to tax, and hence a termination of traditional Indian immunity from state taxation:

> "Congress was fully aware of the means by which termination could be effected. But clear termination language was not employed in the ... Act. This being so, we are not inclined to infer an intention to terminate. . . . A congressional determination to terminate must be expressed on the face of the Act or be clear from the surrounding circumstances and legislative history." Mattz v. Arnett, 412 U.S. 481, 504–505 (1973).

[Reversed.]

NOTES

1.   The reasoning in *Bryan* is drawn in large part from Santa Rosa Band of Indians v. Kings County, 532 F.2d 655 (9th Cir.1975). *Santa Rosa* was essentially based on an analysis of the issues contained in the law review articles by Professor Carole Goldberg proving the occasional power of the professor's pen.

2.   *Bryan* addressed the question of state regulatory and taxing jurisdiction. The absence of such jurisdiction over Indians and Indian property is clear. State regulatory and taxing jurisdiction over non-Indians, however, depends on the same analysis that applies to Indian country in states not covered by Public Law 280.

3.   Is the rule of construction announced at the end of note 14 a principled method of construing Indian statutes enacted in earlier eras of federal policy?

4.   Lower courts, interpreting *Bryan's* exclusion of state taxing and regulatory laws from the civil jurisdiction assumed by Public Law 280 states, developed an approach that sought to determine whether a state law was civil and regulatory in nature, and therefore not applicable to the reservation, or criminal and prohibitory in nature and therefore applicable to the reservation in P.L. 280 states. Where does a court draw the line between regulatory and prohibitory state law? Are state "controlled substances" laws regulatory? Is antitrust legislation prohibitory? In Wisconsin, a law providing for the civil commitment of sexually violent individuals was found to be criminal-prohibitory in nature. In re Commitment of Burgess, 665 N.W.2d 124 (Wis.2003). The Minnesota Supreme Court held that most of the states' traffic laws, except those prohibiting drinking and driving and reckless or dangerous driving, are civil-regulatory laws, and therefore the state lacks jurisdiction

under Public Law 280 to enforce them within reservation boundaries. State v. Stone, 572 N.W.2d 725 (Minn.1997). However, the state law against driving after revocation of a license was held to be criminal-prohibitory. State v. Losh, 755 N.W.2d 736 (Minn 2008). On the other hand, State v. George, 905 P.2d 626 (Idaho 1995), found that Idaho's traffic laws were criminal-prohibitory in nature, and therefore enforceable on reservations within the state.

5. In Lamere v. Superior Court, 131 Cal.App.4th 1059 (2005), the court held that Public Law 280 did not grant the state court jurisdiction over alleged violations of tribal and federal law arising out of a dispute over tribal enrollment. See also Ackerman v. Edwards, 121 Cal.App.4th 946 (2004). Neither of these decisions turned on the *Bryan* analysis, but instead carved out an internal tribal relations exception to Public Law 280.

CAROLE GOLDBERG-AMBROSE, PUBLIC LAW 280 AND THE PROBLEM OF LAWLESSNESS IN CALIFORNIA INDIAN COUNTRY
44 UCLA L.Rev. 1405, 1415–19 (1997).

Public Law 280 has had both direct and indirect effects on the legal regime within the Indian country to which it applies. Both types of consequences have implications for the problem of lawlessness.

* * *

The direct effects of Public Law 280 were twofold: First it extended state criminal jurisdiction and civil judicial jurisdiction over reservation Indians in certain states; second, it eliminated special federal criminal jurisdiction over reservation areas in the states specifically named in the law. Thus, the law substituted state for federal legal authority on all the designated reservations. No mention was made of tribal authority. Historically, states resented the special rights and status of tribes under federal law, and the federal government often intervened to protect the tribes. Public Law 280 did not strip the tribes of most of these rights and did not erase the trust status of their lands. Indeed, there were several exceptions to state jurisdiction built into the law to protect tribal land, water, hunting, and fishing rights. But by giving the states additional authority on reservations, it empowered an often hostile force.

In view of the fact that federal courts were not authorized to hear many civil and criminal disputes arising on reservations in the pre-Public Law 280 era, Public Law 280 also expanded the realm of non-Indian control over reservation activities. State courts could suddenly hear reservation-based civil disputes and criminal cases that federal courts would not have entertained in the past, and that tribes would have treated as within their sole purview.

The direct effects of Public of Public Law 280 were not the only effects, however. Although this law addressed only the question of which governments had power to resolve criminal and civil disputes on reservations, its passage signaled a change in the philosophy shaping federal Indian policy. No longer would the federal government profess (if not discharge) responsibility for the welfare of tribes and tribal members. Instead, states would be asked to assume that responsibility, just as they were assuming responsibility for the education, welfare, and health care of needy non-Indians. Public Law 280 was just a small step toward the realization of that vision. But the federal Indian bureaucracy—the Bureau of Indian Affairs—used it as the rationale for redirecting federal support on a wholesale basis away from tribes in the "Public Law 280 states" and toward all other tribes.

Nowhere was this reallocation of funds more evident than in California, where Congress also singled out forty-one small reservations (out of more than one hundred in the state) for termination—meaning that these tribes would no longer be recognized by the federal government, and lands would no longer enjoy federal trust protection. Together, termination and Public Law 280 formed a toxic brew, eating away at the funds authorized by federal law for Indian welfare, education, and health care in California. Moreover, for California, the advent of Public Law 280 meant that tribes were never "dealt in" to many of the new federal Indian programs that Congress and the Bureau instituted in the 1960s and 1970s, largely in response to social movements of that period.

The most striking illustration of this phenomenon is funding for tribal law enforcement and tribal courts. Until the middle of this century, federal courts of Indian offenses handled dispute resolution on many reservations, ruthlessly imposing non-Indian norms on tribal members. In the 1960s, tribes in the non-Public Law 280 states began to form their own judicial and law enforcement systems, partly to fend off state jurisdiction and partly to express their own sovereignty. Federal funding for tribal courts and police escalated sharply outside of California, fueled by a growing number of United States Supreme Court decisions affirming exclusive tribal jurisdiction over reservation-based disputes. In California, however, the Bureau refused to support tribal justice systems, on the ground that Public Law 280 made tribal jurisdiction unnecessary and perhaps even eliminated such tribal authority. In fact, courts, attorneys general, and federal administrators have affirmed that tribal legal authority survived Public Law 280. But legal authority requires infrastructure and institutions, and Public Law 280 stood in their way.

Even if one accepts the claim that many reservations were lawless at the time Public Law 280 was enacted, a tragic irony is inescapable. Taking account of the direct and indirect effects described above, Public Law 280 has itself become a source of lawlessness on reservations. Two different and distinct varieties of lawlessness are discernable. First, jurisdictional vacuums or gaps have been created, often precipitating the use of self-help remedies that border on or erupt into violence. Sometimes these gaps exist because no government has authority. Sometimes they arise because the government(s) that may have authority in theory has no institutional support or incentive for the exercise of that authority. * * * Second, when state law enforcement does intervene, gross abuses of authority are not uncommon. In other words, power is uncabined by the law that is supposed to constrain it. * * *

NOTES

1.   In 2006, Professors Goldberg and Duane Champagne published a comprehensive study of Public Law 280's effectiveness. See Carole Goldberg & Duane Champagne, *Is Public Law 280 Fit for the Twenty-First Century? Some Data at Last*, 38 Conn.L.Rev. 697 (2006):

> Public Law 280 is out of step with the prevailing federal policy of tribal self-determination and has garnered considerable criticism from tribal communities. * * * [S]tate and county police in Public Law 280 jurisdictions either provide less satisfactory service than those in non-Public Law 280 jurisdictions, or have an assessment of their own effectiveness that is more divergent from community assessments than in non-Public Law 280 jurisdictions.

Id. at 729.

2.   In the 1940s, legislation substantially similar to Public Law 280 ceded criminal jurisdiction to Kansas, North Dakota, and Iowa, but added that: "This section shall not deprive the courts of the United States of jurisdiction over offenses defined by the laws of the United States committed by or against Indians on Indian reservations." The Supreme Court said that the language saving federal jurisdiction over crimes covered by the Major Crimes Act in the 1940 Kansas Act did not make such jurisdiction exclusive in Negonsott v. Samuels, 507 U.S. 99 (1993). The defendant, a Kickapoo tribal member, contended that the state could not prosecute him for an aggravated assault on the Kickapoo Reservation in Kansas. He argued the effect of the Act was to give Kansas jurisdiction only over crimes—essentially misdemeanors—that were not covered by the federal laws comprehended by the saving clause. The Court said that: "the most logical meaning of this proviso, we believe, is that federal courts shall retain their jurisdiction to try all offenses subject to federal jurisdiction under 18 U.S.C. §§ 1152 and 1153, while Kansas courts shall have jurisdiction to try persons for the same conduct when it violates state law." 507 U.S. at 105. What is the effect of the absence of language saving or terminating federal criminal jurisdiction in Public Law 280?

3.   What can tribes do to address the "lawlessness" that Goldberg argues has resulted from Public Law 280? Goldberg makes it clear that Congress was allocating federal and state jurisdiction and not addressing tribal jurisdiction. Tribal jurisdiction, then, should survive to the extent that it exists in non-Public Law 280 states. Tribal criminal jurisdiction, for instance, survived

Public Law 280 but remains concurrent with the state. See Walker v. Rushing, 898 F.2d 672, 674 (8th Cir.1990) where the court stated:

> Public Law 280 did not itself divest Indian tribes of their sovereign power to punish their own members for violations of tribal law. Nothing in the wording of Public Law 280 or its legislative history precludes concurrent tribal authority. F. Cohen, Cohen's Handbook of Federal Indian Law 344. As both the Supreme Court and this court have made clear, limitations on an Indian tribe's power to punish its own members must be clearly set forth by Congress.

See also Hester v. Redwood County, 885 F. Supp. 2d 934, 939 (D.Minn.2012) ("The Lower Sioux Community retains inherent criminal jurisdiction over its own members within its territorial boundaries.") (citing *Walker*).

Indian tribes in Public Law 280 states also retain the authority to operate law enforcement agencies. Cabazon Band of Mission Indians v. Smith, 34 F. Supp. 2d 1195 (C.D.Cal.1998). See also Cabazon Band of Mission Indians v. Smith, 388 F.3d 691 (9th Cir.2004) (holding that state law barring tribal police vehicles from utilizing emergency light bars was invalid).

The *Walker* court's reasoning used to sustain concurrent tribal criminal jurisdiction in Public Law 280 states has been applied to find tribal civil jurisdiction concurrent with the state. E.g., Teague v. Bad River Band of the Lake Superior Tribe of Chippewa Indians, 612 N.W.2d 709 (Wis.2000); Native Village of Venetie I.R.A. Council v. State of Alaska, 944 F.2d 548 (9th Cir.1991); Confederated Tribes of the Colville Reservation v. Superior Court of Okanogan County, 945 F.2d 1138 (9th Cir.1991) (child custody matters).

SECTION D. TRIBAL CRIMINAL JURISDICTION

Indian tribes initially possessed exclusive jurisdiction over crimes committed by one tribal member against another in Indian country—even when the crime was murder, as in Ex parte Crow Dog, 109 U.S. 556 (1883). Tribal criminal jurisdiction over Indians in Indian country derives from inherent sovereignty, so that constitutional limitations on states and the federal governments do not apply. Talton v. Mayes, 163 U.S. 376 (1896). Similarly, since tribal authority over members does not trace to a federal source, double jeopardy does not prohibit concurrent prosecutions by the two sovereigns. United States v. Wheeler, 435 U.S. 313 (1978).

Talton and *Wheeler* are only two instances where the Supreme Court has acknowledged the authority of Indian tribes to prosecute their own members. Others include Ex parte Crow Dog, 109 U.S. 556 (1883) (inherent authority); Westmoreland v. United States, 155 U.S. 545 (1895) (authorized by treaty to prosecute non-Indians who became members of the tribe); Alberty v. United States, 162 U.S. 499 (1896) (same). Congress has acknowledged tribal criminal jurisdiction over tribal members expressly at least since the Trade and Intercourse Act. 18 U.S.C. § 1152 (referencing "any Indian committing any offense in the Indian country who has been punished by the local law of the tribe", first enacted in 1790). The Indian Civil Rights Act imposes limitations and obligations upon tribes in enforcing their laws, including procedural guarantees and sentence limitations.

Note the unfinished chart below noting tribal criminal jurisdiction over crimes committed:

Who was the defendant?	What was the crime?	Jurisdiction (and possible sentence)
Indian		
Nonmember Indian		
Non-Indian		

In the 1970s and 1980s, as tribes began to pass more laws, expand their tribal court systems and assert the right to regulate the conduct of both non-Indians and Indians in Indian country, non-Indian challenges to their sovereignty and jurisdiction increased. However, as the Supreme Court held in 1978, the same year it decided *Wheeler*, tribal criminal jurisdiction over non-Indians in Indian country was relinquished when tribes "submitt[ed] to the overriding sovereignty of the United States." Oliphant v. Suquamish Indian Tribe, 435 U.S. 191 (1978).

1. TRIBAL CRIMINAL JURISDICTION OVER NON-INDIANS

OLIPHANT V. SUQUAMISH INDIAN TRIBE
Supreme Court of the United States, 1978.
435 U.S. 191, 98 S.Ct. 1011, 55 L.Ed.2d 209.

MR. JUSTICE REHNQUIST delivered the opinion of the Court.

* * * Located on Puget Sound across from the city of Seattle, the Port Madison Reservation [of the Suquamish Tribe] is a checkerboard of tribal community land, allotted Indian lands, property held in fee-simple by non-Indians, and various roads and public highways maintained by Kitsap County.[9]

---

[9] According to the District Court's findings of fact, "[T]he Port Madison Indian Reservation consists of approximately 7276 acres of which approximately 63% thereof is owned in fee-simple absolute by non-Indians and the remainder 37% is Indian owned lands subject to the trust status of the United States, consisting mostly of unimproved acreage upon which no persons reside. Residing on the reservation is an estimated population of approximately 2,928 non-Indians living in 976 dwelling units. There lives on the reservation approximately 50 members of the Suquamish Indian Tribe. Within the reservation are numerous public highways of the State of Washington, public schools, public utilities and other facilities in which neither the Suquamish Indian Tribe nor the United States has any ownership or interest." * * *

The Suquamish Indians are governed by a tribal government which in 1973 adopted a Law and Order Code. The Code, which covers a variety of offenses from theft to rape, purports to extend the Tribe's criminal jurisdiction over both Indians and non-Indians. Proceedings are held in the Suquamish Indian Provisional Court. Pursuant to the Indian Civil Rights Act of 1968, 25 U.S.C. § 1302, defendants are entitled to many of the due process protections accorded to defendants in federal or state criminal proceedings. However, the guarantees are not identical. Non-Indians, for example, are excluded from Suquamish tribal court juries.[4]

Both petitioners are non-Indian residents of the Port Madison Reservation. Petitioner Mark David Oliphant was arrested by tribal authorities during the Suquamish's annual Chief Seattle Days celebration and charged with assaulting a tribal officer and resisting arrest. After arraignment before the tribal court, Oliphant was released on his own recognizance. Petitioner Daniel B. Belgarde was arrested by tribal authorities after an alleged high-speed race along the reservation highways that only ended when Belgarde collided with a tribal police vehicle. Belgarde posted bail and was released. Six days later he was arraigned and charged under the tribal code with "recklessly endangering another person" and injuring tribal property. Tribal court proceedings against both petitioners have been stayed pending a decision in this case.

* * * [The District Court and the Ninth Circuit Court of Appeals upheld tribal jurisdiction.] We granted certiorari, 431 U.S. 964, to decide whether Indian tribal courts have criminal jurisdiction over non-Indians. We decide that they do not.

I

Respondents do not contend that their exercise of criminal jurisdiction over non-Indians stems from affirmative congressional authorization or treaty provision. Instead, respondents urge that such jurisdiction flows automatically from the "Tribe's retained inherent powers of government over the Port Madison Indian Reservation." * * *

The Suquamish Indian Tribe does not stand alone today in its assumption of criminal jurisdiction over non-Indians. Of the 127 reservation court systems that currently exercise criminal jurisdiction in the United States, 33 purport to extend that jurisdiction to non-Indians.

* * *

The effort by Indian tribal courts to exercise criminal jurisdiction over non-Indians, however, is a relatively new phenomenon. And where the effort has been made in the past, it has been held that the jurisdiction did not exist. Until the middle of this century, few Indian tribes maintained

---

4   * * * In 1977, the Suquamish Tribe amended its Law and Order Code to provide that only Suquamish tribal members shall serve as jurors in tribal court.

any semblance of a formal court system. Offenses by one Indian against another were usually handled by social and religious pressure and not by formal judicial processes; emphasis was on restitution rather than on punishment. In 1834 the Commissioner of Indian Affairs described the then status of Indian criminal systems: "With the exception of two or three tribes, who have within a few years past attempted to establish some few laws and regulations amongst themselves, the Indian tribes are without laws, and the chiefs without much authority to exercise any restraint." H.R.Rep. No. 474, 23d Cong., 1st Sess., at 91 (1834).

It is therefore not surprising to find no specific discussion of the problem before us in the volumes of United States Reports. But the problem did not lie entirely dormant for two centuries. A few tribes during the 19th century did have formal criminal systems. From the earliest treaties with these tribes, it was apparently assumed that the tribes did not have criminal jurisdiction over non-Indians absent a congressional statute or treaty provision to that effect. For example, the 1830 Treaty with the Choctaw Indian Tribe, which had one of the most sophisticated of tribal structures, guaranteed to the Tribe "the jurisdiction and government of all the persons and property that may be within their limits." Despite the broad terms of this governmental guarantee, however, the Choctaws at the conclusion of this treaty provision "express *a wish* that Congress *may grant* to the Choctaws the right of punishing by their own laws any white man who shall come into their nation, and infringe any of their national regulations."[8] Such a request for affirmative congressional authority is inconsistent with respondents' belief that criminal jurisdiction over non-Indians is inherent in tribal sovereignty. Faced by attempts of the Choctaw Tribe to try non-Indian offenders in the early-1800's the United States Attorneys General also concluded that the Choctaws did not have criminal

---

[8] The history of Indian treaties in the United States is consistent with the principle that Indian tribes may not assume criminal jurisdiction over non-Indians without the permission of Congress. The earliest treaties typically expressly provided that "any citizen of the United States, who shall do an injury to any Indian of the [tribal] nation, or to any other Indian or Indians residing in their towns, and under their protection, shall be punished according to the laws of the United States." See, e.g., Treaty with the Shawnees, Art. III, 7 Stat. 26 (1786). * * * Far from representing a recognition of any inherent Indian criminal jurisdiction over non-Indians settling on tribal lands, these provisions were instead intended as a means of discouraging non-Indian settlements on Indian territory, in contravention of treaty provisions to the contrary. See 5 Annals of Congress 903–904 (April 9, 1796). Later treaties dropped this provision and provided instead that non-Indian settlers would be removed by the United States upon complaint being lodged by the tribe. See, e.g., Treaty with the Sacs and Foxes, 7 Stat. 84 (1804).

As the relationship between Indian tribes and the United States developed through the passage of time, specific provisions for the punishment of non-Indians by the United States, rather than by the tribes, slowly disappeared from the treaties. Thus, for example, none of the treaties signed by Washington Indians in the 1850's explicitly proscribed criminal prosecution and punishment of non-Indians by the Indian tribes. * * * When it was felt necessary to expressly spell out respective jurisdictions, later treaties still provided that criminal jurisdiction over non-Indians would be in the United States. *See, e.g.,* Treaty with the Utah-Tabequache Band, Art. 6, 13 Stat. 674 (1863).

* * *

jurisdiction over non-Indians absent congressional authority. See 2 Opinions of the Attorney General 693 (1834); 7 Opinions of the Attorney General 174 (1855). * * *

At least one court has previously considered the power of Indian courts to try non-Indians and it also held against jurisdiction.[9] * * * Ex parte Kenyon, 14 Fed.Cases 353 (WD Ark.1878). * * * The conclusion of Judge Parker was reaffirmed only recently in a 1970 Opinion of the Solicitor of the Department of the Interior. See 77 I.D. 113 (1970).[11]

While Congress was concerned almost from its beginning with the special problems of law enforcement on the Indian reservations, it did not initially address itself to the problem of tribal jurisdiction over non-Indians. For the reasons previously stated, there was little reason to be concerned with assertions of tribal court jurisdiction over non-Indians because of the absence of formal tribal judicial systems. * * *

It was in 1834 that Congress was first directly faced with the prospect of Indians trying non-Indians. In the Western Territory Bill, Congress proposed to create an Indian territory beyond the western-directed destination of the settlers; the territory was to be governed by a confederation of Indian tribes and was expected ultimately to become a State of the Union. While the bill would have created a political territory with broad governing powers, Congress was careful not to give the tribes of the territory criminal jurisdiction over United States officials and citizens traveling through the area.[13] The reasons were quite practical:

> "Officers, and persons in the service of the United States, and persons required to reside in the Indian country by treaty stipulation, must necessarily be placed under the protection, and subject to the laws of the United States. To persons merely travelling in the Indian country the same protection is extended. The want of fixed laws, of competent tribunals of justice, which must for some time continue in the Indian country, absolutely requires for the peace of both sides that this protection be extended." H.R.Rep. No. 474, 23d Cong., 1st Sess., at 18 (1834).

Congress' concern over criminal jurisdiction in this proposed Indian Territory contrasts markedly with its total failure to address criminal jurisdiction over non-Indians on other reservations, which frequently bordered non-Indian settlements. The contrast suggests that Congress

---

[9] According to Felix Cohen's Handbook of Federal Indian Law (U.S. Dept. of the Interior 1941), "attempts of tribes to exercise jurisdiction over non-Indians * * * have been generally condemned by the federal courts since the end of the treaty-making period, and the writ of habeas corpus has been used to discharge white defendants from tribal custody."

[11] The 1970 Opinion of the Solicitor was withdrawn in 1974 but has not been replaced. No reason was given for the withdrawal.

[13] * * * While the Western Territory bill was resubmitted several times in revised form, it was never passed. * * *

shared the view of the Executive Branch and lower federal courts that Indian tribal courts were without jurisdiction to try non-Indians.

This unspoken assumption was also evident in other congressional actions during the 19th century. [The opinion discusses amendments to the Nonintercourse Act in 1854 and enactment of the Major Crimes Act of 1885.]

* * * While Congress never expressly forbade Indian tribes to impose criminal penalties on non-Indians, we now make express our implicit conclusion of nearly a century ago that Congress consistently believed this to be the necessary result of its repeated legislative actions.

In a 1960 Senate Report, that body expressly confirmed its assumption that Indian tribal courts are without inherent jurisdiction to try non-Indians, and must depend on the Federal Government for protection from intruders.[15] In considering a statute that would prohibit unauthorized entry upon Indian land for the purpose of hunting or fishing, the Senate Report noted:

* * *

> * * * One who comes on such lands without permission may be prosecuted under State law but a non-Indian trespasser on an Indian reservation enjoys immunity. *This is by reason of the fact that Indian tribal law is enforcible against Indians only; not against non-Indians*
>
> *Non-Indians are not subject to the jurisdiction of Indian courts and cannot be tried in Indian courts on trespass charges.* Further, there are no Federal laws which can be invoked against trespassers.

* * *

S.Rep. No. 1686, 86th Cong., 2d Sess., 2–3 (1960) (emphasis added).

II

While not conclusive on the issue before us, the commonly shared presumption of Congress, the Executive Branch, and lower federal courts that tribal courts do not have the power to try non-Indians carries considerable weight. "Indian law" draws principally upon the treaties drawn and executed by the Executive Branch and legislation passed by

---

[15] In 1977, a Congressional Policy Review Commission, citing the lower court decisions in Oliphant and Belgarde, concluded that "[t]here is an established legal basis for tribes to exercise jurisdiction over non-Indians." 1 American Indian Policy Review Commission, Final Report 114, 117, and 152–154 (1977). However, the Commission's report does not deny that for almost two hundred years before the lower courts decided Oliphant and Belgarde, the three branches of the Federal Government were in apparent agreement that Indian tribes do not have jurisdiction over non-Indians. As the Vice-Chairman of the Commission noted in dissent, "such jurisdiction has generally not been asserted and . . . the lack of legislation on this point reflects a congressional assumption that there was no such tribal jurisdiction." Id. at 587.

Congress. These instruments, which beyond their actual text form the backdrop for the intricate web of judicially made Indian law, cannot be interpreted in isolation but must be read in light of the common notions of the day and the assumptions of those who drafted them.

While in isolation the Treaty of Point Elliott, 12 Stat. 927 (1855), would appear to be silent as to tribal criminal jurisdiction over non-Indians, the addition of historical perspective casts substantial doubt upon the existence of such jurisdiction. In the Ninth Article, for example, the Suquamish "acknowledge their dependence on the Government of the United States." As Chief Justice Marshall explained in Worcester v. Georgia, 6 Pet. 515, 551–552, 554 (1832), such an acknowledgement is not a mere abstract recognition of the United States' sovereignty. "The Indian nations were, from their situation, necessarily dependent on [the United States] for their protection from lawless and injurious intrusions into their country." Id., at 555. By acknowledging their dependence on the United States, in the Treaty of Point Elliott, the Suquamish were in all probability recognizing that the United States would arrest and try non-Indian intruders who came within their Reservation. Other provisions of the Treaty also point to the absence of tribal jurisdiction. Thus the Tribe "agree[s] not to shelter or conceal offenders against the laws of the United States, but to deliver them up to the authorities for trial." Read in conjunction with 18 U.S.C. § 1152, which extends federal enclave law to non-Indian offenses on Indian reservations, this provision implies that the Suquamish are to promptly deliver up any non-Indian offender, rather than try and punish him themselves.[17]

By themselves, these treaty provisions would probably not be sufficient to remove criminal jurisdiction over non-Indians if the Tribe otherwise retained such jurisdiction. But an examination of our earlier precedents satisfies us that, even ignoring treaty provisions and congressional policy, Indians do not have criminal jurisdiction over non-Indians absent affirmative delegation of such power by Congress. Indian tribes do retain elements of "quasi-sovereign" authority after ceding their lands to the United States and announcing their dependence on the Federal Government. See Cherokee Nation v. Georgia, 5 Peters 1, 15 (1831). But the tribes' retained powers are not such that they are limited only by specific restrictions in treaties or congressional enactments. As the Court of Appeals recognized, Indian tribes are proscribed from exercising both those powers of autonomous states that are expressly terminated by Congress *and* those powers *"inconsistent with their status."*

---

[17] In interpreting Indian treaties and statutes, "[d]oubtful expressions are to be resolved in favor of the weak and defenseless people who are the wards of the nation, dependent upon its protection and good faith." *McClanahan v. Arizona State Tax Comm'n*, 411 U.S. 164, 174 (1973). But treaty and statutory provisions which are not clear on their face may "be clear from the surrounding circumstances and legislative history." Cf. *DeCoteau v. District Cty. Ct.*, 420 U.S. 425, 444 (1975).

Indian reservations are "a part of the territory of the United States." United States v. Rogers, 4 How. 567, 571 (1846). Indian tribes "hold and occupy [the reservations] with the assent of the United States, and under their authority." Id., at 572. Upon incorporation into the territory of the United States, the Indian tribes thereby come under the territorial sovereignty of the United States and their exercise of separate power is constrained so as not to conflict with the interests of this overriding sovereignty. "[T]heir rights to complete sovereignty, as independent nations [are] necessarily diminished." Johnson v. McIntosh, 8 Wheat. 543, 574 (1823).

We have already described some of the inherent limitations on tribal powers that stem from their incorporation into the United States. In *Johnson v. McIntosh*, supra, we noted that the Indian tribes' "power to dispose of the soil at their own will, to whomsoever they pleased," was inherently lost to the overriding sovereignty of the United States. And in *Cherokee Nation v. Georgia*, supra, the Chief Justice observed that since Indian tribes are "completely under the sovereignty and dominion of the United States, . . . any attempt [by foreign nations] to acquire their lands, or to form a political connexion with them, would be considered by all as an invasion of our territory, and an act of hostility."

Protection of territory within its external political boundaries is, of course, as central to the sovereign interests of the United States as it is to any other sovereign nation from the formation of the Union and the adoption of the Bill of Rights, the United States has manifested an equally great solicitude that its citizens be protected by the United States from unwarranted intrusions on their personal liberty. The power of the United States to try and criminally punish is an important manifestation of the power to restrict personal liberty. By submitting to the overriding sovereignty of the United States, Indian tribes therefore necessarily give up their power to try non-Indian citizens of the United States except in a manner acceptable to Congress. This principle would have been obvious a century ago when most Indian tribes were characterized by a "want of fixed laws [and] of competent tribunals of justice." H.R.Rep. No. 474, 23d Cong., 1st Sess., at 18 (1834). It should be no less obvious today, even though present-day Indian tribal courts embody dramatic advances over their historical antecedents.

In Ex parte Crow Dog, 109 U.S. 556 (1883), the Court was faced with almost the inverse of the issue before us here—whether, prior to the passage of the Major Crimes Act, federal courts had jurisdiction to try Indians who had offended against fellow Indians on reservation land. In concluding that criminal jurisdiction was exclusively in the tribe, it found particular guidance in the "nature and circumstances of the case." The United States was seeking to extend United States "law, by argument and inference only, ... over aliens and strangers; over the members of a community separated by race [and] tradition, ... from the authority and power which seeks to impose upon them the restraints of an external and unknown code ...; which judges them by a standard made by others and not for them.... It tries them, not by their peers, nor by the customs of their people, nor the law of their land, but by ... a different race, according to the law of a social state of which they have an imperfect conception...." Id. at 571.

These considerations, applied here to the non-Indian rather than Indian offender, speak equally strongly against the validity of respondents' contention that Indian tribes, although fully subordinated to the sovereignty of the United States, retain the power to try non-Indians according to their own customs and procedure.

* * *

* * * We recognize that some Indian tribal court systems have become increasingly sophisticated and resemble in many respects their state counterparts. We also acknowledge that with the passage of the Indian Civil Rights Act of 1968, which extends certain basic procedural rights to *anyone* tried in Indian tribal court, many of the dangers that might have accompanied the exercise by tribal courts of criminal jurisdiction over non-Indians only a few decades ago have disappeared. Finally, we are not unaware of the prevalence of non-Indian crime on today's reservations which the tribes forcefully argue requires the ability to try non-Indians. But these are considerations for Congress to weigh in deciding whether Indian tribes should finally be authorized to try non-Indians. They have little relevance to the principles which lead us to conclude that Indian tribes do not have inherent jurisdiction to try and punish non-Indians. The judgments below are therefore

Reversed.

MR. JUSTICE BRENNAN took no part in the consideration or decision of this case.

[MR. JUSTICE MARSHALL's dissent omitted.]

I agree with the court below that the "power to preserve order on the reservation ... is a sine qua non of the sovereignty that the Suquamish originally possessed." In the absence of affirmative withdrawal by treaty or statute, I am of the view that Indian tribes enjoy as a necessary aspect of their retained sovereignty the right to try and punish all persons who commit offenses against tribal law within the reservation. Accordingly, I dissent.

NOTES

1. Recall the language of United States v. Wheeler, 435 U.S. 313 (1978), that reaffirmed the traditional principles of tribal self-government. Although *Oliphant* and *Wheeler* might seem to have emanated from different planets, or at least from different courts in different eras, *Wheeler* was handed down just two weeks after *Oliphant*. See generally Ezekiel J.N. Fletcher, *Trapped in the Spring of 1978: The Continuing Impact of the Supreme Court's Decisions in* Oliphant, Wheeler, *and* Martinez, 55 Fed.Law. 34 (Mar./Apr., 2008).

2. Normally, the Supreme Court has applied a clear statement rule in ascertaining whether the United States has abrogated an aspect of tribal sovereignty, such as criminal jurisdiction. In Ex parte Crow Dog, 118 U.S. 556 (1883) , the Court applied a clear statement rule to find that federal statutory language did not explicitly sustain an assertion of federal criminal jurisdiction over Indian country crime:

> To give to the clauses in the treaty of 1868 and the agreement of 1877 effect, so as to uphold the jurisdiction exercised in this case, would be to reverse in this instance the general policy of the government towards the Indians, as declared in many statutes and treaties, and recognized in many decisions of this court, from the beginning to the present time. *To justify such a departure, in such a case, requires a clear expression of the intention of congress*, and that we have not been able to find.

Id. at 572 (emphasis added). Do the authorities relied upon by the Court constitute a clear statement of federal intent to strip Indian tribes of criminal jurisdiction over non-Indians?

3. In *Oliphant,* Justice Rehnquist invoked a crucial passage from the Court's late nineteenth century decision in *Crow Dog* to illustrate the principle seemingly underlying *Oliphant*: that it is unfair to try "a different race, according to the law of a social state of which they have an imperfect conception." *Oliphant*, 435 U.S. at 211. Compare the original, unedited passage from *Crow Dog,* 118 U.S. at 571, with the edited version quoted in *Oliphant.* Consider Professor Williams' argument that the *Oliphant* Court, far from showing sensitivity to intercultural differences, sought an homogenizing result:

> In its own efficient and subtle ways, Rehnquist's text works to assure that tribal "self-government" will be carried out in a self-policing manner. Tribes must exercise their "rights" to self-determination so as not to conflict with the interests of the dominant sovereign. In effect, this form of discourse enforces a highly efficient process of legal auto-genocide, the ultimate hegemonic effect of which is to instruct the savage to self-extinguish all troublesome expressions of difference that diverge from the white man's own hierarchic, universalized world view.

Robert A. Williams, Jr., *The Algebra of Federal Indian Law: The Hard Trail of Decolonizing and Americanizing the White Man's Indian Jurisprudence*, 1986 Wis.L.Rev. 219, 273–74. See also Robert A. Williams, Jr., Like a Loaded Weapon: The Rehnquist Court, Indian Rights, and the Legal History of Racism in America, ch. 7 (2005). Concerning Justice Rehnquist's history, recent scholarship indicates that the Cherokee Nation long had exercised criminal jurisdiction over non-Indians, and at least in one early 19th century instance, prosecuted a non-Indian referred to the Cherokees by federal officials. See J. Matthew Martin, *The Nature and Extent of the Exercise of Criminal Jurisdiction by the Cherokee Supreme Court: 1823–1835*, 32 N.C. Central L.Rev. 27 (2009).

4.   The Court left open the possibility that Congress could delegate authority to tribes to prosecute non-Indians for crimes committed on the reservation. Although such delegations are relatively rare, in United States v. Mazurie, 419 U.S. 544 (1975) the Court upheld a federal criminal conviction of non-Indian tavern owners on the Wind River Reservation who had failed to obtain a tribal liquor license for their bar that was located on non-Indian land. A federal statute made it unlawful to introduce liquor into Indian country unless it was consistent with tribal regulations, 18 U.S.C. § 1154. In upholding the delegation of authority to the tribe, Justice Rehnquist wrote that constitutional limitations on delegation are "less stringent in cases where the entity exercising the delegated authority itself possesses independent authority over the subject matter." He concluded that:

> Indian tribes are unique aggregations possessing attributes of sovereignty over both their members and their territory * * *
>
> Cases such as *Worcester*, supra, and *Kagama*, supra, surely establish the proposition that Indian tribes within "Indian country" are a good deal more than "private, voluntary organizations" * * *

Id. at 557.

5.   What is the significance of footnote 1 of the opinion? Does it matter that the demographic numbers were not introduced by the habeas petitioners? What about the fact that Oliphant and his co-defendant had driven their vehicle into a tribal police car during the Suquamish holiday, Chief Seattle Days? Are these facts relevant in determining whether a tribe has criminal jurisdiction over non-Indians? See Matthew L.M. Fletcher, *Rebooting Indian Law in the Supreme Court*, 55 S.D.L.Rev. 510, 515 (2010).

6.   There are obvious and important public policy considerations resulting from *Oliphant*. It appears that crimes committed by non-Indians have increased throughout Indian country in the decades since *Oliphant* was decided, while crimes rates nationally have declined. The Indian Law and Order Commission recommended that Indian tribes be authorized to reassume plenary criminal jurisdiction authority over Indian country. *A Roadmap for Making Native America Safer: Report to the President & Congress of the United States* ix (Nov. 2013) ("Congress should clarify that any Tribe that so chooses

can opt out immediately, fully or partially, of Federal Indian country criminal jurisdiction and/or congressionally authorized State jurisdiction, except for Federal laws of general application. Upon a Tribe's exercise of opting out, Congress would immediately recognize the Tribe's inherent criminal jurisdiction over all persons within the exterior boundaries of the Tribe's lands as defined in the Federal Indian Country Act.").

NATION BUILDING NOTE: ENHANCED SENTENCING AND CRIMINAL JURISDICTION OVER CRIMES OF DOMESTIC VIOLENCE

In 2010, the United States significantly altered tribal criminal jurisdiction by authorizing Indian tribes to sentence convicted criminals to up to three years in jail, so long as the tribal conviction meets certain procedural requirements. 25 U.S.C. §§ 1302(b)–(d).

In 2013, the United States acknowledged the authority of Indian tribes to prosecute crimes of domestic violence committed by non-Indians, again so long as the tribal conviction meets certain procedural requirements. 25 U.S.C. § 1304.

Enhanced Sentencing

In the Tribal Law and Order Act (TLOA), Pub.L. 111–211, July 29, 2010, 124 Stat. 2258, the federal government amended the Indian Civil Rights Act to authorize Indian tribes to sentence a convicted criminal (all Indians) to three years of jail time. 25 U.S.C. § 1302(b). The statute mandates that the Indian tribe must guarantee the following rights:

(1)　provide to the defendant the right to effective assistance of counsel at least equal to that guaranteed by the United States Constitution; and

(2)　at the expense of the tribal government, provide an indigent defendant the assistance of a defense attorney licensed to practice law by any jurisdiction in the United States that applies appropriate professional licensing standards and effectively ensures the competence and professional responsibility of its licensed attorneys;

(3)　require that the judge presiding over the criminal proceeding—

(A)　has sufficient legal training to preside over criminal proceedings; and

(B)　is licensed to practice law by any jurisdiction in the United States;

(4)　prior to charging the defendant, make publicly available the criminal laws (including regulations and interpretative documents), rules of evidence, and rules of criminal procedure (including rules governing the recusal of judges in appropriate circumstances) of the tribal government; and

(5)   maintain a record of the criminal proceeding, including an audio or other recording of the trial proceeding.

25 U.S.C. § 1302(c).

Recall that the original version of the so-called Indian Bill of Rights, still codified at 25 U.S.C. § 1302(a), provided for guarantees of rights to any person under tribal jurisdiction, but were not perfect copies of the Bill of Rights. The 2010 Act allows tribes to continue to prosecute under the previous version and to sentence criminals to a year in jail. But in order to utilize the enhanced sentencing option, tribes must guarantee that the tribal judge is a licensed attorney, that the defendant is represented by a licensed attorney who has specialized training or experience in criminal defense, that the tribe's laws are publicly available, and that the tribal court is a court of record. Some of these requirements are not obligatory in state or federal court; for example, state and federal judges need not be licensed attorneys (some estimate that far more than half of state judges, including magistrates, justices of the peace, and family court referees, are not lawyers).

TLOA also clarified an issue that arose periodically when tribal courts sentenced the guilty to consecutive sentences, or what some called "stacked sentences." Defendants charged with separate offenses could be sentenced to jail for more than the one year authorized by the Indian Civil Rights Act so long as the court did not impose a sentence longer than a year for any one offense. E.g., Miranda v. Anchondo, 684 F.3d 844 (9th Cir.2011). The occasional lower court had held that tribes may not utilize consecutive sentencing if the overall sentence exceeded a year. E.g., Spears v. Red Lake Band of Chippewa Indians, 363 F. Supp. 2d 1176 (D.Minn.2005) (holding that consecutive sentence was not authorized by ICRA); Romero v. Goodrich, 2010 WL 8983216 (D.N.M., Mar. 9, 2010) (magistrate judge opinion recommending vacature of tribal court consecutive sentence), withdrawn, 2010 WL 9450759 (D.N.M., Sept. 22, 2010). TLOA allows tribes to utilize consecutive sentencing, so long as the overall sentence does not exceed nine years. 25 U.S.C. § 1302(a)(7)(D).

Domestic Violence Jurisdiction

The 2013 reauthorization of the Violence Against Women Act acknowledged the inherent authority of Indian tribes to prosecute non-Indian lawbreakers. Pub.L. 113–4, tit. IX, § 904, 127 Stat. 54, 120, codified at 25 U.S.C. § 1304. The statute acknowledges tribal authority to prosecute "dating violence" and "domestic violence" perpetrated by non-Indians. 25 U.S.C. §§ 1304(a)(1)–(2). But not all non-Indians are affected; the statute only authorizes tribes to prosecute non-Indians with certain "ties" to the tribal community, including residence, employment, or an intimate relationship with a tribal member or resident nonmember Indian. 25 U.S.C. § 1304(b)(4)(B).

Moreover, Indian tribes must guarantee all the protections of the original Indian Bill of Rights, 25 U.S.C. § 1302(a), the newer procedural requirements contained in TLOA, 25 U.S.C. §§ 1302(b)(d), *and* new requirements on the composition of juries, 25 U.S.C. § 1304(d)(3). The new jury requirements oblige tribes prosecuting non-Indians to empanel juries that "reflect a fair cross section of the community; and * * * do not systematically exclude any distinctive group in the community, including non-Indians * * *." Finally, perhaps as an effort to force eventual challengers of convictions under the statute to first seek "as applied" outcomes rather than "facial" challenges to the entire statute, the new law requires tribes to guarantee "all other rights whose protection is necessary under the Constitution of the United States in order for Congress to recognize and affirm the inherent power of the participating tribe to exercise special domestic violence criminal jurisdiction over the defendant." 25 U.S.C. § 1304(d)(4).

Three tribes participated in an early pilot project to test the viability of the statute—the Pascua Yaqui Tribe of Arizona, the Tulalip Tribes, and the Confederated Tribes of the Umatilla Indian Reservation. In 2014, all other Indian tribes were eligible to be certified by the Attorney General to prosecute non-Indians under § 1304. To date, while a few dozen non-Indians have been prosecuted, mostly by the Pasqua Yaqui Tribe, no federal cases challenging those convictions have been decided under the ICRA habeas statute, 25 U.S.C. § 1303.

The Little Traverse Bay Bands of Odawa Indians are one of three Michigan Indian tribes that have implemented the tribal jurisdictional provisions (the others are the Pokagon Band of Potawatomi Indians and the Nottawaseppi Huron Band of the Potawatomi). The tribe dedicated Chapter 7 of its Criminal Laws to the special jurisdictional provisions. Waganakising Odawa Tribal Code of Law, Title IX, Chapter 7, §§ 9.701–9.713 (2016). The tribe's code provisions mirror the relevant provisions of the Indian Civil Rights Act. The tribe has also dedicated a tribal court staff member, who is a licensed attorney, to serve as a tribal liaison to the court, the tribal council, the prosecutor, and the criminal defenders in domestic violence matters.

Note the partially completed chart below noting tribal criminal jurisdiction over crimes committed:

Who was the defendant?	What was the crime?	Jurisdiction (and possible sentence)
Indian	Any crime	Tribal
Nonmember Indian		
Non-Indian	Any crime Any crime cognizable under 25 U.S.C. § 1304	State or Federal State or Federal, or tribe that complies with § 1304

2. TRIBAL CRIMINAL JURISDICTION OVER NONMEMBER INDIANS

Throughout *Oliphant,* the Court referred to the application of tribal criminal jurisdiction over "non-Indians." In Duro v. Reina, 495 U.S. 676 (1990), the Court further limited the scope of tribal criminal jurisdiction, holding that the retained sovereignty of the tribe to govern its own affairs does not include the authority to impose criminal sanctions against an Indian who is not a tribal member. As in *Oliphant,* the Court reviewed federal authorities, seeking federal law on whether tribes could assert criminal jurisdiction over nonmember Indians:

The brief history of the tribal courts themselves provides somewhat clearer guidance. The tribal courts were established under the auspices of the Indian Reorganization Act.* * * The 60 years preceding the Act had witnessed a calculated policy favoring elimination of tribal institutions, sale of tribal lands, and assimilation of Indians as individuals into the dominant culture. Many Indian leaders and others fought to preserve tribal integrity, however, and the 1930's saw a move toward toleration of Indian self-determination * * * .

The Indian Reorganization Act allowed the expression of retained tribal sovereignty by authorizing creation of new tribal governments, constitutions, and courts. The new tribal courts supplanted the federal courts of Indian offenses operated by the Bureau of Indian Affairs. Significantly, new law and order codes were required to be approved by the Secretary of the Interior * * *. The opinions of the Solicitor of the Department of the Interior on the new tribal codes leave unquestioned the authority of the tribe over its members.

Evidence on criminal jurisdiction over nonmembers is less clear, but on balance supports the view that inherent tribal jurisdiction extends to tribe members only. One opinion flatly declares that "[i]nherent rights of self government may be invoked to justify punishment of members of the tribe but not of non members." 1 Op. Solicitor of Dept. of Interior Relating to Indian Affairs 1917–1974 (Op.Sol.) p. 699 (Nov. 17, 1936). But this opinion refers to an earlier opinion that speaks in broad terms of jurisdiction over Indians generally. 55 I.D. 14, 1 Op.Sol. 445 (Oct. 25, 1934). Another opinion disapproved a tribal ordinance covering all Indians on the ground that the tribal constitution embraced only members. The Solicitor suggested two alternative remedies, amendment of the tribal constitution and delegation of federal authority from the Secretary. 1 Op.Sol. 736 (Mar. 17, 1937). One of these options would reflect a belief that tribes possess inherent sovereignty over nonmembers, while the other would indicate its absence. Two later opinions, however, give a strong indication that the new tribal courts were not understood to possess power over nonmembers. One mentions only adoption of nonmembers into the tribe or receipt of delegated authority as means of acquiring jurisdiction over nonmember Indians. 1 Op.Sol. 849 (Aug. 26, 1938). A final opinion states more forcefully that the only means by which a tribe could deal with interloping nonmember Indians were removal of the offenders from the reservation or acceptance of delegated authority. 1 Op.Sol. 872 (Feb. 17, 1939).

Id. at 690–92 (citations omitted). At least nominally, these authorities, coupled with the authorities described in *Oliphant*, disclaim tribal criminal jurisdiction over nonmember Indians.

Justice Kennedy, writing for the majority, also articulated a theory of tribal authority that limits tribal authority to persons who consent to tribal authority, namely, tribal members. Id. at 693 ("The retained sovereignty of the tribe is but a recognition of certain additional authority the tribes maintain over Indians who consent to be tribal members. Indians like all other citizens share allegiance to the overriding sovereign, the United States. A tribe's additional authority comes from the consent of its members, and so in the criminal sphere membership marks the bounds of tribal authority.").

Duro was overridden by subsequent congressional legislation in 1991, recognizing and affirming the power of tribes to exercise criminal jurisdiction within their reservations over all "Indians," using the same definition for defining federal jurisdiction over crimes covered by the Major Crimes Act. See 25 U.S.C. § 1301(4). This statute is colloquially known as the "Duro fix." Congress had the option of delegating federal authority to Indian tribes to prosecute nonmember Indians, but instead Congress sought to reverse the Court's *Duro* decision by reaffirming the inherent authority of Indian tribes to prosecute nonmember Indians.

UNITED STATES V. LARA

Supreme Court of the United States, 2004.
541 U.S. 193, 124 S.Ct. 1628, 158 L.E.2d 420.

MR. JUSTICE BREYER delivered the opinion of the Court.

This case concerns a congressional statute "recogniz[ing] and affirm[ing]" the "inherent" authority of a tribe to bring a criminal misdemeanor prosecution against an Indian who is not a member of that tribe—authority that this Court previously held a tribe did not possess. Compare 25 U.S.C. § 1301(2) with Duro v. Reina, 495 U.S. 676 (1990). We must decide whether Congress has the constitutional power to relax restrictions that the political branches have, over time, placed on the exercise of a tribe's inherent legal authority. We conclude that Congress does possess this power.

I

Respondent Billy Jo Lara is an enrolled member of the Turtle Mountain Band of Chippewa Indians in north-central North Dakota. He married a member of a different tribe, the Spirit Lake Tribe, and lived with his wife and children on the Spirit Lake Reservation, also located in North Dakota. After several incidents of serious misconduct, the Spirit Lake Tribe issued an order excluding him from the reservation. Lara ignored the order; federal officers stopped him; and he struck one of the arresting officers.

The Spirit Lake Tribe subsequently prosecuted Lara in the Spirit Lake Tribal Court for "violence to a policeman." Lara pleaded guilty and, in respect to that crime, served 90 days in jail.

After Lara's tribal conviction, the Federal Government charged Lara in the Federal District Court for the District of North Dakota with the federal crime of assaulting a federal officer. 324 F.3d, at 636. Key elements of this federal crime mirror elements of the tribal crime of "violence to a policeman." And this similarity between the two crimes would ordinarily have brought Lara within the protective reach of the Double Jeopardy Clause. But the Government, responding to Lara's claim of double jeopardy, pointed out that the Double Jeopardy Clause does not bar successive prosecutions brought by *separate sovereigns,* and it argued that this "dual sovereignty" doctrine determined the outcome here. See Heath v. Alabama, 474 U.S. 82.

The Government noted that this Court has held that an Indian tribe acts as a separate sovereign when it prosecutes its own members. United States v. Wheeler, 435 U.S. 313, 318, 322–323 (1978). The Government recognized, of course, that Lara is not one of the Spirit Lake Tribe's *own* members; it also recognized that, in *Duro v. Reina,* supra, this Court had held that a tribe no longer possessed inherent or sovereign authority to prosecute a "nonmember Indian." Id., at 679. But it pointed out that, soon after this Court decided *Duro,* Congress enacted new legislation specifically authorizing a tribe to prosecute Indian members of a different tribe. That new statute, in permitting a tribe to bring certain tribal prosecutions against nonmember Indians, does not purport to delegate the Federal Government's own *federal* power. Rather, it enlarges the *tribes'* own " 'powers of self-government' " to include "the inherent power of Indian tribes, hereby recognized and affirmed, to exercise criminal jurisdiction over *all* Indians," including nonmembers. 25 U.S.C. § 1301(2) (emphasis added).

In the Government's view, given this statute, the Tribe, in prosecuting Lara, had exercised its own inherent tribal authority, not delegated federal authority; hence the "dual sovereignty" doctrine applies, and since the two prosecutions were brought by two different sovereigns, the second, federal, prosecution does not violate the Double Jeopardy Clause.

An Eighth Circuit * * * en banc Court of Appeals, by a vote of 7 to 4 * * *, held the Tribal Court, in prosecuting Lara, was exercising a federal prosecutorial power; hence the "dual sovereignty" doctrine does not apply; and the Double Jeopardy Clause bars the second prosecution. 324 F.3d 635, 640 (2003). The four dissenting judges, agreeing with the Federal Government, concluded that the Tribal Court had exercised inherent tribal power in prosecuting Lara; hence the "dual sovereignty" doctrine applies and allows the second, federal, prosecution. Id., at 641.

Because the Eighth Circuit and Ninth Circuit have reached different conclusions about the new statute, we granted certiorari. Compare United States v. Enas, 255 F.3d 662 (C.A.9 2001) (en banc), cert. denied, 534 U.S. 1115 (2002). We now reverse the Eighth Circuit.

II

We assume, as do the parties, that Lara's double jeopardy claim turns on the answer to the "dual sovereignty" question. What is "the source of [the] power to punish" nonmember Indian offenders, "inherent *tribal* sovereignty" or delegated federal authority? See *Wheeler,* supra, at 322 (emphasis added).

We also believe that Congress intended the former answer. The statute says that it "recognize[s] and affirm[s]" in each tribe the "inherent" tribal power (not delegated federal power) to prosecute nonmember Indians for misdemeanors. And the statute's legislative history confirms that such was Congress' intent ("The Committee of the Conference notes that . . . this legislation is not a delegation of this jurisdiction but a clarification of the status of tribes as domestic dependent nations").

Thus the statute seeks to adjust the tribes' status. It relaxes the restrictions, recognized in *Duro,* that the political branches had imposed on the tribes' exercise of inherent prosecutorial power. The question before us is whether the Constitution authorizes Congress to do so. Several considerations lead us to the conclusion that Congress does possess the constitutional power to lift the restrictions on the tribes' criminal jurisdiction over nonmember Indians as the statute seeks to do.

First, the Constitution grants Congress broad general powers to legislate in respect to Indian tribes, powers that we have consistently described as "plenary and exclusive." E.g., Washington v. Confederated Bands and Tribes of Yakima Nation, 439 U.S. 463, 470–471 (1979); see *Wheeler,* 435 U.S., at 323.

This Court has traditionally identified the Indian Commerce Clause, U.S. Const., Art. I, § 8, cl. 3, and the Treaty Clause, Art. II, § 2, cl. 2, as sources of that power. E.g., Morton v. Mancari, 417 U.S. 535, 552 (1974). The "central function of the Indian Commerce Clause," we have said, "is to provide Congress with plenary power to legislate in the field of Indian affairs." Cotton Petroleum Corp. v. New Mexico, 490 U.S. 163, 192 (1989).

* * *

Moreover, "at least during the first century of America's national existence . . . Indian affairs were more an aspect of military and foreign policy than a subject of domestic or municipal law." Cohen 208. Insofar as that is so, Congress' legislative authority would rest in part, not upon "affirmative grants of the Constitution," but upon the Constitution's adoption of preconstitutional powers necessarily inherent in any Federal Government, namely powers that this Court has described as "necessary concomitants of nationality." United States v. Curtiss-Wright Export Corp., 299 U.S. 304, 315–322 (1936).

Second, Congress, with this Court's approval, has interpreted the Constitution's "plenary" grants of power as authorizing it to enact legislation that both restricts and, in turn, relaxes those restrictions on tribal sovereign authority. From the Nation's beginning Congress' need for such legislative power would have seemed obvious. After all, the Government's Indian policies, applicable to numerous tribes with diverse cultures, affecting billions of acres of land, of necessity would fluctuate dramatically as the needs of the Nation and those of the tribes changed over time. And Congress has in fact authorized at different times very different Indian policies (some with beneficial results but many with tragic consequences). Congressional policy, for example, initially favored "Indian removal," then "assimilation" and the break-up of tribal lands, then protection of the tribal land base (interrupted by a movement toward greater state involvement and "termination" of recognized tribes); and it now seeks greater tribal autonomy within the framework of a "government-to-government relationship" with federal agencies. 59 Fed.Reg. 22951 (1994).

Such major policy changes inevitably involve major changes in the metes and bounds of tribal sovereignty. The 1871 statute, for example, changed the status of an Indian tribe from a "powe[r] . . . capable of making treaties" to a "power with whom the United States may [not] contract by treaty."

One can readily find examples in congressional decisions to recognize, or to terminate, the existence of individual tribes. See United States v. Holliday, 3 Wall. 407, 419 (1866) ("If by [the political branches] those Indians are recognized as a tribe, this court must do the same"). Indeed, Congress has restored previously extinguished tribal status—by re-recognizing a Tribe whose tribal existence it previously had terminated. 25 U.S.C. §§ 903–903f (restoring the Menominee Tribe). Congress has advanced policies of integration by conferring United States citizenship upon all Indians. Congress has also granted tribes greater autonomy in their inherent law enforcement authority (in respect to tribal members) by increasing the maximum criminal penalties tribal courts may impose [under the ICRA].

Third, Congress' statutory goal—to modify the degree of autonomy enjoyed by a dependent sovereign that is not a State—is not an unusual legislative objective. The political branches, drawing upon analogous constitutional authority, have made adjustments to the autonomous status of other such dependent entities—sometimes making far more radical adjustments than those at issue here. See, e.g., Hawaii—Hawaii v. Mankichi, 190 U.S. 197, 209–210 (1903) (describing annexation of Hawaii by joint resolution of Congress and the maintenance of a "Republic of Hawaii" until formal incorporation by Congress).

Fourth, Lara points to no explicit language in the Constitution suggesting a limitation on Congress' institutional authority to relax restrictions on tribal sovereignty previously imposed by the political branches.

Fifth, the change at issue here is a limited one. It concerns a power similar in some respects to the power to prosecute a tribe's own members— a power that this Court has called "inherent." *Wheeler*, 435 U.S., at 322– 323. In large part it concerns a tribe's authority to control events that occur upon the tribe's own land. And the tribes' possession of this additional criminal jurisdiction is consistent with our traditional understanding of the tribes' status as "domestic dependent nations." See Cherokee Nation v. Georgia, 5 Pet. 1, 17 (1831). Consequently, we are not now faced with a question dealing with potential constitutional limits on congressional efforts to legislate far more radical changes in tribal status. In particular, this case involves no interference with the power or authority of any State. Nor do we now consider the question whether the Constitution's Due Process or Equal Protection Clauses prohibit tribes from prosecuting a nonmember citizen of the United States. See Part III, infra.

Sixth, our conclusion that Congress has the power to relax the restrictions imposed by the political branches on the tribes' inherent prosecutorial authority is consistent with our earlier cases. True, the Court held in those cases that the power to prosecute nonmembers was an aspect of the tribes' external relations and hence part of the tribal sovereignty that was divested by treaties and by Congress. *Wheeler*; *Oliphant*; *Duro*. But these holdings reflect the Court's view of the tribes' retained sovereign status *as of the time* the Court made them. They did not set forth constitutional limits that prohibit Congress from changing the relevant legal circumstances, *i.e.*, from taking actions that modify or adjust the tribes' status.

To the contrary, *Oliphant* and *Duro* make clear that the Constitution does not dictate the metes and bounds of tribal autonomy, nor do they suggest that the Court should second-guess the political branches' own determinations. In *Oliphant,* the Court rested its conclusion about inherent tribal authority to prosecute tribe members in large part upon "the commonly shared presumption of Congress, the Executive Branch, and lower federal courts," a presumption which, "[w]hile not conclusive . . . [,] carries considerable weight." 435 U.S., at 206. The Court pointed out that " 'Indian law' draws principally upon the treaties drawn and executed by the Executive Branch and legislation passed by Congress." Ibid. (emphasis added). It added that those "instruments, . . . form the backdrop for the intricate web of judicially made Indian law." Ibid. (emphasis added).

Similarly, in *Duro,* the Court drew upon a host of different sources in order to reach its conclusion that a tribe does not possess the inherent power to prosecute a nonmember. The Court referred to historic practices, the views of experts, the experience of forerunners of modern tribal courts, and the published opinions of the Solicitor of the Department of the Interior.

* * *

We concede that *Duro,* like several other cases, referred only to the need to obtain a congressional statute that *"delegated"* power to the tribes. See *id.,* at 686; *Bourland*; Montana v. United States, 450 U.S. 544, 564 (1981). But in so stating, *Duro* (like the other cases) simply did not consider whether a statute, like the present one, could constitutionally achieve the same end by removing restrictions on the tribes' inherent authority. Consequently we do not read any of these cases as holding that the Constitution forbids Congress to change "judicially made" federal Indian law through this kind of legislation. *Oliphant,* supra, at 206; cf. County of Oneida v. Oneida Indian Nation of N. Y., 470 U.S. 226, 233–237 (1985).

Wheeler, Oliphant, and *Duro,* then, are not determinative because Congress has enacted a new statute, relaxing restrictions on the bounds of the inherent tribal authority that the United States recognizes. And that fact makes all the difference.

III

Lara makes several additional arguments. First, he points out that the Indian Civil Rights Act of 1968, lacks certain constitutional protections for criminal defendants, in particular the right of an indigent defendant to counsel. See 25 U.S.C. § 1302. And he argues that the Due Process Clause forbids Congress to permit a tribe to prosecute a nonmember Indian citizen of the United States in a forum that lacks this protection.

* * *

[The Court rejected several due process and equal protection challenges to the Lara's convictions by the Spirit Lake Nation, holding without addressing the merits of those challenges that even if Lara prevailed on them, the federal conviction at bar would still stand.]

IV

For these reasons, we hold, with the reservations set forth in Part III, supra, that the Constitution authorizes Congress to permit tribes, as an exercise of their inherent tribal authority, to prosecute nonmember Indians. We hold that Congress exercised that authority in writing this statute. That being so, the Spirit Lake Tribe's prosecution of Lara did not amount to an exercise of federal power, and the Tribe acted in its capacity of a separate sovereign. Consequently, the Double Jeopardy Clause does not prohibit the Federal Government from proceeding with the present prosecution for a discrete federal offense.

The contrary judgment of the Eighth Circuit is

Reversed.

[MR. JUSTICE STEVENS' concurring opinion is omitted.]

MR. JUSTICE KENNEDY, concurring in the judgment.

* * *

Lara, after all, is a citizen of the United States. To hold that Congress can subject him, within our domestic borders, to a sovereignty outside the basic structure of the Constitution is a serious step. The Constitution is based on a theory of original, and continuing, consent of the governed. Their consent depends on the understanding that the Constitution has established the federal structure, which grants the citizen the protection of two governments, the Nation and the State. Each sovereign must respect the proper sphere of the other, for the citizen has rights and duties as to both. Here, contrary to this design, the National Government seeks to subject a citizen to the criminal jurisdiction of a third entity to be tried for conduct occurring wholly within the territorial borders of the Nation and one of the States. This is unprecedented. * * *

The Court resolves, or perhaps avoids, the basic question of the power of the Government to yield authority inside the domestic borders over citizens to a third sovereign by using the euphemistic formulation that in amending the ICRA Congress merely relaxed restrictions on the tribes. . . . The terms of the statute are best understood as a grant or cession from Congress to the tribes, and it should not be doubted that what Congress has attempted to do is subject American citizens to the authority of an extraconstitutional sovereign to which they had not previously been subject. * * *

* * *

* * * Perhaps the Court's holding could be justified by an argument that by enrolling in one tribe Lara consented to the criminal jurisdiction of other tribes, but the Court does not mention the point. And, in all events, we should be cautious about adopting that fiction.

The present case, however, does not require us to address these difficult questions of constitutional dimension. Congress made it clear that its intent was to recognize and affirm tribal authority to try Indian nonmembers as inherent in tribal status. The proper occasion to test the legitimacy of the tribe's authority, that is, whether Congress had the power to do what it sought to do, was in the first, tribal proceeding. There, however, Lara made no objection to the tribe's authority to try him. * * *

MR. JUSTICE THOMAS, concurring in the judgment.

As this case should make clear, the time has come to reexamine the premises and logic of our tribal sovereignty cases. It seems to me that much of the confusion reflected in our precedent arises from two largely incompatible and doubtful assumptions. First, Congress (rather than some other part of the Federal Government) can regulate virtually every aspect of the tribes without rendering tribal sovereignty a nullity. See, e.g., United States v. Wheeler, 435 U.S. 313, 319 (1978). Second, the Indian tribes retain inherent sovereignty to enforce their criminal laws against their own members. See, e.g., id., at 326. These assumptions, which I must accept as the case comes to us, dictate the outcome in this case, and I therefore concur in the judgment.

I write separately principally because the Court fails to confront these tensions, a result that flows from the Court's inadequate constitutional analysis. I cannot agree with the Court, for instance, that the Constitution grants to Congress plenary power to calibrate the "metes and bounds of tribal sovereignty." Unlike the Court, I cannot locate such congressional authority in the Treaty Clause, U.S. Const., Art. II, § 2, cl. 2, or the Indian Commerce Clause, Art. I, § 8, cl. 3. Additionally, I would ascribe much more significance to legislation such as 25 U.S.C. § 71, that purports to terminate the practice of dealing with Indian tribes by treaty. The making of treaties, after all, is the one mechanism that the Constitution clearly provides for the Federal Government to interact with sovereigns other than the States. Yet, if I accept that Congress does have this authority, I believe that the result in *Wheeler* is questionable. In my view, the tribes either are or are not separate sovereigns, and our federal Indian law cases untenably hold both positions simultaneously.

* * *

Although *Wheeler* seems to be a sensible example of federal common lawmaking, I am not convinced that it was correctly decided. To be sure, it makes sense to conceptualize the tribes as sovereigns that, due to their unique situation, cannot exercise the full measure of their sovereign powers. *Wheeler,* at times, seems to analyze the problem in just this way. See, e.g., id., at 323–326.

* * *

Further, federal policy itself could be thought to be inconsistent with this residual-sovereignty theory. In 1871, Congress enacted a statute that purported to prohibit entering into treaties with the "Indian nation[s] or tribe[s]." 25 U.S.C. § 71. Although this Act is constitutionally suspect (the Constitution vests in the President both the power to make treaties, Art. II, § 2, cl. 2, and to recognize foreign governments, Art. II, § 3); it nevertheless reflects the view of the political branches that the tribes had become a purely domestic matter.

To be sure, this does not quite suffice to demonstrate that the tribes had lost their sovereignty. After all, States retain sovereignty despite the fact that Congress can regulate States qua States in certain limited circumstances. See, e.g., Katzenbach v. Morgan, 384, U.S. 641. But the States (unlike the tribes) are part of a constitutional framework that allocates sovereignty between the State and Federal Governments and specifically grants Congress authority to legislate with respect to them, see U.S. Const., Amdt. 14, § 5. And even so, we have explained that "the Framers explicitly chose a Constitution that confers upon Congress the power to regulate individuals, not States." New York v. United States, 505 U.S., 144.

The tribes, by contrast, are not part of this constitutional order, and their sovereignty is not guaranteed by it.

* * *

III

* * *

I do, however, agree that this case raises important constitutional questions that the Court does not begin to answer. The Court utterly fails to find any provision of the Constitution that gives Congress enumerated power to alter tribal sovereignty.

* * *

In the end, the Court resorts to citing past examples of congressional assertions of this or similar power. At times, such history might suffice. But it does not suffice here for at least two reasons. First, federal Indian law is at odds with itself. I find it difficult to reconcile the result in *Wheeler* with Congress' 1871 prospective prohibition on the making of treaties with the Indian tribes. The Federal Government cannot simultaneously claim power to regulate virtually every aspect of the tribes through ordinary domestic legislation and also maintain that the tribes possess anything resembling "sovereignty." * * * In short, the history points in both directions.

* * *

The Court should admit that it has failed in its quest to find a source of congressional power to adjust tribal sovereignty. Such an acknowledgement might allow the Court to ask the logically antecedent question whether Congress (as opposed to the President) has this power. A cogent answer would serve as the foundation for the analysis of the sovereignty issues posed by this case. We might find that the Federal Government cannot regulate the tribes through ordinary domestic legislation and simultaneously maintain that the tribes are sovereigns in any meaningful sense. But until we begin to analyze these questions honestly and rigorously, the confusion that I have identified will continue to haunt our cases.

MR. JUSTICE SOUTER, with whom MR. JUSTICE SCALIA joins, dissenting.

[Omitted.]

NOTES

1.   As you encounter cases in which the Court finds limitations on the inherent powers of Indian tribes consider the potential for a "fix" by Congress to reverse or modify such decisions.

2.   In a widely-noticed case that was heard by the Navajo Supreme Court in 1999, the well-known Oglala Sioux activist and actor, Russell Means, challenged his criminal prosecution by the Navajo Nation, asserting that as a non-member Indian his prosecution in Navajo district court violated his constitutional rights to equal protection of the law. Means was charged with threatening and battering his father-in-law, a member of the Omaha Tribe, and a Navajo Indian in related incidents, while residing on the reservation married to an enrolled member of the Navajo Nation. Rather than rely on the congressional "*Duro*-fix" to justify the tribe's criminal prosecution of a non-member Indian, the Navajo Supreme Court held that the Navajo Nation possessed criminal jurisdiction in the case by virtue of its 1868 treaty with the United States and Means' *hadane* (in-law) status as a "member" of the tribe under Navajo common law. Means v. District Court of the Chinle Judicial District, 26 Indian L.Rep. 6083 (Navajo Supreme Court 1999). Examining the Treaty of 1868, the Court found that Article II had set apart the Navajo reservation "for the use and occupation of the Navajo tribe of Indians, and for such other friendly tribes or individual Indians as from time to time they may be willing, with the consent of the United States, to admit among them." Id. at 6087.

Means filed a petition for a writ of habeas corpus in federal court after losing his appeal in the Navajo courts. As Justice Kennedy noted, perhaps the proper way to challenge the Duro fix was through a direct appeal of the tribal conviction, just as Means did. Means even hired as his counsel the same attorney who represented the non-member Indian petitioner in *Duro v. Reina*. The Ninth Circuit upheld Means' conviction, on the grounds that *Lara* established "definitively" that "an Indian tribe may exercise inherent sovereign judicial power in criminal cases against nonmember Indians for crimes committed on the tribe's reservation." Means v. Navajo Nation, 432 F.3d 924, 931 (9th Cir.2005), cert. denied, 549 U.S. 952 (2006). Did the fact that Means was actually represented by counsel, as well as the fact that at Navajo, nonmember Indians were eligible to serve on tribal court juries, influence the Supreme Court's decision to deny review of the case? See Matthew L.M. Fletcher, *Means Case a Supreme Affirmation of Tribal Authority*, Indian Country Today, Oct. 20, 2006, at A3.

Note the chart below noting tribal criminal jurisdiction over crimes committed:

Who was the defendant?	What was the crime?	Jurisdiction (and possible sentence)
Indian	Any crime	Tribal
Nonmember Indian	Any crime	Tribal
Non-Indian	Any crime Any crime cognizable under 25 U.S.C. § 1904	State or Federal State or Federal, or tribe that complies with § 1904

CHAPTER EIGHT

TRIBAL AND STATE CONFLICTS OVER CIVIL REGULATORY AND ADJUDICATORY JURISDICTION

■ ■ ■

For most Americans, the laws governing matters such as taxation, land use regulation, child custody, domestic relations, and automobile accidents emanate from state or local legislative bodies, and typically disputes are resolved in state courts. Even federal environmental legislation such as the Clean Water Act, Clean Air Act, and the hazardous and solid waste laws delegate most regulatory authority to the states. By now, it should be clear that for Indians in Indian country quite different rules apply. Cases such as Worcester v. Georgia, 31 U.S. 515 (1832), and Williams v. Lee, 358 U.S. 217 (1959), create a doctrinal floor under all of these areas that excludes state jurisdiction. However, throughout American history, the United States has repeatedly encouraged non-Indians to enter Indian lands and further has repeatedly authorized states to assert some forms of jurisdiction in Indian country. As the historical traditions, specific statutes, and concerns of governments and private parties have differed, the courts developed subrules for taxation and regulatory and adjudicatory jurisdiction in Indian country, treated in this chapter, and for Indian hunting and fishing and water rights, which are covered later. In the area child protection matters, Congress has stepped in to extend tribal authority, and that topic is treated in this chapter as well.

SECTION A. CIVIL REGULATORY JURISDICTION IN INDIAN COUNTRY

The Supreme Court's 1978 decision in Oliphant v. Suquamish Indian Tribe, 435 U.S. 191 (1978), did not address the question of the existence and extent of tribal civil regulatory jurisdiction over non-Indians. Three years later, however, the Court applied the General Allotment Act to limit tribal regulation of nonmember activities on nonmember owned reservation fee lands.

MONTANA V. UNITED STATES

Supreme Court of the United States, 1981.
450 U.S. 544, 101 S.Ct. 1245, 67 L.Ed.2d 493.

JUSTICE STEWART delivered the opinion of the Court. [The case involved tribal regulation of duck hunting and trout fishing by non-Indians on their own fee lands within the boundaries of the Crow Reservation. The Court first held that title to the bed of the Big Horn River, a navigable watercourse, passed to the State of Montana at the time of statehood. That portion of the opinion is reprinted at page 290, supra. The Court then turned to the question of tribal regulation of non-Indians on the portion of the Big Horn River within the reservation.]

* * *

III

Though the parties in this case have raised broad questions about the power of the Tribe to regulate hunting and fishing by non-Indians on the reservation, the regulatory issue before us is a narrow one. The Court of Appeals held that the Tribe may prohibit non-members from hunting or fishing on land belonging to the Tribe or held by the United States in trust for the Tribe, 604 F.2d, at 1165–1166, and with this holding we can readily agree. We also agree with the Court of Appeals that if the Tribe permits nonmembers to fish or hunt on such lands, it may condition their entry by charging a fee or establishing bag and creel limits. What remains is the question of the power of the Tribe to regulate non-Indian fishing and hunting on reservation land owned in fee by nonmembers of the Tribe. * * *

A

The purposes of the 1851 Treaty were to assure safe passage for settlers across the lands of various Indian Tribes; to compensate the Tribes for the loss of buffalo, other game animals, timber and forage; to delineate tribal boundaries; to promote intertribal peace; and to establish a way of identifying Indians who committed depredations against non-Indians. As noted earlier, the treaty did not even create a reservation, although it did designate tribal lands. See Crow Tribe v. United States, 284 F.2d 361, 364, 366, 368 (Ct.Cl.). Only Article 5 of that Treaty referred to hunting and fishing, and it merely provided that the eight signatory tribes "do not surrender the privilege of hunting, fishing, or passing over any of the tracts of country heretofore described." 11 Stat. 749. The treaty nowhere suggested that Congress intended to grant authority to the Crow Tribe to regulate hunting and fishing by nonmembers on nonmember lands. Indeed, the Court of Appeals acknowledged that after the treaty was signed non-Indians, as well as members of other Indian tribes, undoubtedly hunted and fished within the treaty-designated territory of the Crows. 604 F.2d, at 1167.

The 1868 Fort Laramie Treaty, 15 Stat. 649, reduced the size of the Crow territory designated by the 1851 Treaty. Article II of the treaty established a reservation for the Crow Tribe, and provided that it be "set apart for the *absolute and undisturbed use and occupation* of the Indians herein named and for such other friendly tribes or individual Indians as from time to time they may be willing, with the consent of the United States, to admit amongst them . . . ," (emphasis added) and that "the United States now solemnly agrees that no persons, except those herein designated and authorized so to do . . . shall ever be permitted to pass over, settle upon or reside in the territory described in this article for the use of said Indians. . . ." The treaty, therefore, obligated the United States to prohibit most non-Indians from residing on or passing through reservation lands used and occupied by the Tribe, and, thereby, arguably conferred upon the Tribe the authority to control fishing and hunting on those lands. But that authority could only extend to land on which the Tribe exercises "absolute and undisturbed use and occupation." And it is clear that the quantity of such land was substantially reduced by the allotment and alienation of tribal lands as a result of the passage of the General Allotment Act of 1887, 25 U.S.C. § 331 et seq., and the Crow Allotment Act of 1920, 41 Stat. 751. If the 1868 Treaty created tribal power to restrict or prohibit non-Indian hunting and fishing on the reservation, that power cannot apply to lands held in fee by non-Indians.

* * *

B

* * * The Court of Appeals * * * identified that power as an incident of the inherent sovereignty of the Tribe over the entire Crow Reservation. But "inherent sovereignty" is not so broad as to support the application of Resolution No. 74–05 to non-Indian lands.

This Court most recently reviewed the principles of inherent sovereignty in United States v. Wheeler, 435 U.S. 313. In that case, noting that Indian tribes are "unique aggregations possessing attributes of sovereignty over both their members and their territory," id., at 323, the Court upheld the power of a tribe to punish tribal members who violate tribal criminal laws. But the Court was careful to note that, through their original incorporation into the United States as well as through specific treaties and statutes, the Indian tribes have lost many of the attributes of sovereignty. Id., at 326. The Court distinguished between those inherent powers retained by the tribes and those divested. * * *

Thus, in addition to the power to punish tribal offenders, the Indian tribes retain their inherent power to determine tribal membership, to regulate domestic relations among members, and to prescribe rules of inheritance for members. Id., at 322, n. 18. But exercise of tribal power beyond what is necessary to protect tribal self-government or to control internal relations is inconsistent with the dependent status of the tribes, and so cannot survive without express Congressional delegation. Since regulation of hunting and fishing by non-members of a tribe on lands no longer owned by the Tribe bears no clear relationship to tribal self-government or internal relations,[13] the general principles of retained inherent sovereignty did not authorize the Crow Tribe to adopt Resolution No. 74–05.

The Court recently applied these general principles in Oliphant v. Suquamish Indian Tribe, 435 U.S. 191, rejecting a tribal claim of inherent sovereign authority to exercise criminal jurisdiction over non-Indians. * * * Though *Oliphant* only determined inherent tribal authority in criminal matters, the principles on which it relied support the general proposition that the inherent sovereign powers of an Indian tribe do not extend to the activities of nonmembers of the tribe. To be sure, Indian tribes retain inherent sovereign power to exercise some forms of civil jurisdiction over non-Indians on their reservations, even on non-Indian fee lands. A tribe may regulate, through taxation, licensing, or other means, the activities of nonmembers who enter consensual relationships with the tribe or its members, through commercial dealing, contracts, leases, or other arrangements. Williams v. Lee, 358 U.S. 217, 223; Morris v. Hitchcock, 194 U.S. 384; Buster v. Wright, 135 F. 947, 950 (CA8); see Washington v. Confederated Tribes of the Colville Indian Reservation, 447 U.S. 134, 153. A tribe may also retain inherent power to exercise civil authority over the conduct of non-Indians on fee lands within its reservation when that conduct threatens or has some direct effect on the political integrity, the economic security, or the health or welfare of the tribe. See Fisher v. District Court, 424 U.S. 382, 386; Williams v. Lee, 358 U.S. 217, 220; Montana Catholic Missions v. Missoula County, 200 U.S. 118, 128–129; Thomas v. Gay, 169 U.S. 264, 273.[15]

No such circumstances, however, are involved in this case. Non-Indian hunters and fishermen on non-Indian fee land do not enter any agreements or dealings with the Crow Tribe so as to subject themselves to tribal civil jurisdiction. And nothing in this case suggests that such non-Indian hunting and fishing so threaten the Tribe's political or economic security as to justify tribal regulation. The complaint in the District Court did not allege that non-Indian hunting and fishing on fee lands imperil the

---

[13] Any argument that Resolution No. 74–05 is necessary to Crow tribal self-government is refuted by the findings of the District Court that the State of Montana has traditionally exercised "near exclusive" jurisdiction over hunting and fishing on fee lands within the reservation, and that the parties to this case had accommodated themselves to the state regulation. *United States v. Montana*, supra, 457 F.Supp., at 610. The Court of Appeals left these findings unaltered and indeed implicitly reaffirmed them, adding that the record reveals no attempts by the Tribe at the time of the Crow Allotment Act to forbid non-Indian hunting and fishing on reservation lands. United States v. Montana, supra, 604 F.2d at 1168 and n. 11A.

[15] As a corollary, this Court has held that the Indian tribes retain rights to river waters necessary to make their reservations livable. *Arizona v. California*, 373 U.S. 546, 599.

subsistence or welfare of the Tribe. Furthermore, the District Court made express findings, left unaltered by the Court of Appeals, that the Crow Tribe has traditionally accommodated itself to the State's "near exclusive" regulation of hunting and fishing on fee lands within the reservation. And the District Court found that Montana's statutory and regulatory scheme does not prevent the Crow Tribe from limiting or forbidding non-Indian hunting and fishing on lands still owned by or held in trust for the Tribe or its members.

* * *

NOTES

1.   In formulating its general rule that tribes do not have inherent regulatory powers over the activities of nonmembers "beyond what is necessary to protect tribal self-government or to control internal relations," the *Montana* Court found two exceptions from prior case law. The first exception, which recognizes tribal regulatory power over the activities of nonmembers who enter consensual relationships with the tribe or its members, was found not to apply in *Montana* because there were no agreements or dealings between non-Indian hunters and fisherman on non-Indian fee land and the Crow Tribe. The second *Montana* exception, recognizing tribal regulatory authority over non-member conduct on fee lands within the reservation where that conduct threatens or has "some direct effect on the political integrity, the economic security, or the health or welfare of the tribe," was also found not to apply in this case by the Court, in part because "at the time of the treaty the Crows were a nomadic tribe dependent chiefly on buffalo, and fishing was not important to their diet or way of life." 450 U.S. at 556. That statement derived from the district court's findings of fact that are now known to be highly suspect, if not outright false. John P. LaVelle, *Beating a Path of Retreat from Treaty Rights and Tribal Sovereignty: The Story of Montana v. United States*, in Indian Law Stories 535, 552–53 (Carole Goldberg, Kevin K. Washburn, and Philip P. Frickey, eds. 2011).

2.   Recall that the Supreme Court in Oliphant v. Suquamish Indian Tribe, 435 U.S. 191 (1978), held that tribes do not retain criminal jurisdiction authority over "non-Indians," whereas the *Montana* Court mixed "nonmembers" and "non-Indians" together in the opinion. However, it is now well established that, for civil jurisdiction purposes, the jurisdictional keystone is membership, not Indian status. For criminal jurisdiction purposes, the jurisdictional boundary remains Indian status as a result of federal statute. See 25 U.S.C. § 1301(4) (referencing 18 U.S.C. § 1153).

3.   Recall that *Montana* involved nonmember owned lands within Indian country. The Supreme Court has treated civil jurisdiction on Indian lands—especially trust lands—much differently.

MERRION V. JICARILLA APACHE TRIBE

Supreme Court of the United States, 1982.
455 U.S. 130, 102 S.Ct. 894, 71 L.Ed.2d 21.

JUSTICE MARSHALL delivered the opinion of the Court.

Pursuant to long-term leases with the Jicarilla Apache Tribe, petitioners, 21 lessees, extract and produce oil and gas from the Tribe's reservation lands. In these two consolidated cases, petitioners challenge an ordinance enacted by the Tribe imposing a severance tax on "any oil and natural gas severed, saved and removed from Tribal lands." We granted certiorari to determine whether the Tribe has the authority to impose this tax, and, if so, whether the tax imposed by the Tribe violates the Commerce Clause.

I

The Jicarilla Apache Tribe resides on a reservation in northwestern New Mexico. Established by Executive Order in 1887, the reservation contains 742,315 acres, all of which is held as tribal trust property. * * *

The Tribe is organized under the Indian Reorganization Act of 1934, which authorizes any tribe residing on a reservation to adopt a constitution and bylaws, subject to the approval of the Secretary of the Interior (Secretary). The Tribe's first Constitution, approved by the Secretary on August 4, 1937, preserved all powers conferred by § 16 of the Indian Reorganization Act of 1934, 25 U.S.C. § 476. In 1968, the Tribe revised its Constitution to specify:

> "The inherent powers of the Jicarilla Apache Tribe, including those conferred by Section 16 of the Act of June 18, 1934 (48 Stat. 984), as amended, shall vest in the tribal council and shall be exercised thereby subject only to limitations imposed by the Constitution of the United States, applicable Federal statutes and regulations of the Department of the Interior, and the restrictions established by this revised constitution." Revised Constitution of the Jicarilla Apache Tribe, Art. XI, § 1.

The Revised Constitution provides that "[t]he tribal council may enact ordinances to govern the development of tribal lands and other resources," Art. XI, § 1(a)(3). It further provides that "[t]he tribal council may levy and collect taxes and fees on tribal members, and may enact ordinances, subject to approval by the Secretary of the Interior, to impose taxes and fees on nonmembers of the tribe doing business on the reservation," Art. XI, § 1(e). The Revised Constitution was approved by the Secretary on February 13, 1969.

To develop tribal lands, the Tribe has executed mineral leases encompassing some 89% of the reservation land. Beginning in 1953, the petitioners entered into leases with the Tribe. The Commissioner of Indian

Affairs, on behalf of the Secretary, approved these leases, as required by the Act of May 11, 1938, 25 U.S.C. §§ 396a–396g. In exchange for a cash bonus, royalties, and rents, the typical lease grants the lessee "the exclusive right and privilege to drill for, mine, extract, remove, and dispose of all oil and natural gas deposits in and under" the leased land for as long as the minerals are produced in paying quantities. Petitioners may use oil and gas in developing the lease without incurring the royalty. In addition, the Tribe reserves the rights to use gas without charge for any of its buildings on the leased land, and to take its royalties in kind. Petitioners' activities on the leased land have been subject to taxes imposed by the State of New Mexico on oil and gas severance and on oil and gas production equipment. See Act of March 3, 1927, 25 U.S.C. § 398c (permitting state taxation of mineral production on Indian reservations) (1927 Act).

Pursuant to its Revised Constitution, the Tribal Council adopted an ordinance imposing a severance tax on oil and gas production on tribal land. The ordinance was approved by the Secretary, through the Acting Director of the Bureau of Indian Affairs, on December 23, 1976. The tax applies to "any oil and natural gas severed, saved and removed from Tribal lands. * * * " Id. * * * Oil and gas consumed by the lessees to develop their leases or received by the Tribe as in-kind royalty payments are exempted from the tax.

In two separate actions, petitioners sought to enjoin enforcement of the tax by either the tribal authorities or the Secretary.

* * *

II

* * *

A

In Washington v. Confederated Tribes of the Colville Indian Reservation, [447 U.S. 134 (1980)] (*Colville*), we addressed the Indian tribes' authority to impose taxes on non-Indians doing business on the reservation. We held that "[t]he power to tax transactions occurring on trust lands and significantly involving a tribe or its members is a fundamental attribute of sovereignty which the tribes retain unless divested of it by federal law or necessary implication of their dependent status." The power to tax is an essential attribute of Indian sovereignty because it is a necessary instrument of self-government and territorial management. This power enables a tribal government to raise revenues for its essential services. The power does not derive solely from the Indian tribe's power to exclude non-Indians from tribal lands. Instead, it derives from the tribe's general authority, as sovereign, to control economic activity within its jurisdiction, and to defray the cost of providing governmental services by requiring contributions from persons or enterprises engaged in economic activities within that jurisdiction.

The petitioners avail themselves of the "substantial privilege of carrying on business" on the reservation. They benefit from the provision of police protection and other governmental services, as well as from "the advantages of a civilized society" that are assured by the existence of tribal government. Numerous other governmental entities levy a general revenue tax similar to that imposed by the Jicarilla Tribe when they provide comparable services. Under these circumstances, there is nothing exceptional in requiring petitioners to contribute through taxes to the general cost of tribal government.[5]

As we observed in *Colville,* supra, the tribe's interest in levying taxes on nonmembers to raise "revenues for essential governmental programs * * * is strongest when the revenues are derived from value generated on the reservation by activities involving the Tribes and when the taxpayer is the recipient of tribal services." This surely is the case here. The mere fact that the government imposing the tax also enjoys rents and royalties as the lessor of the mineral lands does not undermine the government's authority to impose the tax. The royalty payments from the mineral leases are paid to the Tribe in its role as partner in petitioners' commercial venture. The severance tax, in contrast, is petitioners' contribution "to the general cost of providing governmental services." State governments commonly receive both royalty payments and severance taxes from lessees of mineral lands within their borders.

Viewing the taxing power of Indian tribes as an essential instrument of self-government and territorial management has been a shared assumption of all three branches of the Federal Government.

* * *

B

* * *

Petitioners argue that their leaseholds entitle them to enter the reservation and exempt them from further exercises of the Tribe's sovereign authority. Similarly, the dissent asserts that the Tribe has lost the power to tax petitioners' mining activities because it has leased to them the use of the mineral lands and such rights of access to the reservation as might be necessary to enjoy the leases. However, this conclusion is not compelled by linking the taxing power to the power to exclude. Instead, it

---

[5] Through various Acts governing Indian tribes, Congress has expressed the purpose of "fostering tribal self-government." Colville, supra. We agree with Judge McKay's observation that "[I]t simply does not make sense to expect the tribes to carry out municipal functions approved and mandated by Congress without being able to exercise at least minimal taxing powers, whether they take the form of real estate taxes, leasehold taxes or severance taxes." 617 F.2d, at 550 (McKay, J., concurring).

is based on additional assumptions and confusions about the consequences of the commercial arrangement between petitioners and the Tribe.

Most important, petitioners and the dissent confuse the Tribe's role as commercial partner with its role as sovereign. This confusion relegates the powers of sovereignty to the bargaining process undertaken in each of the sovereign's commercial agreements. It is one thing to find that the Tribe has agreed to sell the right to use the land and take from it valuable minerals; it is quite another to find that the Tribe has abandoned its sovereign powers simply because it has not expressly reserved them through a contract.

Confusing these two results denigrates Indian sovereignty. Indeed, the dissent apparently views the tribal power to exclude, as well as the derivative authority to tax, as merely the power possessed by any individual landowner or any social group to attach conditions, including a "tax" or fee, to the entry by a stranger onto private land or into the social group, and not as a sovereign power.

* * *

Indian sovereignty is not conditioned on the assent of a nonmember; to the contrary, the nonmember's presence and conduct on Indian lands is conditioned by the limitations the Tribe may choose to impose.

Viewed in this light, the absence of a reference to the tax in the leases themselves hardly impairs the Tribe's authority to impose the tax. Contractual arrangements remain subject to subsequent legislation by the presiding sovereign. Even where the contract at issue requires payment of a royalty for a license or franchise issued by the governmental entity, the government's power to tax remains unless it "has been specifically surrendered in terms which admit of no other reasonable interpretation."

* * *

No claim is asserted in this case, nor could one be, that petitioners' leases contain the clear and unmistakable surrender of taxing power required for its extinction. We could find a waiver of the Tribe's taxing power only if we inferred it from silence in the leases. To presume that a sovereign forever waives the right to exercise one of its sovereign powers unless it expressly reserves the right to exercise that power in a commercial agreement turns the concept of sovereignty on its head, and we do not adopt this analysis.[14]

---

[14] Petitioners and the dissent also argue that we should infer a waiver of the taxing power from silence in the Tribe's original Constitution. Although it is true that the Constitution in force when petitioners signed their leases did not include a provision specifically authorizing a severance tax, neither the Tribe's Constitution nor the Federal Constitution is the font of any sovereign power of the Indian tribes. Because the Tribe retains all inherent attributes of sovereignty that have not been divested by the Federal Government, the proper inference from silence on this point is that the sovereign power to tax remains intact. The Tribe's Constitution

* * *

IV

In Worcester v. Georgia, 6 Pet. 515, 559 (1832), Chief Justice Marshall observed that Indian tribes had "always been considered as distinct, independent political communities, retaining their original natural rights." Although the tribes are subject to the authority of the Federal Government, the "weaker power does not surrender its independence—its right to self government, by associating with a stronger, and taking its protection." Id., at 561. Adhering to this understanding, we conclude that the Tribe did not surrender its authority to tax the mining activities of petitioners, whether this authority is deemed to arise from the Tribe's inherent power of self-government or from its inherent power to exclude nonmembers. Therefore, the Tribe may enforce its severance tax unless and until Congress divests this power, an action that Congress has not taken to date. Finally, the severance tax imposed by the Tribe cannot be invalidated on the ground that it violates the "negative implications" of the Commerce Clause.

Affirmed.

JUSTICE STEVENS, with whom THE CHIEF JUSTICE and JUSTICE REHNQUIST join, dissenting.

* * *

The power to exclude petitioners would have supported the imposition of a discriminatory tribal tax on petitioners when they sought to enter the Jicarilla Apache Reservation to explore for minerals. Moreover, even if no tax had been imposed at the time of initial entry, a discriminatory severance tax could have been imposed as a condition attached to the grant of the privilege of extracting minerals from the earth. But the Tribe did not impose any tax prior to petitioners' entry or as a condition attached to the privileges granted by the leases in 1953. As a result, the tax imposed in 1976 is not valid unless the Tribe retained its power either to exclude petitioners from the reservation or to prohibit them from continuing to extract oil and gas from reservation lands.

* * *

Petitioners were granted authority by the Tribe to extract oil and gas from reservation lands. The Tribe now seeks to change retroactively the conditions of that authority. These petitioners happen to be prosperous oil companies. Moreover, it may be sound policy to find additional sources of revenue to better the economic conditions of many Indian tribes. If this retroactive imposition of a tax on oil companies is permissible, however, an Indian tribe may with equal legitimacy contract with outsiders for the construction of a school or a hospital, or for the rendition of medical or

_____

was amended to authorize the tax before the tax was imposed, and this is the critical event necessary to *effectuate* the tax.

technical services, and then—after the contract is partially performed—change the terms of the bargain by imposing a gross receipts tax on the outsider. If the Court is willing to ignore the risk of such unfair treatment of a local contractor or a local doctor because the Secretary of the Interior has the power to veto a tribal tax, it must equate the unbridled discretion of a political appointee with the protection afforded by rules of law. That equation is unacceptable to me. Neither wealth, political opportunity, nor past transgressions can justify denying any person the protection of the law.

NOTES

1.   In *Merrion* the Court seemed to rely on the Secretary of Interior's approval of the tribe's Indian Reorganization Act (IRA) constitution and the tax ordinance. The Navajo Tribal Council is not organized under the IRA and its unwritten constitutional practices result in only certain types of ordinances being submitted to the Secretary of the Interior. When it passed an ordinance imposing taxes on all businesses, Indian and non-Indian, on the reservation, the tribal council submitted the ordinance to the Bureau of Indian Affairs for approval. The BIA responded that this was not among the types of ordinances requiring secretarial approval and took no action. A mineral lessee challenged the taxes claiming that they were invalid without the Secretary's approval. In an opinion unanimously upholding the tribal taxes, the Supreme Court sustained the tribe's power to impose taxes on non-Indian businesses. Kerr-McGee Corp. v. Navajo Tribe, 471 U.S. 195 (1985). It rejected the company's argument that the law requires secretarial approval of all tribal government actions:

> Petitioner suggests that the Indian Reorganization Act of 1934 is such a law. Section 16 of the IRA authorizes any tribe on a reservation to adopt a constitution and by-laws, subject to the approval of the Secretary of the Interior. 25 U.S.C. § 476. The Act, however, does not provide that a tribal constitution must condition the power to tax on Secretarial approval. Indeed, the terms of the IRA do not govern tribes, like the Navajo, which declined to accept its provisions. 25 U.S.C. § 478.

> Many tribal constitutions written under the IRA in the 1930's called for Secretarial approval of tax laws affecting non-Indians. See, e.g., Constitution and Bylaws of the Rosebud Sioux Tribe of South Dakota, Art. 4, § 1(h) (1935). But there were exceptions to this practice. For example, the 1937 Constitution and By-laws of the Saginaw Chippewa Indian Tribe of Michigan authorized the Tribal Council, without Secretarial approval, to "create and maintain a tribal council fund by * * * levying taxes or assessments against members or nonmembers." Art. 4, § 1(g). Thus the most that can be said about this period of constitution writing is that the Bureau of Indian Affairs, in assisting the drafting of tribal constitutions, had a

policy of including provisions for Secretarial approval; but that policy was not mandated by Congress.

Nor do we agree that Congress intended to recognize as legitimate only those tribal taxes authorized by constitutions written under the IRA. Long before the IRA was enacted, the Senate Judiciary Committee acknowledged the validity of a tax imposed by the Chickasaw Nation on non-Indians. See S.Rep. No. 698, 45th Cong., 3d Sess., 1–2 (1879). And in 1934, the Solicitor of the Department of the Interior published a formal opinion stating that a tribe possesses "the power of taxation [which] may be exercised over members of the tribe and over nonmembers." Powers of Indian Tribes, 55 I.D. 14, 46. The 73rd Congress, in passing the IRA to advance tribal self-government, see Williams v. Lee, 358 U.S. 217, 220 (1959), did nothing to limit the established, pre-existing power of the Navajos to levy taxes.

Some tribes that adopted constitutions in the early years of the IRA may be dependent on the Government in a way that the Navajos are not. However, such tribes are free, with the backing of the Interior Department, to amend their constitutions to remove the requirement of Secretarial approval. See, e.g., Revised Constitution and Bylaws of the Mississippi Band of Choctaw Indians, Art. 8, § 1(r) (1975).

471 U.S. at 198–99.

2.   Decisions that quickly followed *Montana* and *Merrion* in time seemed to suggest that tribal regulatory authority on all reservation lands would be supported by the Court. For example, in New Mexico v. Mescalero Apache Tribe, 462 U.S. 324 (1983), the Court held that New Mexico's game laws could not be enforced on nonmembers on tribal trust lands, and that tribal (and federal) governance authority controlled. Decisions that predated *Merrion* are also in accord. E.g., Washington v. Confederated Tribes of the Colville Indian Reservation, 447 U.S. 134, 152–53 (1980) (holding that tribes may tax nonmember activities on tribal lands).

3.   Ultimately, however, the Supreme Court appeared to elevate *Montana* to higher status than *Merrion*, likely because the Court began hearing a greater number of disputes arising on nonmember owned reservation lands. Two decisions, Brendale v. Confederated Tribes and Bands of the Yakima Indian Nation, 492 U.S. 408 (1989), and South Dakota v. Bourland, 508 U.S. 679 (1993), more or less applied *Montana* to questions of reservation governance on lands owned by nonmembers, presumably leaving *Merrion* to govern issues arising on tribal and Indian lands. *Brendale* involved a tribe's assertion of civil regulatory jurisdiction over allotted lands held in fee simple by nonmembers within the reservation's exterior boundaries. In *Brendale*, the Court fragmented badly, issuing three opinions that differed on which cases controlled, and in turn divided the Yakama Indian Reservation into "open" and "closed" portions. In the so-called "open" portion of the reservation, which was opened up to allotment, the Court held that the tribe did not have authority to

enforce its zoning regulations on nonmember owned land. Id. at 444–45 (Stevens, J.,) (concurring with Justice White's opinion). In the so-called "closed" area of the reservation, which included lands primarily owned by the tribe and tribal members, the Court held that the tribe does have authority to enforce its zoning laws on nonmember owned lands. Id. at 446–47 (Stevens, J.) (concurring with Justice Blackmun's opinion). After *Brendale*, the Court clarified in *Bourland* that *Montana* was the controlling authority in relation to reservation fee lands owned by nonmembers. Id. at 689–92.

Two critically important lower court decisions affirmed tribal regulatory authority over water quality standards set by tribes in accordance with federal law. City of Albuquerque v. Browner, 97 F.3d 415 (10th Cir.1996), cert. denied, 522 U.S. 965 (1997) (Pueblo of Isleta); State of Montana v. EPA, 137 F.3d 1135 (9th Cir.1997) (Confederated Salish and Kootenai Tribes), cert. denied, 525 U.S. 921 (1998). In both instances, the Environmental Protection Agency recognized tribal authority under the *Montana* rubric to promulgate water quality standards governing the reservation. 33 U.S.C. § 1377. In both instances, the tribal standards would apply to nonmembers, both on and off the reservation, largely upstream water polluters. In *State of Montana*, the court concurred with EPA's determination that "activities of the non-members posed such serious and substantial threats to Tribal health and welfare that Tribal regulation was essential." Id. at 1141.

A later Supreme Court decision, Nevada v. Hicks, 533 U.S. 353 (2001), discussed in greater detail infra, asserted that *Montana* would govern tribal authority over nonmembers even on tribal trust lands. However, that case involved state law enforcement officials, and the tribal governance portion of the *Hicks* opinion may be dicta only. A later case, albeit obliquely, suggested that tribes may retain a form of "plenary jurisdiction" over lands not alienated through allotment or another means. Plains Commerce Bank v. Long Family Land and Cattle Co., 556 U.S. 316, 328 (2008) ("Our cases have made clear that once tribal land is converted into fee simple, the tribe loses plenary jurisdiction over it.").

4.   Also in 2001, the Supreme Court held that an Indian tribe's authority to tax nonmembers on nonmember-owned lands was subject to the *Montana* analysis. See Atkinson Trading Co., Inc. v. Shirley, 532 U.S. 645 (2001). But it took a restrictive view of the exceptions allowing tribes to exercise inherent jurisdiction over non-Indians. It held that the Navajo Nation did not have the authority to tax guests at a non-Indian owned hotel located on fee simple land within the Navajo reservation. The Cameron Trading Post was built in 1916 by a non-Indian trader on land purchased from the United States. In 1934, the boundaries of the Navajo Reservation were extended by Congress to include the trading post. In 1992 the Navajo Nation imposed a hotel occupancy tax of 8% on guests of hotels within the boundaries of the Navajo Nation and applied it to a tourist hotel that had been established at the trading post. In a unanimous decision written by Chief Justice Rehnquist, the Supreme Court held that the Navajo Nation's authority to tax nonmembers "reaches no further than tribal land," unless the Navajo Nation comes within one of the *Montana*

exceptions. Id. at 645–46. The Court then concluded that neither exception applied in this case: "Because respondents have failed to establish that the hotel occupancy tax is commensurately related to any consensual relationship with petitioner or is necessary to vindicate the Navajo Nation's political integrity, the presumption ripens into a holding." Id. at 659.

In 2005, the Supreme Court decided Wagnon v. Prairie Band Potawatomi Nation, 546 U.S. 95 (2005), in which the Court held that a state motor fuel tax was not preempted by federal law and by a tribal motor fuel tax imposed by the Prairie Band Potawatomi Nation on its non-Indian customers at a tribally-owned gas station. Of note, while the Court upheld the state tax, it assumed without discussion that the Nation's tax on its non-Indian customers was valid.

5.   In City of Sherrill v. Oneida Indian Nation, 544 U.S. 197 (2005), the Supreme Court announced a theoretical basis for rejecting reservation governance initiatives by Indian tribes. The theory asserts that some tribal governance activities are too "disruptive" of "justifiable expectations" of non-Indian governments and their nonmember constituents. Id. at 215 (quoting Rosebud Sioux Tribe v. Kneip, 430 U.S. 584, 604–05 (1977)). Sherrill was a tribal tax immunity case where the tribe had purchased fee lands within its reservation boundaries and asserted that the land was protected from local property taxes and state regulation. The Court rejected that argument because the State of New York had primary governance authority over those parcels for two centuries before the tribe re-acquired the land. Id. at 216. The Court also noted that the tribe could ask the Interior Secretary to take the land into trust under 25 U.S.C. § 465.

In 2016, the Supreme Court decided a reservation boundary case, Nebraska v. Parker, 136 S. Ct. 1072 (2016). The underlying dispute was whether the Omaha Tribe had authority (delegated by the federal government) to impose a liquor tax on nonmember businesses on the reservation. That case transformed over time from a tribal regulatory jurisdiction case to a tribal adjudicatory jurisdiction case to a reservation boundaries case. See Village of Pender v. Parker, 2007 WL 2914871 (D.Neb., Oct. 4, 2007) (staying challenge to tribal regulatory authority to allow plaintiffs to exhaust tribal court remedies); Village of Pender v. Morris, No. 08–02 (Omaha Nation in Nebraska & Iowa Tribal Court, Feb. 4, 2013) (affirming the reservation boundaries of the Omaha Reservation and therefore the regulatory authority of the tribe). If the Village of Pender was within the reservation, then the tribe had the authority to impose the liquor tax.

The Supreme Court unanimously held that Congress did not intend for the Omaha Reservation to be diminished, and therefore the Village of Pender remained within the reservation. But the Court's final statement about the case was a suggestion that the Sherrill decision might "curtail" the tribe's power to impose the tax: "Because petitioners have raised only the single question of diminishment, we express no view about whether equitable considerations of laches and acquiescence may curtail the Tribe's power to tax the retailers of Pender in light of the Tribe's century-long absence from the disputed lands." 136 S. Ct. at 1082 (citing *Sherrill*). The statement was plainly a suggestion that Nebraska and the village should consider re-filing the matter again. Keep in mind that the Village is composed of nonmember land within the Omaha Reservation, and absent the federal delegation of authority to impose the tax, the tribe's taxing authority would likely be subject to the *Montana* analysis.

NATION BUILDING NOTE: MONTANA, SHERRILL, AND TRIBAL RESERVATION GOVERNANCE

Montana dramatically impacts reservation governance to this day. The allotment era, in particular, exposed Indian country to the presence of many nonmembers. On many reservations, non-Indians outnumber Indians by a wide margin. Still, for the first decade after the Supreme Court announced *Montana*, the Court acknowledged broad tribal regulatory authority on tribal lands (trust lands, for the most part) within Indian country: "taxes on reservation sales to nonmembers; taxes on nonmember interests on reservation leaseholds; taxes on reservation resources removed by nonmembers; regulation of nonmember hunting and fishing on reservation lands; and even zoning regulation of nonmember-owned fee land in a predominantly tribal portion of an Indian reservation." Matthew L.M. Fletcher, *Contract and (Tribal) Jurisdiction*, 126 Yale L.J.F. 1, 3 (Apr. 11, 2016) (citing several cases).

Sherrill is a new player to the question of tribal regulatory jurisdiction. The *Sherrill* ruling is purely judge-made law allowing states and local governments to raise equitable defenses to defeat tribal tax and regulatory immunities on tribally owned fee lands within reservation boundaries. The Second Circuit has extended *Sherrill's* reasoning to Indian land claims brought under the Nonintercourse Act, 25 U.S.C. § 177, but that is not the issue in this Note. Lower courts have not yet broadly applied *Sherrill's* reasoning to assertions of tribal regulatory powers, but the Supreme Court's invitation in *Nebraska v. Parker*, 136 S.Ct. 1072, 182 (2016), may encourage lower courts to do so.

Judicial decisions in jurisdictional disputes rarely conclude the acrimony between tribes and states. All-or-nothing resolutions in favor of one sovereign or the other tend to fan the flames of disagreement and lead to further tests of the limits of jurisdiction of each. Yet the day-to-day problems of law enforcement, maintaining orderly means for dispute resolution, tax collection, and furnishing government services continue.

As the Supreme Court itself has noted, historically for Indian tribes, "the people of States where they are found are often their deadliest enemies." United States v. Kagama, 118 U.S. 375, 384 (1886). Only in recent times have tribes and states been able to find sufficient common ground in order to work cooperatively in governance matters of mutual concern. See generally Matthew L.M. Fletcher, *Retiring the "Deadliest Enemies" Model of Tribal-State Relations*, 43 Tulsa L.Rev. 73 (2007). Tribal-state cooperation has sometimes been mandated by congressional action such as in the Indian Child Welfare Act and the Indian Gaming Regulatory Act. Increasingly, however, tribes and states have been able to find sufficient common ground and respect for each other's sovereignty to work cooperatively without a federal mandate. In such instances, tribes and states have been able to focus their resources and energies on solving the practical problems of local self-government through compromise and negotiation, as opposed to litigating jurisdictional issues to definitive and final resolution. See Matthew L.M. Fletcher, *Reviving Local Tribal Control in Indian Country*, 53 Fed.Law. 38 (Mar./Apr. 2006).

A few tribes have reached broad settlements on reservation governance with states and local governments, with federal approval, after initiating strategic litigation. In 2005, the Saginaw Chippewa Indian Tribe (SCIT) sued the governor of the State of Michigan and local governments for a judgment on the Tribe's reservation boundaries. A series of treaties created in the nineteenth century guaranteed the reservation for the exclusive use of the Tribe and its members, a guarantee that was routinely disregarded for over 100 years. The SCIT had numerous conflicts with state agencies, Isabella County, and the City of Mount Pleasant over taxes and regulations on fee lands within the reservation, as well as criminal jurisdiction over the Tribe's members. After the Tribe survived a motion to dismiss based on *Sherrill*, Saginaw Chippewa Indian Tribe v. Granholm, 2008 WL 4808823, at *17–24 (E.D.Mich. Oct. 22, 2008), SCIT, the governor, and the local units of government reached a far-ranging settlement regarding criminal jurisdiction, environmental regulation, taxes, land use, and public safety. The defendants received what they wanted—certainty in jurisdictional questions, cooperation from the Tribe, and resources to implement the agreement. This case caused a disruption of established governance structures; the disruption opened an opportunity not only to redefine jurisdictional roles but moreover to clarify previously muddled jurisdictional issues allowing for improved public-service delivery. See Matthew L.M. Fletcher, Kathryn E. Fort, and Dr. Nicholas J. Reo, *Tribal Disruption and Indian Claims*, 112 Mich.L.Rev. First Impressions 65, 70 (2014). See also Matthew L.M. Fletcher, *Tribal Disruption and Federalism*, 76 Mont.L.Rev. 97, 103–09 (2015) (describing the agreements in greater detail).

Another example involves the tribe at issue in the *Sherrill* matter itself, the Oneida Indian Nation of New York. As the Supreme Court suggested, the tribe sought to place its fee properties in trust with the United States, only to be faced with intense opposition. E.g., Town of Verona v. Jewell, 2015 WL 1400291 (N.D.N.Y., Mar. 26, 2015) (affirming Interior Secretary's decision to acquire land in trust for the Oneida Indian Nation). While legal proceedings moved forward, the tribe, the state, local governments, and the federal government negotiated over the governance of the reservation going forward if the tribe's land went into trust. They eventually reached an agreement "couched as a gaming compact that settles the taxation and land disputes between the parties." Fletcher, Fort & Reo, supra, at 71 (citing Settlement

Agreement by the Oneida Nation, the State of New York, the County of Madison, and the County of Oneida (May 20, 2013)).

States and tribes have negotiated numerous cooperative agreements in critical areas of law enforcement, including but not limited to agreements for cross-deputization and extradition, interjurisdictional enforcement of warrants, subpoenas and other forms of legal process, provision of parole and probationary supervisory services, juvenile justice issues, enforcement of child support and custody orders, domestic relations law matters, domestic violence restraint orders, cross recognition of civil judgments, full faith and credit, mutual enforcement of traffic laws, and the sharing of records, information, reports and resources. Other cooperative agreements include a wide range of governance issues involving contract, tort and property laws, land rights, development and zoning, repossessions, taxation, economic development and infrastructure development, environmental issues, hunting and fishing regulations, and water rights. See Conference of Western Attorneys General, American Indian Law Deskbook §§ 1401–1459, at 1009–71 (2014 ed.).

The Conference of State Chief Justices has recognized the importance of tribal-state jurisdictional arrangements and has set to work implementing strategies to promote communication, cooperation and comity between state and tribal courts. See Stanley G. Feldman and David L. Withey, *Resolving State-Tribal Jurisdictional Dilemmas*, 79 Judicature 154 (1995) (intergovernmental agreements "that provide for cross-utilization of facilities, programs, and personnel by state and tribal court systems"). Given the historically antagonistic relationships that exist between many tribes and state and local governments, cooperative agreements are most likely to emerge out of situations where both parties perceive mutual benefits arising from a negotiated resolution of jurisdictional disputes. See Rebecca Tsosie, *Negotiating Economic Survival: The Consent Principle and Tribal-State Gaming Compacts Under the Indian Gaming Regulatory Act*, 29 Ariz.L.J. 25 (1997). Note, *Intergovernmental Compacts in Native American Law: Models for Expanded Usage*, 112 Harv.L.Rev. 922 (1999). The Conference of Western Attorneys General drafted a detailed manual for state negotiators on how to negotiate with tribal leaders, with an emphasis on mutual respect and creativity, with a recommendation to avoid demanding jurisdictional concessions from tribes. See Conference of Western Attorneys General, American Indian Law Deskbook §§ 1412–1424, at 1038–47 (2014 ed.).

In many instances, congressional legislation has indeed served as the catalyst for successful state and tribal negotiations. Tribal-state agreements have become especially commonplace in implementing the Indian Child Welfare Act of 1978, and the Indian Gaming Regulatory Act of 1988. The relationships developing between the Pokagon Band of Potawatomi Indians of southwestern Michigan and the local units of government in the Band's service area provide examples of how the child welfare agreements result from the revenue sharing typical of tribal-state gaming compacts. See Brief of Pokagon Band at 10–13, Taxpayers of Michigan Against Casinos v. Norton, 433 F.3d 852 (D.C.Cir.2006) (No. 05–5206).

SECTION B. CIVIL ADJUDICATORY JURISDICTION IN INDIAN COUNTRY

Neither *Williams* nor *Fisher* involved a suit brought *against* nonmembers of the tribe in a tribal court. The tribal assertion of criminal or civil regulatory jurisdiction over nonmembers of the tribe raises a number of special concerns in federal Indian law. In the following decision the Supreme Court recognized a narrow but potentially significant basis for obtaining federal court review over tribal assertions of jurisdiction over nonmembers who are sued in tribal court. This creates a safety valve of sorts for nonmembers who dispute the existence of tribal jurisdiction over them for their on-reservation conduct and activities.

NATIONAL FARMERS UNION INSURANCE COMPANIES v. CROW TRIBE OF INDIANS

Supreme Court of the United States, 1985.
471 U.S. 845, 105 S.Ct. 2447, 85 L.Ed.2d 818.

JUSTICE STEVENS delivered the opinion for the Court.

* * *

[O]n May 27, 1982, Leroy Sage, a Crow Indian minor, was struck by a motorcycle in the Lodge Grass Elementary School parking lot while returning from a school activity. The school has a student body that is 85% Crow Indian [and] is located * * * within the boundaries of the Crow Indian Reservation. Through his guardian, Flora Not Afraid, Sage initiated a lawsuit in the Crow Tribal Court against the School District, a political subdivision of the State, alleging damages of $153,000, including medical expenses of $3,000 and pain and suffering of $150,000.

On September 28, 1982, process was served by Dexter Falls Down on Wesley Falls Down, the Chairman of the School Board. For reasons that have not been explained, Wesley Falls Down failed to notify anyone that a suit had been filed. On October 19, 1982, a default judgment was entered pursuant to the rules of the Tribal Court, and on October 25, 1982, Judge Roundface entered findings of fact, conclusions of law and a judgment for $153,000 against the School District. Sage v. Lodge Grass School District, 10 Indian L.Rep. 6019 (1982). A copy of that judgment was hand-delivered by Wesley Falls Down to the school Principal who, in turn, forwarded it to National on October 29, 1982.

[National brought suit in federal district court. The court enjoined the tribal defendants from enforcing the default judgment.]

* * *

A divided panel of the Court of Appeals for the Ninth Circuit reversed. 736 F.2d 1320 (1984). * * *

I

Section 1331 of the Judicial Code provides that a federal district court "shall have original jurisdiction of all civil actions arising under the Constitution, laws, or treaties of the United States." It is well settled that this statutory grant of jurisdiction "will support claims founded upon federal common law as well as those of a statutory origin." Federal common law as articulated in rules that are fashioned by court decisions are "laws" as that term is used in § 1331.

Thus, in order to invoke a federal district court's jurisdiction under § 1331, it was not essential that the petitioners base their claim on a federal statute or a provision of the Constitution. It was, however, necessary to assert a claim "arising under" federal law. As Justice Holmes wrote for the Court, a "suit arises under the law that creates the cause of action." Petitioners contend that the right which they assert—a right to be protected against an unlawful exercise of Tribal Court judicial power—has its source in federal law because federal law defines the outer boundaries of an Indian tribe's power over non-Indians.

As we have often noted, Indian tribes occupy a unique status under our law. At one time they exercised virtually unlimited power over their own members as well as those who were permitted to join their communities. Today, however, the power of the Federal Government over the Indian tribes is plenary. Federal law, implemented by statute, by treaty, by administrative regulations, and by judicial decisions, provides significant protection for the individual, territorial, and political rights of the Indian tribes. The tribes also retain some of the inherent powers of the self-governing political communities that were formed long before Europeans first settled in North America.

This Court has frequently been required to decide questions concerning the extent to which Indian tribes have retained the power to regulate the affairs of non-Indians. We have also been confronted with a series of questions concerning the extent to which a tribe's power to engage in commerce has included an immunity from state taxation. In all of these cases, the governing rule of decision has been provided by federal law. In this case the petitioners contend that the Tribal Court has no power to enter a judgment against them. Assuming that the power to resolve disputes arising within the territory governed by the Tribe was once an attribute of inherent tribal sovereignty, the petitioners, in essence, contend that the Tribe has to some extent been divested of this aspect of sovereignty. More particularly, when they invoke the jurisdiction of a federal court under § 1331, they must contend that federal law has curtailed the powers of the Tribe, and thus afforded them the basis for the relief they seek in a federal forum.

The question whether an Indian tribe retains the power to compel a non-Indian property owner to submit to the civil jurisdiction of a tribal court is one that must be answered by reference to federal law and is a "federal question" under § 1331.[14] Because petitioners contend that federal law has divested the Tribe of this aspect of sovereignty, it is federal law on which they rely as a basis for the asserted right of freedom from Tribal Court interference. They have, therefore, filed an action "arising under" federal law within the meaning of § 1331. * * *

II

Respondents contend that, even though the District Court's jurisdiction was properly invoked under § 1331, the Court of Appeals was correct in ordering that the complaint be dismissed because the petitioners failed to exhaust their remedies in the tribal judicial system. They further assert that the underlying tort action "has turned into a procedural and jurisdictional nightmare" because petitioners did not pursue their readily available Tribal Court remedies. Petitioners, in response, relying in part on Oliphant v. Suquamish Indian Tribe, 435 U.S. 191 (1978), assert that resort to exhaustion as a matter of comity "is manifestly inappropriate."

In *Oliphant* we held that the Suquamish Indian Tribal Court did not have criminal jurisdiction to try and to punish non-Indians for offenses committed on the reservation. That holding adopted the reasoning of early opinions of two United States Attorneys General, and concluded that federal legislation conferring jurisdiction on the federal courts to try non-Indians for offenses committed in Indian Country had implicitly preempted tribal jurisdiction. * * *

If we were to apply the *Oliphant* rule here, it is plain that any exhaustion requirement would be completely foreclosed because federal courts would *always* be the only forums for civil actions against non-Indians. For several reasons, however, the reasoning of *Oliphant* does not apply to this case. First, although Congress' decision to extend the criminal jurisdiction of the federal courts to offenses committed by non-Indians

---

[14] We have recognized that federal law has sometimes diminished the inherent power of Indian tribes in significant ways. As we stated in *United States v. Wheeler*, 435 U.S., at 322–326:

"Their incorporation within the territory of the United States, and their acceptance of its protection, necessarily divested them of some aspects of the sovereignty which they had previously exercised. . . . In sum, Indian tribes still possess those aspects of sovereignty not withdrawn by treaty or statute, or by implication as a necessary result of their dependent status.

The areas in which such implicit divestiture of sovereignty has been held to have occurred are those involving the relations between an Indian tribe and nonmembers of the tribe. Thus, Indian tribes can no longer freely alienate to non-Indians the land they occupy. Oneida Indian Nation v. County of Oneida, 414 U.S. 661, 667–668; Johnson v. McIntosh, 8 Wheat. 543, 574. They cannot enter into direct commercial or governmental relations with foreign nations. Worcester v. Georgia, 6 Pet. 515, 559; Cherokee Nation v. Georgia, 5 Pet., [1], at 17–18 [8 L.Ed. 25]; Fletcher v. Peck, 6 Cranch 87, 147 [3 L.Ed. 162] (Johnson, J., concurring). And, as we have recently held, they cannot try nonmembers in tribal courts. Oliphant v. Suquamish Indian Tribe [435 U.S. 191 (1978)]."

against Indians within Indian Country supported the holding in *Oliphant,* there is no comparable legislation granting the federal courts jurisdiction over civil disputes between Indians and non-Indians that arise on an Indian reservation. Moreover, the opinion of one Attorney General on which we relied in Oliphant, specifically noted the difference between civil and criminal jurisdiction. Speaking of civil jurisdiction, Attorney General Cushing wrote:

> "But there is no provision of treaty, and no statute, which takes away from the Choctaws jurisdiction of a case like this, a question of property strictly internal to the Choctaw nation; nor is there any written law which confers jurisdiction of such a case in any court of the United States.

> * * *

> "The conclusion seems to me irresistible, not that such questions are justiciable nowhere, but that they remain subject to the local jurisdiction of the Choctaws.

> * * *

> "Now, it is admitted on all hands ... that Congress has 'paramount right' to legislate in regard to this question, in all its relations. It has legislated, in so far as it sa*w fit, by taking jurisdiction in criminal matters, and omitting to take jurisdiction in civil matters. . . . By all possible rules of construction the inference is clear that jurisdiction is left to the Choctaws themselves of civil controversies arising strictly within the Choctaw Nation."* 7 Op.Atty.Gen. 175, 179–181 (1855) (emphasis added).

Thus, we conclude that the answer to the question whether a tribal court has the power to exercise civil subject-matter jurisdiction over non-Indians in a case of this kind is not automatically foreclosed, as an extension of *Oliphant* would require. Rather, the existence and extent of a tribal court's jurisdiction will require a careful examination of tribal sovereignty, the extent to which that sovereignty has been altered, divested, or diminished, as well as a detailed study of relevant statutes, Executive Branch policy as embodied in treaties and elsewhere, and administrative or judicial decisions.

We believe that examination should be conducted in the first instance in the Tribal Court itself. Our cases have often recognized that Congress is committed to a policy of supporting tribal self-government and self-determination. That policy favors a rule that will provide the forum whose jurisdiction is being challenged the first opportunity to evaluate the factual and legal bases for the challenge.[21] Moreover the orderly administration of justice in the federal court will be served by allowing a full record to be developed in the Tribal Court before either the merits or any question concerning appropriate relief is addressed.[22] The risks of the kind of "procedural nightmare" that has allegedly developed in this case will be minimized if the federal court stays its hand until after the Tribal Court has had a full opportunity to determine its own jurisdiction and to rectify any errors it may have made. Exhaustion of tribal court remedies, moreover, will encourage tribal courts to explain to the parties the precise basis for accepting jurisdiction, and will also provide other courts with the benefit of their expertise in such matters in the event of further judicial review.

III

Our conclusions that § 1331 encompasses the federal question whether a tribal court has exceeded the lawful limits of its jurisdiction, and that exhaustion is required before such a claim may be entertained by a federal court, require that we reverse the judgment of the Court of Appeals. Until petitioners have exhausted the remedies available to them in the Tribal Court system, n. 4, supra, it would be premature for a federal court to consider any relief. Whether the federal action should be dismissed or merely held in abeyance pending the development of further Tribal Court proceedings, is a question that should be addressed in the first instance by the District Court. Accordingly, the judgment of the Court of Appeals is reversed, and the case is remanded for further proceedings consistent with this opinion.

* * *

NOTES

1.   After *National Farmers,* the Supreme Court extended the holding to cases involving federal jurisdiction based on diversity of citizenship. Iowa Mutual Insurance Co. v. LaPlante, 480 U.S. 9 (1987). LaPlante was a member of the Blackfeet Tribe, employed on a ranch located on the reservation, and was injured while driving a cattle truck on the reservation. LaPlante and his wife sued the ranch owners' insurer in the Blackfeet Tribal Court, seeking compensation for injuries and claiming compensatory and punitive damages against Iowa Mutual for a bad faith refusal to settle. Iowa Mutual moved to

---

[21] We do not suggest that exhaustion would be required where an assertion of tribal jurisdiction "is motivated by a desire to harass or is conducted in bad faith," cf. Juidice v. Vail, 430 U.S. 327, 338 (1977), or where the action is patently violative of express jurisdictional prohibitions, or where exhaustion would be futile because of the lack of an adequate opportunity to challenge the court's jurisdiction.

[22] Four days after receiving notice of the default judgment, petitioners requested that the District Court enter an injunction. Crow Tribal Court Rule of Civil Procedure 17(d) provides that a party in a default may move to set aside the default judgment at any time within 30 days. Petitioners did not utilize this legal remedy. * * *

dismiss for lack of subject matter jurisdiction. The tribal court upheld jurisdiction on the ground that the tribe can regulate the conduct of non-Indians engaged in commercial relations with Indians on the reservation. Then Iowa Mutual sued LaPlante, the individual ranch owners, and the ranch company in federal court based on diversity jurisdiction and claimed it had no duty to defend the insured under the policy. The district court dismissed the action, deferring to the tribal court, and the Ninth Circuit affirmed, citing *National Farmers*. The Supreme Court also affirmed:

> Although petitioner alleges that federal jurisdiction in this case is based on diversity of citizenship, rather than the existence of a federal question, the exhaustion rule announced in *National Farmers Union* applies here as well. Regardless of the basis for jurisdiction, the federal policy supporting tribal self-government directs a federal court to stay its hand in order to give the Tribal Court a "full opportunity to determine its own jurisdiction." Ibid. In diversity, as well as federal-question cases, unconditional access to the federal forum would place it in direct competition with the tribal courts, thereby impairing the latter's authority over reservation affairs. Adjudication of such matters by any non-tribal court also infringes upon tribal lawmaking authority, because tribal courts are best qualified to interpret and apply tribal law.

> * * * The federal policy of promoting tribal self-government encompasses the development of the entire tribal court system, including appellate courts. At a minimum, exhaustion of tribal remedies means that tribal appellate courts must have the opportunity to review the determinations of the lower tribal courts.

480 U.S. at 16–18.

2. The *National Farmers/Iowa Mutual* exhaustion doctrine has been invoked in numerous cases in federal and state courts. Although many have been returned to tribal court to exhaust opportunities for jurisdictional determinations, relatively few of the resulting jurisdictional decisions have then been reviewed by the federal courts. *Iowa Mutual* also requires non-members to exhaust their tribal court remedies all the way through the tribal appellate courts as well. The expense of fully litigating a civil suit to a final conclusion in tribal court before suing in federal court over jurisdiction may be sufficient to convince a non-member defendant to settle.

Still, only one Supreme Court case came to the Court after complete exhaustion of tribal remedies, Plains Commerce Bank v. Long Family Land and Cattle Co., 556 U.S. 316 (2008). Three others reached the Court with incomplete exhaustion, a tribal appellate court decision affirming tribal jurisdiction on interlocutory appeal from the tribal court. Strate v. A-1 Contractors, Inc., 520 U.S. 438 (1997); Nevada v. Hicks, 533 U.S. 353 (2001); Dollar General Corp. v. Mississippi Band of Choctaw Indians, 746 F.3d 588 (5th Cir.2014), aff'd by equally divided court, 136 S.Ct. 2159 (2016). A fourth reached the Court after a jurisdictional order from the tribal court, apparently with no tribal appellate court review. El Paso Natural Gas Co. v. Neztsosie, 526 U.S. 473 (1999). Tribal exhaustion is excused where "an assertion of tribal jurisdiction 'is motivated by a desire to harass or is conducted in bad faith,' or where the action is patently violative of express jurisdictional prohibitions, or where exhaustion would be futile because of the lack of an adequate opportunity to challenge the court's jurisdiction." *National Farmers Union*, 471 U.S. at 856 n.21. The Court in *Strate* and *Hicks* invoked what could be called the futility exception to excuse exhaustion. *Strate*, 520 U.S. at 449 & n.7; *Hicks*, 533 U.S. at 369. The Court in *El Paso* invoked the express jurisdictional prohibition. 526 U.S. at 482–83.

Meanwhile, the Court forbids federal courts from looking into whether tribal forums were biased or incompetent. *National Farmers Union*, 471 U.S. at 856 n.21. See also Frank Pommersheim, *Tribal Courts and Federal Courts: A Very Preliminary Set of Notes for Federal Courts Teachers*, 36 Ariz.St.L.J. 63, 72 n.51 (2004).

3.   Following exhaustion, the rule is that, if and when the federal court considers the question of tribal judicial jurisdiction, tribal court determinations of tribal law should be accorded deference, and factual questions would be reviewed using a clearly erroneous standard, and federal questions would be reviewed de novo. *Iowa Mutual* said that: "[u]nless a federal court determines that the Tribal Court lacked jurisdiction, however, proper deference to the tribal court system precludes relitigation" of the merits. 480 U.S. at 978.

This boilerplate description of the law—that federal courts are authorized to only look into the tribal court's jurisdiction—is incomplete. "[S]tate and federal courts. . . make factual assumptions and assert presumptions about [tribal court bias and incompetence] without ever taking evidence on [these factors] to determine whether these factors are present." Matthew L.M. Fletcher, *A Unifying Theory of Tribal Civil Jurisdiction*, 46 Ariz.St.L.J. 779, 831 (2014). The practice of the federal courts, implicitly sanctioned by the Supreme Court, of making assumptions about fairness in tribal courts based on allegations made by nonmembers encourages nonmembers to do exactly that. Id. at 827 (citing Burlington N. R.R. Co. v. Red Wolf, 196 F.3d 1059 (9th Cir.1999), cert. denied, 529 U.S. 1110 (2000); Estates of Red Wolf & Bull Tail v. Burlington N. R.R. Co., No. 94–31 (Crow Ct. App.1996)).

STRATE V. A-1 CONTRACTORS, INC.

Supreme Court of the United States, 1997.
520 U.S. 438, 117 S.Ct. 1404, 137 L.Ed.2d 661.

JUSTICE GINSBURG delivered the opinion of the Court.

This case concerns the adjudicatory authority of tribal courts over personal injury actions against defendants who are not tribal members. * * *

* * *

I

In November 1990, petitioner Gisela Fredericks and respondent Lyle Stockert were involved in a traffic accident on a portion of a North Dakota state highway running through the Fort Berthold Indian Reservation. The highway strip crossing the reservation is a 6.59-mile stretch of road, open to the public, affording access to a federal water resource project. North Dakota maintains the road under a right-of-way granted by the United States to the State's Highway Department; the right-of-way lies on land held by the United States in trust for the Three Affiliated Tribes (Mandan, Hidatsa, and Arikara) and their members.

The accident occurred when Fredericks' automobile collided with a gravel truck driven by Stockert and owned by respondent A-1 Contractors, Stockert's employer. A-1 Contractors, a non-Indian-owned enterprise with its principal place of business outside the reservation, was at the time under a subcontract with LCM Corporation, a corporation wholly owned by the Tribes, to do landscaping work related to the construction of a tribal community building. A-1 Contractors performed all work under the subcontract within the boundaries of the reservation. The record does not show whether Stockert was engaged in subcontract work at the time of the accident. Neither Stockert nor Fredericks is a member of the Three Affiliated Tribes or an Indian. Fredericks, however, is the widow of a deceased member of the Tribes and has five adult children who are tribal members.

Fredericks sustained serious injuries in the accident and was hospitalized for 24 days. In May 1991, she sued respondents A-1 Contractors and Stockert, as well as A-1 Contractors' insurer, in the Tribal Court for the Three Affiliated Tribes of the Fort Berthold Reservation. In the same lawsuit, Fredericks' five adult children filed a loss-of-consortium claim. Together, Fredericks and her children sought damages exceeding $13 million. Respondents and the insurer made a special appearance in the Tribal Court to contest that court's personal and subject-matter jurisdiction. The Tribal Court ruled that it had authority to adjudicate Gisela Fredericks' case, and therefore denied respondents' motion to dismiss the action.[3] Respondents appealed the Tribal Court's jurisdictional ruling to the Northern Plains Intertribal Court of Appeals, which affirmed. Thereafter, pursuant to the parties' stipulation, the Tribal Court dismissed the insurer from the suit.

Before Tribal Court proceedings resumed, respondents commenced this action in the United States District Court for the District of North Dakota. Naming as defendants Fredericks, her adult children, the Tribal

---

[3] Satisfied that it could adjudicate Gisela Fredericks' claims, the Tribal Court declined to address her adult children's consortium claim, App. 25; thus, no ruling on that claim is here at issue.

Court, and Tribal Judge William Strate, respondents sought a declaratory judgment that, as a matter of federal law, the Tribal Court lacked jurisdiction to adjudicate Fredericks' claims. The respondents also sought an injunction against further proceedings in the Tribal Court.

* * * The Court of Appeals concluded that our decision in Montana v. United States, 450 U.S. 544 (1981), was the controlling precedent, and that, under *Montana*, the Tribal Court lacked subject-matter jurisdiction over the dispute.

We granted certiorari and now affirm.

II

Our case law establishes that, absent express authorization by federal statute or treaty, tribal jurisdiction over the conduct of nonmembers exists only in limited circumstances. In Oliphant v. Suquamish Tribe, 435 U.S. 191 (1978), the Court held that Indian tribes lack criminal jurisdiction over non-Indians. *Montana v. United States*, decided three years later, is the pathmarking case concerning tribal civil authority over nonmembers. *Montana* concerned the authority of the Crow Tribe to regulate hunting and fishing by non-Indians on lands within the Tribe's reservation owned in fee simple by non-Indians. * * *

* * *

A

We begin with petitioners' contention that *National Farmers* and *Iowa Mutual* broadly confirm tribal-court civil jurisdiction over claims against nonmembers arising from occurrences on any land within a reservation. * * *

* * *

Recognizing that our precedent has been variously interpreted, we reiterate that *National Farmers* and *Iowa Mutual* enunciate only an exhaustion requirement, a "prudential rule," based on comity. These decisions do not expand or stand apart from *Montana*'s instruction on "the inherent sovereign powers of an Indian tribe." While *Montana* immediately involved regulatory authority, the Court broadly addressed the concept of "inherent sovereignty." Regarding activity on non-Indian fee land within a reservation, *Montana* delineated—in a main rule and exceptions—the bounds of the power tribes retain to exercise "forms of civil jurisdiction over non-Indians." As to nonmembers, we hold, a tribe's adjudicative jurisdiction does not exceed its legislative jurisdiction. Absent congressional direction enlarging tribal-court jurisdiction, we adhere to that understanding. Subject to controlling provisions in treaties and statutes, and the two exceptions identified in *Montana*, the civil authority of Indian tribes and their courts with respect to non-Indian fee lands generally "does not extend to the activities of nonmembers of the tribe."

B

We consider next the argument that *Montana* does not govern this case because the land underlying the scene of the accident is held in trust for the Three Affiliated Tribes and their members. Petitioners and the United States point out that in *Montana*, as in later cases following *Montana*'s instruction the challenged tribal authority related to nonmember activity on alienated, non-Indian reservation land. We "can readily agree," in accord with *Montana*, that tribes retain considerable control over nonmember conduct on tribal land. On the particular matter before us, however, we agree with respondents: The right-of-way North Dakota acquired for the State's highway renders the 6.59-mile stretch equivalent, for nonmember governance purposes, to alienated, non-Indian land.

Congress authorized grants of rights-of-way over Indian lands in 1948 legislation. §§ 25 U.S.C. § 323–328. A grant over land belonging to a tribe requires "consent of the proper tribal officials," § 324, and the payment of just compensation, § 325. The grant involved in this case was made, pursuant to the federal statute, in 1970. Its purpose was to facilitate public access to Lake Sakakawea, a federal water resource project under the control of the Army Corps of Engineers.

In the granting instrument, the United States conveyed to North Dakota "an easement for a right-of-way for the realignment and improvement of North Dakota State Highway No. 8 over, across and upon [specified] lands." * * *

* * *

Forming part of the State's highway, the right-of-way is open to the public, and traffic on it is subject to the State's control. The Tribes have consented to, and received payment for, the State's use of the 6.59-mile stretch for a public highway. They have retained no gatekeeping right. So long as the stretch is maintained as part of the State's highway, the Tribes cannot assert a landowner's right to occupy and exclude. Cf. *Bourland*, 508 U.S. at 689 (regarding reservation land acquired by the United States for operation of a dam and a reservoir, Tribe's loss of "right of absolute and exclusive use and occupation . . . implies the loss of regulatory jurisdiction over the use of the land by others"). We therefore align the right-of-way, for the purpose at hand, with land alienated to non-Indians. Our decision in *Montana*, accordingly, governs this case.

III

Petitioners and the United States refer to no treaty or statute authorizing the Three Affiliated Tribes to entertain highway-accident tort suits of the kind Fredericks commenced against A-1 Contractors and

Stockert. Rather, petitioners and the United States ground their defense of tribal-court jurisdiction exclusively on the concept of retained or inherent sovereignty. *Montana*, we have explained, is the controlling decision for this case. To prevail here, petitioners must show that Fredericks' tribal-court action against nonmembers qualifies under one of *Montana*'s two exceptions.

The first exception to the *Montana* rule covers "activities of nonmembers who enter consensual relationships with the tribe or its members, through commercial dealing, contracts, leases, or other arrangements." The tortious conduct alleged in Fredericks' complaint does not fit that description. The dispute, as the Court of Appeals said, is "distinctly non-tribal in nature." It "arose between two non-Indians involved in [a] run-of-the-mill [highway] accident." Although A-1 was engaged in subcontract work on the Fort Berthold Reservation, and therefore had a "consensual relationship" with the Tribes, "Gisela Fredericks was not a party to the subcontract, and the Tribes were strangers to the accident."

Montana's list of cases fitting within the first exception indicates the type of activities the Court had in mind: Williams v. Lee, 358 U.S. 217 (1959) (declaring tribal jurisdiction exclusive over lawsuit arising out of on-reservation sales transaction between nonmember plaintiff and member defendants); Morris v. Hitchcock, 194 U.S. 384 (1904) (upholding tribal permit tax on nonmember-owned livestock within boundaries of the Chickasaw Nation); Buster v. Wright, 135 F. 947 (C.A.8 1905) (upholding Tribe's permit tax on nonmembers for the privilege of conducting business within Tribe's borders; court characterized as "inherent" the Tribe's "authority . . . to prescribe the terms upon which noncitizens may transact business within its borders"); *Colville*, 447 U.S. at 152–154 (tribal authority to tax on-reservation cigarette sales to nonmembers "is a fundamental attribute of sovereignty which the tribes retain unless divested of it by federal law or necessary implication of their dependent status"). Measured against these cases, the Fredericks-Stockert highway accident presents no "consensual relationship" of the qualifying kind.

The second exception to *Montana*'s general rule concerns conduct that "threatens or has some direct effect on the political integrity, the economic security, or the health or welfare of the tribe." 450 U.S. at 566. Undoubtedly, those who drive carelessly on a public highway running through a reservation endanger all in the vicinity, and surely jeopardize the safety of tribal members. But if *Montana*'s second exception requires no more, the exception would severely shrink the rule. * * *

* * *

Read in isolation, the *Montana* rule's second exception can be misperceived. Key to its proper application, however, is the Court's preface:

"Indian tribes retain their inherent power [to punish tribal offenders,] to determine tribal membership, to regulate domestic relations among members, and to prescribe rules of inheritance for members. . . . But [a tribe's inherent power does not reach] beyond what is necessary to protect tribal self-government or to control internal relations." Neither regulatory nor adjudicatory authority over the state highway accident at issue is needed to preserve "the right of reservation Indians to make their own laws and be ruled by them." *Williams*, 358 U.S. at 220. The *Montana* rule, therefore, and not its exceptions, applies to this case.

Gisela Fredericks may pursue her case against A-1 Contractors and Stockert in the state forum open to all who sustain injuries on North Dakota's highway. Opening the Tribal Court for her optional use is not necessary to protect tribal self-government; and requiring A-1 and Stockert to defend against this commonplace state highway accident claim in an unfamiliar court is not crucial to "the political integrity, the economic security, or the health or welfare of the [Three Affiliated Tribes]." *Montana*, 450 U.S. at 566.[14]

* * *

For the reasons stated, the judgment of the Court of Appeals for the Eighth Circuit is

Affirmed.

NOTES

1.   Gisela Fredericks was not a tribal member, which, as the Court suggested, made the tribe a "stranger" to the case. However Fredericks was married to a tribal member, had tribal member children, and had never lived within the United States anywhere except on the Fort Berthold Reservation (she was a German national and moved to the Reservation at a young age). These facts were legally irrelevant to the Court. Would it matter if the plaintiff in a similar case was a tribal member?

In Wilson v. Marchington, 127 F.3d 805 (9th Cir.1997), cert. denied, 523 U.S. 1074 (1998), a tribal member sued a non-Indian in tribal court for damages sustained in a traffic accident on a state highway within a reservation. The Court of Appeals applied the *Strate* rule, and held that the judgment of the tribal court was not entitled to recognition in United States courts.

---

[14] When, as in this case, it is plain that no federal grant provides for tribal governance of nonmembers' conduct on land covered by Montana's main rule, it will be equally evident that tribal courts lack adjudicatory authority over disputes arising from such conduct. As in criminal proceedings, state or federal courts will be the only forums competent to adjudicate those disputes. See *National Farmers Union Ins. Cos. v. Crow Tribe*, 471 U.S. 845, 854 (1985). Therefore, when tribal-court jurisdiction over an action such as this one is challenged in federal court, the otherwise applicable exhaustion requirement must give way, for it would serve no purpose other than delay. *Cf. National Farmers*, 471 U.S. at 856, n. 21.

2.   The Justices in *Strate* seemed to be concerned about requiring defendants involved in "commonplace" highway accident claims to appear in an unfamiliar forum merely because the highway passed through a reservation. During oral arguments, Justices Souter, Ginsburg, and Breyer all expressed preferences for a rule that would allow for a uniform body of tort law for those traveling on state highways in Indian country.

Several Justices, most especially Justice O'Connor, appeared concerned about the fact that in many tribal courts, the judge and jury will consist entirely of tribal members only. During oral argument in *Strate*, Justice O'Connor asked:

> Well, how about if it goes to trial in the tribal court and the tribe chooses to use as the jury all the friends and relatives of the victim, and they say, yeah, she's really been injured, and we're going to give a heck of a verdict here, and they do, and suppose other errors that might amount to a due process violation in a Federal or State court obtain. There is no way to challenge that as a due process violation later in any State or Federal court, I assume.

Oral Argument at 28, Strate v. A-1 Contractors, 520 U.S. 438 (1997) (No. 95–1872).

One amicus brief filed in *Strate* asserted that non-Indian companies sued in tribal courts faced "outrageous" abuses in tribal courts:

> In 1995, BN was sued in tribal court on the Crow Reservation in Montana by the survivors of two members of the tribe killed in a railroad crossing accident on the reservation. Red Wolf v. Burlington Northern R.R., Civ. No. 94–31 (Crow Tribal Ct.). In 1996 the case was tried to a jury made up entirely of members of the tribe, including some who were relatives of the plaintiffs. During jury selection, many potential jurors expressed a deep-seated bias against the railroad. That bias was echoed by the court itself when a judge (who was not presiding over the case) addressed the venire panel in the Crow language, telling them
>
>> "A train runs through the middle of our land, Crows, you know, I don't have to tell you. Bodies, in the past, bodies are scattered along the railway. Now, this is the day."
>
> Although the evidence showed that the driver and her mother were intoxicated at the time of the accident, the jury found BN 100% liable for wrongful death and awarded the five heirs what the jury described as "compensatory" damages in the astonishing amount of $250 million.

Brief for the American Trucking Associations, Inc. et al., at 3, Strate v. A-1 Contractors, 520 U.S. 438 (1997) (No. 95–1872). No facts like these were entered in the tribal court record in *Strate*—nor could they be, since the plaintiff brought suit in federal court without exhausting tribal court remedies. It is possible that the Supreme Court granted certiorari in *Strate* because the

Eighth Circuit had committed gross error in failing to comply with the rule in *National Farmers Union*. But then might the circumstances of the *Red Wolf* case called to the Court's attention in briefing have influenced it not to return the case to tribal court?

3.   Justice Ginsburg's holding that the state highway located on tribal lands was nonmember land for purposes of applying *Montana* kept open the question of the impact the *Montana* test would have on tribal jurisdiction on Indian lands. The next case involved tribal jurisdiction over events occurring on tribal trust lands but did little to resolve that question.

NEVADA V. HICKS

Supreme Court of the United States, 2001.
533 U.S. 353, 121 S.Ct. 2304, 150 L.Ed.2d 398.

JUSTICE SCALIA delivered the opinion of the Court.

This case presents the question whether a tribal court may assert jurisdiction over civil claims against state officials who entered tribal land to execute a search warrant against a tribe member suspected of having violated state law outside the reservation.

I.

Respondent Hicks is one of about 900 members of the Fallon Paiute-Shoshone Tribes of western Nevada. He resides on the Tribes' reservation of approximately 8,000 acres, established by federal statute in 1908. In 1990 Hicks came under suspicion of having killed, off the reservation, a California bighorn sheep, a gross misdemeanor under Nevada law. A state game warden obtained from state court a search warrant "SUBJECT TO OBTAINING APPROVAL FROM THE FALLON TRIBAL COURT IN AND FOR THE FALLON PAIUTE-SHOSHONE TRIBES." According to the issuing judge, this tribal-court authorization was necessary because "[t]his Court has no jurisdiction on the Fallon Paiute-Shoshone Indian Reservation." A search warrant was obtained from the tribal court, and the warden, accompanied by a tribal police officer, searched respondents yard, uncovering only the head of a Rocky Mountain bighorn, a different (and unprotected) species of sheep.

Approximately one year later, a tribal police officer reported to the warden that he had observed two mounted bighorn sheep heads in respondent's home. The warden again obtained a search warrant from state court; though this warrant did not explicitly require permission from the Tribes, a tribal-court warrant was nonetheless secured, and respondent's home was again (unsuccessfully) searched by three wardens and additional tribal officers.

Respondent, claiming that his sheep-heads had been damaged, and that the second search exceeded the bounds of the warrant, brought suit against the Tribal Judge, the tribal officers, the state wardens in their individual and official capacities, and the State of Nevada in the Tribal Court in and for the Fallon Paiute-Shoshone Tribes. (His claims against all defendants except the state wardens and the State of Nevada were dismissed by directed verdict and are not at issue here.) Respondent's causes of action included trespass to land and chattels, abuse of process, and violation of civil rights specifically, denial of equal protection, denial of due process, and unreasonable search and seizure, each remediable under 42 U.S.C. § 1983. Respondent later voluntarily dismissed his case against the State and against the state officials in their official capacities, leaving only his suit against those officials in their individual capacities.

The Tribal Court held that it had jurisdiction over the claims, a holding affirmed by the Tribal Appeals Court. . . . . The Ninth Circuit [concurred], concluding that the fact that respondent's home is located on tribe-owned land within the reservation is sufficient to support tribal jurisdiction over civil claims against nonmembers arising from their activities on that land. 196 F.3d 1020 (1999). We granted certiorari.

II.

In this case, which involves claims brought under both tribal and federal law, it is necessary to determine, as to the former, whether the Tribal Court in and for the Fallon Paiute-Shoshone Tribes has jurisdiction to adjudicate the alleged tortuous conduct of state wardens executing a search warrant for evidence of an off-reservation crime; and, as to the latter, whether the Tribal Court has jurisdiction over claims brought under 42 U.S.C. § 1983. We address the former question first.

A.

* * *

The principle of Indian law central to this aspect of the case is our holding in Strate v. A-1 Contractors, 520 U.S. 438, 453 (1997): "As to nonmembers . . . a tribe's adjudicative jurisdiction does not exceed its legislative jurisdiction. . . ." That formulation leaves open the question whether a tribe's adjudicative jurisdiction over nonmember defendants *equals* its legislative jurisdiction.[2] We will not have to answer that open question if we determine that the Tribes in any event lack legislative jurisdiction in this case. We first inquire, therefore, whether the Fallon

---

[2] In *National Farmers Union Ins. Cos. v. Crow Tribe*, 471 U.S. 845, 855–856 (1985), we avoided the question whether tribes may generally adjudicate against nonmembers claims arising from on-reservation transactions, and we have never held that a tribal court had jurisdiction over a nonmember defendant. Typically, our cases have involved claims brought against tribal defendants. See, e.g., *Williams v. Lee*, 358 U.S. 217 (1959). In *Strate v. A-1 Contractors*, 520 U.S. 438, 453 (1997), however, we assumed that "where tribes possess authority to regulate the activities of nonmembers, civil jurisdiction over disputes arising out of such activities presumably lies in the tribal courts," without distinguishing between nonmember plaintiffs and nonmember defendants. See also Iowa Mut. Ins. Co. v. LaPlante, 480 U.S. 9, 18 (1987). Our holding in this case is limited to the question of tribal-court jurisdiction.

Paiute-Shoshone Tribes—either as an exercise of their inherent sovereignty, or under grant of federal authority—can regulate state wardens executing a search warrant for evidence of an off-reservation crime.

Indian tribes' regulatory authority over nonmembers is governed by the principles set forth in Montana v. United States, 450 U.S. 544 (1981), which we have called the "pathmarking case" on the subject, *Strate*, supra, at 445. * * * 3

Both *Montana* and *Strate* rejected tribal authority to regulate nonmembers' activities on land over which the tribe could not "assert a landowner's right to occupy and exclude." *Strate*, supra, at 456; *Montana*, supra, at 557. Respondents and the United States argue that since Hicks's home and yard *are* on tribe-owned land within the reservation, the Tribe may make its exercise of regulatory authority over nonmembers a condition of nonmembers' entry. Not necessarily. * * * *Oliphant* itself drew no distinctions based on the status of land. And *Montana*, after announcing the general rule of no jurisdiction over nonmembers, cautioned that "[t]o be sure, Indian tribes retain inherent sovereign power to exercise some forms of civil jurisdiction over non-Indians on their reservations, even on non-Indian fee lands," 450 U.S., at 565—clearly implying that the general rule of *Montana* applies to both Indian and non-Indian land. The ownership status of land, in other words, is only one factor to consider in determining whether regulation of the activities of nonmembers is necessary to protect tribal self-government or to control internal relations. It may sometimes be a dispositive factor. * * * But the existence of tribal ownership is not alone enough to support regulatory jurisdiction over nonmembers.

* * *

B.

* * *

Our cases make clear that the Indians' right to make their own laws and be governed by them does not exclude all state regulatory authority on the reservation. State sovereignty does not end at a reservation's border. Though tribes are often referred to as sovereign entities, it was "long ago" that "the Court departed from Chief Justice Marshall's view that 'the laws of [a State] can have no force' within reservation boundaries." Worcester v. Georgia, 6 Pet. 515, 561 (1832), White Mountain Apache Tribe v. Bracker, 448 U.S. 136, 141 (1980). "Ordinarily," it is now clear, "an Indian

---

[3] *Montana* recognized an exception to this rule for tribal regulation of "the activities of nonmembers who enter consensual relationships with the tribe or its members, through commercial dealing, contracts, leases, or other arrangements." 450 U.S., at 565. Though the wardens in this case "consensually" obtained a warrant from the Tribal Court before searching respondent's home and yard, we do not think this qualifies as an "other arrangement" within the meaning of this passage. Read in context, an "other arrangement" is clearly another private consensual relationship, from which the official actions at issue in this case are far removed.

reservation is considered part of the territory of the State." U.S. Dept. of Interior, Federal Indian Law 510, and n.1 (1958), citing Utah & Northern R. Co. v. Fisher, 116 U.S. 28 (1885).

* * *

While it is not entirely clear from our precedent whether the last mentioned authority entails the corollary right to enter a reservation (including Indian-fee lands) for enforcement purposes, several of our opinions point in that direction. . . . In *Utah & Northern R. Co.*, however, we observed that "[i]t has . . . been held that process of [state] courts may run into an Indian reservation of this kind, where the subject-matter or controversy is otherwise within their cognizance," 116 U.S., at 31. Shortly thereafter, we considered, in United States v. Kagama, 118 U.S. 375 (1886), whether Congress could enact a law giving federal courts jurisdiction over various common-law, violent crimes committed by Indians on a reservation within a State. We expressed skepticism that the Indian Commerce Clause could justify this assertion of authority in derogation of state jurisdiction, but ultimately accepted the argument that the law

> does not interfere with the process of the State courts within the reservation, nor with the operation of State laws upon white people found there. Its effect is confined to the acts of an Indian of some tribe, of a criminal character, committed within the limits of the reservation.

> "It seems to us that this is within the competency of Congress."

Id., at 383.

The Court's references to "process" in *Utah & Northern R. Co.* and *Kagama*, and the Court's concern in *Kagama* over possible federal encroachment on state prerogatives, suggest state authority to issue search warrants in cases such as the one before us. . . . . This makes perfect sense, since, as we explained in the context of federal enclaves, the reservation of state authority to serve process is necessary "to prevent [such areas] from becoming an asylum for fugitives from justice." Fort Leavenworth R. Co. v. Lowe, 114 U.S. 525, 533 (1885).

We conclude today, in accordance with these prior statements, that tribal authority to regulate state officers in executing process related to the violation, off reservation, of state laws is not essential to tribal self-government or internal relations-to "the right to make laws and be ruled by them." The State's interest in execution of process is considerable, and even when it relates to Indian-fee lands it no more impairs the tribe's self-government than federal enforcement of federal law impairs state government. * * *

* * *

III.

We turn next to the contention of respondent and the Government that the tribal court, as a court of general jurisdiction, has authority to entertain federal claims under § 1983. It is certainly true that state courts of "general jurisdiction" can adjudicate cases invoking federal statutes, such as § 1983, absent congressional specification to the contrary. "Under [our] system of dual sovereignty, we have consistently held that state courts have inherent authority, and are thus presumptively competent, to adjudicate claims arising under the laws of the United States," Tafflin v. Levitt, 493 U.S. 455, 458 (1990). * * * This historical and constitutional assumption of concurrent state-court jurisdiction over federal-law cases is completely missing with respect to tribal courts.

Respondents' contention that tribal courts are courts of "general jurisdiction" is also quite wrong. Tribal courts, it should be clear, cannot be courts of general jurisdiction in this sense, for a tribe's inherent adjudicative jurisdiction over nonmembers is at most only as broad as its legislative jurisdiction. It is true that some statutes proclaim tribal-court jurisdiction over certain questions of federal law. See, e.g., 25 U.S.C. § 1911(a) (authority to adjudicate child custody disputes under the Indian Child Welfare Act of 1978); 12 U.S.C. § 1715–z13(g)(5) (jurisdiction over mortgage foreclosure actions brought by the Secretary of Housing and Urban Development against reservation homeowners). But no provision in federal law provides for tribal-court jurisdiction over § 1983 actions.

* * *

IV.

The last question before us is whether petitioners were required to exhaust their jurisdictional claims in Tribal Court before bringing them in Federal District Court. . . . Since it is clear, as we have discussed, that tribal courts lack jurisdiction over state officials for causes of action relating to their performance of official duties, adherence to the tribal exhaustion requirement in such cases "would serve no purpose other than delay," and is therefore unnecessary.

V.

Finally, a few words in response to the concurring opinion of Justice O'Connor, which is in large part a dissent from the views expressed in this opinion.

The principal point of the concurrence is that our reasoning "gives only passing consideration to the fact that the state officials' activities in this case occurred on land owned and controlled by the Tribe." According to Justice O'Connor, "that factor is not prominent in the Court's analysis." Even a cursory reading of our opinion demonstrates that this is not so. To the contrary, we acknowledge that tribal ownership is a factor in the

Montana analysis, and a factor significant enough that it "may sometimes be . . . dispositive." We simply do not find it dispositive in the present case, when weighed against the State's interest in pursuing off-reservation violations of its laws. The concurrence is of course free to disagree with this judgment; but to say that failure to give tribal ownership determinative effect "fails to consider adequately the Tribe's inherent sovereign interests in activities on their land," (opinion of O'Connor, J.), is an exaggeration.

* * *

The judgment of the Court of Appeals is reversed, and the case remanded for further proceedings consistent with our opinion.

It is so ordered.

JUSTICE SOUTER, with whom JUSTICES KENNEDY and THOMAS join, concurring.

* * *

The ability of nonmembers to know where tribal jurisdiction begins and ends, it should be stressed, is a matter of real, practical consequence given "[t]he special nature of [Indian] tribunals," Duro v. Reina, 495 U.S. 676, 693 (1990), which differ from traditional American courts in a number of significant respects. To start with the most obvious one, it has been understood for more than a century that the Bill of Rights and the Fourteenth Amendment do not of their own force apply to Indian tribes. See Talton v. Mayes [, 163 U.S. 376 (1896)]. Although the Indian Civil Rights Act of 1968 (ICRA) makes a handful of analogous safeguards enforceable in tribal courts, 25 U.S.C. § 1302, "the guarantees are not identical," *Oliphant*, 435 U.S., at 194, and there is a "definite trend by tribal courts" toward the view that they "ha[ve] leeway in interpreting the ICRA's due process and equal protection clauses and need not follow the U.S. Supreme Court precedents jot-for-jot," Newton, Tribal Court Praxis: One Year in the Life of Twenty Indian Tribal Courts, 22 Am. Indian L.Rev. 285, 344, n.238 (1998). In any event, a presumption against tribal-court civil jurisdiction squares with one of the principal policy considerations underlying *Oliphant*, namely, an overriding concern that citizens who are not tribal members be "protected . . . from unwarranted intrusions on their personal liberty," 435 U.S., at 210.

Tribal courts also differ from other American courts (and often from one another) in their structure, in the substantive law they apply, and in the independence of their judges. Although some modern tribal courts "mirror American courts" and "are guided by written codes, rules, procedures, and guidelines, tribal law is still frequently unwritten, being based instead on the values, mores, and norms of a tribe and expressed in its customs, traditions, and practices," and is often "handed down orally or by example from one generation to another." Melton, Indigenous Justice

Systems and Tribal Society, 79 Judicature 126, 130–131 (1995). The resulting law applicable in tribal courts is a complex mix of tribal codes and federal, state, and traditional law, National American Indian Court Judges Assn., Indian Courts and the Future 43 (1978), which would be unusually difficult for an outsider to sort out.

Hence the practical importance of being able to anticipate tribal jurisdiction by reference to a fact more readily knowable than the title status of a particular plot of land. One further consideration confirms the point. It is generally accepted that there is no effective review mechanism in place to police tribal courts' decisions on matters of non-tribal law, since tribal-court judgments based on state or federal law can be neither removed nor appealed to state or federal courts. The result, of course, is a risk of substantial disuniformity in the interpretation of state and federal law, a risk underscored by the fact that "[t]ribal courts are often subordinate to the political branches of tribal government," *Duro,* supra, at 693 (quoting Cohen 334–335).

Justice Ginsburg, concurring.

I join the Court's opinion. As the Court plainly states, and as Justice Souter recognizes, the "holding in this case is limited to the question of tribal-court jurisdiction over state officers enforcing state law." The Court's decision explicitly "leave[s] open the question of tribal-court jurisdiction over nonmember defendants in general," including state officials engaged on tribal land in a venture or frolic of their own (a state officers conduct on tribal land "unrelated to [performance of his law-enforcement duties] is potentially subject to tribal control").

* * *

Justice O'Connor, with whom Justice Stevens and Justice Breyer join, concurring in part and concurring in the judgment.

The Court holds that a tribe has no power to regulate the activities of state officials enforcing state law on land owned and controlled by the tribe. The majority's sweeping opinion, without cause, undermines the authority of tribes to "make their own laws and be ruled by them." Strate v. A-1 Contractors, 520 U.S. 438, 459 (1997) (quoting Williams v. Lee, 358 U.S. 217, 220 (1959)). I write separately because Part II of the Court's decision is unmoored from our precedents.

I.

* * *

The majority's rule undermining tribal interests is all the more perplexing because the conduct in this case occurred on land owned and controlled by the Tribes. Although the majority gives a passing nod to land status at the outset of its opinion, that factor is not prominent in the Court's analysis. This oversight is significant. *Montana* recognizes that tribes may retain inherent power to exercise civil jurisdiction when the nonmember conduct "threatens or has some direct effect on the political integrity, the economic security, or the health or welfare of the tribe." 450 U.S., at 566. These interests are far more likely to be implicated where, as here, the nonmember activity takes place on land owned and controlled by the tribe. If *Montana* is to bring coherence to our case law, we must apply it with due consideration to land status, which has always figured prominently in our analysis of tribal jurisdiction.

* * *

II

* * *

To resolve this case, it suffices to answer the questions presented, which concern the civil adjudicatory jurisdiction of tribal courts. Petitioners contend that tribal court jurisdiction over state officials should be determined with reference to officials claims of immunity. I agree and would resolve this case by applying basic principles of official and qualified immunity.

* * *

In this case, the state officials raised their immunity defenses in Tribal Court as they challenged that court's subject matter jurisdiction. Thus the Tribal Court and the Appellate Tribal Court had a full opportunity to address the immunity claims. These defendants, like other officials facing civil liability, were entitled to have their immunity defenses adjudicated at the earliest stage possible to avoid needless litigation. It requires no magic to afford officials the same protection in tribal court that they would be afforded in state or federal court. I would therefore reverse the Court of Appeals in this case on the ground that it erred in failing to address the state official's immunity defenses. It is possible that Hicks' lawsuits would have been easily disposed of on the basis of official and qualified immunity.

* * *

JUSTICE STEVENS, with whom JUSTICE BREYER joins, concurring in the judgment.

* * *

NOTES

1.   The Supreme Court's majority opinion analyzing this strange fact pattern is at least as strange as the facts. The Court held, as would be expected, that the State of Nevada should prevail in the matter, and that the tribal court did not have jurisdiction over the matter. How the Court reached that conclusion is unusual. First, instead of addressing the meatier questions of

whether a tribal court could have jurisdiction over a Section 1983 claim at all, whether Congress intended to allow suits against state officials in tribal court when it enacted Section 1983, and whether the state officer still may have retained qualified immunity from damages, the majority began with a discussion of *Montana*. It is likely that the majority intended to directly rebut the conclusion of the Ninth Circuit, which had recognized broad tribal authority to exclude anyone, even state officers, from tribal lands: "The Tribe's unfettered power to exclude state officers from its land implies its authority to regulate the behavior of non-members on that land." 196 F.3d 1020, 1028 (9th Cir.1999). The Ninth Circuit also held that *Montana* did not apply at all to actions arising on tribal lands. Id. at 1025–30. The majority's rigorous efforts to refute those conclusions apparently led it to focus first on the *Montana-Strate* line of cases. The majority specifically held that *Montana* applies to actions arising on tribal lands, but also held that landownership remained an important, if not dispositive, factor. However, the majority eventually held that state officers may enter Indian country to enforce state law, rendering the *Montana* analysis unnecessary, and arguably dicta.

2.   The South Dakota Supreme Court, distinguishing Nevada v. Hicks, held that state police officers could not engage in fresh pursuit onto the reservation for a traffic violation without a warrant or permission from the tribe. South Dakota v. Cummings, 679 N.W.2d 484 (S.D.2004), cert denied, 543 U.S. 943 (2004). According to the court:

> * * * [I]n *Hicks*, the Tribe was attempting to extend its jurisdiction over state officials by subjecting them to claims in tribal court. Here, the State is attempting to extend its jurisdiction into the boundaries of the Tribe's Reservation without consent of the Tribe or a tribal-state compact allowing such jurisdiction. In other words, in *Hicks*, tribal sovereignty was being used as a sword against state officers. Here, tribal sovereignty is being used as a shield to protect the Tribe's sovereignty from incursions by the State. This is significant because historically, the Federal Government has been highly protective of the Tribes' right to be free from harm and interference by states.

> * * *

> Finally, the question in *Hicks* was whether the tribal court had jurisdiction over state officers acting in their individual or official capacity on tribal land. *Hicks* should be construed to address that question only, and in fact, several federal courts have done so. See e.g., McDonald v. Means, 309 F.3d 530 (9th Cir. 2002); MacArthur v. San Juan County, 309 F.3d 1216 (10th Cir. 2002); United States v. Archambault, 174 F.Supp.2d 1009 (D.S.D.2001); Fidelity and Guaranty Insurance Co. v. Bradley, 212 F.Supp.2d 163 (W.D.N.C. 2002). The question whether a state officer in fresh pursuit for a crime committed off the reservation has jurisdiction to enter the reservation without tribal permission or a warrant was not squarely

before the Court. We decline to usurp the power of the United States
Congress to make laws with respect to Native American rights and
sovereignty and the authority of the Supreme Court to interpret those
laws by relying on dicta from a factually and legally distinguishable
case.

Id. at 487–89.

3.   In Inyo County, California v. Paiute-Shoshone Indians of the Bishop
Community of the Bishop Colony, 538 U.S. 701 (2003), the Supreme Court held
that Indian tribes do not have standing to sue state governments under 42
U.S.C. § 1983, the main civil rights enforcement statute under federal law,
because tribes are not "persons" under the statute. Id. at 711–12. In that case,
county officials served a state court-issued warrant on the tribe, asserting the
right to inspect tribal employment records.

4.   In Plains Commerce Bank v. Long Family Land and Cattle Co., 554
U.S. 316 (2008), the Supreme Court held 5–4 that the Cheyenne River Sioux
Tribal Court did not possess jurisdiction over nonmember owned lands
sufficient to stop a sale of lands formerly owned by tribal members to
nonmembers. The Court also held that the tribal court could not sustain a
judgment of $750,000 against the Bank by the Long Company for breaches of
contract and a race discrimination tort. In important respects, *Plains
Commerce* changes nothing in terms of the *Montana* analysis on nonmember
lands.

The Court focused on the fact that the Long Company's land had been
alienated to nonmembers, rendering all but certain the tribe could not assert
jurisdiction over the Bank under *Montana*. The Court also more closely tied
the *Montana* general rule to the federal legislative allotment of Indian
reservations. The Court noted that the allotment of Indian reservations
leading the alienation of Indian lands to nonmembers also eliminated the
tribe's "plenary" control over the lands:

> [The *Montana*] general rule restricts tribal authority over
> nonmember activities taking place on the reservation, and is
> particularly strong when the nonmember's activity occurs on land
> owned in fee simple by non-Indians-what we have called "non-Indian
> fee land." * * * Thanks to the Indian General Allotment Act of 1887,
> 24 Stat. 388, as amended, 25 U.S.C. § 331 et seq., there are millions
> of acres of non-Indian fee land located within the contiguous borders
> of Indian tribes. * * * The history of the General Allotment Act and
> its successor statutes has been well rehearsed in our precedents. * * *
> Suffice it to say here that the effect of the Act was to convert millions
> of acres of formerly tribal land into fee simple parcels, "fully
> alienable," . . . and "free of all charge or encumbrance whatsoever,"
> 25 U.S.C. § 348 (2000 ed., Supp. V). See F. Cohen, Handbook of
> Federal Indian Law § 16.03[2][b], pp. 1041–1042 (2005 ed.).

Our cases have made clear that once tribal land is converted into fee simple, the tribe loses plenary jurisdiction over it. See *County of Yakima, supra*, at 267–268, 112 S.Ct. 683 (General Allotment Act permits Yakima County to impose ad valorem tax on fee land located within the reservation); Goudy v. Meath, 203 U.S. 146, 149–150, 27 S.Ct. 48, 51 L.Ed. 130 (1906) (by rendering allotted lands alienable, General Allotment Act exposed them to state assessment and forced sale for taxes); In re Heff, 197 U.S. 488, 502–503, 25 S.Ct. 506, 49 L.Ed. 848 (1905) (fee land subject to plenary state jurisdiction upon issuance of trust patent (superseded by the Burke Act, 34 Stat. 182, 25 U.S.C. § 349) (2000 ed.)). Among the powers lost is the authority to prevent the land's sale, *see County of Yakima, supra*, at 263, 112 S.Ct. 683 (General Allotment Act granted fee holders power of voluntary sale)—not surprisingly, as "free alienability" by the holder is a core attribute of the fee simple, C. Moynihan, Introduction to Law of Real Property § 3, p. 32 (2d ed.1988). Moreover, when the tribe or tribal members convey a parcel of fee land "to non-Indians, [the tribe] loses any former right of absolute and exclusive use and occupation of the conveyed lands." South Dakota v. Bourland, 508 U.S. 679, 689, 113 S.Ct. 2309, 124 L.Ed.2d 606 (1993) (emphasis added). This necessarily entails the "the loss of regulatory jurisdiction over the use of the land by others." Ibid. As a general rule, then, "the tribe has no authority itself, by way of tribal ordinance or actions in the tribal courts, to regulate the use of fee land." Brendale v. Confederated Tribes and Bands of Yakima Nation, 492 U.S. 408, 430, 109 S.Ct. 2994, 106 L.Ed.2d 343 (1989) (opinion of White, J.).

Plains Commerce, 554 U.S. 328–29 (citations omitted). Tying the *Montana* rule to Acts of Congress potentially moves the Court away from embracing what Professor and Tribal Judge Frank Pommersheim termed "judicial plenary power" over Indian affairs. Frank Pommersheim, *Tribal Courts and the Federal Judiciary: Opportunities and Challenges for a Constitutional Democracy*, 58 Mont.L.Rev. 313, 328 (1997). If the analysis on divestitures of tribal sovereignty begins and ends with Acts of Congress, then the Supreme Court's past assertions that tribal authority can be implicitly divested by judicial fiat are invalid.*

5.   Even with the application of the *Montana* general rule, *Plains Commerce* was a close case. *Plains Commerce* may be the beginning of a new kind of tribal advocacy modeled to an important extent on legal realism. Instead of relying upon assumptions about tribal court practice, the Court might begin to focus on the practical realities on the ground.

---

*   Note that Pommersheim sat on the Cheyenne River Sioux Tribe's appellate court when it decided *Plains Commerce*, and was the lead author of the opinion. Bank of Hoven (Plains Commerce Bank) v. Long Family Land and Cattle Co., 32 Indian L. Rep. 6001 (Cheyenne River Sioux Tribal Court of Appeals 2004); Frank Pommersheim, Tribal Justice: Twenty-Five Years as a Tribal Appellate Justice 61–76 (2015).

For the first time, the United States, participating as *amicus curiae* in support of the Long Family, argued that tribal common law generally is not unfairly applied by tribal courts to nonmembers:

> Petitioner and some of its amici suggest that tribal common-law claims may present a trap for unwary nonmembers. . . . But this Court has previously "rejected * * * attacks on tribal court jurisdiction" predicated on allegations of "local bias and incompetence," * * * and the facts do not bear out petitioner's concerns. Tribal courts take different forms and draw from varied traditions, but, like the CRST's own courts * * * , many of them look to federal or state law to govern disputes where no established tribal law applies.[15] Indeed, when the Cheyenne River Sioux Tribal Court of Appeals recognized the principle of judicial review, it relied not only on Lakota tradition but also on this Court's opinion in *Marbury v. Madison. See* Cohen's Handbook of Federal Indian Law 274 n.545 (citing Clemente v. LeCompte, 22 Indian L. Rep. 6111 (Chy. R. Sx. Ct. App. 1994)).

Brief of the United States as Amicus Curiae Supporting Respondents 27–28, 2008 WL 742923. The brief came in direct response to Justice Souter's concurrence in *Nevada v. Hicks* that expressed concern about the application of "unfamiliar law" in tribal forums to nonmembers. Justice Souter joined the dissent in *Plains Commerce*.

Tribal amici, including the Cheyenne River Sioux Tribe itself, peppered the Court with briefs detailing the inner workings of tribal courts, and especially the Cheyenne River Sioux tribal court. See generally Frank Pommersheim, Amicus Briefs in Indian Law: The Case of Plains Commerce Bank v. Long Family Land & Cattle Co., 56 S.D.L.Rev. 86 (2011). Of note, the Cheyenne River Sioux Tribe's brief noted that the Bank had invoked tribal court jurisdiction in over 20 cases before challenging the tribal court's jurisdiction in *Plains Commerce.* Amicus curiae Cheyenne River Sioux Tribe argued:

> Of particular significance to this case, the Bank has often prevailed in tribal court or settled cases on favorable terms. In addition, tribal courts have issued numerous judicial orders in favor of the Bank. The Bank also has sought the assistance of tribal courts to obtain relief against tribal members. In fact, in a number of cases, as it did in this case, the Bank has conceded the jurisdiction of the tribal court. And, where the Bank has been successful in litigation in

---

[15] See, e.g., Matthew L.M. Fletcher, Toward a Theory of Intertribal and Intratribal Common Law, 43 Hous. L.Rev. 701, 739 (2006) (noting tribal law "tends to mirror American laws" because Tribes "must be able to function in the American political system in a seamless manner"); id. at 734–735 (discussing tribal-court use of Anglo-American legal constructs and state and federal common law; concluding there is little evidence that tribal courts are unfair to nonmembers); Bethany R. Berger, Justice and the Outsider: Jurisdiction Over Nonmembers in Tribal Legal Systems, 37 Ariz. St. L.J. 1047, 1085 (2005) (finding Navajo common law has been used to provide protections comparable "to those in state courts" even when tribal codes do not).

tribal court (whether against tribal members or nonmembers living on the Reservation), it has accepted the tribal court's jurisdiction without objection.

Brief for Amicus Curiae Cheyenne River Sioux Tribe in Support of Respondents, at 30–31, 2008 WL 782553. With the experience of using the tribal courts for its own advantage, are you surprised that the bank argued that the tribal courts were foreign forums and it should not be subjected to their jurisdiction?

The Tribe also pointed to practices of the Bank that explained why it was important for the tribe to have jurisdiction over it:

> It is an unfortunate but still all-too-common occurrence for Indians living on reservations to experience racial discrimination. They often are victimized by the predatory lending practices of local banks that seek to exploit the disadvantages of reservation economies compared to those of neighboring communities. See, e.g., Bone Shirt v. Hazeltine, 336 F.Supp.2d 976, 1031 (D.S.D. 2004) ("Indians in South Dakota have also been subject to discrimination in lending"), aff'd, 461 F.3d 1011 (8th Cir. 2006). * * *

> Indeed, the Bank and other lenders have not only discriminated against tribes and their members, but also have threatened to withhold loans from CRST members on the Reservation.

Id. at 17–20. What impact does the decision have on individual tribal members, tribes, and tribal courts based on what you have learned from the experience of the Cheyenne River Sioux Tribe in its relations with the Plains Commerce Bank? There are more details on this case in the lawyering note that follows.

6.   In Water Wheel Camp Recreational Area, Inc. v. LaRance, 642 F.3d 802 (9th Cir.2011), the Ninth Circuit held that as a practical matter *Montana*'s exceptions are easily satisfied on tribally owned or controlled lands. There, the Water Wheel camp corporation was a lessor of tribal trust lands. When the lease expired, the corporation refused to leave. The Colorado River Indian Tribes sued in tribal court to force an eviction. Water Wheel denied jurisdiction in tribal court, and also refused to comply with discovery requests on the question of whether the actions of the corporate principal were sufficient to pierce the corporate veil.

The court held that the tribal power over nonmembers is informed by (and possibly superceded by) the tribe's power to exclude nonmembers from tribal lands:

> As a preliminary matter, we consider the relationship between the tribe's inherent authority to exclude and its authority to exercise jurisdiction. The district court stated, and arguably held despite its footnote indicating otherwise, that a tribe's inherent authority to exclude a non-Indian from tribal land is subject to *Montana*. But the Supreme Court has recognized that a tribe's power to exclude exists independently of its general jurisdictional authority. *See* Duro v.

Reina, 495 U.S. 676, 696–97, 110 S.Ct. 2053, 109 L.Ed.2d 693 (1990) (noting that even where tribes lack criminal jurisdiction over a non-Indian defendant, they "possess their traditional and undisputed power to exclude persons whom they deem to be undesirable from tribal lands. * * * Tribal law enforcement authorities have the power to restrain those who disturb public order on the reservation, and if necessary, to eject them. Where jurisdiction to try and punish an offender rests outside the tribe, tribal officers may exercise their power to detain the offender and transport him to the proper authorities"), superseded on other grounds by congressional statute, 25 U.S.C. § 1301.

Montana limited the tribe's ability to exercise its power to exclude only as applied to the regulation of non-Indians on non-Indian land, not on tribal land. See Merrion v. Jicarilla Apache Tribe, 455 U.S. 130, 144–45 * * * (1982)(recognizing a tribe's inherent authority to exclude non-Indians from tribal land, without applying *Montana*); *see also* * * * *Montana*, 450 U.S. at 557 * * * (recognizing a tribe's inherent authority to condition the entry of non-Indians on tribal land as a separate matter from whether a tribe may condition the entry of non-Indians on non-Indian land); Cohen's Handbook of Federal Indian Law § 4.01[2][e], 220 (Nell Jessup Newton et al. eds., 2005) [hereinafter Cohen] (explaining that "[b]ecause the exclusionary power is a fundamental sovereign attribute intimately tied to a tribe's ability to protect the integrity and order of its territory and the welfare of its members, it is an internal matter over which the tribes retain sovereignty") * * * .

Water Wheel, 642 F.3d at 810–11.

Noting that the tribe's adjudicatory jurisdiction is equal to its regulatory jurisdiction, the court also held that the tribal court also retained jurisdiction over the nonmember principal:

> For purposes of determining whether a consensual relationship exists under *Montana*'s first exception, consent may be established "expressly or by [the nonmember's] actions." *Plains Commerce Bank*, 554 U.S. at 337 * * * . There is no requirement that Johnson's commercial dealings with the CRIT be a matter of written contract or lease actually signed by Johnson. See *Montana*, 450 U.S. at 565 * * * (tribes may regulate the activities of nonmembers who enter into "*commercial dealing*, contracts, leases, *or other arrangements*" (emphasis added)). We are to consider the circumstances and whether under those circumstances the non-Indian defendant should have reasonably anticipated that his interactions might "trigger" tribal authority. Id. at 338 * * * .

> Johnson owned and operated Water Wheel on tribal land for more than twenty years and had extensive dealings with the CRIT before the lease expired. Additionally, Johnson was on notice through the leases's explicit terms that Water Wheel, its agents, and employees were subject to CRIT laws, regulations, and ordinances.

These facts adequately support the tribal court's conclusion that Johnson had entered into a consensual relationship with the tribe and could reasonably anticipate that the tribe would exercise its jurisdictional authority. Johnson's subjective beliefs regarding his relationship with the tribe do not change the consensual nature of that relationship for purposes of regulatory jurisdiction. Moreover, the tribe's claims for unpaid rent and related damages arose directly from this relationship.

As noted above, the commercial dealings between the tribe and Johnson involved the use of tribal land, one of the tribe's most valuable assets. Thus, if *Montana* applied to the breach of contract claim, either exception would provide regulatory jurisdiction over Johnson.

As for the trespass claim, there is no legal or logical basis to require a consensual relationship between a trespasser and the offended landowner. This is particularly true when the trespass is to tribal land, the offended owner is the tribe, and the trespasser is not a tribal member. *Merrion*, 455 U.S. at 144 * * * . If tribes lacked authority to evict holdover tenants and their agents, tribes would be discouraged from entering into financially beneficial leases with nonmembers for fear of losing control over tribal land.

Evaluating the trespass claim under *Montana*'s second exception, unpaid rent and percentages of the business's gross receipts here totaled $1,486,146.42 at the time of the tribal court's judgment. Johnson's unlawful occupancy and use of tribal land not only deprived the CRIT of its power to govern and regulate its own land, but also of its right to manage and control an asset capable of producing significant income. Thus, in addition to the tribe's undisputed authority to eject trespassers from its own land, *Montana*'s second exception would provide regulatory jurisdiction.

Id. at 818–19.

7.   The Fifth Circuit in Dolgencorp, Inc. v. Mississippi Band of Choctaw Indians, 746 F.3d 167 (5th Cir.2014), aff'd by an equally divided court, 136 S.Ct. 2159 (2016), held over a strident dissent that a tribal court may take jurisdiction over a civil suit against a nonmember corporation for a tort alleged to have been committed on tribal trust property leased to the corporation. Id. at 169.

The facts are tragic. Dolgencorp entered into a lease agreement with the tribe to operate a store on tribal trust land. The tribe ran a tribal youth job training program on the reservation, which included placing youth in unpaid internships with local businesses, including Dollar General. The plaintiff in the tribal court matter, a Youth Opportunity Program (TOP) employee, alleged that a Dollar General employee had committed an act of sexual assault on the plaintiff in the store. The Fifth Circuit found a sufficient nexus between the lease with the tribe and the alleged tort under a Montana 1 analysis:

> Dolgencorp argues that there is no nexus between its participation in the YOP and Doe's tort claims. We disagree. The conduct for which Doe seeks to hold Dolgencorp liable is its alleged placement, in its Dollar General store located on tribal lands, of a manager who sexually assaulted Doe while he was working there. This conduct has an obvious nexus to Dolgencorp's participation in the YOP. In essence, a tribe that has agreed to place a minor tribe member as an unpaid intern in a business located on tribal land on a reservation is attempting to regulate the safety of the child's workplace. Simply put, the tribe is protecting its own children on its own land. It is surely within the tribe's regulatory authority to insist that a child working for a local business not be sexually assaulted by the employees of the business. The fact that the regulation takes the form of a tort duty that may be vindicated by individual tribe members in tribal court makes no difference. * * * To the extent that foreseeability is relevant to the nexus issue, as Dolgencorp suggests, it is present here. Having agreed to place a minor tribe member in a position of quasi-employment on Indian land in a reservation, it would hardly be surprising for Dolgencorp to have to answer in tribal court for harm caused to the child in the course of his employment.

Dolgencorp, 746 F.3d at 173–74.

The dissent argued that the panel majority's decision was unprecedented in Indian law:

> For the first time ever, a federal court of appeals upholds Indian tribal-court tort jurisdiction over a non-Indian, based on a consensual relationship, without a finding that jurisdiction is "necessary to protect tribal self-government or to control internal relations." Montana v. United States, 450 U.S. 544, 564, 101 S.Ct. 1245, 67 L.Ed.2d 493 (1981). The majority's alarming and unprecedented holding far outpaces the Supreme Court, which has never upheld Indian jurisdiction over a nonmember defendant.

> This ruling profoundly upsets the careful balance that the Supreme Court has struck between Indian tribal governance, on the one hand, and American sovereignty and the constitutional rights of U.S. citizens, on the other hand. The majority's bold announcement is conspicuous for its audacity, given that this court hears few Indian cases and decides little Indian law. I respectfully dissent.

Dolgencorp, 746 F.3d at 173–74 (Smith, C.J., dissenting).

The dissent seems to view Montana 1 as applying to contract claims only, and Montana 2 as applying to tort claims only (when it applies at all). Is this a useful dichotomy?

LAWYERING NOTE: SALVAGING A SUPREME COURT LOSS— BEYOND PLAINS COMMERCE BANK V. LONG FAMILY LAND AND CATTLE CO.

One would think that losing parties in Supreme Court cases simply put their heads down and walk away, disappointed in the outcome but powerless to respond. Not so! In many cases, the parties must return to the starting gate and commence more litigation, with the Supreme Court precedent merely altering the playing field or re-balancing the bargaining positions of each side. Federal Indian law is no exception. The Supreme Court's decision in Plains Commerce Bank v. Long Family Land and Cattle Co., 554 U.S. 316 (2008), is a perfect example.

The facts in *Plains Commerce* are as complex as any Indian law case before it. The Long Family Land and Cattle Company was owned and operated by a mixed family on fee lands within the Cheyenne River Sioux Tribe's reservation. You may recall that the Supreme Court held in Solem v. Bartlett, 465 U.S. 463 (1984), that the exterior boundaries of that reservation remain extant. Kenneth Long, a nonmember, and Maxine Long, a tribal member, owned and operated the company for many years. Their business was ranching, and they ran cattle on more than 2300 acres. They took out operating loans from the Bank of Hoven, acquired later during the pendency of the litigation by Plains Commerce Bank. Ranchers, like farmers, require operating loans to cover high overhead costs during times of low revenue streams. In South Dakota, the winter is a very slow and treacherous time for ranchers, often requiring business owners to spend extra capital to cover food and shelter for cattle.

After doing business for several years with the Bank of Hoven, Maxine Long walked on, and Kenneth followed in 1995. At the time of Kenneth's death, the Long Company had mortgaged its lands to the Bank and owed the Bank $750,000 or so. Ronnie and Lila Long, both tribal members, became the new owners. During 1996, the new owners and the Bank negotiated over new terms of their operating loan arrangements. In December 1996, the Long Company and the Bank reached two new agreements. In the first agreement, the Longs Company deeded their lands to the Bank in lieu of foreclosure, canceled some debt, and established a new operating loan arrangement. In the second agreement, the Long Company leased the 2300 acres from the Bank, with an option to buy in two years.

The winter of 1996–1997 was especially brutal, and the Bank failed to come through with promised operating loans. A tribal court jury would later find that the Bank refused to honor its promises because of race discrimination. Five hundred head of the Long Company's cattle perished, and the company was in dire straits. When the two year lease expired, the Long Company did not have the revenue to exercise the purchase option. The Bank commenced eviction proceedings, first in state court, then in tribal court.

The Bank began to sell off parts of the 2300 acres; two parcels went to nonmembers in 1998 and 1999. By June 1999, the Long Company occupied only 960 acres. In July 1999, the Long Company sued the Bank in the Cheyenne River Sioux Tribal Court. They alleged breach of contract, bad faith, violation of tribal law self-held remedies, and race discrimination under both federal and tribal law. After tribal judge B.J. Jones denied the Bank's motion to dismiss on jurisdictional grounds, the case proceeded to trial on four causes of action, breach of contract, bad faith, violation of self-help remedies, and discrimination. Order, Long Family Land and Cattle Company v. Maciejewski, No. R–120–99 (Cheyenne River Sioux Tribal Court, Sept. 30, 2002).

The Cheyenne River Sioux Tribe court rules allow for nonmembers to invoke the right to be tried by a jury that includes nonmembers, but the Bank did not invoke this right. A seven-member jury reached a general verdict on the four causes of action, holding the Bank liable under each theory. The court issued a judgment ordering the Bank to pay judgment award of $750,000 plus interest. Judgment, Long Family Land and Cattle Company v. Maciejewski, No. R–120–99 (Cheyenne River Sioux Tribal Court, Jan. 18, 2003). The court also authorized Long Company to exercise the option to purchase the lands back from the Bank. Supplemental Judgment, Long Family Land and Cattle Company v. Maciejewski, No. R–120–99 (Cheyenne River Sioux Tribal Court, Feb. 18, 2003). The Cheyenne River Sioux appellate court affirmed. Bank of Hoven (Plains Commerce Bank) v. Long Family Land and Cattle Co., 32 Indian L.Rep. 6001 (Cheyenne River Sioux Tribal Court of Appeals 2004).

Importantly, the appellate court noted that the Bank had appealed the judgment in only one of the four causes of action, the race discrimination claim. Recall that for purposes of tribal court exhaustion under *National Farmers Union* and *Iowa Mutual*, nonmembers must raise their jurisdictional challenges all the way through the tribal appellate court before bringing suit in federal court. Further note that it is hornbook law that in context of a general verdict, any one of a group of causes of action can suffice to support the legal basis of the entire verdict, even where one or more of the individual causes of action is later vacated.

The Bank, now Plains Commerce Bank, sued in federal court to enjoin enforcement of the verdict and seeking a declaratory judgment that the tribal court did not have jurisdiction over the race discrimination claim. The Bank lost at both the federal district court and circuit appellate court levels before securing a grant of certiorari review from the Supreme Court.

As pointed out earlier, the Court held 5–4 that the tribal court (and the tribe) could not exercise jurisdiction over the lands owned by the Bank and the two nonmembers the Bank had sold to. One would think that the Long Company would have dissolved, with Ronnie and Lila Long evicted from their ranch.

Instead, in important respects, the Long Company prevailed. Professor and Tribal Judge Frank Pommersheim, the lead author of the tribal appellate court decision, wrote that the status quo remained in place after the Supreme

Court's decision. Frank Pommersheim, Tribal Justice: Twenty-Five Years as a Tribal Appellate Justice 78 (2015). The question of the $750,000 judgment remained, as three of the four causes of action remained valid due to the Bank's failure to exhaust their remedies on those questions. Eventually, the Long Company brought suit to enforce the judgment in tribal court. The Bank immediately brought suit in federal district court, which then sent the case back to the tribal court to exhaust tribal remedies. Plains Commerce Bank v. Long Family Land and Cattle Co., 910 F.Supp.2d 1188 (D.S.D. 2012). The parties reached a confidential settlement in 2013.

Pommersheim has also noted *Plains Commerce* is the only tort claim against a nonmember that reached the Supreme Court after a full trial on the merits. Pommersheim, *Tribal Justice*, supra, at 79. Other cases have been deemed to exhaust tribal remedies when they reached judgment on interlocutory review of the tribal court's jurisdiction by the tribal appellate court. By comparison, the Supreme Court's grant of certiorari in Dollar General Corp. v. Mississippi Band of Choctaw Indians, 746 F.3d 588 (5th Cir.2014), aff'd by equally divided court, 136 S.Ct. 2159 (2016) (2016), a case in which the Supreme Court deadlocked 4–4, was likely bolstered by the fact that the plaintiff's claim for relief—$2.5 million in compensatory and punitive damages—had not been tried on the merits and remained a potential judgment against nonmember defendants. Matthew L.M. Fletcher, *Contract and (Tribal) Jurisdiction*, 126 Yale L.J.F. 1, 3 (Apr. 11, 2016).

NATION BUILDING NOTE: STATE ADJUDICATORY JURISDICTION OVER MATTERS ARISING IN INDIAN COUNTRY

The Bar on State Jurisdiction in Williams v. Lee

In Williams v. Lee, 358 U.S. 217 (1959), Mr. Lee, a non-Indian trader, entered into a contract for the sale of goods on the Navajo Reservation with Mr. and Mrs. Williams, both Navajos. Payment was not made and Lee sued in the Arizona Superior Court for Apache County. Reversing the Arizona Supreme Court, the U.S. Supreme Court held that "exclusive" jurisdiction was vested in the Navajo Tribe and that the Arizona state court had no subject matter jurisdiction.

The Supreme Court cited the principles of Worcester v. Georgia, 31 U.S. 515 (1832), protecting tribal sovereignty and underscoring the existence of congressional power as displacing state government. The Court explained that:

> Essentially, absent governing Acts of Congress, the question has always been whether the state action infringed on the right of reservation Indians to make their own laws and be ruled by them. * * *

* * *

> There can be no doubt that to allow the exercise of state jurisdiction here would undermine the authority of the tribal courts over Reservation affairs and hence would infringe on the right of the

Indians to govern themselves. It is immaterial that respondent is not an Indian. He was on the Reservation and the transaction with an Indian took place there. The cases in this Court have consistently guarded the authority of Indian governments over their reservations. Congress recognized this authority in the Navajos in the Treaty of 1868, and has done so ever since. If this power is to be taken away from them, it is for Congress to do it.

Williams, 358 U.S. at 220, 223.

As Judge Canby has written, because *Williams* "precludes the state courts from assuming jurisdiction when a non-Indian sues a tribal member (or possibly any Indian) over a claim arising in Indian country, it follows even more strongly that the state has no jurisdiction over such claims when both parties are tribal members." William C. Canby, American Indian Law in a Nutshell, 211–12 (6th ed. 2015). Thus, the Supreme Court, following *Williams*, barred state court jurisdiction in Fisher v. District Court, 424 U.S. 382 (1976), a case involving an adoption proceeding in which all parties were members of the Northern Cheyenne Tribe and residents of the tribe's reservation in Montana. State court jurisdiction, according to the Court, "plainly would interfere with the powers of self-government" exercised by the tribe through its own tribal courts. Id. at 387. State courts have complied with this reasoning. E.g., Gustafson v. Estate of Poitra, 800 N.W.2d 842, 846 (N.D.2011) ("A state court does not have jurisdiction over a civil action if state court jurisdiction undermines tribal authority."); In re Estate of Big Spring, 255 P.3d 121, 133 (Mont.2011) ("Restated, the proper analysis in both regulatory and adjudicatory actions involving tribal members or lands is to ask whether the exercise of jurisdiction by a state court or regulatory body is preempted by federal law or, if not, whether it infringes on tribal self-government.").

However, *Williams* and *Fisher* precedents do not announce a categorical rule that Indians living in Indian country may never be sued in state court without federal consent. Indian parents' obligations to their families may be subject to state court determination where the family involved at least one non-Indian parent or where the family at least partially resided off-reservation. E.g., Lavallie v. Lavallie, 861 N.W.2d 164 (N.D.2011) (child support); Garcia v. Gutierrez, 217 P.3d 591 (N.M.2009) (child custody). State courts might also have jurisdiction over Indian country lands alienated to non-Indians during the allotment era. E.g., McGuire v. Aberle, 826 N.W.2d 353 (S.D.2013).

Additionally, Indian tribes and their business entities routinely consent to state court jurisdiction for business and other purposes. E.g., Stifel, Nicolaus & Co., Inc. v. Lac du Flambeau Band of Lake Superior Chippewa Indians, 807 F.3d 184, 198 (7th Cir.2015) ("Given that the Tribal Entities have consented to the jurisdiction of the Wisconsin courts (federal or state) *to the exclusion of any tribal courts*, and given that the Tribal Entities do not suggest that any other courts have jurisdiction over bond-related disputes, these disputes *must be* resolved in the federal or state courts of Wisconsin.") (emphasis added); Outsource Services Management, LLC v. Nooksack Business Corp., 333 P.3d

380, 383 (Wash.2014) ("The tribe itself—acting through its tribal enterprise—consensually entered into a contract where it both waived its sovereign immunity and consented to jurisdiction in state court for claims related to that contract. It first waived its sovereign immunity with respect to any claim related to the contract.").

Public Law 280 and Similar State Jurisdictional Statutes

The federal government, through the exercise of its Indian affairs power, may more broadly open state courthouses to civil actions originating in Indian country. Public Law 280 is the most obvious example, but there are several other state or reservation specific statutes. The federal government asserted that at least some of these statutes were required to provide a forum for legitimate civil suits where there was no tribal forum available. Since the 1950s, when many of these states came into being, numerous affected Indian tribes have established tribal justice systems, perhaps negating the need for state court jurisdiction. In most instances, it appears that states and tribes have concurrent jurisdiction over these suits. A wide variety of state court doctrines dealing with this jurisdictional hassle have arisen.

New York. New York is governed by a precursor to Public Law 280 enacted in the 1948 and 1950. 25 U.S.C. §§ 232 (criminal jurisdiction), 233 (civil jurisdiction. See generally Robert B. Porter, Note, The Jurisdictional Relationship between the Iroquois and New York State: An Analysis of 25 U.S.C. §§ 233, 233, 27 Harv.J.Legis. 497 (1990). Section 233, the civil jurisdiction provision, does reserve some areas where state court jurisdiction is or could be inapplicable.

Since New York tribes have tribal courts, the state and tribal courts have concurrent jurisdiction over matters arising on New York reservations. The tribes and the state have not resolved these questions preemptively, and so the general practice is a first-to-file, race to the courthouse strategy by litigants. For example, in Aernam v. Nenno, 2006 WL 1644691 (W.D.N.Y., June 9, 2006), a divorce action between a tribal member and a nonmember, both of whom resided on the Seneca reservation, became a hotly contested and difficult question of jurisdiction as the parties brought competing claims in state and tribal court, eventually leading an even more complex Section 1983 federal court action.

The leading case in New York is Bowen v. Doyle, 880 F.Supp. 99 (W.D.N.Y.1995), aff'd, 230 F.3d 525 (2d Cir.2000). That case involved a state court action involving the internal governance of the Seneca Nation of Indians. The court held that state courts would be enjoined from resolving matters of tribal self-government as reserved in treaties. Id. at 112–15. The court held that Section 233 did not express a clear statement of intent from Congress to abrogate that treaty right. Id. at 115–23. Other cases have followed this reasoning. E.g., Cayuga Nation v. Jacobs, 986 N.Y.S.2d 791 (N.Y.Super.2014) (dismissing claim brought by tribal faction asking state court to recognize tribal government), dismissing appeal, 132 A.D.3d 1264 (2015).

Wisconsin. Wisconsin is a mandatory Public Law 280 state (the Menominee Reservation is exempted through its 1973 restoration act), and tribal courts have arisen there as well. The Wisconsin Supreme Court began to address the problem of concurrent jurisdiction in Teague v. Bad River Band of the Lake Superior Tribe of Chippewa Indians, 612 N.W.2d 709 (Wis.2000). There, the court rejected the race-to-the-courthouse analysis, and adopted a complex comity framework requiring state courts to assess a large number of factors to determine whether the state court or the tribal court should have jurisdiction over a particular matter. Eventually, the court fractured badly and did not coalesce into a majority over whether the tribal or state court should have jurisdiction over the underlying case, a wrongful termination suit brought by a nonmember against the tribe. Teague v. Bad River Band of the Lake Superior Tribe of Chippewa Indians, 665 N.W.2d 899 (Wis.2013). Lower courts began to implement the state supreme court's decision, known colloquially as the "Teague protocol."

After lengthy negotiation between the state, state courts, and tribes, the state legislature codified a form of the Teague protocol that created a process by which state and tribal courts would confer over jurisdiction, in addition to considering the Teague factors. Wis. Stat. Ann. § 801.54 (2009). Still, the Wisconsin Supreme Court was deeply fractured when it addressed the first case under the new statute. Kroner v. Oneida Seven Generations Corp., 819 N.W.2d 264 (Wis.2012). The court, again split into pluralities, refused to apply the new statute retroactively. Lower courts have apparently applied the transfer rules in numerous instances, however. E.g., Harris v. Lake of Torches Resort & Casino, 2015 WL 1014778 (Wis.Ct.App., Mar. 10, 2015). State courts have transferred hundreds of cases to tribal courts. Larry Nesper, What's the Extent of Jurisdictional Geography?, 89 Wis.Law. 28 (Jan. 2016).

Minnesota. Minnesota is another mandatory Public Law 280 state (excepting the Red Lake Reservation), and the tribes there have also established tribal justice systems. Minnesota is where Bryan v. Itasca County, 426 U.S. 373 (1976), arose. Minnesota Court Rule 10 governs when recognition of tribal court orders by state courts is mandatory or discretionary. See generally Kevin K. Washburn & Chloe Thompson, A Legacy of Public Law 280: Comparing and Contrasting Minnesota's New Rule for the Recognition of Tribal Court Judgments with the Recent Arizona Rule, 31 Wm. Mitchell L.Rev. 479 (2004).

Unfortunately, the state and tribes have not reached agreement on civil jurisdiction. And despite Bryan, state courts have adopted an expansive body of common law interpreting Public Law 280 to more broadly authorize state civil jurisdiction over reservation Indians. Under Bryan, a state has jurisdiction over Indian country violations of criminal/prohibitory state statutes but not civil/regulatory statutes. E.g., State v. Losh, 755 N.W.2d 736 (Minn.2008) (holding the state may prosecute reservation Indians for driving with a revoked license in violation of state law). However, the court has adopted a rule of analysis that involves (largely) an ad hoc review of the subject area of the state statute and state public policy that would justify the assertion of state civil laws into Indian country. For example, in In re Civil Commitment of Johnson, 800 N.W.2d 134 (Minn.2011), the Minnesota Supreme Court held that Public Law 280 authorized the state to commit tribal members under state statutes providing for the civil commitment of sexually dangerous persons. Civil commitment is a gray area of law involving the regulation of persons who are convicted felons, but by definition is civil/regulatory. The Minnesota Supreme Court has given robust meaning to a line in the United States Supreme Court's decision in California v. Cabazon Band of Mission Indians, 480 U.S. 202 (1987), suggesting that a state may have jurisdiction to enforce a civil statute in Indian country if "exceptional circumstances" are present. *Johnson*, 800 N.W.2d at 145 (quoting *Cabazon*, 480 U.S. at 215). See also Beaulieu v. Minnesota Dept. of Human Services, 825 N.W.2d 716 (Minn.2013) (following Johnson). If a state can assert jurisdiction in "exceptional circumstances" the state itself identifies, and if a state has jurisdiction to investigate violations of state law in Indian country under Nevada v. Hicks, 533 U.S. 353 (2001), then what is left of the *Bryan/Cabazon* civil-regulatory/criminal-prohibitory distinction?

Some tribal and state court judges have begun to work together to negotiate these thorny questions on a case by case basis. The Leech Lake Band of Ojibwe and Cass County courts have begun cooperating by establishing a joint tribal-state court to address these issues. Korey Wahwassuck, The New Face of Justice: Joint Tribal-State Jurisdiction, 47 Washburn L.J. 733 (2008).

SECTION C. PREEMPTION OF STATE LAW

The strong competing assertions of tribal and state interests in taxing and regulating Indian country are understandable, given the economic potential of the 56 million acre reservation land base—and the unique political and legal status of tribes. While tribes are generally free of direct regulation and taxation by states, jurisdictional conflicts can still present particularly difficult obstacles to tribes in achieving reservation development and self-sufficiency. Anxious to protect their own, oftentimes competing, revenue raising or regulatory interests, states persistently seek to assert jurisdictional authority and control over the reservation. As tribes increase the reach and sophistication of their own governmental powers over Indian country, conflicts with neighboring states and local governments are bound to intensify. Much more is at stake in these jurisdictional conflicts and controversies, however, than which governmental entity gets to control a stream of tax revenues or apply its regulatory ordinances on the reservation. Tribal sovereignty and jurisdictional control over Indian country hang in the balance, as courts and legislatures grapple with the foundational principles of federal Indian law in an effort to resolve these intense, high-stakes cross-cultural conflicts.

The most important questions about taxation in Indian country have always been about which governments—tribal or state or both—have jurisdiction to tax property or business activity in Indian country, and under what set of facts might either government be prohibited from exercising taxing authority on the reservation. Tribal authority to tax on-reservation business activity carried on by tribal members and nonmembers alike has been affirmed consistently by the Supreme Court in the modern era. E.g., Washington v. Confederated Tribes of the Colville Indian Reservation, 447 U.S. 134 (1980); Kerr-McGee Corp. v. Navajo Tribe, 471 U.S. 195 (1985). But, tribal authority to tax (or regulate) may not be exclusive. As exemplified in the cases that follow, states have been permitted to tax some nonmember activities based on various factual anomalies. A different analysis applies to questions of whether a tribe can tax a nonmember's reservation activity than applies when a state seeks to tax the same activity. This difference in approach by the Court to tribal versus state power to tax nonmembers in Indian country has resulted in allowing concurrent tribal and state jurisdiction in some cases.

Early cases decided that tribes as sovereigns were immune from state taxation. The question of the states' power to tax Indian property in Indian country first came before the Court in two companion cases, The Kansas Indians, 72 U.S. (5 Wall.) 737 (1867), and The New York Indians, 72 U.S. (5 Wall.) 761 (1867). *The Kansas Indians* involved state attempts to tax tribal land and treaty allotments held by individual Indians. The Supreme Court categorically barred states from taxing these categories of land. Id. at 755–57 ("If the tribal organization of the Shawnees is preserved intact, and recognized by the political department of the government as existing, then they are a 'people distinct from others,' capable of making treaties, separated from the jurisdiction of Kansas, and to be governed exclusively by the government of the Union. * * * While the general government has a superintending care over their interests, and continues to treat with them as a nation, the State of Kansas is estopped from denying their title to it.").

Since the Court's landmark 1959 decision in Williams v. Lee, 358 U.S. 217 (1959), recognizing the "right of reservation Indians to make their own laws and be ruled by them," the Justices have dealt with increasingly intense conflicts between states and tribes competing over the power to tax transactions in Indian country. In Warren Trading Post v. Arizona Tax Commission, 380 U.S. 685 (1965), the Court struck down an attempt by the state of Arizona to levy a 2% transaction privilege tax on the gross receipts of a non-Indian trading post on the Navajo reservation. The company operated under a federal license and an extensive federal regulatory scheme governing Indian traders growing out of a long series of congressional statutes beginning with the first Nonintercourse Act in 1790.

Justice Black, who had authored the Court's 1959 unanimous opinion in *Williams*, also wrote the opinion for a unanimous Court in *Warren*

Trading Post, holding that the state's power to tax the transactions had been barred by Congress. "The apparently all-inclusive regulations and the statutes authorizing them would seem in themselves sufficient to show that Congress has taken the business of Indian trading on reservation so fully in hand that no room remains for state laws imposing additional burdens upon traders." 380 U.S. at 690.

Warren Trading Post has been called the "seminal pre-emption case" in the Supreme Court's Indian law, but its "expansive language" rejecting state taxation of traders selling goods to Indians on the reservation relied exclusively on an extensive federal statutory scheme dating back to the earliest Indian legislation. William C. Canby, American Indian Law in a Nutshell 304 (6th ed. 2015). Because the Indian trader statutes preempted state authority, Justice Black's opinion had no need to discuss the relevance of the tribal sovereignty principles of *Worcester,* or the "infringement" test of *Williams.*

In McClanahan v. Arizona State Tax Commission, 411 U.S. 164 (1973), Arizona argued for the right to impose its state personal income tax on an Indian in Indian country, contending that there were no "governing acts of Congress" dealing specifically with taxing the income of an Indian earned on the reservation. In finding that Arizona could not impose its tax on the reservation, the Court relied heavily on treaty language to conclude that Arizona's taxing power had been preempted.

Is a state's taxation of income earned by a tribal member on the reservation always barred? Suppose the tribal member is employed on the reservation by the tribe itself, but lives outside the reservation and commutes to work? Would the tax affect tribal self-government and federal policies more or less than the tax in *McClanahan?* Based on such facts, but without close analysis of the particular treaties and statutes in question, the Supreme Court held categorically that nonmember Indians residing on an Indian reservation are subject to state income tax. Oklahoma Tax Comm'n v. Chickasaw Nation, 515 U.S. 450 (1995).

WHITE MOUNTAIN APACHE TRIBE V. BRACKER

Supreme Court of the United States, 1980.
448 U.S. 136, 100 S.Ct. 2578, 65 L.Ed.2d 665.

JUSTICE MARSHALL delivered the opinion of the Court.

In this case we are once again called upon to consider the extent of state authority over the activities of non-Indians engaged in commerce on an Indian reservation. The State of Arizona seeks to apply its motor carrier license and use fuel taxes to petitioner Pinetop Logging Co. (Pinetop), an enterprise consisting of two non-Indian corporations authorized to do business in Arizona and operating solely on the Fort Apache Reservation. Pinetop and petitioner White Mountain Apache Tribe contend that the taxes are pre-empted by federal law or alternatively, that they represent an unlawful infringement on tribal self-government. The Arizona Court of Appeals rejected petitioners' claims. We hold that the taxes are pre-empted by federal law, and we therefore reverse.

I.

The 6,500 members of petitioner White Mountain Apache Tribe reside on the Fort Apache Reservation in a mountainous and forested region of northeastern Arizona. The Tribe is organized under a constitution approved by the Secretary of the Interior under the Indian Reorganization Act, 25 U.S.C. § 476. The revenue used to fund the Tribe's governmental programs is derived almost exclusively from tribal enterprises. Of these enterprises, timber operations have proved by far the most important, accounting for over 90% of the Tribe's total annual profits.

The Fort Apache Reservation occupies over 1,650,000 acres, including 720,000 acres of commercial forest. Approximately 300,000 acres are used for the harvesting of timber on a "sustained yield" basis, permitting each area to be cut every 20 years without endangering the forest's continuing productivity. Under federal law, timber on reservation land is owned by the United States for the benefit of the Tribe and cannot be harvested for sale without the consent of Congress. Acting under the authority of 25 CFR § 141.6 (1979) and the tribal constitution, and with the specific approval of the Secretary of the Interior, the Tribe in 1964 organized the Fort Apache Timber Co. (FATCO), a tribal enterprise that manages, harvests, processes, and sells timber. FATCO, which conducts all of its activities on the reservation, was created with the aid of federal funds. It employs about 300 tribal members.

The United States has entered into contracts with FATCO, authorizing it to harvest timber pursuant to regulations of the Bureau of Indian Affairs. FATCO has itself contracted with six logging companies, including Pinetop, which perform certain operations that FATCO could not carry out as economically on its own.3 Since it first entered into agreements with FATCO in 1969, Pinetop has been required to fell trees, cut them to the correct size, and transport them to FATCO's sawmill in return for a contractually specified fee. Pinetop employs approximately 50 tribal members. Its activities, performed solely on the Fort Apache Reservation, are subject to extensive federal control.

* * *

III.

[W]e turn to the respondents' claim that they may, consistent with federal law, impose the contested motor vehicle license and use fuel taxes on the logging and hauling operations of petitioner Pinetop. At the outset we observe that the Federal Government's regulation of the harvesting of

Indian timber is comprehensive. That regulation takes the form of Acts of Congress, detailed regulations promulgated by the Secretary of the Interior, and day-to-day supervision by the Bureau of Indian Affairs. Under 25 U.S.C. §§ 405–407, the Secretary of the Interior is granted broad authority over the sale of timber on the reservation. Timber on Indian land may be sold only with the consent of the Secretary, and the proceeds from any such sales, less administrative expenses incurred by the Federal Government, are to be used for the benefit of the Indians or transferred to the Indian owner. Sales of timber must "be based upon a consideration of the needs and best interests of the Indian owner and his heirs." 25 U.S.C. § 406(a). The statute specifies the factors which the Secretary must consider in making that determination. In order to assure the continued productivity of timber-producing land on tribal reservations, timber on unallotted lands "may be sold in accordance with the principles of sustained yield." 25 U.S.C. § 407. The Secretary is granted power to determine the disposition of the proceeds from timber sales. He is authorized to promulgate regulations for the operation and management of Indian forestry units. 25 U.S.C. § 466.

Acting pursuant to this authority, the Secretary has promulgated a detailed set of regulations to govern the harvesting and sale of tribal timber. Among the stated objectives of the regulations is the "development of Indian forests by the Indian people for the purpose of promoting self-sustaining communities, to the end that the Indians may receive from their own property not only the stumpage value, but also the benefit of whatever profit it is capable of yielding and whatever labor the Indians are qualified to perform." 25 CFR § 141.3(a)(3) (1979). The regulations cover a wide variety of matters: for example, they restrict clear-cutting, § 141.5; establish comprehensive guidelines for the sale of timber, § 141.7; regulate the advertising of timber sales, §§ 141.8, 141.9; specify the manner in which bids may be accepted and rejected, § 141.11; describe the circumstances in which contracts may be entered into, §§ 141.12, 141.13; require the approval of all contracts by the Secretary, § 141.13; call for timber-cutting permits to be approved by the Secretary, § 141.19; specify fire protective measures, § 141.21; and provide a board of administrative appeals, § 141.23. Tribes are expressly authorized to establish commercial enterprises for the harvesting and logging of tribal timber. § 141.6.

Under these regulations, the Bureau of Indian Affairs exercises literally daily supervision over the harvesting and management of tribal timber. In the present case, contracts between FATCO and Pinetop must be approved by the Bureau; indeed, the record shows that some of those contracts were drafted by employees of the Federal Government. Bureau employees regulate the cutting, hauling, and marking of timber by FATCO and Pinetop. The Bureau decides such matters as how much timber will be cut, which trees will be felled, which roads are to be used, which hauling equipment Pinetop should employ, the speeds at which logging equipment may travel, and the width, length, height, and weight of loads.

The Secretary has also promulgated detailed regulations governing the roads developed by the Bureau of Indian Affairs. 25 CFR Part 162 (1979). Bureau roads are open to "[f]ree public use." § 162.8. Their administration and maintenance are funded by the Federal Government, with contributions from the Indian tribes. §§ 162.6–162.6a. On the Fort Apache Reservation the Forestry Department of the Bureau has required FATCO and its contractors, including Pinetop, to repair and maintain existing Bureau and tribal roads and in some cases to construct new logging roads. Substantial sums have been spent for these purposes. In its federally approved contract with FATCO, Pinetop has agreed to construct new roads and to repair existing ones. A high percentage of Pinetop's receipts are expended for those purposes, and it has maintained separate personnel and equipment to carry out a variety of tasks relating to road maintenance.

In these circumstances we agree with petitioners that the federal regulatory scheme is so pervasive as to preclude the additional burdens sought to be imposed in this case. Respondents seek to apply their motor vehicle license and use fuel taxes on Pinetop for operations that are conducted solely on Bureau and tribal roads within the reservation. There is no room for these taxes in the comprehensive federal regulatory scheme. In a variety of ways, the assessment of state taxes would obstruct federal policies. And equally important, respondents have been unable to identify any regulatory function or service performed by the State that would justify the assessment of taxes for activities on Bureau and tribal roads within the reservation.

* * *

Mr. Justice STEVENS, with whom Mr. Justice STEWART and Mr. Justice REHNQUIST join, dissenting.

[omitted]

NOTES

1.   The same day it decided *Bracker*, the Court handed down Central Machinery Co. v. Arizona Tax Comm'n, 448 U.S. 160 (1980). A nonmember corporation chartered by and doing business in Arizona and located off the reservation sold eleven farm tractors to a tribal farming enterprise on the Gila River Reservation in Arizona. The sale of the tractors was approved by the BIA. The Court, in a 5–4 decision, held that Arizona could not impose its transaction privilege tax amounting to $2,916, which was assessed against the company as seller of the tractors, to the transaction. Justice Marshall, who authored the Court's opinion in *Bracker*, also wrote the majority opinion in *Central Machinery*:

There are only two distinctions between *Warren Trading Post*, supra, and the present case: appellant is not a licensed Indian trader, and it does not have a permanent place of business on the reservation. The Supreme Court of Arizona concluded that these distinctions indicated that federal law did not bar imposing the transaction privilege tax on appellant. We disagree.

The contract of sale involved in the present case was executed on the Gila River Reservation, and delivery and payment were effected there. Under the Indian trader statutes, 25 U.S.C. §§ 261–264, this transaction is plainly subject to federal regulation. It is irrelevant that appellant is not a licensed Indian trader. Indeed, the transaction falls squarely within the language of 25 U.S.C. § 264, which makes it a criminal offense for "[a]ny person . . . to introduce goods, or to trade" without a license "in the Indian country, or on any Indian reservation." It is the existence of the Indian trader statutes, then, and not their administration, that pre-empts the field of transactions with Indians occurring on reservations.

* * *

Since the transaction in the present case is governed by the Indian trader statutes, federal law pre-empts the asserted state tax. As we held in *Warren Trading Post*, by enacting these statutes Congress "has undertaken to regulate reservation trading in such a comprehensive way that there is no room for the States to legislate on the subject." It may be that in light of modern conditions the State of Arizona should be allowed to tax transactions such as the one involved in this case. Until Congress repeals or amends the Indian trader statutes, however, we must give them "a sweep as broad as [their] language," United States v. Price, 383 U.S. 787, 801 (1966), and interpret them in light of the intent of the Congress that enacted them.

Id. at 164–66. Is federal supervision of this transaction under the trader statutes sufficient to constitute preemption? Can preemption be sustained solely on the basis of laws and policies favoring Indian economic self-sufficiency and tribal self-governance? The trial court opinion in *Central Machinery*, which struck down the tax on grounds similar to those employed by the Supreme Court, was written by Maricopa County Superior Court Judge Sandra Day O'Connor.

2.   In Wagnon v. Prairie Band Potawatomi Nation, 546 U.S. 95 (2005), the Supreme Court held that the *Bracker* and *Central Machinery* decisions inapplicable where a state imposed its tax on a nonmember's off-reservation activities. There, the legislature of the State of Kansas imposed a tax on off-reservation fuel wholesalers that did business with the tribe. The wholesaler passed on the state tax to the tribe as retailer, which could have passed on the cost to its gasoline customers. But the tribe also imposed its own tax on the

gasoline equivalent to the state tax. In short, there would be double taxation on the gas, making the gas prohibitively expensive to the tribe's customers.

The critical legal and economic analysis in these cases involves the "legal incidence" and the "economic incidence" of the tax. This parlance first appeared in this context in Oklahoma Tax Comm'n v. Chickasaw Nation, 515 U.S. 450, 458–59 (1995). In line with *Kansas Indians* and *Williams v. Lee*, two cases that had held that state taxation and regulatory authority on Indians and tribal lands is categorically barred, *Chickasaw* had held that state taxes on reservation income of tribal members is barred as a bright-line rule. The "incidence" of a tax looks to which individual or entity in the chain of commerce will pay the tax. The legal incidence looks to which individual or entity has been identified in the statute as the taxpayer. The economic incidence looks at the real taxpayer, that is, which person or entity shoulders the cost of the tax. The reality in most instances is that the last individual or entity in the chain of commerce pays the tax, as each taxpayer passes the cost down the line— from manufacturer to wholesaler to retailer to customer.

In *Wagnon*, the tribe did not want to pass the state tax down to its customers, and so argued that the state tax was preempted by the reality that the tribe would pay the tax. If so, then the line of cases from *Kansas Indians* to *Chickasaw* would have held the state tax preempted. But the Kansas legislature had identified an off-reservation entity as the taxpayer upon which the legal incidence of the tax was placed. So the Supreme Court held that the state tax was an off-reservation tax, and therefore could not be preempted under principles of federal Indian law.

3.   The Court also granted certiorari in a companion case, also captioned Wagnon v. Prairie Band Potawatomi Nation, 546 U.S. 1072 (2005) (*Wagnon II*). *Wagnon II* involved the efforts of the Nation to issue its own motor vehicle registrations and titles and to force the State of Kansas to recognize them. 402 F.3d 1015 (10th Cir.2005). The Court issued a GVR, or grant-vacate-and-remand, vacating the earlier Tenth Circuit opinion favoring the Nation on the question and remanding the case back to the appellate court for reconsideration in light of *Wagnon I*. On remand, the Tenth Circuit reaffirmed its holding in favor of the Nation, but on different grounds—that the State's refusal to recognize tribal licenses and titles was illegitimate discrimination against the Nation, a ground asserted by Judge Michael McConnell's concurrence in the earlier panel decision:

> The sole reason offered by Defendants to justify their refusal to recognize the Nation's registration and titling law is that of public safety. * * * Indeed, Defendants conceded at two separate oral arguments that revenue was not at issue; the sole concern was that of safety and protection of a state's police powers. . . . Defendants make much of the fact that the Nation's tribal vehicle registrations do not appear in the national criminal database, thereby endangering the lives of law enforcement personnel by preventing them from obtaining crucial vehicle information * * * . Judge McConnell, in his

well-reasoned concurrence * * * , questioned whether Kansas refused to recognize registrations from other jurisdictions not linked to the same database. * * * The answer to that question is no. The record reveals that Oklahoma tribal registrations-recognized by Kansas-are not included in the database. * * * As Judge McConnell stated: "If nonparticipation in the database is a genuine problem, Kansas could amend its reciprocity statute to recognize only those non-resident registrations that are included in the database, or meet other non-discriminatory public safety criteria." * * * Moreover, although safety is a legitimate concern, we previously commented that Defendants had "exaggerated" the severity of that concern here. * * * Kansas recognizes license plates from other states, Canada, and Mexico, and tribally issued tags from other jurisdictions, including Minnesota and Oklahoma, without any record-supported safety concerns. In addition, Minnesota has signed a reciprocity agreement with the Nation, indicating a lack of concern over safety on the part of the Minnesota government. * * * Defendants have introduced no evidence indicating that a contrary result is warranted.

* * *

Consequently, we hold that Kansas, by recognizing vehicle registrations from other jurisdictions without concern for safety standards but refusing to recognize vehicles registered by Plaintiff due to alleged safety concerns, impermissibly discriminates against similarly situated sovereigns. The limited regulatory power at issue in this case represents an undeniable incident of tribal sovereignty that the State has effectively undermined through its discriminatory treatment.

Prairie Band Potawatomi Nation v. Wagnon, 476 F.3d 818, 826–27 (10th Cir.2007).

NOTE: PREEMPTION IN INDIAN LAW

Preemption is a constitutional doctrine that permits Congress to oust all or some state authority in subject matter areas where states have authority to legislate absent federal action. Where Congress acts, however, state law is displaced if it implicitly conflicts with achievement of the full purposes of the federal legislation. Thus, the Supreme Court has struck down, for example: a state law for training and licensing of hazardous waste site workers, Gade v. National Solid Wastes Management Ass'n, 505 U.S. 88 (1992); a state statute imposing weight limitations on trucks operating under an Interstate Commerce Commission certificate of convenience, Castle v. Hayes Freight Lines, Inc., 348 U.S. 61 (1954); a state law requiring identifying tags on tobacco, Campbell v. Hussey, 368 U.S. 297 (1961); a local ordinance curbing airport noise, City of Burbank v. Lockheed Air Terminal, Inc., 411 U.S. 624 (1973); and a state law regulating oil tankers on Puget Sound, Ray v. Atlantic Richfield Co., 435 U.S. 151 (1978). In each case the state or local law would have been a valid exercise of the police power but for the terms or intent of federal legislation which conflicted with the state law or which was so comprehensive as to occupy the field. Federal preemption, of course, is based on the exercise of constitutional authority (often but not always the Commerce Clause) coupled with the Supremacy Clause of article VI, clause 2. On preemption generally see, e.g., Laurence H. Tribe, American Constitutional Law, vol. 1, 1172–1220 (3d ed. 2000).

It is important to note the contours of the Indian preemption doctrine since it varies in several significant respects from preemption analyses used in other areas of constitutional law. Although generalizations about preemption are dangerous because cases often turn on specific statutory language and congressional intent, some general observations can fairly be made.

Cases rejecting assertions of state law over Indians have repeatedly emphasized the primacy of federal law in the field of Indian policy. Worcester v. Georgia, 31 U.S. 515 (1832), discussed the broad federal power over Indian affairs and its preemptive force, in addition to the tribe's inherent sovereignty, in striking down the operation of state law in Indian country. *Williams* in 1959, *Warren* in 1965, and Kennerly v. District Court, 400 U.S. 423 (1971), expanded the analysis. But it was *McClanahan*, a 1973 case involving state taxation of a reservation Indian, that first used the word "preemption" in a modern era Supreme Court Indian law decision. The *McClanahan* Court also for the first time said that the doctrine of tribal sovereignty was to be used as a "backdrop" against which federal treaties and statutes must be read.

Preemption in Indian law plays its signal role in jurisdictional conflicts in Indian country. The subject matter of the preemption is the field of *government* in a *geographic area,* namely Indian country. Indian preemption can be invoked simply by general federal action recognizing or creating Indian country, "whether the particular territory consists of a formal or informal reservation, allotted lands, or dependent Indian communities." Oklahoma Tax Comm'n v. Sac and Fox Nation, 508 U.S. 114 (1993). In Mescalero Apache Tribe v. Jones, 411 U.S. 145 (1973), decided the same day as *McClanahan,* the Court held that income from a tribally owned ski resort outside the reservation on adjacent National Forest lands leased by the tribe was within the reach of a state gross receipts tax. Distinguishing *McClanahan*, the Court said "tribal activities conducted outside the reservation present different considerations. * * * Absent express federal law to the contrary,* Indians going beyond reservation boundaries have generally been held subject to nondiscriminatory state laws otherwise applicable to all citizens of the state." 411 U.S. at 148–49.

If preemption is found, state governmental authority is excluded in favor of federal or tribal governmental authority. Indian law preemption, then,

---

*   Examples of such express laws are treaties reserving off-reservation fishing rights. See generally Chapter 12 infra.

determines which government—federal, tribal, or state—has jurisdiction in Indian country.

Preemption is not a monolithic doctrine. The Court has viewed preemption in non-Indian, non-reservation settings differently depending upon the subject matter, whether for instance, that subject matter involves taxation, civil rights, foreign affairs, criminal law or labor law. But federal law has typically been found to have "occupied the field" in subject areas which are "traditionally federal," e.g., Hines v. Davidowitz, 312 U.S. 52 (1941) (registration of aliens), or which have been subjected to a comprehensive regulatory scheme, e.g., San Diego Bldg. Trades Council v. Garmon, 359 U.S. 236 (1959) (NLRB a "centralized administrative agency" to regulate labor relations). Otherwise, the modern preemption cases decided by the Court have tended to find in favor of state regulation. See, e.g., Pacific Gas & Electric Co. v. State Energy Resources Conservation & Development Comm'n, 461 U.S. 190, 206, 216 (1983).

A separate body of Indian preemption law, with different roots than other types of preemption, has developed under the Indian Commerce Clause. Indian preemption has grown from the special policies set out in *Worcester,* while other lines of preemption cases have evolved from different considerations. The latter is evident in the Commerce Clause cases, which can be traced to Chief Justice John Marshall's opinions in McCulloch v. Maryland, 17 U.S. (4 Wheat.) 316 (1819), and Gibbons v. Ogden, 22 U.S. (9 Wheat.) 1 (1824). This separate development explains why there has been little cross-citation between Indian preemption cases and other lines of preemption authority.

Issues of federal preemption are pervasive in Indian law. Whether state law has been trumped by federal treaties and other laws has regularly arisen in fields such as hunting and fishing, water, zoning, child welfare, civil and criminal court jurisdiction, licensing, gaming, and environmental regulation. The Court has handed down many Indian law opinions involving state taxes, and the taxation cases demonstrate the nature of the preemption analysis under the Indian Commerce Clause.

The distinctive nature of the Court's approach to preemption in the field of Indian taxation can be seen by contrasting the Court's preemption analyses in tax cases not involving Indian law. Federal lands (Van Brocklin v. Anderson, 117 U.S. 151 (1886)), like Indian lands (The Kansas Indians, 72 U.S. (5 Wall.) 737 (1866)), have long been held to be free of state real property taxes. But, for activities on the federal lands in non-Indian settings, the modern Court has tended to construe strictly any implied immunities from non-discriminatory state taxes; the same limited immunity applies for federal contractors and agents. See, e.g., United States v. City of Detroit, 355 U.S. 466 (1958) (upholding a "nondiscriminatory" city use tax, based on the value of the leased property, levied upon a private corporation that had leased an industrial plant owned by the United States). Also analogous is United States v. County of Fresno, 429 U.S. 452 (1977), where the Court upheld a state possessory interest tax on leasehold interests of United States Forest Service employees who received housing on National Forest land as part of their compensation.

The Court's reasoning was that the tax was nondiscriminatory and that its "legal incidence" did not fall on the federal government or on federal property. On federal preemption of state taxation generally, see L. Tribe, supra, at 1220–1237.

A different "categorical" approach, as the Court itself has described it, is taken concerning state taxation of Indians and tribes in Indian law. The cases seldom turn on whether the state tax is "nondiscriminatory;" rather, state taxes are generally inapplicable as against reservation Indians and reservation lands, unless Congress provides to the contrary. In *McClanahan*, for example, a nondiscriminatory state income tax was struck down even though there was no demonstrable economic impact on the United States or, for that matter, on the Navajo Tribe. In effect, the Court recognized a presumption against state taxation of Indians residing on their own reservations. By contrast, state income taxes, such as the one in *McClanahan*, apply to federal employees on federal lands. See, e.g., Graves v. New York ex rel. O'Keefe, 306 U.S. 466 (1939), and *United States v. County of Fresno*, supra, 429 U.S. at 463 n.11.

The presumption against state taxation of reservation Indians and tribes operating businesses on reservation land was evidenced in the Court's 1995 decision in Oklahoma Tax Comm'n v. Chickasaw Nation, 515 U.S. 450 (1995). In that case, the Court applied a "legal incidence" test to state taxes on the sale of gasoline to non-members by the Chickasaw Nation at tribally-owned convenience stores in Indian country. The majority opinion by Justice Ginsburg reasoned that Oklahoma's fuel tax is levied on retailers, not on distributors or consumers; therefore, "Oklahoma may not apply its motor fuel tax, as currently designed, to fuel sold by the tribe in Indian country. In so holding, we adhere to settled law: when Congress does not instruct otherwise, a State's excise tax is unenforceable if its legal incidence falls on a Tribe or its members for sales made within Indian country." Id. at 453.

Significantly, the Court in *Chickasaw* defended its "categorical approach" (quoting County of Yakima v. Confederated Tribes and Bands of Yakima Nation, 502 U.S. 251 (1992)), in denying state power to tax reservation land and Indians absent federal statutes permitting such taxation by stressing the advantages of a "bright-line standard." From a tax administration perspective, Justice Ginsburg explained, the Court's categorical approach to the question of state taxation of reservation land and Indians "responds to the need for substantial certainty as to the permissible scope of state taxation authority." 515 U.S. at 460.

The second issue dealt with by the *Chickasaw* Court was whether Oklahoma could impose an income tax upon tribal members who were employed by the tribe, but who resided in Oklahoma outside Indian country. This issue represented a variation on the facts in *McClanahan*—where a state tax was sought to be applied to a tribal member who resided on the reservation and whose income is derived from on-reservation sources. But Justice Ginsburg did not apply the *McClanahan* analysis and instead invoked the "well established principle of interstate and international taxation—namely, that a jurisdiction, such as Oklahoma, may tax all the income of its residents, even income earned outside the taxing jurisdiction," in holding against the tribe and its member employees on this issue. Id. at 462–463.

As with off-reservation effects of state law on Indians, Indian law preemption has less force in cases involving tribal regulatory authority over non-members. The Court found that state court jurisdiction is preempted in favor of tribal court authority in Williams v. Lee, 358 U.S. 217 (1959), a case dealing with a lawsuit brought by a non-Indian against an Indian for collection of a debt incurred on the Navajo Reservation. The Court has given greater value to state interests in regulating non-members when they are on non-Indian land within the reservation. For instance in Brendale v. Confederated Tribes and Bands of Yakima Indian Nation, 492 U.S. 408 (1989), recall that state regulation was not preempted even though the tribe had a comprehensive zoning regulatory scheme on those parts of the reservation where there was heavy non-Indian landownership and activity. See page, 546, supra. But comprehensive tribal regulation of non-Indians has been found to preempt state regulation where Indian land is involved. New Mexico v. Mescalero Apache Tribe, 462 U.S. 324 (1983).

In the modern era the Supreme Court has invoked the principle of federal preemption to hold that state gaming laws, see, e.g., California v. Cabazon Band of Mission Indians, 480 U.S. 202 (1987), and state hunting, fishing, and gathering laws, Minnesota v. Mille Lacs Band Chippewa Indians, 526 U.S. 172 (1999), have been preempted by congressional activity in the field of Indian affairs. Though broadly applied, the preemption analysis in Indian law has been articulated in various ways as the doctrine has developed. Once invoked, courts purporting to apply the preemption analysis of *McClanahan* to either tax or regulatory jurisdictional conflicts on the reservation will consider state, federal and tribal interests to determine whether, under the circumstances, Congress intended to preempt state jurisdiction.

> State jurisdiction is preempted by the operation of federal law if it interferes with or is incompatible with federal and tribal interests reflected in federal law, unless the state interests at stake are sufficient to justify the assertion of state authority.

New Mexico v. Mescalero Apache Tribe, supra, at 334. It is important to understand that the Court's traditional approach to finding federal preemption in Indian affairs is not "balancing" in the sense that the court weighs interests of all the government involved and ignores the presumption of tribal jurisdiction and backdrop of tribal sovereignty. Nevertheless, the Supreme Court itself has referred to interest balancing in dicta in some recent cases. E.g., Strate v. A-1 Contractors, 520 U.S. 438, 457–58 (1997); Oklahoma Tax Comm'n v. Chickasaw Nation, 515 U.S. 450, 458 (1995); Dept. of Taxation & Finance v. Milhelm Attea & Bros., 512 U.S. 61, 73 (1994); County of Yakima v. Confederated Tribes & Bands of the Yakima Indian Nation, 502 U.S. 251, 267 (1992). This characterization would seem to license a more subjective judicial role. See, e.g., David Getches, *Conquering the Cultural Frontier: The New Subjectivism of the Supreme Court in Indian Law*, 84 Calif.L.Rev. 1573 (1996) (stating that "the Court has assumed the prerogative of balancing various non-Indian interests in order to prune tribal sovereignty to the Court's own notion of what it ought to look like.").

NATION BUILDING NOTE: SMOKE SHOPS, GAS STATIONS, AND ON-RESERVATION VALUE

Before Indian gaming, before tribal self-determination compacting, before Indian tribes enjoyed significant control over their natural resources, Indian tribes and their people were almost always destitute. Many that have not benefited from the self-determination era economic advances remain impoverished. Enterprising Indian tribes and tribal members began to exploit limited state taxation and regulatory authority over Indian country. In the 1960s and beyond, tribes and tribal members attempted to sell products that states heavily regulated or taxed such as tobacco products and motor fuels. Drawing from specific and general treaty rights language, and Worcester v. Georgia, 31 U.S. 515 (1832), Indian people and tribes opened smoke shops and gas stations and sold those products free from state taxes. For a time, some of these retailers earned a windfall.

A series of Supreme Court decisions beginning with Moe v. Confederated Salish and Kootenai Tribes of the Flathead Reservation, 425 U.S. 463 (1976), and concluding with Wagnon v. Prairie Band Potawatomi Nation, 546 U.S. 95 (2005), effectively eliminated much of the economic value of these early tax-free sales. However, the Court's decisions also left open significant opportunities for reservation economic activity that could be largely free of state taxes and regulation.

The stories of tax-free sales from Indian reservations are legendary and remain in the collective imagination. The drier aspects of these tales are told in Supreme Court decisions. In *Moe*, the State of Montana had arrested a tribal member for selling tobacco products without a license. The Court held that the state could not tax sales by the tribe or tribal members to other reservation Indians on tribal lands. Id. at 480–81. However, the Court held that the state did have taxation authority over sales to nonmembers (the Court was then still using the Indians/non-Indians distinction, but later would clarify that the proper distinction for civil cases is member/nonmember). Id. at 482–83. Moreover, the state could require the tribal member retailer to collect the state's taxes and remit them to the state, reasoning that "the competitive advantage which the Indian seller doing business on tribal land enjoys over all other cigarette retailers, within and without the reservation, is dependent on the extent to which the non-Indian purchaser is willing to flout his legal obligation to pay the tax." Id. at 482.

The Court returned to the question in Washington v. Confederated Tribes of the Colville Indian Reservation, 447 U.S. 134 (1980). There, instead of individual tribal members, Indian tribes themselves had opened tax-free tobacco shops. The Colville, Yakama, Makah, and Lummi tribes argued that, as Indian tribes, they had a greater interest in generating tribal governmental revenue than mere individual tribal members. The Court disagreed, and held that not only could states tax their sales to nonmembers, the states could require the tribal retailers to collect the taxes and remit them to the state. The Court held that Indian tribes cannot merely market an exemption from state taxes without more:

> It is painfully apparent that the value marketed by the smokeshops to persons coming from outside is not generated on the reservations by activities in which the Tribes have a significant interest. Cf. Moe v. Salish & Kootenai Tribes, 425 U.S., at 475–481 * * * ; McClanahan v. Arizona State Tax Comm'n, 411 U.S. 164 * * * (1973). What the smokeshops offer these customers, and what is not available elsewhere, is solely an exemption from state taxation. The Tribes assert the power to create such exemptions by imposing their own taxes or otherwise earning revenues by participating in the reservation enterprises. If this assertion were accepted, the Tribes could impose a nominal tax and open chains of discount stores at reservation borders, selling goods of all descriptions at deep discounts and drawing custom from surrounding areas. We do not believe that principles of federal Indian law, whether stated in terms of pre-emption, tribal self-government, or otherwise, authorize Indian tribes thus to market an exemption from state taxation to persons who would normally do their business elsewhere.

Id. at 155. The Court's first sentence, however, provides tribes with an avenue for economic opportunity: perhaps states do not have authority to tax economic value that is generated from the reservation. The notion that an Indian tribe could generate on-reservation economic activity free from state interference would be an important factor in the rise of Indian gaming following California v. Cabazon Band of Mission Indians, 480 U.S. 202 (1987). However, the Court would ignore that principle in terms of tribal natural resources extraction in Cotton Petroleum v. New Mexico, 490 U.S. 163 (1989). Moreover, the *Colville* Court affirmed the tribe's authority to tax reservation sales to both members and nonmembers.

Indian tribes and tribal members began to focus on specific treaty terms to back up their claims to immunity from state taxation, most controversially in New York State. The Haudenosaunee (Iroquois) nations, most notably the Seneca Nation of New York, argued that state laws and regulations violated their treaty rights. In Dept. of Taxation and Finance of New York v. Milhelm Attea & Bros., Inc., 512 U.S. 61 (1994), the Supreme Court affirmed state regulations on cigarette quality and a state quota on reservation sales as permissible burdens on Indian traders. Haudenosaunee retailers refused to comply with state regulations, leading to a near-tragic confrontation with state authorities that some alleged would have involved an "invasion" of three Haudenosaunee reservations. Martin Kallen, *Indians Not Taxed: Will*

Sovereignty Survive?, 13:2 Native Americas 14 (June 30, 1996) ("In 1995, the State of New York issued an order to plan the military invasion of three Iroquois communities so that 'unpaid' taxes on the sale of gasoline, cigarettes, alcohol, and gaming revenues to non-Natives could be collected by the state. The order, termed 'Gallant Piper,' was dismissed by state officials in early February of this year. Had it been executed, it would have moved up to 10,000 military personnel and State Police onto the St. Regis Mohawk (Akwesasne), Onondaga and Cattaraugus (Seneca) Reservations."). Eventually, the Indian tribes and the state reached an agreement to defer state enforcement of tobacco and fuel regulations and taxes. Joseph J. Heath, *Review of the History of the April 1997 Trade and Commerce Agreement among the Traditional Haudenosaunee Councils of Chiefs and New York State and the Impact Thereof on Haudenosaunee Sovereignty*, 46 Buff.L.Rev. 1011 (1998). That agreement lasted until 2011, when New York again began collecting taxes. Several Haudenosaunee wholesalers and retailers began robust and profitable online and direct mail tobacco businesses. In 2009, Congress enacted the Prevent All Cigarette Trafficking, or PACT Act. Pub. L. 111–154, Mar. 31, 2010, 124 Stat. 1087, codified at 15 U.S.C. § 375 et seq. That statute effectively destroyed the Haudenosaunee wholesale market.

The most recent tobacco and gasoline tax case is *Wagnon*, where the Supreme Court held that Kansas's tobacco and motor fuel taxes imposed on off-reservation wholesalers and manufacturers were not preempted by on-reservation tribal taxes. The Prairie Band's efforts to demonstrate the impact of the state tax on its sovereignty was met with deaf ears from the Court. Justice Souter's first question to the tribe's counsel during oral argument was as follows: "Then what's its gripe? It wants a bigger profit?" Oral Argument, Wagnon v. Prairie Band Potawatomi Nation, 2005 WL 2651392, at *25.

In general, the Supreme Court has been hostile to tribal and Indian tax-free sales, but that theoretical reality often loses its luster on the ground. Tribes and Indians still do make tax-free or reduced-tax sales to both members and nonmembers, though that is a risky venture. In 1991, the Supreme Court acknowledged that states might have a right without a remedy in relation to on-reservation tax collection.

OKLAHOMA TAX COMMISSION V. CITIZEN BAND POTAWATOMI INDIAN TRIBE OF OKLAHOMA

Supreme Court of the United States, 1991.
498 U.S. 505, 111 S.Ct. 905, 112 L.Ed.2d 1112.

CHIEF JUSTICE REHNQUIST delivered the opinion of the Court.

* * *

Respondent, the Citizen Band Potawatomi Indian Tribe of Oklahoma (Potawatomis or Tribe), owns and operates a convenience store in Oklahoma on land held in trust for it by the Federal Government. For many years, the Potawatomis have sold cigarettes at the convenience store without collecting Oklahoma's state cigarette tax on these sales. In 1987, petitioner, the Oklahoma Tax Commission (Oklahoma or Commission), served the Potawatomis with an assessment letter, demanding that they pay $2.7 million for taxes on cigarette sales occurring between 1982 and 1986. The Potawatomis filed suit to enjoin the assessment in the United States District Court for the Western District of Oklahoma.

Oklahoma counterclaimed, asking the District Court to enforce its $2.7 million claim against the Tribe and to enjoin the Potawatomis from selling cigarettes in the future without collecting and remitting state taxes on those sales. The Potawatomis moved to dismiss the counterclaim on the ground that the Tribe had not waived its sovereign immunity and therefore could not be sued by the State. * * *

* * *

I.

* * *

Indian tribes are "domestic dependent nations" that exercise inherent sovereign authority over their members and territories. Cherokee Nation v. Georgia, 5 Pet. 1, 17, 8 L.Ed. 25 (1831). Suits against Indian tribes are thus barred by sovereign immunity absent a clear waiver by the tribe or congressional abrogation. Santa Clara Pueblo v. Martinez, 436 U.S. 49, 58 * * * (1978). Petitioner acknowledges that Indian tribes generally enjoy sovereign immunity, but argues that the Potawatomis waived their sovereign immunity by seeking an injunction against the Commission's proposed tax assessment. It argues that, to the extent that the Commission's counterclaims were "compulsory" under Federal Rule of Civil Procedure 13(a), the District Court did not need any independent jurisdictional basis to hear those claims.

We rejected an identical contention over a half-century ago in United States v. United States Fidelity & Guaranty Co., 309 U.S. 506, 511–512 * * * (1940). In that case, a surety bondholder claimed that a federal court had jurisdiction to hear its state-law counterclaim against an Indian Tribe because the Tribe's initial action to enforce the bond constituted a waiver of sovereign immunity. We held that a tribe does not waive its sovereign immunity from actions that could not otherwise be brought against it merely because those actions were pleaded in a counterclaim to an action filed by the tribe. Id., at 513 * * * . "Possessing * * * immunity from direct suit, we are of the opinion [the Indian tribes] possess a similar immunity from cross-suits." Ibid. Oklahoma does not argue that it received congressional authorization to adjudicate a counterclaim against the Tribe, and the case is therefore controlled by *Fidelity & Guaranty*. We uphold the Court of Appeals' determination that the Tribe did not waive its sovereign immunity merely by filing an action for injunctive relief.

* * *

II.

* * *

Although the doctrine of tribal sovereign immunity applies to the Potawatomis, that doctrine does not excuse a tribe from all obligations to assist in the collection of validly imposed state sales taxes. Washington v. Confederated Tribes of Colville Reservation, 447 U.S. 134 * * * (1980). Oklahoma argues that the Potawatomis' tribal immunity notwithstanding, it has the authority to tax sales of cigarettes to nonmembers of the tribe at the Tribe's convenience store. We agree. In Moe v. Confederated Salish and Kootenai Tribes, 425 U.S. 463 * * * (1976), this Court held that Indian retailers on an Indian reservation may be required to collect all state taxes applicable to sales to non-Indians. We determined that requiring the tribal seller to collect these taxes was a minimal burden justified by the State's interest in assuring the payment of these concededly lawful taxes. Id., at 483 * * * . "Without the simple expedient of having the retailer collect the sales tax from non-Indian purchasers, it is clear that wholesale violations of the law by the latter class will go virtually unchecked." Id., at 482 * * * . Only four years later we reiterated this view, ruling that tribal sellers are obliged to collect and remit state taxes on sales to nonmembers at Indian smoke-shops on reservation lands. *Colville*, supra.

* * *

In view of our conclusion with respect to sovereign immunity of the Tribe from suit by the State, Oklahoma complains that, in effect, decisions such as Moe and Colville give them a right without any remedy. There is no doubt that sovereign immunity bars the State from pursuing the most efficient remedy, but we are not persuaded that it lacks any adequate alternatives. We have never held that individual agents or officers of a tribe are not liable for damages in actions brought by the State. See Ex parte Young, 209 U.S. 123 * * * (1908). And under today's decision, States may of course collect the sales tax from cigarette wholesalers, either by seizing unstamped cigarettes off the reservation, *Colville*, supra, 447 U.S., at 161–162 * * * , or by assessing wholesalers who supplied unstamped cigarettes to the tribal stores, City Vending of Muskogee, Inc. v. Oklahoma Tax Comm'n, 898 F.2d 122 (CA10 1990). States may also enter into agreements with the tribes to adopt a mutually satisfactory regime for the collection of this sort of tax. See 48 Stat. 987, as amended, 25 U.S.C. § 476. And if Oklahoma and other States similarly situated find that none of these alternatives produce the revenues to which they are entitled, they may of course seek appropriate legislation from Congress.

[JUSTICE STEVENS' concurring opinion omitted.]

NOTES

1.   A few years after the Court's decision in *Potawatomi*, the New York legislature enacted a complicated regulatory scheme designed to prevent nonmembers from escaping the state tax on cigarettes purchased on Indian reservations. The law imposed recordkeeping requirements and quantity limitations on cigarette wholesalers who sold untaxed cigarettes to reservation Indians. It also directly regulated reservation Indians by requiring them to have identification certificates to buy tax-exempt cigarettes on the reservations. The Supreme Court, in *Milhelm Attea*, upheld New York's program:

> * * * The state law we found preempted in *Warren Trading Post* was a tax directly "imposed upon Indian traders for trading with Indians." 380 U.S., at 691. See also *Central Machinery*, 448 U.S. at 164. That characterization does not apply to regulations designed to prevent circumvention of "concededly lawful" taxes owed by non-Indians. Although broad language in our opinion in *Warren Trading Post* lends support to a contrary conclusion, we now hold that Indian traders are not wholly immune from state regulation that is reasonably necessary to the assessment or collection of lawful state taxes.

Department of Taxation and Finance of New York v. Milhelm Attea & Bros., Inc., 512 U.S. 61, 71–75 (1994).

If the overriding concern of New York in *Milhelm Attea* was preventing non-Indian purchasers from avoiding their obligation to pay taxes, it presumably could interdict them and make arrests as they left the reservation with untaxed cigarettes. Instead, the state chose its more elaborate scheme, enlisting Indian traders and reservation Indians in the process. Why did the Court in *Milhelm Attea* not insist that alternative measures be pursued by the state as suggested in *Potawatomi*?

The Court had to deal with two distinct barriers to state regulation in *Milhelm Attea*: Indian immunity from state law and preemption of state law under the Indian trader statutes. Moe v. Salish and Kootenai Tribes, 425 U.S. 463 (1976), was concerned with tribal immunity from state law. Once the Court found that non-members were liable for paying state taxes on cigarettes purchased on the reservation, it created a limitation on immunity that would require a tribal cigarette seller to collect the tax from non-member purchasers. According to the Court, this would be a "minimal burden." In *Milhelm Attea*, the Court extended this unique cigarette tax collection exception to Indian immunity from state regulation to include New York's elaborate regulatory schemes for reservation cigarette marketing. In dealing with the trader statute preemption question the Court used the same "minimal burden" rationale to find that the federal purpose of the statute would not be frustrated. This departed from the approach in *Warren Trading Post* where the Court found that the comprehensiveness of the trader statutes allowed no state regulation whatsoever.

Has the Court made a fundamental departure from its Indian law jurisprudence or does it treat cigarette tax cases different from other matters?

2. States typically tax the non-Indian contractors that construct the buildings that house tribal government operations on trust land in Indian country. See Matthew L.M. Fletcher, *The Power to Tax, the Power to Destroy, and the Michigan Tribal-State Tax Agreements*, 82 U.Det. Mercy L.Rev. 1, 27 (2004). Does the on-reservation value generated analysis provide state tax immunity where a tribe, often relying solely on tribal or federal funds, hires off-reservation builders and architects to construct on-reservation government buildings, activities that are certainly fundamental to tribal sovereignty?

3. Preemption is broadly applied where a federal Indian policy is implicated. In Ramah Navajo School Board v. Bureau of Revenue, 458 U.S. 832 (1982), a Navajo tribal organization contracted with the BIA for construction of a new school for Navajo children on the reservation. New Mexico imposed its gross receipts tax on a non-Indian owned construction company hired to build the school. The Supreme Court, in a 6–3 decision written by Justice Marshall, held the tax preempted by federal law. Calling federal policy "both comprehensive and pervasive," the Court cited the Snyder Act, 25 U.S.C. § 13 (1921), the Johnson-O'Malley Act, 25 U.S.C. § 452 et seq. (1934), the Navajo-Hopi Rehabilitation Act, 25 U.S.C. § 631 et seq. (1950), and the Indian Self-Determination and Education Assistance Act, 25 U.S.C. § 450 et seq. (1975). These laws reflected a policy of encouraging the development of Indian-controlled educational institutions on the reservations that would be inhibited if New Mexico's gross receipts tax were applied to the non-Indian construction company building an Indian school.

In Arizona Department of Revenue v. Blaze Construction Company, Inc., 526 U.S. 32 (1999), the Supreme Court distinguished *Ramah* where a tribal contract was involved and held that contracts between the federal government and private contractors that are performed on Indian reservations are subject to state taxation. If Indian tribes have a greater immunity from state taxes than does the United States, can that result be justified? Why is the preemption test different?

COTTON PETROLEUM CORP. v. NEW MEXICO

Supreme Court of the United States, 1989.
490 U.S. 163, 109 S.Ct. 1698, 104 L.Ed.2d 209.

JUSTICE STEVENS delivered the opinion of the Court.

This case is a sequel to Merrion v. Jicarilla Apache Tribe, 455 U.S. 130, 102 S.Ct. 894, 71 L.Ed.2d 21 (1982), in which we held that the Jicarilla Apache Tribe (Tribe) has the power to impose a severance tax on the production of oil and gas by non-Indian lessees of wells located on the Tribe's reservation. We must now decide whether the State of New Mexico can continue to impose its severance taxes on the same production of oil and gas.

* * *

I.

This Court's approach to the question whether a State may tax on-reservation oil production by non-Indian lessees has varied over the course of the past century. At one time, such a tax was held invalid unless expressly authorized by Congress; more recently, such taxes have been upheld unless expressly or impliedly prohibited by Congress. The changed approach to these taxes is one aspect of the evolution of the doctrine of intergovernmental tax immunity that we recently discussed in detail in South Carolina v. Baker, 485 U.S. 505 * * * (1988).

* * *

In sum, it is well settled that, absent express congressional authorization, a State cannot tax the United States directly. * * * It is also clear that the tax immunity of the United States is shared by the Indian tribes for whose benefit the United States holds reservation lands in trust. * * * Under current doctrine, however, a State can impose a nondiscriminatory tax on private parties with whom the United States or an Indian tribe does business, even though the financial burden of the tax may fall on the United States or tribe. * * * Although a lessee's oil production on Indian lands is therefore not "automatically exempt from state taxation," Congress does, of course, retain the power to grant such immunity. * * * Whether such immunity shall be granted is thus a question that "is essentially legislative in character." * * *

The question for us to decide is whether Congress has acted to grant the Tribe such immunity, either expressly or by plain implication. In addition, we must consider Cotton's argument that the "multiple burden" imposed by the state and tribal taxes is unconstitutional.

III.

* * *

The 1938 [Indian Mineral Leasing] Act neither expressly permits state taxation nor expressly precludes it, but rather simply provides that "unallotted lands within any Indian reservation or lands owned by any tribe * * * may, with the approval of the Secretary of the Interior, be leased for mining purposes, by authority of the tribal council * * *, for terms not to exceed ten years and as long thereafter as minerals are produced in paying quantities." 25 U.S.C. § 396a. The Senate and House Reports that accompanied the Act, moreover-even when considered in their broadest possible terms-shed little light on congressional intent concerning state taxation of oil and gas produced on leased lands. See S.Rep. No. 985, 75th Cong., 1st Sess. (1937); H.R.Rep. No. 1872, 75th Cong., 3d Sess. (1938). Both Reports reflect that the proposed legislation was suggested by the Secretary and considered by the appropriate committees, which recommended that it pass without amendment. Beyond this procedural summary, the Reports simply rely on the Secretary's letter of transmittal to describe the purpose of the Act. That letter provides that the legislation was intended, in light of the disarray of federal law in the area, "to obtain uniformity so far as practicable of the law relating to the leasing of tribal lands for mining purposes," and, in particular, was designed to "bring all mineral leasing matters in harmony with the Indian Reorganization Act." Id., at 1, 3; S.Rep. No. 985, supra, at 2, 3. In addition, the letter contains the following passage:

> "It is not believed that the present law is adequate to give the Indians the greatest return from their property. As stated, present law provides for locating and taking mineral leases in the same manner as mining locations are made on the public lands of the United States; but there are disadvantages in following this procedure on Indian lands that are not present in applying for a claim on the public domain. For instance, on the public domain the discoverer of a mineral deposit gets extralateral rights and can follow the ore beyond the side lines indefinitely, while on the Indian lands under the act of June 30, 1919, he is limited to the confines of the survey markers not to exceed 600 feet by 1,500 feet in any one claim. The draft of the bill herewith would permit the obtaining of sufficient acreage to remove the necessity for extralateral rights with all of its attending controversies." Id., at 2; H.R.Rep. No. 1872, supra, at 2 (emphasis added).

Relying on the first sentence in this paragraph, Cotton argues that the 1938 Act embodies a broad congressional policy of maximizing revenues for Indian tribes. Cotton finds support for this proposition in Montana v. Blackfeet Tribe, 471 U.S. 759 * * * (1985). That case raised the question whether the 1938 Act authorizes state taxation of a tribe's royalty interests under oil and gas leases issued to nonmembers. Applying the settled rule that a tribe may only be directly taxed by a State if "Congress has made its intention to [lift the tribe's exemption] unmistakably clear," id., at 765, 105 S.Ct., at 2403, we concluded that "the State may not tax Indian royalty income from leases issued pursuant to the 1938 Act," id., at 768, 105 S.Ct., at 2404. In a footnote we added the observation that direct state taxation of Indian revenues would frustrate the 1938 Act's purpose of "ensur[ing] that Indians receive 'the greatest return from their property,' [S.Rep. No. 985, supra, at] 2; H.R.Rep. No. 1872, supra, at 2." Id., at 767, n. 5, 105 S.Ct., at 2404, n. 5.

To the extent Cotton seeks to give the Secretary's reference to "the greatest return from their property" talismanic effect, arguing that these words demonstrate that Congress intended to guarantee Indian tribes the maximum profit available without regard to competing state interests, it overstates its case. There is nothing remarkable in the proposition that, in authorizing mineral leases, Congress sought to provide Indian tribes with a profitable source of revenue. It is however quite remarkable, indeed unfathomable in our view, to suggest that Congress intended to remove all state-imposed obstacles to profitability by attaching to the Senate and House Reports a letter from the Secretary that happened to include the phrase "the greatest return from their property." Read in the broadest terms possible, the relevant paragraph suggests that Congress sought to remove "disadvantages in [leasing mineral rights] on Indian lands that are not present in applying for a claim on the public domain." S.Rep. No. 985, supra, at 2; H.R.Rep. No. 1872, supra, at 2. By 1938, however, it was established that oil and gas lessees of public lands were subject to state taxation. * * * It is thus apparent that Congress was not concerned with state taxation, but with matters such as the unavailability of extralateral mineral rights on Indian land. Nor do we read the *Blackfeet* footnote, 471 U.S., at 767, n. 5 * * *, to give the Secretary's words greater effect. We think it clear that the footnote simply stands for the proposition that the Act's purpose of creating a source of revenue for Indian tribes provides evidence that Congress did not intend to authorize direct state taxation of Indian royalties.

We thus agree that a purpose of the 1938 Act is to provide Indian tribes with badly needed revenue, but find no evidence for the further supposition that Congress intended to remove all barriers to profit maximization. The Secretary's letter of transmittal, even when read permissively for broad policy goals and even when read to resolve ambiguities in favor of tribal independence, supports no more.

* * *

[T]he factual findings of the New Mexico District Court clearly distinguish this case from both *Bracker*, supra, and *Ramah Navajo School Bd.*, supra. After conducting a trial, that court found that "New Mexico provides substantial services to both the Jicarilla Tribe and Cotton," costing the State approximately $3 million per year. App. to Juris. Statement 16. Indeed, Cotton concedes that from 1981 through 1985 New Mexico provided its operations with services costing $89,384, but argues that the cost of these services is disproportionate to the $2,293,953 in taxes the State collected from Cotton. Brief for Appellants 13–14. Neither *Bracker*, nor *Ramah Navajo School Bd.*, however, imposes such a proportionality requirement on the States. Rather, both cases involved complete abdication or noninvolvement of the State in the on-reservation activity. * * *

We thus conclude that federal law, even when given the most generous construction, does not pre-empt New Mexico's oil and gas severance taxes. This is not a case in which the State has had nothing to do with the on-reservation activity, save tax it. Nor is this a case in which an unusually large state tax has imposed a substantial burden on the Tribe. It is, of course, reasonable to infer that the New Mexico taxes have at least a marginal effect on the demand for on-reservation leases, the value to the Tribe of those leases, and the ability of the Tribe to increase its tax rate. Any impairment to the federal policy favoring the exploitation of on-reservation oil and gas resources by Indian tribes that might be caused by these effects, however, is simply too indirect and too insubstantial to support Cotton's claim of pre-emption. To find pre-emption of state taxation in such indirect burdens on this broad congressional purpose, absent some special factor such as those present in *Bracker* and *Ramah Navajo School Bd.*, would be to return to the pre-1937 doctrine of intergovernmental tax immunity. Any adverse effect on the Tribe's finances caused by the taxation of a private party contracting with the Tribe would be ground to strike the state tax. Absent more explicit guidance from Congress, we decline to return to this long-discarded and thoroughly repudiated doctrine.

IV

Cotton also argues that New Mexico's severance taxes—"insofar as they are imposed without allocation or apportionment on top of Jicarilla Apache tribal taxes"—impose "an unlawful multiple tax burden on interstate commerce." Brief for Appellants 33. In support of this argument, Cotton relies on three facts: (1) that the State and the Tribe tax the same activity; (2) that the total tax burden on Cotton is higher than the burden on its off-reservation competitors who pay no tribal tax; and (3) that the state taxes generate revenues that far exceed the value of the services it provides on the reservation.

[A] multiple taxation issue may arise when more than one State attempts to tax the same activity. If a unitary business derives income from several States, each State may only tax the portion of that income that is attributable to activity within its borders. * * * Thus, in such a case, an apportionment formula is necessary in order to identify the scope of the taxpayer's business that is within the taxing jurisdiction of each State. In this case, however, all of Cotton's leases are located entirely within the borders of the State of New Mexico and also within the borders of the Jicarilla Apache Reservation. Indeed, they are also within the borders of the United States. There are, therefore, three different governmental entities, each of which has taxing jurisdiction over all of the non-Indian wells. * * * The federal sovereign has the undoubted power to prohibit taxation of the Tribe's lessees by the Tribe, by the State, or by both, but since it has not exercised that power, concurrent taxing jurisdiction over all of Cotton's on-reservation leases exists. * * * Unless and until Congress provides otherwise, each of the other two sovereigns has taxing jurisdiction over all of Cotton's leases.

It is, of course, true that the total taxes paid by Cotton are higher than those paid by off-reservation producers. But neither the State nor the Tribe imposes a discriminatory tax. The burdensome consequence is entirely attributable to the fact that the leases are located in an area where two governmental entities share jurisdiction. As we noted in *Merrion*, the tribal tax does "not treat minerals transported away from the reservation differently than it treats minerals that might be sold on the reservation." 455 U.S., at 157–158 * * * . Similarly, the New Mexico taxes are administered in an evenhanded manner and are imposed at a uniform rate throughout the State-both on and off the reservation. * * *

* * *

[JUSTICE BLACKMUN's dissent omitted.]

* * *

NOTES

1. A number of other taxes are regularly imposed by governments in order to capture rents from mineral production. The most common is the severance tax—a tax on the value of minerals extracted from the land. The *Cotton Petroleum* Court considered whether a state mineral severance tax was precluded by the 1938 Act. The *Cotton* Court rejected the argument that the 1938 Indian Mineral Leasing Act asserted comprehensive federal regulatory control sufficient to preempt all state taxes. Although the Act was silent as to taxation, the Court found that because an earlier act (Indian Oil Act of 1927, 25 U.S.C. § 398a) had specifically allowed states to tax, the new act in 1938 was meant to continue the state tax. Was the Court's interpretation of the 1938 Act consistent with the canons of construction? *Expressio unius est exclusio alterius* is the usual rule of statutory construction—when the statute specifies one thing, what is not mentioned is to be excluded. Was the Court correct in implying that when the 1938 Act was adopted, without language expressly allowing state taxation, the previous policy of waiving tribal immunity and allowing state taxation extended to the 1938 Act?

2. The *Cotton Petroleum* Court also spoke to an issue of dual taxation left open in *Merrion*. In holding that New Mexico's severance tax on a non-Indian oil and gas company operating on reservation land was not precluded by the imposition of a tribal tax, the Court reasoned that unless Congress had expressly or impliedly preempted state taxation, a non-Indian lessee producing oil and gas on Indian land was subject to a non-discriminatory state severance tax as well as the tribal tax.

3. *Cotton* also rejected intergovernmental immunity as an outmoded and disfavored doctrine that formerly was invoked whenever a state tax on a private party would burden the federal government economically. Today, said the Court, such taxes are valid unless they are preempted by Congress. As a practical matter, what effect does *Cotton* have on the tribal right to tax recognized in *Merrion*? Is there a point at which the state tax on top of the

tribal tax would be so burdensome as to defeat the purpose of the Act and therefore be grounds for preemption?

MONTANA V. BLACKFEET TRIBE OF INDIANS

Supreme Court of the United States, 1985.
471 U.S. 759, 105 S.Ct. 2399, 85 L.Ed.2d 753.

JUSTICE POWELL delivered the opinion of the Court.

This case presents the question whether the State of Montana may tax the Blackfeet Tribe's royalty interests under oil and gas leases issued to non-Indian lessees pursuant to the Indian Mineral Leasing Act of 1938.

* * *

Congress first authorized mineral leasing of Indian lands in the Act of Feb. 28, 1891, 26 Stat. 795, codified at 25 U.S.C. § 397 (the 1891 Act). The Act authorized leases for terms not to exceed 10 years on lands "bought and paid for" by the Indians. The 1891 Act was amended by the 1924 Act. The amendment provided in pertinent part:

> "Unallotted land . . . subject to lease for mining purposes for a period of ten years under section 397 . . . may be leased . . . by the Secretary of the Interior, with the consent of the [Indian] council . . . , for oil and gas mining purposes for a period of not to exceed ten years, and as much longer as oil or gas shall be found in paying quantities, and the terms of any existing oil and gas mining lease may in like manner be amended by extending the term thereof for as long as oil or gas shall be found in paying quantities: *Provided,* That the production of oil and gas and other minerals on such lands may be taxed by the State in which said lands are located in all respects the same as production on unrestricted lands, and the Secretary of the Interior is authorized and directed to cause to be paid the tax so assessed against the royalty interests on said lands: *Provided, however,* That such tax shall not become a lien or charge of any kind or character against the land or the property of the Indian owner." 25 U.S.C. § 398.

Montana relies on the first proviso in the 1924 Act in claiming the authority to tax the Blackfeet's royalty payments.

In 1938, Congress adopted comprehensive legislation in an effort to "obtain uniformity so far as practicable of the law relating to the leasing of tribal lands for mining purposes." S.Rep. No. 985, 75th Cong., 1st Sess. 2 (1937) (hereafter Senate Report). Like the 1924 Act, the 1938 Act permitted, subject to the approval of the Secretary of the Interior, mineral leasing of unallotted lands for a period not to exceed 10 years and as long thereafter as minerals in paying quantities were produced. The Act also detailed uniform leasing procedures designed to protect the Indians. See

25 U.S.C. §§ 396b–396g. The 1938 Act did not contain a provision authorizing state taxation; nor did it repeal specifically the authorization in the 1924 Act. A general repealer clause was provided in § 7 of the Act: "All Act [sic] or parts of Acts inconsistent herewith are hereby repealed." The question presented by this case is whether the 1924 Act's proviso that authorizes state taxation was repealed by the 1938 Act, or if left intact, applies to leases executed under the 1938 Act.

* * *

In keeping with its plenary authority over Indian affairs, Congress can authorize the imposition of state taxes on Indian tribes and individual Indians. It has not done so often, and the Court consistently has held that it will find the Indians' exemption from state taxes lifted only when Congress has made its intention to do so unmistakably clear. The 1924 Act contains such an explicit authorization. As a result, in British-American Oil Producing Co. v. Board of Equalization, 299 U.S. 159 (1936), the Court held that the State of Montana could tax oil and gas produced under leases executed under the 1924 Act.

The State urges us that the taxing authorization provided in the 1924 Act applies to leases executed under the 1938 Act as well. It argues that nothing in the 1938 Act is inconsistent with the 1924 taxing provision and thus that the provision was not repealed by the 1938 Act. * * *

The State fails to appreciate, however, that the standard principles of statutory construction do not have their usual force in cases involving Indian law. As we said earlier this Term, "[t]he canons of construction applicable in Indian law are rooted in the unique trust relationship between the United States and the Indians." Oneida County v. Oneida Indian Nation, 470 U.S. 226, 247 (1985). Two such canons are directly applicable in this case: first, the States may tax Indians only when Congress has manifested clearly its consent to such taxation; second, statutes are to be construed liberally in favor of the Indians, with ambiguous provisions interpreted to their benefit. When the 1924 and 1938 Acts are considered in light of these principles, it is clear that the 1924 Act does not authorize Montana to enforce its tax statutes with respect to leases issued under the 1938 Act.

* * *

Nothing in either the text or legislative history of the 1938 Act suggests that Congress intended to permit States to tax tribal royalty income generated by leases issued pursuant to that Act. The statute contains no explicit consent to state taxation. Nor is there any indication that Congress intended to incorporate implicitly in the 1938 Act the taxing authority of the 1924 Act.[5] Contrary to the State's suggestion, under the applicable principles of statutory construction, the general repealer clause of the 1938 Act cannot be taken to incorporate consistent provisions of earlier laws. The clause surely does not satisfy the requirement that Congress clearly consent to state taxation. Nor would the State's interpretation satisfy the rule requiring that statutes be construed liberally in favor of the Indians.

Moreover, the language of the taxing provision of the 1924 Act belies any suggestion that it carries over to the 1938 Act.[6] The tax proviso in the 1924 Act states that "the production of oil and gas and other minerals on such lands may be taxed by the State in which said lands are located. . . ." 25 U.S.C. § 398. Even applying ordinary principles of statutory construction, "such lands" refers to "[u]nallotted land . . . subject to lease for mining purposes . . . under section 397 [the 1891 Act]." When the statute is "liberally construed . . . in favor of the Indians," Alaska Pacific Fisheries v. United States, 248 U.S. 78, 89 (1918), it is clear that if the tax proviso survives at all, it reaches only those leases executed under the 1891 Act and its 1924 amendment.

* * *

[JUSTICE WHITE, with whom JUSTICE REHNQUIST and JUSTICE STEVENS join, dissenting.]

NOTES

1.   The 1924 Act construed in *Blackfeet Tribe* dealt specifically with payment of taxes on royalty interests of Indians from oil and gas leases. The Court said in footnote 5 of its opinion that allowing state taxation of royalties would undermine Congress' intent in the 1938 Act of ensuring that Indians receive "the greatest return from their property."

2.   In Crow Tribe of Indians v. Montana, 650 F.2d 1104 (9th Cir.1981), amended 665 F.2d 1390 (9th Cir.1982) (*Crow I*), the Crow Tribe challenged application of Montana's large severance tax on non-Indian lessees of tribal coal interests underlying a "ceded strip" of land. The court held that if the tribe

---

[5]   In fact, the legislative history suggests that Congress intended to replace the 1924 Act's leasing scheme with that of the 1938 Act. As the Court of Appeals recognized, Congress had three major goals in adopting the 1938 Act: (i) to achieve "uniformity so far as practicable of the law relating to the leasing of tribal lands for mining purposes," (ii) to "bring all mineral-leasing matters in harmony with the Indian Reorganization Act;" and (iii) to ensure that Indians receive "the greatest return from their property." As the Court of Appeals suggested, these purposes would be undermined if the 1938 Act were interpreted to incorporate the taxation proviso of the 1924 Act. See 729 F.2d 1192, 1196–1198 (C.A.9 1984).

[6]   The Court of Appeals held that the 1938 Act did not repeal implicitly the 1924 consent to state taxation and thus that this consent continues in force with respect to leases issued under the 1924 or 1891 Acts. See Blackfeet Tribe of Indians v. Montana, 729 F.2d 1192, 1200 (C.A.9 1984). Because the Blackfeet have not sought review on this question, we need not decide whether the Court of Appeals was correct. We assume for purposes of this case that the 1924 Act's authorization remains in effect for leases executed pursuant to that statute.

proved its allegations concerning the effects of the state tax, it would interfere with statutory goals of the 1938 Indian Mineral Leasing Act, 25 U.S.C. §§ 396a–396g, particularly the purpose of encouraging reservation economic development. In addition, the court noted that the tribe's right of self-government could be impermissibly affected by the drain on revenues from tribal resources created by the state tax.

After a trial, the district court found that Montana could tax coal extracted from the ceded strip, but the Ninth Circuit reversed, finding that the tribe had shown the impacts necessary for preemption. It observed that "Congress attaches great significance to the firm federal policy of promoting tribal self-sufficiency and economic development," and therefore "Montana's coal taxes are preempted by federal laws and policies." Crow Tribe of Indians v. Montana, 819 F.2d 895, 898, 903 (9th Cir.1987), affirmed 484 U.S. 997 (1988) (*Crow II*). The Ninth Circuit pointed out that the state's 30% tax was so large that it could not be applied to tribal leases without interfering with tribal economic development. The court also held that the tax interfered with tribal self-government because it was not narrowly tailored to the state's legitimate interests. Among other things, it frustrated the tribe's ability to impose its own tax on coal production.

From 1983 to 1988 taxes collected by Montana were deposited in the court registry. After the ruling in *Crow II*, the funds were released to the tribe. The tribe then sought to recover $58.2 million in taxes that had been collected by Montana between 1975 and 1982, still being held in a state trust fund. The tribe argued that it would be unjust to allow the state to keep the taxes collected in violation of federal law. The Ninth Circuit held that the tribe was entitled to the proceeds. Crow Tribe of Indians v. Montana, 92 F.3d 826, amended 98 F.3d 1194 (9th Cir.1996) (*Crow IV*).

The Supreme Court then held that the Crow Tribe could not recover the revenues. Montana v. Crow Tribe of Indians, 523 U.S. 696 (1998). The Court cited its 1989 decision in *Cotton Petroleum*, supra, which upheld New Mexico's severance taxes on reservation mineral lessees, even where the tribe had its own severance tax. There the Court distinguished *Crow II* in a footnote saying that the Montana tax was "an unusually large state tax [that] has imposed a substantial burden on the tribe." 490 U.S. at 186. Since not all state severance taxes on reservation mineral lessees are preempted, Montana might have lawfully collected some taxes. Consequently, the tribe would be entitled to recover monies collected by the state only to the extent it showed actual damages from the negative impacts of Montana's tax—the basis of the preemption found in *Crow II*. Because the tribe had "argued for total disgorgement" and "did not develop a case for relief of a different kind or size" the Supreme Court said that it would have to seek any further relief in the district court.

3.   In County of Yakima v. Confederated Tribes and Bands of the Yakima Indian Nation, 502 U.S. 251 (1992), the Supreme Court held that a county government in Washington could impose an ad valorem property tax on

lands within the Yakima Indian Reservation patented in fee pursuant to the General Allotment Act of 1887 and now owned by reservation Indians or by the tribe itself. The Court's decision turned on its interpretation of a 1906 amendment to the Allotment Act, known as the Burke Act, 34 Stat. 182, which includes a proviso authorizing the Secretary of the Interior, "whenever he shall be satisfied that any Indian allottee is competent and capable of managing his or her affairs" to issue a patent in fee simple to the allottee, *and thereafter all restrictions as to * * * taxation of said land shall be removed.*" Id. at 183. The Court held that the language of the Burke Act contains the unmistakably clear expression of intent that is necessary to authorize state taxation of Indian lands. The Court dismissed the contention of the tribe and the United States that this explicit statutory conferral of taxing power had been impliedly repealed by the Indian Reorganization Act and its repudiation of the allotment policy, citing the "cardinal rule * * * that repeals by implication are not favored." Id. at 262.

However, the Court did hold that Yakima County could not impose its excise tax on sales of patented reservation land, since the Indian General Allotment Act explicitly authorizes only "taxation of * * * land," but not taxation of transactions involving land. Under the Court's holding, therefore, Yakima County can proceed to foreclose on fee patented properties within the reservation for which ad valorem taxes were past due, including those lands held by the Nation itself or its members. Justice Scalia, writing for the eight-person majority in the case, noted that the Yakima Nation's argument that state jurisdiction over reservation fee land "is manifestly inconsistent with the policies of Indian self-determination and self-governance that lay behind the Indian Reorganization Act and subsequent congressional enactments * * * seems to us a great exaggeration." 502 U.S. at 265. Scalia stated that "the mere power to assess and collect a tax on certain real estate" would not be "significantly disruptive of tribal self-government." He added that: "In any case, these policy objections do not belong in this forum. If the Yakima Nation believes that the objectives of the Indian Reorganization Act are too much obstructed by the clearly retained remnant of an earlier policy, it must make that argument to Congress." Id. at 265.

In his dissent, Justice Blackmun wrote:

> The majority deems any concerns for tribal self-determination to be a "great exaggeration." I myself, however, am "far from convinced that when a State imposes taxes upon reservation members without their consent, its action can be reconciled with trial self-determination." *McClanahan v. Arizona State Tax Comm'n*, 411 U.S., at 179. The majority concludes that, as a practical matter, "mere" property taxes are less disruptive of tribal integrity than cigarette sales taxes and certain personal property taxes (as on automobiles). * * * I cannot agree that paying a few more pennies for cigarettes or a tax on some personal property is more a threat to tribal integrity and self-determination than foreclosing upon and seizing tribal lands.

> Finally, the majority platitudinously suggests that the Yakima "must make [their policy] argument to Congress." I am less confident than my colleagues that the 31 Yakima Indian families likely to be rendered landless and homeless by today's decision are well-positioned to lobby for change in the vast corridors of Congress.

Id. at 277–78.

4.   The Supreme Court has extended *County of Yakima* to any alienable lands held by a tribe, not just those that passed out of trust under legislation expressly stating that the lands would be taxable (like allotments subject to the Burke Act). Cass County v. Leech Lake Band of Chippewa Indians, 524 U.S. 103 (1998). It rejected an argument favoring an exemption for lands authorized to be sold by the Nelson Act of 1889 which did not mention taxability, and that were later reacquired by a tribe, saying that simply making land alienable manifests congressional "intent to render such land subject to state and local taxation." Id. at 115.

NATION BUILDING NOTE: RESOLVING JURISDICTIONAL DISPUTES BY COOPERATIVE AGREEMENT[*]

Beginning in 2001, the federally recognized tribes of Michigan entered into negotiations with the State of Michigan regarding taxes. On December 20, 2002, seven of the twelve tribes signed the uniform tax agreements (collectively referred to as the "Uniform Tax Agreement" or "Agreement") with the State.

The Bay Mills Indian Community, the Hannahville Indian Community, the Little River Band of Ottawa Indians, the Little Traverse Bay Bands of Odawa Indians, the Nottawaseppi Huron Band of Potawatomi Indians, the Pokagon Band of Potawatomi Indians, and the Sault Ste. Marie Tribe of Chippewa Indians entered into the Agreement. The Grand Traverse Band of Ottawa and Chippewa Indians signed in 2004. The Match-E-Be-Nash-She-Wish Band of Pottawatomi Indians entered into a tax agreement with the State in 2008.

After intense negotiations over a period of years, the finalized uniform tax agreement covered six categories of state taxes that include sales and use taxes, income tax, motor fuel tax, tobacco product taxes, and single business tax. Earlier efforts by the state and individual Michigan tribes had largely failed before the uniform agreement. For example, earlier agreements may have been illegal under state law because the state treasury did not have the authority to enter into tax agreements. Interview with John Wernet, Deputy Legal Counsel to the Governor of the State of Michigan, in Lansing, Michigan, Sept. 21, 2009. If a tribe was going to be exempt from a state tax, it was a

---

[*]   The following material is derived from Matthew L.M. Fletcher, Alicia Ivory, Adrea Korthase, and Sheena Oxendine, Tribal-State Relations: Michigan as Case Study, Michigan State University College of Law Indigenous Law and Policy Center Occasional Paper 2009–06 (Sept. 30, 1999). See also Matthew L.M. Fletcher, The Power to Tax, the Power to Destroy, and the Michigan Tribal-State Tax Agreements, 82 U.Det. Mercy L.Rev. 1, 5 (2004).

matter of federal law. In 1995, the State announced that it would no longer enter into agreements that had varying provisions for each tribe.

Therefore, to accomplish a more uniform tax agreement, the "state actually initiated the process by rescinding the individual agreements it had with a number of tribes. The state took the position that those agreements 'compromised' Michigan tax laws and that any deviation from Michigan tax laws required legislation, which required a uniform approach." Interview with Bill Brooks, Tribal Attorney for Nottawaseppi Huron Band of Potawatomi Indians, Sept. 23, 2009. In its attempts to achieve that uniformity, the state entered into agreements with a few of the Michigan Indian tribes in the 1990s. For example, in 1997, Michigan entered into an agreement with the Bay Mills Indian Community, which the state subsequently revoked. Other tribes sought agreements similar to the Bay Mills agreement, but the state declined.

In 1997, the state and the tribes first met to discuss a possible tax agreement. The Michigan Indian tribes caucused in 2000 to come up with a proposed agreement to present to the state. Interview with Bill Brooks, Tribal Attorney for Nottawaseppi Huron Band of Potawatomi Indians, (Sept. 23, 2009). The tribes and the state began face-to-face negotiations in 2001 in which each side presented its uniform proposal. The Tribes were attempting to minimize their tax burdens and maximize the exemptions under the agreement that they had enjoyed under prior agreements, Interview with John Wernet, Deputy Legal Counsel to the Governor of the State of Michigan, Lansing, Michigan, Sept. 21, 2009, that "optimized the Tribe's ability to use sovereignty and tax immunities to develop a reservation economy." Interview with Bill Brooks, Tribal Attorney for Nottawaseppi Huron Band of Potawatomi Indians, Sept. 23, 2009. The State however, was attempting to integrate the Tribes into its tax laws.

During the negotiations, the concept of an "agreement area" was developed to incorporate a form of Indian country because there is a lack of clearly designated Indian land in the state for most tribes. The parties agreed that the state did not have the authority to enforce tax laws on tribal members on tribal lands. Michigan tribes have many members who do not live on tribally owned lands and the Tribes also have numerous parcels of land held in trust. Interview with John Wernet, Deputy Legal Counsel to the Governor of the State of Michigan, in Lansing, Michigan, Sept. 21, 2009. The agreement area became the heart of the tax agreement, in that the area was larger than reservation and trust lands, thereby making the benefits of the agreement available to more tribal members. Id. This broader recognition of exemptions for individuals, governmental functions, and business activities in setting up an "agreement area" was the "key compromise that probably led to the agreement's approval and it continuing to work." Interview with Bill Brooks, Tribal Attorney for Nottawaseppi Huron Band of Potawatomi Indians, (Sept. 23, 2009).

There were six categories of taxation agreements. These categories were chosen because the Treasury had the ability to regulate these areas. Interview with John Wernet, Deputy Legal Counsel to the Governor of the State of Michigan, in Lansing, Michigan, Sept. 21, 2009. They were also the major tax categories that had been "addressed in individual agreements and were the state taxes that were impacted by Indian Country." Interview with Bill Brooks, Tribal Attorney for Nottawaseppi Huron Band of Potawatomi Indians, Sept. 23, 2009. Property taxes were left out of the Agreement because the Treasury could do nothing to modify property taxes. Interview with John Wernet, Deputy Legal Counsel to the Governor of the State of Michigan, in Lansing, Michigan, Sept. 21, 2009. These categories dealt with the major taxes that were common to everyone and were comprehensive and pragmatic. Id.

The Uniform Agreement forced the tribes and the state together, creating a better overall relationship. Even though the state had to recognize that each individual tribe is different, it was important to the Treasury that the basic agreement would be the same for all the tribes, since minute variations would become administratively impossible. Interview with John Wernet, Deputy Legal Counsel to the Governor of the State of Michigan, in Lansing, Michigan, Sept. 21, 2009. Michigan attempted to be reasonably consistent from tribe to tribe and tried to balance competing concerns. The basic rules for the each agreement are the same and the only differing aspects of each agreement were the size and location of the agreement areas. The State was cognizant of the tribes' population and the size of trust lands. The parties anticipated that there may be disagreements in the future and therefore agreed to attend an annual summit, and also agreed to a dispute resolution process.

This Agreement has improved the relationship between the tribes and the State of Michigan. Interview with John Wernet, Deputy Legal Counsel to the Governor of the State of Michigan, Lansing, Michigan, Sept. 21, 2009, . The Uniform Tax Agreement has brought predictability to a controversial issue. This Agreement shows that the Tribes and the State "can set aside intractable disagreements on the law and negotiate, and reach compromises, over policy." Interview with Bill Brooks, Tribal Attorney for Nottawaseppi Huron Band of Potawatomi Indians, Sept. 23, 2009. Overall, the Agreement is working, but the Tribes did have to make some compromises. These compromises, however, are offset by the "relative certainty the agreement provides [no litigation] and the benefits to Tribal citizens in most cases." For the Treasury, the Uniform Tax Agreement has proven to be more expensive than anticipated. Interview with John Wernet, Deputy Legal Counsel to the Governor of the State of Michigan, in Lansing, Michigan, Sept. 21, 2009. The Tax Agreement represents a huge step toward improved relations between the tribes and the state, even though not all of the Michigan Indian tribes participate in the Agreement.

The Uniform Tax Agreement may prove useful in negotiations between the Tribes and the State in areas other than taxes. "There has been suggestion that this approach, reaching agreement on 'substantive outcomes' based on policy negotiations, can work in other areas such that jurisdictional conflicts— whether those are based on disagreements about current federal Indian law, or disputed Reservation boundaries—can become less important and set aside." Interview with Bill Brooks, Tribal Attorney for Nottawaseppi Huron Band of Potawatomi Indians, Sept. 23, 2009. The Agreement may also provide an example for other states and tribes to start negotiations and improve relations between two sovereigns. "States and tribes should begin to think outside the box and get beyond the bottom lines to figure out what really matters." Interview with John Wernet, Deputy Legal Counsel to the Governor of the State of Michigan, in Lansing, Michigan, Sept. 21, 2009.

SECTION D. THE INDIAN CHILD WELFARE ACT OF 1978

Cases involving custody of Indian children had been resolved within the general framework of Indian law principles governing civil jurisdiction. Law in this area was relatively well-defined. When the affected parties were within Indian country, tribal jurisdiction was exclusive. Fisher v. District Court, 424 U.S. 382 (1976). In some cases, however, state jurisdiction was upheld where the Indian child or several of the parties resided outside the reservation. See, e.g., In re Adoption of Doe, 555 P.2d 906 (N.M.Ct.App.1976). The sometimes tragic consequences of some state court judgments in human terms moved Congress to extend tribal jurisdiction, supplanting state authority in an area of intense concern to Indian tribes and cultures.

The dominance of judge-made principles was altered in the area of Indian child welfare by the passage of the Indian Child Welfare Act (ICWA) of 1978, 25 U.S.C. §§ 1901–1963, by any standard one of the most sweeping statutes in the field of Indian law.

The ICWA is now involved in more litigation than any other Indian affairs statute. See Kathryn E. Fort, The Cherokee Conundrum: California Courts and the Indian Child Welfare Act, Michigan State University College of Law Legal Studies Research Paper No. 07–07 (Apr. 20, 2009) (noting that the California courts alone decide hundreds of ICWA cases each year). The impacts of the Act are sufficiently broad, especially in state courts, that many private practitioners and state government lawyers have been drawn into Indian law for the first time. And, as the following materials demonstrate, the subject matter is of profound importance to the future of American Indian tribalism.

BRIEF OF AMICI CURIAE NATIONAL CONGRESS OF AMERICAN INDIANS, ASSOCIATION OF AMERICAN INDIAN AFFAIRS, AND NATIONAL INDIAN CHILD WELFARE ASSOCIATION

National Council for Adoption et al. v. Jewell (E.D. Va. 2015)
(No. 1:15–cv–00675).

* * *

Congress enacted the Indian Child Welfare Act of 1978 (ICWA or the "Act"), 25 U.S.C. § 1901 et seq., in response to wholesale removal of Indian children from their families by State and private child welfare agencies at rates far disproportionate to those of non-Indian families. Studies and Congressional testimony revealed the devastating impact of this displacement on Indian tribes and families and identified significant and pervasive abuses in state child welfare and private adoption practices as contributing to these harms. As a result, ICWA was carefully crafted to protect the rights of Indian children, families, and tribes by establishing federal standards to govern state child welfare proceedings involving Indian children.

After the end of the devastating federal boarding school era, many states took over responsibility for the care of Indian children. Margaret Jacobs, A Generation Removed: The Fostering and Adoption of Indigenous Children in the Postwar World 6 (2014). In Minnesota, for example, seven years after the boarding school closed, American Indian children made up 9.2 percent of the child welfare caseload, despite being only 0.5 percent of the population. Across the country, state social workers routinely removed Indian children from their homes and schools by state social workers based on vague allegations of poverty and neglect. * * * By the time Congress passed ICWA in 1978, between 25 and 35 percent of all Indian children had been taken from their families and placed in adoptive, foster, or institutional care. * * * In passing ICWA, Congress intended to combat this deliberate, collaborative abuse of the child welfare system, to reinstate tribes' inherent authority to determine the best interest of their children, and to restore the integrity of Indian families.

Despite passage of ICWA, the abuse of Indian children and families continues to the present. In 2015, in Oglala Sioux Tribe v. Van Hunnick, the United States District Court for South Dakota found that a South Dakota state judge and the State Department of Social Services

> failed to protect Indian parents' fundamental rights to a fair hearing by not allowing them to present evidence to contradict the State's removal documents. The defendants failed by not allowing the parents to confront and cross-examine DSS witnesses. The defendants failed by using documents as a basis for the court's

decisions which were not provided to the parents and which were not received in evidence at the 48-hour hearings.

[100 F. Supp. 3d 749, 772 (D.S.D. 2015)]. This class action suit demonstrates the continued difficulty states have properly implementing the law and protecting American Indian families.

However, to address this very issue, the BIA in 1979 published its Guidelines for State Courts in Indian Child Custody Proceedings. 44 Fed. Reg. 67,584 (Nov. 26, 1979) ("1979 Guidelines"). Since their publication, the 1979 Guidelines have proven an invaluable tool to state courts applying ICWA in countless child welfare cases across the nation. As useful as the 1979 Guidelines have been, much has changed in the 35 years since they were published. Congress has enacted further legislation affecting state child welfare practices generally, the U.S. Supreme Court has twice been called upon to interpret ICWA's statutory language, and hundreds of state court decisions have inconsistently interpreted or outright ignored ICWA's mandates in contravention of Congress's original intent.

Recognizing these changes, earlier this year the BIA published the first revision of the Guidelines since 1979. Guidelines for State Courts in Indian Child Custody Proceedings, 80 Fed. Reg. 10,146 (Feb. 25, 2015) ("2015 Guidelines"). The 2015 Guidelines synthesize thirty-six years of case law, legislative changes, and evolution in social work practice in order to provide state courts with additional guidance and clarity in implementing the law.

Together with ICWA's statutory language, BIA's 2015 Guidelines provide a critical update to a trusted legal source cited in more than forty state supreme court opinions. Although many of the problems ICWA sought to remediate persist today, largely through misapplication or misinterpretation, *Amici* and other leading mainstream child welfare organizations continue to view the law as the "gold standard" for child protection. * * *

* * *

I.   Congress Enacted ICWA in Response to the Widespread Abuses Committed by State Child Welfare Systems Against Indian Children and Families.

Congress did not enact ICWA in a vacuum. In 1959, the Bureau of Indian Affairs ("BIA") along with Child Welfare League of America ("CWLA") created the "Indian Adoption Project." Claire Palmiste, *From the Indian Adoption Project to the Indian Child Welfare Act: the Resistance of Native American Communities*, Indigenous Policy Journal, Vol II, No. 1, at 1 (Summer 2011). The policy mandated that Indian children were to be adopted out to primarily non-Indian families in order to reduce to reduce the populations of Indian reservations, lower federal education costs, and address the growing demand for adoptive children. * * * Project-approved local state agencies took on the responsibility of enacting this policy of "Indian extraction." Ellen L. Slaughter, *Indian Child Welfare: A Review of the Literature*, Denver University Colorado Research Institute, Children's Bureau, Department of Health, Education, and Welfare (1976) * * * .

During the years prior to the final vote on the Act in 1978, Congressionally-commissioned reports and wide-ranging testimony taken from "the broad spectrum of concerned parties, public and private, Indian and non-Indian," H.R. Rep. No. 95–1386, at 28 (1978) * * * ("House Report 95–1386") wove together a chilling narrative—state and private child welfare agencies, with the backing of many state courts and the collaboration of the federal government, had engaged in the systematic removal of Indian children from their families without evidence of harm or due process of law. By the time of ICWA's passage, state agencies had removed between 25 and 35 percent of all Indian children nationwide from their families, placing about 90 percent of those removed children in non-Indian homes. Of those removals, 99 percent were cited for vague reasons of "neglect" or "social deprivation" and the emotional damage the children might be subject to by continuing to live with their Indian families. H.R. Rep. No. 95–1386, at 10 (1978). *See also* Mississippi Band of Choctaw Indians v. Holyfield, 490 U.S. 30, 32–33 (1989) (citing Indian Child Welfare Program: Hearings before the Subcommittee on Indian Affairs of the Senate Committee on Interior and Insular Affairs, 93rd Cong, 2d Sess., 3 (1974) (statement of William Byler) ("1974 Hearings").

In conducting removals of Indian children, State officials, agencies, and procedures "fail[ed] . . . to take into account the special problems and circumstances of Indian families and the legitimate interest of the Indian tribe in preserving and protecting the Indian family as the wellspring of its own future." House Report 95–1386 at 19; *Holyfield*, 490 U.S. at 45, n.18; see also id. (" 'state courts and agencies and their procedures share a large part of the responsibility' for crisis threatening 'the future and integrity of Indian tribes and Indian families.' ") (citing 124 Cong. Rec. 39,103 (letter of Rep. Morris Udall to Assistant Atty. Gen. Patricia M. Wald)). Many removals by child welfare agencies were conducted with "no basis for intelligently evaluating the cultural and social premises underlying Indian home life and childrearing," which excluded Indian family members as the most appropriate—or even viable—placements. *Holyfield*, 490 U.S. at 34–35 (citing Hearing on S. 1214, 95th Cong. 191–92 (1978) (statement of the Nat'l Tribal Chairmen's Assoc.)).

In fact, Congress found that "many social workers, ignorant of Indian cultural values and social norms, make decisions that are wholly inappropriate in the context of Indian family life and so they frequently discover neglect or abandonment where none exists." House Report 95–1386, at 10; see also id. (" . . . the dynamics of Indian extended families are largely misunderstood. An Indian child may have scores of, perhaps more than a hundred, relatives who are counted as close, responsible members of the family."); 1974 Hearings at 473 (statement of Sen. Abourezk) ("We've had testimony here that in Indian communities throughout the Nation there is no such thing as an abandoned child because when a child does have a need for parents for one reason or another, a relative or friend will take that child in. It's the extended family concept."); *Holyfield*, 490 U.S. at 35, n.4. The legislation ultimately enacted as ICWA thus contained protections that, in the words of one clinical psychologist and hearing witness, "support the general proposition that it is in the best interests of [Indian] children to be raised by their natural family and that every opportunity should be provided to maintain the integrity of the natural family." Hearing on S. 1214 Before the Select Comm. on Indian Affairs, 95th Cong. 142 (1977) (statement of Marlene Echohawk, Ph.D., National Congress of American Indians).

Congress also expressed particular concerns about the failure of both state and private adoption agencies to utilize Indian families for placement. See, e.g., 1974 Hearings at 61 (testimony of Dr. Carl Mindell, Department of Psychiatry and Child Psychiatry, Albany Medical College) ("[W]elfare agencies tend to think of adoption too quickly without having other options available . . . Once you're at the point of thinking about adoption . . . welfare agencies are not making adequate use of the Indian communities themselves. They tend to look elsewhere for adoption type of homes."); id. at 117 (statement of Mel Sampson, Northwest Affiliated Tribes) ("The standards that have been established by adoption agencies have created an additional burden . . . as they are white status quo oriented . . . As you well know, this automatically leaves the Indian out."); 1977 Senate Hearing at 271 (testimony of Virgil Gunn, Chairman of the Health, Education and Welfare Committee of the Colville Tribal Business Council) ("Through various ways, the State of Washington public assistance and private placing agencies can completely go around the issue and place without contact to that child's tribe, until the action is completed and irreversible"); see also 1974 Hearings at 147 (testimony of Leon Cook, Dept. of Indian Work).

The result of this Indian child welfare crisis was dire: "[f]or Indians generally and tribes in particular, the continued wholesale removal of their children by nontribal government and private agencies constitutes a serious threat to their existence as ongoing, self-governing communities." 124 Cong. Rec. 38,103 (1978) (statement of Rep. Lagomarsino); see also, *id.* at 38, 102 (statement of sponsor Rep. Morris Udall) ("Indian tribes and Indian people are being drained of their children and, as a result, their future as a tribe and a people is being placed in jeopardy"); *Holyfield*, 490 U.S. at 34, n.3. Abusive child welfare practices also proved harmful to Indian children. Congress was concerned about "the placement of Indian children in non-Indian homes ... based in part on evidence of the detrimental impact on the children themselves of such placement outside their culture." *Holyfield*, 490 U.S. at 49–50. Congress heard multiple examples of Indian children placed in non-Indian homes later suffering from identity crises when they reached adolescence and adulthood. See, e.g., 1974 Hearings at 114 (statement of James Shore, former Chief, Mental Health Office, Portland Area Indian Health Service, and William Nicholls, Director, Health, Welfare and Social Services, Confederated Tribes of The Warm Springs Reservation.). This phenomenon occurred even when the children had few memories of living as part of an Indian community. Such testimony led Congress to conclude that "[r]emoval of Indians from Indian society has serious long-and short-term effects ... for the individual child ... who may suffer untold social and psychological consequences." S. Rep. No. 95–597, at 43 (1977) (hereinafter "Senate Report 95–597").

Congress explicitly recognized and attempted to remediate this national crisis through ICWA—a statute designed to establish "minimum Federal standards for the removal of Indian children from their families and the placement of such children in foster or adoptive homes," 25 U.S.C. § 1902, to be implemented by state and private agencies and applied by state courts with the intention "to promote the stability and security of Indian tribes and families." Id. The Congressional findings further "make[ ] clear that the underlying principle of the bill is in the best interest of the Indian child." House Report 95–1386 at 19; 25 U.S.C. § 1902 ("Congress hereby declares that it is the policy of this Nation to protect the best interests of Indian children. . . ."). At its core, ICWA "seeks to protect the rights of the Indian child *as an Indian* and the rights of the Indian community and tribe in retaining its children in its society ... by establishing 'a Federal policy that wherever possible, an Indian child should remain in the Indian community.' " *Holyfield*, 490 U.S. at 37 (1989) (quoting House Report 95–1386, at 23) (emphasis added).

II. Because ICWA is Implemented by State Court Systems, the BIA's Guidelines are Necessary for Uniform Interpretation of the Law.

A. ICWA's Procedural and Substantive Provisions

The United States has a "distinctive obligation of trust" to federally recognized tribes, Seminole Nation v. United States, 316 U.S. 286, 296–97 (1942). Indeed, ICWA explicitly recognizes this obligation in no uncertain terms:

> Congress, through statutes, treaties, and the general course of dealing with Indian tribes, has assumed the responsibility for the protection and preservation of Indian tribes and their resources . . . there is no resource that is more vital to the continued existence and integrity of Indian tribes than their children . . . the United States has a direct interest, as trustee, in

protecting Indian children who are members of or are eligible for membership in an Indian tribe.

25 U.S.C. §§ 1901(2)–(3). The findings also explicitly recognize Congress's exclusive constitutional authority to legislate Indian affairs. 25 U.S.C. § 1901(1) * * * .

However, ICWA is unique within the body of federal Indian law in that, while "the main effect" of the statute "is to curtail state authority," the primary responsibility for ICWA's implementation is left to the states. *Holyfield*, 490 U.S. at 45 n.17. Generally, ICWA provides the framework for its application, defining to whom it applies and under what circumstances. It also provides various procedural and substantive mandates to protect Indian families and children under the jurisdiction of state court systems. *Holyfield*, 490 U.S. at 36.

ICWA applies only to child custody proceedings involving an "Indian child." * * * ICWA's application is directly tied to the child's membership in a federally recognized tribe or her eligibility to be enrolled in a federally recognized tribe. * * * Given this broad authority, the fact that some federally recognized tribes might employ blood quantum or descendancy as a means to define membership is therefore irrelevant.

ICWA's mandates apply to four defined types of state child custody proceedings: (1) foster care placement; (2) termination of parental rights; (3) preadoptive placement; and (4) adoptive placement. 25 U.S.C. § 1903(1). The Act also delineates the division of jurisdiction in such proceedings between tribal and state courts, see 25 U.S.C. § 1911, and provides explicit protections for families in state court proceedings that involve the involuntary removal of an Indian child from her parent or Indian custodian. See, e.g., 25 U.S.C. § 1912(d) and (e) (requiring that the party seeking to effect the removal prove to a court that "active efforts have been made to prevent the breakup of the Indian family" and that the continued custody of the child by the parent or Indian custodian is "likely to result in serious emotional or physical damage."). ICWA requires that "[i]n any involuntary proceeding in a State court, where the court knows or has reason to know that an Indian child is involved, the party seeking the foster care placement of, or termination of parental rights to, an Indian child shall notify the parent or Indian custodian and the Indian child's tribe. . . ." 25 U.S.C. § 1912(a).

The "most important substantive requirement imposed on state courts" in the Act are the adoptive placement preferences codified at 25 U.S.C. § 1915. *Holyfield*, 490 U.S. at 36–37. These preferences establish a "Federal policy that, where possible, an Indian child should remain in the Indian community," and that Indian child welfare decisions should not be made according to "white, middle-class standard[s] which, in many cases, foreclose[ ] placement with [an] Indian family." Id. at 37 (quoting House Report 95–1386, at 24).

B.   The Guidelines are Critically Necessary for ICWA's Uniform Application across State Child Welfare Systems.

The *Holyfield* Court explicitly recognized the need for uniformity in the interpretation and application of ICWA's terms:

> [M]ost fundamentally, the purpose of the ICWA gives no reason to believe that Congress intended to rely on state law for the definition of a critical term; quite the contrary. It is clear from the very text of the ICWA, not to mention its legislative history and the hearings that led to its enactment, that Congress was concerned with the rights of Indian families and Indian communities vis-a-vis state authorities.

Holyfield, 490 U.S. at 44. * * * Since 1979, state courts have regularly used the Guidelines to assist their interpretation and implementation of ICWA within their respective child welfare systems. The Guidelines serve as a critical bridge between the BIA, the federal agency charged with overseeing Indian affairs, and the state courts responsible for implementing ICWA and integrating it into the day-to-day mechanics of the state child welfare systems. The revised Guidelines provide much needed clarity in areas where state courts have struggled over the past 35 years to effectively implement ICWA. Four brief examples illustrate this point.

Placement Preferences. ICWA enumerates lists of preferred placements for Indian children removed from their homes and subject to foster care, preadoptive, or adoptive proceedings in state court. 25 U.S.C. § 1915(a)–(b). Sections 1915(a)–(b) mandate that, absent good cause to the contrary, Indian children shall be placed according to the statutes' stated preferences. However, "ICWA does not define good cause, nor does it set forth factors to be considered in determining whether good cause exists." C.L. v. P.C.S., 17 P.3d 769, 773 (Alaska 2001).

The 1979 Guidelines sought to bridge this gap by providing factors for state courts to consider when charged with making this "good cause determination." 1979 Guidelines at 67,594. The Guidelines were written specifically to discourage courts from applying a "best interest" analysis in support of a good cause determination:

> Conspicuously absent from the list of justifications for deviating from the placement preferences is a determination that adherence to the preferences would not be within the child's best interests-presumably because the BIA did not wish to invite state courts to engage in a highly discretionary and potentially biased analysis.

Barbara Ann Atwood, *Flashpoints Under the Indian Child Welfare Act: Toward a New Understanding of State Court Resistance*, 51 Emory L.J.

587, 643–644 (2002); 1979 Guidelines, § D.3 (commentary) ("A child may not be removed simply because there is someone else willing to raise the child who is likely to do a better job or that it would be 'in the best interests of the child' for him or her to live with someone else"); House Report 95–1386, at 19 (noting that "judges too may find it difficult, in utilizing vague standards like 'the best interests of the child,' to avoid decisions resting on subjective values") (quoting Smith v. Offer, 431 U.S. 816, 835 n.36 (1977)).

* * * The 2015 Guidelines provide additional clarity in this regard, recommending that while the "extraordinary physical or emotional needs of the child" may warrant good cause to deviate from the placement preferences, such a determination should not include an "independent consideration of the best interest of the Indian child because the preferences reflect the best interests of an Indian child in light of the purposes of the act." 2015 Guidelines, § F.4. * * *

Jurisdiction. While "[t]ribal jurisdiction over Indian child custody proceedings is not a novelty of the ICWA" *Holyfield*, 490 U.S. at 42, ICWA provides that tribal courts have *exclusive* jurisdiction over custody proceedings involving Indian children domiciled in Indian Country. 25 U.S.C. § 1911(a), see also Fisher v. Dist. Ct., 424 U.S. 382 (1976). In addition, the statute provides that tribal courts have *concurrent* and *presumptive* jurisdiction over Indian child custody cases where the child is domiciled outside of Indian Country. 25 U.S.C. § 1911(b); *Holyfield*, 490 U.S. at 36. At the request of a parent or of the tribe, the state shall transfer jurisdiction of an Indian child welfare case to tribal jurisdiction.

However, the law also allows a state court to deny a tribe's request to transfer if there is "good cause" to do so. Determining what constitutes "good cause" to deny transfer has been the subject of considerable litigation, in part because the 1979 Guidelines permitted denial of a tribe's request to transfer if the matter was at an "advanced stage of the proceedings." With no other guidance, state courts have split on when a proceeding was at an "advanced stage." * * * To address this quandary, the revised Guidelines explicitly state that courts should no longer consider if a case is at an advance stage of the proceedings when a transfer request is made. 2015 Guidelines, § C.3(c).

Notice. Described by the Department of the Interior at the time of passage as "a major element" of the Act, House Report 95–1386 at 31 (Report of the Department of the Interior, June 6, 1978), ICWA requires that a state court in an involuntary proceeding involving an Indian child provide "notice" to the parent or Indian custodian and the Indian child's tribe. 25 U.S.C. § 1912(a). But ICWA does not expressly define what events trigger notice, nor does it enumerate what constitutes adequate notice. The 1979 Guidelines included specific recommendations concerning the provision of, and the information to be included in, notice to tribes. 1979

Guidelines, § B.5. However, despite this guidance, disagreements have arisen in many state courts (and sometimes courts within the same state) concerning when notice is required and what information is to be included in the notice. * * * The 2015 revisions attempt to rectify this confusion by providing additional clarification as to when ICWA's notice requirement is triggered, 2015 Guidelines, § A.3(c)–(d), as well as what types of information the notice should contain. 2015 Guidelines, § B.6.

Active Efforts. As noted above, ICWA requires that "active efforts" be made to "provide remedial services and rehabilitative programs designed to prevent the breakup of an Indian family." 25 U.S.C. 1912(d). The 1979 Guidelines explain that active efforts: "shall take into account the prevailing social and cultural conditions and the way of life of the Indian child's tribe. They shall also involve and use the available resources of the extended family, the tribe, Indian social services agencies, and individual Indian care givers." 1979 Guidelines, § D.2. Many state courts have drawn upon this guidance to find that active efforts require more than the standard services offered parents in non-ICWA cases; however, others have concluded that ICWA's "active efforts" requirement is equivalent to the reunification services offered in a non-ICWA case—"reasonable efforts." See Megan Scanlon, From Theory to Practice: Incorporating the "Active Efforts" Requirement in Indian Child Welfare Act Proceedings, 43 Ariz. St. L.J. 629, 629 (2011) (compiling cases). The 2015 Guidelines address these inconsistencies by providing a clear definition of active efforts, enumerating more than a dozen factors constituting active efforts, and specifically stating that active efforts is a higher standard than "reasonable efforts." 2015 Guidelines, § A.2.

III. Because Social Work Practice and Child Welfare Law Has Progressed Considerably in the Past Thirty-Six Years Revisions to the Guidelines Were Appropriate and Necessary.

Much of child welfare practice has changed since 1979. Despite the advancement and progression in the practice, the Guidelines remained static. This rendered them outdated and incompatible with the current state of child welfare practice and court proceedings.

The 2015 Revisions, therefore, are a critical and necessary resource for the continued informed application and implementation of ICWA.

Not surprisingly, given the passage of time, the 1979 Guidelines contain incorrect statements of law. For example, the 1979 Guidelines define the term "domicile" on the basis that "[t]here is no indication that these state law definitions tend to undermine in any way the purposes of the Act." 1979 Guidelines at 67,585. The Supreme Court, however, expressly overruled this construction of "domicile" in *Holyfield*, yet the invalidated definition remained in the Guidelines up until BIA published is revisions in February 2015. Additionally, the 1979 Guidelines failed to incorporate the Supreme Court's 1978 statement that: "[a] tribe's right to define its own membership for tribal purposes has long been recognized as central to its existence as an independent political community." Santa Clara Pueblo v. Martinez, 436 U.S. 49, 72 n.32 (1978). The continued incorporation of incorrect statements of the law, such as these, further necessitated the revision of the guidelines.

The 1979 Guidelines also have failed to account for significant changes in federal child welfare legislation. The primary responsibility for providing child welfare services rests with the states. Ex parte Burrus, 136 U.S. 586, 593–94 (1890). However, states must conform to federal requirements to be eligible for Federal child welfare funding programs. * * * Federal funding legislation, therefore, prompts state level responses and changes. These responses typically include new state legislation, revision of state agency policy and procedures, and implementation of new child welfare practices and programs.

Since 1979, Congress has passed at least 30 laws addressing child welfare funding that have had a significant impact on state child welfare policy and practice. In addition to changing child welfare practice for all children, these changes also directly affect how states implement ICWA and coordinate its requirements with child welfare practice more generally. * * *

Federal laws have been the primary force driving child welfare change for the past 35 years. Gerard P. Mallon & Peg McCartt Hess, Preface in Child Welfare for the Twenty-First Century: A Handbook of Practices, Policies, and Programs xii (Gerard P. Mallon & Peg McCartt Hess, eds, 2005). Yet practices have also been shaped, to a lesser degree, by changes in social work practice as well as ideological and planning orientations. * * * The most pronounced change in social work practice since 1979 is the use of empirical evidence and the movement towards implementing "evidence-based practices." Id. at xiii. * * *

In addition, the ability of tribes to provide services, implement programs, manage and adjudicate cases has shifted dramatically since the passage of ICWA, and has had a profound impact on ICWA's implementation. Terry L. Cross and Robert J. Miller, *The Indian Child Welfare Act of 1978 and Its Impact on Tribal Sovereignty and Governance*, in Facing the Future: The Indian Child Welfare Act at 30, 13 (Matthew L.M. Fletcher et al., eds., 2009) ("In the years since the passage of the 1979 Guidelines tribal capacity has grown, tribal social service programs have expanded, and the number of tribal courts have increased."). * * *

* * *

NOTE

On June 14, 2016, the Department of the Interior promulgated regulations to govern the implementation of the Indian Child Welfare Act. Indian Child Welfare Act Proceedings, 25 CFR Part 23, 81 Fed. Reg. 38778. The regulations substantially revise and replace the 2015 guidelines referenced in the excerpt above. The Interior Department promises revised guidelines in late 2016. The regulations will go into effect in December 2016, six months after promulgation. Congress initially authorized Interior to promulgate regulations in ICWA itself, 25 U.S.C. § 1952. Regulations, unlike the guidelines documents issued in 1979 and 2015 that are persuasive authority, have the force of law.

MISSISSIPPI BAND OF CHOCTAW INDIANS V. HOLYFIELD

Supreme Court of the United States, 1989.
490 U.S. 30, 109 S.Ct. 1597, 104 L.Ed.2d 29.

JUSTICE BRENNAN delivered the opinion of the Court.

* * *

I

A

* * *

At the heart of the ICWA are its provisions concerning jurisdiction over Indian child custody proceedings. Section 1911 lays out a dual jurisdictional scheme. Section 1911(a) establishes exclusive jurisdiction in the tribal courts for proceedings concerning an Indian child "who resides or is domiciled within the reservation of such tribe," as well as for wards of tribal courts regardless of domicile. Section 1911(b), on the other hand, creates concurrent but presumptively tribal jurisdiction in the case of children not domiciled on the reservation: on petition of either parent or the tribe, state-court proceedings for foster care placement or termination of parental rights are to be transferred to the tribal court, except in cases of "good cause," objection by either parent, or declination of jurisdiction by the tribal court.

* * *

B

This case involves the status of twin babies, known for our purposes as B.B. and G.B., who were born out of wedlock on December 29, 1985. Their mother, J.B., and father, W.J. were both enrolled members of appellant Mississippi Band of Choctaw Indians (Tribe), and were residents and domiciliaries of the Choctaw Reservation in Neshoba County, Mississippi. J.B. gave birth to the twins in Gulfport, Harrison County, Mississippi, some 200 miles from the reservation. On January 10, 1986,

J.B. executed a consent-to-adoption form before the Chancery Court of Harrison County. W.J. signed a similar form. On January 16, appellees Orrey and Vivian Holyfield filed a petition for adoption in the same court, and the chancellor issued a Final Decree of Adoption on January 28. Despite the court's apparent awareness of the ICWA, the adoption decree contained no reference to it, nor to the infants' Indian background.

Two months later the Tribe moved in the Chancery Court to vacate the adoption decree on the ground that under the ICWA exclusive jurisdiction was vested in the tribal court. On July 14, 1986, the court overruled the motion, holding that the Tribe "never obtained exclusive jurisdiction over the children involved herein. . . ." The court's one-page opinion relied on two facts in reaching that conclusion. The court noted first that the twins' mother "went to some efforts to see that they were born outside the confines of the Choctaw Indian Reservation" and that the parents had promptly arranged for the adoption by the Holyfields. Second, the court stated: "At no time from the birth of these children to the present date have either of them resided on or physically been on the Choctaw Indian Reservation."

The Supreme Court of Mississippi affirmed. * * *

* * *

II

Tribal jurisdiction over Indian child custody proceedings is not a novelty of the ICWA. Indeed, some of the ICWA's jurisdictional provisions have a strong basis in pre-ICWA case law in the federal and state courts [citing Fisher v. District Court, 424 U.S. 382 (1976) and other authorities]. In enacting the ICWA Congress confirmed that, in child custody proceedings involving Indian children domiciled on the reservation, tribal jurisdiction was exclusive as to the States.

The state-court proceeding at issue here was a "child custody proceeding." That term is defined to include any " 'adoptive placement' which shall mean the permanent placement of an Indian child for adoption, including any action resulting in a final decree of adoption." 25 U.S.C. § 1903(1)(iv). Moreover, the twins were "Indian children." See 25 U.S.C. § 1903(4). The sole issue in this case is, as the Supreme Court of Mississippi recognized, whether the twins were "domiciled" on the reservation.

A

The meaning of "domicile" in the ICWA is, of course, a matter of Congress' intent. The ICWA itself does not define it. The initial question we must confront is whether there is any reason to believe that Congress intended the ICWA definition of "domicile" to be a matter of state law. * * *

* * *

First, and most fundamentally, the purpose of the ICWA gives no reason to believe that Congress intended to rely on state law for the definition of a critical term; quite the contrary. It is clear from the very text of the ICWA, not to mention its legislative history and the hearings that led to its enactment, that Congress was concerned with the rights of Indian families and Indian communities vis-à-vis state authorities. More specifically, its purpose was, in part, to make clear that in certain situations the state courts did *not* have jurisdiction over child custody proceedings. Indeed, the congressional findings that are a part of the statute demonstrate that Congress perceived the States and their courts as partly responsible for the problem it intended to correct. See 25 U.S.C. § 1901(5) (state "judicial bodies ... have often failed to recognize the essential tribal relations of Indian people and the cultural and social standards prevailing in Indian communities and families"). Under these circumstances it is most improbable that Congress would have intended to leave the scope of the statute's key jurisdictional provision subject to definition by state courts as a matter of state law.

Second, Congress could hardly have intended the lack of nationwide uniformity that would result from state-law definitions of domicile. * * *

* * *

B

It remains to give content to the term "domicile" in the circumstances of the present case. The holding of the Supreme Court of Mississippi that the twin babies were not domiciled on the Choctaw Reservation appears to have rested on two findings of fact by the trial court: (1) that they had never been physically present there, and (2) that they were "voluntarily surrendered" by their parents. 511 So.2d, at 921. The question before us, therefore, is whether under the ICWA definition of "domicile" such facts suffice to render the twins nondomiciliaries of the reservation.

* * *

It is undisputed in this case that the domicile of the mother (as well as the father) has been, at all relevant times, on the Choctaw Reservation. Thus, it is clear that at their birth the twin babies were also domiciled on the reservation, even though they themselves had never been there. The statement of the Supreme Court of Mississippi that "[a]t no point in time can it be said that twins * * * were domiciled within the territory set aside for the reservation," 511 So.2d, at 921, may be a correct statement of that State's law of domicile, but it is inconsistent with generally accepted doctrine in this country and cannot be what Congress had in mind when it used the term in the ICWA.

Nor can the result be any different simply because the twins were "voluntarily surrendered" by their mother. Tribal jurisdiction under

§ 1911(a) was not meant to be defeated by the actions of individual members of the tribe, for Congress was concerned not solely about the interests of Indian children and families, but also about the impact on the tribes themselves of the large numbers of Indian children adopted by non-Indians. See 25 U.S.C. §§ 1901(3) ("[T]here is no resource that is more vital to the continued existence and integrity of Indian tribes than their children"), 1902 ("promote the stability and security of Indian tribes"). The numerous prerogatives accorded the tribes through the ICWA's substantive provisions, e.g., §§ 1911(a) (exclusive jurisdiction over reservation domiciliaries), 1911(b) (presumptive jurisdiction over nondomiciliaries), 1911(c) (right of intervention), 1912(a) (notice), 1914 (right to petition for invalidation of state-court action), 1915(c) (alter presumptive placement priorities applicable to state-court actions), 1915(e) (right to obtain records), 1919 (authority to conclude agreements with States), must, accordingly, be seen as a means of protecting not only the interests of individual Indian children and families, but also of the tribes themselves.

In addition, it is clear that Congress' concern over the placement of Indian children in non-Indian homes was based in part on evidence of the detrimental impact on the children themselves of such placements outside their culture. Congress determined to subject such placements to the ICWA's jurisdictional and other provisions, even in cases where the parents consented to an adoption, because of concerns going beyond the wishes of individual parents. As the 1977 Final Report of the congressionally established American Indian Policy Review Commission stated, in summarizing these two concerns, "[r]emoval of Indian children from their cultural setting seriously impacts a long-term tribal survival and has damaging social and psychological impact on many individual Indian children." Senate Report, at 52.

These congressional objectives make clear that a rule of domicile that would permit individual Indian parents to defeat the ICWA's jurisdictional scheme is inconsistent with what Congress intended. * * * The Supreme Court of Utah expressed this well in its scholarly and sensitive opinion in what has become a leading case on the ICWA:

> "To the extent that [state] abandonment law operates to permit [the child's] mother to change [the child's] domicile as part of a scheme to facilitate his adoption by non-Indians while she remains a domiciliary of the reservation, it conflicts with and undermines the operative scheme established by subsections [1911(a)] and [1913(a)] to deal with children of domiciliaries of the reservation and weakens considerably the tribe's ability to assert its interest in its children. The protection of this tribal interest is at the core of the ICWA, which recognizes that the tribe has an interest in the child which is distinct from but on a parity with the

interest of the parents. This relationship between Indian tribes and Indian children domiciled on the reservation finds no parallel in other ethnic cultures found in the United States. It is a relationship that many non-Indians find difficult to understand and that non-Indian courts are slow to recognize. It is precisely in recognition of this relationship, however, that the ICWA designates the tribal court as the exclusive forum for the determination of custody and adoption matters for reservation-domiciled Indian children, and the preferred forum for nondomiciliary Indian children. [State] abandonment law cannot be used to frustrate the federal legislative judgment expressed in the ICWA that the interests of the tribe in custodial decisions made with respect to Indian children are as entitled to respect as the interests of the parents." In re Adoption of Halloway, 732 P.2d 962, 969–970 (1986).

* * *

III

We are not unaware that over three years have passed since the twin babies were born and placed in the Holyfield home, and that a court deciding their fate today is not writing on a blank slate in the same way it would have in January 1986. Three years' development of family ties cannot be undone, and a separation at this point would doubtless cause considerable pain.

Whatever feelings we might have as to where the twins should live, however, it is not for us to decide that question. We have been asked to decide the legal question of *who* should make the custody determination concerning these children—not what the outcome of that determination should be. The law places that decision in the hands of the Choctaw tribal court. Had the mandate of the ICWA been followed in 1986, of course, much potential anguish might have been avoided, and in any case the law cannot be applied so as automatically to "reward those who obtain custody, whether lawfully or otherwise, and maintain it during any ensuing (and protracted) litigation." *Halloway*, supra, at 972. It is not ours to say whether the trauma that might result from removing these children from their adoptive family should outweigh the interest of the Tribe—and perhaps the children themselves—in having them raised as part of the Choctaw community. Rather, "we must defer to the experience, wisdom, and compassion of the [Choctaw] tribal courts to fashion an appropriate remedy." Ibid.

The judgment of the Supreme Court of Mississippi is reversed and the case remanded for further proceedings not inconsistent with this opinion.

It is so ordered.

JUSTICE STEVENS, with whom THE CHIEF JUSTICE and JUSTICE KENNEDY join, dissenting.

[omitted]

* * *

NOTES

1.   By the time legal proceedings under the Indian Child Welfare Act are brought, the Indian child sometimes has been with the foster parents for several months or even years. This situation may raise serious questions about the impact of disruptive family changes on the child. What options remain for the tribal court in its "experience, wisdom, and compassion," as Justice Brennan described the situation in *Holyfield?* Should the tribal court remove the child from the adoptive home after it has bonded with the family?

Following the Supreme Court's decision in *Holyfield*, the Mississippi Choctaw Tribal Court ultimately granted adoption of the twins to Ms. Holyfield, based on the court's determination that it was in the children's best interest to stay with her. Marcia Coyle, *After the Gavel Comes Down*, National Law Journal, Feb. 25, 1991, at 1.

2.   Several state courts objected to ICWA for policy reasons and created a common law "existing Indian family" exception to the ICWA. This was first articulated in 1982 by the Kansas Supreme Court in Matter of Adoption of Baby Boy L., 643 P.2d 168 (Kan.1982). In *Baby Boy L.*, the court held that ICWA could not apply to a child who was not a member of a tribe, did not live on a reservation or participate in tribal culture, and "probably never would." Id. at 175.

In 2009, that court abandoned the doctrine in In re A.J.S., 204 P.3d 543 (Kan.2009), writing:

> The validity of the existing Indian family doctrine has been called into repeated question by a variety of courts and commentators over the course of the 27 years since *Baby Boy L.* was decided. See, e.g., In re Baby Boy C. Jeffrey A., 27 A.D.3d 34, 46–47, 805 N.Y.S.2d 313 (2005); Atwood, *Flashpoints Under the Indian Child Welfare Act: Toward a New Understanding of State Court Resistance*, 51 Emory L.J. 587, 624–34 (2002); Prim, *The Indian Child Welfare Act and the Existing Indian Family Exception: Rerouting the Trail of Tears?*, 24 Law & Psychol. Rev. 115, 118–19 (2000).

> Although the United States Supreme Court has not addressed the issue before us and has consistently denied review of cases dealing with the constitutionality of ICWA, its 1989 decision in *Mississippi Band of Choctaw Indians v. Holyfield*, underscored the central importance of the relationship between an Indian child and his or her tribe, independent of any parental relationship. *Holyfield*, 490 U.S. at 50 * * * .

In *Holyfield*, the Court vacated an adoption decree entered under state law, holding that ICWA should have been applied to the proceedings when both unmarried parents were Indian, were domiciled on a reservation, and the mother had left the reservation to give birth to twins. The couple consented to the twins' adoption under state law, and the adoption decree was final within a month of the twins' birth. *Holyfield*, 490 U.S. at 37–38, 109 S.Ct. 1597.

The tribe sought to invalidate the adoption, and, although the twins had been living with their adoptive parents for 3 years, the Supreme Court agreed that the proceedings were invalid, that ICWA should have governed, and that the tribe had the right to be involved in the proceeding. . . .

Id. at 546–47. The court continued:

[W]e hereby overrule Baby Boy L., 231 Kan. 199, 643 P.2d 168,and abandon its existing Indian family doctrine. Indian heritage and the treatment of it has a unique history in United States law. A.J.S. has both Indian and non-Indian heritage, and courts are right to resist essentializing any ethnic or racial group. However, ICWA's overall design, including its "good cause" threshold in 25 U.S.C. § 1915, ensures that all interests-those of both natural parents, the tribe, the child, and the prospective adoptive parents-are appropriately considered and safeguarded. ICWA applies to this state court child custody proceeding involving A.J.S., and the Cherokee Nation must be permitted to intervene.

Id. at 551.

Ultimately, a significant majority of state courts rejected the "existing Indian family" exception. The 2015 ICWA Guidelines and the 2016 ICWA Regulations bar the application of the "existing Indian family" exception.

ADOPTIVE COUPLE V. BABY GIRL

Supreme Court of the United States, 2013.
___ U.S. ___, 133 S.Ct. 2552, 186 L.Ed.2d 729.

JUSTICE ALITO delivered the opinion of the Court.

This case is about a little girl (Baby Girl) who is classified as an Indian because she is 1.2% (3/256) Cherokee. Because Baby Girl is classified in this way, the South Carolina Supreme Court held that certain provisions of the federal Indian Child Welfare Act of 1978 required her to be taken, at the age of 27 months, from the only parents she had ever known and handed over to her biological father, who had attempted to relinquish his parental rights and who had no prior contact with the child. The provisions of the federal statute at issue here do not demand this result.

* * *

I

"The Indian Child Welfare Act of 1978 (ICWA), 92 Stat. 3069, 25 U.S.C. §§ 1901–1963, was the product of rising concern in the mid-1970's over the consequences to Indian children, Indian families, and Indian tribes of abusive child welfare practices that resulted in the separation of large numbers of Indian children from their families and tribes through adoption or foster care placement, usually in non-Indian homes." Mississippi Band of Choctaw Indians v. Holyfield, 490 U.S. 30, 32 * * * (1989). Congress found that "an alarmingly high percentage of Indian families [were being] broken up by the removal, often unwarranted, of their children from them by nontribal public and private agencies." § 1901(4). This "wholesale removal of Indian children from their homes" prompted Congress to enact the ICWA, which establishes federal standards that govern state-court child custody proceedings involving Indian children. Id., at 32, 36. * * *

Three provisions of the ICWA are especially relevant to this case. First, "[a]ny party seeking" an involuntary termination of parental rights to an Indian child under state law must demonstrate that "active efforts have been made to provide remedial services and rehabilitative programs designed to prevent the breakup of the Indian family and that these efforts have proved unsuccessful." § 1912(d). Second, a state court may not involuntarily terminate parental rights to an Indian child "in the absence of a determination, supported by evidence beyond a reasonable doubt, including testimony of qualified expert witnesses, that the continued custody of the child by the parent or Indian custodian is likely to result in serious emotional or physical damage to the child." § 1912(f). Third, with respect to adoptive placements for an Indian child under state law, "a preference shall be given, in the absence of good cause to the contrary, to a placement with (1) a member of the child's extended family; (2) other members of the Indian child's tribe; or (3) other Indian families." § 1915(a).

II

In this case, Birth Mother (who is predominantly Hispanic) and Biological Father (who is a member of the Cherokee Nation) became engaged in December 2008. * * * The couple's relationship deteriorated, and Birth Mother broke off the engagement in May 2009. In June, Birth Mother sent Biological Father a text message asking if he would rather pay child support or relinquish his parental rights. Biological Father responded via text message that he relinquished his rights.

Birth Mother then decided to put Baby Girl up for adoption. Because Birth Mother believed that Biological Father had Cherokee Indian heritage, her attorney contacted the Cherokee Nation to determine whether Biological Father was formally enrolled. The inquiry letter misspelled Biological Father's first name and incorrectly stated his birthday, and the Cherokee Nation responded that, based on the information provided, it could not verify Biological Father's membership in the tribal records.

Working through a private adoption agency, Birth Mother selected Adoptive Couple, non-Indians living in South Carolina, to adopt Baby Girl. * * *

It is undisputed that, for the duration of the pregnancy and the first four months after Baby Girl's birth, Biological Father provided no financial assistance to Birth Mother or Baby Girl, even though he had the ability to do so. Indeed, Biological Father "made no meaningful attempts to assume his responsibility of parenthood" during this period. * * *

Approximately four months after Baby Girl's birth, Adoptive Couple served Biological Father with notice of the pending adoption. (This was the first notification that they had provided to Biological Father regarding the adoption proceeding.) Biological Father signed papers stating that he accepted service and that he was "not contesting the adoption." * * * But Biological Father later testified that, at the time he signed the papers, he thought that he was relinquishing his rights to Birth Mother, not to Adoptive Couple.

Biological Father contacted a lawyer the day after signing the papers, and subsequently requested a stay of the adoption proceedings. In the adoption proceedings, Biological Father sought custody and stated that he did not consent to Baby Girl's adoption. Moreover, Biological Father took a paternity test, which verified that he was Baby Girl's biological father.

A trial took place in the South Carolina Family Court in September 2011, by which time Baby Girl was two years old. * * * The Family Court concluded that Adoptive Couple had not carried the heightened burden under § 1912(f) of proving that Baby Girl would suffer serious emotional or physical damage if Biological Father had custody. * * * The Family Court therefore denied Adoptive Couple's petition for adoption and awarded custody to Biological Father. * * * On December 31, 2011, at the age of 27 months, Baby Girl was handed over to Biological Father, whom she had never met.

The South Carolina Supreme Court affirmed the Family Court's denial of the adoption and the award of custody to Biological Father. * * * We granted certiorari. * * *

III

* * *

A

Section 1912(f) addresses the involuntary termination of parental rights with respect to an Indian child. Specifically, § 1912(f) provides that "[n]o termination of parental rights may be ordered in such proceeding in the absence of a determination, supported by evidence beyond a reasonable doubt, * * * that the *continued custody* of the child by the parent or Indian custodian is likely to result in serious emotional or physical damage to the child." (Emphasis added.) The South Carolina Supreme Court held that Adoptive Couple failed to satisfy § 1912(f) because they did not make a heightened showing that Biological Father's "prospective legal and physical custody" would likely result in serious damage to the child. * * * That holding was error.

Section 1912(f) conditions the involuntary termination of parental rights on a showing regarding the merits of "*continued* custody of the child by the parent." (Emphasis added.) The adjective "continued" plainly refers to a pre-existing state. As Justice SOTOMAYOR concedes, * * * "continued" means "[c]arried on or kept up without cessation" or "[e]xtended in space without interruption or breach of conne[ct]ion." Compact Edition of the Oxford English Dictionary 909 (1981 reprint of 1971 ed.) (Compact OED). * * * The phrase "continued custody" therefore refers to custody that a parent already has (or at least had at some point in the past). As a result, § 1912(f) does not apply in cases where the Indian parent never had custody of the Indian child.

* * *

Under our reading of § 1912(f), Biological Father should not have been able to invoke § 1912(f) in this case, because he had never had legal or physical custody of Baby Girl as of the time of the adoption proceedings. As an initial matter, it is undisputed that Biological Father never had physical custody of Baby Girl. And as a matter of both South Carolina and Oklahoma law, Biological Father never had legal custody either. See S.C.Code Ann. § 63–17–20(B) (2010) ("Unless the court orders otherwise, the custody of an illegitimate child is solely in the natural mother unless the mother has relinquished her rights to the child"); Okla. Stat., Tit. 10, § 7800 (West Cum.Supp. 2013) ("Except as otherwise provided by law, the mother of a child born out of wedlock has custody of the child until determined otherwise by a court of competent jurisdiction").

In sum, the South Carolina Supreme Court erred in finding that § 1912(f) barred termination of Biological Father's parental rights.

* * *

B

Section 1912(d) provides that "[a]ny party" seeking to terminate parental rights to an Indian child under state law "shall satisfy the court that active efforts have been made to provide remedial services and rehabilitative programs designed *to prevent the breakup of the Indian family* and that these efforts have proved unsuccessful." (Emphasis added.) The South Carolina Supreme Court found that Biological Father's parental rights could not be terminated because Adoptive Couple had not demonstrated that Biological Father had been provided remedial services in accordance with § 1912(d). * * * We disagree.

Consistent with the statutory text, we hold that § 1912(d) applies only in cases where an Indian family's "breakup" would be precipitated by the termination of the parent's rights. The term "breakup" refers in this context to "[t]he discontinuance of a relationship," American Heritage Dictionary 235 (3d ed. 1992), or "an ending as an effective entity," Webster's 273 (defining "breakup" as "a disruption or dissolution into component parts: an ending as an effective entity"). * * * But when an Indian parent abandons an Indian child prior to birth and that child has never been in the Indian parent's legal or physical custody, there is no "relationship" that would be "discontinu[ed]"—and no "effective entity" that would be "end[ed]"—by the termination of the Indian parent's rights. In such a situation, the "breakup of the Indian family" has long since occurred, and § 1912(d) is inapplicable. * * *

* * *

Section 1912(d) is a sensible requirement when applied to state social workers who might otherwise be too quick to remove Indian children from their Indian families. It would, however, be unusual to apply § 1912(d) in the context of an Indian parent who abandoned a child prior to birth and who never had custody of the child. The decision below illustrates this point. The South Carolina Supreme Court held that § 1912(d) mandated measures such as "attempting to stimulate [Biological] Father's desire to be a parent." * * * But if prospective adoptive parents were required to engage in the bizarre undertaking of "stimulat[ing]" a biological father's "desire to be a parent," it would surely dissuade some of them from seeking to adopt Indian children. And this would, in turn, unnecessarily place vulnerable Indian children at a unique disadvantage in finding a permanent and loving home, even in cases where neither an Indian parent nor the relevant tribe objects to the adoption.

In sum, the South Carolina Supreme Court erred in finding that § 1912(d) barred termination of Biological Father's parental rights.

IV

In the decision below, the South Carolina Supreme Court suggested that if it had terminated Biological Father's rights, then § 1915(a)'s preferences for the adoptive placement of an Indian child would have been applicable. * * * In so doing, however, the court failed to recognize a critical limitation on the scope of § 1915(a).

Section 1915(a) provides that "[i]n any adoptive placement of an Indian child under State law, a preference shall be given, in the absence of good cause to the contrary, to a placement with (1) a member of the child's extended family; (2) other members of the Indian child's tribe; or (3) other Indian families." Contrary to the South Carolina Supreme Court's suggestion, § 1915(a)'s preferences are inapplicable in cases where no alternative party has formally sought to adopt the child. This is because there simply is no "preference" to apply if no alternative party that is eligible to be preferred under § 1915(a) has come forward.

In this case, Adoptive Couple was the only party that sought to adopt Baby Girl in the Family Court or the South Carolina Supreme Court. * * * Biological Father is not covered by § 1915(a) because he did not seek to adopt Baby Girl; instead, he argued that his parental rights should not be terminated in the first place. Moreover, Baby Girl's paternal grandparents never sought custody of Baby Girl. * * * Nor did other members of the Cherokee Nation or "other Indian families" seek to adopt Baby Girl, even though the Cherokee Nation had notice of—and intervened in—the adoption proceedings. * * *

The Indian Child Welfare Act was enacted to help preserve the cultural identity and heritage of Indian tribes, but under the State Supreme Court's reading, the Act would put certain vulnerable children at a great disadvantage solely because an ancestor—even a remote one—was an Indian. As the State Supreme Court read §§ 1912(d) and (f), a biological Indian father could abandon his child in utero and refuse any support for the birth mother—perhaps contributing to the mother's decision to put the child up for adoption—and then could play his ICWA trump card at the eleventh hour to override the mother's decision and the child's best interests. If this were possible, many prospective adoptive parents would surely pause before adopting any child who might possibly qualify as an Indian under the ICWA. Such an interpretation would raise equal protection concerns, but the plain text of §§ 1912(f) and (d) makes clear that neither provision applies in the present context. Nor do § 1915(a)'s rebuttable adoption preferences apply when no alternative party has formally sought to adopt the child. We therefore reverse the judgment of the South Carolina Supreme Court and remand the case for further proceedings not inconsistent with this opinion.

It is so ordered.

JUSTICE THOMAS, concurring.

I join the Court's opinion in full but write separately to explain why constitutional avoidance compels this outcome. Each party in this case has put forward a plausible interpretation of the relevant sections of the Indian Child Welfare Act (ICWA). However, the interpretations offered by respondent Birth Father and the United States raise significant constitutional problems as applied to this case. Because the Court's decision avoids those problems, I concur in its interpretation.

* * *

JUSTICE BREYER, concurring.

[omitted]

JUSTICE SCALIA, dissenting.

* * * The Court's opinion, it seems to me, needlessly demeans the rights of parenthood. It has been the constant practice of the common law to respect the entitlement of those who bring a child into the world to raise that child. We do not inquire whether leaving a child with his parents is "in the best interest of the child." It sometimes is not; he would be better off raised by someone else. But parents have their rights, no less than children do. This father wants to raise his daughter, and the statute amply protects his right to do so. There is no reason in law or policy to dilute that protection.

JUSTICE SOTOMAYOR, with whom JUSTICE GINSBURG and JUSTICE KAGAN join, and with whom JUSTICE SCALIA joins in part, dissenting.

A casual reader of the Court's opinion could be forgiven for thinking this an easy case, one in which the text of the applicable statute clearly points the way to the only sensible result. In truth, however, the path from the text of the Indian Child Welfare Act of 1978 (ICWA) to the result the Court reaches is anything but clear, and its result anything but right.

The reader's first clue that the majority's supposedly straightforward reasoning is flawed is that not all Members who adopt its interpretation believe it is compelled by the text of the statute, see * * * THOMAS, J., concurring[ ]; nor are they all willing to accept the consequences it will necessarily have beyond the specific factual scenario confronted here, see * * * BREYER, J., concurring[ ]. The second clue is that the majority begins its analysis by plucking out of context a single phrase from the last clause of the last subsection of the relevant provision, and then builds its entire argument upon it. That is not how we ordinarily read statutes. The third clue is that the majority openly professes its aversion to Congress' explicitly stated purpose in enacting the statute. The majority expresses concern that reading the Act to mean what it says will make it more difficult to place Indian children in adoptive homes, * * * but the Congress that enacted the statute announced its intent to stop "an alarmingly high percentage of Indian families [from being] broken up" by, among other things, a trend of "plac[ing] [Indian children] in non-Indian * * * adoptive homes." 25 U.S.C. § 1901(4). Policy disagreement with Congress' judgment is not a valid reason for this Court to distort the provisions of the Act. Unlike the majority, I cannot adopt a reading of ICWA that is contrary to both its text and its stated purpose. I respectfully dissent.

I

Beginning its reading with the last clause of § 1912(f), the majority concludes that a single phrase appearing there—"continued custody"—means that the entirety of the subsection is inapplicable to any parent, however committed, who has not previously had physical or legal custody of his child. Working back to front, the majority then concludes that § 1912(d), tainted by its association with § 1912(f), is also inapplicable; in the majority's view, a family bond that does not take custodial form is not a family bond worth preserving from "breakup." Because there are apparently no limits on the contaminating power of this single phrase, the majority does not stop there. Under its reading, § 1903(9), which makes biological fathers "parent[s]" under this federal statute (and where, again, the phrase "continued custody" does not appear), has substantive force only when a birth father has physical or state-recognized legal custody of his daughter.

When it excludes noncustodial biological fathers from the Act's substantive protections, this textually backward reading misapprehends ICWA's structure and scope. Moreover, notwithstanding the majority's focus on the perceived parental shortcomings of Birth Father, its reasoning necessarily extends to all Indian parents who have never had custody of their children, no matter how fully those parents have embraced the financial and emotional responsibilities of parenting. The majority thereby transforms a statute that was intended to provide uniform federal standards for child custody proceedings involving Indian children and their biological parents into an illogical piecemeal scheme.

* * *

B

The majority also does not acknowledge the full implications of its assumption that there are some ICWA "parent[s]" to whom §§ 1912(d) and (f) do not apply. Its discussion focuses on Birth Father's particular actions, but nothing in the majority's reasoning limits its manufactured class of semiprotected ICWA parents to biological fathers who failed to support their child's mother during pregnancy. Its logic would apply equally to noncustodial fathers who have actively participated in their child's upbringing.

Consider an Indian father who, though he has never had custody of his biological child, visits her and pays all of his child support obligations. Suppose that, due to deficiencies in the care the child received from her custodial parent, the State placed the child with a foster family and proposed her ultimate adoption by them. Clearly, the father's parental rights would have to be terminated before the adoption could go forward. On the majority's view, notwithstanding the fact that this father would be a "parent" under ICWA, he would not receive the benefit of either § 1912(d) or § 1912(f). Presumably the court considering the adoption petition would have to apply some standard to determine whether termination of his parental rights was appropriate. But from whence would that standard come?

Not from the statute Congress drafted, according to the majority. The majority suggests that it might come from state law. * * * But it is incongruous to suppose that Congress intended a patchwork of federal and state law to apply in termination of parental rights proceedings. Congress enacted a statute aimed at protecting the familial relationships between Indian parents and their children because it concluded that state authorities "often failed to recognize the essential tribal relations of Indian people and the cultural and social standards prevailing in Indian communities and families." 25 U.S.C. § 1901(5). It provided a "minimum Federal standar[d]," § 1902, for termination of parental rights that is more demanding than the showing of unfitness under a high "clear and convincing evidence" standard that is the norm in the States, see 1 J. Hollinger, Adoption Law and Practice § 2.10 (2012). * * *

* * *

II

C

The majority also protests that a contrary result to the one it reaches would interfere with the adoption of Indian children. * * * This claim is the most perplexing of all. A central purpose of ICWA is to "promote the stability and security of Indian * * * families," 25 U.S.C. § 1902, in part by countering the trend of placing "an alarmingly high percentage of [Indian] children * * * in non-Indian foster and adoptive homes and institutions." § 1901(4). The Act accomplishes this goal by, first, protecting the familial bonds of Indian parents and children * * * ; and, second, establishing placement preferences should an adoption take place, see § 1915(a). ICWA does not interfere with the adoption of Indian children except to the extent that it attempts to avert the necessity of adoptive placement and makes adoptions of Indian children by non-Indian families less likely.

The majority may consider this scheme unwise. But no principle of construction licenses a court to interpret a statute with a view to averting the very consequences Congress expressly stated it was trying to bring about. * * *

The majority further claims that its reading is consistent with the "primary" purpose of the Act, which in the majority's view was to prevent the dissolution of "intact" Indian families. * * * As we observed in *Holyfield*, ICWA protects not only Indian parents' interests but also those of Indian tribes. * * * A tribe's interest in its next generation of citizens is adversely affected by the placement of Indian children in homes with no connection to the tribe, whether or not those children were initially in the custody of an Indian parent.

[T[he majority's focus on "intact" families, * * * begs the question of what Congress set out to accomplish with ICWA. In an ideal world, perhaps all parents would be perfect. They would live up to their parental responsibilities by providing the fullest possible financial and emotional support to their children. They would never suffer mental health problems, lose their jobs, struggle with substance dependency, or encounter any of the other multitudinous personal crises that can make it difficult to meet these responsibilities. In an ideal world parents would never become estranged and leave their children caught in the middle. But we do not live in such a world. Even happy families do not always fit the custodial-parent mold for which the majority would reserve ICWA's substantive protections; unhappy families all too often do not. They are families nonetheless. Congress understood as much. ICWA's definitions of "parent" and "termination of parental rights" provided in § 1903 sweep broadly. They should be honored.

* * *

III

* * *

The majority casts Birth Father as responsible for the painful circumstances in this case, suggesting that he intervened "at the eleventh hour to override the mother's decision and the child's best interests[.]". I have no wish to minimize the trauma of removing a 27-month-old child from her adoptive family. It bears remembering, however, that Birth Father took action to assert his parental rights when Baby Girl was four months old, as soon as he learned of the impending adoption. As the South Carolina Supreme Court recognized, " '[h]ad the mandate of * * * ICWA been followed [in 2010], * * * much potential anguish might have been avoided[;] and in any case the law cannot be applied so as automatically to "reward those who obtain custody, whether lawfully or otherwise, and maintain it during any ensuing (and protracted) litigation.' " * * *

The majority's hollow literalism distorts the statute and ignores Congress' purpose in order to rectify a perceived wrong that, while heartbreaking at the time, was a correct application of federal law and that in any case cannot be undone. Baby Girl has now resided with her father for 18 months. However difficult it must have been for her to leave Adoptive Couple's home when she was just over 2 years old, it will be equally devastating now if, at the age of 3½, she is again removed from her home and sent to live halfway across the country. Such a fate is not foreordained, of course. But it can be said with certainty that the anguish this case has caused will only be compounded by today's decision.

NOTES

1.   Shortly after the Supreme Court decided *Adoptive Couple*, the Birth Father, his wife, and his parents each filed court papers in Oklahoma to adopt Baby Girl. A week later, the South Carolina Supreme Court ordered that the Adoptive Couple's adoption of Baby Girl be immediately concluded. The court held: "The Supreme Court has articulated the federal standard, and its application to this case is clear: the ICWA does not authorize Birth Father's retention of custody. Therefore, we reject Birth Father's argument that § 1915(a)'s placement preferences could be an alternative basis for denying the Adoptive Couple's adoption petition." 746 S.E.2d 51, 52 (S.C.2013). Is the South Carolina Supreme Court correct?

2.   On the same day the South Carolina Supreme Court issued its order, but a few hours earlier, the Cherokee Nation District Court granted an emergency guardianship order in favor of awarding temporary custody of Baby Girl to her stepmother and parental grandparents. See Adrea Korthase, *Cherokee Nation Tribal Court Grants Custody to Father's Wife and Father's Parents in Baby Veronica Matter*, Turtle Talk blog post (July 22, 2013).

3.   Justice Thomas concurred in the result (and joined the majority) but wrote separately to argue that his understanding of Congressional powers under the Indian Commerce Clause does not allow for Congress enact ICWA at all, arguments similar to those he raised in United States v. Lara, 541 U.S. 193 (2004), and later in United States v. Bryant, 136 S. Ct. 1954 (2016). Compare *Adoptive Couple*, 133 S. Ct. at 2556–57 (Thomas, J., concurring) ("Although this Court has said that the 'central function of the Indian Commerce Clause is to provide Congress with plenary power to legislate in the field of Indian affairs,' * * * neither the text nor the original understanding of the Clause supports Congress' claim to such 'plenary' power."), with *Lara*, 541 U.S. at 224 ("The Court utterly fails to find any provision of the Constitution that gives Congress enumerated power to alter tribal sovereignty. The Court cites the Indian Commerce Clause and the treaty power. * * * I cannot agree that the Indian Commerce Clause 'provide[s] Congress with plenary power to legislate in the field of Indian affairs.' ") (Thomas, J., concurring in result), and *Bryant*, 136 S. Ct. at 1968 ("Congress' purported plenary power over Indian tribes rests on even shakier foundations.").

NATION BUILDING NOTE: ENFORCING TRIBAL COURT JUDGMENTS IN STATE AND FEDERAL COURTS

The U.S. Constitution, art. IV, § 1, states that: "Full Faith and Credit shall be given in each State to the public Acts, Records, and judicial Proceedings of every other State." By its terms, then, the clause applies only as between states. Congress has passed implementing legislation requiring that: "Acts, records and judicial proceedings * * * [as] authenticated, shall have the same full faith and credit in every court within the United States and its Territories and Possessions as they have by law or usage in the courts of such State, Territory or Possession from which they are taken." 28 U.S.C. § 1738.

Congress has additionally provided that some tribal court orders must be given full faith and credit by state, federal, and other tribal courts. The Court in Santa Clara Pueblo v. Martinez, 436 U.S. 49, 65 n.21 (1978), said in dictum that tribal court judgments "have been regarded in some circumstances as entitled to full faith and credit in other courts," citing Mackey v. Coxe, 59 U.S. 100 (1855). The Indian Child Welfare Act expressly requires all jurisdictions to grant full faith and credit to tribal court orders and judgments in regard to proceedings covered by the Act, 25 U.S.C. § 1911(d), as does the Full Faith and Credit for Child Support Orders Act, 28 U.S.C. § 1738B, and the Violence Against Women Act, 18 U.S.C. § 2265.

However, absent Congressional mandate, state, federal, and tribal courts generally enforce each other's judgments and orders under principles of comity. Comity is another device employed by courts for recognition and enforcement of judgments of courts in other jurisdictions. "Comity, in the legal sense, is neither a matter of absolute obligation, on the one hand, nor of mere courtesy and good will, upon the other. But it is the recognition which one nation allows within its territory to the legislative, executive or judicial acts of another nation, having due regard both to international duty and convenience, and to the rights of its own citizens or of other persons who are under protection of its laws." Hilton v. Guyot, 159 U.S. 113, 163–64 (1895). The doctrine is typically used by American courts in recognizing a foreign judgment where the foreign court accords sufficient due process.

Dean Stacy L. Leeds, who is a former Justice on the Cherokee Nation Supreme Court, published an empirical study in 2000 of tribal court judges that found wide variations in state courts as to outcomes in the enforcement of tribal court orders:

> Fifty-six percent of the respondent judges report at least one occasion in which another jurisdiction refused to recognize their tribal court orders, often in direct violation of state policy or federal law. Of those tribes indicating non-recognition, eighty percent report that their difficulties arose in a state forum, and twenty percent report problems with other tribal courts.

> But the most striking result of the study is the extent to which states fail to recognize tribal court judgments even when required by federal law to do so. Of the respondents indicating that a state court has failed to recognize an order of their tribal court, over forty percent involved subject matters covered by the federal full faith and credit mandates of Violence Against Women Act and the Child Support Orders Act. Roughly one-third of the total reported instances of non-recognition involved custody disputes between parents. Twenty-seven percent of the courts that reported instances of non-recognition involved domestic violence orders after the enactment of Violence Against Women Act. The remaining instances of non-recognition cover a broad range of subject matter from state agencies refusing to

recognize tribal court orders for purposes of vital statistics records to money judgments in consumer debt cases.

Stacy L. Leeds, *Cross-Jurisdictional Recognition and Enforcement of Judgments: A Tribal Court Perspective*, 76 N.D.L.Rev. 311, 349–50 (2000).

In several states, Indian tribes and state courts have adopted formal court rules after negotiation and consultation to address these issues.* Michigan Court Rule 2.615 is typical. In 1889, the Michigan Supreme Court decided a case in favor of a Native American in the Upper Peninsula of Michigan. Kobogum v. Jackson Iron Co., 43 N.W. 602 (Mich.1889). An Ojibwe woman, Kobogum, was trying to collect on a note promised to her deceased father from a mining company he led to an iron ore deposit. See Matthew L.M. Fletcher, *Laughing Whitefish: A Tale of Justice and Anishinaabe Custom*, in Robert Traver, Laughing Whitefish vii–xxiii (1965) (Michigan State University Press reprint, 2011). According to Kathryn Tierney, attorney for the Bay Mills Indian Community, this case set the stage for Michigan's state-tribal relations and is an example that as far back as the 19th Century, Michigan showed a respect to tribes when issues arose. Telephone interview with Kathryn Tierney, Attorney for Bay Mills Indian Community, Sept. 3, 2009. In deciding the case, and in response to the attempt by the defense to claim they did not have to pay out on a note to plaintiff's father because he was a polygamist, the court recognized that the Constitution sets tribes apart from the State. The court also recognized that tribal laws, customs and traditions should be recognized by the State courts. See *Kobogum*, 43 N.W. at 605 ("They were placed by the constitution of the United States beyond our jurisdiction, and we had no more right to control their domestic usages than those of Turkey or India.").

In a 1999 address, Michigan Supreme Court Justice Michael F. Cavanagh points to an even earlier indication of the State of Michigan's commitment to its tribes. In 1850, the Michigan legislature petitioned to set aside an order from President Zachary Taylor for the removal of Chippewa Indians from the Upper Peninsula. Justice Cavanagh, while still recognizing hardship and injustice that all Native Americans have experienced throughout history, believes that Michigan has managed to remain free of problems that other jurisdictions face even today. Hon. Michael F. Cavanagh, *Michigan's Story: State and Tribal Courts Try to do the Right Thing*, 76 U.Det. Mercy L.Rev. 709, 712 (1999).

Judge Michael Petoskey, tribal court judge for various tribes in Michigan, agrees with Justice Cavanagh and Ms. Tierney. Judge Petoskey says that the history of state-tribal relations in Michigan is fairly devoid of contentions issues because many Michigan tribes were historically ignored by the federal government and thus invisible to the State, at least until treaty fishing rights

---

* The following material is derived from Matthew L.M. Fletcher, Alicia Ivory, Adrea Korthase, and Sheena Oxendine, Tribal-State Relations: Michigan as Case Study, Michigan State University College of Law Indigenous Law and Policy Center Occasional Paper 2009–06 (Sept. 30, 1999).

issues arose. Interview with Michael Petoskey, Tribal Court Judge, East Lansing, MI, Sept. 2, 2009.

The road to greater visibility began in 1992 when seven state and tribal judges met for an Indian Tribal Court/State Court Forum. The seven judges were Hon. Michelle Boyer, Hon. Bradley Dakota, Hon. William Ervin, Hon. Michael W. MacDonald, Hon. Michael Petoskey, Hon. Thomas A. Van Tiem, and Hon. Garfield Hood, who chaired the Forum. Both Judge Petoskey and Ms. Tierney credit Justice Cavanagh with bringing everyone together. Both agree that Justice Cavanagh saw it as the right thing to do among little fanfare. Judge Michael Petoskey says that the "stars were aligned" for the development of the rule and Kathryn Tierney labels the timing "serendipitous." Both credited Justice Cavanagh many times for his commitment and efforts. They also give a lot of credit to Judge Garfield Hood, retired judge of Michigan's 12th District. The forum was funded by the State Justice Institute, and by the National Center for State Courts. Hon. Michael F. Cavanagh, *The First Tribal/State Court Forum and the Creation of MCR 2.615*, Michigan State University College of Law Indigenous Law & Policy Center, Working Paper 2007–16, at 3 (2007). Justice Cavanagh says that "[a]s its first priority, the Forum indicated the need for a measure to ensure mutual recognition of state and tribal judgments." Cavanagh, *Michigan's Story*, supra, at 713. The Forum discussed various ways to approach the measure, deciding on full faith and credit while still considering other ways of implementation, including statutory enactment or a rule based on comity. Id.

After the Forum, the court rule was considered from two different angles. The State Bar of Michigan American Indian Law Committee (created by the Forum itself) asked the State Bar to submit a proposal to the Michigan Supreme Court, which published the proposal for comment. Id. Justice Cavanagh talked about the Court's decision as to whether the rule should come from them or from the legislature, concluding with: "In the end, we determined that it was an appropriate exercise of our constitutional authority. And a prudent one. To be honest, we were also aware that this is a procedural problem that we could probably handle better than the Legislature." Cavanagh, *First Tribal/State Court Forum*, supra, at 11.

Several models of the rule were considered. According to Justice Cavanagh, the decision makers felt that a reciprocal agreement would offer a better chance of enforcement and "omit much of the temptation to second-guess the other jurisdiction's order." Id. at 9–10. North Dakota Rule 7.2, a non-reciprocal rule, was among the model rules considered. Kathryn Tierney points out that the result is a broader rule than a standard full faith and credit rule because it deals with orders and warrants as well as judgments. Telephone interview with Kathryn Tierney, Attorney for Bay Mills Indian Community (Sept. 3, 2009).

Kathryn Tierney says that up until the 1990s, the relationships the tribal courts had were mostly local and cordial. There were efforts to make sure that there were not competing orders for divorces and similar matters. She sees the stakeholders of the process as the Court members themselves, recognizing that individuals do not necessarily know how to bring about uniformity and it is the judges' responsibility to do that. Telephone interview with Kathryn Tierney, Attorney for Bay Mills Indian Community, Sept. 3, 2009.

Judge Petoskey feels that the tribal governments are the larger stakeholders because they benefited from the adoption of the court rule. He says that "the two most significant challenges for tribal courts and for tribal judges was garnering respect from within the community itself and credibility from outside of the community so we were seen as credible institutions." He continues by saying that when you look at MCR 2.615 it says that any judgment, order, subpoena, or warrant coming out of the tribal court is just as valid as if it came out of a State Court and as significant. It enhanced the stature of tribal courts and increased their visibility. Interview with Michael Petoskey, Judge, East Lansing, MI, Sept. 2, 2009.

Petoskey remembers that shortly after the court rule was in place, the Grand Traverse Band needed to compel the appearance of an inmate at the Michigan Department of Corrections. When the subpoena or writ was sent down to the prison, the first reaction to the subpoena was one of confusion and perhaps even stalling. Once the tribal attorney pointed to the court rule, however, things got easier. Petoskey says that the court rule has made many things easier. In the beginning, he says, some tribal communities were reluctant to adopt a rule that would require them to recognize and enforce State Court orders and judgments because they saw it as an infringement of their sovereignty. As they saw the results for other tribes who adopted the rule, though, they began to view the rule as an expansion of their sovereignty and a recognition of the validity of their governments.

The court rule has assisted in the procedural development of tribal courts as well. As an example, Petoskey talks about what happens if someone wants to file a garnishment action and outlines the two-step process:

In terms of a foreign judgment coming to the tribal court for recognition and enforcement, we've adopted court rules that lay out a procedure and provide for objection periods. So if you have a money judgment against an individual, first you have to register and file the foreign judgment and have it recognized by the tribal court and just like the grounds of objection in the Michigan Court Rule, most tribes have those same reasons. . . Secondly. . .we have them file the garnishment action once the judgment is recognized and then we have a garnishment process and procedure. [Interview with Michael Petoskey, Judge, in East Lansing, MI, Sept. 2, 2009.]

Before the rule there was no formal process for such situations and Judge Petoskey thinks the rule has helped to lay one out.

MCR 2.615 does not exist in isolation because visibility, something the rule promotes, is crucial to the rule's power. The 1992 Forum developed several other ideas that were implemented prior to the court rule and continue to work alongside MCR 2.615 to promote the State's relationship with tribal courts.

The Michigan Bar Journal Directory lists tribal courts in Michigan and includes information ranging from the structure of the court systems to the Tribes' territorial jurisdiction. Judge Petoskey stated that for the first year, tribal courts were listed with federal courts, but following the advisement of Forum members, they were listed separately.

Additionally, the State Bar of Michigan has both an American Indian Law Committee and an American Indian Law Section. The State Library and Hall of Justice, where the Michigan Supreme Court is housed, both contain information about Michigan tribal courts in its learning center. The Michigan Judicial Institute helps to train tribal judges and includes information about tribal courts when training new state court judges. The rule is only one component of the way that the 1992 Forum helped to create a tribal court presence in the framework of the state.

The court rule is not all encompassing, of course. Although both Judge Petoskey and Ms. Tierney agree that the court rule has also helped with tribe-to-tribe relations, Ms. Tierney points out that there are a lot of matters that really need to be taken into account between different tribal jurisdictions. Telephone interview with Kathryn Tierney, Attorney for Bay Mills Indian Community (Sept. 3, 2009). According to Tierney, Bay Mills Indian Community has an acknowledged reciprocal agreement with Sault Ste. Marie Chippewa tribe. The Model Codes Project of the Michigan Indian Judicial Association encouraged reciprocal recognition and enforcement between the Michigan tribes themselves. Furthermore, Tierney acknowledges that there are many interfaces between jurisdictions. Certain federal laws mandate "full faith and credit" recognition and enforcement of state and tribal court orders and thus pre-empt the "comity" requirements of the Michigan Court Rule. In any event, the rule itself opens the door for relationships that go beyond the court systems and promote a sense of understanding and unity in Michigan communities.

CHAPTER NINE

THE NATION BUILDING CHALLENGE: MODERN TRIBAL ECONOMIES

■ ■ ■

Looking back on the development of federal Indian law and policy during the past half-century, one fact stands out: no one could have predicted that out of the policy wreckage of the post-World War II termination era, modern American Indian tribalism would emerge as a potent political, legal, cultural, and economic force in the life of the nation. As Indian tribes enter the twenty-first century together with the rest of United States society, the heightened public profile of tribes becomes evident simply by watching the nightly news, surfing the Internet, or reading national newspapers like the *New York Times* or *Wall Street Journal*.

With strong and educated leaders and lawyers knowledgeable in Indian law, tribes today are actively engaged in the political process at all levels and branches of government. They affect Indian policy wherever it is being made, with their own sophisticated tribal institutions of self-governance, effective lobbyists, highly trained and educated specialists in diverse fields, and many other important human and reservation resources to draw on. National political figures, as well as state and local politicians, now court reservation Indians like other blocs of voters.

In the courts, Indian tribes remain active as ever in protecting their rights, litigating numerous cases in the federal and state court systems each year and fighting to protect the victories won in earlier precedent-setting cases. As the United States faces an uncertain future, Indian tribes will likely encounter even fiercer resistance from non-Indian political and economic interests that may be in competition with the assertion of those hard-earned Indian rights.

But it is perhaps in the areas of economic and community development that Indian tribes have made their most significant advances over the past half-century. At the same time, creating and sustaining safe, healthy and prosperous Indian tribes on their reservation homelands will be among the most difficult—and promising—challenges confronting tribes in the century ahead.

SECTION A. TRIBAL ECONOMIC DEVELOPMENT

American Indian communities engaged in local and regional trade before contact with other nations and people. For example, the Odawa people were known best as regional traders, traveling by canoe to markets that reached far up the St. Lawrence River to the east and into the Northern Plains to the west. In general, Indian traders living near rivers, major lakes, and seas could and did travel great distances to visit other communities and engage in trade. In Chaco Canyon, New Mexico, for example, researchers have unearthed evidence that the communities there grew and developed as trading centers, with people living there for no other reason than to facilitate trade. There is evidence of similar trading centers all over the North American continent.

After contact, in the Great Lakes, the Haudenosaunee and the Anishinaabek participated in the fur trade as suppliers for the almost unlimited European demand for furs. Great Lakes Indians often stopped their long-standing economic activities in order to pursue the fur trade and its rewards. In the Great Plains, the arrival of the horse and then later modern weaponry—both results of contact with Europeans—pushed the Lakota people toward hunting the bison in a manner much different than before. Some Great Plains Indian cultures moved more toward following the bison herds, until they became far more dependent on these animals than before.

Through the Indian Commerce Clause, the Framers of the Constitution elevated commerce with Indian tribes to be the primary means of regulating affairs (calling it "intercourse") between Americans and Indians. The Trade and Intercourse Acts, enacted and reenacted from the First Congress until made permanent in 1834, established the primacy of trade as the means with which to deal with Indian affairs. Of course, the overriding American Indian policy was to acquire lands and resources from Indian tribes (as opposed to Indian people) at the lowest cost possible.

In his deeply influential work, American Indians, Time, and the Law (1987), Charles Wilkinson coined the term "measured separatism" to describe much of federal Indian law and policy throughout American history. In part, measured separatism was an economic plan. Under this concept, both Americans and Indians likely presumed that shared economic activities would be extremely limited. Indians would have hoped for the opportunity to be left alone to pursue economic, political, and social activities without the interference of American citizens and others. Americans would have hoped to keep the Indians away from their ongoing pursuit of expansion and economic growth.

Of course, measured separatism never lasted long. There would never be enough resources and space to satisfy the overwhelming numbers of American people and businesses, creating demand for Indian land and resources preserved in treaty negotiations as soon as the ink dried on them, if not earlier. Great Lakes tribes retained their on and off-reservation hunting, fishing, and gathering rights, but still were forced to enter the local labor market. Great Plains Indians, often forced to live on worthless land, literally fenced in, often depended entirely on American military rations guaranteed by treaty.

Other reservation economies flourished, only to be undermined by federal administrative action. Felix Cohen's famous rendition of the ways that the Bureau of Indian Affairs employees destroyed a successful cattle ranching operation at Blackfeet is but one example. Felix S. Cohen, *The Erosion of Indian Rights, 1950–1953: A Case Study in Bureaucracy*, 62 Yale L.J. 348, 368–69 (1953). Other examples include Bureau activities to use reservation water supplies to benefit non-Indians over the intended beneficiaries (the Indians) and simple corruption in land tenure and use. In short, before tribal self-determination, tribal economies were in a shambles.

STEPHEN CORNELL AND JOSEPH P. KALT, AMERICAN INDIAN SELF-DETERMINATION: THE POLITICAL ECONOMY OF A SUCCESSFUL POLICY

Joint Occasional Papers on Native Affairs Working Paper No. 1, at 4–14.
(Native Nations Institute for Leadership, Management, and Policy & The Harvard Project on American Indian Economic Development 2010).

* * *

Tribes now commonly refer to themselves as "nations." This does not signify status as nation-states; and tribes lack powers under the U.S. federal system to maintain their own military forces, issue currency, enter into agreements with foreign nation-states, or otherwise exercise powers superior to the federal government. Paralleling the status of a U.S. state's citizens, tribal citizens are also voting citizens of the United States, subject to federal taxes, laws, and regulations. When working and residing on reservations, tribal citizens are governed by tribal and federal law, and generally are not subject to state law and taxation—just as a resident citizen of, say, Nevada, is not subject to California law and taxation when that Nevadan is in Nevada. By the same token, just as the State of Massachusetts, as owner of one of the largest and most successful gambling businesses in the United States (i.e., the Massachusetts State Lottery), is not subject to taxation on such a business by the federal government or other states, tribal government-owned businesses are free of such taxation. And just as the State of Massachusetts employs its tax and business revenues for state governmental purposes, so too do tribal governments employ their revenues to run schools, build infrastructure, support citizens' incomes, address social problems, and so on.

* * *

The diversity of Indian societies persists to the present. As noted, Indian nations range from the very small to the quite large in both geography and population. Many reservations are quite rural, while others have become engulfed by major cities (as is the case with many of the tribes in and around Southern California; Seattle, Washington; Phoenix, Arizona; and Minneapolis, Minnesota). Economic systems range from the manufacturing economy of the Mississippi Choctaw in central Mississippi, to the predominantly gaming economy of the Mashantucket Pequot Tribal Nation in Connecticut, to the retail trade economy of the Tulalip Tribes in Washington state. Cultural diversity, too, is marked, with widely varying rates of Indigenous language use * * *, and religious practices that range from the stalwartly traditional to the devoutly Christian.

* * *

In terms of standards of material living, for decades American Indians on reservations have been the poorest identifiable group in the United States. Notwithstanding the much publicized growth and success of the casino gaming enterprises owned by many tribal governments, gaming incomes have been concentrated in a relatively small number of tribes near major metropolitan patron populations, and, on average, American Indians residing in Indian Country remain the poorest group in America * * *. Income per American Indian household on reservations in 2000 (the date of the last available systematic data) was $24,249, compared to $41,994 for the average U.S. household. Not surprisingly, accompanying Indian poverty have been concomitant indicators of social stress—high rates of suicide, ill-health, poor housing, crime, school dropouts, and the like. Recent years, however, have seen sharp absolute and relative economic progress that shows signs of being sustained.

* * *

Although per capita incomes of Indians on reservations remain less than half the U.S. average, the per capita income of American Indians on reservations has been growing approximately three times more rapidly than the United States as a whole since the early 1990s. This holds true for both tribes with much-publicized casino gambling and for non-gaming tribes * * *. This burst of economic development is starting from a low base, but is manifesting itself in improving social conditions and other indicators of development. Housing is improving; educational attainment through at least high school is approaching par with the U.S. average; health measures such as infant mortality, deaths due to accident, infectious disease rates, and tuberculosis show sharp trends toward improvement. Particularly in tribes with substantial tribal government-owned gaming or other business revenues, the switch from federal administration to tribal administration is being manifested in investment in long-neglected infrastructure, as streets, water systems, schools, health clinics, and the like are rapidly being upgraded.

* * *

Roots of the Social, Economic, and Political Renaissance of Indian America

A. Isolating Causal Factors

* * *

The development boom that is underway in Indian Country raises the question of where it has come from. While the answer to that question is, of course, exceedingly complicated and involves strands of politics, economics, social change, and the like, the development boom is not the product of massive or even substantial infusions of resources from the national government of the United States. In fact, federal U.S. budget spending on Indian affairs peaked in real dollars in the mid-1970s— approximately coincident with the advent of the major legislation in Congress that made tribal self-determination the core principle of U.S. Indian policy. By the early 2000s, the U.S. Commission on Civil Rights labeled the spending levels in Indian Country a "quiet crisis." The Commission reported that while American Indians were marked by the most severe poverty in America and had suffered treaty violations and other forms of deprivation over the centuries at the hand of the federal government, governmental spending in Indian America was dramatically and disproportionately below levels of funding provided to other groups in the United States and the general U.S. population. * * *

In short, the rapid changes and development progress we see in Indian Country is not the product of injections of resources from outside governments. Importantly, research also consistently finds that the economic, social, and political transformation that is occurring across the Indian nations is not the product of cultural change, or at least is not the product of the cultural assimilation of Native Americans into non-Indian society and norms. Thus, for example, performance in both the economic arena and in public administration is positively correlated with natural measures of lack of cultural assimilation, such as rates of Native language use (which are strongly related to adherence to traditional Native religious and associated cultural practices).

* * * Prior to the 1970s—indeed into the 1980s—the Indian nations of the United States were subjected to essentially uniform, one-size-fits-all policies and micro-administration by federal agencies and agents. Tribal governments generally operated under boilerplate constitutions that had emanated from the federal government in the 1930s. What self-rule there was on reservations typically took the form of advising and complaining about decisions and policies under the control of the federal Bureau of

Indian Affairs ("BIA") and similar federal agencies tasked with administering life on reservations, under policies and programs applied on a roughly common basis across all tribes.

With its start marked most saliently by the passage in 1975 of the Indian Self-Determination and Education Assistance Act (US Public Law 95–638), the era of formal policies of tribal self-determination began with halting steps. The vast majority of tribes embarked on strategies of meaningful self-rule under conditions of stark poverty, utilizing externally designed governmental systems, lacking meaningful experience in business and governmental decision making among the living population, and bearing legacies of federally-imposed systems of education. By the second half of the 1980s, however, self-determination had become a widespread and systematic restructuring of tribal governments and their relations with the federal government. This restructuring has acquired a name as the "nation building" movement. It is being manifested by wholesale changes in tribal institutions and policies as the Indian nations themselves rewrite their constitutions, generate increasing shares of their revenues through their own taxes and business enterprises, establish their own courts and law enforcement systems, remake school curricula, and so on, across the panoply of functions commonly associated in the United States with state governments.

B. Tribal Self-Government and the Reasons for Development Progress

Not only is the pace of development remarkable, but also its character in the current era of federal policies of self-determination is dramatic compared to what preceded it. The Tohono O'odham Nation outside of Tucson, Arizona, for example, funded, built, and now operates the first either Native or non-Native elder care facility to achieve the highest level of federal quality rating for health care provision. The Citizen Potawatomi Nation ("CPN") in Oklahoma has engaged in constitutional reform over the last two decades that has resulted in a judicial system of trial and appeals courts that function at a level of sufficiently high quality such that it has attracted tens of millions of dollars of capital to the Nation's business enterprises and induced a neighboring non-Indian township to opt into the Potawatomi system and out of the State of Oklahoma system for its municipal court services. While a number of tribes operate well-known casino gambling and related resort enterprises, less well-known are the tribes, such as the Chickasaw Nation, whose Chickasaw Nation Industries provides program management, information technology, technical and administrative support, medical and dental staffing, aviation and space technical support, construction, manufacturing, property management, and logistics to government and commercial clients. A number of tribes across the United States have organized themselves, their education systems, and their allocation of resources so as to reverse decades of language loss to the point that the childhood population on some reservations now utilizes Native language at a higher rate than the adult population * * * .

These and many, many other examples were essentially unheard of prior to the era of self-determination. Indeed, it is difficult to imagine such pattern-breaking accomplishments in the era in which federally recognized tribes and their affairs were managed as de facto federal programs. In fact, the Indian nations that have not adopted the nation building strategies of taking programs and policies over from the federal government are uniformly marked with little to no signs of development progress. Both the nature and reasons for this success mirror those applicable to state and local governments elsewhere in the United States and internationally. Just as some state/provincial and local governments have performed better than others under the devolution to them of powers and functions of the national government, so have some Indian nations performed better than others. At the same time, however, the overall pattern of results in Indian Country is quite positive, and the reasons lie in the facts that local decision making and administration (1) improve accountability and (2) allow on-the ground programs and policies to better reflect local values. Consider, for example:

Overall Economic Growth: * * * [P]er capita incomes among Native citizens on reservations have been growing rapidly. The same pattern is seen in household incomes. Over 1990–2000, real Indian household incomes on reservations without gaming grew 33 percent, and grew 24 percent on reservations with gaming. By comparison, for the US as a whole, real median household income grew only 4 percent during the entire decade of 1990–2000. As noted, this pattern of differential economic performance appears to have continued through to at least the current worldwide recession.

Industrial Performance: Statistical research on 75 tribes finds that, among those tribes that have employed contracting and compacting to take over control of timber management, each high-skilled position that is transferred from federal BIA forestry to tribal forestry results in a productivity increase of 38,000 board feet of timber output, and the price received in the marketplace for that output rises by 4.5 percent. This is accomplished within "allowable cuts" (i.e., maximum sustainable harvest levels) and with the quality of logs harvested held constant. The result is hundreds of thousands of dollars per year in additional income for the typical reservation forestry operation.

Business Performance: Growing numbers of cases of business success in Indian Country are well-documented. Leading cases include:

- The Winnebago of Nebraska Tribe's Ho-Chunk, Inc. and its conglomerate of dot-com, financial service, construction, consulting, and retailing businesses now yields more than $100 million a year in revenues. Over the last decade, reservation unemployment has been lowered from around 70 percent to the point where every reservation citizen able and willing to work has a job. Company earnings are systematically plowed back into the community, and Ho-Chunk, Inc.'s non-profit arm is now building an entire town from scratch.

- The Tulalip Tribes' creation of the municipality of Quil Ceda Village and the Village's heavy investments in otherwise-absent municipal infrastructure and services are the source of value upon which a thriving commercial center is built. In the process, the Tribes have become the second largest employer in the county where they are located, north of Seattle, Washington.

- In the late 1970s, the material assets of the Citizen Potawatomi Nation * * * consisted of 2½ acres of trust land, $550 in the bank, and an old trailer that served as the tribal headquarters. Today, CPN's assets include a bank, a golf course, a recently-opened casino, restaurants, a large discount food retail store, a tribal farm, a radio station, and more than 4,000 acres purchased by the Nation. CPN eschews per capita payments and, instead, channels its resources into services for citizens—from health care to educational and child development support, from a pharmacy to an award-winning small business development program. The directory of CPN businesses lists scores and scores of private citizen businesses, and CPN is the economic engine of the Shawnee, Oklahoma region.

Program Performance: For many years, the BIA in the U.S. Department of the Interior has been widely regarded by pundits and researchers alike as the worst-run federal agency. It has recently been successfully sued for billions of dollars in monetary damages for its mismanagement of funds and gross neglect of its trust responsibilities pursuant to its mishandling and failure to account for more than a century's collection and putative investment of monies collected through its leasing of Indian minerals and other real property on behalf of Indians as its trust clients.

In addition to the improved management of now-tribally-run forestry operations noted above, social service delivery shows systematic improvement under tribal government control. The National Indian Health Board, for example, finds in research on 83 tribal health facilities that measures of patient satisfaction improve markedly under contracting and compacting relative to federal Indian Health Service ("IHS") management. Under self-governance compacting, for example, 86 percent of programs report that waiting times—a common measure of the ability of health care providers to effectively serve their patients—improved upon tribal assumption of management responsibility, and none reported a worsening of waiting times. Tribes still served by the IHS were less satisfied with the quality of their health care than tribes under contracts, and the latter were not as satisfied as those operating under compacts (where local discretion is generally highest). The number and integration of programs and facilities in operation, the prioritization of preventative programs, and total payments collected from third parties were higher in those Indian nations that managed their own health care programs. Similar patterns are found in policing: Tribal assumption of management of reservation policing under contracting and compacting results in tribal citizens reporting systematically greater satisfaction with the police service they receive.

AMERICAN LAW INSTITUTE, TRIBAL ECONOMIC ENTERPRISES
Restatement of the Law of American Indians § 58, comments
(Addendum to Preliminary Draft No. 4) (Feb. 4, 2016).

* * * *a. Indian tribes and unincorporated subdivisions, agencies, and instrumentalities of Indian tribes.* Indian tribes engage in economic activities within and outside of Indian country in their own capacity and through subdivisions, agencies, or instrumentalities over which their tribal governments maintain ownership and control. Indian tribes and their subdivisions, agencies, and instrumentalities have sovereign immunity from suit for actions to enforce economic obligations unless certain conditions are met. * * * Under certain circumstances, state courts may have subject-matter jurisdiction over actions to enforce economic obligations entered into by Indian tribes or their unincorporated subdivisions, agencies, or instrumentalities. * * * Federal courts generally lack subject-matter jurisdiction to enforce economic obligations entered into by Indian tribes or by their subdivisions, agencies, or instrumentalities. * * * Tribal courts or other tribal adjudicatory forums generally have subject-matter jurisdiction over actions to enforce economic obligations entered into by Indian tribes or their subdivisions, agencies, or instrumentalities arising within Indian country. * * *

b. Federally chartered corporations. Indian tribes engage in economic activities within and outside of Indian country through federally chartered corporations pursuant to Section 17 of the Indian Reorganization Act (the "IRA"), 25 U.S.C. § 477 ("IRA Section 17 corporations"). Indian tribes within the State of Oklahoma may charter corporations under Section 17 of the IRA pursuant to 25 U.S.C. § 503, a provision of the Oklahoma Indian Welfare Act, and such corporations have the same status as IRA Section 17 corporations. IRA Section 17 corporations have sovereign immunity from suit for actions to enforce economic obligations unless certain conditions are met. * * * Under certain circumstances, state courts may have subject-matter jurisdiction over actions to enforce economic obligations entered into by IRA Section 17 corporations. * * * Where the conditions for diversity of citizenship are met, federal courts have subject-matter jurisdiction pursuant to 28 U.S.C. § 1332 to enforce economic obligations entered into by IRA Section 17 corporations. * * * Tribal courts or other tribal adjudicatory forums generally have subject-matter jurisdiction over actions to enforce economic obligations entered into by IRA Section 17 corporations arising within Indian country. * * *

c. Tribal corporations and other business associations. Indian tribes may establish corporations or other business associations pursuant to tribal law to engage in economic activities within and outside of Indian country. If certain conditions are met, such tribal corporations and other business associations will have sovereign immunity from suit for actions to enforce economic obligations. * * * Under certain circumstances, state courts may have subject-matter jurisdiction over actions to enforce economic obligations entered into corporations or business associations formed by Indian tribes pursuant to tribal law. * * * Where the conditions for diversity of citizenship are met, federal courts have subject-matter jurisdiction pursuant to 28 U.S.C. § 1332 to enforce economic obligations entered into by corporations or other business associations formed by Indian tribes pursuant to tribal law. * * * Tribal courts or other tribal adjudicatory forums generally have subject-matter jurisdiction over actions to enforce economic obligations entered into by tribal corporations or business associations arising within Indian country. * * *

d. State corporations and other business associations. Indian tribes may establish corporations or other business associations under state law to engage in economic activities within and outside of Indian country. Such state corporations or business associations generally will not have sovereign immunity from suit unless certain conditions are met. * * * Under certain circumstances, state courts may have subject-matter jurisdiction over actions to enforce economic obligations entered into by corporations or business associations formed by Indian tribes pursuant to state law. * * * Where the conditions for diversity of citizenship are met, federal courts have subject-matter jurisdiction pursuant to 28 U.S.C. § 1332 to enforce economic obligations entered into by corporations or other business associations formed by Indian tribes pursuant to state law. * * * Tribal courts or other tribal adjudicatory forums generally have subject-matter jurisdiction over actions to enforce economic obligations entered into by state corporations or business associations arising within Indian country. * * *

NOTES

1. Congress first expressly authorized the Secretary of Interior to charter federal corporations in Section 17 of the Indian Reorganization Act of 1934. 25 U.S.C. § 477. These corporations are often called "Section 17 corporations." Since Congress intended tribes to utilize Section 17 corporations for business purposes (while protecting core tribal assets), the charters for the corporations typically include a "sue and be sued" clause. Until recent decades, federal courts found that these charters constituted a waiver of immunity. However, tribes now typically expressly reserve tribal immunity in all cases under tribal constitution or corporate code provisions, and more recent cases recognize that the immunity of Section 17 is likely to be decided by tribal corporate codes, tribal immunity statutes, or tribal constitutional provisions.

2. Indian tribes also routinely charter corporate entities under tribal corporate codes or state law. Tribal corporations chartered under tribal law are usually immune from suit, and any waivers of immunity depend on tribal law. Tribally-owned corporations chartered under state law, in contrast, are usually not immune from suit, and immunity determinations are dependent on state law. Tribes also purchase companies (corporate and non-corporate) initially formed or chartered by non-Indians. So long as the tribe wholly owns and controls the business entity under tribal law, immunity will apply.

In Cash Advance and Preferred Cash Loans v. State of Colorado ex rel. Suthers, 242 P.3d 1099 (Colo.2010), the Attorney General for the State of Colorado sought to investigate payday lender franchises owned by Section 17 corporations suspected of doing business with Colorado residents over the internet in violation of state consumer protection laws. The Attorney General's subpoenas targeted the Section 17 corporations owned by the Miami Tribe of Oklahoma and the Santee Sioux Tribe of Nebraska. The Colorado Supreme Court followed the "arm of the tribe" analysis and ordered the trial court on remand to determine: "(1) whether the tribes created the entities pursuant to tribal law; (2) whether the tribes own and operate the entities; and (3) whether the entities' immunity protects the tribes' sovereignty." *Cash Advance*, 242 P.3d at 1110, 1111. The first two factors can easily be determined as a factual matter by a court, while the third factor is more subjective and all but meaningless.

Other courts have adopted even more factor-intensive tests that include the two objective *Cash Advance* factors but include numerous other subjective factors. E.g., Breakthrough Management Group, Inc. v. Chukchansi Gold Casino and Resort, 629 F.3d 1173 (10th Cir.2010) (applying six-factor test to determine whether tribe organized the entity under tribal law and whether the tribe controlled the entity, and several additional subjective public policy factors), cert. denied, 132 S. Ct. 64 (2011).

NATION BUILDING NOTE: TRIBAL ECONOMIC DEVELOPMENT OR MARKETING EXEMPTIONS?

In recent decades, tribal economic fortunes have depended heavily on the ability of tribally owned businesses to access and control valuable natural resources, access a profitable gaming market, or take advantage of immunities from federal, state, and local taxes and regulations in commercial areas like tobacco products, motor fuels, and other areas. Tribal economies have also benefitted from the federal government's turn to self-governance and self-determination, which allows tribes to administer their own federal programs. In recent years, some Indian tribes have profited mightily from the rise in oil, gas, and coal prices, and may suffer the most as those prices rise and fall based on market forces far beyond their control. A significant number of Indian tribes have benefitted from the rise of Indian gaming, some extraordinarily so, but most Indian tribes do not even operate a gaming enterprise.

Tribes without significant natural resources or access to a profitable gaming market continue to struggle in significant ways. There are 229 Alaska Native nations, none of which have gaming operations and have little control over their natural resources, which mostly are owned by Alaska Native corporations. And there are about 100 or so more Indian tribes in the lower 48 states that also have little in the way of resources or gaming operations.

Several tribes have turned to online lending as a means of generating governmental revenue. Online lending, which may include payday lending or car title lending, or any of a multitude of forms, has many of the classic features of earlier versions of tribal economic activity: a highly regulated commercial area in which tribes generally have immunity from most state and local regulations, and which the federal government has not yet regulated comprehensively. The tribes merely need access to the internet to start, though start-up requirements may be complicated and require sophisticated legal help.

Advocates for Indian tribes facing severe economic situations argue that tribes should be allowed to engage in self-regulate online lending as a means of generating much needed government revenue and reservation economic activity. For example, the Lac Vieux Desert Band of Lake Superior Chippewa Indians, local in the rural Upper Peninsula of Michigan, depends heavily on online lending:

> [A] tribe of 684 members—the Lac Vieux Desert Band of Lake Superior Chippewa Indians—depends on the lending revenues, which account for 42 percent of the annual budget, tribal officials say, and have filled a shortfall that otherwise would have brought many of the tribe's health-care and education services to a halt. She sees how lending has brought a handful of decent jobs to one of America's most remote regions, Michigan's Upper Peninsula, where winter temperatures often fall to 20 below zero.

Lending has allowed the tribe to subsidize propane costs during winters, preventing members from facing a choice "between heat and food," tribal Chairman James Williams Jr. said. Lending allowed the tribe to cover the combined $60,000 shipping costs for 12 old Federal Emergency Management Agency trailers—government hand-me-downs, including a few used in the Hurricane Katrina aftermath, that will soon turn into permanent housing. For McGeshick, lending proceeds even helped get her an affordable prefab home. She pays a $300 per month mortgage. Tribal subsidies cover the rest.

Chico Harlan, *Indian Tribes Gambling on High-Interest Loans to Raise Revenue*, Wash. Post, Mar. 1, 2015.

Tribal advocates also have argued that Indian country residents suffer from a lack of access to banks and credit, and that tribal online lending (also called sovereign lending) is a partial solution to that problem. In 2008, the National Congress of American Indians noted (in another context) that reservation residents may be exploited by predatory lending given their desperate economic outlooks and lack of a financial services market:

There is no doubt that there is a need for micro lending backed by income or assets in Indian country and other parts of America; however, there is also no doubt that protections should be provided to consumers. There are no other aspects of the financial services industry—from investments to all other forms of lending—that forego the obligation of performing due diligence prior to a customer investing or borrowing money.

The issue of predatory lending in Indian country is complex because, as with most issues, there are underlying causes that make tribal populations vulnerable to disproportionately using small payday loans to fulfill fundamental financial needs including high-interest, high fee, short-term loans with minimal due diligence. These loans are used not because they offer a great competitive alternative, but because they are simply one of only a few options available.

Because of the persistent lack of economic opportunity, a sustainable financial services market, and tribal jurisdictional issues, there have only been a handful of banks or credit unions that serve tribal communities. As a result, tribal citizens continue to lack basic financial services or financial choices that most Americans have come to take for granted. Tribal members have limited access when financing a home, starting a business or purchasing necessary property like cars needed to make a living accessing a line of credit to meet short term capital needs.

Predatory Lending in Indian Country, Hearing before the Senate Committee on Indian Affairs, 110th Cong., 2d Sess. 76 (June 5, 2008) (Prepared Statement of the National Congress of American Indians).

Other observers are concerned that online lending subject to no regulation or tribal regulation is exploitative and abusive, lamenting that tribal sovereign immunity is used to preclude state regulatory investigation of tribal online lending business operations:

> Internet payday lending is growing quickly and many online lenders claim to be immune from State laws. Even where States have won cases holding that online lenders must comply with State laws, lenders often fail to do so. State regulators have again garnered precious resources to enforce their laws, often to no avail. The most recent survey by the Consumer Federation of America (CFA) notes that lenders continue to claim choice of law from lax jurisdictions, to locate off-shore, or to claim tribal sovereign immunity to avoid complying with State consumer protection laws.

> The trial sovereign immunity loophole is particularly troubling, as it pits two traditionally disadvantaged groups, Native Americans and low-income consumers, against one another in a complex battle over who needs protection more. Under this model, lenders team up with Indian tribes to avoid State laws. Tribes engaged in off-reservation activities must comply with nondiscriminatory State laws, as must anybody else. Despite this requirement, tribes are immune from suit because they are separate sovereigns. Thus, while they must obey State laws, they can't be sued to enforce the laws or compel their compliance. This motivates lenders to seek out tribal partners as this industry Web site explains:

>> Due to the strict regulations that are hitting the payday loan industry hard, many lenders are now turning to Indian Tribes to help them out. The American Indian Tribes throughout the United States have been granted sovereign immunity which means that they are not held subject to the laws that payday loans are currently going up against. There are 12 States which have banned payday lending but as long as their (sic) is an Indian tribe who runs the operation on this sovereign land, the lenders can continue their business even where payday loans have already been banned. Similar to the Casino boom, payday loans are the new financial strategy that many are using as a loophole through the strict payday loan laws. The revenue is quite high and promising for these tribes who often find themselves struggling. There are approximately 35 online cash advance and payday loan companies that are owned by American Indian tribes. * * * It is no surprise that many lending companies are currently seeking out American Indian Tribes in an effort to save their businesses by escaping U.S. lending laws. Tribal leaders are paid a few thousand dollars a month for allowing a payday lender to incorporate on tribal land. The more lenders that tribes allow to move onto their reservation, the larger the profit that they make.

Often, as this excerpt clearly articulates, the lenders using this model are not tribes. Proving that the lenders are not entitled to tribal sovereign immunity is not easy, however. A simple Federal interest rate cap would eliminate this loophole as even tribes are bound by Federal law.

Are Alternatives Financial Products Serving Consumers?, Hearing before the Subcommittee on Financial Institutions and Consumer Protection of the Committee on Banking, Housing, and Urban Affairs, 113th Cong., 2d Sess. 52 (Mar. 16, 2014) (Prepared Statement of Nathalie Martin).

Litigation over tribal online lending has exploded, with Indian tribes bringing suit to challenge state assertions of jurisdiction over tribal enterprises, e.g., Otoe-Missouria Tribe of Indians v. New York State Dept. of Financial Services, 769 F.3d 105 (2d Cir.2013) (rejecting tribal petition for injunction against state regulation); states suing to force investigations of tribal business practices, e.g., Cash Advance and Preferred Cash Loans v. State, 242 P.3d 1099 (Colo.2010) (holding tribal immunity precludes state investigation); and individuals suing to avoid tribal lending obligations, e.g., Everette v. Mitchem, 2015 WL 7351498 (D.Md., Nov. 20, 2015) (dismissing class action challenge to tribal online lending regime).

In one highly public case, the Federal Trade Commission successfully forced an online lender headed by race car driver Scott Tucker and partially backed by Miami Nation Enterprises to pay $21 million in fines to the federal government. Federal Trade Commission v. AMG Services, Inc., No. 2:12–CV–00536–GMN (D.Nev., Jan. 15, 2015). See also Federal Trade Commission v. AMG Services, Inc., 2013 WL 7870795 (D.Nev., July 16, 2013) (rejecting all defenses based on tribal immunity).

One additional wrinkle is that tribal online lenders are self-regulating, and tribal lenders may require borrowers to bring complaints to tribal forums such as tribal courts or arbitration under tribal law. For the most part, there are few challenges to tribal jurisdiction. However, one notorious lender operating under the name Western Sky Financial, located on the Cheyenne River Sioux Tribe's reservation, exploited this tactic to great effect and profit for several years. Western Sky, not affiliated with any tribe and operating with companies such as CashCall, Inc. or Payday Financial, LLC, required its customers to seek redress through arbitration under Cheyenne Sioux Tribe arbitration even though no such legal mechanism existed. At least three federal circuits have held that these arbitration clauses were unenforceable. E.g., Moses v. CashCall, Inc., 781 F.3d 63, 67 (4th Cir.2015); Inetianbor v. CashCall, Inc., 768 F.3d 1346, 1354 (11th Cir.2014); Jackson v. Payday Financial, LLC, 764 F.3d 765, 779 (7th Cir.2014), cert. denied, 135 S. Ct. 1894 (2015).

These cutting edge legal questions may have helped create bad law. For example, the Seventh Circuit also held that under the *Montana* line of cases the tribal court would not have jurisdiction even if the arbitration clause was valid. *Jackson*, 764 F.3d at 781–86. This holding would seem to conflict with other cases that held nonmembers can consent to tribal jurisdiction in commercial matters.

Given the demonstrated need for tribal economic development, and the demonstrated need for adequate consumer protection, is tribal online lending regulated by the tribes themselves justified?

SECTION B. INDIAN GAMING

Indian gaming has produced perhaps the most dramatic *positive* political and financial development in the history of federal Indian law and policy. Since the Supreme Court's 1987 decision in California v. Cabazon Band of Mission Indians, 480 U.S. 202 (1987), and Congress's reaction in enacting the Indian Gaming Regulatory Act (IGRA), 25 U.S.C.A. §§ 2701–2721, in 1988, the literal fortunes of hundreds of Indian tribes nationwide changed. Prior to developing gaming enterprises, many tribes had only a minimal governmental revenue base with budgets composed almost entirely by federal appropriations and grants. They were able to provide few governmental services on the reservation. The tribes that turned to gaming were generally able to use of the new revenues to expand their governmental services and other exercises of sovereignty. But with this influx of gaming revenues came both benefits and detriments.

Gaming revenues have been unevenly distributed among tribes and within them. A few Indian tribes became wealthy but increasing tribal revenues did not always mean relieving the poverty of individual Indians. Many members of gaming tribes, however, did move from poverty to the lower middle class and in some tribes members become the beneficiaries of enormous per capita distributions. At the same time, state governments became intensely interested capturing a share of tribal gaming revenues. And changes—such as in the public perception of Indian tribes—were felt throughout Indian country, even for tribes that have very limited or no gaming activities. See generally Steven Andrew Light & Kathryn R. L. Rand, Indian Gaming and Tribal Sovereignty: The Casino Compromise (2005); Jessica R. Cattelino, High Stakes: Florida Seminole Gaming and Sovereignty (2008).

Before the decision in *Cabazon*, Indian tribes in California, Florida, Maine, New York, and Wisconsin had been operating on-reservation bingo halls since the early 1970s and perhaps even as far back as the late 1960s. See generally Matthew L.M. Fletcher, *Bringing Balance to Indian Gaming*, 44 Harv. J. Legis. 39, 45–55 (2007). As former Dean Kevin Washburn wrote, Indian gaming likely would not exist but for legal and policy choices by state governments, which have treated gambling as a vice and have strictly regulated the industry. See Kevin K. Washburn, *Federal Law, State Policy, and Indian Gaming*, 4 Nev.L.J. 285 (2003–2004). And since states generally had no authority to prohibit or regulate on-reservation activities, even gaming, the market for Indian gaming mushroomed. This is not to say that gambling was legal in Indian country—the Johnson Act banned most gaming on reservations. See Kathryn R. L. Rand & Steven Andrew Light, Indian Gaming Law and Policy 65–67 (2006). But states had no authority to enforce the Johnson Act.

As tribal gaming was growing in the early 1980s, Congress considered Indian gaming legislation as early as 1983. Still, federal statements on federal Indian policy encouraged Indian tribes to engage in creative means of generating governmental revenue. In his 1983 federal Indian policy statement, President Reagan said, "It is important to the concept of self-government that tribes reduce their dependence on Federal funds by providing a greater percentage of the cost of their self-government." President Ronald Reagan, Statement on Indian Policy (Jan. 24, 1983). This fit the President's goal of reducing the size of government and cutting federal appropriations. This agenda indirectly fueled the movement toward Indian gaming. Eventually, the challenge to on-reservation gaming reached the Supreme Court, arising from a challenge by a Public Law 280 state, California.

1. THE SUPREME COURT'S APPLICATION OF PUBLIC LAW 280'S REGULATORY-PROHIBITORY DISTINCTION

CALIFORNIA V. CABAZON BAND OF MISSION INDIANS

Supreme Court of the United States, 1987.
480 U.S. 202, 107 S.Ct. 1083, 94 L.Ed.2d 244.

* * *

JUSTICE WHITE delivered the opinion of the Court.

The Cabazon and Morongo Bands of Mission Indians, federally recognized Indian Tribes, occupy reservations in Riverside County, California. Each Band, pursuant to an ordinance approved by the Secretary of the Interior, conducts bingo games on its reservation.[2] The Cabazon Band has also opened a card club at which draw poker and other card games are played. The games are open to the public and are played predominantly by non-Indians coming onto the reservations. The games

---

[2] The Cabazon ordinance authorizes the Band to sponsor bingo games within the reservation "[i]n order to promote economic development of the Cabazon Indian Reservation and to generate tribal revenues" and provides that net revenues from the games shall be kept in a separate fund to be used "for the purpose of promoting the health, education, welfare and well being of the Cabazon Indian Reservation and for other tribal purposes." The ordinance further provides that no one other than the Band is authorized to sponsor a bingo game within the reservation and that the games shall be open to the public, except that no one under 18 years old may play. The Morongo ordinance similarly authorizes the establishment of a tribal bingo enterprise and dedicates revenues to programs to promote the health, education, and general welfare of tribal members. It additionally provides that the games may be conducted at any time but must be conducted at least three days per week, that there shall be no prize limit for any single game or session, that no person under 18 years old shall be allowed to play, and that all employees shall wear identification.

are a major source of employment for tribal members, and the profits are the Tribes' sole source of income. The State of California seeks to apply to the two Tribes Cal.Penal Code Ann. § 326.5 (West Supp.1987). That statute does not entirely prohibit the playing of bingo but permits it when the games are operated and staffed by members of designated charitable organizations who may not be paid for their services. Profits must be kept in special accounts and used only for charitable purposes; prizes may not exceed $250 per game. Asserting that the bingo games on the two reservations violated each of these restrictions, California insisted that the Tribes comply with state law. * * *

* * *

In Pub. L. 280, Congress expressly granted six States, including California, jurisdiction over specified areas of Indian country within the States and provided for the assumption of jurisdiction by other States. In § 2, California was granted broad criminal jurisdiction over offenses committed by or against Indians within all Indian country within the State. Section 4's grant of civil jurisdiction was more limited. In Bryan v. Itasca County, 426 U.S. 373 (1976), we interpreted § 4 to grant States jurisdiction over private civil litigation involving reservation Indians in state court, but not to grant general civil regulatory authority. * * * Accordingly, when a State seeks to enforce a law within an Indian reservation under the authority of Pub.L. 280, it must be determined whether the law is criminal in nature, and thus fully applicable to the reservation under § 2, or civil in nature, and applicable only as it may be relevant to private civil litigation in state court.

* * *

Following its earlier decision in Barona Group of Capitan Grande Band of Mission Indians, San Diego County, Cal. v. Duffy, 694 F.2d 1185 (1982), cert. denied, 461 U.S. 929 (1983), which also involved the applicability of § 326.5 of the California Penal Code to Indian reservations, the Court of Appeals * * * drew a distinction between state "criminal/prohibitory" laws and state "civil/regulatory" laws: if the intent of a state law is generally to prohibit certain conduct, it falls within Pub. L. 280's grant of criminal jurisdiction, but if the state law generally permits the conduct at issue, subject to regulation, it must be classified as civil/regulatory and Pub.L. 280 does not authorize its enforcement on an Indian reservation. The shorthand test is whether the conduct at issue violates the State's public policy. Inquiring into the nature of § 326.5, the Court of Appeals held that it was regulatory rather than prohibitory. * * *

We are persuaded that the prohibitory/regulatory distinction is consistent with Bryan's [Bryan v. Itasca County, 426 U.S. 373 (1976), page 565, supra] construction of Pub. L. 280. It is not a bright-line rule, however;

and as the Ninth Circuit itself observed, an argument of some weight may be made that the bingo statute is prohibitory rather than regulatory. * * *

[However,] California does not prohibit all forms of gambling. California itself operates a state lottery, Cal. Gov't Code Ann. § 8880 et seq. (West Supp.1987), and daily encourages its citizens to participate in this state-run gambling. California also permits parimutuel horse-race betting. Cal.Bus. & Prof.Code Ann. § 19400–19667 (West 1964 and Supp.1987). Although certain enumerated gambling games are prohibited under Cal.Penal Code Ann. § 330 (West Supp.1987), games not enumerated, including the card games played in the Cabazon card club, are permissible. The Tribes assert that more than 400 card rooms similar to the Cabazon card club flourish in California, and the State does not dispute this fact. Also, as the Court of Appeals noted, bingo is legally sponsored by many different organizations and is widely played in California. * * * In light of the fact that California permits a substantial amount of gambling activity, including bingo, and actually promotes gambling through its state lottery, we must conclude that California regulates rather than prohibits gambling in general and bingo in particular.[10]

California argues, however, that high stakes, *unregulated* bingo, the conduct which attracts organized crime, is a misdemeanor in California and may be prohibited on Indian reservations. But that an otherwise regulatory law is enforceable by criminal as well as civil means does not necessarily convert it into a criminal law within the meaning of Pub.L. 280. Otherwise, the distinction between § 2 and § 4 of that law could easily be avoided and total assimilation permitted. * * * Accordingly, we conclude that Pub.L. 280 does not authorize California to enforce Cal. Penal Code Ann. § 326.5 (West Supp.1987) within the Cabazon and Morongo Reservations.

California and Riverside County also argue that the Organized Crime Control Act (OCCA) authorizes the application of their gambling laws to the tribal bingo enterprises. The OCCA makes certain violations of state and local gambling laws violations of federal law.[12] The Court of Appeals

---

[10] Nothing in this opinion suggest that cock fighting, tattoo parlors, nude dancing, and prostitution are permissible on Indian reservations within California. The applicable state laws governing an activity must be examined in detail before they can be characterized as regulatory or prohibitory. The lower courts have not demonstrated an inability to identify prohibitory laws. For example, in *United States v. Marcyes,* 557 F.2d 1361, 1363–1365 (C.A.9 1977), the Court of Appeal adopted and applied the prohibitory/regulatory distinction in determining whether a state law governing the possession of fireworks was made applicable to Indian reservations by the Assimilative Crimes Act, 62 Stat. 686, 18 U.S.C. § 13. The Court concluded that, despite limited exceptions to the statute's prohibition, the fireworks law was prohibitory in nature. See also *United States v. Farris,* 624 F.2d 890 (C.A.9 1980).

[12] 2 OCCA, 18 U.S.C. § 1955, provides in pertinent part:

(a) Whoever conducts, finances, manages, supervises, directs, or owns all or part of an illegal gambling business shall be fined not more than $20,000 or imprisoned not more than five years, or both.

(b) As used in this section—

rejected appellants' argument * * * The court explained that whether a tribal activity is "a violation of the law of a state" within the meaning of OCCA depends on whether it violates the "public policy" of the State, the same test for application of state law under Pub.L. 280, and similarly concluded that bingo is not contrary to the public policy of California.

* * * And because enforcement of OCCA is an exercise of federal rather than state authority, there is no danger of state encroachment on Indian tribal sovereignty. This latter observation exposes the flaw in appellants' reliance on OCCA. That enactment is indeed a federal law that, among other things, defines certain federal crimes over which the district courts have exclusive jurisdiction. There is nothing in OCCA indicating that the States are to have any part in enforcing federal criminal laws or are authorized to make arrests on Indian reservations that in the absence of OCCA they could not effect. We are not informed of any federal efforts to employ OCCA to prosecute the playing of bingo on Indian reservations, although there are more than 100 such enterprises currently in operation, many of which have been in existence for several years, for the most part with the encouragement of the Federal Government. * * *

* * *

Because the state and county laws at issue here are imposed directly on the Tribes that operate the games, and are not expressly permitted by Congress, the Tribes argue that the judgment below should be affirmed without more. They rely on the statement in McClanahan v. Arizona State Tax Comm'n, 411 U.S. 164, 170–171 (1973), that "[s]tate laws generally are not applicable to tribal Indians on an Indian reservation except where Congress has expressly provided that State laws shall apply" (quoting U.S. Dept. of the Interior, Federal Indian Law 845 (1958)). Our cases, however, have not established an inflexible *per se* rule precluding state jurisdiction over tribes and tribal members in the absence of express congressional consent. "[U]nder certain circumstances a State may validly assert authority over the activities of nonmembers on a reservation, and . . . in exceptional circumstances a State may assert jurisdiction over the on-reservation activities of tribal members." New Mexico v. Mescalero Apache Tribe, 462 U.S. 324, 331–332 (1983).

* * *

This case also involves a state burden on tribal Indians in the context of their dealings with non-Indians since the question is whether the State may prevent the Tribes from making available high stakes bingo games to

---

(i) is a *violation of the law of a State or political subdivision* in which it is conducted;

(ii) involves five or more persons who conduct, finance, manage, supervise, direct, or own all or part of such a business; and

(iii) has been or remains in substantially continuous operations for a period in excess of thirty days or has a gross revenue of $2,000 in any single day." (Emphasis added.)

non-Indians coming from outside the reservations. Decision in this case turns on whether state authority is pre-empted by the operation of federal law; and "[s]tate jurisdiction is pre-empted ... if it interferes or is incompatible with federal and tribal interests reflected in federal law, unless the state interests at stake are sufficient to justify the assertion of state authority." *Mescalero*, 462 U.S., at 333, 334. The inquiry is to proceed in light of traditional notions of Indian sovereignty and the congressional goal of Indian self-government, including its "overriding goal" of encouraging tribal self-sufficiency and economic development.

These are important federal interests. They were reaffirmed by the President's 1983 Statement on Indian Policy. More specifically, the Department of the Interior, which has the primary responsibility for carrying out the Federal Government's trust obligations to Indian tribes, has sought to implement these policies by promoting tribal bingo enterprises. Under the Indian Financing Act of 1974, 25 U.S.C. § 1451 et seq. (1982 ed. and Supp.III), the Secretary of the Interior has made grants and has guaranteed loans for the purpose of constructing bingo facilities. The Department of Housing and Urban Development and the Department of Health and Human Services have also provided financial assistance to develop tribal gaming enterprises. Here, the Secretary of the Interior has approved tribal ordinances establishing and regulating the gaming activities involved. The Secretary has also exercised his authority to review tribal bingo management contracts under 25 U.S.C. § 81, and has issued detailed guidelines governing that review.

These policies and actions, which demonstrate the Government's approval and active promotion of tribal bingo enterprises, are of particular relevance in this case. The Cabazon and Morongo Reservations contain no natural resources which can be exploited. The tribal games at present provide the sole source of revenues for the operation of the tribal governments and the provision of tribal services. They are also the major sources of employment on the reservations. Self-determination and economic development are not within reach if the Tribes cannot raise revenues and provide employment for their members. The Tribes' interests obviously parallel the federal interests.

California seeks to diminish the weight of these seemingly important tribal interests by asserting that the Tribes are merely marketing an exemption from state gambling laws. * * * Here, however, the Tribes are not merely importing a product onto the reservations for immediate resale to non-Indians. They have built modern facilities which provide recreational opportunities and ancillary services to their patrons, who do not simply drive onto the reservations, make purchases and depart, but spend extended periods of time there enjoying the services the Tribes provide. The Tribes have strong incentive to provide comfortable, clean, and attractive facilities and well-run games in order to increase attendance at the games. The tribal bingo enterprises are similar to the resort complex, featuring hunting and fishing, that the Mescalero Apache Tribe operates on its reservation through the "concerted and sustained" management of reservation land and wildlife resources. *New Mexico v. Mescalero Apache Tribe,* 462 U.S., at 341.

* * *

The sole interest asserted by the State to justify the imposition of its bingo laws on the Tribes is in preventing the infiltration of the tribal games by organized crime. To the extent that the State seeks to prevent any and all bingo games from being played on tribal lands while permitting regulated, off-reservation games, this asserted interest is irrelevant and the state and county laws are pre-empted. Even to the extent that the State and county seek to regulate short of prohibition, the laws are pre-empted. The State insists that the high stakes offered at tribal games are attractive to organized crime, whereas the controlled games authorized under California law are not. This is surely a legitimate concern, but we are unconvinced that it is sufficient to escape the pre-emptive force of federal and tribal interests apparent in this case. California does not allege any present criminal involvement in the Cabazon and Morongo enterprises, and the Ninth Circuit discerned none. * * *

We conclude that the State's interest in preventing the infiltration of the tribal bingo enterprises by organized crime does not justify state regulation of the tribal bingo enterprises in light of the compelling federal and tribal interests supporting them. State regulation would impermissibly infringe on tribal government, and this conclusion applies equally to the county's attempted regulation of the Cabazon card club. We therefore affirm the judgment of the Court of Appeals and remand the case for further proceedings consistent with this opinion.

It is so ordered.

JUSTICE STEVENS, with whom JUSTICE O'CONNOR and JUSTICE SCALIA join, dissenting.

Unless and until Congress exempts Indian-managed gambling from state law and subjects it to federal supervision, I believe that a State may enforce its laws prohibiting high-stakes gambling on Indian reservations within its borders. Congress has not pre-empted California's prohibition against high-stakes bingo games and the Secretary of the Interior plainly has no authority to do so. While gambling provides needed employment and income for Indian tribes, these benefits do not, in my opinion, justify tribal operation of currently unlawful commercial activities. Accepting the majority's reasoning would require exemptions for cock fighting, tattoo parlors, nude dancing, houses of prostitution, and other illegal but profitable enterprises. As the law now stands, I believe tribal entrepreneurs, like others who might derive profits from catering to non-Indian customers, must obey applicable state laws.

* * *

NOTES

1.   Like California, all other Public Law 280 states allow gambling under certain circumstances and subject to certain limits. In *Cabazon*, the two tribes conducted bingo games and draw poker which were permitted by state law under strictly defined conditions, including volunteer staffing of bingo games and a maximum $250 prize. The tribes did not comply with these conditions and, according to the Court, they need not. Suppose a California tribe conducts card games besides poker and the few others permitted under California state law. For instance, if a tribe operated a casino with every form of gambling found in Las Vegas, would the Court allow it? Once a state allows a little regulated gambling, perhaps a lottery or low-stakes church bingo or free plays for winners in pinball games, is the door open to unlimited gambling on Indian reservations under the Court's decision in *Cabazon*? See Lac du Flambeau Band of Indians v. Wisconsin, 743 F.Supp. 645 (W.D.Wis.1990).

2.   In the absence of Public Law 280's consent to state jurisdiction, how do the principles of tribal sovereignty and preemption discussed in *Cabazon* apply?

2.   THE CONGRESSIONAL RESPONSE TO *CABAZON*: THE INDIAN GAMING REGULATORY ACT

In the wake of *Cabazon*, Congress responded to state concerns and passed the Indian Gaming Regulatory Act (IGRA), 25 U.S.C. §§ 2701–2721. The Act recited Congress's reading of the *Cabazon* holding as its predicate: "Indian tribes have the exclusive right to regulate gaming activity on Indian lands if the gaming activity is not specifically prohibited by Federal law and is conducted within a State which does not, as a matter of criminal law and public policy, prohibit such gaming activity." Id. § 2701(5). It goes on to limit and regulate the authority that tribes would have under the immunities from state law recognized in *Cabazon*. IGRA's reference to whether a state's policy prohibited gambling was borrowed directly from *Cabazon*'s application of Public Law 280 under which criminal jurisdiction, but not civil regulatory jurisdiction, in Indian country had been extended to California. Thus, state policy attitudes became the key point of reference under IGRA and states were given an expanded role in allowing tribally-sanctioned gaming within their boundaries.

IGRA, which is extraordinarily complex and detailed, is designed to deal with gaming enterprises going beyond bingo, lotto, and card games. Indian gaming under IGRA is divided into three classes. Class I games include "social games" for prizes with nominal value and traditional tribal gaming. These games are subject solely to the jurisdiction of the Indian tribe.

Class II games include bingo, instant bingo, lotto, punch boards, tip jars, pull-tabs, and other games similar to bingo. Class II also includes manually conducted card games which are legal and played anywhere in a state and are not played against the house. Accordingly, blackjack (21), baccarat, and chemin de fer are excluded from Class II. Class II card games are fully subject to the laws and regulations of the state governing hours of operation as well as wager and pot size limitations. Class II games are regulated by Indian tribes jointly with the National Indian Gaming Commission established within the Department of the Interior. A tribe may conduct or license and regulate Class II gambling if it occurs in "a State that permits such gaming for any purpose by any person" and it is not prohibited by federal law.

Class III games include all other gambling, such as electronic or electromechanical facsimiles of permissible Class III games, card games which are played against the house such as blackjack and baccarat, casino games, pari-mutuel racing, and jai alai. Class III gaming activity may be conducted or licensed and regulated by a tribe "in a State that permits such gaming," subject to an allocation of regulatory authority between the state and tribe set forth in a tribal-state compact. The compact may provide for enforcement of agreed rules and regulations, cross-deputization, tribal taxes equal to those of the state, and procedural remedies for breach of the compact.

IGRA also establishes the National Indian Gaming Commission which has broad regulatory and investigative authority to assure that Indian gaming is not subject to the influences of organized crime. The Commission is funded by an assessment on Indian Class II gaming enterprises. The assessment cannot exceed 5% of the gross revenues in excess of $1,500,000.00. A compact may authorize a state to levy an assessment upon tribes that engage in Class III gaming in an amount equal to the state's costs of regulating tribal gaming.

The requirement that tribes and states negotiate a compact in order for a tribe to conduct Class III gaming activities has triggered a number of high-stakes lawsuits. Under IGRA as enacted by Congress in 1988, a tribe, in order to initiate the state-tribal compact procedure, contacts the state with a request to enter into negotiations. Following the request, the parties are given 180 days to arrive at the terms of the compact. In the event that an agreement is not reached within such period, the tribe is authorized by IGRA to file an action in United States District Court to determine whether or not the state has negotiated in "good faith." Under IGRA, the state has the burden of proving it negotiated in good faith. If the court finds the state failed to do so, a mediator is appointed who, after reviewing the positions of both the tribe and the state, presents a "last offer" to the state which the state may either accept or reject. If the state rejects the last offer, the Secretary of the Interior is empowered unilaterally to determine and impose the terms of the compact upon consultation with only the Indian tribe.

The complicated and tenuous compromise that IGRA proposed between tribes, state governments, and the United States came to an abrupt conclusion in 1996 when the Supreme Court undermined a major component of the statute. As a result, the law now operates much differently from what Congress expected.

FLORIDA V. SEMINOLE TRIBE OF FLORIDA

Supreme Court of the United States, 1996.
517 U.S. 44, 116 S.Ct. 1114, 134 L.Ed.2d 252.

* * *

CHIEF JUSTICE REHNQUIST delivered the opinion of the Court.

The Indian Gaming Regulatory Act provides that an Indian tribe may conduct certain gaming activities only in conformance with a valid compact between the tribe and the State in which the gaming activities are located. 102 Stat. 2475, 25 U.S.C. § 2710(d)(1)(C). The Act, passed by Congress under the Indian Commerce Clause, U.S. Const., Art. I, § 8, cl. 3, imposes upon the States a duty to negotiate in good faith with an Indian tribe toward the formation of a compact, § 2710(d)(3)(A), and authorizes a tribe to bring suit in federal court against a State in order to compel performance of that duty, § 2710(d)(7). We hold that notwithstanding Congress' clear intent to abrogate the States' sovereign immunity, the Indian Commerce Clause does not grant Congress that power, and therefore § 2710(d)(7) cannot grant jurisdiction over a State that does not consent to be sued. We further hold that the doctrine of Ex parte Young, 209 U.S. 123 * * * (1908), may not be used to enforce § 2710(d)(3) against a state official.

* * *

II

* * *

B

We begin our inquiry into whether Congress has the power to abrogate unilaterally the States' immunity from suit is narrowly focused on one question: Was the Act in question passed pursuant to a constitutional provision granting Congress the power to abrogate? * * * Previously, in conducting that inquiry, we have found authority to abrogate under only two provisions of the Constitution. [W]e recognized that the Fourteenth Amendment, by expanding federal power at the expense of state autonomy, had fundamentally altered the balance of state and federal power struck by the Constitution. * * * We noted that § 1 of the Fourteenth Amendment contained prohibitions expressly directed at the States and that § 5 of the Amendment expressly provided that "The Congress shall have power to enforce, by appropriate legislation, the provisions of this article." * * * We held that through the Fourteenth Amendment, federal power extended to intrude upon the province of the Eleventh Amendment and therefore that § 5 of the Fourteenth Amendment allowed Congress to abrogate the immunity from suit guaranteed by that Amendment.

In only one other case has congressional abrogation of the States' Eleventh Amendment immunity been upheld. In Pennsylvania v. Union Gas Co., 491 U.S. 1 * * * (1989), a plurality of the Court found that the Interstate Commerce Clause, Art. I, § 8, cl. 3, granted Congress the power to abrogate state sovereign immunity, stating that the power to regulate interstate commerce would be "incomplete without the authority to render States liable in damages." * * * Justice White added the fifth vote necessary to the result in that case, but wrote separately in order to express that he "[did] not agree with much of [the plurality's] reasoning." * * *

In arguing that Congress through the Act abrogated the States' sovereign immunity, petitioner does not challenge the Eleventh Circuit's conclusion that the Act was passed pursuant to neither the Fourteenth Amendment nor the Interstate Commerce Clause. Instead, accepting the lower court's conclusion that the Act was passed pursuant to Congress' power under the Indian Commerce Clause, petitioner now asks us to consider whether that Clause grants Congress the power to abrogate the States' sovereign immunity.

Petitioner begins with the plurality decision in Union Gas and contends that "[t]here is no principled basis for finding that congressional power under the Indian Commerce Clause is less than that conferred by the Interstate Commerce Clause." Brief for Petitioner 17. Noting that the Union Gas plurality found the power to abrogate from the "plenary" character of the grant of authority over interstate commerce, petitioner emphasizes that the Interstate Commerce Clause leaves the States with some power to regulate, * * * whereas the Indian Commerce Clause makes "Indian relations * * * the exclusive province of federal law." County of Oneida v. Oneida Indian Nation of N.Y., 470 U.S. 226, 234 * * * (1985). Contending that the Indian Commerce Clause vests the Federal Government with "the duty of protect[ing]" the tribes from "local ill feeling" and "the people of the States," United States v. Kagama, 118 U.S. 375, 383–384 * * * (1886), petitioner argues that the abrogation power is necessary "to protect the tribes from state action denying federally guaranteed rights." Brief for Petitioner 20.

Respondents dispute petitioner's analogy between the Indian Commerce Clause and the Interstate Commerce Clause. They note that we have recognized that "the Interstate Commerce and Indian Commerce Clauses have very different applications," Cotton Petroleum Corp. v. New Mexico, 490 U.S. 163, 192 * * * (1989), and from that they argue that the two provisions are "wholly dissimilar." Brief for Respondents 21. Respondents contend that the Interstate Commerce Clause grants the power of abrogation only because Congress' authority to regulate interstate commerce would be "incomplete" without that "necessary" power. * * * The Indian Commerce Clause is distinguishable, respondents contend, because it gives Congress complete authority over the Indian tribes. Therefore, the abrogation power is not "necessary" to Congress' exercise of its power under the Indian Commerce Clause.

* * *

Following the rationale of the Union Gas plurality, our inquiry is limited to determining whether the Indian Commerce Clause, like the Interstate Commerce Clause, is a grant of authority to the Federal Government at the expense of the States. The answer to that question is obvious. If anything, the Indian Commerce Clause accomplishes a greater transfer of power from the States to the Federal Government than does the Interstate Commerce Clause. This is clear enough from the fact that the States still exercise some authority over interstate trade but have been divested of virtually all authority over Indian commerce and Indian tribes. * * * [I]f the States' partial cession of authority over a particular area includes cession of the immunity from suit, then their virtually total cession of authority over a different area must also include cession of the immunity from suit. * * * We agree with petitioner [there is] no principled distinction in favor of the States to be drawn between the Indian Commerce Clause and the Interstate Commerce Clause.

* * *

Never before the decision in *Union Gas* had we suggested that the bounds of Article III could be expanded by Congress operating pursuant to any constitutional provision other than the Fourteenth Amendment. Indeed, it had seemed fundamental that Congress could not expand the jurisdiction of the federal courts beyond the bounds of Article III. Marbury v. Madison, 1 Cranch 137, 2 L.Ed. 60 (1803). The plurality's citation of prior decisions for support was based upon what we believe to be a misreading of precedent. * * *

* * *

In the five years since it was decided, *Union Gas* has proved to be a solitary departure from established law. * * * Reconsidering the decision in *Union Gas*, we conclude that none of the policies underlying stare decisis require our continuing adherence to its holding. The decision has, since its issuance, been of questionable precedential value, largely because a majority of the Court expressly disagreed with the rationale of the plurality. * * * The case involved the interpretation of the Constitution and therefore may be altered only by constitutional amendment or revision by this Court. Finally, both the result in *Union Gas* and the plurality's rationale depart from our established understanding of the Eleventh Amendment and undermine the accepted function of Article III. We feel bound to conclude that *Union Gas* was wrongly decided and that it should be, and now is, overruled.

* * *

In overruling *Union Gas* today, we reconfirm that the background principle of state sovereign immunity embodied in the Eleventh Amendment is not so ephemeral as to dissipate when the subject of the suit is an area, like the regulation of Indian commerce, that is under the exclusive control of the Federal Government. Even when the Constitution vests in Congress complete law-making authority over a particular area, the Eleventh Amendment prevents congressional authorization of suits by private parties against unconsenting States. The Eleventh Amendment restricts the judicial power under Article III, and Article I cannot be used to circumvent the constitutional limitations placed upon federal jurisdiction. Petitioner's suit against the State of Florida must be dismissed for a lack of jurisdiction.

III

Petitioner argues that we may exercise jurisdiction over its suit to enforce § 2710(d)(3) against the Governor notwithstanding the jurisdictional bar of the Eleventh Amendment. Petitioner notes that since our decision in Ex parte Young, 209 U.S. 123 * * * (1908), we often have found federal jurisdiction over a suit against a state official when that suit seeks only prospective injunctive relief in order to "end a continuing violation of federal law." * * * The situation presented here, however, is sufficiently different from that giving rise to the traditional *Ex parte Young* action so as to preclude the availability of that doctrine.

* * *

Where Congress has created a remedial scheme for the enforcement of a particular federal right, we have, in suits against federal officers, refused to supplement that scheme with one created by the judiciary. * * * Here, of course, the question is not whether a remedy should be created, but instead is whether the Eleventh Amendment bar should be lifted, as it was in *Ex parte Young*, in order to allow a suit against a state officer. Nevertheless, we think that the same general principle applies: Therefore, where Congress has prescribed a detailed remedial scheme for the enforcement against a State of a statutorily created right, a court should hesitate before casting aside those limitations and permitting an action against a state officer based upon *Ex parte Young*.

* * *

Here, Congress intended § 2710(d)(3) to be enforced against the State in an action brought under § 2710(d)(7); the intricate procedures set forth in that provision show that Congress intended therein not only to define, but also to limit significantly, the duty imposed by § 2710(d)(3). For example, where the court finds that the State has failed to negotiate in good faith, the only remedy prescribed is an order directing the State and the Indian tribe to conclude a compact within 60 days. And if the parties disregard the court's order and fail to conclude a compact within the 60-day period, the only sanction is that each party then must submit a proposed compact to a mediator who selects the one which best embodies the terms of the Act. Finally, if the State fails to accept the compact selected by the mediator, the only sanction against it is that the mediator shall notify the Secretary of the Interior who then must prescribe regulations governing class III gaming on the tribal lands at issue. By contrast with this quite modest set of sanctions, an action brought against a state official under Ex parte Young would expose that official to the full remedial powers of a federal court, including, presumably, contempt sanctions. If § 2710(d)(3) could be enforced in a suit under *Ex parte Young*, § 2710(d)(7) would have been superfluous; it is difficult to see why an Indian tribe would suffer through the intricate scheme of § 2710(d)(7) when more complete and more immediate relief would be available under *Ex parte Young*.

Here, of course, we have found that Congress does not have authority under the Constitution to make the State suable in federal court under § 2710(d)(7). Nevertheless, the fact that Congress chose to impose upon the State a liability that is significantly more limited than would be the liability imposed upon the state officer under *Ex parte Young* strongly indicates that Congress had no wish to create the latter under § 2710(d)(3). Nor are we free to rewrite the statutory scheme in order to approximate what we think Congress might have wanted had it known that § 2710(d)(7) was beyond its authority. If that effort is to be made, it should be made by Congress, and not by the federal courts. We hold that *Ex parte Young* is inapplicable to petitioner's suit against the Governor of Florida, and therefore that suit is barred by the Eleventh Amendment and must be dismissed for a lack of jurisdiction.

* * *

NOTES

1.   While calling the Court's holding in *Seminole* "remarkable," Professor Martha Field, a leading scholar of federalism, like a number of other

commentators, has stated that the case will not have "much impact at all" on Indians and their interests:

> *Seminole* is probably not of major significance in regard to federal-Indian-state relations. It is designed to be, and is, a major decision about the meaning of the Eleventh Amendment and about federal-state relations, judicial and congressional. The decision does, obviously, affect the IGRA. But the scheme that replaces the one held unconstitutional in *Seminole* could prove more advantageous to Native Americans rather than less.

Martha A. Field, *The* Seminole *Case, Federalism, and the Indian Commerce Clause*, 29 Ariz.St L.J. 3, 3–4 (1997).

The scheme referred to by Professor Field as replacing the one held unconstitutional in *Seminole* was described by Justice Stevens, in his dissent:

> If each adversary adamantly adheres to its understanding of the law, if the District Court determines that the State's inflexibility constitutes a failure to negotiate in good faith, and if the State thereafter continues to insist that it is acting within its rights, the maximum sanction that the Court can impose is an order that refers the controversy to a member of the Executive Branch of the Government for resolution. 25 U.S.C. § 2710(d)(7)(B). As the Court of Appeals interpreted the Act, this final disposition is available even though the action against the State and its Governor may not be maintained. 11 F.3d 1016, 1029 (C.A.11 1994) (The Court does not tell us whether it agrees or disagrees with that disposition.)

Seminole Tribe, 517 U.S. at 99.

2.   Technological advances have created an interesting market in so-called Class II "slot machines" in the wake of *Seminole Tribe*. In states where the government refuses to negotiate a Class III gaming compact in good faith, tribes and their business partners developed "technologic aids" to make Class II bingo and pull-tab games more marketable. IGRA defines Class II games as including "the game of chance commonly known as bingo (whether or not electronic, computer, or other technologic aids are used in connection therewith). . . ." 25 U.S.C. § 2703(7)(A)(i).

The National Indian Gaming Commission and the United States Department of Justice frequently litigated the question of whether electronic "aids" that transformed standard paper bingo into an electronic form of bingo that resembled electronic slot machines were actually electronic "facsimiles" if Class III games, and therefore *not* Class II games. The litigation came to a head when the Tenth Circuit decided Seneca-Cayuga Tribe of Oklahoma v. National Indian Gaming Commission, 327 F.3d 1019 (10th Cir.2003), in favor of the tribe, and when the Eighth Circuit decided United States v. Santee Sioux Tribe of Nebraska, 324 F.3d 607 (8th Cir.2003) (en banc), also in favor of the tribe. The United States Department of Justice petitioned the Supreme Court to grant certiorari in both cases, but the Court denied the petition in both cases.

See Ashcroft v. Seneca-Cayuga Tribe of Oklahoma, 540 U.S. 1218 (2004); United States v. Santee Sioux Tribe of Nebraska, 540 U.S. 1229 (2004).

INDIAN LAWYERING NOTE: CASINO-STYLE GAMING AFTER SEMINOLE TRIBE

The Indian Gaming Regulatory Act (IGRA) is a great compromise of federal, state, and tribal interests. *Seminole Tribe* undid that compromise, but opened up other avenues for creative tribal lawyering.

IGRA's legislative history provides that the tribal-state compacting process "is a viable mechanism for settling various matters between two equal sovereigns." S. Rep. No. 100–446, at 13 (1988). Congress balanced "the strong concerns of states [regarding] state laws and regulations relating to sophisticated forms of class III gaming * * * against the strong tribal opposition to any imposition of State jurisdiction over activities on Indian lands." Id.

Seminole Tribe was the culmination of a series of cases in which Indian tribes sued states for failure to negotiate Class III gaming compacts, and those states asserted immunity from those suits under the Eleventh Amendment. Indian tribes in Connecticut and Michigan were able to secure Class III gaming compacts prior to *Seminole Tribe* through negotiated settlement, but agreed to revenue sharing. In each instance, the tribes agreed to pay 25 and 10 percent, respectively, to state or local governments in exchange for a complete monopoly over casino-style gaming in the state.

Other tribes were not so successful. After *Seminole Tribe*, Indian tribes no longer had a legal recourse through federal court litigation. No tribe was able to finalize a gaming compact for over two years after the *Seminole Tribe* decision. Some tribes responded by threatening to close down roads in order to force negotiations. Other tribes sought to amend state law via public referendum to force negotiations.

Ultimately, both states and tribes had reasons to seek agreement. Indian gaming had too much potential to generate revenue and economic activity for states to ignore it. While the states could still afford to reject gaming in most instances, Indian tribes could not because they often did not have a sufficient alternative tax base. The financial advantage for the states was obvious—they could generate revenue without doing much to earn it. Additionally, after *Seminole Tribe*, states could dictate terms to the tribes. Not surprisingly, many states attempted to extort Indian tribes. They demanded a cut of the profits from class III gaming. Other states demanded abrogation or abandonment of treaty rights or tax concessions.

Tribal and state negotiations and compacts after *Seminole Tribe* have one major commonality—revenue sharing with states and state subdivisions. Complicating all this is IGRA, which flatly bars states from taxing or otherwise benefitting from Indian gaming revenues. 25 U.S.C. § 2710(d)(4). Moreover, the Secretary of the Interior is charged with reviewing all Class III gaming compacts. 25 U.S.C. § 2719)(d)(3)(B). The Secretary likely will approve a compact that involves a "meaningful concession" from the state to the tribe in exchange for revenue sharing. The "meaningful concessions" test arises not from the text of IGRA but from federal agency statements and the common law of gaming compact revenue sharing arrangements. See generally Ezekiel J.N. Fletcher, *Negotiating Meaningful Concessions from States in Gaming Compacts to Further Tribal Economic Development: Satisfying the "Economic Benefits" Test*, 54 S.D.L.Rev. 419 (2009).

A recent United States Government Accountability Office report details the number of Class III gaming compacts that contain revenue sharing, and the Interior Department's process in determining whether to approve, reject, or acquiesce to Class III compacts:

> Based on our analysis of compacts about 61 percent (169 of 276) of all compacts in effect as of October 2014 contained revenue sharing provisions between the tribes and states. These revenue sharing provisions include various payment structures that may require, for example, tribes to pay states a fixed amount or a flat percentage of all gaming revenues or an increasing percentage as gaming revenues rise. Of the 169 compacts that include revenue sharing provisions, most (164) involve payments tied to gaming revenues and include a maximum payment, ranging from 3.5 percent to 25 percent of all or a portion of gaming revenues * * * .

> * * * Based on decision letters we reviewed, Interior conducts a two-pronged analysis to determine whether the revenue sharing provision violates IGRA. First, Interior evaluates whether the state has offered a "meaningful concession" in exchange for the tribe's revenue sharing. For example, a state can offer a tribe exclusivity— the sole right to conduct gaming in the state, or a specific geographic area within the state. Second, Interior determines whether the concessions offered by the state provide a substantial economic benefit for the tribe.

United States Government Accountability Office, Indian Gaming: Regulation and Oversight by the Federal Government, States, and Tribes 18–19 (June 2015).

Gaming operations in the United States have exploded since IGRA's enactment. While states were able to offer meaningful concessions and economic benefits in the 1990s and 2000s, the saturation of the gaming market has severely undermined their efforts now. In 2010, a split panel of the Ninth Circuit held that California Governor Schwarzenegger had acted in bad faith by demanding revenue sharing during compact negotiations without satisfying the so-called "meaningful concessions" test. See Rincon Band of Luiseno Mission Indians of Rincon Reservation v. Schwarzenegger, 602 F.3d 1019 (9th Cir.2010), cert. denied, 131 S.Ct. 3055 (2011).

Following *Rincon*, the Interior Department has been forced to reject some proposed revenue sharing agreements. E.g., Letter from Larry Echo Hawk, Assistant Secretary—Indian Affairs to Hon. Sherry Treppa, Chairperson, Habematolel Pomo of Upper Lake (Aug. 17, 2010). However, IGRA allows for the approval by default of a proposed gaming compact if Interior does not act within 45 days. The Department has allowed difficult revenue sharing provisions to become effective through this route on occasion. E.g., Letter from Donald E. Laverdure, Acting Assistant Secretary—Indian Affairs to Hon. Jerry Brown, Governor, State of California (July 13, 2012) (Graton Rancheria compact).

There might be another avenue for tribes as well. After the decision in *Seminole Tribe*, the Secretary of the Interior sought to reshape the Secretary's role under the new legal regime. Following the understanding of congressional staffers familiar with the negotiations leading up to the enactment of IGRA, such as now-Professor Alex Skibine, former deputy counsel on Indian Affairs for the House Interior Committee, the Secretary promulgated a rule, now codified at 25 CFR Part 291. The rule allows a tribe to invoke a secretarial procedure akin to that of 25 U.S.C. § 2710(d)(7)(B)(vii) if a state refuses to negotiate a class III gaming compact in good faith and invokes its Eleventh Amendment immunity from suit. However, the Secretary's authority to promulgate the rule has been challenged by states.

If Part 291 is a valid exercise of the Secretary's authority, the procedure would be a very effective tool that tribes could use to avoid the intransigence of a state refusing to engage in good faith compact negotiations. However, nothing in the text of IGRA allows the tribe or the Secretary to bypass the requirement of IGRA that a federal court make a determination that the state "has failed to negotiate in good faith with the Indian tribe to conclude a Tribal-State compact governing the conduct of gaming activities * * * ." § 2710(d)(7)(B)(3). As the Secretary asserted in promulgating the final rule, Part 291 restores a critical portion of IGRA and fulfills Congressional intent, but is that enough to authorize the rule?

In Texas v. United States, 497 F.3d 491 (5th Cir.2007), cert. denied sub nom., Kickapoo Traditional Tribe of Texas v. Texas, 129 S.Ct. 32 (2008), the Fifth Circuit held over a strong dissent that the Secretarial procedures in 25 CFR Part 291 were not authorized by IGRA and struck them down. See id. at 509. The majority reasoned that Congress never would have intended the Secretary to have so much power under IGRA:

> The role the Secretary plays and the power he wields under the Procedures bear no resemblance to the secretarial power expressly delegated by Congress under IGRA. First, IGRA interposes, before any secretarial involvement, the requirement that an impartial factfinder determine whether the state has negotiated in good faith. See § 2710(d)(7)(B)(iii). Under the Secretarial Procedures, however, it matters not that a state undertook good-faith negotiations with the tribe: The Secretary may prescribe Class III gaming irrespective of a

state's good faith. See 25 C.F.R. § 291.7–.8. This result contravenes the plain language of IGRA.

Second, under IGRA, if mediation is ordered, it is undertaken by a neutral, judicially-appointed mediator who objectively weighs the proposals submitted by the state and tribe. See § 2710(d)(7)(B)(iv). Under the Procedures, however, the Secretary selects the mediator. 25 C.F.R. § 291.9. In light of the Secretary's statutory trust obligation to protect the interests of Indian tribes, this aspect of the Procedures is stacked against the objective interest-balancing Congress intended and creates the strong impression of a biased mediation process. See, e.g., Kickapoo Tribe of Indians of Kickapoo Reservation in Kan. v. Babbitt, 43 F.3d 1491, 1499 (D.C.Cir.1995) (noting that "the Secretary was not in a position to champion the State's position in view of his trust obligations to the tribe." (citing Heckman v. United States, 224 U.S. 413, 444–45 * * * (1912))). Common sense dictates that the Secretary cannot play the role of tribal trustee and objective arbiter of both parties' interests simultaneously. Congress did not intend this incoherent result.

Third, whereas under IGRA's remedial scheme the court-appointed mediator essentially defines the regulations that the Secretary may promulgate, the Procedures enable the Secretary to disregard not only the mediator's proposal, but also the proposals of the state and tribe. IGRA's remedial process makes clear that Congress did not intend to delegate to the Secretary unbridled power to prescribe Class III regulations.

Fourth, the Secretarial Procedures contemplate Class III gaming in the absence of a tribal-state compact-directly in derogation of Congress's repeated and emphatic insistence. See, e.g., S.Rep. No. 100–446, at 6 (1988), as reprinted in 1988 U.S.C.C.A.N. 3071, 3076 ("[IGRA] does not contemplate and does not provide for the conduct of class III gaming activities on Indian lands in the absence of a tribal-State compact."). The only exception to the compact requirement Congress envisioned was the promulgation of procedures after a bad-faith determination and in concert with the proposal selected by a court-appointed mediator. Yet in spite of this single statutory exception-the product of IGRA's complex and balanced remedial scheme-Appellees maintain it is equally reasonable to assume that Congress intended a waiver of liability under the Johnson Act and 18 U.S.C. § 1166 even *without* a judicial determination of bad faith; *without* the participation of a court-appointed mediator; and *without* the requirement that the regulations ultimately promulgated be "consistent with the proposed compact selected by the [court-appointed] mediator." § 2710(d)(7)(b)(vii)(I).

Id. at 508–09. Circuit Judge Dennis dissented, noting that states had a "veto" power over Indian gaming after *Seminole*. Id. at 522 (citing Matthew L.M. Fletcher, *Bringing Balance to Indian Gaming*, 44 Harv.J. on Legis. 39, 75 (2007)).

NATION BUILDING NOTE: GAMING ON AFTER-ACQUIRED LANDS

The Indian Gaming Regulatory Act generally bars gaming on lands acquired by an Indian tribe after the passage of the Act on October 17, 1988. 25 U.S.C. § 2719(a). However, there are an enormous number of exceptions to this rule, as a review of the statute makes clear:

(a) * * * Except as provided in subsection (b), gaming regulated by this chapter shall not be conducted on lands acquired by the Secretary in trust for the benefit of an Indian tribe after October 17, 1988, unless—

(1) such lands are located within or contiguous to the boundaries of the reservation of the Indian tribe on October 17, 1988; or

(2) the Indian tribe has no reservation on October 17, 1988, and—

(A) such lands are located in Oklahoma and—

(i) are within the boundaries of the Indian tribe's former reservation, as defined by the Secretary, or

(ii) are contiguous to other land held in trust or restricted status by the United States for the Indian tribe in Oklahoma; or

(B) such lands are located in a State other than Oklahoma and are within the Indian tribe's last recognized reservation within the State or States within which such Indian tribe is presently located.

(b) Exceptions

(1) Subsection (a) will not apply when—

(A) the Secretary, after consultation with the Indian tribe and appropriate State and local officials, including officials of other nearby Indian tribes, determines that a gaming establishment on newly acquired lands would be in the best interest of the Indian tribe and its members, and would not be detrimental to the surrounding community, but only if the Governor of the State in which the gaming activity is to be conducted concurs in the Secretary's determination; or

(B) lands are taken into trust as part of—

(i)   a settlement of a land claim,

(ii) the initial reservation of an Indian tribe acknowledged by the Secretary under the Federal acknowledgment process, or

(iii) the restoration of lands for an Indian tribe that is restored to Federal recognition.

Gaming on after-acquired lands has become one of the most controversial areas of federal Indian law. Gaming opponents charge Indian tribes with "reservation shopping" and claim they are exploiting federal law to access lucrative gaming markets. However, relatively few Indian tribes have been successful in opening up gaming facilities off-reservation, excepting Indian tribes that the United States has federally recognized in recent decades. Those tribes have been able to invoke the initial reservation exception, see 25 U.S.C. § 2719(b)(1)(B)(ii), or the restored tribes—restored land exception, see 25 U.S.C. § 2719(b)(1)(B)(iii), for example, have been reasonable successful in establishing gaming rights.

The history of the Turtle Creek Casino owned and operated by the Grand Traverse Band of Ottawa and Chippewa Indians is instructive.[*] On June 14, 1996, the Grand Traverse Band opened the Turtle Creek Casino in Whitewater Township, just east of Acme, Michigan, and the Grand Traverse Bay. On that day, the tribe filed a lawsuit in federal court in Grand Rapids seeking an order that the operation of the casino was legal and in accordance with the Indian Gaming Regulatory Act. The United States government, the defendant in the case, sought to prove that the operation of the casino was illegal, as did the State of Michigan, which intervened in the lawsuit.

The tribe purchased the land upon which Turtle Creek was located in 1989, shortly after the passage of the gaming act by Congress, and placed the land into trust. The purpose for the land was to provide a location from which the tribe could provide services to tribal members living in and around Grand Traverse, Antrim, and Charlevoix counties, and for economic development. Tribal leaders believed the location was on or near the Grand Traverse Reservation boundaries created in the 1836 Treaty of Washington. For several years, the location had served as a satellite office for the tribal government, providing services to local tribal members, but the tribe had always kept open the possibility of using the location for economic development. Eventually, the tribe opened satellite offices in Traverse City and outside of Charlevoix, rendering the Whitewater Township office somewhat redundant.

The Whitewater Township parcel's 1989 purchase date was important under the Indian Gaming Regulatory Act because the act generally prohibited gaming on lands acquired after October 1988, when it became operative. The

---

[*]   The material on the Turtle Creek Casino is excerpted from Matthew L.M. Fletcher, The Eagle Returns: The Legal History of the Grand Traverse Band of Ottawa and Chippewa Indians (2011).

Grand Traverse Band believed that the parcel met an exception that would become known as the "restored lands/restored tribes" exception. The major weakness in this theory was that no court had ever decided a case interpreting the "restored lands/restored tribes" exception, so it was an unknown. Moreover, the tribe would have to hire expert witnesses to prove that the tribe was a "restored tribe," and especially, to prove that the lands upon which Turtle Creek rested were "restored lands." The fact that the theory was untested in federal court and would require the tribe to invest a large amount of resources to conduct the historical research counseled against asserting the theory unless as a last resort.

A federal court judge in Grand Rapids, Judge David W. McKeague, issued a ruling in a gaming case involving the Keweenaw Bay Indian Community that provided the second legal theory the Grand Traverse Band could use to open a casino at the Whitewater Township location. The case, Keweenaw Bay Indian Community v. United States, 914 F.Supp. 476 (W.D.Mich.1996), stood for the proposition that the State of Michigan agreed in the 1993 gaming compacts to allow any of the compacting tribes to commence gaming on any lands then part of the tribe's reservation. The Grand Traverse Band, similarly, believed that the Whitewater Township parcel, purchased and placed into trust in 1989, was part of the Grand Traverse Band's reservation lands when the compacts were signed in 1993. Because the second legal theory actually had the stamp of approval from a federal court, the Grand Traverse Band believed that it was the stronger legal theory.

Using this second legal theory, the Grand Traverse Band was able to avoid a preliminary ruling from the federal court shutting down the casino. However, in 1998, the Sixth Circuit reversed Judge McKeague's ruling on the second legal theory, Keweenaw Bay Indian Community v. United States, 136 F.3d 469 (6th Cir.), cert. denied, 525 U.S. 929 (1998), forcing the Grand Traverse Band to rely upon the first theory, the unknown.

In 1999, in a major preliminary ruling, Judge Douglas W. Hillman decided that the Turtle Creek Casino could continue operating, but asked the National Indian Gaming Commission to issue an opinion on whether the casino was authorized by the Indian Gaming Regulatory Act. Grand Traverse Band of Ottawa and Chippewa Indians v. Office of the United States Attorney for the Western District of Michigan, 46 F. Supp. 2d 689 (W.D.Mich.1999). He tentatively accepted the tribe's theory on the "restored lands/restored tribes" exception.

Judge Hillman believed that the Whitewater Township parcel met criteria he read into the statute relating to the question of whether the land was "restored" as understood in the gaming act. First, the land met "geographic" criteria, meaning that the land was located well within the traditional territory of the Grand Traverse Band. While there was some question as to whether the parcel was located within the 1836 reservation boundaries, it was still part of the tribe's historical lands. Second, the land met "temporal" criteria, meaning the tribe had purchased the land for economic development purposes within a few short years of receiving reaffirmation of its federal recognition. In fact, while the United States had extended federal recognition to the tribe in 1980, because of a dispute over the tribe's constitution the United States had refused to take much land into trust for the tribe until 1988. As such, the United States took the Whitewater Township parcel into trust within a year or so of the tribe's first land purchases, around the same time the government took into trust several parcels that now constitute the bulk of the Grand Traverse Reservation. This land, Judge Hillman concluded, was intended to be part of the restoration of the lands of the Grand Traverse Reservation. Third, Judge Hillman thought it very important that the Whitewater Township parcel was probably located within the exterior boundaries of the 1836 reservation.

Judge Hillman also concluded that the Grand Traverse Band met the definition of a "restored tribe" for purposes of the gaming act. He noted that the plain meaning of the term "restored" was "brought back or put back into a former position or condition." Since the Grand Traverse Band once had been federally recognized, at least until the 1870s, then administratively terminated, and then extended federal recognition in 1980, that the Grand Traverse Band's federal recognition had been "restored."

According to the terms of Judge Hillman's order, the parties would have to ask for an opinion from the National Indian Gaming Commission on how to interpret the "restored lands/restored tribes" exception, and whether the specific facts of the Grand Traverse Band fit the exception. Once again, the tribe, the United States, and the State of Michigan submitted mountains of papers and evidence on the question, this time to the general counsel of the National Indian Gaming Commission, Kevin K. Washburn.

It was the first time that a federal court had asked the commission to opine on the "restored lands/restored tribes" exception, but the Solicitor's Office in the Department of the Interior had issued opinions called "Indian Lands Opinions" in the cases of the Little Traverse Bay Bands of Odawa Indians and the Pokagon Band of Potawatomi Indians.

General Counsel Washburn adopted Judge Hillman's general framework for determining whether the Whitewater Township parcel constituted "restored lands" under the Indian Gaming Regulatory Act. He relied upon the tribe's exhaustive ethnohistory of the eastern shore of Grand Traverse Bay that demonstrated a significant presence of Grand Traverse Band people from before treaty times and on through to the present day. He also found that the tribe had purchased the land and put it into trust with the United States during the first major push the tribe made to restore as much land as possible to tribal ownership and control in the Grand Traverse Bay region. He concluded, as Judge Hillman presupposed, that the Turtle Creek Casino rested on lands that constituted restored lands, as that term was used in the gaming act. He also agreed with Judge Hillman that the Grand Traverse Band was a tribe that had been restored to federal recognition.

General Counsel Washburn released the opinion letter in August 2001. Shortly thereafter, the United States Department of Justice, which had been prosecuting the case, accepted the opinion and asked to be dismissed from the litigation. This left only the State of Michigan, which continued to oppose the Turtle Creek Casino. The Grand Traverse Band sought, and received, an expedited trial schedule for January 2002 before Judge Hillman, sitting without a jury.

The tribe prevailed at trial, and again on appeal to the Sixth Circuit. Grand Traverse Band of Ottawa and Chippewa Indians v. Office of the United States Attorney for the Western District of Michigan, 198 F.Supp. 2d 920 (W.D.Mich.2002), aff'd, 369 F.3d 960 (6th Cir.2004).

Still, similarly situated tribes might now be forced to navigate new objections to their eligibility for trust lands acquisition raised in the aftermath of Carcieri v. Salazar, 555 U.S. 379 (2009). E.g., Big Lagoon Rancheria v. State of California, 789 F.3d 947 (9th Cir.2015) (en banc); Confederated Tribes of Grand Ronde Community of Oregon v. Jewell, 75 F. Supp. 3d 387 (D.D.C.2014), on appeal (D.C.Cir.) (No. 14–5326).

Indian tribes that have been federally recognized have also faced difficulties in moving off-reservation in their efforts to seek better gaming markets.

MICHIGAN V. BAY MILLS INDIAN COMMUNITY

Supreme Court of the United States, 2014.
___ U.S. ___, 134 S.Ct. 2024, 188 L.Ed.2d 1071.

* * *

JUSTICE KAGAN delivered the opinion of the Court.

* * *

Pursuant to the [Indian Gaming Regulatory] Act, Michigan and Bay Mills, a federally recognized Indian Tribe, entered into a compact in 1993. * * * The compact empowers Bay Mills to conduct class III gaming on "Indian lands"; conversely, it prohibits the Tribe from doing so outside that territory. * * * The compact also contains a dispute resolution mechanism, which sends to arbitration any contractual differences the parties cannot settle on their own. * * * Since entering into the compact, Bay Mills has operated class III gaming, as authorized, on its reservation in Michigan's Upper Peninsula.

In 2010, Bay Mills opened another class III gaming facility in Vanderbilt, a small village in Michigan's Lower Peninsula about 125 miles from the Tribe's reservation. Bay Mills had bought the Vanderbilt property with accrued interest from a federal appropriation, which Congress had made to compensate the Tribe for 19th-century takings of its ancestral lands. See Michigan Indian Land Claims Settlement Act, 111 Stat. 2652. Congress had directed that a portion of the appropriated funds go into a "Land Trust" whose earnings the Tribe was to use to improve or purchase property. According to the legislation, any land so acquired "shall be held as Indian lands are held." § 107(a)(3), id., at 2658. Citing that provision, Bay Mills contended that the Vanderbilt property was "Indian land" under IGRA and the compact; and the Tribe thus claimed authority to operate a casino there.

Michigan disagreed: The State sued Bay Mills in federal court to enjoin operation of the new casino, alleging that the facility violated IGRA and the compact because it was located outside Indian lands. The same day Michigan filed suit, the federal Department of the Interior issued an opinion concluding (as the State's complaint said) that the Tribe's use of Land Trust earnings to purchase the Vanderbilt property did not convert it into Indian territory. * * * The District Court entered a preliminary injunction against Bay Mills, which promptly shut down the new casino and took an interlocutory appeal. * * * Although no injunction is currently in effect, Bay Mills has not reopened the Vanderbilt casino.

* * *

III

IGRA partially abrogates tribal sovereign immunity in § 2710(d)(7)(A)(ii)—but this case, viewed most naturally, falls outside that term's ambit. The provision, as noted above, authorizes a State to sue a tribe to "enjoin a class III gaming activity located on Indian lands and conducted in violation of any Tribal-State compact." * * * A key phrase in that abrogation is "on Indian lands"—three words reflecting IGRA's overall scope (and repeated some two dozen times in the statute). A State's suit to enjoin gaming activity on Indian lands * * * falls within § 2710(d)(7)(A)(ii); a similar suit to stop gaming activity off Indian lands does not. And that creates a fundamental problem for Michigan. After all, the very premise of this suit—the reason Michigan thinks Bay Mills is acting unlawfully—is that the Vanderbilt casino is outside Indian lands. * * * By dint of that theory, a suit to enjoin gaming in Vanderbilt is correspondingly outside § 2710(d)(7)(A)(ii)'s abrogation of immunity.

Michigan first attempts to fit this suit within § 2710(d)(7)(A)(ii) by relocating the "class III gaming activity" to which it is objecting. True enough, Michigan states, the Vanderbilt casino lies outside Indian lands. But Bay Mills "authorized, licensed, and operated" that casino from within its own reservation. Brief for Michigan 20. According to the State, that necessary administrative action—no less than, say, dealing craps—is "class III gaming activity," and because it occurred on Indian land, this suit to enjoin it can go forward.

But that argument comes up snake eyes, because numerous provisions of IGRA show that "class III gaming activity" means just what it sounds like—the stuff involved in playing class III games. For example, § 2710(d)(3)(C)(i) refers to "the licensing and regulation of [a class III gaming] activity" and § 2710(d)(9) concerns the "operation of a class III gaming activity." Those phrases make perfect sense if "class III gaming activity" is what goes on in a casino—each roll of the dice and spin of the wheel. But they lose all meaning if, as Michigan argues, "class III gaming activity" refers equally to the off-site licensing or operation of the games. (Just plug in those words and see what happens.) See also §§ 2710(b)(2)(A), (b)(4)(A), (c)(4), (d)(1)(A) (similarly referring to class II or III "gaming activity"). The same holds true throughout the statute. Section 2717(a)(1) specifies fees to be paid by "each gaming operation that conducts a class II or class III gaming activity"—signifying that the gaming activity is the gambling in the poker hall, not the proceeds of the off-site administrative authority. And §§ 2706(a)(5) and 2713(b)(1) together describe a federal agency's power to "clos[e] a gaming activity" for "substantial violation[s]" of law—e.g., to shut down crooked blackjack tables, not the tribal regulatory body meant to oversee them. Indeed, consider IGRA's very first finding: Many tribes, Congress stated, "have licensed gaming activities on Indian lands," thereby necessitating federal regulation. § 2701(1). The "gaming activit[y]" is (once again) the gambling. And that means § 2710(d)(7)(A)(ii) does not allow Michigan's suit even if Bay Mills took action on its reservation to license or oversee the Vanderbilt facility.

Stymied under § 2710(d)(7)(A)(ii), Michigan next urges us to adopt a "holistic method" of interpreting IGRA that would allow a State to sue a tribe for illegal gaming off, no less than on, Indian lands. Brief for Michigan 30. Michigan asks here that we consider "IGRA's text and structure as a whole." * * * But (with one briefly raised exception) Michigan fails to identify any specific textual or structural features of the statute to support its proposed result. Rather, Michigan highlights a (purported) anomaly of the statute as written: that it enables a State to sue a tribe for illegal gaming inside, but not outside, Indian country. "[W]hy," Michigan queries, "would Congress authorize a state to obtain a federal injunction against illegal tribal gaming on Indian lands, but not on lands subject to the state's own sovereign jurisdiction?" Reply Brief 1. That question has no answer, Michigan argues: Whatever words Congress may have used in IGRA, it could not have intended that senseless outcome. See Brief for Michigan 28.

But this Court does not revise legislation, as Michigan proposes, just because the text as written creates an apparent anomaly as to some subject it does not address. Truth be told, such anomalies often arise from statutes, if for no other reason than that Congress typically legislates by parts—addressing one thing without examining all others that might merit comparable treatment. Rejecting a similar argument that a statutory anomaly (between property and non-property taxes) made "not a whit of sense," we explained in one recent case that "Congress wrote the statute it wrote"—meaning, a statute going so far and no further. * * * The same could be said of IGRA's abrogation of tribal immunity for gaming "on Indian lands." This Court has no roving license, in even ordinary cases of statutory interpretation, to disregard clear language simply on the view that (in Michigan's words) Congress "must have intended" something broader. Brief for Michigan 32. And still less do we have that warrant when the consequence would be to expand an abrogation of immunity, because (as explained earlier) "Congress must 'unequivocally' express [its] purpose" to subject a tribe to litigation. * * *

In any event, IGRA's history and design provide a more than intelligible answer to the question Michigan poses about why Congress would have confined a State's authority to sue a tribe as § 2710(d)(7)(A)(ii) does. Congress adopted IGRA in response to this Court's decision in California v. Cabazon Band of Mission Indians, 480 U.S. 202, 221–222 * * * (1987), which held that States lacked any regulatory authority over gaming on Indian lands. Cabazon left fully intact a State's regulatory power over tribal gaming outside Indian territory—which, as we will soon show, is capacious. * * * So the problem Congress set out to address in IGRA (Cabazon's ouster of state authority) arose in Indian lands alone. And the solution Congress devised, naturally enough, reflected that fact. * * * Everything—literally everything—in IGRA affords tools (for either state or federal officials) to regulate gaming on Indian lands, and nowhere else. Small surprise that IGRA's abrogation of tribal immunity does that as well.

And the resulting world, when considered functionally, is not nearly so "enigma[tic]" as Michigan suggests. * * * True enough, a State lacks the ability to sue a tribe for illegal gaming when that activity occurs off the reservation. But a State, on its own lands, has many other powers over tribal gaming that it does not possess (absent consent) in Indian territory. Unless federal law provides differently, "Indians going beyond reservation boundaries" are subject to any generally applicable state law. * * * So, for example, Michigan could, in the first instance, deny a license to Bay Mills for an off-reservation casino. See Mich. Comp. Laws Ann. §§ 432.206–432.206a (West 2001). And if Bay Mills went ahead anyway, Michigan could bring suit against tribal officials or employees (rather than the Tribe itself) seeking an injunction for, say, gambling without a license. See § 432.220; see also § 600.3801(1)(a) (West 2013) (designating illegal gambling facilities as public nuisances). As this Court has stated before, analogizing to Ex parte Young, 209 U.S. 123 * * * (1908), tribal immunity does not bar such a suit for injunctive relief against individuals, including tribal officers, responsible for unlawful conduct. * * * And to the extent civil remedies proved inadequate, Michigan could resort to its criminal law, prosecuting anyone who maintains—or even frequents—an unlawful gambling establishment. See Mich. Comp. Laws Ann. §§ 432.218 (West 2001), 750.303, 750.309 (West 2004). In short * * *, the panoply of tools Michigan can use to enforce its law on its own lands—no less than the suit it could bring on Indian lands under § 2710(d)(7)(A)(ii)—can shutter, quickly and permanently, an illegal casino.

Finally, if a State really wants to sue a tribe for gaming outside Indian lands, the State need only bargain for a waiver of immunity. Under IGRA, a State and tribe negotiating a compact "may include * * * remedies for breach of contract," 25 U.S.C. § 2710(d)(3)(C)(v)—including a provision allowing the State to bring an action against the tribe in the circumstances presented here. States have more than enough leverage to obtain such terms because a tribe cannot conduct class III gaming on its lands without a compact, see § 2710(d)(1)(C), and cannot sue to enforce a State's duty to negotiate a compact in good faith * * * . So as Michigan forthrightly acknowledges, "a party dealing with a tribe in contract negotiations has the power to protect itself by refusing to deal absent the tribe's waiver of sovereign immunity from suit." Brief for Michigan 40. And many States have taken that path. See Brief for Seminole Tribe of Florida et al. as Amici Curiae 12–22 (listing compacts with waivers of tribal immunity). To be sure, Michigan did not: As noted earlier, the compact at issue here, instead of authorizing judicial remedies, sends disputes to arbitration and expressly retains each party's sovereign immunity. * * * But Michigan—like any State—could have insisted on a different deal (and indeed may do so now for the future, because the current compact has expired and remains in effect only until the parties negotiate a new one * * * . And in that event, the limitation Congress placed on IGRA's abrogation of tribal immunity—whether or not anomalous as an abstract matter—would have made no earthly difference.

* * *

NOTES

1.   The Vanderbilt casino tract at issue in *Bay Mills*, purchased in 2010, is after-acquired land under IGRA. Moreover, it was (and remains, as of this writing) fee land. The Bay Mills Indian Community prevailed in this matter by asserting its immunity from suit. But assuming a court reached the merits of the validity of the casino, what exceptions to the bar on after-acquired lands could the tribe invoke?

The tribe stated its reliance on the Michigan Indian Land Claims Settlement Act, Pub. L. No. 105–143, 111 Stat. 2652 (1997). The tribe claimed to have purchased lands using a trust fund established by the Act. Section 107(a)(3) of the statute provided, "Any land acquired with funds from the Land Trust shall be held as Indian lands are held." Does this provision automatically transform land purchased using trust fund money gaming eligible as "Indian lands?" See 25 U.S.C. § 2703(4) (defining "Indian lands").

The 1997 Act is a land settlement act. Does the purchase of lands using settlement funds automatically transform the land into gaming-eligible land under the so-called settlement of a land claim exception to the bar on gaming on after-acquired lands? See 25 U.S.C. § 2719(b)(1)(B)(i).

The Vanderbilt area is located more than 100 miles from the Bay Mills reservation. Could this parcel qualify as lands within the boundaries of the tribe's former reservation? See 25 U.S.C. § 2719(a)(2)(i). The Little Traverse Bay Bands of Odawa Indians sued Bay Mills even before the State of Michigan hoping to shut down the casino, arguing that the Vanderbilt area was primarily their traditional territory.

2. The Sault Ste. Marie Tribe of Chippewa Indians, along with three other Michigan tribes, is a beneficiary of the Michigan Indian Land Claims Settlement Act. The Sault Tribe's portion of the statute provides that land acquired by the tribe from settlement funds "shall" be held in trust by the Secretary of the Interior. See Pub. L. No. 105–143, § 108(f) ("Any lands acquired using amounts from interest or other income of the Self-Sufficiency Fund shall be held in trust by the Secretary for the benefit of the tribe."). This is a markedly different, and apparently stronger, provision than the statute applicable to Bay Mills purchases.

In 2014, the Sault Tribe, which is a neighbor to the Bay Mills Indian Community in the Upper Peninsula of Michigan, petitioned the Secretary of Interior to take land into trust for gaming purposes in Lansing, Michigan, and also near the Detroit Metro Airport in Wayne County, Michigan. What are the tribe's chances of successfully opening a gaming facility in those locations?

NATION BUILDING NOTE: HOUSING

As Indian people suffered through a history of loss of their homelands, the federal government induced tribes to give up their old homes with the assurance of building new ones. This promise was fulfilled only sporadically, and even when housing was provided, HUD and the BIA constructed substandard housing without regard for deep-rooted tribal customs.

Indian people continue to face some of the worst housing conditions in the country. According to the National Congress of American Indians, 40% of on-reservation housing is considered substandard (compared to 6% outside of Indian country) and nearly one-third of homes on reservations are overcrowded. Less than half of the homes on reservations are connected to public sewer systems, 16% lack indoor plumbing, and 7.5% lack kitchen utilities. Seventy percent of the existing housing stock in Indian country is in need of upgrades and repairs, many of them extensive. HUD recently paid out $12.4 million to 18 tribes to address dangerous mold in over 1,000 homes.

Increasingly, tribes are exercising their tribal sovereignty to design and implement their own housing and community development infrastructure for their citizens. As a beginning, the tribes made a significant breakthrough in 1974 when they succeeded in persuading Congress to include tribes as governments eligible to compete for HUD block grant funds. In response to tribal initiatives and lobbying, Congress passed the Native American Housing and Self-Determination Act (NAHASDA) of 1996, which consolidated federal housing funds through grants to the tribes and their Tribal Designated Housing Entities (TDHEs). Tribes, now in charge of their own housing programs, are building sustainable and culturally relevant homes and renovating existing ones. There are almost 500 TDHEs in Indian country today. These laws have not only provided significant and flexible funding, but have also lessened the tribes' sole reliance on the BIA.

Gaming revenue allows some tribes to develop housing in a more expansive and self-sufficient way. An example is the Fond du Lac Band of Lake Superior Chippewa, which has invested large amounts of gaming revenue for construction of family homes for low-income families and a state-of-the-art assisted living community for senior citizens. With the help of gaming revenue, the Band is able to do a much better job meeting the community needs than when it relied solely on government programs.

Acting as a self-sufficient government in housing does not mean refusing federal financial assistance. Executive Director of Minnesota Chippewa Tribes Gary Frazer explains:

> "Some think if you are self-sufficient you don't need government funds anymore. That's not the point. The point is to use the government funds like any county, city or municipality. They all use government funds. That does not mean they are not self-sufficient. Self-sufficiency means you are able to provide for those on your reservation, and one of the ways to provide for them is to use your sovereignty and seek program funding."

Housing remains a significant problem in Indian country—it amounts to overcoming more than a century of neglect—but now the tribal role is deeper and broader as tribal housing authorities are spearheading development. As tribes reclaim responsibility for housing programs, they are able to exercise their sovereignty in a way that far better addresses the needs of their people.

For more details, see generally A Quiet Crisis: Federal Funding and Unmet Needs in Indian Country, U.S. Comm'n on Civil Rights (2003); Fiscal Year 2016 Budget Request: Promoting Self-Determination, Modernizing the Trust Relationship, Nat'l Cong. of Am. Ind., 119–21 (2015); Sharon Schmickle, Casino Profits Give Tribes a Surge of Confidence, MinnPost, Dec. 13, 2012; David S. Edmunds et al., Tribal Housing, Codesign, and Cultural Sovereignty, Sci.Tech. & Hum. Values, Nov. 2013; Nate Seltenrich, Healthier Tribal Housing: Combining the Best of Old and New, 120 Envtl. Health Persp. 12 (Dec. 2012).

CHAPTER TEN

INDIAN RELIGION AND CULTURE

■ ■ ■

American Indian tribes have rich spiritual traditions that explain humans' place in the world, foster connections with the supernatural, and develop values to guide community behavior. In many Indian cultures, religion is interwoven with relationships, rituals, stories, and places. Navajos, for example, have many practices identified as elements of the Navajo "religion" such as a spiritual ethic, cosmology, deities, creation story, ceremonial chantways, daily rituals, and sacred sites. But in the Navajo language, it may be more meaningful to describe these practices as an entire way of living in harmony with one's surroundings, relatives, and circumstances. James Zion explains that one of the fundamental principles of Navajo life is the phrase "*sa'ah naaghai bik'eh hozho*, which states that 'the conditions for health and well-being are harmony within and connection to the physical/spiritual world.'" James W. Zion, *Navajo Therapeutic Jurisprudence*, 18 Touro L.Rev. 563, 603 (2002) (quoting Elizabeth L. Lewton & Victoria Bydone, *Identity and Healing in Three Navajo Religious Traditions: Sa'ah Naaghai Bik'eh Hozho*, 14 Med. Anthropology Q. 476, 478 (2000)).

American Indian religious experiences are quite diverse and they are evolving. These religions have also been poorly understood by outsiders. Former Cherokee Principal Chief Wilma Mankiller once said that "stereotypes . . . particularly with regard to spirituality" persist "because of the dearth of accurate information about Native people." Wilma Mankiller, Every Day is a Good Day: Reflections by Contemporary Indigenous Women 13 (2004). The hundreds of tribal religions and cultures are often lumped into generalities about Indian relationships with the natural world, including the common impression that for Indians, "everything is sacred." On the other hand, when scholars examine the specifics of any traditional tribal religion, they must take care to develop adequate cultural familiarity and respect particular privacy norms. See Kristen A. Carpenter, *Limiting Principles and Empowering Practices in American Indian Religious Freedoms*, 45 Conn.L.Rev. 387 (2012) (describing Indian religions and legal challenges to them).

"Traditional tribal religions" are those associated with the indigenous spiritual experience of each tribe, that is, Navajo, Euchee, Wenatchee, and so on. These religions often begin with a creation story that traces the group's origin as a distinct people to a place of emergence or migration. Some sacred sites mark a location where the people have interacted with the creator or other sacred elements. A creation story or cycle of stories often situates the tribe in a particular place in the natural landscape and sets forth a way of life—including values and practices—that allows the people to thrive there. In many such stories, the people and natural world are mutually dependent, with humans having obligations or covenants that they must perform in order to live in harmony with the plants, animals, waters, mountains, and other features of the natural world. The traditional religion often pervades identity, kinship, governance, subsistence, and social order and often serves as a way to define and maintain the tribal existence, even in contemporary times. As Hopi clan leaders declared in 1951, "Our land, our religion, and our life are one." John D. Loftin, Religion And Hopi Life 116 (2d ed. 2003).

Depending on the tribe, so called traditional tribal religious and cultural practices today may include prayers, dances, and songs that take place at ceremonial grounds and sacred sites in the tribe's natural landscape. Certain rituals are recurring (e.g., sun dances among certain Plains tribes and stomp dances among some Oklahoma tribes) while others mark occasions (i.e., a coming of age, marriage, or burial). To this very day traditional religious practices are undertaken for the collective of the tribe, as much as for any individual purposes. For example, a Navajo Nation Resolution provides:

> This religion, Beauty Way of Life, holds this land sacred and that we, the Navajo People, must always care for it. Through this sacred covenant, this sacred ancestral homeland is the home and hogan of all Navajo people. Further, if the Navajo left their homelands, all prayers and religion would be ineffective and lost forever.

Navajo Nation Council Res. CD–107–94 (Dec. 13, 1994). Tribes, unlike the federal and state governments of the United States, are not necessarily bound by the Free Exercise or Establishment Clauses of the federal Constitution. While tribes may choose to adopt laws along these lines, others intertwine secular and sacred practices.

Some tribal religious practices are led by medicine men or women, while others by chiefs and traditionalists. In some communities, the people take medicine to heal or to promote insight and understanding. American Indians across a number of tribes participate in the peyote religion which has roots in ancient traditions. Indigenous use of peyote dates back to at least 1600 C.E., by the Huichol and Tarahumara Indians of Northern Mexico, and possibly back to the Aztecs in 8000 B.C.E. In North America, Kiowa-Apaches, Kiowas, and Comanches used religious peyote in the 1860s, and the Native American Church (NAC) was officially chartered in

1918 foster and promote the religious beliefs of the several tribes of Indians with the practice of the "Peyote Sacrament." Practitioners attest to the healing power of the plant, the fellowship among peyotists, and the moral code of the NAC. Some view the peyote religion as a syncretic one, drawing from indigenous and Christian beliefs and practices.

Some Indian people are members of organizations that draw from tribal and Christian practices, such as Cherokee Baptist churches where, for example, Christian hymns may be sung with Cherokee lyrics that invoke concepts from both worldviews. Still other Indians are practicing Catholics, Methodists, Latter Day Saints, Muslims, Buddhists, Jews, and so on. In some instances, religious institutions have established missions in tribal communities, while in other instances, individuals have gravitated to a particular faith just like anyone else in the United States might.

Notwithstanding the ancient origins of many tribal religions, Indians were often perceived as godless savages by early Europeans. As described in earlier chapters, religion was a flashpoint in the conquest and colonization of North America. From the fourteenth century, monarchs invoked Christian theology and papal law in justification of their New World policies, using indigenous "heathenry" as a justification for military incursions and land seizures, for example. At the same time, some Catholic thinkers argued that Indians were human beings entitled to a measure of natural law protection from the Spanish, if only the right to be conquered and converted for their own benefit. In the sixteenth and seventeenth centuries, French and Spanish colonization efforts worked closely with churches to establish missions across tribal communities, while some of the English colonies and colonists isolated Indians in "praying towns" so they could be instructed away from whites.

Once the United States gained independence, federal lawmakers quickly grasped that the eradication of Indian cultures was a key step in breaking up tribes and paving the way for political and geographic domination by states and the federal government. At the same time, policymakers believed that encouraging Indians to "put aside all savage ways" would help them achieve "salvation" through Christianity. Report of Commissioner of Indian Affairs W.A. Jones (Oct. 16, 1902), reprinted in 2 Wilcomb E. Washburn, The American Indian And The United States: A Documentary History 724, 727 (1973). These measures targeted individual Indians and whole tribes alike. Beginning in 1869, President Grant's "Peace Policy" provided contracts to Christian missions, assigning them to reservations and granting federal funding for the purpose of bringing civilization to the Indians. Federally funded boarding schools with a mission to "Kill the Indian in him and Save the Man" targeted the children of traditional Indian communities for removal from their families and educated them in English, Christianity, and manual labor skills.

In 1883, the Commissioner of Indian Affairs issued rules for the "Courts of Indian Offenses," applicable on reservations nationwide. As reissued in 1892, the rules prohibited Indian religious dances (punishable by 10 days withholding of rations or 10 days' imprisonment) and the practices of medicine men (10–30 days' imprisonment for the first offense, not more than 6 months' imprisonment for subsequent offenses). See House Exec. Doc no. 1, 52d. Cong, 2d Sess., serial 3088, pp. 28–31, reprinted in Francis Paul Prucha, ed., Documents of United States Indian Policy 185–187 (3d. ed. 2000). In 1890, the Seventh Cavalry of the U.S. Army famously attacked and killed over 200 Indians engaged in a religious revival ceremony called the Ghost Dance. See James Mooney, The Ghost Dance Religion and Wounded Knee, in Fourteenth Annual Report of the Bureau of Ethnology, Part 2, 867–72 (1973 reprint).

In 1902, the federal Indian Commissioner issued an order to reservation-based Indian agents providing: "Indian dances and so-called Indian feasts should be prohibited. In many cases, these dances and feasts are simply subterfuges to cover degrading acts and to disguise immoral purposes. You are directed to use your best efforts in the suppression of these evils." Report of Commissioner of Indian Affairs W.A. Jones, supra, at 725. In 1904, the federal government criminalized Indian religious dances, making, for example, the practice of the Sun Dance punishable by ten days in prison or ten days' denial of food rations. Around the same time, Indian Affairs declared peyote to be a narcotic and waged an assault on the peyote religion; in 1908 and 1909, for example, an Indian Affairs "investigator" reported that he had destroyed 176,400 peyote buttons, an act of incredible offense, sacrilege, and waste to the practitioners for whom it was a holy sacrament.

As late as 1921, the Commissioner of Indian Affairs advocated a sweeping governmental policy of suppression of traditional Indian religious and cultural practices:

> The sun-dance, and all other similar dances and so-called religious ceremonies are considered "Indian offences" under existing regulations, and corrective penalties are provided. I regard such restrictions as applicable to any dance which * * * involves the reckless giving away of property * * * frequent or prolonged periods of celebration * * * in fact any disorderly or plainly excessive performance that promotes superstitious cruelty, licentiousness, idleness, danger to health, and shiftless indifference to family welfare.

Quoted in Felix Cohen, Handbook of Federal Indian Law 175 (1941).

While some support for Indian cultural traditions surfaced in the 1930s, federal policy began to change in earnest in the 1960s and 1970s. Inspired both by tribal activism and federal policy changes, tribes nationwide started to revitalize their political, economic, and cultural institutions. In 1970, President Richard M. Nixon announced a federal policy in favor of tribal "self-determination," inspiring dozens of new statutes and programs to support tribal autonomy over education, economics, government, and culture. The practice of tribal religions was an important component, particularly in light of historic persecution of Indian religions described above.

In 1978, Congress passed the American Indian Religious Freedom Act (AIRFA), expressly repudiating past policies and declaring:

> [I]t shall be the federal policy of the United States to protect and preserve for American Indians their inherent right of freedom to believe, express, and exercise the traditional religions of the American Indian, Eskimo, Aleut, and Native Hawaiians, including but not limited to access to sites, use and possession of sacred objects, and the freedom to worship through ceremonials and traditional rites.

Other statutes, such as the Native American Grave Protection and Repatriation Act of 1990, protecting the cemeteries, human remains, and sacred objects of tribes, followed.

Today, American Indians continue to encounter a complex set of contending forces when attempting to assert their basic human rights of religious and cultural self-expression. The dark years of Indian removal, assimilation, and allotment cast a long shadow, such that many sacred sites are outside of tribal territories and religious objects still being sold illegally. Moreover, tribal religion and culture still remain exotic and incomprehensible to many courts, legislators, and agency officials. Long-held racial stereotypes of Indian beliefs, customs, and practices continue to be perpetuated by the dominant society's media industries and cultural institutions. See generally Philip J. Deloria, Playing Indian (1998); Devon Mihesuah, American Indians: Stereotypes and Realities (1996).

Is it any wonder, then, that Indians have had to struggle so hard to protect their religion and culture within the alien institutions and categories of an externally imposed legal and political system? The very categories suggested by the separate treatment of "religion" and "culture" and "property" reflects the inadequacies of the dominant society's categories in trying to accommodate Indian spiritual beliefs and value systems. For most tribal Indians, culture is conterminous with religion, as both concepts encompass the spiritual dimension of a human being living in harmony with all persons and nature. See generally Vine Deloria, The World We Used to Live In: Remembering the Powers of the Medicine Man (2006).

The historical inability of federal and state courts to fit claims of Indian "religious freedom" into the pigeonholes of the Bill of Rights creates a continuing tension. The framework for evaluating Indian appeals for legal protection of traditional spiritual practices and beliefs has origins and purposes that are deeply rooted in European-derived values and traditions. In that Westernized framework, organized churches represent religion, and government's role is to remain apart from and not hamper the individual pursuit of a church-based religion. Statements of the Founding Fathers, such as Thomas Jefferson's declaration that the First Amendment's Establishment Clause had built "a wall of separation between Church and State," *Letter from President Thomas Jefferson to the Danbury Baptists*, Jan. 1, 1802, in 15 The Writings of Thomas Jefferson 281–82 (Albert E. Bergh ed. 1904), show that the institutions of the United States' political and legal system were not focused on protecting the "religion" of indigenous tribal peoples whose essential spirituality pervades all aspects of their beings and understandings.

Recall as well that the Founding Fathers believed that the "Savage as the Wolf" would ultimately vanish from the cultural landscape of the United States as the country became more "civilized." They would have found it hard to believe that more than two centuries after the creation of the American Republic, Indian tribes were still fighting to protect their basic human rights to cultural survival and religious freedom, and calling upon the legal and political system the Founders created for support in this historic struggle. See Allison M. Dussias, *Ghost Dance and Holy Ghost: The Echoes of Nineteenth-Century Christianization Policy in Twentieth-Century Native American Free Exercise Cases*, 49 Stan.L.Rev. 773 (1997).

In the summer and fall of 2016, thousands of Indians camped out along the Cannonball River in North Dakota to show solidarity with the Standing Rock Sioux Tribe's challenge to construction of the Dakota Access Pipeline, a $3.8 billion project that would transport half a million barrels of crude oil per day across five states to other other lines and refineries in the Gulf of Mexico. The pipeline was slated to be built within a half mile of the Standing Rock Sioux Reservation, traveling across treaty-guaranteed lands, under the tribe's main source of drinking water, and through sacred sites. Lawyers for the tribe agrued that an oil spill at the site would threaten to the tribe's culture and way of life. As this casebook goes to print, the Obama administration has issued a halt to construction in certain contested areas, and called on the relevant federal departments and agencies to assess both the adequacy of consultation with tribes regarding this project and long term reform to the tribal-federal consultation process. In this and many other cases, Indian people's tenacious insistence on maintaining distinctive spiritual traditions struggles to find meaningful expression or legal protection in the categories of religious belief and property rights recognized by U.S. law.

SECTION A. PROTECTION OF AMERICAN INDIAN SACRED LANDS AND SITES

LYNG V. NORTHWEST INDIAN CEMETERY PROTECTIVE ASSOCIATION

Supreme Court of the United States, 1988.
485 U.S. 439, 108 S.Ct. 1319, 99 L.Ed.2d 534.

JUSTICE O'CONNOR delivered the opinion of the Court.

This case requires us to consider whether the First Amendment's Free Exercise Clause prohibits the Government from permitting timber harvesting in, or constructing a road through, a portion of a National Forest that has traditionally been used for religious purposes by members of three American Indian tribes in northwestern California. We conclude that it does not.

I

As part of a project to create a paved 75-mile road linking two California towns, Gasquet and Orleans, the United States Forest Service has upgraded 49 miles of previously unpaved roads on federal land. In order to complete this project (the G-O road), the Forest Service must build a 6-mile paved segment through the Chimney Rock section of the Six Rivers National Forest. That section of the forest is situated between two other portions of the road that are already complete.

In 1977, the Forest Service issued a draft environmental impact statement that discussed proposals for upgrading an existing unpaved road that runs through the Chimney Rock area. In response to comments on the draft statement, the Forest Service commissioned a study of American Indian cultural and religious sites in the area. The Hoopa Valley Indian Reservation adjoins the Six Rivers National Forest, and the Chimney Rock area has historically been used for religious purposes by Yurok, Karok, and Tolowa Indians. The commissioned study, which was completed in 1979, found that the entire area "is significant as an integral and indispens[able] part of Indian religious conceptualization and practice." Specific sites are used for certain rituals, and "successful use of the [area] is dependent upon and facilitated by certain qualities of the physical environment, the most important of which are privacy, silence, and an undisturbed natural setting." The study concluded that constructing a road along any of the available routes "would cause serious and irreparable damage to the sacred areas which are an integral and necessary part of the belief systems and lifeway of Northwest California Indian peoples." Accordingly, the report recommended that the G-O road not be completed.

In 1982, the Forest Service decided not to adopt this recommendation, and it prepared a final environmental impact statement for construction of the road. The Regional Forester selected a route that avoided archeological sites and was removed as far as possible from the sites used by contemporary Indians for specific spiritual activities. Alternative routes that would have avoided the Chimney Rock area altogether were rejected because they would have required the acquisition of private land, had serious soil stability problems, and would in any event have traversed areas having ritualistic value to American Indians. At about the same time, the Forest Service adopted a management plan allowing for the harvesting of significant amounts of timber in this area of the forest. The management plan provided for one-half mile protective zones around all the religious sites identified in the report that had been commissioned in connection with the G-O road.

After exhausting their administrative remedies, respondents—an Indian organization, individual Indians, nature organizations and individual members of those organizations, and the State of California— challenged both the road-building and timber-harvesting decisions in the United States District Court for the Northern District of California. Respondents claimed that the Forest Service's decisions violated the Free Exercise Clause, the Federal Water Pollution Control Act (FWPCA), 86 Stat. 896, as amended, 33 U.S.C. § 1251 et seq., the National Environment Policy Act of 1969 (NEPA), 83 Stat. 852, 42 U.S.C. § 4321 et seq., several other federal statutes, and governmental trust responsibilities to Indians living on the Hoopa Valley Reservation.

After a trial, the District Court issued a permanent injunction prohibiting the Government from constructing the Chimney Rock section of the G-O road or putting the timber-harvesting management plan into effect. See *Northwest Indian Cemetery Protective Assn. v. Peterson*, 565 F. Supp. 586 ([N.D. Cal.] 1983). * * *

* * *

A panel of the Ninth Circuit affirmed in part. *Northwest Indian Cemetery Protective Assn. v. Peterson*, 795 F. 2d 688 (1986). * * *

By a divided decision, the District Court's constitutional ruling was also affirmed. Relying primarily on the Forest Service's own commissioned study, the majority found that construction of the Chimney Rock section of the G-O road would have significant, though largely indirect, adverse effects on Indian religious practices. The majority concluded that the Government had failed to demonstrate a compelling interest in the completion of the road, and that it could have abandoned the road without thereby creating "a religious preserve for a single group in violation of the establishment clause." The majority apparently applied the same analysis to logging operations that might be carried out in portions of the Chimney Rock area not covered by the California Wilderness Act. ("Because most of the high country has now been designated by Congress as a wilderness area, the issue of logging becomes less significant, although it does not disappear").

* * *

III

* * *

The Free Exercise Clause of the First Amendment provides that "Congress shall make no law . . . prohibiting the free exercise [of religion]." It is undisputed that the Indian respondents' beliefs are sincere and that the Government's proposed actions will have severe adverse effects on the practice of their religion. Those respondents contend that the burden on their religious practices is heavy enough to violate the Free Exercise Clause unless the Government can demonstrate a compelling need to complete the G-O road or to engage in timber harvesting in the Chimney Rock area. We disagree.

In *Bowen v. Roy*, 476 U. S. 693 (1986), we considered a challenge to a federal statute that required the States to use Social Security numbers in administering certain welfare programs. Two applicants for benefits under these programs contended that their religious beliefs prevented them from acceding to the use of a Social Security number for their two-year-old daughter because the use of a numerical identifier would " 'rob the spirit' of [their] daughter and prevent her from attaining greater spiritual power." Id., at 696. Similarly, in this case, it is said that disruption of the natural environment caused by the G-O road will diminish the sacredness of the area in question and create distractions that will interfere with "training and ongoing religious experience of individuals using [sites within] the area for personal medicine and growth * * * and as integrated parts of a system of religious belief and practice which correlates ascending degrees of personal power with a geographic hierarchy of power." ("Scarred hills and mountains, and disturbed rocks destroy the purity of the sacred areas, and [Indian] consultants repeatedly stressed the need of a training doctor to be undistracted by such disturbance"). * * *

The building of a road or the harvesting of timber on publicly owned land cannot meaningfully be distinguished from the use of a Social Security number in *Roy*. In both cases, the challenged Government action would interfere significantly with private persons' ability to pursue spiritual fulfillment according to their own religious beliefs. In neither case, however, would the affected individuals be coerced by the Government's action into violating their religious beliefs; nor would either governmental action penalize religious activity by denying any person an equal share of the rights, benefits, and privileges enjoyed by other citizens.

* * *

* * * This does not and cannot imply that incidental effects of government programs, which may make it more difficult to practice certain religions but which have no tendency to coerce individuals into acting contrary to their religious beliefs, require government to bring forward a compelling justification for its otherwise lawful actions. The crucial word in the constitutional text is "prohibit": "For the Free Exercise Clause is written in terms of what the government cannot do to the individual, not in terms of what the individual can exact from the government." *Sherbert* [*v. Verner*, 374 U.S. 398 (1963)], at 412 (Douglas, J., concurring).

Whatever may be the exact line between unconstitutional prohibitions on the free exercise of religion and the legitimate conduct by government of its own affairs, the location of the line cannot depend on measuring the effects of a governmental action on a religious objector's spiritual development. The Government does not dispute, and we have no reason to doubt, that the logging and road-building projects at issue in this case could have devastating effects on traditional Indian religious practices. Those practices are intimately and inextricably bound up with the unique features of the Chimney Rock area, which is known to the Indians as the "high country." Individual practitioners use this area for personal spiritual development; some of their activities are believed to be critically important in advancing the welfare of the Tribe, and indeed, of mankind itself. The Indians use this area, as they have used it for a very long time, to conduct a wide variety of specific rituals that aim to accomplish their religious goals. According to their beliefs, the rituals would not be efficacious if conducted at other sites than the ones traditionally used, and too much disturbance of the area's natural state would clearly render any meaningful continuation of traditional practices impossible. To be sure, the Indians themselves were far from unanimous in opposing the G-O road, and it seems less than certain that construction of the road will be so disruptive that it will doom their religion. Nevertheless, we can assume that the threat to the efficacy of at least some religious practices is extremely grave.

Even if we assume that we should accept the Ninth Circuit's prediction, according to which the G-O road will "virtually destroy the . . . Indians' ability to practice their religion," 795 F.2d, at 693 (opinion below), the Constitution simply does not provide a principle that could justify upholding respondents' legal claims. However much we might wish that it were otherwise, government simply could not operate if it were required to satisfy every citizen's religious needs and desires. * * *

One need not look far beyond the present case to see why the analysis in *Roy*, but not respondents' proposed extension of *Sherbert* and its progeny, offers a sound reading of the Constitution. Respondents attempt to stress the limits of the religious servitude that they are now seeking to impose on the Chimney Rock area of the Six Rivers National Forest. While defending an injunction against logging operations and the construction of a road, they apparently do not *at present* object to the area's being used by recreational visitors, other Indians, or forest rangers. Nothing in the principle for which they contend, however, would distinguish this case from another lawsuit in which they (or similarly situated religious objectors) might seek to exclude all human activity but their own from sacred areas of the public lands. The Indian respondents insist that "[p]rivacy during the power quests is required for the practitioners to maintain the purity needed for a successful journey." Similarly: "The practices conducted in the high country entail intense meditation and require the practitioner to achieve a profound awareness of the natural environment. Prayer seats are oriented so there is an unobstructed view, and the practitioner must be surrounded by *undisturbed* naturalness." (emphasis added). No disrespect for these practices is implied when one notes that such beliefs could easily require *de facto* beneficial ownership of some rather spacious tracts of public property. Even without anticipating future cases, the diminution of the Government's property rights, and the concomitant subsidy of the Indian religion, would in this case be far from trivial: the District Court's order permanently forbade commercial timber harvesting, or the construction of a two-lane road, anywhere within an area covering a full 27 sections (*i.e.* more than 17,000 acres) of public land.

The Constitution does not permit government to discriminate against religions that treat particular physical sites as sacred, and a law forbidding the Indian respondents from visiting the Chimney Rock area would raise a different set of constitutional questions. Whatever rights the Indians may have to the use of the area, however, those rights do not divest the Government of its right to use what is, after all, *its* land. * * *

B

Nothing in our opinion should be read to encourage governmental insensitivity to the religious needs of any citizen. The Government's rights to the use of its own land, for example, need not and should not discourage it from accommodating religious practices like those engaged in by the Indian respondents. It is worth emphasizing, therefore, that the Government has taken numerous steps in this very case to minimize the impact that construction of the G–O road will have on the Indians' religious activities. First, the Forest Service commissioned a comprehensive study of the effects that the project would have on the cultural and religious value of the Chimney Rock area. * * *

Although the Forest Service did not in the end adopt the report's recommendation that the project should be abandoned, many other ameliorative measures were planned. No sites where specific rituals take place were to be disturbed. In fact, a major factor in choosing among alternative routes for the road was the relation of the various routes to religious sites. * * *

Except for abandoning its project entirely, and thereby leaving the two existing segments of road to dead-end in the middle of a National Forest, it is difficult to see how the Government could have been more solicitous. Such solicitude accords with "the policy of the United States to protect and preserve for American Indians their inherent right of freedom to believe, express, and exercise the traditional religions of the American Indian * * * including but not limited to access to sites, use and possession of sacred objects, and the freedom to worship through ceremonials and traditional rites." American Indian Religious Freedom Act (AIRFA), Pub.L. 95–341, 92 Stat. 469, 42 U.S.C. § 1996.

Respondents, however, suggest that AIRFA goes further and in effect enacts their interpretation of the First Amendment into statutory law. Although this contention was rejected by the District Court, they seek to defend the judgment below by arguing that AIRFA authorizes the injunction against completion of the G-O road. This argument is without merit. After reciting several legislative findings, AIRFA "resolves" upon the policy quoted above. A second section of the statute, 92 Stat. 470, required an evaluation of federal policies and procedures, in consultation with native religious leaders, of changes necessary to protect and preserve the rights and practices in question. The required report dealing with this evaluation was completed and released in 1979. Nowhere in the law is there so much as a hint of any intent to create a cause of action or any judicially enforceable individual rights.

What is obvious from the face of the statute is confirmed by numerous indications in the legislative history. The sponsor of the bill that became AIRFA, Representative Udall, called it "a sense of Congress joint resolution," aimed at ensuring that "the basic right of the Indian people to exercise their traditional religious practices is not infringed without a clear decision on the part of the Congress or the administrators that such religious practices must yield to some higher consideration." 124 Cong.Rec. 21444 (1978). Representative Udall emphasized that the bill would not "confer special religious rights on Indians," would "not change any existing State or Federal law," and in fact "has no teeth in it."

* * *

IV

The decision of the court below, according to which the First Amendment precludes the Government from completing the G-O road or from permitting timber harvesting in the Chimney Rock area, is reversed. In order that the District Court's injunction may be reconsidered in light of this holding, and in the light of any other relevant events that may have intervened since the injunction issued, the case is remanded for further proceedings consistent with this opinion.

It is so ordered.

* * *

JUSTICE BRENNAN, with whom JUSTICE MARSHALL and JUSTICE BLACKMUN join, dissenting.

* * *

I

For at least 200 years and probably much longer, the Yurok, Karok, and Tolowa Indians have held sacred an approximately 25-square-mile area of land situated in what is today the Blue Creek Unit of Six Rivers National Forest in northwestern California. As the Government readily concedes, regular visits to this area, known to respondent Indians as the "high country," have played and continue to play a "critical" role in the religious practices and rituals of these Tribes. Those beliefs, only briefly described in the Court's opinion, are crucial to a proper understanding of respondents' claims.

As the Forest Service's commissioned study, the Theodoratus Report, explains, for Native Americans religion is not a discrete sphere of activity separate from all others, and any attempt to isolate the religious aspects of Indian life "is in reality an exercise which forces Indian concepts into non-Indian categories." D. Theodoratus, Cultural Resources of the Chimney Rock Section, Gasquet-Orleans Roads, Six Rivers National Forest (1979). Thus, for most Native Americans, "[t]he area of worship cannot be delineated from social, political, cultur[al], and other areas o[f] Indian lifestyle." American Indian Religious Freedom, Hearings on S. J. Res. 102 Before the Senate Select Committee on Indian Affairs, 95th Cong., 2d Sess., 86 (1978) (statement of Barney Old Coyote, Crow Tribe). A pervasive feature of this lifestyle is the individual's relationship with the natural world; this relationship, which can accurately though somewhat incompletely be characterized as one of stewardship, forms the core of what might be called, for want of a better nomenclature, the Indian religious experience. While traditional Western religions view creation as the work of a deity "who institutes natural laws which then govern the operation of physical nature," tribal religions regard creation as an on-going process in which they are morally and religiously obligated to participate. U.S. Federal Agencies Task Force, American Indian Religious Freedom Act Report 11 (1979) (Task Force Report). Native Americans fulfill this duty through ceremonies and rituals designed to preserve and stabilize the earth and to protect humankind from disease and other catastrophes. Failure to conduct these ceremonies in the manner and place specified, adherents believe, will result in great harm to the earth and to the people whose welfare depends upon it.

In marked contrast to traditional Western religions, the belief systems of Native Americans do not rely on doctrines, creeds, or dogmas. Established or universal truths—the mainstay of Western religions—play no part in Indian faith. Ceremonies are communal efforts undertaken for specific purposes in accordance with instructions handed down from generation to generation. Commentaries on or interpretations of the rituals themselves are deemed absolute violations of the ceremonies, whose value lies not in their ability to explain the natural world or to enlighten individual believers but in their efficacy as protectors and enhancers of tribal existence. Where dogma lies at the heart of Western religions, Native American faith is inextricably bound to the use of land. The site-specific nature of Indian religious practice derives form the Native American perception that land is itself a sacred, living being. See Suagee, American Indian Religious Freedom and Cultural Resources Management: Protecting Mother Earth's Caretakers, 10 Am. Ind. L. Rev. 1, 10 (1982). Rituals are performed in prescribed locations not merely as a matter of traditional orthodoxy, but because land, like all other living things, is unique, and specific sites possess different spiritual properties and significance. Within this belief system, therefore, land is not fungible; indeed, at the time of the Spanish colonization of the Americans Southwest, "all * * * Indians held in some form a belief in a sacred and indissoluble bond between themselves and the land in which their settlements were located." E. Spicer, Cycles of Conquest: The Impact of Spain, Mexico, and the United States on the Indians of the Southwest, 1533–1960, p. 576 (1962).

For respondent Indians, the most sacred of lands is the high country where, they believe, prehuman spirits moved with the coming of humans to the Earth. Because these spirits are seen as the source of religious power, or "medicine," many of the tribes' rituals and practices require frequent journeys to the area. * * *

* * *

II

The Court does not for a moment suggest that the interests served by the G-O road are in any way compelling, or that they outweigh the destructive effect construction of the road will have on respondents' religious practices. Instead, the Court embraces the Government's contention that its prerogative as landowner should always take precedence over a claim that a particular use of federal property infringes religious practices. Attempting to justify this rule, the Court argues that the First Amendment bars only outright prohibitions, indirect coercion, and penalties on the free exercise of religion. All other "incidental effects of government programs," it concludes, even those "which may make it more difficult to practice certain religions but which have no tendency to coerce individuals into acting contrary to their religious beliefs," simply do not give rise to constitutional concerns. Since our recognition nearly half a century ago that restraints on religious conduct implicate the concerns of the Free Exercise Clause, see *Prince v. Massachusetts*, 321 U. S. 158 (1944), we have never suggested that the protections of the guarantee are limited to so narrow a range of governmental burdens. The land-use decision challenged here will restrain respondents from practicing their religion as surely and as completely as any of the governmental actions we have struck down in the past, and the Court's efforts simply to define away respondents' injury as nonconstitutional are both unjustified and ultimately unpersuasive.

* * *

III

Today, the Court holds that a federal land-use decision that promises to destroy an entire religion does not burden the practice of that faith in a manner recognized by the Free Exercise Clause. Having thus stripped respondents and all other Native Americans of any constitutional protection against perhaps the most serious threat to their age-old religious practices, and indeed to their entire way of life, the Court assures us that nothing in its decision "should be read to encourage governmental insensitivity to the religious needs of any citizen." I find it difficult, however, to imagine conduct more insensitive to religious needs than the Government's determination to build a marginally useful road in the face of uncontradicted evidence that the road will render the practice of respondents' religion impossible. Nor do I believe that respondents will derive any solace from the knowledge that although the practice of their religion will become "more difficult" as a result of the Government's actions, they remain free to maintain their religious beliefs. Given today's ruling, that freedom amounts to nothing more than the right to believe that their religion will be destroyed. The safeguarding of such a hollow freedom not only makes a mockery of the " 'policy of the United States to protect and preserve for American Indians their inherent right of freedom to believe, express, and exercise the[ir] traditional religions,' " (quoting AIRFA), it fails utterly to accord with the dictates of the First Amendment.

I dissent.

NOTES

1. The *Lyng* Court never reached the "compelling governmental interest" test normally applied by United States courts under the First Amendment. Notwithstanding the lower court's acceptance of an expert report opining that the road would "destroy" the Indians' practice of

religion because the area was "indispensable" to their religion, the government's actions were not sufficient to "prohibit" the free exercise of their religion. Justice O'Connor said that "incidental effects of government programs, which may make it more difficult to practice certain religions but which have no tendency to coerce individuals into acting contrary to their religious beliefs [do not] require government to bring forward a compelling justification for its otherwise lawful actions." Id. at 450–51. Had the government's conduct been found to be within the First Amendment's protection against "prohibition" of free exercise, the government would have been subject to heightened scrutiny for its alleged interests in building the highway. One commentator has argued that the free exercise analysis used by the Court in *Lyng* discriminates against Indian tribal religions:

> By focusing on the form of impact the challenged government action creates, rather than the impairment of religious exercise, the Court has drawn a line that discriminates against American Indian religious practitioners. As a result of the free exercise analysis developed by the Supreme Court, persons practicing Western religious traditions are protected from even relatively minor burdens on their religious practices, while American Indians are not protected from government actions that essentially destroy entire religious traditions.

Scott Hardt, Comment, *The Sacred Public Lands: Improper Line Drawing in the Supreme Court's Free Exercise Analysis,* 60 U.Colo.L.Rev. 601, 657 (1989).

2.   With its refusal to treat the government's "indirect" destruction of Indian religion as within the First Amendment's protections, the *Lyng* Court effectively placed federal public lands management decisions affecting Indian religious sites beyond free exercise review. *Lyng* created a hierarchy in which the government's property rights trump religious freedoms at Indian sacred sites located on the federally-owned lands. See Kristen Carpenter, *A Property Rights Approach to Sacred Sites Cases: Asserting a Place for Indians as Nonowners,* 52 UCLA L.Rev. 1061 (2005). More broadly, *Lyng* has been cited by federal courts in rejecting free exercise claims in a number of non-Indian cases. See, e.g., United States v. Turnbull, 888 F.2d 636, 638 (9th Cir.1989), cert. denied 498 U.S. 825 (1990); Messiah Baptist Church v. County of Jefferson, 859 F.2d 820, 824 (10th Cir.1988), cert. denied 490 U.S. 1005 (1989); Warner v. City of Boca Raton, 64 F.Supp.2d 1272, 1288–90 (S.D.Fla.1999).

3.   When the *Lyng* opinion hit the banks of the Klamath River, the tribal communities were shocked, devastated, and despondent. This was their first major defeat since the cultural and religious revitalization began in the early 1960s. Yurok tribal member Abby Abinanti remembers that, prior to the Supreme Court proceeding, the Indian communities had felt confident about the case. The tribal witnesses had offered strong testimony

on the sacredness of the High Country. The lawyers and the plaintiffs in the case had had built a strong record regarding the burden placed upon the religion. It was a record the Supreme Court had to rely on, as a matter of law, in making its decision. Three lower courts had ruled in their favor. The Indians felt confident that the Supreme Court would afford constitutional protection to tribal religions—but it did not.

Abinanti remembers the community's disbelief and pain. How could the Indians on the Klamath River be ineligible for the protections of the Constitution? The Supreme Court justices "must not have understood," she explained, "because if they did how could they have allowed an ancient religion to be completely destroyed just to permit the construction of a road?" She continues, "I have to believe they didn't get it, because I can't be a citizen of a government that treats its people with such disregard for their religious freedom. I have to believe they didn't understand." Traditional leader Chris Peters elaborated: "We were shocked at the extent of the damage. They (the Supreme Court) just went so far. My phone began ringing off the hook. Reporters and community members wanted to know what was next—what were we going to do."

The litigation process had exhausted the financial resources of the tribal communities, environmental groups, California Indian Legal Services, and the individual Indian plaintiffs. They decided to focus remaining resources on educating others about the lack of constitutional protection for Native American sacred sites and religion. Other Indian groups, tribes, and Native Hawaiians came to the Klamath River to learn about the case. The lawyers and the plaintiffs spoke on college campuses throughout the United States. The protection of Indian sacred sites began to command political attention on the national stage.

Two years after the Supreme Court handed down the *Lyng* decision, Congress passed the Smith River National Recreation Area Act of 1990. While Indian people supported the legislation, they were not directly involved in the lobbying process. Some tribal leaders speculate the Act was passed to avoid widespread protest in Northern California. Chris Peters explains: "If the road was built, an occupation would have happened." The Act protected the *entire* High Country, including the proposed site of the G-O Road, from development by adding it to the Siskiyou Wilderness Area. The High Country was *safe*, at last. For additional detail on the tribal perspectives and lawyering strategy before, during, and after the Lyng case, see Amy Bowers and Kristen A. Carpenter, *Lyng v. Northwest Indian Cemetery Protective Association: Challenging the Narrative of Conquest, in* Indian Law Stories (C. Goldberg et al. eds.) (2010) (explaining cultural revitalism during the self-determination era, as well as tribal legal strategy during the administrative and judicial stages of the case). See also Abby Abinanti, *A Letter to Justice O'Connor*, 1 Indigenous Peoples' J.L. Culture & Resist. 1, 21 (2004) ("I lived complying with your decision, but I never accepted it as anything but bending to brute, irresistible, and immoral force.")

INDIAN LAWYERING NOTE: LEGISLATIVE AND ADMINISTRATIVE ADVOCACY FOLLOWING LYNG

Besides closing off the Constitution's Free Exercise Clause as an avenue of challenge to government action that did not amount to a prohibition, *Lyng* also confirmed that the American Indian Religious Freedom Act of 1978 (AIRFA), 42 U.S.C.A. § 1996, as Justice O'Connor's opinion recited, "has no teeth in it."

Congressional and Executive Branch Responses to the Lyng Decision

After a decade of congressional neglect in following up on AIRFA's purposes, and the repeated setbacks for the Act's proponents in the courts that culminated in the *Lyng* decision, the American Indian Religious Freedom Coalition was formed in 1988. The Coalition, with human rights and environmental groups, drafted an omnibus "Native American Cultural Rights Act" to remedy the many deficiencies in AIRFA. As described above, a significant legislative victory was achieved in 1990 when Congress designated public lands which included the sacred High Country involved in the *Lyng* decision for permanent wilderness protection under the Smith River National Recreation Area Act. 16 U.S.C. § 460bbb (2000).

Congress failed to overturn *Lyng* expressly, but the Coalition and other supporters of Indian religious freedom did succeed in convincing Congress to amend several federal statutes, most significantly the National Historic Preservation Act of 1966 (NHPA), 16 U.S.C. § 470 et seq. Under the NHPA, the Secretary of the Interior, acting through the National Park Service (NPS), is authorized by Congress to include historically and culturally significant properties on the National Register of Historic Places. At the behest of Indian support groups like the American Indian Religious Freedom Coalition and the Association of American Indian Affairs, Congress amended the Act in 1992 to provide that "properties of traditional religious and cultural importance to an Indian tribe * * * may be determined to be eligible for inclusion in the National Register." See National Historic Preservation Act Amendments of 1992, 16 U.S.C. § 470a(d)(6)(A). Congress also amended Section 106 of NHPA by adding Indian tribes to the federal agency consultation process that must take place with states and other interested parties when federal agency actions threaten to affect any historic properties. Id. at § 470a (d)(6)(B). See generally Martin Nie, *The Use of Co-Management and Protected Land-Use Designations to Protect Tribal Cultural Resources and Reserved Treaty Rights on Federal Lands*, 48 Nat. Resources J. 585 (2008).

The legislative actions taken by Congress following *Lyng* were bolstered considerably by President Clinton's Executive Order 13,007, 61 Fed. Reg. 26,771 (May 24, 1996). The order, entitled "Indian Sacred Sites," directed federal agencies to "accommodate access to and ceremonial use of Indian sacred sites by Indian religious practitioners" on federal land, and sent a clear signal to federal land use managers that their role must include accommodation of Indian religious practices and protection of those sacred sites. The order also directs agencies to "avoid adversely affecting the physical integrity of such sacred sites" by providing notice of proposed activities that may impact sacred sites identified by an Indian tribe or individual authorized to represent an Indian religion. Federal agency heads are directed to report to the President on the implementation of the order, including changes necessary to accommodate access to and ceremonial use of sacred sites and to avoid adversely affecting the physical integrity of the sites. Agencies also must develop procedures to facilitate consultation with tribes and religious leaders and to resolve disputes relating to agency actions on federal lands expeditiously. See generally Michelle Kay Albert, *Obligations and Opportunities to Protect Native American Sacred Sites Located on Public Lands*, 40 Colum.Hum.Rts.L.Rev. 479 (2009); Marcia Yablon, *Property Rights and Sacred Sites: Federal Regulatory Responses to American Indian Religious Claims on Public Land*, 113 Yale L.J. 1623 (2004).

Devils Tower Voluntary Climbing Ban

The increased federal emphasis on tribal consultation encouraged by congressional legislation such as the 1992 amendments to the NHPA and President Clinton's Executive Order resulted in several historic agreements negotiated between federal land use agencies and Indian tribes, seeking to protect Indian sacred sites located on public lands. Perhaps the best known of these agreements, and the most exhaustively litigated, involves the National Park Service plan to accommodate Native American religious practices at the Devils Tower National Monument in Wyoming.

Devils Tower was the first national monument in the United States, dedicated by President Theodore Roosevelt in 1906. Made even more famous by the 1977 movie, *Close Encounters of the Third Kind* and Richard Dreyfus's mashed potato vision quest, Devils Tower is also within the aboriginal territory of the Sioux tribes and is regarded as a sacred site by a number of Indian tribes. Indians have traveled to and conducted ceremonies at Devils Tower for centuries.

N. Scott Momaday, the Pulitzer Prize-winning Kiowa writer, tells the story of how this sacred place, called *Tsoai* (the "Rock Tree") by the Kiowa, came about in the world. A boy and his seven sisters were at play. The boy turned into a terrifying bear, and his sisters all ran in fear of their lives, with the bear in hot pursuit.

> They came to the stump of a great tree, and the tree spoke to them. It bade them climb upon it, and as they did so it began to rise into the air. The bear came to kill them, but they were just beyond its reach. It reared against the tree and scored the bark all around with its claws.

N. Scott Momaday, The Man Made of Words 122–23 (1997). As Momaday, the master Native American storyteller tells us, the seven sisters lifted into the sky by *Tsoai*, the Rock Tree, became the seven stars of the Big Dipper. Id.

NPS regulations for Devils Tower require the conservation of a number of values, including archeological resources, cultural landscapes, ethnographic resources and historic sites. Activities that impair the integrity of park resources or values are generally prohibited. NPS's most recent policies fully reflect the force of the post-*Lyng* legislative measures and Executive Branch mandates in recognizing and encouraging the importance of tribal consultation on management decisions affecting sacred sites in our national parks. NPS has specifically acknowledged that "site-specific worship is vital to Native American religious practices." Management policies for such sites "will be as unrestrictive as possible in permitting Native American tribes access to park areas to perform traditional religious, ceremonial, or other customary activities at places that have been used historically for such purposes * * * ." See Sandra B. Zellmer, *Sustaining Geographies of Hope: Cultural Resources on Public Lands*, 73 U.Colo.L.Rev. 413, 458 (2002).

Besides its tremendous religious significance to the Indians of the Plains, Devils Tower is also considered a premier rock climbing destination, and many commercial climbing operations and businesses rely on the monument's use for this purpose. In 1995, the Park Service, after consulting with Indian groups, announced a plan that denied commercial rock climbing licenses at Devils Tower during the month of June, when the most significant tribal ceremonial activities take place. Under the 1995 NPS Plan, the visitor center at the monument provides information on the sacred significance of Devils Tower, and signs are posted, indicating that Devils Tower is sacred to American Indians and encouraging visitors to stay on designated paths.

Soon after the plan was announced, a group of climbers filed suit against the Park Service in federal district court, alleging that the mandatory climbing ban under the plan established Indian religious practices at the monument in violation of the First Amendment. The Cheyenne River Sioux Tribe and four of its religious leaders intervened in the lawsuit in support of the Park Service plan. Federal district court Judge William Downes granted a preliminary injunction in June, 1996 against the Park Service, forcing it to issue commercial climbing permits (No. 96–CV–063 D (D.Wyo. June 8, 1996)). Downes' ruling said the ban appeared to favor one group over another for religious purposes, in violation of the First Amendment's Establishment Clause. The Park Service then revised its rules to provide that it would ask rock climbers not to scale the tower during June. In April, 1998, Judge Downes dismissed a lawsuit filed by several rock climbers challenging the new "voluntary climbing ban" as coercive and an unconstitutional endorsement of American Indian religious ceremonies. Judge Downes held that the Park Service's voluntary program sought to remove barriers to religious worship occasioned by public ownership of the tower, and therefore did not violate the Constitution. See Bear Lodge Multiple Use Ass'n v. Babbitt, 2 F.Supp.2d 1448 (D.Wyo.1998), affirmed, 175 F.3d 814 (10th Cir.1999), cert. denied 529 U.S. 1037 (2000).

On appeal, the Tenth Circuit upheld the district court ruling. After recognizing the increased federal emphasis on protection of Indian religious rights and cultural forms of expression over the course of the century, the court of appeals had little difficulty in finding that the NPS could manage Devils Tower in a manner that accommodated Indian religious practices at the National Monument.

> Starting in the 1930's federal policy toward Indians changed, and over the past 65 years, has valued and protected tribal governments and cultures. In 1978, Congress enacted the American Indian Religious Freedom Act creating a government-wide policy to protect Indian sacred sites and traditional forms of worship. See 42 U.S.C. § 1996 (1994). In 1990, Congress passed the Native American Graves and Repatriation Act (NAGPRA) requiring federal land managers, including the NPS, to protect Indian graves, consult with Indian tribes concerning religious and cultural sites and objects, and to repatriate cultural and religious items found on federal lands. See 25 U.S.C. § 3001 (1995). Under the National Historical Preservation Act Amendments of 1992, "properties of traditional religious and cultural importance to an Indian tribe . . . may be determined eligible for inclusion on the National Register" and federal agencies, including the NPS are directed to consult "with any tribe . . . that attaches religious and cultural significance to [such] properties." 16 U.S.C. § 470a(d)(6)(A)–(B) (1985 & 1998 Supp.) The federal government acknowledges that site specific worship is vital to Indian religious practices. Recently the executive branch has ordered federal agencies to: (1) accommodate access to and ceremonial use of Indian sacred sites by Indian religious practitioners and (2) avoid aversely affecting the physical integrity of such sacred sites. See Exec. Order 13,007, 61 Fed.Reg. 26771 (1996). Numerous other laws generally protect Indian religion and allow access to and/or temporary closure of specific tribal sacred sites located on federal lands.[6]

175 F.3d at 817–18.

---

[6] See, e.g., 16 U.S.C. § 460uu–47 (1993 & 1998 Supp.) (authorizing access to and temporary closures of El Malpais National Monument for traditional cultural and religious purposes); 16 U.S.C. § 410pp–6 (1992 & 1998 Supp.) (authorizing temporary closures of Cibola Historical Park for Indian religious services); 16 U.S.C. § 228i(c) (1992) (preserving access to Grand Canyon National Park for Indian religious purposes); 16 U.S.C. § 41011–4 (1992) (preserving access to federal park lands or archaeological sites for traditional Indian religious purposes); 25 U.S.C. §§ 640d–20 (1995) (providing the Navajo and Hopi tribes with rights to use and access sacred sites).

Other Federal-Tribal Sacred Sites
Agreements and Litigation

Building on the successful defense of the agreement in *Bear Lodge*, the NPS entered into a site management agreement for Rainbow Bridge National Monument that included full closure of the area and unrestricted and non-permitted access for Native American religious practices, and voluntary limits on use by other visitors. In drafting the site plan for Rainbow Bridge, the NPS assembled a panel of representatives from interested tribes. The role of the panel was to generate a Memorandum of Agreement to address concerns over natural and cultural resource management at the Monument. The Programmatic Agreement included stipulations for the Park Service to consult the tribes on a variety of issues: interpretation programs, trail maintenance, construction of wayside exhibits, interpreter training, revegetation, visitor traffic control, and measures to reduce resource degradation. In 2002 the Natural Arch and Bridge Society brought suit in federal court challenging the constitutionality of the agreement. The Tenth Circuit in an unreported decision upheld the plan, citing to the *Bear Lodge* case and pointing to the voluntary nature of the accommodations in the plan. See Natural Arch and Bridge Society v. Alston, 209 F.Supp.2d 1207 (D. Utah 2002), affirmed, 2004 WL 569888 (10th Cir.2004) (unreported decision).

The Forest Service's tribal consultation process for Indian sacred sites was once again at the center of the litigation over the Historic Preservation Plan (HPP) for the Medicine Wheel National Historic Landmark and Medicine Mountain, negotiated in 1996. See Wyoming Sawmills, Inc. v. United States Forest Service, 179 F.Supp.2d 1279 (D.Wyo.2001), affirmed, 383 F.3d 1241 (10th Cir.2004). The Medicine Wheel National Historic Landmark is located within the Big Horn National Forest in Wyoming. The prehistoric site consists of a circular structure of rocks, eighty feet in diameter, and a large rock pile in the center of the circle with twenty-eight spokes of rocks radiating from the center to the circle's edge. Archeological evidence indicates that people have been present in the area for at least 7,500 years, and the Wheel is considered a sacred site by numerous Indian tribes. See 179 F.Supp.2d at 1286.

In 1994, the Forest Service, after a lengthy consultation process mandated by the NHPA, reached agreement with two American Indian groups, the Big Horn County Commissioner and the Federal Aviation Administration which operates a radar site on Medicine Mountain. The HPP for the Medicine Wheel has as its "selected management priority" protection of traditional cultural values. See Historic Preservation Plan for Medicine Wheel National Historic Landmark and Vicinity, USDA Forest Service, R-2 Bighorn National Forest, Sept. 1996, at p. 5. The HPP also includes a "values" statement which describes the religious nature of the Medicine Wheel and the entire mountain it is on. "[T]he Medicine Wheel is most important currently as a place for conducting traditional sacred ceremonies for Indian people. It is valuable also as a place where visitors can experience the powerful sanctity and learn about the nature of Indian religions and the central importance that religion has in traditional practitioners' lives." Id. at 10–11. Under the plan, the Forest Service must consult with affiliated tribes before permitting activities that might harm the spiritual values associated with the site. Id. at 24. The Plan also closes a road within view of the Medicine Wheel. Id. at 33.

When a logging association filed suit against the Plan, alleging that the Forest Service had violated the Establishment Clause in "promoting" Indian religion, as well as other statutory requirements, the federal district court dismissed the complaint. The court said it was unable to provide redress for any of the logging association's First Amendment claims and found that the Forest Service had complied with applicable rules and regulations in promulgating the Plan. As the court explained, the Historic Preservation Plan was not the cause of the injuries alleged by the logging association; rather, it was "Congress' decision to designate Medicine Wheel as a National Monument," an act which the association did not challenge. 179 F.Supp.2d at 1296. See Access Fund v. U.S. Dept. of Agriculture, 499 F.3d 1036 (9th Cir.2007) (upholding climbing ban on Washoe sacred site on grounds that it preserved cultural resources, and therefore had a secular purpose, against Establishment Clause challenge). See also Albert, supra, at 509 (noting that so long as federal land managers can assert a secular purpose for initiating action that results in the protection of a sacred site, courts appear unwilling to hold that they have violated the Establishment Clause).

Does the "voluntary" nature of the accommodations agreed to by tribes and Indian religious leaders undermine or lessen the value or significance of these agreements with the federal government? Consider what one commentator has written:

> The courts and Congress have left sacred sites protection in the hands of land management agencies, and although many feared this decision would be disastrous, land agencies have actually embraced their role and sought to accommodate Indian religions and protect their sacred sites. Furthermore, agency accommodation is actually better for society as a whole than the broader judicial and legislative protections typically advocated by sacred sites supporters. Agency accommodation avoids the disadvantages of broad categorical protection while still serving as a strong method for preserving sacred sites. Although land agencies have had the role of sacred sites protectors thrust upon them, they seem to have turned out to be ideally suited for the job.

M. Yablon, supra, at 1661.

From a broader perspective, how do you assess the move toward expanded consultation and cooperative agreements between Indian tribes and federal land use managers that resulted as a response to judicial defeats like *Lyng* and the failure to secure congressional legislation directly overturning that much-criticized decision? Does this approach adequately respect the status of Indians as "peoples" maintaining longstanding relationships with sacred sites on the public lands? Does it meet human rights standards, such as the UN Declaration's requirement that states respect tribes' traditional lands and religions, and obtain indigenous peoples' "consent" to certain measures affecting them? Kristen A. Carpenter, *Real Property and Peoplehood*, 27 Stan.Env.L.J. 313 (2008) (arguing for a more robust approach to tribal-agency consultation and agreement in the sacred sites realm). *See generally* Kristen A. Carpenter, Sonia K. Katyal, and Angela R. Riley, In Defense of Property, 118 Yale L.J. 1022 (2009); Dean B. Suagee, *Tribal Voices in Historic Preservation: Sacred Landscapes, Cross-Cultural Bridges, and Common Ground*, 21 Vt.L.Rev. 145 (1996); Robert A. Williams, Jr., *Large Binocular Telescopes, Red Squirrel Pinatas, and Apache Sacred Mountains: Decolonizing Environmental Law in a Multicultural World*, 96 W.Va.L.Rev. 1133 (1994).

SECTION B.   PROTECTION OF AMERICAN INDIAN RELIGIOUS PRACTICES AND BELIEFS

EMPLOYMENT DIVISION, DEPARTMENT OF HUMAN RESOURCES OF OREGON v. SMITH

Supreme Court of the United States, 1990.
494 U.S. 872, 110 S.Ct. 1595, 108 L.Ed.2d 876.

JUSTICE SCALIA delivered the opinion of the Court.

* * *

I

Oregon law prohibits the knowing or intentional possession of a "controlled substance" unless the substance has been prescribed by a medical practitioner. * * * [T]he drug peyote, a hallucinogen derived from the plant *Lophophora williamsii Lemaire*[, is a controlled substance].

Respondents Alfred Smith and Galen Black (hereinafter respondents) were fired from their jobs with a private drug rehabilitation organization because they ingested peyote for sacramental purposes at a ceremony of the Native American Church, of which both are members. When respondents applied to petitioner Employment Division (hereinafter petitioner) for unemployment compensation, they were determined to be ineligible for benefits because they had been discharged for work-related "misconduct." * * *

* * * The Oregon Supreme Court reasoned, however, that the criminality of respondents' peyote use was irrelevant to resolution of their constitutional claim—since the purpose of the "misconduct" provision under which respondents had been disqualified was not to enforce the

State's criminal laws but to preserve the financial integrity of the compensation fund, and since that purpose was inadequate to justify the burden that disqualification imposed on respondents' religious practice. Citing our decisions in *Sherbert v. Verner*, 374 U. S. 398 (1963), and *Thomas v. Review Board of Indiana Employment Security Div.*, 450 U. S. 707 (1981), the court concluded that respondents were entitled to payment of unemployment benefits. We granted certiorari.

Before this Court in 1987, petitioner continued to maintain that the illegality of respondents' peyote consumption was relevant to their constitutional claim. We agreed, concluding that "if a State has prohibited through its criminal laws certain kinds of religiously motivated conduct without violating the First Amendment, it certainly follows that it may impose the lesser burden of denying unemployment compensation benefits to persons who engage in that conduct." *Employment Div., Dept. of Human Resources of Oregon v. Smith*, 485 U. S. 660, 670 (1988) *(Smith I)*. * * * [W]e vacated the judgment of the Oregon Supreme Court and remanded for further proceedings.

On remand, the Oregon Supreme Court held that respondents' religiously inspired use of peyote fell within the [criminal] prohibition of the Oregon statute, which "makes no exception for the sacramental use" of the drug. 307 Ore. 68, 72–73, 763 P. 2d 146, 148 (1988). It then considered whether that prohibition was valid under the Free Exercise Clause, and concluded that it was not. The court therefore reaffirmed its previous ruling that the State could not deny unemployment benefits to respondents for having engaged in that practice.

We again granted certiorari.

II

Respondents' claim for relief rests on our decisions in *Sherbert v. Verner, supra, Thomas v. Review Bd. of Indiana Employment Security Div., supra,* and *Hobbie v. Unemployment Appeals Comm'n of Florida*, 480 U. S. 136 (1987), in which we held that a State could not condition the availability of unemployment insurance on an individual's willingness to forgo conduct required by his religion. As we observed in *Smith I*, however, the conduct at issue in those cases was not prohibited by law. We held that distinction to be critical, for "if Oregon does prohibit the religious use of peyote, and if that prohibition is consistent with the Federal Constitution, there is no federal right to engage in that conduct in Oregon," and "the State is free to withhold unemployment compensation from respondents for engaging in work-related misconduct, despite its religious motivation." 485 U. S., at 672. Now that the Oregon Supreme Court has confirmed that Oregon does prohibit the religious use of peyote, we proceed to consider whether that prohibition is permissible under the Free Exercise Clause.

A

The Free Exercise Clause of the First Amendment, which has been made applicable to the States by incorporation into the Fourteenth Amendment, see *Cantwell v. Connecticut*, 310 U. S. 296, 303 (1940), provides that "Congress shall make no law respecting an establishment of religion, or *prohibiting the free exercise thereof. . . .*" U. S. Const., Amdt. 1 (emphasis added). The free exercise of religion means, first and foremost, the right to believe and profess whatever religious doctrine one desires. Thus, the First Amendment obviously excludes all "governmental regulation of religious *beliefs* as such." *Sherbert v. Verner, supra,* at 402. The government may not compel affirmation of religious belief, punish the expression of religious doctrines it believes to be false, impose special disabilities on the basis of religious views or religious status, or lend its power to one or the other side in controversies over religious authority or dogma.

But the "exercise of religion" often involves not only belief and profession but the performance of (or abstention from) physical acts: assembling with others for a worship service, participating in sacramental use of bread and wine, proselytizing, abstaining from certain foods or certain modes of transportation. It would be true, we think (though no case of ours has involved the point), that a State would be "prohibiting the free exercise [of religion]" if it sought to ban such acts or abstentions only when they are engaged in for religious reasons, or only because of the religious belief that they display. It would doubtless be unconstitutional, for example, to ban the casting of "statues that are to be used for worship purposes," or to prohibit bowing down before a golden calf.

Respondents in the present case, however, seek to carry the meaning of "prohibiting the free exercise [of religion]" one large step further. They contend that their religious motivation for using peyote places them beyond the reach of a criminal law that is not specifically directed at their religious practice, and that is concededly constitutional as applied to those who use the drug for other reasons. * * *

* * * We have never held that an individual's religious beliefs excuse him from compliance with an otherwise valid law prohibiting conduct that the State is free to regulate. On the contrary, the record of more than a century of our free exercise jurisprudence contradicts that proposition. * * * We first had occasion to assert that principle in *Reynolds v. United States*, 98 U. S. 145 (1879), where we rejected the claim that criminal laws against polygamy could not be constitutionally applied to those whose religion commanded the practice. "Laws," we said, "are made for the government of actions, and while they cannot interfere with mere religious belief and opinions, they may with practices. . . . Can a man excuse his practices to the contrary because of his religious belief? To

permit this would be to make the professed doctrines of religious belief superior to the law of the land, and in effect to permit every citizen to become a law unto himself."

* * *

B

Respondents argue that even though exemption from generally applicable criminal laws need not automatically be extended to religiously motivated actors, at least the claim for a religious exemption must be evaluated under the balancing test set forth in *Sherbert v. Verner*, 374 U. S. 398 (1963). Under the *Sherbert* test, governmental actions that substantially burden a religious practice must be justified by a compelling governmental interest. Applying that test we have, on three occasions, invalidated state unemployment compensation rules that conditioned the availability of benefits upon an applicant's willingness to work under conditions forbidden by his religion. We have never invalidated any governmental action on the basis of the *Sherbert* test except the denial of unemployment compensation. * * * In *Lyng v. Northwest Indian Cemetery Protective Assn.* , 485 U. S. 439 (1988), we declined to apply *Sherbert* analysis to the Government's logging and road construction activities on lands used for religious purposes by several Native American Tribes, even though it was undisputed that the activities "could have devastating effects on traditional Indian religious practices." * * *

* * *

Whether or not the decisions are that limited, they at least have nothing to do with an across-the-board criminal prohibition on a particular form of conduct. Although, as noted earlier, we have sometimes used the *Sherbert* test to analyze free exercise challenges to such laws, we have never applied the test to invalidate one. We conclude today that the sounder approach, and the approach in accord with the vast majority of our precedents, is to hold the test inapplicable to such challenges. The government's ability to enforce generally applicable prohibitions of socially harmful conduct, like its ability to carry out other aspects of public policy, "cannot depend on measuring the effects of a governmental action on a religious objector's spiritual development." *Lyng, supra,* at 451. To make an individual's obligation to obey such a law contingent upon the law's coincidence with his religious beliefs, except where the State's interest is "compelling"—permitting him, by virtue of his beliefs, "to become a law unto himself," *Reynolds v. United States*, 98 U. S., at 167—contradicts both constitutional tradition and common sense.[2]

---

[2]　JUSTICE O'CONNOR seeks to distinguish *Lyng v. Northwest Indian Cemetery Protective Assn.*, 485 U.S. 439 (1988), and *Bowen v. Roy*, 476 U. S. 693 (1986), on the ground that those cases involved the government's conduct of "its own internal affairs," which is different because, as Justice Douglas said in *Sherbert,* " 'the Free Exercise Clause is written in terms of what the

The "compelling government interest" requirement seems benign, because it is familiar from other fields. But using it as the standard that must be met before the government may accord different treatment on the basis of race, or before the government may regulate the content of speech, is not remotely comparable to using it for the purpose asserted here. What it produces in those other fields—equality of treatment and an unrestricted flow of contending speech—are constitutional norms; what it would produce here—a private right to ignore generally applicable laws—is a constitutional anomaly.

Nor is it possible to limit the impact of respondents' proposal by requiring a "compelling state interest" only when the conduct prohibited is "central" to the individual's religion. Cf. *Lyng v. Northwest Indian Cemetery Protective Assn.*, 485 U. S., at 474–476 (BRENNAN, J., dissenting). It is no more appropriate for judges to determine the "centrality" of religious beliefs before applying a "compelling interest" test in the free exercise field, than it would be for them to determine the "importance" of ideas before applying the "compelling interest" test in the free speech field. * * *

If the "compelling interest" test is to be applied at all, then, it must be applied across the board, to all actions thought to be religiously commanded. Moreover, if "compelling interest" really means what it says (and watering it down here would subvert its rigor in the other fields where it is applied), many laws will not meet the test. Any society adopting such a system would be courting anarchy, but that danger increases in direct proportion to the society's diversity of religious beliefs, and its determination to coerce or suppress none of them. Precisely because "we are a cosmopolitan nation made up of people of almost every conceivable religious preference," *Braunfeld v. Brown*, 366 U. S., at 606, and precisely because we value and protect that religious divergence, we cannot afford the luxury of deeming *presumptively invalid,* as applied to the religious objector, every regulation of conduct that does not protect an interest of the highest order. The rule respondents favor would open the prospect of constitutionally required religious exemptions from civic obligations of almost every conceivable kind—ranging from compulsory military service, to the payment of taxes; to health and safety regulation such as manslaughter and child neglect laws, compulsory vaccination laws, drug laws, and traffic laws; to social welfare legislation such as minimum wage laws, child labor laws, animal cruelty laws, environmental protection laws,

---

government cannot do to the individual, not in terms of what the individual can exact from the government.' " (O'Connor, J., concurring in judgment). But since Justice Douglas voted with the majority in *Sherbert*, that quote obviously envisioned that what "the government cannot do to the individual" includes not just the prohibition of an individual's freedom of action through criminal laws but also the running of its programs (in *Sherbert*, state unemployment compensation) in such fashion as to harm the individual's religious interests. Moreover, it is hard to see any reason in principle or practicality why the government should have to tailor its health and safety laws to conform to the diversity of religious belief, but should not have to tailor its management of public lands, *Lyng, supra,* or its administration of welfare programs, *Roy, supra.*

and laws providing for equality of opportunity for the races. The First Amendment's protection of religious liberty does not require this.

Values that are protected against government interference through enshrinement in the Bill of Rights are not thereby banished from the political process. Just as a society that believes in the negative protection accorded to the press by the First Amendment is likely to enact laws that affirmatively foster the dissemination of the printed word, so also a society that believes in the negative protection accorded to religious belief can be expected to be solicitous of that value in its legislation as well. It is therefore not surprising that a number of States have made an exception to their drug laws for sacramental peyote use. See, e.g., Ariz. Rev. Stat. Ann. §§ 13–3402(B)(1)–(3) (1989); Colo. Rev. Stat. § 12–22–317(3) (1985); N. M. Stat. Ann. § 30–31–6(D) (Supp. 1989). But to say that a nondiscriminatory religious-practice exemption is permitted, or even that it is desirable, is not to say that it is constitutionally required, and that the appropriate occasions for its creation can be discerned by the courts. It may fairly be said that leaving accommodation to the political process will place at a relative disadvantage those religious practices that are not widely engaged in; but that unavoidable consequence of democratic government must be preferred to a system in which each conscience is a law unto itself or in which judges weigh the social importance of all laws against the centrality of all religious beliefs.

* * *

Because respondents' ingestion of peyote was prohibited under Oregon law, and because that prohibition is constitutional, Oregon may, consistent with the Free Exercise Clause, deny respondents unemployment compensation when their dismissal results from use of the drug. The decision of the Oregon Supreme Court is accordingly reversed.

* * *

JUSTICE O'CONNOR, with whom JUSTICE BRENNAN, JUSTICE MARSHALL, and JUSTICE BLACKMUN join as to Parts I and II, concurring in the judgment.*

Although I agree with the result the Court reaches in this case, I cannot join its opinion. In my view, today's holding dramatically departs from well-settled First Amendment jurisprudence, appears unnecessary to resolve the question presented, and is incompatible with our Nation's fundamental commitment to individual religious liberty.

* * *

* * * [T]he Court today suggests that the disfavoring of minority religions is an "unavoidable consequence" under our system of government

---

* Although JUSTICE BRENNAN, JUSTICE MARSHALL, and JUSTICE BLACKMUN join Part I and II of this opinion, they do not concur in the judgment.

and that accommodation of such religions must be left to the political process. In my view, however, the First Amendment was enacted precisely to protect the rights of those whose religious practices are not shared by the majority and may be viewed with hostility. The history of our free exercise doctrine amply demonstrates the harsh impact majoritarian rule has had on unpopular or emerging religious groups such as the Jehovah's Witnesses and the Amish. Indeed, the words of Justice Jackson in *West Virginia State Bd. of Ed. v. Barnette* (overruling *Minersville School Dist. v. Gobitis,* 310 U. S. 586 (1940)) are apt:

> "The very purpose of a Bill of Rights was to withdraw certain subjects from the vicissitudes of political controversy, to place them beyond the reach of majorities and officials and to establish them as legal principles to be applied by the courts. One's right to life, liberty, and property, to free speech, a free press, freedom of worship and assembly, and other fundamental rights may not be submitted to vote; they depend on the outcome of no elections." 319 U.S., at 638.

See also *United States v. Ballard,* 322 U. S. 78, 87 (1944) ("The Fathers of the Constitution were not unaware of the varied and extreme views of religious sects, of the violence of disagreement among them, and of the lack of any one religious creed on which all men would agree. They fashioned a charter of government which envisaged the widest possible toleration of conflicting views"). The compelling interest test reflects the First Amendment's mandate of preserving religious liberty to the fullest extent possible in a pluralistic society. For the Court to deem this command a "luxury," is to denigrate "[t]he very purpose of a Bill of Rights."

* * *

[JUSTICE BLACKMUN, with whom JUSTICE BRENNAN and JUSTICE MARSHALL join, dissenting.]

NOTES

1.   One constitutional law scholar suggests that the Court's decision to leave accommodation of religious practices to the political process abdicates a traditionally perceived purpose of judicial review of legislative actions: to protect minority rights from majoritarian tyranny. See Jesse H. Choper, *The Rise and Decline of the Constitutional Protection of Religious Liberty,* 70 Neb.L.Rev. 651, 685–88 (1991). Other commentators have been equally harsh in their criticism of the decision. See Frank S. Ravitch, *A Funny Thing Happened on the Way to Neutrality: Broad Principles, Formalism and the Establishment Clause,* 38 Ga.L.Rev. 489 (2004); Craig J. Dorsay & Lea Ann Easton, *Employment Division v. Smith: Just Say "No" to the Free Exercise Clause,* 59 UMKC L.Rev. 555 (1991); Douglas Laycock, *The Remnants of Free Exercise,* 1990 Sup.Ct.Rev. 1, 2, 29–44, 55–56; Ira C. Lupu, *Reconstructing the*

Establishment Clause: The Case Against Discretionary Accommodation of Religion, 140 U.Pa.L.Rev. 555, 572 n. 56 (1991). In the years following Smith, scholars have analyzed the extent to which various legislative and administrative measures have meaningfully accommodated tribal and other collective Indian religious practices. See Kristen A. Carpenter, *Limiting Principles and Empowering Practices in American Indian Religious Freedoms,* 45 Conn.L.Rev. 387 (2012).

2. *Smith* was controversial because it provided that states could outlaw peyote possession even for religious use. True, as Professor Marci Hamilton often points out, many states legislated in favor of peyote exemptions following *Smith* But this hardly ensured widespread religious liberty for NAC members. To the contrary, these laws created a "patchwork" effect in which twenty-eight states had an exemption for religious use and the rest made peyote possession a felony. As Walter Echo-Hawk argued, "NAC members became subject in twenty-two states to arrest, incarceration, and discrimination solely because of their form of worship." Walter R. Echo-Hawk, In the Courts of the Conqueror: The 10 Worst Indian Law Cases Ever Decided 317 (2010) Not only were peyote practitioners forbidden from practicing *in* those states, but they could not transport peyote *across* those states. Given that peyote grows only in Texas (and Mexico), it became very difficult to obtain the sacrament. Moreover, the state rules varied, with some, like Texas, imposing a "25 percent Indian blood-quantum requirement" and others using different measures of eligibility. As a result of outright prohibitions, legal uncertainty, and continuing societal ignorance about peyote, NAC members were left to "pray in fear" after *Smith.*

3. In the aftermath of *Smith,* American Indians leaders and members of the Native American Church reach out to religious institutions across the country to push for legislative measures to from a broad variety of faiths to push for peyote is the sacrament of the NAC, deeply revered for its spiritual and healing powers. After the broad-based coalition of religious and secular organizations declined to push for peyote-specific protections, well-known peyote leaders such as Reuben Snake partnered with legal services organizations and the Native American Religious Freedom Project to push remedial legislation. The coalition ultimately failed to address peyote but did manage to restore earlier judicial standards on religious liberty. Congress enacted the Religious Freedom Restoration Act of 1993 (RFRA), 42 U.S.C. §§ 2000bb to 2000bb–4. As explained by President Clinton in signing RFRA into law, "this Act reverses the Supreme Court's decision in *Employment Division v. Smith* and reestablishes a standard that better protects all Americans of all faiths in the exercise of their religion." Religious Freedom Restoration Act Signing Ceremony, Fed. News Service (Nov. 16, 1993).

In passing RFRA, Congress restored the "compelling interest" test that the Supreme Court had historically applied prior to *Smith,* through statutory language declaring that "Government shall not substantially burden a person's exercise of religion even if the burden results from a rule of general applicability," unless it can be demonstrated that "application of the burden to the person: (1) is in furtherance of a compelling governmental interest; and (2) is the least restrictive means of furthering that compelling interest." 42 U.S.C. §§ 2000bb–1(a) and (b). Relying on its enforcement powers under the Fourteenth Amendment, Congress extended application of RFRA to state and local laws and practices, as well as to the federal government.

4.   In City of Boerne v. Flores, 521 U.S. 507 (1997), a non-Indian case, the United States Supreme Court struck down RFRA as to its applicability to the states, holding that Congress had exceeded its constitutional authority to enforce the due process and equal protection clauses against the states under the Fourteenth Amendment. Since that authority is limited to remedial action, the Court reasoned, imposing a "compelling interest" test on the state when an individual's religious freedom is "substantially burdened" by a neutral rule of general applicability, particularly when there is little evidence of widespread religious discrimination, is disproportionate to the injury suffered and improperly legislates a change in substantive rights.

In a case involving the use of *hoasca* tea containing DMT, a controlled substance, by members of a religious group with roots in Brazil the Supreme Court held RFRA's congressionally-imposed "compelling interest" test still applies to federal agency enforcement of the Controlled Substances Act. See Gonzales v. O Centro Espirita Beneficente Uniao do Vegetal, 546 U.S. 418 (2006) (court ruled government failed to demonstrate a compelling interest in banning sacramental use of *hoasca*). See also Guam v. Guerrero, 290 F.3d 1210 (9th Cir.2002) (Although Guam's statute criminalizing importation of marijuana could be enforced against marijuana for sacramental use in Rastafarianism, the statute did not substantially burden the practice of Ratsafariamisn under RFRA).

5.   Some tribes have attempted to use RFRA to protect sacred lands and sites. In Navajo Nation v. United States Forest Service, 535 F.3d 1058 (2008) (en banc), cert. denied 556 U.S. 1281 (2009), the Ninth Circuit, sitting *en banc*, rejected a lawsuit brought by six Indian tribes to stop a federally-approved plan for using treated sewage effluent to create snow for skiing on the San Francisco Peaks in northern Arizona. The tribes asserted that the site is sacred and that the use of wastewater on the mountains would spiritually contaminate the area and devalue the religious experience. Invoking RFRA, the Court's opinion established a robust standard for demonstrating that the tribal plaintiffs suffered a "substantial burden" on their religious freedom:

> The Supreme Court's decisions in *Sherbert* and *Yoder*, relied upon and incorporated by Congress into RFRA, lead to the following conclusion: Under RFRA, a "substantial burden" is imposed only when individuals are forced to choose between following the tenets of their religion and receiving a governmental benefit (*Sherbert*) or coerced to act contrary to their religious beliefs by the threat of civil or criminal sanctions (*Yoder*). Any burden imposed on the exercise of religion short of that described by *Sherbert* and *Yoder* is not a "substantial burden" within the meaning of RFRA, and does not

require the application of the compelling interest test set forth in those two cases.

* * *

Applying *Sherbert* and *Yoder,* there is no "substantial burden" on the Plaintiffs' exercise of religion in this case. The use of recycled wastewater on a ski area that covers one percent of the Peaks does not force the Plaintiffs to choose between following the tenets of their religion and receiving a governmental benefit, as in *Sherbert.* The use of recycled wastewater to make artificial snow also does not coerce the Plaintiffs to act contrary to their religion under the threat of civil or criminal sanctions, as in *Yoder.* The Plaintiffs are not fined or penalized in any way for practicing their religion on the Peaks or on the Snowbowl. Quite the contrary: the Forest Service "has guaranteed that religious practitioners would still have access to the Snowbowl" and the rest of the Peaks for religious purposes. *Navajo Nation,* 408 F.Supp.2d at 905.

The only effect of the proposed upgrades is on the Plaintiffs' subjective, emotional religious experience. That is, the presence of recycled wastewater on the Peaks is offensive to the Plaintiffs' religious sensibilities. To plaintiffs, it will spiritually desecrate a sacred mountain and will decrease the spiritual fulfillment they get from practicing their religion on the mountain. Nevertheless, under Supreme Court precedent, the diminishment of spiritual fulfillment-serious though it may be-is not a "substantial burden" on the free exercise of religion.

Navajo Nation, 535 F.3d at 1067, 1069–70.

6. Federal law and Indian religious practice also are in tension when Indians engage in the ceremonial use of eagle feathers and parts. Although taking (including possession) of eagles and their parts is prohibited by the Bald Eagle Protection Act, the Act expressly authorizes the Secretary of the Interior to permit the taking of bald and golden eagles "for the religious purposes of Indian tribes" if compatible with the statute's conservation purpose. 16 U.S.C. § 668A. Regulations governing such permits are designed to ensure that eagle parts are used only in bona fide tribal religious ceremonies. 50 C.F.R. § 22.22 (1985).

Prior to RFRA, most eagle feather cases dealt with Indian claims that treaty hunting rights entitle tribal members to hunt for eagles. See United States v. Dion, 476 U.S. 734 (1986), page 344, supra. The issue of whether the federal prohibitions constitute a violation of the free exercise clause had occasionally arisen. In United States v. Top Sky, 547 F.2d 483 (9th Cir.1976), an Indian craftsman who made articles for use in Indian religious ceremonies claimed that his conviction for violation of the Bald Eagle Protection Act interfered with his free exercise of religion. The court upheld the conviction, ruling that the defendant had no standing to raise free exercise issues. The prosecution was based upon the sale of a feather fan and bustle to non-Indians who were undercover federal agents and the court found that the defendant had asserted only a commercial interest in the feathers. Therefore, the defendant could not make the necessary showing that the law operated coercively against him in the exercise of his religion. See also United States v. Thirty Eight (38) Golden Eagles, 649 F.Supp. 269 (D.Nev.1986), affirmed 829 F.2d 41 (9th Cir.1987) (conviction of an Indian religious leader who sold eagle feathers to an undercover agent upheld; first amendment freedoms must yield to compelling governmental interest). See generally Britt Banks, Comment, *Birds of a Feather: Cultural Conflict and the Eagle in American Society*, 59 U.Colo.L.Rev. 639 (1988); Tina S. Boradiansky, Comment, *Conflicting Values: The Religious Killing of Federally Protected Wildlife*, 30 Nat. Resources J. 709 (1990).

In United States v. Hardman, 297 F.3d 1116 (10th Cir.2002), RFRA was interpreted by the Tenth Circuit as having been violated by the federal government's seizure of eagle feathers from a Chiricahua Apache Indian in New Mexico, whose tribe had been terminated in the nineteenth century. The government argued that only members of federally recognized tribes can use eagle feathers under the federal permitting system established to accommodate Indian religious practitioners. The appeals court held, however, that the Chiricahua Apache had a religious right to possess eagle feathers, pursuant to RFRA. The case was remanded to determine if the government's permitting system of regulation for eagle feathers was the least restrictive means of accomplishing its conservation, trust obligation, and accommodation purposes.

The Ninth Circuit, however, declined to follow *Hardman* in a case involving a Canadian Indian tribal member who was ineligible to receive a federal permit and who was convicted for exchanging eagle parts acquired in his home country for money and goods in the United States as part of a potlatch ceremony. United States v. Antoine, 318 F.3d 919 (9th Cir.2003), cert. denied 540 U.S. 1221 (2004). The appeals court found that the government's permit requirement excluding non-federally recognized Indian tribes was the least restrictive means of protecting eagles, and therefore did not violate RFRA.

In United States v. Friday, 525 F.3d 938 (10th Cir.2008), cert. denied 555 U.S. 1176 (2009), the Tenth Circuit rejected facial and as-applied challenges under RFRA to the Bald and Golden Eagle Protection Act, which created the National Eagle Repository. The Repository is the only avenue for Native American practitioners of the Sun Dance to acquire a whole (and unprocessed) bald eagle, critical for the ceremonies.

The Tenth Circuit was not persuaded that the difficulty in obtaining a permit (especially since Mr. Friday never applied for a permit in the first place) amounted to a constitutional violation:

> In *United States v. Hardman,* we concluded that Native Americans charged with violating the Eagle Act could make an as-applied challenge to the Act's permitting system without applying for

permits if they demonstrated that "it would have been futile . . . to apply for permits." 297 F.3d 1116, 1121 (10th Cir.2002) (en banc). Citing our decision in *Hardman,* the district court here found "futility in the application process." On this basis the court concluded that the Eagle Act, without an effective permitting system, substantially burdened Mr. Friday's religion in a manner more restrictive than is necessary. Examining the record and reviewing this conclusion de novo, *see Bose,* 466 U.S. at 501, 508, 104 S.Ct. 1949, we disagree.

* * *

It is simply not "clear that [Mr. Friday] would not have" received a permit if he had applied, and therefore it is not clear that he "would not have been accommodated by applying" for one. Govt. App. 191. We therefore conclude that it was not futile for Mr. Friday to apply for a permit.

525 F.3d at 953–55.

7.　At the time of *Smith,* federal regulations on unlawful drugs provided (and still continue to provide) an exemption for "the non-drug use of peyote in bona fide religious ceremonies of the Native American Church" (21 CFR § 1307.31 (1985)). Following *Smith,* Congress passed the American Indian Religious Freedom Act Amendments of 1994, 42 U.S.C.A. § 1996a, to prohibit any state from penalizing an Indian who used peyote in a traditional manner for religious purposes, subject to certain governmental restrictions on peyote use, e.g., situations involving law enforcement, public transportation, the military, and prisons.

8.　Prior to *Smith,* the leading case on Native American religious use of peyote was People v. Woody, 394 P.2d 813 (Cal.1964). In *Woody,* the California Supreme Court overturned a conviction for peyote use by a Native American Church member on First Amendment grounds. Justice Tobriner found: "[T]he statutory prohibition of the use of peyote results in a virtual inhibition of the practice of defendants' religion. To forbid the use of peyote is to remove the theological heart of Peyotism." 394 P.2d at 818. He went on to weigh the religious freedom with the asserted compelling state interest in controlling feared drug abuse, finding that the balance tipped toward constitutional protection:

> On the other hand, the right to free religious expression embodies a precious heritage of our history. In a mass society, which presses at every point toward conformity, the protection of a self-expression, however unique, of the individual and the group becomes ever more important. The varying currents of the subcultures that flow into the mainstream of our national life give it depth and beauty. We preserve a greater value than an ancient tradition when we protect the rights of the Indians who honestly practiced an old religion in using peyote one night at a meeting in a desert hogan near Needles, California.

Id. at 821–22. *People v. Woody* was followed in State v. Whittingham, 504 P.2d 950 (Ariz.Ct.App.1973), cert. denied 417 U.S. 946 (1974) and Whitehorn v. State, 561 P.2d 539 (Okla.Crim.App.1977), but was rejected in State v. Soto, 537 P.2d 142 (Or.Ct.App.1975), cert. denied 424 U.S. 955 (1976), where the court found that the use of mescaline by a member of the Native American Church was not based on religious belief but rather was constitutionally unprotected conduct. See generally John Rhodes, *An American Tradition: The Religious Persecution of Native Americans*, 52 Mont.L.Rev. 13 (1991); Russel Lawrence Barsh, *Grounded Visions: Native American Conceptions of Landscape and Ceremony*, 13 St. Thomas L.Rev. 127 (2000).

9.   Indians have challenged government prohibitions on traditional hair styles as violative of their religious tenets. In New Rider v. Board of Education, 480 F.2d 693 (10th Cir.1973), cert. denied 414 U.S. 1097 (1973), Pawnee Indian school children who wore their hair in braids in the traditional manner and their parents challenged a public school hair length regulation that prevented male students from wearing long hair. The court held that the record did not establish that the hair length regulation impinged on the free exercise of religion and, following an earlier precedent, that hair style was not a form of constitutionally protected free expression.

Justice Douglas, joined by Justice Marshall, dissented from the Supreme Court's denial of certiorari in *New Rider,* challenging the Court of Appeals' premise that wearing long hair cannot be constitutionally protected. Certainly it would not matter to the Indian litigants which constitutional pigeonhole is used to protect their activities. But the struggle to categorize neatly what Indians are moved to do by their traditions as either an exercise of free speech or an exercise of religion illustrates the difficulty our legal system has in applying constitutional protections to a differing culture's value system and spiritual life. Justice Douglas' lengthy dissent from the denial of certiorari in *New Rider* viewed the challenged school regulation as symptomatic of a homogenizing force which has impeded the success of Indian education.

Is Indian religion so odd, so enigmatic, that it falls outside the Bill of Rights' meaning of "religion?" Can its exercise be protected only as individual expression?

10.   Courts have divided over Indian challenges to prison hair length and style regulations which are claimed as denying Indian religious freedom rights. See, e.g., Teterud v. Burns, 522 F.2d 357 (8th Cir.1975) (State prison regulation unlawfully prohibited an Indian inmate from wearing long braided hair). But see Pollock v. Marshall, 845 F.2d 656 (6th Cir.1988), cert. denied 488 U.S. 897 (1988) (reasons given by prison superintendent for policy against long hair outweighed the minor infringement on Indian religious freedom). In Sample v. Borg, 675 F.Supp. 574 (E.D.Cal.1987), vacated as moot 870 F.2d 563 (9th Cir.1989), the district court ordered the California prison system to alter regulations to allow Native American inmates to wear headbands, but not hairwraps. Regarding other religious practices, the court allowed participation in pipe ceremonies and possession of tobacco ties, but upheld restrictions on

participation in drum ceremonies and possession of a medicine bag. In Standing Deer v. Carlson, 831 F.2d 1525 (9th Cir.1987), the court held that when a prison regulation impinges on inmates' constitutional rights, the regulation is valid if it is reasonably related to legitimate penological interests. Thus, the court upheld a ban on headbands and further ruled that the prison officials do not bear the burden of disproving the availability of alternatives to the challenged regulations. See also SapaNajin v. Gunter, 857 F.2d 463 (8th Cir.1988) (prison policy of bringing in only one official religious medicine man whose beliefs and practices were known to differ significantly from Sioux prisoner violated his rights).

11. More recently, Indian inmates have attempted to use the RFRA, as well as the Religious Land Use and Institutionalized Persons Act (RLUIPA), to secure the right to practice their religion by wearing their hair long in prison. Two federal courts have come to different conclusions on the issue of hair length under RLUIPA; in Warsoldier v. Woodford, 418 F.3d 989 (9th Cir.2005), the Ninth Circuit held that the hair length restriction could not be justified, but the Fifth Circuit came to the opposite holding in Longoria v. Dretke, 507 F.3d 898 (5th Cir.2007).

In Fowler v. Crawford, 534 F.3d 931 (8th Cir.2008), the court upheld a denial of an inmate's request for permission to use a sweat lodge against a RLUIPA challenge. In Hyde v. Fisher, 203 P.3d 712 (Idaho App.2009), an inmate was denied permission to use a sweat lodge, but the court held that a complete ban on smudging ceremonies had not been demonstrated to be the least restrictive means by which to achieve the compelling state interest of safety and security at the prison. In Alvarez v. Hill, 518 F.3d 1152 (9th Cir.2008), an American Indian inmate denied rights to use a sweat lodge was found to have satisfied RLUIPA in his appeal, and the case was remanded by the Ninth Circuit.

SECTION C. PROTECTION OF AMERICAN INDIAN CULTURAL RESOURCES

In the past, Indian religious beliefs and practices have been suppressed, and even outlawed by the dominant society in the United States. Modern era cases such as *Lyng* and *Smith,* and the tribal focus on federal laws such as AIRFA and the National Historic Preservation Act, are manifestations of the increasing pressures American Indians feel on their tribal traditions and culture and their hope that legal protections will vindicate rights in this area as they have in other areas of Indian law.

Native Americans are similarly frustrated in their desires to protect another vital aspect of their traditional heritage: sacred artifacts and other cultural resources, including the burial sites and remains of their ancestors and tribal intellectual property rights. Here, the problems often relate to commercial exploitation and cultural insensitivity on the part of non-Indian collectors, archaeologists, and museums. American Indian advocacy demanding the right to control and protect their cultural resources have resulted in a number of recent federal acts and initiatives.

1. THE NATIVE AMERICAN GRAVE PROTECTION AND REPATRIATION ACT (NAGPRA)

Like people around the world, American Indians conduct funeral rites and care for the gravesites of deceased relatives. For example, some Native Hawaiians express an intergenerational relationship between the ancestors and living human beings. Ancestors nourish the earth through the *mana* or power contained in their bones, while the living have obligations to care for gravesites, bring offerings to the ancestors, and recite personal lineages going back for generations. Since the mid-nineteenth century, however, Native peoples have struggled to protect gravesites against encroaching settlers—who acquired their lands including cemeteries—and gravediggers—who excavated Native graves for their scientific or curiosity value.

Indian graves have also been looted by governments. During the 1800s, federal agencies were directed to collect Indian human remains as scientific specimen, and in 1868, the U.S. Surgeon General ordered army personnel to collect Indian skulls for craniology studies taking place at the Army Medical Museum. In another instance, the Nebraska State Historical Society came to possess the remains of over 400 dead Pawnee Indians.

Well into the twentieth century, government-sponsored and private parties looted Indian graves in the name of art, science, and education. Early legal advocacy to protect gravesites and recover cultural patrimony met many hurdles. See Onondaga Nation v. Thacher, 189 U.S. 306, 306–08 (1903) (rejecting Onondaga Nation's attempt to recover wampum belts from state custody). Federal law, such as the Archaeological Resources Protection Act, treated Indian artifacts on public lands as nationally owned property, and state cemetery protection laws rarely extended to Indian burial sites. In one powerful story, Lyda Burton Conley, ca. 1869–1946, a Wyandotte woman, spent her entire life trying to save the tribal cemetery from sale and excavation. The first female member of the Kansas bar, Conley ultimately argued pro se before the Supreme Court and held midnight watch, armed with a shotgun, to protect her mother's grave. Kim Dayton, *"Trespassers, Beware!": Lyda Burton Conley and the Battle for Huron Place Cemetery*, 8 Yale J.L. & Feminism 1 (1996).

By the late 1980s, thousands of human skeletons and many more funerary artifacts were housed in federally funded museums and other locations. The National Museum of Natural History possesses 19,250 human skeletal remains of Native Americans. Many museums had in their collections tribal religious objects such as rattles, drums, figurines, shirts, robes and other items. American Indian advocates, led by Walter Echo-

Hawk, Suzan Harjo, and others, convened tribal leaders in a a campaign to address these religious, cultural, and dignitary harms through federal legislation. They testified both to the basic human rights and interests, shared by peoples across the world, associated with laying people to rest after their deaths. They also explained that in many American Indian cultures, the disinterment of graves brings about personal and collective grief, and that the loss of religious and cultural items makes it difficult or impossible to perform contemporary ceremonies.

In response to these efforts, Congress passed the Native American Grave Protection and Repatriation Act (NAGPRA), 25 U.S.C. §§ 3001–3013 (Supp. 1991). Passed in 1990, NAGPRA was hailed as landmark legislation to protect American Indian heritage. One commentator claimed that it "established as a national policy the repatriation requirements to correct the long-standing practices of abuse and disrespect of American Indian remains." Julia A. Cryne, *NAGPRA Revisited: A Twenty-Year Review of Repatriation Efforts*, 34 Am. Indian L.Rev. 99, 109 (2010). Another commentator has stated that the statute "was the product of a national consensus concerning the dignity and respect due American Indians, their property, and their cultures." Steven J. Gunn, *The Native Americans Graves Protection and Repatriation Act at Twenty: Reaching the Limits of Our National Consensus*, 36 Wm. Mitchell L.Rev. 503, 505 (2010).

NAGPRA provides a process for museums and Federal agencies to return certain Native American cultural items, including human remains, funerary objects, sacred objects, or objects of cultural patrimony, to lineal descendants, and culturally affiliated Indian tribes and Native Hawaiian organizations. The law prohibits trade, transport, or sale of Native American human remains and directs federal agencies and museums to take inventory of any Native American or Native Hawaiian remains and, if identifiable, the agency or museum is to return them to the tribal descendants. NAGPRA mandates that the Secretary of Interior establish a committee to monitor the return of remains and objects and authorizes the Secretary to make grants for assisting museums with compliance. The Act prohibits remains and objects from being considered archaeological resources, prohibits disturbing sites without tribal consent, and imposes criminal penalties for unauthorized excavation, removal, damage or destruction.

NAGPRA's criminal provisions, 25 U.S.C.A. § 3001 (3) (D), have been upheld as applied to trafficking in Navajo ceremonial adornment masks, United States v. Corrow, 119 F.3d 796 (10th Cir.1997); Hopi masks and priest's robes from Acoma Pueblo, United States v. Tidwell, 191 F.3d 976 (9th Cir.1999); and a prayer-stick bundle containing a sun disk, bird feather, and a tablita, United States v. Kramer, 168 F.3d 1196 (10th Cir.1999). See generally *Symposium: The Native American Graves Protection and Repatriation Act of 1990 and State Repatriation-Related*

Legislation, 24 Ariz.St.L.J. 1 (1992); Kelly E. Yasaitis, *NAGPRA: A Look Back Through the Litigation,* 25 J. Land Resources & Envtl.L. 259 (2005).

Some museums, art dealers, archaeologists, and others initially opposed NAGRPA, fearing that human skeletons and other objects with scientific, educational, and aesthetic value to the public would be returned wholesale to tribes, leaving museums, labs, and other institutions empty of their most precious resources. There are also significant costs associated with inventory and reptariation. Yet in many instances, NAGPRA has facilitated cooperation among museums and tribes, and among scientists and tribes. See, e.g., Miranda J. Brady, *A Dialogic Response to the Problematized Past,* in Contesting Knowledge: Museums and Indigenous Perspectives 133–37 (Susan Sleeper-Smith ed. 2009). Such interactions are characterized by a substantial investment in time and the development of mutual respect among the parties.

Enforcement of the Act's provisions on burial protections has generated a number of highly-publicized controversies between Indian tribes and non-Indian museums and scientific researchers. One of the most widely publicized battles over NAGPRA involved the discovery in 1996 of the "Kennewick Man," a 9,300-year-old human skeleton found on the banks of the Columbia River. Surprisingly, the skeleton is reported to have Caucasian features said by scientific experts not to exist in Native American anthropological history. See Note, *Property Rights in Ancient Human Skeletal Remains,* 70 S.Cal.L.Rev. 805, 816–19 (1997).

Indian tribes from the area of the Columbia River where Kennewick Man was found made a claim of ownership under NAGPRA, and opposed scientific study of the bones. When federal officials, seeking to comply with NAGPRA, determined that the remains should be granted to the tribes, a group of prominent scientists sued for the right to study the bones. They claimed their findings would reveal important information about the early inhabitants of North America and where they came from. The Ninth Circuit upheld a federal district court order that the remains be turned over to the scientists on the grounds that no cognizable link could be found to exist between Kennewick Man and modern Columbia River Indian tribes. See Bonnichsen v. United States, 367 F.3d 864 (9th Cir.2004). See generally Jack F. Trope and Walter R. Echohawk, *The Native American Graves Protection and Repatriation Act: Background and Legislative History,* 24 Ariz.St.L.J. 35 (Spring 1992); C. Timothy McKeown and Sherry Hutt, *In the Smaller Scope of Conscience: The Native American Graves Protection & Repatriation Act Twelve Years After,* 21 UCLA J.Envtl L. & Pol'y 153 (2003).

2. THE NATIONAL MUSEUM OF THE AMERICAN INDIAN ACT

The National Museum of the American Indian Act, 20 U.S.C. §§ 80q to 80q–15 (Supp.1990), provided for the creation of a new National Museum of the American Indian of the Smithsonian Institution, which opened in September 2004 on the Mall in Washington, D.C. In addition, the statute provided for repatriation to tribes of some of the Smithsonian's collection of the remains of an estimated 19,000 Native Americans. The Smithsonian must inventory and identify the origins of human remains and funerary objects under its control, "in consultation and cooperation with traditional Indian religious leaders and government officials of Indian tribes." 20 U.S.C. § 80q–9 (Supp.1990). If Indian human remains are identified as those of a particular individual or as those of an individual culturally affiliated with a particular Indian tribe, the Secretary of the Smithsonian, "upon the request of the descendants of such individual or of the Indian tribe shall expeditiously return such remains (together with any associated funerary objects) to the descendants or tribe, as the case may be." 20 U.S.C. § 80q–9(c). The law also provides for the return of funerary objects not associated with specific human remains if the object can be identified as coming from a particular burial site. 20 U.S.C. § 80q–11. The Act also covers Native Hawaiian remains.

3. THE ARCHEOLOGICAL RESOURCES PROTECTION ACT

The Archaeological Resources Protection Act, 16 U.S.C. §§ 470aa–470mm, is an extension of the Antiquities Act of 1906, 16 U.S.C.A. §§ 431–33. The Act prohibits the excavation, removal, alteration, or destruction of archeological resources on federal and tribal lands, and includes protections for graves and human remains. Once excavated, archaeological resources defined as "any material remains of past human life or activities" of at least 100 years of age, are deemed to be the property of the United States if removed from public lands. The Act itself references NAGPRA in regulating the disposition of Native American remains or cultural objects excavated on public lands. Tribes must be notified by federal land managers when issuing permits in public lands that might harm "any religious or cultural site." See 16 U.S.C. § 470cc(b)–(c).

Many tribes have moved to establish their own programs designed to protect graves and human remains located on sacred lands and sites. In 2005, the Harvard Project on American Indian Economic Development honored the Tribal Monitors Program of the Standing Rock Sioux, a program designed to identify and monitor sacred sites on tribal lands through the Tribe's Historic Preservation Office. One of the program's goals is to ensure that any exposed artifacts or human remains are dealt with in a culturally appropriate manner. See Honoring Nations: Directory of Honored Programs, Sept. 2007 p. 32 http://hpaied.org/images/resources/general/Dir_web.pdf.

4. OTHER FEDERAL, STATE, AND TRIBAL LAWS PROTECTIVE OF INDIAN CULTURE

In 1990, Congress amended the Native American Languages Act, 25 U.S.C. §§ 2901–2906. The amendments recite that Native American cultures and languages have unique status and that the United States has the responsibility to act with the tribes to promote the rights and freedom of Native Americans to use, practice, and develop Native American languages, including using them as a medium of instruction in all schools funded by the Secretary of Interior. In this area of cultural revitalization as well, tribes have taken the lead in preserving and developing tribal languages. In 2005, the Harvard Project on American Indian Economic Development honored the Cherokee Language Revitalization Project for its commitment to keeping its language alive through immersion programs for children and community activities providing language instruction to adults. See Honoring Nations, supra, pp. 32–33.

Congress passed a related measure, the Native American Languages Act of 1992, and in 2006 passed the Esther Martinez Native American Languages Preservation Act, which expanded funding for the preservation of Native American languages and authorized grants for a variety of programs, including the creation and expansion of language nests for children and parents, language survival schools for children, and demonstration programs designed to provide assistance to the nests and survival schools. The Act did not, however, mandate action be taken to preserve languages, nor did it specify a dollar amount to be put toward the programs. See Allison M. Dussias, *Indigenous Languages Under Siege: The Native American Experience*, 3 Intercultural Hum.Rts.L.Rev. 5 (2008).

The Indian Arts and Crafts Act, 18 U.S.C.A. §§ 1158–1159, 25 U.S.C.A. § 305 et seq., promotes Indian art by giving the federal Indian Arts and Crafts Board to identify and support Indian arts and crafts, expand marketing opportunities, and ensure truth-in-advertising . The IACB administers a broad set of programs setting forth best practices for labelling and buying Indian art. See https://www.doi.gov/iacb/Act. The Act also prohibits the misrepresentation of goods and products as Indian made, allowing the federal government, Indian tribes, and Indian organizations to bring enforcement actions. See Native American Arts, Inc. v. Bud K Worldwide, Inc., 2012 WL 1833877 (M.D.Ga. May 18, 2012) (by offering testimony regarding lost profits and business opportunities caused by defendant's sale of fake Indian arts and crafts, Native American organization showed sufficient standing to survive motion to dismiss IACA action). Professor Naomi Mezey identifies one potential problem with the

Act; "[t]he problem with certifying authentic Indian stuff is that it requires certifying authentic Indians." Naomi Mezey, *The Paradoxes of Cultural Property*, 107 Colum.L.Rev. 2004, 2015 (2007).

Professor Angela Riley has argued that tribal law itself must play the major role in the protection of indigenous cultural property:

> It is now apparent that a tiered system of laws—international, national, and tribal—will best protect the cultural property of indigenous groups. However, tribal law, which provides vital cultural context, must serve as the foundation. Because it is suited to indigenous groups' particular cultures and normative framework, tribal law is inimitably capable of capturing and accommodating the unique features of the tribal community. Tribal cultures are not all alike; tribal laws reflect a tribe's economic system, cultural beliefs, and sensitive sacred knowledge in nuanced ways that top-down national and international regimes simply cannot.

Angela R. Riley, *"Straight Stealing": Toward an Indigenous System of Cultural Property Protection*, 80 Wash.L.Rev. 69, 73–74 (2005).

Several states have enacted their own cultural resources protection legislation. In 1976, California enacted legislation prohibiting any public agency or private person using public lands from interfering with the free exercise of Indian religion or from causing irreparable damage to an Indian religious site located on public property, "except on a clear and convincing showing that the public interest and necessity so require." Cal.Pub.Res.Code § 5097.9 (West 1984). The state's Native American Heritage Commission is empowered to: (1) assist state agencies to negotiate with federal agencies to protect Indian sacred places located on federal lands; (2) file court actions to prevent severe damage and assure Indian access to religious sites and cemeteries; and (3) recommend the state's acquisition of private lands on which Indian sacred sites are located. The statute was unsuccessfully challenged by a California archaeologist who sought to resist a commission subpoena to return Indian artifacts. The court rejected claims that the statute was void for vagueness and violated the due process and equal protection clauses of the constitution. See People v. Van Horn, 267 Cal.Rptr. 804 (Ct.App.1990).

NOTE

In Chilkat Indian Village v. Johnson, 870 F.2d 1469 (9th Cir.1989), a Tlingit Indian village in Alaska, organized as a tribe under the Indian Reorganization Act, sued Michael Johnson and sixteen others in federal district court for the return of Tlingit artifacts. The artifacts at issue in the case were four carved wooden posts and a rain screen long coveted by art dealers and museums. The tribe alleged that: 1) the artifacts were owned by the tribe and were removed by the defendants without permission; and 2) defendants violated a village ordinance and federal law by removing the artifacts. The Ninth Circuit reversed the district court's dismissal of the tribe's claim against Johnson, a non-Indian, for lack of subject matter jurisdiction, holding that it arose under federal law. It cited *National Farmers Union,* see page 618, supra, in which the Supreme Court stated that federal law defines the jurisdiction of Indian tribes over non-members. "In our case the state of the law is such that the heart of the controversy over the claim will be the Village's power, under federal law, to enact its ordinance and apply it to non-Indians." *Chilkat Indian Village v. Johnson,* 870 F.2d at 1474.

5. INTELLECTUAL PROPERTY RIGHTS

Intellectual property law includes a broad range of protected legal interests. Extensive statutory schemes exist to protect trade secrets, copyrights, patents, and trademarks as property rights under United States law. Intellectual property law has generated a rich variety of disputes and controversies that have involved Indians and Indian issues. Invariably, it seems, these legal battles raise broader issues about the persistence and perpetuation of certain racial stereotypes of Indians that have little connection to present-day realities of Indian life in the United States. Scholars have argued that these cases reveal the ways in the U.S. legal system has facilitated and normalized the taking of *all* things Indian for others' use. *See* Angela R. Riley and Kristen A. Carpenter, *Owning* Red: *A Theory of Indian Appropriation,* 94 Tex.L.Rev. 859 (2016) (linking the historic dispossession of Indian lands and resources to contemporary appropriation of Indian culture and religion).

The controversy over the use of Native American names and mascots by high schools, colleges, and professional sports teams has received a great deal of publicity and notoriety in recent years. See Gavin Clarkson, *Racial Imagery and Native Americans: A First Look at the Empirical Evidence Behind the Indian Mascot Controversy,* 11 Cardozo J.Int'l & Comp.L. 393 (2003). At the college level, momentum began to move in the direction of limiting the use of Indian mascots began over a decade ago. The NCAA issued a 2005 decision to "prohibit NCAA colleges and universities from displaying hostile and abusive racial/ethnic/national origin mascots, nicknames or imagery at any of the 88 NCAA championships." Citing the NCAA's principles of "cultural diversity and gender equity," "sportsmanship and ethical conduct," and "nondiscrimination," the NCAA policy provides that schools with Indian mascots or logos may continue to use them without penalty if they seek and receive consent from the relevant Indian tribe. However, if the relevant tribe does not consent, the offending institution must either change the mascot or be prevented from hosting NCAA postseason championship events.

When first announced, NCAA's mascot policy was controversial. At the University of North Dakota, certain alumni threatened to withdraw funding if the institution abandoned the "Fighting Sioux" mascot, and some American Indian students experienced racial hostility and backlash. The University ultimately decided to retire the name when it could not obtain the necessary consent from one of the two tribes it was required to consult. By contrast, the longstanding relationship between Florida State University and Seminole Tribe of Florida, in which the tribe has consented to university's mascot usage, appears to have been enhanced by the NCAA policy. The team consults with the tribe regularly regarding depictions of Seminole history, and culture. The relationship stretches beyond athletics to include a new Seminole history course, honorary degrees for tribal leaders, and gifts between the university and tribal council. See andré douglas pond cummings and Seth E. Harper, *Wide Right: Why the NCAA's Policy on the American Indian Mascot Issue Misses the Mark*, 9 U.Md.L.J. Race, Religion, Gender & Class 135 (2009).

In professional sports, the most highly publicized case involves the legal challenge to several trademark registrations held by the Pro-Football corporation, the owner of the Washington "Redskins" of the National Football League.[10] The term "r-skin" was widely used in the nineteenth century to describe the skins of Indians, for which various governments offered and paid bounties incentivizing whites to kill them. American Indian advocates argue that the term has evolved into a racial slur used to intimidate, humiliate, and harm contemporary American Indians, which is thus "disparaging" under the Lanham Act. Yet, supporters of the marks, including the Washington team owner and team fans, have vigilantly defended them against in a series of lawsuits alleging rights based on the First and Fifth Amendments, as well as other defenses.

Section 2(a) of the Lanham Act provides that trademark registration may be denied or cancelled if a mark "consists of or comprises immoral, deceptive or scandalous matter," or brings persons, living or dead, "into contempt or disrepute." 15 U.S.C. § 1052(a). In 1992, a group American Indians, led by Suzan Harjo filed *Harjo et al v. Pro Football, Inc.*, filed an action before the U.S. Patent and Trademark Office Trial Trademark and Appeal Board to cancel the federal trademark registrations for names and images using the r-skins name and imagery. The TTAB ruled in favor of their petition in 1999.

The Board found the marks "may disparage" Native Americans or "bring them into contempt, or disrepute," in violation of the Lanham Act. Harjo v. Pro-Football, Inc., 50 U.S.P.Q.2d 1705, 1749 (T.T.A.B.1999). The

---

[10] For subsequent references to the team name, the editors use the abbreviation "R-skins," following the practices of media outlets and others that have stopped using the term based on their understanding that it is a racial epithet. David Uberti, Journalism Says Goodbye to Redskins: A List of News Organizations That No Longer Use the Team Name, Colum. Journalism Rev., Nov./Dec. 2014.

Board's finding cited dictionary definitions of the word "r-skins" sworn deposition testimony of "linguistic experts," "voluminous excerpts from newspapers, including cartoons, headlines, editorials and articles from the 1940s to the present," a telephone survey "purporting to measure the views, at the time of the survey in 1996, of the general population and separately of Native Americans towards the word 'red skin' as a reference to Native Americans," and other evidence presented to the Board.

In Pro-Football, Inc. v. Harjo, 284 F.Supp.2d 96 (D.D.C.2003), however, a federal district court reversed the Board on an *appeal* de novo. Declining to rule on whether the word "r-skin" was insulting to Native Americansthe district court found that the Board had relied upon partial, dated and irrelevant evidence and therefore restored the trademarks to the team. The court also ruled that because of the substantial delay in bringing a challenge to the trademarks (25 years from the first trademark registered in 1967 for r-skins laches was available as a defense to the team. The D.C. Circuit Court of Appeals overturned this decision in Pro-Football, Inc. v. Harjo, 415 F.3d 44 (D.C.Cir.2005), but on remand, the district court again held that Romero's claim was barred by laches on the theory that he waited for eight years after the age he reached majority to file suit, causing economic and procedural prejudice to Pro-Football, Inc.as a result. See Pro-Football, Inc. v. Harjo, 567 F. Supp. 2d 46 (D.D.C.2008). The D.C. Circuit affirmed on those grounds. See Pro Football, Inc. v. Harjo, 565 F.3d 880 (D.C.Cir.2009).

The next phase of litigation was filed by Amanda Blackhorse and others who had recently reached the age of majority, on the theory that their claim would not be barred by laches. Again the TTAB decided to cancel the marks using the r-skins term and imagery pursuant to the Lanham Act. Pro-Football, Inc. v. Blackhorse, 112 F.Supp.3d 439, 490 (E.D.Va.2015). This time the federal court upheld the TTAB's cancellation, drawing on "(1) dictionary evidence, (2) literary, scholarly, and media references, and (3) statements of individuals and groups in the referenced group" to conclude that the r-skins marks "consisted of matter that 'may disparage' a substantial composite of Native Americans during the relevant time period (1967, 1974, 1978, and 1990)."

The case is now on appeal, where the parties are arguing myriad issues including the constitutionality of the Lanham Act's disparagement provision. On this point, the district court rejected Pro-Football's free speech claims, treating trademark registration as government speech subject to a lower level of protection. The court also noted that even if the federal trademark registrations are cancelled, Pro-Football, will still be fully free to use the name and mascot; it will just not be able to claim federal trademark infringement. *See Blackhorse*, 112 F.Supp.3d at 464. *But see* In re Tam, 808 F.3d 1321 (Fed.Cir.2015) (holding Section 2(a) of the Lanham Act is a content-based regulation of speech that violates the First

Amendment). For a discussion of the norms of expression and anti-discrimination in trademark law, see Sonia K. Katyal, *Trademark Intersectionality*, 57 UCLA L.Rev. 1601, 1632–38 (2010).

NATION-BUILDING NOTE: THE MOVEMENT TO ADDRESS INDIAN SPORTS MASCOTS[11]

The movement to challenge the mascot of the Washington Football team has brought together a cross-section of leaders in the American Indian community making an unprecedented impact on public awareness on these issues. This experience speaks volumes about Indian advocacy in the contemporary era and the role of tribal nations in this movement.

Suzan Harjo is a Cheyenne tribal member. She has been a radio host, tribal lands advocate, and director of the National Congress of American Indians. She has been awarded a Presidential Medal of Freedom. Forty years ago, Harjo was a young woman who had recently moved to D.C. and attended a Washington R-skins football game. As she recently explained to the New York Times, "Fans sitting nearby, apparently amused that American Indians were in their midst, pawed their hair and poked them, 'not in an unfriendly way, but in a scary way.'" She decided to do something about it.

Harjo became the lead plaintiff in the first case to challenge the trademark registrations. She and others explained the racially discriminatory roots of the name in the practice of putting a bounty on Indians' "red skins" as an incentive for murder, and explained how they had contemporarily experienced the term as a racial epithet. As described above, the trademark board ruled that the marks were disparaging racial designations for American Indians, but reviewing courts reversed on grounds that the plaintiffs had waited too long to assert their claims. Undeterred, Harjo reached out to the next generation of Indian leaders, recruiting Amanda Blackhorse and others. As described above, that case is still pending

Meanwhile, an entire generation of young people have taken the anti-mascot campaign to social media and other contemporary outlets. High school students, led by Dahkota Kicking Bear, and college athletes such as Bronson Koenig of the Wisconsin Badgers, are speaking out publicly to explain how Indian mascots foster experiences of humiliation, fear, and discrimination among young people. Bloggers, including Jessica Metcalfe of Beyond Buckskin and Adrienne Keene of Native Appropriations post real-time discussions, debates, and news stories on mascots and other cultural property issues. Groups such as The 1491s, Native Voice Network, and Buffalo Nickel Creative have produced videos satirizing the team, its fans, and its sponsors for what appears to be their blithe ignorance in continuing to use a "dictionary defined racial slur" in their activities. The #notyourmascot hashtag and the "Proud to

---

[11]   This section is derived from Angela R. Riley and Kristen A. Carpenter, Owning Red: A Theory of Indian Appropriation, 94 Tex.L.Rev. 859 (2016).

Be" advertisement against the R-skins have flooded Twitter, Facebook, and other social-media platforms.

In support of these claims, Indian tribes have put their resources behind efforts to educate and to advocate for the name change. The Oneida Indian Nation of New York and the Yocha Dehe Wintun Nation of California have both recently emerged from hundreds of years of land loss and poverty to engage in economic development, political advocacy, and cultural recovery. Both tribes have invested substantial funds in the campaign to end offensive Indian mascot use. Yocha Dehe paid for an advertisement entitled Proud to Be to run on television during the National Basketball Association finals in 2014. The ad showed sixty seconds of Indian people, in each instance "proud to be" strong, brave, or resilient; Hopi, Navajo, or Cherokee; an athlete, lawyer, or mother, but never a "r-skin." The Oneida Nation's "Change the Name" initiative works with the National Congress of American Indians on high-level outreach to National Football League players, and also opposes use of the r-skins name in forums ranging from local high schools to army bases to discount retail chains.

Why do these tribes spend their precious resources to fight the r-skins? Tribal leaders say this cause is essential to the well-being of Indian people. According to Yocha Dehe chairman Marshall McKay, tribal members face discrimination based on misperceptions of Indian race and culture. They cannot thrive in school, at work, or in public places when they are called racial epithets, denied jobs, or physically assaulted. Oneida Nation representative Ray Halbritter cites the need to end the dehumanizing use of the r-skins term as critical to disrupting the cycles of poverty, alcoholism, and suicide that plague Indian people. Halbritter believes that "[c]hange will come . . . 'not because of the benevolence of a team owner, but because a critical mass of Americans will no longer tolerate, patronize, and cheer on bigotry.' "

Together with the legal claims, these various forms of advocacy appear have had a palpable impact on mainstream media, entertainment, and politics. The New Yorker, South Park and The Daily Show have all lampooned the NFL, the team, its owner, and its fans for their insensitivity in continuing to use the name. Shareholder actions and divestment campaigns are now targeted at FedEx, the owner of the stadium where the R-skins play. In politics, President Obama, Attorney General Holder, and fifty U.S. Senators have all weighed in, favoring a name change. Everyone from school children to a federal judge, several major newspapeers and at least one NFL referee have said they will not use the name.

The strategy to end racist sports mascots is diffuse and pervasive, including legal and non-legal methods, and venues as diverse as the Indian community itself. Indians have joined the cause as individuals, organizations, and as nations. The resilience of long-time activists, creativity of young people, and resources of tribal government have all coalesced. As a result, the legal status of the Washington Team's trademarks remains contested, but the time when people can use racial epithets for American Indians without rebuttal appears to be ending.

NOTE

1.   In Hornell Brewing Co. v. Rosebud Sioux Tribal Court, 133 F.3d 1087 (8th Cir.1998), the family of Tasunke Witko, known in English as "Crazy Horse," attempted to bring a lawsuit on behalf of Crazy Horse's estate in tribal court to stop the brewery from using the revered Lakota political and spiritual leader's name to market "Crazy Horse Beer." The family requested damages for violation of the estate's right of publicity, and negligent and intentional infliction of emotional distress. With no evidence that the Company had ever marketed the beer through an on-reservation liquor store, the Eighth Circuit applied the *Montana* rule and its exceptions, and found that the tribal court lacked jurisdiction over the makers of Crazy Horse Beer for activities occurring outside the reservation:

> The mere fact that a member of a tribe or a tribe itself has a cultural interest in conduct occurring outside a reservation does not create jurisdiction of a tribal court under its powers of limited inherent sovereignty. . . . As *Montana* emphasizes, "exercise of tribal power beyond what is necessary to protect tribal self-government or to control internal relations is inconsistent with the dependent status of the tribes, and so cannot survive without express Congressional delegation."

Id. at 1091–92. The Eighth Circuit said, however, that the estate and other interested parties may assert their claims in federal district court.

Suppose the brewery had distributed Crazy Horse Malt Liquor to an on-reservation liquor store that sold the beverage to tribal members, but the store was owned by a non-Indian and was located on non-Indian fee land, and the breweries' delivery trucks had entered the reservation by driving solely on state-maintained roads? Could the estate, under the reasoning of *Strate v. A-1 Contractors*, and *Montana*, then bring its suit in tribal court, or would it still have to sue in federal district court?

2.   American Indian and other indigenous peoples often possess valuable traditional knowledge, including information about the nutritional and medicinal properties of plants and animals within their territories. According to the World Intellectual Property Organization, "traditional knowledge" (TK) constitutes the "knowledge, know-how, skills and practices that are developed, sustained and passed on from generation to generation within a community, often forming part of its cultural or spiritual identity." Traditional Knowledge, World Intell. Prop. Org., http://www.wipo.int/tk/en/tk/.

Conflicts arise when universities and corporations enter indigenous communities, harvest information and materials, and use these in their applications for patents to medicines and foods, sometimes without adequate notice or compensation to the Indian tribe. Some argue that indigenous peoples should seek their own patents so that they can establish and exploit their own resources. This may be easier said than done. Patent law requires that the applicant demonstrate that the invention is patentable subject matter, as defined by Congress, useful, novel, and not previously disclosed. These factors may be difficult to demonstrate in the context of collective, intergenerational knowledge production. Indigenous cultural norms giving rise to traditional knowledge, such as collective stewardship of resources, reciprocity with the natural world, and religious privacy, may prevent the kinds of disclosure and use required to establish a patent.

U.S. tribes and other leaders are involved in negotiations at WIPO regarding these issues. The Tulalip Tribes from Washington have led these efforts arguing, for example, that the Tribe's treaty rights to hunt, fish, and gather extend to the right to regulate and protect the TK associated with lands. While WIPO has not fully resolved its position on these issues, it offers technical assistance for documentation of TK and a set of model laws for nation states regarding the protection of folklore. Negotiations are ongoing regarding a new international instrument to protect traditional knowledge, cultural expressions, and genetic resources.

The Convention on Biodiversity and the U.N. Declaration on the Rights of Indigenous People may bear on these negotiations. UNDRIP Article 31 provides: Indigenous peoples have the right to maintain, control, protect and develop their cultural heritage, traditional knowledge and traditional cultural expressions. * * * They also have the right to maintain, control, protect and develop their intellectual property over such cultural heritage, traditional knowledge, and traditional cultural expressions. Indigenous leaders have called for the UNDRIP's provisions on "free, prior, and informed consent" to govern in transactions and relationships among indigenous peoples, governments, and others who seek to obtain their traditional knowledge.

Suppose you represent a tribe in which certain elders maintain knowledge and ceremonial practices around the medicinal qualities of plants in their territory. These elders know and use a method for treating persistent headaches using a compound they make from a particular tree leaf, which is administered to the patient, along with a set of ritual incantations. How might you work with the tribe to implement international norms on traditional knowledge as a matter of tribal law and practice? How do you frame the conversation with your client regarding the potential interests of the elders, tribe, pharmaceutical industry, and society-at-large?

CHAPTER ELEVEN

WATER RIGHTS

■ ■ ■

Perhaps the overriding natural resource issue in the western United States is the allocation of water rights. Basically, it is a physical problem. The West is semi-arid and the areas with the greatest needs—cities, fertile farmlands, mines—are often located far from water sources. Seasonal fluctuations and changing climate patterns exacerbate the problem.

In the early West, competitors for water for mining and agriculture sometimes resolved their disputes with violence. A simple scheme of water rights was developed to allocate the best rights to precious water to those who first put water to a beneficial use. "First in time, first in right" summarizes the fundamental role of most western states' water laws. The rights of later users produce less dependable supplies, as rights on paper do not guarantee delivery in dry years. In a drought some water rights are meaningless, and all but the most senior appropriators live in fear that they will not see delivery of the water on which their livelihood is based.

The uncertainties caused by climate are compounded by the existence of undefined Indian rights that exist under federal law. Indian water rights allow reservation water users to preempt others who have been using water for years, disturbing the apparent order of the first in time, first in right regime. A doctrine stemming from the early case of *Winters v. United States*, page 819, infra, assures tribes the right to use sufficient water to fulfill the purposes of their reservations. This right is prior to all uses that began after the reservation was established. It does not matter when the Indian use begins; the reserved right can take priority over and displace those who have been using water for many years under state water rights. The rationale of the old, court-made doctrine is that neither the Indians in ceding vast land areas, nor Congress in approving the arrangement, could have intended that tribes would be left with a useless wasteland; therefore, they impliedly reserve sufficient water to make productive the lands set aside in treaties, agreements, and executive orders—and to fulfill the government's plan implicit in those documents to "civilize" Indians.

Nearly all of the western states are embroiled in reserved water rights issues. Under a federal statute commonly referred to as the McCarran Amendment, states can initiate lawsuits to determine all water rights in a watershed and can force the federal government to participate as representative of Indian tribes claiming water rights. Only one such adjudication has run the gamut from state trial and appellate courts to a U.S. Supreme Court test (*Big Horn I,* page 850, infra). The cost and inflexibility in judicial quantification of reserved rights has led many states and tribes to negotiate rather than litigate the extent of reserved rights, and then to ask Congress or the courts to approve their agreements. The United States Supreme Court has tried to ameliorate the harsh potential of the reserved rights doctrine for non-Indian water users by limiting the ability of tribes to expand rights after they have been quantified, even if they were inadequately represented by the United States at the time of quantification. The Court's insistence on the finality of reserved rights determinations has made it incumbent on tribes to hire their own lawyers and experts to participate as tribal rights are determined.

Many significant issues concerning the nature and extent of Indian reserved water rights have not been decided. The broad, judicially-developed standard for measuring Indian water rights when a reservation has been set aside for agricultural purposes—sufficient water to irrigate all "practicably irrigable acreage" (PIA) within the reservation—leaves room for technical theories and legal advocacy. Courts in different states have issued conflicting rulings on whether the practicably irrigable acreage formula must be applied in all such cases and on whether tribes possess instream, non-consumptive rights for reservation fisheries and for religious purposes. Moreover, some courts have begun to recognize that the measure of Indian water rights should not be limited to PIA, but rather should be more broadly defined as the amount needed to sustain a homeland. In times when economic sustainability of tribal nations may depend on operating business ventures, resource development, attracting tourism, and creating viable residential communities, agricultural purposes should not dominate the determination of rights.

Another important and as yet unresolved question is whether tribes or states control the non-Indian use of water within Indian reservations. Several Indian tribes have established their own water administration agencies, with trained personnel and sophisticated management techniques. Tribal water codes that include comprehensive water management schemes are coming into conflict with state water laws purporting to regulate all water use within state boundaries. This is the classic tribal-state jurisdictional conflict, but cast in the setting of water resources management. It is one of the most vital Indian sovereignty issues today, and gives rise to questions about how the modern era Supreme Court cases concerning jurisdiction over non-Indians should be applied to Indian reserved water rights.

SECTION A. WATER LAW IN THE WEST

The doctrine of prior appropriation is the keystone of western water rights. It creates the framework in which Indian reserved rights operate. The following article explains the doctrine's development and effects.

HAROLD A. RANQUIST, THE *WINTERS* DOCTRINE AND HOW IT GREW: FEDERAL RESERVATION OF RIGHTS TO THE USE OF WATER
1975 BYU.L.Rev. 639, 642–46.

When the federal government acquired western lands through the Louisiana Purchase and the Treaty of Guadalupe Hidalgo, little was known of the area. It was considered desert land incapable of crop production except along the rivers of the Great Plains and on the coastal strip bordering the Pacific Ocean. The area was unpopulated except for Indian communities: agricultural pueblos along the Rio Grande, farming communities of the Navajo and Pima-Maricopa Tribes, seed collecting cultures of California, fishing-based cultures of the Northwest, and nomad hunters of the Great Plains. By the mid-1800's, there was also a small irrigated colony in the Salt Lake Valley and surrounding areas established by the Mormon pioneers under Brigham Young.

With the discovery of gold in the West and the race to expand the number of both free and slave states in the Midwest, the settlement of the West increased rapidly. Miners swarmed over the uninhabited land, occupying the public domain and operating their mines with the silent acquiescence of the United States Government. To bring order out of the resulting chaos, the miners and the pioneers established customs and rules which regulated the ownership and operation of the mines and the right to the use of water. In essence, these rules provided that the first to locate the mining claim and the first to use the water held a prior right and would be protected against the claims of others.

The United States owned all western lands not privately held under previous sovereigns and possessed the power to dispose of these lands and the water, together or separately. By its acquiescence, the United States permitted those persons whose rights were recognized by the developing customs and rules to possess the public lands and waters and to divert those waters out of their watersheds and across the public lands to distant mining claims and irrigated tracts. The existence of federal authority to dispose of the water on one hand, and the actual disposition of that water under the growing doctrine of prior appropriation on the other, resulted in conflict between the first appropriator of water and the federal patentee who claimed an unencumbered title.

Shortly after the close of the Civil War, legislative proposals were made to have Congress withdraw the mines from the public domain of the West and either operate or sell them to obtain revenue to retire the Civil War debt. The opposition of western Senators and Congressmen resulted, however, in the enactment of legislation in 1866 which expressly confirmed both the rights of the miners and the rights of the appropriators of water.

> *** What it did was to take cognizance of the customs and usages that had grown up on the public lands under State and Territorial sanction and to make compliance therewith essential to the enjoyment of the Federal grant. ***

Thus, the conflict between prior appropriators and federal patentees was resolved in favor of the former. Not only were appropriators protected against grantees of the federal government, they could also appropriate water on the entire public domain of the Western States, not just arid or desert lands.

A second conflict developed between the common law riparian concepts of water rights and the developing appropriation doctrine. Each western state, either in its constitution or by legislation, sought to resolve the clash between these two systems of water law. Generally, the states followed one of three approaches. Some, such as California and Washington, adopted a dual system known as the *California doctrine* in which appropriative rights and riparian rights continued to coexist. Others, such as Oregon, recognized riparian rights which had actually been exercised by making beneficial use of the water prior to adoption of a comprehensive statutory water system with a priority as of the date of entry; all rights arising thereafter had to be established in compliance with the statutory system that used the appropriation concept. The third approach, followed in Colorado, recognized only appropriative rights. Those eight western states that always recognized only appropriative rights are said to be following the *Colorado doctrine*. California, Oregon, and Washington all transitioned from riparian law to prior appropriation law, which is now dominant in those three states.

* * *

Early state water law legislation was generally incomplete. The water law systems created thereby, however, developed into elaborate and detailed schemes that erected a ladder of priorities establishing the measure and extent of each right, the place and nature of its use, the manner in which rights could be acquired and used, and the method of giving notice to the public of each use.[21] Because the states created and

---

[21] The same basic legal concepts are found in each state system: (1) beneficial use is the measure of the existence and scope of the right; (2) the right may, but need not necessarily, be appurtenant to the land; (3) ownership of the land itself is not considered a basis for a water right; (4) the appropriated water may be applied at any place where it is needed, regardless of the distance from the stream; (5) diversions out of a watershed and interstate diversions are protected;

enforced comprehensive systems of water law, a pattern of reliance on state law developed and the role of federal law was ignored for many years. No one considered what right the federal sovereign had to make use of the unappropriated water to fulfill its own purposes. Further, no one considered how such a right might be established and recorded. But in 1908 the United States Supreme Court thrust upon the scene the federal reserved water right with the claim to an early priority and a right to expand the use of water in the future as the need arose, but with no known means of establishing the amount of use or allowable types of uses. The painful howls of protest from the states and from their water users were at least understandable. This response resulted in part from the failure to recognize the already established principle that the source of the authority to administer the use of water was the federal sovereign. It also demonstrated a failure to fully appreciate the concept of federal supremacy as applied to the fulfillment of the federal sovereign's objectives.

SECTION B. NATURE AND EXTENT OF INDIAN RESERVED WATER RIGHTS

WINTERS V. UNITED STATES

Supreme Court of the United States, 1908.
207 U.S. 564, 28 S.Ct. 207, 52 L.Ed. 340.

MR. JUSTICE MCKENNA * * * delivered the opinion of the court.

* * *

[The Fort Belknap Reservation in Montana is a vestige of a huge area set aside by Congress in 1874 for the Gros Ventre, Piegan, Blood, Blackfeet, and River Crow Indians. In order to open the area for settlement by non-Indians, the government entered into an 1888 agreement in which the tribes ceded all the lands set aside for them except the Fort Belknap Reservation. The 1888 agreement described the northern boundary of the

---

(6) the rights of the prior appropriator must be filled before a junior appropriator is permitted to take water, and the burden of shortage falls on those who have the latest right; (7) in time of shortage, there is no proration; (8) the holder of the prior right can take no more water than is necessary for his original need; (9) the rights of the various users among themselves are very carefully regulated by means of court decrees, state administration practices, and a bevy of water masters and ditch riders who operate a system of diversions through canals, headgates, and ditches; (10) the right to the water is intended to be good as against the whole world except against someone with an earlier priority; (11) each right is recorded in detail on a use-by-use basis; and (12) mining, irrigation, municipal and sanitary purposes, and industrial power production are recognized as beneficial uses. [1881] Colo.Laws 142; [1879] Colo.Laws 94; [1881] Idaho Laws 267, 273; ch. 115, [1886] Kans.Laws Spec.Sess. 154; [1885] Mont.Laws 130; ch. 68, [1889] Nebr.Laws 503; ch. 20, [1880] Utah Laws 36; ch. 61, [1886] Wyo.Laws 294.

Some of the states are beginning to recognize that recreation and the maintenance of minimum stream flows are beneficial uses. See, e.g., Wash.Rev.Code Ann. § 90.22.010 (Supp.1974). In addition, the constitutions of some states have given a preference to some water uses over others. See, e.g., Idaho Const. art. XV, § 3 (domestic use preferred over all other uses, and agricultural use preferred over manufacturing).

reservation as the middle of the Milk River. Settlers came into the ceded area and acquired title under the homestead and desert land laws. In 1895, the settlers began filing and posting their water claims on the Milk River according to Montana water law. This was their only supply of water, without which the lands would be useless. The reservation had been diverting small quantities of water at least since 1887. Then, in 1898 a government irrigation project on the reservation began taking 5,000 miners' inches for irrigation of reservation lands. In a drought year, the upstream diversions by the settlers deprived the Indians of water from the Milk River. The United States sued on behalf of the Indians and the lower court enjoined the defendants from interfering with water use on the reservation.]

The case, as we view it, turns on the agreement of May, 1888, resulting in the creation of Fort Belknap Reservation. In the construction of this agreement there are certain elements to be considered that are prominent and significant. The reservation was a part of a very much larger tract which the Indians had the right to occupy and use and which was adequate for the habits and wants of a nomadic and uncivilized people. It was the policy of the Government, it was the desire of the Indians, to change those habits and to become a pastoral and civilized people. If they should become such the original tract was too extensive, but a smaller tract would be inadequate without a change of conditions. The lands were arid and, without irrigation, were practically valueless. And yet, it is contended, the means of irrigation were deliberately given up by the Indians and deliberately accepted by the Government. The lands ceded were, it is true, also arid; and some argument may be urged, and is urged, that with their cession there was the cession of the waters, without which they would be valueless, and "civilized communities could not be established thereon." And this, it is further contended, the Indians knew, and yet made no reservation of the waters. We realize that there is a conflict of implications, but that which makes for the retention of the waters is of greater force than that which makes for their cession. The Indians had command of the lands and the waters—command of all their beneficial use, whether kept for hunting, "and grazing roving herds of stock," or turned to agriculture and the arts of civilization. Did they give up all this? Did they reduce the area of their occupation and give up the waters which made it valuable or adequate? And, even regarding the allegation of the answer as true, that there are springs and streams on the reservation flowing about 2,900 inches of water, the inquiries are pertinent. If it were possible to believe affirmative answers, we might also believe that the Indians were awed by the power of the Government or deceived by its negotiators. Neither view is possible. The Government is asserting the rights of the Indians. But extremes need not be taken into account. By a rule of interpretation of agreements and treaties with the Indians, ambiguities occurring will be resolved from the standpoint of the Indians. And the rule should certainly be applied to determine between two inferences, one of which would support the purpose of the agreement and the other impair or defeat it. On account of their relations to the Government, it cannot be supposed that the Indians were alert to exclude by formal words every inference which might militate against or defeat the declared purpose of themselves and the Government, even if it could be supposed that they had the intelligence to foresee the "double sense" which might some time be urged against them.

Another contention of appellants is that if it be conceded that there was a reservation of the waters of Milk River by the agreement of 1888, yet the reservation was repealed by the admission of Montana into the Union, February 22, 1889, c. 180, 25 Stat. 676, "upon an equal footing with the original States." The language of counsel is that "any reservation in the agreement with the Indians, expressed or implied, whereby the waters of Milk River were not to be subject of appropriation by the citizens and inhabitants of said State, was repealed by the act of admission." But to establish the repeal counsel rely substantially upon the same argument that they advance against the intention of the agreement to reserve the waters. The power of the Government to reserve the waters and exempt them from appropriation under the state laws is not denied, and could not be. The United States v. The Rio Grande Dam & Irrigation Co., 174 U.S. 690, 702; United States v. Winans, 198 U.S. 371. That the Government did reserve them we have decided, and for a use which would be necessarily continued through years. This was done May 1, 1888, and it would be extreme to believe that within a year Congress destroyed the reservation and took from the Indians the consideration of their grant, leaving them a barren waste—took from them the means of continuing their old habits, yet did not leave them the power to change to new ones. * * *

* * *

Decree affirmed.

MR. JUSTICE BREWER dissents.

NOTES

1.   Who did the reserving—the tribe or the United States—in *Winters*? What was the tribe's priority date? 1874? 1888? A point in pre-history when the Indians first occupied the area? As a practical matter, does it make any difference?

2.   The doctrine of reserved rights emerged three years before *Winters* in a case involving off-reservation fishing rights of the Yakima Indians. *United States v. Winans*, page 906, infra.

3.   Together, *Winans* and *Winters* put to rest the argument that the "equal footing" doctrine gave newly-admitted states the same general police power over all lands within states, including Indian country, that the original thirteen states possessed. An earlier Supreme Court case held that Indian

treaty rights generally had been extinguished by admission of the state (Wyoming) to the Union. Ward v. Race Horse, 163 U.S. 504 (1896). *Ward* was factually limited to the particular treaty which the court found created a temporary privilege (rather than a perpetual right) extending to certain "hunting districts" where the rights could be extinguished with a change in federal ownership or jurisdiction. But the Court in *Ward* seemed to revive the "equal footing doctrine" as a way to abrogate Indian treaties, stating in an alternate holding that the federal treaty promise could not survive statehood if it put special obligations or limits on the new state. That doctrine had already been rejected in The Kansas Indians, 72 U.S. (5 Wall.) 737, 755–56 (1866). *Winans* and *Winters* removed any lingering doubts about the continuing vitality of the "equal footing" doctrine with respect to Indian country and impliedly overruled that part of *Ward*. See also Menominee Tribe v. United States, 391 U.S. 404, 411 n.12 (1968). See generally Felix S. Cohen, *Handbook of Federal Indian Law* 511 n.93 (2005 ed.). The Supreme Court has recently stated that *Ward* was based on the "false premise" that treaty rights cannot coexist with state sovereignty, and affirmed that *Winans* had long ago repudiated the rationale of *Ward*. See Minnesota v. Mille Lacs Band of Chippewa Indians, 526 U.S. 172, 204–05 n.7 (1999).

4.   The *Winters* doctrine offered the possibility that reservation water could be developed and tribes would move closer to self-sufficiency. What actually occurred is summarized in the following excerpt from the final report of the National Water Commission:

> Following *Winters,* more than 50 years elapsed before the Supreme Court again discussed significant aspects of Indian water rights. During most of this 50-year period, the United States was pursuing a policy of encouraging the settlement of the West and the creation of family-sized farms on its arid lands. In retrospect, it can be seen that this policy was pursued with little or no regard for Indian water rights and the *Winters* doctrine. With the encouragement, or at least the cooperation, of the Secretary of the Interior—the very office entrusted with protection of all Indian rights—many large irrigation projects were constructed on streams that flowed through or bordered Indian Reservations, sometimes above and more often below the Reservations. With few exceptions the projects were planned and built by the Federal Government without any attempt to define, let alone protect, prior rights that Indian tribes might have had in the waters used for the projects. * * * In the history of the United States Government's treatment of Indian tribes, its failure to protect Indian water rights for use on the Reservations it set aside for them is one of the sorrier chapters.

United States National Water Comm'n, Water Policies for the Future—Final Report to the President and to the Congress of the United States, 474–75 (1973). See also United States v. Ahtanum Irrigation Dist., 236 F.2d 321, 330 n.12, 337 (9th Cir.1956), cert. denied 352 U.S. 988 (1957).

Thus, the tribes lacked the capacity to build water projects and the United States chose to use federal monies to fund projects benefiting non-Indians. Most tribes were simply unable to utilize their *Winters* rights effectively. Despite a hiatus in Supreme Court activity, the *Winters* doctrine was the basis of several cases on behalf of tribes brought by the government around the West. During this period, Congress episodically debated the controversial doctrine and its potential impact on appropriative water rights. Lawyer-historian John Shurts has documented the active concern with and application of the doctrine in the early part of the century. John Shurts, Indian Reserved Water Rights: The *Winters* Doctrine in its Social and Legal Context, 1880s–1930s (2000). Yet when the following decision was handed down in 1963, it was greeted with surprise and viewed by some as creating inequity for established non-Indian uses. *Winters* was reaffirmed in a most difficult context—the longstanding struggle among Arizona, California, and five other western states over rights to the Colorado River in the parched Southwest.

ARIZONA V. CALIFORNIA
Supreme Court of the United States, 1963.
373 U.S. 546, 83 S.Ct. 1468, 10 L.Ed.2d 542.

MR. JUSTICE BLACK delivered the opinion of the Court.

In 1952 the State of Arizona invoked the original jurisdiction of this Court by filing a complaint against the State of California and seven of its public agencies. Later, Nevada, New Mexico, Utah, and the United States were added as parties either voluntarily or on motion. The basic controversy in the case is over how much water each State has a legal right to use out of the waters of the Colorado River and its tributaries. After preliminary pleadings, we referred the case to [a Special Master]. * * * The Master conducted a trial lasting from June 14, 1956, to August 28, 1958, during which 340 witnesses were heard orally or by deposition, thousands of exhibits were received, and 25,000 pages of transcript were filled. Following many motions, arguments, and briefs, the Master in a 433-page volume reported his findings, conclusions, and recommended decree, received by the Court on January 16, 1961. The case has been extensively briefed here and orally argued twice, the first time about 16 hours, the second, over six. * * * [The relevant congressional legislation] can be better understood when [it] is set against its background—the gravity of the Southwest's water problems; the inability of local groups or individual States to deal with these enormous problems; the continued failure of the States to agree on how to conserve and divide the waters; and the ultimate action by Congress at the request of the States creating a great system of dams and public works nationally built, controlled, and operated for the purpose of conserving and distributing the water.

The Colorado River itself rises in the mountains of Colorado and flows generally in a southwesterly direction for about 1,300 miles through

Colorado, Utah, and Arizona and along the Arizona-Nevada and Arizona-California boundaries, after which it passes into Mexico and empties into the Mexican waters of the Gulf of California. On its way to the sea it receives tributary waters from Wyoming, Colorado, Utah, Nevada, New Mexico, and Arizona. The river and its tributaries flow in a natural basin almost surrounded by large mountain ranges and drain 242,000 square miles, an area about 900 miles long from north to south and 300 to 500 miles wide from east to west—practically one-twelfth the area of the continental United States excluding Alaska. Much of this large basin is so arid that it is, as it always has been, largely dependent upon managed use of the waters of the Colorado River System to make it productive and inhabitable. The Master refers to archaeological evidence that as long as 2,000 years ago the ancient Hohokam tribe built and maintained irrigation canals near what is now Phoenix, Arizona, and that American Indians were practicing irrigation in that region at the time white men first explored it. * * *

During the latter part of the nineteenth and the first part of the twentieth centuries, people in the Southwest continued to seek new ways to satisfy their water needs, which by that time were increasing rapidly as new settlers moved into this fast-developing region. But none of the more or less primitive diversions made from the mainstream of the Colorado conserve enough water to meet the growing needs of the basin. The natural flow of the Colorado was too erratic, the river at many places in canyons too deep, and the engineering and economic hurdles too great for small farmers, larger groups, or even States to build storage dams, construct canals, and install the expensive works necessary for a dependable year-round water supply. * * *

It is not surprising that the pressing necessity to transform the erratic and often destructive flow of the Colorado River into a controlled and dependable water supply desperately needed in so many States began to be talked about and recognized as far more than a purely local problem which could be solved on a farmer-by-farmer, group-by-group, or even state-by-state basis, desirable as this kind of solution might have been. * * *

The prospect that the United States would undertake to build as a national project the necessary works to control floods and store river waters for irrigation was apparently a welcome one for the basin States. But it brought to life strong fears in the northern basin States that additional waters made available by the storage and canal projects might be gobbled up in perpetuity by faster growing lower basin areas, particularly California, before the upper States could appropriate what they believed to be their fair share. These fears were not without foundation, since the law of prior appropriation prevailed in most of the Western States. Under that law the one who first appropriates water and puts it to beneficial use thereby acquires a vested right to continue to divert and use that quantity of water against all claimants junior to him in point of time. "First in time, first in right" is the short hand expression of this legal principle. * * *

[In the Colorado River Compact of 1922, the states agreed to what they expected would be an essentially equal division of water between the Upper Basin states—Colorado, Utah, Wyoming, and New Mexico—and the Lower Basin states—Arizona, California, and Nevada, with each entitled to take 7.5 million acre-feet (MAF) per year. In 1948, the Upper Basin states signed a compact dividing among them the Upper Basin's apportionment according to percentage shares. California, Arizona, and Nevada, however, were unable to agree upon a division of the Lower Basin share.

In this lengthy opinion, the Court held that the Boulder Canyon Project Act of 1928, 43 U.S.C.A. §§ 617–617f, had effectively apportioned the water among the three states—2.8 MAF to Arizona, 4.4 MAF to California, and 300,000 AF to Nevada. The Court then turned to the question of Indian water rights.]

The Government, on behalf of five Indian Reservations in Arizona, California, and Nevada, asserted rights to water in the mainstream of the Colorado River.[97] The Colorado River Reservation, located partly in Arizona and partly in California, is the largest. It was originally created by an Act of Congress in 1865, but its area was later increased by Executive Order. Other reservations were created by Executive Orders and amendments to them, ranging in dates from 1870 to 1907. The Master found both as a matter of fact and law that when the United States created these reservations or added to them, it reserved not only land but also the use of enough water from the Colorado to irrigate the irrigable portions of the reserved lands. The aggregate quantity of water which the Master held was reserved for all the reservations is about 1,000,000 acre-feet, to be used on around 135,000 irrigable acres of land. Here, as before the Master, Arizona argues that the United States had no power to make a reservation of navigable waters after Arizona became a State; that navigable waters could not be reserved by Executive Orders; that the United States did not intend to reserve water for the Indian Reservations; that the amount of water reserved should be measured by the reasonably foreseeable needs of the Indians living on the reservation rather than by the number of irrigable acres; and, finally, that the judicial doctrine of equitable apportionment should be used to divide the water between the Indians and the other people in the State of Arizona.

The last argument is easily answered. The doctrine of equitable apportionment is a method of resolving water disputes between States. It was created by this Court in the exercise of its original jurisdiction over controversies in which States are parties. An Indian Reservation is not a

---

[97]　The Reservations were Chemehuevi, Cocopah, Yuma, Colorado River and Fort Mohave.

State. And while Congress has sometimes left Indian Reservations considerable power to manage their own affairs, we are not convinced by Arizona's argument that each reservation is so much like a State that its rights to water should be determined by the doctrine of equitable apportionment. Moreover, even were we to treat an Indian Reservation like a State, equitable apportionment would still not control since, under our view, the Indian claims here are governed by the statutes and Executive Orders creating the reservations.

Arizona's contention that the Federal Government had no power, after Arizona became a State, to reserve waters for the use and benefit of federally reserved lands rests largely upon statements in *Pollard's Lessee v. Hagan*, 3 How. 212 (1845), and *Shively v. Bowlby*, 152 U.S. 1 (1894). Those cases and others that followed them gave rise to the doctrine that lands underlying navigable waters within territory acquired by the Government are held in trust for future States and that title to such lands is automatically vested in the States upon admission to the Union. But those cases involved only the shores of and lands beneath navigable waters. They do not determine the problem before us and cannot be accepted as limiting the broad powers of the United States to regulate navigable waters under the Commerce Clause and to regulate government lands under Art. IV, § 3, of the Constitution. We have no doubt about the power of the United States under these clauses to reserve water rights for its reservations and its property.

Arizona also argues that, in any event, water rights cannot be reserved by Executive Order. Some of the reservations of Indian lands here involved were made almost 100 years ago, and all of them were made over 45 years ago. In our view, these reservations, like those created directly by Congress, were not limited to land, but included waters as well. Congress and the Executive have ever since recognized these as Indian Reservations. Numerous appropriations, including appropriations for irrigation projects, have been made by Congress. They have been uniformly and universally treated as reservations by map makers, surveyors, and the public. We can give but short shrift at this late date to the argument that the reservations either of land or water are invalid because they were originally set apart by the Executive.[102]

Arizona also challenges the Master's holding as to the Indian Reservations on two other grounds: first, that there is a lack of evidence showing that the United States in establishing the reservations intended to reserve water for them; second, that even if water was meant to be reserved the Master has awarded too much water. We reject both of these contentions. Most of the land in these reservations is and always has been arid. If the water necessary to sustain life is to be had, it must come from

---

[102] See *United States v. Midwest Oil Co.*, 236 U.S. 459, 469–475 (1915); *Winters v. United States*, 207 U.S. 564 (1908).

the Colorado River or its tributaries. It can be said without overstatement that when the Indians were put on these reservations they were not considered to be located in the most desirable area of the Nation. It is impossible to believe that when Congress created the great Colorado River Indian Reservation and when the Executive Department of this Nation created the other reservations they were unaware that most of the lands were of the desert kind—hot, scorching sands—and that water from the river would be essential to the life of the Indian people and to the animals they hunted and the crops they raised. In the debate leading to approval of the first congressional appropriation for irrigation of the Colorado River Indian Reservation, the delegate from the Territory of Arizona made this statement:

> "Irrigating canals are essential to the prosperity of these Indians. Without water there can be no production, no life; and all they ask of you is to give them a few agricultural implements to enable them to dig an irrigating canal by which their lands may be watered and their fields irrigated, so that they may enjoy the means of existence. You must provide these Indians with the means of subsistence or they will take by robbery from those who have. During the last year I have seen a number of these Indians starved to death for want of food." Cong.Globe, 38th Cong., 2d Sess. 1321 (1865).

* * *

The Court in *Winters* concluded that the Government, when it created that Indian Reservation, intended to deal fairly with the Indians by reserving for them the waters without which their lands would have been useless. *Winters* has been followed by this Court as recently as 1939 in *United States v. Powers*, 305 U.S. 527. We follow it now and agree that the United States did reserve the water rights for the Indians effective as of the time the Indian Reservations were created. This means, as the Master held, that these water rights, having vested before the Act became effective on June 25, 1929, are "present perfected rights" and as such are entitled to priority under the Act.

We also agree with the Master's conclusion as to the quantity of water intended to be reserved. He found that the water was intended to satisfy the *future as well as the present needs* of the Indian Reservations and ruled that enough water was reserved to irrigate all the practicably irrigable acreage on the reservations. Arizona, on the other hand, contends that the quantity of water reserved should be measured by the Indians' "reasonably foreseeable needs," which, in fact, means by the number of Indians. How many Indians there will be and what their future needs will be can only be guessed. We have concluded, as did the Master, that the only feasible and fair way by which reserved water for the reservations can be measured is irrigable acreage. The various acreages of irrigable land which the Master found to be on the different reservations we find to be reasonable. * * *

* * *

NOTES

1.   Is the opinion consistent with *Winters*? Is the "practicably irrigable acreage" standard too expansive? Should the same rationale for reserved rights apply where, as in *Arizona v. California*, there are no treaties and a reservation is established by executive order?

The Court entered its decree, setting out with specificity all adjudicated rights, one year after the decision. See Arizona v. California, 376 U.S. 340 (1964). For treatments of water issues on the Colorado River, see New Courses for the Colorado River: Major Issues for the Next Century (Gary D. Weatherford & F. Lee Brown, eds. 1986); David H. Getches, *Colorado River Governance: Sharing Federal Authority as an Incentive to Create a New Institution*, 68 U.Colo.L.Rev. 573 (1997); David H. Getches, *Competing Demands for the Colorado River,* 56 U.Colo.L.Rev. 413 (1985).

2.   *Groundwater. Winters* rights extend to streams, lakes, and springs which arise upon, border, or traverse a reservation. The United States Supreme Court has not directly ruled on whether *Winters* rights also extend to groundwater that underlies the reservation. In Cappaert v. United States, 426 U.S. 128 (1976), the Supreme Court upheld the right of the federal government to enjoin pumping from wells near Death Valley National Monument because it tended to lower the water level in Devil's Hole, a small limestone cavern within the monument, threatening the existence of the rare Devil's Hole pupfish. At stake for the government was the future of the pupfish, which exists nowhere else; at stake for the Cappaerts was a $7 million investment in a 123,000 acre cattle ranch. It was not clear until the defendants actually began using water that there was a hydrologic connection between the cavern and the Cappaerts' wells. The Court affirmed a ruling that the government had impliedly reserved sufficient water for survival of the pupfish and that the Cappaerts must curtail pumping.

Cappaert dealt specifically with a national monument. State and federal courts seem to agree that the *Winters* doctrine applies to groundwater needed for Indian reservations. See In re General Adjudication of All Rights to Use Water in the Gila River Sys. and Source, 989 P.2d 739 (Ariz. 1999) (federal reserved rights can be invoked to protect groundwater sources, including percolating *groundwater*, although such groundwater is treated differently under state law); Agua Caliente Band of Cahuilla Indians v. Coachella Valley Water District, 2015 WL 1600065 (W.D.Cal.2015). See also United States v. Orr Water Ditch Co., 600 F.3d 1152 (9th Cir.2010) (Orr Ditch Decree recognizing that a tribe's senior water rights protects the tribe from allocations of groundwater that would adversely affect its decreed water rights and *Winters* doctrine would provide equivalent protection in absence of decree). But see In re General Adjudication of All Rights to Use Water in the Big Horn River

Sys., 753 P.2d 76 (Wyo. 1988), aff'd on other grounds by an equally divided court, 492 U.S. 406 (1989) (*Big Horn I*), page 850, infra (rejecting reserved groundwater right for Indian reservation). See John D. Leshy, *The Federal Role in Managing the Nation's Groundwater*, 14 Hastings W.–N.W.J.Env.L. & Pol'y 1323 (2008); Judith Royster, *Indian Tribal Rights to Groundwater*, 15 Kan.J.L.&Pub. Pol'y 489 (2006).

3.   *Water Quality.* The courts have not yet decided whether the *Winters* doctrine enables a tribe to insist upon a certain water quality. The United States alleged in *Winters* that it was necessary for the purposes for which the reservation was created to ensure that the waters of the stream flowed "undeteriorated in quality," 207 U.S. at 567, but the Court did not discuss the allegation.

Agricultural uses and maintenance of fisheries often depend upon protecting water quality. Under a 1935 consent decree, the San Carlos Apache Tribe has a right to use 6,000 acre-feet of water during irrigation season. Because of the irrigation practices, groundwater pumping, and return flows of upstream non-Indians, the water reaching the reservation is too saline to irrigate most crops traditionally grown by the tribe. In United States v. Gila Valley Irrigation District, 920 F.Supp. 1444 (D.Ariz.1996), the court ruled that upstream users must forgo uses as necessary to deliver water of sufficient quality to the tribe. In another case, a federal court ordered non-Indians to leave sufficient water in a stream to ensure water temperatures low enough to support a salmon fishery. United States v. Anderson, 6 Indian L.Rep. F–129 (1979).

4.   *Pueblo Water Rights.* The Indian pueblos of New Mexico have been situated in their present locations for many hundreds of years. The pueblos were ruled by the Kingdom of Spain prior to 1821, and by the Republic of Mexico between the years 1821 and 1848 when, by the Treaty of Guadalupe Hidalgo, 9 Stat. 922, Mexico ceded the area to the United States. Pueblo land titles had long been recognized by the Spanish and Mexican governments, and in 1858 they were confirmed by Congress. 11 Stat. 374. There has been major water rights litigation concerning certain tributaries of the Rio Grande. In State of New Mexico v. Aamodt, 537 F.2d 1102 (10th Cir.1976), cert. denied 429 U.S. 1121 (1977), the court of appeals reversed a district court ruling that pueblo rights were governed by state law and held that they were prior and paramount to rights of most of the non-Indian parties. Although the appellate court stated that the *Winters* doctrine was not technically applicable, it seemed to hold that rights to the use of water were reserved with priorities no later than the acts confirming the pueblos' titles. The case was remanded to the district court with the suggestion that Spanish or Mexican law may be controlling.

The district court held that the pueblos "are entitled to a first right * * * to enough water for their needs," or the "irrigation of the lands," and have an "immemorial" priority water right. But it also stated, without citing authority, that these Winters—like rights would only attach to lands actually irrigated between 1846–1924. Applying this rule, the district court's quantification was only one-tenth the amount recommended by a special master appointed to report on factual matters. See Findings and Conclusions Regarding Pueblos' Historically Irrigated Acreage, Apr. 29, 1987. The court of appeals rejected the pueblos' interlocutory appeal. See Richard W. Hughes, *Indian Law,* 18 N.M.L.Rev. 403, 422 (1988).

Application of Spanish law in other situations has led to results comparable to an application of the *Winters* doctrine. The Spanish had several laws and policies that recognized a continuing right to sufficient water to meet Indian needs. See translations in Frederic Hall, The Laws of Mexico 61–64 (1885). California recognizes similar "pueblo water rights" for municipalities, tracing to Spanish and Mexico law. The Treaty of Guadalupe Hidalgo assures continued respect for property rights vested prior to 1848. Thus, those whose title traces to Spanish land grants have a *Winters*-type water right. The California grants were for pueblos that were to produce agricultural supplies for the presidios. In City of Los Angeles v. City of San Fernando, 537 P.2d 1250 (Cal.1975), the California Supreme Court looked to the purpose of the pueblo (now Los Angeles) to find that Spanish law provided rights to sufficient water for its present and future municipal needs:

> The pueblo was deliberately located to take maximum advantage of the Los Angeles River as a source of water for irrigation and the orders for the pueblo's founding included detailed provisions for an irrigation dam and canals. These circumstances strongly suggest a governmental policy of assuring the pueblo a supply of water sufficient for its maintenance and growth, at least in the absence of any other town or settlement of comparable importance competing for the same water supply.

537 P.2d at 1275. Contra, State ex rel. Martinez v. City of Las Vegas, 89 P.3d 47 (N.M. 2004) (Pueblo rights doctrine is inconsistent with New Mexico's system of prior appropriation and not protected by the Treaty of Guadalupe Hidalgo).

5. *Federal Reserved Rights.* In *Arizona v. California,* the Court recognized reserved rights for federal, as well as Indian, lands. See 373 U.S. at 601. In *Cappaert,* supra, also involving public lands, the Supreme Court said that Congress impliedly reserved "only that amount of water necessary to fulfill the purpose of the reservation, no more." 426 U.S. at 141. In United States v. New Mexico, 438 U.S. 696 (1978), the federal government claimed reserved water rights in the Gila National Forest for various purposes including minimum stream flows for fish preservation, recreation, and aesthetics. The Supreme Court carefully examined the specific purposes for which Congress set aside public lands for national forests and held that they did not include such uses:

> The legislative debates surrounding the Organic Administration Act of 1897 and its predecessor bills demonstrate that Congress intended national forests to be reserved for only two purposes—"[t]o

conserve the water flows and to furnish a continuous supply of timber for the people." 30 Cong.Rec. 967 (1897) (Cong. McRae). See United States v. Grimaud, 220 U.S. 506, 515 (1911). National forests were not to be reserved for aesthetic, environmental, recreational, or wildlife-preservation purposes. * * *

Id. at 707. The point of departure for the four dissenting Justices in *New Mexico* was their view that "the forests" included not only the trees but all wildlife and vegetation inhabiting them.

Would a strict application of the doctrine as applied to federal reservations in *New Mexico* potentially limit the Indians' *Winters* rights?

In *Winters* the Supreme Court said the reservation's purpose was to make the Indians "a pastoral and civilized people;" the Court said that, without water, the reservation would have been "practically valueless" and "civilized communities could not be established thereon." Congress intended to school the Indians in the "habits of industry and civilization." This view is consistent with the broad public policy recognized in other cases that saw the purpose of most Indian reservations as providing a place where the Indians could exist as self-governing communities and become economically self-sustaining. See *McClanahan v. Arizona State Tax Comm'n*, page 421, supra; *Warren Trading Post v. Arizona State Tax Comm'n*, page 654, supra; United States v. Shoshone Tribe of Indians, 304 U.S. 111, 117–18 (1938), page 282, supra; United States v. McGowan, 302 U.S. 535, 537 (1938); Alaska Pacific Fisheries v. United States, 248 U.S. 78, 88–89 (1918). But the Wyoming Supreme Court in *Big Horn I,* infra, applied *New Mexico* and rejected the broad "homeland" purpose of the reservation that would allow quantification for such water uses. Portions of the Wyoming Supreme Court's opinion in the *Big Horn I* case are reprinted at page 850, infra.

Some courts have said that *New Mexico* is not applicable to Indian reservations. See State ex rel. Greely v. Confederated Salish and Kootenai Tribes of the Flathead Reservation, 712 P.2d 754, 766–67 (Mont.1985) ("Unlike Indian reserved rights, which include water for future needs and changes in use, federal reserved rights are quantified on the basis of the original, primary purposes of the reservation."); In re General Adjudication of all Rights to Use Water in the Gila River System, 35 P.3d 68 (Ariz.2001) (primary-secondary test applies only to non-Indian federal reservations where rights are quantified only to meet original purposes).

6. The reserved rights doctrine was created by the Supreme Court to provide tribes with water for their reservations even if non-Indian neighbors had begun using water first—the key to gaining superior rights under the prior appropriation doctrine that prevails in most western states. Can tribes in eastern states that follow the riparian doctrine—recognizing water rights in landowners along a stream—assert the *Winters* doctrine? In one case a court said yes, if a tribe showed that riparian law did not provide a sufficient quantity or quality of water to meet its needs, but that the tribe had not made such a showing. See Mattaponi Indian Tribe v. Commonwealth, 72 Va.Cir. 444

(2007) (tribe did not show necessity). See also Hope M. Babcock, *Reserved Water Rights in Riparian Jurisdictions: Water, Water Everywhere, Perhaps Some Drops for Us,* 91 Cornell L.Rev. 1203, (2006) (analyzing whether non-federally recognized eastern tribes should be able to claim *Winters* rights in riparian jurisdictions).

UNITED STATES V. ADAIR

United States Court of Appeals, Ninth Circuit, 1983.
723 F.2d 1394, cert. denied sub nom. Oregon v. United States,
467 U.S. 1252, 104 S.Ct. 3536, 82 L.Ed.2d 841 (1984).

Before KILKENNY, GOODWIN and FLETCHER, CIRCUIT JUDGES.

FLETCHER, CIRCUIT JUDGE:

* * *

I

Background

A.   *History of the Litigation Area*

* * *

The Klamath Indians have hunted, fished, and foraged in the area of the Klamath Marsh and upper Williamson River for over a thousand years. In 1864 the Klamath Tribe entered into a treaty with the United States whereby it relinquished its aboriginal claim to some 12 million acres of land in return for a reservation of approximately 800,000 acres in south-central Oregon. This reservation included all of the Klamath Marsh as well as large forested tracts of the Williamson River watershed. Treaty between the United States of America and the Klamath and Moadoc Tribes and Yahooskin Band of Snake Indians, Oct. 14, 1864, 16 Stat. 707. Article I of the treaty gave the Klamath the exclusive right to hunt, fish, and gather on their reservation. Article II provided funds to help the Klamath adopt an agricultural way of life. 16 Stat. 708.

* * *

B.   *Proceedings in the District Court*

In September of 1975, the United States filed suit in federal district court seeking a declaration of water rights within the Williamson River drainage [within the former Klamath Reservation]. In January of 1976, the State of Oregon initiated formal proceedings under state law to determine water rights in the Klamath Basin including that portion of the Williamson River drainage covered by the Government's suit. * * * The district court * * * significantly limited the nature of the federal proceeding. The district court did not agree to decide any question concerning the actual quantification of water rights. * * *

III

Water Rights

The district court declared reserved water rights within the litigation area to the Klamath Tribe, the Government, individual Indians, and non-Indian successors to Indian land owners. * * *

* * *

A. A Reservation of Water to Accompany the Tribe's Treaty Right to Hunt, Fish, and Gather

Article I of the 1864 treaty with the Klamath Tribe reserved to the Tribe the exclusive right to hunt, fish, and gather on its reservation. This right survived the Klamath Termination Act. The issue presented for decision in this case is whether, as the district court held, these hunting and fishing rights carry with them an implied reservation of water rights.

1. Reservation of Water in the 1864 Treaty

* * * *New Mexico* and *Cappaert,* while not directly applicable to *Winters* doctrine rights on Indian reservations, see F. Cohen, *Handbook of Federal Indian Law* 581–85 (1982 ed.), establish several useful guidelines. First, water rights may be implied only "[w]here water is necessary to fulfill the very purposes for which a federal reservation was created," and not where it is merely "valuable for a secondary use of the reservation." Second, the scope of the implied right is circumscribed by the necessity that calls for its creation. The doctrine "reserves only that amount of water necessary to fulfill the purpose of the reservation, no more."

* * *

Article I of the Klamath Treaty expressly provides that the Tribe will have exclusive on-reservation fishing and gathering rights. * * * In view of the historical importance of hunting and fishing, and the language of Article I of the 1864 Treaty, we find that one of the "very purposes" of establishing the Klamath Reservation was to secure to the Tribe a continuation of its traditional hunting and fishing lifestyle. This was at the forefront of the Tribe's concerns in negotiating the treaty and was recognized as important by the United States as well.

At the same time, as the State and individual defendants argue, Articles II through V of the 1864 Treaty evince a purpose to convert the Klamath Tribe to an agricultural way of life. Article II provides that monies paid to the Tribe in consideration for the land ceded by the treaty "shall be expended . . . to promote the well-being of the Indians, advance them in civilization, *and especially agriculture,* and to secure their moral improvement and education." A similar focus on agriculture is reflected in the language of Articles III, IV and V. It is apparent that a second essential purpose in setting aside the Klamath Reservation, recognized by both the

Tribe and the Government, was to encourage the Indians to take up farming.

Neither *Cappaert* nor *New Mexico* requires us to choose between these activities or to identify a single essential purpose which the parties to the 1864 Treaty intended the Klamath Reservation to serve. In fact, in *Colville Confederated Tribes v. Walton,* 647 F.2d 42 (9th Cir.), cert. denied, 454 U.S. 1092 (1981), this court found that provision of a "homeland for the Indians to maintain their agrarian society," *id.* at 47, as well as "preservation of the tribe's access to fishing grounds," *id.* at 48, were dual purposes behind establishment of the Colville Reservation. Consequently the court found an implied reservation of water to support both of these activities. President Grant established the Colville Reservation in a one-paragraph Executive Order that stated only that the land would be "set apart as a reservation for said Indians." Thus the court in *Colville* discovered the purposes of the reservation and implied water rights from a much less explicit text than that provided by the 1864 Klamath Treaty, Articles I through V. We therefore have no difficulty in upholding the district court's finding that at the time the Klamath Reservation was established, the Government and the Tribe intended to reserve a quantity of the water flowing through the reservation not only for the purpose of supporting Klamath agriculture, but also for the purpose of maintaining the Tribe's treaty right to hunt and fish on reservation lands.

A water right to support game and fish adequate to the needs of Indian hunters and fishers is not a right recognized as a part of the common law doctrine of prior appropriation followed in Oregon. Indeed, one of the standard requirements of the prior appropriation doctrine is that some diversion of the natural flow of a stream is necessary to effect a valid appropriation. But diversion of water is not required to support the fish and game that the Klamath Tribe take in exercise of their treaty rights. Thus the right to water reserved to further the Tribe's hunting and fishing purposes is unusual in that it is basically non-consumptive. The holder of such a right is not entitled to withdraw water from the stream for agricultural, industrial, or other consumptive uses (absent independent consumptive rights). Rather, the entitlement consists of the right to prevent other appropriators from depleting the streams' waters below a protected level in any area where the non-consumptive right applies. * * *

* * *

2.   *Effect of the Klamath Termination Act on the Tribe's Hunting and Fishing Water Rights*

In 1954, Congress terminated federal supervision of the Klamath Tribe. The state and individual appellants now argue that the Termination Act also abrogated any water rights reserved by the 1864 Treaty to accompany the Tribe's right to hunt and fish. Appellants contend that when federal supervision was terminated, former reservation lands were sold at full market value without limitations on use. They conclude that recognition of a reserved water right to sustain the Tribe's hunting and fishing rights would impose a servitude or limitation on the use of former reservation lands in contravention of the Termination Act policy of unencumbered sale.

Appellants' argument, however, overlooks the substantive language of the Termination Act, the canons of construction for legislation affecting Indian Tribes, and the implications of our [previous] decision. Section 564m(a) of the Termination Act provides, "[n]othing in sections 564–564w of this title shall abrogate any water rights of the tribe and its members." This provision admits no exception, nor can it be read to exclude reserved water rights. Congress presumably was aware of the importance of such rights to Indian tribes at the time it drafted section 564m of the Klamath Termination Act. * * *

* * *

* * * In sum, we agree with the district court that the water rights reserved to the Klamath Tribe by Treaty in 1864 were not abrogated by enactment of the Klamath Termination Act in 1954.

3.   Priority of the Water Right Reserved to Accompany the Tribe's Treaty Right to Hunt and Fish

The district court found that the Tribe's water right accompanying its right to hunt and fish carried a priority date for appropriation of time immemorial. The State and individual appellants argue that an implied reservation of water cannot have a priority date earlier than establishment of the reservation. The Government and the Tribe argue that a pre-reservation priority date is appropriate for tribal water uses that pre-date establishment of the reservation. We have been unable to find any decisions that squarely address this issue. We therefore begin our analysis by turning to well-established principles of Indian treaty interpretation and Indian property rights for guidance.

Foremost among these is the principle that "the treaty is not a grant of rights to the Indians, but a grant of rights from them—a reservation of those not granted." Further, Indian treaties should be construed as the tribes would have understood them. And any ambiguity in a treaty must be resolved in favor of the Indians. A corollary of these principles, also recognized by the Supreme Court, is that when a tribe and the Government negotiate a treaty, the tribe retains all rights not expressly ceded to the Government in the treaty so long as the rights retained are consistent with the tribe's sovereign dependent status.

In 1864, at the time the Klamath entered into a treaty with the United States, the Tribe had lived in Central Oregon and Northern California for more than a thousand years. This ancestral homeland encompassed some 12 million acres. * * *

With this background in mind, we examine the priority date attaching to the Klamath Tribe's reservation of water to support its hunting and fishing rights. In Article I of the 1864 Treaty the Tribe expressly ceded "all [its] right, title and claim" to most of its ancestral domain. In the same article, however, the Tribe reserved for its exclusive use and occupancy the lands that became the Klamath Reservation, the same lands that are the subject of the instant suit. There is no indication in the treaty, express or implied, that the Tribe intended to cede any of its interest in those lands it reserved for itself. Nor is it possible that the Tribe would have understood such a reservation of land to include a relinquishment of its right to use the water as it had always used it on the land it had reserved as a permanent home. Further, we find no language in the treaty to indicate that the United States intended or understood the agreement to diminish the Tribe's rights in that part of its aboriginal holding reserved for its permanent occupancy and use. Accordingly, we agree with the district court that within the 1864 Treaty is a recognition of the Tribe's aboriginal water rights and a confirmation to the Tribe of a continued water right to support its hunting and fishing lifestyle on the Klamath Reservation.

The Tribe's water rights necessarily carry a priority date of time immemorial. The rights were not created by the 1864 Treaty, rather, the treaty confirmed the continued existence of these rights. To assign the Tribe's hunting and fishing water rights the later, 1864, priority date argued for by the State and individual appellants would ignore one of the fundamental principles of prior appropriations law—that priority for a particular water right dates from the time of first use. Furthermore, an 1864 priority date might limit the scope of the Tribe's hunting and fishing water rights by reduction for any pre-1864 appropriations of water. This could extinguish rights the Tribe held before 1864 and intended to reserve to itself thereafter. Thus, we are compelled to conclude that where, as here, a tribe shows its aboriginal use of water to support a hunting and fishing lifestyle, and then enters into a treaty with the United States that reserves this aboriginal water use, the water right thereby established retains a priority date of first or immemorial use. * * *

In its opinion discussing the Tribe's hunting and fishing water rights, the district court stated "[t]he Indians are still entitled to as much water on the Reservation lands as they need to protect their hunting and fishing rights." We interpret this statement to confirm to the Tribe the amount of water necessary to support its hunting and fishing rights as currently exercised to maintain the livelihood of Tribe members, not as these rights once were exercised by the Tribe in 1864. We find authority for such a construction of the Indians' rights in the Supreme Court's decision in *Washington v. Fishing Vessel Ass'n*, 443 U.S. 658 (1979). There, citing

Arizona v. California, 373 U.S. 546 (1963), a reserved water rights case, the court stated "that Indian treaty rights to a natural resource that once was thoroughly and exclusively exploited by the Indians secures so much as, but not more than, is necessary to provide the Indians with a livelihood—that is to say, a moderate living." 443 U.S. at 686, 99 S.Ct. at 3075. Implicit in this "moderate living" standard is the conclusion that Indian tribes are not generally entitled to the same level of exclusive use and exploitation of a natural resource that they enjoyed at the time they entered into the treaty reserving their interest in the resource, unless, of course, no lesser level will supply them with a moderate living. As limited by the "moderate living" standard enunciated in *Fishing Vessel*, we affirm the district court's decision that the Klamath Tribe is entitled to a reservation of water, with a priority date of immemorial use, sufficient to support exercise of treaty hunting and fishing rights.

* * *

B. Water Rights of Successors-in-interest to Klamath Indian Allottees

* * *

1. Indian Successors to Allotted Reservation Lands

* * * The scope of Indian irrigation rights is well settled. It is a right to sufficient water to "irrigate all the practicably irrigable acreage on the reservation." Individual Indian allottees have a right to use a portion of this reserved water. Moreover, the full measure of this right need not be exercised immediately. As with rights reserved to the Tribe, water may be used by Indian allottees for present and future irrigation needs.[25]

This right is limited here only by section 14 of the Klamath Termination Act, 25 U.S.C. § 564m (1976). This section provides, first, that "[n]othing in [The Termination Act] shall abrogate any water rights of the tribe and its members," and second, that "the laws of the State of Oregon with respect to abandonment of water rights by non-use shall not apply to the tribe and its members until fifteen years after the date of the proclamation [of termination]." *Id.* The State and individual appellants argue that the second part of section 564m was meant to apply all Oregon water law, except that respecting abandonment of water rights by non-use, to the Tribe immediately upon the proclamation of termination.

---

[25] The water rights of Indian irrigators, as the district court noted, are subordinate to the Tribe's right to water for support of its hunting and fishing lifestyle. 478 F.Supp. at 346. This hierarchy among Indian water rights arises, not from any implication in the 1864 treaty that the purpose of hunting and fishing should predominate over any of the other purposes for which the Klamath Reservation was established, but rather from the analytically separate question of what priority date for appropriation the various water rights reserved in the treaty carry. Analysis of this latter question, under the unique circumstances of this case, leads to the conclusion that the Tribe's hunting and fishing water rights carry an earlier priority date for appropriation, because of historical use, than do water rights for irrigation.

* * *

In order to effectuate the Termination Act's explicit command that Klamath water rights survive unimpaired, we must interpret the second part of section 564m to mean that starting in 1976, fifteen years after the proclamation of termination in 1961, reserved water actually appropriated for use by members of the Tribe on allotments, could be lost under Oregon laws "with respect to abandonment of water rights by non-use." However, no other provision of Oregon water law that might preclude appropriation of the full measure of Klamath reserved water rights may be applied to the Tribe or its members consistently with the unequivocal language of protection in the first sentence of section 564m. To hold otherwise would sanction destruction of treaty rights in the absence of the required express Congressional approval.

2. *Non-Indian Successors to Allotted Reservation Lands*

The district court held that:

a non-Indian successor to an Indian allottee acquires an appurtenant right to water for the actual acreage under irrigation when he gets title from his Indian predecessor. The priority date of that right is 1864.

The non-Indian also acquires a right, with an 1864 priority date, to water for additional acreage which he, with reasonable diligence, may place under irrigation.

The sole claim raised by the Tribe in its cross-appeal is to this aspect of the district court's decision.

The claim, however, is foreclosed by our recent decision in *Colville Confederated Tribes v. Walton,* 647 F.2d at 42. There we held that "[t]he full quantity of water available to the Indian allottee thus may be conveyed to the non-Indian purchaser." The limitations on this transfer, recognized in *Colville* are, first, that the non-Indian successor's right to water is "limited by the number of irrigable acres [of former reservation lands that] he owns," and second, that the non-Indian purchaser may lose the right to that quantity of water through non-use. Thus, citing the district court's opinion in the instant case, in *Colville,* we limited a non-Indian successor to lands allotted to a member of the Colville Tribe to the amount of water used by the Indian predecessor plus additional water that "he or she appropriates with reasonable diligence after the passage of title." * * *

* * *

NOTES

1.   The context of *Adair* was difficult because the tribe had lost its reservation through termination, yet the treaty right to hunt and fish—along

with the attendant right to sufficient water to sustain a fishery—survived termination and loss of title to the land. The same court refused to find that the Skokomish Tribe had impliedly reserved water rights for its *on-reservation* fishery based on an express reservation of *off-reservation* fishing rights under a treaty that recognized such rights in common with others at places along the river—the same river that runs through the tribe's reservation. Skokomish Indian Tribe v. United States, 401 F.3d 979 (9th Cir.2005) (*en banc*). Applying *New Mexico*, the court held that the tribe failed to show that fishing was a "primary purpose" of the reservation. It distinguished *Adair* saying that the basis for implying water rights for the fishery there had been the existence of reserved water rights based on treaty provisions recognizing the Klamath Tribe's exclusive fishing rights on its now-extinguished reservation. Did the court actually follow or depart from *Adair* and the precedent on which it was based?

2. A number of cases have held that tribes may hold reserved water rights to minimum instream flows, typically for preservation of fishing rights secured by treaty. In addition to *Colville,* cited in *Adair*, and later proceedings in that case, Colville Confederated Tribes v. Walton, 752 F.2d 397 (9th Cir.1985), cert. denied 475 U.S. 1010 (1986), see Muckleshoot Indian Tribe v. Trans-Canada Enterprises, Ltd., 713 F.2d 455 (9th Cir.1983), cert. denied 465 U.S. 1049 (1984); Joint Bd. of Control of the Flathead, Mission and Jocko Irrigation Districts v. United States, 832 F.2d 1127 (9th Cir.1987), cert. denied 486 U.S. 1007 (1988). The issues are extremely sensitive because instream flows for fisheries may compete with established consumptive water users seeking to withdraw water from the streams. See also United States v. Washington, Phase II, 759 F.2d 1353 (9th Cir.1985) (en banc), cert. denied 474 U.S. 994 (1985). Cf. Carson-Truckee Water Conservancy District v. Clark, 741 F.2d 257 (9th Cir.1984), cert. denied 471 U.S. 1065 (1985) (Secretary of the Interior may allocate all the water from a federal reclamation project to protect endangered species in Pyramid Lake on which the Pyramid Lake Paiute Tribe depends for its livelihood from fishing). See generally, Julia Guarino, *Protecting Traditional Water Resources: Options for Preserving Tribal Non-consumptive Water Use*, 37 Pub. Land & Resources L.Rev. 89 (2016).

For many tribes, Winters rights, and even instream flows, are too narrow to address the cultural and spiritual aspects that Indian people value in water. In the Murray-Darling Basin of Australia, traditional aboriginal people have been proposing, with some success, what they term "cultural flows." See Jessica Weir, *Cultural Flows in Murray River County*, 48 Austl.Human.Rev. 131 (2010). Cultural rights are defined as "water entitlements that are legally and beneficially owned by the Indigenous Nations and are of a sufficient and adequate quantity and quality to improve the spiritual, cultural, environmental, social and economic conditions of those Indigenous Nations." S. E. Jackson, *The Cultural Politics of Environmental Water Management in Australia*, in *Water and Society III* 37 (C. A. Brebbia ed. 2015).

3. The special master's report upon which the decision in *Arizona v. California* is based, stated that use of irrigable acreage as a measure of the

Indians' rights "does not necessarily mean, however, that water reserved for Indian Reservations may not be used for purposes other than agriculture and related uses." Simon Rifkind, Report of the Special Master in Arizona v. California 265 (1962). He explained that the measure had been used because agriculture had been the initial purpose of the reservations, but added that the government could use the right for any purpose that may benefit the Indians. In United States v. Finch, 548 F.2d 822 (9th Cir.1976), reversed on other grounds 433 U.S. 676 (1977), the right to use reservation waters for fishery purposes was upheld, although the only purpose referred to in documents contemporaneous with the reservation's establishment was agriculture. The court said: "We find it inconceivable that the United States intended to withhold from Indians the right to sustain themselves from any source of food which might be available on their reservation." 548 F.2d at 832. But see In re Rights to Use Water in Big Horn River System (*Big Horn II*), page 859, infra.

4.   Are Indians entitled to a reserved right to use as much water as they need to advance them as far along the economic and social spectrum as their "new habits" enable them? Or are they limited to a bare subsistence? Or to the national median income? How fully should reservation purposes be satisfied?

Adair cites Washington v. Washington State Commercial Passenger Fishing Vessel Association, page 911, infra, where the Supreme Court analogized reserved water rights to off-reservation treaty fishing rights and held that Washington Indian tribes had reserved a right to take up to half of the harvests of fish from fishing areas in the lands they gave up by treaty. The Court added that the Indians' 50 percent share could be limited to prevent them from taking more than they needed for their livelihood; "that is to say, a moderate living." 443 U.S. at 686. Is this consistent with the *Arizona v. California* Court's express rejection of equitable apportionment or "reasonably foreseeable needs" as measures for the Indian reserved water right? Is it an appropriate rule? Is the fishing right different from the water right?

5.   Another contribution of *Adair* to the field of water law was its decision that where there is evidence of pre-historic Indian water use, the tribe's priority date for reserved water rights is "time immemorial." Could this apply to agricultural water on those reservations where irrigation had been established before contact with non-Indians? This would be mostly in the Southwest; irrigated farming elsewhere occurred after the government settled hunting and fishing tribes on reservations. United States v. Gila Valley Irrig. Dist., Globe Equity Decree No. 59 (D.Ariz. June 29, 1935).

6.   The *Adair* court's decision that the tribe, Indian allotment holders, and non-Indian successors to allotments all hold water rights with priority dates as of the date the reservation was created, can lead to conflict among these three rights holders in times of shortage. A later decision from the same court held that the rights holders must curtail their uses on a pro rata basis under such circumstances. Colville Confederated Tribes v. Walton, 752 F.2d 397 (9th Cir.1985), cert. denied 475 U.S. 1010 (1986). Is it consistent with the reservation purposes to require a tribe to limit its water use to allow water to

be used by a non-Indian allotment purchaser? Is such a result consistent with the purposes of the General Allotment Act? What support is there in law or policy for the *Walton* court's ruling that: 1. Indian allottees (and their purchasers) own a pro rata share of waters reserved for irrigation of an Indian reservation? 2. The water rights of Indian allottees (and their purchasers) have a priority date as of the date the reservation was created? 3. Non-Indian purchasers take a reserved right to all water being put to use on the land and to water appropriated with reasonable diligence after title passes? Commentators disagree on the correct approach to be taken on each of these points. See, e.g., Richard B. Collins, *Indian Allotment Water Rights*, 20 Land & Water L.Rev. 421 (1985), and David H. Getches, *Water Rights on Indian Allotments*, 26 S.D.L.Rev. 405 (1981).

7. Establishing the standard for determining reserved water rights based on the purpose of the reservation is only the first step in adjudicating a tribe's rights. In *Adair*, the court said that it was up to Oregon forums to quantify the amount of water necessary for the purposes of the reservation so long as the state forums complied with the substantive standards set forth by the Ninth Circuit. Oregon had created an administrative system for such adjudications, subject to later judicial appeals (Oregon, alone among the western states, holds its general stream adjudications in the state water agency rather than state courts). The Oregon Water Resources Department initiated a general stream adjudication using an administrative process, which was created by state statute. The department gave notice that anyone who claimed a right to water from the river must file a claim. Some 5,000 claims were submitted, including those of the tribes. The complex proceeding moved slowly and included a petition to federal court on preliminary matters. This system of primacy of federal substantive law and deference to state adjudicative processes in Indian water law cases, under the McCarran amendment is explained in the next section.

Finally, in 2013, the administrative law judge rendered an opinion unlike any seen before in that it decreed large numbers of detailed and sweeping senior instream flow rights based on the needs of natural vegetation, non-game fish, and furbearing animals. The agency opinion was faithful to *Adair* in every respect, including the time immemorial priority date. The state proceedings are summarized in Rachael Paschal Osborn, *Native American Winters Doctrine and Stevens Treaty Water Rights: Recognition, Quantification, Management*, 2 Am. Indian L.J. 76, 89–91 (2013).

There was widespread doubt as to whether the state would enforce the order. Western water law had never seen anything like it before, and consumptive water users and many state water officials considered instream flows as suspect at best. The idea that these rights had a priority date of "time immemorial" seemed radical and unfair to existing users who had always assumed that they were the ultimate seniors. Further, 2013 was a dry year and former seniors might get shut down if the tribes made calls based on their rights. But Governor John Kitzhaber announced that he would order the Oregon Water Resources Department to enforce the calls if any were made.

Finally, late in the irrigation season, the tribes did make a number of calls on former senior users and the state enforced the calls, shutting down 100,000 irrigated acres that supported an estimated 70,000 cattle. See Tony Barboza, *Severe Drought Forces a Moment of Truth for the Klamath*, High Country News, Aug. 19, 2013.

The widely-feared violence never occurred and within months the irrigators, who had long proclaimed that they would never negotiate with the tribes, entered into negotiations. By the spring of 2014 the tribes, irrigators, and state and federal agencies reached a comprehensive agreement. Among other things, ranchers will retire 30,000 acre-feet of water per year. An ambitious riparian management program will return large amounts of water to the streams, to the benefit of both the tribes and the ranchers. See Office of Governor John Kitzhaber, "Historic Agreement Reached on Upper Klamath Basin Water," Mar. 5, 2014. Some ranchers have filed exceptions with the state circuit court and those appeals are expected to take many years to resolve. In the meantime, there is a new and very different status quo in the Klamath River basin.

SECTION C. QUANTIFICATION

Water users on heavily appropriated western streams see the existence of Indian reserved rights as a time bomb. A tribe's reserved right with an early priority date leaves all junior rights holders on the same stream uncertain of whether they will have the benefit of their long-established uses if and when the tribe begins using water. Of course, the most junior rights holders are in the greatest jeopardy, but how far up the ladder of priorities the jeopardy extends depends on the size of the tribe's right and the amount of water flowing in the stream in a particular year. For that reason, states and non-Indian water users have pressed for quantification of Indian reserved rights. The quantification process has proved difficult and expensive.

1. JURISDICTION

Reserved Indian water rights are creatures of federal common law. Their existence and application are independent of state laws, and their effect is to preempt rights determined by state forums. But by means of the McCarran Amendment, enacted in 1952, Congress has consented to joinder of the United States in state court adjudications of water rights in river systems where the government owns rights. 43 U.S.C.A. § 666. May rights still be adjudicated in federal court? Does the statutory consent concerning federally-owned water rights include Indian rights?

COLORADO RIVER WATER CONSERVATION DISTRICT V. UNITED STATES

Supreme Court of the United States, 1976.
424 U.S. 800, 96 S.Ct. 1236, 47 L.Ed.2d 483.

MR. JUSTICE BRENNAN delivered the opinion of the Court.

The McCarran Amendment, 66 Stat. 560, 43 U.S.C. § 666, provides that "consent is hereby given to join the United States as a defendant in any suit (1) for the adjudication of rights to the use of water of a river system or other source, or (2) for the administration of such rights, where it appears that the United States is the owner of or is in the process of acquiring water rights by appropriation under State law, by purchase, by exchange, or otherwise, and the United States is a necessary party to such suit." The questions presented by this case concern the effect of the McCarran Amendment upon the jurisdiction of the federal district courts under 28 U.S.C. § 1345 over suits for determination of water rights brought by the United States as trustee for certain Indian tribes and as owner of various non-Indian Government claims.

I

It is probable that no problem of the Southwest section of the Nation is more critical than that of scarcity of water. As southwestern populations have grown, conflicting claims to this scarce resource have increased. To meet these claims, several Southwestern States have established elaborate procedures for allocation of water and adjudication of conflicting claims to that resource. In 1969, Colorado enacted its Water Rights Determination and Administration Act in an effort to revamp its legal procedures for determining claims to water within the State.

Under the Colorado Act, the State is divided into seven Water Divisions, each Division encompassing one or more entire drainage basins for the larger rivers in Colorado. Adjudication of water claims within each Division occurs on a continuous basis. Each month, Water Referees in each Division rule on applications for water rights filed within the preceding five months or refer those applications to the Water Judge of their Division. Every six months the Water Judge passes on referred applications and contested decisions by Referees. A State Engineer and engineers for each Division are responsible for the administration and distribution of the waters of the State according to the determinations in each Division.

Colorado applies the doctrine of prior appropriation in establishing rights to the use of water. * * *

The reserved rights of the United States extend to Indian reservations, *Winters v. United States*, 207 U.S. 564 (1908), and other federal lands, such as national parks and forests, *Arizona v. California*, 373 U.S. 546 (1963). The reserved rights claimed by the United States in this case affect waters within Colorado Water Division No. 7. On November 14, 1972, the Government instituted this suit in the United States District Court for the District of Colorado, invoking the court's jurisdiction under 28 U.S.C.A. § 1345. The District Court is located in Denver, some 300 miles from Division 7. The suit, against some 1,000 water users, sought declaration of the Government's rights to waters in certain rivers and their tributaries located in Division 7. In the suit, the Government asserted reserved rights on its own behalf and on behalf of certain Indian tribes, as well as rights based on state law. It sought appointment of a water master to administer any waters decreed to the United States.

* * *

Shortly after the federal suit was commenced, one of the defendants in that suit filed an application in the state court for Division 7, seeking an order directing service of process on the United States in order to make it a party to proceedings in Division 7 for the purpose of adjudicating all of the Government's claims, both state and federal. On January 3, 1973, the United States was served pursuant to authority of the McCarran Amendment. Several defendants and intervenors in the federal proceeding then filed a motion in the District Court to dismiss on the ground that under the Amendment, the court was without jurisdiction to determine federal water rights. Without deciding the jurisdictional question, the District Court, on June 21, 1973, granted the motion in an unreported oral opinion stating that the doctrine of abstention required deference to the proceedings in Division 7. On appeal, the Court of Appeals for the Tenth Circuit reversed, *United States v. Akin*, 504 F.2d 115 (1974) holding that the suit of the United States was within district-court jurisdiction under 28 U.S.C.A. § 1345, and that abstention was inappropriate. We granted certiorari to consider the important questions of whether the McCarran Amendment terminated jurisdiction of federal courts to adjudicate federal water rights and whether, if that jurisdiction was not terminated, the District Court's dismissal in this case was nevertheless appropriate. We reverse.

II

We first consider the question of district-court jurisdiction under 28 U.S.C.A. § 1345. That section provides that the district courts shall have original jurisdiction over all civil actions brought by the Federal Government "[e]xcept as otherwise provided by Act of Congress." It is thus necessary to examine whether the McCarran Amendment is such an Act of Congress excepting jurisdiction under § 1345.

The McCarran Amendment does not by its terms, at least, indicate any repeal of jurisdiction under § 1345. * * *

* * *

* * * Not only do the terms and legislative history of the McCarran Amendment not indicate an intent to repeal § 1345, but also there is no irreconcilability in the operation of both statutes. The immediate effect of the Amendment is to give consent to jurisdiction in the state courts concurrent with jurisdiction in the federal courts over controversies involving federal rights to the use of water. There is no irreconcilability in the existence of concurrent state and federal jurisdiction. Such concurrency has, for example, long existed under federal diversity jurisdiction. Accordingly, we hold that the McCarran Amendment in no way diminished federal-district-court jurisdiction under § 1345 and that the District Court had jurisdiction to hear this case.

III

We turn next to the question whether this suit nevertheless was properly dismissed in view of the concurrent state proceedings in Division 7.

A

First, we consider whether the McCarran Amendment provided consent to determine federal reserved rights held on behalf of Indians in state court. * * *

United States v. District Court for Eagle County, 401 U.S. 520 (1971), and *United States v. District Court for Water Div. 5*, 401 U.S. 527 (1971), held that the provisions of the McCarran Amendment, * * * subject federal reserved rights to general adjudication in state proceedings for the determination of water rights. * * * Though *Eagle County* and *Water Div. 5* did not involve reserved rights on Indian reservations, viewing the Government's trusteeship of Indian rights as ownership, the logic of those cases clearly extends to such rights. Indeed, *Eagle County* spoke of non-indian rights and Indian rights without any suggestion that there was a distinction between them for purposes of the Amendment.

Not only the Amendment's language, but also its underlying policy, dictates a construction including Indian rights in its provisions. *Eagle County* rejected the conclusion that federal reserved rights in general were not reached by the Amendment for the reason that the Amendment "[deals] with an all-inclusive statute concerning 'the adjudication of rights to the use of water of a river system.'" This consideration applies as well to federal water rights reserved for Indian reservations. * * *

* * *

Thus, bearing in mind the ubiquitous nature of Indian water rights in the Southwest, it is clear that a construction of the Amendment excluding those rights from its coverage would enervate the Amendment's objective.

* * *

The Government argues that because of its fiduciary responsibility to protect Indian rights, any state-court jurisdiction over Indian property should not be recognized, however, that an action for the destruction of personal property may be brought against an Indian tribe where "[a]uthority to sue * * * is implied." *Turner v. United States*, 248 U.S. 354, 358 (1919). Moreover, the Government's argument rests on the incorrect assumption that consent to state jurisdiction for the purpose of determining water rights imperils those rights or in some way breaches the special obligation of the Federal Government to protect Indians. Mere subjection of Indian rights to legal challenge in state court, however, would no more imperil those rights than would a suit brought by the Government in district court for their declaration, a suit which, absent the consent of the Amendment, would eventually be necessitated to resolve conflicting claims to a scarce resource. The Government has not abdicated any responsibility fully to defend Indian rights in state court, and Indian interests may be satisfactorily protected under regimes of state law. The Amendment in no way abridges any substantive claim on behalf of Indians under the doctrine of reserved rights. Moreover, as *Eagle County* said, "questions [arising from the collision of private rights and reserved rights of the United States], including the volume and scope of particular reserved rights, are federal questions which, if preserved, can be reviewed [by the Supreme Court] after final judgment by the Colorado court."

* * *

Next, we consider whether the District Court's dismissal was appropriate under the doctrine of abstention. We hold that the dismissal cannot be supported under that doctrine in any of its forms.

* * *

Although this case falls within none of the abstention categories, there are principles unrelated to considerations of proper constitutional adjudication and regard for federal-state relations which govern in situations involving the contemporaneous exercise of concurrent jurisdictions, either by federal courts or by state and federal courts. These principles rest on considerations of "[w]ise judicial administration, giving regard to conservation of judicial resources and comprehensive disposition of litigation." * * *

* * *

* * * Turning to the present case, a number of factors clearly counsel against concurrent federal proceedings. The most important of these is the McCarran Amendment itself. The clear federal policy evinced by that legislation is the avoidance of piecemeal adjudication of water rights in a river system. This policy is akin to that underlying the rule requiring that jurisdiction be yielded to the court first acquiring control of property, for the concern in such instances is with avoiding the generation of additional litigation through permitting inconsistent dispositions of property. This concern is heightened with respect to water rights, the relationships among which are highly interdependent. * * *

* * *

Beyond the congressional policy expressed by the McCarran Amendment and consistent with furtherance of that policy, we also find significant (a) the apparent absence of any proceedings in the District Court, other than the filing of the complaint, prior to the motion to dismiss, (b) the extensive involvement of state water rights occasioned by this suit naming 1,000 defendants, (c) the 300-mile distance between the District Court in Denver and the court in Division 7, and (d) the existing participation by the Government in Division 4, 5, and 6 proceedings. We emphasize, however, that we do not overlook the heavy obligation to exercise jurisdiction. We need not decide, for example, whether, despite the McCarran Amendment, dismissal would be warranted if more extensive proceedings had occurred in the District Court prior to dismissal, if the involvement of state water rights were less extensive than it is here, or if the state proceeding were in some respect inadequate to resolve the federal claims. But the opposing factors here, particularly the policy underlying the McCarran Amendment, justify the District Court's dismissal in this particular case.

The judgment of the Court of Appeals is reversed and the judgment of the District Court dismissing the complaint is affirmed for the reasons here stated.

* * *

NOTES

1.　Most western states were admitted to the Union on the condition that they disclaim all "right and title" to Indian property. These disclaimers were included in state enabling acts and constitutions and typically stated that "until the title of such Indians or Indian tribes shall have been extinguished the same shall be and remain subject to the disposition and under the absolute jurisdiction and control of the Congress of the United States."

In Arizona v. San Carlos Apache Tribe, 463 U.S. 545 (1983), several tribes and the United States brought federal actions to adjudicate tribal reserved water rights in Arizona, New Mexico, and Montana—states that have disclaimers. When the United States was served with process in state general stream adjudications in those disclaimer states pursuant to the McCarran Amendment, it challenged the state courts' jurisdiction. The government and the tribes attempted to distinguish *Colorado River Water Conservation District* based on Colorado's being exceptional because it was not subject to a disclaimer.

The Supreme Court rejected this argument saying:

[O]ur many recent decisions recognizing crucial limits on the power of the States to regulate Indian affairs have rarely either invoked reservations of jurisdiction contained in statehood enabling acts by anything more than a passing mention or distinguished between disclaimer States and nondisclaimer States.

* * * Congress clearly would have had the right to distinguish between disclaimer and nondisclaimer States in passing the McCarran Amendment. But the Amendment was designed to deal with a general problem arising out of the limitations that federal sovereign immunity placed on the ability of the States to adjudicate water rights, and nowhere in its text or legislative history do we find any indication that Congress intended the efficacy of the remedy to differ from one State to another. Moreover, we stated in *Colorado River* that "bearing in mind the ubiquitous nature of Indian water rights in the Southwest, it is clear that a construction of the Amendment excluding those rights from its coverage would enervate the Amendment's objective." * * *

Id. at 551.

Having dealt with the tribes' principal argument, the Court continued:

The United States and the various Indian respondents raise a series of arguments why dismissal or stay of the federal suit is not appropriate when it is brought by an Indian tribe and only seeks to adjudicate Indian rights. (1) Indian rights have traditionally been left free of interference from the States. (2) State courts may be inhospitable to Indian rights. (3) The McCarran Amendment, although it waived United States sovereign immunity in state comprehensive water adjudications, did not waive *Indian* sovereign immunity. It is therefore unfair to force Indian claimants to choose between waiving their sovereign immunity by intervening in the state proceedings and relying on the United States to represent their interests in state court, particularly in light of the frequent conflict of interest between Indian claims and other federal interests and the right of the Indians under 28 U.S.C. § 1362 to bring suit on their own behalf in federal court. (4) Indian water rights claims are generally based on federal rather than state law. (5) Because Indian water claims are based on the doctrine of "reserved rights," and take priority over most water rights created by state law, they need not as a practical matter be adjudicated *inter sese* with other water rights, and could simply be incorporated into the comprehensive state decree at the conclusion of the state proceedings.

Each of these arguments has a good deal of force. We note, though, that very similar arguments were raised and rejected in *Eagle County* and *Colorado River*. More important, all of these arguments founder on one crucial fact: If the state proceedings have jurisdiction over the Indian water rights at issue here, as appears to be the case, then concurrent federal proceedings are likely to be duplicative and wasteful, generating "additional litigation through permitting inconsistent dispositions of property." Moreover, since a judgment by either court would ordinarily be res judicata in the other, the existence of such concurrent proceedings creates the serious potential for spawning an unseemly and destructive race to see which forum can resolve the same issues first—a race contrary to the entire spirit of the McCarran Amendment and prejudicial, to say the least, to the possibility of reasoned decision making by either forum. * * *

* * *

Colorado River, of course, does not require that a federal water suit must always be dismissed or stayed in deference to a concurrent and adequate comprehensive state adjudication. Certainly, the federal courts need not defer to the state proceedings if the state courts expressly agree to stay their own consideration of the issues raised in the federal action pending disposition of that action. Moreover, it may be in a particular case that, at the time a motion to dismiss is filed, the federal suit at issue is well enough along that its dismissal would itself constitute a waste of judicial resources and an invitation to duplicative effort. Finally, we do not deny that, in a case in which the arguments for and against deference to the state adjudication were otherwise closely matched, the fact that a federal suit was brought by Indians on their own behalf and sought only to adjudicate Indian rights should be figured into the balance. But the most important consideration in *Colorado River,* and the most important consideration in any federal water suit concurrent to a comprehensive state proceeding, must be the "policy underlying the McCarran Amendment," and, despite the strong arguments raised by the respondents, we cannot conclude that water rights suits brought by Indians and seeking adjudication only of Indian rights should be excepted from the application of that policy or from the general principles set out in *Colorado River.* * * *

Id. at 567–70.

After *San Carlos,* under what circumstances may a federal court adjudicate Indian reserved water rights? In *Adair,* the federal court first assumed jurisdiction to determine the nature of the tribes' water rights but deferred to the later initiated—state court action for quantification. As shown by *Colorado River,* this is not always the result where the federal action begins before the state general stream adjudication. Not surprisingly, the abstention policy of the McCarran Amendment was not an impediment to federal court jurisdiction in a case that had been pending for 60 years (*Globe Equity*), noted at page 840 supra. In re the General Adjudication of all Rights to use Water in the Gila River System and Source, 134 P.3d 375 (Ariz.2006).

2.   Aside from sovereign immunity and other legal arguments, why would a tribe be concerned about adjudication of its water rights in a state forum?

2.   ADJUDICATION

IN RE GENERAL ADJUDICATION OF ALL RIGHTS TO USE WATER IN THE BIG HORN RIVER SYSTEM

Supreme Court of Wyoming, 1988.
753 P.2d 76, affirmed sub nom. Wyoming v. United States,
492 U.S. 406, 109 S.Ct. 2994, 106 L.Ed.2d 342 (1989).

I   Introduction

This appeal is from the district court's order adjudicating rights to use water in the Big Horn River System and all other sources within the State's Water Division No. 3. The district court modified the special master's recommended decree. All parties have appealed from the district court's amended judgment and decree. We affirm in part and reverse in part.

* * *

The history of the Big Horn Basin for purposes of this case begins in the early 1800's when explorers, trappers and traders began traveling into northwestern Wyoming, part of the vast hunting grounds of the peripatetic Shoshone Indians. Neither group encroached on the other and relations were friendly. Nonetheless, in 1865, the United States, hoping to preserve the peace and stability, reached an agreement delineating the area within which the Eastern Shoshone roamed, a 44,672,000-acre region comprising parts of Wyoming, Colorado and Utah. Following the Civil War, as the westward movement gained momentum, the United States government realized the size of the region set aside for Indians only was unrealistic, and on July 3, 1868, executed the Second Treaty of Fort Bridger with the Shoshone and Bannock Indians, establishing the Wind River Indian Reservation.

During their first years on the reservation, the Shoshone Indians were still dependent on the buffalo as the mainstay of their life, but as the supply rapidly decreased, they began to rely upon an agricultural economy. During the 1870's the Shoshone Indians increased their efforts in both farming and ranching. The Shoshone ceded lands beyond the Popo Agie back to the United States in the 1872 Brunot Agreement. The Arapahoe moved to the reservation in 1878. By the 1880's it was evident that the agricultural economy of the Indians was failing, and by 1895, the Indians on the Wind River Indian Reservation were totally dependent on the government for food, clothing and shelter. These economic misfortunes compelled them to sell more of their land to the United States. The First McLaughlin Agreement, or Thermopolis Purchase, was concluded in 1897; the Big Horn

Hot Springs was the main feature of the lands ceded to the United States for cash payment. An additional 1,480,000 acres of reservation land were ceded to the Government in the Second McLaughlin Agreement in 1904–1905. The revenue derived helped to develop the remaining reservation lands (which came to be known as the "diminished reservation"). The United States Government offered the ceded lands for sale to others, under the provisions of the homestead, townsite, coal and mineral land laws, and reimbursed the Tribes or expended for the benefit of the Tribes the money raised by the sales.

The earliest non-Indian settlements in northwestern and north central Wyoming were near the gold and silver fields in the South Pass area of the Wind River Range. These mining camps soon expanded into permanent farming and ranching communities which relied primarily on cattle ranching and dryland or easily-irrigated farming for sustenance. By the mid-1800's, many small communities had been established by settlers who had obtained their land under the Congressional land disposal acts. By the early 1900's most of the best land in the region was occupied by ranches or irrigated farms. Yet the settlers continued to arrive, forcing gradual expansion onto the dry basin floors and prompting the development of many irrigation projects, often sponsored jointly by private citizens and the United States. The arrival of the homesteaders in the Wind River Basin significantly altered the Indian's economic base. As the number of settlers and their farms increased, the number of Indians working their own farms and ranches decreased, and they began to rent and eventually to sell their land while hiring themselves out as laborers.

In 1934, all remaining lands which had been ceded to the United States by the 1904 agreement were reserved from non-Indian settlement. In 1940, the Secretary of Interior began a series of restorations of certain undisposed lands to tribal ownership. These lands again became part of the existing Wind River Reservation. In addition, the United States later reacquired, in trust for the Tribes, additional ceded land and certain lands within the diminished reservation which previously had passed into private ownership. Since 1953, the size of the reservation has remained fairly stable.

* * *

On January 22, 1977, Wyoming enacted § 1–1054.1, W.S.1957 (now § 1–37–106, W.S.1977), authorizing the State to commence system-wide adjudications of water rights. The State of Wyoming filed the complaint commencing this litigation and naming the United States as a defendant on January 24, 1977, in the District Court of the Fifth Judicial District of Wyoming.

* * *

The special master signed his 451-page Report Concerning Reserved Water Right Claims by and on Behalf of the Tribes in the Wind River Reservation on December 15, 1982, covering four years of conferences and hearings, involving more than 100 attorneys, transcripts of more than 15,000 pages and over 2,300 exhibits.

The report recognized a reserved water right for the Wind River Indian Reservation and determined that the purpose for which the reservation had been established was a permanent homeland for the Indians. A reserved water right for irrigation, stock watering, fisheries, wildlife and aesthetics, mineral and industrial, and domestic, commercial, and municipal uses was quantified and awarded.

* * *

The State of Wyoming, the United States, the Shoshone and Arapahoe Tribes, and numerous private parties presented objections to the master's report, and on May 10, 1983, Judge Joffe entered his Findings of Fact, Conclusions of Law and Judgment approving that portion of the master's report awarding reserved water rights for practicably irrigable acreage within the Wind River Indian Reservation and refusing to accept that portion of the master's report recommending an award of reserved water rights for other than agricultural purposes.

* * *

The treaty establishing the Wind River Indian Reservation, signed on July 3, 1868, ratified on February 16, 1869, and proclaimed on February 24, 1869, Treaty of Ft. Bridger, 15 Stat. 673 (1869), is silent on the subject of water for the reservation. Yet both the district court and the special master found an intent to reserve water. We affirm.

* * *

IV   Purposes of the Wind River Indian Reservation

The government may reserve water from appropriation under state law for use on the lands set aside for an Indian reservation. *Winters v. United States,* supra, 207 U.S. 564. A reserved water right is implied for an Indian reservation where water is necessary to fulfill the purposes of reservation. *United States v. Adair,* 723 F.2d 1394, 1409 (9th Cir.1983), cert. denied sub nom. *Oregon v. United States,* 467 U.S. 1252 (1984). The quantity of water reserved is the amount of water sufficient to fulfill the purpose of the lands set aside for the reservation. * * * We have already decided that Congress intended to reserve water for the Wind River Indian Reservation when it was created in 1868, and we accept the proposition that the amount of water impliedly reserved is determined by the purposes for which the reservation was created.

* * *

* * * The district court ascertained the purpose of the reservation from the treaty itself, stating: "On the very face of the Treaty, it is clear that its purpose was purely agricultural." This legal determination is fully reviewable by this court.

* * *

A.   The Treaty

[The court quoted excerpts from The Treaty with the Shoshones and the Bannocks, July 3, 1868.] Considering the well-established principles of treaty interpretation, the treaty itself, the ample evidence and testimony addressed, and the findings of the district court, we have no difficulty affirming the finding that it was the intent at the time to create a reservation with a sole agricultural purpose. Indian treaties should be interpreted generously * * * and should not be given a crabbed or restrictive meaning. *McClanahan v. State Tax Commission of Arizona,* supra 411 U.S. at 176. Nor should treaties be improperly construed in favor of Indians, for " '[W]e cannot remake history,' " *Rosebud Sioux Tribe v. Kneip,* supra 430 U.S. at 615, and courts should not distort the words of a treaty to find rights inconsistent with its language. *Ward v. Race Horse,* 163 U.S. 504.

Article 7 of the treaty refers to "said agricultural reservations." Article 6 authorizes allotments for farming purposes; Article 8 provides seeds and implements for farmers; in Article 9 "the United States agreed to pay each Indian farming a $20 annual stipend, but only $10 to 'roaming' Indians"; and Article 12 establishes a $50 prize to the ten best Indian farmers. The treaty does not encourage any other occupation or pursuit. The district court correctly found that the reference in Article 4 to "permanent homeland" does nothing more than permanently set aside lands for the Indians; it does not define the purpose of the reservation. Rather, the purpose of the permanent-home reservation is found in Articles 6, 8, 9, and 12 of the treaty.

The emphasis on education for Indians settled on "said agricultural reservations," in Article 7 also helps to define the purpose of the reservation. Those words do not refer only to the farm tracts selected by individual Indians under Article 6, but to the two Indian reservations authorized by the treaty—for the Shoshone in Wyoming (Wind River) and for the Bannock in Utah (Fort Hall). Other treaties have emphasized the importance of education in somewhat different language. The thrust of all these provisions is that education is especially important for those Indians who are settled and engaged in agriculture and are no longer roaming. Thus, while Article 7 of the instant treaty emphasizes the importance of education for Indians engaged in farming, "said agricultural reservations" does have a broader meaning—that the two Indian reservations were to be agricultural.

Although the treaty did not force the Indians to become farmers and although it clearly contemplates that other activities would be permitted (hunting is mentioned in Article 4, lumbering and milling in Article 3, roaming in Article 9), the treaty encouraged only agriculture, and that was its primary purpose. The Court in *United States v. Shoshone Tribe of Indians,* supra 304 U.S. 111, discussing the purpose of this treaty, stated:

> "Provisions in aid of teaching children and of adult education in farming, and to secure for the tribe medical and mechanical service, to safeguard tribal and individual titles, when taken with other parts of the treaty, plainly evidence purpose on the part of the United States to help to create an independent permanent farming community upon the reservation." *Id.,* 304 U.S. at 117–118.

The Court, while recognizing that the Tribes were the beneficial owners of the reservation's timber and mineral resources, and that it was known to all before the treaty was signed that the Wind River Indian Reservation contained valuable minerals, nonetheless concluded that the purpose of the reservation was agricultural. The fact that the Indians fully intended to continue to hunt and fish does not alter that conclusion. October 4, 1868 Report to the President of the Indian Peace Commission; Report of Wyoming Territory Superintendent of Indian Affairs, October 11, 1870. See also Williams, Personal Recollections of Wash-A-Kie, Chief of the Shoshones, 1 Utah Historical Quarterly 101, 104 (1928) (the Shoshone left the reservation both before and after the treaty for better hunting and fishing grounds in Utah).

Agreements subsequent to the treaty acknowledge the continuance of non-agricultural activities on the reservation. The reports of the Indian agents are replete with descriptions of and plans for other activities. Yet not one of the cited reports neglects to report also on the progress of the farming and ranching operations. The primary activity was clearly agricultural.

B.   Fisheries

Reserved water rights for fisheries have been recognized where a treaty provision explicitly recognized an exclusive right to take fish on the reservation or the right to take fish at traditional off-reservation fishing grounds, in common with others.

Instream fishery flows have also been recognized where the Indians were heavily, if not totally, dependent on fish for their livelihood. *United States v. Adair,* supra 723 F.2d at 1409; *Colville Confederated Tribes v. Walton,* supra 647 F.2d at 48. In the case at bar, the Tribes introduced evidence showing that fish had always been part of the Indians' diet. The master, erroneously concluding that a reserved right for fisheries should be implied when the tribe is "at least partially dependent upon fishing," awarded an instream flow right for fisheries. The district court, however, finding neither a dependency upon fishing for a livelihood nor a traditional lifestyle involving fishing, deleted the award. The district court did not err. The evidence is not sufficient to imply a fishery flow right absent a treaty provision.

C.　Mineral and Industrial

The Tribes were denied a reserved water right for mineral and industrial development. All parties to the treaty were well aware before it was signed of the valuable mineral estate underlying the Wind River Indian Reservation. The question of whether, because the Indians own the minerals, the intent was that they should have the water necessary to develop them must be determined, of course, by the intent in 1868. Neither the Tribes nor the United States has cited this court to any provision of the treaty or other evidence indicating that the parties contemplated in 1868 that a purpose of the reservation would be for the Indians to develop the minerals. The fact that the Tribes have since used water for mineral and industrial purposes does not establish that water was impliedly reserved in 1868 for such uses. The district court did not err in denying a reserved water right for mineral and industrial uses.

D.　Municipal, Domestic and Commercial

A reserved water right for municipal, domestic and commercial uses was included within the agricultural reserved water award. Domestic and related use has traditionally been subsumed in agricultural reserved rights. Practicably irrigable acreage (PIA) was established as the measure of an agricultural reserved water right in *Arizona v. California,* supra 373 U.S. at 601. The special master there indicated that PIA was the measure of water necessary for agriculture and related purposes. The court properly allowed a reserved water right for municipal, domestic, and commercial use.

E.　Livestock

For the reasons stated above, the district court did not err in finding a sole agricultural purpose for the reservation or in subsuming livestock use within that purpose.

F.　Wildlife and Aesthetics

The special master awarded 60% of historic flows for wildlife and aesthetic uses, consistent with his determination that the purpose of the reservation was to be a permanent homeland. The district court deleted this award, reciting not only that the purpose was solely agricultural, but that insufficient evidence had been presented to justify an award for these uses. The district court did not err in holding that the Tribes and the United States did not introduce sufficient evidence of a tradition of wildlife and aesthetic preservation which would justify finding this to be a purpose for which the reservation was created and for which water was impliedly reserved.

The district court did not err in finding a sole agricultural purpose in the creation of the Wind River Indian Reservation. The Treaty itself evidences no other purpose, and none of the extraneous evidence cited is sufficient to attribute a broader purpose.

V   Scope of the Reserved Water Right

A.   Groundwater

The logic which supports a reservation of surface water to fulfill the purpose of the reservation also supports reservation of groundwater. See *Tweedy v. Texas Company*, 286 F.Supp. 383, 385 (D.Mont.1968) ("whether the [necessary] waters were found on the surface of the land or under it should make no difference"). Certainly the two sources are often interconnected. See § 41–3–916, W.S.1977 (where underground and surface waters are "so interconnected as to constitute in fact one source of supply," a single schedule of priorities shall be made); Final Report to the President and to the Congress by the National Water Commission, Water Policies for the Future 233 (1973) (groundwater and surface water "often naturally related"); *Cappaert v. United States*, supra 426 U.S. at 142–143 (citing additional authority to this effect).

Acknowledging the above, we note that, nonetheless, not a single case applying the reserved water doctrine to groundwater is cited to us. The ninth circuit indicated that groundwater was reserved in *United States v. Cappaert*, 508 F.2d 313, 317 (9th Cir.1974). The United States Supreme Court, however, found the water in the pool reserved for preservation of the pupfish was not groundwater but surface water, protected from subsequent diversions from either surface or groundwater supplies. Nor have the other cases cited to us granted a reserved right in underground water. In *Colville Confederated Tribes v. Walton*, supra 647 F.2d 42, there is slight mention of the underground aquifer and of pumping wells, but the opinion does not indicate that "their wells" are a source of reserved water or even discuss a reserved groundwater right. *Tweedy v. Texas Company*, supra 286 F.Supp. 383, did not recognize a reserved groundwater right. Pueblo water rights, which include not only surface water but also groundwater "interrelated to the surface water as an integral part of the hydrologic cycle," *State of New Mexico ex rel. Reynolds v. Aamodt*, 618 F.Supp. 993, 1010 (D.N.M.1985), do not apply here.

The district court did not err in deciding there was no reserved groundwater right. Because we hold that the reserved water doctrine does not extend to groundwater, we need not address the separate claim that the district court erred in determining that the State owns the groundwater. The State has not appealed the decision that the Tribes may continue to satisfy their domestic and livestock needs (part of the agricultural award) from existing wells at current withdrawal rates; therefore, we do not address that question.

B. *Exportation*

The district court held that "[t]he Tribes can sell or lease any part of the water covered by their reserved water rights but the said sale or lease cannot be for exportation off of the Reservation." The Tribes did not seek permission to export reserved water, and the United States concedes that no federal law permits the sale of reserved water to non-Indians off the reservation. Because of our holding on the groundwater issue, we need not address the separate constitutional attack on the prohibition of exportation of groundwater.

NOTES

1. Two judges dissented separately in the Wyoming Supreme Court decision in *Big Horn I*. Justice Thomas disagreed with the majority's application of the practicably irrigable acreage (PIA) standard, and would have reduced the tribes' award on that basis, but he also objected to the majority's narrow view of the purposes of the reservation.

> The purpose of establishing an Indian reservation, such as the Wind River Indian Reservation, is to provide a homeland for Indian peoples. If one is to assume that, pursuant to the reserved rights doctrine relating to water, there is an implied reservation of those waters essential to accomplish the purpose of the reservation of land, then I cannot agree that the implied reservation of water with respect to the Wind River Indian Reservation should be limited, as the majority has held in approving the judgment of the district court. The fault that I find with such a limitation is that it assumes that the Indian peoples will not enjoy the same style of evolution as other people, nor are they to have the benefits of modern civilization. I would understand that the homeland concept assumes that homeland will not be a static place frozen in an instant of time but that the homeland will evolve and will be used in different ways as the Indian society develops. For that reason, I would hold that the implied reservation of water right attaching to an Indian reservation assumes any use that is appropriate to the Indian homeland as it progresses and develops. The one thing that I would not assume is that using the reserved water as a salable commodity was contemplated in connection with the implied reservation of the water. I would limit its use to the territorial boundaries of the reservation.

753 P.2d at 119.

District Judge Hanscum, sitting on the court by designation, agreed that water was impliedly reserved for all purposes consistent with a homeland, going the additional step of endorsing off-reservation water marketing by the tribes.

2.   The U.S. Supreme Court granted certiorari in *Big Horn I* limited to
the question: "In the absence of any demonstrated necessity for additional
water to fulfill Reservation purposes and in the presence of substantial state
water rights long in use on the Reservation, may a reserved water right be
implied for all practicably irrigable lands within a Reservation?" The Supreme
Court was equally divided and affirmed without an opinion. This caused much
speculation about the effect of the decision on the PIA standard for quantifying
Indian reserved water rights set by the Supreme Court in *Arizona v.
California,* page 823, supra. Of course, the evenly-split decision cannot change
existing law, so the mission of courts quantifying water rights for reservations
set aside for agricultural purposes is still to determine the amount of water
needed for all the PIA within a reservation. Yet we now know that the Court
came within a day of issuing a decision that would have narrowed the
application of the PIA standard.

Justice Sandra Day O'Connor had circulated a draft opinion that was
joined by a majority of the Court. She wrote that the amount of water awarded
to a tribe under the PIA standard should be curtailed as necessary to reflect
"sensitivity to the impact on state and private appropriators of scarce water
under state law" including "a practical assessment—a determination apart
from the theoretical and economic and engineering feasibility—of the
reasonable likelihood that future [Indian] irrigation projects, will actually be
built." The draft opinion and the memoranda exchanged among the Justices
were discovered in previously confidential files made available to researchers
upon the death of Justice Thurgood Marshall. See David H. Getches,
*Conquering the Cultural Frontier: The New Subjectivism of the Supreme Court
in Indian Law,* 84 Calif.L.Rev. 1573, 1640–41 (1996); Andrew C. Mergen &
Sylvia F. Liu, *A Misplaced Sensitivity: The Draft Opinions in Wyoming v.
United States,* 68 U.Colo.L.Rev. 683 (1997).

Justice O'Connor's opinion was abandoned, however, when she circulated
a memorandum to her fellow Justices shortly before the decision was to be
rendered, saying that she was disqualifying herself in the case because her
family ranch was joined "in a river water suit brought by an Indian tribe
affecting the Gila River, which adjoins a portion of the ranch." Thus, the Court
was left without a majority for reversal and so the Wyoming court was affirmed
on the 4–4 division among the remaining Justices.

3.   The tribes won confirmation of their rights to over 400,000 acre-feet
of water, the majority of the river's annual flow. The tribes, however, had
several concerns with the state supreme court decision and cross-petitioned for
certiorari. For instance, the court held that the purpose of the reservation was
"purely agricultural," rather than the broader purpose of creating a
"permanent homeland." See Peg Rogers, Note, *In re Rights to Use Water in the
Big Horn River,* 30 Nat. Resources J. 439 (1990); Berrie Martinez, *From
Quantification to Qualification: A State Court's Distortion of the Law* In re
General Adjudication of All Rights to Use Water in the Big Horn River System,
68 Wash.L.Rev. 435 (1993). The tribes' cross-petition was denied.

4. Following *Big Horn I,* litigation over the administration and use of the tribes' reserved water rights continued to rage. The tribes adopted a Wind River Interim Water Code, created the Wind River Water Resources Control Board, and authorized the dedication of water in the Wind River for "fisheries restoration and enhancement, recreational uses, ground water recharge, and downstream benefits to irrigators and other water users."

Shortly after the tribal water board issued an instream flow permit, the tribes complained to the state engineer that the upstream diversion of water by holders of state-awarded water rights interfered with the permit by diminishing Wind River flows to less than that amount specified in the permit. The state engineer informed the tribes that their permit was unenforceable because the tribes had been awarded only the right to divert water for future agricultural uses in *Big Horn I*. When the tribes contested the state engineer's failure to enforce the instream flow rights, the state district court ruled in their favor.

The Wyoming Supreme Court reversed the district court in a decision that produced five separate and divergent opinions (from the five-member court). A majority of the justices agreed that the tribes were not authorized to change their reserved right to divert future project water (water not yet used in agriculture) to instream flows for fishery purposes, except in accordance with Wyoming state water law. In re General Adjudication of All Rights to Use Water in the Big Horn River System *(Big Horn II),* 835 P.2d 273 (Wyo.1992). State water law in Wyoming and other western states requires that changes in the place, purpose, or manner of water use not injure any other appropriators in terms of their ability to use water rights. Can this principle operate to negate the utility or value of tribal water that has not yet been put to use? How can the state court determine whether a change in use from agriculture to fishery purposes injures other water users when, in fact, the tribe's water has not yet been put to any use? Perhaps the court must make assumptions about where, when, and how much water might be used for agriculture, and then measure the extent of injury caused by "changing" to instream flow uses relative to that hypothetical agricultural use. Is *any* use by a tribe of previously unused agricultural water—even for agriculture—a "change" that would be subject to the no injury rule under the reasoning of *Big Horn II*? The final decree in the Big Horn adjudication was filed in 2014, 37 years after the proceeding began. The Wyoming Law Review has dedicated an issue to it. *Big Horn General Stream Adjudication Symposium,* 15 Wyo.L.Rev. 231–516 (2015).

5. As noted at pages 828–829, supra, courts that have considered the matter have generally held that the *Winters* doctrine applies to groundwater.

NOTE: RESERVATION PURPOSES AND THE QUANTIFICATION PROCESS

The special master in *Arizona v. California* found in his 1963 report that: "The reservations of water were made for the purpose of enabling the Indians to develop a viable agricultural economy * * * ." Having so defined the purpose of the reservations, the master recommended, and the Supreme Court approved, a method for determining tribal water entitlements based on the amount of practicably irrigable acreage (PIA) on the reservations, multiplied by the amount of water needed to irrigate each acre. This formulation was upheld, albeit narrowly, in *Big Horn I.*

Most claims asserted by tribes, or by the United States on behalf of tribes in cases like *Big Horn I,* are based on an agricultural purpose for the reservation in question. Consequently, it is necessary to determine the PIA.

Expert Evidence and PIA

How does the tribe or the government prove its claim? At least four disciplines are involved: soil science, hydrology, engineering, and economics. The first step is to conduct a soils survey to classify the reservation lands for irrigation suitability. This task separates potentially irrigable lands, i.e., those lands capable of supporting sustained agricultural development without long term deterioration in quality, from those that are nonirrigable. Such a determination may depend on drainage, slope, topography, chemical composition, soil structure, soil depth, and the like.

The next step is to determine whether surface or groundwater of adequate quantity and quality is available to serve the potentially irrigable lands. This requires an analysis to determine surface water flow, and it may involve drilling of test wells to determine groundwater availability.

The third task is to determine the feasibility of constructing a water delivery system to bring the water to the land at a reasonable cost. Further calculations are required to determine the consumptive irrigation requirements of particular crops and the prevailing climate and growing season.

Finally, it is necessary to demonstrate that the proposed agricultural development is economically feasible. The agricultural economist must (in consultation with other experts such as agronomists and horticulturists) select an appropriate demonstration cropping plan and then gather information concerning the costs of agricultural practices required to grow these crops, analyze expected yields and prices, and determine other economic benefits.

Economics is perhaps the most controversial component in the prima facie case. If the tribal claim were confined to historically irrigated acreage or to an amount necessary to support a subsistence economy, a strong case could be made for excluding economic considerations. Claims presently being asserted by the tribes and by the United States on their behalf, however, envisage full development of the irrigable land base utilizing modern technology. But how efficient must irrigation be to be practicable? If economics were no constraint, almost any land could be made irrigable. Rock could be crushed into fine particles, and soils could be amended and made irrigable.

Special Master Tuttle, in the reopened *Arizona v. California* case to determine water rights of Colorado River tribes, see pages 870–871, infra found that economic feasibility was one ingredient in the determination of practicably irrigable acreage, but that profitability was not required. He noted in his 1982 report that many of the lands that the 1962 master's report found to be practicably irrigable could not be cultivated at a profit even under the most favorable circumstances. Thus, he rejected state claims that the benefits of Indian water use must exceed costs by a set margin, finding that a benefit-cost ratio equal to or greater than unity (i.e., benefits are equal to costs) was sufficient. He also refused to accept the argument that practicability should be determined based on nineteenth century farming technology. The tribes urged him to consider subsidies available to Indians (e.g., exemption from irrigation project repayment, 25 U.S.C.A. § 386a), but he refused to do so. The master's findings on these points were not challenged so the Supreme Court did not review his approach. The court did, however, approve the master's findings on expanded practicably irrigable acreage on the Cocopah and Fort Mojave Reservations. Arizona v. California, 460 U.S. 605, 640–41 (1983). Many uncertainties remain, such as how to evaluate future benefits to an Indian tribe with perpetual existence that may be extremely important but that would have a discounted present value of zero. See H.S. Burness, Ronald Cummings, W.D. Gorman & R.R. Lansford, *The "New" Arizona v. California: Practicably Irrigable Acreage and Economic Feasibility*, 22 Nat. Resources J. 517 (1982); H.S. Burness, Ronald Cummings, W.D. Gorman & R.R. Lansford, *Practicably Irrigable Acreage and Economic Feasibility: The Role of Time, Ethics, and Discounting*, 23 Nat. Resources J. 289 (1983).

When faced with a disagreement among experts as to the economic feasibility of a proposed reservation development plan, what is the proper inquiry for the court? Should the court examine the feasibility of irrigating each acre claimed or undertake a marginal analysis to determine at what point, overall, the plan becomes infeasible?

Is it relevant to compare the economic feasibility of non-Indian irrigation projects funded by the Congress? Most non-Indian irrigation projects built in the western United States received substantial federal subsidies. The government determined as a matter of policy that it was desirable to develop parts of the arid West for irrigation, and projects were designed and built accordingly. Only a small part of project costs have been repaid by project water users. See generally Richard W. Wahl, *Markets for Federal Water: Subsidies, Property Rights, and the Bureau of Reclamation* (1989). If a proposed Indian water development has costs per acre or costs per acre foot of water similar to projects actually built for non-Indians, is that enough to prove that the Indian claim is economically feasible?

Non-agricultural Reservation Purposes

Adair, page 832, supra, held that where an essential purpose of the reservation was hunting and fishing, water rights were impliedly reserved to fulfill those purposes. The Ninth Circuit said that the tribes have a right to "prevent other appropriators from depleting the streams and waters below a protected level in any area where the non-consumptive [water] right applies." *Adair*, 723 F.2d at 1411. Quantification of the rights described in *Adair* was left to state court proceedings under the McCarran Amendment. Is there any way besides quantification to protect the tribes' rights?

Alternatives to PIA

Because irrigation is one of the most intensive uses of water, quantification of reserved rights for Indian reservations using PIA can result in recognition of rights to substantial amounts of water, as it did in *Arizona v. California*, page 823, supra, and *Big Horn I*, page 850, supra. In the absence of express purposes for establishing a reservation other than agriculture, did the Supreme Court make PIA the exclusive standard for quantifying reserved rights? The United States and several tribes took this position in a major adjudication of water rights in Arizona, but the Arizona Supreme Court disagreed. *In re* the General Adjudication of All Rights to Use Water in The Gila River, 35 P.3d 68 (Ariz.2001).

The *Gila River* court said: "The *Winters* doctrine retains the concept of 'minimal need' by reserving 'only that amount of water necessary to fulfill the purpose of the reservation, no more.' *Cappaert*, 426 U.S. at 141. The method utilized in arriving at such an amount, however, must satisfy both present and future needs of the reservation as a livable homeland." Expounding on the "flaws" of the PIA standard, the court said:

> The first objection to an across-the-board application of PIA lies in its potential for inequitable treatment of tribes based solely on geographical location. Arizona's topography is such that some tribes inhabit flat alluvial plains while others dwell in steep, mountainous areas. This diversity creates a dilemma that PIA cannot solve. As stated by two commentators:
>
>> There can be little doubt that the PIA standard works to the advantage of tribes inhabiting alluvial plains or other relatively flat lands adjacent to stream courses. In contrast, tribes inhabiting mountainous or other agriculturally marginal terrains are at a severe disadvantage when it comes to demonstrating that their lands are practicably irrigable.
>
> Mergen & Liu, *A Misplaced Sensitivity: The Draft Opinions in Wyoming v. United States*, 68 U.Colo.L.Rev. 683 (1997) at 695. Tribes who fail to show either the engineering or economic feasibility of proposed irrigation projects run the risk of not receiving any reserved water under PIA. *See, e.g., State ex rel. Martinez v. Lewis*, 116 N.M. 194, 861 P.2d 235, 246–51 (Ct.App. 1993) (denying water rights to the Mescalero Apache Tribe, situated in a mountainous region of southern New Mexico, for failure to prove irrigation projects were economically feasible). This inequity is unacceptable and inconsistent with the idea of a permanent homeland.
>
> Another concern with PIA is that it forces tribes to pretend to be farmers in an era when "large agricultural projects . . . are risky, marginal enterprises. This is demonstrated by the fact that no federal

project planned in accordance with the Principles and Guidelines [adopted by the Water Resources Council of the Federal Government] has been able to show a positive benefit/cost ratio in the last decade [1981 to 1991]." A permanent homeland requires water for multiple uses, which may or may not include agriculture. The PIA standard, however, forces "tribes to prove economic feasibility for a kind of enterprise that, judging from the evidence of both federal and private willingness to invest money, is simply no longer economically feasible in the West."

Limiting the applicable inquiry to a PIA analysis not only creates a temptation for tribes to concoct inflated, unrealistic irrigation projects, but deters consideration of actual water needs based on realistic economic choices. We again agree with the analysis of Justice Richard V. Thomas in *Big Horn I*:

> I would be appalled . . . if the Congress . . . began expending money to develop water projects for irrigating these Wyoming lands when far more fertile lands in the midwestern states now are being removed from production due to poor market conditions. I am convinced that . . . those lands which were included as practicably irrigable acreage, based upon the assumption of the construction of a future irrigation project, should not be included for the purpose of quantification of the Indian peoples' water rights. They may be irrigable academically, but not as a matter of practicality. . . .

753 P.2d at 119 (Thomas, J.).

> The PIA standard also potentially frustrates the requirement that federally reserved water rights be tailored to minimal need. Rather than focusing on what is necessary to fulfill a reservation's overall design, PIA awards what may be an overabundance of water by including every irrigable acre of land in the equation.

35 P.3d at 78–79.

The *Gila River* court affirmed that a "fact-intensive inquiry must be made on a reservation-by-reservation basis" in order to determine the amount of water necessary to accomplish a reservation's purpose. The court identified factors that should be part of this inquiry: a history of water uses of cultural significance, the tribal land's geography, topography, and natural resources, "groundwater availability," the optimal manner of "creating jobs and income for the tribes and the most efficient use of water," the tribe's economic infrastructure, historic uses of water, present and projected population, and other relevant information.

If you were the judge in the lower court charged with quantifying reserved rights, what evidence would you consider relevant? Did the state or the tribes win the *Gila River* case? Is a tribe with a small number of residents (perhaps because of a lack of economic opportunity) but with a large land area that could be irrigated with a substantial infusion of capital better off or worse off under the *Gila River* formulation than under a PIA standard? A tribe with a large number of residents and little irrigable acreage?

3. FINALITY OF ADJUDICATION

NEVADA V. UNITED STATES
Supreme Court of the United States, 1983.
463 U.S. 110, 103 S.Ct. 2906, 77 L.Ed.2d 509.

JUSTICE REHNQUIST delivered the opinion of the Court.

In 1913 the United States sued to adjudicate water rights to the Truckee River for the benefit of the Pyramid Lake Indian Reservation and the planned Newlands Reclamation Project. Thirty-one years later, in 1944, the United States District Court for the District of Nevada entered a final decree in the case pursuant to a settlement agreement. In 1973 the United States filed the present action in the same court on behalf of the Pyramid Lake Indian Reservation seeking additional water rights to the Truckee River. The issue thus presented is whether the Government may partially undo the 1944 decree, or whether principles of res judicata prevent it, and the intervenor Pyramid Lake Paiute Tribe, from litigating this claim on the merits.

* * *

The origins of the cases before us are found in two historical events involving the Federal Government in this part of the country. First, in 1859 the Department of the Interior set aside nearly half a million acres in what is now western Nevada as a reservation for the area's Paiute Indians. In 1874 President Ulysses S. Grant by executive order confirmed the withdrawal as the Pyramid Lake Indian Reservation. The Reservation includes Pyramid Lake, the land surrounding it, the lower reaches of the Truckee River, and the bottom land alongside the lower Truckee.

Then, with the passage of the Reclamation Act of 1902, the Federal Government was designated to play a more prominent role in the development of the West. That Act directed the Secretary of the Interior to withdraw from public entry arid lands in specified western States, reclaim the lands through irrigation projects, and then to restore the lands to entry pursuant to the homestead laws and certain conditions imposed by the Act itself. Accordingly, the Secretary withdrew from the public domain approximately 200,000 acres in western Nevada, which ultimately became the Newlands Reclamation Project. The Project was designed to irrigate a substantial area in the vicinity of Fallon, Nevada, with waters from both the Truckee and the Carson Rivers.

* * *

Before the works contemplated by the Project went into operation, a number of private landowners had established rights to water in the Truckee River under Nevada law. The Government also asserted on behalf of the Indians of the Pyramid Lake Indian Reservation a reserved right under the so-called "implied-reservation-of-water" doctrine set forth in *Winters v. United States*. The United States therefore filed a complaint in the United States District Court for the District of Nevada in March, 1913, commencing what became known as the *Orr Ditch* litigation. The Government, for the benefit of both the Project and the Pyramid Lake Reservation, asserted a claim to 10,000 cubic feet of water per second for the Project and a claim to 500 cubic feet per second for the Reservation. The complaint named as defendants all water users on the Truckee River in Nevada. The Government expressly sought a final decree quieting title to the rights of all parties.

Following several years of hearings, a Special Master issued a report and proposed decree in July of 1924. The report awarded the Reservation an 1859 priority date in the Truckee River for 58.7 second feet and 12,412 acre feet annually of water to irrigate 3,130 acres of Reservation lands. The Project was awarded a 1902 priority date for 1,500 cubic feet per second to irrigate, to the extent the amount would allow, 232,800 acres of land within the [Newlands Reclamation] Project. * * * [Twenty years later a settlement agreement embodying the recommendations of the report, but allowing an increase in the tribe's rights to irrigate an additional 2,745 acres, was signed and adopted by the Court.]

* * *

On December 21, 1973 [after the tribe commenced an action to compel the United States to protect its water rights, see Pyramid Lake Paiute Tribe v. Morton, page 393, supra] the Government instituted the action below seeking additional rights to the Truckee River for the Pyramid Lake Indian Reservation; the Pyramid Lake Paiute Tribe was permitted to intervene in support of the United States. The Government named as defendants all persons presently claiming water rights to the Truckee River and its tributaries in Nevada. The defendants include the defendants in the *Orr Ditch* litigation and their successors, approximately 3800 individual farmers that own land in the Newlands Reclamation Project, and the [Truckee-Carson Irrigation District]. * * *

In its complaint the Government purported not to dispute the rights decreed in the *Orr Ditch* case. Instead, it alleged that *Orr Ditch* determined only the Reservation's right to "water for irrigation," not the claim now being asserted for "sufficient waters from the Truckee River . . . [for] the maintenance and preservation of Pyramid Lake, [and for] the maintenance of the lower reaches of the Truckee River as a natural spawning ground for fish." The complaint further averred that in establishing the Reservation the United States had intended that the Pyramid Lake fishery be maintained. Since the additional water now being claimed is allegedly necessary for that purpose, the Government alleged that the executive order creating the Reservation must have impliedly reserved a right to this water.

The defendants below asserted res judicata as an affirmative defense, saying that the United States and the Tribe were precluded by the *Orr Ditch* decree from litigating this claim. * * *

* * *

Both the briefs of the parties and the opinion of the Court of Appeals focus their analysis of res judicata on provisions relating to the relationship between private trustees and fiduciaries, especially those governing a breach of duty by the fiduciary to the beneficiary. While these undoubtedly provide useful analogies in a case such as this, they cannot be regarded as finally dispositive of the issues. This Court has long recognized "the distinctive obligation of trust incumbent by the Government" in its dealings with Indian tribes, *see, e.g.*, *Seminole Nation v. United States*, 316 U.S. 286, 296 (1942). These concerns have been traditionally focused on the Bureau of Indian Affairs within the Department of the Interior. *Poafpybitty v. Skelly Oil Co.*, 390 U.S. 365, 374 (1968). See 25 U.S.C. § 1.

But Congress in its wisdom, when it enacted the Reclamation Act of 1902, required the Secretary of the Interior to assume substantial obligations with respect to the reclamation of arid lands in the western part of the United States. Additionally, in § 26 of the Act of April 21, 1904, ch. 1402, 33 Stat. 225, Congress provided for the inclusion of irrigable lands of the Pyramid Lake Indian Reservation within the Newlands Project, and further authorized the Secretary, after allotting five acres of such land to each Indian belonging to the Reservation, to reclaim and dispose of the remainder of the irrigable Reservation land to settlers under the Reclamation Act.

Today, particularly from our vantage point nearly half a century after the enactment of the Indian Reorganization Act of 1934, it may well appear that Congress was requiring the Secretary of the Interior to carry water on at least two shoulders when it delegated to him both the responsibility for the supervision of the Indian tribes and the commencement of reclamation projects in areas adjacent to reservation lands. But Congress chose to do this, and it is simply unrealistic to suggest that the Government may not perform its obligation to represent Indian tribes in litigation when Congress has obliged it to represent other interests as well. In this regard, the Government cannot follow the fastidious standards of a private fiduciary, who would breach his duties to his single beneficiary solely by representing potentially conflicting interests without the beneficiary's consent. The Government does not "compromise" its obligation to one interest that Congress obliges it to represent by the mere fact that it simultaneously performs another task for another interest that Congress has obligated it by statute to do.

* * *

Simply put, the doctrine of res judicata provides that when a final judgment has been entered on the merits of a case, "[i]t is a finality as to the claim or demand in controversy, concluding parties and those in privity with them, not only as to every matter which was offered and received to sustain or defeat the claim or demand, but as to any other admissible matter which might have been offered for that purpose." *Cromwell v. County of Sac,* 94 U.S. 351 (1876). The final "judgment puts an end to the cause of action, which cannot again be brought into litigation between the parties upon any ground whatever." *Commissioner v. Sunnen,* 333 U.S. 591, 597 (1948).

To determine the applicability of res judicata to the facts before us, we must decide first if the "cause of action" which the Government now seeks to assert is the "same cause of action" that was asserted in *Orr Ditch;* we must then decide whether the parties in the instant proceeding are identical to or in privity with the parties in *Orr Ditch.* We address these questions in turn.

* * *

[In *Orr Ditch,* the Government alleged:]

* * *

"On or about or prior to the 29th day of November, 1859, the Government of the United States * * * being desirous of protecting said Indians and their descendants in their homes, fields, pastures, fishing, and their use of said lands and waters, and in affording to them an opportunity to acquire the art of husbandry and other arts of civilization, and to become civilized, did reserve said lands from any and all forms of entry or sale and for the sole use of said Indians, and for their benefit and civilization. * * *

"The United States by setting aside said lands for said purposes and creating said reservation, and by virtue of the matters and things in this paragraph set forth, did on, to wit, the 29th day of November, 1859, reserve from further appropriation, appropriate and set aside for its own use in, on, and about said Indian reservation, and the land thereof, from and of the waters of the said Truckee River, five hundred (500) cubic feet of water per second of time."

This cannot be construed as anything less than a claim for the full "implied-reservation-of-water" rights that were due the Pyramid Lake Indian Reservation.

* * *

Having decided that the cause of action asserted below is the same cause of action asserted in the *Orr Ditch* litigation, we must next determine which of the parties before us are bound by the earlier decree. * * *

There is no doubt but that the United States was a party to the *Orr Ditch* proceeding, acting as a representative for the Reservation's interests and the interests of the Newlands Project, and cannot relitigate the Reservation's "implied-reservation-of-water" rights with those who can use the *Orr Ditch* decree as a defense. We also hold that the Tribe, whose interests were represented in *Orr Ditch* by the United States, can be bound by the *Orr Ditch* decree.[14] This Court left little room for an argument to the contrary in *Heckman v. United States*, 224 U.S. 413 (1912), where it plainly said that "it could not, consistently with any principle, be tolerated that, after the United States on behalf of its wards had invoked the jurisdiction of its courts . . . these wards should themselves be permitted to relitigate the question." Id., at 446. See also Restatement (Second) of Judgments § 41(d) (1982). We reaffirm that principle now.[15]

We then turn to the issue of which defendants in the present litigation can use the *Orr Ditch* decree against the Government and the Tribe. There

---

[14] We, of course, do not pass judgment on the quality of representation that the Tribe received. In 1951 the Tribe sued the Government before the Indian Claims Commission for damages, basing its claim of liability on the Tribe's receipt of less water for the fishery than it was entitled to. *Northern Paiute Tribe v. United States*, 30 Ind.Cl.Comm. 210 (1973). In a settlement the Tribe was given $8,000,000 in return for its waiver of further liability on the part of the United States.

[15] This Court held in *Hansberry v. Lee*, 311 U.S. 32, 44 (1940), that persons vicariously represented in a class action could not be bound by a judgment in the case where the representative parties had interests that impermissibly conflicted with those of persons represented. See also Restatement (Second) of Judgments § 42(d) (1982). The Tribe seeks to take advantage of this ruling, arguing that the Government's primary interest in *Orr Ditch* was to obtain water rights for the Newlands Reclamation Project and that by definition any water rights given to the Tribe would conflict with that interest. We reject this contention.

We have already said that the Government stands in a different position than a private fiduciary where Congress has decreed that the Government must represent more than one interest. When the Government performs such duties it does not by that reason alone compromise its obligation to any of the interests involved.

* * *

The record suggests that the BIA alone may have made the decision not to press claims for a fishery water right, for reasons which hindsight may render questionable, but which did not involve other interests represented by the Government. For instance, in a 1926 letter to a federal official on the Pyramid Lake Reservation, the Commissioner of Indian Affairs explained:

We feel that the Indians would be wise to assume that Truckee River water will be used practically as far as it can be for irrigation, and that the thing for the Indians to do is, if possible, instead of trying to stop such development to direct it so that is will inure to their benefit . . . [I]f their ultimate welfare depends in part on their being able to hold their own in a civilized world . . . they should look forward to a different means of livelihood, in part at least, from their ancestral one, of fishing and hunting. * * *

The District court's finding [that the government did not have an impermissible conflict of interest] reflects the nature of a democratic government that is charged with more than one responsibility; it does not describe conduct that would deprive the United States of the authority to conduct litigation on behalf of diverse interests.

is no dispute but that the *Orr Ditch* defendants were parties to the earlier decree and that they and their successors can rely on the decree. * * *

* * *

At least by 1926, when the [Truckee Carson Irrigation District (TCID)] came into being, and very likely long before, when conveyances of the public domain to settlers within the Reclamation Project necessarily carried with them the beneficial right to appropriate water reserved to the Government for this purpose, third parties entered into the picture. The legal relationships were no longer simply those between the United States and the Paiute Tribe, but also those between the United States, the TCID, and the several thousand settlers within the Project who put the Project water to beneficial use. We find it unnecessary to decide whether there would be adversity of interests between the Tribe, on the one hand, and the settlers and TCID, on the other, if the issue were to be governed by private law respecting trusts. We hold that under the circumstances described above, the interests of the Tribe and the Project landowners were sufficiently adverse so that both are now bound by the final decree entered in the *Orr Ditch* suit.

We turn finally to those defendants below who appropriated water from the Truckee subsequent to the *Orr Ditch* decree. * * *

* * * Nonparties such as the subsequent appropriators in this case have relied just as much on the *Orr Ditch* decree in participating in the development of western Nevada as have the parties of that case. We agree with the Court of Appeals that under "these circumstances it would be manifestly unjust . . . not to permit subsequent appropriators" to hold the Reservation to the claims it made in *Orr Ditch;* "[a]ny other conclusion would make it impossible ever finally to quantify a reserved water right."

* * *

JUSTICE BRENNAN concurring.

The mere existence of a formal "conflict of interest" does not deprive the United States of authority to represent Indians in litigation, and therefore to bind them as well. If, however, the United States actually causes harm through a breach of its trust obligations the Indians should have a remedy against it. I join the Court's opinion on the understanding that it reaffirms that the Pyramid Lake Paiute Tribe has a remedy against the United States for the breach of duty that the United States has admitted.

In the final analysis, our decision today is that thousands of small farmers in northwestern Nevada can rely on specific promises made to their forebears two and three generations ago, and solemnized in a judicial decree, despite strong claims on the part of the Pyramid Lake Paiutes. The availability of water determines the character of life and culture in this region. Here, as elsewhere in the West, it is insufficient to satisfy all claims. In the face of such fundamental natural limitations, the rule of law cannot avert large measures of loss, destruction, and profound disappointment, no matter how scrupulously even-handed are the law's doctrines and administration. Yet the law can and should fix responsibility for loss and destruction that should have been avoided, and it can and should require that those whose rights are appropriated for the benefit of others receive appropriate compensation.

NOTES

1. In *Pyramid Lake Paiute Tribe of Indians v. Morton*, page 393, supra, the court found that the United States was obliged to assert and protect the tribe's water rights. The principal competitor for the water was the Newlands Project, a federal reclamation project primarily for the benefit of non-Indian irrigators. The district court in *Pyramid Lake* found that the federal government's operation of the reclamation project was not consistent with the fiduciary duties it owed to the tribe. Part of the federal response was the commencement of litigation that resulted in *Nevada v. United States*. The United States also revised its regulations as required by the district court. Then, when the irrigation district intentionally diverted more water than the new regulations permitted, the Secretary of the Interior terminated the district's contract to operate the Newlands Project. Truckee-Carson Irrigation District v. Secretary of the Department of the Interior, 742 F.2d 527 (9th Cir.1984), cert. denied 472 U.S. 1007 (1985). The Pyramid Lake Paiute Tribe continued its efforts to assert rights to sufficient water to restore water levels in the lake to sustain the fishery. At least six more cases reached the Ninth Circuit Court of Appeals after 1986. Many issues that had been in litigation or headed for litigation were ultimately resolved legislatively in 1990. The settlement is discussed at page 875, infra.

2. The United States' failure to assist Indian tribes in developing the practical ability to exercise their water rights, even as it extended substantial subsidies for federal reclamation projects to assist non-Indians in the development of some of the same water supplies contributed to the uncertainty over the extent of Indian water rights. See National Water Commission, quoted at pages 822–823, supra. As Indian rights languished in their unused, undefined state, non-Indians built up important reliance interests in the supplies that tribes might need to tap. The federal government has encouraged non-Indians (like the defendants in *Winters* and the district in *Nevada*) to build their livelihoods on waters that would later be claimed by Indians. Does the complicity of the government in denying Indian uses change the equities? At what point should water users who depend on bodies of water connected with Indian lands be considered to have had notice of potentially adverse Indian claims?

3. How final should a quantification of reserved rights be? The Supreme Court in *Arizona v. California*, page 823, supra, said that water was reserved

"to satisfy the future as well as the present needs of the Indian Reservations." If Indian rights have been quantified to satisfy present needs can the quantification be expanded (or reduced) in the future to meet changed needs? Can quantification be changed if technology—pumping systems, land reclamation, drip irrigation, or new fertilization and cultivation techniques—becomes available that would make it feasible to put lands into agriculture that were not claimed as PIA in a judicial quantification? What is the impact of a changing climate on the finality of a quantification?

In 1979, fifteen years after the original decree, the tribes involved in *Arizona v. California* moved to intervene, claiming water for additional acreage. They said that the decree had been based on errors and that circumstances had changed since 1964. They also asserted that the United States had not represented their interests adequately in the original adjudication. A special master was appointed. A 315-page Report of the Special Master, Senior Circuit Judge Elbert P. Tuttle, concluded that the United States had not presented the maximum possible claims on behalf of the tribes and that therefore the new claims should be heard, including those resulting from resolution of several boundary disputes. The master's report recommended expansion of the allocations by about 35 percent over the 1964 allocation.

The Supreme Court accepted the master's recommendations only as to enlarged entitlements that were due to final determinations of boundary disputes left open in the 1964 decree. Arizona v. California, 460 U.S. 605 (1983). Most of the Indian claims to greater acreage—those that arose from the failure of the United States to claim as PIA all of the acreage that was actually irrigable—were denied. The Court premised its ruling largely on the "strong interest in finality" in water rights adjudications, noting the problems of cost and potential for inconsistent decisions. It concluded:

> * * * Certainty of rights is particularly important with respect to water rights in the Western United States. The development of that area of the United States would not have been possible without adequate water supplies in an otherwise water-scarce part of the country. The doctrine of prior appropriation, the prevailing law in the western states, is itself largely a product of the compelling need for certainty in the holding and use of water rights.

460 U.S. at 620.

The surviving claims of the tribes for more water rights, mostly based on boundary changes, occupied extensive proceedings before a succession of special masters and several hearings before the Court. Ultimately, the Supreme Court accepted modifications of the original decree that modestly expanded tribal rights, but addressed some omissions that were important to smaller reservations. The Court then entered a consolidated decree embodying the multiple proceedings and decisions in the case that spanned more than forty years. Arizona v. California, 547 U.S. 150 (2006).

Two tribes later claimed that the United States had breached its trust obligation to them because government attorneys failed to claim the full extent of practicably irrigable acreage. The tribes sought damages for the value of the water rights that were not claimed. The Court acknowledged that the Justice Department lawyers could have claimed their water rights but said that the tribes had not demonstrated that the attorneys acted in bad faith or as a result of a conflict of interest. Fort Mojave Indian Tribe v. United States, 32 Fed. Cl. 29 (Fed.Cl.1994).

4. NON-JUDICIAL QUANTIFICATION

The disadvantages of litigating reserved rights cases can be substantial. Clear answers to practical questions about how water can be used may be lacking and only paper decrees—no "wet water"—may result without large investments in delivery systems. Yet the judgment will be binding under principles of res judicata. One sure thing for all litigants is that the process will be expensive and lengthy. The Special Master in *Big Horn I* estimated that the Wyoming litigation cost well over $20 million.

The National Water Commission, in the course of recommending that the United States assist tribes in quantifying their reserved rights, litigating cases when warranted, also suggested several practical approaches to accommodate Indian and non-Indian uses. For instance, it recommended that the United States make a standing offer to lease unused Indian rights at market value. U.S. National Water Commission, Water Policies for the Future, Final Report to the President and Congress 477–81 (1973).

Some commentators argue for articulation of guidelines for quantifying Indian water rights that would apply to litigation and settlements. See Gina McGovern, *Settlement or Adjudication: Resolving Indian Reserved Rights*, 36 Ariz.L.Rev. 195 (1994). Yet others caution that because of the wide differences among tribes concerning the cultural and economic importance of water, varied climates, and different levels of competing non-Indian demands, a blanket solution to all tribes' reserved water rights claims would be difficult. See generally Charles DuMars & Helen Ingram, *Congressional Quantification of Indian Reserved Water Rights: A Definitive Solution or a Mirage?*, 20 Nat. Resources J. 17 (1980).

One way of resolving the uncertainties presented by Indian reserved water rights, while heeding the differences among tribes and their situations, is through negotiations leading to agreements between tribes and other users. See generally Robert T. Anderson, *Indian Water Rights: Litigation and Settlements,* 42 Tulsa L.Rev. 23 (2006). Although nearly all Indian water rights disputes arise in the context of litigation, most current issues in fact are destined for negotiation. And the negotiated agreements almost invariably become the subject of federal legislation. This is because they involve federal spending and because Indian water rights, as a form of trust property, are likely subject to the Non-Intercourse Act.

The advantages of negotiation over litigation include savings in time, money, and effort. Negotiation should also enable parties to tailor a solution to fit the needs of water users in individual watersheds. Litigation, on the other hand, subjects all parties to the much rougher cut demanded by legal rules of general applicability. See also, Celene Hawkins, *Beyond Quantification: Implementing and Sustaining Tribal Water Settlements*, 16 U.Den. Water L.Rev. 229 (2013), arguing that, although the process of achieving settlement is onerous, the process of implementing water settlements promotes tribal self-determination, tribal sovereignty, and tribal governmental capacity.

The obstacles to negotiated settlements of water quantification suits, however, are formidable. First, negotiations can be surprisingly expensive. A tremendous amount of technical information is necessary before the parties can make a reasonable assessment of the extent of a tribe's *Winters* claim. These technical studies are typically prepared by expert consultants.

Negotiation may be impeded by political barriers to compromise. No matter how favorable an agreement appears to be, some factions in a tribe may contend that tribal leaders and attorneys who propose the settlement are "selling out." State officials typically face hostile water users opposed to "giving" water rights to Indians who have not complied with the requirements of the prior appropriation system. Some state and tribal officials may perceive it as easier to have a court enter an order allocating water than to assume personal responsibility for a particular agreement.

Notwithstanding these barriers, politics often favor negotiated settlements. Significant federal financial assistance can sometimes be obtained to facilitate Indian water rights settlements. In Washington's Yakima Valley, for example, the state, the federal government, and local water users negotiated a proposed solution to several collateral problems. Although the tribes' basic water claims were resolved in a McCarran Amendment proceeding, Congress passed the Yakima River Basin Water Enhancement Act to address concerns dealing with instream flows. Pub.L.No. 103–434, §§ 1201–1212, 108 Stat. 4550–4565 (1994). And in settling the claims of the San Carlos Apache Tribe, Congress relieved beneficiaries of the Central Arizona Project of the burden of paying for a portion of project water, earmarking it for the tribe.

Attempts to negotiate Indian water claims sometimes take as long as litigation and can produce enormous complications before they produce results. Consider the arduous saga of one tribe's settlement. The Ak-Chin Indian Community agreed in 1978 to forgo substantial water claims against non-Indians in return for a promise of 85,000 acre-feet of irrigation water to be furnished by the Secretary of the Interior from a federal wellfield project. As it turned out, the wells threatened to deplete groundwater beneath the Tohono O'Odham Nation reservation. The Department of the Interior then looked elsewhere to find water to make good on its promise to the tribe. The department renegotiated an existing water service contract with an irrigation district for water that it did not need from the Colorado River; the excess water was then delivered to the tribe. The settlement act was then amended in 1984 and 1992. See Pub.L.No. 95–328, 42 Stat. 409 (1978); Pub.L.No. 98–530, 98 Stat. 2698 (1984). Pub.L.No. 102–497, 106 Stat. 3258 (1992). The 1992 amendment enabled the tribe to lease or market its water off the reservation.

While the Ak-Chin machinations proceeded, the San Xavier district of the Tohono O'Odham Nation settled its claims against groundwater users in the Tucson area in 1982. The first bill approving the San Xavier settlement was vetoed by the President because the federal government had not been significantly involved in the negotiating process. In the view of the President, the government was being called upon to fund "a multimillion dollar bailout * * * of the mining companies and local water users" who would be relieved of the Indian claims. A second bill was approved. Pub.L.No. 97–293, Title III, 96 Stat. 1274 (1982). Like the Ak-Chin settlement, the San Xavier negotiations resulted in the tribe receiving valuable consideration for water rights foregone, including apparently credible promises of delivered water.

The Fort Peck-Montana Compact allowed the Assiniboine and Sioux Tribes to divert over 1 million acre-feet of water a year from the Missouri River and groundwater sources and to consume over half a million acre-feet. The compact was negotiated under the auspices of a nine-member Reserved Water Rights Compact Commission created by state statute to pursue "compacts for the equitable division and apportionment of waters between the state and its people and the several Indian tribes claiming reserved water rights within the state." The commission was authorized to negotiate with Indian tribes and the federal government while water adjudication activities were suspended. See Mont.Code Ann. 2–15–212 (1983). Of the seven Indian reservations in Montana, only one has rejected the concept of negotiations.

Possibly the most comprehensive of the settlements was the Fallon Paiute-Shoshone Truckee-Carson-Pyramid Lake Water Rights Settlement Act, Pub.L.No. 101–618 (1990). Litigation regarding the allocation of the water that flows out of the California Sierras through the Truckee River system has gone on for decades. See *Pyramid Lake Paiute Tribe of Indians v. Morton*, page 393, supra, and *Nevada v. United States*, page 864, supra. The dispute was initially over the water claims of the Pyramid Lake Paiute Tribe as against conflicting non-Indian uses under the Newlands Irrigation Project. The settlement act also dealt with the claims of another tribe and many other issues besetting the entire region. It confirmed an apportionment of waters of the Truckee, Carson, and Lake Tahoe basins as between the states of California and Nevada. In so doing, it required the Secretary of Interior and the two states to reach agreement with other interests for the storage and exchange of water in Truckee River reservoirs consistent with the terms of an agreement that had been reached between the Pyramid Lake Tribe and the Sierra Pacific Power Company. It also provided for water rights purchases for wetlands enhancement and protection of endangered fish. It required increased water-use efficiency at the Fallon Naval Air Station. Settlement funds were set up for the Pyramid Lake Tribe to conserve and protect the Pyramid Lake fishery and for the economic development of the two tribes. For a chronicle of this saga and the 1990 settlement, see Barbara Cosens, *Farmers, Fish, Tribal Power, and Poker; Reallocating Water in the Truckee River Basin, Nevada and California*, 14 Hastings W.–N.W.J.Env.L. & Pol'y 1243 (2008).

Another settlement notable for its comprehensiveness grew out of the Snake River Basin Adjudication in Idaho. Pub.L.No. 108–447, 108 Stat. 3431 (2004). The Nez Perce Tribe's claims in the expansive adjudication extended not only to on-reservation consumptive uses, but also to instream flows for a fishery and to rights to springs on formerly tribal lands outside the reservation. The settlement also resolved matters relating to land transfers, endangered species, and the management of two fish hatcheries. See the seven articles dealing with the settlement in 42 Idaho L.Rev. No. 3 (2006).

The Navajo Indian Reservation encompasses 17 million acres in three states in the Colorado River Basin and therefore could have vast water rights. However, the Navajo Nation was not among the five tribes whose water rights were quantified in *Arizona v. California*, page 823, supra. Instead, the recognition and resolution of water rights have been dealt with piecemeal. In 1968, the nation consented to limiting the use of water on a portion of the reservation to 50,000 acre-feet a year for up to fifty years to facilitate construction of a coal-burning power plant at Page, Arizona upon the promise of jobs for Navajos and increased tribal revenues. The Navajos also consented to the use of 34,100 acre-feet of that water by the power plant. By another agreement made in 1957, the Navajos waived their 1868 priority date on the San Juan River in exchange for congressional approval of the Navajo Indian Irrigation Project. Congress then allowed the Navajo project to proceed at the same time as the San Juan-Chama Project, sought by non-Indian interests, that would draw on the same river because the tribe effectively agreed to share shortages with non-Indians. Both agreements resulted in disappointments. Neither the number of jobs nor the revenues from the Page power plant approached the expectations voiced in negotiations. The Navajo Indian Irrigation Project encountered economic problems and mismanagement and turned out to be best suited for large-scale farms rather than the family farms that the Navajos were equipped to operate, and its construction was delayed for many years.

In 2009, the Navajo Nation's water rights claims for the New Mexico portion of the reservation were resolved and embodied in federal legislation that allocated 600,000 acre-feet per year to the Navajo Nation, as well as authorizing $870 million for badly needed water delivery infrastructure.

Following a decade of negotiation, Arizona, federal, and municipal interests and the Hopi Tribe (which has competing claims) resolved their differences and agreed to submit a package settling claims for the Arizona portion of the reservation to their respective governing bodies. The settlement included construction of a huge pipeline from Lake Powell to the reservation which could also serve non-Indian communities. Consideration by the Navajo Tribal council and other entities was incomplete at the time of publication.

One of the largest quantities of water secured in any tribal water settlement was for the Gila River Indian Community in Arizona. About one million acre-feet of water was put under the control of the tribe, allowing expansion of irrigation by 100,000 acres for Gila River Farms, a tribal agricultural operation. The settlement included $400 million for repair and extension of irrigation infrastructure. The source of most of the water is Central Arizona Project water and water from surface sources that was committed to non-Indian irrigation. The tribe, in turn, can then lease a large quantity of water to nearby growing cities.

Some common threads run through many Indian water rights settlements. They include: (1) a federal investment in water development facilities or acquisition of water to enable tribes to put their water to use without infringement on established non-Indian uses; (2) non-federal cost sharing—state and local contributions toward the costs of construction and other elements of the settlement; (3) creation of substantial Indian trust funds from federal and non-federal monies that may be used by the tribes to develop their water and for other purposes; (4) limited off-reservation water marketing, allowing tribes to gain economic benefits from their water resources and non-Indians to use water that would otherwise be unavailable if tribes put it all to use on the reservations; (5) deference to states and to interstate water compacts (such as the "Law of the River" when the Colorado River system is involved); (6) emphasis on efficient management, conservation, and environmental concerns and; (7) a strategy of tying Indian water delivery projects to proposed projects that are beneficial to non-Indian interests. See generally Bonnie G. Colby, John E. Thorson, Sarah Britton, Negotiating Tribal Water Rights: Fulfilling Promises in the Arid West (2006); Daniel McCool, Native Waters: Contemporary Indian Water Settlements and the Second Treaty Era (2002); David H. Getches, Indian Water Rights Conflicts in Perspective, in

Indian Water in the New West (William B. Lord & Thomas R. McGuire, eds. 1993). For an historical overview of Indian water settlements from 1910 through 1989, see Lloyd Burton, American Indian Water Rights and the Limits of Law 63–86 (1991).

Settlements affecting more than 40 Indian reservations have been negotiated. Almost all were facilitated by the hope of federal funding for tribal water systems and economic development. Fulfillment of settlements depends on annual congressional appropriations, however, and therefore is subject to the vicissitudes of the federal budgeting process. Even when appropriations have been made they sometimes have been offset with reductions in other parts of the Bureau of Indian Affairs budget through earmarks—effectively at the expense of tribes that do not benefit from the settlements.

Tribal water settlements can be exceptions to the modern wisdom that the era of building large federal water projects is over. The era ended after the Executive and Congress reacted to the staggering economic costs and environmental consequences of these projects. But tribes in the West were notoriously left out when water projects were built by the Bureau of Reclamation and the U.S. Army Corps of Engineers to benefit others. This was recognized by the National Water Commission in its findings quoted at pages 822–823, supra. Indeed, sometimes tribes suffered lasting harm from those projects. The impact of the operation of the Newlands Reclamation Project on the Pyramid Lake Paiute Tribe is one example. In other cases reservations were flooded when huge reservoirs were built to serve non-Indians. Tribes may now argue, based on the history of federal water development, that there should be serious consideration of building government-sponsored water projects, and perhaps re-operating existing federal projects in order to benefit their reservations. See Kaylee Ann Newell, *Federal Water Projects, Native Americans and Environmental Justice: The Bureau of Reclamation's History of Discrimination*, 20 Environs 40 (June 1997). Thus, water project development and reallocation of water from existing projects has become a key to facilitating settlements.

The willingness of Congress to consider water project construction and extension of water user subsidies to tribes in order to correct for the past injustices to tribes has enabled non-Indians to gain as well. New water projects that would be politically infeasible can be "wrapped in an Indian blanket" and thereby gain congressional support and funding. Water from existing projects can be reallocated to tribes to relieve non-Indian users of repayment obligations.

In 2000 Congress authorized construction of the Animas-La Plata Project, a 120,000 acre-foot reservoir costing $278 million, as part of the Colorado Ute Indian Water Rights Settlement. The reservoir, Lake Nighthorse, began filling in 2009 and should reach capacity in 2011. The size of the project was drastically reduced from its mid-twentieth century conception as a mammoth Bureau of Reclamation irrigation project, and was cut by about two-thirds in cost from the project contemplated by the settlement authorized in 1988 to which serious environmental objections had been raised. Notwithstanding these changes, it is highly unlikely that a project of this kind could have been built with federal funds without the tribes' agreement to settle their water claims. Over half of the annual water depletions for the project will be available to the Southern Ute and the Ute Mountain Ute tribes although no funding is provided expressly for facilities to deliver that water. No water from the project is to be used for irrigation; it is now a project primarily to supply growing towns near the reservations with municipal water. The tribes understand that they are to use a $40 million development fund included in the settlement "in partnership with adjacent non-Indian communities or entities in the area." See Animas-La Plata Project, U.S. Bureau of Reclamation http://www.usbr.gov/uc/progact/animas/.

Non-Indians also support Indian water settlements when they allow for tribal water marketing specifically to benefit off-reservation communities. Most notably, in Arizona tribal water settlements allow for off-reservation water marketing. The scope of marketing is more limited than what non-Indians can do with water rights held under state law. Typically, a tribe can market water by leasing it to off-reservation users only in specified areas. The particularity as to permissible markets is designed to procure a source of water for economic and population expansion in the growing urban areas. A major source of the water is the Central Arizona Project (CAP), a federal Bureau of Reclamation project. By transferring rights to CAP water away from non-Indian farmers to the tribes, the irrigation districts are relieved of repayment obligations that they cannot afford and then the water can be marketed to cities by the tribes, usually under 100-year leases. This provides a means for the cities to comply with a state law requiring them to demonstrate the availability of a 100-year water supply from sources other than groundwater before they can expand. Cities like Phoenix, Scottsdale, and Tucson have procured rights to use a significant amount of water from the Ak-Chin Community, the Fort McDowell Tribe, the Salt River Pima-Maricopa Community, the Yavapai-Prescott Tribe, and San Carlos Apache Tribe.

Tribal Water Settlements

Date	Reservation	Funding*	Water Uses	Marketing
1982 1992	Tohono O'odham, AZ	$25.7	66,000 af of CAP and reclaimed water and 10,000 af of groundwater	Yes (in Tucson area only)

Tribal Water Settlements

Date	Reservation	Funding*	Water Uses	Marketing
1985	Fort Peck, MT	none	Tribal-state compact gave tribe 525,236 af of water for irrigation and instream flows	Yes (limited to 50,000 af/y unless state authorized
1978 1984 1992	Ak-Chin, AZ	$28.9 + U.S. constructs irrigation works.	75,000 af from CAP for irrigation	Yes (leasing in defined areas)
1987	Seminole Tribe, FL	$7.25 from state and local governments	15% of water from South Florida Water Management District	No
1988	Bands of Mission Indians, CA	$30	16,000 af	No
1988	Salt River, AZ	$47.47 + $96 from local governments	122,400 af for irrigation	Yes (limited to 13,00 af in Phoenix area)
1988 2000	Ute Mountain Ute and Southern Ute, CO	$89.5 + $16 state and local + $250 construction	20,000 af per tribe	Yes subject to state law
1990	Fallon Paiute-Shoshone and Pyramid Lake Paiute, NV	$83 + $25 for fisheries for PL Paiute		
1990	Fort Hall, ID	$23 +$0.5 from state	Guaranteed 581,031 af diversion, 354,239 consumption	Yes, on and off reservation
1990 2006	Fort McDowell, AZ	$33 + $44 from state, local and tribal	35,950 af from Verde River and CAP	Yes in defined areas

Tribal Water Settlements

Date	Reservation	Funding*	Water Uses	Marketing
1992	Northern Cheyenne, MT	$21.5 + $43 to improve dam + $21.8 from state	91,000 af	Yes (after 10 years)
1992	Jicarilla Apache, NM	$6		Yes subject to state law
1992	Uintah-Ouray Ute, UT	$198.5		Yes subject to state law
1992	San Carlos Apache, AZ	$38.4 +$3 from state	76,435 af	Yes (100 yr contracts for CAP water)
1994	Yavapai-Prescott Tribe, AZ	Up to $1.02 + $0.2 from the state	1000 af surface and 550 af CAP	Yes (only surface water from reservations)
1997	Warm Springs, OR		324,000 af consumptive use	Yes subject to state and federal law
1999	Rocky Boys, MT	$48	20,000 af (10,000 af stored in federal reservoir)	Yes with federal and state approval
2000	Shivwits Paiute, UT	$36.75 + $1.5 state and local for construction	4,000 af from the Virgin and Santa Clara River Systems as well as 100 af of groundwater	Yes subject to state and federal law
2001	Fort Belknap, MT	None	645 cfs from Milk River. Tribes can divert hydrologically connected groundwater	
2003	Zuni Pueblo, NM and AZ	$26.5; $19.25 from federal gov't.	1500 af groundwater; 35000 af of surface water can be purchased	Yes but only to Zuni fee land. After that, it is subject to state law

Tribal Water Settlements

Date	Reservation	Funding*	Water Uses	Marketing
2004	Gila River Indian Community	$24	655,000 af from CAP and the Gila, Salt, and Verde Rivers	Yes in-state
2004	Nez Perce, ID	$23 + acquisition of BLM land worth $7	50,000 af	Allows leasing
2008	Soboba Band of Luiseno Indians, CA	$29 ($18 from water districts + 128 acres of land)	9000 af	Yes (100 yr contracts)
2009	Navajo Nation, NM	Construction of a $870 pipeline	600,000 af	Yes (only with NM)
2009	Duck Valley-Shoshone and Paiute, NV	$12	111,476 af from East Fork Owyhee River + full flow of springs and creeks on reservation	Yes (only 265 af to upstream users)
2010	Taos Pueblo, NM	$121	11,927 af from specific rivers	Yes subject to state and federal law
2010	Aamodt (Nambe, Pojoaque San Ildefonso, and Tesuque Pueblos), NM	$168	2500 af from Rio Grande	Yes within the Pojoaque basin
2010	White Mountain Apache, AZ (under framework of Gila River Settlement)	$113.5	27,000 af from Salt and Little Colorado; 25,000 af from CAP	Yes (leases of 22,500 af CAP water to cities for 100 year terms)
2010	Crow Tribe, MT	$527 for water projects on and off the reservation	300,000 af in Bighorn Lake and 500,000 af from Bighorn River	Yes (limited to contracts for 50,000 af)

* All figures are in millions and are federal funds except as specified.

There are several negotiated settlements that will not become final until Congress has acted. In some cases action is stalled because of the difficulty of appropriating money. In the case of the Crow and Blackfeet tribes, for example some policy makers have expressed concerns about the precedent that the large settlements—over $500 million each—could set for future Indian water rights settlements. Three other settlements have passed the House but not the Senate.

5. MARKETING TRIBAL WATER

Tribal water marketing proposals raise a variety of legal concerns. Absent congressional consent, alienation of Indian water rights, like other property rights, is barred by the Nonintercourse Act, 25 U.S.C.A. § 177. See page 281, supra. Limited water leasing has been allowed in the context of congressionally approved Indian reserved water rights settlements. From time to time, legislation has been proposed that would allow tribes to lease their water rights, but none has been enacted. A variety of other potential schemes for marketing Indian water are conceivable. Indian water could be sold as a commodity to non-Indian users on- or off-reservation. The rights to Indian water might be leased or even sold. Non-Indians with rights junior to Indians could pay Indians simply to defer using their quantified water rights. Indeed, non-Indians may be willing to pay a tribe not to perfect and use unquantified rights. The Gila River Indian Community in Arizona made such a deferral agreement with the Kennecott Copper Company.

A federal statute authorizes Indian tribes to lease tribal lands for a specified maximum term to be used for various purposes, "including the development or utilization of natural resources in connection with operations under such leases," with approval by the Secretary of the Interior. 25 U.S.C.A. § 415. This seems to imply that water rights may be included in a lease of land. See Skeem v. United States, 273 F. 93 (9th Cir.1921) (lessee of Indian land may exercise water rights of allottee). The statute, however, does not address the question of water leasing apart from the land for on-or off-reservation uses.

Although there are no legal prohibitions on tribes seeking to permit some of their water to be used outside reservations, neither the Supreme Court nor Congress has acknowledged the existence and parameters of tribal water marketing authority. The unpublished O'Connor opinion in *Big Horn I*, see page 850, supra, noted that the Supreme Court "has never determined the specific attributes of reserved water rights—whether such rights are subject to forfeiture for nonuse or *whether they may be sold or leased for use on or off the reservation*." In the end, the most substantial practical obstacle to marketing of Indian water rights may be the concern of purchasers that, as property interests tied to the land and subject to the

Non-Intercourse Act, any transfer would be voidable without the specific approval of Congress or some enabling legislation.

Some commentators have argued against the transferability of Indian water rights, saying they "were created as an adjunct to the land and have no existence apart from the land." Jack D. Palma II, *Considerations and Conclusions Concerning the Transferability of Indian Water Rights*, 20 Nat. Resources J. 91 (1980). Thus, off-reservation uses of water would be precluded—at least uses unrelated to reservation resources. Another perspective is that Indian reserved water rights were recognized not simply to enhance land value, but to fulfill the congressional policy to "encourage Indian peoples to become tribally independent, industrious, and self-supporting American citizens" and that off-reservation transfers of water should be allowed if the transfers are consistent with applicable state law. See Lee Herold Storey, *Leasing Indian Water off the Reservation: A Use Consistent with the Reservation's Purpose*, 76 Calif.L.Rev. 179, 208–12 (1988). If the overall purpose of Indian reservations is to provide a permanent homeland where the tribe can be economically self-sufficient, this purpose could conceivably be promoted by allowing the sale or lease of water off-reservation. See also, Justin Nyber, *The Promise of Indian Water Leasing: An Examination of One Tribe's Success at Brokering Its Surplus Water Rights*, 55 Nat. Resources J. 181 (2015).

Many state and industry leaders, however, support the idea of off-reservation marketing because it eliminates uncertainty and opens up a potential source of secure water rights for development:

> The urban sector initially opposed off-reservation leasing. Because of the early priority of Indian reserved rights, it is urban users with junior or "late" priorities who may face shortages if tribes exercise their reserved rights. As urban purveyors evaluate options for new water supply, the initial opposition to off-reservation leasing is changing.

Peter W. Sly, *Urban and Interstate Perspectives on Off-Reservation Tribal Water Leases*, 10 Nat. Resources & Env't. 43 (1996).

Although urban opposition to intrastate marketing has diminished, opposition to tribal *interstate* water marketing continues. Interstate marketing implicates an array of difficult issues such as the disruption of interstate water compacts, possible abuse of the privilege by private entrepreneurs, and potential dormant commerce clause violations. Nonetheless, there are strong incentives to marketing tribal water across state boundaries, including economic benefits to tribes, delivery of scarce water to growing cities, providing instream flows to depleted western rivers, and easing pressures on the federal budget. In 1994, the Bureau of Reclamation circulated proposed regulations in which it claimed to have the authority to approve and regulate limited off-reservation water marketing in the lower Colorado River Basin, based on the powers conferred on the Bureau under the Boulder Canyon Project Act. 43 U.S.C.A. §§ 617 et seq. See David H. Getches, *Colorado River Governance: Sharing Federal Authority as an Incentive to Create a New Institution*, 68 U.Colo.L.Rev. 573, 609–23 (1997). Those regulations were not pursued after outcries of opposition from the basin states.

Tribes also must weigh several policy considerations in authorizing Indian water rights to be transferred to or used by non-Indians. Tribes may be better off receiving payments instead of water, and many companies may be quite willing to pay for the assurance of a supply not subject to interruption by the exercise of reserved rights. But even if other water users have formally acknowledged Indian rights, will the "leased" water later be available to the tribes for their own uses should they need it? And what are the tradeoffs in terms of coherent social structure and community life? A community can be built on a developed agricultural use of water but can it be founded on a common interest in collection and distribution of periodic payments in lieu of such uses? What additional issues are raised when a tribe proposes to market its water that are not present when non-Indian holders of water rights under the prior appropriation doctrine market water?

SECTION D. REGULATION AND ADMINISTRATION OF WATER IN INDIAN COUNTRY

A question bound to arise with increasing frequency is the extent to which state and tribal governments have jurisdiction to regulate water use by non-Indians within reservation boundaries. The immunity of tribes and reservation Indians from state regulation is clear. Recent Supreme Court decisions concerning regulation of non-Indians in other contexts, however, raise questions about when and if non-Indian water use on reservations can be controlled by the respective sovereigns. Several tribes have enacted ordinances and codes that attempt to extend tribal authority over all water resources and all water users on a reservation. States continue to assert authority over non-Indians with water rights on Indian reservations and even over Indians who hold rights pursuant to state law. In the final analysis, the determination of which governmental entity decides and enforces policies concerning water use on Indian reservations may be as important as which court decides on the quantity of reserved rights held by a tribe.

UNITED STATES V. ANDERSON

United States Court of Appeals, Ninth Circuit, 1984.
736 F.2d 1358.

J. BLAINE ANDERSON, CIRCUIT JUDGE:

* * *

The plaintiffs sought an adjudication of water rights in the Chamokane Basin, a hydrological system including Chamokane Creek, its tributaries and its ground water basin. The waters of the Chamokane Basin are not wholly within the Spokane Indian Reservation; Chamokane Creek originates north of the reservation and flows south along the eastern boundary. The creek leaves the reservation by discharging into the Spokane River which, in turn, joins with the Columbia River and flows into the Pacific Ocean. * * *

The Spokane Indian Reservation is not exclusively owned and resided upon by Indians. Non-Indian settlement has occurred there, encouraged by various federal programs authorizing allotment of reservation lands to individual Indians and opening excess land to homesteading by non-Indians. * * *

* * *

In the case before us, the district court determined that it was permissible for the State of Washington to exercise regulatory jurisdiction over non-Indian use of excess Chamokane Basin waters on lands owned by non-Indians within the Spokane Indian Reservation. The Spokane Tribe takes issue with this determination, arguing that it, not the state, has jurisdiction by virtue of our decision in *Colville Confederated Tribes v. Walton*. * * *

Regulatory jurisdiction of a state over non-Indian activities on a tribal reservation "may be barred either because it is pre-empted by federal law, or because it unlawfully infringes on the right of reservation Indians to self-government." *Walton*, 647 F.2d at 51. These barriers to regulation, although independent, are related by the concept of tribal sovereignty.

* * *

Recent case law has affirmed tribal exercise of civil jurisdiction over nonmembers. Where nonmembers have transacted business with the tribe or entered onto the tribal lands for other purposes, the Supreme Court has upheld the imposition of taxes or the assessment of special fees. * * *

* * *

Applying these standards, we conclude that the State, not the Tribe, has the authority to regulate the use of excess Chamokane Basin waters by non-Indians on non-tribal, i.e., fee, land. Our review reveals no consensual agreement between the non-Indian water users and the Tribe which would furnish the basis for implication of tribal regulatory authority. We find no conduct which so threatens or has such a "direct effect on the political integrity, the economic security, or the health or welfare of the Tribe," as to confer tribal jurisdiction. *Montana v. United States*, 450 U.S. at 566. The water rights adjudication which furnishes the basis for the instant inquiry quantifies and preserves tribal water rights. The district court appointed a federal water master whose responsibility is to administer the available waters in accord with the priorities of all the water rights as adjudicated. The district court recognized the importance of the tribal fishery and has awarded non-consumptive water rights to preserve it. The tribe is, of course, entitled to utilize its water for *any* lawful purpose. *Colville Confederated Tribes v. Walton*, 647 F.2d 42, 48 (9th Cir.1981). If the tribe chooses to use water reserved for irrigation in a non-consumptive manner, it does not thereby relinquish any of its water rights to state permittees or subject the exercise of its rights to state regulation. The state may regulate only the use, by non-Indian fee owners, of excess water. Any permits issued by the state would be limited to excess water. If those permits represent rights that may be empty, so be it.

It is evident, however, that the political and economic welfare of the Tribe will not suffer adverse impact from the state-regulated use of surplus waters by nonmembers on non-Indian lands. Instead the factual situation points in favor of state regulation. First, no direct federal preemption of state regulation has occurred. No federal statute or regulatory scheme expressly or impliedly governs water use by non-Indians on the Spokane Reservation. Second, the balance of interest weighs most heavily in favor of the state.

The instant situation is contrary to that addressed by this circuit in *Colville Confederated Tribes v. Walton*, 647 F.2d 42 (1981). In *Walton,* we determined that state regulation of the water system was preempted when viewed in light of the Colville's right to self-government. The *Walton* decision recognized the general rule of deference to state water law. *Walton* rested on a determination that "deference is not applicable to water use on a federal reservation, at least where such use has no impact off the reservation." Although recognizing that the usual policy of deference stems in part from the need to permit western states to fashion water rights regimes that are responsive to local needs and in part from the "legal confusion that would arise if federal water law and state water law reigned side by side in the same locality," the *Walton* court found neither rationale applicable to the matter. In accordance with its determination that neither of the policy considerations supporting deference to state jurisdiction would be fulfilled by permitting state regulation of the No Name System, the *Walton* court held such jurisdiction preempted by the creation of the Colville Reservation.

The *Walton* decision was compelled by the geography and hydrology of the No Name Basin and its relationship to the Colville Reservation. The reservation lands in question were allotted, not opened for entry and settlement. The No Name hydrological system is non-navigable and is located *entirely* within the reservation. Validation of the state-issued permits claimed by Walton could have jeopardized the agricultural use of downstream tribal users as well as the existence of the tribal fishery. In essence, the interest of the Tribe in regulation of the waters of the No Name Basin was "critical to the lifestyle of its residents and the development of its resources."

The district court noted, and we agree, that because water per se lies within the exterior boundaries of an Indian reservation does not necessarily negate a state's interest in overseeing its usage along with the other in-state water systems. Washington is obligated to regulate and conserve water consumption for the benefit of all its citizens, including those who own land within a reservation in fee. Therefore, the state's special concern is shared with, not displaced by, similar tribal and federal interests when water is located within the boundaries of both the state and the reservation. The weight of the state's interest depends, in large part, on the extent to which waterways or aquifers transcend the exterior boundaries of Indian country.

* * *

* * * Central to our decision is the fact that the interest of the state in exercising its jurisdiction will not infringe on the tribal right to self-government nor impact on the Tribe's economic welfare because those rights have been quantified and will be protected by the federal water master. Additionally, in view of the hydrology and geography of the Chamokane Creek Basin, the State of Washington's interest in developing a comprehensive water program for the allocation of surplus waters weighs heavily in favor of permitting it to extend its regulatory authority to the excess waters, if any, of the Chamokane Basin. State permits issued for any such excess water will be subject to all preexisting rights and those preexisting rights will be protected by the federal court decree and its appointed water master. We do not believe there is any realistic infringement on tribal rights and protected affairs. If there is any intrusion, it is minimal and permissible under all of the circumstances of this case.

* * *

NOTES

1. Is the decision consistent with Supreme Court cases involving tribal jurisdiction to regulate nonmembers on non-Indian land? See pages 601–617, supra.

2.   The court in the principal case cited the state's interest in having a comprehensive water management program. Although *Walton* may be distinguishable because the stream in question was entirely on the reservation, could the following statement from *Walton* be applied to streams that cross or border both reservation and non-reservation land?

> A water system is a unitary resource. The actions of one user have an immediate and direct effect on other users. The Colvilles' complaint in the district court alleged that the Waltons' appropriations from No Name Creek imperiled the agricultural use of downstream tribal lands and the trout fishery, among other things.

> Regulation of water on a reservation is critical to the life-style of its residents and the development of its resources. Especially in arid and semi-arid regions of the West, water is the lifeblood of the community. Its regulation is an important sovereign power.

647 F.2d at 52.

Both the state and the tribe may have substantial interests in the management of shared waters. How can both interests be respected and reconciled? If the interests of the state and the tribe are essentially equal, which has regulatory jurisdiction? Is tribal regulatory jurisdiction affected by the provision in the McCarran Amendment, 43 U.S.C.A. § 666, quoted on page 857, supra, waiving sovereign immunity "in any suit * * * for the administration" of reserved rights?

3.   What arguments support the exclusive application of a tribal water code to Indians and non-Indians on a reservation? See New Mexico v. Mescalero Apache Tribe, (1983), page 895, infra. Concurrent application of tribal and state water laws? Can arguments for applying either exclusive or concurrent tribal water code jurisdiction to non-Indians on fee lands on the Yakima Indian Reservation prevail after the Supreme Court's decision in Brendale v. Confederated Tribes and Bands of the Yakima Indian Nation, discussed at pages 612–613, supra. The Ninth Circuit had ruled prior to *Brendale* that the Yakima Nation Water Code could not be applied to control use by non-Indians of excess waters on or passing through the Yakima Indian Reservation. Holly v. Confederated Tribes & Bands of the Yakima Indian Nation, 655 F.Supp. 557 (E.D.Wash.1985), affirmed sub nom. Holly v. Totus, 812 F.2d 714 (9th Cir.1987), cert. denied 484 U.S. 823 (1987).

4.   A number of tribes have enacted or are developing comprehensive water management codes. The Navajo Nation administers its water code through a Department of Water Resources with responsibility for water planning, development, permitting, and regulation. See Title 22, Navajo Tribal Code Annotated (2005). The tribal government also provides irrigators with assistance such as irrigation system operation, soil conservation programs, well development, and group marketing services. The code also protects the health and safety of the Navajo people through the Navajo Nation Safe Drinking Water Act, 22 Navajo Tribal Code Annotated, Chapter 13 (2005).

The Umatilla Tribe in Oregon began with a research and data gathering program, then established a technical advisory committee on water administration, and then enacted an interim water code. The code created a permit system for water use, a licensing system for well-drillers, and a regulatory scheme for water administration, including enforcement provisions. Numerous other tribal governments have promulgated water codes and instituted their own management systems. See generally Steven J. Shupe, *Water in Indian Country: From Paper Rights to a Managed Resource*, 57 U.Colo.L.Rev. 561 (1986); Thomas W. Clayton, Comment, *The Policy Choices Tribes Face when Deciding Whether to Enact a Water Code*, 17 Am. Indian L.Rev. 523 (1992).

5. Tribal efforts to adopt and enforce water codes are inhibited by Department of the Interior policy. Many tribes, especially those with IRA constitutions, require secretarial approval of ordinances. In 1975, the Secretary reacted to mounting state concerns over the enactment of Indian water codes and issued a moratorium on approval of the codes to allow time for him to develop guidelines for approval. Proposed rules were published in 1977 and 1981 (42 Fed.Reg. 14885; 46 Fed.Reg. 944), but they never became final.

The secretarial moratorium has not been lifted. The moratorium applies to all tribes having constitutional provisions mandating that tribal laws be approved by the Secretary. On what legal grounds could the Secretary refuse to approve a tribal water code? See generally Susan M. Williams, *Indian Winters Water Rights Administration: Averting New War*, 11 Pub. Land L.Rev. 53 (1990). The Navajo code was adopted by the Navajo Tribal Council in 1984. Navajo law did not require approval by the Secretary of the Interior. See 22 Navajo Tribal Code Annotated § 1101 (2005). The Secretary has approved water codes extending tribal control over non-Indian water use, however, in response to congressional legislation specifically authorizing the exercise of such jurisdiction. In addition, former Secretary Bruce Babbitt announced that he would approve tribal constitutional amendments that eliminated the requirement of secretarial approval of tribal laws. A tribe could then enact a water code and avoid the necessity of presenting it to the Secretary.

6. Robert Anderson, in *Water Rights, Water Quality, and Regulatory Jurisdiction in Indian Country*, 34 Stan.Envtl.L.J. 195–245 (2015), addressed tribal water regulation of quantity and quality in comprehensive and compelling fashion. He convincingly doubted the persuasive value of *Anderson* as opposed to *Walton*. More importantly, Anderson demonstrated how nation building can elevate the level and quality of tribal participation in some of the most sensitive and far-reaching concerns affecting tribal and non-tribal communities. He offered an enlightening discussion of these issues of water regulation, all wrapped in matters of land, law, governmental authority, history, and communities, and showed that tribal nations have proved their capacity for complex regulation and for finding common ground and reaching durable collaborative agreements with federal, state, and corporate offices involving large public issues. Anderson urged this:

There are few reported decisions dealing with the tribal-versus-state authority to regulate on-reservation water use. Nevertheless, many tribes assert ownership and control over all resources within their reservations as a general matter, and forty-nine tribes are recognized by the EPA as having inherent jurisdiction over reservation waters—including jurisdiction over non-members and water use on non-member fee lands. The fact that such tribes may clearly regulate non-members under the CWA, and may complement that authority with a comprehensive water code, makes a powerful case for tribal authority over the use of all reservation waters. Under these circumstances, tribes and states should consider the following propositions.

First, all parties should recognize that Indian tribes and their members have paramount rights to the use of some if not all reservation water resources. Second, many non-Indians have acquired fee simple land within Indian reservations and use water under tribal or state law, or both. Third, scarcity of water for new uses and controversy over changes in existing uses involve sensitive issues for policy-makers to consider. Tribal governments are best positioned to make such policy judgments and enforce local regulations within their reservation homelands. This is consistent with the original promises embodied in treaties, executive orders, and other agreements setting aside tribal lands for permanent tribal occupation. At the same time, vacillating federal policies resulted in non-Indian land ownership within reservations. Where non-members have acquired water permits or other claims to water under state law, tribes should honor those claims to the extent consistent with tribal water rights and policies. This may be a relaxation of full tribal sovereignty over water uses, but it may be worth it as a way to avoid lengthy and costly litigation—litigation that may resolve only the particular case and leave future outcomes uncertain. Through such a process, tribes could bring non-Indian water users into a comprehensive tribal system designed to allow for water use consistent with settled expectations, but be mindful of the need for environmental protection and changing needs of reservation communities. Of course, state cooperation (or at least non-opposition) will be necessary for such a regime to work, and not devolve into litigation.

The Secretary of the Interior should lift the moratorium on tribal water code approval, but in doing so could suggest that the approval process will consider how a tribal applicant will treat currently exercised state water rights—if any exist. This would move the discussion over tribal regulatory power from a judicially supervised contest to a process that considers the interests of the parties, rather than simply their legal positions. It would also put the Secretary in the proper position of facilitating tribal self-determination, and promoting effective water management as opposed to standing as an obstacle to these ends.

At the end of the day, it is tribal governments that must decide whether to assert some or all of their regulatory authority over water use and water quality. States must decide whether it is in their interest to cooperate with tribal efforts, or enter the labyrinth of litigation over tribal regulatory power. The EPA's current position regarding inherent tribal authority argues in favor of recognizing tribal authority where it is asserted. But any regulatory regime requires a substantial commitment of resources, and can be aided by efforts at inter-governmental cooperation. Reconciliation of interests in this area should be the goal to ensure efficient use of scarce reservation water resources while maintaining water quality.

CHAPTER TWELVE

FISHING AND HUNTING RIGHTS

■ ■ ■

Fishing and hunting have always been vitally important to Indians. For most aboriginal cultures harvesting food was a cultural activity as well as a livelihood. The ancestors of today's Indian people found such a pervasive practical and spiritual value in fish and wildlife resources that they frequently insisted on expressly reserving special rights to hunt and fish in treaties with the United States. As the Supreme Court has put it, such rights "were not much less necessary to the existence of the Indians than the atmosphere they breathed." *United States v. Winans*, page 163, supra.

The cultural and economic significance of Indian fishing and hunting remains great today. Some tribes have expanded their traditional commerce in fish by operating fishing fleets and packing companies. Many tribes license lucrative recreational hunting and fishing on their reservations by non-Indians. The personal involvement of Indians in fishing and hunting—in modern business enterprises and scientific management, as well as in subsistence harvesting and religious ceremonies—holds deep cultural significance. See generally Michael J. Chiarappa and Kristin M. Szylvian, Fish for All: An Oral History of Multiple Claims and Divided Sentiment on Lake Michigan 1–99 (2003); Vine Deloria, Jr., Indians of the Pacific Northwest: From the Coming of the White Man to the Present Day (1977); Charles Wilkinson, Messages From Frank's Landing: A Story of Salmon, Treaties, and the Indian Way (2000). Indian legal claims to special rights in fish and wildlife have been the crucible for some of the most intense historic battles over the sovereignty of tribes. States have vigorously resisted assertions of Indian rights to fish and hunt free of state regulation and they have challenged the authority of tribes over non-Indians who fish and hunt on reservations. Compelling policy arguments can be made that Indian rights conflict with consistent, unified wildlife management that is essential to conservation. But evidence does not sustain contentions that Indian treaty hunting and fishing or wildlife management practices are generally harmful. Opponents of Indian rights raise familiar legal arguments that special rights for Indians violate equal protection guarantees and contend that state jurisdiction is absolute.

Although Indians have prevailed in most challenges to their rights to fish and hunt, conflicts persist. This can be explained in part by the economic and social importance that wildlife resources have for non-Indians as well as Indians. In a few states, particularly in the Northwest and the Great Lakes areas, commercial fishing is a major part of the economy. In addition, sport fishing and hunting account for millions of dollars in income from license fees and from the accompanying business that recreationists generate. Indians threaten this economic base by fishing and hunting outside of state management regimes and, more recently, by developing their own agencies and businesses to capture fish and wildlife revenues.

The numbers of people involved in fishing and hunting also mean that there is a powerful political constituency for favorable state policies. States once argued that they owned, and therefore had the inherent right to control, wildlife within their boundaries, Geer v. Connecticut, 161 U.S. 519 (1896). The Supremacy Clause of the Constitution, Art. VI, cl. 2, however, makes federal laws dominant. Missouri v. Holland, 252 U.S. 416 (1920); Kleppe v. New Mexico, 426 U.S. 529 (1976); Hughes v. Oklahoma, 441 U.S. 322 (1979) (expressly overruling *Geer*). Therefore, Indian treaties, agreements, executive orders, and statutes may override state law and establish rights to take fish and game without a state license, free of state regulation. Nevertheless, legal contests have continued, placing the controversies ignited by the assertion of Indian fishing and hunting rights among the leading federalism disputes of the past century.

Factors other than the economic importance of hunting and fishing animate resistance to Indian rights. Many non-Indian hunters and fishers rightfully pride themselves as people who treasure wildlife; some anglers return all or most of their catch. Commercial fishers are an independent breed who depend upon fishing for their livelihood. And, like their counterparts in the water rights struggle, they are not lawyers or historians who had actual notice of treaties which reserved Indian fishing rights more than a century ago. In their eyes, Indian fishing rights appeared only recently and these special rights strike them as unfair.

The strength of non-Indian opposition has tested the fortitude of Indians. The importance of traditional pursuits to Indians has been demonstrated in their willingness to fight for recognition of rights that their ancestors insisted upon having included in treaties. They have been undeterred by decades of violence, hostile publicity, arrests, criminal prosecutions, and gear seizures resulting from their attempted exercises of rights secured by federal treaties. They also have held firm through seemingly interminable and expensive litigation and relitigation of complex legal issues.

SECTION A. REGULATION OF ON-RESERVATION FISHING AND HUNTING

The existence of on-reservation fishing and hunting rights does not depend on express language in a treaty. The Supreme Court has inferred their existence from a treaty reserving lands "to be held as Indian lands are held." *Menominee Tribe v. United States*, page 238, supra, (quoting the 1854 Treaty of Wolf River). Once a reservation has been set aside by a federal treaty, agreement, statute, or executive order for the use and occupation of a tribe, state jurisdiction over hunting or fishing within the reservation generally is preempted as an incident of the creation of Indian country. See Chapter 8A, supra.

NEW MEXICO V. MESCALERO APACHE TRIBE

Supreme Court of the United States, 1983.
462 U.S. 324, 103 S.Ct. 2378, 76 L.Ed.2d 611.

* * *

JUSTICE MARSHALL delivered the opinion of the Court.

We are called upon to decide in this case whether a State may restrict an Indian Tribe's regulation of hunting and fishing on its reservation. * * *

I

The Mescalero Apache Tribe (Tribe) resides on a reservation located within Otero County in south central New Mexico. The reservation, which represents only a small portion of the aboriginal Mescalero domain, was created by a succession of Executive Orders promulgated in the 1870's and 1880's. The present reservation comprises more than 460,000 acres, of which the Tribe owns all but 193.85 acres. Approximately 2,000 members of the Tribe reside on the reservation, along with 179 non-Indians, including resident federal employees of the Bureau of Indian Affairs and the Indian Health Service.

* * * The Tribe has constructed a resort complex financed principally by federal funds, and has undertaken a substantial development of the reservation's hunting and fishing resources. These efforts provide employment opportunities for members of the Tribe, and the sale of hunting and fishing licenses and related services generates income which is used to maintain the Tribal government and provide services to Tribe members.[4]

---

[4] Income from the sale of hunting and fishing licenses, "package hunts" which combine hunting and fishing with use of the facilities at the Inn, and campground and picnicking permits totaled $269,140 in 1976 and $271,520 in 1977. The vast majority of the nonmember hunters and fishermen on the reservation are not residents of the State of New Mexico.

Development of the reservation's fish and wildlife resources has involved a sustained, cooperative effort by the Tribe and the Federal Government. Indeed, the reservation's fishing resources are wholly attributable to these recent efforts. Using federal funds, the Tribe has established eight artificial lakes which, together with the reservation's streams, are stocked by the Bureau of Sport Fisheries and Wildlife of the U.S. Fish and Wildlife Service, Department of the Interior, which operates a federal hatchery located on the reservation. None of the waters are stocked by the State. The United States has also contributed substantially to the creation of the reservation's game resources. Prior to 1966 there were only 13 elk in the vicinity of the reservation. In 1966 and 1967 the National Park Service donated a herd of 162 elk which was released on the reservation. Through its management and range development the Tribe has dramatically increased the elk population, which by 1977 numbered approximately 1,200. New Mexico has not contributed significantly to the development of the elk herd or the other game on the reservation, which includes antelope, bear and deer.

The Tribe and the Federal Government jointly conduct a comprehensive fish and game management program. Pursuant to its Constitution and to an agreement with the Bureau of Sport Fisheries and Wildlife, the Tribal Council adopts hunting and fishing ordinances each year. The tribal ordinances, which establish bag limits and seasons and provide for licensing of hunting and fishing, are subject to approval by the Secretary under the Tribal Constitution and have been so approved. The Tribal Council adopts the game ordinances on the basis of recommendations submitted by a Bureau of Indian Affairs range conservationist who is assisted by full-time conservation officers employed by the Tribe. The recommendations are made in light of the conservation needs of the reservation, which are determined on the basis of annual game counts and surveys. Through the Bureau of Fish and Wildlife, the Secretary also determines the stocking of the reservation's waters based upon periodic surveys of the reservation.

Numerous conflicts exist between State and tribal hunting regulations. For instance, tribal seasons and bag limits for both hunting and fishing often do not coincide with those imposed by the State. The Tribe permits a hunter to kill both a buck and a doe; the State permits only buck to be killed. Unlike the State, the Tribe permits a person to purchase an elk license in two consecutive years. Moreover, since 1977, the Tribe's ordinances have specified that State hunting and fishing licenses are not required for Indians or non-Indians who hunt or fish on the reservation. The New Mexico Department of Game and Fish has enforced the state's regulations by arresting non-Indian hunters for illegal possession of game killed on the reservation in accordance with tribal ordinances but not in accordance with State hunting regulations.

* * *

II

New Mexico concedes that on the reservation the Tribe exercises exclusive jurisdiction over hunting and fishing by members of the Tribe and may also regulate the hunting and fishing by nonmembers. New Mexico contends, however, that it may exercise concurrent jurisdiction over nonmembers and that therefore its regulations governing hunting and fishing throughout the State should also apply to hunting and fishing by nonmembers on the reservation. Although New Mexico does not claim that it can require the Tribe to permit nonmembers to hunt and fish on the reservation, it claims that, once the Tribe chooses to permit hunting and fishing by nonmembers, such hunting and fishing is subject to any state-imposed conditions. Under this view the State would be free to impose conditions more restrictive than the Tribe's own regulations, including an outright prohibition. The question in this case is whether the State may so restrict the Tribe's exercise of its authority.

Our decision in *Montana v. United States*, 450 U.S. 544 (1981), does not resolve this question. Unlike this case, *Montana* concerned lands located within the reservation but *not* owned by the Tribe or its members. We held that the Crow Tribe could not as a general matter regulate hunting and fishing on those lands. But as to "lands belonging to the Tribe or held by the United States in trust for the Tribe," we "readily agree[d]" that a Tribe may "prohibit nonmembers from hunting or fishing * * * [or] condition their entry by charging a fee or establish bag and creel limits." We had no occasion to decide whether a Tribe may only exercise this authority in a manner permitted by a State.

* * *

In *White Mountain Apache Tribe v. Bracker*, 448 U.S. 136 (1980), we reviewed our prior decisions concerning tribal and state authority over Indian reservations and extracted certain principles governing the determination whether federal law preempts the assertion of state authority over nonmembers on a reservation. We stated that that determination does not depend "on mechanical or absolute conceptions of state or tribal sovereignty, but call[s] for a particularized inquiry into the nature of the state, federal, and tribal interests at stake."

We also emphasized the special sense in which the doctrine of preemption is applied in this context. * * * By resting pre-emption analysis principally on a consideration of the nature of the competing interests at stake, our cases have rejected a narrow focus on congressional intent to pre-empt State law as the sole touchstone. They have also rejected the proposition that pre-emption requires "an express congressional statement to that effect." *Bracker, supra*, 448 U.S., at 144. State jurisdiction is preempted by the operation of federal law if it interferes or is incompatible with federal and tribal interests reflected in federal law, unless the State interests at stake are sufficient to justify the assertion of State authority. *Bracker, supra*.[16] * * *

Certain broad considerations guide our assessment of the federal and tribal interests. The traditional notions of Indian sovereignty provide a crucial "backdrop," *Bracker, supra*, 448 U.S., at 143, citing *McClanahan*, 411 U.S., at 172, against which any assertion of state authority must be assessed. Moreover, both the tribes and the Federal Government are firmly committed to the goal of promoting tribal self-government, a goal embodied in numerous federal statutes. We have stressed that Congress' objective of furthering tribal self-government encompasses far more than encouraging tribal management of disputes between members, but includes Congress' overriding goal of encouraging "tribal self-sufficiency and economic development." *Bracker, supra*, 448 U.S., at 143. In part as a necessary implication of this broad federal commitment, we have held that tribes have the power to manage the use of * * * territory and resources by both members and nonmembers, to undertake and regulate economic activity within the reservation, and to defray the cost of governmental services by levying taxes. Thus, when a tribe undertakes an enterprise under the authority of federal law, an assertion of State authority must be viewed against any interference with the successful accomplishment of the federal purpose. * * *

Our prior decisions also guide our assessment of the state interest asserted to justify State jurisdiction over a reservation. The exercise of State authority which imposes additional burdens on a tribal enterprise must ordinarily be justified by functions or services performed by the State in connection with the on-reservation activity. Thus a State seeking to impose a tax on a transaction between a Tribe and non-members must point to more than its general interest in raising revenues. A State's regulatory interest will be particularly substantial if the State can point to off-reservation effects that necessitate State intervention.

III

With these principles in mind, we turn to New Mexico's claim that it may superimpose its own hunting and fishing regulations on the Mescalero Apache Tribe's regulatory scheme.

A

It is beyond doubt that the Mescalero Apache Tribe lawfully exercises substantial control over the lands and resources of its reservation, including its wildlife. As noted [above], and as conceded by New Mexico, the sovereignty retained by the Tribe under the Treaty of 1852 includes its

---

[16] The exercise of State authority may also be barred by an independent barrier—inherent tribal sovereignty—if it "unlawfully infringe[s] 'on the rights of reservation Indians to make their own laws and be ruled by them.' " *White Mountain Apache Tribe v. Bracker.*

right to regulate the use of its resources by members as well as nonmembers. In *Montana v. United States*, supra, we specifically recognized that tribes in general retain this authority.

* * *

B

Several considerations strongly support the Court of Appeals' conclusion that the Tribe's authority to regulate hunting and fishing preempts state jurisdiction. It is important to emphasize that concurrent jurisdiction would effectively nullify the Tribe's authority to control hunting and fishing on the reservation. Concurrent jurisdiction would empower New Mexico wholly to supplant tribal regulations. The State would be able to dictate the terms on which nonmembers are permitted to utilize the reservation's resources. The Tribe would thus exercise its authority over the reservation only at the sufferance of the State. The tribal authority to regulate hunting and fishing by non-members, which has been repeatedly confirmed by federal treaties and laws and which we explicitly recognized in Montana v. United States, supra, would have a rather hollow ring if tribal authority amounted to no more than this.

Furthermore, the exercise of concurrent State jurisdiction in this case would completely "disturb and disarrange" the comprehensive scheme of federal and tribal management established pursuant to federal law. * * *

Concurrent state jurisdiction would supplant this regulatory scheme with an inconsistent dual system: members would be governed by tribal ordinances, while nonmembers would be regulated by general State hunting and fishing laws. This could severely hinder the ability of the Tribe to conduct a sound management program. Tribal ordinances reflect the specific needs of the reservation by establishing the optimal level of hunting and fishing that should occur, not simply a maximum level that should not be exceeded. State laws in contrast are based on considerations not necessarily relevant to, and possibly hostile to, the needs of the reservation. For instance, the ordinance permitting a hunter to kill a buck and a doe was designed to curb excessive growth of the deer population on the reservation. Enforcement of the State regulation permitting only buck to be killed would frustrate that objective. Similarly, by determining the tribal hunting seasons, bag limits, and permit availability, the Tribe regulates the duration and intensity of hunting. These determinations take into account numerous factors, including the game capacity of the terrain, the range utilization of the game animals, and the availability of tribal personnel to monitor the hunts. Permitting the State to enforce different restrictions simply because they have been determined to be appropriate for the State as a whole would impose on the Tribe the possibly insurmountable task of ensuring that the patchwork application of State and tribal regulations remains consistent with sound management of the reservation's resources.

* * * Requiring tribal ordinances to yield whenever State law is more restrictive would seriously "undermine the Secretary's [and the Tribe's] ability to make the wide range of determinations committed to [their] authority." *Bracker, supra*, 448 U.S., at 149.

The assertion of concurrent jurisdiction by New Mexico not only would threaten to disrupt the federal and tribal regulatory scheme, but would also threaten Congress' overriding objective of encouraging tribal self-government and economic development. The tribe has engaged in a concerted and sustained undertaking to develop and manage the reservation's wildlife and land resources specifically for the benefit of its members. The project generates funds for essential tribal services and provides employment for members who reside on the reservation. This case is thus far removed from those situations, such as on-reservation sales outlets which market to nonmembers goods not manufactured by the tribe or its members, in which the tribal contribution to an enterprise is *de minimis*. The tribal enterprise in this case clearly involves "value generated on the reservation by activities involving the Trib[e]." The disruptive effect that would result from the assertion of concurrent jurisdiction by New Mexico would plainly "stan[d] as an obstacle to the accomplishment of the full purposes and objectives of Congress".

C

The State has failed to "identify any regulatory function or service . . . that would justify" the assertion of concurrent regulatory authority. The hunting and fishing permitted by the Tribe occur entirely on the reservation. The fish and wildlife resources are either native to the reservation or were created by the joint efforts of the Tribe and the Federal Government. New Mexico does not contribute in any significant respect to the maintenance of these resources, and can point to no other "governmental functions it provides," in connection with hunting and fishing on the reservation by nonmembers that would justify the assertion of its authority.

The State also cannot point to any off-reservation effects that warrant State intervention. Some species of game never leave tribal lands, and the State points to no specific interest concerning those that occasionally do. Unlike *Puyallup Tribe v. Washington Game Dept.*, [433 U.S. 165 (1977),] this is not a case in which a Treaty expressly subjects a tribe's hunting and fishing rights to the common rights of nonmembers and in which a State's interest in conserving a scarce, common supply justifies State intervention. The State concedes that the Tribe's management has "not had an adverse impact on fish and wildlife outside the reservation."

We recognize that New Mexico may be deprived of the sale of state licenses to nonmembers who hunt and fish on the reservation, as well as some federal matching funds calculated in part on the basis of the number of state licenses sold. However, any financial interest the State might have in this case is simply insufficient to justify the assertion of concurrent jurisdiction. The loss of revenues to the State is likely to be insubstantial given the small numbers of persons who purchase tribal hunting licenses.[29] * * *

* * *

* * * Given the strong interests favoring exclusive tribal jurisdiction and the absence of state interests which justify the assertion of concurrent authority, we conclude that the application of the State's hunting and fishing laws to the reservation is pre-empted.

NOTES

1. In *Mescalero Apache,* New Mexico conceded that the tribe had exclusive jurisdiction over fishing and hunting by tribal members. Courts have consistently held that Indians may fish and hunt within their reservation free of state regulation. As in other Indian country jurisdiction matters involving tribal members, the actual land ownership pattern is not determinative. For example, in Mattz v. Arnett, 412 U.S. 481 (1973), the Supreme Court held that areas of the Klamath River Reservation that had been opened for unrestricted homestead entry were Indian country, thus excluding state jurisdiction over Indian fishing. See also Leech Lake Band of Chippewa Indians v. Herbst, 334 F.Supp. 1001 (D.Minn.1971) (Nelson Act, which provided for "a complete extinguishment of the Indian title" to the lands of the Leech Lake Reservation, did not abrogate the treaty fishing and hunting rights).

2. The more difficult situation arises when a tribe asserts control over non-Indian fishing and hunting within areas of a reservation that are not Indian-owned. In South Dakota v. Bourland, 508 U.S. 679 (1993), the Supreme Court applied the rule in *Montana v. United States,* page 602, supra, to abrogate tribal treaty rights to regulate non-Indian fishing and hunting on a large area of land within the Cheyenne River Reservation taken from the tribe for use by the federal government in constructing the huge Oahe Dam and Reservoir Project on the Missouri River. Although Congress did not provide for the taken lands to be conveyed to non-Indians, it opened them to public use and made hunting and fishing subject to federal regulation. Thus, the Court held that "when Congress has broadly opened up such land to non-Indians, the effect of the transfer is the destruction of pre-existing Indian rights to regulatory control." 508 U.S. at 692.

The Court in *Bourland* did not disturb its rule in *Mattz v. Arnett,* supra, that there is no state jurisdiction to regulate Indian fishing and hunting unless

---

[29] In recent years the Tribe sold 10 antelope licenses compared to 3,500 for the State, 50 elk licenses compared to 14,000 by the State, and 500 deer licenses compared to 100,000 for the State.

a close examination of the Act opening up a reservation and congressional intent reveal a clear purpose to disestablish the reservation. Although the Cheyenne River Reservation lands in *Bourland* were almost all owned by the government, not by non-Indians as in *Montana,* the Court said the *Montana* rule applied to preclude tribal jurisdiction over non-Indians because the lands were "broadly opened" to the public. If the law had not resulted in such a non-Indian presence, and commensurate limitations on Indian use and occupancy, would the rule of exclusive tribal jurisdiction in *Mescalero Apache* have applied to the federal lands on the Cheyenne River Reservation?

Even where there has been a "broad" opening of federal lands on the reservation, an exception under *Montana* says the tribe's inherent sovereignty over non-Indians has not been abrogated if the non-Indian activity is consensual or "threatens or has some direct effect on the political integrity, economic security, or the health or welfare of the tribe." On remand from the Supreme Court, the Eighth Circuit held in *Bourland* that the latter exception did not apply. South Dakota v. Bourland, 39 F.3d 868 (8th Cir.1994). In an appropriate case could the tribe's interest in a comprehensive scheme of tribal fish and game management be so disturbed by non-Indian activity on non-Indian (or open-to-the-public federal) land that it would fit the *Montana* exception?

3.   A federal statute bolsters tribal control over fishing and hunting on Indian land. Title 18 U.S.C.A. § 1165 makes it a crime for anyone "without lawful authority or permission [to go] upon any land that belongs to any Indian or Indian tribe, band, or group * * * [and which is] held by the United States * * * for the purpose of hunting, trapping, or fishing * * *." A few courts have construed § 1165 as a conferral or acknowledgement of tribal authority to grant, withhold, or condition non-Indian entry as a means of controlling reservation fishing and hunting. See Confederated Tribes of the Colville Indian Reservation v. Washington, 412 F.Supp. 651 (E.D.Wash.1976), reversed 591 F.2d 89 (9th Cir.1979), and Quechan Tribe v. Rowe, 531 F.2d 408 (9th Cir.1976). In United States v. Pollmann, 364 F.Supp. 995 (D.Mont.1973), it was held that a non-Indian's fishing from a boat on the portion of Flathead Lake which is within the Flathead Reservation constituted going upon "land" within the statute's meaning. The defendant was acquitted, however, because the statute requires that violations be made willfully and knowingly, and Pollmann had relied on his attorney's advice that the lake was not "land."

4.   The authority of the Secretary of Interior to adopt an interim game code for on-reservation hunting and fishing was upheld over the challenge of the Arapahoe Tribe of Indians. The Shoshone Tribe shares the Wind River Reservation with the Arapahoe Tribe and requested adoption of the federal code after the tribes failed to agree on an appropriate game code to govern the reservation. Northern Arapahoe Tribe v. Hodel, 808 F.2d 741 (10th Cir.1987).

NOTE: COOPERATIVE WILDLIFE MANAGEMENT AGREEMENTS

Wild animals and fish do not respect political boundaries and thus wise resource management often demands coordination of goals and regulatory approaches. Action taken by the states or tribes in pursuit of their objectives can affect the numbers and well-being of fish and wildlife throughout their ranges. Without coordination with the other government's actions, neither will be totally successful at achieving its goal.

In seeking broad, consistent management, tribes and states have sought to expand their exclusive authority to control resources as far as possible. Litigation has often resulted in a collage of jurisdiction that is sensitive to legal principles but not to the realities of wildlife management. Consequently, some states and tribes have worked out management agreements in the wake of litigation. Cooperative agreements typically contain two elements: a clarification of jurisdiction, and an arrangement for interaction of wildlife managers and coordination of resource management goals.

In the *Leech Lake* case, cited in note 1, supra, after the federal district court ruled in favor of the tribe's reserved fishing and hunting rights, appeals and cross-appeals were filed. The state and the tribe then decided to enter into an agreement that was ratified by the Minnesota legislature, Minn.Stat. § 97A.151 and Minn. Stat. § 97A.155 (Amendments to Leech Lake Indian Reservation Agreement) (2003), and incorporated into a consent judgment in the federal court case. The agreement acknowledged that tribal members were free from state regulation while hunting, fishing, trapping, or gathering rice on the reservation. The tribe agreed to prohibit commercial taking of game, fish, or rice, and to adopt a conservation code. In lieu of a tribal licensing program, the state adopted a licensing system whereby a supplemental fee is collected from non-Indians for their right to hunt, fish, and gather rice on the reservation. The state rebates the supplemental fees to the tribe. The supplemental amount charged non-Indians is determined by a tribal committee and the proceeds are used by the tribe for resource management.

Minnesota established a similar revenue-sharing mechanism in response to a litigation victory by the White Earth Chippewas. See State v. Clark, 282 N.W.2d 902 (Minn.1979), cert. denied 445 U.S. 904 (1980); White Earth Band of Chippewa Indians v. Alexander, 683 F.2d 1129 (8th Cir.1982), cert. denied 459 U.S. 1070 (1982). The legislature authorized the Minnesota commissioner of natural resources to distribute to the tribes a percentage of the proceeds from the sale of all hunting, fishing, and trapping licenses sold in Minnesota, two and one-half percent for the White Earth Tribe and five percent for the Leech Lake Tribe. Minn.Stat., § 97A.161 (2003).

In connection with the Maine Indian Claims Settlement, the State of Maine granted the Passamaquoddy and Penobscot tribes exclusive authority within their reservations to promulgate hunting and fishing regulations, Me.Rev.Stat.Ann. tit. 30, § 6207 (West 1993). However, tribal ordinances that require the registration of wildlife killed during the hunt must be substantially similar to the Maine procedures. If the Commissioner of Inland Fisheries and

Wildlife determines that a tribal ordinance or the lack of one may result in adverse effects on fish stocks outside the reservation, the Commissioner consults with the tribes on remediation measures. If no agreement with the tribes is possible, the state may impose remedial measures. Me.Rev.Stat.Ann. tit. 30, § 6207(6) (West 1993).

Not all cooperative agreements have followed court decisions. The first such agreement between the state of Colorado and the Southern Ute Tribe in 1962 arose out of concern that a rapidly expanding deer herd was severely damaging the range and food supply. The deer migrated in and out of the reservation, and both the state and the tribe were aware of the problem. The agreement outlined a management plan for the herd that opened the reservation to non-Indian hunting. A later agreement responded to Indian claims of immunity from prosecution for hunting in Indian country by recognizing Indian treaty rights and providing for cooperation in game and fish management.

In Minnesota, the Department of Natural Resources and the Grand Portage Band of Chippewa reached an agreement after extended negotiations concerning Lake Superior fishing. The agreement recognized tribal fishing rights in the lake. The tribe consented to limit the number of fish taken by members, to regulate netting practices, and to create a limited season for netting. In return, Minnesota continued to stock the lake with fish and train tribal wildlife management officers.

Decreasing riparian habitat in New Mexico caused the Department of Game and Fish to look to Sandia Pueblo lands for a needed wildlife study. The tribe and the state reached a five-year limited agreement to allow state officials access to the reservation so that the study could go forward.

Other tribal-state hunting and fishing cooperative agreements include compacts between: the state of Arizona and the Fort Mohave Tribe, Hualapai Tribe, San Carlos Apache Tribe, Navajo Nation, and White Mountain Apache Tribe; the state of Montana, the Fort Belknap Community Council, and the Fort Peck Tribe; the states of Oregon and Washington and the Nez Perce Tribe, Confederated Tribes of the Umatilla Reservation, Confederated Tribes of the Warm Springs Reservation, and Confederated Tribes and Bands of the Yakima Indian Nation; the state of South Dakota and the Cheyenne River Sioux Tribe; the state of Washington and the Hoh and Quinault Tribes, the Nisqually Tribe, and the Port Gamble, Klallam, Skokomish, and Suquamish Tribes; and the state of Wisconsin and the Winnebago Tribe. See generally Mary Christina Wood, *The Tribal Property Right to Wildlife Capital (Part I): Applying Principles of Sovereignty To Protect Imperiled Wildlife Populations*, 37 Idaho L.Rev. 1 (2000); Shelly D. Stokes, *Ecosystem Co-Management Plans: A Sound Approach or a Threat to Tribal Rights?* 27 Vt.L.Rev. 421 (2003).

Acceptance of negotiated agreements can be tenuous. In Confederated Salish & Kootenai Tribes v. Montana, 750 F.Supp. 446 (D.Mont.1990), the court found the tribe had exclusive regulatory jurisdiction over both member and non-member fishing and hunting on the south half of Flathead Lake. The tribes then adopted an ordinance asserting exclusive jurisdiction over the entire reservation. The tribes and the state negotiated an agreement to provide for unitary management and regulation of fish and wildlife. Although the state legislature passed a bill approving the agreement and the governor signed it into law, the governor refused to sign the agreement itself and sought some changes. The tribes then decided to enforce the exclusive jurisdiction ordinance. The state responded by saying it would enforce its fishing regulations against all non-members of the tribes within the reservation. The tribe brought suit to enjoin state enforcement but the court granted a preliminary injunction only as to the south half of Flathead Lake saying that allowing state jurisdiction over non-members elsewhere—where 85% of the population were non-members—would preserve the status quo. The court did announce its intention to reconsider the portion of its ruling favoring the state if the state failed to adopt emergency regulations at least as restrictive as the tribal regulations.

SECTION B. OFF-RESERVATION FISHING AND HUNTING

1.   PACIFIC NORTHWEST

States generally are free to regulate Indians outside of Indian country. A major exception is Indian off-reservation treaty hunting and fishing. Some tribes in the Pacific Northwest and in the Great Lakes region reserved off-reservation fishing rights by treaty. In a few instances, tribes reserved off-reservation hunting rights.

The earliest and most numerous court cases involved the off-reservation fishing rights of tribes of the Pacific Northwest. In various treaties, tribes in western Washington reserved rights to fish at traditional locations on the many streams that flow into Puget Sound, in Puget Sound itself, and in the Pacific Ocean. On the Columbia River, litigation has dealt with the off-reservation rights of the Yakima tribe of Washington, the Warm Springs and Umatilla tribes of Oregon, and the Nez Perce tribe of Idaho. Major disputes also have arisen on the Klamath River in northern California.

The fish that have "caused" the controversy in the Pacific Northwest are six species of anadromous fish that are among the great wonders of nature. Anadromous fish are born in fresh water streams often hundreds, and sometimes even a thousand, miles from the ocean. They go to the ocean as young fish and live most of their lives in salt water. They then return to the streams in which they were born in order to spawn. Included are five species of Pacific salmon—the Chinook, the sockeye the silver or Coho, the pink, and the chum or dog salmon. They are of varying importance to sport anglers and commercial fishers. The sixth species of anadromous fish is the steelhead, which is the most prized sport fish in the Northwest.

Commercial fishing for steelhead has been banned by state legislatures in California, Oregon, and Washington. More recently, the "fish" that have become the subject of intense dispute between Indians and non-Indians are not fish at all, but shellfish, especially the commercially valuable geoducks, and Dungeness crabs.

Almost all the Indian take is for commercial purposes, although the small catch for ceremonial fishing is of cultural and religious importance. Indians take virtually no anadromous fish for sport. Non-Indian commercial fishers are divided into four groups: "gillnetters," who use nets in bays and rivers; "reefnetters," who fish near artificial reefs in Puget Sound; "purse seiners," who drop weighted nets on schools of fish in the ocean and in the sounds; and "trollers," who fish with multiple-hook rigs in the ocean. Sport fishing occurs both on the ocean and in the rivers.

Obviously, the technological and legal problems in allocating the millions of fish that annually attempt to run the gamut of user groups as they move in their spawning migration from the oceans up into the streams have strained almost everyone's competence and patience. See generally Charles F. Wilkinson & Daniel Keith Conner, *The Law of the Pacific Salmon Fishery: Conservation and Allocation of a Transboundary Common Property Resource,* 32 Kan.L.Rev. 17 (1983).

States have consistently opposed the rights of some Indians to fish free of state conservation laws outside the reservations

UNITED STATES V. WINANS

Supreme Court of the United States, 1905.
198 U.S. 371, 25 S.Ct. 662, 49 L.Ed. 1089.

[The opinion is reproduced at page 163, supra.]

NOTE

Winans is a turn-of-the-century case that continues to have broad ramifications for state authority over wildlife resources valued by a variety of non-Indian commercial and recreational interest groups. In *Winans,* Justice McKenna, who also authored the Supreme Court's *Winters* decision on reserved water rights, page 819, supra, announced tribal reserved rights in the area of off-reservation hunting and fishing regulations.

At least since *Winans,* there has been no question of federal power to enter into treaties that would preserve rights capable of surviving subsequent statehood. One might have expected that *Winans* would have paved the way for treaty Indians to exercise their reserved fishing rights unmolested. Instead, it was followed by over seventy years of litigation.

In order to determine what rights were intended, courts have had to review the treaties and the negotiation process. Treaty language relative to off-reservation fishing and hunting varies considerably. It is the task of courts (assisted by the research, documentary evidence, and expert witnesses produced by counsel) to find the meaning, scope and intent of such phrases as: "the right of taking fish at all usual and accustomed places, in common with citizens of the territory" (Treaty with the Yakimas, 12 Stat. 951); "the privilege of hunting * * * on open and unclaimed lands" (Treaty of Medicine Creek, 10 Stat. 1132); "[t]he right to hunt on the unoccupied lands of the United States so long as game may be found thereon, and so long as peace subsists among the whites and the Indians on the borders of the hunting districts" (Treaty with the Eastern Band of Shoshone and Bannock Tribe of Indians, 15 Stat. 673); and the "right of hunting on the land ceded with other usual privileges of occupancy" (Treaty with the Ottawas, 7 Stat. 491). To attribute meaning to these cryptic phrases, courts have drawn from history, including contemporaneous writings, treaty minutes, and other available information. Testimony of anthropologists and historians produced by both sides has been an indispensable aid.

Until relatively recent times Indians have lacked the necessary financial and legal resources to assert fully their treaty rights as a bar to application of state laws. Many cases have been criminal prosecutions in which individual Indian defendants were unable to mount a winning treaty defense, replete with historical research, anthropological experts, biological evidence, and lawyers able to press the case through the trial and appellate process. Since the late 1960s, however, the federal government has acted on a number of fronts, often by bringing the complex litigation necessary to assert tribal rights. Further, Indians have had access to attorneys funded by government agencies and private foundations. Additional resources have been needed outside of court, too. In an area so politically charged—involving the role of powerful state and federal agencies, sophisticated conservation programs, and major commercial industries—litigation cannot be a final answer.

For the most part, the Indian litigation offensive has been successful. Rights effectively inchoate for a century have gained legal definition and enforcement. Tribes are experiencing new pride as members work together to exercise rights finally recognized after years of legal conflict. There also has been a lessening of the poverty of many fishing tribes as their traditional and culturally based livelihood has been resumed. Significantly, tribes have developed their own wildlife and fishery management and regulatory programs.

But a current of resistance to Indian fishing and hunting rights still runs strong. Many non-Indians (and a few elected officials) today remain unconvinced of the necessity to honor treaties negotiated during the nineteenth century in which the United States acquired virtually all the lands of the Pacific Northwest in return for the Indians' continued (but diminished) right to fish in the ceded area. The late Judge George H. Boldt, author of the district court decision in Washington v. Washington State Commercial Passenger Fishing Vessel Association, 443 U.S. 658 (1979), page 911, infra, (the "Boldt Decision") was the subject of a campaign calling for his impeachment and was hanged in effigy. Tens of thousands of signatures were gathered on petitions to Congress calling for abrogation of Indian treaties, and such proposals have been introduced in Congress. To be sure, judicial acknowledgment of Indian fishing and hunting rights has contributed significantly to a "backlash" movement against Indian rights. See Fay G. Cohen, Treaties on Trial 15 (1986); Charles F. Wilkinson, *To Feel the Summer in the Spring: The Treaty Fishing Rights of the Wisconsin Chippewa*, 1991 Wis.L.Rev. 375 (1991).

Winans teaches that "the treaty was not a grant of rights to the Indians, but a grant of rights from them—a reservation of those not granted." 198 U.S. at 381. Thus, to the extent Indians refrain from ceding rights, the rights are retained. Similarly, the Supreme Court has held that a treaty silent as to hunting and fishing rights impliedly reserves them. *Menominee Tribe v. United States*, page 238, supra. But what if there is no treaty? Are all rights reserved, except those taken away by congressional action? In State v. Coffee, 556 P.2d 1185 (Idaho 1976), a Kootenai Indian convicted of killing deer out of season contrary to state law contended that she was exercising an aboriginal right that never had been extinguished because the Kootenai had no treaty with the United States. The court did not deal with the aboriginal rights issue, but instead found that the Kootenai were the beneficiaries of rights under the Treaty of Hellgate, 12 Stat. 975 (1855). Although the tribe was not a party to it, the treaty had been effective in taking title to lands that the tribe had occupied, and consequently Kootenai Indians should not be deprived of the treaty's benefits. The conviction was upheld, however, because the treaty right did not apply on private lands.

The Supreme Court had suggested the possibility of state regulation of off-reservation Indian treaty fishing rights in Tulee v. Washington, 315 U.S. 681 (1942). An Indian was arrested for netting salmon without a license. He had been fishing under the same Yakima Treaty involved in *Winans*. The Court ruled that the treaty "forecloses the state from charging the Indians a [license] fee of the kind in question here," but added: "it is clear that their regulatory purpose could be accomplished otherwise. * * * ", that the imposition of license fees is not indispensable to the effectiveness of a state conservation program. Even though this method may be both convenient and, in its general impact, fair, it acts upon the Indians as a charge for exercising the very right their ancestors intended to reserve. We believe that such exaction of fees as a prerequisite to the enjoyment of fishing in the "usual and accustomed places" cannot be reconciled with a fair construction of the treaty. We therefore hold the state statute invalid as applied in this case. 315 U.S. at 685.

After *Tulee,* the State of Washington conceded that it could not charge a license fee of Indians engaged in treaty fishing, but continued to regulate Indian off-reservation treaty fishing based on the assumption that it was "indispensable" to the regulatory program. Indian resistance to state regulation grew. The State of Washington then sued the Puyallup and Nisqually Tribes and several of their individual members to enjoin further fishing inconsistent with state law.

In Puyallup Tribe v. Department of Game, 391 U.S. 392 (1968), the Supreme Court ruled for the first time that states could lawfully exercise some forms of control over the federal treaty rights of Indian tribes. The treaty at issue in *Puyallup* guaranteed to the Indians the "right of taking fish, at all usual and accustomed grounds and stations * * * in common with all citizens of the Territory." As Justice Douglas explained in his opinion for the Court, the tribes' use of set nets to take salmon and steelhead for their own needs as well as for commercial purposes was illegal under Washington state law. The Court went on to hold:

> The treaty right is in terms the right to fish "at all usual and accustomed places." We assume that fishing by nets was customary at the time of the Treaty; and we also assume that there were commercial aspects to that fishing as there are at present. But the *manner* in which the fishing may be done and its purpose, whether or not commercial, are not mentioned in the Treaty. We would have quite a different case if the Treaty had preserved the right to fish at the "usual and accustomed places" *in the "usual and accustomed" manner*. But the Treaty is silent as to the mode or modes of fishing that are guaranteed. Moreover, the right to fish at those respective places is not an exclusive one. Rather, it is one "in common with all citizens of the Territory." Certainly the right of the latter may be regulated. And we see no reason why the right of the Indians may not also be regulated by an appropriate exercise of the police power of the State. The right to fish "at all usual and accustomed" places may, of course, not be qualified by the State, even though all Indians born in the United States are now citizens of the United States. * * * But the manner of fishing, the size of the take, the restriction of commercial fishing, and the like may be regulated by the State in the interest of conservation, provided the regulation meets appropriate standards and does not discriminate against the Indians.

Id. at 398.

Because the question of whether the prohibition of the use of set nets was a "reasonable and necessary" conservation measure had not been decided by the Washington courts, the Supreme Court remanded the case, with the added instruction "that any ultimate findings on the conservation issue must also cover the issue of equal protection implicit in the phrase 'in common with.' " Id. at 403.

Both Indians and the state claimed victory and admitted defeat in the aftermath of the first *Puyallup* case (*Puyallup I*). The state's power to regulate federal treaty fishing was established—a power strenuously resisted by Indians on Supremacy Clause grounds. But the Court also upheld the Indians' claims that their treaty rights were superior to the privilege of non-Indians to fish. The state had long denied any special status for Indians. After *Puyallup I*, state regulations affecting Indian fishing were allowed only if they were "necessary for the conservation of fish." Because a treaty right is involved, the less stringent due process standard of reasonableness normally required for exercises of state police power is not sufficient. 391 U.S. at 401–02 n.14. It was later held that these special standards applied not only to Indian treaties, but also to an agreement between the United States and a tribe. Antoine v. Washington, 420 U.S. 194 (1975).

The late Professor Ralph W. Johnson criticized *Puyallup I*'s holdings on state power to regulate a federal Indian treaty rights in these terms:

> No valid basis for the existence of such state power can be found. The Constitution of the United States provides that treaties are the "supreme law of the land." Because agreements with the Indians are treaties, the Indians are not subject to state regulation unless the treaty so provides or unless Congress so legislates. The treaties with the Indians do not provide for state regulation and Congress has never authorized such regulation.

Ralph W. Johnson, *The States Versus Indian Off-Reservation Fishing: A United States Supreme Court Error,* 47 Wash.L.Rev. 207, 208 (1972).

Professor Johnson went on to call the *Puyallup I* standard for allowing state regulation of Indian treaty fishing—that the regulation must be a "reasonable and necessary" conservation measure—"notoriously vague." He predicted that its application would portend "a continuing series of clashes between the Indians and the states, each seeking to carve out the broadest possible claim in this legal thicket." 47 Wash.L.Rev. at 208–09. The accuracy of his prediction was demonstrated on the remand of *Puyallup I* to the Washington Supreme Court, which ruled that the state properly could ban all Indian net fishing for steelhead because after sport fishing only enough fish for spawning escapement remained in the stream. Thus, the state insisted that the ban against nets (like all of the other elements of its regulatory program) was "necessary for conservation." The dispute over the propriety of this prohibition became *Puyallup II,* Department of Game v. Puyallup Tribe, 414 U.S. 44 (1973). The Supreme Court had little difficulty reaching the conclusion that the priority for hook-and-line sport fishing was improper because virtually all Indian fishing was by net: "There is discrimination here because all Indian net fishing is barred and only hook-and-line fishing, entirely preempted by non-Indians, is allowed." Id. at 48. But Justice Douglas also responded to the state's arguments about conservation, warning that "the Treaty does not give the Indians a federal right to pursue the last living steelhead until it enters their nets." Id. at 49.

As of the early 1970s, a critical question remained unresolved: Do the treaties entitle the tribes to a numeric share of the marine resources and, if so, what should that share be? This was in the midst of the angry and sometimes violent "fish wars" over tribal fishing rights and aggressive state regulation. District Court Judge Robert Belloni first addressed the issue in the fishing rights cases on the Columbia River, holding that the tribes were entitled to a "fair share" of the salmon runs. Sohappy v. Smith, 302 F.Supp. 899 (D.Or.1969). The Northwest Washington tribes were determined however, to have a more specific definition of their rights. The federal government agreed and, in 1970, filed *United States v. Washington* in Federal District Court in Western Washington. The tribes then intervened on behalf of the United States. Four years later, the district court handed down the landmark opinion commonly known as the "Boldt decision" after its author, District Judge George H. Boldt.

The Boldt decision upheld the right of tribes to have an opportunity to harvest up to 50 percent of the runs, after allowing for escapement. See United States v. Washington, 384 F.Supp. 312 (W.D.Wash.1974). The Ninth Circuit Court of Appeals substantially affirmed 520 F.2d 676 (9th Cir.1975), and the Supreme Court denied certiorari, 423 U.S. 1086 (1976). Literally hundreds of post-judgment orders followed, as disputes arose over allocation of individual runs of salmon and steelhead. West Publishing Company issued a special volume collecting the reported decisions. The state and non-Indian fishing interests continued to attack the original ruling collaterally, arguing that the issue was of such significance that the public would not consider it final until the United States Supreme Court had actually ruled on the merits. Finally, the Court granted certiorari in collateral proceedings and resolved the underlying issues in the following historic decision.

WASHINGTON V. WASHINGTON STATE COMMERCIAL PASSENGER FISHING VESSEL ASSOCIATION
Supreme Court of the United States, 1979.
443 U.S. 658, 99 S.Ct. 3055, 61 L.Ed.2d 823.

MR. JUSTICE STEVENS delivered the opinion of the Court.

To extinguish the last group of conflicting claims to lands lying west of the Cascade Mountains and north of the Columbia River in what is now the State of Washington, the United States entered into a series of treaties with Indian tribes in 1854 and 1855. The Indians relinquished their interest in most of the territory in exchange for monetary payments. In addition, certain relatively small parcels of land were reserved for their exclusive use, and they were afforded other guarantees, including protection of their "right of taking fish, at usual and accustomed grounds and stations * * * in common with all citizens of the Territory."

The principal question presented by this litigation concerns the character of that treaty right to take fish.

* * *

One hundred and twenty-five years ago when the relevant treaties were signed, anadromous fish were even more important to most of the population of western Washington than they are today. At that time, about three-fourths of the approximately 10,000 inhabitants of the area were Indians. Although in some respects the cultures of the different tribes varied—some bands of Indians, for example, had little or no tribal organization[5] while others, such as the Makah and the Yakima, were highly organized—all of them shared a vital and unifying dependence on anadromous fish.

Religious rites were intended to insure the continual return of the salmon and the trout; the seasonal and geographic variations in the runs of the different species determined the movements of the largely nomadic tribes. Fish constituted a major part of the Indian diet, was used for commercial purposes, and indeed was traded in substantial volume. The Indians developed food-preservation techniques that enabled them to store fish throughout the year and to transport it over great distances. They used a wide variety of methods to catch fish, including the precursors of all modern netting techniques. Their usual and accustomed fishing places were numerous and were scattered throughout the area, and included marine as well as fresh-water areas.

All of the treaties were negotiated by Isaac Stevens, the first Governor and first Superintendent of Indian Affairs of the Washington Territory, and a small group of advisers. Contemporaneous documents make it clear that these people recognized the vital importance of the fisheries to the Indians and wanted to protect them from the risk that non-Indian settlers might seek to monopolize their fisheries. There is no evidence of the precise understanding the Indians had of any of the specific English terms and phrases in the treaty. It is perfectly clear, however, that the Indians were vitally interested in protecting their right to take fish at usual and accustomed places, whether on or off the reservations, and that they were invited by the white negotiators to rely and in fact did rely heavily on the good faith of the United States to protect that right.

Referring to the negotiations with the Yakima Nation, by far the largest of the Indian tribes, the District Court found:

> "At the treaty council the United States negotiators promised, and the Indians understood, that the Yakimas would forever be able to continue the same off-reservation food gathering and fishing practices as to time, place, method, species and extent as they had or were exercising. The Yakimas relied on these promises and they formed a material and basic part of the treaty and of the Indians' understanding of the meaning of the treaty." Id., at 381 (record citations omitted).

* * *

The Indians understood that non-Indians would also have the right to fish at their off-reservation fishing sites. But this was not understood as a significant limitation on their right to take fish. Because of the great

---

[5]   Indeed, the record shows that the territorial officials who negotiated the treaties on behalf of the United States took the initiative in aggregating certain loose bands into designated tribes and even appointed many of the chiefs who signed the treaties. 384 F.Supp., at 354–355, 366.

abundance of fish and the limited population of the area, it simply was not contemplated that either party would interfere with the other's fishing rights. The parties accordingly did not see the need and did not intend to regulate the taking of fish by either Indians or non-Indians, nor was future regulation foreseen.

Indeed, for several decades after the treaties were signed, Indians continued to harvest most of the fish taken from the waters of Washington, and they moved freely about the Territory and later the State in search of that resource. The size of the fishery source continued to obviate the need during the period to regulate the taking of fish by either Indians or non-Indians. Not until major economic developments in canning and processing occurred in the last few years of the 19th century did a significant non-Indian fishery develop. It was as a consequence of these developments, rather than of the treaty, that non-Indians began to dominate the fisheries and eventually to exclude most Indians from participating in it—a trend that was encouraged by the onset of often discriminatory state regulation in the early decades of the 20th century.

In sum, it is fair to conclude that when the treaties were negotiated, neither party realized or intended that their agreement would determine whether, and if so how, a resource that had always been thought inexhaustible would be allocated between the native Indians and the incoming settlers when it later became scarce.

* * *

Unfortunately, that resource has now become scarce, and the meaning of the Indians' treaty right to take fish has accordingly become critical. The United States Court of Appeals for the Ninth Circuit and the Supreme Court of the State of Washington have issued conflicting decisions on its meaning. In addition, their holdings raise important ancillary questions that will appear from a brief review of this extensive litigation.

The federal litigation was commenced in the United States District Court for the Western District of Washington in 1970. The United States, on its own behalf and as trustee for seven Indian tribes, brought suit against the State of Washington seeking an interpretation of the treaties and an injunction requiring the State to protect the Indians' share of the anadromous fish runs. Additional Indian tribes, the State's Fisheries and Game Departments, and one commercial fishing group, were joined as parties at various stages of the proceedings, while various other agencies and groups, including all of the commercial fishing associations that are parties here, participated as amici curiae.

During the extensive pretrial proceedings, four different interpretations of the critical treaty language were advanced. * * *

The District Court agreed with the parties who advocated an allocation to the Indians, and it essentially agreed with the United States as to what that allocation should be. It held that the Indians were then entitled to a 45% to 50% share of the harvestable fish that will at some point pass through recognized tribal fishing grounds in the case area. The share was to be calculated on a river-by-river, run-by-run basis, subject to certain adjustments. Fish caught by Indians for ceremonial and subsistence purposes as well as fish caught within a reservation were excluded from the calculation of the tribes' share. In addition, in order to compensate for fish caught outside of the case area, i.e., beyond the State's jurisdiction, the court made an "equitable adjustment" to increase the allocation to the Indians. The court left it to the individual tribes involved to agree among themselves on how best to divide the Indian share of runs that pass through the usual and accustomed grounds of more than one tribe, and it postponed until a later date the proper accounting for hatchery-bred fish. With a slight modification, the Court of Appeals for the Ninth Circuit affirmed, 520 F.2d 676, and we denied certiorari, 423 U.S. 1086.

The injunction entered by the District Court required the Department of Fisheries (Fisheries) to adopt regulations protecting the Indians' treaty rights. After the new regulations were promulgated, however, they were immediately challenged by private citizens in suits commenced in the Washington state courts. The State Supreme Court, in two cases that are here in consolidated form * * * ultimately held that Fisheries could not comply with the federal injunction.

As a matter of federal law, the state court first accepted the Game Department's and rejected the District Court's interpretation of the treaty and held that it did not give the Indians a right to a share of the fish runs, and second concluded that recognizing special rights for the Indians would violate the Equal Protection Clause of the Fourteenth Amendment. * * * Because we are * * * satisfied that the constitutional holding is without meritt[20] our review of the state court's judgment will be limited to the treaty issue.

When Fisheries was ordered by the state courts to abandon its attempt to promulgate and enforce regulations in compliance with the federal court's decree—and when the Game Department simply refused to comply—the District Court entered a series of orders enabling it, with the aid of the United States Attorney for the Western District of Washington

---

[20] The Washington Supreme Court held that the treaties would violate equal protection principles if they provided fishing rights to Indians that were not also available to non-Indians. The simplest answer to this argument is that this Court has already held that these treaties confer enforceable special benefits on signatory Indian tribes, e.g. *Tulee v. Washington,* 315 U.S. 681 (1942); *United States v. Winans,* 198 U.S. 371 (1905), and has repeatedly held that the peculiar semi-sovereign and constitutionally recognized status of Indians Justifies special treatment on their behalves when rationally related to the Government's "unique obligation toward the Indians." *Morton v. Mancari,* 417 U.S. 535.

and various federal-law enforcement agencies, directly to supervise those aspects of the State's fisheries necessary to the preservation of treaty fishing rights. The District Court's power to take such direct action and, in doing so, to enjoin persons who were not parties to the proceeding was affirmed by the United States Court of Appeals for the Ninth Circuit. * * * Subsequently, the District Court entered an Enforcement Order regarding the salmon fisheries for the 1978 and subsequent seasons * * * .

Because of the widespread defiance of the District Court's orders, this litigation has assumed unusual significance. We granted certiorari in the state and federal cases to interpret this important treaty provision and thereby to resolve the conflict between the state and federal courts regarding what, if any, right the Indians have to a share of the fish, to address the implications of international regulation of the fisheries in the area, and to remove any doubts about the federal court's power to enforce its orders.

* * *

The treaties secure a "right of taking fish." The pertinent articles provide:

> "The right of taking fish, at all usual and accustomed grounds and stations, is further secured to said Indians, in common with all citizens of the Territory, and of erecting temporary houses for the purpose of curing, together with the privilege of hunting, gathering roots and berries, and pasturing their horses on open and unclaimed lands: *Provided, however,* That they shall not take shell fish from any beds staked or cultivated by citizens."

* * *

A treaty, including one between the United States and an Indian tribe, is essentially a contract between two sovereign nations. When the signatory nations have not been at war and neither is the vanquished, it is reasonable to assume that they negotiated as equals at arms length. There is no reason to doubt that this assumption applies to the treaty at issue here.

Accordingly, it is the intention of the parties, and not solely that of the superior side, that must control any attempt to interpret the treaties. When Indians are involved, this Court has long given special meaning to this rule. It has held that the United States, as the party with the presumptively superior negotiating skills and superior knowledge of the language in which the treaty is recorded, has a responsibility to avoid taking advantage of the other side. "[T]he treaty must therefore be construed, not according to the technical meaning of its words to learned lawyers, but in the sense in which they would naturally be understood by the Indians." *Jones v. Meehan*, 175 U.S. 1, 11. This rule, in fact, has thrice been explicitly relied on by the Court in broadly interpreting these very treaties in the Indians' favor. *Tulee,* supra; *Seufert Bros. v. United States,* 249 U.S. 194 (1919); *Winans,* supra.

Governor Stevens and his associates were well aware of the "sense" in which the Indians were likely to view assurances regarding their fishing rights. During the negotiations, the vital importance of the fish to the Indians was repeatedly emphasized by both sides, and the Governor's promises that the treaties would protect that source of food and commerce were crucial in obtaining the Indians' assent. It is absolutely clear, as Governor Stevens himself said, that neither he nor the Indians intended that the latter "should be excluded from their ancient fisheries," and it is accordingly inconceivable that either party deliberately agreed to authorize future settlers to crowd the Indians out of any meaningful use of their accustomed places to fish. That each individual Indian would share an "equal opportunity" with thousands of newly arrived individual settlers is totally foreign to the spirit of the negotiations.[22] Such a "right," along with the $207,500 paid the Indians, would hardly have been sufficient to compensate them for the millions of acres they ceded to the Territory.

It is true that the words "in common with" may be read either as nothing more than a guarantee that individual Indians would have the same right as individual non-Indians or as securing an interest in the fish runs themselves. If we were to construe these words by reference to 19th century property concepts, we might accept the former interpretation, although even "learned lawyers" of the day would probably have offered differing interpretations of the three words. But we think greater importance should be given to the Indians likely understanding of the other words in the treaty and especially the reference to the "right of *taking* fish"—a right that had no special meaning at common law but that must have had obvious significance to the tribes relinquishing a portion of their preexisting rights to the United States in return for this promise. * * *

This interpretation is confirmed by additional language in the treaty. The fishing clause speaks of "securing" certain fishing rights, a term the Court has previously interpreted as synonymous with "reserving" rights previously exercised. Because the Indians had always exercised the right to meet their subsistence and commercial needs by taking fish from treaty area waters, they would be unlikely to perceive a "reservation" of that right

---

[22] The state characterizes its interpretation of the treaty language as assuring Indians and non-Indians an "equal opportunity" to take fish from the State's waters. * * *

In light of the far superior numbers, capital resources, and technology of the non-Indians, the concept of the Indians' "equal *opportunity*" to take advantage of a scarce resource is likely in practice to mean that the Indians' "right of taking fish" will net them virtually no catch at all. For the "opportunity" is at best theoretical. Indeed, in 1974, before the District Court's injunction took effect, and while the Indians were still operating under the "equal opportunity" doctrine, their take amounted to approximately 2% of the total harvest of salmon and trout in the treat area. The State characterizes its interpretation of the treaty language as assuring Indians and non-Indians an "equal opportunity to take fish from the state's waters." * * *

as merely the chance, shared with millions of other citizens, occasionally to dip their nets into the territorial waters. Moreover, the phrasing of the clause quite clearly avoids placing each individual Indian on an equal footing with each individual citizen of the State. The referent of the "said Indians" who are to share the right of taking fish with "all citizens of the Territory" is not the individual Indians but the various signatory "tribes and bands of Indians" listed in the opening article of each treaty. Because it was the tribes that were given a right in common with non-Indian citizens, it is especially likely that a class right to a share of fish, rather than a personal right to attempt to land fish, was intended.

In our view, the purpose and language of the treaties are unambiguous; they secure the Indians' right to take a share of each run of fish that passes through tribal fishing areas. But our prior decisions provide an even more persuasive reason why this interpretation is not open to question. For notwithstanding the bitterness that this litigation has engendered, the principal issue involved is virtually a "matter decided" by our previous holdings.

The Court has interpreted the fishing clause in these treaties on six prior occasions. In all of these cases the Court placed a relatively broad gloss on the Indians' fishing rights and—more or less explicitly—rejected the State's "equal opportunity" approach; in the earliest and the three most recent cases, moreover, we adopted essentially the interpretation that the United States is reiterating here.

In *United States v. Winans*, 198 U.S. 371, the respondent, having acquired title to property on the Columbia River and having obtained a license to use a "fish wheel"—a device capable of catching salmon by the ton and totally destroying a run of fish—asserted the right to exclude the Yakimas from one of their "usual and accustomed" places. The Circuit Court for the District of Washington sustained respondent, but this Court reversed. The Court initially rejected an argument that is analogous to the "equal opportunity" claim now made by the State. * * *

But even more significant than the language in *Winans* is its actual disposition. The Court not only upheld the Indians' right of access to respondent's private property but also ordered the circuit court on remand to devise "some adjustment and accommodation" that would protect them from total exclusion from the fishery. * * * In short, it assured the Indians a share of the fish.

In the more recent litigation over this treaty language between the Puyallup Tribe and the Washington Department of Game, the Court in the context of a dispute over rights to the run of steelhead trout on the Puyallup River reaffirmed both of the holdings that may be drawn from *Winans*— the treaty guarantees the Indians more than simply the "equal opportunity" along with all of the citizens of the State to catch fish, and it in fact assures them some portion of each relevant run. But the three *Puyallup* cases are even more explicit; they clearly establish the principle that neither party to the treaties may rely on the State's regulatory powers or on property law concepts to defeat the other's right to a "fairly apportioned" share of each covered run of harvestable anadromous fish.

* * *

The purport of our cases is clear. Non treaty fishermen may not rely on property law concepts, devices such as the fish wheel, license fees, or general regulations to deprive the Indians of a fair share of the relevant runs of anadromous fish in the case area. Nor may treaty fishermen rely on their exclusive right of access to the reservations to destroy the rights of other "citizens of the Territory." Both sides have a right, secured by treaty, to take a fair share of the available fish. That, we think, is what the parties to the treaty intended when they secured to the Indians the right of taking fish in common with other citizens.

* * *

We also agree with the Government that an equitable measure of the common right should initially divide the harvestable portion of each run that passes through a "usual and accustomed" place into approximately equal treaty and nontreaty shares, and should then reduce the treaty share if tribal needs may be satisfied by a lesser amount. * * *

The division arrived at by the District Court is also consistent with our earlier decisions concerning Indian treaty rights to scarce natural resources. In those cases, after determining that at the time of the treaties the resource involved was necessary to the Indians' welfare, the Court typically ordered a trial judge or special master, in his discretion, to devise some apportionment that assured that the Indians' reasonable livelihood needs would be met. *Arizona v. California*, 373 U.S. 546 (1963), *Winters v. United States*, 207 U.S. 564 (1908). This is precisely what the District Court did here, except that it realized that some ceiling should be placed on the Indians' apportionment to prevent their needs from exhausting the entire resource and thereby frustrating the treaty right of "all [other] citizens of the Territory."

Thus, it first concluded that at the time the treaties were signed, the Indians, who comprised three-fourths of the territorial population, depended heavily on anadromous fish as a source of food, commerce, and cultural cohesion. Indeed, it found that the non-Indian population depended on Indians to catch the fish that the former consumed. Only then did it determine that the Indian's present-day subsistence and commercial needs should be met, subject, of course, to the 50% ceiling.

It bears repeating, however, that the 50% figure imposes a maximum but not a minimum allocation. As in *Arizona v. California* and its predecessor cases, the central principle here must be that Indian treaty rights to a natural resource that once was thoroughly and exclusively exploited by the Indians secures so much as, but not more than, is necessary to provide the Indians with a livelihood—that is to say, a moderate living. Accordingly, while the maximum possible allocation to the Indians is fixed at 50%[27], the minimum is not; the latter will, upon proper submissions to the District Court, be modified in response to changing circumstances. If, for example, a tribe should dwindle to just a few members, or if it should find other sources of support that lead it to abandon its fisheries, a 45% or 50% allocation of an entire run that passes through its customary fishing grounds would be manifestly inappropriate because the livelihood of the tribe under those circumstances could not reasonably require an allotment of a large number of fish.

In addition to their challenges to the District Court's basic construction of the treaties, and to the scope of its allocation of fish to treaty fishermen, the State and the commercial fishing associations have advanced two objections to various remedial orders entered by the District Court. It is claimed that the District Court has ordered a state agency to take action that it has no authority to take as a matter of state law and that its own assumption of the authority to manage the fisheries in the State after the state agencies refused or were unable to do so was unlawful.

These objections are difficult to evaluate in view of the representations to this Court by the Attorney General of the State that definitive resolution of the basic federal question of construction of the treaties will both remove any state-law impediment to enforcement of the State's obligations under the treaties, and enable the State and its Fisheries to carry out those obligations. Once the state agencies comply, of course, there would be no issue relating to federal authority to order them to do so nor any need for the District Court to continue its own direct supervision of enforcement efforts.

The representations of the Attorney General are not binding on the courts and legislature of the State, although we assume they are authoritative within its executive branch. Moreover, the State continues to argue that the District Court exceeded its authority when it assumed control of the fisheries in the State, and the commercial fishing groups continue to argue that the District Court may not order the state agencies

---

[27] Because the 50% figure is only a ceiling, it is not correct to characterize our holding "as guaranteeing the Indians a specified percentage" of the fish. See Powell, J., dissenting, *post.* The logic of the 50% ceiling is manifest. For an equal division—especially between parties who presumptively treated with each other as equals—is suggested, if not necessarily dictated, by the word "common" as it appears in the treaties. Since the days of Solomon, such a division has been accepted as a fair apportionment of a common asset, and Anglo-American common law has presumed that division when, as here, no other percentage is suggested by the language of the agreement or the surrounding circumstances, e.g., 2 American Law of Property § 6.5, at 19 (A. Casner ed. 1952); E. Hopkins, Handbook on the Law of Real Property § 209, at 336 (1896).

to comply with its orders when they have no state-law authority to do so. * * * State-law prohibition against compliance with the District Court's decree cannot survive the command of the Supremacy Clause of the United States Constitution. It is also clear that Game and Fisheries, as parties to this litigation, may be ordered to prepare a set of rules that will implement the Court's interpretation of the rights of the parties even if state law withholds from them the power to do so. Once again the answer to a question raised by this litigation is largely dictated by our Puyallup trilogy. There, this Court mandated that state officers make precisely the same type of allocation of fish as the District Court ordered in this case.

Whether Game and Fisheries may be ordered actually to promulgate regulations having effect as a matter of state law may well be doubtful. But the District Court may rescind that problem by assuming direct supervision of the fisheries if state recalcitrance or state-law barriers should be continued. It is therefore absurd to argue as do the fishing associations, both that the state agencies may not be ordered to implement the decree and also that the District Court may not itself issue detailed remedial orders as a substitute for state supervision. The federal court unquestionably has the power to enter the various orders that state official and private parties have chosen to ignore, and even to displace local enforcement of those orders if necessary to remedy the violations of federal law found by the court. Even if those orders may have been erroneous in some respects, all parties have an unequivocal obligation to obey them while they remain in effect.

In short, we trust that the spirit of cooperation motivating the Attorney General's representation will be confirmed by the conduct of state officials. But if it is not, the District Court has the power to undertake the necessary remedial steps and to enlist the aid of the appropriate federal law enforcement agents in carrying out those steps. Moreover, the comments by the Court of Appeals strongly imply that it is prepared to uphold the use of stern measures to require respect for federal-court orders.[36]

* * *

[Dissenting opinion of JUSTICE POWELL, joined by JUSTICES STEWART and REHNQUIST, has been omitted.]

---

[36] "The state's extraordinary machinations in resisting the [1974] decree have forced the district court to take over a large share of the management of the state's fishery in order to enforce its decrees. Except for some desegregation cases [citations omitted], the district court has faced the most concerted official and private efforts to frustrate a decree of a federal court witnessed in this century. The challenged orders in this appeal must be reviewed by this court in the context of events forced by litigants who offered the court no reasonable choice." 573 F.2d, at 1126.

NOTES

1. The Supreme Court in the principal case upheld a maximum percentage allocation of the anadromous fish harvests to the Puget Sound tribes, but it found that the allocation could be reduced "in response to changing circumstances" in order to ensure that the tribes cannot harvest any more fish than are necessary to provide them with a "moderate living." What is the legal basis for the limitation? Did the Court assume that the Indian or federal representatives who negotiated the treaties understood that Indian fishing rights would decline as the tribes began to prosper? What constitutes a "moderate living?"

2. The right to "fish" is limited by a provision in the Stevens treaties: "Provided, however, that they shall not take shellfish from any beds staked or cultivated by citizens." Today, most tidelands where shellfish are found in the treaty area are privately owned. The state and commercial growers, asserting that the proviso was clear and broad on its face, argued that tribal gatherers had no right to harvest on private tidelands. The state also contended that tribes had no treaty right to harvest "deep-water" species of shellfish that were not harvested in shallower waters or tidelands. In a proceeding under the continuing jurisdiction ordered by Judge Boldt, tribes asserted rights to the shellfish harvested from tidelands and deep-water areas. In United States v. Washington, 157 F.3d 630 (9th Cir.1998), cert. denied 526 U.S. 1060 (1999), the Ninth Circuit applied the Indian law canons of construction to uphold broad tribal rights to harvest shellfish. The growers, as acknowledged by the tribes, have the exclusive right to harvest from beds, created by growers, on tidelands that did not support natural sustainable commercial production before the treaties. For natural beds where natural production was enhanced by growers, the growers were entitled to harvest all of the enhanced production. The tribes, however, had the right to harvest 50% of the natural production on these private lands. Mariel J. Combs, *United States v. Washington: The Boldt Decision Reincarnated*, 29 Envtl.L. 683 (1999).

The court in the shellfish case also ruled that tribes could fish in deep-water areas and that the right extended to all shellfish, broadly defined:

> The State of Washington argues that the Tribes' right to take shellfish is limited to those species of fish actually harvested by the Tribes prior to the signing of the Treaties. Specifically, Washington contends that the tribes have no Treaty right to certain "deep-water" species of shellfish that were not historically harvested in shallower waters and on tidelands. We respectfully reject this contention because it is plainly inconsistent with the language of the Treaties, the law of the case, and the intent and understanding of the signatory parties. [Citing authority].
>
> With all deference to the State, there is no language in the Treaties to support its position: The Treaties make no mention of any species-specific or technology-based restrictions on the Tribes' rights. The district court aptly noted that, had the Treaty parties intended

to limit the harvestable species, the parties would not have chosen the word "fish." The word "fish" has "perhaps the widest sweep of any word the drafters could have chosen." *Id*. Thus, the district court correctly chose not to "deviate from [the Treaties'] plain meaning." Id. at 643.

These rulings have proved to be of great importance to the tribes by clarifying that the Boldt decision extends far beyond salmon. Species such as Dungeness crab, shrimp, native littleneck, manila and geoduck clams, Pacific oysters, and other shellfish are now covered by the treaties. Tribes re entitled to harvest throughout Puget Sound and ocean coastal waters where tribes fished before the treaties. Since the shellfish decision, tribes have considerably expanded their fleets. As for financial returns, Dungeness crab revenues now exceed those for salmon, especially given the decline in the salmon runs.

3.   Salmon fishing, protected by seven treaties negotiated in 1854 and 1855, continues to be important to the western Washington tribes. However, the despoliation of Washington streams has severely reduced the number of fish available for the taking. Some of the historic runs have been destroyed altogether. A primary cause of this destruction has been environmental change accompanying non-Indian settlement of the Pacific Northwest.

The critical habitat needs of salmon have been severely impacted by economic development in western Washington. Over 141 dams have blocked access to large areas of former salmon habitat. Effluent from agricultural, industrial, and sewage disposal has degraded the water quality in salmon runs. Logging and irrigation practices have reduced streamside vegetation and withdrawn water, subjecting salmon to intolerably high summer water temperatures and smothering spawning beds under increased sediment loads. Direct gravel removal operations have reduced the amount of suitable spawning habitat. Road and industrial pollution have degraded the general aquatic ecosystem on which immature salmon depend for food. Finally, river channelization projects, through the smoothing of stream bottoms, have decreased available shelter needed by salmon. See, e.g., Michael C. Blumm and Andy Simrin, *The Unraveling of the Parity Promise: Hydropower, Salmon, and Endangered Species in the Columbia Basin,* 21 Envtl.L. 657 (1991).

Beginning in the late 1970s, the Northwest tribes began pursuing claims asserting an "environmental right" in the treaties that had been bifurcated from the original *United States v. Washington* litigation. Eventually, as recounted in the following opinion, the proceeding evolved into a challenge to the State of Washington's permitting and and construction of culverts, alleging that these structures blocked or impeded the passage of fish, destroyed fish habitat, and greatly reduced the size of Northwest Washington salmon runs.

UNITED STATES V. WASHINGTON

United States Court of Appeals, Ninth Circuit, 2016.
827 F.3d 836.

Before: WILLIAM A. FLETCHER and RONALD M. GOULD, CIRCUIT JUDGES, and DAVID A. EZRA, DISTRICT JUDGE.

Opinion by JUDGE W. FLETCHER

In 1854 and 1855, Indian tribes in the Pacific Northwest entered into a series of treaties, now known as the "Stevens Treaties," negotiated by Isaac I. Stevens, Superintendent of Indian Affairs and Governor of Washington Territory. * * *

In 2001, pursuant to an injunction previously entered in this long-running litigation, twenty-one Indian tribes ("tribes"), joined by the united states, filed a "request for determination"—in effect, a complaint—in the federal district court for the western district of Washington. * * *

The Tribes contended that Washington State had violated, and was continuing to violate, the Treaties by building and maintaining culverts that prevented mature salmon from returning from the sea to their spawning grounds; prevented smolt (juvenile salmon) from moving downstream and out to sea; and prevented very young salmon from moving freely to seek food and escape predators. * * * In 2013, the court issued an injunction ordering Washington to correct its offending culverts.

We affirm the decision of the district court.

I. Historical Background

For over a hundred years, there has been conflict between Washington and the Tribes over fishing rights under the Treaties. We recount here some of the most salient aspects of this history.

* * *

[The Court explained how, beginning soon after the treaties, non-Indian fisherman forced tribal fishers off the best fishing spots and introduced mechanized devices, such as fish wheels, all quickly leading to "domination of the prime fisheries of the region" by the whites. Beginning in the early 1900s, the state began regulating off-reservation Indian fishing, making it increasingly difficult for the tribes to exercise their off-reservation treaty fishing rights. In spite of the treaties, the state claimed jurisdiction over Indian fishers. By the 1950s, the Indian share of the salmon fishery was just 6%. In the 1960s, tribes reacted to the state's "military-style campaign" of enforcement, which included "tear gas, billy clubs, and guns," with demonstrations and other activism. The conflicts, sometimes leading to violence, came to be called "the fish wars.]

In 1970, in an effort to resolve the persistent conflict between the State and the Indians, the United States brought suit against the State on behalf of the Tribes. The dispute now before us is part of that litigation.

II.   Anadromous Fisheries and Washington's Barrier Culverts

Anadromous fish, such as salmon, hatch and spend their early lives in fresh water, migrate to the ocean to mature, and return to their waters of origin to spawn. Washington is home to several anadromous fisheries, of which the salmon fishery is by far the most important. Before the arrival of white settlers, returning salmon were abundant in the streams and rivers of the Pacific Northwest. Present-day Indian tribes in the Pacific Northwest eat salmon as an important part of their diet, use salmon in religious and cultural ceremonies, and fish for salmon commercially.

Roads often cross streams that salmon and other anadromous fish use for spawning. Road builders construct culverts to allow the streams to flow underneath roads, but many culverts do not allow fish to pass easily. Sometimes they do not allow fish passage at all. A "barrier culvert" is a culvert that inhibits or prevents fish passage. Road builders can avoid constructing barrier culverts by building roads away from streams, by building bridges that entirely span streams, or by building culverts that allow unobstructed fish passage.

Four state agencies are responsible for building and managing Washington's roads and the culverts that pass under them. * * *

Of these, [Washington State Department of Transportation "WSDOT"], is the agency responsible for Washington's highways, builds and maintains by far the most roads and culverts.

III. Earlier Proceedings

In 1970, the United States, on its own behalf and as trustee for Pacific Northwest tribes, sued Washington in federal court in the Western District of Washington. The United States sought declaratory and injunctive relief based on the fishing clause of the Treaties. *United States v. State of Washington*, 384 F. Supp. 312 (W.D. Wash. 1974) ("Washington I"). In what has come to be known as the "Boldt decision," District Judge George H. Boldt divided the case into two phases. Phase I was to determine what portion, if any, of annually harvestable fish were guaranteed to the Tribes by the fishing clause. Phase II was to determine whether the fishing clause extends to hatchery fish, and whether it requires Washington to prevent environmental degradation within the Case Area.

In Phase I, Judge Boldt held that the phrase "the right of taking fish . . . in common with all citizens" gives the Tribes the right to take up to fifty percent of the harvestable fish in the Case Area, subject to the right of non-treaty fishers to do the same. *Id.* The Supreme Court affirmed in

Washington v. Washington State Commercial Passenger Fishing Vessel Ass'n, 443 U.S. 658 (1979) ("*Fishing Vessel*"). * * *

In 1976, the United States initiated Phase II of the litigation, asking for a declaratory judgment clarifying the Tribes' rights with respect to * * * the "environmental" issue.

Sitting en banc, we affirmed in part and vacated in part. *United States v. State of Washington*, 759 F.2d 1353 (9th Cir.1985) (en banc) ("*Washington III*"). * * *

We vacated the court's decision on the environmental issue. We held that the issue was too broad and varied to be resolved in a general and undifferentiated fashion, and that the issue of human-caused environmental degradation must be resolved in the context of particularized disputes. * * *

Although we vacated the district court's decision with respect to the environmental issue, we made clear that we were not absolving Washington of environmental obligations under the fishing clause. We concluded the section of our opinion devoted to the environmental issue by emphasizing that Washington "is bound by the treaty." *Id.*

Judge Boldt's 1974 decision authorized the parties to invoke the continuing jurisdiction of the district court to resolve disputes "concerning the subject matter of this case." * * *

In 2001, the Tribes filed a Request for Determination ("Request"), seeking "to enforce a duty upon the State of Washington to refrain from constructing and maintaining culverts under State roads that degrade fish habitat so that adult fish production is reduced." The Tribes sought a permanent injunction from the district court "requiring Washington to identify and then to open culverts under state roads and highways that obstruct fish passage, for fish runs returning to or passing through the usual and accustomed grounds and stations of the plaintiff tribes." [The United States joined the Tribes' request.]

* * *

The district court granted summary judgment in favor of the Tribes and the United States, concluding that the dispute involved the kind of "concrete facts" that were lacking in *Washington III*. * * * It held, second, that "the State of Washington currently owns and operates culverts that violate this duty."

The district court conducted a bench trial in 2009 and 2010 to determine the appropriate remedy. After failed efforts to reach a settlement, the court issued both a Memorandum and Decision and a Permanent Injunction. In its Memorandum and Decision, issued in 2013, the court found that Governor Stevens had assured the Tribes that they would have an adequate supply of salmon forever. The court wrote:

> During the negotiations leading up to the signing of the treaties, Governor Isaac Stevens and other negotiators assured the Tribes of their continued access to their usual fisheries. Governor Stevens assured the Tribes that even after they ceded huge quantities of land, they would still be able to feed themselves and their families forever. As Governor Stevens stated, "I want that you shall not have simply food and drink now but that you may have them forever."

(Emphasis added.)

The court found that salmon stocks in the Case Area have declined "alarmingly" since the Treaties were signed, and "dramatically" since 1985. The court wrote, "A primary cause of this decline is habitat degradation, both in breeding habitat (freshwater) and feeding habitat (freshwater and marine areas) . . . .One cause of the degradation of salmon habitat is . . . culverts which do not allow the free passage of both adult and juvenile salmon upstream and downstream." The "consequent reduction in tribal harvests has damaged tribal economies, has left individual tribal members unable to earn a living by fishing, and has caused cultural and social harm to the Tribes in addition to the economic harm."

The court ordered the State * * * , in consultation with the Tribes and the United States, to prepare within six months a current list of all state-owned barrier culverts within the Case Area. It ordered WSDNR, State Parks, and WDFW-to correct certain listed culverts by the end of October 2016 and many of its barrier culverts within seventeen years, and to correct the remainder only at the end of the culverts' natural life or in connection with independently undertaken highway projects. * * *

* * *

V.   Discussion

* * *

A.   Washington's Duty under the Treaties

The fishing clause of the Stevens Treaties guarantees to the Tribes a right to engage in off-reservation fishing. * * *

Washington concedes that the clause guarantees to the Tribes the right to take up to fifty percent of the fish available for harvest, but it contends that the clause imposes no obligation on the State to ensure that any fish will, in fact, be available.

In its brief to us, Washington denies any treaty-based duty to avoid blocking salmon-bearing streams:

[T]he Tribes here argue for a treaty right that finds no basis in the plain language or historical interpretation of the treaties. On its face, the right of taking fish in common with all citizens does not include a right to prevent the State from making land use decisions that could incidentally impact fish. Rather, such an interpretation is contrary to the treaties' principal purpose of opening up the region to settlement.

At oral argument, Washington even more forthrightly denied any treaty-based duty. Washington contended that it has the right, consistent with the Treaties, to block every salmon-bearing stream feeding into Puget Sound:

The Court: Would the State have the right, consistent with the treaty, to dam every salmon stream into Puget Sound?

Answer: Your honor, we would never and could never do that. . . .

The Court: . . . I'm asking a different question. Would you have the right to do that under the treaty?

Answer: Your honor, the treaty would not prohibit that[.]

The Court: So, let me make sure I understand your answer. You're saying, consistent with the treaties that Governor Stevens entered into with the Tribes, you could block every salmon stream in the Sound?

Answer: Your honor, the treaties would not prohibit that[.]

The State misconstrues the Treaties.

We have long construed treaties between the United States and Indian tribes in favor of the Indians. Chief Justice Marshall wrote in the third case of the Marshall Trilogy, "The language used in treaties with the Indians should never be construed to their prejudice." *Worcester v. Georgia*, 31 U.S. 515, 582 (1832). [Discussion of further authority on the canons of construction.]

The Supreme Court has interpreted the Stevens Treaties on several occasions. In affirming Judge Boldt's decision, the Court wrote:

[I]t is the intention of the parties, and not solely that of the superior side, that must control any attempt to interpret the treaties. When Indians are involved, this Court has long given special meaning to this rule. It has held that the United States, as the party with the presumptively superior negotiating skills and superior knowledge of the language in which the treaty is recorded, has a responsibility to avoid taking advantage of the other side.

> "[T]he treaty must therefore be construed, not according to the
> technical meaning of its words to learned lawyers, but in the sense
> in which they would naturally be understood by the Indians."
> *Jones v. Meehan,*175 U.S. 1, 11. This rule, in fact, has thrice been
> explicitly relied on by the Court in broadly interpreting these very
> treaties in the Indians' favor. *Tulee v. Washington,* 315 U.S. 681
> [1947]; *Seufort Bros. Co. v. United States,* 249 U.S. 194 [1919];
> *United States v. Winans,* 198 U.S. 371 [1905]. See also
> *Washington v. Yakima Indian Nation,* 439 U.S. 463, 484 [1979].

Fishing Vessel, 443 U.S. at 675–76.

Washington has a remarkably one-sided view of the Treaties. In its
brief, Washington characterizes the "treaties' principal purpose" as
"opening up the region to settlement." Opening up the Northwest for white
settlement was indeed the principal purpose of the United States. But it
was most certainly not the principal purpose of the Indians. Their
principal purpose was to secure a means of supporting themselves once the
Treaties took effect.

Salmon were a central concern. An adequate supply of salmon was
"not much less necessary to the existence of the Indians than the
atmosphere they breathed." *Winans,* 198 U.S. at 381. Richard White, an
expert on the history of the American West and Professor of American
History at Stanford University, wrote in a declaration filed in the district
court that, during the negotiations for the Point-No-Point Treaty, a
Skokomish Indian worried aloud about "how they were to feed themselves
once they ceded so much land to the whites." Professor White wrote, to the
same effect, that during negotiations at Neah Bay, Makah Indians "raised
questions about the role that fisheries were to play in their future." In
response to these concerns, Governor Stevens repeatedly assured the
Indians that there always would be an adequate supply of fish. Professor
White wrote that Stevens told the Indians during negotiations for the
Point Elliott Treaty, "I want that you shall not have simply food and drink
now but that you may have them forever." During negotiations for the
Point-No-Point Treaty, Stevens said, "This paper is such as a man would
give to his children and I will tell you why. This paper gives you a home.
Does not a father give his children a home? . . . This paper secures your fish.
Does not a father give food to his children?" *Fishing Vessel,* 443 U.S. at 667
n.11.

The Indians did not understand the Treaties to promise that they
would have access to their usual and accustomed fishing places, but with
a qualification that would allow the government to diminish or destroy the
fish runs. Governor Stevens did not make, and the Indians did not
understand him to make, such a cynical and disingenuous promise. The
Indians reasonably understood Governor Stevens to promise not only that

they would have access to their usual and accustomed fishing places, but also that there would be fish sufficient to sustain them. They reasonably understood that they would have, in Stevens' words, "food and drink . . . forever." * * *

Even if Governor Stevens had not explicitly promised that "this paper secures your fish," and that there would be food "forever," we would infer such a promise. In *Winters v. United States*, 207 U.S. 564 (1908), the treaty creating the Fort Belknap Reservation in Montana did not include an explicit reservation of water for use on the reserved lands, but the Supreme Court inferred a reservation of water sufficient to support the tribe. The purpose of the treaty was to reserve land on which the Indians could become farmers. Without a reservation of water, the "lands were arid, and . . . practically valueless." *Id.* at 576. "[B]etween two inferences, one of which would support the purpose of the agreement and the other impair or defeat it," the Court chose the former. *Id.* at 577.

* * *

Thus, even if Governor Stevens had made no explicit promise, we would infer, as in *Winters* and *Adair*, a promise to "support the purpose" of the Treaties. * * *

In *Washington III*, we vacated the district court's declaration of a broad and undifferentiated obligation to prevent environmental degradation. We did not dispute that the State had environmental obligations, but, in the exercise of discretion under the Declaratory Judgment Act, we declined to sustain the sweeping declaratory judgment issued by the district court. * * *

Salmon now available for harvest are not sufficient to provide a "moderate living" to the Tribes. *Fishing Vessel*, 443 U.S. at 686. The district court found that "[t]he reduced abundance of salmon and the consequent reduction in tribal harvests has damaged tribal economies, has left individual tribal members unable to earn a living by fishing, and has caused cultural and social harm to the Tribes in addition to the economic harm." The court found, further, that "[m]any members of the Tribes would engage in more commercial and subsistence salmon fisheries if more fish were available."

We therefore conclude that in building and maintaining barrier culverts within the Case Area, Washington has violated, and is continuing to violate, its obligation to the Tribes under the Treaties.

[The Court also ruled that the United States was not barred from bringing this action by waiver, latches, or estoppel; and that the State was barred by federal sovereign immunity from bringing a "cross-request"—in effect, a counterclaim—against the United States.]

* * *

D. Injunction

The district court held a trial in 2009 and 2010 to determine the appropriate remedy for Washington's violation of the Treaties. At the time of trial, there were 1,114 state-owned culverts in the Case Area. At least 886 of them blocked access to "significant habitat," defined as 200 linear meters or more of salmon habitat upstream from the culvert to the first natural passage barrier. More barrier culverts were identified or constructed within the Case Area after 2009. * * *

In 1997,* * * WSDOT reported to the Washington State legislature that WSDOT culverts blocked 249 linear miles of stream, comprising over 1.6 million square meters of salmon habitat, which they estimated was sufficient to produce 200,000 adult salmon per year. Based on * * * records, the district court found that at the time of trial, state-owned barrier culverts in the Case Area blocked access to approximately 1,000 miles of stream, comprising almost 5 million square meters of salmon habitat.

The district court issued a permanent injunction in 2013, on the same day it issued its Memorandum and Decision. * * *

* * *

* * * Washington now objects on several grounds to the injunction that was formulated without its participation. Washington specifically objects (1) that the injunction is too "broad," (2) that the district court did not "defer to the State's expertise," (3) that the court did not properly consider costs and equitable principles, (4) and that the injunction "impermissibly and significantly intrudes into state government operations.". Finally, Washington objects that its four specific objections support a contention that the court's injunction is inconsistent with "federalism principles.". We consider the State's objections in turn.

1. Breadth of the Injunction

Washington contends in its brief that "[t]he Tribes *presented no evidence* that state-owned culverts are a significant cause of the decline [in salmon]. . . . Despite that *complete failure of proof*, the district court found that state-owned culverts 'have a significant total impact on salmon production.'"). Washington contends, further, that the district court "ordered replacement of nearly every state-owned barrier culvert within the case area without any specific showing that those culverts have significantly diminished fish runs or tribal fisheries, or that replacing them will meaningfully improve runs."

Washington misrepresents the evidence and mischaracterizes the district court's order.

Contrary to the State's contention, the Tribes presented extensive evidence in support of the court's conclusion that state-owned barrier culverts have a significant adverse effect on salmon. The 1997 report prepared for the Washington State Legislature by two of the defendants in this case, WDFW [Washington Department of Fish and Wildlife]and WSDOT, stated, "Fish passage at human made barriers such as road culverts is one of the most recurrent and correctable obstacles to healthy salmonid stocks in Washington." The report concluded:

A total potential spawning and rearing area of 1,619,839 m² (249 linear miles) is currently blocked by WSDOT culverts on the 177 surveyed streams requiring barrier resolution; this is enough wetted stream area to produce 200,000 adult salmonids annually. These estimates would all increase when considering the additional 186 barriers that did not have full habitat assessments.

* * *

Based on later WDFW figures, the district court found that at the time of trial state-owned barrier culverts in the Case Area blocked access to approximately 1,000 linear miles of stream, comprising almost 5 million square meters of salmon habitat. These figures, taken together with the 1997 figures supplied by WDFW and WSDOT, indicate that the total habitat blocked by state-owned barrier culverts in the Case Area is capable of producing several times the 200,000 mature salmon specified in the 1997 report.

Witnesses at trial repeatedly described benefits to salmon resulting from correction of barrier culverts. One example is evidence presented by Mike McHenry, habitat program manager for the Lower Elwha Klallam Tribe. In his written testimony, McHenry described several studies. One was a 2003 study of culvert removal projects on the Stillaguamish River that opened up 19 linear kilometers of salmon habitat. According to the study, over 250 adult coho salmon were observed spawning in the newly accessible habitat in each of the two years immediately after the completion of the projects. Based on his own experience as habitat manager for the tribe, McHenry wrote that removal of barrier culverts on the Lower Elwha River had had a similar effect. In McHenry's view, "The systematic correction of barrier culverts is an important place to focus restoration efforts." He wrote, further, "The correction of human caused barriers is generally recognized as the second highest priority for restoring habitats used by Pacific salmon (following the protection of existing functional habitats)."

* * *

The district court's injunction took into account the facts that culvert correction is not the only factor in salmon recovery; that some culverts block more habitat than others; and that some culverts are more expensive to correct than others. The court ordered correction of high-priority culverts—those blocking 200 linear meters or more of upstream habitat—within seventeen years. For low-priority culverts—those blocking less than 200 linear meters of upstream habitat—the court ordered correction only at the end of the useful life of the existing culvert, or when an independently undertaken highway project would require replacement of the culvert. Further, recognizing the likelihood that accelerated replacement of some high-priority culverts will not be cost-effective, the court allowed the State to defer correction of high-priority culverts accounting for up to ten percent of the total blocked upstream habitat, and to correct those culverts on the more lenient schedule of the low-priority culverts. Wagner's evidence indicates that if the sole criterion for choosing deferred culverts is the amount of blocked habitat, there will be approximately 230 deferred culverts. If cost of correction of particular culverts is added as a criterion, there will be a somewhat smaller number of deferred culverts.

In sum, we disagree with Washington's contention that the Tribes "presented no evidence," and that there was a "complete failure of proof," that state-owned barrier culverts have a substantial adverse effect on salmon * * * We also disagree with Washington's contention that the court ordered correction of "nearly every state-owned barrier culvert" without "any specific showing" that such correction will "meaningfully improve runs." The State's own evidence shows that hundreds of thousands of adult salmon will be produced by opening up the salmon habitat that is currently blocked by the State's barrier culverts. Finally, we disagree with Washington's contention that the court's injunction indiscriminately orders correction of "nearly every state-owned barrier culvert" in the Case Area. The court's order carefully distinguishes between high- and low-priority culverts based on the amount of upstream habitat culvert correction will open up. The order then allows for a further distinction, to be drawn by WSDOT in consultation with the United States and the Tribes, between those high-priority culverts that must be corrected within seventeen years and those that may be corrected on the more lenient schedule applicable to the low-priority culverts.

2.   Deference to the State's Expertise

Washington contends that the district court made a clearly erroneous finding of fact, concluding that correction of human-caused barriers is the highest priority in habitat restoration. It contends, further, that this finding led the court to ignore the expert testimony presented by both the State and the Tribes. * * *

Contrary to Washington's contention, the district court had a sophisticated record-based understanding of the various causes of the decline of salmon in the Case Area, of what could be achieved by the correction of state-owned barrier culverts, and of the limitations on what could be achieved by culvert correction. The court's injunction is carefully crafted to reflect that understanding.

3.   Costs and Equitable Principles

Washington contends that the district court's injunction fails properly to take costs into account, and that its injunction is inconsistent with equitable principles.

a.   Costs

Washington writes in its brief that correction of WSDOT barrier culverts will cost approximately $1.88 billion over the course of the seventeen-year schedule ordered by the court, or "roughly $ 117 million per year of the injunction." (Using Washington's own estimates, a correct calculation is actually $110.6 million per year rather than $ 117 million.) Washington's estimated total cost is based on an assumption of 817 corrected culverts, at an average correction cost of $2.3 million per culvert.

Washington's cost estimates are not supported by the evidence. Washington contended at trial, as it now contends to us, that the average cost to replace a WSDOT barrier culvert would be $2.3 million. But the district court did not accept this estimate. The court found that "the actual cost of construction for twelve WSDOT stream simulation culvert projects completed prior to the 2009 trial ranged from $413,000 to $1,674,411; the average cost for the twelve was $658,639 each." * * *

* * *

b.   Equitable Principles

Washington makes one specific objection based on equitable principles. It objects that the court abused its discretion in requiring that "the State alone," rather than State in conjunction with the United States, be "burdened with the entire cost of culvert repair. We disagree. The court's order required correction of only those barrier culverts that were built and maintained by the State. It was not an abuse of discretion to require the State to pay for correction of its own barrier culverts.

Further, we note more generally that the district court did consider equitable principles, and concluded that those principles favored the Tribes and the citizens of the State. The court wrote:

> The Tribes and their individual members have been harmed economically, socially, educationally, and culturally by the greatly reduced salmon harvests that have resulted from State-created or State-maintained fish passage barriers.

> This injury is ongoing, as efforts by the State to correct the barrier culverts have been insufficient. . . . Remedies at law are

inadequate as monetary damages will not adequately compensate the Tribes and their individual members for these harms. . . .

The balance of hardships tips steeply toward the Tribes in this matter. The promise made to the Tribes that the Stevens Treaties would protect their source of food and commerce was crucial in obtaining their assent to the Treaties' provisions. . . . Equity favors requiring the State of Washington to keep the promises upon which the Tribes relied when they ceded huge tracts of land by way of the Treaties.

. . .

The public interest will not be disserved by an injunction. To the contrary, it is in the public's interest, as well as the Tribes' to accelerate the pace of barrier correction. All fishermen, not just Tribal fishermen, will benefit from the increased production of salmon. . . . The general public will benefit from the enhancement of the resource and the increased economic return from fishing in the State of Washington. The general public will also benefit from the environmental benefits of salmon habitat restoration.

5.   Federalism Principles

Washington contends, based on the four specific objections just reviewed, that the district court's injunction violates principles of federalism. Washington asserts four principles of federalism:

First, the remedy must be no broader than necessary to address the federal law violation. Second, courts must grant deference to a state's institutional competence and subject matter expertise. Third, courts must take cost into consideration and not substitute their budgetary judgment for that of the state. And finally, relief must be fashioned so that it is the least intrusive into state governmental affairs. The district court's injunction here contravenes all of these principles.

We will not quarrel here with these principles, stated at this level of generality. However, for the reasons given above, we have concluded that the district court's injunction violates none of them.

Further, a federalism-based objection to an injunction enforcing Indian treaty rights should not be viewed in the same light as an objection to a more conventional structural injunction. * * *

The district court in *Fishing Vessel* had entered a series of detailed injunctions implementing its holding that the Treaties entitled the Tribes to take up to fifty percent of harvestable salmon in any given year. Washington strenuously resisted, with the result that the district court effectively took over much of the State's management of the salmon fishery. Washington objected both to the district court's interpretation of the Treaties, and to the court's intrusion into its affairs. The Supreme Court affirmed the district court's holding on the meaning of the Treaties. It then rejected, in no uncertain terms, federalism-based objections to the injunctions enforcing the Treaties:

> Whether [Washington] Game and Fisheries may be ordered actually to promulgate regulations having effect as a matter of state law may well be doubtful. But the District Court may prescind that problem by assuming direct supervision of the fisheries if state recalcitrance or state-law barriers should be continued. *It is therefore absurd to argue . . . both that the state agencies may not be ordered to implement the decree and also that the District Court may not itself issue detailed remedial orders as a substitute for state supervision.*

Fishing Vessel, 443 U.S. at 695 (emphasis added).

Conclusion

In sum, we conclude that in building and maintaining barrier culverts Washington has violated, and continues to violate, its obligation to the Tribes under the fishing clause of the Treaties. The United States has not waived the rights of the Tribes under the Treaties, and has not waived its own sovereign immunity by bringing suit on behalf of the Tribes. The district court did not abuse its discretion in enjoining Washington to correct most of its high-priority barrier culverts within seventeen years, and to correct the remainder at the end of their natural life or in the course of a road construction project undertaken for independent reasons.

AFFIRMED.

NOTES

1.   As of publication of this edition, Washington has the option of petitioning for a hearing en banc by the full Ninth Circuit and pursuing a petition for certiorari to the Supreme Court.

2.   The traditional canons of construction in Indian law play a major role here, as they did in the original Boldt decision. The court stated that Isaac Stevens had "explicitly promised that 'this paper secures your fish.'" Does Stevens' language as quoted in the decision support that conclusion? Does that language justify the "environmental right" announced by the court? The opinion also says that, even without such a promise, the court "would infer such a promise." Do you agree with that? As a general matter, does this case demonstrate the value of the canons of construction or does it show that they are dangerous, with the potential of creating sweeping rights such as those announced in the Boldt decision and the culvert case?

3.   How would you balance the interests in determining whether to grant equitable relief? The Ninth Circuit approved the trial court's conclusion that "the balance of hardship tips steeply toward the Tribes in this matter." Does this give fair weight to the broad interests of the citizenry? How much weight would you give to the environmental benefits received by the citizenry? How much weight would you give to the costs of complying with the injunction, which must be borne by Washington state citizens?

4.   At their essence, both the Boldt decision and the culvert case conclude that under these circumstances tribal sovereignty, as fortified by federal treaties, trumps state sovereignty. Wildlife management has always been considered to be a matter usually left to state police power. Here there are few if any words in existing federal statutes or treaties that speak specifically to a 50% tribal share or an environmental right. Is it dangerous to leave so much to judicial rulings when matters are this sensitive? Put another way, it may be there is no basis in existing American law for reaching results of this kind and magnitude except for Indian treaties. If that is true, have these courts simply taken Indian law too far?

5.   The culvert case is one example of how tribes have put a great amount of energy into protecting their treaty rights by taking actions to protect and restore fisheries habitat. The tribes and their intertribal council, the Northwest Indian Fisheries Commission, have developed impressive scientific and management expertise. They have participated in many watershed restoration projects. In time it became necessary to take on the dams found on the rivers of the Pacific Northwest.

In the past two decades, the field of natural resources management has evolved to include the once-unthinkable notion of using dam removal as a way to achieve environmental objectives. The Pacific Northwest, facing the impacts of dams on migrating salmon, has been especially active and tribes have played a major role. See, Michael C Blumm and Andrew B. Erickson, *Dam Removal in the Pacific Northwest: Lessons for the Nation,* 42 Envtl.L. 1043 (2014). The most dramatic removals to date took place on the Olympic Peninsula in 2011 when the two dams on the Elwha River were breached, allowing the legendary Elwha salmon runs to return to the rich habitat in the high mountains of the Olympic National Park for the first time in a century. The Lower Elwha Klallam Tribe took a leadership role in the removals. Julia Guarino, *Tribal Advocacy and the Art of Dam Removal: The Lower Elwha Klallam and the Elwha Dams,* 42 Am. Indian L.Rev. 114 (2013). The Yakama nation accomplished the removal of another major impoundment, Condit Dam on the White Salmon River, also in 2011.

If accomplished, the removal of four dams on the Klamath River in Southern Oregon and Northwest California would apparently amount to the largest dam removal in history. The effort also called for extensive habitat restoration throughout the watershed. Three tribes, the Yurok and Karuk in California and the Klamath in Oregon, joined forces and have leadership roles in a coalition of some 50 entities, including the states of Oregon and California, several federal agencies, agricultural associations, tribes, counties, commercial fishing organizations, and conservation groups to restore the once-robust salmon runs in the Klamath. See, e.g., Blumm & Erickson, supra, at 1084–94.

The ambitious effort has had a number of fits and starts, but continues to hold great promise. The 2014 agreement between the Klamath Tribes and irrigators in connection with the Klamath River Basin Adjudication has already established significant instream flows and irrigation reductions in the upper watershed. The dam removal proponents, in spite of the large and influential coalition, have found it challenging to move the proposal in Congress. Progress, however has been made and, as of the printing of this edition, success seems more probable than not. See, Bettina Boxall, *Pact reached to remove four Klamath River dams that block salmon migration*, L.A. Times, Apr. 6, 2016; Office of the Secretary, U.S. Department of the Interior, Press Release, "Two new Klamath Basin Agreements carve out the path for dam removal and Provide Key Benefits for Irrigators" Apr. 6, 2016.

2. GREAT LAKES

Litigation similar to the Washington dispute concerning Indian fishing rights in the Great Lakes resulted in years of judicial proceedings. Three years after the Washington state Indian fishing rights litigation began, the United States sued the state of Michigan on behalf of the Bay Mills Indian Community to protect the tribe's rights to fish in waters of the Great Lakes vested in the tribe by virtue of the Treaty of 1836 with the Ottawa and Chippewa Nations. United States v. Michigan, 471 F.Supp. 192 (W.D.Mich.1979). Article XIII of the 1836 treaty reads: "The Indians stipulate for the right of hunting on the lands ceded, with the other usual privileges of occupancy, until the land is required for settlement."

Particularly at issue was the Indians' right to fish with gill nets contrary to state law. The district court held in 1979 that, unlike the treaty involved in the *Puyallup* cases, the absence of "in common" language in the relevant treaties indicated that the fishing right was not to be shared with non-Indian state citizens. Thus, "the State of Michigan does not have any right to regulate Ottawa and Chippewa Indian fishing on the Great Lakes in exercise of their rights." Id. at 270. Having found that the state had no power to limit Indian fishing rights in any way, the district court enjoined Michigan officials from interfering with Indian gill net fishing and enjoined state judges from proceeding any further in related cases.

The United States Court of Appeals for the Sixth Circuit stayed the lower court's injunctions, reasoning "that unless the order is stayed there is a strong possibility that the fishery, the fish supply and spawning grounds in Grand Traverse Bay will be irreparably damaged or destroyed by continued intensive gill net fishing." United States v. Michigan, 623 F.2d 448, 449 (6th Cir.1980). Secretary of the Interior Cecil Andrus then issued comprehensive regulations governing Indian fishing in the Great

Lakes. Consequently, the circuit court modified its stay of the lower court's injunction to allow treaty fishing under the Secretary of the Interior's regulations and remanded the matter to the district court to consider the regulations. When Interior Secretary James Watt announced his decision not to renew the federal regulations upon their expiration in deference to the state's regulatory authority, the state requested the Sixth Circuit to set aside the earlier remand order. The tribes responded by adopting the federal regulations as part of their conservation codes.

The Sixth Circuit rebuked the Secretary for letting the regulations lapse, saying that "protection of [Indian treaty] rights is the solemn obligation of the federal government and no principle of federalism requires the federal government to defer to the states in connection with the protection of those rights." United States v. Michigan, 653 F.2d 277, 279 (6th Cir.1981). In the absence of federal regulations, the court said that "[o]nly upon a finding of necessity, irreparable harm and the absence of effective Indian tribal self-regulation should the District Court sanction and permit state regulation of gill net fishing." Id. at 279. Upon remand, a weary federal district court judge declared as follows:

> [T]he inability of the parties to negotiate, or to litigate in the District Court, has meant that this Court must continue to assume a role in Great Lakes fishing. The initiation of "hostile flanking actions," state prosecutions of treaty fishers for compliance with federal court orders, various attempts to avoid the court system by seeking political solutions in Washington, and the frequent trips to the Sixth Circuit Court have only served to postpone and delay these already lengthy proceedings. While not wanting to become a "perpetual fish master," this court must continue its role in this dispute, if the need arises.

United States v. Michigan, 520 F.Supp. 207, 211 n.5 (W.D.Mich.1981), cert. denied 454 U.S. 1124 (1981).

As in the *Washington* case, the court and the parties finally realized that the most important question to be determined was the portion of the fishery to which the Indians were entitled. The district judge appointed a special master with the mission of resolving the issues in the case. In 1985, intense negotiations produced an agreement among representatives for all parties, including the tribes, the state and federal governments, and several sport and commercial fishing interests. One of the tribal parties did not ratify the agreement but after a trial the court adopted the terms of the agreement as its order, making it binding on all parties.

The order provided for an allocation of the fisheries in Lakes Michigan, Huron, and Superior among state-licensed commercial fishers and the Sault Ste. Marie Tribe of Chippewa Indians, the Bay Mills Indian Community, and the Grand Traverse Band of Ottawa and Chippewa

Indians. Sport fishing for lake trout and coho salmon was accommodated by setting aside certain refuges that are closed to commercial fishing. State-licensed commercial fishers and tribal fishers were required to curtail fishing in several other areas.

Under the 1985 agreement, the State of Michigan was required to close some areas to non-Indian commercial fishing and to reduce the allowable catch in order to carry out the court's decision. State-issued commercial fishing licenses were greatly reduced in value. For a time the state voluntarily compensated the adversely affected commercial fishers. The holders of commercial licenses then sued the state claiming a breach of contract to make payments and denial of equal protection. The plaintiffs lost on all points, the court holding that the rights of the Chippewa are superior to all other fishers. Bigelow v. Michigan Dep't of Natural Resources, 727 F.Supp. 346 (W.D.Mich.1989), vacated by 970 F.2d 154 (6th Cir.1992) (plaintiffs failed to exhaust state remedies). After 15 years of dissatisfaction and difficulties with the 1985 decree, the State of Michigan and the tribes both agreed to a new consent decree in 2000, which recognizes the Chippewa Ottawa's Resource Authority as an inter-tribal regulatory agency with authority over the exercise of Indian treaty rights. See *Seven Sovereigns Sign 2000 Consent Decree*, 3 Tribal Fishing 1 (2000).

In 2007, the State of Michigan and the five federally recognized tribes that were signatories to the 1836 Treaty of Washington entered into a consent decree relating to *inland* usufructuary rights to hunt, fish, and gather on lands within the ceded territories. The agreement defined the lands that are available for the exercise of the inland right. *See* 2007 Consent Decree § VII. The area in which Indian treaty rights practitioners may engage in off-reservation hunting, fishing, and gathering includes virtually all public lands within the ceded territory (the ceded territory is about one-third of the entire State of Michigan). Within this land area are thousands of acres of public lands. The 2007 Consent Decree easily amounts to the largest land area in which Indians may engage in treaty rights in the eastern half of the United States. Moreover, unlike the other agreements in Michigan relating to treaty rights, the 2007 Consent Decree does not expire.

Like tribes in the Northwest and in Michigan, six bands of Chippewa (Anishinabe) located in northern Wisconsin have pursued lengthy litigation over their off-reservation hunting, fishing and gathering rights under their treaties of 1837, 1842, and 1854 with the United States government. Under these treaties, the Chippewa ceded roughly 27 million acres in northern Wisconsin, Minnesota, and upper Michigan to the United States, in exchange for reservations for individual bands on much smaller parcels of land. In addition, the Chippewa received cash, annuities, goods, and most importantly, off-reservation subsistence rights. Under the treaties, the Chippewa reserved "[t]he privilege of hunting, fishing, and gathering the wild rice, upon the lands, the rivers and the lakes included in the territory ceded." These off-reservation rights were guaranteed to the Chippewa "during the pleasure of the President of the United States," a term the Indians understood as meaning that so long as "they behaved themselves," they would not be disturbed. United States v. Bouchard, 464 F.Supp. 1316, 1327 (W.D.Wis.1978), reversed 700 F.2d 341, cert. denied 464 U.S. 805 (1983), quoting Benjamin Armstrong, Early Life Among the Indians 12 (1892).

Despite the treaty language, Wisconsin state officials sought to confine the Chippewa Indians to resources on their reservations as more whites began to populate the northern parts of the state at the turn of the century. Under the Wisconsin Supreme Court's decision in State v. Morrin, 117 N.W. 1006 (Wis. 1908), that the Chippewa's off-reservation fishing rights had been abrogated by Wisconsin statehood (a decision that flew squarely in the face of *Winans,* supra), any Indian who ventured off the reservation to exercise treaty rights risked criminal prosecution by state authorities.

Buoyed by the rising national tide of Indian activism, the accompanying revival of tribal culture and traditions occurring throughout Indian country, and several favorable federal court rulings in other states, the Chippewa went to court in the 1970s seeking to challenge Wisconsin's long-standing denial of their rights under their treaties.

In the first stage of the litigation, *United States v. Bouchard,* supra, Judge James Doyle (who later became as notorious and vilified by non-Indians in Wisconsin as Judge Boldt, in Washington) first held that the 1854 Treaty reserving lands for the Chippewa in Wisconsin had extinguished the usufructuary rights of several bands to the ceded lands created in the 1837 and 1842 treaties, 464 F.Supp. 1316 (W.D.Wis.1978). In Lac Courte Oreilles Band v. Voigt, 700 F.2d 341 (7th Cir.1983), (*LCO I*), the Seventh Circuit reversed, holding that the treaty rights of the Wisconsin Chippewa had not been extinguished. It found that an 1850 removal order by President Zachary Taylor, purporting to remove the tribes in exercise of the "Presidential pleasure" reserved in the treaties exceeded the scope of presidential authority under the 1837 and 1842 treaties, and was therefore invalid. A shock wave ran through Wisconsin. Local opposition took the form of protest, ranging from nonviolent to confrontational. Physical and verbal racial assaults took place. Non-Indians angered by the decision marketed "Treaty Beer" to raise money for litigation to overturn the decision and for lobbying Congress to abrogate the 1837 and 1842 treaties.

The United States Supreme Court declined to review the *LCO I* holding. 464 U.S. 805 (1983). On remand, Judge Doyle held that the holding concerning treaty rights and privately owned property meant that the tribes could exercise usufructuary rights only on lands not sold to private parties prior to the date of the decision. In *LCO II*, the 7th Circuit rejected this approach and held that treaty rights could be exercised on all public lands within Wisconsin, regardless of past ownership, 760 F.2d 177 (7th Cir.1985).

On the next remand, Judge Doyle, who was fast becoming an expert on Chippewa treaties, dealt with the issue of the nature and scope of the treaty rights to off-reservation resources. The court determined that the treaty rights extended to all forms of animal and plant life which had been historically utilized. These materials could be sold to non-Indians, and harvested using modern distribution and sales methods. The judge refused to allocate resources on a percentage basis as was done in the Washington litigation, as no showing had been made that the resources were scarce. The court also held that the state could impose conservation restrictions if they were necessary and reasonable to conserve resources, 653 F.Supp. 1420 (W.D.Wis.1987) (*LCO III*).

Then, in *LCO IV*, Judge Barbara Crabb, who had replaced Judge Doyle after his death, determined that state regulation was proper not only for conservation but also for health and safety reasons. She also said that the tribes' rights to collect resources was limited to the amount needed to provide a "modest" standard of living. Lac Courte Oreilles Band v. Wisconsin, 668 F.Supp. 1233 (W.D.Wis.1987).

LCO V involved issues of whether the tribes could regulate themselves with regard to the harvesting of muskellunge and walleye, both revered sport fish. The court held that they could do so as long as the tribes adopted regulations that incorporated biological conditions that would preserve the species in each lake in which they occurred, and provided a sufficient margin of safety. 707 F.Supp. 1034 (W.D.Wis.1989).

The allocation of small game, deer, and fur-bearing mammals was dealt with in *LCO VI*, 740 F.Supp. 1400 (W.D.Wis.1990). *LCO VI* also returned to the allocation question for all of the disputed resources. Judge Crabb applied Washington v. Washington Commercial Passenger Fishing Vessel Ass'n, supra page 911, to hold that the harvest should be shared equally between the Chippewa and the state, as the bargain between the parties under the treaties, "included competition for the harvest." Id. at 1416. Under the decision, the allocation of the harvest can be adjusted if the Indians' moderate living needs declined to a level where they could be satisfied with less than 50% of the harvest. She also held that the tribes could not hunt or trap on private lands, could not use lights to hunt deer, hunt them at night, or in the summer.

The court subsequently held in *LCO VII*, 758 F.Supp. 1262 (W.D.Wis.1991), that the tribes had no off-reservation treaty rights to log timber, as the tribes had not logged at the time of the treaties. The tribes did, however, retain rights to gather forest products, including maple sap and firewood.

The history and background of the *LCO* litigation is discussed in Charles F. Wilkinson, *To Feel the Summer in the Spring: The Treaty Fishing Rights of the Wisconsin Chippewa,* 1991 Wis.L.Rev. 375.

Like the Wisconsin Chippewa bands, a number of Chippewa bands in Minnesota who were also beneficiaries of the same 1837 treaty involved in the *LCO* litigation initiated their own litigation over off-reservation treaty hunting and fishing rights. In 1999, the United States Supreme Court issued its decision in a closely watched Indian treaty fishing rights case.

MINNESOTA V. MILLE LACS BAND OF CHIPPEWA INDIANS
Supreme Court of the United States, 1999.
526 U.S. 172, 119 S.Ct. 1187, 143 L.Ed.2d 270.

JUSTICE O'CONNOR delivered the opinion of the Court.

In 1837, the United States entered into a Treaty with several Bands of Chippewa Indians. Under the terms of this Treaty, the Indians ceded land in present-day Wisconsin and Minnesota to the United States, and the United States guaranteed to the Indians certain hunting, fishing, and gathering rights on the ceded land. We must decide whether the Chippewa Indians retain these usufructuary rights today. The State of Minnesota argues that the Indians lost these rights through an Executive Order in 1850, an 1855 Treaty, and the admission of Minnesota into the Union in 1858. After an examination of the historical record, we conclude that the Chippewa retain the usufructuary rights guaranteed to them under the 1837 Treaty.

I.

A.

* * * In the first two articles of the 1837 Treaty, the Chippewa ceded land to the United States in return for 20 annual payments of money and goods. The United States also, in the fifth article of the Treaty, guaranteed to the Chippewa the right to hunt, fish, and gather on the ceded lands:

"The privilege of hunting, fishing, and gathering the wild rice, upon the lands, the rivers and the lakes included in the territory ceded, is guarantied [sic] to the Indians, during the pleasure of the President of the United States." 1837 Treaty with the Chippewa, 7 Stat. 537.

* * *

In the late 1840's, pressure mounted to remove the Chippewa to their unceded lands in the Minnesota Territory. On September 4, 1849, Minnesota Territorial Governor Alexander Ramsey urged the Territorial

Legislature to ask the President to remove the Chippewa from the ceded land.

* * *

Whatever the impetus behind the removal effort, President Taylor responded to this pressure by issuing an Executive Order on February 6, 1850. The order provided:

> "The privileges granted temporarily to the Chippewa Indians of the Mississippi, by the Fifth Article of the Treaty made with them on the 29th of July 1837, 'of hunting, fishing and gathering the wild rice, upon the lands, the rivers and the lakes included in the territory ceded' by that treaty to the United States; and the right granted to the Chippewa Indians of the Mississippi and Lake Superior, by the Second Article of the treaty with them of October 4th 1842, of hunting on the territory which they ceded by that treaty, 'with the other usual privileges of occupancy until required to remove by the President of the United States,' are hereby revoked; and all of the said Indians remaining on the lands ceded as aforesaid, are required to remove to their unceded lands."

The officials charged with implementing this order understood it primarily as a removal order, and they proceeded to implement it accordingly.

The Government hoped to entice the Chippewa to remove to Minnesota by changing the location where the annuity payments—the payments for the land cessions—would be made. The Chippewa were to be told that their annuity payments would no longer be made at La Pointe, Wisconsin (within the Chippewa's ceded lands), but, rather, would be made at Sandy Lake, on unceded lands, in the Minnesota Territory. The Government's first annuity payment under this plan, however, ended in disaster. The Chippewa were told they had to be at Sandy Lake by October 25 to receive their 1850 annuity payment. By November 10, almost 4,000 Chippewa had assembled at Sandy Lake to receive the payment, but the annuity goods were not completely distributed until December 2. In the meantime, around 150 Chippewa died in an outbreak of measles and dysentery; another 230 Chippewas died on the winter trip home to Wisconsin.

The Sandy Lake annuity experience intensified opposition to the removal order among the Chippewa as well as among non-Indian residents of the area. In the face of this opposition, Commissioner of Indian Affairs Luke Lea wrote to the Secretary of the Interior recommending that the President's 1850 order be modified to allow the Chippewa "to remain for the present in the country they now occupy." According to Commissioner Lea, removal of the Wisconsin Bands "is not required by the interests of the citizens or Government of the United States and would in its consequences in all probability be disastrous to the Indians." Three months later, the Acting Commissioner of Indian Affairs wrote to the Secretary to inform him that 1,000 Chippewa were assembled at La Pointe, but that they could not be removed from the area without the use of force. He sought the Secretary's approval "to suspend the removal of these Indians until the determination of the President upon the recommendation of the commissioner is made known to this office." Two days later, the Secretary of the Interior issued the requested authorization, instructing the Commissioner "to suspend the removal of the Chippeway [sic] Indians until the final determination of the President." Commissioner Lea immediately telegraphed the local officials with instructions to "[s]uspend action with reference to the removal of Lake Superior Chippewas for further orders." As the State's own expert historian testified, "[f]ederal efforts to remove the Lake Superior Chippewa to the Mississippi River effectively ended in the summer of 1851."

* * *

Although the United States abandoned its removal policy, it did not abandon its attempts to acquire more Chippewa land.

* * * [I]n December 1854, Minnesota's territorial delegate to Congress recommended to Commissioner Manypenny that he negotiate a treaty with the Mississippi, Pillager, and Lake Winnibigoshish Bands of Chippewa Indians. Commissioner Manypenny summoned representatives of those Bands to Washington, D.C., for the treaty negotiations, which were held in February 1855. The purpose and result of these negotiations was the sale of Chippewa lands to the United States. To this end, the first article of the 1855 Treaty contains two sentences:

> "The Mississippi, Pillager, and Lake Winnibigoshish bands of Chippewa Indians hereby cede, sell, and convey to the United States all their right, title, and interest in, and to, the lands now owned and claimed by them, in the Territory of Minnesota, and included within the following boundaries, viz: [describing territorial boundaries]. And the said Indians do further fully and entirely relinquish and convey to the United States, any and all right, title, and interest, of whatsoever nature the same may be, which they may now have in, and to any other lands in the Territory of Minnesota or elsewhere."

Article 2 set aside lands in the area as reservations for the signatory tribes. The Treaty, however, makes no mention of hunting and fishing rights, whether to reserve new usufructuary rights or to abolish rights guaranteed by previous treaties. The Treaty Journal also reveals no discussion of hunting and fishing rights.

A little over three years after the 1855 Treaty was signed, Minnesota was admitted to the Union. See Act of May 11, 1858, 11 Stat. 285. The admission Act is silent with respect to Indian treaty rights.

* * *

II.

We are first asked to decide whether President Taylor's Executive Order of February 6, 1850, terminated Chippewa hunting, fishing, and gathering rights under the 1837 Treaty. The Court of Appeals began its analysis of this question with a statement of black letter law: " 'The President's power, if any, to issue the order must stem either from an act of Congress or from the Constitution itself.' " 124 F.3d, at 915 (quoting Youngstown Sheet & Tube Co. v. Sawyer, 343 U.S. 579, 585 (1952)). The court considered whether the President had authority to issue the removal order under the 1830 Removal Act (hereinafter Removal Act). The Removal Act authorized the President to convey land west of the Mississippi to Indian tribes that chose to "exchange the lands where they now reside, and remove there." According to the Court of Appeals, the Removal Act only allowed the removal of Indians who had consented to removal. Because the Chippewa had not consented to removal, according to the court, the Removal Act could not provide authority for the President's 1850 removal order.

* * *

Because the Removal Act did not authorize the 1850 removal order, we must look elsewhere for a constitutional or statutory authorization for the order. In this Court, only the landowners argue for an alternative source of authority; they argue that the President's removal order was authorized by the 1837 Treaty itself. There is no support for this proposition, however. The Treaty makes no mention of removal, and there was no discussion of removal during the Treaty negotiations. * * * Because the parties have pointed to no colorable source of authority for the President's removal order, we agree with the Court of Appeals' conclusion that the 1850 removal order was unauthorized.

* * *

When the 1850 order is understood as announcing a removal policy, the portion of the order revoking Chippewa usufructuary rights is seen to perform an integral function in this policy. The order tells the Indians to "go," and also tells them not to return to the ceded lands to hunt and fish. The State suggests that President Taylor might also have revoked Chippewa usufructuary rights as a kind of "incentive program" to encourage the Indians to remove had he known that he could not order their removal directly. The State points to no evidence, however, that the President or his aides ever considered the abrogation of hunting and fishing rights as an "incentive program." Moreover, the State does not explain how this incentive was to operate. * * *

* * *

We conclude that President Taylor's 1850 Executive Order was ineffective to terminate Chippewa usufructuary rights under the 1837 Treaty. The State has pointed to no statutory or constitutional authority for the President's removal order, and the Executive Order, embodying as it did one coherent policy, is inseverable. We do not mean to suggest that a President, now or in the future, cannot revoke the Chippewa usufructuary rights in accordance with the terms of the 1837 Treaty. All we conclude today is that the President's 1850 Executive Order was insufficient to accomplish this revocation because it was not severable from the invalid removal order.

III

The State argues that the Mille Lacs Band of Chippewa Indians relinquished its usufructuary rights under the 1855 Treaty with the Chippewa. Specifically, the State argues that the Band unambiguously relinquished its usufructuary rights by agreeing to the second sentence of Article 1 in that Treaty:

> "And the said Indians do further fully and entirely relinquish and convey to the United States, any and all right, title, and interest, of whatsoever nature the same may be, which they may now have in, and to any other lands in the Territory of Minnesota or elsewhere."

This sentence, however, does not mention the 1837 Treaty, and it does not mention hunting, fishing, and gathering rights. The entire 1855 Treaty, in fact, is devoid of any language expressly mentioning—much less abrogating—usufructuary rights. Similarly, the Treaty contains no language providing money for the abrogation of previously held rights. These omissions are telling because the United States treaty drafters had the sophistication and experience to use express language for the abrogation of treaty rights. In fact, just a few months after Commissioner Manypenny completed the 1855 Treaty, he negotiated a Treaty with the Chippewa of Sault Ste. Marie that expressly revoked fishing rights that had been reserved in an earlier Treaty. See Treaty with the Chippewa of Sault Ste. Marie, Art. 1, 11 Stat. 631 ("The said Chippewa Indians surrender to the United States the right of fishing at the falls of St. Mary's . . . secured to them by the treaty of June 16, 1820").

The State argues that despite any explicit reference to the 1837 Treaty rights, or to usufructuary rights more generally, the second sentence of Article 1 nevertheless abrogates those rights. But to determine whether this language abrogates Chippewa Treaty rights, we look beyond the written words to the larger context that frames the Treaty, including "the history of the treaty, the negotiations, and the practical construction adopted by the parties." *Choctaw Nation v. United States,* 318 U.S. 423. In this case, an examination of the historical record provides insight into how the parties to the Treaty understood the terms of the agreement. This insight is especially helpful to the extent that it sheds light on how the Chippewa signatories to the Treaty understood the agreement because we interpret Indian treaties to give effect to the terms as the Indians themselves would have understood them. See *Washington v. Washington State Commercial Passenger Fishing Vessel Assn.*, 443 U.S. 658, 675–676 (1979); United States v. Winans, 198 U.S. 371, 380–381.

The 1855 Treaty was designed primarily to transfer Chippewa land to the United States, not to terminate Chippewa usufructuary rights. It was negotiated under the authority of the Act of December 19, 1854. This Act authorized treaty negotiations with the Chippewa "for the extinguishment of their title to all the lands owned and claimed by them in the Territory of Minnesota and State of Wisconsin." Ch. 7, 10 Stat. 598. The Act is silent with respect to authorizing agreements to terminate Indian usufructuary privileges, and this silence was likely not accidental. During Senate debate on the Act, Senator Sebastian, the chairman of the Committee on Indian Affairs, stated that the treaties to be negotiated under the Act would "reserv[e] to them [i.e., the Chippewa] those rights which are secured by former treaties."

* * *

Like the authorizing legislation, the Treaty Journal, recording the course of the negotiations themselves, is silent with respect to usufructuary rights. The journal records no discussion of the 1837 Treaty, of hunting, fishing, and gathering rights, or of the abrogation of those rights. *Id.*, at 297–356. This silence suggests that the Chippewa did not understand the proposed Treaty to abrogate their usufructuary rights as guaranteed by other treaties. It is difficult to believe that in 1855, the Chippewa would have agreed to relinquish the usufructuary rights they had fought to preserve in 1837 without at least a passing word about the relinquishment.

* * *

IV.

Finally, the State argues that the Chippewa's usufructuary rights under the 1837 Treaty were extinguished when Minnesota was admitted to the Union in 1858. In making this argument, the State faces an uphill battle. Congress may abrogate Indian treaty rights, but it must clearly express its intent to do so. United States v. Dion, 476 U.S. 734, 738–740 (1986). There must be "clear evidence that Congress actually considered the conflict between its intended action on the one hand and Indian treaty rights on the other, and chose to resolve that conflict by abrogating the treaty." *United States v. Dion*, supra, at 740. There is no such "clear evidence" of congressional intent to abrogate the Chippewa Treaty rights here. The relevant statute—Minnesota's enabling Act—provides in relevant part:

"[T]he State of Minnesota shall be one, and is hereby declared to be one, of the United States of America, and admitted into the Union on an equal footing with the original States in all respects whatever." Act of May 11, 1858, 11 Stat. 285.

This language, like the rest of the Act, makes no mention of Indian treaty rights; it provides no clue that Congress considered the reserved rights of the Chippewa and decided to abrogate those rights when it passed the Act. The State concedes that the Act is silent in this regard, and the State does not point to any legislative history describing the effect of the Act on Indian treaty rights.

With no direct support for its argument, the State relies principally on this Court's decision in Ward v. Race Horse, 163 U.S. 504 (1896). In *Race Horse*, we held that a Treaty reserving to a Tribe " 'the right to hunt on the unoccupied lands of the United States, so long as game may be found thereon, and so long as peace subsists among the whites and Indians on the borders of the hunting districts' " terminated when Wyoming became a State in 1890. Id., at 507, (quoting Art. 4 of the Treaty). This case does not bear the weight the State places on it, however, because it has been qualified by later decisions of this Court.

The first part of the holding in *Race Horse* was based on the "equal footing doctrine," the constitutional principle that all States are admitted to the Union with the same attributes of sovereignty (i.e., on equal footing) as the original 13 States. As relevant here, it prevents the Federal Government from impairing fundamental attributes of state sovereignty when it admits new States into the Union. According to the *Race Horse* Court, because the Treaty rights conflicted irreconcilably with state regulation of natural resources—"an essential attribute of its governmental existence," *Race Horse*, supra—the Treaty rights were held an invalid impairment of Wyoming's sovereignty. Thus, those rights could not survive Wyoming's admission to the Union on "equal footing" with the original States. But *Race Horse* rested on a false premise. As this Court's subsequent cases have made clear, an Indian tribe's treaty rights to hunt, fish, and gather on state land are not irreconcilable with a State's sovereignty over the natural resources in the State. See, e.g., *Washington v. Washington State Commercial Passenger Fishing Vessel Assn.* Rather, Indian treaty rights can coexist with state management of natural resources. Although States have important interests in regulating wildlife and natural resources within their borders, this authority is shared with the Federal Government when the Federal Government exercises one of its enumerated constitutional powers, such as treaty making. U.S. Const., Art. VI, cl. 2. Here, the 1837 Treaty gave the Chippewa the right to hunt, fish, and gather in the ceded territory free of territorial, and later state, regulation, a privilege that others did not enjoy. Today, this freedom from state regulation curtails the State's ability to regulate hunting, fishing, and gathering by the Chippewa in the ceded lands. But this Court's cases have also recognized that Indian treaty-based usufructuary rights do not guarantee the Indians "absolute freedom" from state regulation. Oregon Dept. of Fish and Wildlife v. Klamath Tribe, 473 U.S., at 765, n. 16. We have repeatedly reaffirmed state authority to impose reasonable and necessary nondiscriminatory regulations on Indian hunting, fishing, and gathering rights in the interest of conservation. See Puyallup Tribe v. Department of Game of Wash., 391 U.S. 392, 398 (1968). This "conservation necessity" standard accommodates both the State's interest in management of its natural resources and the Chippewa's federally guaranteed treaty rights. Thus, because treaty rights are reconcilable with state sovereignty over natural resources, statehood by itself is insufficient to extinguish Indian treaty rights to hunt, fish, and gather on land within state boundaries.

* * *

The Chief Justice reads *Race Horse* to establish a rule that "temporary and precarious" treaty rights, as opposed to treaty rights "which were 'of such a nature as to imply their perpetuity,'" are not intended to survive statehood. But the "temporary and precarious" language in *Race Horse* is too broad to be useful in distinguishing rights that survive statehood from those that do not. In *Race Horse*, the Court concluded that the right to hunt on federal lands was temporary because Congress could terminate the right at any time by selling the lands. 163 U.S., at 510. Under this line of reasoning, any right created by operation of federal law could be described as "temporary and precarious," because Congress could eliminate the right whenever it wished. In other words, the line suggested by *Race Horse* is simply too broad to be useful as a guide to whether treaty rights were intended to survive statehood.

The focus of the *Race Horse* inquiry is whether Congress (more precisely, because this is a treaty, the Senate) intended the rights secured by the 1837 Treaty to survive statehood. The 1837 Treaty itself defines the circumstances under which the rights would terminate: when the exercise of those rights was no longer the "pleasure of the President." There is no suggestion in the Treaty that the President would have to conclude that the privileges should end when a State was established in the area. Moreover, unlike the rights at issue in *Race Horse*, there is no fixed termination point to the 1837 Treaty rights. The Treaty in *Race Horse* contemplated that the rights would continue only so long as the hunting grounds remained unoccupied and owned by the United States; the happening of these conditions was "clearly contemplated" when the Treaty was ratified. By contrast, the 1837 Treaty does not tie the duration of the rights to the occurrence of some clearly contemplated event. Finally, we note that there is nothing inherent in the nature of reserved treaty rights to suggest that they can be extinguished by implication at statehood.

Treaty rights are not impliedly terminated upon statehood. Wisconsin v. Hitchcock, 201 U.S. 202, 213–214 (1906). * * *

Accordingly, the judgment of the United States Court of Appeals for the Eighth Circuit is affirmed.

CHIEF JUSTICE REHNQUIST, with whom JUSTICE SCALIA, JUSTICE KENNEDY and JUSTICE THOMAS join, dissenting.

* * *

Rather than engage in the flawed analysis put forward by the Court, I would instead hold that the Executive Order constituted a valid revocation of the Chippewa's hunting and fishing privileges. Pursuant to a Treaty, the President terminated the Indians' hunting and fishing privileges in an Executive Order which stated, in effect, that the privilege to come onto federal lands and hunt was terminated, and that the Indians move themselves from those lands.

* * *

* * * [B]ecause the 1837 Treaty, in conjunction with the Presidential power over public lands gave the President the power to order removal in conjunction with his termination of the hunting rights, the Court's severability analysis is unnecessary. In sum, there is simply no principled reason to invalidate the 150-year-old Executive Order, particularly in view of the heightened deference and wide latitude that we are required to give orders of this sort.

* * *

IV.

Finally, I note my disagreement with the Court's treatment of the equal footing doctrine, and its apparent overruling sub silentio of a precedent of 103 years' vintage. In Ward v. Race Horse, 163 U.S. 504 (1896), we held that a Treaty granting the Indians "the right to hunt on the unoccupied lands of the United States, so long as game may be found thereon, and so long as peace subsists among the whites and the Indians on the borders of the hunting districts" did not survive the admission of Wyoming to the Union since the Treaty right was "temporary and precarious." Id., at 515.

But the Court, in a feat of jurisprudential legerdemain, effectively overrules *Ward* sub silentio. First, the Court notes that Congress may only abrogate Indian treaty rights if it clearly expresses its intent to do so. Next, it asserts that Indian hunting rights are not irreconcilable with state sovereignty, and determines that "because treaty rights are reconcilable with state sovereignty over natural resources, statehood by itself is insufficient to extinguish Indian treaty rights to hunt, fish, and gather on land within state boundaries." And finally, the Court hints that *Ward* rested on an incorrect premise—that Indian rights were inconsistent with state sovereignty.

Without saying so, this jurisprudential bait-and-switch effectively overrules *Ward*, a case which we reaffirmed as recently as 1985 in Oregon Dept. of Fish and Wildlife v. Klamath Tribe, 473 (1985). *Ward* held merely that treaty rights which were only "temporary and precarious," as opposed to those which were "of such a nature as to imply their perpetuity," do not survive statehood. 163 U.S., at 515. Here, the hunting privileges were clearly, like those invalidated in *Ward*, temporary and precarious: The privilege was only guaranteed "during the pleasure of the President"; the legally enforceable annuity payments themselves were to terminate after 20 years; and the Indians were on actual notice that the President might end the rights in the future, App. 78 (1837 Journal of Treaty Negotiations).

* * *

The Court today invalidates for no principled reason a 149-year-old Executive Order, ignores the plain meaning of a 144-year-old treaty provision, and overrules sub silentio a 103-year-old precedent of this Court. I dissent.

[JUSTICE THOMAS' dissenting opinion is omitted.]

NOTE: INTERPRETATION OF INDIAN TREATY LANGUAGE

American Indian treaty interpretation, until recent years, has focused almost entirely on the understanding of the treaty language as described in contemporaneous accounts generated by the American treaty negotiators and commentators, in spite of the dictum from the federal courts that treaty language is to be interpreted the way that the Indians would have understood. The expectation was that there was little or no way to discern how the Indians understood the treaty language, and so reliance upon American treaty negotiators was presumed, except in rare cases. That is changing.

In *United States v. Washington*, Judge Boldt found that the Stevens Treaties were written in English, translated by an American interpreter into a trade jargon, and then reinterpreted into the various Coast Salish dialects. See *United States v. Washington*, 384 F.Supp. 312, 356 (W.D.Wash.1974). Judge Boldt found that many tribal treaty negotiators would not have been able to understand the legal subtleties of the treaty language using this method of translation:

> The Makah could neither read, write nor speak English. Governor Stevens and his party had the assistance of a Clallam Indian who spoke the Makah language, though Makah is totally different and unrelated to Clallam. The treaty appears to have been translated into Chinook jargon, which has a limited vocabulary and was used primarily for trade purposes, but is inadequate to convey concepts of tenure and tenancy in a legal document. Governor

Stevens spoke to the Makah in English which was translated into
Chinook by B. F. Saw, the official interpreter.

Id. at 364. The circumstances made it relatively easy for Judge Boldt to at least
hold that treaty language ambiguity should be interpreted to the benefit of the
Indians.

During the negotiations in the 2007 consent decree in *United States v.
Michigan* that established the parameters of the so-called "inland" right to
hunt, fish, and gather, the tribe's expert witnesses described how the parties
to the 1836 Treaty of Washington would have understood the relevant treaty
language—Article XIII, which stated: "The Indians stipulate for the right of
hunting on the lands ceded, with the other privileges of *occupancy, until the
land is required for settlement*." (emphasis added). The experts established that
federal treaty negotiators understood what "settlement" meant, and how they
explained it to the Michigan *ogimaag* (leaders) in a manner that satisfied the
Anishinaabek about the permanence of the treaty rights.

However, "settlement" is not a word that the Anishinaabek would have
understood without context—there simply is no obvious conjugate in
Anishinaabemowin to this word or notion. See generally Frederic Baraga, A
Dictionary of the Ojibway Language (English-Otchipwe) 225 (1878)
(Minnesota Historical Society Press 1992) (definitions of "settle" involving
interpersonal relationships). The concept of "settlement" is far more complex
for the Anishinaabe than for the Americans. Ultimately, the consent decree
experts agreed that "settlement," according to the American negotiators,
meant actual residences and permanent agriculture, not mere timber clear-
cutting and mining activities. The Anishinaabek would have concurred in such
an understanding, probably, and the result left more than 60 percent of the
1836 ceded territory "unsettled," as defined by the treaty.

The other key word, "occupancy," is a word that likely had more meaning
for the Anishinaabek than "settlement." In Anishinaabemowin, to "occupy" is
"abiitan," or to live in a place. See generally John D. Nichols & Earl Nyholm,
A Concise Dictionary of Minnesota Ojibwe 220 (1995) (defining "occupy" as
"abiitan"); *id.* at 3 (defining "abiitan" as "to live in"); Baraga, supra, at 4
(defining "abitan" as "I inhabit it"). Occupancy was still more complicated for
the Anishinaabek, given that the Indians of this region moved from place to
place seasonally, and could be said to have at least three permanent homes.

What is clear from the great weight of ethnohistorical authority is that
the 1836 tribal negotiators successfully preserved their rights to hunt, fish,
and gather on the ceded territories in Michigan and on the Great Lakes
through reliance on the distinction between "occupancy" and "settlement," as
understood in Anishinaabemowin. *See* Matthew L.M. Fletcher, "Occupancy"
and "Settlement": Anishinaabemowin and the Interpretation of Michigan
Indian Treaty Language, Michigan State University Legal Studies Research
Paper No. 08–04 (Apr. 9, 2010); Gregory E. Dowd, *The Meaning of Article 13 of
the Treaty of Washington, March 28, 1836,* Expert Report prepared for the
Chippewa Ottawa Resource Authority *in* United States v. Michigan, No. 2:73

CV 26 (W.D.Mich., Oct. 11, 2004). A large portion of the 1836 cession area has never been "required for settlement," as the treaty negotiators would have understood that term: "Settlement is equated with occupation with, in the case of whites, good land. 'Good' in this context undoubtedly means agricultural land." Susan E. Gray, *Article 13 in the Treaty of Washington and Land Use in the Session, 1836 to the Present* 25, Expert Report prepared for the Chippewa Ottawa Resource Authority *in* United States v. Michigan, No. 2:73 CV 26 (W.D.Mich., Oct. 19, 2004).

PART THREE

THE FRONTIERS OF INDIGENOUS PEOPLES' RIGHTS

■ ■ ■

In the preceding parts of the book we have explored the nature and effects, historical and modern, of American laws with ancient roots. Enduring principles, many derived from the Enlightenment-era Law of Nations, are invoked to protect the American Indians' self-governing authority, their land base, and a special relationship with the United States. Some interpretations of those European-derived international legal principles, however, seem disingenuous and constraining. The scope of tribal sovereignty has been impliedly limited beyond express treaty terms or statute. Indian land bases have been eroded with a singular respect for legal formality. And the special trust relationship is marked by tensions and distrust. Yet the doctrines of federal Indian law have been utilized by American Indians to secure certain advantages not possessed by other minorities within the United States. The special legal and political status of American Indian tribes has been a foil against the forces of assimilation. The struggle to protect and develop tribal cultures has been difficult, but the use of law by American Indian peoples has been of immense value in achieving some success in those efforts.

Until relatively recently, the United States was unusual among nations in its painstaking concern for rationalizing the rights of indigenous peoples with its constitutional and other domestic legal principles. The Supreme Court has continually referred to old and revered international law principles as the basis for the nation's special political and legal relationship with American Indians. Yet most other nations established by European colonization historically ignored the same international law principles that recognized the sovereignty, territorial rights, and special status of indigenous peoples. Some countries did not even bother to consider the rights of indigenous peoples and regarded the lands they had occupied for centuries and even millennia as *terra nullius*, empty territory that was freely available to European colonizers. Indigenous peoples in these countries and throughout the world are now pressing for broader recognition of their rights and, like their counterparts in the United States, have sought to utilize the domestic and international law adopted by their colonizers to achieve success in their efforts.

Even as indigenous peoples in other nations pursue their rights, a large number of Native Americans here in the United States—Native Hawaiians in particular—have been denied the rights of self-government, a reserved land base, and a special trust relationship with the United States recognized as belonging to other Native Americans. The value of those special rights is currently underscored by the situation of Alaska Natives, whose status as indigenous tribal peoples possessed of pre-existing aboriginal sovereignty over their lands, resources, and internal affairs was ignored by the Alaska Native Claims Settlement Act. The Act is a complex legal device designed to settle native claims to land by endowing a network of instantly created corporations with land titles and money. Meanwhile, Alaska Natives seek to secure their rights as recognized by the enduring principles of United States federal Indian law.

The questions raised by comparing federal Indian law with the legal treatment of indigenous peoples not fully recognized as Indian tribes in the United States, or with native law in other countries and the emerging principles of indigenous peoples' human rights under international law, are many. But it is clear that a global transformation in legal consciousness about the rights of indigenous peoples in the modern world is occurring, and the voices of indigenous peoples are a vital part of that movement. How those voices will continue to shape the domestic and international law of their colonizers represents one of the most important issues raised by the comparative study of indigenous peoples' rights.

CHAPTER THIRTEEN

RIGHTS OF ALASKA NATIVES AND NATIVE HAWAIIANS

■ ■ ■

For historical and other reasons unique to their situations, certain native groups in the United States have not been able to rely on the doctrines of American Indian law to protect their sovereignty, territories, and special status as indigenous peoples. Alaska Natives, partly because of Alaska's late incorporation into the United States, did not enter into treaties with the federal government. From the start, Congress has legislated specially concerning Alaska Natives and included them in general Indian legislation. During the period of Indian reform in the 1930s, for example, the Bureau of Indian Affairs was authorized by Congress to organize Alaska Native villages under the Indian Reorganization Act (IRA). Although few reservations were ever established in Alaska, there was little pressure for non-Indian settlement of the remote lands occupied by Alaska Native villages. Therefore, it was unnecessary for many years for the United States to conclude formal agreements confining Alaska Natives to specific lands and extinguishing their title to others.

Though not "tribal" peoples, Native Hawaiians were the native inhabitants of Hawaii at the time of formal annexation by the United States in 1898. But the overthrow of the Hawaiian monarchy five years earlier by a group of American sugar planters and missionary families, supported by a contingent of United States marines, provided an excuse for avoiding recognition of their native rights and status as indigenous peoples when the United States took possession of their former territory.

The struggles of the native peoples of Alaska and Hawaii to protect their self-determining rights as indigenous peoples and secure a land and natural resource base to exercise those rights are important parts of the historic struggle of all Native Americans. For these native groups, however, maintaining and developing their cultural heritage has been made more difficult and complicated by doubts on the part of United States courts and policymakers about the wisdom and costs of extending further the principles of federal Indian law and the unique aspects of the federal-tribal trust relationship to cover the indigenous peoples of Alaska and Hawaii.

SECTION A. ALASKA NATIVES: LOOKING FORWARD TO THE PAST?

1. HISTORICAL BACKGROUND

The aboriginal inhabitants of Alaska, who settled there at least 11,000 years ago, can be divided into three groups. Aleuts inhabit the Alaska Peninsula and the Aleutian Islands in southwestern Alaska. Western and northern Alaska is inhabited by the Yupik and Inupiat peoples of related groups collectively referred to in the past by the foreign term, "Eskimos," ethnically related to other Inuit ("the people") located across northern Canada and in Greenland. Ethnologically, these groups are not considered Indians but they have always been treated as such for the purposes of federal Indian policy. See, e.g., 53 Interior Dec. 593 (1932). The final group of Alaska Natives is comprised of tribal Indians—Tlingits and Haidas in southeastern Alaska, and Athabascans who live in interior Alaska.

Exclusive aboriginal possession was not broken until the arrival of the Russians in the mid-1700s. Russia claimed Alaska, but its settlements were always small and scattered. The average Russian population of Alaska was only about 550 persons and the only substantial permanent settlements were at Kodiak and Sitka.

The United States succeeded to Russia's interests when Alaska was purchased by the Treaty of Cession in 1867. The treaty said only that the "uncivilized tribes" were to be "subject to such laws and regulations as the United States may, from time to time, adopt in regard to aboriginal tribes of that country." But in 1884 Congress stated in the Organic Act for the Territory of Alaska that:

> the Indians or other persons in said district shall not be disturbed in the possession of any lands actually in their use or occupation or now claimed by them but the terms under which such persons may acquire title to such lands is reserved for future legislation by Congress.

23 Stat. 24 § 8.

The Supreme Court rejected an argument that the Organic Act recognized absolute ownership in the Alaska Natives but found that it acknowledged the continuing existence of aboriginal rights. *Tee-Hit-Ton Indians v. United States*, page 296, supra. Native land rights were similarly preserved in several other acts relating to Alaska.

There was little pressure to settle the vast lands of the territory because of Alaska's harsh climate and remote location. Consequently, the motivation that had existed in the lower 48 states to negotiate with native peoples to extinguish title simply was not present in Alaska for nearly a century. That situation changed with statehood in 1958 and ended with the discovery of huge oil reserves a few years later.

The Act admitting Alaska to the Union allowed the state to select 103.5 million acres of federally owned land for itself, 72 Stat. 339, by far the largest grant of public land to any new state. The Act also required the state to disclaim any rights or jurisdiction in lands "the right or title to which may be held by any Indians, Eskimos or Aleuts." The requirement of respect for native land rights became a bar to state selection of lands that were subject to aboriginal title as recognized by *Johnson v. McIntosh*, page 74, supra, and other cases—virtually all the land in the state. Moved by economic exigency, the state started choosing the lands it wanted. Predictably, the first selections were of lands valuable for oil and gas and other natural resources. Native groups had filed protective blanket claims on all public lands, but the federal government processed the state's selections anyway. This mobilized and unified Alaska Natives. They organized, first regionally and ultimately statewide. Native villages protested and this moved Secretary of the Interior Stewart L. Udall to halt the processing of state selections in 1966 (the "Freeze). Then, in 1969 Udall issued his sweeping formal withdrawal from state land selections, mineral leases and claims, and homesteading on Alaska's federal public lands— about 90 percent of the state. However, Udall's controversial "Deep Freeze" did not prevent the sale of oil and gas leases on previously selected state lands, the most notable of which was the $900 million Prudhoe Bay sale in September, 1969.

Recovery of huge profits from oil exploration on Alaska's North Slope hinged on finding a way to transport crude oil out of the Arctic. The Prudhoe Bay field was adjacent to the Beaufort Sea, but ice prevented ship access during most of the year. About one year before the lease sale, a consortium of major oil companies developed a scheme to move Prudhoe Bay oil 800 miles through a pipeline to be built across federal lands (impressed by native claims) to Valdez, an ice-free port in the south. Thus, besides being fraught with gigantic technological and environmental problems, the pipeline was on a collision course with Alaska Native land claims. When the oil companies sought a right of way for a haul road associated with the pipeline, they met objections from several native villages. A federal court enjoined the Department of the Interior from issuing the right of way across land claimed by a native village of 66 residents that was organized under the IRA. Provisions of environmental and mineral leasing laws later also became obstacles to the pipeline. But the project—along with oil company investments and the state's visions of wealth—ultimately depended on clearing the cloud of native title from the land. Almost overnight oil companies joined a movement to settle Alaska Native land claims in a convergence of interests that was to alter dramatically the legal rights and status of Alaska's indigenous tribal communities.

2.   THE ALASKA NATIVE CLAIMS SETTLEMENT ACT

An unlikely alliance of native leaders and oil company lobbyists, sometimes assisted by organized labor and civil rights groups, worked for two agonizing years to produce the Alaska Native Claims Settlement Act (ANCSA), which became law on December 18, 1971. See 43 U.S.C.A. §§ 1601–1628. In return for relinquishing their claims to aboriginal title to most of the state (365 million acres), Alaska Natives agreed to accept land selection rights to 44 million acres (an area about the size of the State of Missouri) along with money payments totaling $962.5 million. This allowed state land selections and mineral development to resume. To complicate matters, however, the "(d)(2)" provision of ANCSA, 43 U.S.C.A. § 1616(d)(2), authorized the Secretary of the Interior to withdraw 80 million acres of land that might merit inclusion in the four "national interest" systems (national parks, wildlife refuges, national forests, and wild and scenic rivers). The issue of national interest lands was resolved in 1980, when the Alaska National Interest Lands Conservation Act (ANILCA), 16 U.S.C.A. §§ 3101–3133, was signed into law. ANILCA allocated 110 million acres, mostly former Bureau of Land Management (BLM) lands, to the federal conservation systems mentioned above. The settling of the boundaries for the national interest lands clarified the areas available for final selections by the state and by Alaska Natives.

ANCSA amounted to one of the greatest land transactions in history. In some respects, it is similar to the treaties that tribes in the lower forty-eight states executed with the United States: the tribes relinquished aboriginal claims to vast amounts of land and, in return, received recognized title to lesser amounts of land. In other respects, however, the ANCSA transaction differed from treaty making in the lower forty-eight states. Land title was received by corporations chartered under state law, not by Indian tribes with governmental powers. Children born after the passage of ANCSA in 1971 would not become shareholders in the corporations. Stock held by natives would become fully transferable, even to non-natives, as of 1991. Tribal organizations then in existence—and their future role—were virtually ignored. ANCSA also made no provision for special hunting, fishing, or water rights. As Professor Monroe E. Price explained; "The spectacular aspect of the Claims Act is its embrace of this corporate ideology. If the General Allotment Act of 1887 had the small farmer as its ideal and goal for the Indian family, the Alaska legislation has the corporate shareholder as its model." Monroe E. Price, *A Moment in History: The Alaska Native Claims Settlement Act*, 8 UCLA-Alaska L.Rev. 89, 99 (1979). See also Gigi Berardi, *The Alaska Native Claims Settlement*

Act (ANCSA)—Whose Settlement Was it? An Overview of Salient Issues, 25 J. Land Resources & Envtl.L. 131 (2005).

These are the basic provisions of ANCSA as originally enacted in 1971:

1.   Alaska Natives were entitled to select about 44 million acres of land in their aboriginal territory. The surface estate of 22 million acres was to be transferred to some 200 village corporations designated in ANCSA. Twelve regional corporations, generally defined by ethnic and traditional use boundaries, received title to the subsurface estate in the 22 million acres selected by the village corporations; in addition, six of the twelve regional corporations were entitled to select another 16 million acres of land. The remaining lands were set aside for pending native allotment applications, townsites, historic sites, and other purposes; any such lands not conveyed were to be allocated to the regional corporations based on population. As noted, the village and regional corporations are chartered under state law. No lands were to be selected by a thirteenth regional corporation, which was comprised of natives living outside of Alaska.

2.   An Alaska Native Fund was established by ANCSA to distribute $962.5 million to native corporations. The fund was comprised of $462.5 million appropriated by Congress over an eleven-year period and $500 million from annual revenues collected by the state and federal government from mineral leases on lands in Alaska. Payments from the Alaska Native Fund were made to the regional corporations pursuant to a detailed formula. Approximately 50 percent of all money from the fund had to be redistributed from regional corporations (including the thirteenth regional corporation) to their stockholders and to village corporations within each region.

3.   Each Alaska Native alive on December 18, 1971, the date on which ANCSA was passed, was entitled to 100 shares of stock in a regional corporation and, depending on his or her residence, to become a shareholder in a village corporation as well. Alaska Natives born after December 18, 1971 ("afterborns") could become shareholders only by inheritance. With very limited exceptions, corporate stock in regional and village corporations could not be sold or otherwise disposed of until December 18, 1991. On that date, all stock in regional and village corporations was to be cancelled and new shares issued. The new stock would be without the restrictions on alienation required of shares originally issued under ANCSA. These provisions were substantially changed by the "1991 Amendments" to the Act as discussed below.

4.   All of the eight reserves previously set aside by executive orders for Alaska Natives, except for the Annette Island Reserve of the Metlakatla Indian Community, were revoked by ANCSA. The other villages with reserves created prior to ANCSA could choose to retain their reserve lands in lieu of other rights to land and money provided under the Act.

5.   All lands selected by the native corporations were to be received in fee simple with few restrictions on alienation. However, state taxation was limited: lands held by corporations and not developed or leased to third parties were exempt from state and local real property taxes for 20 years. The period was to expire on December 18, 1991 but this was changed by an amendment.

6.   ANCSA expressly provided that "any aboriginal hunting or fishing rights that may exist, are hereby extinguished." 43 U.S.C.A. § 1603(b). ANCSA also extinguished aboriginal title rights in all "submerged land underneath all water areas" in Alaska.

7.   The Act stated that it was not intended to establish any "permanent racially defined institutions" or "lengthy wardship or trusteeship," 43 U.S.C.A. § 1601(b). Those phrases were not elucidated elsewhere in ANCSA or in the legislative history, leaving ambiguity about the nature of the relationship between the United States and Alaska Natives.

Although all reserves except one were revoked, no attempt was made in ANCSA to limit the tribal governing authority of the native villages, either the many villages that had organized pursuant to the IRA or those that had traditionally governed themselves according to their inherent authority. The provisions of ANCSA were declared to "constitute compensation for the extinguishment of claims to land, and shall not be deemed to substitute for any governmental programs otherwise available to the native people of Alaska as citizens of the United States and the state of Alaska." 43 U.S.C.A. § 1626(a). Since ANCSA, federal agencies such as the Bureau of Indian Affairs and the Indian Health Service have continued to provide special Indian services to Alaska Natives. Further, in major Indian legislation since ANCSA, Congress has specifically included Alaska Natives, tribes, villages, and corporations among those Indian entities eligible for programs.

By the early 1980s, Alaska Natives began to realize fully the many problems that ANCSA had wrought. They called in Thomas Berger, a distinguished Canadian judge, to investigate the impacts of the statute on Alaska Native communities, subsistence rights, and lands. Berger held hearings in 62 villages, where 1600 native people offered testimony. The result, Thomas R. Berger, Village Journey: The Report of the Alaska Native Review Commission (1985), faithfully documented the many concerns among Alaska Natives and made many recommendations designed to address ANCSA's assaults on native land, subsistence, and sovereign rights. The Berger Commission helped galvanize native determination to engage in a multi-faceted effort to remedy the effects of ANCSA.

As a result, dozens of amendments to ANCSA have been enacted by Congress since the Act's passage in 1971. The most important set of amendments focused on the 1991 deadline under the original legislation, when the bans on stock alienation and property taxation would be lifted and it was feared that natives would be vulnerable to loss of their land. For a comprehensive analysis of the amendments to ANCSA, see J. Tate London, *The "1991 Amendments" to the Alaska Native Claims Settlement Act: Protection for Native Lands?*, 8 Stan.Envtl.L.J. 200 (1989). Congress addressed these concerns in 1987 amendments by shifting the decision-making authority on many issues to shareholders. Regional and village corporations were permitted to amend their articles of incorporation to issue stock to natives born after December 18, 1971, those who were eligible to enroll but who did not, and other natives age 65 or older. The corporations could elect to make these additional shares of stock cancelable on the death of the shareholders. The corporations may also amend their articles to give themselves a right to purchase stock passing by intestate succession to non-natives and to impose certain other restrictions on stock alienation and rights designed to keep the corporations under native control. Unless the corporations amend their articles to the contrary, the restrictions on alienability of stock that would have expired on December 18, 1991 are continued until removed by the board of directors. Because of the potential change in rights and possible dilution of interests of existing shareholders, the amendments set statutes of limitations for constitutional challenges and placed jurisdiction in a three-judge federal district court. They were not challenged. Earlier, provisions added by ANILCA allowed corporations to provide for a first right to purchase stock exercisable by the corporation or by the shareholder's family.

Under the amendments, property tax exemptions for lands conveyed to natives and native corporations were extended indefinitely unless the land is developed or leased. The amendments also protected undeveloped native corporation lands from being seized by creditors or court judgment, lost through bankruptcy or involuntary distributions, or taken by squatters. Several new sections were added and former sections removed, dealing with the complexities of land selection and conveyance, a process that was still not complete twenty years after passage of ANCSA.

Elements of traditional federal Indian policy and law remain in Alaska. Land title is in corporate ownership, but the tribal governments that predated ANCSA continue in existence. Special subsistence hunting and fishing rights have been reorganized, not under a reservation system but by an amalgam of state and federal statutes. Most federal services continue to be provided to Alaska Natives in much the same manner as they are provided to Indians in the lower 48 states. Nevertheless, as discussed in the next section, native villages cannot yet define their post-ANCSA status with precision; several of the crucial elements of this unique legal system remain undefined and unadapted to the social and economic situation of Alaska Natives. In the following case, the Supreme Court made it clear, however, that corporately-held lands selected by Alaska Natives under ANCSA's settlement provisions cannot be governed as "Indian country." The Court's first-ever decision on Alaska Native self-governing rights under ANCSA raises a host of important questions on the meaning and scope of tribal sovereignty in Alaska, jurisdiction over Native-controlled lands and village life, and the sovereign immunity of Alaska Native governments. On ANCSA, ANILCA, and the legal status of Alaska Natives generally, see David S. Case and David A. Voluck, Alaska Natives and American Laws (3d ed. 2012); Felix S. Cohen, Handbook of Federal Indian Law § 4.07[3], at 326–56 (2012 ed.).

3.   NATIVE LANDS IN ALASKA

One of the most foundational of all ANCSA reform issues involved sovereign tribal jurisdiction over Alaska Native lands. Except for scattered trust allotments, all native land was held by the state-chartered corporations, not tribal governments. There seemed to be no basis for tribal jurisdiction under the definition of "Indian country" in 18 U.S.C. § 1151. Then, native leaders saw promise in a strategy developed during the Berger Commission hearings. Native leaders in the Village of Venetie, within one of the reservations revoked by ANCSA, took action. The Venetie village corporation transferred all of its land to the IRA-recognized Venetie tribal government. Among other sovereign measures, the tribe adopted a business-activities tax and in time applied it to a construction firm doing business on tribal land. The Ninth Circuit Court of Appeals ruled for the tribe and then the case went to the Supreme Court.

ALASKA V. NATIVE VILLAGE OF VENETIE

Supreme Court of the United States, 1998.
522 U.S. 520, 118 S.Ct. 948, 140 L.Ed.2d 30.

JUSTICE THOMAS delivered the opinion of the Court.

* * *

Pursuant to ANCSA [43 U.S.C.A. §§ 1601 et seq.], two Native corporations were established for the Neets'aii Gwich'in, one in Venetie, and one in Arctic Village. In 1973, those corporations elected to make use of a provision in ANCSA allowing Native corporations to take title to former reservation lands set aside for Indians prior to 1971, in return for forgoing the statute's monetary payments and transfers of nonreservation land. See § 1618(b). The United States conveyed fee simple title to the land constituting the former Venetie Reservation to the two corporations as tenants in common; thereafter, the corporations transferred title to the land to the Native Village of Venetie Tribal Government (the Tribe).

In 1986, the State of Alaska entered into a joint venture agreement with a private contractor for the construction of a public school in Venetie, financed with state funds. In December 1986, the Tribe notified the contractor that it owed the Tribe approximately $161,000 in taxes for conducting business activities on the Tribe's land. When both the contractor and the State, which under the joint venture agreement was the party responsible for paying the tax, refused to pay, the Tribe attempted to collect the tax in tribal court from the State, the school district, and the contractor.

* * *

The * * * District Court * * * held that the Tribe's ANCSA lands were not Indian country within the meaning of 18 U.S.C. § 1151(b), which provides that Indian country includes all "dependent Indian communities within the borders of the United States"; as a result, "the Tribe [did] not have the power to impose a tax upon non-members of the tribe such as the plaintiffs." [The Court of Appeals for the Ninth Circuit reversed. 101 F.3d 1286 (1996). The Supreme Court granted certiorari to determine whether the court of appeals had correctly determined that the Tribe's land is Indian country.]

"Indian country" is currently defined at 18 U.S.C. § 1151. In relevant part, the statute provides:

> The term "Indian country" . . . means (a) all land within the limits of any Indian reservation under the jurisdiction of the United States Government . . . , (b) all dependent Indian communities within the borders of the United States whether within the original or subsequently acquired territory thereof, and whether within or without the limits of a state, and (c) all Indian allotments, the Indian titles to which have not been extinguished, including rights-of-way running through the same.

* * *

Because ANCSA revoked the Venetie Reservation, and because no Indian allotments are at issue, whether the Tribe's land is Indian country depends on whether it falls within the "dependent Indian communities" prong of the statute, § 1151(b). We now hold that it refers to a limited category of if Indian lands that are neither reservations nor allotments, and that satisfy two requirements—first they must have been set aside by the Federal Government for the use of the Indians as Indian land; second they must be under federal superintendence. * * *

Before § 1151 was enacted, we held in three cases that Indian lands that were not reservations could be Indian country and that the Federal Government could therefore exercise jurisdiction over them. See United States v. Sandoval, 231 U.S. 28 (1913); United States v. Pelican, 232 U.S. 442 (1914); United States v. McGowan, 302 U.S. 535 (1938). * * *

* * *

In each of these cases, therefore, we relied upon a finding of both a federal set-aside and federal superintendence in concluding that the Indian lands in question constituted Indian country and that it was permissible for the Federal Government to exercise jurisdiction over them. Section 1151 does not purport to alter this definition of Indian country * * * .

We therefore must conclude that in enacting § 1151(b), Congress indicated that a federal set-aside and a federal superintendence requirement must be satisfied for a finding of a "dependent Indian community" * * * . The federal set-aside requirement ensures that the land in question is occupied by an "Indian community"; the federal superintendence requirement guarantees that the Indian community is sufficiently "dependent" on the Federal Government that the Federal Government and the Indians involved, rather than the States, are to exercise primary jurisdiction over the land in question.

B

The Tribe's ANCSA lands do not satisfy either of these requirements. * * *

With respect to the federal set-aside requirement, it is significant that ANCSA, far from designating Alaskan lands for Indian use, revoked the existing Venetie Reservation, and indeed revoked all existing reservations in Alaska *"set aside* by legislation or by Executive or Secretarial Order for *Native use,"* save one. 43 U.S.C. § 1618(a) (emphasis added). In no clearer fashion could Congress have departed from its traditional practice of setting aside Indian lands.

The Tribe argues—and the Court of Appeals majority agreed—that the ANCSA lands were set apart for the use of the Neets'aii Gwich'in, "as such," because the Neets'aii Gwich'in acquired the lands pursuant to an ANCSA provision allowing Natives to take title to former reservation lands in return for forgoing all other ANCSA transfers (citing 43 U.S.C. § 1618(b)). The difficulty with this contention is that ANCSA transferred reservation lands to private, state-chartered Native corporations, without any restraints on alienation or significant use restrictions, and with the goal of avoiding "any permanent racially defined institutions, rights, privileges, or obligations." § 1601(b); see also §§ 1607, 1613. By ANCSA's very design,

Native corporations can immediately convey former reservation lands to non-Natives, and such corporations are not restricted to using those lands for Indian purposes. Because Congress contemplated that non-Natives could own the former Venetie Reservation, and because the Tribe is free to use it for non-Indian purposes, we must conclude that the federal set-aside requirement is not met.

Equally clearly, ANCSA ended federal superintendence over the Tribe's lands. As noted above, ANCSA revoked the Venetie Reservation along with every other reservation in Alaska but one, and Congress stated explicitly that ANCSA's settlement provisions were intended to avoid a "lengthy wardship or trusteeship." § 1601(b). After ANCSA, federal protection of the Tribe's land is essentially limited to a statutory declaration that the land is exempt from adverse possession claims, real property taxes, and certain judgments as long as it has not been sold, leased, or developed. See § 1636(d). These protections, if they can be called that, simply do not approach the level of superintendence over the Indians' land that existed in our prior cases. In each of those cases, the Federal Government actively controlled the lands in question, effectively acting as a guardian for the Indians. Finally, it is worth noting that Congress conveyed ANCSA lands to state-chartered and state-regulated private business corporations, hardly a choice that comports with a desire to retain *federal* superintendence over the land.

The Tribe contends that the requisite federal superintendence is present because the Federal Government provides "desperately needed health, social, welfare, and economic programs" to the Tribe. The Court of Appeals majority found this argument persuasive. Our Indian country precedents, however, do not suggest that the mere provision of "desperately needed" social programs can support a finding of Indian country. * * *

The Tribe's federal superintendence argument, moreover, is severely undercut by its view of ANCSA's primary purposes, namely, to effect Native self-determination and to end paternalism in federal Indian relations. See Brief for Petitioner (noting that ANCSA's land transfers "fostered greater tribal self-determination" and "renounced BIA [Bureau of Indian Affairs] paternalism"). The broad federal superintendence requirement for Indian country cuts against these objectives, but we are not free to ignore that requirement as codified in 18 U.S.C. § 1151. Whether the concept of Indian country should be modified is a question entirely for Congress.

NOTES

1.   For an argument in favor of establishing Indian country in Alaska, See Gregory D. Strommer and Stephen D. Osborne, *"Indian Country" and The Nature and Scope of Tribal Self-Government in Alaska*, 22 Alaska L.Rev. 1 (2005).

2.   An early case held that "federal officers are obligated to protect aboriginal lands 'against intrusion by third parties' until such time as Congress acts to extinguish possessory rights therein." Edwardsen v. Morton, 369 F.Supp. 1359 (D.D.C.1973). That decision found that when federal officers allowed oil companies and others to use the aboriginal lands of the Inupiat people on the North Slope of Alaska under permits and licenses for oil exploration, it gave the Natives a cause of action in trespass and for breach of fiduciary duty against the government officers who had effectively authorized trespass by third parties. The trespasses resulted in physical damage to the land, damage to fish and game, and interference with whaling.

But in United States v. Atlantic Richfield Co., 612 F.2d 1132 (9th Cir.1980), cert. denied 449 U.S. 888 (1980), the court held that ANCSA had validated pre-existing permits and had "extinguished not only the aboriginal titles of all Alaska Natives, but also every claim 'based on' aboriginal title in the sense that the past or present existence of aboriginal title is an element of the claim." Thus, the court did not disagree that the breach of a fiduciary duty to protect lands held by aboriginal title may have given the Inupiats a cause of action against the federal government. Rather, the court found that ANCSA had extinguished all such causes of action in which aboriginal title is an ingredient, including pre-Act claims of trespass.

Atlantic Richfield left open the question of what compensation might be due under the Fifth Amendment for extinguishment of native property interests and claims by the operation of the Act. The court in *Atlantic Richfield* suggested that compensation claims would be resolved in a suit that had been filed by the Inupiats in the Court of Claims. The Inupiats were later denied relief in their Court of Claims suit against the government. Inupiat Community of the Arctic Slope v. United States, 680 F.2d 122 (Ct.Cl.1982), cert. denied 459 U.S. 969 (1982). The court adopted the reasoning of *Atlantic Richfield* to hold that the Inupiats' claims that the United States was liable for allowing others to trespass were "based on" aboriginal title and therefore had been extinguished by ANCSA. The claim that the government was liable for extinguishment of trespass claims that had matured prior to enactment of ANCSA was also rejected. The court said, because the Inupiats' land was in aboriginal title, that:

> * * * [ANCSA] terminated not only the [aboriginal] title, but any claims based upon that title. The right to sue for trespass was merely one aspect of the protection Congress provided for their aboriginal title. The extent and measure of that protection lay within the discretion of Congress to determine.

> * * * Congress's authority to extinguish aboriginal title without payment also authorized it without payment to extinguish the trespass claims based on that title.

680 F.2d at 126. The court concluded that Congress's action in extinguishing trespass claims was "a political decision not subject to judicial reexamination."

Is the *Atlantic Richfield* decision an expansion of the rule in *Tee-Hit-Ton*? See page 296, supra. Would the same reasoning allow extinguishment of an unsatisfied judgment for trespass to aboriginal land? Do you think the court would have been so willing to deny relief in *Inupiat Community* if Congress had provided no compensation at all in ANCSA?

3.   Did ANCSA extinguish the fiduciary duty to manage property for the benefit of Alaska Natives prior to conveyance to native corporations? Suppose the United States failed to put lands selected by, but not conveyed to, a native corporation to any productive use for several years or it allowed assets to be wasted or destroyed? Does the corporation have any recourse? The trust duty has been found applicable when federal agencies administer statutory programs for Alaska Natives, such as for housing. See, e.g., Eric v. Department of Housing and Urban Development, 464 F.Supp. 44 (D.Alaska 1978).

4.   For Alaska Natives, the *Venetie* decision was perhaps the most painful setback since ANCSA itself. They decided, based upon the Court's repeated reference to land under federal "superintendence," that is, trust land, to find a way to have Alaska Native land taken into trust under the ongoing fee-into-trust program administered by the BIA. The problem was that the department had adopted a regulation, the so-called "Alaska Exception" that removed Alaska tribal governments from eligibility for fee-into-trust transactions. The tribes requested the Interior Department to delete the "Alaska Exception" but were unsuccessful. Then, in 2006, they filed suit.

The District Court held in Akiachak Native Community v. Salazar, 935 F. Supp. 2d 195 (D.D.C.2013), that ANCSA did not repeal the Secretary's authority under the IRA, 25 U.S.C. § 465 and 25 U.S.C. § 473a, to take land into trust for Alaska Natives. The State of Alaska argued that ANCSA impliedly repealed the IRA provisions. The court emphasized the preference against implied repeals, but also concluded that the plain meaning of ANCSA did not support a repeal:

The State points first to ANCSA's extinguishment of "[a]ll claims against the United States, the State [of Alaska], and all other persons that are based on claims of aboriginal right, title, use, or occupancy of land . . . or that are based on any statute or treaty of the United States relating to Native use and occupancy." ANCSA, § 4(c) (codified at 43 U.S.C. § 1603(c)). If a petition to have Alaska land taken into trust is indeed such a "claim," then ANCSA forecloses the Secretary's authority to grant it. But, as the plaintiffs argue, petitions to have land taken into trust are not "claims," because to grant or deny those petitions is within the discretion of the Secretary. See 25 U.S.C. § 465, and a "claim" is necessarily an assertion of right. [Citing authority]. Evidence from the legislative history of ANCSA indicates that Congress understood the word in this way. . . . And that the Claims Settlement Act speaks of "claims *against* the United States, the State [of Alaska], and all other persons," ANCSA, § 4(c) (codified at 43 U.S.C. § 1603(c)) (emphasis added), strengthens the conclusion by emphasizing that a claim is necessarily adverse to the interests of another party.

The State does not argue with any particular force that petitions to have land taken into trust are "claims" within the usual meaning of that word, and the court concludes that, because they are not, the Secretary's authority to consider them is unaffected by ANCSA § 4(c).

The court also found that the exclusion of Alaska Natives from the fee-into-trust program was void under 25 U.S.C. § 467(g), which nullifies regulations that discriminate among Indian Tribes. In 2014, the Department of Interior then published a final rule deleting the "Alaska Exclusion," 25 C.F.R. § 151.1, for taking land into trust. 79 FR 76.888–02.

On the appeal of the District Court decision, the Court of Appeals dismissed Alaska's appeal on the ground that a case or controversy no longer exists: "After the district court held that Interior's interpretation was contrary to law, the Department, following notice and comment, revised its regulations and dismissed its appeal. The State of Alaska disagrees with both the district court and Interior, and now seeks to prevent any new efforts by the United States to take tribal land in trust within the State's borders. Unfortunately for Alaska, which intervened in the district court as a defendant and brought no independent claim for relief, the controversy between the tribes and the Department is now moot. We therefore dismiss Alaska's appeal for lack of jurisdiction." Akiachak Native Community v. United States Department of the Interior, 827 F.3d 100, 101–02 (D.C.Cir.2016).

In its opinion, the Court of Appeals noted that Alaska could still challenge the District Court ruling in an APA proceeding. If the lower court decision is upheld, will Alaska Native tribes be eligible to transfer fee land into trust? If so, will such land be Indian country under § 1151 and the *Venetie* opinion? See Oklahoma Tax Comm'n v. Citizen Band of Potawatomi Indian Tribe, 498 U.S. 505 (1991).

4. ALASKA NATIVE TRIBAL SOVEREIGNTY

Even without "Indian country" status following *Venetie*, Alaska Natives, largely organized at the village level, continue to assert their sovereignty, self-governing status, and other rights under principles of federal Indian law. There are more than 200 federally recognized Alaska Native tribes. Approximately 150 of these tribal communities operate under traditional governments and 75 of these Native villages have organized tribal councils and governments under the IRA. 25 U.S.C.A. § 473(a). See D. Case and D. Voluck, supra, at 327.

ANCSA did not address the status of Alaska Native IRA or traditional governments. The amendments to ANCSA in 1987 addressing the so-called "1991 issues" also consciously avoided the sovereignty issue by declaring that the Act cannot be construed as determining whether any federally recognized tribe "has or does not have governmental authority over lands * * * or persons within the State of Alaska." 30 U.S.C.A. § 1601. What does this tell us about congressional intent?

Prior to the U.S. Supreme Court's decision in *Venetie*, Alaska's Supreme Court had taken the position that an Alaska Native village organized under the IRA was "not self-governing or in any meaningful sense sovereign." Native Village of Stevens v. Alaska Management and Planning, 757 P.2d 32, 34 (Alaska 1988). The case involved a contract dispute between Stevens Village, an Alaska Native village organized as a tribe under the IRA, and a private business engaged in rural development projects. Stevens Village moved to dismiss the state court action on the ground that the suit was barred by the doctrine of tribal sovereign immunity. The court held that Stevens Village did not have sovereign immunity, as "there is nothing in the legislative history of ANCSA which remotely suggests that IRA villages are to be recognized as having a government role." Id. at 40–41.

The Ninth Circuit, however, took a different approach on the existence of Alaska Native sovereignty rights under ANCSA and principles of federal Indian law. In Alaska v. Native Village of Venetie, 856 F.2d 1384 (9th Cir.1988), the court held that while organization of a Native village under the Indian Reorganization Act did not automatically establish sovereignty, sovereignty could be established by a showing of federal reorganization, or alternatively, by other historical factors. Native Village of Noatak v. Hoffman, 896 F.2d 1157 (9th Cir.1990) held that one village with an IRA constitution and another village listed in ANCSA, qualified as "tribes" for purposes of securing federal question jurisdiction under 28 U.S.C.A. § 1362. The villages, therefore, could sue the state of Alaska because, under the Ninth Circuit's analysis, the state's Eleventh Amendment immunity was overcome by the state's consent to the U.S. Constitution in which federal authority over Indian affairs is supreme. *Hoffman*'s holding as to the state's Eleventh Amendment immunity was overturned by the United States Supreme Court in Blatchford v. Native Village of Noatak & Circle Village, 501 U.S. 775 (1991). The Supreme Court's holding on state immunity from suit by Indian tribes under the Eleventh Amendment has implications for all Indian tribes, but the decision does not seem to affect the general thrust of the Ninth Circuit's holding on Alaska Native village tribal status for purposes of establishing federal question jurisdiction under 28 U.S.C.A. § 1362.

In January 1993, just days prior to a new presidential administration assuming office in Washington, the Solicitor of the Department of the Interior issued an opinion on the tribal status and governmental powers of Alaska Native villages. 58 Fed. Reg. 54365 (1993). The opinion concluded that while Alaska Native villages are recognized as Native American tribes, "with the immunities and privileges available to other federally acknowledged Indian tribes," they lack any territorial powers enjoyed by tribes in the lower 48 states. Since then, however, the Department of the Interior has acknowledged the existence of some 228 tribes in Alaska. See

80 Fed. Reg. 1942 (2015). In the following landmark decision, the Alaska Supreme Court held that the secretarial action provided the federal recognition that the Court found lacking in *Stevens Village*.

JOHN V. BAKER

Supreme Court of Alaska, 1999.
982 P.2d 738, cert. denied, 528 U.S. 1182, 120 S.Ct. 1221, 145 L.Ed.2d 1121 (2000).

FABE, JUSTICE.

I.   Introduction

Seeking sole custody of his two children, John Baker, a member of Northway Village, filed a custody petition in the Northway Tribal Court. Anita John, the children's mother and a member of Mentasta Village, consented to Northway's jurisdiction. After the tribal court issued an order granting shared custody, Mr. Baker filed an identical suit in state superior court. Although Ms. John moved to dismiss based on the tribal court proceeding, the superior court denied the motion and awarded primary physical custody to Mr. Baker. Ms. John appeals, arguing that as a federally recognized tribe, Northway Village has the inherent sovereignty to adjudicate custody disputes between its members and that the superior court therefore should have dismissed the state case.

This appeal raises a question of first impression. We must decide whether the sovereign adjudicatory authority of Native tribes exists outside the confines of Indian country. After reviewing evidence of the intent of the Executive Branch, as well as relevant federal statutes and case law, we conclude that Native tribes do possess the inherent sovereign power to adjudicate child custody disputes between tribal members in their own courts. We therefore reverse and remand to the superior court to determine whether the tribal court's custody determination should be recognized by the superior court under the doctrine of comity.

* * *

Shortly after we initially held oral argument in this appeal, the United States Supreme Court decided *Alaska v. Native Village of Venetie Tribal Government*. We then requested supplemental briefing, asking the parties to address how the Venetie decision affects the issues presented. * * *

We have previously held that tribal status is a non-justiciable political question.[47] We therefore will defer to the determinations of Congress and the Executive Branch on the question of tribal status.[48] If Congress or the

---

[47]   See Atkinson v. Haldane, 569 P.2d 151, 163 (Alaska 1977).

[48]   See Native Village of Stevens v. Alaska Management & Planning, 757 P.2d 32, 34–35 (Alaska 1988).

Executive Branch recognizes a group of Native Americans as a sovereign tribe, we "must do the same."[49]

Prior to 1993, no such recognition of Alaska villages had occurred. In *Native Village of Stevens v. Alaska Management & Planning*, we conducted an historical analysis and concluded that the federal government had never recognized Alaska villages as sovereign tribes.

* * *

II. Discussion
* * *

In 1993, however, the Department of the Interior issued a list of federally recognized tribes that included Northway Village and most of the other Native villages in Alaska. In the list's preamble, the Department of Interior explained that it was issuing the list in order to clarify confusion over the tribal status of various Alaska Native entities. The Department believed that previous lists had been interpreted to mean that Native villages in Alaska, although qualifying for federal funding, were not recognized as sovereign tribes. It sought to rectify this misunderstanding and to reaffirm the sovereign status of the recognized tribes. In particular, the Department emphasized that the list included those Alaskan entities that the federal government historically had treated as tribes.

* * *

And for those who may have doubted the power of the Department of the Interior to recognize sovereign political bodies, a 1994 act of Congress appears to lay such doubts to rest. In the Federally Recognized Tribe List Act of 1994,[60] Congress specifically directed the Department to publish annually "a list of all Indian tribes which the Secretary recognizes to be eligible for the special programs and services provided by the United States to Indians because of their status as Indians." The Department published tribal lists for 1995 through 1998, all of which include Alaska Native villages such as Northway, based on this specifically delegated authority. * * *

Through the 1993 tribal list and the 1994 Tribe List Act, the federal government has recognized the historical tribal status of Alaska Native villages like Northway. In deference to that determination, we also recognize such villages as sovereign entities.

The fact that Northway Village is a federally recognized tribe answers only part of the question posed by this case. Alaska Native villages such as Northway are in a unique position: Unlike most other tribes, Alaska Native villages occupy no reservations and for the most part possess no Indian

---

[49]   United States v. Holliday, 70 U.S. (3 Wall.) 407, 419, 18 L.Ed. 182 (1865).

[60]   25 U.S.C. § 479a et seq. (West Supp.1998).

country. Mr. Baker and the dissent argue that the existence of tribal land—Indian country—is the cornerstone of tribal court jurisdiction and that Congress necessarily withdrew such jurisdiction from Alaska Native villages when it enacted ANCSA.

To evaluate this argument, we must decide how much authority tribes retain in the absence of reservation land. We must, in other words, determine the meaning of "sovereignty" in the context of Alaska's post-ANCSA landscape by asking whether ANCSA, to the extent that it eliminated Alaska's Indian country, also divested Alaska Native villages of their sovereign powers.

* * *

In determining whether Tribes retain their sovereign powers, the United States Supreme Court looks to the character of the power that the tribe seeks to exercise, not merely the location of events. * * * Because Northway Village's status as a federally recognized tribe is undisputed and its adjudication of child custody disputes over member children is necessary "to protect tribal self-government or to control internal relations," its tribal courts require no express congressional delegation of the right to determine custody of tribal children.

* * *

Ample evidence exists that Congress did not intend for ANCSA to divest tribes of their powers to adjudicate domestic disputes between members. Congress intended ANCSA to free Alaska Natives from the dictates of "lengthy wardship or trusteeship," not to handicap tribes by divesting them of their sovereign powers. As a principal author of the law has explained, ANCSA "rejected the paternalism of the past and gave Alaska Natives an innovative way to retain their land and culture without forcing them into a failed reservation system." But nowhere does the law express any intent to force Alaska Natives to abandon their sovereignty.

Outside of ANCSA, too, ample evidence exists that Congress did not intend for ANCSA to divest tribes of their powers to adjudicate domestic disputes between members. Post-ANCSA congressional actions such as the Tribe List Act, ICWA, and the Tribal Justice Act indicate that Congress intended for post-ANCSA Alaska Natives to continue to regulate their internal affairs.

* * *

4.   *Federal case law suggests that post-ANCSA, Alaska's tribes retain non-territorial sovereignty that includes power over child custody disputes.*

* * *

The federal decisions discussing the relationship between Indian country and tribal sovereignty indicate that the nature of tribal sovereignty stems from two intertwined sources: tribal membership and tribal land. The United States Supreme Court has recognized the dual nature of Indian sovereignty for more than a century and a half; the Court has explained that, under federal law, "Indian tribes are unique aggregations possessing attributes of sovereignty over both their members and their territory."[96] Tribes not only enjoy the authority to exercise control within the boundaries of their lands, but they also possess the inherent "power of regulating their internal and social relations."[97]

* * *

Decisions of the United States Supreme Court support the conclusion that Native American nations may possess the authority to govern themselves even when they do not occupy Indian country. The federal decisions contain language supporting the existence of tribal sovereignty based on either land or tribal status. Indian law jurisprudence stresses the central importance of membership and the fundamental powers of tribes to adjudicate internal family law affairs like child custody disputes. * * *

   5.   *Alaska's state courts retain concurrent jurisdiction over this dispute.*

Although we recognize Northway's jurisdiction to adjudicate child custody disputes between village members, its jurisdiction is not exclusive. The State of Alaska can also exercise jurisdiction over such disputes. This is so because villages like Northway presumably do not occupy Indian country, and federal law suggests that the only bar to state jurisdiction over Indians and Indian affairs is the presence of Indian country. Outside Indian country, all disputes arising within the State of Alaska, whether tribal or not, are within the state's general jurisdiction.[143] Thus the state, as well as the tribe, can adjudicate such disputes in its courts. A tribe's inherent jurisdiction does not give tribal courts priority, or presumptive authority, in disputes involving tribal members.

* * *

For example, the fact that many of Alaska's Native villages are located far from the courtrooms of our state trial courts limits our state judicial system's ability to respond to the needs of many Alaska Natives. Moreover, we have recognized that Alaska is home to "uniquely divergent cultures," including many "Native cultures which remain today much as they were prior to the infusion of Anglo-American culture."[150] Because of this great diversity, barriers of culture, geography, and language combine to create a judicial system that remains foreign and inaccessible to many Alaska

---

[96]   United States v. Mazurie, 419 U.S. 544, 557 (1975) (citing Worcester v. Georgia, 6 Pet. 515, 557 (1832)).

[97]   Id. (quoting United States v. Kagama, 118 U.S. 375, 381–82 (1886)).

[143]   See AS 22.10.020(a).

[150]   Calista Corp. v. Mann, 564 P.2d 53, 61 (Alaska 1977).

Natives. These differences have "created problems in administering a unified justice system sensitive to the needs of Alaska's various cultures."[152] By acknowledging tribal jurisdiction, we enhance the opportunity for Native villages and the state to cooperate in the child custody arena by sharing resources. Recognizing the ability and power of tribes to resolve internal disputes in their own forums, while preserving the right of access to state courts, can only help in the administration of justice for all.

D. TRIBAL LAW APPLIES TO CHILD CUSTODY DISPUTES ADJUDICATED BY TRIBAL COURTS.

Ms. John and the amici argue that Northway should be able to apply its own law, including tribal law and custom, in resolving a custody dispute that falls within its jurisdiction. We agree.

Decisions addressing tribal power to adjudicate internal matters state that tribes have the "power to make their own substantive law in internal matters and to enforce that law in their own forums."[158] Similarly, the Supreme Court has stressed that tribal sovereignty is valuable precisely because it enables Native Americans "to control their own internal relations, and to preserve their own unique customs and social order."[159] Because Alaska Native tribes have inherent sovereignty to adjudicate internal tribal disputes, the tribes must be able to apply their tribal law to those disputes. Thus, tribal sovereignty over issues like family relations includes the right to enforce tribal law in resolving disputes.

E. THE DOCTRINE OF COMITY PROPERLY GOVERNS STATE RECOGNITION OF TRIBAL COURT DECISIONS.

We must also determine whether the superior court should have dismissed Mr. Baker's identical state suit. After examining whether states should afford tribal court judgments full faith and credit, we conclude that the comity doctrine provides the proper framework for deciding when state courts should recognize tribal court decisions.

* * *

* * * Although Indian tribes, as domestic dependent nations, differ from foreign countries, we agree with the Ninth Circuit that comity affords the best "analytical framework for recognizing tribal judgments."[173] Numerous state courts have reached the same conclusion. We therefore hold that, as a general rule, our courts should respect tribal court decisions under the comity doctrine.

---

[152] *Calista*, 564 P.2d at 61.

[158] Santa Clara Pueblo v. Martinez, (1978).

[159] Duro v. Reina, 495 U.S. 676, 685–86 (1990).

[173] Wilson v. Marchington, 127 F.3d 805, 810 (9th Cir.1997).

* * *

NOTES

1.   As a result of the U.S. Supreme Court's decision in *Venetie* holding that Alaska Native villages like Northway Village that occupy ANCSA lands are not within "Indian country," Public Law 280 was held not to apply in *John* by the Alaska Supreme Court. Of course, neither did the Indian Child Welfare Act (ICWA), as *John* involved a custody dispute between parents. See pages The Alaska Supreme Court has held that under ICWA, cases involving Native children should be transferred to Native courts absent good cause to the contrary under 25 U.S.C. § 1911(b). See In re CRH, 29 P.3d 849 (Alaska 2001). In holding that full faith and credit be given to a Native court's adoption judgment, the Ninth Circuit in Kaltag Tribal Council v. Jackson, 344 Fed. Appx. 324 (9th Cir.2009), applied Venetie's holding in finding that neither the ICWA nor Public Law 280 prevented the tribal court from exercising jurisdiction. The Ninth Circuit reiterated Venetie's finding that reservation status is not a requirement of jurisdiction because "[a] Tribe's authority over its reservation or Indian country is incidental to its authority over its members." *Venetie*, 944 F.2d at 559 n.12.

2.   The Alaska Supreme Court has continued to apply the principles of John v. Baker. In Healy Lake Village v. Mt. McKinley Bank, 322 P.3d 866 (2014), the court held that a dispute involving a tribal election must be dismissed: "Because the state has no interest in determining the outcome of this internal tribal dispute, the tribal election and membership dispute in this case remains within the 'tribe's retained inherent sovereign powers.' In Simmonds v. Parks, 329 P.3d 995 (Alaska 2014), a proceeding under ICWA, a father failed to exhaust his tribal remedies by failing to appeal a Minto Village tribal court decree, which terminated his parental rights, to the Minto Tribal Court of Appeals. The Alaska Supreme Court held that there was no denial of due process in the tribal court and that the father could not proceed in state court, which was bound to give full faith and credit to the tribal court decree: "We have recognized that tribal court judgments in ICWA-defined child custody proceedings are entitled to full faith and credit to the same extent as a judgment of a sister state." See generally Heather Kendall-Miller, *State of Alaska v. Native Village of Tanana: Enhancing Tribal Power by Affirming Concurrent Tribal Jurisdiction to Initiate ICWA Defined Child Custody Proceedings, Both Inside and Outside of Indian Country*, 28 Alaska L.Rev. 217–44 (2011); Ryan Fortson, *Advancing Tribal Court Criminal Jurisdiction in Alaska*, 32 Alaska L.Rev. 93 (2015)

3.   The applicability of Indian country jurisdictional principles in Alaska is limited in any event because it is a Public Law 280 state. Alaska was added to the list of mandatory states in 1958. See page 558, supra. Generally speaking, in Indian country the state has broad criminal jurisdiction, with tribes retaining concurrent jurisdiction over Indians. State regulatory laws do not apply to the tribe and its members but do apply to non-members. Tribes

have regulatory jurisdiction, including concurrent jurisdiction over nonmembers, except that the rule of *Montana v. United States*, see Chapter 7D, supra, applies to nonmembers on fee land. One decision upheld a conviction of an Indian hunting deer out of season as defined by Alaska law because, assuming that the native allotment where it occurred was Indian country, the law was "prohibitory" and not "regulatory" and therefore covered by the more extensive grant of criminal jurisdiction under Public Law 280. *Jones v. State*, 936 P.2d 1263 (Alaska Ct. App. 1997).

4.   The Violence Against Women Act Amendments of 2013 (see pages 586–575) included a provision in section 910 that excluded Alaska Tribes (other than Metlakatla). Congress amended the statute in 2014 to repeal section 910, extending VAWA to all Alaska Tribes. Pub. L. No. 113–275.

5. NATIVE CULTURE AND SUBSISTENCE RIGHTS

The corporate form selected by Congress for administering ANCSA had little connection to the institutions of self-governance or subsistence traditions which Alaska Natives had developed over generations. ANCSA made the primarily rural, often non-English speaking natives involuntary participants in the corporate world. Inexperience in managing a corporation, poor investments, exploitation by "scavenger" consultants, enormous administrative burdens, under-capitalization, and hostile litigation were not unexpectedly among the major difficulties encountered by the native corporations. The corporations probably spent more than the $465 million they received in legal and accounting fees and other office overhead expenses since the Act's inception. See Hal Bernton, *Alaska's Native Corporations at 20: Mixed Results Amid Sharp Divisions*, Wash. Post, Jan. 2, 1992, at A3. See also Ben Summit, *The Alaska Native Claims Settlement Act (ANCSA): Friend or Foe in the Struggle to Recover Alaska Native Heritage*, 14 T.M. Cooley L.Rev. 607, 621 (1997).

In 1985, Haida Corporation became the first village corporation to file for bankruptcy; the following year, the first regional corporation also filed for protection from creditors. See 5 Alaska Bus. Monthly, § 1, at 24, Dec.1988. A few others followed, but all have since emerged after bankruptcy reorganization.

The difficulties in the transition to the corporate form cannot be explained simply by a lack of business experience on the part of the natives, or even the vast structural complexities of ANCSA. William Iggiagruk Hensley played an important role in the passage of ANCSA as one of the founders of the Alaska Federation of Natives. After helping to win passage of ANCSA, Hensley spent twenty years working for the Inuit-owned NANA Regional Corporation established by the legislation. Here are some of his reflections on his experiences with the corporate form established by ANCSA, and the challenges of managing this Westernized institution according to Alaska Native traditional knowledge, values and culture:

In the beginning, we had little idea what a corporation was or what it could become. But we put our spirit, goodwill, and communal effort into designing NANA's structure, adding some important elements of our traditional approach to getting things done. Our past livelihood had always depended upon the recognition that achieving success required the effort of all our people. So the corporation we created was not a typically hierarchical arrangement. There were checks and balances, and ways of recognizing special talents. Those who had good Inupiaq language skills ratcheted up in importance and became a bridge to the older generation and more traditional people. Those well versed in naluagmiut knowledge—accounting and finance, for instance—did the grunt work of corporate bureaucracy.

* * *

At NANA, we worked hard on developing cooperative relationships with other local entities as we did on making investments and generating profits. We took satisfaction in using our institutions to foster basic human values—cooperation, sharing, hard work, and humility, among others—that had sustained our people in another, fast disappearing age. During my years at NANA, I often reflected on those lessons I had learned as a boy in the bush. They still applied, even in business: Know your environment. Know your partners. Plan ahead. Use only as much manpower and resources as necessary. Make sure your efforts benefit the whole community.

So much had changed, and yet the essence was the same.

William L. Iggiagruk Hensley, Fifty Miles from Tomorrow: A Memoir of Alaska and the Real People 172–74 (2008).

Hensley's observations about NANA apply generally to the other regional corporations, most of which have improved their economic conditions considerably, in some cases dramatically, since the difficult beginnings. While some village corporations have done well, most have struggled. A piece about the Alaska economy generally, Naomi Klouda, *The Alaska Economy: Past, Present, and Future*, Alaska Bus. Monthly Jan. 2015, included an assessment of the Alaska Native corporations:

Of the Alaskan-owned companies that self-report gross revenue to Alaska Business Monthly, the top four are all Alaska Native Corporations, with Arctic Slope Regional Corporation remaining in the lead with its $2.5 billion in gross revenue. Following closely is the Bristol Bay Native Corporation (BBNC)in the second slot ($1.8 billion), NANA Regional in the third ($1.7 billion), and Chenega Corporation in fourth ($1 billion). In fact, of the twenty highest grossing Alaska Business Monthly Top 49er companies, fifteen are Alaska Native Corporations formed under the 1971 Alaska Native Claims Settlement Act.

Alaska Native Corporations saw a lot of changes in the past thirty years to build today's present rate of success, says Jason Metrokin, president and CEO of the BBNC. One of the most important moves was the ability to find diverse investments to buffer against downturns in any one segment. Today, there is a new shift at BBNC and other corporations to add home-grown investment opportunities into the mix.

"We've all had the experience in the Lower 48 and even internationally in finding opportunities to diversify our portfolios. Now there's a sharper focus on small business growth and expansion, such as the Alaska cottage industry businesses that have done well."

BBNC's investment in Peak Oil Field Services was one of the biggest Native corporation acquisitions. Investing in-state makes sense. The expertise and resources are here, while Outside investments may prove difficult to manage from afar, Metrokin says.

"This doesn't mean we're turning our backs on our business emphasis of diversification," he says. "Other Native corporations are following a similar strategy, looking for new opportunities. Oil field support is going to be a boon for Alaska, given our new tax structure. You'll see several regional corporations are building new commercial real estate complexes, such as Calista and CIRI. One of the big areas of investment is government contracting. On the flip side, the federal government is looking for ways to pull back spending. There are regulatory challenges. We are having to look at new ways to contract for the federal government."

Alaska Natives depend on the availability of animal and fish resources, and subsistence uses remain vital to their culture, survival, and religious practices. The following case arose before the enactment of ANILCA, but it demonstrates that state judicial remedies are available to Alaska Natives for disputes arising under state fish and game laws. The Alaska state constitution governs religious freedom in Article I section 4, which states "No law shall be made respecting an establishment of religion, or prohibiting the free exercise thereof." The standard for free exercise claims under Article I section 4 of the Alaska is established in the following decision.

FRANK V. STATE OF ALASKA
Supreme Court of Alaska, 1979
604 P.2d 1068.

MATTHEWS, JUSTICE.

In October of 1975, Delnor Charlie, a young man from Minto, died. Immediately preparations were made for a ritual that had been performed countless times in Minto and other Central Alaska Athabascan villages. It is called the funeral potlatch, a ceremony of several days' duration culminating in a feast, eaten after burial of the deceased, which is shared by members of the village and others who come from sometimes distant locations.

Delnor Charlie's burial, as is traditional, was delayed until friends and relatives living elsewhere could reach Minto and until the foods necessary for the potlatch could be prepared. With the food preparation under way, Carlos Frank and twenty-five to thirty other men from the village formed several hunting parties for the purpose of taking a moose. It was their belief that there was insufficient moose meat available for a proper potlatch. One cow moose was shot, which Frank assisted in transporting to Minto. Some 200 to 250 people attended the final feast.

[State officials] charged Frank with unlawful transportation of game illegally taken. The season for moose hunting was closed and in any event there was no open season for cow moose in 1975.

* * *

On appeal [from a district court decision adverse to Frank] Superior Court Judge Van Hoomissen also determined "that the potlatch is an activity rooted in religious belief and a very integral part of the religious tenets of the Athabascan Indian. . . . The sincerity of the natives of Minto in their religious beliefs is not doubted." However, he agreed with Judge Clayton that fresh moose meat was not such an "absolute necessity . . . as to override the compelling state interest of the State of Alaska in the management and control of its game for the benefit of all its people, native and white," and affirmed the conviction.

We have concluded that the free exercise clauses of the first amendment to the United States Constitution, and Article I, section 4 of the Alaska Constitution, protect Frank's conduct and that the state has not demonstrated reasons which justify prohibiting it. * * *

I

No value has a higher place in our constitutional system of government than that of religious freedom. The freedom to believe is protected absolutely. The freedom to act on one's religious beliefs is also protected, but such protection may be overcome by compelling state interests. A law imposing criminal or other penalties on the performance of acts which conscience compels, pressures the underlying beliefs and infringes to that extent the freedom to believe. * * *

Because of the close relationship between conduct and belief and because of the high value we assign to religious beliefs, religiously impelled actions can be forbidden only where they pose "some substantial threat to public safety, peace or order," or where there are competing governmental interests that are "of the highest order and [are] not otherwise served."

* * * In certain cases the free exercise clause requires government to accommodate religious practices by creating exemptions from general laws. *Wisconsin v. Yoder* involved a conflict between respondents' belief, rooted in the religion of the old order Amish, that children should not attend public school beyond the eighth grade, and a Wisconsin statute requiring all children to attend public schools through the age of sixteen. The court held that an exemption must be granted. Other courts have also required exceptions to facially neutral laws in order to protect religiously based conduct.

II

The free exercise clause may be invoked only where there is a religion involved, only where the conduct in question is religiously based, and only where the claimant is sincere. These requirements are readily present here. We shall examine them in order.

The appellant presented impressive evidence concerning the religion of the Central Alaskan Athabascan people. Several Athabascans and expert anthropologists testified and anthropological works were received in evidence. The evidence was unrefuted. * * *

Athabascan culture is highly individualized. From a complex belief system individual selection is tolerated and is the norm. Yet, there is a distinct belief system recognizable in Athabascan villages many miles apart. These beliefs have blended comfortably with Christianity which was introduced in the 19th century.

Death is the life crisis receiving the greatest attention in current Athabascan culture. While it may be awaited with equanimity, it is an event of predominant significance, whose repercussions are long felt in the village.

The funeral potlatch is the most important institution in Athabascan life. It is mandatory. Peter John, seventy-six, a former tribal chief in Minto, could not remember a death that was not followed by a funeral potlatch. It is apparently an obscenity to suggest that possibility. While a potlatch may be held to celebrate secular occasions, the funeral potlatch is distinguished by its fundamentally sacred aspect. The ritual has its origins in antiquity and it has not changed in any important respect since anthropologists first began to describe it.

Food is the cornerstone of the ritual. From the moment the death is learned of, food preparation begins. People begin to arrive in the village from nearby and remote places. * * * The body will not be buried until a sufficient quantity of the proper food is prepared for the post burial feast. In the case of Delnor Charlie this took four to five days.

Athabascans believe that the funeral potlatch is the last meal shared by the living with the deceased. It is a communion meal. The deceased is discussed and songs of eulogy are sung. The deceased is thought to partake of the meal and this helps his spirit on its journey.

The funeral potlatch serves other functions. The grief of the family is to be eased. The community becomes involved and the sharing of food is the communal tie. Prayers are said for the dead and the living. All who have come and contributed are thanked. It is hoped that the funeral potlatch and one that is to follow, often more than a year later, the memorial potlatch, will assuage the spirits and prevent future deaths.

From the foregoing it is clear, and consistent with the findings of the courts below, that the funeral potlatch is a religious ceremony. The role of moose meat in that ceremony must next be examined.

Native foods comprise almost all of the foods served at the funeral potlatch. In a culture without many formal rules this is an absolute requirement. Native food means moose, bear, caribou, porcupine, fish, duck, and berry dishes.

Of the native foods moose is at the apex. * * * As the district court found, it is the staff of life; it is the meat which the people regard as most important for their sustenance. However, the district court found that although the evidence indicated that moose is the most desirable of foods to be served, it is not "an essential requirement."

The district court's finding that moose was not essential for a funeral potlatch is based primarily on the following testimony of Chief Peter John:

Q. Could there be a potlatch without wild meat?

A. Well, it could be, maybe, but then I don't think I'll enjoy it.

However, John also stated that he had been to hundreds of potlatches and had never attended one in which there was no moose meat, a recollection shared by Catherine Attla, fifty-two, and Carlos Frank. Barbara Lane, an anthropologist, provided this gloss on John's statements:

A. If a Roman Catholic priest were in some bush area up here and found himself without the proper wafers and wine, he could still perform his function with some substitute, but it wouldn't do in the sense—If at all possible to have the proper foods, that's what you would use.

Q.   But nevertheless it could be accomplished?

A.   I believe so. As a dire strait, in some unusual circumstance.

Other witnesses stated that moose meat is a necessary requirement having the sacramental equivalent to the wine and wafer in Christianity. Frank and all of the Athabascan witnesses, including Peter John, testified that they could not risk showing disrespect to the dead by failing to provide moose for the post burial ritual.

     * * *

We think the evidence is inescapable that the utilization of moose meat at a funeral potlatch is a practice deeply rooted in the Athabascan religion. While moose itself is not sacred, it is needed for proper observance of a sacred ritual which must take place soon after death occurs. Moose is the centerpiece of the most important ritual in Athabascan life and is the equivalent of sacred symbols in other religions.

The question of sincerity requires no extended discussion. * * * That conclusion is abundantly supported in the record.

III

Having established that protected religious conduct is involved, we turn next to an evaluation of the competing state interest. There can be no question but that there is a very strong state interest underlying hunting restrictions. The game resources of Alaska occupy a place in the lifestyle of Alaskans which is unparalleled elsewhere in the United States. Rural Alaska natives are acutely aware of this. * * *

It is not enough, however, simply to conclude that there is a compelling state interest in maintaining a healthy moose population. The question is whether that interest, or any other, will suffer if an exemption is granted to accommodate the religious practice at issue. * * *

The state contends that widespread civil disobedience will result if Athabascans are allowed to take moose out of season when necessary for a funeral potlatch. As the state's brief colorfully puts it: "Alaskans seem to have a marked tendency to come unglued over fish and wildlife allocation issues." The state predicts as a result, general non-observance of the game laws, a "downward spiral into anarchy", "poaching and creek robbing," and "tragic confrontations" between recreational hunters and Athabascans.

We give no credence to this argument. It is, first of all, not supported by any evidence. Moreover, its prediction of general lawlessness is an extreme and unwarranted comment on the general character of the state's citizens. Interests which justify limitations on religious practices must be far more definite than these. Justifications founded only on fear and apprehension are insufficient to overcome rights asserted under the First Amendment.

* * * The burden of demonstrating a compelling state interest which justifies curtailing a religiously based practice lies with the state. On this record, that burden has not been met.

IV

Finally, we turn to the state's argument that granting an exemption in this case would amount to an establishment of religion contravening the establishment clauses of the United States Constitution and the Alaska Constitution. Accommodating the religious beliefs of Athabascans by permitting the killing of a moose for a funeral potlatch does not rise to [a violation]. The purpose of such an accommodation is merely to permit the observance of the ancient traditions of the Athabascans. As such, the exemption "reflects nothing more than the governmental obligation of neutrality in the face of religious differences, and does not represent that involvement of religious with secular institutions which it is the object of the Establishment Clause to forestall."

V

If the reason the state did not urge that exemptions for funeral potlaches will endanger moose populations is that such a showing cannot be made, the state may be well advised to adopt regulations governing the taking of moose for such purposes. Carefully designed regulations would have the effect of guarding against abuses and aid in record keeping, which would be of value in determining the impact of the exemption on moose populations. There exist models for similar religious accommodations. For example, 16 U.S.C.A. § 668(a), authorizes the Secretary of the Interior to allow eagles to be taken "for the religious purposes of Indian tribes," upon a finding that the taking is compatible with the preservation of the species. Regulations have been published implementing this. 50 C.F.R. § 22.22 (1978). * * *

The judgment is reversed and this case is remanded with instructions to dismiss the complaint.

CONNOR, JUSTICE, dissenting.

On the record I am unable to conclude that a freshly killed moose was necessary to conduct the funeral potlatch. While it is traditional that as many native foods as possible should be served, it has not been established by the evidence in this case that fresh moose meat is indispensable for such a ceremony. It is merely desirable that such meat be served at those functions. For this particular potlatch there was already on hand a moose hind quarter, bear meat, and fish. * * * To the extent that moose meat was desirable because it had magico-religious, i.e., symbolic significance, it was already available.

Unless the use of fresh moose meat rises to the level of a cardinal religious principle, unless it is central to a religious observance, it cannot qualify as a practice protected by the "free exercise" clauses of either the state or federal constitutions.

Because there was not a sufficient showing made here, a case for the application of those clauses was not made out.

NOTES

1.   *Frank* sets out a three-step process to determine when government action must meet the compelling interest standard: (1) religion must be involved, (2) the conduct in question in religiously based and (3) the claimant is sincere. The court here accepted the lower court's finding of religious basis for Frank's claim, but did not expand on how courts should arrive at the first step of the test. How should a court approach a case where the religious basis for a claim is less clear?

2.   *Frank* upheld a claim of protection of religion in spite of a compelling government interest that only indirectly burdened the religious practice. Although the balancing test is fact-specific, the court has reaffirmed the *Frank* standard. See Herning v. Eason, 739 P.2d 167 (Alaska 1987); Sands v. Living Ward Fellowship, 34 P.3d 955 (Alaska 2001).

3.   In Phillip v. State of Alaska, 347 P.3d 128 (Alaska Ct.App.2015), thirteen Yup'ik fishermen, all living a subsistence lifestyle, were charged with violating a state emergency fish and game order restricting fishing for king salmon with gillnets in the Kuskokwim River. The fishermen claimed a religious exemption under the free exercise clause of the Alaska Constitution. The Alaska Court of Appeals applied *Frank*, and found that even though fishing was a valid religious activity the state interest in maintaining a healthy and sustainable king salmon population would be harmed if a religious exemption was granted. The court compared the taking of just one moose in *Frank* with the need for "unfettered subsistence fishing" by the defendants, and found the threat to the population was greater than in *Frank*. The emergency order in *Phillip* was a result of unexpectedly low run numbers, which some attributed to climate change.

Phillip can be viewed as a reminder of the distinct threat of climate change to native people and subsistence. "If Yup'ik people do not fish for King Salmon, the King Salmon spirit will be offended and it will not return to the river." Many Native Villages are at risk of relocation due to erosion or other consequences of melting icepack, which also affects the migratory patterns of animals that rural Alaskans depend on. *See* Elizabeth Ristroph, *Alaska Tribes' Melting Subsistence Rights* 1 Ariz.J.Envtl.L.&Pol'y 47 (2010). Several coastal Alaska Native villages are at the front edge of climate change due to rapid melting of sea ice as temperatures have risen from 2 to as much as 5 degrees Fahrenheit in some parts of the Arctic region. With the sea already having claimed significant areas of land, the Native Village of Kivalina, 80 miles north of the Arctic Circle, brought suit, alleging that "fossil fuel emissions by various energy-related multi-national companies had resulted in global warming, severely eroding the land where the City of Kivalina sits and threatening it with imminent destruction." Native Village of Kivalina v. Exxon Mobil Corp., 696 F.3d 849 (9th Cir.2012), ruled that the Village's nuisance claim had been displaced by the Clean Air Act and EPA actions taken pursuant to it. For a powerful presentation of the Alaska Natives' dilemma, see Adam Weymouth, *When Global Warming Kills Your God*, The Atlantic, June 3, 2014.

NOTE: SURVIVAL OF ALASKA NATIVE SUBSISTENCE RIGHTS UNDER ANILCA AND ALASKA STATE LAW

When Congress passed the Alaska National Interest Lands Conservation Act (ANILCA) in 1980, identifying public lands to continue in federal ownership and opening others to selection by the state under the Statehood Act, as anticipated by ANCSA, it included provisions to protect continued subsistence uses on federal public lands in Alaska. See 16 U.S.C.A. §§ 3101–3133. At the time of ANCSA, Congress expected that the Secretary of the Interior would act to protect native subsistence hunting and fishing uses on the federal lands, but that did not happen. Therefore, ANILCA imposed specific obligations on federal officials managing the lands and conditioned state fish and game management on giving priorities to subsistence users.

To understand the political volatility surrounding ANILCA and the issue of subsistence in Alaska, familiarity with the geography of the state as well as an examination of the meaning of subsistence is helpful. Alaska totals over 570,000 square miles, while its population consists of about 737,000 persons. Though population density averages a little more than one person per square mile, Alaskans are largely concentrated in a few major population centers. Outside urban areas, however, there are still over two hundred villages, many of them remote, and some with only a few families. Alaska has fewer road miles than New Hampshire, and many Alaska villages are accessible only by plane, boat, snow machine, or dogsled. These villages, varying in size from more than one thousand to less than one hundred residents, are predominantly occupied by natives. And, while technology and a cash economy are increasingly permeating these villages, traditional native values, culture, and lifestyles still largely prevail.

For Alaska Natives, subsistence is not limited to the physical, "sustenance" dimension of hunting, fishing, and gathering, but rather, describes an entire way of life. Subsistence encompasses a rich social and spiritual component of native culture in Alaska.

As natives interact with each other and their environment, they pass on knowledge about local resources, preserve traditional customs and ceremonies associated with seasonal fishing and hunting, and maintain their ties to the land and water. Subsistence living strengthens the links within the community and between the generations. It etches the values, skills, and merits associated with an adaptive, interdependent lifestyle based on a complex system of unwritten rules, knowledge, and customs into the interstices of the community. As recognized by many commentators and by Alaska Natives themselves, subsistence is not only an absolute necessity for the economic survival of modern native families, it is the cultural nucleus of native life. Sophie Theriault, Ghislain Otis, Gerald Duhaime, and Christopher Furgal, *The Legal Protection of Subsistence: A Prerequisite of Food Security for the Inuit of Alaska*, 22 Alaska L.Rev. 35, 36–37 (2005).

Non-Alaskans, the courts, and Congress all have struggled to comprehend the transcendent importance of subsistence activity to the social and cultural relations of Alaska Natives apart from economic harm from loss of fishing and hunting resources. Yet in 1997, the Ninth Circuit Court of Appeals could write, in denying damages to Alaska Natives resulting from The Exxon Valdez oil spill, that the natives had not suffered injury of a different kind from the general public (as required to state a claim under public nuisance law); "While the oil spill may have affected Alaska Natives more severely than other members of the public, 'the right to obtain and share wild food, enjoy uncontaminated nature, and cultivate traditional, cultural, spiritual, and psychological benefits in pristine natural surroundings' is shared by all Alaskans." In re The Exxon Valdez, 104 F.3d 1196 (9th Cir.1997).

———————

ANILCA, enacted in 1980, offered the state the prerogative of maintaining its control of fish and game on Alaska's vast public lands provided the state's laws afford "long-term protection to the subsistence way of life." Bowing to political pressures, Congress did not limit the subsistence preference to natives, however, but extended it to others in rural Alaska who had relied on hunting and fishing for subsistence. ANILCA expressly required that a state-law subsistence priority be based on:

(1)   customary and direct dependence upon the population [of fish and wildlife] as the mainstay of livelihood;

(2)   local residency; and

(3)   the availability of alternative resources.

16 U.S.C. § 3114.

The failure of ANILCA to articulate that subsistence preference should be specific to native people and the state's insistence on treating native and non-natives the same have fomented a high-pitched battle over how to manage access to fish and game on federal public lands in Alaska. Several attempts by the state to implement the preference have fallen short. They were followed by federal regulations that address the issue in ways that are politically controversial in the state, resulting in continuing litigation.

An Alaska statute passed in 1978 gave subsistence uses priority over commercial and sport hunting and fishing whenever the resources fall short of meeting all needs and it becomes necessary to restrict the overall take. Attempting to apply this as consistent with ANILCA, the state agency interpreted it as a preference for rural residents. But the state supreme court set aside the rural preference as not authorized by statute. Madison v. Alaska Dep't of Fish and Game, 696 P.2d 168 (Alaska 1985).

Then, in a renewed attempt to comply with ANILCA, the legislature amended the state's subsistence law in 1986 to state a rural residency requirement. The statute and implementing regulations were attacked from all sides.

State regulations defined the term "rural" to include only areas dominated by a subsistence economy, thereby excluding most of the state. Alaska Natives challenged the regulations on a number of grounds. Indians of the Kenai Peninsula, an area that was outside the definition, challenged the rule. Kenaitze Indian Tribe v. State of Alaska, 860 F.2d 312 (9th Cir.1988), cert. denied 491 U.S. 905 (1989).

In Bobby v. State of Alaska, 718 F.Supp. 764 (D.Alaska 1989), native residents of Lime Village objected to provisions of subsistence regulations setting seasons and bag limits on the taking of caribou and moose. The court held that the seasons were arbitrary for failing to accommodate the village's customary harvesting of moose and caribou throughout the year and the bag limits on subsistence hunting by village residents were struck down as inconsistent with the communal sharing of moose and caribou by villagers.

As the federal courts were dealing with native challenges to the regulations, the state Supreme Court, in an extraordinary ruling, threw out the entire statutory preference for rural residents to take fish and game for subsistence purposes on state constitutional grounds. See McDowell v. Alaska, 785 P.2d 1 (Alaska 1989). *McDowell* held that the rural residency requirement improperly disqualified "non-rural" residents citing state constitutional provisions that said fish and wildlife were reserved "for common use" and that natural resources laws "shall apply equally to all persons similarly situated with reference to the subject matter." This strained interpretation put the Alaska law at odds with ANILCA. Thus, Alaska was not in compliance with ANILCA and the state lost the right to regulate fish and wildlife on federal public lands. See, Jack B. McGee, *Subsistence Hunting and Fishing in Alaska: Does ANCILA's Rural Subsistence Priority Really Conflict with the Alaska Constitution*, 27 Alaska L.Rev. 221 (2010), arguing that there is no conflict between ANILCA and Alaska's Constitution.

The Alaska legislature then tried a backhanded way of accomplishing the same result. It passed a 1992 law requiring the state Boards of Fisheries and Game to designate "non-subsistence areas" where a dependence on subsistence activity is not a principal characteristic of the economy and culture, and no preference is applied. See A.S. 16.05.258. The State Supreme Court upheld this classification defining areas where no preference applied, but struck down under *McDowell* a provision that extended the preference, i.e., eligibility to receive subsistence permits, partly based on "proximity of the domicile" of the user to the fish or game population. Alaska v. Kenaitze Indian Tribe *(Kenaitze II)*, 894 P.2d 632 (Alaska 1995). This left standing state law criteria for subsistence users that consider their "customary and direct dependence" on fish or game as a mainstay of their livelihood and their ability to obtain other food. With "non-subsistence" areas being those closest to cities, the state agency tried to limit the preference, as a practical matter, primarily to rural residents. But urban residents could still receive a subsistence permit if they can meet the two remaining qualifications in the statute.

In the meantime, the federal agencies were moving forward to fill the regulatory void created by McDowell. The regulations to implement this new approach were then litigated in the three "Katie John" cases. The namesake of this trilogy is the venerable Athabascan elder, Katie John. She grew up near the Batzulnetas traditional fish camp; now part of a national park. Until her death at 97 she was a powerful and effective advocate for Native subsistence rights on many fronts. Katie John raised 20 children, including 6 adopted children, to whom she passed on generations-old customary and traditional subsistence practices. At the time of her death she counted more than 250 descendants. She was determined that her children and grandchildren be able to feed themselves and carry on the age-old practices she had learned from her parents.

Responding to native frustration with the state's awkward and unsuccessful attempts to meet the requirements of ANILCA, the U.S. Department of the Interior promulgated regulations, effectively taking over the task. 55 Fed. Reg. 27, 114 (1990). ANILCA defined the term "Federal land" to mean "lands the title to which is in the United States," 16 U.S.C. § 3102(2) and the term "land" to mean "lands, waters, and interests therein." 16 U.S.C. § 3102(1) The federal regulations defined public lands where the subsistence regulations applied as including "navigable waters" in which the federal government has reserved water rights. After years of intense litigation and public controversy, the Ninth Circuit ruled that the federal government's definition of public lands in this way was reasonable, and that it was the government's responsibility to identify those waters. Alaska v. Babbitt, 72 F.3d 698 (9th Cir.1995), cert. denied 517 U.S. 1187 (1996) ("*Katie John I*").

Then, in regulations adopted in 1999, the federal government elaborated upon the earlier regulations to identify those public lands and waters to which ANILCA applies. 64 Fed. Reg. 1276 (1999) (codified at 36 C.F.R. § 242, 50 C.F.R. § 100). These regulations were critical as a matter of water law because they added considerable specificity to the federal reserved water rights. Under the previous regulations, the federal agencies confirmed that the reserved rights generally applied on all federal lands and "adjacent" waters where the rural preference applied. The 1999 regulations went much further and identified the specific bodies of water to which the water rights attached.

The Ninth Circuit upheld the 1999 regulations in John v. United States, 247 F.3d 1032 (9th Cir.2001) (en banc) in a narrow per curium opinion that did not address in any detail the merits of the regulations ("Katie *John II*"). The decision of Alaska Governor Tony Knowles not to appeal the *Katie John II* decision upholding the federal regulations was so controversial that it resulted in calls for his impeachment.

The state and the natives, inspired by Katie John, returned to court to obtain a comprehensive ruling on the 1999 regulations, which was handed down in John v. United States, 720 F.3d 1214 (9th Cir.2013), cert. denied 134 S. Ct. 1759 (2014) ("Katie John III"). The court, finding that the federal agencies had proceeded in a principal way, upheld the regulation.

Although the court rejected Katie John's attempt to further expand the definition of public lands, this opinion upheld federal jurisdiction, including the right to set in the stream flows, over 60% of Alaska's navigable inland waters. The decision was roundly approved in the Alaska native community; it would take time before the federal reserved rights would be fully qualified and enforced, but Katie John III laid the foundation for substantial instream flows for salmon. The state's petition for certiorari was denied.

Resource management in Alaska, under ANILCA and many other federal and state laws, is a crazy quilt of formal and informal relationships among the federal government, the state, and tribal governments. Alaska manages subsistence practices on state and private lands, which include those owned by Native Corporations. There is no preference for rural residents under state law and all Alaskans are entitled to some amount of subsistence fishing. There is no preference specifically for Native Alaskans under either regime. However federal statutes of general applicability and certain Migratory Bird Treaties make exceptions for Alaska Native subsistence hunting and fishing and expressly preempt Alaska state law. The Endangered Species Act permits endangered or threatened species to be taken for subsistence purposes by Alaska Natives. 16 U.S.C.A. § 1539(e). The Marine Mammal Protection Act includes a similar exception for coastal Native Alaskan whaling for creation of Native artifacts and non-wasteful subsistence. 16 U.S.C.A. 1371(b). Alaska Natives hunt bowhead whale under co-management between the Alaska Eskimo Whaling Commission, the federal government, and the International Whaling Commission. The Reindeer Act intended to secure a means of subsistence for Alaska Natives, by putting the reindeer herding industry under Native control. 25 U.S.C.A § 500 et seq. Nonnative reindeer herders appealed an IBIA decision that prohibited nonnative entry into the reindeer industry in Alaska in Williams v. Babbitt. 115 F.3d 657 (9th Cir.1997). The Court of Appeals held that the Reindeer Industry Act did not preclude nonnatives in Alaska from owning and importing reindeer. The court noted interpreting the Act otherwise would raise serious constitutional issues. On the applicability of these federal statutes to Alaska natives, see generally, Case & Voluck, Alaska Natives and American Laws, 281–90 (3d ed. 2012). For an analysis of the framework for Alaska native rights to Marine fisheries including evolving examples of comanagement, see Jordan Dimond, et al., *Rights and Roles: Alaska Natives and Ocean and Coastal Subsistence Resources*, 8 Fla. A&M U.L.Rev. 219 (2013).

Regulations promulgated by the Alaska Board of Game establish two different systems of subsistence hunting for moose and caribou in Alaska's Copper Basin region: (1) community hunts for groups following a hunting pattern similar to the one traditionally practiced by members of the Ahtna Tene Nene' community; and (2) individual hunts. The community hunts were based on traditional Athabascan hunting patterns of community and sharing, but the permits were available to any Alaskans hunting in this way. A private outdoors group challenged the regulatory framework for violation of the equal access and equal protection clauses of the Alaska Constitution by establishing a preference for a certain user group in Alaska Fish and Wildlife Conservation Fund v. State, 347 P.3d 97 (Alaska 2015). The court found in favor of the state and upheld the regulations. *Frank v. Alaska*, page 981–986, supra, is another example of the recognition of native traditions in Alaska state law.

In addition to its requirement of preference for subsistence hunting and fishing on public lands, ANILCA imposes responsibilities on federal land managers that are designed to protect resources and habitats important to subsistence users:

> In determining whether to withdraw, reserve, lease, or otherwise permit the use, occupancy, or disposition of public lands under any provision of law authorizing such actions, the head of the Federal agency having primary jurisdiction over such lands or his designee shall evaluate the effect of such use, occupancy, or disposition on subsistence uses and needs, the availability of other lands for the purposes sought to be achieved, and other alternatives which would reduce or eliminate the use, occupancy, or disposition of public lands needed for subsistence purposes. No such withdrawal, reservation, lease, permit, or other use, occupancy or disposition of such lands which would significantly restrict subsistence uses shall be effected until the head of such Federal agency—
>
> > (1) gives notice to the appropriate State agency and the appropriate local committees and regional councils established pursuant to section 3115 of this title;
> >
> > (2) gives notice of, and holds, a hearing in the vicinity of the area involved; and
> >
> > (3) determines that (A) such a significant restriction of subsistence uses is necessary, consistent with sound management principles for the utilization of the public lands, (B) the proposed activity will involve the minimal amount of public lands necessary to accomplish the purposes of such use, occupancy, or other disposition, and (C) reasonable steps

will be taken to minimize adverse impacts upon subsistence uses and resources resulting from such actions.

16 U.S.C.A. § 3120(a).

ANILCA's requirement in § 3120 that the Secretary "shall evaluate" the impacts of public land development on subsistence was the basis of a lawsuit by Alaska Natives seeking an injunction against oil and gas leasing on the outer continental shelf. In Amoco Production Co. v. Village of Gambell, 480 U.S. 531 (1987), cited in *John*, the United States Supreme Court held that the outer continental shelf was not within the boundary of Alaska as defined by ANILCA and therefore was not subject to the subsistence provisions of ANILCA. The Court's holding on the limited territorial reach of ANILCA has drawn criticism for its failure to consider the heavy dependence of Alaska Natives on use of the sea for subsistence hunting and fishing. See Marlyn J. Twitchell, *Amoco Production Co. v. Village of Gambell: Federal Subsistence Protection Ends at Alaska's Border*, 18 Envtl.L. 635 (1988). The Ninth Circuit rejected a claim by five Alaska Native villages to non-exclusive aboriginal hunting and fishing rights in the areas of the outer continental shelf they have traditionally used. Native Village of Eyak v. Blank, 688 F.3d 619 (9th. Cir.2012). Oil and gas development in areas of the outer continental shelf used by Alaska Natives continues. See Resisting Environmental Destruction on Indigenous Lands v. EPA, 716 F.3d 1155 (9th Cir.2013).

NOTE: POLITICAL ENGAGEMENT OF ALASKA NATIVES

About 20 distinct Native languages are spoken in Alaska. Native Alaskans strive to protect and preserve native languages as an important part of culture, but they also demand a meaningful right to vote in elections that affect them. Alaska Natives sued the State of Alaska for violating the Voting Rights Act and the voting guarantees of the Fourteenth and Fifteenth Amendments to the U.S. Constitution by failing to provide translations of voting materials to voters whose primary language is Gwich'in or Yup'ik in certain census areas. The court held the State had indeed denied the voters the information they need to cast an informed ballot. After nine months of negotiations, a judicially approved settlement agreement was reached in late 2015. Materials will now be translated into multiple Native languages and dialects and increased language assistance will be provided. This will lead to stronger election procedures and continued engagement by Native Alaskans in the political and legal system where they fight to protect their rights. See Rachel d'Oro, *Settlement reached in Alaska Native voting rights case* Alaska Dispatch News Sept. 10, 2015.

SECTION B. HAWAII: KINGDOM, OVERTHROW, AND REVIVAL

Kanaka Maoli, the Native Hawaiian people, trace their ancestry to the aina (land), the natural forces of the world, and to taro, the staple food of the Hawaiian people. The following passage is excerpted from *Native Hawaiian Law: A Treatise*, edited by Melody Kapilialoha MacKenzie (2015):

> The Hawaiian people are the living descendants of Papa, the earth mother, and Wakea, the sky father. They also trace their origins through Kane of the living waters found in streams and springs; Lono of the winter rains and the life force for agricultural crops; Kanaloa of the deep foundation of the earth, the ocean and its currents; Ku of the thunder, war, fishing, and planting; Pele of the volcano; and thousands of deities of the forest, the ocean, the winds, the rains, and the various other elements of nature. . . . This unity of humans, nature and the gods formed the fore of the Hawaiian people's philosophy, world view, and spiritual belief system.

Native Hawaiians are Polynesians, but Hawaii's isolation and environment resulted in a unique culture and society tied to the land. There are several historical distinctions that separate Native Hawaiians from other Native Americans, although none of them explains adequately the federal government's failure to assume comparable responsibilities for the protection of Hawaiian native people, their land, and their political status. Indeed, the history of the United States' conduct in Hawaii makes a particularly compelling case for redress of claims, yet Native Hawaiians remain the only major group of Native Americans with whom the nation has not reconciled historic claims.

1. HISTORIC CLAIMS AND CONTEMPORARY WRONGS

a. Traditional Land Tenure. The distant Hawaiian Islands were isolated from outside contact for centuries before 1778, when Captain James Cook arrived. High chiefs each controlled a district of an island or an entire island. Other chiefs controlled specific lands, and commoners worked the land for the benefit of the chiefs. Lands were typically divided into parcels enclosed by boundaries that radiated from a point on a mountaintop to the sea so as to enclose a drainage area. The parcel was known as an *ahupua'a,* an economically self-sufficient tract of land, which usually included farmland, water, and access to the sea. Operation of the Hawaiian land tenure system somewhat resembled the feudal arrangements that prevailed in early England because a portion of all that was produced went to the chiefs. But lands were held for the common benefit. If commoners believed that they were not being treated fairly, they could move to another *ahupua'a* as they were not tied to the land. The chiefs of the various islands fought for control of one another's fiefdoms, causing periodic instability.

The islands became unified under a single king, Kamehameha I, shortly after the first European contact. Political unification proved to be instrumental in dealing with the onslaught of foreigners who came to trade beginning in the nineteenth century. The unified Hawaiian Kingdom preserved the land tenure system based on agriculture. It also furnished governmental leadership with which foreigners could deal. It was not long, however, before substantial foreign influence was felt in the Hawaiian government. Outsiders gave advice to the government, often unsought and often in the shadow of a foreign military presence. The first foreigners to become involved with the king were traders seeking commercial advantages and missionaries seeking acceptance of their religion.

b.   *The Great Mahele.* The land tenure system came under pressure as foreigners sought land for themselves. There were originally no individual land titles because the interests of the king, the chiefs, and commoners were intertwined. Pressure from whites who desired to own land in fee simple led to a series of developments that transformed Hawaiian land tenure relationships. In 1840, on the advice of westerners, King Kamehameha III promulgated a written constitution, declaring that the monarchy controlled the land of the kingdom for the benefit of the chiefs and the people, who owned the land collectively. The "Great Mahele" of 1848, dividing up the lands so that clear title could be determined and transferred, followed this initial formal declaration clarifying land ownership in the kingdom. The king quitclaimed his interest in about 1.5 million acres of *ahupua'a* and other lands to 245 chiefs. A land commission then confirmed grants of these lands to the chiefs, subject to a reservation of "the rights of the people." The chiefs quitclaimed to the king any interest they had in the remaining 2.5 million acres. The king in turn was to transfer some of the lands that had been quitclaimed to him to the commoners who cultivated it. Instead, he designated approximately 1.5 million acres for "the chiefs and people of my Kingdom" (government lands) and another million acres were "set apart for me and for my heirs and successors forever, as my own property exclusively" (crown lands). This process vested title in the king and the chiefs.

The common people never received lands as originally anticipated by the land commission that had recommended the *mahele*. In fact, very little land ever reached individual commoners. An intended remedy for the concentration of land outside commoners' hands was the provision of an 1850 act that allowed tenants to apply for *kuleana*—small parcels that they cultivated, and a houselot. Many of those eligible for *kuleana* did not get them because they could not afford the survey costs or meet other requirements of the law. Less than one percent of Hawaii's land was actually distributed as *kuleana*.

Not only did the *mahele* fail to distribute land widely among natives, it ultimately resulted in large amounts of some of the best Hawaiian land passing to foreigners. The *mahele* and the laws passed soon after it effectively lifted the restriction on alienation of property that had been imposed by the 1840 Constitution. Government lands and crown lands then were sold whenever the king approved. The chiefs had incurred large debts that they paid with land. Some attempted plantation farming but failed and lost their land through mortgage foreclosure. The king was free to sell, lease, or mortgage his crown lands as he pleased and the government sold considerable acreage, often at low prices. To check the loss of lands the Hawaiian legislature, following a court decision ruling that crown lands would descend only to the successors of the king, declared in 1865 that crown lands were inalienable.

By 1890 foreigners, mostly Americans owned over a million acres in Hawaii. They controlled another three-quarters of a million acres under leases procured at bargain rates from the government and the king. The overthrow of the Hawaiian monarchy in 1893 wrested all remaining government and crown lands from Hawaiian control and put them into the hands of a provisional government, and eventually of the United States government.

Throughout the latter part of the nineteenth century, Americans, in Washington, D.C. and in Hawaii itself, were involved intimately in the day-to-day political life of the kingdom, and in the eventual overthrow of the monarchy as well. The United States considered Hawaii vital to the protection of its interests and power in the Pacific and treaty relations focused on assuring commercial access. In 1826, the first treaty of peace and friendship was negotiated between the United States and Hawaii. Treaty with Hawaii on Commerce, Dec. 23, 1826, United States-Hawaii, 3 Charles I. Bevans, Treaties and Other International Agreements of the United States, 1776–1949, at 861 (1971). Though the Senate never formally ratified it, the State Department regarded the document as an agreement between nations arising under international law. President John Tyler assigned a minister to Hawaii in 1848. In 1849, the first ratified treaty between the United States and Hawaii was entered, dealing with friendship, commerce, and navigation, 9 Stat. 977, followed by the commercial reciprocity treaty of 1875, 19 Stat. 625.

Notwithstanding a history of continual nation-to-nation transaction, American Presidents and Secretaries of State had come to view Hawaii as part of the "American system," meaning that the kingdom had come under the virtual suzerainty of the United States. It was a colony in substance, if not in form, and efforts by another foreign power, such as England or

Japan, to colonize the islands would have been regarded as acts of war against United States' strategic interests in the Pacific.

A number of American Presidents as far back as Ulysses S. Grant, and other officials of the government had suggested the idea of voluntary annexation of the kingdom by the United States, but it was American merchant interests and missionary family residents on the islands that actually initiated the chain of events by which Hawaii formally became a territory of the United States. In 1887, an opposition group made up mostly of Americans pressed for adoption of a constitution that would reduce the king to a ceremonial figurehead, with all power to reside in a cabinet that was responsible to the legislature. King Kalakaua unsuccessfully sought United States protection from this powerful group. He was ultimately forced to sign the 1887 Constitution that became known as the "bayonet constitution."

Under the 1887 Constitution, the king was stripped of power and a United States-dominated cabinet ran the Hawaiian government. King Kalakaua's displeasure with the bayonet constitution moved him to propose restoration of his power. Attempts to reach that goal were all unsuccessful. The presence of American military forces in Hawaii helped to discourage these efforts, and American and European ministers directly intervened to pressure the king to retreat from his position. The king's successor, Queen Liliuokalani, began testing the limits of her authority under the constitution and was rumored to have proposed a new constitution.

   c.   Annexation. With strong encouragement from Washington, D.C., a group opposed to the queen worked hard for annexation of Hawaii to the United States. The Annexation Club, a secret group, formed a "Committee of Safety." With assurances of support from the United States minister, the committee plotted the overthrow of the monarchy. On orders of the United States minister, American troops landed in Honolulu on January 16, 1893 according to plans devised by the insurrectionists. Although the stated reason for the invasion was to protect the U.S. consulate and "the lives and property of American Citizens," the troops took up a position between the queen's palace and the government building. The insurrectionists then occupied the building.

Even before the takeover of the Hawaiian government was complete, the United States minister recognized the new "Provisional government as the de facto government of the Hawaiian Islands." On January 17, 1893, the queen, beloved by her people, was forced to abdicate but did so under protest and subject to a later review of the situation by the American government. To ensure order, the military later took custody of the government building and raised the American flag over it.

An investigation of the overthrow revealed facts that led President Grover Cleveland, a Democrat who had run on a platform opposed to high tariffs, free silver, and imperialism, to call for restoration of the monarchy. In a lengthy and eloquent message to Congress, the President observed that the overthrow was not "by the people of the islands." Rather "the Provisional Government owes its existence to an armed invasion by the United States." He concluded that the United States' role was opposed to established American foreign policy, to morality, and to principles of international law. Consequently, he said, the United States "cannot allow itself to refuse to redress an injury inflicted through an abuse of power by officers clothed with its authority and wearing its uniform; the United States cannot fail to vindicate its honor and its sense of justice by an earnest effort to make all possible reparation." H.R.Exec. Doc. No. 47, 53d Cong., 2d Sess. (1893). Cleveland left office in 1897 and his successor, President William McKinley, a Republican who favored annexation, ultimately obtained Senate approval of annexation in 1898.

Upon annexation, most Hawaiian land laws remained in effect, but control of the crown lands and government lands that had been seized by the provisional government passed to the United States. Thus, an estimated 1.75 million acres in which Native Hawaiians were to have an interest following the *mahele* became United States property. Congress in turn entrusted management of the lands to a territorial legislature established by the Organic Act of 1900, which set up a government for the Territory of Hawaii.

d.   Hawaiian Homes Commission Act. Early in the twentieth century, Congress was made aware of deteriorating social and economic conditions among Native Hawaiians. Recognizing that the situation was related to loss of the Hawaiian land base and the associated culture, Congress enacted limited measures to remedy the natives' plight. An amendment to the Organic Act in 1910 was designed to ease the ability of Native Hawaiians to take up homesteads under an 1895 law of the Republic of Hawaii. It required that crown lands be made available when groups of Hawaiian citizens so requested. This posed a potential threat to sugar growers whose long-term leases on plantation lands obtained from the Hawaiian Kingdom were about to expire. Increased pressure from Native Hawaiians for special legislative attention to their needs coincided with the planters' demands for protection from homesteaders. The result was passage of the Hawaiian Homes Commission Act of 1921 (HHCA), allowing native homesteads on specific lands. 42 Stat. 108, ch. 42.

By developing the HHCA, executive branch and congressional leaders apparently had the impression that the federal government was assuming fiduciary responsibilities similar to those it had historically exercised in managing Indian affairs. In the hearings on the legislation, Secretary of the Interior Lane, testified as follows: "One thing that impressed me * * * was the fact that the natives of the islands who are our wards, I should say, and for whom in a sense we are trustees, are falling off rapidly in numbers, and many of them are in poverty." H.R.Rep. No. 839, 66th Cong., 2d Sess. 4 (1920).

The House Committee Report on HHCA defended the bill against the charge that it was "unconstitutional class legislation" by noting that Congress had the authority to provide special benefits for unique groups such as "Indians, soldiers and sailors. * * * " (The United States Supreme Court would address constitutional arguments, half a century later, to uphold legislation benefiting Indians as a group. See *Morton v. Mancari*, page 257, supra.)

The model provided by the history of federal Indian policy in establishing reservations was also in the minds of the Congressmen who voted for the Hawaiian Homes Commission legislation. Recognizing that the Hawaiians "were deprived of their lands without any say on their part," the chairman of the House Committee on Territories noted that the motivations behind the legislation were the same as those supporting similar land trust legislation relating to Indian tribes "[b]ecause we came to this country and took their land away from them * * * [a]nd if we can afford to [provide lands in trust] for the Indians * * * why can we not do the same for the Hawaiians?" Proposed Amendments to the Organic Act of the Territory of Hawaii, Hearings on H.R. 7257 Before the House Comm. on the Territories, 67th Cong. 1st Sess. 141 (1921).

Under the Hawaiian Homes Commission Act as passed in 1921, Congress designated a trust of some 200,000 acres of public lands as available for Native homesteads. The Act has generally failed to provide agricultural or residential lands to large numbers of people or to achieve its lofty goal of "rehabilitating" Native Hawaiians having at least 50 percent native blood. The lands set aside were some of the poorest, largely unsuitable for farming, and lacking in necessary irrigation water. Many of the ostensibly available lands actually have been used for ordinary government purposes or leased to private interests. The way in which the agency in charge of carrying out the Act has administered the land has sparked intense criticism.

The Hawaiian Homes Commission Act was remarkably similar in purpose and effect to the General Allotment Act. Both statutes submerged Congress's good intentions in the ambitions of others who coveted the lands. Both were poorly carried out, often giving their purported beneficiaries parcels of unarable land.

e.   Admission Act. The terms of the Act admitting Hawaii to statehood in 1959 obligated the state to hold the lands entrusted to it and the income from them "as a public trust for the support of the public schools * * * , for the betterment of the conditions of native

Hawaiians * * * , for the development of farm and home ownership on as widespread basis as possible, for the making of public improvements, and for the provision of lands for public use." The Act says that departure from the prescribed purposes is a breach of trust. Hawaii Admission Act 1959, sec. 5(f), Pub.L.No. 86–3, 73 Stat. 4. The language of trust in the Act arguably reflects a continuing interest of Hawaiian people in the so-called "5(f)" lands transferred to the state by the United States. This would give rise to a claim for income from the lands or for the value of lands the state has appropriated to its own uses.

Until the 2000 census, the U.S. Census Bureau lacked a separate category for Native Hawaiians. The 2010 census counted 135,422 "Native Hawaiians and Other Pacific Islanders" in the state. When added to those who said they were mixed race people—part Hawaiian or Pacific Islander—the total was 327,433, amounting to 25 percent of the state's population of 1.3 million. Moreover, the birth rate of Native Hawaiians is high and population is rapidly growing.

f.   Modern Advocacy. Today Native Hawaiians are severely disadvantaged. Studies reveal that in terms of health, education, crime, and employment, Native Hawaiians are worse off than any other ethnic group in the state. See generally Kathryn Nalani Setsuko Hong, *Understanding Native Hawaiian Rights: Mistakes and Consequences of Rice v. Cayetano,* 15 Asian Am.L.J. 9 (2008).

Native Hawaiians feel that they are being squeezed out of an economy where only the rich can afford to own property. The ancient, land-centered Hawaiian culture has been strained by Hawaii's heavy dependence on tourists. Issues of access to traditional sacred places, to water for taro crop production, and to beaches where fish and other resources can be gathered, persist. One of the most intriguing and legally distinctive aspects of Hawaii state law is the incorporation of traditional law tracing to ancient times. As shown in cases such as Reppun v. Board of Water Supply, page 1003, infra, and PASH v. Hawaii County Planning Commission, p. 1011, infra, and the notes following, this respect for native customs is the source of protection for subsistence uses, beach access, and water rights as customary prerogatives of Hawaiians.

Contacts with Native Americans on the mainland and in Alaska, and with indigenous peoples in other parts of the world, have made Hawaiians aware of a disparity in the way they have been treated. More Hawaiians are becoming politically active and numerous Native Hawaiian groups have been formed in recent years to promote awareness about Hawaiian sovereignty and self-determination. Such increased activism on the part of the Native Hawaiian community has led to even greater calls for the state and federal governments to take action to redress past American conduct.

g. *Office of Hawaiian Affairs.* Most notably, several state constitutional amendments dealing with Native Hawaiian rights were adopted by Hawaii voters in 1978. The amendments implicitly acknowledged that the special requirements of the Admission Act had not been fully observed by the state. The result is an Office of Hawaiian Affairs (OHA) managed by a Native Hawaiian board of trustees that receives and expends the portion of income from trust lands that is allocable to Hawaiians and operates programs to benefit Hawaiians. Hawaii Constitution, article XII, §§ 4–6 (1978).

Other measures undertaken by the state ranged from the largely symbolic order of then-Governor John Waihee, himself of Native Hawaiian ancestry, to fly only the Kingdom of Hawaii's flag over the state capital building on the 100th anniversary of the overthrow of the Hawaiian monarchy, to legislation the same year acknowledging and recognizing "the unique status that the native Hawaiian people bear to the State of Hawaii and to the United States." The Act called for a vote "to determine the will of the native Hawaiian people for self-governance of their own choosing." A majority of voters in the 1996 election that followed favored electing delegates to draft a proposed constitution that would create a "native Hawaiian government." See Hawaii Organic Act § 2, 1993 Haw.Sess. Laws 359 (as amended by 1994 Hawaii Sess. Laws 200 and 1996 Haw.Sess. Laws 140). This effort later was eclipsed by efforts to enact federal legislation— the Akaka Bill, discussed below, that would reorganize native Hawaiians as Native Americans. This effort has again shifted to a push for government-to-government relationship with a Native Hawaiian governing body.

h. *Apology Resolution.* The federal government began to take notice of Native claims in the 1980s. A congressionally-mandated Native Hawaiians Study Commission released a 1983 report extensively surveying the facts and issues concerning Native Hawaiians. In 1993, Congress passed a joint resolution acknowledging the 100th anniversary of the January 17, 1893 overthrow of the kingdom of Hawaii, "with the participation of agents and citizens of the United States," and offering "an apology to Native Hawaiians on behalf of the United States." Pub.L.No. 103–150, 107 Stat. 1510 (1993). Congress was careful to state that nothing in the Apology Resolution served as a settlement of claims (§ 3). As Hawaii v. OHA, page 1045, infra, shows, attempts to breathe substance into the Resolution have failed. In 2000 the DOI and DOJ published "From Makua to Makai: The River of Justice Must Flow Freely" a report on the reconciliation process between the Federal Government and Native Hawaiians. The report recommended federal recognition, an Office of Native Hawaiian Affairs at Interior, Assignment of Office of Tribal Justice, Native Hawaiian Advisory Commission, and true reconciliation. In 2004, Congress created an Office of Native Hawaiian Relations based in

Washington D.C. thereby highlighting the special relationship between the U.S. government and Native Hawaiians.

i.   Akaka Bill. An important development in recent years was the pursuit of federal legislation that would federally recognize a Native Hawaiian governing body that would be similar to an Indian tribe in several respects, and would create a framework for negotiation of Native claims. This proposed legislation, known as the "Akaka Bill" after Senator Daniel Akaka of Hawaii and introduced in various forms since 2000, was propelled by the United States Supreme Court decision in Rice v. Cayetano, page 1030, infra, which threw the constitutionality of OHA and other Native Hawaiian programs into doubt. The struggle to enact the Akaka Bill triggered an avalanche of litigation. One strain of cases challenges the state's management of the Hawaiian Home Lands under the Hawaiian Homes Commission Act. Another attacks the existence of Native Hawaiian programs as impermissibly race-based. Yet, several cases claim that such programs are not exclusive enough, seeking to limit the class of beneficiaries to half-blood or greater Hawaiian as defined in the Hawaiian Homes Commission Act of 1921 and some other legislation. An important case attempted to halt all state transfers of certain lands ceded by the Kingdom of Hawaii until Hawaiian land claims are resolved. See Hawaii v. OHA, page 1045, infra. The Akaka Bill was last introduced in 2013 and for now seems to have died in Congress. Although recognition has been unsuccessful through federal legislation, activists continue to work at the state level and are continuing to make progress.

j.   Act 195. Growing Native Hawaiian advocacy led Hawaii to enact Act 195 in 2011 to recognize Native Hawaiians as the only indigenous, aboriginal, maoli population of Hawaii. Discussed in further detail below, Act 195 establishes a new chapter in the Hawaii revised statutes titled "Native Hawaiian Recognition" which contemplates a process leading to Native Hawaiian self-organization. In September 2016, the Department of the Interior adopted regulations has issued a notice of proposed rulemaking for procedures to re-establish a government-to-government relationship with the Native Hawaiian community as part of the reconciliation process called for in the Apology Resolution.

On the historical development of laws relating to Native Hawaiians, see generally Melody Kapilialoha MacKenzie, Native Hawaiian Law: A Treatise 5–74, (2015); Davianna Pōmaika'i McGregor and Melody Kapilialoha MacKenzie, *Mo'olelo Ea O Na Hawai'i: History of Native Hawaiian Governance in Hawai'i* (Office of Hawaiian Affairs, 2014);. See also Senate Select Committee on Indian Affairs, Improving the Education Status of Native Hawaiians, Senate Report 100–36, 100th Cong., 1st Sess. 12–17 (1987).

2. NATIVE RIGHTS UNDER HAWAIIAN COMMON AND STATUTORY LAW

Hawaii has a unique body of common law and statutes dating back to the Hawaiian Kingdom. These early laws recognized certain traditional rights that then had to be reconciled with land dispositions and the onslaught of non-Native residents. Some important legal principles survive and remain the basis for significant Native rights under state law. Hawaiian water law is an example of how state law has embraced ancient Native Hawaiian customs and adopted them, not just as a means of preserving rights of Native Hawaiians, but as the core of a common law of water rights. The same kind of evolution has taken place in other areas of Hawaiian natural resources law.

REPPUN V. BOARD OF WATER SUPPLY

Supreme Court of Hawai'i, 1982.
65 Haw. 531, 656 P.2d 57, cert. denied,
471 U.S. 1014, 105 S.Ct. 2016, 85 L Ed.2d 298 (1985).

RICHARDSON, CHIEF JUSTICE.

I.   Introduction

The geological structure of the Koolau Mountains of Oahu enables parts thereof to act as natural reservoirs of fresh water; these natural storage compartments are called dike complexes or systems. The seepage and overflow from one such dike complex or system serve as the primary source of the Waihee stream. Competing claims to the waters of the stream and competing ownership claims to the waters at its source are advanced in this appeal.

The Board of Water Supply of the City and County of Honolulu (hereinafter BWS) maintains a tunnel and inclined shafts to facilitate the withdrawal of water from the Waihee dike system; it also pumps water therefrom. This substantial withdrawal of water by the BWS naturally diminishes the flow of the Waihee stream. Six taro farmers who claim appurtenant and riparian rights to the waters of the stream initiated this case, alleging that they are entitled at least to a flow of water sufficient to maintain their crops. Conversely, the BWS claims its predecessor in interest purchased the bulk of the rights to the waters in question. It contends the withdrawals of water cannot be deemed a legal wrong subject to injunction since it draws water from the underground source rather than the stream. It further asserts that the "public use doctrine" precludes the issuance of an injunction here.

II.   Statement of the Case

The natural flow of the Waihee stream is approximately 6 to 8 million gallons per day (mgd). In 1955 the BWS drilled a tunnel into the dike system feeding the stream. Water was subsequently withdrawn via the tunnel, thereby reducing the stream flow to approximately 4 mgd. In 1974 and 1976 the BWS increased the amount of withdrawable water by constructing inclined wells and pumping water from the dike system. When the wells were operative the flow of the Waihee stream was reduced to a summer average of 2.3 mgd in 1975 and 2.03 mgd in 1976.

The plaintiffs utilize the waters of the Waihee stream to irrigate their crops. Their method of irrigation involves a diversion of the waters from the stream to flood and flow through their taro[2] patches or lois, which approximates the traditional means of taro cultivation[3]. Until 1975 the stream's flow was sufficient to satisfy their needs. However, in the summer of 1975, one of the farmers sustained crop losses from a fungal growth known as pythium[4] that causes rot in the root or corm of the taro plants. In subsequent years all the plaintiffs save one suffered losses attributable to pyhthium. Plaintiffs believed, and the trial court subsequently agreed, that the proliferation of pythium was related to the diminution of the flow of the Waihee stream, as the spread of the fungus can be retarded or halted by a flow of cool fresh water through the taro lois and such a flow was rendered impossible by the actions of the BWS. This suit was therefore initiated in 1976 to enjoin the BWS from diverting any of the stream's waters.[5]

A.

The plaintiffs' claims to the waters of the Waihee stream stem from their status as landowners or lessees of riparian lands and from the fact that much of their lands were devoted to the cultivation of taro at the time of the Great Mahele, when the lands were granted in fee to their occupants. They assert they are thus entitled to 1) riparian rights to the natural flow of the Waihee stream, and 2) appurtenant rights to water required in the cultivation of taro on all lands that were being utilized for such purpose at the time of the Mahele.

The BWS counters by claiming it purchased virtually all of the rights now being asserted by plaintiffs. * * *

---

[2]   "Taro (Colocasia escylenta) is a kind of aroid cultivated since ancient times for food spreading widely from the tropics of the Old World. In Hawaii taro has been the staple from earliest times . . . and its culture developed greatly including more than 300 forms. All parts of the plant are eaten, its starch root principally as poi, and its leaves as lu'au. It is a perennial herb consisting of a cluster of long-stemmed, heart shaped leaves rising a foot or more from underground tubers or corms." Pukui & Elbert, Hawaiian Dictionary, 115 (1971).

[3]   As to the traditional means of cultivating wet land taro see, Handy & Handy, Native Planters in Old Hawaii, 90–102 (1972).

[4]   Pythium infestation causes "the transformation of the normally firm flesh of the corm into a soft, mushy, often evil-smelling mass, unfit for human consumption." Parris, Diseases of Taro in Hawaii and their Control, 9 (1941).

[5]   Plaintiffs also claim to be entitled to injunctive relief because of alleged BWS violations of various environmental statutes and regulations. Each of these claims were either dismissed or remanded by the trial court. We see no basis for reversing the trial court on these matters.

Thus, a critical issue in this case is whether most of the water rights theretofore attaching to the plaintiff taro farmers' lands were effectively severed and transferred by deed to the BWS. The trial court, interpreting our opinion in *McBryde v. Robinson,* McBryde Sugar Co. v. Robinson, 504 P.2d 1330 (Haw. 1973), affirmed on rehearing 517 P.2d 26 (Haw. 1973), cert. denied 417 U.S. 962 (1974), as precluding the severance of such rights, held that the water rights of the plaintiffs could not be severed from the land to which they appertained and the deed by which the Koolau Company conveyed certain lands and all water rights that it owned in Waihee to the BWS was therefore a nullity with respect to any attempted conveyance of water rights. This conclusion is of course contested by the BWS.

* * *

IV. Discussion

A. Severance of Riparian and Appurtenant Rights

* * *

The plaintiff taro farmers' claims to the waters of the Waihee stream are premised on *McBryde v. Robinson, supra.* There, we held, inter alia, that 1) HRS § 7–1, originally enacted in 1850 as section 7 of our Kuleana Act, imposed the "natural flow" doctrine of riparianism upon the waters of our state; 2) that riparian water rights appertain only to land adjoining a natural watercourse for its use; and 3) that the right to the use of water by virtue of its application to the land at the time of the Mahele, *i.e.,* appurtenant water rights, may be used only in connection with those particular parcels of land to which that right appertains. Plaintiffs read *McBryde* as stating that neither appurtenant nor riparian rights can be severed from the land. Thus they contend the deed by which the BWS claims to have purchased their rights was a nullity and all water rights in the ahupuaa of Waihee are still intact.

The BWS contends *McBryde* is not subject to being so interpreted and applied. It not only argues against any reading that would forbid the severance of water rights, but urges this court to overrule *McBryde* and reinstitute what it regards as prior Hawaii water law on surplus and appurtenant water rights.

i.   Applicability of *McBryde v. Robinson*

We decline the invitation to overrule *McBryde v. Robinson, supra.* We find that the rules of law posited in that opinion are applicable here.

McBryde has been criticized as an unjustifiable deviation from pre-existing water law[10]. But a re-examination of the development of the laws governing water in this jurisdiction convinces us of its soundness. Our local system of water rights is "based upon and is an outgrowth of

---

[10]   See Robinson v. Ariyoshi, 441 F. Supp. 559 (D.Haw.1977).

ancient Hawaiian customs and methods of Hawaiians in dealing with the subject of water." *Territory v. Gay.* 31 Haw. 376, 395 (1930). In ancient times there was no resource more precious. Although there is a belief that at some point this resource was transformed into a freely transferable private commodity, we do not find this to be so. For in *McBryde* we reexamined what some believed to be the foundation of certain private rights and interests in water and found them to be fatally flawed. We therefore set about to correct these errors of the past, as it was both our duty and prerogative to do.

Our understanding of the necessity for the holdings in *McBryde* begins with the native system of water allocation. This system has been recently described as follows:

> Perhaps the essential feature of the ancient water system was that water was guaranteed to those natives who needed it, provided they helped in the construction of the irrigation system. Because agriculture was a matter of great importance to the Hawaiians, they were, in general, willing to contribute their efforts to the water system. The konohikis aimed to secure equal rights to all makaainana and to avoid disputes. Beneficial use of water by the makaainana were also essential to the continued delivery of water. The natives were subject to compulsory maintenance work on the auwais under the supervision of the konohiki. The konohiki, on the other hand, was reluctant to impose unreasonable burdens on the tenants because they were normally free to leave a particular plot if unhappy with the konohiki. Hence a "spirit of mutual dependence and helpfulness prevailed, alike among the high and low, with respect to the use of water." (Citations omitted.)

Van Dyke, Chang, Aipa, Higham, Marsden, Sur, Tagamori and Yukimoto, *Water Rights in Hawaii*, in Land and Water Resource Management in Hawaii 141 (1977). The foregoing characterization is uncontroverted.

The system based on this "spirit of mutual dependence" was a stable one. While the authority for the distribution of water ultimately rested in the King, the chiefs, or their agents (konohiki), "the aim of the konohiki and all others in authority was to secure equal rights to all and to avoid quarrels." Perry, *A Brief History of Hawaiian Water Rights* 7 (1912). This benevolent attitude was not a product of indifference to the application of water nor of overabundance. On the contrary, the cooperative nature of the system appears to have stemmed from the critical import of water in the lives of the people.

For example, the Hawaiian word "kanawai" denoting law or laws related originally to regulations regarding water. *Id.* at 3. Interference with existing auwais was punishable by death, and the body of the offender was used to repair whatever damage done to deter further offenses. Nakuina, *Ancient Hawaiian Water Rights*, in Thrums Hawaiian Annual 79 (1894). Failure to keep one's auwai in repair was a ground for the cutting off of water privileges. *Id.* at 82. And the completion of a new watercourse was the occasion for religious thanksgiving and celebration. *Id.*

As with the ownership of land, there were no fixed rights to water. Hutchins, *The Hawaiian System of Water Rights*, 21, 22 (1946). Rather, water privileges were earned through participation in the construction of the irrigation systems and retained only by the productive application of the waters to which one was thereby entitled. Handy and Handy, *Native Planters in Old Hawaii* 31 (1972). Inasmuch as the prosperity of the landlord was dependent upon the productivity of all of his assigned lands, he necessarily attempted to insure that maximum benefit was achieved through the application of the vital resource. *Id.* at 279. In times of plenty, all shared in nature's munificence; in times of scarcity, allocation was resorted to in order to insure the survival of all.

The nature of the activity to which water was applied reinforced the cooperative aspects of its allocation. *Id.* See also, Earl, *Control Hierarchies in the Traditional Irrigation Economy of the Halelea District, Kauai, Hawaii*, 160 (1973). The principal crop requiring irrigation was taro, the staple of the native Hawaiian lifestyle. The irrigation of taro called for flowing water, most of which was not consumed by the land. Hence, a cooperative system whereby unused waters were returned to their source or allowed to flow into lower adjoining patches maximized the application of the resource. Handy & Handy, Native Planters in *Old Hawaii, supra.*

The limitations of technology also fostered cooperation, for the irrigational systems required in the culture of taro could only be constructed through the joint efforts of those who would benefit thereby. That the labor of the commoners would be rewarded by the just application of the resource to their land was insured by the fact that they were not "serfs" tied to the land by any particular obligation to the landlord, but were free to leave at any time and begin their efforts anew in virtually any uncultivated area. Van Dyke et al., *Water Rights in Hawaii, supra.*

Finally, it was entirely to the advantage of the konohiki or landlord that water be allocated according to industry and need. Prior to the imposition of western ways water had little value apart from its application. Thus, it was considered strictly a resource to be used when required, not a commodity. In an agrarian society where technological capacity for storage or long range transport was nonexistent, there was simply no value in hoarding water or in even fixing an amount to which any person would be entitled. This was, of course, to change.

* * *

The western doctrine of "property" has traditionally implied certain rights. Among these are the right to the use of the property, the right to exclude others and the right to transfer the property with the consent of the "owner". In conformance with creation of private interests in land, each of these rights were embodied in the delineation of post- Mahele judicial water rights. Ostensibly, this judge-made system of rights was an outgrowth of Hawaiian custom in dealing with water. However, the creation of private and exclusive interests in water, within a context of western concepts regarding property, compelled the drawing of fixed lines of authority and interests which were not consonant with Hawaiian custom.

Thus, the distinction drawn between "rights" and "supplies by permission" or "favors" in *Horner,* while making perfect sense within the western understanding of "property", would make no sense at all under the ancient system of allocation. Under the ancient system both the self-interest and responsibility of the konohikis would have created a duty to share and to maximize benefits for the residents of the ahupuaa. In other words, under the ancient system the "right" of the konohiki to control water was inseparable from his "duty" to assist each of the deserving tenants. The private division of land and the subsequent division of water allowed for the separation of this "right" from the concomitant "duty".

The pattern of isolating a traditional "right" from its correlative duties and obligations continued to serve as a basis for the evolution of private interests in water. Thus, in 1896 the court condoned the sale and transfer of appurtenant water on the grounds that interahupuaa transfers were made in ancient times, ignoring the fact that such transfers were undoubtedly made to satisfy some particular communal purpose and not for the exclusive benefit of a particular transferor or transferee. Similarly, in 1904, surplus water was deemed the property of the konohiki of the ahupuaa of its origin since "no limitation . . . existed or was supposed to exist to his power to use the surplus waters as he saw fit." Again, the essential nature of the konohiki's customary powers over the waters of his ahupuaa was disregarded, and an individual was granted a personal "right" to profit, presumably by virtue of ancient authority, from the sale and application of water without regard for the consequences to those who historically would have been within his charge.

We cannot continue to ignore what we firmly believe were fundamental mistakes regarding one of the most precious of our resources. *McBryde* was a necessary and proper step in the rectification of basic misconceptions concerning water "rights" in Hawaii.

ii. Severability of Riparian Rights

Having acknowledged and ratified *McBryde's* vitality, we turn to the question of whether the riparian rights of the plaintiffs were effectively severed and transferred by the language of the various deeds of title purporting to do so. We conclude they were not.

BWS argues, and we agree, that even the "natural flow" theory of riparianism does not, in most jurisdictions, prohibit the annulment or severance of riparian rights by contract. *See,* 1 Clark, *Waters and Water Rights,* 70 (1967). But riparian rights in Hawaii are of statutory rather than common law origin. The privileges and rights attaching to riparian land should therefore be determined consistently with the statute to which their genesis is traceable.

Riparian rights in Hawaii are a product of the people's statutory rights to "flowing" and "running" water currently embodied in HRS § 7–1 (1976). HRS § 7–1 was originally enacted in 1850 as section 7 of what has come to be known as the Kuleana Act. The first six sections of the Act enabled the common people of Hawaii to secure fee simple title to the lands they actually cultivated. The seventh section contained the rights that were to accompany a commoner's tenancy. The section was drafted at the behest of the King and was reported to reflect his concern that "[a] little bit of land even with allodial title, if they be cut off from all other privileges would be of very little value." Privy Council Minutes, July 13, 1850. Thus, it appears that the riparian water rights of HRS § 7–1 were established to enable tenants of ahupuaas to make productive use of their lands.

Riparian rights in Hawaii are thus analogous to the federally reserved water rights accruing to Indian reservations pursuant to *Winters v. United States,* 207 U.S. 564, 28 S.Ct. 207, 52 L.Ed. 340 (1908). In words reminiscent of Hawaii's King, the Supreme Court has described that decision as follows: "The Court in *Winters* concluded that the Government, when it created [an] Indian Reservation, intended to deal fairly with the Indians by reserving for them the waters without which their lands would have been useless." *Arizona v. California,* 373 U.S. 546, 600, 83 S. Ct. 1468, 1497 10 L.Ed.2d 542 (1963). The Court in *Winters* thus implied from a treaty establishing the Fort Belknap Indian Reservation a reservation of enough unappropriated waters to fulfill the purposes of the treaty.

* * *

Summary

Our holdings as summarized are reiterated below:

1. Riparian rights.

    a.   Water rights attaching to riparian lands by virtue of HRS § 7–1 cannot be severed or extinguished by a riparian land owner's grantor. The riparian rights of each plaintiff taro farmer were therefore unaffected by language in their deeds that purported to reserve such water rights.

b.   Riparian landowners are entitled to make reasonable use of the quantity and flow of a natural watercourse and may prevent diversions that interfere with such use.

1)   The agricultural activities of the plaintiffs' taro farmers constitute a reasonable use of the waters of the Waihee Stream as their mode of irrigation approximates that which has been historically utilized for the cultivation of taro. Plaintiffs are therefore entitled to the use of the waters of the Waihee Stream for the cultivation of their riparian lands with the quantity and flow that existed prior to the reduction of the flow that contributed to the damaging of their crops.

2.   Appurtenant rights.

a.   Appurtenant water rights are incidents of the ownership of land which, by virtue of their appurtenant nature, may not be transferred or applied to lands other than those to which the rights appertain. They may, however, be extinguished by the grantor of such lands.

b.   When the same parcels of land are being utilized to cultivate traditional products by means approximating those utilized at the time of the Mahele, there is sufficient evidence to establish a presumption that the amount of water diverted for such cultivation adequately approximates the quantity of the appurtenant water rights to which that land is entitled.

c.   Plaintiffs' lands possessing appurtenant water rights that were not extinguished by their grantors are therefore entitled to the quantity and flow of water which was utilized to irrigate crops prior to the diminution of the stream that damaged the crops.

* * *

NOTES

1.   A 1978 constitutional amendment recognized the state's trust obligation to assure water resource use for the public benefit. A series of unsuccessful constitutional challenges followed, and in 1987 the state adopted a permit system. Haw.Rev.Stat. § 174C–59 (1987). In administering the permit system, the Commission on Water Resource Management is charged with protecting traditional and customary Native Hawaiian rights as a public trust purpose. See In re Contested Case Filed by Kukui, 174 P.3d 320 (Haw.2007) (applicant has burden of showing action will not harm Hawaiian rights). The Department of Hawaiian Home Lands has reserved water rights for future use, and protection of those rights is a public trust purpose that can preclude a new water user from obtaining a permit. See In re Wai'ola O Moloka'i, Inc., 83 P.3d 664 (Haw.2004); Kauai Springs, Inc. v. Planning Comm'n of the County of Kaua'i, 324 P.3d 951 (Haw.2014) ("The public trust protects the use of water in 'the exercise of Native Hawaii and traditional and customary rights.' * * *

Private commercial use is not protected by the public trust. "[T]he public trust has never been understood to safeguard rights of exclusive use for private commercial gain. The very meaning of the public trust is to recognize separate and enduring public rights in trust resources superior to any private interest.")

2.   Despite the nature of Hawaiian water law as written in the court decision and statute pages—a body of law that is considerably more favorable to natives than in the other states—Native Hawaiians do suffer from some of the attitudes found in mainland water agencies. Hawaii's water officials tend to be utilitarian and often are less than enamored with claims based on cultural and public trust concerns. In addition, water rights disputes tend to be long and drawn out, with the result that Native Hawaiians wanting to enforce their traditional water rides may face lengthy delays and high costs. Elizabeth Ann Ho-oipo Kala'ena'auao Pa Martin, et al., *Cultures in Conflict in Hawai'i: The Law and Politics of Native Hawaiian Water Rights*, 18 U.Haw.L.Rev. 71 (1996).

The situation is steadily improving, but actual water management in Hawaii still does not fully square with the water law on the books. As one example, in the mid-19th-century the sugar industry began transporting by tunnel large amounts of water from East Maui over to sugar plantations in Central Maui. Traditional taro farmers in East Maui strenuously objected, but to no avail. Today, much of sugar in Central Maui has been replaced by housing subdivisions, big-box retailers, and golf courses. In 2001, taro farmers, by then represented by the non-profit Native Hawaiian Legal Corporation, with a strong case based on public trust obligations, obtained from the state Water Resources Commission a temporary order that restored some water to some of the streams in East Maui. The overall situation, however, remained very much in limbo. Numerous rulings, appeals, and hearings followed over the next decade and a half. In a major development in 2016, the Water Resources Commission did restore a considerable amount of water on a permanent basis although several streams have yet to be restored. Wendy Osher, "historic release—water to flow at multiple East Maui streams" Apr. 21 2016. The wheels of justice are still turning—slowly.

PUBLIC ACCESS SHORELINE HAWAII (PASH) V. HAWAI'I COUNTY PLANNING COMMISSION

Supreme Court of Hawaii, 1995.
79 Hawai'i 425, 903 P.2d 1246, cert. denied,
517 U.S. 1163, 116 S.Ct. 1559, 134 L.Ed.2d 660.

KLEIN, JUSTICE.

* * *

* * * [T]his case . . . concerns a challenge by Public Access Shoreline Hawaii (PASH) and Angel Pilago to the Hawai'i County Planning Commission's (HPC) decision denying them standing to participate in a contested case hearing on an application by Nansay Hawai'i, Inc. (Nansay) for a Special Management Area (SMA) use permit.

In order to pursue development of a resort complex on land within a SMA on the island of Hawai'i (Big Island), Nansay applied to the HPC for a SMA use permit. PASH, an unincorporated public interest membership organization based in Kailua-Kona, and Pilago opposed the issuance of the permit and requested contested case hearings before the HPC. The HPC denied the requests on the ground that, under its rules, neither PASH nor Pilago had standing to participate in a contested case. The HPC subsequently issued a SMA use permit to Nansay. * * *

* * *

The HPC received a SMA use permit application from Nansay for a resort development on the Big Island. Nansay sought approval of its plans to develop a community complex including: two resort hotels with over 1,000 rooms; 330 multiple family residential units; 380 single family homes; a golf course; a health club; restaurants; retail shops; an artisan village; a child care center; and other infrastructure and improvements over a 450-acre shoreline area in the ahupua'a of Kohanaiki on the Big Island. On September 18, 1990, the HPC held a public hearing on Nansay's permit application, as required by the agency's rules. * * *

* * *

* * * Although the HPC Rules allow formal intervention through specified procedures, PASH was denied standing to participate in a contested case hearing because the agency found that its asserted interests were "substantially similar" to those of the general public. The HPC's restrictive interpretation of standing requirements is not entitled to deference.[12] * * * Accordingly, we review *de novo* whether PASH has demonstrated its interests were injured.

* * * Through unrefuted testimony, PASH sufficiently demonstrated that its members, as "native Hawaiian[s] who [have] exercised such rights as were customarily and traditionally exercised for subsistence, cultural, and religious purposes on undeveloped lands[,] [have] an interest in a proceeding for the approval of [a SMA permit] for the development of lands within the ahupua'a which are [sic] clearly distinguishable from that of the general public." *Id.* at 252, 900 P.2d at 1319. Although we hold that PASH sufficiently demonstrated standing to participate in a contested case, at least for the purposes of the instant appeal, we observe that "[o]pportunities shall be afforded all parties to present evidence and

---

[12] An "ahupua'a" is a land division usually extending from the mountains to the sea along *rational* lines, such as ridges or other natural characteristics. *In re Boundaries of Pulehunui*, 4 Haw. 239, 241 (1879) (acknowledging that these "rational" lines may also be based upon tradition, culture, or other factors).

argument on all issues involved" in the contested case hearing held on remand. HRS § 91–9(c).

* * *

IV. The Obligation to Preserve and Protect
Culture and Historic Resources

* * *

* * * [T]he HPC is obligated to protect customary and traditional rights to the extent feasible under the Hawai'i Constitution and relevant statutes. Article XII, section 7 of the Hawai'i Constitution (1978) provides:

> The State reaffirms and *shall protect all rights, customarily and traditionally exercised for subsistence, cultural and religious purposes* and possessed by ahupua'a tenants who are descendants of native Hawaiians who inhabited the Hawaiian Islands prior to 1778, *subject to the right of the State to regulate such rights.*

(Emphasis added.) HRS § 1–1 (Supp. 1992) provides:

> The common law of England, as ascertained by English and American decisions, is declared to be the common law of the State of [Hawai'i] in all cases, except as otherwise expressly provided by the Constitution or laws of the United States, or by the laws of the State, or fixed by Hawaiian judicial precedent, *or established by Hawaiian usage*; provided that no person shall be subject to criminal proceedings except as provided by the written laws of the United States or of the State.

(Emphasis added).

The aforementioned provisions were discussed by this court, in the context of an individual's asserted gathering rights, in *Kalipi v. Hawaiian Trust Co.*, 66 Haw. 1, 656 P.2d 745 (1982). Ten years later, in *Pele Defense Fund v. Paty*, (73 Haw. 578, 837 P.2d 1247 (1992)), we recognized that ancient Hawaiian gathering rights may have extended beyond the boundaries of individual ahupua'a in certain cases. 73 Haw. at 620, 837 P.2d at 1272. Nevertheless, neither *Kalipi* nor *Pele* precluded further inquiry concerning the extent that traditional practices have endured under the laws of this State. "In *Kalipi*, we foresaw that '[t]he precise nature and scope of the rights retained by § 1–1 would, of course, depend upon the particular circumstances of each case.'" *Pele*, 73 Haw. at 619, 837 P.2d at 1271 (quoting *Kalipi*, 66 Haw. at 12, 656 P.2d at 752).

In order to determine whether the HPC must protect traditional and customary rights of the nature asserted in this case, we shall first review our analysis of gathering rights in *Kalipi* and *Pele*. Then we shall clarify the status of customary rights in general, as a result of relevant judicial and legislative developments in Hawaiian history. Finally, we will provide the HPC with some specific, although not necessarily exhaustive, guidelines to aid its future deliberations in the event that Nansay elects to pursue its challenges to the legitimacy of PASH's claims.

1. *Kalipi v. Hawaiian Trust Co.: judicial recognition of traditional Hawaiian gathering rights based upon residency in a particular ahupua'a.*

Kalipi involved an individual's attempt to gain access to private property on the island of Moloka'i in order to exercise purportedly traditional Hawaiian gathering rights. The court prefaced its consideration of Kalipi's claims with a discussion of the State's obligation to preserve and enforce traditional Hawaiian gathering rights under article XII, section 7 of the Hawai'i Constitution:

> We recognize that permitting access to private property for the purpose of gathering natural products may indeed conflict with the exclusivity traditionally associated with fee simple ownership of land. But *any argument for extinguishing of traditional rights based simply upon the possible inconsistency of purported native rights with our modern system of land tenure must fail.*

66 Haw. at 4, 656 P.2d at 748 (emphasis added).

The court then began its analysis of Kalipi's asserted gathering rights by interpreting HRS § 7–1 (1985)[22] so as to essentially "*conform* these traditional rights born of a culture which knew little of the rigid exclusivity associated with the private ownership of land, with a modern system of land tenure in which the right to exclude is perceived to be an integral part of fee simple title." *Id.* at 7, 656 P.2d at 749 (emphasis added). Accordingly, the court fashioned a rule permitting "lawful occupants of an [ahupua'a] . . . [to] enter undeveloped lands within the [ahupua'a] to gather those items enumerated in the statute [HRS § 7–11]." *Id.* at 7–8, 652 P.2d at 749.

> The requirement that these rights be exercised on undeveloped land is not, of course, found within the statute. However, if this limitation were not imposed, there would be nothing to prevent residents from going anywhere within the [ahupua'a], including fully developed property, to gather the enumerated items. *In the context of our current culture this result*

---

[22] HRS § 7–1, which has not undergone significant change since the 1851 enactment that amended an earlier version of the statute, provides:

> Building materials, water, etc.: landlords' title subject to tenants' use. Where the landlords have obtained, or may hereafter obtain, allodial titles to their lands, the people on each of their lands shall not be deprived of the right to take firewood, house-timber, aho cord, thatch, or ki leaf, from the land on which they live, for their own private use, but they shall not have a right to take such articles to sell for profit. The people shall also have a right to drinking water, and running water, and the right of way. The springs of water, running water, and roads shall be free to all, on all lands granted in fee simple; provided that this shall not be applicable to wells and watercourses, which individuals have made for their own use.

would so conflict with understandings of property, and potentially lead to such disruption, that we could not consider it anything short of absurd and therefore other than that which was intended by the statute's framers. Moreover, it would conflict with our understanding of the traditional Hawaiian way of life in which cooperation and non-interference with the well-being of other residents were integral parts of the culture.

Similarly, the requirement that the rights be utilized to practice native customs represents, we believe, a reasonable interpretation of the Act as applied to our current context. The gathering rights of § 7–1 were necessary to insure the survival of those who, in 1851, sought to live in accordance with the ancient ways. They thus remain, to the extent provided in the statute, available to those who wish to continue those ways.

Id. at 8–9, 656 P.2d at 749–50 (emphasis added).

Because Kalipi did not actually reside within the subject ahupua'a, the court held that he was not entitled to exercise HRS § 7–1 gathering rights there. *Id.* at 9, 656 P.2d at 750. Nevertheless, the court specifically refused to decide the ultimate scope of traditional gathering rights under HRS § 1–1 because there was "an *insufficient basis* to find that such rights would, or should, accrue to persons who did not actually reside within the [ahupua'a] in which such rights are claimed." *Id.* at 12, 656 P.2d at 752 (emphasis added). In other words, *Kalipi* did not foreclose the possibility of establishing, in future cases, traditional Hawaiian gathering and access rights in one ahupua'a that have been customarily held by residents of another ahupua'a.

2.   *Pele Defense Fund v. Paty: judicial recognition of traditional access and gathering rights based upon custom*

Pele involved, inter alia, the assertion of customarily and traditionally exercised subsistence, cultural, and religious practices in the Wao kele 'O Puna Natural Area Reserve on the Big Island. For the purposes of summary judgment, we held that there was a sufficient basis to find that gathering rights can be claimed by persons who do not reside in the particular ahupua'a where they seek to exercise those rights. *Pele,* 73 Haw. at 621, 837 P.2d at 1272 (reversing summary judgment and remanding for trial on this issue). We specifically held that "native Hawaiian rights protected by article XII, § 7 may extend beyond the ahupua'a in which a native Hawaiian resides." In so holding, we explicated the discussion of gathering rights in *Kalipi* by recognizing that a claim based on practiced customs raises different issues than assertions premised on mere land ownership.

Unlike Kalipi, [Pele Defense Fund] members assert native Hawaiian rights based on the traditional access and gathering patterns of native Hawaiians in the Puna region. Because Kalipi based his claims entirely on land ownership, rather than on the practiced customs of Hawaiians on [Moloka'i], the issue facing us is somewhat different from the issue in *Kalipi*.

Pele, 73 Haw. at 618–19, 837 P.2d at 1271.

Although we later mentioned "other requirements of *Kalipi*" with approval—implicitly referring to the "undeveloped lands" and "no actual harm" requirements of *Kalipi*—our holding in *Pele* was not intended to foreclose argument regarding those requirements in future, unrelated cases involving assertions of customary and traditional rights under HRS § 1–1. "In *Kalipi*, we foresaw that '[t]he precise nature and scope of the rights retained by § 1–1 would, of course, depend upon the particular circumstances of each case.'" *Pele*, 73 Haw. at 619, 837 P.2d at 1271 (quoting *Kalipi*, 66 Haw. at 12, 656 P.2d at 752).

3.   *The "other requirements of Kalipi"*

In addition to creating the "undeveloped land" requirement, the court in *Kalipi* made the following observations concerning claims of traditional gathering rights under HRS § 1–1:

> We perceive the Hawaiian usage exception to the adoption of the common law to represent an attempt on the part of the framers of the statute to avoid results inappropriate to the isles' inhabitants by permitting the continuance of native understandings and practices which did not unreasonably interfere with the spirit of the common law. The statutory exception is thus *akin to the English doctrine of custom* whereby practices and privileges unique to particular districts continued to apply to the residents of those districts even though in contravention of the common law. *This is not to say that we find that all the requisite elements of the doctrine of custom were necessarily incorporated in § 1–1. Rather we believe that the retention of a Hawaiian tradition should in each case be determined by balancing the respective interests and harm once it is established that the application of the custom has continued in a particular area.*
>
> In this case, Plaintiff's witnesses testified at trial that there have continued in certain [ahupua'a] a range of practices associated with the ancient way of life which required the utilization of the undeveloped property of others and which were not in § 7–1. Where these practices have, without harm to anyone, been continued, we are of the opinion that the reference to Hawaiian usage in § 1–1 insures their continuance for so long as no actual harm is done thereby. * * *

* * *

* * * Traditional and customary rights are properly examined against the law of property as it has developed in this state. Thus, the regulatory power provided in article XII, section 7 does not justify summary extinguishment of such rights by the State merely because they are deemed inconsistent with generally understood elements of the western doctrine of "property."

4.   *The development of private property rights in Hawai'i*

Some of the generally understood western concepts of property rights were discussed in Reppun v. Board of Water Supply, 65 Haw. 531, 656 P.2d 57 (1982). * * *

Although the court in *Reppun* focused on interests in water, its discussion of the development of Hawaiian property rights is enlightening.

[The court cites influence of Hawaiian property rights to water interests in Hawaii discussed in Reppun.]

* * *

After the Mahele, the Privy Council considered the rights of tenants under the new system of private land ownership and proposed a resolution providing that:

> the rights of the makaainanas [sic] to firewood, timber for house, grass for thatching, ki leaf, water for household purposes in said land, and the privilege of making salt and taking certain fish from the seas adjoining said lands shall be and is hereby sacredly reserved and confirmed to them for their private use [should they need them] but not for sale . . . provided, that before going for firewood, timber for houses and grass for thatching, said makaainanas [sic] shall give notice to the Lord or his luna resident therein. 3B *Privy Council Records* 681, 687 (1850).[35]

The King responded, however, by expressing his concern that "a little bit of land even with allodial title, if they were cut off from all other privileges, would be of very little value[.]" Accordingly, the final resolution was passed with the comment that "the proposition of the King, which he inserted as the seventh clause of the law, a rule for the claims of the common people to go to the mountains, and the seas attached to their own particular land exclusively, is agreed to[.]" Provisions of the law requiring the landlord's consent were repealed the following year because "many difficulties and complaints have arisen from the bad feeling existing on

---

[35]   The word "maka'āinana" is defined as "[c]ommoner, populace, people in general; citizen, subject . . . people that attend the land." Pukui & Elbert, *Hawaiian Dictionary* 224 (2nd ed. 1986). Our observations concerning the interpretation of "hoa'āina" and "tenant" as incorporating traditional Hawaiian cultural attitudes toward the land are further supported by this legislative history. *See also* Kent, *Treasury of Hawaiian Words* 386 (1986) (defining "maka'āinana" as, inter alia, the "laboring class, which was resident on the land they worked and transferred with it when ownership changed"). * * *

account of the Konohiki's [sic] forbidding the tenants on the lands enjoying the benefits that have been by law given them."

Given the preservation of Hawaiian usage in conjunction with the transition to a new system of land tenure, it is doubtful that "accept[ance]" of traditional and customary rights was required or that recognition of such rights would have "fundamentally violat[ed] the new system." *Kalipi.*

Our examination of the relevant legal developments in Hawaiian history leads us to the conclusion that the western concept of exclusivity is not universally applicable in Hawai'i. In other words, the issuance of a Hawaiian land patent confirmed a limited property interest as compared with typical land patents governed by western concepts of property. Cf. *United States v. Winans*, 198 U.S. 371 (1905) (observing that the United State Congress was competent "to secure to the Indians such a remnant of the great rights they possessed").

Although this premise clearly conflicts with common "understandings of property" and could theoretically lead to disruption, the non-confrontational aspects of traditional Hawaiian culture should minimize potential disturbances. In any event, we reiterate that the State retains the ability to reconcile competing interests under article XII, section 7. We stress that unreasonable or non-traditional uses are not permitted under today's ruling. *See, e.g., Winans* (noting that the trial court found "that it would 'not be justified in issuing process to compel the defendants to permit the Indians to *make a camping ground of their property while engaged in fishing* '") (emphasis added).

There should be little difficulty accommodating the customary and traditional Hawaiian rights asserted in the instant case with Nansay's avowed purposes. A community development proposing to integrate cultural education and recreation with tourism and community living represents a promising opportunity to demonstrate the continued viability of Hawaiian land tenure ideals in the modern world.

5. *Customary Rights under Hawai'i law*

The Kalipi court properly recognized that "all the requisite elements of the doctrine of custom were [not] necessarily incorporated in § 1–1." Accordingly, HRS § 1–1 represents the codification of the doctrine of custom *as it applies in our State*. One of the most dramatic differences in the application of custom in Hawai'i is that passage of HRS § 1–1's predecessor fixed November 25, 1892 as the date Hawaiian usage must have been established in practice.

Other differences in the doctrine's applicability are readily discernible. For example, under English common law, "a custom for every inhabitant of an ancient messuage [meaning '[d]welling-house with the adjacent buildings and curtilage[,]' see *Black's Legal Dictionary* 990 (6th ed. 1990)] within a parish to take a profit *a prendre* in the land of an individual is bad." Blackstone's Commentaries, at 78 n. 18. Strict application of the English common law, therefore, would apparently have precluded the exercise of traditional Hawaiian gathering rights. (As such, this element of the doctrine of custom could not apply in Hawai'i).

In light of the confusion surrounding the nature and scope of customary Hawaiian rights under HRS § 1–1, the following subsections of this opinion discuss applicable requirements for establishing such rights *in the instant case.*

a.

Nansay argues that the recognition of rights exercised by persons who do not actually reside in the subject ahupua'a "represents such a departure from existing law . . . [that *Pele*] should be overruled or strictly limited to its specific facts." Nansay contends further that *Pele* is inconsistent with the fundamental nature of Hawaiian land tenure, which allegedly recognizes only three classes: government, landlord, and tenant.

We decline Nansay's invitation to overrule *Pele*; on the contrary, we reaffirm it and expressly deem the rules of law posited therein to be applicable here. In *Pele*, we held that article XII, section 7, which, inter alia, obligates the State to protect customary and traditional rights normally associated with tenancy in an ahupua'a, may also apply to the exercise of rights beyond the physical boundaries of that particular ahupua'a. *Pele*, 73 Haw. at 620, 837 P.2d at 1272. Although it is not clear that customary rights should be limited by the term "tenant," we are nonetheless aware that the "tenant" class includes at least one sub-class. *See 2 Revised Land Laws of Hawaii* (1925), at 2124, 2126 (mentioning a "lowest class of tenants," "lower orders" and "sub-tenants," apparently from the Hawaiian terms "lopa ma lalo," "hoa'aina ma lalo," and "lopa"). Therefore, we hold that common law rights ordinarily associated with tenancy do not limit customary rights existing under the laws of this state.

* * *

We have stated previously that rights of access and collection will not necessarily prevent landowners from developing their lands. Our analysis in the instant case is consistent with these cases.

* * *

Depending on the circumstances of each case, once land has reached the point of "full development" it may be inconsistent to allow or enforce the practice of traditional Hawaiian gathering rights on such property. However, legitimate customary and traditional practices must be protected to the extent feasible in accordance with article XII, section 7. Although access is only *guaranteed* in connection with undeveloped lands, and article XII, section 7 does not *require* the preservation of such lands, the State does not have the unfettered discretion to regulate the rights of ahupua'a tenants out of existence.

Thus, to the extent feasible, we hold that HPC must protect the reasonable exercise of customary or traditional rights that are established by PASH on remand.

V.   None of Nonsay's Property Interests Have Been Taken

It is a fundamental rule under the United States and Hawai'i Constitutions that the uncompensated taking of private property is prohibited. The recognition and protection of Hawaiian rights give rise to potential takings claims under two theories: judicial taking and regulatory taking.

A.   Judicial Taking

* * *

In the instant case, Nansay argues that the recognition of traditional Hawaiian rights beyond those established in *Kalipi* and *Pele* would fundamentally alter its property rights. However, Nansay's argument places undue reliance on western understandings of property law that are not universally applicable in Hawai'i. Moreover, Hawaiian custom and usage have always been a part of the laws of this State. Therefore, our recognition of customary and traditional Hawaiian rights * * * does not constitute a judicial taking.

B.   Regulatory Taking

A regulatory taking occurs when the government's application of the law to a particular landowner denies all economically beneficial use of his or her property without providing compensation. *Lucas v. South Carolina Coastal Council*, 505 U.S. 1003 (1992). However, not every limitation on the use of private property will constitute a "taking." For instance, the government "assuredly [can] . . . assert a permanent easement that [reflects] a pre-existing limitation upon the landowner's title." *Lucas*, 112 S.Ct. at 2900. Furthermore, conditions may be placed on development without effecting a "taking" so long as the conditions bear an "essential nexus" to legitimate state interests and are "roughly proportional" to the impact of the proposed development. *Dolan v. City of Tigard*, 114 S.Ct. 2309, 2317–19 (1994).

In the instant case, the HPC must consider PASH's alleged customary rights on remand. * * * No determination as to the extent of any applicable limitations on Nansay's ability to develop its land may be made until the HPC holds a contested case hearing in accordance with this opinion. For that reason, we agree with Nansay that any claim alleging a regulatory taking would be premature at this time.

* * *

NOTES

1.   Notice the Hawaii Supreme Court's assimilation of traditional Hawaiian law and Indian law principles in this case. Is this unusual for a state court in considering rights of Native peoples?

2.   The ability to use Hawaii's beaches to fish, gather other foods, travel around the islands, and reach spiritual places often located along the coast is essential to Native Hawaiian culture. Natives have organized to resist development that obstructs beach access and alters areas that have been used by them and their ancestors for centuries. Litigants generally have been successful in asserting rights to use the beaches. The Hawaii Supreme Court has held that the "upper reaches of the wash of the waves" is the boundary between private and public land. County of Hawaii v. Sotomura, 517 P.2d 57 (Haw.1973); see also In re Ashford, 440 P.2d 76 (Haw.1968). The court has said that "public policy * * * favors extending to public use and ownership as much of Hawaii's shoreline as is reasonably possible." Id. at 61–62. The Hawaii decisions are grounded in Native Hawaiian customary rights, but the beneficiaries of those rights are all members of the public. See Michael D. Tom, Comment, *Hawaiian Beach Access: A Customary Right,* 26 Hastings L.J. 823 (1975); Michael Town & William Yuen, *Public Access to Beaches in Hawaii: "A Social Necessity,"* 10 Haw.B.J. 5 (1973); and Asami Miyazawa, *Public Beach Access: A Right for All? Opening the Gate to Iroquois Point Beach*, 30 U.Haw.L.Rev. 495 (2008):

> Whether by using common law or the Native Hawaiian doctrine of customs, claimants must show that the exercised customary rights are "ancient." The two doctrines differ on the definitions of "ancient": under the common law, a customary right is considered ancient if it existed prior to the beginning of a state's political history, which in Hawai'i would be 1846. The date under the Native Hawaiian doctrine is November 25, 1892. Either way, it would be necessary to prove, most likely by use of *kama' ina* testimony, that the descendants of Native Hawaiians have been practicing their traditional customary rights at Iroquois Point. The customs need not be limited to fishing and gathering; it may include other activities such as swimming, as long as they relate to subsistence, religious or cultural uses, and are non-commercial.

3. ENFORCING NATIVE RIGHTS UNDER FEDERAL LEGISLATION

DAY V. APOLIONA
United States Court of Appeals, Ninth Circuit, 2007.
496 F.3d 1027.

BERZON, CIRCUIT JUDGE:

The Hawaii Admission Act, Pub.L. No. 86–3, 73 Stat. 4 (1959) ("Admission Act") granted Hawaii title to most of the federal government's public land within the state, and required the state to hold that land and profits from it in "public trust" for five purposes. One such purpose is "for the betterment of the conditions of Native Hawaiians." The other purposes-for public schools, development of farm and home ownership, public improvements, and the provision of land for public use-are not limited to Native Hawaiians.

The plaintiffs in this case, whom we call "Day" after the first-named of them, are Native Hawaiians, defined under federal law as "descendant[s] of not less than one-half part of the blood of the races inhabiting the Hawaiian Islands previous to 1778." Hawaiian Homes Commission Act, Pub.L. No. 67–34, 42 Stat. 108 (1921) ("HHCA"); *see generally Rice v. Cayetano,* 528 U.S. 495, 507, 120 S.Ct. 1044, 145 L.Ed.2d 1007 (2000).[1] Based on the Admission Act and state law, these Native Hawaiians contend that the defendants, current and former trustees of the state's Office of Hawaiian Affairs ("OHA"), have not properly considered ethnic distinctions in spending the assets of the Admission Act trust ("§ 5(f) trust"). To enforce their asserted right to ensure that the § 5(f) trust funds are spent in accordance with the Admission Act's specifications, Day filed suit under 42 U.S.C. § 1983 [providing a right of action for "deprivation of any rights, privileges, or immunities secured by the Constitution and laws," Eds.].

* * *

I. PROCEDURAL HISTORY

State law assigns to the OHA the promotion of "[t]he betterment of conditions of Native Hawaiians . . . [and] Hawaiians." Haw.Rev.Stat. § 10–3. To effectuate this assignment, OHA receives a portion of the § 5(f) trust monies, which it is to devote "to the betterment of the conditions of Native

---

[1] Hawaii state law similarly defines the term "Native Hawaiians." Hawaii separately defines the term "Hawaiians" as any descendants-regardless of exact ancestry or "blood" quantum-of certain aboriginal peoples inhabiting the Hawaiian Islands in 1778. Haw.Rev.Stat. § 10–2. We use the terms "Native Hawaiian" and "Hawaiian" as they are defined in federal and state law, respectively.

Hawaiians," *id.* at § 10–3(1).3[3] The agency receives other funds as well, which it uses to fund projects that do not meet the § 5(f) restrictions.

In this case, Day alleges that OHA misspent § 5(f) trust funds in two ways: (1) by lobbying in favor of a federal bill (the "Akaka Bill") "that purports to create a Native Hawaiian Governing Entity to be established by persons . . . without regard to the blood quantum requirements set out under HHCA," and (2) by supporting three social service programs whose "funds are not subject to the limitation that they may be expended only for the betterment of the conditions of 'native Hawaiians.' " Such expenditures, the amended complaint alleges, are inconsistent with the purposes listed in § 5(f) and constitute a violation of (1) the Admissions Act and the HHCA, enforceable by 42 U.S.C. § 1983. * * *

The district court dismissed the amended complaint. Ruling on an argument raised not by the defendants but by the state of Hawaii in an amicus curiae brief, the court held that the complaint failed to allege any Admission Act violation enforceable under § 1983. * * *

II. ANALYSIS

The question in this case, whether a violation of § 5(f) of the Admission Act is enforceable via § 1983, is not new to this court. Over the last two decades, we have established the broad contours of Native Hawaiians' right to sue for breach of the state's § 5(f) trust obligations and held that § 5(f) does not create an implied private right of action for breach of the § 5(f) trust, but does create a right enforceable via 42 U.S.C. § 1983, *see Price v. Akaka,* 3 F.3d 1220 (9th Cir.1993) ("*Akaka II*"); *Keaukaha-Panaewa Cmty. Ass'n v. Hawaiian Homes Comm'n,* 739 F.2d 1467 (9th Cir.1984) ("*Keaukaha II*"). We have repeatedly applied this latter holding.

The district court concluded, however, that *Akaka II*'s holding is no longer good law because it has been effectively overruled by *Gonzaga University v. Doe,* 536 U.S. 273, 122 S.Ct. 2268, 153 L.Ed.2d 309 (2002). * * *

---

[3]   The § 5 grant included approximately "200,000 acres [formerly] set aside [as "Hawaiian homelands" to benefit Native Hawaiians] under the Hawaiian Homes Commission Act and almost 1.2 million additional acres of land." *Rice,* 528 U.S. at 507, 120 S.Ct. 1044. OHA receives twenty percent of the revenue from the 1.2 million additional acres. Haw.Rev.Stat. § 10–13.5. A different agency, the Department of Hawaiian Home Lands, administers the 200,000 acres that were set aside by the HHCA. Haw.Rev.Stat. § 26–17; *see generally Rice,* 528 U.S. at 509, 120 S.Ct. 1044. We have not previously decided whether the HHCA lands may be used for the purposes specified in § 5(f) or only for the more restricted uses specified in the HHCA. *See* Admission Act § 4, 73 Stat. at 5; *Keaukaha-Panaewa Cmty. Ass'n v. Hawaiian Homes Comm'n,* 588 F.2d 1216, 1218–19 & n. 2 (9th Cir.1979) ("*Keaukaha I*"); *see also Akaka I,* 928 F.2d at 826 n. 1 ("A 'compact' between Hawaii and the United States strictly limits the manner in which Hawaii may manage the homelands and the income they produce."). We do not decide that question today either, as Day challenges only the use of funds managed by the OHA.

A. Breach of trust actions under the Admission Act

Before explaining our conclusion regarding the impact of *Gonzaga*, we set the scene by describing our existing case law regarding the enforcement of the § 5(f) trust by beneficiaries in some detail.

Section 5(f) of the Admissions Act provides that the relevant lands and income from them

> *shall be held by said State as a public trust* for the support of the public schools and other public educational institutions, for the betterment of the conditions of Native Hawaiians, as defined in the Hawaiian Homes Commission Act, 1920, as amended, for the development of farm and home ownership on as widespread a basis as possible for the making of public improvements, and for the provision of lands for public use. Such lands, proceeds, and income shall be managed and disposed of for one or more of the foregoing purposes in such manner as the constitution and laws of said State may provide, and *their use for any other object shall constitute a breach of trust for which suit may be brought by the United States.*

73 Stat. at 6 (emphasis added).

Prior to *Gonzaga,* we twice explicitly held that because it creates a trust, § 5(f) also creates a right enforceable under § 1983 by the trust's beneficiaries. In *Keaukaha II,* we reached that conclusion by relying on "a presumption that a federal statute creating enforceable rights may be enforced in a section 1983 action." 739 F.2d at 1470. Our primary concern was whether the § 1983 remedy was foreclosed by the statute's public remedy. Earlier, in *Keaukaha I,* 588 F.2d 1216, we had concluded that the Admission Act did not create an implied private cause of action in part because the Act allowed the United States to sue for breach of trust. *Id.* at 1223–24. But in *Keaukaha II,* we concluded that the public remedy did not foreclose a § 1983 action because of the presumption in favor of a § 1983 remedy where a statute creates enforceable rights. 739 F.2d at 1470.

Keaukaha II recognized that "[t]here remains a question . . . whether the Admission Act created a federal 'right' enforceable under section 1983." *Id.* at 1471. While we observed that "[t]he Admission Act clearly mandates establishment of a trust for the betterment of native Hawaiians," we did not discuss the question in any detail, because "[t]he defendants [did] not seriously contend that plaintiffs have no enforceable rights." *Id.*

Our next substantive discussion of the issue was in *Akaka I,* 928 F.2d at 826–27. *Akaka I* considered Native Hawaiians' claim that OHA trustees violated § 5(f) by comingling § 5(f) trust funds with other funds, and by not spending the trust funds to benefit Native Hawaiians or to serve the other § 5(f) purposes. We did not directly address the question of whether the statute created an enforceable right. But we did discuss the plaintiffs' rights, in explaining why they had standing even though the trustees could legally spend the § 5(f) funds for purposes other than to benefit Native Hawaiians:

> We recently considered this very question, and determined that allegations such as those Price has made are sufficient to show an 'injury in fact.' *See Price* [*v. State of Hawaii*, 764 F.2d 623, 630 (9th Cir.1985)]. In addition, allowing Price to enforce § 5(f) is consistent with the common law of trusts, in which one whose status as a beneficiary depends upon the discretion of the trustee nevertheless may sue to compel the trustee to abide by the terms of the trust.

Akaka I, 928 F.2d at 826–27.

Drawing directly on *Akaka I,* we explicitly returned in *Akaka II,* 3 F.3d 1220, to the enforceable rights question identified in *Keaukaha II.* * * *

Akaka II * * * explained why § 5(f) created an enforceable right by citing to *Akaka I:*

> The instant case involves a public trust, and under basic trust law principles, beneficiaries have the right to "maintain a suit (a) to compel the trustee to perform his duties as trustee; (b) to enjoin the trustee from committing a breach of trust; [and] (c) to compel the trustee to redress a breach of trust." Restatement 2d of the Law of Trusts, § 199; *see also id.* § 200, comment a. We have accordingly held that "allowing Price to enforce § 5(f) is consistent with the common law of trusts, in which one whose status as a beneficiary depends upon the discretion of the trustee nevertheless may sue to compel the trustee to abide by the terms of the trust." *Akaka I,* 928 F.2d at 826–27.
>
> * * * Congress enacted the Admission Act, a federal public trust, which by its nature creates a federally enforceable right for its beneficiaries to maintain an action against the trustee in breach of the trust. As a beneficiary, Price may therefore bring a § 1983 action under the Hawaii Admission Act against the trustees.

Id. at 1224–25 (internal parenthetical omitted).

Akaka II's reliance on trust law was not unique. Unifying most of our § 5(f) case law is the understanding that because they are designated as a "public trust," § 5(f) funds are governed by a set of trust law principles that have procedural as well as substantive implications. * * * If nothing else, the words "public trust" in the Admission Act "betoken the State's duty to avoid deviating from section 5(f)'s purpose." *Price v. Hawaii,* 921 F.2d at 955–56. *But see id.* at 955 (concluding that because the Hawaii Admission

Act "confers a broad authority upon the State," it does not impose any duties on the state regarding the management of the § 5(f) funds). And we have implied that the "body of law [applicable] for the purpose of enforcing" this duty likely draws on the common law of trusts. * * *

* * *

B.   The effect of recent Supreme Court cases

After *Akaka II* was decided, two Supreme Court cases—*Blessing v. Freestone,* 520 U.S. 329, 117 S.Ct. 1353, 137 L.Ed.2d 569 (1997), and *Gonzaga,* 536 U.S. 273, 122 S.Ct. 2268—summarized, explained, and, on some points, refined the law regarding when a statute creates a right enforceable under § 1983.

[The Court reviewed the changes in the law created by the two cases and found that they did not affect the rights of beneficiaries to sue to enforce provisions of the 5(f) trust created by the Admission Act. Eds.]

* * *

C.   The district court's analysis

Our analysis of this issue differs not only in result but also in approach from that of the district court. The district court held that after *Gonzaga, Akaka II*'s reaffirmance that § 5(f) established a right enforceable under § 1983 was no longer good law, because that conclusion is irreconcilable with the Ninth Circuit's earlier holding in *Keaukaha I* that there was no implied private right of action under the Admission Act. This conclusion was based on a misunderstanding of *Gonzaga.*

The court read *Gonzaga* to equate the availability of an implied private right of action with the availability of a right enforceable under § 1983. But *Gonzaga* endorsed no such equation. To the contrary, *Gonzaga* stressed that "whether a statutory violation may be enforced through § 1983 is a different inquiry than that involved in determining whether a private right of action can be implied from a particular statute. But the inquiries overlap in one meaningful respect-in either case we must first determine whether Congress *intended to create a federal right.*" *Gonzaga,* 536 U.S. at 283, 122 S.Ct. 2268 (quotation marks and citation omitted). In other words, under *Gonzaga,* the inquiry into whether there is a federal *right* is the same in the context of private rights of action and § 1983 rights. The inquiry into whether there is a private right *of action* is different, however, from the inquiry of whether there is a private right *enforceable* through § 1983 because an implied private right of action requires "not just a private right but also a private remedy." *Alexander v. Sandoval,* 532 U.S. 275, 286, 121 S.Ct. 1511, 149 L.Ed.2d 517 (2001).

Keaukaha I's holding that the Admission Act created no implied private right of action is thus fully consistent with *Akaka II,* after *Gonzaga* as before. The former did not disavow the existence of a private right; to the contrary, *Keaukaha I* suggested there was such a right, but held that there was no private right of action because the statute created no *remedy* for the right. * * * .

Because it is based on a misreading of *Gonzaga,* the district court's conclusion that *Gonzaga* so conflicts with this court's precedents as to require deviation from those precedents cannot stand.

CONCLUSION

We thus reaffirm what we have already held and reaffirmed: that each Native Hawaiian plaintiff, as a beneficiary of the trust created by § 5(f), has an individual right to have the trust terms complied with, and therefore can sue under for violation of that right. Violations of this right may include, at minimum, wrongs of the type of which Day complains: expenditure of funds for purposes not enumerated under § 5(f). We leave to the district court to interpret those § 5(f) purposes to determine in the first instance not only whether Day's allegations are true, but also whether the described expenditures in fact violate § 5(f). In doing so, we recognize the sore lack of judicial guidance on this point and the uncertainty that lack of guidance has injected into the policymaking environment. Cases related to the OHA's expenditure of funds for Native Hawaiians have reached our court on numerous prior occasions, but we and the district court have shed little light on the merits of § 5(f) claims. *See generally Arakaki v. Lingle,* 477 F.3d 1048, 1052–53 (9th Cir.2007) (citing cases). Absent further foundational issues with Day's claim, today's affirmance of our existing precedent should permit much-needed elucidation of the substance of § 5(f).

AFFIRMED in part, REVERSED in part, and REMANDED

NOTES

1.   *Day* was brought by Native Hawaiian plaintiffs objecting to OHA's use of funds to benefit those having less than the "half-blood" formula in § 5(f) of the Admissions Act. Those who legally qualify as "Native Hawaiians" having at least 50 percent Hawaiian blood are pitted against the mere "Hawaiians" whose blood quantum is less. Meanwhile, as shown by Rice v. Cayetano, page 1030, infra, there are non-Hawaiians who consistently challenge legislation or programs that distinctively benefit Hawaiians. Do you think divisions among Hawaiians that were originally created by the governments of the dominant society—help or hinder the "Native Hawaiian" and "Hawaiian" communities in their efforts to protect and assert their rights as Hawaii's indigenous peoples?

2.   After remand, the Ninth Circuit affirmed the district court's summary judgment for OHA. Day v. Apoliona, 616 F.3d 918 (9th Cir.2010) it said that while the individual plaintiffs had a federal right to have the funds expended according to any of the § 5(f) purposes, only one of those purposes

was specific to half-blood Native Hawaiians. The challenged expenditures were, it said, at the discretion of the OHA trustees and there is no federal right to examine the entire state law scheme for carrying out the trust. Unless an expenditure was outside all of the five purposes of the trust, the court would not find it an unreasonable exercise of discretion.

3.   The multiple cases in which Hawaiians have sought to challenge the state's administration of § 5(f), many of them cited in the principal case, have often languished on procedural obstacles. But they embody a variety of claims besides whether benefits should be shared beyond half-blood Native Hawaiians.

The *Keaukaha* cases were brought against the Hawaiian Homes Commission and challenged the commission's administration of the Hawaiian Homes Commission Act. The plaintiffs alleged a breach of trust arising out of the loss of 25 acres of Hawaiian Homes Commission Act lands. The ruling in *Keaukaha II* encouraged Native Hawaiians to challenge Hawaii's administration of trust lands under the Admission Act in several other federal cases.

A persistent group of plaintiffs challenged the use of income from trust lands as being outside the five § 5(f) purposes and requested an accounting and an order that an appropriate portion be dedicated to Native Hawaiians. But the claims were eclipsed again by procedural issues. Even after *Keaukaha II* allowed such plaintiffs to proceed under § 1983, the *Price* plaintiffs sought other avenues to federal court, asserting jurisdiction under 28 U.S.C. § 1331 (federal question) and 28 U.S.C. § 1362 (federal question jurisdiction for Indian tribes). Price v. Hawaii, 764 F.2d 623 (9th Cir.1985). The Ninth Circuit denied the group—claiming to be a tribe under the name "Hou Hawaiians"— jurisdiction as a tribe, saying that the federal government had not recognized them as such and so "we will not intrude on the traditionally executive or legislative prerogative of recognizing tribe's existence." The court held, however, that federal question jurisdiction would exist on the same rationale as § 1983 jurisdiction—a federal right under the Admission Act. That Act created a trust for the plaintiffs' benefit and was effectively a compact between the new state and the federal government and the right is now embodied in the state constitution that "incorporated the spirit of the Hawaiian Homes Commission Act looking to the continuance of the Hawaiian homes projects." Id. at 729.

But then the plaintiffs had to deal with the Eleventh Amendment objections when they claimed that the Admission Act was violated by the state's management of the § 5(f) lands in ways that did not benefit Hawaiians. The court said that—while plaintiffs' allegations of commingling and improper expenditures could be considered by the federal court—the suit was barred as being directly against the state. The federal court could not require "that the State adopt a particular approach to management and holding of the ceded lands or of the income from those lands." Price v. State of Hawaii, 921 F.2d 950 (9th Cir.1990). The court noted that the Admission Act was too vague to impose the same exacting trust obligations that apply to the United States in dealing with Indians. See also Ulaleo v. Paty, 902 F.2d 1395 (9th Cir.1990) (Eleventh Amendment prevented suit challenging an exchange of trust land). Once the plaintiffs amended their complaint to name individual trustees, not the state per se, the Ninth Circuit held that the suit was not barred by the Eleventh Amendment and allowed a claim challenging the use of trust funds for a referendum on whether there should be a single definition of Hawaiians. Price v. Akaka, 928 F.2d 824 (9th Cir.1990), cert. denied 502 U.S. 967 (1991). The court later held that OHA was entitled to qualified immunity from the claim asserted. Price v. Akaka, 3 F.3d 1220 (9th Cir.1993).

4.   Native Hawaiians have also sought to enforce their rights in Hawaii state courts. In Ahuna v. Department of Hawaiian Home Lands, 640 P.2d 1161 (Haw.1982), the Hawaii Supreme Court imposed a trust duty on the Department of Hawaiian Home Lands, the state agency created to administer the program created by Congress in 1921 under the HHCA. Citing *Cherokee Nation v. Georgia*, see page 128, supra, Chief Justice Richardson wrote that in dealing with eligible Native Hawaiians under the program, the department "must adhere to high fiduciary duties normally owed by a trustee to its beneficiaries." Richardson's opinion elaborated on the state's trust responsibility:

> One specific trust duty is the obligation to administer the trust solely in the interest of the beneficiary. * * *

> A second fundamental trust obligation is to use reasonable skill and care to make trust property productive, * * * or simply to act as an ordinary and prudent person would in dealing with his own property. * * *

> Given these two basic duties of a trustee, we now impose them on the Hawaiian Homes Commission, the individual commissioners, and the Department to determine whether there has been a breach of fiduciary duties.

Id. at 1169.

Notwithstanding these principles, challenges to practices of the Hawaiian Homes Commission and of the State of Hawaii over trust lands are often unsuccessful. See, e.g., Ahia v. Department of Transportation, 751 P.2d 81 (Haw.1988) (lease of Hawaiian Home Lands to state Department of Transportation was not incompatible with the mandate to promote the interests of Native Hawaiians; preferential treatment of Hawaiians was not mandated when leasing to a government agency). See also Trustees of Office of Hawaiian Affairs v. Yamasaki, 737 P.2d 446 (Haw.1987) (disputes as to legislative determinations on division of income derived from public trust lands raised non-justiciable policy questions, given the lack of judicially discoverable and manageable standards for resolving the disputes). However, in Bush v. Watson, 918 P.2d 1130 (Haw.1996), the Hawaii Supreme Court held that the Hawaiian Homes Commission violated the terms of the HHCA by approving the leasing of Native Hawaiian homelands to nonnative third parties while there was a long waiting list of Native Hawaiians awaiting homestead assignments. The *Day* plaintiffs also sued in Kealoha v. Machado, 315 P.3d 213 (Haw.2013), claiming that OHA violated its trust obligations by expending funds for lobbying in favor of the Akaka Bill. The Hawaii Supreme Court upheld the dismissal of the action on the basis of OHA's broad discretion.

4. NATIVE HAWAIIANS AS NATIVE AMERICANS

RICE V. CAYETANO
Supreme Court of the United States, 2000.
528 U.S. 495, 120 S.Ct. 1044, 145 L.Ed.2d 1007.

JUSTICE KENNEDY delivered the opinion of the Court.

A citizen of Hawaii comes before us claiming that an explicit, race-based voting qualification has barred him from voting in a statewide election. The Fifteenth Amendment of the Constitution of the United States, binding on the National Government, the States, and their political subdivisions, controls the case.

* * *

In 1978 Hawaii amended its Constitution to establish the Office of Hawaiian Affairs, Haw. Const., Art. XII, § 5 which has as its mission "[t]he betterment of conditions of native Hawaiians ... [and] Hawaiians," Haw.Rev.Stat. § 10–3 (1993). * * *

Implementing statutes and their later amendments vested OHA with broad authority to administer two categories of funds: a 20 percent share of the revenue from the 1.2 million acres of lands granted to the State pursuant to § 5(b) of the Admission Act, which OHA is to administer "for the betterment of the conditions of native Hawaiians," Haw.Rev.Stat § 10–13.5, and any state or federal appropriations or private donations that may be made for the benefit of "native Hawaiians" and/or "Hawaiians," Haw.Const., Art. XII, § 6. * * *

OHA is overseen by a nine-member board of trustees, the members of which "shall be Hawaiians" and—presenting the precise issue in this case—shall be "elected by qualified voters who are Hawaiians, as provided by law." Haw.Const., Art. XII, § 5; see Haw.Rev.Stat. §§ 13D–1, 13D–3(b)(1) (1993). The term "Hawaiian" is defined by statute:

> " 'Hawaiian' means any descendant of the aboriginal peoples inhabiting the Hawaiian Islands which exercised sovereignty and subsisted in the Hawaiian Islands in 1778, and which peoples thereafter have continued to reside in Hawaii." § 10–2.

The statute defines "native Hawaiian" as follows:

> " 'Native Hawaiian' means any descendant of not less than one-half part of the races inhabiting the Hawaiian Islands previous to 1778, as defined by the Hawaiian Homes Commission Act, 1920, as amended; provided that the term identically refers to the descendants of such blood quantum of such aboriginal peoples which exercised sovereignty and subsisted in the Hawaiian Islands in 1778 and which people thereafter continued to reside in Hawaii." Ibid.

Petitioner Harold Rice is a citizen of Hawaii and a descendant of pre-annexation residents of the islands. * * * He is not, as we have noted, a descendant of pre-1778 natives, and so he is neither "native Hawaiian" nor "Hawaiian" as defined by the statute. * * * Rice applied in March 1996 to vote in the elections for OHA trustees. To register to vote for the office of the trustee he was required to attest: "I am also Hawaiian and desire to register to vote in OHA elections." Rice marked through the words "am also Hawaiian and," then checked the form "yes." The State denied his application.

Rice sued Benjamin Cayetano, the Governor of Hawaii, in the United States District Court for the District of Hawaii. Rice contested his exclusion from voting in elections for OHA trustees and from voting in a special election relating to native Hawaiian sovereignty which was held in August 1996.

* * * Surveying the history of the islands and their people, the District Court determined that Congress and the State of Hawaii have recognized a guardian-ward relationship with the native Hawaiians, which the court found analogous to the relationship between the United States and the Indian tribes. Rice v. Cayetano, 941 F.Supp. 1529, 1551–1554 (1996). On this premise, the court examined the voting qualification with the latitude that we have applied to legislation passed pursuant to Congress' power over Indian affairs. Finding that the electoral scheme was "rationally related to the State's responsibility under the Admission Act to utilize a portion of the proceeds from the § 5(b) lands for the betterment of Native Hawaiians," the District Court held that the voting restriction did not violate the Constitution's ban on racial classifications 963 F.Supp. at 1554–1555.

The Court of Appeals affirmed. * * *

We granted certiorari, and now reverse.

III

The purpose and command of the Fifteenth Amendment are set forth in language both explicit and comprehensive. The National Government and the States may not violate a fundamental principle: They may not deny or abridge the right to vote on account of race. Color and previous condition of servitude, too, are forbidden criteria or classifications, though it is unnecessary to consider them in the present case.

Enacted in the wake of the Civil War, the immediate concern of the Amendment was to guarantee to the emancipated slaves the right to vote, lest they be denied the civil and political capacity to protect their new freedom. Vital as its objective remains, the Amendment goes beyond it. Consistent with the design of the Constitution, the Amendment is cast in fundamental terms, terms transcending the particular controversy which was the immediate impetus for its enactment. The Amendment grants protection to all persons, not just members of a particular race.

The design of the Amendment is to reaffirm the equality of races at the most basic level of the democratic process, the exercises of the voting franchise. A resolve so absolute required language as simple in command as it was comprehensive in reach. Fundamental in purpose and effect and self-executing in operation, the Amendment prohibits all provisions denying or abridging the voting franchise of any citizen or class of citizens on the basis of race. "[B]y the inherent power of the Amendment the word white disappeared" from our voting laws, bringing those who have been excluded by reason of race within "the generic grant of suffrage made by the State." Guinn v. United States, 238 U.S. 347, 363 (1915). * * *

* * *

* * * [T]he voting structure now before us is neither subtle nor indirect. It is specific in granting the vote to persons of defined ancestry and to no others. The State maintains this is not a racial category at all but instead a classification limited to those ancestors who were in Hawaii at a particular time, regardless of their race. The State points to theories of certain scholars concluding that some inhabitants of Hawaii as of 1778 may have migrated from the Marquesas Islands and the Pacific Northwest, as well as from Tahiti. Furthermore, the State argues, the restriction in its operation excludes a person whose traceable ancestors were exclusively Polynesian if none of these ancestors resided in Hawaii in 1778; and, on the other hand, the vote would be granted to a person who could trace, say, one sixty-fourth of his or her ancestry to a Hawaiian inhabitant on the pivotal date. These factors, it is said, mean the restriction is not a racial classification. We reject this line of argument.

Ancestry can be a proxy for race. It is that proxy here. Even if the residents of Hawaii in 1778 had been of more diverse ethnic backgrounds and cultures, it is far from clear that a voting test favoring their descendants would not be a race-based qualification. But that is not this case. For centuries Hawaii was isolated from migration. The inhabitants shared common physical characteristics, and by 1778 they had a common culture. Indeed, the drafters of the statutory definition in question emphasized the "unique culture of the ancient Hawaiians" in explaining their work. Hawaii Senate Journal, Standing Committee Rep. No. 784, at 1354. The provisions before us reflect the State's effort to preserve that commonality of people to the present day. In the interpretation of the Reconstruction era civil rights law we have observed that "racial discrimination" is that which singles out "identifiable classes of person . . . solely because of their ancestry or ethnic characteristics." Saint Francis College v. Al-Khazraji, 481 U.S. 604 (1987). The very object of the statutory definition in question and of its earlier congressional counterpart in the Hawaiian Homes Commission Act is to treat the early Hawaiians as a distinct people, commanding their own recognition and respect. The State, in enacting the legislation before us, has used ancestry as a racial definition and for a racial purpose.

* * *

The ancestral inquiry mandated by the State is forbidden by the Fifteenth Amendment for the further reason that the use of racial classifications is corruptive of the whole legal order democratic elections seek to preserve. The law itself may not become the instrument for generating the prejudice and hostility all too often directed against persons whose particular ancestry is disclosed by their ethnic characteristics and cultural traditions. "Distinctions between citizens solely because of their ancestry are by their very nature odious to a free people whose institutions are founded upon the doctrine of equality." Hirabayashi v. United States, 320 U.S. 81, 100 (1943). Ancestral tracing of this sort achieves its purpose by creating a legal category which employs the same mechanisms, and causes the same injuries, as laws or statutes that use race by name. The State's electoral restriction enacts a race-based voting qualification.

IV

The State offers three principal defenses of its voting law, any of which it contends, allows it to prevail even if the classification is a racial one under the Fifteenth Amendment. We examine, and reject, each of these arguments.

A

The most far reaching of the State's arguments is that exclusion of non-Hawaiians from voting is permitted under our cases allowing the differential treatment of certain members of Indian tribes. * * * The *Mancari* case, and the theory upon which it rests, are invoked by the State to defend its decision to restrict voting for the OHA trustees, who are charged so directly with protecting the interests of native Hawaiians.

If Hawaii's restriction were to be sustained under *Mancari* we would be required to accept some beginning premises not yet established in our case law. Among other postulates, it would be necessary to conclude that

Congress, in reciting the purposes for the transfer of lands to the State—and in other enactments such as the Hawaiian Homes Commission Act and the Joint Resolution of 1993—has determined that native Hawaiians have a status like that of Indians in organized tribes, and that it may, and has, delegated to the State a broad authority to preserve that status. These propositions would raise questions of considerable moment and difficulty. * * * We can stay far off that difficult terrain, however.

The State's argument fails for a more basic reason. Even were we to take the substantial step of finding authority in Congress, delegated to the State, to treat Hawaiians or native Hawaiians as tribes, Congress may not authorize a State to create a voting scheme of this sort.

Of course, as we have established in a series of cases, Congress may fulfill its treaty obligations and its responsibilities to the Indian tribes by enacting legislation dedicated to their circumstances and needs. As we have observed, "every piece of legislation dealing with Indian tribes and reservations . . . single[s] out for special treatment a constituency of tribal Indians." *Mancari,* supra, at 552.

Mancari, upon which many of the above cases rely, presented the somewhat different issue of a preference in hiring and promoting at the federal Bureau of Indian Affairs (BIA), a preference which favored individuals who were " 'one-fourth or more degree Indian blood and . . . member[s] of a Federally-recognized tribe.' " 417 U.S., at 553, n. 24 (quoting 44 BIAM 335, 3.1 (1972)). Although the classification had a racial component, the Court found it important that the preference was "not directed towards a 'racial' group consisting of 'Indians,' but rather only to members of 'federally recognized' tribes." 417 U.S., at 553, n. 24. "In this sense," the Court held, "the preference [was] political rather than racial in nature." Id. at 554. * * * Because the BIA preference could be "tied rationally to the fulfillment of Congress' unique obligation toward the Indians," and was "reasonably and rationally designed to further Indian self-government," the Court held that it did not offend the Constitution. Id., at 555. The opinion was careful to note, however, that the case was confined to the authority of the BIA, an agency described as "sui generis." Id., at 554.

Hawaii would extend the limited exception of *Mancari* to a new and larger dimension. The State contends that "one of the very purposes of OHA—and the challenged voting provision—is to afford Hawaiians a measure of self-governance," and so it fits the model of *Mancari.* It does not follow from *Mancari,* however, that Congress may authorize a State to establish a voting scheme that limits the electorate for its public officials to a class of tribal Indians, to the exclusion of all non-Indians citizens.

The tribal elections established by the federal statutes the State cites illuminate its error (citing, e.g., the Menominee Restoration Act, 25 U.S.C.

§ 903b, and the Indian Reorganization Act, 25 U.S.C. § 476). If a non-Indian lacks a right to vote in tribal elections, it is for the reason that such elections are the internal affair of a quasi-sovereign. The OHA elections, by contrast, are the affair of the State of Hawaii. OHA is a state agency, established by the State Commission, responsible for the administration of state laws and obligations. See Haw.Const., Art. XII, §§ 5–6. * * *

* * *

The validity of the voting restriction is the only question before us. As the court of appeals did, we assume the validity of the underlying administrative structure and trusts, without intimating any opinion on that point. Nonetheless, the elections for OHA trustee are elections of the State, not of a separate quasi-sovereign, and they are elections to which the Fifteenth Amendment applies. To extend *Mancari* to this context would be to permit a State, by racial classification, to fence out whole classes of its citizens from decision making in critical state affairs. The Fifteenth Amendment forbids this result.

B

Hawaii further contends that the limited voting franchise is sustainable under a series of cases holding that the rule of one person, one vote does not pertain to certain purpose districts such as water or irrigation districts. * * *

The question before us is not the one-person, one-vote requirement of the Fourteenth Amendment, but the race neutrality command of the Fifteenth Amendment. Our special purpose district cases have not suggested that compliance with the one-person, one-vote rule of the Fourteenth Amendment somehow excuses compliance with the Fifteenth Amendment. We reject that argument here. * * *

C

Hawaii's final argument is that the voting restriction does no more than ensure an alignment of interests between the fiduciaries and the beneficiaries of a trust. Thus, the contention goes, the restriction is based on beneficiary status rather than race.

As an initial matter, the contention founders on its own terms, for it is not clear that the voting classification is symmetric with the beneficiaries of the programs OHA administers. Although the bulk of the funds for which OHA is responsible appears to be earmarked for the benefit of "native Hawaiians," the State permits both "native Hawaiians" and "Hawaiians" to vote for the office of trustee. The classification thus appears to create, not eliminate, a differential alignment between the identity of OHA trustees and what the State calls beneficiaries.

Hawaii's argument fails on more essential grounds. The State's position rests, in the end, on the demeaning premise that citizens of a particular race are somehow more qualified than others to vote on certain matters. That reasoning attacks the central meaning of the Fifteenth Amendment. * * * Under the Fifteenth Amendment voters are treated not as members of a distinct race but as members of the whole citizenry. Hawaii may not assume, based on race, that petitioner or any other of its citizens will not cast a principled vote. To accept the position advanced by the State would give rise to the same indignities, and the same resulting tensions and animosities, the Amendment was designed to eliminate. The voting restriction under review is prohibited by the Fifteenth Amendment.

* * *

When the culture and way of life of a people are all but engulfed by a history beyond their control, their sense of loss may extend down through generations; and their dismay may be shared by many members of the larger community. As the State of Hawaii attempted to address these realities, it must, as always, seek the political consensus that begins with a sense of shared purpose. One of the necessary beginning points is this principle: The Constitution of the United States, too, has become the heritage of all the citizens of Hawaii.

In this case the Fifteenth Amendment invalidates the electoral qualification based on ancestry. The judgment of the Court of Appeals for the Ninth Circuit is reversed.

It is so ordered.

* * *

JUSTICE STEVENS, with whom JUSTICE GINSBURG joins as to Part II, dissenting.

The Court's holding today rests largely on the repetition of glittering generalities that have little, if any, application to the compelling history of the State of Hawaii. When that history is held up against the manifest purpose of the Fourteenth and Fifteenth Amendments, and against two centuries of this Court's federal Indian law, it is clear to me that Hawaii's election scheme should be upheld.

* * *

That conclusion is in keeping with three overlapping principles. First, the Federal Government must be, and has been, afforded wide latitude in carrying out its obligations arising from the special relationship it has with the aboriginal peoples, a category that includes the native Hawaiians, whose lands are now a part of the territory of the United States. In addition, there exists in this case the State's own fiduciary responsibility—arising from its establishment of a public trust—for administering assets granted it by the Federal Government in part for the benefit of native Hawaiians. Finally, even if one were to ignore the more than two centuries of Indian law precedent and practice on which this case follows, there is simply no invidious discrimination present in this effort to see that indigenous peoples are compensated for past wrongs, and preserve a distinct and vibrant culture that is as much a part of this Nation's heritage as any.

* * *

Critically, neither the extent of Congress' sweeping power nor the character of the trust relationship with indigenous peoples has depended on the ancient racial origins of the people, the allotment of tribal lands, the coherence or existence of tribal self-government, or the varying definitions of "Indian" Congress has chosen to adopt. Rather, when it comes to the exercise of Congress' plenary power in Indian affairs, this Court has taken account of the "numerous occasions" on which "legislation that singles out Indians for particular and special treatment" has been upheld, and has concluded that as "long as the special treatment can be tied rationally to the fulfillment of Congress' unique obligation towards the Indians, such legislative judgments will not be disturbed." Morton v. Mancari, 417 U.S. 535, 554–555 (1974). * * *

* * *

* * * Among the many and varied laws passed by Congress in carrying out its duty to indigenous peoples, more than 150 today expressly include native Hawaiians as part of the class of Native Americans benefited. By classifying native Hawaiians as "Native Americans" for purposes of these statutes, Congress has made clear that native Hawaiians enjoy many of "the same rights and privileges accorded to American Indian, Alaska Native, Eskimo, and Aleut communities." 42 U.S.C. § 11701(19).

While splendidly acknowledging this history—specifically including the series of agreements and enactments the history reveals—the majority fails to recognize its import. The descendants of the native Hawaiians share with the descendants of the Native Americans on the mainland or in the Aleutian Islands not only a history of subjugation at the hands of colonial forces, but also a purposefully created and specialized "guardian-ward" relationship with the Government of the United States. It follows that legislation targeting the native Hawaiians must be evaluated according to the same understanding of equal protection that this Court has long applied to the Indians on the continental United States: that "special treatment . . . be tied rationally to the fulfillment of Congress' unique obligation" toward the native peoples.

* * *

* * * Under this standard, as with the BIA preferences in Mancari, the OHA voting requirement is certainly reasonably designed to promote "self-government" by the descendants of the indigenous Hawaiians, and to make OHA "more responsive to the needs of its constituent groups." Mancari, 417 U.S., at 554. The OHA statute provides that the agency is to be held "separate" and "independent of the [State] executive branch," Haw.Rev.Stat. § 10–4 (1993); OHA executes a trust, which, by its very character, must be administered for the benefit of Hawaiians and native Hawaiians, §§ 10–2, 10–3(*l*), 10–13.5; and OHA is to be governed by a board of trustees that will reflect the interests of the trust's native Hawaiian beneficiaries, Haw. Const., Art. XII, § 5 (1993); Haw.Rev.Stat. § 13D–3(b) (1993). OHA is thus "directed to participation by the governed in the governing agency." Mancari, 417 U.S., at 554. In this respect among others, the requirement is "reasonably and directly related to a legitimate, nonracially based goal." Ibid.

The foregoing reasons are to me more than sufficient to justify the OHA trust system and trustee election provision under the Fourteenth Amendment.

III

It * * * is likewise wrong to conclude that the OHA voting scheme is likely to "become the instrument for generating the prejudice and hostility all too often directed against persons whose particular ancestry is disclosed by their ethnic characteristics and cultural traditions." The political and cultural concerns that motivated the nonnative majority of Hawaiian voters to establish OHA reflected an interest in preserving through the self-determination of a particular people ancient traditions that they value. The fact that the voting qualification was established by the entire electorate in the State—the vast majority of which is not native Hawaiian—testifies to their judgment concerning the Court's fear of "prejudice and hostility" against the majority of state residents who are not "Hawaiian," such as petitioner. Our traditional understanding of democracy and voting preferences makes it difficult to conceive that the majority of the State's voting population would have enacted a measure that discriminates against, or in any way represents prejudice and hostility toward, that self-same majority. Indeed, the best insurance against that danger is that the electorate here retains the power to revise its laws.

IV

The Court today ignores the overwhelming differences between the Fifteenth Amendment case law on which it relies and the unique history of the State of Hawaii. The former recalls an age of abject discrimination against an insular minority in the old South; the latter at long last yielded the "political consensus" the majority claims it seeks—a consensus determined to recognize the special claim to self-determination of the indigenous peoples of Hawaii. * * *

* * *

Accordingly, I respectfully dissent.

NOTES

1.   Were the voters of Hawaii motivated by, as Justice Kennedy asserts, a "demeaning premise" about the qualifications of voters for OHA trustees? The *Rice* decision seems consistent with a philosophy that eschews race conscious decision-making by government officials, and subjects all race-based classifications to strict scrutiny. At some point does color-blind justice inhibit efforts to do justice for some uniquely situated minority groups? Can you think of an argument for special treatment by Congress for Native Hawaiians that the *Rice* Court might find convincing?

2.   *Rice* has been followed and extended to qualifications for candidates to be OHA trustees. Arakaki v. Hawaii, 314 F.3d 1091 (9th Cir.2002); see also Office of Hawaiian Affairs v. Cayetano, 6 P.3d 799 (Haw.2000) (construing effect of *Rice* on trustees elected before decision).

3.   Prior to *Rice*, when the issue came before the federal courts, the constitutionality of special legislation to benefit Native Hawaiians was upheld, though not in the Fifteenth Amendment context. For example, in Naliielua v. Hawaii, 795 F.Supp. 1009 (D.Haw.1990), aff'd on other grounds 940 F.2d 1535 (9th Cir.1991), the court rejected the constitutional challenge to the Hawaiian Home Lands program established under federal legislation but administered by the state, because "Native Hawaiians are people indigenous to the State of Hawaii, just as American Indians are indigenous to the mainland United States." Id. at 1013. Does this generalization survive *Rice*?

4.   The decision in *Rice* touched off more litigation by non-Hawaiians attempting to extend its reach by invoking the Fifth and Fourteenth Amendments to challenge state programs for Native Hawaiians as racially discriminatory and thus to subject the programs to strict scrutiny. The courts have shied away from confronting the merits of these cases.

In Arakaki v. Lingle, 305 F.Supp.2d 1161 (D.Haw.2004) the court dismissed a claim that OHA programs for Natives are unconstitutional as not presenting a judicial question. The court quoted language of the Supreme Court in *Rice*: " '[i]t is a matter of some dispute . . . whether Congress may treat the native Hawaiians as it does Indian tribes.' The Supreme Court said it 'could stay far off that difficult terrain.' Accordingly, the Supreme Court decision in *Rice* supports the proposition that another branch of government should make the decision as to whether Hawaiians should be treated as Indians for purposes of the *Morton* analysis." Id at 1174. Similar challenges have also confronted procedural impediments. See, e.g., Carroll v. Nakatani, 342 F.3d 934 (9th Cir.2003) (non-Natives lack standing to challenge OHA business loan program and Hawaiian Homes program).

In later decisions, the Ninth Circuit ruled that the equal protection claims in the case were justiciable. Without ever reaching the merits, the *Arakaki* litigation ultimately produced two dozen orders and six court of appeals decisions, one of which was vacated and remanded by the United States Supreme Court. On remand from the Supreme Court, the Court of Appeals concluded that the plaintiffs lacked taxpayer standing to challenge state programs for Native Hawaiians. Arakaki v. Lingle, 477 F.3d 1048 (9th Cir.2007). The district court then denied leave to amend the complaint noting the lengthy course of unsuccessful litigation and the potential injustice to other parties of prolonging it rather than filing a new case. The plaintiffs and others then did pursue cases in state courts alleging that the Hawaiian Homes Commission Act violates equal protection and that the tax exemption for Hawaiian homesteads was unconstitutional. The consolidated cases were argued before the Supreme Court of Hawaii in August 2010.

5.   Kamehameha Schools, an institution of great importance to Native Hawaiians, was founded by Princess Bernice Pauahi Bishop, the great-granddaughter and last royal descendant of King Kamehameha. The Schools, a private institution but able through its endowment to provide high-quality education to children at essentially no cost to parents, educate Native Hawaiians from grades kindergarten through 12, with a current enrollment of approximately 5,000 students. A non-Native Hawaiian student brought suit challenging the school's admissions policy of accepting only students of native Hawaiian ancestry. After a federal court decision upheld the admissions policy, a divided panel of the Ninth Circuit Court of Appeals, citing *Rice v. Cayetano*, held that the admissions policy operates as a "racial classification" constituting unlawful race discrimination in violation of federal civil rights laws. The court of appeals granted hearing en banc and reversed because the schools were private, receiving no federal funds, and because "specific, significant imbalances in educational achievement currently affect Native Hawaiians in Hawaii and the Schools aim to remedy that imbalance." Doe v. Kamehameha Schools, 470 F.3d 827 (9th Cir.2006) (en banc), *cert. denied*, 550 U.S. 931 (2007).

6.   In recent years, Congress has included Native Hawaiians among the beneficiaries of more than 100 federal statutes providing services to other Native Americans. See, e.g., Native Hawaiian Health Care Act of 1988, Pub.L. No. 100–579; Native American Programs Act, 42 U.S.C.A. § 2991a. In addition, Congress has enacted numerous statutes specifically for the benefit of Native Hawaiians. E.g., Hawaiian Homelands Homeownership Act of 2000, Pub. L. 106–568, 114 Stat. 2872–2903, sec. 202(13)(2) (Dec. 27, 2000); 2002 Native Hawaiian Education Act, 20 U.S.C. § 7512(1); Native Hawaiian Health Care Act of 1988, 42 U.S.C. §§ 11701–11714. Some courts have said these statutes are sufficient to establish a trust relationship with Native Hawaiians. E.g., John Doe v. Kamehameha Schools/Bernice Pauahi Bishop Estate, 295 F.Supp.2d 1141, 1168–74 (D.Haw.2003). Is such federal legislation vulnerable under *Rice*? To what extent is there room to apply *Mancari* to federal laws

benefiting Native Hawaiians for special treatment so long as they do not implicate voting qualifications?

7.   The U.S. Department of the Interior's regulations allowing Indian tribes to seek recognition of the federal government do not extend to Native Hawaiian groups. Confronting a claim that this practice violated the equal protection clause of the Fifth Amendment, the Ninth Circuit refused to apply the strict scrutiny required under *Rice* because the claim related to a political classification, not individual rights:

> Although we conclude that the Department of Interior's exclusion of Hawaiians passes constitutional muster, we recognize that, in many ways, the result is less than satisfactory. We would have more confidence in the outcome if the Department of Interior had applied its expertise to parse through history and determine whether native Hawaiians, or some native Hawaiian groups, could be acknowledged on a government-to-government basis. It would have been equally rational, if perhaps not more so, for the Department to have decided to undertake that inquiry in the first instance. However, under equal protection rational basis review, it is not for us "to judge the wisdom, fairness, or logic" of the choices made. [citing cases] Thus, in the end, we must commit this question to Congress to apply its wisdom in deciding whether or not native Hawaiians should be included among those eligible to apply for federal tribal recognition.

Kahawaiolaa v. Norton, 386 F.3d 1271, 1283 (9th Cir.2004).

NOTE: TOWARD FEDERAL RECOGNITION OF NATIVE HAWAIIANS

Ever since the decision in *Rice v. Cayetano*, Hawaii's congressional delegation has attempted to craft legislation that would recognize Hawaiians as Native Americans and lead to resolution of their claims concerning land and status. The persistent litigation over trust responsibilities, land rights, and the power of Congress and the state to enact legislation to recognize and benefit Hawaiians is likely to continue until such legislation passes or another solution is reached.

Now-retired Senator Akaka led a charge in Congress to pass "The Akaka Bill" which would have formally recognized Native Hawaiian sovereignty; reestablished a government-to-government relationship with the newly-organized Native Hawaiian government; and reaffirmed a federal trust relationship. His proposed bill also would have set in motion a process for transferring land and resources to the Native Hawaiian governing entity. A version of the Akaka Bill was introduced in almost every session of Congress from 2000–2012 and was constantly stalled. The last version of the bill died in Congress when the 112th session adjourned in January 2013 and with the subsequent retirement of Senator Akaka.

The federal recognition process established under the Akaka Bill would have prepared a membership roll to elect an Interim Governing Council to propose a constitution or other governing documents. The Native Hawaiian governing entity would be elected by the membership under the Constitution. According to the proposed legislation, at that point "the special political and legal relationship between the United States and the Native Hawaiian governing entity is hereby reaffirmed and the United States extends Federal recognition to the Native Hawaiian governing entity as the sovereign representative governing body of the Native Hawaiian people." The Akaka Bill would not have effected a settlement of Native claims. Instead, after recognition and affirmation have occurred, it is anticipated that the Native Hawaiian governing entity would enter into critical three-way negotiations with the state and federal governments over such key issues as the transfer of land and the exercise of civil and criminal jurisdiction. The governing entity would have many other responsibilities, including researching, negotiating, and perhaps litigating claims on behalf of the Native Hawaiian government.

Even with the failure of the Akaka Bill in Congress, Native Hawaiian advocacy at the state level persists. Act 195, signed into law in 2011, includes a state recognition of Native Hawaiians to "provide for and to implement the recognition of the Native Hawaiian people by means and methods that will facilitate their self-governance, including the establishment of, or the amendment to, programs, entities, and other matters pursuant to law that relate, or affect ownership, possession, or use of lands by the Native Hawaiian people, and by further promoting their culture, heritage, entitlements, health, education, and welfare." SB 1520 Article III Section 2 (2011). The Act authorizes the creation of a Native Hawaiian role commission to maintain a roll of qualified Native Hawaiians. The Roll Commission would be dissolved after fulfilling its purpose of facilitating the process under which qualified Native Hawaiians may independently commence the organization of a convention of qualified Native Hawaiians, established for the purpose of organizing themselves. At the convention, the Native Hawaiian community would organize itself and create governing documents. The governing body would be positioned to negotiate with the state and federal governments, but nothing in Act 195 is "intended to serve as a settlement of any claims against the State of Hawaii, or affect the rights of the Native Hawaiian people under state, federal, or international law."

On the federal level, Department of Interior furthering the establishment of a Native Hawaiian government. After robust public comment, in September of 2016 the Department promulgated a regulation for reestablishing a government-to-government relationship with the Native Hawaiian community. The rule "established an administrative procedure and criteria that the Secretary would use if the Native Hawaiian community forms a unified government that then seeks a formal government-to-government relationship with the United States. Consistent with the Federal policy of indigenous self-determination and Native self-governance, the Native

Hawaiian community itself would determine whether and how to reorganize its government."

Kana'iolwalu is the organization of the Native Hawaiian Role Commission, which compiled a roll of eligible members. The nonprofit organization Na'i Aupuni, with funding from OHA, was conducting elections for delegates of the Native Hawaiian convention in 2015, when the vote was challenged in court. Akina v. Hawaii, 2015 WL 6560634 (D.Haw.2015). The plaintiffs in the case brought claims that the race-based election violated equal protection, due process, and the first amendment. Plaintiffs also moved for a preliminary injunction to stop the voting. The district court denied the motion. The 9th Circuit denied an emergency application for an injunction and the plaintiffs appealed to the Supreme Court. In December of 2015, Justice Kennedy enjoined Hawaii from counting election votes or certifying winners pending further orders.

In response to the injunction and a court battle that might last years, Na'i Aupuni cancelled the election, and offered all 196 delegates who ran a seat for delegate at the convention. Plaintiffs filed a motion with the Supreme Court to hold Na'i Aupuni in contemt which was denied in January of 2016. The convention took place in February of 2016 and produced a 15-page document to serve as the blueprint for the future structure and function of a Native Hawaiian government. If ratified, it will be the basis of the governing body that will negotiate with the state and federal government for potential recognition or other goals. Na'i Aupuna is waiting to hold the ratification vote until the legal claims against them, including the appeal of the original lawsuit, are resolved. If the governing documents are ratified, a Native Hawaiian governing body could be formally established.

Varied opposition has arisen to federal and state actions designed to recognize Native Hawaiian sovereignty. Some opponents argue that Congress lacks constitutional authority to recognize a Native Hawaiian government. They reject the idea that Congress can legislate on behalf of Native Hawaiians. In their view, it would be racially discriminatory legislation.

Of course, the Supreme Court has held that Congress can legislate for the benefit of federally recognized "tribes" subject only to rational basis review because such legislation is not fundamentally race-based, but instead stems from a relationship that historically has been political. *Morton v. Mancari*, page 257, supra.

One version of the argument against congressional power contends that Native Hawaiians do not constitute an "Indian tribe, under the Commerce Clause." Therefore, "for constitutional purposes, there is no 'special relationship' between Native Hawaiians and the federal government pursuant to which programs singling out Native Hawaiians would be subject to rational basis review." See Stuart Minor Benjamin, *Equal Protection and the Special Relationship: The Case of Native Hawaiians*, 106 Yale L.J. 537, 539–40 (1996). Using strict scrutiny review, Benjamin concludes that "under the Supreme

Court's case law, legislation such as the HHCA treating Native Hawaiians specially is presumptively invalid."

The Supreme Court has continually sustained the broad power of Congress to to "recognize and affirm" powers of Native governments. In United States v. Lara, 541 U.S. 193 (2004), discussed at page 589, supra, the Court sustained legislation reversing the decision in *Duro v. Reina*, 495 U.S. 676 (1990), which had extended to non-member Indians the holding in *Oliphant* denying tribes criminal jurisdiction over non-Indians. *Lara*, referring to the restoration of the previously terminated Menominee Tribe of Wisconsin, stated that "indeed, Congress has restored previously extinguished tribal status—by re-recognizing a Tribe whose tribal existence it previously had terminated." 541 U.S. at 203. The opinion in *Lara* explained that the Constitution authorizes Congress to "enact legislation that both restricts and, in turn, relaxes those restrictions on tribal sovereign authority." The Court quoted an older case to the effect that "[I]f [by the political branches] those Indians are recognized as a tribe, this court must do the same." Id.

There is some opposition to the federal recognition or a Native Hawaiian government-to-government relationship with the United States among Hawaiians. A vocal minority of Native Hawaiians raise diverse objections to the legislation. One objection is it is too permissive by extending status and rights to Hawaiians with less than 50 percent Hawaiian blood. Other opponents challenge the wisdom of seeking recognition from the United States rather than demanding total independence. They advocate decolonization of Hawaii from the United States. Some have self-proclaimed the restoration or continued existence of the Hawaiian Kingdom. The independence movement includes groups such as Nation of Hawaii, which considers itself a sovereign nation operating within the illegally U.S.-occupied Hawaiian Islands. They believe that accepting recognition implicitly validates the annexation of Hawaii and statehood, and ends the "right" of Native Hawaiians to establish a nation on their own terms. Some believe that it will have the effect of extinguishing all Native Hawaiian claims against the United States. Feelings are strong in these groups and some individuals have either renounced their American citizenship or claimed dual citizenship.

As the struggle to deal with Native status and claims continues, and legislative efforts are prolonged in Congress and at the state level, Hawaiians worry that lands subject to their claims will be alienated by the state agencies charged with managing them. In Office of Hawaiian Affairs v. Housing and Community Development Corp. of Hawaii, 177 P.3d 884 (Haw.2008), the Supreme Court of Hawaii, relying primarily on the Apology Resolution as the legal basis for its decision, ordered a lower court to enjoin the Housing and Community Development Corporation from alienating ceded lands to third parties until the claims of Hawaiians were resolved. Citing trial court testimony of one of the editors of this book, the Hawaii Supreme Court held that transfer of lands would cause irreparable injury to Hawaiians because of the special cultural and historical significance of the lands to them. It further said that such transfers would be contrary to the public interest because the continued diminishment of trust land would make settlement of Hawaiian land claims more difficult. In the following decision the Supreme Court reversed.

HAWAII V. OFFICE OF HAWAIIAN AFFAIRS

United States Supreme Court, 2009.
556 U.S. 163, 129 S.Ct. 1436, 173 L.Ed.2d 333.

JUSTICE ALITO delivered the opinion of the Court.

This case presents the question whether Congress stripped the State of Hawaii of its authority to alienate its sovereign territory by passing a joint resolution to apologize for the role that the United States played in overthrowing the Hawaiian monarchy in the late 19th century. Relying on Congress' joint resolution, the Supreme Court of Hawaii permanently enjoined the State from alienating certain of its lands, pending resolution of native Hawaiians' land claims that the court described as "unrelinquished." We reverse.

* * *

III

Turning to the merits, we must decide whether the Apology Resolution "strips Hawaii of its sovereign authority to sell, exchange, or transfer" (Pet. for Cert. i) the lands that the United States held in "absolute fee" (30 Stat. 750) and "grant[ed] to the State of Hawaii, effective upon its admission into the Union" (73 Stat. 5). We conclude that the Apology Resolution has no such effect.

A

"We begin, as always, with the text of the statute." The Apology Resolution contains two substantive provisions. See 107 Stat. 1513–1514. Neither justifies the judgment below.

The resolution's first substantive provision uses six verbs, all of which are conciliatory or precatory. Specifically, Congress "acknowledge[d] the historical significance" of the Hawaiian monarchy's overthrow, "recognize[d] and commend[ed] efforts of reconciliation" with native Hawaiians, "apologize[d] to [n]ative Hawaiians" for the monarchy's overthrow, "expresse[d] [Congress's] commitment to acknowledge the ramifications of the overthrow," and "urge[d] the President of the United States to also acknowledge the ramifications of the overthrow...." § 1. Such terms are not the kind that Congress uses to create substantive rights-especially those that are enforceable against the cosovereign States.

The Apology Resolution's second and final substantive provision is a disclaimer, which provides: "Nothing in this Joint Resolution is intended to serve as a settlement of any claims against the United States." § 3. By its terms, § 3 speaks only to those who may or may not have "claims *against the United States.*" The court below, however, held that the only way to save § 3 from superfluity is to construe it as a congressional recognition—and preservation—of claims *against Hawaii* and as "the *foundation* (or starting point) for reconciliation" between the State and native Hawaiians. 117 Hawai'i, at 192, 177 P.3d, at 902.

* * * The Supreme Court of Hawaii erred in reading § 3 as recognizing claims inconsistent with the title held in "absolute fee" by the United States (30 Stat. 750) and conveyed to the State of Hawaii at statehood. See *supra,* at 1440–1441.

B

Rather than focusing on the operative words of the law, the court below directed its attention to the 37 "whereas" clauses that preface the Apology Resolution. See 107 Stat. 1510–1513. "Based on a plain reading of" the "whereas" clauses, the Supreme Court of Hawaii held that "Congress has clearly recognized that the native Hawaiian people have unrelinquished claims over the ceded lands." 117 Hawai'i, at 191, 177 P.3d, at 901. That conclusion is wrong for at least three reasons.

First, "whereas" clauses like those in the Apology Resolution cannot bear the weight that the lower court placed on them. * * *

Second, even if the "whereas" clauses had some legal effect, they did not "chang[e] the legal landscape and restructur[e] the rights and obligations of the State." 117 Hawai'i, at 190, 177 P.3d, at 900. * * * The Apology Resolution reveals no indication—much less a "clear and manifest" one—that Congress intended to amend or repeal the State's rights and obligations under Admission Act (or any other federal law); nor does the Apology Resolution reveal any evidence that Congress intended *sub silentio* to "cloud" the title that the United States held in "absolute fee" and transferred to the State in 1959. On that score, we find it telling that even respondent OHA has now abandoned its argument, made below, that "Congress . . . enacted the Apology Resolution and thus . . . change[d]" the Admission Act.

Third, the Apology Resolution would raise grave constitutional concerns if it purported to "cloud" Hawaii's title to its sovereign lands more than three decades after the State's admission to the Union. We have emphasized that "Congress cannot, after statehood, reserve or convey submerged lands that have already been bestowed upon a State." *Idaho v. United States,* 533 U.S. 262, 280, n. 9, 121 S.Ct. 2135, 150 L.Ed.2d 326 (2001). And that proposition applies *a fortiori* where virtually all of the State's public lands—not just its submerged ones—are at stake. In light of those concerns, we must not read the Apology Resolution's nonsubstantive "whereas" clauses to create a retroactive "cloud" on the title that Congress granted to the State of Hawaii in 1959.

* * *

When a state supreme court incorrectly bases a decision on federal law, the court's decision improperly prevents the citizens of the State from addressing the issue in question through the processes provided by the State's constitution. Here, the State Supreme Court incorrectly held that Congress, by adopting the Apology Resolution, took away from the citizens of Hawaii the authority to resolve an issue that is of great importance to the people of the State. Respondents defend that decision by arguing that they have both state-law property rights in the land in question and "broader moral and political claims for compensation for the wrongs of the past." Brief for Respondents 18. But we have no authority to decide questions of Hawaiian law or to provide redress for past wrongs except as provided for by federal law. The judgment of the Supreme Court of Hawaii is reversed, and the case is remanded for further proceedings not inconsistent with this opinion.

It is so ordered.

NOTES

1.   To uphold an injunction the Hawaii Supreme Court had to find that the plaintiffs were likely to succeed on the merits. If the Apology Resolution was insufficient, were there other possible legal grounds that would have been more likely to succeed?

2.   Following the decision, the Hawaii Legislature passed S.B. 1667 requiring a two-thirds majority vote of the legislature before a state agency could sell or give away ceded lands and that notice be given to OHA. The legislature's stated purpose for the new law was to "carry out its fiduciary responsibilities to all the people of Hawai'i, and ensure[ ] the preservation of the public land trust corpus for the benefit of the Native Hawaiian people." OHA settled the case based on the new statute but an individual plaintiff chose to pursue the injunction. Hawaii's Supreme Court found that he had standing to do so but such a claim would not be ripe until the legislature had approved a transfer as required in the legislation. However, it rejected a claim by the state that he lacked standing because he did not allege that he qualified as a "native Hawaiian" with at least 50 percent Hawaiian blood. Office of Hawaiian Affairs v. Housing & Community. Dev. Corp., 219 P.3d 1111 (2009).

CHAPTER FOURTEEN

COMPARATIVE AND INTERNATIONAL LEGAL PERSPECTIVES ON INDIGENOUS PEOPLES' RIGHTS

■ ■ ■

The historian J.G.A. Pocock has suggested that the struggle for indigenous rights in the countries colonized and settled by the western nation-states involves a dialogue between two peoples, who find that history itself is heavily biased in favor of one people. Stated another way, the struggle for indigenous rights is, in part, an effort to give voice to indigenous peoples' vision of history, and rewrite that history so as to substantiate their claims in the jurisprudence of their colonizers. See J.G.A. Pocock, *Tangata Whenua and Enlightenment Anthropology*, 6 N.Z.J.Hist. 28, 45–49 (1992).

Over the past several decades, the law, both domestic and international, relating to indigenous peoples' rights has been rewritten quite rapidly. In a number of countries, there has been a move toward greater recognition of indigenous peoples' historical legal claims against the dominant society. But as in the United States in recent decades, the increasing demands for recognition and enforcement of long-denied rights belonging to indigenous peoples has engendered intense reaction and resistance in many of these countries. The global struggle for recognition and protection of indigenous peoples' rights raises fundamental questions about the ability of domestic and international legal systems to respond to demands for justice and redress of native claims.

This chapter first traces several of the major developments in Canada, Australia, and New Zealand, which, like the United States, have inherited the English common law tradition with its related set of rules and principles derived from the doctrine of discovery and Chief Justice Marshall's 1823 *Johnson v. McIntosh* opinion. It then turns to the emerging voices and significant advances of indigenous peoples in the international human rights process. As this chapter illustrates, the continuing struggles for indigenous survival around the world are united by common themes and concerns with the legacies of colonialism, racism, and the human rights vision of indigenous peoples. See Robert A. Williams, Jr., *The Sixth Annual McDonald Lecture on Constitutional Studies—Sovereignty, Racism, Human Rights: Indian Self-Determination and the Postmodern World*

Legal System, 2 Rev.Const.Stud./Revue d'etudes Constitutionnelles 146 (1995).

SECTION A. NATIVE LAW IN OTHER NATIONS

1. CANADA

DOUGLAS SANDERS, ABORIGINAL RIGHTS IN CANADA: AN OVERVIEW
2 Law and Anthropology 177, 177–85 (1987).

THE POPULATIONS

Indigenous peoples live in all parts of Canada. They are more evenly distributed, geographically, than the non-Indian populations, which are heavily concentrated near the southern borders of the country. * * *

* * *

The Indian peoples belong to 10 separate language groups. Cultural patterns vary greatly. These diverse societies were brought under a uniform national system of units recognized by the Indian Act. Most recognized bands have one or more "reserves" for their use. In most of Canada, the reserves were intended to be an agricultural land base for the Indian communities. Often reserves were not established in the non-agricultural northern areas. A variant reserve system was established on the west coast, where seasonal village sites and numerous fishing stations were made into reserves. The result is a pattern of multiple reserves per band, giving British Columbia more reserves than the rest of Canada.

* * *

THE HISTORY OF DEALINGS

* * *

The Royal Proclamation of 1763 is the first major written constitutional document for Canada. While its exact legal status seems unclear, it is routine to say that it has the force of statute and that its Indian provisions have never been repealed. The document did not create the treaty process. It confirmed a process seen at the time as well established, though not without problems caused by "great frauds and abuses." The document did not give any legal status to Indian territorial rights, other than recognizing them as being in existence and as something to be acquired by the treaty process. * * *

The next significant constitutional provision came in 1867 with the creation of Canada as a federal state. The national government was given jurisdiction over "Indians, and Land reserved for Indians" in § 91(24) of the Constitution (originally the British North America Act 1867 (UK)). It is generally accepted that the reason for national jurisdiction in 1867 was the protection of the Indians against local settlers, a theme articulated in both Britain and Upper Canada earlier in the 19th century.

The present land mass of Canada was put together in stages from 1867 to 1949. There are references to Indian rights in various constitutional documents over those years. * * *

The end result is that constitutional provisions which involve the recognition of some substantive Indian rights exist for about half the land mass of Canada. Treaties also exist for about half the land mass of Canada, but the two geographical areas are not identical.

THE MOVE AWAY FROM RECOGNITION

* * *

In the last decades of the 19th century Canada was at an earlier stage of western settlement than the United States. Canada continued to sign treaties with western tribes. There were real possibilities of Indian resistance and it was wise to try to establish relations with the tribes on the basis of agreement. There were government fears of Cree support for the Metis resistance in 1885. There were fears of the strength of the Blackfoot Confederacy, of the tribes on the route to the Klondike Gold Rush and of possible Indian wars in British Columbia.

But continuity started to break down. British Columbia joined Canada in 1871. Fourteen treaties had been signed for small areas on Vancouver Island in the 1850s, but treaty making had been abandoned as official government policy. The Canadian government wanted to continue treaty making through to the coast, but was stopped by the opposition of the provincial government. After a number of disputes over the issue, the federal government abandoned the idea of treaties for the area. No treaties were signed in the Yukon or in the Inuit areas in the north.

* * *

THE MOVE BACK TO RECOGNITION

Canadian Indian policy largely slept through the 1930s, ignoring the innovations of the "Indian New Deal" in the United States. US policy, always more volatile, swung into termination in the 1950s, when Canada was gradually rediscovering its indigenous peoples. The ideological hostility to special status or collective rights that was manifested in the US termination policy simply did not find fertile ground in Canada, where limited patterns of French language rights and Catholic school rights were familiar and accepted. But if the French-Catholics made Canada more accepting of collective minority rights, Indian policy could also be affected by changes to French-English relations. The 1960s saw the rise of a strong French-Canadian nationalism.

* * *

CONSTITUTIONAL AMENDMENT

While the issues of termination and land claims are familiar in other countries, the Canadian events connected with the "patriation" of the constitution are difficult for outsiders to comprehend. For particular political reasons, the Government of Canada decided in 1978 to attempt major amendments to the Canadian constitution. The initiative was essentially a response to the issues of French-Canadian nationalism. The amendments were to secure (a) rights to English or French language school instruction in all parts of Canada, (b) a domestic amending formula (in place of the odd colonial holdover that major parts of the Constitution could only be amended by the Parliament of the United Kingdom), and (c) a bill of rights.

In 1978 the National Indian Brotherhood of Canada defined constitutional reform as an Indian issue, seeking (a) the recognition of aboriginal and treaty rights, (b) an Indian role in the constitutional reform process, and (c) the requirement of Indian consent to any constitutional amendment affecting Indian rights. The response of Canadian political leaders was accommodative. Indigenous rights were added to the list of agenda items. Indians were promised "participation" in the process. * * * By the beginning of 1981 the federal Government was openly bargaining with interest groups and opposition parties in attempts to bolster support for its proposals. The bargaining led to provisions on indigenous peoples, women and the handicapped. The final provisions on indigenous people include three elements. Section 35 entrenches existing aboriginal and treaty rights. Section 25 protects indigenous rights against the general provisions of the Charter of Rights and Freedom. Section 37 redeemed the promise of "participation" by providing for future First Minister's Conferences on aboriginal constitutional issues.

NOTES

1.   As Professor Sanders notes, Canada's national government was placed in charge of Indian affairs under the British North American Act of 1867 (UK). It began signing treaties with Indians in 1871, continuing the practice until the 1920s. Canadian judges of the period, however, took a dim view of the status of Indian treaties and the rights they supposedly secured to Canada's First Nations. The result was that, even more so than in the United States, many Indian treaty rights lay largely dormant and unenforced.

In perhaps the most notorious Canadian Indian law case of the period, R. v. Syliboy, [1929] 1 D.L.R. 307 (Co.Ct.1928), the court held that hunting and fishing rights guaranteed to the Indians of Nova Scotia were unenforceable because Indians did not have the capacity to conclude a valid treaty as understood in international law. Judge Patterson, writing for the court, dismissed the legal significance of Indian treaties under Canadian law in the following terms:

> But the Indians were never regarded as an independent power. A civilized nation first discovering a country of uncivilized people or savages held such country as its own until such time as by treaty it was transferred to some other civilized nation. The savages' rights of sovereignty even of ownership were never recognized. Nova Scotia had passed to Great Britain not by gift or purchase from or even by conquest of the Indians but by treaty with France, which had acquired it by priority of discovery and ancient possession; and the Indians passed with it.

* * *

> In my judgment the Treaty of 1752 is not a treaty at all and is not to be treated as such; it is at best a mere agreement made by the Governor and council with a handful of Indians giving them in return for good behaviour food, presents, and the right to hunt and fish as usual—an agreement that, as we have seen, was very shortly after broken.

[1929] 1 D.L.R. at 313–14.

2.   Canada's Indian Act of 1876, Act of April 12, 1876, ch. 18, 1876 Can.Stat. 43, which dictated an assimilationist Indian policy for the country, helps explain a good deal of the judicial hostility to the assertion of Indian rights against the government. The Act defined who was an Indian, provided for delivery of education and other services to Indians, and determined how Indian lands and resources were to be managed. In addition, the Indian Act effectively allowed provinces to abrogate Indian treaties. Subsequent amendments to the Act made it a federal crime to prosecute Indian claims in court, to raise money to pursue Indian claims, or to organize to pursue Indian claims. See From Recognition to Reconciliation: Essays on the Constitutional Entrenchment of Aboriginal and Treaty Rights (Patrick Macklem & Douglas Sanderson eds. 2016); Peter Scott Vicaire, *Two Roads Diverged: A Comparative Analysis of Indigenous Rights in a North American Constitutional Context*, 58 McGill L.J. 607 (2013).

A 1951 amendment to the Act, 3 Can.Rev.Stat. ch. 149 (1952), ended provincial authority to abrogate Indian treaties, but did make Indians on reserves subject to provincial law to the extent not covered by federal law. An attempt to repeal the Indian Act in the late 1960s was defeated by Indian activists who saw the proposal as the Canadian equivalent of termination. Existing treaty rights and aboriginal rights were affirmed, though not defined, in section 35 of Canada's 1982 Constitution Act:

> (1)   The existing aboriginal and treaty rights of the aboriginal peoples of Canada are hereby recognized and affirmed.

> (2)   In this Act, "aboriginal peoples of Canada" includes the Indian, Inuit and Métis peoples of Canada.

(3) For greater certainty, in subsection (1) "treaty rights" includes rights that now exist by way of land claims agreements or may be so acquired.

(4) Notwithstanding any other provision of this Act, the aboriginal and treaty rights referred to in subsection (1) are guaranteed equally to male and female persons.

3.   Commentators agree that section 35 of the Canadian Constitution is a substantive guarantee of the aboriginal as well as treaty rights of the aboriginal peoples of Canada. Compare this constitutional protection of aboriginal rights with the United States' approach to aboriginal rights as set out in the United States Supreme Court's decision in *Tee-Hit-Ton Indians v. United States*, page 296, supra. Section 52 of the Constitution Act of 1982 declares that the Constitution is the "supreme law of Canada." Accordingly, aboriginal and treaty rights of the aboriginal peoples of Canada therein are constitutionalized. See Thomas Isaac, *The Constitution Act, 1982 and the Constitutionalization of Aboriginal Self-Government in Canada: Cree-Naskapo (of Quebec) Act*, 1991 Can. Native L.Rep. 1; Andrew Erueti, *The Demarcation of Indigenous Peoples' Traditional Lands: Comparing Domestic Principles of Demarcation with Emerging Principles of International Law*, 23 Ariz.J.Int'l&Comp.Law 543, 561–70, 576–79 (2006).

4.   A number of important questions regarding Indian rights remained unaddressed in Canadian law, even after the Constitution Act of 1982, but the formal recognition of aboriginal and treaty rights in section 35(1) worked a profound effect on judicial attitudes and prior precedents. Guerin v. The Queen, [1984] 2 S.C.R. 335, involved the Musqueam Indian Reserve, described by the Supreme Court as being located upon "the most potentially valuable 400 acres in Vancouver today." Id. at 342.

In 1958, the Musqueam Band surrendered 162 acres of its valuable reserve lands to the Crown for lease to a golf club. The terms obtained by the Crown were much less favorable than those approved by the band three months earlier at a "surrender meeting" with government agents. In arguing to the Court, the Crown asserted that the surrender document imposed on it no obligation to lease to the golf club on the terms discussed at the surrender meeting, nor did it impose any duty on the Crown to obtain the approval of the Band in respect of the terms of the lease ultimately entered into by the government on the Band's behalf. The Court disagreed, upholding the trial court's award of $10,000,000 (Canadian) in damages to the band:

> * * * [T]he nature of Indian title and the framework of the statutory scheme established for disposing of Indian land places upon the Crown an equitable obligation, enforceable by the courts, to deal with the land for the benefit of the Indians. This obligation does not amount to a trust in the private law sense. It is rather a fiduciary duty. If, however, the Crown breaches this fiduciary duty it will be liable to the Indians in the same way and to the same extent as if such a trust were in effect.

The fiduciary relationship between the Crown and the Indians has its roots in the concept of aboriginal, native or Indian title. The fact that Indian bands have a certain interest in lands does not, however, in itself give rise to a fiduciary relationship between the Indians and the Crown. The conclusion that the Crown is a fiduciary depends upon the further proposition that the Indian interest in the land is inalienable except upon surrender to the Crown.

* * *

In obtaining without consultation a much less valuable lease than that promised, the Crown breached the fiduciary obligation it owed the band. It must make good the loss suffered in consequence.

Id. at 389.

Following *Guerin*, in Simon v. The Queen, [1985] 2 S.C.R. 387, the Canadian Supreme Court overruled the infamous *Syliboy* decision. See note 1, supra. Citing a United States Supreme Court decision, United States v. Santa Fe Pacific Railroad, 314 U.S. 339 (1941), as authority for the proposition that extinguishment of an Indian treaty right "cannot be lightly implied," the Canadian Supreme Court held that "strict proof" would be demanded to prove an intent to extinguish Indian treaty rights. As for the earlier views expressed in *Syliboy* on Indian capacity to understand a treaty, Chief Judge Dickson of the Canadian Supreme Court stated in *Simon:*

It should be noted that the language used by Patterson J., * * * reflects the biases and prejudices of another era in our history. Such language is no longer acceptable in Canadian law and indeed is inconsistent with a growing sensitivity to native rights in Canada. With regard to the substance of [Judge] Patterson's words, leaving aside for the moment the question of whether treaties are international-type documents, his conclusions on capacity are not convincing.

[1985] 2 S.C.R. at 399.

It wasn't until 1997, however, that a First Nation finally succeeded in presenting a live aboriginal title claim in traditional lands and territory to Canada's highest court. In the following case, still widely regarded and relied upon as the most important decision on Indian land claims in the country's history, Canada's Supreme Court overturned a lower court decision dismissing the evidentiary relevance of Indian testimony relating the oral history of traditional land tenure and rights in proving aboriginal title.

DELGAMUUKW V. BRITISH COLUMBIA
Supreme Court of Canada, 1997.
[1997] 3 S.C.R. 1010.

THE CHIEF JUSTICE.

I.   Introduction

This appeal is the latest in a series of cases in which it has fallen to this Court to interpret and apply the guarantee of existing aboriginal rights found in s. 35(1) of the *Constitution Act, 1982.* Although that line of decisions, commencing with *R. v. Sparrow*, [1990] 1 S.C.R. 1075, proceeding through the *Van der Peet* trilogy (*R. v. Van der Peet*, [1996] 2 S.C.R. 507, *R. v. N.T.C. Smokehouse Ltd.*, [1996] 2 S.C.R. 672, and *R. v. Gladstone*, [1996] 2 S.C.R. 723), and ending in *R. v. Pamajewon*, [1996] 2 S.C.R. 821, *R. v. Adams*, [1996] 3 S.C.R. 101, and *R. v. Côté*, [1996] 3 S.C.R. 139, have laid down the jurisprudential framework for s. 35(1), this appeal raises a set of interrelated and novel questions which revolve around a single issue—the nature and scope of the constitutional protection afforded by s. 35(1) to common law aboriginal title.

* * *

II.   Facts

At the British Columbia Supreme Court, McEachern C.J. heard 374 days of evidence and argument. Some of that evidence was not in a form which is familiar to common law courts, including oral histories and legends. Another significant part was the evidence of experts in genealogy, linguistics, archeology, anthropology, and geography.

* * *

A.   The Claim at Trial

This action was commenced by the appellants, who are all Gitksan or Wet'suwet'en hereditary chiefs, who, both individually and on behalf of their "Houses" claimed separate portions of 58,000 square kilometres in British Columbia. For the purpose of the claim, this area was divided into 133 individual territories, claimed by the 71 Houses. This represents all of the Wet'suwet'en people, and all but 12 of the Gitksan Houses. Their claim was originally for "ownership" of the territory and "jurisdiction" over it. (At this Court, this was transformed into, primarily, a claim for aboriginal title over the land in question.) The province of British Columbia counterclaimed for a declaration that the appellants have no right or interest in and to the territory or alternatively, that the appellants' cause of action ought to be for compensation from the Government of Canada.

* * *

At trial, the appellants' claim was based on their historical use and "ownership" of one or more of the territories. The trial judge held that these are marked, in some cases, by physical and tangible indicators of their association with the territories. He cited as examples totem poles with the Houses' crests carved, or distinctive regalia. In addition, the Gitksan Houses have an "adaawk" which is a collection of sacred oral tradition about their ancestors, histories and territories. The Wet'suwet'en each have a "kungax" which is a spiritual song or dance or performance which ties them to their land. Both of these were entered as evidence on behalf of the appellants.

The most significant evidence of spiritual connection between the Houses and their territory is a feast hall. This is where the Gitksan and Wet'suwet'en peoples tell and retell their stories and identify their territories to remind themselves of the sacred connection that they have with their lands. The feast has a ceremonial purpose, but is also used for making important decisions. The trial judge also noted the *Criminal Code* prohibition on aboriginal feast ceremonies, which existed until 1951.

* * *

V.   Analysis

* * *

This appeal requires us to * * * adapt the laws of evidence so that the aboriginal perspective on their practices, customs and traditions and on their relationship with the land, are given due weight by the courts. In practical terms, this requires the courts to come to terms with the oral histories of aboriginal societies, which, for many aboriginal nations, are the only record of their past. Given that the aboriginal rights recognized and affirmed by s. 35(1) are defined by reference to pre-contact practices or, as I will develop below, in the case of title, pre-sovereignty occupation, those histories play a crucial role in the litigation of aboriginal rights.

* * *

Many features of oral histories would count against both their admissibility and their weight as evidence of prior events in a court that took a traditional approach to the rules of evidence. * * *

Notwithstanding the challenges created by the use of oral histories as proof of historical facts, the laws of evidence must be adapted in order that this type of evidence can be accommodated and placed on an equal footing with the types of historical evidence that courts are familiar with, which largely consists of historical documents. This is a long-standing practice in the interpretation of treaties between the Crown and aboriginal peoples. To quote Dickson C.J., given that most aboriginal societies "did not keep written records", the failure to do so would "impose an impossible burden of proof" on aboriginal peoples, and "render nugatory" any rights that they have (*Simon v. The Queen*, [1985] 2 S.C.R. 387, at p. 408). This process must be undertaken on a case-by-case basis. I will take this approach in my analysis of the trial judge's findings of fact.

* * *

The general principle of appellate non-interference applies with particular force in this appeal. The trial was lengthy and very complex. There were 318 days of testimony. There were a large number of witnesses, lay and expert. The volume of evidence is enormous. To quote the trial judge:

> A total of 61 witnesses gave evidence at trial, many using translators from their native Gitksan or Wet'suwet'en language; "word spellers" to assist the official reporters were required for many witnesses; a further 15 witnesses gave their evidence on commission; 53 territorial affidavits were filed; 30 deponents were cross-examined out of court; there are 23,503 pages of transcript evidence at trial; 5,898 pages of transcript of argument; 3,039 pages of commission evidence and 2,553 pages of cross-examination on affidavits (all evidence and oral arguments are conveniently preserved in hard copy and on diskettes); about 9,200 exhibits were filed at trial comprising, I estimate, well over 50,000 pages; the plaintiffs' draft outline of argument comprises 3,250 pages, the province's 1,975 pages, and Canada's over 1,000 pages; there are 5,977 pages of transcript of argument in hard copy and on diskettes. All parties filed some excerpts from the exhibits they referred to in argument. The province alone submitted 28 huge binders of such documents. At least 15 binders of reply argument were left with me during that stage of the trial.

The result was a judgment of over 400 pages in length.

* * *

* * * [T]he appellants have alleged that the trial judge made a number of serious errors relating to the treatment of the oral histories of the appellants. * * *

(b) *Adaawk and Kungax*

The adaawk and kungax of the Gitksan and Wet'suwet'en nations, respectively, are oral histories of a special kind. They were described by the trial judge as a "sacred 'official' litany, or history, or recital of the most important laws, history, traditions and traditional territory of a House". The content of these special oral histories includes its physical representation, totem poles, crests and blankets. The importance of the adaawk and kungax is underlined by the fact that they are "repeated, performed and authenticated at important feasts". At those feasts, dissenters have the opportunity to object if they question any detail and, in this way, help ensure the authenticity of the adaawk and kungax. Although they serve largely the same role, the trial judge found that there are some differences in both the form and content of the adaawk and the kungax. For example, the latter is "in the nature of a song . . . which is intended to represent the special authority and responsibilities of a chief. . . ." However, these differences are not legally relevant for the purposes of the issue at hand.

It is apparent that the adaawk and kungax are of integral importance to the distinctive cultures of the appellant nations. At trial, they were relied on for two distinct purposes. First, the adaawk was relied on as a component of and, therefore, as proof of the existence of a system of land tenure law internal to the Gitksan, which covered the whole territory claimed by that appellant. In other words, it was offered as evidence of the Gitksan's historical use and occupation of that territory. For the Wet'suwet'en, the kungax was offered as proof of the central significance of the claimed lands to their distinctive culture. As I shall explain later in these reasons, both use and occupation, and the central significance of the lands occupied, are relevant to proof of aboriginal title.

* * *

The trial judge, however, went on to give these oral histories no independent weight at all. He held that they were only admissible as "direct evidence of facts in issue . . . in a few cases where they could constitute confirmatory proof of early presence in the territory". His central concern [was] that the adaawk and kungax could not serve "as evidence of detailed history, or land ownership, use or occupation". I disagree with some of the reasons he relied on in support of this conclusion.

Although he had earlier recognized, when making his ruling on admissibility, that it was impossible to make an easy distinction between the mythological and "real" aspects of these oral histories, he discounted the adaawk and kungax because they were not "literally true", confounded "what is fact and what is belief", "included some material which might be classified as mythology", and projected a "romantic view" of the history of the appellants. He also cast doubt on the authenticity of these special oral histories because, *inter alia*, "the verifying group is so small that they cannot safely be regarded as expressing the reputation of even the Indian community, let alone the larger community whose opportunity to dispute territorial claims would be essential to weight". Finally, he questioned the utility of the adaawk and kungax to demonstrate use and occupation because they were "seriously lacking in detail about the specific lands to which they are said to relate".

Although he framed his ruling on weight in terms of the specific oral histories before him, in my respectful opinion, the trial judge in reality based his decision on some general concerns with the use of oral histories as evidence in aboriginal rights cases. In summary, the trial judge gave no independent weight to these special oral histories because they did not accurately convey historical truth, because knowledge about those oral histories was confined to the communities whose histories they were and because those oral histories were insufficiently detailed. However, as I mentioned earlier, these are features, to a greater or lesser extent, of all oral histories, not just the adaawk and kungax. The implication of the trial judge's reasoning is that oral histories should never be given any independent weight and are only useful as confirmatory evidence in aboriginal rights litigation. I fear that if this reasoning were followed, the oral histories of aboriginal peoples would be consistently and systematically undervalued by the Canadian legal system, in contradiction of the express instruction to the contrary in *Van der Peet* that trial courts interpret the evidence of aboriginal peoples in light of the difficulties inherent in adjudicating aboriginal claims.

(c)   *Recollections of Aboriginal Life*

* * *

In my opinion, the trial judge expected too much of the oral history of the appellants, as expressed in the recollections of aboriginal life of members of the appellant nations. He expected that evidence to provide definitive and precise evidence of pre-contact aboriginal activities on the territory in question. However, as I held in *Van der Peet*, this will be almost an impossible burden to meet. Rather, if oral history cannot conclusively establish pre-sovereignty (after this decision) occupation of land, it may still be relevant to demonstrate that current occupation has its origins prior to sovereignty. This is exactly what the appellants sought to do.

* * *

(e)   *Conclusion*

The trial judge's treatment of the various kinds of oral histories did not satisfy the principles I laid down in *Van der Peet*. These errors are particularly worrisome because oral histories were of critical importance to the appellants' case. They used those histories in an attempt to establish their occupation and use of the disputed territory, an essential requirement for aboriginal title. The trial judge, after refusing to admit, or giving no independent weight to these oral histories, reached the conclusion that the appellants had not demonstrated the requisite degree of occupation for "ownership". Had the trial judge assessed the oral histories correctly, his conclusions on these issues of fact might have been very different.

In the circumstances, the factual findings cannot stand. However, given the enormous complexity of the factual issues at hand, it would be impossible for the Court to do justice to the parties by sifting through the record itself and making new factual findings. A new trial is warranted, at which the evidence may be considered in light of the principles laid down in *Van der Peet* and elaborated upon here. * * *

C.   *What is the content of aboriginal title, how is it protected by s. 35(1) of the Constitution Act, 1982, and what is required for its proof?*

(1)   Introduction

* * *

Although cases involving aboriginal title have come before this Court and Privy Council before, there has never been a definitive statement from either court on the *content* of aboriginal title. In *St. Catherine's Milling*, the Privy Council, as I have mentioned, described the aboriginal title as a "personal and usufructuary right", but declined to explain what that meant because it was not "necessary to express any opinion upon the point." Similarly, in *Calder*, *Guerin*, and *Paul*, the issues were the extinguishment of, the fiduciary duty arising from the surrender of, and statutory easements over land held pursuant to, aboriginal title, respectively; the content of title was not at issue and was not directly addressed.

Although the courts have been less than forthcoming, I have arrived at the conclusion that the content of aboriginal title can be summarized by two propositions: first, that aboriginal title encompasses the right to exclusive use and occupation of the land held pursuant to that title for a variety of purposes, which need not be aspects of those aboriginal practices, customs and traditions which are integral to distinctive aboriginal cultures; and second, that those protected uses must not be irreconcilable with the nature of the group's attachment to that land. * * *

* * *

(d)   *Aboriginal Title under s. 35(1) of the Constitution Act, 1982*

Aboriginal title at common law is protected in its full form by s. 35(1). This conclusion flows from the express language of s. 35(1) itself, which states in full: "[t]he *existing* aboriginal and treaty rights of the aboriginal peoples of Canada are hereby recognized and affirmed" (emphasis added). On a plain reading of the provision, s. 35(1) did not create aboriginal rights; rather, it accorded constitutional status to those rights which were "existing" in 1982. The provision, at the very least, constitutionalized those rights which aboriginal peoples possessed at common law, since those rights existed at the time s. 35(1) came into force. Since aboriginal title was a common law right whose existence was recognized well before 1982 (e.g., *Calder*, *supra*), s. 35(1) has constitutionalized it in its full form.

* * *

The acknowledgement that s. 35(1) has accorded constitutional status to common law aboriginal title raises a further question—the relationship of aboriginal title to the "aboriginal rights" protected by s. 35(1). * * *

Because aboriginal rights can vary with respect to their degree of connection with the land, some aboriginal groups may be unable to make out a claim to title, but will nevertheless possess aboriginal rights that are recognized and affirmed by s. 35(1), including site-specific rights to engage in particular activities. * * *

* * *

(ii) The Test for the Proof of Aboriginal Title

In order to make out a claim for aboriginal title, the aboriginal group asserting title must satisfy the following criteria: (i) the land must have been occupied prior to sovereignty, (ii) if present occupation is relied on as proof of occupation pre-sovereignty, there must be a continuity between present and pre-sovereignty occupation, and (iii) at sovereignty, that occupation must have been exclusive.

* * *

(f) *Infringements of Aboriginal Title: the Test of Justification*

(i) Introduction

The aboriginal rights recognized and affirmed by s. 35(1), including aboriginal title, are not absolute. Those rights may be infringed, both by the federal (e.g., *Sparrow*) and provincial (e.g., *Côté*) governments. However, s. 35(1) requires that those infringements satisfy the test of justification. In this section, I will review the Court's nascent jurisprudence on justification and explain how that test will apply in the context of infringements of aboriginal title.

(ii) General Principles

The test of justification has two parts, which I shall consider in turn. First, the infringement of the aboriginal right must be in furtherance of a legislative objective that is compelling and substantial. I explained in *Gladstone* that compelling and substantial objectives were those which were directed at either one of the purposes underlying the recognition and affirmation of aboriginal rights by s. 35(1), which are (at para. 72):

> . . . the recognition of the prior occupation of North America by aboriginal peoples or . . . the reconciliation of aboriginal prior occupation with the assertion of the sovereignty of the Crown.

I noted that the latter purpose will often "be most relevant" at the stage of justification. I think it important to repeat why (at para. 73) that is so:

> Because . . . distinctive aboriginal societies exist within, and are a part of, a broader social, political and economic community, over which the Crown is sovereign, there are circumstances in which, in order to pursue objectives of compelling and substantial

importance to that community as a whole (taking into account the fact that aboriginal societies are a part of that community), some limitation of those rights will be justifiable. *Aboriginal rights are a necessary part of the reconciliation of aboriginal societies with the broader political community of which they are part; limits placed on those rights are, where the objectives furthered by those limits are of sufficient importance to the broader community as a whole, equally a necessary part of that reconciliation.* [Emphasis added; "equally" emphasized in original.]

* * *

The second part of the test of justification requires an assessment of whether the infringement is consistent with the special fiduciary relationship between the Crown and aboriginal peoples. What has become clear is that the requirements of the fiduciary duty are a function of the "legal and factual context" of each appeal (*Gladstone, supra*). *Sparrow* and *Gladstone*, for example, interpreted and applied the fiduciary duty in terms of the idea of *priority*. The theory underlying that principle is that the fiduciary relationship between the Crown and aboriginal peoples demands that aboriginal interests be placed first. * * *

* * *

(iii) Justification and Aboriginal Title

The general principles governing justification laid down in *Sparrow*, and embellished by *Gladstone*, operate with respect to infringements of aboriginal title. In the wake of *Gladstone*, the range of legislative objectives that can justify the infringement of aboriginal title is fairly broad. Most of these objectives can be traced to the *reconciliation* of the prior occupation of North America by aboriginal peoples with the assertion of Crown sovereignty, which entails the recognition that "distinctive aboriginal societies exist within, and are a part of, a broader social, political and economic community." In my opinion, the development of agriculture, forestry, mining, and hydroelectric power, the general economic development of the interior of British Columbia, protection of the environment or endangered species, the building of infrastructure and the settlement of foreign populations to support those aims, are the kinds of objectives that are consistent with this purpose and, in principle, can justify the infringement of aboriginal title. Whether a particular measure or government act can be explained by reference to one of those objectives, however, is ultimately a question of fact that will have to be examined on a case-by-case basis.

* * *

Moreover, the other aspects of aboriginal title suggest that the fiduciary duty may be articulated in a manner different than the idea of priority. * * * There is always a duty of consultation. Whether the aboriginal group has been consulted is relevant to determining whether the infringement of aboriginal title is justified, in the same way that the Crown's failure to consult an aboriginal group with respect to the terms by which reserve land is leased may breach its fiduciary duty at common law: *Guerin*. The nature and scope of the duty of consultation will vary with the circumstances. In occasional cases, when the breach is less serious or relatively minor, it will be no more than a duty to discuss important decisions that will be taken with respect to lands held pursuant to aboriginal title. Of course, even in these rare cases when the minimum acceptable standard is consultation, this consultation must be in good faith, and with the intention of substantially addressing the concerns of the aboriginal peoples whose lands are at issue. In most cases, it will be significantly deeper than mere consultation. Some cases may even require the full consent of an aboriginal nation, particularly when provinces enact hunting and fishing regulations in relation to aboriginal lands.

* * * The economic aspect of aboriginal title suggests that compensation is relevant to the question of justification as well, a possibility suggested in *Sparrow* and which I repeated in *Gladstone*. Indeed, compensation for breaches of fiduciary duty are a well-established part of the landscape of aboriginal rights: *Guerin*. In keeping with the duty of honour and good faith on the Crown, fair compensation will ordinarily be required when aboriginal title is infringed. The amount of compensation payable will vary with the nature of the particular aboriginal title affected and with the nature and severity of the infringement and the extent to which aboriginal interests were accommodated. Since the issue of damages was severed from the principal action, we received no submissions on the appropriate legal principles that would be relevant to determining the appropriate level of compensation of infringements of aboriginal title. In the circumstances, it is best that we leave those difficult questions to another day.

* * *

[The Court went on to hold that the province of British Columbia lacked the power to extinguish the rights of the province's aboriginal peoples, including rights to aboriginal title, after it joined Canada in confederation in 1871.]

* * *

VI. Conclusion and Disposition

For the reasons I have given above, I would allow the appeal in part, and dismiss the cross-appeal. Reluctantly, I would also order a new trial.

* * *

* * * [T]his litigation has been both long and expensive, not only in economic but in human terms as well. By ordering a new trial, I do not necessarily encourage the parties to proceed to litigation and to settle their dispute through the courts. As was said in *Sparrow*, s. 35(1) "provides a solid constitutional base upon which subsequent negotiations can take place". Those negotiations should also include other aboriginal nations which have a stake in the territory claimed. Moreover, the Crown is under a moral, if not a legal, duty to enter into and conduct those negotiations in good faith. Ultimately, it is through negotiated settlements, with good faith and give and take on all sides, reinforced by the judgments of this Court, that we will achieve what I stated in *Van der Peet*, *supra*, at para. 31, to be a basic purpose of s. 35(1)—"the reconciliation of the pre-existence of aboriginal societies with the sovereignty of the Crown". Let us face it, we are all here to stay.

NOTES

1.   Sparrow v. R., [1990] 1 S.C.R. 1075, discussed and cited repeatedly throughout the *Delgamuukw* decision, is another seminal decision in modern Canadian Native rights law. In *Sparrow*, a member of the Musqueam Indian Band was charged with violating Canada's *Fisheries Act* by fishing with a drift net longer than that permitted by the terms of the band's government-issued Indian food fishing license. The Musqueam band member argued that he was exercising an existing aboriginal right to fish and that the net length restriction contained in the band's license was invalidated by section 35(1) of the Constitution.

At trial, the Crown argued that the Musqueam Band's aboriginal right to fish had been extinguished by validly imposed regulations under the *Fisheries Act*. The Supreme Court of Canada, however, rejected that argument, stating that it "confuses regulation with extinguishment. That the right is controlled in great detail by the regulations does not mean that the right is thereby extinguished." Id. at 1097. The Court then held that the sovereign's intention must be clear and plain in order to extinguish an aboriginal right, and that nothing in the *Fisheries Act* or its detailed regulations demonstrated a clear and plain intention to extinguish the Indian aboriginal right to fish. The permitting system used by the government was "simply a manner of controlling the fisheries, not defining underlying rights," according to the Court. Id. at 1099.

Having found that the Musqueam Band's aboriginal fishing rights had not been extinguished by the extensive regulations promulgated under the federal Fisheries Act, the *Sparrow* Court next turned to the Crown's argument that it could justifiably regulate those rights by imposition of the net length restriction. In response to this argument, the Court set out, for the first time, the "justification" test, cited in *Delgamuukw*, for government infringement of existing aboriginal rights protected under section 35(1) of Canada's Constitution:

Section 35(1) suggests that while regulation affecting aboriginal rights is not precluded, such regulation must be enacted according to a valid objective. Our history has shown, unfortunately all too well, that Canada's aboriginal peoples are justified in worrying about government objectives that may be superficially neutral but which constitute *de facto* threats to the existence of aboriginal rights and interests. By giving aboriginal rights constitutional status and priority, Parliament and the provinces have sanctioned challenges to social and economic policy objectives embodied in legislation to the extent that aboriginal rights are affected. Implicit in this constitutional scheme is the obligation of the legislature to satisfy the test of justification. The way in which a legislative objective is to be attained must uphold the honour of the Crown and must be in keeping with the unique contemporary relationship, grounded in history and policy, between the Crown and Canada's aboriginal peoples. The extent of legislative or regulatory impact on an existing aboriginal right may be scrutinized so as to ensure recognition and affirmation.

* * *

To determine whether the fishing rights have been interfered with such as to constitute a *prima facie* infringement of s. 35(1), certain questions must be asked. First, is the limitation unreasonable? Second, does the regulation impose undue hardship? Third, does the regulation deny to the holders of the right their preferred means of exercising that right? The onus of proving a *prima facie* infringement lies on the individual or group challenging the legislation. In relation to the facts of this appeal, the regulation would be found to be a *prima facie* interference if it were found to be an adverse restriction on the Musqueam exercise of their right to fish for food. * * *

If a *prima facie* interference is found, the analysis moves to the issue of justification. This is the test that addresses the question of what constitutes legitimate regulation of a constitutional aboriginal right. The justification analysis would proceed as follows. First, is there a valid legislative objective? Here the court would inquire into whether the objective of Parliament in authorizing the department to enact regulations regarding fisheries is valid. The objective of the department in setting out the particular regulations would also be scrutinized. An objective aimed at preserving s. 35(1) rights by conserving and managing a natural resource, for example, would be valid. Also valid would be objectives purporting to prevent the exercise of s. 35(1) rights that would cause harm to the general populace or to aboriginal peoples themselves, or other objectives found to be compelling and substantial.

* * *

Id. at 1110–13.

The Court explained that under this form of justification test, any allocation of fish by the government made "after valid conservation measures have been implemented must give top priority to Indian food fishing." Even if conservation needs required a reduction in the number of fish to be caught in a given year, and that number equaled the number required for Indian food fishing, "then all the fish available after conservation would go to the Indians according to the constitutional nature of their fishing right," the Court explained. Sport fishing and commercial fishing interests would be denied any of the catch under such circumstances. Id. at 1116. The *Sparrow* Court ordered a new trial on the question of infringement and whether any such infringement was justified under Section 35(1) of the Constitution.

2.   *Sparrow* did not address the question of an aboriginal right to fish for commercial purposes. In R. v. Gladstone, [1996] 2 S.C.R. 723, Canada's Supreme Court did find that prior to contact, Heiltsuk Band Indians engaged in an extensive trade of herring spawn for commercial purposes, and found the existence of a constitutionally protected commercial fishing right. On aboriginal rights in Canada and their definition by the courts generally, see John Borrows, *Frozen Rights in Canada: Constitutional Interpretation and the Trickster*, 22 Am. Indian L.Rev. 37 (1997).

3.   In November 2004, the Supreme Court of Canada issued rulings in two major cases involving resource development on "Crown" or government-owned lands subject to aboriginal title and rights claims, Haida Nation v. British Columbia, [2004] 3 S.C.R. 511 and Taku River Tlingit First Nation v. British Columbia, [2004] 3 S.C.R. 550. In both cases, the Court ruled that the government has a legal duty to consult First Nations about the use of such lands, and when appropriate, to accommodate their interests. As the Court said in *Haida*, the duty to consult arises "when the Crown has knowledge, real or constructive, of the potential existence of the Aboriginal right or title and contemplates conduct that might adversely affect it." Id. at para. 35. The scope of this duty, the Court, explained, is proportionate to the strength of the case that supports the aboriginal right or title and to the severity of the potentially adverse effects upon the right or title claimed. Id. at para. 39.

Following its reasoning in *Haida*, the Court held in *Taku River* that the government's environmental review process for a proposed 160 kilometer mining road running through the traditional territory of the Taku River Tlingit First Nation (TRTFN) fulfilled the Crown's duty to consult and accommodate. The Court noted that TRTFN, while objecting to the final outcome, participated "fully" in the government review process, and the final project approval contained measures designed to address First Nation concerns; "The Province was not under a duty to reach agreement with the TRTFN, and its failure to do so did not breach the obligations of good faith that it owed the TRTFN." 3 S.C.R. 550, at para. 22. The Court did state the expectation that, throughout the remaining stages of the permitting, approval and licensing process for the mine, as well as in the development of a land use strategy, "the Crown will continue to fulfill its honourable duty to consult and, if appropriate, accommodate the TRTFN." Id. at para. 26. Then in 2014, the Court issued the following historic decision, which recognized and affirmed, for the first time ever under Canadian domestic law, the aboriginal title and rights of a Canadian First Nation in its traditional lands and territory.

TSILHQOT'IN NATION V. BRITISH COLUMBIA
Supreme Court of Canada, 2014
[2014] 2 S.C.R. 256.

THE CHIEF JUSTICE.

* * *

For centuries, people of the Tsilhqot'in Nation—a grouping of six bands sharing common culture and history—have lived in a remote valley bounded by rivers and mountains in central British Columbia. They lived in villages, managed lands for the foraging of roots and herbs, hunted and trapped. They repelled invaders and set terms for the European traders who came onto their land. From the Tsilhqot'in perspective, the land has always been theirs.

Throughout most of Canada, the Crown entered into treaties whereby the indigenous peoples gave up their claim to land in exchange for reservations and other promises, but, with minor exceptions, this did not happen in British Columbia. The Tsilhqot'in Nation is one of hundreds of indigenous groups in British Columbia with unresolved land claims.

The issue of Tsilhqot'in title lay latent until 1983, when the Province granted Carrier Lumber Ltd. a forest licence to cut trees in part of the territory at issue. The Xeni Gwet'in First Nations government (one of the six bands that make up the Tsilhqot'in Nation) objected and sought a declaration prohibiting commercial logging on the land. The dispute led to the blockade of a bridge the forest company was upgrading. The blockade ceased when the Premier promised that there would be no further logging without the consent of the Xeni Gwet'in. Talks between the Ministry of Forests and the Xeni Gwet'in ensued, but reached an impasse over the Xeni Gwet'in claim to a right of first refusal to logging. In 1998, the original claim was amended to include a claim for Aboriginal title on behalf of all Tsilhqot'in people.

The claim is confined to approximately five percent of what the Tsilhqot'in—a total of about 3,000 people—regard as their traditional territory. The area in question is sparsely populated. About 200 Tsilhqot'in people live there, along with a handful of non-indigenous people who support the Tsilhqot'in claim to title. There are no adverse claims from other indigenous groups. The federal and provincial governments both oppose the title claim.

* * * The trial judge spent time in the claim area and heard extensive evidence from elders, historians and other experts. He found that the Tsilhqot'in people were in principle entitled to a declaration of Aboriginal title to a portion of the claim area as well as to a small area outside the claim area. However, for procedural reasons which are no longer relied on by the Province, he refused to make a declaration of title (2007 BCSC 1700, [2008] 1 C.N.L.R. 112).

In 2012, the British Columbia Court of Appeal held that the Tsilhqot'in claim to title had not been established, but left open the possibility that in the future, the Tsilhqot'in might be able to prove title to specific sites within the area claimed. For the rest of the claimed territory, the Tsilhqot'in were confined to Aboriginal rights to hunt, trap and harvest (2012 BCCA 285, 33 B.C.L.R. (5th) 260).

* * * The Tsilhqot'in ask this Court to restore the trial judge's finding, affirm their title to the area he designated, and confirm that issuance of forestry licences on the land unjustifiably infringed their rights under that title.

* * *

V.   Is Aboriginal Title Established?

The Test for Aboriginal Title

How should the courts determine whether a semi-nomadic indigenous group has title to lands? This Court has never directly answered this question. The courts below disagreed on the correct approach. We must now clarify the test.

As we have seen, the *Delgamuukw* test for Aboriginal title to land is based on "occupation" prior to assertion of European sovereignty. To ground Aboriginal title this occupation must possess three characteristics. It must be *sufficient*; it must be *continuous* (where present occupation is relied on); and it must be *exclusive*.

* * *

The trial judge in this case held that "occupation" was established for the purpose of proving title by showing regular and exclusive use of sites or territory. On this basis, he concluded that the Tsilhqot'in had established title not only to village sites and areas maintained for the harvesting of roots and berries, but to larger territories which their ancestors used regularly and exclusively for hunting, fishing and other activities.

The Court of Appeal disagreed and applied a narrower test for Aboriginal title—site-specific occupation. It held that to prove sufficient occupation for title to land, an Aboriginal group must prove that its ancestors *intensively* used a definite tract of land with reasonably defined boundaries at the time of European sovereignty.

For semi-nomadic Aboriginal groups like the Tsilhqot'in, the Court of Appeal's approach results in small islands of title surrounded by larger territories where the group possesses only Aboriginal rights to engage in activities like hunting and trapping. By contrast, on the trial judge's approach, the group would enjoy title to all the territory that their ancestors regularly and exclusively used at the time of assertion of European sovereignty.

Against this backdrop, I return to the requirements for Aboriginal title: sufficient pre-sovereignty occupation; continuous occupation (where present occupation is relied on); and exclusive historic occupation.

* * *

* * * Sufficiency of occupation is a context-specific inquiry. * * * The intensity and frequency of the use may vary with the characteristics of the Aboriginal group asserting title and the character of the land over which title is asserted. Here, for example, the land, while extensive, was harsh and was capable of supporting only 100 to 1,000 people. The fact that the Aboriginal group was only about 400 people must be considered in the context of the carrying capacity of the land in determining whether regular use of definite tracts of land is made out.

To sufficiently occupy the land for purposes of title, the Aboriginal group in question must show that it has historically acted in a way that would communicate to third parties that it held the land for its own purposes. This standard does not demand notorious or visible use akin to proving a claim for adverse possession, but neither can the occupation be purely subjective or internal. There must be evidence of a strong presence on or over the land claimed, manifesting itself in acts of occupation that could reasonably be interpreted as demonstrating that the land in question belonged to, was controlled by, or was under the exclusive stewardship of the claimant group. As just discussed, the kinds of acts necessary to indicate a permanent presence and intention to hold and use the land for the group's purposes are dependent on the manner of life of the people and the nature of the land. Cultivated fields, constructed dwelling houses, invested labour, and a consistent presence on parts of the land may be sufficient, but are not essential to establish occupation. The notion of occupation must also reflect the way of life of the Aboriginal people, including those who were nomadic or semi-nomadic.

* * *

* * * [W]hat is required is a culturally sensitive approach to sufficiency of occupation based on the dual perspectives of the Aboriginal group in question—its laws, practices, size, technological ability and the character of the land claimed—and the common law notion of possession as a basis for title. It is not possible to list every indicia of occupation that might apply in a particular case. The common law test for possession—which requires an intention to occupy or hold land for the purposes of the occupant—must be considered alongside the perspective of the Aboriginal group which, depending on its size and manner of living, might conceive of possession of land in a somewhat different manner than did the common law. * * *

* * *

What Rights Does Aboriginal Title Confer?

As we have seen, *Delgamuukw* establishes that Aboriginal title "encompasses the right to exclusive use and occupation of the land held pursuant to that title for a variety of purposes" (para. 117), including non-traditional purposes, provided these uses can be reconciled with the communal and ongoing nature of the group's attachment to the land. Subject to this inherent limit, the title-holding group has the right to choose the uses to which the land is put and to enjoy its economic fruits (para. 166). * * *

The Incidents of Aboriginal Title

Aboriginal title confers ownership rights similar to those associated with fee simple, including: the right to decide how the land will be used; the right of enjoyment and occupancy of the land; the right to possess the land; the right to the economic benefits of the land; and the right to pro-actively use and manage the land.

Aboriginal title, however, comes with an important restriction—it is collective title held not only for the present generation but for all succeeding generations. This means it cannot be alienated except to the Crown or encumbered in ways that would prevent future generations of the group from using and enjoying it. Nor can the land be developed or misused in a way that would substantially deprive future generations of the benefit of the land. Some changes—even permanent changes—to the land may be possible. Whether a particular use is irreconcilable with the ability of succeeding generations to benefit from the land will be a matter to be determined when the issue arises. * * *

Justification of Infringement

To justify overriding the Aboriginal title-holding group's wishes on the basis of the broader public good, the government must show: (1) that it discharged its procedural duty to consult and accommodate; (2) that its actions were backed by a compelling and substantial objective; and (3) that the governmental action is consistent with the Crown's fiduciary obligation to the group: *Sparrow*. * * *

Where Aboriginal title is unproven, the Crown owes a procedural duty imposed by the honour of the Crown to consult and, if appropriate, accommodate the unproven Aboriginal interest. By contrast, where title has been established, the Crown must not only comply with its procedural duties, but must also ensure that the proposed government action is substantively consistent with the requirements of s. 35 of the *Constitution Act, 1982*. This requires both a compelling and substantial governmental objective and that the government action is consistent with the fiduciary duty owed by the Crown to the Aboriginal group.

* * *

As *Delgamuukw* explains, the process of reconciling Aboriginal interests with the broader interests of society as a whole is the *raison d'être* of the principle of justification. Aboriginals and non-Aboriginals are "all here to stay" and must of necessity move forward in a process of reconciliation (para. 186). To constitute a compelling and substantial objective, the broader public goal asserted by the government must further the goal of reconciliation, having regard to both the Aboriginal interest and the broader public objective.

* * *

If a compelling and substantial public purpose is established, the government must go on to show that the proposed incursion on the Aboriginal right is consistent with the Crown's fiduciary duty towards Aboriginal people.

* * *

In summary, Aboriginal title confers on the group that holds it the exclusive right to decide how the land is used and the right to benefit from those uses, subject to one carve-out—that the uses must be consistent with the group nature of the interest and the enjoyment of the land by future generations. Government incursions not consented to by the title-holding group must be undertaken in accordance with the Crown's procedural duty to consult and must also be justified on the basis of a compelling and substantial public interest, and must be consistent with the Crown's fiduciary duty to the Aboriginal group.

* * *

With the declaration of title, the Tsilhqot'in have now established Aboriginal title to the portion of the lands designated by the trial judge * * * . This gives them the right to determine, subject to the inherent limits of group title held for future generations, the uses to which the land is put and to enjoy its economic fruits. As we have seen, this is not merely a right of first refusal with respect to Crown land management or usage plans. Rather, it is the right to proactively use and manage the land.

Breach of the Duty to Consult

The alleged breach in this case arises from the issuance by the Province of licences permitting third parties to conduct forestry activity and construct related infrastructure on the land in 1983 and onwards, before title was declared. During this time, the Tsilhqot'in held an interest in the land that was not yet legally recognized. The honour of the Crown required that the Province consult them on uses of the lands and accommodate their interests. The Province did neither and breached its duty owed to the Tsilhqot'in.

* * *

Conclusion

I would allow the appeal and grant a declaration of Aboriginal title over the area at issue, as requested by the Tsilhqot'in. I further declare that British Columbia breached its duty to consult owed to the Tsilhqot'in through its land use planning and forestry authorizations.

NOTES

1.   Commentators were quick to jump on the Supreme Court's decision in *Tsilhqot'in* as significantly altering the legal landscape in favor of First Nations with respect to land claims and ownership and control of resource entitlements throughout the country. Depending on the strength of the claim, governments in Canada, at the federal and provincial levels, must now justify their infringements on Aboriginal title, act consistently with their fiduciary duties, and risk judicial shutdown of projects if they do not obtain the prior consent of the Aboriginal titleholder claimants. Industry will have to meaningfully engage with Aboriginal title holders when proposing to conduct business on their territories. See, e.g., Harry Swain and James Baillie, *Tsilhquotin Nation v. British Columbia: Aboriginal Title and Section 35* 56 Can.Bus.L.J. 265, 274 (2015).

2.   On Canada's Atlantic coast, the Mi'kmaq have been engaged in a decades long struggle to secure their rights under their treaties with the Crown. Two major and related decisions on Indian treaty rights issued by the Supreme Court of Canada in 1999, recognizing the Mi'kmaq Indians' treaty rights to obtain "necessaries" through hunting, fishing, and trading the products of those traditional activities, sent shock waves throughout Canadian society. In R. v. Marshall, [1999] 3 S.C.R. 456, a Mi'kmaq Indian was charged with violating fishing regulations of the province of Nova Scotia. The Court agreed that the Mi'kmaq treaty rights, dating back to 1760–61, constituted a defense to the charge of fishing for eels without a license.

The majority opinion in *Marshall* cautioned that Mi'kmaq treaty rights are subject to federal regulation. According to the Court; "Catch limits that could reasonably be expected to produce a moderate livelihood for individual Mi'kmaq families at present-day standards can be established by regulation and enforced without violating the treaty rights." Id. at para. 61. However, the potential scope of the ruling's effect on the countless Native rights claims working their way through the federal and provincial courts rocked Canadian society. Government officials, major non-Native newspapers, and Native leaders in the province and across Canada rushed to give their own interpretations to the Supreme Court's *Marshall* decision, and violent protests that included the destruction of Mi'kmaq lobster traps stirred an emotional outpouring of public and private recriminations and soul-searching throughout Canadian society by Natives and non-Natives alike.

Much of the controversy surrounding the first *Marshall* decision centered around the statement in the majority opinion that the treaties "affirm the right of the Mi'kmaq people to continue to provide for their own sustenance by taking the products of their hunting, fishing and other gathering activities, and trading for what in 1760 was termed 'necessities.' " Id. at para. 4. Both sides to the controversy made claims that the broadly-worded language of the Court's opinion gave the Mi'kmaqs the right to an open, unregulated season in the coastal fisheries. Commercial fishing interests warned that Nova Scotia's highly prized and regulated lobster fishery, salmon, crab, cod, and even moose and other wildlife resources were covered by the Court's holding. The Native Council of Nova Scotia and the Union of New Brunswick Indians made the alarming assertion in subsequent filings in the case that the "economic treaty right" they read as being affirmed in *Marshall* potentially might cover all resources harvested from the sea, forests and the land, including minerals and offshore natural gas deposits. See R. v. Marshall, [1999] 3 S.C.R. 533, at para. 19 [hereinafter *Marshall II*]. It was widely recognized in Canada that the Court's liberal approach to interpreting Native treaty rights claims, if applied to other Indian treaties in Canada, could have ominous, even revolutionary consequences for the Canadian economy, and for the legal, economic, and political status of First Nations in Canadian society as a whole.

It did not take long for Canada's Supreme Court to close ranks and respond to the tumultuous reaction to its September 1999 landmark decision. On November 17, 1999, the Court seized upon the opportunity provided by a motion filed by an intervenor in the *Marshall* case [hereinafter referred to as *Marshall I*], a fisherman's coalition, for a rehearing, stay of judgment, and new trial. It issued a new opinion, *Marshall II*, supra, in which a now unanimous Supreme Court (*Marshall I* had been decided 5–2) denied the motion for reconsideration, and sought to clear up what it called the "misconceptions about what the September 17 majority judgment decided and what it did not decide." Id. at para. 2.

In its *Marshall II* elaboration of its *Marshall I* decision, the Court said the government of Canada could lawfully restrict the Mi'kmaq treaty right to earn a moderate livelihood from the fishery if "such regulation is shown by the Crown to be justified on conservation or other grounds of public importance." Id. at para. 6. As the Court noted, under Canadian law, those other grounds might include economic and regional fairness, and recognition of the historical reliance upon, and participation in, the fishery by non-aboriginal groups.

The Court also took pains to note that its *Marshall I* decision extends only so far as its limited facts; "As stated, this was a prosecution of a private citizen. It required the Court to determine whether certain precise charges relating to the appellant's participation in the eel fishery could be sustained. The majority judgment of September 17, 1999 was limited to the issues necessary to dispose of appellant's guilt or innocence." *Marshall II*. The Court said that its original decision was only related to treaty rights "to fish and wildlife or to the type of things traditionally 'gathered' by the Mi'kmaq in a 1760 aboriginal lifestyle," and that trade in logging or minerals, or the exploitation of off-shore natural gas deposits as part of the Mi'kmaq treaty right was never discussed in evidence and never addressed in *Marshall I*. "The issues were much narrower and the ruling was much narrower." *Marshall II*. Id. at para. 20.

The Court in *Marshall II* also advised the parties that the process of accommodation of the Mi'kmaq treaty right may best be resolved by "a process of negotiation and reconciliation that properly considers the complex and competing interests at stake." Id. at para. 22. Since the *Marshall* decisions were handed down, the government has in fact negotiated fishing rights agreements with Native reserve communities in Nova Scotia.

2.   NEW ZEALAND

J.G.A. POCOCK, LAW, SOVEREIGNTY, AND HISTORY IN A DIVIDED CULTURE: THE CASE OF NEW ZEALAND AND THE TREATY OF WAITANGI

The Iredell Memorial Lecture, Lancaster University, 20–23, 10 October 1991.

* * *

The historical circumstances are these. As part of the process of establishing the Crown's sovereignty over New Zealand in 1840, a treaty was drawn up and signed by the Crown's representative Captain Hobson and the chiefs of a number of independent *iwi* or tribes, at Waitangi in the north of the North Island. It was subsequently proffered to the chiefs of other *iwi,* and accepted by most if not all of them in both islands. It was not a treaty with the Maori people as a whole, and that people did not then or subsequently form a single unit or confederation for purposes of legal or political action; the word "Maori" was only just coming into general use to distinguish the indigenous Polynesians from the European settlers, and the tribe or *iwi* remains for most the group of identification. However, since nearly all *iwi* have entered into the Treaty relationship, it is reasonable to see its provisions as underlying the relations of Maori to the Crown wherever they can be found.

It can be debated just what role the Treaty has in the establishment of Crown sovereignty in New Zealand. A claim could be made on the grounds of prior discovery, which gave Britain a right not shared with any European nation to pre-empt land from the indigenous inhabitants, and this right of pre-emption has been exercised, in ways often hard to reconcile with the language of the Treaty, to purchase and sometimes confiscate land or dispose of it by legislative or executive action. The Crown's sovereignty can be defined as an exclusive right to acquire and dispose of the title to it by sale or grant, and this is claimed exclusively of other nations on the grounds of discovery. But a series of proclamations, instructions to royal officials, and private memoranda belonging to the period make it quite clear that the Crown had no intention of proclaiming sovereignty without the consent of the inhabitants, and give us a number of clues as to how this consent was to be granted. In written statements by Lord John Russell the prime minister and Lord Glenelg the colonial secretary it is confirmed that the inhabitants of New Zealand are not "savages living by the chase"—i.e., not hunter-gatherers with no relation to the soil; this is to assign them a fairly advanced place in the scheme of history worked out in the recent Enlightenment; but that they are capable of occupying the land and apportioning it between them. It would be interesting to know whether Russell and Glenelg had been informed, by missionaries or others, that the Maori were turning to agriculture and beginning to plant and harvest cereals, as some of them were; whether they recognised in them some other capacity for occupation and apportionment, such as is claimed and conceded today; or whether the Crown's intent was to attribute to them a capacity for property as a preliminary to a capacity for alienation.

These documents further state that though the tribes or *iwi* do not constitute a sovereign state, in the sense that there is no supreme authority which rules them all and can speak on their behalf, they nevertheless possess a "sovereignty" (the word used) which cannot be subordinated to another without their consent; and this appears to state the judicial basis on which the meetings occurred at Waitangi and the Treaty was drawn up and signed. A good deal could certainly be said about the motives of the British ministers in using this language. They were trying to establish a negotiating position in advance of the French (always a prudent thing to do); and if we take the view that their intention already was—as it soon afterwards became—that of investing the Crown with a title to New Zealand land which it might dispose of in parcels to settlers, we can add with much plausibility that their purpose in attributing sovereignty to the *iwi* was to invest them with the capacity to transfer it to the Crown. Nevertheless their language did attribute to the indigenous people a capacity to enter into treaties and to possess land and rights before they began to negotiate it; and we must add that this attributed to them a history, a previous and inherent existence, a past, a present and a future. The language of European jurisprudence had that effect, and it further attributed to the Treaty itself the status of a historical document, a document performing an authoritative act in history, to which reference could be made in the future by actors who saw it as exerting authority in their present arising from their past. Much of the subsequent history of the

Treaty recounts the attempts of *pakeha* [New Zealander of European descent] jurisprudence to deprive it of that status, and the counter-attempts of contemporary bicultural jurisprudence to restore it.

* * *

Where the minds of the two cultures came close enough to meeting at Waitangi to engender misunderstandings—divergent interpretations of the same events or utterances—was over the conceptualisation of title to land. The British desired sovereignty not just in the form of a protectorate defending control over New Zealand against external or foreign competitors, but in the form of a civil government with authority to effect and regulate the transfer of lands from indigenous occupants to immigrant or settler owners. The *iwi* so far involved in this process knew that they were effecting such transfers, but did not expect to be dispossessed as a result of doing so; and such language is inadequate in so far as it is too European to express the Maori perception of what the occupancy of land was. The *iwi* for their part had difficulty in grasping that the Crown was proposing to acquire a pre-emptive sovereignty, a sovereign role for itself in acquiring title to land from indigenous occupants and transferring it to settler owners.

* * *

The Treaty (or *te Tiriti*) was bilingually conducted and texts were drawn up for signature in both English and Maori. Literacy was developing among Maori and the texts had been orally debated; the issue is not therefore that the chiefs did not know what they were signing, but that no satisfactorily final text existed or ever did. The redactors of the Maori text were themselves *pakeha*—a term I shall use from now on when speaking of Europeans in the New Zealand bicultural setting; they were missionaries, with interests of their own not identical with those of the Maori or necessarily of the Crown; and they employed what is known as "missionary Maori", a vocabulary which contains Maori terms adapted or created to express *pakeha* legal, political and religious concepts. More than one Maori text of *te Tiriti* exists, and was presented to various *iwi* for signature after the gathering of Waitangi; these texts are not identical with one another, and philologically exact English translations of them do not always reinforce the official English text recorded by the officers of the Crown. It is therefore possible to understand both the radical Maori view that *te Tiriti* is a fraudulent document, and the extreme *pakeha* view that the Treaty has no binding or legal force. In circumstances I shall presently describe, however, it has attained the status of a fundamental text, possessing authority and open to interpretation; and both the lawyer and the historian will recognise the problems in reconstituting a past and assessing its authority in the present which must next arise. Law is being made in a context of disputed authority and disputed interpretation; that is how law is made and history is written. It is less common, though not unknown, for this to happen in a context of bilingual documents and bicultural interpretation.

The crucial area in the several texts has come to be one in which something is ceded to the Crown which in Maori is termed *kawanatanga* and in English "sovereignty", and something is retained by the chiefs and *iwi* which in Maori is termed *rangatiratanga* and in English "full, exclusive and undisturbed possession of their lands and estates".

* * *

Kawanatanga is missionary Maori, an attempt at a rendering of the English word "government"; similarly, and rather potently, the Treaty itself is sometimes called a *kawanata* or covenant. The English text renders *kawanatanga* as "sovereignty", by which the Maori signatories may have understood in the first instance something like a "protectorate", though they would also have understood that the Crown intended, and was being empowered, to maintain this exclusively of others Europeans or Americans who might seek it. What is less clear is how far they understood the extensions of the English word "sovereignty" into the powers of civil government: to keeping the peace among the *iwi* and *hapu*—the tribes and sub-tribes—or to adjudicating disputes over land between them. It is perfectly clear, however, that they did not think they were conceding to the Crown any ultimate authority over or title to the lands of the two major islands; it is the question of Crown title which has in the end become crucial. On the other hand, the distinction between *kawanatanga* and *rangatiratanga* itself makes quite clear that they were intent on retaining some ultimate authority over land, and were aware of the dichotomy between something which they were retaining and something which they were conceding.

* * *

The crucial term in Maori understanding of *te Tiriti* both was and has become *rangatiratanga;* in full *te tino rangatiratanga.* This is much nearer being an authentic Maori term, though it was already capable of missionary usage; significantly, it was being employed as a Christian sacred term, in translating the words "thy kingdom come" in the Lord's Prayer. *Rangatira* was the word for a chief, and the suffix *tanga* gives us English-speakers the word "chieftainship", which by no means inappropriately suggests that the signatories intended to retain authority as well as possession, *dominium* as well as *usus*. *Rangatiratanga* connotes not only "possession of the land", but "possession according to Maori ways, according to the structures of authority and value inherent in *iwi* society"; the chiefs had no intention that they or their peoples should become mere subjects of the Crown, whose possession of the land was protected by Crown law indeed, but only by the kind of law the Crown was accustomed to administer. *Rangatiratanga* connoted their own authority as *rangatira,* and at least one of them announced that he would never sign the Treaty for fear of finding himself subject to a power not his own. For these reasons, modern Maori interpretation reads into *rangatiratanga* the Treaty's recognition of a right to possession, not of lands, forests and fisheries alone, but of the norms and values, the social structure and culture, inherent in the occupancy of land as the *iwi* then recognised themselves as occupying it; the possession of themselves, their identity as people. They claim to have been dispossessed of this identity, contrary to the provisions of *te Tiriti;* and they claim that the dispossession was unjust, and that the Treaty entitles them to repossession of both land and cultural identity (which are inseparable) where repossession is possible, and to compensation and resources to use in building a new identity where it is not. A new problem instantly arises. Claims under a treaty, or under a common law, are in principle negotiable; claims to a unique and all-inclusive cultural or spiritual identity easily become non-negotiable. In the terms being used in this lecture, the question becomes whether the Maori and the *pakeha* occupy a single history of interaction, or two histories incompatible with one another; and this problem is occasioned by the fact that *kawanatanga* and *rangatiratanga* are each translatable as "sovereignty" * * * . "Sovereignty" begins to denote the power to constitute one's own history, on the level of conceptualisation and possession and on that of authority and action. Even to write history may entail a claim to make it; but to what or whom can that claim be addressed?

* * *

It is a premise on which this lecture is being based that sovereignty, legislative and political, is among other things a mode by which a human community seeks to command its own history: to take actions which shape its policies in the present, and even—since a great deal of history has in fact been written in this way—to declare the shape of the historic past and process out of which it deems itself to be issuing. Neither of these modes of self-determination ever has been or will be in the absolute power of any sovereign community; but this does not prevent us asking what may become of a community's capacity either to make or to write its own history if its political sovereignty should be surrendered to forces without or radically challenged by forces within. With respect to the latter possibility, what has happened in recent New Zealand politics may be described as follows. * * *

There has come into being the Waitangi Tribunal, a body judicial in character and even authority, empowered to hear claims by Maori arising out of performance or non-performance of the Treaty's provisions. Though its proceedings are judicial in character and distinguished judges—several of them Maori learned in the law—have sat on and presided over it, its findings are not binding at law and take the form of recommendations of such authority that courts and parliament do well to give them attention. This authority derives from the circumstance that the Treaty which the Tribunal interprets states the preconditions under which the sovereignty of the Crown, and therefore of courts and parliament, came to be established and New Zealand came into existence and later became a sovereign nation. The Tribunal therefore does more than hear cases against the Crown; it investigates whether the Crown has or has not been discharging conditional obligations subject to which sovereignty was transferred to it in the first place. This is why its recommendations cannot be binding at law, but are such that the law is well advised to give them attention; it has, in the last analysis, a real if limited capacity to query the legitimacy of the sovereign's jurisdiction.

* * * There has also occurred a significant retreat from the position laid down by Chief Justice Prendergast in *Wi Parata versus the Bishop of Wellington* (1877), viz. that the Treaty was of no legal force because only nations already possessed of legislative sovereignty possessed the federative capacity to enter into binding treaties. What is noteworthy here is that Prendergast's judgment is now seen as resting upon a strongly positivist jurisprudence, which made so much of full political sovereignty as to relegate to the condition of savagery any social form not possessed of it. New Zealand's newly bicultural jurisprudence is now withdrawing from these 19th-century presuppositions towards those of the more naturalist *jus gentium* of the 16th through 18th centuries, which conceived of the acquisition of property, rights and sovereignty as taking place by stages in the process of history as then conceived. It of course has to do so it if it is to make sense of the Treaty at all; we have seen that this was specifically based on the presumption that the Maori were not savages and were sufficiently possessed of sovereignty to be capable of transferring it to the Crown. Whether this means that the Treaty can check the sovereign parliament in its legislative course is a question it may be wise to leave unanswered.

NOTES

1. Demographic estimates suggest that prior to European colonization in the early nineteenth century, the Maori numbered between 125,000 and 135,000. At the time of the Treaty of Waitangi, Maori society was organized in an extended kinship order constituted by *hapu* (sub-tribes), which in turn were made up of *whanau* (family groups). The people of several hapu were simply "the people" or *iwi*. Political and economic power was vested with the hapu, which were responsible for resource management and welfare functions. Hapu were large enough to organize effectively for war, gift exchange, and the harvesting of resources but were fluid, not fixed groups.

The European encounter introduced a number of new diseases that devastated the Maori, and at the time of the signing of the 1840 Treaty of

Waitangi, the population had decreased to about 90,000. The next fifty years of English colonization brought rapid population declines. An 1886 census recorded only 42,650 Maori.

The New Zealand colonial government's official concerns were reflected in an 1856 statement by the Superintendent of New Zealand's Wellington Province: "The Maoris are dying out, and nothing can save them. Our plain duty, as good compassionate colonists, is to smooth down their dying pillow. Then history will have nothing to reproach us with." Quoted in David Williams, *Aboriginal Rights in Aotearoa (New Zealand),* 2 L.& Anthropology 423, 424 (1987). During the past century Maori population has steadily increased, both in terms of absolute numbers and as a proportion of New Zealand's population as a whole. Most recent census figures show that today, Maori compose slightly less than fifteen percent of New Zealand's four and a half million people.

2.   Without question, the most significant event in the history of Maori-*pakeha* (settler) legal and political relations is the signing of the Treaty of Waitangi in 1840. By the treaty, New Zealand came under the asserted sovereignty of the British Crown, and evolved from a Crown colony, to self-governing colony, to independent nation status. The evolution of Maori status emerging out of the Treaty of Waitangi, however, as discussed in Professor Pocock's lecture, is a much more complex subject. First, there is the problem presented by the two versions of the Treaty, or *te Tiriti* as the Maori refer to the document. The English version of the treaty was signed by only thirty-nine Maori chiefs. The Maori version was signed by 512 chiefs. By Article I of the English version of the treaty, the Maori were purported to cede "sovereignty" to the Crown, while retaining possession of their lands and resources. But the Maori version of Article I cedes "Kawanatanga" to the Crown, which, as explained by Professor Pocock, is missionary Maori for "government." Thus, the interpretive issue raised by Article I depends on whether the Maori understanding of "government" contained by the term *Kawanatanga* is best rendered by the English term "sovereignty" or, as the Maori assert today, by the term "protectorate."

The Maori assert that Article II of the Treaty demonstrates that the Crown was to protect, not take, Maori proprietary rights under the agreement. The original English version of Article II provides that the Crown "confirms and guarantees" to the Maori "the full exclusive and undisturbed possession of their Lands and Estates, Forests, Fisheries and other properties which they may collectively or individually possess so long as it is their wish and desire to retain the same in their possession." The Crown, under this version, is granted "the exclusive right of Preemption over such lands as the proprietors thereof may be disposed to alienate." The Maori language version of Article II, however, uses the key term "te tino rangatirantanga," which, when rendered back into English, confirms in the Maori "the entire chieftainship of their lands, their villages, and all their property," which may be sold to the Crown on terms agreeable to the Maori.

Thus, the Maori have always felt that based on the Maori version and their interpretation of the Treaty of Waitangi, they possess not only ownership, but a recognized management authority (*rangatiratanga*) over their lands and resources as well. See generally, Michael C. Blumm, *Native Fishing Rights and Environmental Protection in North America and New Zealand: A Comparative Analysis of Profits À Prendre and Habitat Servitudes,* 8 Wisc.Int'l L.J. 1, 30–32 (1989).

3.   As in Canada, courts in New Zealand in the late nineteenth century dismissed treaties with indigenous tribes as having no legal significance. Wi Parata v. Bishop of Wellington, 3 JUR. (N.S.) 72 (1877), cited by Professor Pocock, viewed the Maori as incompetent to exercise sovereignty under then-accepted principles of international law, and declared the Treaty of Waitangi a legal nullity. What rights the Maori had originated under the common law doctrine of discovery or were recognized by the legislature.

The dispossession of Maori customary land was accomplished through a series of legislative acts. The Maori Land Court was established in 1862 to transform Maori customary rights of occupation into Crown-recognized fee titles that could be sold to *pakeha*. The Native Land Act of 1909 expressly made Maori customary title unenforceable against the Crown, thus settling the issue under New Zealand law that Maori land rights depended only on statutory recognition. See Blumm, supra, at pages 32–33. Due to this history, there are almost no Maori customary land holdings in New Zealand, unlike the U.S. or Canada, which had different colonial experiences. Maori now own about 6% of the total landmass of New Zealand, all in freehold title. See Jacinta Ruru, *Indigenous Restitution in Settling Water Claims: The Developing Cultural and Commercial Redress Opportunities in Aotearoa, New Zealand*, 22 Pac. Rim L.&Pol'y 311, 318 (2013).

4.   After decades of dispossession and marginalization in New Zealand, Maori political resurgence in the 1970s culminated in the Treaty of Waitangi Act of 1975. The Act authorized a Waitangi Tribunal to investigate legislative or executive actions that violate the principles of the treaty, to report its findings, and make recommendations. Its investigative powers have been extended to include historic claims. See generally P.G. McHugh, *The Constitutional Role of the Waitangi Tribunal*, 1985 N.Z.L.J. 224. The tribunal is not a court, and has no sanctioning or enforcement powers, but its recommendations have influenced executive and legislative actions and judicial decisions which recognize the Maori interpretation of the Treaty of Waitangi as protecting their customary and traditional rights.

5.   Many Acts of Parliament in New Zealand now contain a clause stipulating that the concerned Act will not be interpreted in a manner violating the Treaty of Waitangi. For example, New Zealand's State-Owned Enterprises Act of 1986, which authorizes transfer of Crown land to state-created enterprises, was amended to include a stipulation that "nothing in this act shall permit the Crown to act in a manner that is inconsistent with the principles of the Treaty of Waitangi." In New Zealand Maori Council v.

Attorney General, [1987] 1 N.Z.L.R. 641 (CA), described by the New Zealand Court of Appeal as a case that was "as important for the future of our country as any that has come before a New Zealand court," the Treaty of Waitangi was described as signifying "a partnership between races" that required their "utmost good faith". Id. at 663–64. The Crown's responsibilities were "analogous to fiduciary duties," and extend to the "active protection of Maori people in the use of their lands and waters to the fullest extent practicable." Id. at 664. Thus the Crown was required to adopt a system guaranteeing the protection of Maori claims prior to land transfer.

In Huakina Development Trust v. Waikato Valley Authority, [1988] 2 N.Z.L.R. 188 (1987), the court held in a Maori water rights case that the treaty is part of the "fabric of New Zealand society," and that therefore it was appropriate to consider Maori spiritual and cultural values protected under the treaty as interpreted by the Waitangi Tribunal.

> The expertise of the Waitangi Tribunal lies in its understanding of Maori values in the context of the Treaty of Waitangi as the Tribunal interprets that Treaty. A moment's reflection upon the provisions of the Treaty of Waitangi Act, its extremely important statutory functions, the constitution of the Waitangi Tribunal and its reported findings must lead to the conclusion that it is an expert source within its field for instruction in Maori values. While, so far as the present case is concerned, no report of that Tribunal is in any way binding on this Court, its considered opinions, within the area of its expert functions, ought to be accorded due weight in this Court. The way in which the Waitangi Tribunal has dealt with the concept of Maori spiritual values in regard to water establishes, sufficiently for the determination of this branch of the appellant's case, that those values cannot be dismissed in a general sort of way by referring to them as personal to the individual or as something which the community at large may trample upon, at least not in the context of the indigenous population of this country which places great value upon the principles of the Treaty of Waitangi. Nor should the benefit of all New Zealanders be given a degree of absolute emphasis so as to exclude, in a branch of the law which has an affinity with the Treaty, Maori spiritual values.

[1988] 2 N.Z.L.R. at 223.

6.   In Te Weehi v. Regional Fisheries Offices, [1986] 1 NZLR 680 (HC), the Maori succeeded in convincing New Zealand's High Court that the quota management system for commercial fishing enacted by the federal Fisheries Act of 1983 ignored Maori customary fishing rights recognized by the common law of aboriginal title. In 1992, following six years of litigation and negotiations, the federal government and Maori leaders executed a settlement agreement resulting in passage of implementing legislation by Parliament, the Treaty of Waitangi (Fisheries Claims) Settlement Act 1992, No. 121. The Settlement Act terminated all past, present, and future Maori commercial

fishing claims and rights, and pledged the government to pay $150 million to assist the Maori in a joint venture purchase of Sealords, New Zealand's largest fishing company and holder of twenty-six percent of the country's total fishing quota.

Under the settlement agreement, the Maori also receive twenty percent of future commercial quotas for all new species brought under New Zealand's fisheries quota management system, while keeping ten percent of the total fishing quota agreed to with the government. Traditional rights to take fish for personal and customary use were retained by the Maori under the Act, to be exercised in designated coastal fishing "reserves" to be regulated by the government with Maori participation. Under the legislation, the Maori agree that the Treaty of Waitangi has been honored with respect to commercial fishing rights by the Act's full and final settlement of Maori commercial fishing claims.

The Fisheries Settlement Act has been called "the most comprehensive settlement of both commercial and non-commercial fishing claims by a native people" anywhere in the world. See Michael A. Burnett, *The Dilemma of Commercial Fishing Rights of Indigenous Peoples: A Comparative Study of the Common Law Nations*, 19 Suffolk Transnat'l L.Rev. 389, 427 (1996). The settlement, not surprisingly, has not worked perfectly to the satisfaction of all Maori. Urban and individual Maori have pursued their complaints about their exclusion from this historic Maori fishing rights agreement before New Zealand's High Court, the Privy Council in England, and the United Nations Human Rights Committee.

New Zealand's High Court ruled that urban and individual Maori not members of a hapu could be excluded from the settlement. The court noted that at the time of the Treaty of Waitangi, Maori commercial fishing rights were under the control of kin groups, usually whanau or hapu. The beneficiaries of the settlement, the Court therefore reasoned, are "mainly the hapu who have succeeded to the Treaty or customary rights." See Te Waka Hi Ika o Te Arawa v. Treaty of Waitangi Fisheries Commission, [2000] 1 NZLR 285 (HC & CA) at 310.

Under New Zealand's legal system at the time, the Privy Council, sitting nearly 12,000 miles away in England, heard the final domestic appeal in the case. The Privy Council also upheld the settlement agreement, noting "that no scheme could be proposed that would be in accordance with the Commission's overriding duty to benefit all Maori." See Manukau Urban Maori Authority and Others v. Treaty of Waitangi Fisheries Commission and Others, [2002] 2 NZLR 17 (PC); [2001] UKPC 32, para. 17–19. New Zealand established its own Supreme Court and stopped sending appeals to the Privy Council in 2004.

7.   Though the Court ruled that Maori land rights are enforceable only under a statute, and not as a customary right, the Court of Appeal in Attorney General v. Ngati Apa, [2003] 3 NZLR 643 (CA) upheld the Maori customary title to seabed and foreshore on the ground that the government did not extinguish it by act of parliament. By virtue of this decision, Maoris could bring

claims to the Waitangi Tribunal for customary title to seabed and foreshore. In 2004, the New Zealand Parliament enacted the Foreshore and Seabed Act in an attempt to extinguish any claims the Maori could bring regarding the seabed and the foreshore. See Sarah M. Stevenson, *Indigenous Land Rights and the Declaration on the Rights of Indigenous Peoples: Implications for Maori Land Claims in New Zealand* 32 Fordham Int'l L.J. 298, 306–8 (2008–2009). The Foreshore and Seabed Act was repealed and replaced by the Marine and Coastal Area (Takutai Moana) Act 2011, which allows Maori to bring claims of customary title to specific areas of foreshore and seabed. While the 2011 legislation is an improvement on the earlier Foreshore and Seabed Act, it still sets a very high evidentiary standard for Maori claimant groups, requiring a showing of "exclusive use and occupation since 1840 without substantial interruption." Jacinta Ruru, *Finding* Support *for a Changed Property Discourse for Aotearoa New Zealand in the United Nations Declaration on the Rights of Indigenous Peoples,* Symposium: The Future of International Law in Indigenous Affairs: The Doctrine of Discovery, the United Nations, and the Organization of American States, 15 Lewis & Clark L.Rev. 951, 966 (2011).

3. AUSTRALIA

MABO V. QUEENSLAND

107 A.L.R. 1 (1992) (Australian High Court).

BRENNAN J.

The Murray Islands lie in the Torres Strait. * * *

EARLY CONTACT WITH EUROPEANS

The Meriam people were in occupation of the Islands for generations before the first European contact. They are a Melanesian people (perhaps an integration of differing groups) who probably came to the Murray Islands from Papua New Guinea. Their numbers have fluctuated, probably no more than 1,000, no less than 400.

* * *

ANNEXATION OF THE MURRAY ISLANDS

* * *

In September 1879, Captain Pennefather on the instructions of HM Chester visited the Murray Islands where (as he reported) he "mustered the natives" and informed them "that they would be held amenable to British law now the island was annexed."

* * * At the same time, he reported:

> "The natives are very tenacious of their ownership of the land and the island is divided into small properties which have been handed down from father to son from generation to generation,

they absolutely refuse to sell their land at any price, but rent small portions to the beche-de-mer men and others. These natives, though lazy like all Polynesians on their islands, build good houses and cultivate gardens, they are a powerful intelligent race and a white man is as safe if not safer residing amongst them, as in Brisbane."

Moynihan J. [the trial court judge] found that there was apparently no concept of public or general community ownership among the people of Murray Island, all the land of Murray Island being regarded as belonging to individuals or groups. In about February, 1882, the Queensland Government "reserved" Murray Island for native inhabitants.

* * *

THE THEORY OF UNIVERSAL AND ABSOLUTE CROWN OWNERSHIP

* * * The legal consequences of these events are in issue in this case. Oversimplified, the chief question in this case is whether these transactions had the effect on 1 August 1879 of vesting in the Crown absolute ownership of, legal possession of and exclusive power to confer title to, all land in the Murray Islands. The defendant submits that that was the legal consequence of the Letters Patent and of the events which brought them into effect. If that submission be right, the Queen took the land occupied by Meriam people on 1 August 1879 without their knowing of the expropriation; they were no longer entitled without the consent of the Crown to continue to occupy the land they had occupied for centuries past.

* * *

The proposition that, when the Crown assumed sovereignty over an Australian colony, it became the universal and absolute beneficial owner of all the land therein, invites critical examination. * * * According to the cases, the common law itself took from indigenous inhabitants any right to occupy their traditional land, exposed them to deprivation of the religious, cultural and economic sustenance which the land provides, vested the land effectively in the control of the Imperial authorities without any right to compensation and made the indigenous inhabitants intruders in their own homes and mendicants for a place to live. Judged by any civilised standard, such a law is unjust and its claim to be part of the common law to be applied in contemporary Australia must be questioned. This Court must now determine whether, by the common law of this country, the rights and interests of the Meriam people of today are to be determined on the footing that their ancestors lost their traditional rights and interests in the land of the Murray Islands on 1 August 1879.

* * *

The peace and order of Australian society is built on the legal system. It can be modified to bring it into conformity with contemporary notions of justice and human rights, but it cannot be destroyed. It is not possible, a priori, to distinguish between cases that express a skeletal principle and those which do not, but no case can command unquestioning adherence if the rule it expresses seriously offends the values of justice and human rights (especially equality before the law) which are aspirations of the contemporary Australian legal system. If a postulated rule of the common law expressed in earlier cases seriously offends those contemporary values, the question arises whether the rule should be maintained and applied. Whenever such a question arises, it is necessary to assess whether the particular rule is an essential doctrine of our legal system and whether, if the rule were to be overturned, the disturbance to be apprehended would be disproportionate to the benefit flowing from the overturning.

* * *

THE ACQUISITION OF SOVEREIGNTY

* * *

* * * By the common law, the law in force in a newly-acquired territory depends on the manner of its acquisition by the Crown. Although the manner in which a sovereign state might acquire new territory is a matter for international law, the common law has had to march in step with international law in order to provide the body of law to apply in a territory newly acquired by the Crown.

International law recognised conquest, cession, and occupation of territory that was terra nullius as three of the effective ways of acquiring sovereignty. * * * The great voyages of European discovery opened to European nations the prospect of occupying new and valuable territories that were already inhabited. As among themselves, the European nations parcelled out the territories newly discovered to the sovereigns of the respective discoverers (*Worcester v. Georgia* (1832) 6 Pet. 515 at 543–544 [31 U.S. 350 at 369]), provided the discovery was confirmed by occupation and provided the indigenous inhabitants were not organised in a society that was united permanently for political action (Lindley, *The Acquisition and Government of Backward Territory in International Law,* (1926), Chs. III and IV). To these territories the European colonial nations applied the doctrines relating to acquisition of territory that was terra nullius. They recognised the sovereignty of the respective European nations over the territory of "backward peoples" and, by State practice, permitted the acquisition of sovereignty of such territory by occupation rather than by conquest (see Lindley, p. 47). Various justifications for the acquisition of sovereignty over the territory of "backward peoples" were advanced. The benefits of Christianity and European civilization had been seen as a sufficient justification from medieval times. (See Williams, *The American*

Indian in Western Legal Thought, (1990), pp. 78ff; and *Johnson v. McIntosh* (1823) 8 Wheat 543 at 573 [21 U.S. 240 at 253].) Another justification for the application of the theory of terra nullius to inhabited territory—a justification first advanced by Vattel at the end of the 18th century—was that new territories could be claimed by occupation if the land were uncultivated, the Europeans had a right to bring lands into production if they were left uncultivated by the indigenous inhabitants. (Vattel, *The Law of Nations* (1797), BK I, pp. 100–101. See Castles, *An Australian Legal History,* (1982), pp. 16–17.)

* * *

When British colonists went out to other inhabited parts of the world, including New South Wales, and settled there under the protection of the forces of the Crown, so that the Crown acquired sovereignty recognised by the European family of nations under the enlarged notion of terra nullius, it was necessary for the common law to prescribe a doctrine relating to the law to be applied in such colonies, for sovereignty imports supreme internal legal authority. (See A. James, *Sovereign Statehood,* (1986), pp. 3ff, 203–209.) The view was taken that, when sovereignty of a territory could be acquired under the enlarged notion of terra nullius, for the purposes of the municipal law that territory (though inhabited) could be treated as a "desert uninhabited" country. The hypothesis being that there was no local law already in existence in the territory, the law of England became the law of the territory (and not merely the personal law of the colonists). Colonies of this kind were called "settled colonies." Ex hypothesi, the indigenous inhabitants of a settled colony had no recognised sovereign, else the territory could have been acquired only by conquest or cession. The indigenous people of a settled colony were thus taken to be without laws, without a sovereign and primitive in their social organisation.

* * *

THE BASIS OF THE THEORY OF UNIVERSAL AND ABSOLUTE CROWN OWNERSHIP

It is one thing for our contemporary law to accept that the laws of England, so far as applicable, became the laws of New South Wales and of the other Australian colonies. It is another thing for our contemporary law to accept that, when the common law of England became the common law of the several colonies, the theory which was advanced to support the introduction of the common law of England accords with our present knowledge and appreciation of the facts.

* * *

The facts as we know them today do not fit the "absence of law" or "barbarian" theory underpinning the colonial reception of the common law of England. That being so, there is no warrant for applying in these times rules of the English common law which were the product of that theory. It would be a curious doctrine to propound today that, when the benefit of the common law was first extended to Her Majesty's indigenous subjects in the Antipodes, its first fruits were to strip them of their right to occupy their ancestral lands. Yet the supposedly barbarian nature of indigenous people provided the common law of England with the justification for denying them their traditional rights and interests in land.

* * * The theory that the indigenous inhabitants of a "settled" colony had no proprietary interest in the land thus depended on a discriminatory denigration of indigenous inhabitants, their social organisation and customs. As the basis of the theory is false in fact and unacceptable in our society, there is a choice of legal principle to be made in the present case. This Court can either apply the existing authorities and proceed to inquire whether the Meriam people are higher "in the scale of social organisation" than the Australian Aborigines whose claims were "utterly disregarded" by the existing authorities or the court can overrule the existing authorities, discarding the distinction between inhabited colonies that were terra nullius and those which were not.

* * *

If the international law notion that inhabited land may be classified as terra nullius no longer commands general support, the doctrines of the common law which depend on the notion that native peoples may be "so low in the scale of social organisation" that it is "idle to impute to such people some shadow of the rights known to our law" (*In re Southern Rhodesia* [1919] AC, at 233–234) can hardly be retained. If it were permissible in past centuries to keep the common law in step with international law, it is imperative in today's world that the common law should neither be nor be seen to be frozen in an age of racial discrimination.

The fiction by which the rights and interests of indigenous inhabitants in land were treated as nonexistent was justified by a policy which has no place in the contemporary law of this country. * * * Whatever the justification advanced in earlier days for refusing to recognise the rights and interests in land of the indigenous inhabitants of settled colonies, an unjust and discriminatory doctrine of that kind can no longer be accepted. The expectations of the international community accord in this respect with the contemporary values of the Australian people. The opening up of international remedies to individuals pursuant to Australia's accession to the [United Nations] Optional Protocol to the International Covenant on Civil and Political Rights (see Communication 78/1980 in *Selected Decisions of the Human Rights Committee under the Optional Protocol*, vol. 2, p. 23) brings to bear on the common law the powerful influence of the Covenant and the international standards it imports. The common law does not necessarily conform with international law, but international law is a legitimate and important influence on the development of the common law, especially when international law declares the existence of universal human rights. A common law doctrine founded on unjust discrimination in the enjoyment of civil and political rights demands reconsideration. It is contrary both to international standards and to the fundamental values of our common law to entrench a discriminatory rule which, because of the supposed position on the scale of social organization of the indigenous inhabitants of a settled colony, denies them a right to occupy their traditional lands.

* * *

However, recognition by our common law of the rights and interests in land of the indigenous inhabitants of a settled colony would be precluded if the recognition were to fracture a skeletal principle of our legal system. The proposition that the Crown became the beneficial owner of all colonial land on first settlement has been supported by more than a disregard of indigenous rights and interests. It is necessary to consider these other reasons for past disregard of indigenous rights and interests and then to return to a consideration of the question whether and in what way our contemporary common law recognises such rights and interests in land.

* * *

THE NATURE AND INCIDENTS OF NATIVE TITLE

Native title has its origin in and is given its content by the traditional laws acknowledged by and the traditional customs observed by the indigenous inhabitants of a territory. The nature and incidents of native title must be ascertained as a matter of fact by reference to those laws and customs.

* * *

First, unless there are pre-existing laws of a territory over which the Crown acquires sovereignty which provide for the alienation of interests in land to strangers, the rights and interests which constitute a native title can be possessed only by the indigenous inhabitants and their descendants. Native title, though recognised by the common law, is not an institution of the common law and is not alienable by the common law. Its alienability is dependent on the laws from which it is derived. If alienation of a right or interest in land is a mere matter of the custom observed by the indigenous inhabitants, not provided for by law enforced by a sovereign power, there is no machinery which can enforce the rights of the alienee.

* * *

Of course, since European settlement of Australia, many clans or groups of indigenous people have been physically separated from their traditional land and have lost their connection with it. But that is not the universal position. It is clearly not the position of the Meriam people. Where a clan or group has continued to acknowledge the laws and (so far as practicable) to observe the customs based on the traditions of that clan or group, whereby their traditional connection with the land has been substantially maintained, the traditional community title of that clan or group can be said to remain in existence. The common law can, by reference to the traditional laws and customs of an indigenous people, identify and protect the native rights and interests to which they give rise. However, when the tide of history has washed away any real acknowledgment of traditional law and any real observance of traditional customs, the foundation of native title has disappeared. A native title which has ceased with the abandoning of laws and customs based on tradition cannot be revived for contemporary recognition. Australian law can protect the interest of members of an indigenous clan or group, whether communally or individually, only in conformity with the traditional laws and customs of the people to whom the clan or group belongs and only where members of the clan or group acknowledge those laws and observe those customs (so far as it is practicable to do so). Once traditional native title expires, the Crown's radical title expands to a full beneficial title, for then there is no other proprietor than the Crown.

* * *

* * * Once the Crown acquires sovereignty and the common law becomes the law of the territory, the Crown's sovereignty over all land in the territory carries the capacity to accept a surrender of native title. The native title may be surrendered on purchase or surrendered voluntarily, whereupon the Crown's radical title is expanded to absolute ownership, a plenum dominium, for there is then no *other* owner (*St. Catherine's Milling & Lumber Co. v. The Queen* (1888) 14 App Cas, at 55). If native title were surrendered to the Crown in expectation of a grant of a tenure to the indigenous title holders, there may be a fiduciary duty on the Crown to exercise its discretionary power to grant a tenure in land so as to satisfy the expectation (see *Guerin v. The Queen* (1984) 13 DLR (4th) 321), but it is unnecessary to consider the existence or extent of such a fiduciary duty in this case.

* * *

Secondly, native title, being recognized by the common law (though not as a common law tenure), may be protected by such legal or equitable remedies as are appropriate to the particular rights and interests established by the evidence, whether proprietary or personal and usufructuary in nature and whether possessed by a community, a group or an individual.

* * *

THE EXTINGUISHING OF NATIVE TITLE

Sovereignty carries the power to create and to extinguish private rights and interests in land within the Sovereign's territory (*Joint Tribal Council of the Passamaquoddy Tribe v. Morton* (1975) 528 Fed.2d 370 at 376 n. 6). It follows that, on a change of sovereignty, rights and interests in land that may have been indefeasible under the old regime become liable to extinction by exercise of the new sovereign power. The sovereign power may or may not be exercised with solicitude for the welfare of indigenous inhabitants but, in the case of a common law countries, the courts cannot review the merits, as distinct from the legality, of the exercise of sovereign power (*United States v. Santa Fe Pacific Railroad Co* (1941) 314 U.S. 339 at 347; *Tee-Hit-Ton Indians v. United States* (1955) 348 U.S. 272 at 281–285).

* * *

However, the exercise of a power to extinguish native title must reveal a clear and plain intention to do so, whether the action be taken by the legislature or by the Executive. This requirement, which flows from the seriousness of the consequences to indigenous inhabitants of extinguishing their traditional rights and interests in land, has been repeatedly emphasized by courts dealing with the extinguishing of the native title of Indian bands in North America. It is unnecessary for our purposes to consider the several juristic foundations—proclamation, policy, treaty or occupation—on which native title has been rested in Canada and the United States but reference to the leading cases in each jurisdiction reveals that, whatever the juristic foundation assigned by those courts might be, native title is not extinguished unless there be a clear and plain intention to do so (*Calder v. Attorney-General of British Columbia* [1973] SCR, at 404; (1973) 34 DLR (3d) at 210; *Hamlet of Baker Lake v. Minister of Indian Affairs* (1979) 107 DLR (3d) 513 at 552; *R v. Sparrow* [1990] 1 SCR 1075 at 1094; (1990) 70 DLR (4th) 385 at 401; *United States v. Santa Fe Pacific Railroad Co.* (1941) 314 U.S., at 353, 354; *Lipan Apache Tribe v. United States* (1967) 180 Ct.Cl. 487 at 492). That approach has been followed in New Zealand (*Te Weehi v. Regional Fisheries Officer* [1986] 1 NZLR 680 at 691–692). It is patently the right rule.

A clear and plain intention to extinguish native title is not revealed by a law which merely regulates the enjoyment of native title (*R v. Sparrow*) [1990] 1 SCR, at 1097; (1990) 70 DLR (4th), at 400 or which creates a regime of control that is consistent with the continued enjoyment of native title (*United States v. Santa Fe Pacific Railroad Co.* (1941) 314 U.S., at 353–354). A fortiori, a law which reserves or authorizes the reservation of land from sale for the purpose of permitting indigenous inhabitants and their descendants to enjoy their native title works no extinguishment.

The Crown did not purport to extinguish native title to the Murray Islands when they were annexed in 1879. In 1882, in purported exercise of powers conferred by the *Crown Lands Alienation Act* 1876 (Qld) the Murray Islands were reserved from sale.

* * * The power to reserve and dedicate land to a public purpose and the power to grant interests in land are conferred by statute on the Governor in Council of Queensland and an exercise of these powers is, subject to the *Racial Discrimination Act,* apt to extinguish native title. The Queensland Parliament retains, subject to the Constitution and to restrictions imposed by valid laws of the Commonwealth (*Mabo v. Queensland* (1988) 166 CLR 186), a legislative power to extinguish native title. This being so, it is necessary to consider the effect which the granting of leases over parts of the Murray Islands has had on native title before the *Racial Discrimination Act* came into force.

A Crown grant which vests in the grantee an interest in land which is inconsistent with the continued right to enjoy a native title in respect of the same land necessarily extinguishes the native title.

* * *

* * * Where the Crown grants land in trust or reserves and dedicates land for a public purpose, the question whether the Crown has revealed a clear and plain intention to extinguish native title will sometimes be a question of fact, sometimes a question of law and sometimes a mixed question of fact and law. Thus, if a reservation is made for a public purpose other than for the benefit of the indigenous inhabitants, a right to continued enjoyment of native title may be consistent with the specified purpose—at least for a time—and native title will not be extinguished. But if the land issued and occupied of the public purpose and the manner of occupation is inconsistent with the continued enjoyment of native title, native title will be extinguished. A reservation of land for future use as a school, a courthouse or a public office will not by itself extinguish native title: construction of the building, however, would be inconsistent with the continued enjoyment of native title which would thereby be extinguished. But where the Crown has not granted interests in land or reserve and dedicated land inconsistently with the right to continued enjoyment of native title by the indigenous inhabitants, native title survives and is legally enforceable.

As the Governments of the Australian Colonies and, latterly, the Governments of the Commonwealth, States and Territories have alienated or appropriated to their own purposes most of the land in this country during the last 200 years, the Australian Aboriginal peoples have been substantially dispossessed of their traditional lands. They were dispossessed by the Crown's exercise of its sovereign powers to grant land to whom it chose and to appropriate to itself the beneficial ownership of parcels of land of the Crown's purposes. Aboriginal rights and interests were not stripped away by operation of the common law on first settlement by British colonists, but by the exercise of a sovereign authority over land exercised recurrently by Governments. To treat the dispossession of the Australian Aborigines as the working out of the Crown's acquisition of ownership of all land on first settlement is contrary to history. Aborigines were dispossessed of their land parcel by parcel, to make way for expanding colonial settlement. Their dispossession underwrote the development of the nation. But, if this be the consequence in law of colonial settlement, is there any occasion now to overturn the cases which held the Crown to have become the absolute beneficial owner of land when British colonists first settled here? Does it make any difference whether native title failed to survive British colonisation or was subsequently extinguished by government action? In this case, the difference is critical: except for certain transactions next to be mentioned, nothing has been done to extinguish native title in the Murray Islands. There, the Crown has alienated only part of the land and has not acquired for itself the beneficial ownership of any substantial area. And there may be other areas of Australia where native title has not been extinguished and where an Aboriginal people, maintaining their identity and their customs, are entitled to enjoy their native title. Even if there be no such areas, it is appropriate to identify the events which resulted in the dispossession of the indigenous inhabitants of Australia, in order to dispel the misconception that it is the common law rather than the action of governments which made many of the indigenous people of this country trespassers on their own land.

* * *

As the Crown holds the radical title to the Murray Islands and as native title is not a title created by grant nor is it a common law tenure, it may be confusing to describe the title of the Meriam people as conferring "ownership", a term which connotes an estate in fee simple or at least an estate of freehold. Nevertheless, it is right to say that their native title is effective as against the State of Queensland and as against the whole world unless the State, in valid exercise of its legislative or executive power, extinguishes the title. * * *

* * *

NOTES

1.   Justice Brennan's opinion for the Court was joined by Chief Justice Mason and Justice McHugh. Justices Deane and Gaudron wrote a separate opinion, agreeing that the common law of Australia recognized native title, but concluding further that legislative extinguishment of native rights would require compensation. Justice Toohey also agreed that native title is recognized under Australian common law, and that remedies that may have been available against the Crown for extinguishment may have lapsed by

operation of statutes of limitation. Justice Dawson dissented from the Court's judgment, concluding that absent recognition by the Crown, any pre-existing native title does not survive. Thus, while six justices recognized native title, only three justices supported a general proposition that its extinguishment by inconsistent Crown grant is compensable. The majority of the Court therefore held that the common law does not recognize a right of compensation for extinguishment of native title. Does this aspect of the decision therefore align Australian aboriginal law with the *Tee-Hit-Ton* rule announced by the United States Supreme Court, page 296, supra?

2.   It is worth mentioning that Chief Justice Mason and Justice McHugh wrote a separate prefatory note to Justice Brennan's opinion for the Court in *Mabo*. They noted the operation of Australia's Racial Discrimination Act of 1975 as a possible qualification on the general proposition that the common law did not recognize compensatory damages for extinguishment of native title, thus implying that the Act might provide a basis for protecting aboriginal lands from extinguishment by the legislature. The Act was designed to implement the United Nations Convention on the Elimination of All Forms of Racial Discrimination. *Mabo* arose out of a challenge under the Act to Queensland legislation declaring that the state owned all land occupied by the aboriginal peoples of Murray Island. Mabo v. Queensland, [1988] 83 ALR 14, cited in the most recent *Mabo* decision, was a High Court ruling on a preliminary procedural question arising during the litigation. That case declared Queensland's legislation unlawful under the Act for abrogating

> the immunity of the Meriam people from arbitrary deprivation of their legal rights in and over the Murray Islands. The Act thus impaired their human rights while leaving unimpaired the corresponding human rights of those whose rights in and over the Murray Islands did not take their origin from the laws and customs of the Meriam people.

The 1988 *Mabo* decision based on the Act thus rejected Queensland's defense that state law resolved the aboriginal challenge, opening the way for the Court's 1992 landmark decision recognizing native title under Australian law.

3.   The High Court's decision in *Mabo* prompted new land rights legislation for Australia's native peoples. Following a lengthy and acrimonious political debate, the federal government passed the Native Title Act, 1993 (Austl.). The complicated legislation and its implications for native title claims in Australia are analyzed in Beth Ganz, *Indigenous Peoples and Land Tenure: an Issue of Human Rights and Environmental Protection*, 9 Geo.Int'l Envtl.L.Rev. 173 (1997):

> The NTA is Commonwealth legislation, but many states and territories also passed legislation to deal with native title claims pursuant to the provisions of this Act. The main purposes of the Act are:

(i) to recognize and protect native title, (ii) to establish and set standards to deal with future issues involving native title, (iii) to establish a mechanism to determine native title claims, and (iv) to validate past acts that native title has now invalidated.

Native title is defined by the Act where:

(a)   the rights and interests [in the land] are possessed under the traditional laws acknowledged, and the traditional customs observed, by the Aboriginal peoples or Torres Strait Islanders; and

(b)   the Aboriginal peoples or Torres Strait Islanders, by those laws and customs, have a connection with the land or waters; and

(c)   the rights and interests are recognized by the common law of Australia.

Although *Mabo* alludes to the requirement, this statute's definition does not seem to require a physical connection to the land. Under section 27(2), the Act establishes an "arbitral body"—the National Native Title Tribunal (NNTT)—where claimants can pursue their claims. Claimants can also pursue land claims at a state or territory arbitration tribunal which can be established under the standards set by the NTA.

The NTA also establishes an application process to claim native title. In establishing these procedures, the government seemed hopeful that negotiations between the parties will be successful. However, the Act provides each party with the opportunity to challenge a determination of native title in the Federal Court, for a final redress. Perhaps most importantly, the NTA provides procedural safeguards for the potential future extinguishment of native title. Native title holders receive notification and procedural rights and are compensated if their native title is extinguished by the government.

The Act provides a system by which an indigenous community can claim title to their traditional lands. Recognition of this land claim could be in jeopardy, however, if the government has previously extinguished the title or if there is a competing interest. In these cases, negotiations between the indigenous community and the competing interest must ensue. This allowance for previous extinguishment of native title claims will obviously harm some indigenous communities. However, many communities will be protected by the procedural safeguards awarded by the Act for potential future extinguishments of title.

Id. at 188–90.

4.   In 1996, the High Court issued another historic and highly controversial decision on aboriginal rights and native title, Wik Peoples v. Queensland, [1996] 141 ALR 129. The High Court's 4–3 decision in *Wik* held

that native title can coexist with pastoral leases granted for livestock raising and related purposes by the Crown, but where the two conflict, the pastoralist's interests override native title.

Australia's powerful pastoral and mining industries were fiercely opposed to *Wik*'s underlying principle that native title is extinguished by a Crown grant only to the extent that the rights conferred by the grant are inconsistent with the native titleholder's rights. The result of their opposition was that Australia's Native Title Act was amended significantly in 1998 over fierce opposition of Australia's indigenous communities. The amendments severely limited the circumstances in which native title over land and waters could be claimed, and 80 of the 115 claims that had been filed before the National Native Title Tribunal were subsequently dismissed. See Larissa Behrendt, Achieving Social Justice: Indigenous Rights and Australia's Future 4 (2003).

The Australian government's 1998 amendments to the 1993 Native Title Act were criticized by the United Nations (UN) Committee on the Elimination of Racial Discrimination (CERD) as violating Australia's obligations under the International Convention on the Elimination of All Forms of Racial Discrimination. The Committee noted that the amended Native Title Act appeared to create legal certainty for governments and third parties at the expense of indigenous title. The Committee was particularly concerned that the amendments had the effect of winding back the protections of the *Mabo* decision. In particular, CERD criticized the lack of effective participation by indigenous communities in formulating the amendments, and called on the Australian government to address its concerns as a matter of utmost urgency by suspending the amendments and entering into negotiations with representatives of the Aboriginal and Torres Strait Islander peoples. Committee on the Elimination of All Forms of Racial Discrimination, Decision 2 (54) on Australia, Fifty-fourth session (18 Mar. 1999), A/54/18, para. 21(2). (Decision), CERD/C/54/Misc.40/Rev.2.

The Australian government responded by rejecting the observations of CERD as an unbalanced and wide-ranging attack that intruded unreasonably into Australia's domestic affairs and declaring it impossible to suspend the amendments. See Australian Parliament Joint Committee on Native Title and the Aboriginal and Torres Strait Islander Land Fund, Sixteenth Report, "Consistency of the Native Title Amendment Act with Australia's international obligations under the Convention on the Elimination of all Forms of Racial Discrimination (CERD)." 28 June 2000.

The UN CERD has continued to express concerns regarding the amendments to the 1993 Native Title Act:

> The Committee reiterates its view that the *Mabo* case and the 1993 Native Title Act constituted a significant development in the recognition of indigenous peoples' rights, but that the 1998 amendments roll back some of the protections previously offered to indigenous peoples and provide legal certainty for Government and

third parties at the expense of indigenous title. CERD/C/AUS/CO/14/Add.1, para. 21 (2006).

In the official government response to the 2006 report, Australia noted that it "does not consider that Australia has an international obligation to obtain the 'informed consent' of a particular group in order to exercise executive or legislative power," and that "the proposed reforms to the native title system and the ALRA are consistent with the Government of Australia's commitment to preserving native title and land rights." CERD/C/AUS/CO/14/Add.1, para. 27 (2006).

    5.   Two important cases decided in 2002 by the High Court represented major setbacks for native title claimant groups in Australia. In Ben Ward and Others (on behalf of the Miriuwung and Gajerrong people) v. State of Western Australia and Others, [2002] HCA 28 (2002), the Court's 297-page decision held that native title rights and interests are not "underlying" property rights but consist of a "bundle of rights" that must be individually proven and that can be extinguished by Crown grants one by one. Importantly, the High Court held that native title rights do not include a right to sub-surface mineral or petroleum resources in Western Australia.

Justice McHugh, writing separately in the *Ben Ward* case, said of the Court's holding, "The deck is stacked against the native title holders whose fragile rights must give way to the superior rights of the landholders wherever the two classes of rights conflict. * * * It may be that the time has come to think of abandoning the present system, a system that simply seeks to declare and enforce the rights of the parties, irrespective of their merits." Id. at para. 561.

Soon after *Ben Ward*, the High Court issued its opinion in Members of the Yorta Yorta Aboriginal Community v. State of Victoria, 2002 HCA 58 (2002). *Yorta Yorta* was the first native title claim to go to trial after the implementation of the Native Title Act. The High Court held that the ancestors of the present day members of the Yorta Yorta community had lost their traditional connection to their land sometime before the end of the nineteenth century. In ruling that the native title rights of the Yorta Yorta people to 2000 square kilometers of land and waterways in Victoria no longer existed, the Court approved the trial judge's finding that:

> The tide of history has indeed washed away any real acknowledgment of their traditional laws and any real observance of their traditional customs. The foundation of the claim to native title in relation to the land previously occupied by those ancestors having disappeared, the native title rights and interests previously enjoyed are not capable of revival. This conclusion effectively resolves the application for a determination of native title.

Members of the Yorta Yorta Aboriginal Community v. Victoria [1998] FCA 1606, at para. 129.

    Summarizing these recent cases one of Australia's leading native title experts, Professor Lisa Strelein, states:

The current inquiry into extinguishment fails to acknowledge that * * * the system of laws and customs that sustain native title has its own internal consistency and is not bound by, and may not adjust to or recognize, the "extinguishing acts" under Australian law * * * the idea of native title as a recognition space or an intersection of two legal systems is a misleading metaphor. The courts have repeatedly shown that, in the absence of extinguishing acts, exclusive possession title is the most meaningful translation of the central relationship between Indigenous peoples and their country. But, as soon as extinguishment comes into play, the courts have sought to "unbundle" or disaggregate the rights conferred by native title to rebuild the title from the fragments. This * * * fails to pay due respect and to provide due recognition and protection to native title as the interest first in time, under which the rights and interests enjoyed are as extensive as the law can allow, subject to the rights taken away by the Crown.

Lisa Strelein, Compromised Jurisprudence: Native Title Cases Since Mabo 125 (2nd ed. 2009).

6.   Australian courts have squarely rejected any attempt by aboriginal peoples to argue that they possess sovereignty over any territory or the continent. See Coe v. Commonwealth, 53 A.L.J.R. 403 (Austl.1979), in which the Court held that claims intended to dispute the validity of the British Crown's and the Commonwealth of Australia's assertions of sovereignty over the continent of Australia in the face of sovereignty allegedly possessed by the aboriginal nation "are not a matter of municipal law, but of the law of nations and are not cognisable in a court exercising jurisdiction under that sovereignty which is sought to be challenged. As such they are embarrassing and cannot be allowed."

The concept of self-government for Australia's aboriginal peoples is not something that has been strongly promoted by recent governments. The Australian Parliament issued an apology in 2008 to the Aboriginal and Torres Strait Islander peoples for "laws and policies of successive Parliaments and governments that have inflicted profound grief, suffering and loss," *Apology to Australia's Indigenous Peoples*, Government Business, Motion No. 1, see http://www.chineseworldnet.org/Text/1124691451962–7684/uploadedFiles/1202 945147435–2304.pdf. But the apology was issued amidst the controversy and dismay engendered among aboriginal leaders and communities by the Northern Territory Emergency Response (NTER), a government plan implemented in 2007 and designed to address what were described as "emergency" conditions faced by Aboriginal peoples in the Northern Territory. The state suspended Australia's Racial Discrimination Act, cited in *Mabo*, in order to assert a virtual plenary power in decision-making for Aboriginal communities in the Northern Territory. The "emergency" plan included a variety of restrictive measures relating to income management, access to and use of alcohol, and loss of power over communities. Despite a change in government in 2008, the NTER and its policies have persisted to the present. S. James Anaya, United Nations Special Rapporteur on the situation of human rights and fundamental freedoms of indigenous people, issued a highly critical report on the NETR, finding it violated the human rights of the Aboriginal communities in Australia's Northern Territory. See Report by the Special Rapporteur on the Situation of Human Rights and Fundamental Freedoms of Indigenous People, Addendum: Situation of Indigenous Peoples in Australia, U.N. Doc. A/HRC/15/37/Add. 4, June 1, 2010.

SECTION B. EMERGING VOICES: INDIGENOUS RIGHTS AND INTERNATIONAL LAW

1. THE UNITED NATIONS HUMAN RIGHTS SYSTEM

On September 13, 2007, after nearly four decades of intense and concerted human rights advocacy efforts by indigenous peoples before the United Nations and other international bodies, the United Nations General Assembly adopted the United Nations (UN) Declaration on the Rights of Indigenous Peoples, (U.N. Doc. A/61/L.67, Adopted September 13, 2007) by a majority vote of 144 states in favor, 4 votes against (Australia, Canada, New Zealand, and the United States) and 11 abstentions (Azerbaijan, Bangladesh, Bhutan, Burundi, Colombia, Georgia, Kenya, Nigeria, Russian Federation, Samoa, and Ukraine).

It is interesting to note that the four countries that originally voted against the UN Declaration—the United States, Canada, Australia, and New Zealand—all share in the same English common law legal heritage that has embraced the doctrine of discovery first declared by Chief Justice John Marshall in *Johnson v. McIntosh* in 1823. Recall from Chapter 2 that the highest courts of Canada, Australia, and New Zealand all cited, approved and followed the United States Supreme Court decision in *Johnson v. McIntosh* in their early decisions on indigenous peoples' rights in their respective legal systems. See pages 72, supra. It is not surprising, therefore, that the UN Declaration would be seen initially as representing a significant human rights challenge to overcome for any country that continues to adhere to *Johnson v. McIntosh* as binding precedent in its fundamental laws on indigenous peoples' rights. The four countries at the time based their opposition to the Declaration on the broad argument that its text created new rights for indigenous peoples previosuly unrecognized in international law and therefore not binding on their governments.

From beginning to end, the Declaration indeed represents a direct repudiation in international law of the modern-day legal systems created under the doctrine of discovery by these four countries to define and decide the rights of indigenous peoples. The Declaration's opening preambular language affirms "that indigenous peoples are equal to all other peoples" and states unequivocally that all "doctrines, policies and practices based on or advocating superiority of peoples or individuals on the basis of national origin or racial, religious, ethnic or cultural differences are racist."

The Declaration goes on to recognize the human rights obligations of UN member states to recognize and protect indigenous peoples':

- right to self-determination and to determine and develop priorities and strategies for exercising their right to development.

- right to maintain and develop their distinct political, economic, social and cultural identities and characteristics as well as their legal systems;

- right not to be subjected to genocide or ethnocide, or actions aimed at or affecting their integrity as distinct peoples, their cultural values and identities, including the dispossession of land, forced relocation, assimilation or integration, the imposition of foreign lifestyles and propaganda;

- right to observe, teach and practice tribal spiritual and religious traditions;

- right to maintain and protect manifestations of their cultures, their language, archaeological and historical sites and artifacts;

- right to restitution of spiritual property taken without their free and informed consent, including the right to repatriate Indian human remains, and protection of sacred places and burial sites.

Even the Declaration's closing paragraph directing that its 46 separate articles "shall be interpreted in accordance with the principles of justice, democracy, respect for human rights, equality, non-discrimination, good governance and good faith," would be nearly impossible to implement consistently in a modern-day legal system that continued to cite and abide by the principles of the doctrine of discovery and *Johnson v. McIntosh* in ruling on the rights of indigenous peoples.

But is this resistance to the Declaration as creating new types of rights for indigenous peoples that depart from the regime of indigenous peoples' rights created under the doctrine of discovery by these four English common law settler states reasonable, or even justifiable under international law? As then UN Special Rapporteur S. James Anaya explained in 2008 in his first report on the significance of this major new development in international human rights law, the Declaration is built on a foundation of existing human rights principles applied generally throughout the international legal system, See S. James Anaya, *The*

Human Rights of Indigenous Peoples, in Light of the New Declaration, and the Challenge of Making Them Operative A/HRC/9/9 (Aug. 5, 2008).

During the last three decades, the demands for recognition of indigenous peoples   across the world have led to the gradual emergence of a common body of opinion regarding the content of the rights of these peoples on the basis of long-standing principles of international human rights law and policy. This common normative understanding has been promoted by international and regional standard-setting processes;   by   the   practice   of international human rights bodies, mechanisms and specialized agencies; and by a significant number of international conferences and expert   meetings.   The   emergence   of   this   common understanding has further been reflected in and supported by widespread State practice and constitutional, legislative and institutional reforms at the domestic level. The Declaration on the Rights of Indigenous Peoples is the most important of these developments globally, encapsulating as it does the widely shared understanding about the rights of indigenous peoples that has been building over decades on a foundation of previously existing sources of international human rights law.

* * *

The United Nations Declaration on the Rights of Indigenous Peoples represents an authoritative common understanding, at the global level, of the minimum content of the   rights   of indigenous peoples, upon a foundation of various sources of international human rights law. The product of a protracted drafting process involving the demands voiced   by   indigenous peoples themselves, the Declaration reflects and builds upon human rights norms of general applicability, as interpreted and applied by United Nations and regional treaty bodies, * * * and other relevant instruments and processes.

Accordingly, the Declaration does not attempt to bestow indigenous peoples with a set of special or new human rights, but rather provides a contextualized elaboration of general human rights principles and rights as they relate to the specific historical, cultural and social circumstances of indigenous peoples. The standards affirmed in the Declaration share an essentially remedial character, seeking to redress the systemic obstacles and discrimination that indigenous peoples have faced in their enjoyment of basic human rights. From this perspective, the standards of the Declaration   connect   to   existing   State obligations under other human rights instruments. * * *

As Professor Robert A. Williams, Jr. explains in his book, Savage Anxieties: The Invention of Western Civilization (2012), the Declaration's newly pronounced international standards built upon well-recognized international law foundations have significantly influenced the work of international human rights bodies and other institutions throughout the UN system. The UN Human Rights Committee and the UN Committee on the Elimination of Racial Discrimination, for example, now regularly cite and apply the principles reflected in the UN Declaration when they monitor human rights situations involving indigenous groups.

Even beyond the formal human rights process, this new language of indigenous human rights now affects the lending processes of the World Bank, the Inter-American Development Bank, the European Union, and the domestic legislation and policies and judge-made law of countries throughout the world. All of these important developments reflect the inventiveness and dedication of indigenous tribal peoples in negotiation the ever-increasing interdependencies, ever-improving communications technologies, and burgeoning international institutions that characterize the contemporary international legal system and its human rights regime of substantive norms and related procedures.

Id. at 230–31.

Not surprisingly, the Declaration's provisions on indigenous peoples' rights to consultation and recognition of their rights in their traditional lands and resources have been among the most fiercely contested and resisted by the States that originally opposed adoption of the Declaration, and also by many of the States that originally voted in favor of it as well.

The most important articles in the Declaration speaking to the rights of consultation belonging to indigenous peoples include:

Article 10

Indigenous peoples shall not be forcibly removed from their lands or territories. No relocation shall take place without the free, prior and informed consent of the indigenous peoples concerned and after agreement on just and fair compensation and, where possible, with the option of return.

Article 18

Indigenous peoples have the right to participate in decision-making in matters which would affect their rights, through representatives chosen by themselves in accordance with their own procedures, as well as to maintain and develop their own indigenous decision-making institutions.

Article 19

States shall consult and cooperate in good faith with the indigenous peoples concerned through their own representative institutions in order to obtain their free, prior and informed consent before adopting and implementing legislative or administrative measures that may affect them.

The Declaration's most important provisions on indigenous peoples' rights in their traditional lands include:

Article 26

1.   Indigenous peoples have the right to the lands, territories and resources which they have traditionally owned, occupied or otherwise used or acquired.

2.   Indigenous peoples have the right to own, use, develop and control the lands, territories and resources that they possess by reason of traditional ownership or other   traditional occupation or use, as well as those which they have otherwise acquired.

3.   States shall give legal recognition and protection to these lands, territories and resources. Such recognition shall be conducted with due respect to the customs, traditions and land tenure systems of the indigenous peoples concerned.

Article 27

States shall establish and implement, in conjunction with indigenous peoples concerned, a fair, independent, impartial, open and transparent process, giving due recognition to indigenous peoples' laws, traditions, customs and land tenure systems, to recognize and adjudicate the rights of indigenous peoples pertaining to their lands, territories and resources, including those which were traditionally owned or otherwise occupied or used. Indigenous peoples shall have the right to participate in this process.

Article 28

1.   Indigenous peoples have the right to redress, by means that can include restitution or, when this is not possible, just, fair and equitable compensation, for the lands, territories and resources which they have traditionally owned or otherwise occupied or used, and which have been confiscated, taken, occupied, used or damaged without their free, prior and informed consent.

2.   Unless otherwise freely agreed upon by the peoples concerned, compensation shall take the form of lands, territories and resources equal in quality, size and legal status or of monetary compensation or other appropriate redress.

The United Nations (UN) Working Group on Indigenous Populations, established in 1982, focused international attention on indigenous peoples' human rights through its drafting of the early versions of the text of the UN Declaration. See Robert A. Williams, Jr., *Encounters on the Frontiers of International Human Rights Law: Redefining the Terms of Indigenous Peoples' Survival in the World,* 1990 Duke L.J. 660, 668–72. See also Russel

Lawrence Barsh, *Indigenous North America and Contemporary International Law,* 62 Or.L.Rev. 73 (1983); S. James Anaya, International Human Rights and Indigenous Peoples (2009).

NOTES

1.   Within the United Nations the breadth of focus on the rights of indigenous peoples has expanded markedly in recent decades. In 2000, the Economic and Social Council established the Permanent Forum on Indigenous Issues. The forum consists of 16 members, eight each to be nominated by governments and by the council, with the council's nominations to be of indigenous peoples. The Permanent Forum serves as an advisory body to the council with a mandate to focus on indigenous issues pertaining to economic development, culture, education, human rights, and health. See S. James Anaya, International Human Rights and Indigenous Peoples (2009) at 20–22. A year later the Human Rights Council established the Special Rapporteur on the situation of human rights and fundamental freedoms of indigenous peoples. The mandate of the Special Rapporteur includes working cooperatively with states, the United Nations, indigenous peoples, regional, bodies, and non-governmental organizations with the objective of the realization of full enjoyment of rights for indigenous peoples. In addition, the Special Rapporteur investigates allegations of human rights violations against indigenous peoples, and provides recommendations for resolution to States and to the Human Right Council. See Report of the Special Rapporteur on the situation of human rights and fundamental freedoms of indigenous people, 11 Aug. 2008, UN Doc. A/HRC/9/9 at paras. 14–17. In 2007, the Human Rights Council created a second mechanism focused on indigenous issues, the Expert Mechanism on the Rights of Indigenous Peoples. The Expert Mechanism consists of a five-member group of experts that is charged with providing the Human Rights Council with studies that reflect particular themes relating to the rights of indigenous peoples. See S. James Anaya, International Human Rights and Indigenous Peoples (2009) at 112–13.

2.   In April 2009, Australia formally announced it was endorsing the Declaration. Exactly one year later, New Zealand announced before the Permanent Forum that it also was endorsing the Declaration. In 2010, Prime Minister Steven Harper of Canada and President Barack Obama of the United States announced that their governments had also reviewed their positions and had both decided to endorse the Declaration.

As was noted at the beginning of this section, all four of these countries that had originally voted against the UN Declaration have all shared in the same English common law legal heritage that has embraced the doctrine of discovery first declared by Chief Justice John Marshall in *Johnson v. McIntosh.* Now, however, all four of these governments have reversed their votes in the UN General Assembly and declared their support for the Declaration. None, however, in caselaw, by statute, or through executive decree, has renounced or repudiated the doctrine of discovery. Given the Declaration's strong statements on, for example, indigenous peoples' rights to consultation and recognition of their property rights in their traditional lands, how long do you think this fundamental contradiction can or will endure in the domestic law of these countries?

NOTE: ARTICLE 27 OF THE INTERNATIONAL COVENANT ON CIVIL AND POLITICAL RIGHTS AND INDIGENOUS PEOPLES' HUMAN RIGHTS

Article 27 of the United Nations International Covenant on Civil and Political Rights (which has been ratified by the United States), has been the basis for several decisions favorable to indigenous peoples by international human rights bodies. The full text of the article reads as follows:

> In those States in which ethnic, religious or linguistic minorities exist, persons belonging to such minorities shall not be denied the right, in community with the other members of their group to enjoy their own culture, to profess and practice their own religion, or to use their own language.

The Covenant on Civil and Political Rights is part of the International Bill of Rights. The International Bill of Rights consists of the human rights provisions of the United Nations Charter (Articles 1(3), 55, and 56), that declare promotion and encouragement of human rights as one of the purposes of the UN, and pledge member states to the achievement of universal respect for, and observance of, human rights and fundamental freedoms; the Universal Declaration of Human Rights; the Covenant on Economic, Social and Cultural Rights, as well as the Covenant on Civil and Political Rights. Additionally, the Covenant on Civil and Political Rights is supplemented by a treaty, the Optional Protocol to the Covenant on Civil and Political Rights, which establishes procedures for implementing the Covenant.

The Universal Declaration of Human Rights was adopted by the UN General Assembly in 1948. While not a treaty in the formal sense in that it was originally intended as recommendatory and non-binding on the member states of the UN, it is today widely regarded as legally binding as customary international law, or as an authoritative interpretation of the UN Charter's human rights commitments. The two Human Rights Covenants were adopted by the UN in 1966. They were brought into force in 1976, when the required number of states ratified both instruments. The covenants created legal obligations on the more than 140 countries that have ratified the two instruments. The Covenant on Civil and Political Rights established an 18-member Human Rights Committee to implement the covenant. Under the Optional Protocol, the Committee can receive individual complaints filed against state parties to the covenant which have separately ratified the protocol. See Siân Lewis-Anthony, *Treaty-Based Procedures for Making Human Rights Complaints Within the UN System* in Guide to International Human Rights Practice 41–49 (Hurst Hannum, ed. 1992 ed.); Thomas Buergenthal, Dinah Shelton, and David Stewart, International Human Rights in a Nutshell 27–70 (2002).

The Human Rights Committee first considered Article 27 in the context of indigenous rights in the case of Sandra Lovelace. See Views of the Human Rights Committee under Article 5(4) of the Optional Protocol to the International Covenant on Civil and Political Rights Concerning Communication No. R 6/24 (1981). Lovelace was a Canadian Indian woman (Canada has ratified the Optional Protocol) who challenged Section 12(1)(b) of Canada's Indian Act (see page 1053, supra) which denied Indian status and benefits to any female Indian who married a non-Indian. The *Lovelace* case therefore raised sex discrimination issues in the context of tribal membership, but unlike the United States Supreme Court case of Santa Clara Pueblo v. Martinez, page 434, supra, the Canadian government, and not the tribe, was enforcing the discriminatory membership rule and the consequences were more severe (loss of membership). There were other differences between the two cases as well. Under Canada's Indian Act, Indian men who married non-Indian women not only did not lose their membership status but their non-Indian wives gained status.

While Lovelace raised claims under articles of the covenant relating to sex discrimination, the committee considered Article 27, relating to minority rights, as "most directly applicable" to her situation, because Canada's Indian Act denied her the benefit of living on the Tobique Reserve with other members of the minority community to which she belonged. "[I]n the opinion of the Committee the right of Sandra Lovelace to access to her native culture and language in community with the other members of her group, has in fact been, and continues to be interfered with, because there is no place outside the Tobique Reserve where such a community exists."

While the principle of the *Lovelace* case might appear to apply to the *Santa Clara* decision, the Committee suggested that the reach of Article 27 is more limited where an indigenous group itself has made the decision to deny membership benefits or status to an individual, and the national government, through legislation, recognizes the group's authority in the matter.

In a 1988 case, Kitok v. Sweden, Communication No. 197/1985, U.N. Human Rights Committee, CCPR/C/33/D/197/1985, the Committee considered a communication on a claim involving the rights of the indigenous people of Scandinavia, the Sami. Ivan Kitok was a person of Sami origin and a citizen of Sweden (which has signed the Optional Protocol). Kitok's family had been active in reindeer herding for more than a century. Kitok had engaged previously in reindeer husbandry, but was forced to find another occupation due to economic misfortunes. Under Sweden's reindeer herding laws, a Sami who undertakes another occupation for three years loses membership rights to herd reindeer. That person can regain those rights if the other members vote him or her back in. Kitok sought to re-enter the village herding collective as a full-time herder but was denied membership by the village organization.

After Kitok's denial of membership by the village organization was upheld by the courts of Sweden, he submitted a communication to the Human Rights Committee alleging violations of the covenant, including a violation of his right to enjoy his own culture under Article 27. The committee upheld Sweden's legislation vesting Sami broad control over reindeer herding. The committee noted the conflict between the legislation, which protected the rights of the Sami as a whole, and its application to a Sami individual. It referred specifically to its earlier opinion in *Lovelace* stating that "a restriction upon the right of an individual member of a minority must be shown to have a reasonable and objective justification and to be necessary of the continued viability and welfare of the minority as a whole." Kitok v. Sweden, § 9.8.

The committee in *Kitok* recognized that collective survival for an indigenous group may take priority over the individual rights of a single member. Thus, when the continued viability and welfare of the minority group as a whole is threatened, a restriction upon an individual member may be allowable under Article 27. See Douglas Sanders, *Collective Rights,* 13 Hum.Rts.Q. 368, 380 (1991). Under this interpretation, what might the committee's opinion have been in the *Santa Clara* case, had Mrs. Martinez been able to present a communication under the Optional Protocol? What is the effect of such decisions, and the impact of international oversight of membership decisions, on indigenous communities?

The committee has also applied Article 27 to indigenous peoples in the case of Ominayak and the Lubicon Lake Band v. Canada, 1990 Annual Report of the Human Rights Committee, U.N. Doc. A/45/40, Vol. II, App. A (1990). The committee found that Canada violated the cultural integrity guarantees of Article 27 by permitting the provincial government of Alberta to grant leases for mineral exploration and timber development within the Lubicon Lake Band's aboriginal territory. The committee recognized that the band's survival as a distinct cultural community was tied to deriving sustenance from its lands. See Dominic McGoldrick, *Canadian Indians, Cultural Rights and the Human Rights Committee,* 40 Int'l &Comp.L.Q. 658 (1991).

2. THE INTER-AMERICAN HUMAN RIGHTS SYSTEM

S. JAMES ANAYA & ROBERT A. WILLIAMS, JR., THE PROTECTION OF INDIGENOUS PEOPLES' RIGHTS OVER LANDS AND NATURAL RESOURCES UNDER THE INTER-AMERICAN HUMAN RIGHTS SYSTEM

14 Harv.Hum.Rts.J. 33, 33–37, 41–43, 45–63, 68, 72–74 (2001).

I. INTRODUCTION

One of the most notable features of the contemporary international human rights regime has been the recognition of indigenous peoples as special subjects of concern. A discrete body of international human rights law upholding the collective rights of indigenous peoples has emerged and is rapidly developing.[13]

In 1948, the Organization of American States General Assembly took initial steps toward recognition of indigenous peoples as special subjects of international concern in article 39 of the Inter-American Charter of Social Guarantees. It required states in the Inter-American system to take "necessary measures" to protect indigenous peoples' lives and property, "defending them from extermination, sheltering them from oppression and exploitation." This regional recognition was followed by the adoption of the first multilateral treaty devoted specifically to recognizing and protecting indigenous peoples' human rights, International Labour Organization Convention No.107 of 1957.[3]

* * *

New international standards concerning the rights of indigenous peoples have significantly influenced the work of several international human rights bodies and other international institutions. The U.N. Human Rights Committee and the U.N. Committee on the Elimination of Racial Discrimination now regularly apply the prevailing understandings of indigenous peoples' rights reflected in the newly articulated standards. They draw heavily on these understandings when they monitor human rights situations involving indigenous groups. Even beyond the formal human rights process, the discourse of indigenous human rights now affects the lending processes of the World Bank, the Inter-American Development Bank, the European Union, and the domestic legislation and policies and judge-made law of states. All of these important developments reflect the ever-increasing interdependencies, ever-improving communications technologies, and burgeoning international institutions that characterize the contemporary international system and its human rights regime of norms and related procedures.

At the regional level in the Americas, where a large part of the world's indigenous peoples live and struggle for cultural survival, the Inter-American system for the protection of human rights, which functions within the Organization of American States (OAS), has responded to the concerns of indigenous peoples. The OAS Inter-American Commission on Human Rights, in consultation with OAS member states and indigenous peoples' representatives, has prepared a Proposed American Declaration

---

[13] See S. James Anaya, Indigenous Peoples in International Law (1996); Robert A. Williams, Jr., *Encounters on the Frontiers of International Human Rights Law: Redefining the Terms of Indigenous Peoples' Survival in the World,* 1990 Duke L.J. 660.

[3] Convention concerning the Protection and Integration of Indigenous Populations and Other Tribal and Semi-Tribal Populations in the Independent Countries, Jun. 2, 1959, 107 I.L.O. 1957 [hereinafter Convention No. 107].

on the Rights of Indigenous Peoples.[9] In reporting on the human rights conditions of particular OAS member states over the last several years, the Commission has focused on the concerns of indigenous peoples. Further, it has accepted several important human rights complaints, which it is currently investigating, brought by indigenous peoples against various OAS member states. The Commission has gone so far as to prosecute one of those cases, the *Awas Tingni* Case from Nicaragua, before the OAS Inter-American Court of Human Rights, which has the authority to issue decisions that are binding on states as a matter of international law.[12]

* * *

III.   PROTECTION OF INDIGENOUS PEOPLES' RIGHTS TO LAND AND NATURAL RESOURCES BY INTER-AMERICAN HUMAN RIGHTS INSTRUMENTS AND U.N. TREATIES

Various human rights instruments of the OAS govern the adjudication of these cases now working through the Inter-American human rights system. In the *Awas Tingni* case, which arises from Nicaragua, the most important instrument is the American Convention on Human Rights, since Nicaragua is a party to that multilateral treaty, as are a majority of the OAS member states. The American Convention establishes both the procedures and substantive rights that govern the adjudication of complaints by the Inter-American Commission and Inter-American Court in relation to state parties to the Convention. * * * [For] OAS member states that are not parties to the American Convention, * * * the principal instrument for determining the applicable substantive rights for those countries in proceedings before the Inter-American Commission is the American Declaration on the Rights and Duties of Man. The Inter-American Court considers the American Declaration to articulate general human rights obligations of OAS member states under the OAS Charter, an organic multilateral treaty with the force of law.

Although neither the American Convention nor the American Declaration specifically mentions indigenous peoples, both include general human rights provisions that protect traditional indigenous land and resource tenure. These include provisions explicitly upholding the rights to property and to physical well being and provisions implicitly affirming the right to the integrity of culture. Thus, provisions of the American Declaration and the American Convention affirm rights of indigenous peoples to lands and natural resources on the basis of traditional patterns of use and occupancy, especially when viewed in light of other relevant

---

[9]   See Proposed American Declaration on the Rights of Indigenous Peoples, Art. XVIII, approved by the Inter-American Commission on Human Rights at its 133rd session on February 26, 1997, in OEA/ser L/V/II. 95. doc.7, rev. 1997.

[12]   [Case of the Mayagna (Sumo) Awas Tingni Community v. Nicaragua, Inter-Am. Ct. H.R. Case No. 11.577, Judgment of August 31, 2001, see page 1116, infra].

human rights instruments and international developments concerning indigenous peoples.

Other human rights instruments that bear directly on an assessment of the rights and corresponding obligations of the parties include two major U.N. human rights treaties, the International Covenant on Civil and Political Rights and the International Convention on the Elimination of All Forms of Discrimination. * * * Both of these UN human rights treaties include provisions that protect indigenous peoples' rights over land and natural resources. The Inter-American Commission on Human Rights has frequently interpreted the obligations of states under the American Convention and the American Declaration by reference to obligations arising from other international instruments. The Commission has found a basis for this approach in article 29 of the American Convention, which states that "[n]o provision of this Convention shall be interpreted as . . . restricting the enjoyment or exercise of any right or freedom recognized by virtue of the laws of any State Party or by virtue of another convention to which one of the said states is a party."

Interpretation of the American instruments by reference to other applicable treaties is supported by the pro homine principle, which favors integrating the meaning of related human rights obligations that derive from diverse sources.

A.   The Right to Property

Indigenous peoples' traditional land and resource tenure is protected by Article 21 of the American Convention on Human Rights, which provides: "Everyone has the right to the use and enjoyment of his property." Similarly, article XXIII of the American Declaration on the Rights and Duties of Man affirms the right of every person "to own such private property as meets the essential needs of decent living and helps to maintain the dignity of the individual and the home." The right to property affirmed in these two instruments must be understood to attach to the property regimes that derive from indigenous peoples' own customary or traditional systems of land tenure independently of whatever property regimes derive from or are recognized by official state enactments. The Inter-American Commission on Human Rights has supported this interpretation of the right to property in its Proposed American Declaration on the Rights of Indigenous Peoples:

1.   Indigenous peoples have the right to the legal recognition of their varied and specific forms and modalities of their control, ownership, use and enjoyment of territories and property.

2.   Indigenous peoples have the right to the recognition of their property and ownership rights with respect to lands, territories and resources they have historically occupied, as well as to the use

of those to which they have historically had access for their traditional activities and livelihood.

Excluding indigenous property regimes from the property protected by the American Convention and American Declaration would perpetuate the long history of discrimination against indigenous peoples. Such discriminatory application of the right to property would be in tension with the principle of non-discrimination that is part of the Inter-American human rights system's foundation.

* * *

Examined in light of the fundamental principle of non-discrimination enshrined in both the American Declaration and the American Convention, the right to property in these same instruments necessarily includes protection for those forms of property that are based on indigenous peoples' traditional patterns of land tenure. Failure to afford such protection to the property rights of indigenous peoples would accord illegitimate discriminatory treatment to their customary land tenure, in violation of the principle of equality under the law.

B. Rights to Physical Well-Being and Cultural Integrity

* * *

Indigenous peoples' agricultural and other land use patterns provide means of subsistence, and, further, are typically linked with familial and social relations, religious practices, and the very existence of indigenous communities as discrete social and cultural phenomena. Several rights articulated in the American Convention and the American Declaration support the enjoyment of such critical aspects of indigenous peoples' cultures, in addition to the right to property discussed above. These rights include the rights to life (American Declaration, article I, American Convention, article 4), the right to preservation of health and physical integrity (American Declaration, article XI, American Convention, article 5.1), the right to religious freedom (American Declaration, article III, American Convention, article 12), the right to family and protection thereof (American Declaration, articles V–VI, American Convention, article 17), and rights to freedom of movement and residence (American Declaration, article VIII; American Convention, article 22). The Inter-American Commission on Human Rights has observed that, "[f]or indigenous peoples, the free exercise of such rights is essential to the enjoyment and perpetuation of their culture."

The right to cultural integrity is made explicit by article 27 of the [United Nations Covenant on Civil and Political Rights, which states: "In those States in which ethnic, religious or linguistic minorities exist, persons belonging to such minorities shall not be denied the right, in community with the other members of their group, to enjoy their own culture, to profess and practice their own religion, or to use their own language."[67] Relying especially on article 27, the Inter-American Commission on Human Rights has affirmed that international law protects minority groups, including indigenous peoples, in the enjoyment of all aspects of their diverse cultures and group identities. According to the Commission, the right to the integrity of, in particular, indigenous peoples' culture covers "the aspects linked to productive organization, which includes, among other things, the issue of ancestral and communal lands."

In its Proposed Declaration on the Rights of Indigenous Peoples, the Commission once again articulated the obligation of states to respect the cultural integrity of indigenous peoples, expressly linking property rights and customs to the survival of indigenous cultures. Article VII of the Proposed Declaration, entitled "Right to Cultural Integrity" states:

1.   Indigenous peoples have the right to their cultural integrity, and their historical and archeological heritage, which are important both for their survival as well as for the identity of their members.

2.   Indigenous peoples are entitled to restitution in respect of the property of which they have been dispossessed, and where that is not possible, compensation on a basis not less favorable than the standard of international law.

3.   The states shall recognize and respect indigenous ways of life, customs, traditions, forms of social, economic and political organization, institutions, practices, beliefs and values, use of dress, and languages.

The United Nations Human Rights Committee has confirmed the Commission's interpretation of the reach of the cultural integrity norm, as displayed in its General Comment on article 27 of the Covenant of Civil and Political Rights:

[C]ulture manifests itself in many forms, including a particular way of life associated with the use of land resources, especially in the case of indigenous peoples. That right may include such traditional activities as fishing or hunting and the right to live in reserves protected by law. The enjoyment of these rights may require positive measures of protection and measures to ensure the effective participation of members of minority communities in decisions which affect them.[71]

---

[67] International Covenant on Civil and Political Rights, December 16, 1966, G.A. Res. 2200 (XXI), 999 U.N.T.S. 171 (entered into force Mar. 23, 1976), Art. 27.

[71] U.N. Hum. Rts. Comm., General Comment No. 23 (50) (Art. 27), HRI/GEN/1/Rev.1 at 38, adopted Apr. 6, 1994 [hereinafter HRC General Comment on Art. 27], para. 7.

Indigenous peoples' traditional land use patterns are included by the Committee as cultural elements that states must take affirmative measures to protect under article 27 regardless of whether states recognize indigenous peoples' ownership rights over lands and resources subject to traditional uses.

* * *

Critical to the viable continuation of indigenous peoples' cultures is the link the Human Rights Committee and Inter-American Commission have recognized between the economic and social activities of indigenous peoples and their traditional territories. Both the Human Rights Committee and the Inter-American Commission have concluded that, under international law, the states' obligation to protect indigenous peoples' right to cultural integrity necessarily includes the obligation to protect traditional lands because of the inextricable link between land and culture in this context. Thus, rights to lands and resources are property rights that are prerequisites for the physical and cultural survival of indigenous communities, and they are protected by the American Declaration, the American Convention, and other international human rights instruments, such as the Convention of the Elimination of All Forms of Racial Discrimination and the Covenant on Civil and Political Rights.

IV. INTERNATIONAL AND DOMESTIC LEGAL PRACTICE: EMERGING CUSTOMARY INTERNATIONAL LAW

* * * As demonstrated by an expanding body of literature, it is evident that indigenous peoples have achieved a substantial level of international concern for their interests, and there is substantial movement toward a convergence of international opinion on the content of indigenous peoples' rights, including rights over lands and natural resources. Developments toward consensus about the content of indigenous rights simultaneously give rise to expectations that the rights will be upheld, regardless of any formal act of assent to the articulated norms. The discourse of indigenous peoples and their rights has been part of multiple international institutions and conferences in response to demands made by indigenous groups over several years backed by an extensive record of justification. The pervasive assumption has been that the articulation of norms concerning indigenous peoples is an exercise in identifying standards of conduct that are required to uphold widely shared values of human dignity. The multilateral processes that build a common understanding of the content of indigenous peoples' rights, therefore, also build expectations of behavior in conformity with those rights.

Under modern legal theory, processes that generate consensus about indigenous peoples' rights build customary international law. As a general matter, norms of customary law arise when a preponderance of states and other authoritative actors converge upon a common understanding of the norms' content and generally expect future behavior in conformity with the norms. The traditional points of reference for determining the existence and contours of customary norms include the relevant patterns of actual conduct of state actors. Today, however, actual state conduct is not the only or necessarily determinative indicia of customary norms. With the advent of modern inter-governmental institutions and enhanced communications media, states and other relevant actors increasingly engage in prescriptive dialogue. Especially in multilateral settings, explicit communication may itself bring about a convergence of understanding and expectation about rules, establishing in those rules a pull toward compliance, even in advance of a widespread corresponding pattern of physical conduct. It is thus increasingly understood that explicit communication, of the sort that is reflected in the numerous international documents and decisions cited below, builds customary rules of international law. Conforming domestic laws and related practice reinforces such customary rules of international law. Non-conforming domestic practice undermines the apparent direction of the international norm-building only to the extent the international regime holds out and eventually accepts as legitimate the non-conformity.

Although international and domestic practice varies somewhat in its recognition and protection of indigenous peoples' land and resource rights, just as state practice varies in its treatment of property rights in general, it nonetheless entails a sufficiently uniform and widespread acceptance of core principles to constitute a norm of customary international law. The relevant practice of states and international institutions establishes that, as a matter of customary international law, states must recognize and protect indigenous peoples' rights to land and natural resources in connection with traditional or ancestral use and occupancy patterns. This new and emerging customary international law, along with treaty obligations arising from outside the Inter-American system, inform an understanding of the rights that are protected by the American Convention and American Declaration.

* * *

NOTES

1. The Inter-American Commission on Human Rights (IACHR), discussed in the the Anaya and Williams article, is an OAS charter organ charged with "the observance and protection of human rights" (OAS Charter, as amended, arts. 51 and 112(1)). The Commission can receive and act on individual petitions alleging a violation of any of the rights enumerated under the American Declaration. The Commission has no direct enforcement authority, but instead relies on its prestige and credibility, and the public opinion generated by its recommendations. The Inter-American Court is an autonomous judicial body that, along with the Inter-American Commission, forms the protective system for human rights within the OAS. The Court has

two principal functions: 1) adjudicatory, allowing it to hear and rule on alleged human rights violation cases that are referred to it; and 2) advisory, permitting it to issue opinions on legal matters that member states or OAS bodies might bring to its attention.

2.   The OAS approved its own Declaration on the Rights of Indigenous Peoples in 2016. See Inter-American Declaration on the Rights of Indigenous Peoples, agreed upon by the Permanent Council at its meeting of June 7, 2016. The American Declaration adopts many of the basic principles found in the UN Declaration on the Rights of Indigenous Peoples. See generally S. James Anaya, *The Protection of Indigenous People's Rights Over Land and Natural Resources Under the Inter-American Human Rights System*, 14 Harv.Hum.Rts.J. 33 (2001); Jo Pasqualucci, *International Indigenous Land Rights: A Critique of the Jurisprudence of the Inter-American Court of Human Rights in Light of the United Nations Declaration on the Rights of Indigenous Peoples*, 27 Wis.Int'l L.J. 51 (2009). For a comprehensive analysis of indigenous human rights in contemporary international law, see S. James Anaya, Indigenous Peoples in International Law (2nd ed. 2004).

3.   The Inter-American Court is part of the Organization of American States (OAS), and has the authority to issue legally binding decisions against state members of the OAS, like Nicaragua, that have ratified the American Convention on Human Rights and acceded to the Court's jurisdiction.

CASE OF THE MAYAGNA (SUMO) AWAS TINGNI COMMUNITY V. NICARAGUA

Inter-Am. Ct. H.R., Case No. 11.577.
Judgment of August 31, 2001.

[The substance of the complaint of the Awas Tingni community charged that Nicaragua had approved destructive logging concessions on indigenous communal lands without consultation with or agreement of the affected communities and that Nicaragua had failed to carry out its legal obligation to demarcate and legally secure indigenous lands, in violation of the American Convention on Human Rights.]

* * *

VIII

VIOLATION OF ARTICLE 25

Right to Judicial Protection

* * *

111. The Court has noted that article 25 of the [American] Convention [on Human Rights] has established, in broad terms,

> the obligation of the States to offer, to all persons under their jurisdiction, effective legal remedy against acts that violate their fundamental rights. It also establishes that the right protected

therein applies not only to rights included in the Convention, but also to those recognized by the Constitution or the law.

112. The Court has also reiterated that the right of every person to simple and rapid remedy or to any other effective remedy before the competent judges or courts, to protect them against acts which violate their fundamental rights, "is one of the basic mainstays, not only of the American Convention, but also of the Rule of Law in a democratic society, in the sense set forth in the Convention".

* * *

114. This Court has further stated that for the State to comply with the provisions of the aforementioned article, it is not enough for the remedies to exist formally, since they must also be effective.

* * *

   a) *Existence of a procedure for indigenous land titling and demarcation:*

116. Article 5 of the 1995 Constitution of Nicaragua states that:

* * *

> The State recognizes the existence of the indigenous peoples, who have the rights, duties and guarantees set forth in the Constitution, and especially those of maintaining and developing their identity and culture, having their own forms of social organization and managing their local affairs, as well as maintaining communal forms of ownership of their lands, and also the use and enjoyment of those lands, in accordance with the law. An autonomous regime is established in the [. . .] Constitution for the communities of the Atlantic Coast.

> The various forms of property: public, private, associative, cooperative, and communitarian, must be guaranteed and promoted with no discrimination, to produce wealth, and all of them while functioning freely must carry out a social function.

117. Article 89 of the Constitution further states that:

> The Communities of the Atlantic Coast are an inseparable part of the Nicaraguan people, and as such they have the same rights and the same obligations.

> The Communities of the Atlantic Coast have the right to maintain and develop their cultural identity within national unity; to have their own forms of social organization and to manage their local affairs according to their traditions.

The State recognizes the communal forms of land ownership of the Community of the Atlantic Coast. It also recognizes the use and enjoyment of the waters and forests on their communal lands.

118. Article 180 of said Constitution states that:

The Communities of the Atlantic Coast have the right to live and develop under the forms of social organization which correspond to their historical and cultural traditions.

The State guarantees these communities the enjoyment of their natural resources, the effectiveness of their communal forms of property and free election of their authorities and representatives.

It also guarantees preservation of their cultures and languages, religions and customs.

* * *

120. Decree No. 16–96 of August 23, 1996, pertaining to the creation of the National Commission for the Demarcation of the Lands of the Indigenous Communities of the Atlantic Coast, established that "the State recognizes communal forms of property of the lands of the Communities of the Atlantic Coast", and pointed out that "it is necessary to establish an appropriate administrative body to begin the process of demarcation of the traditional lands of the indigenous communities". To this end, the decree entrusts that national commission, among other functions, with that of identifying the lands which the various indigenous communities have traditionally occupied, to conduct a geographical analysis process to determine the communal areas and those belonging to the State, to prepare a demarcation project and to seek funding for this project.

121. Law No. 14, published on January 13, 1986 in La Gaceta No. 8, Official Gazette of the Republic of Nicaragua, called "Amendment to the Agrarian Reform Law", establishes in article 31 that:

The State will provide the necessary lands for the Miskito, Sumo, Rama, and other ethnic communities of the Atlantic of Nicaragua, so as to improve their standard of living and contribute to the social and economic development of the [N]ation.

122. Based on the above, the Court believes that the existence of norms recognizing and protecting indigenous communal property in Nicaragua is evident.

123. Now then, it would seem that the procedure for titling of lands occupied by indigenous groups has not been clearly regulated in Nicaraguan legislation. According to the State, the legal framework to carry out the process of land titling for indigenous communities in the country is that set forth in Law No. 14, "Amendment to the Agrarian Reform Law", and that process should take place through the Nicaraguan

Agrarian Reform Institute (INRA). Law No. 14 establishes the procedures to guarantee property to land for all those who work productively and efficiently, in addition to determining that property may be declared "subject to" agrarian reform if it is abandoned, uncultivated, deficiently farmed, rented out or ceded under any other form, lands which are not directly farmed by their owners but rather by peasants through *medieria*, sharecropping, *colonato*, squatting, or other forms of peasant production, and lands which are being farmed by cooperatives or peasants organized under any other form of association. However, this Court considers that Law No. 14 does not establish a specific procedure for demarcation and titling of lands held by indigenous communities, taking into account their specific characteristics.

124. The rest of the body of evidence in the instant case also shows that the State does not have a specific procedure for indigenous land titling. Several of the witnesses and expert witnesses * * * who rendered testimony to the Court at the public hearing on the merits in the instant case, expressed that in Nicaragua there is a general lack of knowledge, an uncertainty as to what must be done and to whom should a request for demarcation and titling be submitted.

125. In addition, a March, 1998 document, "General diagnostic study on land tenure in the indigenous communities of the Atlantic Coast", prepared by the Central American and Caribbean Research Council and supplied by the State in the present case, recognizes " [. . .] lack of legislation assigning specific authority to INRA to grant title to indigenous communal lands" and points out that it is possible that the existence of "legal ambiguities has [. . .] contributed to the pronounced delay in the response by INRA to indigenous demands for communal titling". That diagnostic study adds that

> * * * there is an incompatibility between the specific Agrarian Reform laws on the question of indigenous lands and the country's legal system. That problem brings with it legal and conceptual confusion, and contributes to the political ineffectiveness of the institutions entrusted with resolving this issue.

* * *

> * * * in Nicaragua the problem is the lack of laws to allow concrete application of the Constitutional principles, or [that] when laws do exist (case of the Autonomy Law) there has not been sufficient political will for them to be regulated.

* * *

> [Nicaragua] lacks a clear legal delimitation on the status of national lands in relation to indigenous communal lands.

* * *

* * * [B]eyond the relation between national and communal land, the very concept of indigenous communal land lacks a clear definition.

126. On the other hand, it has been proven that since 1990 no title deeds have been issued to indigenous communities.

127. In light of the above, this Court concludes that there is no effective procedure in Nicaragua for delimitation, demarcation, and titling of indigenous communal lands.

b)   *Administrative and judicial steps:*

[The Inter-American Court next held that Nicaragua's domestic courts failed to reach their decisions on legal actions filed by the indigenous communities to prevent the logging "within a reasonable time," thereby violating Article 25, Right to Judicial Protection, of the American Convention.]

* * *

138. The Court believes it necessary to make the rights recognized by the Nicaraguan Constitution and legislation effective, in accordance with the American Convention. Therefore, pursuant to article 2 of the American Convention, the State must adopt in its domestic law the necessary legislative, administrative, or other measures to create an effective mechanism for delimitation and titling of the property of the members of the Awas Tingni Mayagna Community, in accordance with the customary law, values, customs and mores of that Community.

139. From all the above, the Court concludes that the State violated article 25 of the American Convention, to the detriment of the members of the Mayagna (Sumo) Awas Tingni Community, in connection with articles 1(1) and 2 of the Convention.

IX

VIOLATION OF ARTICLE 21

Right to Private Property

* * *

Considerations of the Court

142. Article 21 of the Convention declares that:

1.   Everyone has the right to the use and enjoyment of his property. The law may subordinate such use and enjoyment to the interest of society.

2.   No one shall be deprived of his property except upon payment of just compensation, for reasons of public utility or social interest, and in the cases and according to the forms established by law.

3.   Usury and any other form of exploitation of man by man shall by prohibited by law.

143. Article 21 of the American Convention recognizes the right to private property. * * *

* * *

148. Through an evolutionary interpretation of international instruments for the protection of human rights, taking into account applicable norms of interpretation and pursuant to article 29(b) of the Convention—which precludes a restrictive interpretation of rights—it is the opinion of this Court that article 21 of the Convention protects the right to property in a sense which includes, among others, the rights of members of the indigenous communities within the framework of communal property, which is also recognized by the Constitution of Nicaragua.

149. Given the characteristics of the instant case, some specifications are required on the concept of property in indigenous communities. Among indigenous peoples there is a communitarian tradition regarding a communal form of collective property of the land, in the sense that ownership of the land is not centered on an individual but rather on the group and its community. Indigenous groups, by the fact of their very existence, have the right to live freely in their own territory; the close ties of indigenous people with the land must be recognized and understood as the fundamental basis of their cultures, their spiritual life, their integrity, and their economic survival. For indigenous communities, relations to the land are not merely a matter of possession and production but a material and spiritual element which they must fully enjoy, even to preserve their cultural legacy and transmit it to future generations.

* * *

151. Indigenous peoples' customary law must be especially taken into account for the purpose of this analysis. As a result of customary practices, possession of the land should suffice for indigenous communities lacking real title to property of the land to obtain official recognition of that property, and for consequent registration.

152. As has been pointed out, Nicaragua recognizes communal property of indigenous peoples, but has not regulated the specific procedure to materialize that recognition, and therefore no such title deeds have been granted since 1990. Furthermore, in the instant case the State has not objected to the claim of the Awas Tingni Community to be declared owner, even though the extent of the area claimed is disputed.

153. It is the opinion of the Court that, pursuant to article 5 of the Constitution of Nicaragua, the members of the Awas Tingni Community have a communal property right to the lands they currently inhabit, without detriment to the rights of other indigenous communities.

Nevertheless, the Court notes that the limits of the territory on which that property right exists have not been effectively delimited and demarcated by the State. This situation has created a climate of constant uncertainty among the members of the Awas Tingni Community, insofar as they do not know for certain how far their communal property extends geographically and, therefore, they do not know until where they can freely use and enjoy their respective property. Based on this understanding, the Court considers that the members of the Awas Tingni Community have the right that the State

   a)   carry out the delimitation, demarcation, and titling of the territory belonging to the Community; and

   b)   abstain from carrying out, until that delimitation, demarcation, and titling have been done, actions that might lead the agents of the State itself, or third parties acting with its acquiescence or its tolerance, to affect the existence, value, use or enjoyment of the property located in the geographical area where the members of the Community live and carry out their activities.

Based on the above, and taking into account the criterion of the Court with respect to applying article 29(b) of the Convention, the Court believes that, in light of article 21 of the Convention, the State has violated the right of the members of the Mayagna Awas Tingni Community to the use and enjoyment of their property, and that it has granted concessions to third parties to utilize the property and resources located in an area which could correspond, fully or in part, to the lands which must be delimited, demarcated, and titled.

154. Together with the above, we must recall what has already been established by this court, based on article 1(1) of the American Convention, regarding the obligation of the State to respect the rights and freedoms recognized by the Convention and to organize public power so as to ensure the full enjoyment of human rights by the persons under its jurisdiction. According to the rules of law pertaining to the international responsibility of the State and applicable under International Human Rights Law, actions or omissions by any public authority, whatever its hierarchic position, are chargeable to the State which is responsible under the terms set forth in the American Convention.

155. For all the above, the Court concludes that the State violated article 21 of the American Convention, to the detriment of the members of the Mayagna (Sumo) Awas Tingni Community, in connection with articles 1(1) and 2 of the Convention.

* * *

164. For the aforementioned reason, pursuant to article 2 of the American Convention on Human Rights, this Court considers that the State must adopt the legislative, administrative, and any other measures required to create an effective mechanism for delimitation, demarcation, and titling of the property of indigenous communities, in accordance with their customary law, values, customs and mores. Furthermore, as a consequence of the aforementioned violations of rights protected by the Convention in the instant case, the Court rules that the State must carry out the delimitation, demarcation, and titling of the corresponding lands of the members of the Awas Tingni Community, within a maximum term of 15 months, with full participation by the Community and taking into account its customary law, values, customs and mores. Until the delimitation, demarcation, and titling of the lands of the members of the Community has been carried out, Nicaragua must abstain from acts which might lead the agents of the State itself, or third parties acting with its acquiescence or its tolerance, to affect the existence, value, use or enjoyment of the property located in the geographic area where the members of the Awas Tingni Community live and carry out their activities.

* * *

NOTES

1.   The Court, by seven votes to one (*ad hoc* Judge Montiel Argüello of Nicaragua, was the lone dissenter) found Nicaragua in violation of the right to judicial protection contained in Article 25 of the Convention and of the right to property contained in Article 21. The same judges imposed, "as reparation for moral damages," a total of $50,000 in damages to be invested by Nicaragua "in public works and services" for the benefit of the Awas Tingni Community and $30,000 for legal costs associated with the proceeding. The Court unanimously decided that Nicaragua must adopt within its domestic legal system "measures of a legislative, administrative, and whatever other character necessary to create an effective mechanism for official delimitation, demarcation, and titling of the indigenous communities' properties, in accordance with the customary law, values, usage and customs of these communities" and "officially recognize, demarcate, and issue title for those lands belonging to the members of the Mayagna (Sumo) Community of Awas Tingni and, until this official delimitation, demarcation, and titling is performed, refrain from acts which could cause agents of the State, or third parties acting with its acquiescence or tolerance, to affect the existence, value, use or enjoyment of that property located in the geographic area in which members of the Mayagna (Sumo) Community of Awas Tingni live and carry out their activities." See Id. at para. 174(4).

NATION BUILDING NOTE: USING INTERNATIONAL LAW TO ADVANCE INDIGENOUS HUMAN RIGHTS IN DOMESTIC LEGAL SYSTEMS

The proceedings within the OAS produced important results for the indigenous peoples of the Atlantic Coast. The offending logging concession was canceled by the Nicaraguan government. The World Bank conditioned a financial aid package to Nicaragua on its development of legislation to demarcate indigenous lands. On December 14, 2008 the Government of Nicaragua officially handed over title to some 74,000 hectares of densely forested aboriginal territory to the Awas Tingni. S. James Anaya, *Nicaragua's Titling of Communal Lands Marks Major Step for Indigenous Rights,* Indian Country Today, Jan. 5, 2009. The Inter-American Court's decision in the *Awas Tingni* case, the separate opinions of the principal pleadings, and the full transcript of the historic hearing that took place at the Court's headquarters in San Jose, Costa Rica have been published in a Symposium on the *Awas Tingni* Case, 19 Ariz.J. of Int'l&Comp.L. 1–456 (2002).

The *Awas Tingni* case originated in the Inter-American Commission on Human Rights with a petition filed in 1996. The Commission ruled favorably on the merits of the petition and recommended appropriate remedial action to the Nicaraguan government in 1998. When Nicaragua continued in its refusal to demarcate Awas Tingni and other indigenous traditional lands, despite domestic constitutional and statutory provisions requiring the state to guarantee indigenous communal lands, the Inter-American Commission itself took the case to the Inter-American Court of Human Rights, in accordance with article 51 of the American Convention on Human Rights.

Because the Inter-American Court possesses the power to require states that have consented to its jurisdiction (as has Nicaragua) to take remedial measures for the violation of human rights, the *Awas Tingni* case establishes an important legal precedent on indigenous land rights under Inter-American and international law.

The Inter-American Commission on Human Rights, which originally heard the petition in the *Awas Tingni* case, has been particularly active in following up on the precedent established by the Inter-American Court's landmark decision on indigenous rights in cases involving member-states, which unlike Nicaragua are not parties to the American Convention on Human Rights. However, under the Commission's Statute and Regulations, the Commission may adjudicate petitions against OAS Member States that are not parties to the Convention by reference to the American Declaration on the Rights and Duties of Man. Thus, the petitions in each of these cases allege violations of the American Declaration, as well as of other sources of international human rights law.

In 2004, relying closely upon the decision in the *Awas Tingni* cases, the Inter-American Commission found that Belize, an OAS Member State, had violated the human rights of Mayan Indian indigenous communities in southern Belize by granting logging and oil concessions to over 700,000 acres of rain forest in Maya traditional territories, while failing to recognize and protect Maya traditional land and resource rights.

In finding that Belize had violated the human rights of the Maya, the Commission specifically cited Article XXIII of the American Declaration, protecting indigenous peoples' right to property, and stated that Belize had failed to take effective measures to recognize the communal property rights to the lands traditionally occupied and used by the Maya. Further, Belize was found to have violated Article XXIII, "by granting logging and oil concessions to third parties to utilize the property and resources that could fall within the lands that must be delimited, demarcated and titled or otherwise clarified and protected, in the absence of effective consultations and the informed consent of the Maya people." The Commission found that indigenous property rights protected by the inter-American human rights system "are not limited to those property interests that are already recognized by states or that are defined by domestic law, but rather that the right to property has an autonomous meaning in international human rights law. In this sense, the jurisprudence of the system has acknowledged that the property rights of indigenous peoples are not defined exclusively by entitlements within a state's formal legal regime, but also include that indigenous communal property that arises from and is grounded in indigenous custom and tradition." Maya Indigenous Communities of the Toledo District v. Belize (24 Oct. 2003), case 12.053, report No. 96/03, at para. 116.

The Inter-American Commission issued its final report in the Belize case in 2004, finding for the Maya and reiterating to the State of Belize that it must:

> 1. Adopt in its domestic law, and through fully informed consultations with the Maya people, the legislative, administrative, and any other measures necessary to delimit, demarcate and title or otherwise clarify and protect the territory in which the Maya people have a communal property right, in accordance with their customary land use practices, and without detriment to other indigenous communities.

Maya Indigenous Communities of the Toledo District v. Belize (Oct. 12, 2004), case 12.053, report No. 40/04.

In 2007, the Supreme Court of Belize issued a landmark decision in the consolidated cases of *Maya Village of Santa Cruz v. Belize* and *Maya Village of Conejo v. Belize*, recognizing the rights of the Maya in their traditional lands. Chief Justice Conteh stated for the Court:

> "I have no doubt that the claimants' rights to and interests in their lands in accordance with Maya customary land tenure, form a kind or species of property that is deserving of the protection the Belize Constitution accords to property in general. There is no doubt this form of property, from the evidence, nurtures and sustains the claimants and their very way of life and existence."

Relying upon the 2004 Inter-American Commission report, the Court recognized Mayan title based on the longstanding use and occupancy of the land and an agreement signed between local Mayan leaders and Belize officials in 2000. Cal et al. v. Attorney General, Claims no. 171 & 172 of 2007, Belize S. Ct. Judgment of Oct. 18, 2007.

That decision was ultimately appealed to the Caribbean Court of Justice, Belize's highest court of appeal, which affirmed the existence of Maya customary land tenure in 2015. Under a consent order accompanying the judgement, the government of Belize is now required to take measures to identify and protect Maya property and other rights arising from customary land tenure and to abstain from interference with these rights unless consultation occurs in order to obtain Maya consent. The Maya Leaders Alliance and The Toledo Alcaldes Association v. The Attorney General of Belize, CCJ Appeal No. BZCV2014/002, [2015] CCJ 15 (AJ) (Caribbean Court of Justice).

In a pair of decisions involving Paraguay, the Inter-American Court of Human Rights articulated the responsibilities of OAS member States that have been found to violate the land rights of indigenous peoples. Case of the Yakye Axa Indigenous Community v. Paraguay, Inter-American Ct. of H.R., Judgment of June 17, 2005, involved a claim by an indigenous petitioner to restitution for ancestral lands taken by the state and held by a private owner. The court held that the state is obligated to recognize the property rights of indigenous peoples even when their ancestral indigenous lands have been granted by the state to private individual owners. Otherwise, the court warned, the state's failure to recognize and protect indigenous peoples' property rights in their lost traditional lands "could affect other basic rights such as the right to cultural identity and the very survival of the indigenous communities and their members." Id. at para. 147.

The Court in *Yakye Axa* went on to explain that when a state cannot return ancestral lands to indigenous peoples, it should, with the agreement of the interested people, attempt to find them alternative lands, "of quality and legal status at least equal to that of the lands previous occupied by them, suitable to provide for their present needs and their development" if alternative land is not available or acceptable, with their agreement the people should be given compensation for the land. That compensation should principally take into account "the meaning that the land has for them." Furthermore, the state is not relieved of this obligation to provide restitution where, for objective and fundamental reasons, it is impossible "to adopt measures to return traditional lands and communal resources to the indigenous populations." Id. at paras. 149, 150.

In Case of the Sawhoyamaxa Indigenous Community v. Paraguay, Inter-American Court of H.R., Judgment of Mar. 29, 2006, the Inter-American Court noted that when the members of indigenous peoples lose possession of their traditional lands for reasons outside their will, they still maintain their rights to the property, even when they do not have legal title, except when the lands have been legitimately transferred in good faith to third persons. Even in that situation, however, the Court was careful to note that members of indigenous communities that involuntarily lost possession of their lands which have been legitimately transferred to innocent third parties have the right to recover them or to obtain other lands of equal size and quality.

The brief survey of comparative and international law materials from the Americas signals important advances made by the Inter-American human right system in contributing t to the protection of indigenous peoples' rights in a number of OAS member-states. But what about Indian tribes in the United States? The record there is less encouraging.

In 2002, shortly after the Inter-American Court issued its decision in the *Awas Tingni* case, supra, the Inter-American Commission, relying substantially upon that decision, ruled that the United States had violated the human rights of Mary and Carrie Dann, two traditional Western Shoshone indigenous women ranchers, to property under Article XXIII of the American Declaration, to judicial protection under Article XVIII of the Declaration, and equality under the law under Article II of the Declaration. See page 1100, supra.

The Commission's 2002 Report on the *Dann* case finding the United States in violation of the Dann sisters' human rights recognized that the special connection of indigenous peoples to their lands and resources is crucial to the free and full enjoyment of their other human rights and their indigenous culture. The Commission found, under principles of international human rights law, that indigenous peoples have the right to state recognition of their permanent and inalienable title to their traditional lands. It suggested that this right implies that the United States should provide an effective procedure for delimiting, demarcating, and securing indigenous title. See Mary and Carie Dann v. United States (27 Dec. 2002), Inter-American Commission on Human Rights, case 11.140, report No. 75/02, Annual Report of the Inter-American Commission on Human Rights: 2002, OAS Doc. OEA/Ser.L/V/II. 117/doc. 1, rev. 1.

In its 2006 annual report, the UN Committee on the Elimination of Racial Discrimination (CERD), following up on the IACHR report on the *Dann* case, provided a series of recommendations for the United States, which included freezing any plans to privatize the ancestral lands of the Western Shoshone to corporations, cease charging Western Shoshones with grazing fees, stop imposing horse and livestock impoundments, and stop restrictions of hunting, fishing, and gathering activities of Western Shoshone people. The recommendations further called for the State to adhere to international human rights norms and begin a dialogue with the Western Shoshone aimed at creating a solution that will be acceptable to the Western Shoshone. Report of the Committee on the Elimination of Racial Discrimination, at paras. 8–11. U.N. Doc. GEN/ G06/440/88/Supplement 18/A/61/18 (2006). No solution has been proposed by the United States to date to resolve the outstanding human rights issues presented by the *Dann* case.

Will the United States, which has not looked to other nations' legal treatment of their indigenous peoples or to international human rights law for guidance during the modern era, feel the influence of the global movement for protection of indigenous peoples' human rights? Professor Robert A. Williams, Jr. has suggested that Indian law scholars and advocates ask the Justices of the United States Supreme Court "to re-imagine a much different vision of how Indian law can work to better protect Indian rights" by looking, as Chief Justice Marshall himself did, to international law "for guidance in defining the basic rights of tribal Indians as indigenous peoples." Robert A. Williams, Jr., Like a Loaded Weapon: The Rehnquist Court, Indian Rights and the Legal History of Racism in America 165–66 (2005). What arguments would you make to the Justices on the current Court that might convince them to look to contemporary international law for guidance in developing the rules and principles of federal Indian law for the 21st century?

INDEX

References are to Pages